When should I travel to get the best airfare?
Where do I go for answers to my travel questions?
What's the best and easiest way to plan and book my trip?

frommers.travelocity.com

Frommer's, the travel guide leader, has teamed up with **Travelocity.com**, the leader in online travel, to bring you an in-depth, easy-to-use resource designed to help you plan and book your trip online.

At **frommers.travelocity.com**, you'll find free online updates about your destination from the experts at Frommer's plus the outstanding travel planning and purchasing features of Travelocity.com. Travelocity.com provides reservations capabilities for 95 percent of all airline seats sold, more than 47,000 hotels, and over 50 car rental companies. In addition, Travelocity.com offers more than 2,000 exciting vacation and cruise packages. Travelocity.com puts you in complete control of your travel planning with these and other great features:

> **Expert travel guidance from Frommer's** - over 150 writers reporting from around the world!
>
> **Best Fare Finder** - an interactive calendar tells you when to travel to get the best airfare
>
> **Fare Watcher** - we'll track airfare changes to your favorite destinations
>
> **Dream Maps** - a mapping feature that suggests travel opportunities based on your budget
>
> **Shop Safe Guarantee** - 24 hours a day / 7 days a week live customer service, and more!

Whether traveling on a tight budget, looking for a quick weekend getaway, or planning the trip of a lifetime, Frommer's guides and Travelocity.com will make your travel dreams a reality. You've bought the book, now book the trip!

AUSTRALIA
FROM $50 A DAY

The Ultimate Guide to Comfortable Low-Cost Travel

by Marc Llewellyn, Natalie Kruger & Lee Mylne

Hungry Minds™

Best-Selling Books • Digital Downloads • e-Books
Answer Networks • e-Newsletters • Branded Web Sites • e-Learning
New York, NY • Indianapolis, IN • Cleveland, OH

ABOUT THE AUTHORS

Sydney resident **Marc Llewellyn** (chapters 2, 3, 4, 5, 8, 9, 10, 11, 12, 13, 14, 15 and Appendix: Australia in Depth) is one of Australia's premier travel writers and a regular contributor to all of Australia's leading newspaper travel sections and travel magazines. As a member of the Australian Society of Travel Writers, he keeps his suitcase ready packed beneath his bed. He is also the author of *Frommer's Portable Sydney*, and co-author of *Frommer's Australia 2002*.

Natalie Kruger (chapters 10 and 11), contributes travel pieces to Australia's top newspapers and magazines, including the *Weekend Australian*, and is a member of the Australian society of Travel Writers. She is co–author of *Frommer's Australia 2002*.

Lee Mylne (chapters 6 and 7) is a Brisbane-based freelance travel writer who writes for a broad range of Australian and international publications, including the national travel trade magazine *Travel Week Australia*. She has lived in Queensland for the past 15 years, and is president of the Australian Society of Travel Writers.

Published by:

HUNGRY MINDS, INC.

909 Third Avenue
New York, NY 10022
www.frommers.com

ISBN 0-7645-6454-4
ISSN 8755-5425

Editor: Kathleen Warnock
Production Editor: Donna Wright
Design by Michele Laseau
Cartographer: John Decamillis
Photo Editor: Richard Fox
Production by Hungry Minds Indianapolis Production Services
Front cover photo: Matthias Kulka / Stock Market
Back cover photo: courtesy of The Russell Hotel

SPECIAL SALES

For general information on Hungry Minds' products and services please contact our Customer Care department; within the U.S. at 800-762-2974, outside the U.S. at 317-572-3993 or fax 317-572-4002. For sales inquiries and reseller information, including discounts, bulk sales, customized editions, and premium sales, please contact our Customer Care department at 800-434-3422.

Manufactured in the United States of America

5 4 3 2 1

Contents

List of Maps   x

1   The Best of Australia   1

1 The Top Travel Experiences   2

2 The Best Outdoor Adventures   3

3 The Best Places to View Wildlife   4

4 The Best Places to Experience the Outback   5

5 The Best Beaches   6

6 The Best Affordable Diving & Snorkeling Sites   6

7 The Best Places to Bushwalk (Hike)   7

8 The Best Places to Learn About Aboriginal Culture   8

9 The Best of Small-Town Australia   9

10 The Best Museums   10

11 The Best Moderately Priced Accommodations   10

12 The Best Alternative Accommodations   11

13 The Best Places to Stay on a Shoestring   12

14 The Best Worth-a-Splurge Restaurants   12

15 The Best Dining Bargains   13

2   Planning an Affordable Trip to Australia   15

1 The Regions in Brief   15

2 How This Guide Can Save You Money   20

3 Fifty Money-Saving Tips   21

4 Planning an Affordable Trip Online   25

5 Visitor Information   27

6 Entry Requirements & Customs   28

The Australian Dollar, the U.S. Dollar & the British Pound   31

7 Money   31

8 When to Go   32

Australia Calendar of Events   35

9 The Active Vacation Planner   37

10 Health & Insurance   44

11 Tips for Travelers with Special Needs   46

12 Booking a Package or Escorted Tour   48

13 Getting Around Australia   51

14 Tips on Accommodations   62

Fast Facts: Australia   65

3   Settling Into Sydney   70

1 Orientation   70

Neighborhoods in Brief   75

2 Getting Around   79

Fast Facts: Sydney   85

3 Accommodations You Can Afford   88

4 Great Deals on Dining   99
The Best Places for a Picnic   104

Family-Friendly Restaurants   105
Something Fishy   109

4   What to See & Do in Sydney   116

Suggested Itineraries   116

1 The Opera House & Sydney Harbour   117

2 Attractions at Darling Harbour   121
A Walk on the Wild Side: Climbing the Harbour Bridge   122

3 Other Top Attractions   123

4 Where to See Aussie Wildlife   124

5 Hitting the Beach   125

6 Museums, Galleries, Historic Houses & More   127

7 Parks & Gardens   130

8 Especially for Kids   132

9 A Stroll Through the Rocks 132
Walking Tour: On The Rocks   133

10 Harbor Cruises & Other Organized Tours   136

11 Staying Active   138

12 Shopping   141

13 Sydney After Dark   147
Cocktails with a View   152

5   New South Wales   155

1 The Blue Mountains   156

2 The Hunter Valley: Wine Tasting & More   168
Something Special: A Cattle Station in the Upper Hunter   173

3 Port Stephens: Dolphin & Whale-Watching   175

4 North of Sydney Along the Pacific Highway: Australia's Holiday Coast   178

5 South of Sydney along the Princes Highway   188

6 The Snowy Mountains: Australia's Ski Country   194
Following in the Footsteps of the Man from Snowy River   196

7 Outback New South Wales   196

6   Brisbane   203

1 Orientation   204
Neighborhoods in Brief   207

2 Getting Around   208
Fast Facts: Brisbane   209

3 Accommodations You Can Afford   212

4 Great Deals on Dining   216
Family-Friendly Restaurants   219

5 Exploring Brisbane   220

Cheap Thrills: What to See & Do for Free (or Almost) in Brisbane 222

6 River Cruises & Other Organized Tours   224

7 Outdoor Pursuits in Brisbane 225

8 The Shopping Scene   226

9 Brisbane After Dark   227

10 Moreton Bay & Islands   230

7	**Queensland & the Great Barrier Reef 235**

*Cheap Thrills: What to See &
Do for Free (or Almost) in
Queensland*   239

1 Exploring the Great Barrier Reef
241

Budget Snorkeling & Diving   247

2 Cairns   251

Where's the Beach?   262

3 Port Douglas, Daintree & the
Cape Tribulation Area   271

*Worth a Splurge: Restaurants in
the Rain Forest*   279

4 The North Coast: Mission Beach,
Townsville & the Islands   281

5 The Whitsunday Coast &
Islands   293

Come Sail with Me   296

6 The Capricorn Coast & the
Southern Reef Islands   307

*Up Close & Personal with a
Turtle*   314

7 Fraser Island: Eco–Adventures &
4WD Fun   317

8 The Sunshine Coast   320

9 The Gold Coast   328

10 The Gold Coast Hinterland:
Back to Nature   340

11 Outback Queensland   345

Can You Be a Survivor   346

8	**The Red Centre 352**

1 Alice Springs   355

*A Degree from Didgeridoo
University*   359

Dinner in the Desert   367

2 Road Trips from Alice Springs
368

3 Kings Canyon   372

4 Uluru-Kata Tjuta National Park
(Ayers Rock/The Olgas)   374

5 En Route to Darwin from Alice
Springs   381

9	**The Top End 383**

1 Darwin   386

2 Kakadu National Park   396

*Never Smile at a
You-Know-What*   398

3 Katherine   403

4 The Kimberley: A Far-Flung
Wilderness   407

10	**Perth & Western Australia 421**

1 Perth   425

Neighborhoods in Brief   428

Fast Facts: Perth   430

2 Side Trips from Perth   447

3 Margaret River & the Southwest:
Wine Tasting & Underground
Wonders   454

4 The Goldfields   459

5 The Midwest & the Northwest:
Where the Outback Meets the
Sea   462

11   Adelaide & South Australia   469

1 Adelaide   470

The Adelaide Festival & Other Special Events   472

Fast Facts: Adelaide   474

A Trip to the Seaside   484

2 Side Trips from Adelaide   487

3 Kangaroo Island   494

Culling Koalas on Kangaroo Island—A National Dilemma   499

4 Outback South Australia   503

A Fabulous Four-Wheel-Drive Adventure   508

5 The Coorong   508

12   Melbourne   511

1 Orientation   512

Neighborhoods in Brief   514

A City Center Walk   516

2 Getting Around   516

Fast Facts: Melbourne   518

3 Accommodations You Can Afford   519

4 Great Deals on Dining   524

5 Seeing the Sights   530

6 Enjoying the Great Outdoors or Catching an Aussie Rules Football Match   535

7 Shopping   537

8 Melbourne After Dark   540

9 Side Trips from Melbourne   544

13   Victoria   554

1 Ballarat: Gold Rush City   556

2 The Great Ocean Road: One of the World's Most Scenic Drives   559

3 The Murray River   563

4 The Southeast Coast   566

5 The High Country   568

6 The Northwest: Grampians National Park   573

14   Canberra   575

1 Orientation   575

2 Getting Around   578

Fast Facts: Canberra   579

3 Accommodations You Can Afford   580

4 Great Deals on Dining   582

5 Seeing the Sights   583

6 Outdoor Pursuits   587

7 Shopping   588

8 Canberra After Dark   588

15   Tasmania   589

1 Hobart   593

2 Port Arthur: Discovering Tasmania's Convict Heritage   604

3 Freycinet National Park   606

4 Hobart to Launceston: The Heritage Highway   607

5 Launceston   609

How to Catch a Tiger   611

6 Cradle Mountain & Lake St. Clair National Park   614

7 The West Coast   617

8 Northwest Coast   619

9 The Central Highlands Lakes
   620

Appendix: Australia in Depth   622

1 Australia's Natural World   622

2 The People of Oz   625

3 History 101   627
   Dateline   627

4 Oz Art   630

5 Aussie Eats & Drinks   631
   Witchetty Grubs, Lilli–Pillies &
   Other Good Things to Eat   632

6 The After-Dark Scene   634

7 Australia in Print & on the Silver
   Screen   635

Index   638

List of Maps

Australia   16
Greater Sydney   71
Sydney at a Glance   76
Sydney Transportation Systems   80
Central Sydney Accommodations   90
Central Sydney Dining   100
Central Sydney Attractions   118
Walking Tour: On the Rocks   134
New South Wales   157
The Blue Mountains   159
The Hunter Valley   169
Greater Brisbane   205
Brisbane   210
Moreton Bay & Islands   231
Queensland   236
The Great Barrier Reef   243
Cairns   253
Port Douglas, Daintree &
   Cape Tribulation   273
The Whitsunday Islands   295
The Sunshine Coast   321
The Gold Coast   329

The Red Centre   353
Alice Springs   357
The Northern Territory   385
Darwin   387
The Kimberley Region   409
Western Australia   423
Perth   427
South Australia   471
Adelaide Accommodations, Dining
   & Attractions   475
Adelaide Hills   491
Kangaroo Island   496
Greater Melbourne   513
Melbourne Accommodations   521
Melbourne Dining   525
Melbourne Attractions   531
Side Trips from Melbourne   545
Victoria   555
Canberra   577
Tasmania   591
Hobart   595

An Invitation to the Reader

In researching this book, we discovered many wonderful places—hotels, restaurants, shops, and more. We're sure you'll find others. Please tell us about them, so we can share the information with your fellow travelers in upcoming editions. If you were disappointed with a recommendation, we'd love to know that, too. Please write to:

Frommer's Australia from $50 a Day, 12th Edition
Hungry Minds, Inc.
909 Third Avenue
New York, NY 10022

An Additional Note

Please be advised that travel information is subject to change at any time—and this is especially true of prices. We therefore suggest that you write or call ahead for confirmation when making your travel plans. The authors, editors, and publisher cannot be held responsible for the experiences of readers while traveling. Your safety is important to us, however, so we encourage you to stay alert and be aware of your surroundings. Keep a close eye on cameras, purses, and wallets, all favorite targets of thieves and pickpockets.

What the Symbols Mean

✪ Frommer's Favorites

Our favorite places and experiences—outstanding for quality, value, or both.

The following abbreviations are used for credit cards:

AE	American Express	ER	EnRoute
BC	Bankcard	EC	Eurocard
CB	Carte Blanche	JCB	Japan Credit Bank
DC	Diners Club	MC	MasterCard
DISC	Discover	V	Visa

Find Frommer's Online

www.frommers.com offers up-to-the-minute listings on almost 200 cities around the globe—including the latest bargains and candid, personal articles updated daily by Arthur Frommer himself. No other Web site offers such comprehensive and timely coverage of the world of travel.

The Best of Australia

M aybe we shouldn't say so, being Aussies ourselves, but Australia has a lot of bests. It's got some of the wildest natural scenery, the weirdest wildlife, certainly some of the most brilliant scuba diving, the best beaches (shut up, California), the oldest rain forest (110 million years and counting), the world's oldest human civilization (some archaeologists say 40,000 years, some say 120,000), the best wines (stop browsing the Napa and come see what we mean), the world's most laid-back people when they're not from Melbourne and watching Aussie Rules football, the best weather (ignoring the Wet Season up north), the most innovative east-meets-west-meets-someplace-else cuisine—all lit by world's most pervasive white sunlight.

"Best" means different things to different people, but scarcely a visitor lands without having the Great Barrier Reef at the top of their "Things to See" list. It really is the Eighth Wonder of the World. Also high on most folks' list is Ayers Rock. This monolith must have some kind of magnet inside it to attract planeloads of tourists. We're not saying the Rock isn't special, but we think the Australian desert all around it is even more special. The third attraction on most visitors' lists is Sydney, the Emerald City that glitters in the Antipodean sunshine on—another "best"—the best harbor spanned by the best bridge in the world (sorry, San Francisco).

These "big three" attractions are understandably popular with travelers. What the TV commercials or the travel agent window displays don't show, however, is how much else there is to see. There are the World Heritage wetlands and Aboriginal rock art of Kakadu National Park, the second Great Barrier Reef on the western coast, and the snowy mountain hiking trails of Tasmania. As planes zoom overhead delivering visitors to the Reef, the Rock, and Sydney, Aussies in charming country towns, on far-flung beaches, on rustic sheep stations, in rain forest villages, and in mountain lodges shake their heads and say, "They don't know what they're missin'." You will no doubt find your own "bests" as you travel, as well as ours below, and we would like to hear about them. In the listing below, NSW stands for New South Wales, QLD for Queensland, NT for the Northern Territory, WA for Western Australia, SA for South Australia, VIC for Victoria, TAS for Tasmania, and ACT for the Australian Capital Territory.

1 The Top Travel Experiences

- **Experiencing Sydney** (NSW): Consistently voted one of the best cities in the world by almost every major travel publication, Sydney is more than just the magnificent Harbour Bridge and Opera House. No other major city has beaches in abundance like Sydney, and few have such a magnificently scenic harbor. My advice: Get aboard a ferry, walk across the bridge, and plan on spending at least a week, because you'll need every minute. See chapters 3 and 4.
- **Discovering the Great Barrier Reef** (QLD): It is hard to believe God would create such a glorious underwater fairyland, a 2,000-kilometer (1,250-mile) coral garden with electric colors and bizarre fish life, *and* have the grace to stick it all somewhere with warm water and year-round sunshine. This is what you came to Australia to see. See chapter 7.
- **Exploring the Wet Tropics Rain Forest** (QLD): Folks from skyscraper lands like Manhattan or Los Angeles can't get over the moisture-dripping ferns, the neon blue butterflies, the primeval peace of this World Heritage patch of rain forest stretching north, south, and west from Cairns. Hike it, 4WD it, or glide over the treetops in the Skyrail gondola from Cairns. See chapter 7.
- **Bareboat Sailing in the Whitsundays** (QLD): Bareboat means unskippered—that's right, even if you think port is an after-dinner drink you can charter a yacht, pay for a day's instruction from a skipper, then take over the helm and explore these 74 island gems. Anchor in deserted bays, snorkel over reefs, fish for coral trout from the deck, and feel the wind in your sails. See chapter 7.
- **Exploring the Olgas (Kata Tjuta) and Ayers Rock (Uluru)** (NT): Just why everyone comes thousands of miles to see the big red stone of Ayers Rock is a mystery—that's probably why they come, because the Rock *is* a mystery. Just 50 kilometers (31 miles) from Ayers Rock are the round red heads of the Olgas, a second rock formation more significant to Aborigines and more intriguing to many visitors than Uluru. See chapter 8.
- **Taking an Aboriginal Culture Tour** (Alice Springs, NT): Eating female wasps, contemplating a hill as a giant resting caterpillar, and seeing in the stars the face of your grandmother smiling down at you will give you a new perspective on your own culture. See what we mean on a half-day tour from the Aboriginal Art and Culture Centre in Alice Springs. See chapter 8.
- **Listening to the "Sounds of Silence"** (Ayers Rock, NT): Billed as a "million star restaurant" because it's outdoors under the Milky Way, this culinary treat is a fabulous way to soak up the desert. Sip champagne to the twang of a didgeridoo as the sun sets, then settle down to a "bush tucker" feast of emu, kangaroo, and crocodile at white-clothed tables in the sand. Then it's lights out, the music stops, and everyone listens to the eerie sound of silence. See chapter 8.
- **Exploring Kakadu National Park** (NT): Australia's biggest national park is a wild wonderland of lily-clad wetlands, looming red escarpment, Aboriginal rock art, fern-fringed waterholes, countless birds, big barramundi (that's a fish), and menacing crocs. Cruise it, hike it, 4WD it, fish it. See chapter 9.
- **Cruising the Kimberley** (WA): Australia's last frontier, the Kimberley is a cocktail of giant South Sea pearls, red soil, crocodiles, Aboriginal rock art called "Wandjina," and million-acre farms in a never-ending wilderness. Cross it by 4WD on the Gibb River Road, stay at a cattle station (ranch), base yourself on the beach in Broome, or cruise its dramatic red coastline. See chapter 9.
- **Rolling in Wildflowers** (WA): Imagine Texas three times over and covered in wildflowers. That's what the state of Western Australia looks like every spring

from August to mid-November when pink, mauve, red, white, yellow, and blue wildflowers bloom their hearts out. See chapter 10.

- **Drinking in the Barossa Valley** (SA): One of Australia's largest wine-producing areas, this German-speaking region less than an hour's drive from Adelaide is also the prettiest. Adelaide's restaurants are some of the country's best, so test out your wine purchases on the city's terrific food. See chapter 11.
- **Following the Great Ocean Road** (VIC): This 106-kilometer (64.5-mile) coastal road carries you past wild and stunning beaches, forests, and dramatic cliff top scenery—including the Twelve Apostles, 12 pillars of red rock standing in splendid isolation in the foaming Southern Ocean. See chapter 13.
- **Driving Around Tasmania:** The island-state is one of Australia's prettiest, a picturesque Eden of lavender fields, wineries, snow-topped granite tors, whitewater wildernesses, and haunting historic prisons. A bonus is that it's small enough to drive around in a few days. See chapter 15.

2 The Best Outdoor Adventures

- **Horse Trekking in the Snowy Mountains** (NSW): The film *Man from Snowy River* alerted travelers to the natural beauty of these ranges, where you can stay in bush lodges, or go camping under the stars. See chapter 5.
- **Abseiling in the Blue Mountains** (NSW): Careering backwards down a cliff face with the smell of gum trees in your nostrils is not everyone's idea of fun, but you sure know you're alive. Several operators welcome both novices and the more experienced. See chapter 5.
- **White-Water Rafting on the Tully River** (Mission Beach, QLD): The Grade 3 to 4 rapids of the Tully River swoosh between lush, rain forested banks. The guides are professional, the scenery is pretty, and the rapids are just hairy enough to be fun. See chapter 7.
- **Canoeing the Top End** (NT): Paddling down the sun-drenched ochre walls of Katherine Gorge sharpens the senses, especially when a freshwater crocodile pops its head up! Head downriver to the rarely explored Flora and Daly River systems to meet Aboriginal communities, shower under waterfalls, and camp in swags along the riverbanks. See chapter 9.
- **Surfing in Margaret River** (WA): A surfing lesson with four-time Western Australia champ **Josh Parmateer** (☎ **04/1895 8264**) is a great introduction to the sport—if only to hear Josh's ripper of an Aussie accent! From July to September, Josh shifts his classes to Cable Beach in Broome. See chapters 9 and 10.
- **Sea Kayaking with Sea Lions** (WA): Snorkel with sea lions and watch penguins feeding on a sea-kayaking day trip from Perth with **Rivergods** (☎ **08/9259 0749**). They also run multi-day sea kayak expeditions past whales, dolphins, and sharks in Shark Bay, and over the brilliant coral of Ningaloo Reef on the Northwest Cape in Western Australia. See chapter 10.
- **Skiing in the Victorian Alps** (VIC): Skiing in Australia? You bet. Where else can you swish down the mountain between gum trees? See chapter 13.
- **Going on Camel Safari** (SA and NT): Trek the Flinders Ranges in South Australia with **Kev's Kamel Kapers** (☎ **04/1983 9288**). You can either trot through the semi-desert range on a two-hour sunset trip or take an overnight safari, camping beside a gumwood fire. See chapter 11. You can also amble on camelback down a dry riverbed in the center of Alice Springs, and roll up to Ayers Rock astride one, à la Lawrence of Arabia. See chapter 8.

- **Hiking Cradle Mountain National Park** (TAS): The 80-kilometer (48-mile) Overland Track is known as the best bushwalking (hiking) trail in Australia. The trek, from Lake St. Clair to Cradle Mountain, takes anywhere from 5 to 10 days, depending on your fitness level. Shorter walks, some lasting just half an hour, are also accessible. See chapter 15.

3 The Best Places to View Wildlife

- **Montague Island** (Narooma, NSW): This little island on the south coast is a haven for seabirds, but it's the water around it that's home to the main attractions. Dolphins are common, fairy penguins, and during the whale-watching season you are almost sure to spot humpback and southern right whales, some with their calves. See chapter 5.
- **Jervis Bay** (NSW): This is probably the nearest place to Sydney where you are certain to see kangaroos in the wild and where you can pat them, too. The national park here is home to hundreds of bird species, including black cockatoos, as well as plenty of possums. See chapter 5.
- **Lone Pine Koala Sanctuary** (Brisbane, QLD): Cuddle a koala (and have your photo taken doing it) at this Brisbane park, the world's first and largest koala sanctuary. Lots of other Aussie wildlife—including lizards, frogs, 'roos, wallabies (which you can hand-feed), and colorful parakeets—are on show. See chapter 6.
- **Australian Butterfly Sanctuary** (Kuranda, near Cairns, QLD): Walk through the biggest butterfly "aviary" in Australia and see some of Australia's most gorgeous butterflies, including the electric-blue Ulysses. See many species of butterfly feed, lay eggs, and mate, and inspect caterpillars and pupae. Wearing pink, red, or white encourages the butterflies to land on you. See chapter 7.
- **Wait-A-While Environmental Tours** (Cairns, QLD): Head into the Wet Tropics rain forest behind Cairns or Port Douglas with this eco-tour operator to spotlight big-eyed possums, lizards, pythons, the bizarre bats—even a platypus, which are so shy that 95 percent of Aussies have never seen one in the wild. About once a month on average, one lucky group will spot the rare and bizarre Lumholtz's tree kangaroo. See chapter 7.
- **Mon Repos Turtle Rookery** (Bundaberg, QLD): Most nights from November to January, giant green, loggerhead and hawksbill turtles crawl up Mon Repos Beach to lay their eggs. From late January to March, the babies hatch and scamper down the beach to the water. Rangers lead group tours down to the beach nightly from the visitor center. Heron Island in Queensland and the Northwest Cape in Western Australia are two other excellent turtle-viewing sites. See chapters 7 and 10.
- **Currumbin Wildlife Sanctuary** (The Gold Coast, QLD): Tens of thousands of unbelievably pretty red, blue, green, and yellow rainbow lorikeets have been screeching into this park for generations to be hand-fed by delighted visitors every morning and afternoon. There are 'roos, wombats, and other Australian animals at the sanctuary, too, but the birds steal the show. See chapter 7.
- **Lamington National Park** (The Gold Coast Hinterland, QLD): Every day brilliant black-and-gold Regent bowerbirds, satin bowerbirds, crimson and cobalt rosellas, and loads of other wild rain forest birds feed right out of your hand at **O'Reilly Rainforest Guesthouse,** located in this mountainous national park a 90-minute drive inland from the Gold Coast. Hike the trails and soak up the cool mountain air while you're here. See chapter 7.

- **Kakadu National Park** (NT): One-third of Australia's bird species live in Kakadu; so do dingoes, snakes, frogs, and lots of dangerous saltwater crocs. A cruise on the Yellow Waters billabong is like a wetlands theme park. It is at its best later in the "Dry Season" around September and October, when wildlife converges around this shrinking water source. See chapter 9.
- **Northwest Cape** (WA): Go snorkeling with a whale shark. No one knows where they come from, but these mysterious monsters up to 18 meters (60 ft.) long surface in these remote waters every March to mid-June. Snorkelers can swim alongside the sharks as they feed (on plankton, not snorkelers). See chapter 10.
- **Monkey Mia** (WA): Just about every day, wild bottlenose dolphins come into this Outback shore to say hello. You have to join the queue, as this place gets worldwide publicity, but it's worth it when the gentle creatures cruise past and look up at you. While you're here, don't miss a cruise on the *Shotover* catamaran to see dugongs (manatees), turtles, sea snakes, and sharks. See chapter 10.
- **Kangaroo Island** (SA): You are sure to see more native animals here—including koalas, wallabies, birds, echidnas, reptiles, seals, and sea lions in their natural habitat than anywhere else in the country. Another plus: The distances between major points of interest are not great, so you won't spend half the day just getting from place to place. See chapter 11.

4 The Best Places to Experience the Outback

- **Broken Hill** (NSW): There's no better place to experience real Outback life than in Broken Hill. There's the city itself, with its thriving art scene and the Royal Flying Doctor service; a ghost town on its outskirts; a national park with Aboriginal wall paintings; an opal mining town nearby; and plenty of kangaroos, emus, and giant wedge-tailed eagles. See chapter 5.
- **Uluru-Kata Tjuta National Park** (Ayers Rock, NT): Sure, this magical monolith will enthrall you with its eerie beauty, but the nearby Olgas are more soothing, more interesting, and actually taller than the Rock, so make the time to wander through them, too. Don't go home until you've stood still in all that sand and felt the powerful heartbeat of the desert. See chapter 8.
- **The MacDonnell Ranges** (NT): The Aborigines say these red rocky hills were formed by the Caterpillar Dreaming that wriggled from the earth and came to rest here. To the west of Alice Springs are dramatic gorges, idyllic (and bloody cold) waterholes, and cute wallabies. To the east are Aboriginal rock carvings, and the Ross River Homestead, where you can crack a stock whip, throw a boomerang, feast on damper and billy tea, and ride a horse through the bush. See chapter 8.
- **Kings Canyon** (NT): Anyone who saw the cult flick *The Adventures of Priscilla, Queen of the Desert* will remember that scene where the transvestites climb a soaring cliff and survey the desert floor. That was Kings Canyon, about 320 kilometers (200 miles) from Alice Springs in one direction and Ayers Rock in the other. Trek the dramatic rim or take the easier shady route along the bottom. Don't forget your lipstick! See chapter 8.
- **Finke Gorge National Park** (NT): If you like your wilderness scenic and ancient, come here. Finke Gorge is home to "living fossil" palm trees, survivors of the ice ages and to what scientists think may be the world's oldest river. Camp, hike, and just soak up the timeless bush. Visit for a day from Alice Springs or camp out. Access is by four-wheel-drive (4WD) vehicle only. See chapter 8.

- **Elsey Station** (NT): This vast farm was the subject of the book *We of the Never Never*, an account of isolated Outback life written in 1902 by the station's owner, Mrs. Jeannie Gunn. The title originated in visitors' desire to "never never" leave such remote beauty. Visit for a day and meet the resident Aboriginal kids, or stay longer and canoe the Roper River to Red Lily Lagoon. See chapter 9.

5 The Best Beaches

- **Palm Beach** (Sydney): At the end of a string of beaches stretching north from Sydney, Palm Beach is long and very white, with some good surfing and a golf course. See chapter 4.
- **Hyams Beach** (Jervis Bay, NSW): This beach in pretty, off-the-beaten-path Jervis Bay is said to be the whitest in the world. You need to wear sun block if you decide to stroll along it, because the reflection from the sun, even on a cloudy day, can give you a nasty sunburn. The beach also squeaks as you walk. See chapter 5.
- **Four Mile Beach** (Port Douglas, QLD): The sea is turquoise, the sun is warm, the palms sway, and the low-rise hotels starting to line this country beach can't spoil the feeling that it is a million miles from anywhere. But isn't there always a serpent in paradise? The "serpent" in this case is north Queensland's seasonal— and potentially deadly—marine stingers. Come from June to September to avoid them, or swim in the stinger net. See chapter 7.
- **Mission Beach** (QLD): Azure blue sea, islands dotting the horizon, and lush white sand edged by dense tangled vine forests make this beach a real winner. So does the fact that hardly anyone ever comes here. Cassowaries (giant emu-like birds) hide out in the rain forest, and the tiny town of Mission Beach politely makes itself invisible behind the leaves. Visit from June to September to avoid deadly marine stingers. See chapter 7.
- **Whitehaven Beach** (The Whitsunday Islands, QLD): It's not a surf beach, but this 6-kilometer (3¾-mile) stretch of silica sand on Whitsunday Island is pristine, peaceful, and as white as snow. Bring a book, curl up under the rain forest lining its edge, and fantasize that the cruise boat is going to leave without you. See chapter 7.
- **Main Beach** (Sunshine Coast, QLD): The trendy shops of Hastings Street line the white sand and gently rolling surf of this pretty beach. Dust off your designer swimsuit for this one. When you get tired of the scene, you can hike the green walking trails of nearby Noosa National Park. See chapter 7.
- **Surfers Paradise Beach** (Gold Coast, QLD): All the beaches on the 30-kilometer (19-mile) Gold Coast strip in south Queensland are worthy of inclusion. Every one of them has clean sand, great surf, and fresh breezes. Just ignore the tacky high-rises behind you. Surfers will like Kirra and Burleigh Heads. See chapter 7.
- **Cable Beach** (Broome, WA): Is it the South Sea pearls they pull out of the Indian Ocean, the camels loping along the sand at sunset, the surf, or the red earth that comes down to meet the green water that gives this beach its exotic appeal? Maybe it's the 22 kilometers (14 miles) of glorious white sand. June to September is the only time to swim here, because of deadly marine stingers. See chapter 9.

6 The Best Affordable Diving & Snorkeling Sites

- **Port Douglas** (QLD): Many fabulous dive sites can be found off the shores of Port Douglas, north of Cairns, including Split-Bommie, with its delicate fan corals and schools of colorful fusiliers; Barracuda Pass, with its coral gardens and giant clams; the swim-through coral spires of the Cathedrals; and numerous rib-bon reefs renowned for their variety of coral and fish life. See chapter 7.

- **Green Island** (QLD): This island is made of coral, so you'd expect the snorkel-ing to be good. Plunge off the beach just about anywhere around the island and marvel at the scenes before you. Come over for the day from Cairns or stay at the island's upscale resort. Divers will like it here, too. See chapter 7.

- **Cairns** (QLD): In addition to Green Island (see above), Moore, Norman, Hardy, Saxon, and Arlington reefs and Michaelmas and Upolu cays—all about 90 min-utes off Cairns—offer great snorkeling and endless dive sites. Explore on a day trip from Cairns or on a 3-day sailing adventure. See chapter 7.

- *Yongala* **wreck** (Off Townsville, QLD): Sunk by a cyclone in 1911, the 120-meter (394-ft.) SS *Yongala* lies in the Coral Sea off Townsville. Big schools of trevally, kingfish, barracuda, and batfish surround the wreckage; giant Queens-land grouper live under the bow, lionfish hide under the stern, turtles graze on the hull, and hard and soft corals make their home on her. Extended live-aboard dive trips run from Townsville and Cairns. See chapter 7.

- **The Whitsunday Islands** (QLD): These 74 breathtaking islands offer countless dive sites among the islands themselves and on the Outer Great Barrier Reef 90 minutes away. Bait Reef on the Outer Reef is popular for its cascading dropoffs. The underwater life is as varied and stunning here as anywhere else along the Great Barrier Reef, and when you're not diving or snorkeling, the above-the-water landscape is a beautiful playground. See chapter 7.

- **Rottnest Island** (WA): Just 19 kilometers (12 miles) off Perth, excellent snor-keling and more than 100 dive sites await you in the sheltered bays of this for-mer prison island. Wrecks, limestone overhangs, and myriad fish will keep you entertained. There are no cars on the island, so rent a bike and snorkel gear, grab a map of snorkel trails, and find your own private coral garden. See chapter 10.

- **Ningaloo Reef** (WA): A stunningly well kept secret is how we'd describe Aus-tralia's second great barrier reef stretching some 260 kilometers (163 miles) along the Northwest Cape halfway up Western Australia. Dazzling coral starts right on shore, not 90 minutes out to sea like at the Great Barrier Reef. You can snorkel or dive with manta rays, and dive to see sharks, angelfish, turtles, eels, grouper, potato cod, and much more. See chapter 10.

7 The Best Places to Bushwalk (Hike)

- **Blue Mountains** (NSW): Many bushwalks in the Blue Mountains National Park offer awesome views of valleys, waterfalls, cliffs, and forest. They are all easily reached from Sydney. See chapter 5.

- **Whitsunday Islands** (QLD): Most people think of snorkeling and water sports when they come to these 74 tropical national park islands clad in dense rain for-est and bush, but every resort island we recommend in chapter 8, except Day-dream Island, also has hiking trails. Some are flat; some are hilly. Wallabies and butterflies are common sights en route. South Molle has the best network of trails and 360° island views from its peak. See chapter 7.

- **Lamington National Park** (Gold Coast hinterland, QLD): Few other national parks in Australia have such a well-marked network of trails as this one—160 kilometers (100 miles) of them, all up. Revel in dense subtropical rain forest, marvel at mossy 2,000-year-old Antarctic beech trees, watch for blue and white Lamington Spiny Crayfish in the streams, and soak up the cool mountain air 900 meters (3,000 ft.) above sea level. See chapter 7.

- **Larapinta Trail** (The Red Centre, NT): Soon you will be able to start at Alice Springs and walk this entire 220-kilometer (138-mile) semi-desert trail that winds through the stark crimson MacDonnell Ranges. The trail is still under construction, but plenty of day-length and overnight sections are ready for your boots now. See chapter 8.
- **Kakadu National Park** (NT): Whether you want a pleasant wetlands stroll or a tough overnight hike, you can find it in this World Heritage-listed park. Hike past red cliffs, cycads straight from a dinosaur movie set, lily-filled lagoons hiding human-eating crocodiles, and what looks like Australia's entire bird population. There's some good Aboriginal rock art here, too. See chapter 9.
- **Cape-to-Cape** (WA): Rugged sea cliffs, china blue sea, eucalyptus forest, white beaches, and coastal heath are what you will experience hiking between Cape Naturaliste and Cape Leeuwin, in the southwest corner of Western Australia. Walk a short section or tackle the whole 6-day extravaganza. In season you will see whales and wildflowers. See chapter 10.
- **Freycinet National Park** (TAS): The trek to Wine Glass Bay passes warty pink granite outcrops, with views over an ocean sliced by a crescent of icy sand. It's prehistorically beautiful. See chapter 15.

8 The Best Places to Learn About Aboriginal Culture

- **Native Guide Safari Tours** (Port Douglas, QLD): Hazel Douglas, an Aborigine who was brought up in the 110-million-year-old rain forest of the Daintree and Cape Tribulation area, takes you on a full-day 4WD rain forest safari to explain Aboriginal legends, point out what different plants are used for, and teach you stuff like how to know when a crocodile is in the water. See chapter 7.
- **The Umbarra Aboriginal Cultural Centre** (Wallaga Lake, near Narooma, NSW): This center offers boomerang and spear throwing instruction, painting with natural ochres, discussions on Aboriginal culture, and guided walking tours of Aboriginal sacred sites. See chapter 5.
- **Tjapukai Aboriginal Cultural Park** (Cairns, QLD): This multimillion-dollar center showcases the history of the local Tjapukai people—their Dreamtime creation history and their often harrowing experiences since the white man arrived—using a film, a superb theatrical work, and a dance performance. Its Aboriginal art and crafts gift shop is one of the country's best. See chapter 7.
- **Aboriginal Art and Culture Centre** (Alice Springs, NT): You'll taste bush food, see traditional houses, throw boomerangs and spears, and learn about Aboriginal family values in a half-day tour of this Aborigine-owned center. Be sure to visit the museum and art gallery where you can take a didgeridoo lesson. See chapter 8.
- **Anangu Tours** (Ayers Rock, NT): The Anangu are the owners of Ayers Rock, or Uluru, as it is called in their native tongue. Join them for walks around the Rock as you learn about the poisonous snake men who fought battles here, pick bush food off the trees, throw spears, visit rock paintings, and watch the sunset over the monolith. Their Uluru-Kata Tjuta Cultural Centre near the base of the Rock has good displays of cultural and Dreamtime life. See chapter 8.
- **Mangarrayi People** (Katherine, NT): Mike Keighley of **Far Out Adventures** (☎ 08/8972 2552) takes tours to the beautiful Elsey Station where you get to visit with the children of the local Mangarrayi people. You'll get to sample bush tucker, learn a little bush medicine, and swim in a vine-clad natural "spa-pool" in the Roper River. See chapter 9.

- **Yamatji Bitja Aboriginal Bush Tours** (Kalgoorlie, WA): Geoffrey Stokes, who was brought up living a traditional Aboriginal life out in the bush near Kalgoorlie, takes you out tracking animals, foraging for bush food, and even hunting a 'roo for dinner (with a gun, not a boomerang!). Explore the bush, learn about creation myths, and find out what his childhood was like. See chapter 10.
- **Tandanya Aboriginal Cultural Institute** (Adelaide, SA): This is a great place to experience Aboriginal life through Aboriginal eyes. You might catch one of the dance or other performances, although there are plenty of other opportunities to find out more about Aboriginal culture. See chapter 11.

9 The Best of Small-Town Australia

- **Central Tilba** (NSW): Just inland from Narooma on the south coast, this hamlet is one of the cutest you'll ever see, complete with its own blacksmiths and leatherwork outlets. The ABC Cheese Factory offers visitors free tastings, while you can spend hours browsing for antiques or admiring the period buildings. See chapter 5.
- **Broken Hill** (NSW): Known for its silver mines, the quirky town of Broken Hill has more pubs per capita than just about anywhere else. It's also the home of the School of the Air—a "classroom" transmitting lessons by radio to isolated communities spread over thousands of miles of Outback. You'll also find the eccentric Palace Hotel, featured in the movie *The Adventures of Priscilla, Queen of the Desert*, as well as colonial mansions and heritage homes. See chapter 5.
- **Mission Beach** (QLD): You'd never know this tidy village, hidden in lush rain forest off the highway, existed if you weren't a well-informed traveler. Aussies know it's here, but few of them bother to patronize its dazzling beach, cute restaurants, and secluded rain forest trails, so you'll have the place all to yourself. There's great white-water rafting on the nearby Tully River, too. See chapter 7.
- **Broome** (WA): This romantic pearling port on the far-flung Kimberley coast on the Indian Ocean blends Australian corrugated-iron architecture with red pagoda roofs left by the Chinese pearl divers who settled here. The town combines a sophisticated international ambience with a rough Outback attitude. Beautiful Cable Beach (see "The Best Beaches" above) is just outside town. This is the place to add to your South Sea pearl collection. See chapter 9.
- **Kalgoorlie** (WA): Vibrant Kalgoorlie sits on what used to be the richest square mile of gold-bearing earth ever. Have a drink in one of the 19th-century pubs (especially at night when the miners come on shift), peer into the open-cut gold mine (the world's biggest), descend an old-fashioned mine shaft and pan for riches, and wander the ghost town streets of Coolgardie. See chapter 10.
- **Hahndorf** (SA): A group of Lutheran settlers founded this German-style town, located in the Adelaide Hills, just outside the Adelaide, in the 1830s. You'll love the churches, the wool factory and craft shops, and the delicious German food served up in the local cafes, restaurants, and bakeries. See chapter 11.
- **Coober Pedy** (SA): For a *fair dinkum* (that means "genuine") Outback experience, few places are as weird and wonderful as this opal-mining town in the middle of nowhere. You can visit mines, wacky museums, and stay in a hotel underground—which is not really that unusual considering all the locals live like moles anyway. See chapter 11.
- **Launceston** (TAS): Tasmania's second city is not much larger than your average European or American small town, but it's packed with Victorian and Georgian

architecture and plenty of remnants of Australia's convict days. Spend a couple of days here discovering the town and the local scenery, and splurge a little on a stay in a historic hotel. See chapter 15.

10 The Best Museums

- **National Maritime Museum** (Sydney, NSW): The best things about this museum are the ships and submarines often docked in the harbor out front. You can climb aboard and explore what it's like to be a sailor. Inside are some fascinating displays relating to Australia's dependence on the oceans. See chapter 4.
- **Telegraph Station Historical Reserve** (Alice Springs, NT): It's not called a museum, but that's what this restored telegraph repeater station out in the picturesque hills by a spring—Alice Springs—really is. From the hot biscuits turned out of the wood-fired oven to the old telegraph equipment tapping away, this 1870s settlement is as real as history can get. See chapter 8.
- **Australian Aviation Heritage Centre** (Darwin, NT): The pride of this hangar is a B-52 bomber on permanent loan from the U.S. But there's loads more, not just planes, engines, and aviation paraphernalia, but detailed stories, jokes, and anecdotes associated with the exhibits—put together by enthusiastic members of the Aviation Historical Society of the Northern Territory. See chapter 9.
- **Warradjan Aboriginal Cultural Park** (Kakadu National Park, NT): This circular building was built in the shape of a pignose turtle at the direction of the Aboriginal owners. Exhibits about the bush tucker, Dreamtime creation myths and lifestyles of the local Bininj Aboriginal people are on display. See chapter 9.
- **Western Australian Museum** (Perth, WA): Skip the natural history displays and head straight to the country's best display of Aboriginal culture. Evocative photographs, artifacts, and display boards paint a sad and thoughtful portrait of Australia before and after the arrival of Europeans. See chapter 10.
- **York Motor Museum** (York, WA): This multimillion-dollar collection of veteran, vintage, classic, and racing cars is one of the most wide-ranging in the country. If you're a car buff, head for the historic town of York and make a day of it. See chapter 10.
- **Migration Museum** (Adelaide, SA): This fascinating museum gives visitors insight into the people who came to Australia, how and where they settled, and how many suffered getting here. Full of interactive activities and exhibits, the museum gives visitors much more to do than just look and read. See chapter 11.
- **Australian War Memorial** (Canberra, ACT): Given its name, you might think this museum is a bleak sort of place, but you'd be wrong. The museum gives important insight into the Anzac (Australian and New Zealand Army Corps) spirit, including an evocative exhibit on the tragic battle of Gallipoli. There's also a pretty good art collection. See chapter 14.

11 The Best Moderately Priced Accommodations

- **Explorers Inn** (☎ 1800/623 288 in Australia or 07/3211 3488) and **Hotel George Williams** (☎ 1800/064 858 in Australia or 07/3308 0700) both in Brisbane, QLD: These two hotels around the corner from each other in Brizzie are shining examples of what cheap hotels should be—trendy, clean, and bright with useful facilities like electronic keys, and an inexpensive restaurant. See chapter 6.
- **Kuranda Rainforest Resort** (Kuranda, QLD; ☎ 1800/806 996 in Australia or 07/4093 7555): Tucked away in the rain forest in the mountaintop village of

Kuranda, these cozy timber slab cabins are a good alternative to staying among the tacky souvenir shops of Cairns. A free shuttle bus takes you into Cairns every day to meet up with Great Barrier Reef cruises and other tours. See chapter 7.

- **Bahia Beachfront Apartments** (the Gold Coast, QLD; ☎ 07/5538 3322): They're no shakes in the glamour-puss stakes, but these comfortable apartments are big and airy, and most have great views of the beach—all for just A$115 (U.S.$80.50) for a double in high season. See chapter 7.
- **Archipelago Studio Apartments** (Port Douglas, QLD; ☎ 07/4099 5387): They may be tiny, but these pretty apartments have a homey atmosphere and are just seconds from spectacular Four Mile Beach. Some units have sea views. The solicitous proprietor is a mine of advice on things to see and do. See chapter 7.
- **Miss Maud Swedish Hotel** (Perth, WA; ☎ 1800/998 022 in Australia or 08/9325 3900): Staying at this slightly musty hotel in the heart of Perth is like staying at grandma's—even if your grandma's house doesn't have Swedish murals on the walls. Friendly staff members who actually look pleased to see you and great food complete the picture. See chapter 10.
- **North Adelaide Heritage Apartments and Cottages** (Adelaide, SA; ☎ 08/8272 1355): These accommodations actually consist of 18 separate fabulous properties in North Adelaide and Eastwood. The former Friendly Meeting Chapel Hall resembles a small church stocked with Victorian antiques. Another memorable place is the George Lowe, Esq. apartment done up in the style of a 19th-century gentleman's bachelor pad. See chapter 11.
- **York Mansions** (Launceston, TAS; ☎ 03/6334 2933): If you feel that where you stay is as important to your visit as what you see, then don't miss out on a night or two here. This National Trust-classified building has five spacious apartments, each with a distinct character. It's like living the high life in the Victorian age. See chapter 15.

12 The Best Alternative Accommodations

- **Underground Motel** (White Cliffs, NSW; ☎ 1800/02 1154 in Australia or 08/8091 6677): All but two of this motel's rooms are underground in this fascinating opal-mining town. Rooms are reached by a maze of spacious tunnels dug out of the rock. See chapter 5.
- **Whitsunday Wilderness Lodge** (The Whitsunday Islands, QLD; ☎ 07/4946 9777): The 10 beachfront cabins are basic, but your vacation at this island retreat will be anything but. Activities include sea kayaking, sailing, snorkeling, hiking rain forest trails, dining outside under the Milky Way, and swimming with Myrtle, the pet kangaroo. Considering you won't put your hand in your wallet except for wine and maybe a seaplane trip to the Reef, this is a great value. See chapter 7.
- **Binnaburra Mountain Lodge** (☎ 1800/074 260 in Australia or 07/5533 3622) and **O'Reilly's Rainforest Guesthouse** (☎ 1800/688 722 in Australia or 07/5544 0644), both in the Gold Coast Hinterland, QLD: Tucked snugly almost 1,000 meters (3,280 ft.) up on rain forested ridges behind the Gold Coast, these retreats offer fresh mountain air and instant access to Lamington National Park. At O'Reilly's you can hand-feed brilliantly colored rain forest birds every morning. See chapter 7.
- **Emma Gorge Resort** (The Kimberley, WA; ☎ 08/9169 1777): At this spick-and-span settlement on the 1-million acre El Questro cattle station, guests stay in safari tents with wooden floors and electric lights, eat at a rustic gourmet

restaurant, and join in hikes, bird-watching tours, river cruises, and more. A hike up Emma Gorge takes you to an Edenic swimming hole surrounded by red cliffs. See chapter 9.

- **Prairie Hotel** (Flinders Ranges, SA; ☎ **08/8648 4844**): This remarkable tin-roofed, stone-walled Outback pub in the Flinders Ranges has quaint rooms, a great bar out front where you can meet the locals, and some of the best food in Australia. See chapter 11.
- **Freycinet Lodge** (Freycinet National Park, Coles Bay, TAS; ☎ **03/6257 0101**): These eco-friendly bush cabins are right next to one of the nation's best walking tracks. The ocean views from the magnificent restaurant and the surrounding balconies are spectacular. See chapter 15.

13 The Best Places to Stay on a Shoestring

- **Sydney Central YHA** (Sydney, NSW; ☎ **02/9281 9111**): One of the biggest, busiest youth hostels in the world, this place has a popular night spot, a bistro selling cheap meals, a convenience store, pool tables, a movie room, a heated swimming pool, and a sauna—all in the center of Sydney. See chapter 3.
- **Holiday Village Backpackers** (Byron Bay, NSW; ☎ **02/6685 8888**): For a bohemian kind of place, this Byron Bay lodging is loaded with comforts. You can stay in a dorm room if you want, but for a couple of dollars more you can get a fully self-contained unit with a bedroom, lounge, and kitchen area. There's also a volleyball court, a spa and pool, and a TV and video lounge. Cool. See chapter 5.
- **Halse Lodge** (Sunshine Coast, QLD; **1800/242 567** in Australia, or 07/5447 3377): How many backpacker lodges do you know located in Heritage-listed Queenslander houses, with neat private rooms, meals for less than A$7.15 (U.S.$5), a wide verandah with attractive furniture and garden views, an atmospheric bar and courtyard, and free surfboards to use at the (excellent) beach just a stroll away? Well, now you know this one. See chapter 7.
- **Beachcomber Coconut Caravan Village** (Mission Beach, QLD; ☎ **07/4068 8129**): Right across the road from what is arguably the prettiest beach in Australia, this oh-so-pretty campground has freshly painted cabins with little balconies, en suite bathrooms, cooking facilities, and even separate bedrooms for you and the kids. Cassowaries wander out of the dense jungle at the back and come right up to you. See chapter 7.
- **The Kimberley Club** (Broome, WA; ☎ **08/9192 3233**): Low-slung Outback architecture, trendy blue walls and yellow curtains in the private rooms, a rustic open-sided bar and restaurant serving great food, and a rock-lined swimming pool make this one of the coolest places to stay in pricey Broome. See chapter 9.

14 The Best Worth-a-Splurge Restaurants

- **Mezzaluna** (Sydney, NSW; ☎ **02/9357 1988**): Come here for truly exquisite food, flawless service, and a great view across the city's western skyline. The main dining room opens onto a huge, all-weather terrace kept warm in winter by giant, overhead fan heaters. Don't miss it. See chapter 3.
- **Fishlips Bar & Bistro** (Cairns, QLD; ☎ **07/4041 1700**): Clever ways with fresh seafood and other Aussie ingredients—such as crocodile—make this cheerful blue beachhouse on a busy Cairns highway a real winner. This place is the pick of the bunch in Cairns. See chapter 7.

- **Zouí Alto** (Townsville, QLD; ☎ **07/4721 4700**): Townsville is not a place that springs to mind when compiling a "Best Restaurants" list, but this rooftop venue fully deserves to be here for faultless Mediterranean fare and fab views of the bay. It's one of the best places to eat on the Queensland coast. See chapter 7.
- **Fraser's** (Perth, WA; ☎ **08/9481 7100**): The city center and Swan River sparkling in the sunshine seem so close that you can almost reach out and touch them from the terrace of this parkland restaurant. Superb Mod Oz food turned out with flare and flavor is what you come here for; seafood is a specialty. Go for a bike ride in Kings Park afterwards to work it off. See chapter 10.
- **Newtown House** (Vasse, near Margaret River, WA; ☎ **08/9755 4485**): Chef Stephen Reagan makes intelligent, flavorsome food that beautifully partners the premium Margaret River wines being made all around him. Stay in his homestead B&B overnight and explore the wineries the next day. See chapter 10.
- **Prairie Hotel** (Flinders Ranges, SA; ☎ **08/8648 4895**): Chef Darren ("Bart") Brooks serves up some very high-class cuisine in the middle of nowhere. His "feral" foods, such as kangaroo tail soup and a mixed grill of emu sausages, camel steak, and kangaroo, is remarkable. See chapter 11.
- **The Tryst** (Canberra, ACT; ☎ **02/6239 4422**): Canberra has far grander and more expensive restaurants, but this place has found a spot in our hearts for its constantly delicious food. It's also relaxed, feeling almost communal on busy nights. See chapter 14.

15 The Best Dining Bargains

- **Returned Services League (RSL) Clubs:** RSL clubs, or their equivalent, can be found in most cities and towns in Australia. Just sign in at the door and you enter a world of cheap drinks and inexpensive meals. You'll probably find a couple of pool or billiards tables too, as well as an atmosphere unique to Australia.
- **The Great Aussie BBQ:** Australian parks are full of public barbecues, often in scenic settings, that are free or cost just a couple of dollars to coin operate. Stock up on meat, veggies, paper plates, plastic glasses, and cheap cooking utensils you can buy from the supermarket, and get ready to cook up a storm. Hand the utensils on to someone else if you can't be bothered carrying them in your suitcase.
- **Govindas** (Sydney, NSW; ☎ **02/9380 5155**): Eat as much as you want at this Hare Krishna vegetarian restaurant in Kings Cross, and then take in a free movie in the theatre upstairs. See chapter 3.
- **No Names** (Sydney, NSW; ☎ **02/9360 4711**). Choose between plates of spaghetti, fish, or meats and fill yourself up on the cheap at this Italian-style cafeteria. Just order your meal off the blackboard. Be sure to bring your own wine, or quaff the free fruit cordial drinks. See chapter 3.
- **Bowen Mangoes:** Queensland produces the best mangoes in Australia, and Bowen, a small coastal town between the Whitsundays and Townsville, produces the best mangoes in Queensland. Look for the mangoes in supermarkets. If you are lucky enough to be driving through north Queensland in summer, you might snare some from roadside sellers at a good price: A$3 (U.S.$2.10) per mango is expensive, A$2 (U.S.$1.40) is fine, A$1 (U.S.70¢) is a steal. See chapter 7.
- **The Pioneer Barbecue and Bar** (Ayers Rock Resort, NT; ☎ **1800/089 622** in Australia, or 08/8956 2170): Forget the expensive eats at Ayers Rock Resort and join the happy throng at this rollicking bar-cum-shearer's mess. Throw your shrimp, steak, or emu sausage on your own barbie, have a beer or two, and you're still looking at a tab of less than A$28.60 (U.S.$20). See chapter 8.

- **A Picnic on the Grounds of the Old Telegraph Station** (Alice Springs, NT): What could be more enjoyable (and affordable) than an alfresco spread on the grounds of this historic site. You'll be surrounded by river red gums, green lawns, and a few historic cottages. Admission to the picnic grounds is free. See chapter 8.
- **Mindil Beach Markets** (Darwin, NT): Every Thursday night between May and October, thousands of Darwin folk pack wine and beach blankets and flock to this city beach to feast at food stalls from every Asian cuisine you can name, and a few you can't. Eat Vietnamese, Cambodian, Singaporean, Malaysian, Indonesian, and more, and then shop the 200 arts-and-crafts stalls, get a Chinese head massage, or have your tarot cards read. See chapter 9.
- **Queen Victoria Market** (Melbourne, VIC): The markets are the heart of this vibrant city, and there's nowhere better to pick up a satisfying snack. The pizzas on sale at Café Bianca are some of the best in Australia, and there are plenty of stalls selling fresh bread and deli produce for a sandwich to take away. See chapter 12.
- **Chinatown** (Melbourne, VIC): Head to this colorful part of town, centered on Little Bourke Street, for super-cheap ethnic eats. You'll be hard-pressed to find a lunch costing more than A$5 (U.S.$3.50). This is where the locals go, so you know it's got be good (and authentic). See chapter 12.

Planning an Affordable Trip to Australia

2

by Marc Llewellyn

This chapter aims to answer all those practical questions that pop up as you plan your trip—How will I get there? How much will it cost? What should I see? How will I get around? Australia's a big country, and you probably won't be able to see all of it, so in this chapter and the rest of the book we give you no-nonsense advice on what's worth your time and money and what's not. We've done the legwork—finding the best deals on airfares, package deals, outdoor adventures, accommodations, and more—so you won't have to.

1 The Regions in Brief

People who have never visited Australia always wonder why such a huge country has a population of just 18 million people. In fact, Australia can barely support that many. The majority of Australia is harsh **Outback** country, characterized by salt bush plains, arid brown crags, shifting sand deserts, and salt lake country. The soil in the Outback is poor; it hardly ever rains, and the rivers barely make it to the ocean. Nearly 90% of Australia's population lives in an area that covers only 2.6% of the continent. Climatic and physical land conditions ensure that the only decent rainfall occurs along a strip of land around Australia's eastern coastal fringe.

If Australia knows the harsh hand of Mother Nature, though, it also knows her bounty. The Queensland coast is blessed with one of the greatest natural attractions in the world: the **Great Barrier Reef.** The Reef stretches some 2,000-plus kilometers (1,250 miles) from off Gladstone in Queensland, to the Gulf of Papua, near New Guinea. It's home to approximately 1,500 kinds of fish and 400 species of corals.

Australia is made up of six states: New South Wales, Queensland, Victoria, South Australia, Western Australia, and Tasmania—and two internal "territories"—the Australian Capital Territory (ACT) and the Northern Territory. The capital is Canberra, located in the ACT.

This book isn't organized along state and territory lines, however. It's organized more in accordance with the way Australians think of the country and travelers will experience it.

NEW SOUTH WALES Australia's most populated state is also the one most visited. Mostly, they come to Sydney, one of the most glamorous cities in the world. The Sydney Harbour Bridge and the Sydney Opera House are major draws, but no one leaves without remarking

Australia

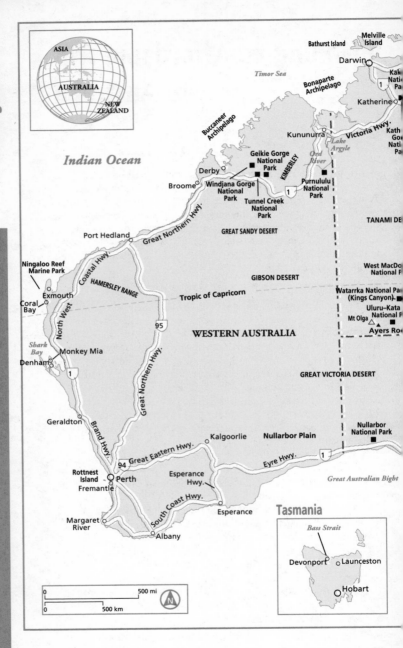

ASIA

AUSTRALIA

NEW ZEALAND

Timor Sea

Bathurst Island

Melville Island

Darwin

Kak Nati Pa

Katherine

Bonaparte Archipelago

Buccaneer Archipelago

Kununurra

Victoria Hwy.

Kath Go Nati Pa

Indian Ocean

Geikie Gorge National Park

Derby

Ord River

Lake Argyle

KIMBERLEY

Broome

Windjana Gorge National Park

Tunnel Creek National Park

Purnululu National Park

GREAT SANDY DESERT

TANAMI DE

Port Hedland

Great Northern Hwy.

Coastal Hwy.

Ningaloo Reef Marine Park

HAMERSLEY RANGE

GIBSON DESERT

West MacDo National F

Exmouth

Tropic of Capricorn

Watarrka National Pa (Kings Canyon)

Coral Bay

North West

95

WESTERN AUSTRALIA

Uluru–Kata National P

Mt Olga

Ayers Roc

Shark Bay

Monkey Mia

Denham

Great Northern Hwy.

GREAT VICTORIA DESERT

Geraldton

Brand Hwy.

Kalgoorlie

Nullarbor Plain

Nullarbor National Park

Rottnest Island

Perth

94

Great Eastern Hwy.

Eyre Hwy.

Fremantle

Esperance Hwy.

Margaret River

South Coast Hwy.

Esperance

Great Australian Bight

Albany

Tasmania

Bass Strait

Devonport

Launceston

Hobart

0 — 500 mi

0 — 500 km

N

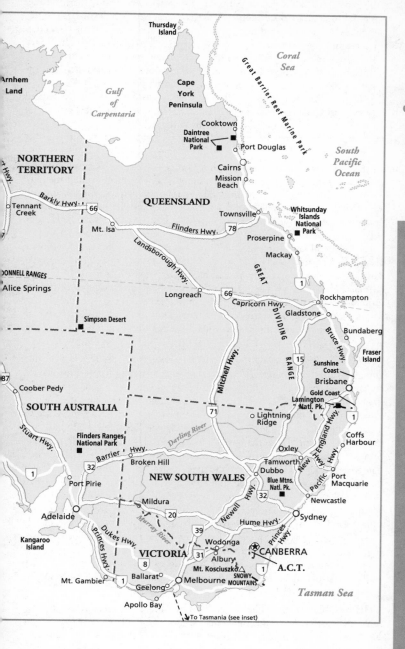

Thursday Island

Coral Sea

Arnhem Land

Gulf of Carpentaria

Cape York Peninsula

Great Barrier Reef Marine Park

Cooktown
Daintree National Park
Port Douglas

South Pacific Ocean

NORTHERN TERRITORY

Barkly Hwy.

Cairns
Mission Beach

Tennant Creek

66

Mt. Isa

QUEENSLAND

Landsborough Hwy.

Flinders Hwy. 78

Townsville

Whitsunday Islands National Park

Proserpine

Mackay

DONNELL RANGES
Alice Springs

Longreach 66

Capricorn Hwy.

GREAT DIVIDING RANGE

Rockhampton
Gladstone

Simpson Desert

Bundaberg

Bruce Hwy.

15

Fraser Island

Sunshine Coast

87
Coober Pedy

SOUTH AUSTRALIA

Mitchell Hwy.

71

Brisbane
Gold Coast
Lamington Natl. Pk.

1

Stuart Hwy.

Flinders Ranges National Park

Lightning Ridge

Coffs Harbour

Barrier Hwy.
Broken Hill

Darling River

Oxley

New England Hwy.

Pacific Hwy.

32

1
Port Pirie

NEW SOUTH WALES

Tamworth
Dubbo
Blue Mtns. Natl. Pk.

Port Macquarie

Mildura

20

Newell Hwy.

32

Newcastle

Adelaide

Murray River

Hume Hwy.

Sydney

39

Kangaroo Island

Dukes Hwy.

Princes Hwy.

Wodonga
Albury

31

CANBERRA
A.C.T.

Mt. Gambier

1

Ballarat

8

VICTORIA

Geelong

Melbourne

Mt. Kosciuszko
SNOWY MOUNTAINS

1

Princes Hwy.

Apollo Bay

To Tasmania (see inset)

Tasman Sea

In September 2001 Ansett Australia, the country's second-largest airline, serving international and domestic destinations, and its subsidiaries (Hazelton Airlines, Kendell Airlines, Skywest Airlines, and Aeropelican) suspended operations. New owners reorganized the company, dubbed "Ansett, Mark II," packaging it as a budget/no frills airline, and resumed domestic service (including on its regional subsidiaries) in October. The Australian government guaranteed tickets purchased on the airline through early 2002.

Contact Ansett (☎ **13 13 00** in Australia, **888/426-7388** in the United States and Canada; www.ansett.com.au) for the latest updates, prices and bookings to cities and regions served by Ansett Mark II.

on the beauty of the dozens of harbor and ocean beaches around the city, and the dramatic mixture of bushland and city development around the harbor itself. You could spend months getting to know Sydney, and set aside at least a week for all the major tourist attractions. Sydney is also a good base to discover inland areas like the Blue Mountains and the wineries of the Hunter Valley.

Farther afield is a string of beachside towns stretching down the southern coast into Victoria. Along the north coast are areas of rain forest, national parks, and a more tropical air, in laid-back hangouts such as Coffs Harbour.

Inland New South Wales is dry and sparsely forested. Intriguing regions to explore are the area around Broken Hill in the western part of the state, for its wildlife and Aboriginal influences, and the Outback opal-mining towns of White Cliffs and Lightning Ridge, which exist in a wacky underground world.

QUEENSLAND   Without a doubt, the biggest draw in Queensland is the Great Barrier Reef. Coming to Australia and not visiting the Reef is a bit like going to Paris and bypassing the Eiffel Tower. Ogling the tropical fish, weird sea creatures, and rainbow-hued corals will be a highlight of your Aussie holiday. The Reef stretches some 2,000-plus kilometers (1,240 miles) along Queensland's coast, and anywhere from Bundaberg north is a good place to see it. Alluring island resorts are dotted along the Reef, and while most are expensive, we clue you in the ones that won't break the bank.

Aside from the Reef, Queensland is also known for its white sand beaches. The best are on the Gold Coast in the state's south, though the Sunshine Coast has some lovely ones. Cairns and Port Douglas in the north have more than their fair share of beaches too, but unfortunately, deadly box jellyfish call a halt to all ocean swimming from October to May anywhere north of Gladstone. Queensland also offers the 74 tropical Whitsunday Islands. These mostly uninhabited islands are a paradise for water sports, sea kayaking, diving, fishing, hiking through rain forest, and best of all, sailing.

Away from the coast, the biggest attraction in the state is the lush 110-million-year-old Daintree Rain Forest, just north of Port Douglas. The capital, Brisbane, has Australia's largest koala sanctuary.

THE RED CENTRE   The eerie silence of Uluru, also called Ayers Rock, is what pulls everyone to the sprawling crimson sands of the Red Centre, the heart of the Northern Territory. Most folks discover that they like the nearby towering domes of Kata Tjuta, also known as the Olgas, even more than Ayers. A half-day's drive from the Rock brings you to Kings Canyon, a sheer orange desert gorge popular with hikers. If you visit the Red Centre, try to schedule some time in Alice Springs. This Outback town has the best Aboriginal arts and crafts shopping in Australia, some fun Aboriginal tours, a desert wildlife park, wonderful scenery, a little local history to explore, hikes through the stark MacDonnell Ranges, and, of all things, camel rides down a dry river bed.

Don't make the common mistake of flying into the Rock one day and flying out the next. Give yourself time to soak up the timeless peace of the Aussie desert. One of the best ways to appreciate it is on a 3-day 4WD safari, where you camp out under the Southern Cross and cook around a campfire.

THE TOP END The northwest reaches of Oz, from the dramatic Kimberley in Western Australia to the northern third of the Northern Territory, encompass what Aussies dub "the Top End." This is Mick "Crocodile" Dundee territory, a remote, vast, hot semi-desert region. Near Darwin, the Territory's capital, is Kakadu National Park, where you can cruise past crocodiles, bird-watch, and visit ancient Aboriginal rock art sites. Closer to Darwin is Litchfield National Park, where you can take a dip in fern-fringed water holes surrounded by red cliffs. You can cruise the orange walls of Katherine Gorge, a few hours south of Darwin, or explore them by canoe. You can even make your own dot painting at an Aboriginal community near Katherine.

In the Western Australia section of the Top End, you can visit ancient Geikie and Windjana gorges, pearl farms where the world's best South Sea pearls grow, and the charming—in a corrugated-iron sort of way—town of Broome. This tract of the country is under-explored, even by Aussies. Near Kununurra, on the eastern edge of the Kimberley, is a 1-million-acre cattle station, El Questro, where you can camp in safari tents, fish for barramundi, hike the bush to Aboriginal rock art, and dine on modern Oz cuisine. In Kununurra you can cruise on the bird-rich and croc-infested Ord River and tour the Argyle Diamond Mine, the world's biggest.

WESTERN AUSTRALIA One of the least-visited states (largely because distance and airfares work against it), Western Australia is also the state with the most untamed natural beauty. The seas here teem with whales, and thrill-seekers can swim alongside gentle giant whale sharks on the Northwest Cape every fall (Mar–June). Snorkelers gawk at corals and fish on Rottnest Island, 19 kilometers (12 miles) off Perth, and in World Heritage-listed Shark Bay, tourists greet wild dolphins at Monkey Mia.

In the southwest "hook" of the continent lies the Margaret River wine region. Along with wild forests, thundering surf, dramatic cliffs, rich bird life and wild 'roos, it's also one of the country's most attractive wine regions. The state capital, Perth, provides an interesting visit, with excellent beaches and the restored 19th-century port of Fremantle. One- or two-hour drives brings you to lovely towns, like York, the state's oldest inland settlement, and the monastery town of New Norcia. Inland, the state is mostly fields and desert, but if you have the time and inclination, head west 600 kilometers (373 miles) from Perth to the gold-mining town of Kalgoorlie. With its gracious old pubs lining the bustling streets, it's just what you think an Aussie country town should be.

SOUTH AUSTRALIA Stretched out between Western Australia and Victoria is the nation's bread basket, South Australia. The capital, Adelaide, is known for its conservatism, parks, and churches. It's a delightful stopover, offering magnificent accommodation options, and as a base for exploring the giant water bird sanctuary called the Coorong—the south's version of Kakadu. The other attraction is the South Australian Outback, where you can stay in an underground hotel in the offbeat opal-mining town of Coober Pedy, or ride a camel through the craggy, ancient arid Flinders Ranges.

The greatest of South Australia's attractions is Kangaroo Island, likely the best place in Australia to see native animals. In a single day—with the right guide—you can spot wallabies, rare birds, sea eagles, echidnas, seals, penguins, and walk along a beach loaded with sea lions. It's a must-see.

VICTORIA   Australia's second largest city, Melbourne, is the capital of Victoria. Melbourne is more stately than Sydney (it feels more Old World than Californian) and offers an exciting mix of cultures and fashion. Around Melbourne there's plenty to see and to do, including Phillip Island, famous for its Penguin Parade, where hundreds of tiny penguins dash up the beach to their burrows at dusk; and the gold-mining city of Ballarat. Victoria is also the site of one of Australia's great road trips along the Great Ocean Road, which stretches for 106 kilometers (64½ miles) along some of the most scenic coastline you will ever experience. Then there's inland, which in Victoria is mostly high country, the stuff of legends, à la *The Man from Snowy River*. The skiing's pretty good as well, if you're around in the Down Under winter.

AUSTRALIAN CAPITAL TERRITORY (ACT)   Surrounded entirely by New South Wales is the tiny Australian Capital Territory. The ACT is made up of bush land and the nation's capital, Canberra, an architecturally orchestrated city similar in concept to Washington, D.C. Many outsiders may consider the capital boring, but Canberra can surprise you. It has the country's best museums, so don't automatically exclude it from your itinerary.

TASMANIA   Finally, there's the last port before Antarctica, Hobart: capital of the island state of Tasmania, which offers beautiful parks, enormous stretches of wilderness, the world's best trout fishing, and a relaxed pace. You can tackle the most well-known hiking trail in Australia, the Overland Track, an 85-kilometer (53-mile) route between Cradle Mountain and Lake St. Clair that passes through highland moors and dense rain forests and traverses several mountains. Another option is a visit to Port Arthur, Australia's version of Devil's Island, where thousands of convicts were imprisoned and died. All Tasmania is spectacular, but at the top of the list is Freycinet National Park, with its pink granite outcrops set against an emerald-green sea.

2 How This Guide Can Save You Money

You might find it hard to believe that you can really travel and stay comfortably around this huge country for as little as $50 a day, but it can be done. In fact, Australia's abundance of family-run motels, authentic country pubs, cute B&Bs, and inexpensive ethnic restaurants offer a wide variety of great eating, welcoming accommodation and some of the most amazing sights you'll ever see, without sacrificing fun, comfort and adventure to a budget.

The "fifty-dollars-a-day" premise is based on the assumption of two adults traveling together who, between the two of them, have at least U.S.$100, or U.S.$50 per person, to spend per day on accommodations and meals. (We used a calculation of A$1 equals U.S.$.65. Recently, the Australian dollar has been faring badly against the U.S. dollar, at times as low as A$1 to U.S.$.50—so you may get more value for your money.) Sightseeing, entertainment, and transportation costs are extra, but we have unearthed loads of free and next-to-free ways for you to see the sights and get around without breaking the bank. Because airfare is likely to be the most expensive part of your trip, we provide tips on finding low-cost deals and packages.

But make no mistake: this isn't a backpacker's guide to Oz. Although the book includes the best backpacker-style accommodations and hostels, its aim is to suggest the best places to stay and dine at the best price. In fact, if you frequent the places recommended and follow our money-saving tips on transportation and sightseeing, you'll be traveling the same way most average Australians do. They would rather stay in a mid-priced country guesthouse that has a bit of charm, and eat at the cheap, fabulous Thai nosh-house, than pay a fortune to sit around a five-star resort's swimming pool eating $15 hamburgers.

3 Fifty Money-Saving Tips

Here's a handy roundup of 50 tips to help keep your travel costs to a minimum:

GENERAL TRAVEL

1. Even if you never set foot in a youth hostel, an all-time great buy is membership in the Australian Youth Hostels Association (AYHA), or its U.S. counterpart, Hostelling International-American Youth Hostels. It entitles you to a huge array of discounts. See "Youth Hostels and Backpacker Lodges" in "Tips on Accommodations," later in this chapter.

2. Try to buy a discounted ticket. Many companies, particularly airline ticket consolidators ("bucket shops") that buy tickets wholesale and some Australian tour companies, offer discounts for booking direct with them, rather than through a travel agent, to whom they must pay commission. Do check with the travel agent, too, to make sure you're getting the best deal, or if you have complex traveling needs.

3. When booking a hotel room at a major chain or renting a car from a major agency, be sure to mention which frequent-flier programs you belong to and ask whether you qualify for miles. If you have acquired a load of frequent-flier miles, they may be redeemable for award travel, lodging and other travel-related needs.

4. If you are a senior or student, be sure to ask about discounts at every opportunity—booking your airfare, hotel, rental car, sightseeing tour; when purchasing theater tickets; or visiting any museum or attraction.

5. Hotels, museums, cafes, and other places displaying the **International Youth Travel Card** (ITYC) logo offer discounts to cardholders. The card is available to anyone under 26, and is issued by the Federation of International Youth Travel Organizations for U.S.$17. Get it from STA Travel (☎ **800/781-4040** in the U.S., 800/836-4115 in Canada, 020/7361-6262 in the U.K., and 1300/360 960 in Australia).

6. Full-time students should have an **International Student Identification Card** (ISIC), available from STA Travel (see no. 5 above). For just U.S.$22, you get free or discounted access to tours, attractions, action pursuits, and even cafes.

7. Before you purchase travel insurance, check that you do not already have it as part of your credit card agreement or existing health insurance policy. If your current health insurance covers you fully for medical treatment and evacuation anywhere in the world and if your credit card company insures you against travel accidents if you buy plane, train, or bus tickets with its card (see "Health & Insurance" later in this chapter). Your homeowner's insurance should cover stolen luggage. However, if you have paid a large portion of your vacation expenses up front, it might be a good idea to buy trip cancellation insurance.

AIR TRAVEL

8. In terms of airfare, the off-season runs from mid-April to the end of August. This is not only the cheapest time to fly from America, but it's also the best time to visit Australia! That's because Down Under winter (June, July, and Aug), when the days are balmy and nice, is more pleasant than the too-hot summer (Dec, Jan, and Feb).

9. Traveling on certain days of the week can save you money. Monday to Thursday departures can shave an extra U.S.$60 off your Qantas airfare.

10. Consider a package. Whether you opt for an independent or group tour, package deals are terrific values because they typically include airfare (usually from Los Angeles), decent accommodations, some or all meals, tours, transfers, and other extras. The per-day price of a package (including airfare) can work out to be about the same as a night's accommodation in a midrange hotel.

11. Look for travel agents and consolidators specializing in cheap fares to Australia. See "Flying to Australia," later in this chapter for a list.

12. The quickest way between two points is not always the cheapest. Sometimes airlines and travel agents release spot specials for people prepared to travel via a lengthier route, or at short notice. If this is you, scour the travel sections of newspapers, and visit airline websites for the latest deals. Canada 3000 is such an airline; it flies to Australia via Honolulu and Fiji, and in the low season, it may be worth heading to Vancouver to catch Canada 3000's Sydney-bound flight.

13. The cheapest fares are usually the ones with the most restrictions. With Qantas's 21-day advance purchase Super-Apex fare, for example, you must pay for the ticket within 21 days after booking, stay at least a week and no more than a month in Australia, can't make stopovers, and you cannot change the routing once you have paid for the ticket. For many people, these conditions are fine for the trip they are planning.

14. Flying within Australia is expensive—but not if you prepurchase coupons from Qantas. The coupons can cost less than half the regular fares. Only non-Australians can buy them, and must buy them before you leave home.

15. Because air travel within Australia is so expensive, Qantas offers discounts of around 30% off regular fares for non-Australian passport holders. To obtain the discount, quote your passport number when booking your flight.

16. If you belong to a frequent-flier club, use your miles to contribute toward your airfare, or take advantage of any offers to buy miles at a reduced rate to reach an award level. If you are not already a frequent flier, join when you buy your ticket. The flight to Australia may earn you another trip!

17. To get even more frequent-flier miles, pay for your airline ticket on a credit card that gives you miles for every dollar you spend. Just be sure you don't get zapped with sky-high interest charges.

ACCOMMODATIONS

18. Airfare and accommodations will take the biggest bite out of your budget, so investigate package tours that include both plane ticket and five or more nights' accommodations—often at substantial savings for both.

19. If you get an apartment with a full kitchen, you can save money by not eating out at every meal. Australian cities and holiday destinations are awash with this kind of accommodation. Even if you only make breakfast every morning, you could save enough to splurge on a really special meal.

20. Try to avoid visiting Australia during the country's school holidays (see "When to Go" section later in this chapter). Hotel and apartment rates in popular vacation spots like the Gold Coast, the Sunshine Coast, and Cairns in Queensland go way up during the Australian school vacations.

21. Many accommodation chains offer discounted rates for customers of a particular car-rental company with which the hotel chain is partnered. When making your reservation or checking in, it never hurts to ask whether you qualify for a discount.

22. Bed-and-breakfasts are a friendly alternative to a cheerless motel room, and in Oz they're often quite cheap. Many pretty B&Bs charge A$75 (U.S.$48.75) or less for a double room with breakfast—about the same as a motel room without breakfast. We recommend many B&Bs; see later in this chapter for details on how to find more.

23. Youth hostels and backpacker lodges are not just for the young. Some are almost as good as resorts, with a pool, a tour desk, Internet access, and they often offer inexpensive meals. Many have basic but clean private rooms for well under A$50 (U.S.$32.50) for a double. As long as you can handle sharing a bathroom, these rooms are often the cheapest comfortable beds in town.

24. **YWCA** (☎ **1800/249 124** in Australia, or 03/9329 3363; www.travel-ys. com) has seven comfortable budget hotels around Australia with private rooms a cut above the average backpacker digs. Rates range from A$40 to $89 (U.S.$26–$57.85) double.

25. Many pubs, especially those in the country, offer lodging. Staying in a pub can be a money-saving option if you don't mind sharing a bathroom (some have private bathrooms, but don't expect it) and coping with the din of farmers drinking in the bar downstairs (often until midnight Friday and Saturday). The quality varies, but most rooms have a measure of historical charm. Rates can be as little as A$40 (U.S.$26) for a double and are rarely more than A$75 (U.S.$48.75); most include breakfast.

26. Most hotels accommodate kids up to age 12 (and even older) free of charge in your room if they use existing beds; if a hotel does charge extra for a child, it's usually only A$10 to 20 (U.S.$6.50–$13) at most.

LOCAL TRANSPORTATION

27. Bus travel in Oz is quite comfortable—the buses are clean, the seats are comfortable, and you sometimes even get a video onboard. Passes from the two national coach companies, Greyhound Pioneer and McCafferty's, represent great value, especially as some of them include tours.

28. Train fares in Australia cost about the same as bus fares, if you travel in a sitting berth (the seats recline somewhat). If you want a sleeper cabin, fares get expensive fast. Check out the money saving passes Rail Australia offers, outlined in "Getting Around," later this chapter.

29. Countrylink, which oversees rail travel in New South Wales, Victoria, and Queensland, offers advance-purchase discounts of up to 40%.

30. Before you book a rental car in Australia, consider whether you really need one. In major tourist towns like Alice Springs and Cairns, travelers fall into the trap of renting a car and then letting it sit outside their hotel the whole vacation, because every local tour company picked them up at the door. If you need a car only to drive into town for dinner, take a cab.

31. Fill up your rental car at a nearby gas station before you return it, not at the much-more-expensive car rental depot's pump.

32. Gas in cities is often cheaper on Mondays because most people fill up their tanks before the weekend.

33. Whether you go by air, rail, bus, or car, try not to backtrack. In a country as big as Australia, you can waste a lot of money retracing your steps.

34. Don't buy maps. Most visitor centers dispense free or next-to-free maps of the area. If you are a member of an automobile club with which the Australian Automobile Association (AAA) has a reciprocal agreement, you can often obtain free state, regional, and city road maps. The American Automobile Association, and the Automobile Associations in the U.K., Canada and New Zealand, have such an arrangement with Australia. Pick up the maps before you leave, or collect them at the AAA offices in Australia. See "Getting Around: By Car" for locations.

WINING & DINING

35. The letters to look for when dining out in Oz are BYO, which stands for Bring Your Own: buy wine or beer at the cheapest bottle shop ("liquor store" to Americans, "off-license" to Brits) you can find, and take it to the restaurant to drink with your meal. That way you avoid the markup of 100%, 200%, or more that restaurateurs are so fond of adding. All you pay is a corkage charge of around A$1 to $3 (U.S.65¢–$1.95) per person.

36. Go ethnic and you're almost guaranteed great food at low prices—Indian, Cambodian, Malaysian, Vietnamese, Italian, and Thai are all pretty sure bets. The smarter Chinese restaurants are good, but often a tad pricey, and not always BYO.

37. An advantage of going out for Asian food is that dishes are usually shared, so small eaters can get away with not ordering a whole meal for themselves (great for families). Because one Asian main course is often enough for two people, the golden rule is to order and eat one dish first, then order a second if you need it.

38. In cities, head to an Italian sidewalk cafe for tasty pasta and stylish sandwiches. A foccacia sandwich with salami, provolone cheese, sun-dried tomatoes, and arugula will set you back around A$8 (U.S.$5.20) and keep you going 'til dinner.

39. Backpacker lodges, youth hostels, and universities (colleges) almost always have restaurants or cafes attached, which serve up big portions of tasty, healthy food for not much money.

40. Tipping is not necessary, although it is common to tip 5% to 10% in restaurants and round cab fares up to the nearest A$1 (U.S.65¢). Plenty of Aussies don't tip, so don't feel embarrassed about hanging on to your coins.

41. If you are traveling by car, keep a box of cereal and long-life milk in the trunk and use the hotel coffee cups as bowls. It beats paying A$10 (U.S.$6.50) for the same thing in the hotel restaurant.

42. RSL (Returned and Services League) clubs and League clubs (as in Rugby League football) serve hearty meals—along the roast, chicken kiev, and steak lines, with vegetables or salad, and bread and potato included—for around A$10 (U.S.$6.50). You will have to sign in before you enter the club and put up with their uniquely lurid brand of neon-lit decor, but that's part of the fun. Kids' meals are about A$5 (U.S.$3.25).

TOURS & SIGHTSEEING

43. Australian city councils are big on providing free entertainment—for example, Sydney has free dance performances or concerts at Darling

Harbour many weekends, and free lunchtime concerts in Martin Place most days; Brisbane has street performers at South Bank Parklands most weekends; and Darwin has free Sunday Jazz by the sea at the MGM Grand Casino in Dry Season. Check local newspapers for details.

44. You can often get half-price theater tickets on the day of the performance. We've listed half-price ticket agencies in the "After Dark" sections of each chapter, where relevant. Matinees are often around A$8 (U.S.$5.20), cheaper than evening shows.

45. Walking tours can be half the price of bus tours, and they give you a good close-up view of the city and sights.

SHOPPING

46. Skincare products, cosmetics, perfume, electronics, imported designer accessories, liquor, cigarettes and other luxury items attract high duty in Australia. If you need to buy these products, get them in duty-free stores, which can be found in capital cities and major tourist destinations. You will need to show your airline ticket and passport to enter the store.

47. If you buy anything expensive—jewelry, for example—ask if there is a tax-free price for international travelers. Most non-duty-free stores selling jewelry, electronic equipment, and other high-ticket items offer tax-free prices to international travelers who show their airline ticket and passport.

48. Aboriginal artifacts make great souvenirs and gifts, but look for the shops just a block or two away from the center of town, which sell the same items a good bit cheaper than the ones on the main shopping streets.

NIGHTLIFE

49. There's no cover charge at pubs, and drinks here are cheaper than in nightclubs. Some have live entertainment, pool, and sports video screens.

50. Aussies love beer any time, but it never tastes better than during happy hour, that idyllic period from around 4 to 6pm when many city bars and pubs mark drinks down to half price or less. Happy hours are especially common Thursday and Friday, but any time of the week you are never far from a pub that makes an art form of brand-based specials.

4 Planning an Affordable Trip Online

Internet users can tap into the travel-planning databases that were once accessible only to travel agents. Sites such as **Travelocity, Expedia,** and **Orbitz** allow you to comparison shop for airfares, book flights, learn of last-minute bargains, and reserve hotel rooms and rental cars.

But don't fire your travel agent just yet! Although online booking sites offer tips and data, they can't endow you with the experience that makes a seasoned travel agent an invaluable resource, even in the Internet age. And for consumers with a complex itinerary, a trusty travel agent is still the best way to arrange the most direct flights to and from the best airports.

The benefits of researching your trip online can be well worth the effort:

- Some sites will send you **e-mail notification** when a cheap fare becomes available. Some will also tell you when fares to a place are lowest.

- All major airlines offer **incentives**—bonus frequent-flier miles, Internet-only discounts, sometimes even free cell phone rentals—when you purchase online or buy an e-ticket. You might also check to see if you can purchase frequent-flier miles from an airline if you are close to the number needed for award travel.

For an excellent travel planning resource, we highly recommend **Arthur Frommer's Budget Travel Online** (www.frommers.com). We're a little biased, but we guarantee you'll find the travel tips, reviews, monthly vacation giveaways, and online-booking capabilities thoroughly indispensable. Among the features are **Ask the Expert** bulletin boards, where Frommer's authors answer your questions via online postings; **Arthur Frommer's Daily Newsletter,** for the latest travel bargains and inside travel secrets; and Frommer's **Destinations archive,** where you'll get travel tips, hotel and dining recommendations, and advice on the sights for more than 200 destinations around the globe Once your research is done, the **Online Reservation System** (www.frommers.com/booktravelnow) takes you to Frommer's favorite sites for booking your vacation at affordable prices.

TRAVEL PLANNING & BOOKING SITES

The best travel-planning and booking sites cast a wide net, offering domestic and international flights, hotel and rental-car bookings, news, destination information, and deals on cruises and packages. Keep in mind that free (one-time) registration is often required. Because several airlines are no longer willing to pay commissions on tickets sold by online travel agencies, be aware that these online agencies will either charge a $10 surcharge if you book a ticket on that carrier or will not carry those airlines' offerings.

This section isn't intended to be a comprehensive list, but a discriminating selection of sites to get you started. Recognition is given to sites based on their content value and ease of use and isn't paid for—unlike some rankings, which are based on payment. Remember: This is a press-time snapshot of leading websites—some will have evolved or moved by the time you read this.

- **Travelocity** (www.travelocity.com or www.frommers.travelocity.com) and **Expedia** (www.expedia.com) are the most longstanding and reputable sites, each offering excellent selections and searches for complete vacation packages. Travelers search by destination and dates coupled with how much they're willing to spend.
- The latest buzz in online travel is about **Orbitz** (www.orbitz.com), launched by United, Delta, Northwest, American, and Continental airlines. It shows all possible fares for your trip, with fares lower than those available through travel agents. (At press time, travel-agency associations were waging an antitrust battle against this site.)
- **Qixo** (www.qixo.com) is another powerful search engine that allows you to search for flights and hotel rooms on 20 other travel-planning sites (such as Travelocity) at once. Qixo sorts results by price, after which you can book your travel directly through the site.

SMART E-SHOPPING

The savvy traveler is one armed with good information. Here are a few tips to help you navigate the Internet successfully and safely:

- **Know when sales start.** Last-minute deals may vanish in minutes. If you have a favorite booking site or airline, find out when last-minute deals are released to the public.
- **Shop around.** Compare results from different sites and airlines—and against a travel agent's best fare. If possible, try a range of times and alternate airports before you make a purchase.

- **Follow the rules of the trade.** Book in advance and choose an off-peak time and date if possible. Some sites will tell you when fares to a destination are cheapest.
- **Stay secure.** You should book only through secure sites (some airline sites aren't secure). Look for a key icon (Netscape) or a padlock (Internet Explorer) at the bottom of your web browser before you enter credit card information or other personal data.
- **Avoid online auctions.** Sites that auction airline tickets and frequent-flier miles are the number-one perpetrators of Internet fraud, according to the National Consumers League.
- **Maintain a paper trail.** If you book an e-ticket, print out a confirmation or write down your confirmation number and keep it safe and accessible—or your trip could be a virtual one!

ONLINE TRAVELER'S TOOLBOX

Veteran travelers usually carry some essential items to make their trips easier. Following is a selection of online tools to bookmark and use:

- **Visa ATM Locator** (www.visa.com/pd/atm) or **MasterCard ATM Locator** (www.mastercard.com/atm). Find ATMs in hundreds of cities in the U.S. and around the world.
- **Intellicast** (www.intellicast.com). Weather forecasts for all 50 states and cities around the world. *Note:* Temperatures are in Celsius for many international destinations.
- **Mapquest** (www.mapquest.com). The best of the mapping sites lets you choose a specific address or destination and will quickly return a map and detailed directions.
- **Cybercafes.com** (www.cybercafes.com) or **Net Cafè Guide** (www. netcafeguide.com/mapindex.htm). Locate Internet cafes at hundreds of places around the globe. Answer your e-mail and log onto the Web for a few dollars per hour.
- **Universal Currency Converter** (www.xe.net/currency). See what your dollar or pound is worth in more than 100 other countries.
- **U.S. State Department Travel Warnings** (www.travel.state.gov/travel_warnings.html). Reports on places where health concerns or unrest might threaten U.S. travelers. It also lists the locations of U.S. embassies around the world.

5 Visitor Information

The Australian Tourist Commission (ATC) is the best source of information on traveling Down Under. Its excellent website, **www.australia.com**, has more than 10,000 pages of listings for tour operators, hotels, car-rental companies, specialist travel outfitters, public holidays, maps, distance charts, suggested itineraries, and much more. It provides you with information tailored to travelers from your country of origin, including good-value packages, and deals. By signing up for the free online Travel Club, you will be e-mailed news of hot deals, major events, and the like on a regular basis. The ATC operates only a website to dispense information on Australia, not telephone lines.

The ATC publishes a general brochure called the *Australian Vacation Planning Kit,* but you may find it too general to be of much use.

The ATC maintains a network of **"Aussie Specialist"** travel agents in cities across the United States, Canada, the United Kingdom, New Zealand, and other countries. These agents receive continuous training and updates on destinations, hotels, deals, tours and the like in Oz. Get a referral to the nearest two Aussie Specialists by hitting the "Aussie Specialist" button on the main page on the ATC's website; or search the whole list by hitting the "Useful Resources" tab, also on the main page, then the "Contact Us" tab.

If you are online, you can contact the ATC's **Travel Counsellors** for help in piecing together an itinerary, or for answers to any other question about traveling in Australia. They attempt to reply within 48 hours.

Via phone, you can contact the ATC's **Aussie Helpline** numbers below to order brochures:

- **United States/Canada:** ☎ **800/333-4305** to locate an Aussie Specialist, or 661/775-2000 for recorded information on visas and other aspects of visiting Australia. You can be transferred to an operator who will give you the nearest two Aussie Specialists, and request an *Australian Vacation Planner.*
- **United Kingdom:** ☎ **09068/633 235** (charged at 60p/minute)
- **Ireland:** ☎ **01/402 6896**
- **New Zealand:** ☎ **1800/650 303** (toll-free outside Auckland) or 09/527 1629 (Both are called "Aussie Infolines" in New Zealand)

In the United Kingdom and Ireland, the letter they send you will contain a full list of Aussie Specialists in your country. The ATC also has brochure-ordering lines in many other countries.

The guide you are holding in your hand is an excellent source of information on Down Under, too! Do check with a travel agent. Don't forget to pump friends and neighbors who have been to Australia for their tips, as word-of-mouth recommendations (and warnings!) are always worth having. To snare the greatest amount of specific, i.e., useful, information, write to the local tourism bureaus of all the places you are keen to visit, requesting an information pack. The main drawback to this strategy is that some bureaus in small towns may not have the resources to mail you huge wads of brochures.

Another excellent information source are the websites of Australia's official state tourism marketing offices. You can contact them at:

- **Canberra Tourism:** www.canberratourism.com.au.
- **Northern Territory Tourist Commission:** www.Ntholidays.com, or www.insidetheoutback.com, which is written for North Americans.
- **South Australian Tourism Commission:** www.southaustralia.com.
- **Tourism New South Wales:** www.visitnsw.com.au, or www.seesydney.com if you live in the U.S., or www.sydneyaustralia.co.uk if you live in Great Britain.
- **Tourism Queensland:** www.queensland-holidays.com.au; or www.destinationqueensland.com, which is written for North Americans.
- **Tourism Tasmania:** www.discovertasmania.com.au.
- **Tourism Victoria:** www.visitvictoria.com.
- **Western Australian Tourism Commission:** www.westernaustralia.net

6 Entry Requirements & Customs

ENTRY REQUIREMENTS   Along with a current passport valid for the duration of your stay, the Australian government requires a visa from visitors of every nation (New Zealand citizens are issued a visa on arrival). The Australian government has streamlined the visa process with the **Electronic Travel Authority (ETA)**—an electronic or "paperless" visa that takes the place of a rubber stamp in your passport.

To get an ETA, give your passport details in person or over the phone to your travel agent, or the salesperson who books your plane ticket. This information will be entered into the airline's reservations system, which is linked to the Australian Department of Immigration and Multicultural Affairs' computer system. Assuming you are not wanted by Interpol, your ETA should be approved in a few seconds while you wait. You can also apply for an ETA at Australian embassies, high commissions, and consulates (see below).

Visa fees below are in Australian dollars; the exact amount charged by the Australian embassy, consulate or high commission in your country will depend on the foreign currency exchange rate.

Tourists should apply for a **Tourist ETA.** It's free and is valid for as many visits to Australia as you like of up to 3 months each within a 1-year period. Tourists may not work in Australia, so if you are visiting for business, you have two choices: apply for a free **Short Validity Business ETA,** which is valid for a single visit of 3 months within a 1-year period, or pay A$60 (U.S.$39) to apply for a **Long Validity Business ETA,** which entitles you to as many 3-month stays in Australia as you like for the life of your passport.

There are still some situations in which you will need to apply for a visa the old-fashioned way—by taking or mailing your passport, a completed visa application form, and the appropriate payment to your nearest Australian embassy or consulate: if your travel agent, airline, or cruise ship (if you arrive in Australia by sea) is not connected to the ETA system. In the United States, Canada, the United Kingdom, Ireland, and other countries, most agents and airlines are ETA-compatible, but cruise lines are not yet. You will also need to apply for a visa the old-fashioned way if you plan to enter Australia as something other than a tourist or a business traveler—for example, as a full-time, long-term student; a long-term resident; a sportsperson; a performer; or a member of a social group or cultural exchange.

If you are into one of the above, you will need to apply for a **Temporary Residence visa.** There is a A$60 (U.S.$39) processing fee for non-ETA tourist and business visas for stays of up to 3 months, and A$150 (U.S.$97.50) for business visas for stays between 3 months and 4 years. Non-ETA visa application fees for other kinds of travelers vary, from nil to thousands of dollars. Before you write a check, ask the nearest Australian embassy, consulate or high commission what forms of payment they accept.

Apply for non-ETA visas at Australian embassies, consulates, and high commissions. In the **United States,** your state of residence determines where you apply. In California, Arizona, New Mexico, Hawaii, Idaho, Montana, Nevada, New Mexico, Oregon, Utah and Washington, apply to the Australian Consulate-General, 2049 Century Park E., Level 19, Los Angeles, CA 90067-3238 (☎ **310/229-4800**). Anywhere else in the U.S., apply to the Australian Embassy, 1601 Massachusetts Ave. NW, Washington, DC 20036-2273 (☎ **202/797-3000**). The Australian Embassy website is **www.aust.emb.nw. dc.us.** In **Canada,** contact the Australian High Commission, 50 O'Connor St., no. 710, Ottawa, ON K1P 6L2 (☎ **613/783-7665**). For business visa inquiries in the United States and Canada call ☎ **800/579-7664.** In the **United Kingdom,** contact the Australian High Commission, Australia House, The Strand, London WC2B 4LA (☎ **09001/600 333** for 24-hour recorded information, or 020/7379 4334); or the Australian Consulate, Chatsworth House, Lever Street, Manchester M1 2QL (☎ **0161/228 1344**). In **Ireland,** contact the Australian Embassy, Fitzwilton House, Wilton Terrace, Dublin 2, Ireland (☎ **1/676 1517**). Travelers from Northern Ireland can lodge their applications in Dublin. The Australian government maintains a website tailored for a British audience at **www.australia.org.uk**.

You can get an application for a non-ETA visa at the **Australian Department of Immigration and Multicultural Affair's website** (www.immi.gov.au). This site also has a good explanation of the ETA system.

Allow at least a month for processing of non-ETA visas.

CUSTOMS & QUARANTINE   Anyone over 18 can bring into Australia no more than 250 cigarettes or 250 grams of cigars or other tobacco products, 1.125 liters (41 fl. oz.) of alcohol, and "dutiable goods" to the value of A$400 (U.S.$260), or A$200 (U.S.$130) if you are under 18. Broadly speaking, **"dutiable goods"** are luxury items like perfume concentrate, watches, jewelry, furs, plus gifts of any kind. Keep this in mind if you are bringing presents for family and friends in Australia; gifts given to you also count towards the dutiable limit. Your own personal goods that you're taking with you when you leave are usually exempt from duty. Customs officers do not collect duty of less than A$50 (U.S.$32.50) as long as you declared the goods in the first place. This means that it's technically legal to bring in two bottles of medium-priced booze—such as Johnny Walker Red—but you must declare them on your customs form and go through the red channel at the airport, and have nothing else of dutiable value which above the A$50 (U.S.$32.50) limit. If you have something you think might be dutiable but are not sure, contact the nearest Australian embassy or consulate (see above). You can also call the **Australian Customs Service** in Canberra, Australia (☎ **02/6275 6666**; www.customs.gov.au).

Many **firearms** and other weapons are prohibited from entry into Australia; any weapons that are not prohibited will require an import permit, which you must obtain before you arrive.

Cash in any currency, and other currency instruments such as traveler's checks, under a value of A$10,000 (U.S.$6,500) need not be declared.

Australia is a signatory to the Convention on International Trade in Endangered Species (CITES), which restricts or bans the import of products made from **protected wildlife.** Examples of restricted items are coral, giant clam, wild cats, monkey, zebra, crocodile or alligator, bear, some types of caviar, American ginseng, and orchid products. You will need an export license from the product's country of origin *and* an import license from Australia to bring restricted items into Australia. Banned items include ivory, tortoise (marine turtle) shell, products from rhinoceros or tiger, and sturgeon caviar. Bear this in mind if you stop in other countries en route to Australia where souvenirs made from banned or restricted items may be sold. Australian authorities may seize and not return the items to you.

Australia is an island, free of many agricultural and livestock diseases. To keep it that way, strict quarantine applies to importing plants, animals and their products, including food. Some items may be held for treatment and returned to you; others may be confiscated; others may be held for you to take with you when you leave. Amnesty trash bins are available before you reach the immigration counters in airport arrivals halls for items such as fruit. Don't be alarmed if, just before landing, the flight attendants spray the aircraft cabin (with products approved by the World Health Organization) to kill potentially disease-bearing insects. For more information on what is and is not allowed entry, contact the nearest Australian embassy or consulate, or the **Australian Quarantine and Inspection Service** (☎ **02/6272 3933**; www.aqis.gov.au).

The Australian Dollar, the U.S. Dollar & the British Pound

For U.S. Readers The rate of exchange used to calculate the dollar values given in this book was approximately A$1.54 (or A$1 = U.S.65¢).

For British Readers The rate of exchange used to calculate the pound values in the accompanying table was 1 British pound = A$2.50 (or A$1 = 40p).

Note: International exchange rates can fluctuate markedly. Check the latest rate when you plan your trip. The table below, and all the prices in this book, should only be used as a guide.

A$	U.S.$	U.K.£	A$	U.S.$	U.K.£
0.25	0.16	0.10	30.00	19.50	12.00
0.50	0.33	0.20	35.00	22.75	14.00
1.00	0.65	0.40	40.00	26.00	16.00
2.00	1.30	0.80	45.00	29.25	18.00
3.00	1.95	1.20	50.00	32.50	20.00
4.00	2.60	1.60	55.00	35.75	22.00
5.00	3.25	2.00	60.00	39.00	24.00
6.00	3.90	2.40	65.00	42.25	26.00
7.00	4.55	2.80	70.00	45.50	28.00
8.00	5.20	3.20	75.00	48.75	30.00
9.00	5.85	3.60	80.00	52.00	32.00
10.00	6.50	4.00	85.00	55.25	34.00
15.00	9.75	6.00	90.00	58.50	36.00
20.00	13.00	8.00	95.00	61.75	38.00
25.00	16.25	10.00	100.00	65.00	40.00

7 Money

CASH & CURRENCY The Australian dollar is divided into 100 cents. Coins come in 5¢, 10¢, 20¢, and 50¢ pieces (all silver in color) and $1 and $2 pieces (gold in color). The 50-cent piece is 12-sided. Prices in Australia often end in a variant of 1¢ and 2¢ (for example, 78 cents or $2.71), a relic from the days before 1-cent and 2-cent pieces were phased out (prices are rounded up or down to the nearest 5¢). Bank notes come in denominations of $5, $10, $20, $50, and $100.

ATMS The fastest, safest, and easiest method of managing money Down Under is to withdraw money from your home bank account at an Australian automatic teller machine (ATM). It's a way to get cash when banks and currency exchanges are closed, and your money is safe in your bank account at home until you withdraw it. You also get the bank exchange rate, not the higher commercial rate charged at currency exchanges. You will be charged a fee for each withdrawal, usually A$4 (U.S.$2.60) or so. It's your bank back home that charges this, not the Aussie bank, so ask your bank what the fee is.

All of the major banks in Australia—**ANZ, Commonwealth, National, and Westpac**—are connected to the Cirrus network, which has 465,000 ATMs around the world—and the Plus network, which has 265,000 ATMs.

Travel Tip

In Outback areas carry **cash** (several hundred dollars) and a credit card. ATMs are widely available in cities and towns, but they can be conspicuous by their absence in small country towns. Small merchants in remote parts may not cash traveler's checks.

Both **Cirrus** (☎ 800/424-7787; www.mastercard.com) and **Plus** (☎ 800/843-7587; www.visa.com) have automated ATM locators that list the banks in each country that will accept your card. You can also ask your bank at home for a directory of international ATM locations where your card is accepted. Most ATMs in Australia accept both 4- and 6-digit PINs (personal identification numbers), but it's a good idea to use a 4-digit PIN, as these are the most common, not just in Australia, but the rest of the world.

Few ATMs have letters on the keypads, so memorize your PIN by number.

CREDIT CARDS   **Visa** and **MasterCard** are universally accepted in Australia, but American Express and Diners Club much less so. Always carry some cash, as many merchants will not take cards for purchases under A$10 (U.S.$6.50) or so. If your credit card is linked to your bank account or you have a PIN for cash advances, you can get cash from an ATM (just keep in mind that interest starts accruing right away). Visa Cards are not accepted in Australia by taxi companies, so when you arrive and want to take a taxi, have some cash or another card handy.

TRAVELER'S CHECKS   Traveler's checks are a bit of an anachronism from the dark days before ATMs. Major towns and all cities in Australia have 24-hour ATMs, and virtually every establishment, even remote Outback gas stations, accepts credit cards. Traveler's checks are not as widely accepted.

If you do buy traveler's checks, get them in **Australian dollars.** Checks in U.S. dollars are accepted at banks, big hotels, currency exchanges, and shops in major tourist regions, but chances are shops, restaurants and any other kind of business will have no idea what the current exchange rate is when you present a U.S. check. Two of the largest Aussie banks, **ANZ** and **Westpac,** cash them for free. It will cost you around A$5 to $7 (U.S.$3.25–$4.55) to cash checks in foreign currency at an Australian bank.

THEFT   Almost every credit card company has an emergency toll-free number you can call if your wallet or purse is stolen. The Australia-wide numbers for the three major cards are **American Express** (☎ 1800/230 100), **MasterCard** (☎ 1800/120 113), and **Visa** (☎ 1800/125 440).

If you opt to carry traveler's checks, keep a record of their serial numbers, separately from the checks. To report a lost or stolen **American Express traveler's checks** call ☎ 1800/25 1902 anywhere in Australia.

Report your stolen wallet to the police, as your credit-card company or insurer may require a police report number.

8 When to Go

When the Northern Hemisphere has winter, Australia has summer in the Southern Hemisphere, and vice versa. That means mid-winter in Australia is July and August, and the hottest months are November to March. Unlike in the Northern Hemisphere, the farther *south* you go in Australia, the colder it gets.

Australia's Average Temperatures (°F) and Rainfall

	Jan	Feb	Mar	Apr	May	June	July	Aug	Sept	Oct	Nov	Dec
Adelaide												
Max	86	86	81	73	66	61	59	62	66	73	79	83
Min	61	62	59	55	50	47	45	46	48	51	55	59
Days of rain	2.8	2.5	8.5	9.4	10.3	8.4	7.6	7.6	6	4.9	3.2	3.2
Alice Springs												
Max	97	95	90	81	73	67	67	73	81	88	93	96
Min	70	69	63	54	46	41	39	43	49	58	64	68
Days of rain	4.8	3.9	8.6	7.8	8	2.6	2.1	2.1	0.6	1.9	3.5	4.4
Brisbane												
Max	85	85	82	79	74	69	68	71	76	80	82	85
Min	69	68	66	61	56	51	49	50	55	60	64	67
Days of rain	12.4	12.3	12.8	11.2	10.4	7.6	6.8	6.1	5.4	7	9.6	10.6
Cairns												
Max	90	89	87	85	81	79	78	80	83	86	88	90
Min	74	74	73	70	66	64	61	62	64	68	70	73
Days of rain	18.5	18.2	19.7	16.1	11.8	8.2	5.4	5.7	4.9	6.0	10.0	14.7
Canberra												
Max	82	82	76	67	60	53	52	55	61	68	75	80
Min	55	55	5	44	37	34	33	35	38	43	48	53
Days of rain	5.2	4.8	9.8	9.2	9.4	6.6	5.9	6.8	4.6	6.2	5.4	5.4
Darwin												
Max	90	90	91	92	91	88	87	89	91	93	94	92
Min	77	77	77	76	73	69	67	70	74	77	78	78
Days of rain	18	16.9	15.5	11.3	8.0	1.5	1.3	1.5	1.2	5.7	11.4	15.2
Hobart												
Max	71	71	68	63	58	53	52	55	59	63	66	69
Min	53	53	51	48	44	41	40	41	43	46	48	51
Days of rain	5.2	4.4	9.4	9.5	9.4	6.8	6.6	6.1	6.0	6.5	6.7	5.6
Melbourne												
Max	78	78	75	68	62	57	56	59	63	67	71	75
Min	57	57	55	51	47	44	42	43	46	48	51	54
Days of rain	5.2	5.0	9.8	9.9	9.7	6.6	6.1	6.1	6.5	7.2	6.5	6.1
Perth												
Max	85	85	81	76	69	64	63	67	70	76	81	73
Min	63	63	61	57	53	50	48	48	50	53	57	61
Days of rain	1.5	1.8	8.3	9.3	12.4	13.8	13.4	12.4	9.0	6.2	2.2	2.0
Sydney												
Max	78	78	76	71	66	61	60	63	67	71	74	77
Min	65	65	63	58	52	48	46	48	51	56	60	63
Days of rain	8.3	9.1	12.3	12.5	12.3	11.0	11.0	8.4	7.9	7.7	7.9	7.2

Source: Australian Tourist Commission Australia Vacation Planner.

HIGH & LOW TRAVEL SEASONS

HIGH SEASON   The peak travel season in the most popular parts of Australia is **winter.** In much of the country—Queensland from around Townsville and northwards, the Top End and the Red Centre, and most of Western Australia—summer is too darn hot, humid, wet, or all three. The most pleasant time to travel here is April to September—daytime temperatures are 19°C to 31°C (66°F–89°F) and it rarely rains. June, July, and August are the busiest months here: book accommodations and tours way in advance then, and you will pay higher rates then, too.

If I had to pick the one best month to visit Australia, I'd say **September,** when it's warm enough to hit the beach in the southern states on a good day, cool enough to tour Ayers Rock, and the humidity and rains have not yet come to Cairns and the Top End.

Travel and accommodation are much more expensive in Australia from **Boxing Day (Dec 26) to the end of January,** when Aussies take their summer vacations. Hotel rooms and seats on planes are harder to come by, and it's a rare airline or hotel that will discount even one dollar off their full tariffs.

LOW SEASON From **October to March,** intense heat can make touring outdoors all but impossible in the Red Centre, the Top End and anywhere in Western Australia except Perth and the Southwest. The Top End, the Kimberley and North Queensland including Cairns, suffer an intensely hot, humid **Wet Season** from November or December to March or April. In the Top End and Kimberley, this is preceded by an even stickier "build-up" in October and November. Some attractions and tour companies close up shop; floodwaters render others off-limits; and hotels drop their rates.

On the other hand, summer (Dec, Jan, Feb) is a nice time to visit the **southern states**—New South Wales, Victoria, South Australia, Western Australia from Perth on south, and Tasmania. Even in winter, temperatures rarely dip below freezing, snow only falls in parts of Tasmania, in the ski slopes of Victoria, and in the Snowy Mountains in New South Wales.

HOLIDAYS

In addition to the period from December 26 to the end of January, when Aussies take their vacations (see "High Season," above), the 4 days at **Easter** (Good Friday through Easter Monday) and all **school holiday periods** (see below) are very busy, so book ahead. Almost everything shuts down on **Boxing Day** (Dec 26) and **Good Friday,** and much is closed New Year's Day, Easter Sunday and Easter Monday. Most things are closed until 1pm, if not all day, on **Anzac Day** (Apr 25), which commemorates World War I.

MAJOR NATIONAL HOLIDAYS

New Year's Day	January 1
Australia Day	January 26
Labor Day	First Monday in March (WA)
Eight Hours Day	First Monday in March (TAS)
Labor Day	Second Monday in March (VIC)
Canberra Day	Third Monday in March (ACT)
Good Friday	Varies
Easter Sunday	Varies
Easter Monday	Varies
Anzac Day	April 25
May Day	First Monday in May (NT)
Labour Day	First Monday in May (QLD)
Adelaide Cup	Third Monday in May (SA)
Foundation Day	First Monday in June (WA)
Queen's Birthday	Second Monday in June (except WA)
Royal National Show Day	Second or third Wednesday in August (QLD)
Queen's Birthday	Monday in late September/early October (WA)
Labour Day	First Monday in October (NSW, SA)

Melbourne Cup Day	First Tuesday in November (Melbourne only)
Christmas Day	December 25
Boxing Day	December 26 (usually celebrated on the next Monday if 26th falls on a weekend; if Christmas Day is a Saturday and Boxing Day a Sunday, then both the following Monday and Tuesday are holidays.)

SCHOOL HOLIDAYS

The school year in Australia is broken into four semesters, with 2-week holidays falling around the last half of April, the last week of June and the first week of July, and the last week of September and the first week of October. Some states break at slightly different dates. There's a 6-week summer/Christmas vacation from mid-December to the end of January.

Australia Calendar of Events

January

✪ **New Year's Eve.** Watching the Sydney Harbour Bridge light up with fireworks is a treat. The main show is at 9pm, not midnight, so kids don't miss out. Pack a picnic and snag a Harbourside spot by 4pm, or even earlier at the best vantage points—Mrs. Macquarie's Chair in the Royal Botanic Gardens and the Sydney Opera House.

• **Sydney Festival.** The highlight of Sydney's visual and performing arts festival are the free jazz, opera, and classical music concerts held outdoors Saturday nights in the Domain near the Botanic Gardens (take a picnic). Contact booking agent **Ticketek** (☎**02/9266 4020;** fax 02/9267 4460) or www.sydneyfestival.org.au. For 3 weeks in January.

• **Tamworth Country Music Festival,** Tamworth (459 kilometers/287 miles northwest of Sydney), New South Wales. It may look like an Akubra Hat Convention, but this 10-day gathering of rural folk and rural folk wannabes is Australia's biggest country music festival. Tamworth. The **Tamworth Information Centre** (☎ **02/6755 4300;** fax 02/6755 4312) takes bookings. Second half of January.

• **Australia Day.** Australia's answer to Independence Day marks the landing of the First Fleet at Sydney Cove in 1788. Most Aussies celebrate by heading to the beach; in Sydney, there are ferry races and tall ships on the harbor, and fireworks in the evening. January 26.

• **Heineken Classic.** One of the country's richest golf tournaments with A$1.6 million (U.S.$1.04 million) in prizes. Contact the Classic's office (☎ **08/9297 3399;** fax 08/9297 3311; www.heinekenclassic.com). In 2002 it shifts to Melbourne (from Perth) for four years.

February

✪ **Sydney Gay & Lesbian Mardi Gras.** A spectacular street parade of floats, costumes, and dancers, cheered on by several hundred thousand onlookers, followed by a giant gay-only warehouse party. Contact Sydney Gay & Lesbian Mardi Gras, 21–23 Erskineville Rd., Erskineville, NSW 2042 (☎ **02/9557 4332;** fax 02/9516 4446; www.mardigras. com.au). Usually the last Saturday night in February; occasionally the first Saturday in March.

March

✪ **Adelaide Festival of Arts.** This major international arts event features performance art, music, dance, and outdoor concerts, as well as a writers' week. A party atmosphere takes over Adelaide's city streets every night until late. For tickets and information, contact **BASS** (☎ **08/8400 2205;** fax 08/8216 8956; www.adelaidefestival.org.au). Over 2½ weeks in March every second year (the dates are Mar 1–10, 2002).

✪ **Qantas Australian Formula One Grand Prix,** Melbourne. The first Grand Prix of the year on the international FIA Formula One World Championship circuit is battled out on one of its fastest circuits, in Melbourne. Qantas offices worldwide sell tickets; in Australia call **Ticketmaster** (☎ **13 16 41**); contact Australian Grand Prix Corporation (☎ **03/9258 7100;** fax 03/9699 3727); or order online at www.grand prix.com.au). Four days in the first or second week of March.

April

• **Australian Surf Life Saving Championships,** Kurrawa Beach, Gold Coast, Queensland. Up to 6,000 Aussie and international men and women swim, ski paddle, sprint relay, pilot rescue boats, perform march-pasts, and resuscitate "drowning" swimmers in front of 10,000 spectators. Contact Surf Life Saving Australia (☎ **02/9597 5588;** fax 02/9599 4809; www.slsa.asn.au). Over 4 days in late March or early April.

June

• **Sydney Film Festival.** World and Australian premieres of Aussie and international flicks are shown in the ornate State Theatre and other venues. Contact Sydney Film Festival, PO Box 950, Glebe, NSW 2037 (☎ **02/9660 3844;** fax 02/9692 8793; www.sydfilm-fest.com.au). Two weeks from first or second Friday in June.

August

• *Sun-Herald* **City to Surf,** Sydney. Fifty thousand Sydneysiders pound the pavement (or walk, or wheelchair it) in this 14-kilometer (9-mile) "fun run" from the city to Bondi Beach. For an entry form, write to the *Sun-Herald* City to Surf, 201 Sussex St., Sydney, NSW 2000 (☎ **1800/ 55 5514** in Australia, or 02/9282 2833), or enter on the day of the race. Usually the second Sunday in August.

September

• **Floriade,** Canberra. A million tulips, daffodils, hyacinths and other blooms bring the banks of Canberra's Lake Burley Griffin to life in stunning themed designs at this spring celebration, to which a little spice is added with performing arts and the like. Contact Canberra Tourism & Events Corporation (☎ **02/6205 0044;** fax 02/6205 0776; www. canberratourism.com.au), or see www.floriadeaustralia.com. Runs about a month from the second or third week of September.

✪ **Henley-on-Todd Regatta,** Alice Springs. Sounds sophisticated, doesn't it? It's actually a harum-scarum race down the dry bed of the Todd River in homemade "boats" made from anything you care to name—an old 4WD chassis, or beer cans lashed together. The only rule is the craft has to look vaguely like a boat. Contact the organizers at P.O. Box 1385, Alice Springs, NT 0871 (☎ /fax **08/8955 1253;** www.henleyontodd. com.au). One Saturday in late September or early October.

• **Honda Indy 300 Carnival,** Surfers Paradise, Queensland. The world's best Indy-car drivers race on the streets around Surfers Paradise on the glitzy Gold Coast, as part of the international FedEx Championship champ car motorsport series. Contact **Ticketek** in Brisbane (☎ **13 19 31** in Queensland or 07/3404 6644, fax 07/3404 6666; or order online at www.indy.com.au. Four days in mid-October.

November

- **Melbourne Cup.** If you're not glued to the TV to watch this A$1-million-plus 3,200-meter (2-mile) horse race in Melbourne, well, you're probably not Australian. Women wear hats to the office, desks are cleared for chicken and champagne, and don't even think about flagging a cab at 3:40pm race time. First Tuesday in November.
- **Gay Games VI.** Sydney hosts the games in 2002, with opening ceremonies on Nov. 2, running through Nov. 9. Athletes will compete in 31 official sports, and additional Exhibition Events. An arts festival runs concurrently with the Games, which are expected to draw 14,000 participants, and more than 40,000 visitors. ☎ **02/9380 8202;** www. sydney2002.org.au.

December

- **Sydney-to-Hobart Yacht Race.** Find a clifftop spot near the Heads to watch the glorious show of spinnakers as a hundred or so yachts leave Sydney Harbour for this grueling world-class event. Contact Tourism New South Wales (☎ **02/9931 1111;** fax 02/9931 1490; www.tourism. nsw.gov.au). Starts December 26.

9 The Active Vacation Planner

Australia's generally warm dry climate and wide-open spaces are made for active vacationers. Most operators and outfitters listed below specialize in adventure vacations for small groups. Meals, accommodation, equipment rental, and guides are included as a rule. International airfares are usually not. Where you end up spending the night can vary depending on the package—for example, on a sea-kayaking trip you usually camp on the beach, on a hiking expedition you may stay at a wilderness lodge, while on a biking trip you often stop over at B&B-style lodgings. If your trip is camping-based, you may need to bring your own sleeping bag, or rent one from the adventure operator.

Additional information on outdoor activities can be found in the relevant regional chapters. Before you head out, review the safety tips in this section.

SCUBA DIVING

Diving Down Under is one of the best travel experiences you can have anywhere. Don't think all of Australia's dive spots are on the Great Barrier Reef, though. Good sites are found all around the coastline. A second barrier reef in **Ningaloo Reef Marine Park** stretches 260 kilometers (163 miles) off the coast of Western Australia (see chapter 10). For a rundown on the country's truly outstanding dive areas, see "The Best Affordable Diving & Snorkeling Sites" in chapter 1, "The Best of Australia."

Wherever you find coral in Australia—which is a lot of places—you will find dive companies offering learn-to-dive courses, day trips, and in some cases, extended journeys on live-aboard vessels. Most international dive certificates, including PADI, NAUI, SSI, and BSAC, are recognized. It's easy to rent gear and wetsuits wherever you go, or bring your own.

Beginners' courses are known as "open-water certification" and usually require 2 days of theory in a pool at the dive company's premises on land, followed by 2 or 3 days on a live-aboard boat where you make between 4 and 9 dives, including a night dive if you opt for the 5-day course. Open-water certification courses range from an intensive 3 days to a more relaxed 5 days, for which you can expect to pay between A$350 and A$600 (U.S.$227.50 and U.S.$390). Most operators offer courses up to instructor level. If you are pressed for time, a PADI Referral course might suit you. It allows you to do your theory work at home, a few hours of pool work at a PADI dive center in your home country, and then spend just 2 or 3 days in the Australian ocean doing your qualifying dives. Remember to allow time in your itinerary for a medical exam in Australia, and expect the dive instructor to grill you on your theory again before you hit the water.

If you are a certified diver, remember to bring your "C" card and log book. If you are going to do a dive course, you will need a medical certificate by an Australian doctor that meets Australian standard AS4005.1 that states you are fit for scuba diving (an all-purpose physical is not enough). Virtually all dive schools will arrange the exam for you; expect to pay around A$50 (U.S.$32.50) for it. Some courses take as little as 3 days, but 5-day courses are generally regarded as best. Remember, you can fly before you dive, but you must complete your last dive 24 hours *before* you fly. This catches a lot of people off guard when they are preparing to go on to their next destination (or home) after a visit to the Reef. You won't be able to helicopter off the Reef back to the mainland, either. Check to see if your travel insurance covers diving.

If you've never dived, you can see what all the fuss is about on an "introductory" dive. Section 1, "Exploring the Great Barrier Reef," in chapter 7, contains more information on diving the Great Barrier Reef.

For information on dive regions, operators, and courses, contact the **Australian Tourist Commission** (see "Visitor Information" earlier in this chapter) for diving anywhere in Australia. **Tourism Queensland's** website (www.queensland-holidays.com.au) contains plentiful information on dive operators working the Great Barrier Reef. If you know exactly where you want to dive, you may obtain an even more detailed list of operators by bypassing the Australian Tourist Commission and contacting the nearest local tourist office for a list of local dive operators. **Dive Queensland** (the Queensland Dive Tourism Association) (☎ **07/4051 1510;** fax 07/4051 1519; www.greatbarrier-reef.net.au) is a one-stop shop for getting in touch with member dive operators in that state who stick to a code of ethics.

Peter Stone's Dive Australia, is a comprehensive 608-page guidebook to more than 2,000 dive sites, plus operators, all over Australia. It is published by Oceans Enterprises (☎ **03/5182 5108;** fax 03/5182 5823; www.oceans. com.au). For U.S. readers, the fourth edition (1999) costs US$36 (U.S.$23), direct from the publisher, including airmail postage. Oceans Enterprises posts online updates (additions, closings).

BUSHWALKING (HIKING)

With so much unique scenery and so many rare animals and plants to protect, it's not surprising Australia is full of national parks crisscrossed with hiking trails. You're never far from a park with a bushwalk, whether it's an easy stroll to a lookout, or a 963-kilometer (601-mile) odyssey on the Bibbulmun Track in Western Australia.

The best place to get information about bushwalking before you leave home is the **National Parks & Wildlife Service,** or its equivalent, in each state, which are listed below. A good Australian bushwalking Web page is at **www.bushwalking.org.au**.

- **NSW National Parks & Wildlife Service** (☎ **02/9585 6333;** fax 02/ 9585 6527; www.npws.nsw.gov.au/).
- **Environmental Protection Agency (QLD Parks & Wildlife Service)** (☎ **07/3227 8197;** fax 07/3227 8749; www.env.qld.gov.au).
- **Parks & Wildlife Commission of the Northern Territory** (☎ **08/ 8999 5511;** fax 08/8932 3849; www.nt.gov.au/paw). The Northern Territory Tourist Commission (see "Visitor Information" this chapter) is the official source for information on parks and wildlife matters.
- Western Australian **Department of Conservation and Land Management (CALM)** (☎ **08/9442 0300;** fax 08/9386 1578; www.calm. wa.gov.au).
- South Australian **Department for Environment and Heritage** (☎ **08/8204 1910;** fax 08/8204 1919; www.denr.sa.gov.au).
- **Parks Victoria** (☎ **03/9816 7066;** fax 03/9816 6897; www.parkweb. vic.gov.au).
- **Tasmania Parks and Wildlife Service** (☎ **03/6191 3382;** fax 03/ 6223 2158; www.parks.tas.gov.au).

Some parks charge a daily or one-time entry fee; it's usually around A$5 to $8 (U.S.$3.25–$5.20), but is can be as much as A$16 (U.S.$10.40).

MORE ACTIVE VACATIONS FROM A TO Z

ABSEILING   Rappelling is another name for this sport that involves backing down vertical cliff faces on a rope and harness. The **Blue Mountains** near Sydney are Australia's abseiling capital. In the **Margaret River region** in Western Australia, you can do it as mighty breakers crash on the cliffs below. You can even do it in the heart of **Brisbane** on riverside cliffs.

BIKING   Australia's flat countryside is ideal for cycling, as Aussies call biking, but consider the heat and the vast distances before attempting long trips. The rain forest hills behind **Cairns** hosted the world mountain-biking championships in 1996, and Sydney's **Blue Mountains** have good mountain-biking trails. On **Rottnest Island** off Perth, it's the only mode of transport. All major towns and most resorts rent regular and mountain bikes.

If you are interested in taking an extended biking trip, get a copy of *Cycling Australia: Bicycle Touring Throughout the Sunny Continent,* by Australian Ian Duckworth (Bicycle Books). This 224-page touring guide outlines eight long trips with maps and detailed route descriptions. Any large bookstore can order it, or it is available for U.S.$14.95 from the **Adventurous Traveler Bookstore** (☎ **800/282-3963** in the U.S. and Canada; www.adventuroustraveler.com), or for £9.95 from the **Quayside Bookshop** in the U.K. (☎ **01626/77-5436;** or order at www.cycling.uk.com).

BIRD-WATCHING   Australia's location ensures it has many unique species. It is probably best known for its many brilliant **parrots,** but you will see species from the wetlands, savannah, mulga scrub, desert, oceans, dense bushland, rain forest, mangroves, rivers, and other habitats. More than half the country's species have been spotted in the **Daintree Rain Forest** in north Queensland, and one-third of Australia's species live in wetlands-rich **Kakadu National Park** in the Top End. **The Coorong** in South Australia and **Broome** in the Top End are home to marvelous waterfowl populations.

To get in touch with bird-watching clubs all over Australia, contact **Birds Australia** (formerly the Royal Australasian Ornithologists' Union), 415 Riversdale Rd., Hawthorn East, VIC 3123 (☎ **03/9882 2622;** fax 03/9882 2677; www.birdsaustralia.com.au).

Australia has one of the world's largest camel populations. Camels were imported to negotiate deserts in the 1900s, but were later set free. They are now making a comeback as a popular way to trek the country. Short rambles of an hour or two in **Alice Springs** and at **Ayers Rock** are a novel way to see the Outback. Several companies in **Broome** lead guided rides along Cable Beach. You can also camel trek through **Flinders Ranges National Park** in South Australia.

Kirrama Wildlife Tours, P.O. Box 133, Silkwood (near Cairns), QLD 4856 (☎ **07/4065 5181;** fax 07/4065 5197; www.gspeak.com.au/kirrama/), operates birding expeditions to remote regions in northern Australia. Broome ornithologist George Swann of **Kimberley Birdwatching, Wildlife & Natural History Tours** (☎ /fax **08/9192 1246,** kimbird@tpg.com.au) designs trips from 3 hours to 21 days throughout the Kimberley.

CANOEING & SEA KAYAKING   Katherine Gorge in the Northern Territory offers spectacular flat canoeing. You'll find delightful canoeing on the magnificent bird-rich **Ord River** in the Top End, too. Katherine Gorge and the Ord are full of generally harmless freshwater crocodiles, but *never* canoe in saltwater crocodile territory. Whitewater canoeing can be found in **Barrington Tops National Park** north of Sydney.

Australia's coastline and rich, warm seas are tailor-made for sea kayaking. Several companies rent kayaks or offer guided expeditions in the **Whitsunday Islands** in north Queensland; to **Dunk Island** off Mission Beach, south of Cairns; and in **Perth, Monkey Mia,** and the **Northwest Cape** in Western Australia.

CAVING   **Australia doesn't have a lot of caves, but the ones it has are spectacular. The best are the **Jenolan Caves in the Blue Mountains west of Sydney, a honeycomb of caverns bursting with intricate stalactites and stalagmites; and the 350 limestone caves in the **Margaret River region** in Western Australia. Five are open to the public.

FISHING   **Reef, game, deep sea, beach, estuary, river, and trout fishing—Australia's massive coastline lets you do it all. Drop a line for coral trout on the **Great Barrier Reef; hook a fighting "barra," short for barramundi, in the **Northern Territory** or the **Kimberley;** or cast for trout in **Tasmania's** highland lakes.

GOLF   **Australians are almost as passionate about golf as they are about football and cricket—after all, before Greg Norman was a Yank he was an Aussie! **Queensland has the lion's share of the most stunning resort courses, like the **Sheraton Mirage** in Port Douglas, **Laguna Quays Resort** near the Whitsundays, and **Hyatt Regency Sanctuary Cove Resort** on the Gold Coast. The Gold Coast is studded with more than 40 courses. The **Novotel Vines** near Perth is another outstanding resort course. One of the world's best desert courses is at Alice Springs. You can play a round of **"bush golf"** in Broken Hill—it's played at night when it's cool with fluorescent golf balls; or hit the links in Lightning Ridge where the "greens" are dusty "browns."

Most courses rent clubs for around A$30 (U.S.$19.50). Greens fees start at around A$20 (U.S.$13) for 18 holes but average A$65 (U.S.$42.25) or more on a championship course.

HORSEBACK RIDING   Horseback-riding operators are everywhere in Australia. A particularly pleasant vacation is a multi-day riding and camping trek in the **Snowy Mountains** in New South Wales.

SAILING   The 74 island gems of the **Whitsundays** in Queensland are an out-of-this-world backdrop for sailing. And you don't have to know how to sail—plenty of operators charter "bareboat" (unskippered) yachts by the day or week, even to folks without any sailing experience. Perth and Sydney are mad-keen sailing cities; head down to the nearest yacht club and see what onboard places are going, especially during summer twilight races. The clubs are often short of sailors and most will welcome out-of-towners.

SURFING   You'll have no trouble finding a good surf beach all along the Australian coast; **Perth** and **Sydney** have loads of good ones right in the city. Other popular spots include the **Gold Coast** in Queensland, the legendary Southern Ocean swells along **Victoria's southern coast,** and the magnificent sets off **Margaret River** in Western Australia. Don't take your board north of the Sunshine Coast in Queensland—the Great Barrier Reef puts a stop to the swell from there all the way to the northern tip of Queensland.

WHITE-WATER RAFTING   The best rapids are the Grade 5 torrents on the **Nymboida** and **Gwydir rivers** behind Coffs Harbour in New South Wales. More Grade 5 rapids await you on the **Johnstone River** in north Queensland, although they must be accessed by helicopter. Loads of tourists who have never held a paddle hurtle down the Grade 3 to 4 **Tully River** near Mission Beach in north Queensland and the gentler Grade 2 to 3 **Barron River** near Cairns. The **Snowy River National Park** in Victoria is another spot popular with rafters. See also "Canoeing & Sea Kayaking," above.

OUTFITTERS & ADVENTURE-TRAVEL OPERATORS
AUSTRALIA-BASED OPERATORS

The Adventure Company (☎ 800/388-7333 in the U.S., or 07/4051 4777; fax 07/4051 4888; www.adventures.com.au) does one-day and extended trips that incorporate hiking, biking, canoeing, rafting, sea kayaking, scuba diving, and four-wheel-driving in wilderness areas of North Queensland and on the Great Barrier Reef.

   MudMaps Australia (☎ 888/MUD-MAPS in the United States, or 02/6257 4796; fax 02/6257 4823; www.mudmaps.com), offers 1- to 4-day wilderness tours from Canberra, Sydney, and Melbourne in the Snowy Mountains. The groups are small, your guide is a bushman, the transport is 4WD or minicoach, accommodations are farms and B&B-style.

   Peregrine Adventures (via Himalayan Travel in the U.S. ☎ 800/225-2380), 01728/86 2222 in the U.K., or 03/9663 8611; fax 03/9663 8618; www.peregrine.net.au) runs rafting expeditions in Victoria and on the Franklin River in Tasmania. It is represented in Canada by several companies,

---

Skiing, Anyone?

Most people don't think of Australia as a place to hit the slopes, but in the Aussie winter, you can try Thredbo and Perisher Valleys in the **Snowy Mountains** in New South Wales or the **High Country** of inland Victoria. The season is short—June to September—with the best falls in July and August.

including WestCan Treks (☎ **800/663-5132** in British Columbia, or 604/734-1066).

Remote Outback Cycle Tours (☎ **08/9244 4614;** fax 08/9244 4615; www.cycletours.com.au) takes bikers of all levels on extended tours through the Red Centre, to Kakadu National Park in the Top End, along the Gibb River Road in the Kimberley, through the vast saltbush plains and into an underground opal mining town in South Australia, or across part of the Nullarbor Plain desert to the Margaret River wine region in southern Western Australia. 4WD vehicles are used some of the time.

Rivergods (☎ **08/9259 0749;** fax 08/9259 0902; www.rivergods.com.au), offers one-day and multi-day sea kayaking, canoeing, and whitewater rafting adventures on Western Australia's pristine ocean and rivers, in which whales, sharks, dugongs (manatees), sea snakes, turtles, and dolphins abound. Their "sea kayak with seals" daytrip from Perth is popular.

Tasmanian Expeditions (☎ **03/6334 3477;** fax 03/6334 3463; www. tas-ex.com/tas-ex) conducts hiking, cycling, rafting, abseiling, canoeing, and rock-climbing trips through Tasmania's national parks and country roads.

U.S.-BASED OPERATORS

The **Great Outdoor Recreation Pages (G.O.R.P.)** site at www.gorp.com has links to many adventure tour operators to Australia, and contains articles; sells books and maps; and has links to sites in Australia with an action slant.

Adventure Express (☎ **800/443-0799** or 415/442-0799; fax 415/901 1025; www.adventureexpress.com) sells scuba-diving packages and custom-built itineraries on the Great Barrier Reef. The company claims to meet or beat any competitor's price.

Down Under Answers (☎ **800/788-6685** or 425/895-0895; fax 425/895 8929; www.adventour.com), sells diving and sea kayaking packages in North Queensland, and biking trips in scenic locales throughout the country. A 7-day package combines canoeing, hiking, biking, and snorkeling.

Outer Edge Expeditions (☎ **800/322-5235** or 517/552 5300; fax 517/ 552 5400; www.outer-edge.com) offers ecologically minded camping, diving, hiking, mountain biking, canoeing, and sea kayaking packages to the Great Barrier Reef, Ayers Rock, and Kangaroo Island off South Australia.

The World Outside (☎ **800/488-8483** or 303/413-0938; fax 303/413 0926; www.theworldoutside.com) runs a 7-day combined hiking, mountain-biking, canoeing, snorkeling, sea kayaking, and diving packages on the Great Barrier Reef and in the North Queensland rain forest.

DOWN UNDER HEALTH, SAFETY & OUTDOOR ETIQUETTE

Australia has a lot of rough, remote territory typified by high temperatures, scarce water or none at all, little shade, flash floods, and bushfires. Add to that the deadly snakes and spiders you might meet, and that the nearest gas station, telephone, or person could be hundreds of miles away, and it's a wonder anyone ventures ten miles from the airport! Extreme heat and ultraviolet rays can lead to exhaustion, dehydration, sunstroke, and severe sunburn quickly, even if you are expending only a small amount of energy.

SOME GENERAL RULES OF THUMB

- Don't disturb wildlife, take plant cuttings, or remove rocks, shells, coral, or other pieces of the wilderness. It's bad form to impact on the environment like this, and it is an offense in national and marine parks.

- Tell someone where you are going, whether it's on a 2-hour hike or a 3-week 4WD safari across the country. If you are hiking in a national park, register in the National Parks & Wildlife Service logbook if there is one placed at the start of the walk (don't forget to de-register, or a search party will be out looking for you while you're back at your hotel). On longer trips, leave travel plans with friends, relatives, or the police.
- Carry extra water. It's easy to dehydrate in Australia's arid conditions. Two liters per person per day should be your minimum; one liter per person per hour is the rule in the Outback and the Top End in summer.
- Don't feed animals, birds, and fish. It makes them unhealthy and causes them to lose their hunting skills.
- Obey fire restrictions. Bushfires are a major threat across Australia. In hot, dry weather, a total fire ban may apply, which means you cannot light a naked flame. Many national parks only permit camp-ovens, not campfires. If you use a campfire, burn only fallen wood, not standing dead trees that could house animals. Extinguish all campfires thoroughly.
- Look at, but don't touch, historic Aboriginal sites such as rock art walls and middens (shell mounds). It can be an offense to disturb them.

BASICS FOR BUSHWALKERS

- Stay on the track. Short cuts can damage vegetation and cause erosion.
- Whatever you take in, take out. Leave nothing, not even organic stuff like an apple core (it takes a long time to degrade, it's not the right food for native animals, and it might take root and become a pest among native vegetation). For the same reason, don't bury your rubbish.
- Check track conditions and the weather forecast before you go.
- Wear a broad-brimmed hat, sunglasses, sunscreen, sturdy shoes, and a comfortable backpack. Insect repellent is essential: flies can reach plague proportions in dry areas and mosquitoes are common in rain forests.

BEACH SAVVY FOR SWIMMERS & SURFERS

- To signal for "help" in the water, raise one arm high above your head.
- Never swim alone at beaches not patrolled by lifesavers (lifeguards).
- Always swim between the red and yellow flags denoting a safe swimming zone. Crossed flagpoles or a red flag mean the beach is closed due to extremely dangerous swimming conditions. A yellow flag means conditions are dangerous and swimming is not advised.
- "Rips" are powerful currents that can carry even strong swimmers out to sea. If caught in one, remain calm, raise one arm high above your head, and wait for help. Try to swim diagonally against the current to shore.
- If you get a cramp, raise one arm and keep the cramped part still.

DANGEROUS AUSSIE WILDLIFE

"If you knew the danger out there, you'd never leave the safety of your hotel," a tourist said to me as he went for a swim off Sydney's Manly Beach the day after a helicopter flew in to fire warning shots across the noses of a school of 3-meter (9.8 feet) hammerhead sharks that had come too close to bathers for comfort. Shark attacks are extremely rare, with only 190 people killed, and 263 people injured by sharks since the first death in 1791.

For a list of animals to avoid, from red-back **spiders** to estuarine (saltwater) **crocodiles**, and where they're found outside of zoos and aquariums, check out Appendix: Australia in Depth at the end of this book.

10 Health & Insurance

Hygiene standards are high, hospitals are modern, and doctors and dentists are well trained, so there's no real need for special health precautions when traveling to Australia. The country's immense distances mean you can sometimes be a long way from a hospital or a doctor, but help is never far away thanks to the **Royal Flying Doctor Service.** No vaccinations are needed to enter the country unless you have been in a yellow fever danger zone—that is, South America or Africa—in the past six days.

You may wish to bring along remedies, or consult with your doctor about how to treat common traveler's ailments like motion sickness, insomnia, jet lag, constipation, and diarrhea.

IF YOU GET SICK AWAY FROM HOME

You may want to consider medical travel insurance (see the section on travel insurance in this chapter). In most cases, your existing health plan will provide all the coverage you need. Be sure to carry your identification card with you.

If you suffer from a chronic illness, consult your doctor before your departure. For conditions like epilepsy, diabetes, or heart problems, wear a **Medic Alert Identification Tag** (☎ 800/IDALERT; www.medicalert.com), which will immediately alert doctors to your condition and give them access to your records through Medic Alert's 24-hour hot line. Membership is U.S.$35, then U.S.$15 for annual renewal.

Pack prescription medications in your carry-on luggage. Carry written prescriptions in generic, not brand name, form and keep all prescription medications in their original containers. Bring along copies of your prescriptions in case you lose your pills or run out. Usually a 3-month supply is the maximum quantity of prescription drugs you are permitted to carry, so if you are carrying large amounts of medication, contact the Australian embassy or consulate in your home country to assure your supply does not exceed the max. If you need more medication in Australia, you will need to get an Australian doctor to write the prescription for you.

If you wear contact lenses, pack an extra pair in case you lose one.

The **International Association for Medical Assistance to Travelers (IAMAT)** (☎ 716/754-4883 in the U.S. or 519/836-0102 in Canada; www.sentex.net/~iamat) offers tips on travel and health concerns in the countries you'll be visiting. Membership is free. The **United States Centers for Disease Control and Prevention** (☎ 877/FYI-TRIP; www.cdc.gov) provides up-to-date information on necessary vaccines and health hazards by region or country. By mail, their "Yellow Book" guide is $25 (call the Government Printing Office ☎ 202/512-1800 to order it and quote stock no: 017-023-00202-3); on the Internet, it's free. If you do get sick, you may want to ask the concierge at your hotel to recommend a local doctor. If you can't find a doctor right

A Word About Smoking

Smoking in many public areas is restricted if not banned. Few Oz restaurants totally ban smoking; they just have smoking and nonsmoking sections. Aussie pubs (bars) are a territorial victory for smokers; after a night in one, nonsmokers go home smelling as if they smoked the whole pack. Most hotels have smoking and nonsmoking rooms. Australian aircraft on all domestic and international routes are nonsmoking.

away, try the emergency room at the local hospital. Doctors are listed under "M" for Medical Practitioners in the Australian Yellow Pages.

WARNING: SUNSHINE MAY BE HAZARDOUS TO YOUR HEALTH

Australians have the world's highest death rate from skin cancer: it's from the country's intense sunlight. Especially during the first few days of your trip, limit your exposure to the sun from 11am to 3pm in summer and 10am to 2pm in winter. Scattered UV rays can bounce off surfaces such city walls, water, and even the ground, and burn you. Use a broad-spectrum sunscreen with a high protection factor (SPF 30+). Wear a broad-brimmed hat that covers the back of your neck, ears, and face (*not* a baseball cap); and a long-sleeved shirt to cover your forearms. Kids need more protection than adults do.

Don't come to Oz without sunglasses or you'll spend your entire vacation squinting against Australia's jewel-sharp "diamond light."

INSURANCE

There are three kinds of travel insurance: **trip cancellation, medical,** and **lost luggage coverage.** The first is a good idea if you have paid a large portion of your vacation expenses up front. The other two types of insurance, however, don't make sense for most travelers. Rule number one: check your existing policies before you buy any additional coverage.

Your existing **health insurance** should cover you if you get sick on vacation (if you belong to an HMO, check to see whether you are fully covered when away from home). If you need hospital treatment, most health insurance plans and HMOs will cover out-of-country hospital visits and procedures, at least to some extent. However, most make you pay up front, and you'll be reimbursed when you file the paperwork. Make sure your policy covers evacuation by helicopter or Australia's Royal Flying Doctor Service airlift—you might well need this if you become sick or injured in the Outback. Your policy should also cover the cost to fly you back home in a stretcher. A stretcher takes up three coach class seats, plus you may need extra seats for a nurse and medical equipment. Medicare does not cover U.S. citizens in Australia.

Australia has a reciprocal medical-care agreement with Great Britain and New Zealand and a limited agreement with Ireland, under which travelers are covered by Australia's national health system for most medical expenses for immediate treatment (but not evacuation, ambulances, funerals, dental care, and other expenses). It's still a good idea to buy insurance, though, as Australia's national healthcare system typically only covers 85%, sometimes much less, of treatment. Foreign students must take out the Australian government's Overseas Student Health Cover as a condition of entry.

For independent travel health insurance providers, see below.

Your **homeowner's insurance** should cover **stolen luggage.** Airlines are responsible for a maximum A$1,600 (U.S.$1,040) on domestic flights in Australia for lost luggage, or U.S.$1,250 on flights within the United States; if you plan to carry anything more valuable than that, keep it in your carry-on.

The differences between **travel assistance** and **insurance** are often blurred, but in general the former offers on-the-spot assistance and 24-hour hotlines (mostly addressing medical problems), while the latter reimburses you for travel problems (medical, travel, or otherwise) after you have filed the paperwork. The coverage you should consider depends on how much protection is contained in your existing health insurance or other policies. Some credit card companies may insure you against travel accidents if you buy plane, train, or bus tickets with their cards. **American Express** offers its cardholders a free 24-hour **Global Assist hotline** (☎ **800/554-AMEX** in the U.S. or call collect 312/935-3600 from overseas or in Illinois). Before purchasing additional insurance, read your policies and agreements over carefully. Call your insurers or credit/charge card companies if you have any questions.

If you require additional insurance, try one of the firms below. But don't pay for more than you need. For example, if you need only trip cancellation insurance, don't purchase coverage for lost or stolen property. Trip cancellation insurance costs approximately 6% to 8% of the total value of your vacation.

Among the reputable issuers of **travel insurance** are:

- **Access America** (☎ **800/284-8300;** www.accessamerica.com)
- **Travel Guard International** (☎ **800/826-1300;** www.travel-guard.com)
- **Travel Insured International** (☎ **800/243-3174;** www.travel insured.com)
- **Columbus Direct** (☎ **020/7375 0011** in London; www.columbus direct.com) insures United Kingdom residents and British passport holders only
- **International SOS Assistance** (☎ **800/523-8930,** or 215/244-1500 in the U.S., 514/874-7674 in Canada, 208/762-8000 in the U.K.; www.intsos.com) is strictly an assistance company
- **Travelex Insurance Services** (☎ **888/457-4602;** www.travelex-insurance.com)

Companies specializing in **accident** and **medical care** include:

- **MEDEX** (☎ **888/MEDEX-00;** www.medexassist.com)
- **Travel Assistance International** (Worldwide Assistance Services, Inc.) (☎ **800/821-2828;** www.worldwideassistance.com)
- **The Divers Alert Network (DAN)** (☎ **800/446-2671;** www.divers alertnetwork.org) insures scuba divers and provides a diving medical emergency hotline.

11 Tips for Travelers with Special Needs

FOR TRAVELERS WITH DISABILITIES   The majority of public hotels, major stores, museums, attractions, and public rest rooms have wheelchair access. Many smaller lodges and even B&Bs are starting to cater to guests with disabilities. National parks make an effort to include wheelchair-friendly pathways, too. Taxi companies in bigger cities can usually supply a cab equipped for wheelchairs. TTY facilities are still limited largely to government services, unfortunately.

For information on all kinds of facilities and services in Australia for people with disabilities (not just travel-related organizations), contact **National Information Communication Awareness Network (NICAN),** P.O. Box 407, Curtin, ACT 2605 (☎ **1800/806 769** voice and TTY in Australia, or 02/6285 3713; fax 02/6285 3714; www.nican.com.au). This free service can put you in touch with accessible accommodations and attractions throughout Australia, as well as with travel agents and tour operators who understand your needs.

A World of Options, a huge book of resources for travelers with disabilities, costs U.S.$35 (U.S.$30 for members) from **Mobility International USA,** P.O. Box 10767, Eugene, OR 97440 (☎ **541/343-1284,** voice and TTY; www.miusa.org). **Twin Peaks Press,** P.O. Box 129, Vancouver, WA 98666-0129

(☎ **360/694-2462;** http://home.pacifier.com/~twinpeak), publishes travel-related books for people with disabilities.

FOR GAY & LESBIAN TRAVELERS   Sydney is one of the most openly gay cities in the world, and across most of Australia, the gay community has a high profile and lots of support services. The annual **Sydney Gay & Lesbian Mardi Gras,** culminating in a huge street parade and gay-only party on the last Saturday in February, is a high point on the city's calendar.

The **International Gay & Lesbian Travel Association (IGLTA)** (☎ **800/ 448-8550** or 954/776-2626; www.iglta.com), links gay travelers up with gay-friendly hotels, travel agents, and other travel organizations.

Some services you may find useful are the **Gay & Lesbian Counseling Service of NSW** (☎ **02/9207 2888** for the administration office), which runs a hotline from 4pm to midnight daily (☎ **1800/805 379** in Australia, or 02/9207 2800, fax 02/9207 2828). The **Albion Street Centre** (☎ **1800/ 451 600** in Australia outside Sydney, 02/9332 4000 in Sydney for the information line, 02/9332 1090 for administration) in Sydney is an AIDS clinic and information service.

FOR SENIORS   Seniors—often referred to as "pensioners" by Aussies—from other countries don't always qualify for the discounted prices to tours, attractions, and events that Australian seniors enjoy, but mostly they do. The best ID to bring is something that shows your date of birth, or something that marks you as an "official" senior, like a membership card from the **American Association of Retired Persons (AARP)** (☎ **800/424-3410** in the U.S.; www.aarp.org). Membership in AARP is open to working or retired people over 50 and costs U.S.$8 a year. AARP has a Purchase Privileges program that entitles members to discounts of 10% to 50% on a wide range of travel operators including airlines, many hotels, cruise lines, rental cars, and more.

Elderhostel (☎ **877/426-8056** toll-free in the U.S. and Canada; www.elderhostel.org) is a nonprofit organization that sells educational package tours, including ones to Australia, for travelers 55 years and over. Recent itineraries in Australia included Great Barrier Reef study cruises, Outback camping trips, bushwalking tours in Tasmania, and visits to Lord Howe Island off the east coast of Australia and Kangaroo Island off the south coast.

FOR FAMILIES   Australians travel widely with their own kids, so facilities for families, including family passes to attractions, are common. A great accommodation option for families is serviced or unserviced apartments. Both are widely available almost everywhere you go. Not only do they offer a living room, kitchen, often two bathrooms and the blissful privacy of a separate bedroom for adults, they often cost considerably less than a hotel room. Most hotels in Australia will arrange babysitting given a day's notice.

International airlines and domestic airlines within Australia charge 67% of the adult fare for kids under 12. Most charge 10% for infants under 2 not occupying a seat. As a general rule, Australian transport companies, attractions and tour operators charge around half-price or 60% for kids.

Rascals in Paradise (☎ **800/U RASCAL** in the U.S. and Canada; www.rascalsinparadise.com), sells family vacation packages to Australia.

These places have great **kids clubs:** Mercure Resort Surfers Paradise on the Gold Coast, and Daydream Island Resort and South Molle Island Resort, which are both in the Whitsunday Islands (see chapter 7).

FOR SINGLES   When it comes to accommodations for singles, pricing policies in Australia vary. Most hotels charge a "single rate," about three-quarters of the full rate. Pubs and hostels can be a good choice as they often charge a flat "per person" rate whether there is one, two, or more of you in the room. Another value-for-money option is B&Bs, which usually charge less for a single than a couple, and offer you the company and security of living with a host. Many package tour and adventure tour operators are happy to pair you up with another solo traveler in a twin-bed room, if you do not mind rooming with someone you've just met. That way each of you pays for the whole tour at the "double" rate, not the more expensive "single" rate.

FOR STUDENTS   STA Travel (☎ **800/781-4040** in the U.S., 020/7361 6144 in the U.K., and 1300/360 960 in Australia; www.statravel.com) and **Council Travel** (☎ **800/2-COUNCIL** in the U.S.; www.counciltravel.com) specialize in affordable airfares, bus and rail passes, accommodation, insurance, tours and packages for students and young travelers. Both issue **International Student Identity Cards (ISIC).** This is the most widely recognized proof in Australia that you really are a student. As well as getting you discounts on a huge range of travel, tours, and attractions, it comes with a 24-hour emergency help line and a global voice/fax/e-mail messaging system with discounted international telephone calls. Available to any full-time student over 12, in the United States it costs $20.

Ask STA Travel for a list of its many offices across Australia so you can keep the discounts flowing (and aid lines open) as you travel.

12 Booking a Package or Escorted Tour

It's possible to buy a package tour to Australia that includes airfare and, say, five nights' accommodation in a decent hotel for less than the cost of the airfare alone. Because each element of a package—airfare, hotel, tour, car rental—costs the package company much less than if you had booked the components yourself, packages are a terrific value and worth investigating.

There are two kinds of "packages"—independent and escorted—and each has pros and cons. **Independent packages** usually include some combination of airfare, lodging, and car rental, with an occasional tour or shopping discount voucher book thrown in. The main advantage is that you travel at your own pace and follow your own interests, rather than sticking to a group schedule. Your car and hotel arrangements are already booked, leaving you free to get on with your day instead of finding a hotel for the night.

Escorted tours have different advantages—you don't have to carry your own luggage, for starters. Nor do you need to constantly plan ahead, and if you have free time, there is someone to advise you on fun things to do and even make your tour bookings for you. A favorable argument for escorted tours is that you usually have a well-informed guide who knows the country, so that you'll probably learn more than you would on your own. You also get to meet and travel with other people. Escorted tours tend to be more expensive because you're paying for the guide, but most meals are included.

If you fancy an independent tour, think about whether you really want to book your own activities, do all the driving yourself (on the wrong side of the road!), and shlep your own luggage. If you're considering an escorted tour, do you really want your bush walk in the Blue Mountains cut short because the at noon we have to be back in Sydney for opal shopping? And can you stand the thought of traveling with the same strangers for days or weeks on end?

The airlines can be a good source of package tours. Check newspaper ads, the Internet, or your travel agent. **Austravel** (☎ **800/633-3404** in the U.S.

and Canada, or 0870/055 0239 in the U.K.; www.austravel.net) and **Inta-Aussie South Pacific** (☎ 800/531-9222 in the U.S.; www.inta-oz.com) are American companies offering independent packages.

Escorted tours are available from **Collette Tours** (☎800/340-5158 in the U.S., 416/626-1661 in Canada, or 0189/581 2333 in the U.K. through Adventures Unlimited, Inc.; www.collettetours.com), and **Maupintour** (☎800/255-4266 in the U.S. and Canada; www.maupintour.com). Collette Tours has an office in Australia. **Connections** (call Adventure Plus ☎510/654-1879 in the U.S., Goway ☎800/387-8850 in Canada, The Imaginative Traveller ☎ 020/8742 8612 in the U.K., or 07/3839 7877 in Australia; www.connections1835.com.au) and **Contiki** (☎800/CONTIKI in the U.S. and Canada, 020/8290 6777 in the U.K., or 02/9511 2200 in Australia; www.contiki.com) has escorted tours for 18 to 35 year olds. These attract a lot of Australians, so they are a good way to meet locals. Connections also does a Connections Plus range of active holidays for people of any age.

These companies offer both independent and escorted tours: **ATS Tours** (☎ 800/423-2880 in the U.S. and Canada; www.atstours.com), **Goway** (☎800/387-8850 in the U.S. and Canada; www.goway.com), **Qantas Vacations** (☎800/348-8139 in the U.S. and 800/268-7525 in Canada; www.qantasvacations.com), **Sunbeam Tours** (☎ 800/955-1818 in the U.S. and Canada; www.sunbeamtours.com), **Swain Australia Tours** (☎ 800/22-SWAIN in the U.S. and Canada; www.swaintours.com), Swain Australia's budget travel division, **Downunder Direct** (☎ 800/642-6224 in the U.S. and Canada); and **United Vacations** (☎ 800/917-9246 in the U.S. and Canada; www.unitedvacations.com). Swain Australia is owned and largely staffed by Aussies. Sunbeam Tours, Swain Australia and Goway have offices in Australia. **ANZA Travel** (☎800/269-2166 in the U.S., or 800/667-4329 in Canada; www.anza-travel.com) specializes in special-interest vacations with an active bent, such as golfing, sailing, and fishing.

FLYING TO AUSTRALIA

Australia is a *looong* flight from anywhere except New Zealand. Sydney is a 14-hour nonstop flight from Los Angeles, longer if your flight stops in Honolulu. From the East Coast, add 5½ hours. If you're coming from the states via Auckland, add transit time in New Zealand plus another 3 hours for the Auckland-Sydney leg. If you are coming from the United Kingdom, brace yourself for a flight of more or less 12 hours from London to Asia; then possibly a long day in transit, as flights to Australia have a nasty habit of arriving in Asia early in the morning and departing around midnight; and finally the 8 to 9 hour flight to Australia.

Sydney, Cairns, Melbourne, Brisbane, Adelaide, Darwin, and Perth are all international gateways, most airlines fly only to Sydney, but some fly to Melbourne.

THE MAJOR CARRIERS

Here are toll-free reservations numbers and websites for the major international airlines serving Australia. The "13" prefix in Australia means the number is charged at the cost of a local call from anywhere in the country.

Major Carriers Flying from North America

- **Air New Zealand** (☎800/262-1234 in the U.S., 800/663-5494 in English and 800/799-5494 in French, or 604/606-0150 in Vancouver in Canada, or 13 24 76 in Australia; www.airnz.com)

- **Canadian Airlines** (☎ **800/665-1177** in Canada, 800/363-7530 in French in Canada outside Quebec, 800/426-7000 in the U.S. or 1300/ 655 767 in Australia; www.cdnair.ca)
- **Qantas** (☎ **800/227-4500** in the U.S. and Canada, or 13 13 13 in Australia; www.qantas.com.au)
- **United Airlines** (☎ **800/241-6522** in the U.S. and Canada, or 13 17 77 in Australia; www.ual.com)

Major Carriers Flying from the U.K.
- **British Airways** (☎ **0845/773-3377** in the U.K., 1800/626 747 in Ireland, or 02/8904 8800 in Sydney, 07/3223 3133 in Brisbane, 1300/ 134 001 in Canberra, 03/9603 1133 in Melbourne, 08/8238 2138 in Adelaide, and 08/9425 7711 in Perth; www.britishairways.com)
- **Cathay Pacific** (☎ **0345/581 581** in the U.K. or 13 17 47 in Australia; www.cathaypacific.com)
- **Malaysia Airlines** (☎ **020/7341 2020** in the U.K., 1/676 2131 in Ireland, 13 26 27 in Australia; www.malaysiaairlines.com.my)
- **Qantas** (☎ **0345/747 767** in the U.K., or 13 13 13 in Australia; www.qantas.com.au)
- **Singapore Airlines** (☎ **0870/608 8886** in the U.K., 1/671 0722 in Ireland, or 13 10 11 in Australia; www.singaporeair.com)
- **Thai Airways International** (☎ **020/7499 9113** in the U.K., or 1300/651 960 in Australia; www.thaiair.com)

FINDING THE BEST AIRFARE

If you are flying from North America, keep in mind that the airlines' low season is mid-April to the end of August—this is when you'll find the cheapest fares. This happens to be the best time to travel most parts of Australia. High season is December through February, and shoulder season is September through November, and again from March to mid-April. Look for special deals offered throughout the year. Unexpected lows in airline passenger loads often lead airlines to put cheap offers on the market. The catch is these usually have a short lead time, requiring you to travel in the next 6 weeks or so. Some deals involve taking a circuitous route, via Fiji or Japan for instance. Canada 3000 has good rates from Vancouver in low season and often has promotional specials. **Austravel** (☎ **800/633-3404** in the U.S. and Canada) publishes a quarterly guide to airfares, carriers, stopovers, and flying times to Australia. Some travel agents and wholesalers specializing in cheap fares to Australia include **Austravel** (☎ **800/633-3404** in the U.S. and Canada, or 0870/055 0239 in the United Kingdom; www.austravel.com); **Downunder Direct,** which is a division of Swain Australia (☎ **800/642-6224** in the U.S. and Canada; www.downunderdirect.com); and **Goway** (☎ **800/387-8850** in the U.S. and Canada; www.goway.com).

   Consolidators, also known as "bucket shops," are another source for low fares. Consolidators buy seats in bulk from the airlines and then sell them back to the public at low prices, sometimes even below even the airlines' discounted rates. Their ads usually run in Sunday travel sections. Before you pay, however, ask for a confirmation number from the consolidator and then call the airline itself to confirm your seat. Be prepared to book your ticket with a different consolidator—there are many to choose from—if the airline can't confirm your reservation. Consolidator tickets are usually nonrefundable or have stiff cancellation penalties, often as high as 50% to 75% of the ticket price.

   Another source of good deals are "rebators" such as **Travel Avenue** (☎ **800/ 333-3335** in the U.S. or 312/876-6866; www.travelavenue.com), which rebate part of their commissions to you.

For hints on finding deals on the Internet, see "Planning an Affordable Trip Online," earlier in this chapter.

IN-FLIGHT COMFORT

To relieve the discomfort on this long-distance flight, your clothing and shoes should be comfortable and roomy, because your feet will swell. Drink plenty of water and go easy on the free alcohol. Requesting a bulkhead or exit door seat will give you more legroom. Some airlines allow you to request seats when you book, but others allocate seats only at check-in—in that case be early to beat savvy Aussies queuing for the same thing!

Jet lag is a foregone conclusion, so don't plan to climb Ayers Rock the first morning you arrive, or book opera tickets for your first evening. There is no "cure" for jet lag, but you can fight it by getting plenty of sleep on the flight and not overeating. Try to acclimatize yourself to the local time as quickly as possible. Stay up as long as you can the first day, then try to get up at a normal hour the next morning.

On such a long journey, it makes sense to break the trip with a 1-night stopover if you can. Coming from America, this will probably be Honolulu or maybe Fiji; from Europe, you have any number of Asian cities—Bangkok, Singapore, Hong Kong—in which to spend a night or two. If you're coming from Europe and you have a long layover in Asia, I strongly recommend you book a day room at a hotel with a 6pm checkout. Wandering around a humid, crowded city at 2pm when your body thinks it's 3am is not fun.

13 Getting Around Australia

One big mistake tourists make Down Under (apart from getting sunburned) is failing to comprehend the vast distances between the most popular locations. Every Sydney hotelier has a tale to tell about the tourist who complains their room doesn't have a view of Ayers Rock, 2,841 kilometers (1,765 miles) away, or asking what time the afternoon boat to the Great Barrier Reef leaves. Don't try to cram too much in one trip.

Flying is the best way to cover long distances in Australia. People who go by train, bus, or car are often disappointed at the flat, unchanging vistas of desert, fields, and gum trees—scenery that goes on for days. A good compromise is fly for long trips and save the land travel for short hops. Backtracking is time-consuming and expensive, so try not to cross your own path too many times.

BY PLANE

Australia is a big country with a small population to support its air routes, hence big airfares. This section contains some tips to help you beat them.

Domestic travel is almost entirely operated by **Qantas** (☎ **800/227-4500** in the U.S. and Canada, 0345/747 767 in the U.K., 0800/808 767 in New Zealand, and 13 13 13 in Australia; www.qantas.com).

In September 2001 Ansett Australia, the country's second-largest airline suspended operations. New owners reorganized the company, dubbed "Ansett Mark II," packaging it as a budget/no frills airline, and resumed domestic service (including on its regional subsidiaries) in October. Contact Ansett (☎ **13 13 00** in Australia, **888/426-7388** in the United States and Canada; www.ansett.com.au) for the latest updates, prices and bookings to cities and regions served by Ansett Mark II."

Contact Qantas (☎ **13 13 13** in Australia, 800/227-4500 in the United States and Canada, 457/747 767 in the UK and the local tourist bureaus of areas where you are planning to travel for the latest on regional air service.

Sample Flying Times & Airfares

Listed below are some commonly flown routes to give you an idea of typical flying times and costs. The times are those on the shortest route available and the fares are one-way at the full coach rate (21-, 14- and 7-day advance-purchase fares, air pass coupons, or fares for international travelers are much cheaper):

Route	Travel Time	Fare
Sydney–Cairns	3 hr.	A$599 (U.S.$389.35)
Cairns–Ayers Rock	3 hr., 45 min.	A$516 (U.S.$335.40)
Sydney–Melbourne	1 hr., 5 min.	A$288 (U.S.$187.20)
Alice Springs–Darwin	2 hr.	A$392 (U.S.$254.80)
Perth–Broome	2 hr., 45 min.	A$537 (U.S.$349.05)

An independent carrier that remains in Australia's domestic air market is **Virgin Blue** (☎ **13 67 89** in Australia; www.virginblue.com.au, an offshoot of Virgin Atlantic), which made its debut in 2000, and flies from Brisbane to Sydney, Sydney to Melbourne, Melbourne and Adelaide, and Sydney-Adelaide.

Virgin Blue sells cheap fares by offering little in the way of in-flight service, meals or entertainment. To get the best deal, book online. Fares booked over the phone are higher, but you will still be way ahead, because they are usually equal to, or lower than, the lowest fares sold by Qantas, and they mostly come without the advance-purchase, "no date change" or "non-transferable" conditions that Qantas places on their lowest-cost fares.

FARES FOR INTERNATIONAL TRAVELERS   Qantas typically offers international travelers a discount of around 30% off domestic fares. So, if the full fare for Australians is A$1,000, international visitors pay only around A$700 (U.S.$455). To qualify for these fares in Australia, give your passport number and international ticket number when you buy your ticket.

AIR PASSES   If you are planning on whipping around to more than one city, purchasing an Air Pass from Qantas is much cheaper than buying regular fares. You must buy these passes before you arrive in Australia; residents of Australia and New Zealand cannot purchase them.

With **Qantas's Boomerang Pass,** for example, you must purchase a minimum of two coupons (and a maximum 10) priced at U.S.$155/C$230 or U.S.$185/C$270 per coupon for travel within a zone, or U.S.$195/C$290 or U.S.$235/C$345 per coupon for travel between zones. The difference between the higher and lower fares depends on the airline's yield management system, so your coupons may cost the lower or higher amount depending on the day you buy them. Air passes are a great value when you consider that the regular Sydney–Cairns fare is A$599, which works out to U.S.$389.35, compared to the coupon fare of just U.S.$155 or $185. Coupons are also good for travel to/from New Zealand and to the most popular South Pacific nations. Zone 1 covers Western Australia; Zone 2 covers the Red Centre and Darwin; Zone 3 covers major towns in South Australia, Tasmania, Victoria, New South Wales, and Queensland; and Zone 4 covers many small towns in the east coast states, including island gateways like Hayman Island, Hamilton Island, Gladstone, and Rockhampton. You must book your first coupon destination before you arrive, but you can book the rest as you go. Another beauty of these fares is that they are refundable and changeable; you will incur a U.S.$45/C$50 fee to make changes after the coupons have been ticketed.

BY TRAIN

The rail network in Australia is mostly good for long-distance travel between state capitals and the towns in between. Australia's trains are clean, comfortable, and safe, and service and facilities are perfectly adequate.

Most long-distance trains have sleepers with big windows, electric outlets, wardrobes, sinks, and fresh linens. First-class sleepers have en suite bathrooms, and meals are often included. Second-class sleepers use shared shower facilities, and meals are not included; some second-class sleepers are private cabins, on other trains you share with strangers. Single cabins are usually of broom-closet dimensions but quite liveable. The food ranges from OK to pretty good. You can smoke in some trains in the club cars, rarely in the dining car or in your sleeper, and on some trains smoking is prohibited.

Australian rail schedules are no match for the snappy frequency of European rail travel—some trains only operate once a week—so check the timetable before you get your other travel arrangements in place.

Australia's rail routes are managed either by the private enterprise **Great Southern Railway** (☎ **13 21 47** in Australia, or 08/8213 4592; www.gsr. com.au), which runs the *Indian Pacific,* the *Overland* (Melbourne to Adelaide), and the *Ghan* (Sydney–Melbourne–Adelaide–Alice Springs) or by one of the following government bodies: **Queensland Rail** (☎ **13 22 32** in Australia, or 07/3235 1000; www.qr.com.au, or check the unofficial site www.qroti.bit. net.au), which handles rail within that state; **Countrylink** (☎ **13 22 32** in Australia, or 02/9379 1298; www.countrylink.nsw.gov.au), which manages travel within New South Wales and to Canberra, Melbourne, and Brisbane; and **Westrail** (☎ **13 10 53** in Western Australia or 1800/099 150 from elsewhere in Australia, or 08/9326 2222), which operates in Western Australia. Outside Australia, **Rail Australia** (www.railaustralia.com.au) handles inquiries and makes reservations for all long-distance trains, with the exception of Westrail. Call Rail Australia's overseas agents: **ATS Tours** (☎ **800/ 423-2880**) in the United States, **Goway** (☎ **800/387-8850**) in Canada, **Leisurail** (☎ **0870/750-0222**) in the United Kingdom, and **Tranz Rail** (☎ **03/372-8209**) in New Zealand.

Possibly the most luxurious train in the world, the ***Great South Pacific Express*** is an opulent new locomotive with lavish turn-of-the-last-century decor, rich timber paneling and silk upholstery. It is a joint venture between the Queensland government and Venice Simplon–Orient-Express. It plies the Brisbane–Cairns route weekly, incorporating the scenic rail trip to Kuranda (see chapter 7) and a side-trip by seaplane or helicopter to a private pontoon on the Great Barrier Reef. The route extends to or from Sydney around once a month. The scenery is dull; you make this trip for the train itself. Fares range from A$2,830 to $4,690 (U.S.$1,839.50–$3,048.50) per person, twin-share, for the Brisbane–Cairns leg. Contact Venice Simplon–Orient-Express (☎ **630/954-2945** in the U.S., 020/7805 5100 in the U.K.), Walshes World in New Zealand (☎ **09/379-3708**), or Orient-Express Trains and Cruises in Australia (☎ **1800/000 395** in Australia, or 07/3247 6595; fax 07/3247 6565); www.orient-expresstrains.com and www.gspe.com.

The only train linking Sydney, Adelaide, and Perth is the ✪ *Indian Pacific,* which makes a 3-day Outback run. Most folks take it for the "experience" rather than as a way to get to Perth. The luxurious *Great South Pacific*

Express plies the Sydney–Cairns route. The *Overland* links Adelaide and Melbourne. The *Ghan* traverses a loop in the desert between Sydney, Melbourne, Adelaide, and Alice Springs. Countrylink runs fast *XPTs* (Express Passenger Trains, which despite their name stop at points en route) linking Sydney with Melbourne, Canberra, Brisbane, and the New South Wales town of Dubbo, trains from Sydney to the farming town of Griffith and the Outback town of Broken Hill, and *Xplorer* trains linking Sydney with Canberra and the New South Wales towns of Tamworth, Armidale and Moree. In Queensland, the *Queenslander* runs Brisbane to Cairns with an all first-class-sleepers configuration, while the *Sunlander* does the same route with seats and economy sleepers. The economy-seat only *Spirit of the Tropics* runs Brisbane–Townsville, and the high-speed *Tilt* train does the Brisbane–Rockhampton route.

RAIL PASSES   National and state rail passes are available from **Rail Australia** (see above) at its overseas agents. National passes must be bought before you arrive and are only available to non-Australian residents. Unfortunately for parents, only the Sunshine Railpass offers a discount for kids, who must be aged 4 to 15 years.

The national **Austrail Pass** is good for economy seats and sleepers on intrastate, interstate, and even suburban city train networks around the country. It comes in 14-, 21- and 30-day versions and costs between A$660 (U.S.$429) and A$1,035 (U.S.$672.75). You can buy 7-day extensions for A$340 (U.S.$221). An alternative pass, the **Austrail Flexipass,** allows you to travel for any 8, 15, 22, or 29 days, consecutive or not, within a 6-month period. An 8-day Flexipass is A$550 (U.S.$357.50), with the price going up to A$1,440 (U.S.$936) for a 29-day Flexipass. *Note:* You cannot use the 8-day pass on the Adelaide–Perth route or the Sydney–, Melbourne– or Adelaide–Alice Springs routes.

State passes are available in New South Wales, Victoria, Queensland, and Western Australia, and can be purchased after you arrive in Australia. The **New South Wales Discovery Pass** is good for unlimited travel for one calendar month on all long-distance trains in New South Wales in economy-class seats (not sleepers); it costs A$249 (U.S.$161.85) or A$199 (U.S.$129.35) for YHA (Youth Hostels Association/Hostelling International) members.

Queensland's **Sunshine Railpass** is valid for 14-, 21-, and 30-day periods; it costs between A$294 (U.S.$191.10) and $427 (U.S.$277.55) and is valid on intrastate and suburban economy-class seats; and between A$427 (U.S.$277.55) and A$640 (U.S.$416) for a first-class sleeper. Queensland's **Roadrail Pass** is good for travel in economy-class sitting berths (not sleepers) on intrastate long-distance and McCafferty's coaches; it costs A$296 (U.S.$192.40) for 10 journeys over a 60-day period, or A$374 (U.S.$243.10) for 20 journeys over a 90-day period. Its use is subject to availability during Queensland school holidays. Unlike the Sunshine Railpass, it cannot be used on suburban trains or the Kuranda Scenic Railway.

The **East Coast Discovery Pass** allows you to travel one-way (north or south) in economy-class seats between Melbourne, Sydney, Brisbane, and Cairns; you can hop on and off as you please within a 6-month period. You buy this pass in sectors: The cheapest is the Sydney–Brisbane or Sydney–Melbourne sector for A$93.50 (U.S.$60.80), most expensive is the entire Melbourne–Cairns run for A$328.90 (U.S.$213.80). Some legs are only available to non-Australian residents.

Upgrades to an economy-class sleeper on Queensland Rail and Great Southern Railway trains are available for a surcharge of between A$35 and A$114 (U.S.$22.75and $74.10) per journey.

RAIL PACKAGES Both **Countrylink** and **Queensland Rail** (see above) offer a range of rail packages that include accommodations and sightseeing throughout New South Wales, as far west as Broken Hill and Lightning Ridge, as far south as Canberra and Melbourne, and throughout Queensland.

BY BUS

Bus travel in Australia is a step up from the low-rent affair it can be in the United States. Terminals are centrally located and well lit, the coaches are clean and air-conditioned, you sit in comfy adjustable seats, videos are shown on board, and the drivers are polite and may even comment on points of interest. Some buses have rest rooms. Unlike Australia's train service, there are few places the bus network can't take you. Buses are totally nonsmoking.

Greyhound Pioneer Australia (☎ **13 20 30** in Australia, or 07/3258 1600, fax 07/3258 1930; www.greyhound.com.au; no relation to Greyhound in the U.S.) and **McCafferty's** (☎ **13 14 99** in Australia, or 07/4690 9888; fax 07/ 4638 2178; www.mccaffertys.com.au) are the two big national coach operators. As well as point-to-point services, both coach companies offer a range of tours at popular locations on their networks. McCafferty's has many international agents, including **Inta-Aussie South Pacific** (☎ **310/568-2060**) in the United States, **Goway** (☎ **800/387-8850**) in Canada, and **Bridge the World** (☎ **020/7911 0900**) in the United Kingdom.

BUS PASSES Bus passes are a great value. **Day Passes** are good for 7, 10, 15, 21 days of travel (and 30 days in McCaffertys' case), consecutive or not, within a 1- to 2-month period depending on how many days you buy. McCaffertys' fares range from A$560 (U.S.$364) for a 7-day pass to A$1,345 (U.S.$874.25) for a 30-day pass. The passes are valid for travel in any direction, and backtracking is allowed. Purchase McCafferty's pass before you arrive in Australia. Greyhound Pioneer's passes are only available in Oz.

If you know where you are going and are willing to obey a "no backtracking" rule, a better deal is a **Travel Australia** (McCafferty's) or **Aussie Explorer** (Greyhound Pioneer) pass. These allow unlimited stops in a generous time frame on a pre-set one-way route (you are sometimes permitted to travel the route in either direction). Some routes allow backtracking on specific legs— Darwin to Kakadu National Park, say. You must book the next leg of your trip

---

Sample Travel Times & Bus Fares

Here are some sample bus fares and travel times. McCafferty's and Greyhound's fares are usually almost identical, to within a couple of dollars. All fares and travel times are one-way.

Route	Travel Time	Fare
Broome–Darwin	26½ hr.	A$234.40 (U.S.$152.40)
Sydney–Brisbane	17 hr.	A$82.50 (U.S.$53.65)
Cairns–Brisbane	28½ hr.	A$108.70 (U.S.$70.65)

Note: These are the fares you'll pay if you buy your ticket in Australia— fares and passes will be considerably cheaper if you're a student, a senior, a backpacker cardholder, or a YHA/Hostelling International member. Take note—you may have to buy them before you leave home to qualify for discounts.

Sample Driving Distances & Times

Here are a few sample road distances between popular points and the minimum time it takes to drive between them.

Route	Distance	Approx. Driving Time
Cairns–Sydney	2,495km (1,559 miles)	29 hr. (allow 4–5 days)
Sydney–Melbourne	873km (546 miles)	15 hr. (allow 1–2 days)
Sydney–Perth	4,131km (2,581 miles)	51 hr. (allow 6–7 days)
Adelaide–Darwin	3,024km (1,890 miles)	31 hr. (allow 4–6 days)
Perth–Darwin	4,163km (2,602 miles)	49 hr. (allow 6–8 days)

24 hours ahead. Choose from a dazzling array of routes with names like "Best of the East and Centre," "Reef & Rock," "Follow the Sun," "Outback Wanderer," and "Top End Safari."

McCafferty's "Sun and Centre" pass takes in Ayers Rock, Alice Springs, Kings Canyon, Katherine, Darwin, Kakadu National Park, Mt. Isa, Cairns, and the east coast down to Sydney. The pass is valid for 6 months and costs A$725 (U.S.$471.25) for travel only, or A$810 (U.S.$526.50) with some tours at popular destinations. McCafferty's does not serve Western Australia, so if you want a pass that covers the whole country, go for Greyhound Pioneer's **All Australian Pass** for A$1,722 (U.S.$1,119.30); it's valid for a year.

Greyhound Pioneer has an **Aussie Kilometre Pass** that allows unlimited stops in any direction within the mileage you buy. Passes are available in increments of 1,000 kilometers (625 miles). Prices range from A$226 (U.S.$146.90) for 2,000 kilometers (1,250 miles)—enough to get you from Cairns to Brisbane—to A$1,617 (U.S.$1,051.05) for a whopping 20,000 kilometers (12,500 miles). McCafferty's has a similar product called an **Australian Roamer Pass,** which is only available to students, holders of selected backpacker cards, and members of YHA/Hostelling International.

BY CAR

Not only are Australia's roads not great, there are not many of them. The taxes of 18 million people get spread pretty thin when it comes to maintaining roads in a country roughly the size of the continental United States. Most highways are two-lane affairs with the occasional rut and pothole, often no outside line markings and sometimes no shoulders to speak of.

When you are studying the map, remember that what looks like a road may be an unsealed (unpaved) track suitable for 4WD vehicles only. Many roads in the Top End are passable only in the Dry Season (about April to November). If you plan to do serious long-distance driving, get a decent road map (see below for sources).

You cannot drive across the middle of the country (except along the north-south Stuart Highway linking Adelaide and Darwin) because it's mostly desert. You can travel around the edge on Highway 1.

Your current **driver's license** or an **international driver's permit** is fine in every Australian state. You must carry your license when driving. The driving age is 16 or 17, depending on which state you are in, but some rental car companies require you to be 21, or even 26 to rent a 4WD vehicle.

CAR RENTALS

Think twice about renting a car in tourist hotspots such as Cairns. In these areas, most tour operators pick you up and drop you back at your hotel door, so having a car isn't worth the expense.

The "big four" car rental companies have extensive networks in Australia:

- **Avis** (☎ **1800/22 5533** in Australia; 800/230-4898 in the U.S.; 800/272-5871 in Canada; 0870/590-0500 in the United Kingdom; 21/28 1111 in Ireland; 09/526 2847 in New Zealand; www.avis.com)
- **Budget** (☎ **1300/36 2848** in Australia; 800/527-0700 in the U.S.; 800/268-8900 in Canada; 0645/60 6060 in the U.K.; 09/375-2222 in New Zealand; www.drivebudget.com)
- **Hertz** (☎ **13 30 39** in Australia; 800/654-3001 in the U.S.; 800/263-0600 in English, 800/263-0678 in French in Canada, or 416/620-9620 in Toronto; 0870/844-8844 in the U.K.; 1/676 7476 in Ireland; 0800/654 321 in New Zealand; www.hertz.com)
- **Thrifty** (☎ **1300/367 227** in Australia; 800/THRIFTY in the U.S. and Canada; 0800/96 3163 in the U.K.; 1800/51 5800 in Ireland; 09/309 1111 in New Zealand; www.thrifty.com)

A small sedan good for zipping around a city or touring a wine region will cost around A$70 (U.S.$45.50) a day. A feistier vehicle with enough grunt to get you hundreds of miles from state to state, will cost around A$85 to $100 (U.S.$55.25–$65) a day. Rentals of a week or longer usually reduce by A$5 (U.S.$3.25) a day or so.

A regular car will get you to most places in Australia, but in areas with many unsealed roads, it can make sense to rent a **four-wheel-drive (4WD) vehicle.** The major car rental companies all have them. They are more expensive than a regular car at around A$150 (U.S.$97.50) per day, or around A$130 (U.S.$84.50) a day for rentals of a week or longer.

Rates quoted here are only a guide. Many local companies, and the big guys, do competitive specials, especially in tourist areas with distinct off-seasons. Advance purchase rates, usually 7 to 21 days, can offer significant savings.

INSURANCE Insurance for loss of, or damage to, the car, and third party property insurance are usually included, but *read the rental agreement* before you set off, as the fine print contains key information the smiling front desk staff never tell you. For example, damage to the car body may be covered, but not damage to the windshield or tires, or damage caused by water.

The deductible, known as "excess" in Australia, on insurance may be as high as A$2,000 (U.S.$1,300) for regular cars and up to $5,500 (U.S.$3,575) on 4WDs and campervans. Reduce or avoid it by paying a surcharge of around A$7 to $16 (U.S.$4.55–$10.40) per day on a car or 4WD, and between A$22 to $44 (U.S.$14.30–$28.60) per day on a camper. The rate depends on the vehicle type and the extent of reduction you choose. The rental company may add in personal accident insurance and baggage insurance, but since your own travel insurance policy may cover these, make sure you're not duplicating coverage. And check the conditions; some excess reduction payments do not reduce excesses on single-vehicle accidents, for example.

ONE-WAY RENTALS Australia's great distances often make one-way rentals a necessity, for which car rental companies can charge a hefty penalty amounting to hundreds of dollars. A one-way fee usually applies to campervan

---

Insurance Alert

Damage to a rental car caused by an **animal** (hitting a kangaroo, for instance) is not covered by car rental companies' insurance policies, nor is driving on an unpaved road—and Australia has a lot of those.

Cut an average of 30% off your car rental by joining the Australian Youth Hostels Association (YHA), the Aussie arm of Hostelling International (see "For Students" under "Tips for Travelers with Special Needs" earlier in this chapter). Membership entitles you discounts from Avis, Budget, and Hertz.

renters too—for example, Maui charges a A$165 (U.S.$107.25) fee on most routes, and Britz charges A$200 (U.S.$130).

CAMPERVANS   Campervans (as Aussies call motor homes) are popular in Australia. Generally a good deal smaller than RVs in the United States, they come in two-, three-, four-, or six-berth versions, and usually have everything you need, such as a refrigerator, microwave, gas stove, cooking and cleaning utensils, linen, and touring information like maps and campground guides. All have showers and toilets, except for some two-berthers. Four-wheel-drive campers are available, but they are small and usually lack hot water, a toilet, a shower, and air-conditioned sleeping quarters. This is a necessity in most of the country from November to March. The minimum driver age is usually 21.

Australia's biggest campervan-rental company is **Britz Campervan Rentals and Tours** (☎ **1800/331 454** in Australia, or 03/9417 1888, fax 03/9416 2933; 805/373-8320 in the United States; 08705/143 609 in the United Kingdom; 0800/83 1900 in New Zealand; 0990/143 609 in the United Kingdom; www.britz.com); other major operators include **Maui** (☎ **1800/227 279** in Australia, or 02/9556 6100, fax 02/9556 3900; www.maui-rentals. com), and **Hertz Campervans** (☎ **1800/33 5888** in Australia, or Auto-Rent Hertz on ☎ 1800/030 500 in Tasmania, or 08/8271 8281; fax 08/8271 8546; or your nearest Hertz office; www.hertz.com).

For a two-berth campervan with shower or toilet, Britz's 2000/2001 rates were between A$106 (U.S.$68.90) and A$203 (U.S.$131.95) per day, over a 4 to 20 day rental period. For a four-berth with shower and toilet, you are looking at between A$150 (U.S.$97.50) and A$265 (U.S.$172.25) per day. Rates vary with the seasons. May and June are the slowest months; December and January are the busiest. It is sometimes possible to get better rates by booking in your home country before departure. Renting for longer than 3 weeks knocks around A$10 (U.S.$6.50) or more off the daily rate. Most companies will demand a minimum 4- or 5-day rental. It is wise to give the company your itinerary before booking, as some routes, such as the ferry across to Tasmania, or in a 4WD campervan's case the Gibb River Road in the Kimberley, may need the company's special permission. Campervan rental companies may not permit you to drive your 2-wheel drive campervan on unsealed roads.

Most local officials take a dim view of you pulling over by the roadside to camp for the night. I think this is absurd in Australia's wide open spaces. Instead, you will likely have to stay in a campground.

ON THE ROAD IN AUSTRALIA

GAS   The price of petrol (gasoline) will elicit a groan from Americans and a whoop of delight from Brits. Prices go up and down a lot, but you're looking at roughly around A80¢ a liter (or U.S.$1.96 per U.S. gallon) for unleaded petrol in New South Wales, as little as A60¢ a liter (or U.S.$1.47 per U.S. gallon) in Queensland, and A95¢ a liter (or U.S.$2.33 per U.S. gallon), or more, in the Outback. One U.S. gallon equals 3.78 liters. Most rental cars take unleaded gas, and campervans run on diesel which costs around A70¢ to $1 a liter (U.S.$1.72–$2.45 per U.S. gallon), depending on your location. Petrol stations (also called "roadhouses" in rural areas) can be few and far between in the Outback, so fill up at every opportunity.

DRIVING RULES   Australians drive on the left, which means you give way to the right. Left turns on a red light are *not* permitted unless a sign says so. Roundabouts are common at intersections; approach these slow enough to stop if you have to, and give way to all traffic on the roundabout. You are supposed to flash your indicator light as you leave the roundabout—even if you're going straight ahead as technically that's a left turn—but most Aussies never bother and it is not widely enforced. The only odd driving rule is Melbourne's requirement that drivers turn *right* from the *left* lane. This allows the city's trams to carry on uninterrupted in the right lane. Pull into the left lane opposite the street you are turning into, and make the turn when the traffic-light in the street you are turning into becomes green.

The maximum blood alcohol level when driving is 0.05, about two 200 milliliter (6.6 fl. oz.) drinks in the first hour for men, one for women, and one drink per hour for both sexes after that. The police set up random breath-testing units (RBTs) in cunningly disguised and unlikely places all the time, so it is easy to get caught. You will face a court appearance if you do.

The **speed limit** is 60 kilometers per hour (37.5 mph) in urban areas and 100 kilometers per hour (63 mph) or 110 kilometers per hour (69 mph) in most country areas. Speed limit signs are black numbers circled in red on a white background.

Drivers and passengers, including taxi passengers, must wear a **seatbelt** at all times, if a belt is fitted in the car, or face a fine. Young children are required to sit in the rear seat in a child-safety seat or harness; car rental companies will rent these to you, but book them ahead. Tell the taxi company you have a child when you call a cab, so they can send a car with the right restraints.

MAPS   Maps published by the state automobile clubs listed in "Auto Clubs" will likely be free if you are a member of an affiliated auto club at home. These don't usually have much tourism information on them, and you will probably have to wait until you arrive Down Under to collect them.

Two of the biggest map publishers in Australia are **HEMA Maps** (☎ 07/ **3290 0322;** fax 07/3290 0478; www.hemamaps.com.au) and **Universal Press** (☎ **02/9857 3700;** fax 02/9888 9074; sales@unipress.com.au). Both publish a big range of state and city maps. HEMA has an especially strong list of regional maps ("Gold Coast" and "The Red Centre" are just a few), while Universal produces a complete range of street directories by city, region or state under the "UBD" and "Gregory's" labels. HEMA produces maps to Kakadu and Lamington National Parks, and a Wine Map of Australia.

"Handy" versions, and its Both companies produce a range of national atlases. HEMA's 112-page "Australia Touring Atlas" doubles as a good road atlas, in a ring-bound form or a lighter bound version. It also publishes a dedicated "Australia Road Atlas" with a 4WD section—good if you plan to go off the trails covered by *Frommer's Australia*—and hasan Australian atlas on CD-ROM. I think Universals' best is the 180-page ring-bound "UBD Motoring Atlas of Australia", which helpfully publishes street maps of small regional towns in each state. A new "Gregory's Road Atlas of Australia" will be available from Universal in 2001. I find HEMA's maps easiest to read.

Both HEMA and Universal Press maps are distributed in the U.S. by **Map Link** (☎ **805/692-6777;** www.maplink.com). HEMA maps are sold by

Barnes & Noble and most specialist map stores in the United States and Canada. Universal Press maps are distributed in the United Kingdom by Edward Stanford's, (☎ 020/7240 3611; fax 020/7836 0189).

In Australia, auto clubs, many newsagents and bookstores are the best source of maps. Petrol stations stock a limited range relating to the route they are on.

ROAD SIGNS Australians navigate by road name, not road number. The easiest way to get where you're going is to familiarize yourself with the major towns along your route and follow the signs towards them.

AUTO CLUBS Every state and territory in Australia has its own auto club. Your auto association back home probably has a reciprocal agreement with Australian clubs, possibly entitling you to free maps, accommodation guides and roadside assistance. Don't forget to bring your membership card. Even if you are not a member, the clubs are a good source of advice on local traffic regulations, touring advice, road conditions, traveling in remote areas, and other motoring questions you may have. They sell maps, accommodation guides, and camping guides to nonmembers at reasonable prices. You can drop into numerous regional offices as well as the head office locations listed here. None will mail maps overseas; you'll have to pick those up on arrival.

- **New South Wales & ACT:** National Roads and Motorists' Association (NRMA), 74–76 King St. at George Street, Sydney, NSW 2000 (☎ **13 21 32** in New South Wales or 02/9848 5201; fax 02/9292 8472)
- **Victoria:** Royal Automobile Club of Victoria (RACV), 550 Princes Hwy., Noble Park, VIC 3174 (☎ **13 19 55** in Australia, or 03/9790 2211; fax 03/9790 2955). Another office is at 360 Bourke St., Melbourne.
- **Queensland:** Royal Automobile Club of Queensland (RACQ), 300 St. Pauls Terrace, Fortitude Valley, QLD 4006 (☎ **13 19 05** in Australia, or 07/3361 2444; fax 07/3252 3587). A more convenient city office is in the General Post Office building at 261 Queen St., Brisbane.
- **Western Australia:** Royal Automobile Club of WA (RAC), 228 Adelaide Terrace, Perth, WA 6000 (☎ **08/9421 4444;** fax 08/9221 2708)
- **South Australia:** Royal Automobile Association of South Australia (RAA), 41 Hindmarsh Sq., Adelaide, SA 5000 (☎ **08/8202 4600;** fax 08/8202 4520)
- **Northern Territory:** Automobile Association of the Northern Territory (AANT), 79–81 Smith St., Darwin, NT 0800 (☎ **08/8981 3837;** fax 08/8941 2965)
- **Tasmania:** Royal Automobile Club of Tasmania (RACT), Corner of Murray and Patrick Streets, Hobart, TAS 7000 (☎ **13 27 22** in Tasmania or 03/6232 6300; fax 03/6232 6330)

These clubs (except AANT) can be reached on the Web at **www.aaa.asn.au**.

DRIVING SAFETY Long distances, unsealed roads, and wildlife are all driving hazards. The most common dangers and ways to avoid them:

Fatigue Fatigue is the number three killer on Australia's long roads, after driving while intoxicated and speeding. Be sure to take a 20-minute break every 2 hours, even if you do not feel tired.

Kangaroos & Other Wildlife It's a sad fact, but Skippy is a road hazard. Avoid driving between dusk and dawn in country areas, as this is when 'roos are most active. If you hit one, stop and check its pouch for live joeys (baby kangaroos) as females usually have one in the pouch. Wrap the joey tightly in a towel or old sweater, don't feed or overhandle it, and take it to a vet in the nearest town or call one of the following wildlife care groups: **Wildlife Information & Rescue Service** (WIRES) in New South Wales (☎ 1800/641 188 or 02/8977 3333); **Wildlife Care Network** in Victoria (☎ 0500/540 000); **Wildcare** in Queensland (☎ 07/5530 6634); **RSPCA Wildlife** in the ACT (☎ 02/6287 8100); **FAWNA Inc.** in Western Australia (☎ 08/9753 2118); **Wildcare Inc.** in the Northern Territory (☎ 08/8999 5511); the **Kangaroo (& Wildlife) Information & Rescue Service** (KRIS) (☎ 017/869 891 is a mobile telephone) or **Fauna Rescue of S.A.** (☎ 08/8289 2920) in South Australia; or **Wildcare** in Tasmania (☎ 03/6233 6556). Most vets will treat native wildlife free of charge.

Some major highways run through unfenced stations (ranches), where sheep and cattle pose a threat. Cattle like to rest on the warm bitumen road at night, so put your lights on high beam to spot them. If an animal does loom up before you, slow down but never swerve or you may roll, and, if you have to, hit it. Tell station owners within 24 hours if you have hit their livestock.

Car rental companies will not insure for animal damage to the car, which should give you an inkling of how common an occurrence this is.

Road Trains   Road trains consist of as many as three big truck carriages linked together to make a "train" up to 53.5-meters (175-ft.) long. If you're in front of one, give it plenty of warning when you brake, as the driver needs a lot of distance to slow down. Allow at least one clear kilometer (over half a mile) before you pass one, but don't expect the driver to make it easy for you— "truckies" are notorious for their lack of concern for motorists.

Unsealed Roads   Many of Australia's country roads are unsealed (unpaved). They are usually bone-dry which makes them a lot more slippery than they look, so travel at a moderate speed on these—35 kilometers per hour (20 mph) is not too cautious and anything over 60 kilometers per hour is dangerous—and don't overcorrect if you veer to one side. Keep well behind any vehicles in front as the dust they throw up can block your vision.

Floods   Floods are common in the Top End and north of Cairns from November or December to March or April (the Wet Season). Never cross a flooded road unless you are sure of its depth. Crocodiles may be in the water, so do not wade in to test it! Fast-flowing water is dangerous. When in doubt, stay put and wait for the water to drop, as most flash floods subside in 24 hours. Check road conditions ahead at least once a day in the Wet Season.

What to Do if Your Vehicle Breaks Down   If you break down or get lost, NEVER leave your vehicle. Many a motorist, often an Aussie who should know better, has died wandering off for help or water, knowing full well that neither is to be found for hundreds of miles. Most people who get lost do so in hot Outback spots; if that happens to you, conserve your body moisture level by doing as little as possible and staying in the shade of your car. Put out distress signals in patterns of three—three yells, three columns of smoke, and so on. The traditional Outback call for help is "coo-*ee*", with the accent on the "ee" and yodeled in a high pitch; it travels a surprisingly long way.

The auto clubs listed above provide free **breakdown emergency assistance** to members of many affiliated automobile associations around the world.

TIPS FOR FOUR-WHEEL DRIVERS   Always keep to the 4WD track and leave gates as you found them (open or closed). On an extended trip or in remote areas, carry 5 liters (1.3 gal.) of drinking water per person per day

Emergency Breakdown Assistance

The emergency breakdown assistance telephone number for every Australian auto club is ☎ **13 11 11** from anywhere in Australia. It is billed as a local call. If you are not a member of an auto club that has a reciprocal agreement with the Australian clubs, you'll have to join the Australian club on the spot before they will come. This costs around A$60 (U.S.$39), not a big price when you're stranded. In the Outback the charge may be much higher. Most car rental companies also have emergency assistance numbers.

(dehydration occurs fast in the Australian heat); enough food to last 3 or 4 days more than you think you will need; a first-aid kit; spare fuel; a good jack and two spare tires; spare fan belts, radiator hoses and air-conditioner hoses; a tow rope; and a good map that marks all gas stations. In seriously remote areas, or if you plan to travel off-road, carry a high frequency and CB radio (even if you have a cell phone, it may not work in the Outback). Obtain permission from the owners before venturing on to private station (ranch) roads. Advise a friend, your hotel manager, the local tourist bureau, or a police station of your route and your expected time of return or arrival at your destination. If you get bogged, let some of the air out of your tires to obtain more traction.

14 Tips on Accommodations

You'll find loads of inexpensive accommodation choices in Australia, even in the cities. Some of the terms used in Australia may not be familiar to international visitors, so here's a brief rundown.

HOTELS   Most rooms have reverse-cycle air-conditioning for heating and cooling, a phone, TV, clock-radio, mini-refrigerator if not a minibar, an iron and ironing board, and self-serve tea and coffee. Private bathrooms are standard, although often there's a shower, not a tub.

SERVICED APARTMENTS   This type of accommodation is very popular with Aussies: you get a furnished apartment with one, two, or three bedrooms and a living room, a full kitchen and often two bathrooms. So you're getting all the facilities and more of a hotel suite—and often for less than the cost of a standard hotel room. Serviced apartments are great for families, and for anyone prepared to save money by cooking their own meals. The Australian apartment inventory ranges from clean and comfortable to luxurious, and rates vary accordingly. You can find a nice two-bedroom apartment for A$120 (U.S.$78). Most can be rented for just one night, but some proprietors may insist on a minimum 3-night stay, or even a week in high season in popular vacation spots. **Medina Serviced Apartments** (☎ **1300/300 232** in Australia, or 02/9360 1699; fax 02/9360 7769; www.medinaapartments.com.au) has a chain of mid-range to upscale properties in Sydney, Melbourne, Brisbane and Canberra.

MOTELS & MOTOR INNS   You can usually rely on Australia's plentiful motels to be neat and clean, if a little dated. Count on air-conditioning, a phone, TV, clock-radio, a minirefrigerator or minibar, and self-serve tea and coffee. Most have showers, not bathtubs. Some have a restaurant attached, and many have a swimming pool. Motor inns offer a greater range of facilities, and fancier rooms than motels, without losing their down-to-earth touch or affordability. Rates average A$70 to $90 (U.S.$45.50–$58.50) double, although in low season you can score rooms for as low as A$50 (U.S.$32.50) double.

BED-&-BREAKFAST INNS   B&Bs in Australia are a fabulous value—it is easy to find charming rooms for A$75 (U.S.$48.75) or less for a double, and rarely will you pay more than A$100 (U.S.$65) for a double per night. Some B&Bs are modest suburban homes whose owners rent out a room to travelers; others are charming historical houses converted to accommodations; still others are purpose-built homes with several rooms designed for traveling guests, often with private bathrooms. Some larger commercial inns, with maybe 10 or 15 rooms, also call themselves B&Bs. Whatever the style, the accommodation is usually cozy and the welcome warm. Staying in B&Bs is a terrific way to meet other travelers, and of course you get to meet your Aussie hosts. Some considerations to take into account: you probably won't have access to a phone unless the hosts let you use theirs; you may not have a TV, clock-radio, minibar, or other amenities standard in hotels and motels; they may not take credit cards; and your hosts, who have their own lives, may not be there to receive you 24 hours a day. Bath facilities are often shared, although many B&Bs these days have private bathrooms.

Travel agents rarely list B&Bs because the establishments are not big enough to pay commission, so they can be hard to find. A great source is *The Australian Bed & Breakfast Book* (Moonshine Press, Sydney ☎ 02/9981 3247) which lists hundreds of high-quality B&B's across Australia. In Australia it is widely available in bookshops and newsagents. In the U.S. it's distributed by **South Pacific Traveler's Booksource,** P.O. Box 55, Wooster, OH 44691-0055 (☎ **800/234-4552;** ☎/fax 330/262-7821), and retails for U.S.$15.95. In the United Kingdom, contact Moonshine Press, 16 Blenheim St., Hebden Bridge, West Yorkshire, HX7 8BU (☎ **01422/845 085;** fax 01422/845 874). It retails for 9.95 British pounds (make cheques payable to "The New Zealand Bed and Breakfast Book", which this British company also distributes, even though it is the Aussie book you're buying). The entire book is posted on the Web at www.bnb.co.nz.

What Next? Productions Pty. Ltd., 24 Mitford St., St. Kilda, Melbourne, VIC 3182 (☎ **03/9537 0833;** fax 03/9537 0922; jhawley@micronica.com.au), publishes two exquisite color guides: *Beautiful B&Bs & Small Hotels,* with a Tasmania edition featuring 104 properties and a Victoria/South Australia edition featuring 240 properties. The places listed are more upscale than most, roughly in the A$100 to $200 (U.S.$65–$130) price range for a double; each book contains six 10% discount vouchers. A guide to New South Wales should be added to the series by the time you read this. The guides sell for A$26.95 (U.S.$17.50) in Australian bookstores.

The Northern Territory Bed & Breakfast Council's website has a list of **Australian B&B directories** on the Web: www.bed-and-breakfast.au.com/dirdir.htm (*note*: the address reads "au.com", *not* "com.au").

PUBS   Many Aussie pubs offer rooms upstairs, usually with shared facilities. Because most pubs are over 100 years old, the rooms are often quaint in an old-fashioned way: wrought-iron beds, lace bedcovers, dark wood furniture, French doors opening onto wide verandahs—or just plain old. Pub accommodations are dying out in cities, but are common enough in the country. Australians are rowdy drinkers, so sleeping over the front bar can be noisy, but a pub's saving grace is low rates. Most charge per person, not per room, and you will rarely pay more than A$50 (U.S.$32.50) per person a night. It is not hard to find a bed for as little as A$20 (U.S.$13) a night.

MEET THE AUSSIES

If you want to see an Australian Rules football game with a knowledgeable local in the game's birthplace of Melbourne, swim at Bondi Beach with a Sydneysider, or meet a Brisbanite for shopping and coffee, get in touch with **Friends Overseas—Australia,** 68–01 Dartmouth St., Forest Hills, NY 11375 (☎ **718/261-0534;** awhyte@mail.idt.net). This program is designed to match visitors to Oz with friendly Aussies of like age and interest, so you can spend time with them, without staying in their homes. Australian program members live in and around Sydney, Melbourne, Canberra, Brisbane, Adelaide, Perth, Hobart, and Cairns. The most unusual member lives on Old Andado, a cattle station in the Red Centre. Send a stamped, self-addressed envelope to the above address. The membership fee is U.S.$25.

If you want to stay with an Aussie family and really get involved in their life, even down to sitting at their table, **Homestay Network,** 5 Locksley St., Killara, NSW 2071 (☎ **02/9498-4400;** fax 02/9498 8324; thenetwork@bigpond. com; www.sydney.citysearch.com.au, click on Visiting Sydney, then Where to Stay, then Guesthouses), can place you in one of some 2,000 homes in the Sydney area. They can try to match your bridge mania, opera fetish or other penchant to hosts with similar tastes. Prices vary, but as a guide expect to pay about A$150 (U.S.$97.50) per double with breakfast.

FARMSTAYS The Aussie answer to the dude ranch is a farmstay, where you get involved in farm duties, tour the property, or just relax under a gum tree. Accommodations on farms can be anything from a basic bunkhouse (ask if it's air-conditioned, most farms are in very hot areas) to rustically luxurious digs that would do Ralph Lauren proud. Do some research on your chosen farm— a lot of activities are seasonal, some farmers will not want you around dangerous jobs, not all will offer horse-riding, and "farm" can mean different things in different parts of Australia. If you like green fields and dairy cows, Victoria is the place for you. If checking fences on a dusty 500,000 acre Outback station (ranch) sounds wildly romantic, not only are you crazy, but you should head to Western Australia or the Northern Territory.

Australian Farm & Country Tourism, Level M2, Rialto North Tower, 525 Collins St., Melbourne, VIC 3000 (☎ **03/9614 0892;** fax 03/9614 0895; www.factv.com) has free brochures, one per state, that detail accommodation, activities, and rates at a range of farmstay properties in Victoria, New South Wales, Queensland, South Australia, and Western Australia. Rates vary, but expect to pay about A$85 (U.S.$55.25) for a double without meals.

YOUTH HOSTELS & BACKPACKER LODGES Australia has oodles of backpacker hostels. Some are little more than grim dormitories (without air-conditioning); others are spiffy new complexes with cheerily painted rooms, a pool, tour desk, restaurant and bar, communal kitchens, and Internet access. If you like the idea of traveling cheap, but aren't wild about bunking with strangers, opt for one of the many that offer private double rooms or family rooms. Some hostels will impose a maximum stay of 3 nights, others are happy to accommodate you for a week or more. Blankets and pillows are provided, but you may need to rent bed linens for an extra two or three dollars per stay; bring your own towel. Look for hostels that have lockers, as the backpacker circuit has more than its fair share of petty thieves. Hostels typically charge between A$11 to $18 (U.S.$7.15–11.70) per dorm bed per night, and between A$40 to $45 (U.S.$26–$29.25) for a twin/double private room. Private rooms are in high demand, so book ahead.

The **Australian Youth Hostels Association** (YHA), 422 Kent St., Sydney, NSW 2000 (☎ **02/9261 1111,** fax 02/9261 1969; www.yha.org.au) is the Australian arm of Hostelling International, and has more than 140 hostels in Australia. People of any age can stay at them. Quality and facilities vary, but YHA hostels are clean, and have communal kitchens and 24-hour access. You don't have to join the association to stay at a hostel, but members receive discounted rates and are entitled to myriad other discounts: on car rental, bus travel, and tours, for example; that can more the cover the membership fee.

In the United States, contact **Hostelling International/American Youth Hostels,** 733 15th St. NW, Suite 840, Washington, DC 20005 (☎ **202/783-6161;** www.hiayh.org) or join at any hostel in the United States. The 12-month membership is free if you are 17 or under, U.S.$25 if you are 18 to 54, and U.S.$15 if you are 55 years or older. Hostelling International sells a directory of all Australian youth hostels for U.S.$5.50.

In Canada, contact **Hostelling International-Canada,** 205 Catherine St., Suite 400, Ottawa, Ontario, K2P 1C3 (☎ **613/237-7884;** www.hostelling intl.ca). In England and Wales, contact **Youth Hostels Association (England and Wales)**, Trevelyan House, 8 St. Stephen's Hill, St. Albans, Hertfordshire AL1 2DY (☎ **1727/855 215**). In Scotland, contact the **Scottish Youth Hostels Association,** 7 Glebe Crescent, Stirling FK8 2JA (☎ **1786/891 400**). In Ireland, contact **Hostelling International-Northern Ireland,** 22 Donegall Rd., Belfast BT12 5JN (☎ **1232/315 435**). All of these offices are accessible at www.iyhf.org. *Note:* YHA properties are nonsmoking.

YWCA (☎ **1800/249 124** in Australia, or 03/9329 3363; www.travel-ys.com; info@travel-ys.com) has eight comfortable budget hotels with private rooms, and sometimes dormitories that are a cut above the average backpacker hostel. There's a Y in Alice Springs, Brisbane, Darwin, a couple in Melbourne, Sydney and Toowoomba.

CAMPING & CARAVAN PARKS   Australians camp year-round, even in remote desert outposts and in winter. The only places you might want to avoid are Tasmania and the mountainous areas of New South Wales and Victoria in winter, when it's a bit nippy, and the Top End in the summer Wet Season.

Campsites are attached to nearly all the country's numerous caravan (camper) parks, and many lodges offer associated campgrounds. Camping in national parks does entail some restrictions: you can camp only at designated campsites; occasionally bookings may be required 24 hours in advance. Open fires are often banned, so you will need to rely on a gas barbecue or, if none is supplied, your own camping stove.

Expect to pay A$3 to $8 (U.S.$1.95–$5.20) per adult in a tent, A$8 to $11 (U.S.$5.20–$7.15) for a powered campsite, and about half price for kids. Definitely book ahead during school vacations and peak season.

Fast Facts: Australia

American Express   For all travel-related customer inquiries including reporting a lost card, call ☎ **1800/230 100.** To report lost or stolen traveler's checks there is a separate line (☎ **1800/251 902**).

Business Hours   Banks are open Monday to Thursday 9:30am to 4pm, and until 5pm on Friday. General business hours are Monday through Friday 8:30am to 5:30pm. Shopping hours are usually 8:30am to 5pm weekdays and 9am to 4pm or 5pm on Saturday. Many shops close

Sundays, although major department stores and shops aimed at tourists, like opal stores, are open seven days.

Car Rentals   See "Getting around Australia" earlier in this chapter.

Climate   See "When to Go" earlier in this chapter.

Currency   See "Money" earlier in this chapter.

Customs   See "Entry Requirements & Customs" in this chapter.

Dates   Australians write their dates day, month, year: January 5, 1968, is 05/01/68.

Documents Required   See "Entry Requirements &Customs" earlier in this chapter.

Driving Rules   See "Getting around Australia" earlier in this chapter.

Drugstores   Called "chemists" or "pharmacies." Australian pharmacists may only fill prescriptions written by Australian doctors.

Electricity   The current is 240 volts AC, 50 Hertz. Sockets take two or three flat, not rounded, prongs. North Americans and Europeans should bring a converter. Some hotels have 110V outlets for electric shavers or dual-voltage, and some will lend converters, but don't count on it. Power does not start automatically when you plug in an appliance; you need to flick the switch located beside the socket.

Embassies/Consulates   Most diplomatic posts are in Canberra, the nation's capital: **British High Commission,** Commonwealth Avenue, Canberra, ACT 2600 (☎ 02/6270 6666); **Embassy of Ireland,** 20 Arkana St., Yarralumla, ACT 2600 (☎ 02/6273 3022); **High Commission of Canada,** Commonwealth Avenue, Yarralumla, ACT 2600 (☎ 02/6270 4000); **New Zealand High Commission,** Commonwealth Avenue, Canberra, ACT 2600 (☎ 02/6270 4211); and the **United States Embassy,** 21 Moonah Place, Yarralumla, ACT 2600 (☎ 02/6214 5600). Embassies or consulates with posts in state capitals are listed in "Fast Facts" in the relevant state chapters.

For Australian embassies abroad, see "Entry Requirements & Customs" earlier in this chapter.

Emergencies   Dial ☎ **000** anywhere in Australia for police, ambulance, or the fire department. This is a free call from public and private telephones, and needs no coins.

Etiquette   Australia's laid-back disposition means it's first names from the start, handshakes all round, and no standing on ceremony, mate. Always return the courtesy of a "shout" (round) at the pub, and don't butt in if there's a queue (line). Try not to use a cellphone in a restaurant (although plenty of diners do) and definitely turn it off in the theater.

Holidays   See "When to Go" earlier in this chapter.

Liquor Laws   Pub (bar) hours vary, but most are open daily from around 10am to 10pm or midnight. The minimum drinking age is 18. Random breath tests to catch drunk drivers are common, and drunk-driving laws are strictly enforced. An arrest for drunk driving will mean a court appearance, not just a fine. The maximum permitted blood alcohol level is 0.05. Alcohol is sold in liquor stores, or "bottle shops" attached to a pub, and rarely in supermarkets.

Mail   Australia's postal service, Australia Post (☎ **13 13 18** in Australia) has a post office in every suburb. Every state capital has a central General Post Office (GPO) offering a complete range of services. Some newsagents sell stamps. A postcard costs A$1 (U.S.65¢) to the United States, Canada, the United Kingdom, or New Zealand.

Newspapers/Magazines   National papers are *The Australian* (Monday through Friday), *The Weekend Australian* (Saturday), the *Australian Financial Review* (Monday through Saturday). *Time* magazine publishes an Australian edition. *The Bulletin* is Australia's weekly news magazine.

Pets   Leave 'em at home. You will be back home planning your next vacation before Fluffy clears quarantine in Oz.

Police   Dial ☎ **000** anywhere in Australia. This is a free call from public and private telephones, and requires no coins.

Safety   Violent crime is uncommon. Guns are strictly controlled. Purse-snatchers are the same threat in capital cities and tourist areas that they are all over the world.

Taxes   In 2000, Australia introduced a 10% Goods and Services Tax (GST) on most products and services. Your international airline ticket to Australia is not taxed, nor are your domestic airline tickets for travel within Australia *if you bought them outside Australia*. Any airline tickets or other travel purchased in Australia will be taxed.

At press time, it was planned that international visitors would be able to claim a refund of the GST paid on a purchase of more than A$300 (U.S.$195) from a single outlet. More than one item may be included in that A$300. For example, you can claim back the GST you paid on 10 T-shirts each worth $31, as long as they were bought at one time in one store. You claim a refund by showing your receipt, called a "tax invoice", to the Customs desk at the airport as you leave Australia. So keep your receipts handy on the day you leave.

Items bought in duty-free stores will not attract GST. Nor will items you export—such as an Aboriginal painting that you buy in a gallery in Alice Springs and have shipped straight to your home outside Australia.

Basic groceries are not GST-taxed, but restaurant meals are.

Other taxes include departure tax of A$30 (U.S.$19.50), which was included in the price of your airline ticket when you bought it; landing and departure taxes at some airports, also included in the ticket price; and "reef tax", (the Environmental Management Charge), of A$4 (U.S.$2.60) for every person over the age of 4 every time he or she enters the Great Barrier Reef Marine Park (this charge goes towards park upkeep).

Telephone & Fax   **From North America:** Dial the international access code (**011**); Australia's country code (**61**); then the area code (we've given the area code for every number listed in this book); then the local number. The local area codes found throughout this book all begin with "0"; drop the "0" if you're calling from outside Australia, but dial it as part of the area code if you're calling from another city or town within Australia. So, to call the Sydney Opera House (☎ **02/9250 7111**) from the United States, dial ☎ **011-61-2-9250-7111**.

To call Australia from the United Kingdom: Dial the international access code **00**, and then follow the instructions above.

Not only do hotels in Australia charge for local calls, most routinely add outrageous surcharges onto all phone calls made from your room. It'll be a lot cheaper to use your own calling card (although some hotels will charge you for this, too) or find a pay phone.

To make an international call from Australia: Dial the international access code **0011** (*note* it has two zeros, not one like the international access code from North America); then the country code, then the area code, and finally the local number. To find out the per-minute international charges to any country, dial ☎ **12552.** To find out a country code, call ☎ **1222** or look in the back of the Australian White Pages. Common country codes are: USA and Canada, 1; United Kingdom, 44; Ireland, 353; New Zealand, 64.

To make an international credit card or collect call from Australia: Dial one of the following access codes to your country:

- **United States: AT&T Direct** (☎ 1800/881 011), **Sprint** (☎ 1800/ 881 877), **MCI** (☎ 1800/881 100), **Worldcom** (☎ 1800/881 212), or **Verizon** (☎ 1800/881 152)
- **United Kingdom: BT** (☎ 1800/881 440, or 1800/881 441, automated service only) or **Mercury** (☎ 1800/881 417)
- **Ireland:** ☎ 1800/881 353
- **New Zealand:** ☎ 1800/881 640

To use a calling card from some pay phones, you will need to deposit A40¢, but this is usually refunded when you hang up.

To make a long-distance call within Australia: Dial the area code, including the initial zero, followed by the number you are calling. Australia's area codes are: New South Wales and the ACT, 02; Victoria and Tasmania, 03; Queensland, 07; and South Australia, Western Australia, and the Northern Territory, 08. Long-distance calls within Australia on Telstra's network are cheaper before 7am and after 7pm Monday through Friday and anytime on weekends.

Australia's toll-free numbers: Australian phone numbers beginning 1800 are toll-free; numbers starting with 13 or 1300 are charged at the local fee of 25¢ from anywhere in Australia. 1900 (or 1901, 1902, etc. numbers) are pay-for-service lines (like 900 numbers in the U.S.); charges are as much as A$5 (U.S.$3.25) a minute.

Local Calls: Local calls in Australia are untimed and cost a flat A40¢ from a public telephone, or A25¢ from a private phone in a home or office. At presstime, telephone companies were throwing around the idea of introducing timed local calls.

To avoid digging for change at pay phones, consider buying a Telstra **Smart Phonecard** (which you swipe in the pay phone; not all public telephones take swiped Phonecard or credit cards yet) or a **PhoneAway card,** used by dialing access codes printed on the card. Both contain a prepaid allotment of time for local, long-distance, international and cell phone calls. PhoneAway cards have a personal Voicemail and fax box. Both are widely sold at newsagents, Telstra shops, tourist information booths and other outlets. PhoneAway cards are sold at post offices, Traveland travel agencies and some duty-free stores.

Mobile Calls: Australia has the world's biggest per capita uptake of cellular or "mobile" telephones. They are available for daily rental at major airports and in big cities. Before you bring your cell phone, check with your provider to see if it will work in Australia. Call rates to mobile telephones vary a lot with the telephone company; they are charged on a per-second or per-minute basis, and can add up quickly.

Operator Assistance: To reach the operator for help making a call, dial ☎ **1234**. To make a collect call, dial the operator on ☎ **12550**. To find out a telephone number, call Directory Assistance at ☎ **1223** for numbers within Australia, or ☎ **1225** for overseas numbers.

Time   Australia crosses three time zones—**Eastern Standard Time** (EST, also written as AEST sometimes) covers Queensland, New South Wales, the Australian Capital Territory, Victoria and Tasmania; **Central Standard Time** covers the Northern Territory and South Australia; and **Western Standard Time** (WST) is used in Western Australia. When it is noon in New South Wales, the A.C.T, Victoria, Queensland, and Tasmania, it is 11:30am in South Australia and the Northern Territory and 10am in Western Australia. All states except Queensland, the Northern Territory, and Western Australia observe daylight saving time from the last Sunday in October (the first Sunday in October in Tasmania's case) to the last Sunday in March. Not all states switch over to daylight saving on the same day or in the same week.

The east coast of Australia is GMT (Greenwich Mean Time) plus 10 hours. When it is noon on the east coast, it is 2am in London that morning, and 6pm in Los Angeles and 9pm in New York the previous night. Allow for daylight saving in the Australian summer, or in the country you are calling. New Zealand is two hours ahead of the east coast of Australia.

For the exact **local time** in the state you are calling from within Australia, call ☎ **1194**. For national and international time zones, ring ☎ **1900/937 106** at 95c per minute.

Tipping   It is customary to tip 5% or round up to the nearest A$10 for a substantial meal in a restaurant (but not for a snack). Waiters get paid decently enough that you are not expected to supplement their income. Some passengers round up to the nearest dollar in a cab, but it's OK to insist on every last 5-cent piece of change back from the driver. Tipping bellboys and porters is sometimes done, but not really expected. No one tips bar staff, barbers, or hairdressers.

Water   Water is fine to drink everywhere except Port Douglas, where you should stick to the bottled variety. In the Outback, the taps may carry warm brackish water from underground called "bore water" for showers and laundry, while drinking water is collected in rainwater tanks.

Weather   For the weather forecast for the state in Australia in which you are in, call ☎ **1196**. This costs A25¢ from a fixed telephone, A40¢ from a public telephone, more from a mobile (cell) phone.

3

Settling into Sydney

by Marc Llewellyn

1 Orientation

SYDNEY

Sunny, sexy, and sophisticated, Sydney basks in its worldwide recognition as the shining star of the southern hemisphere. The "Emerald City" is one of the most attractive metropolises on earth. Some people compare it to San Francisco—but the gateway to Australia is far from a clone of any American or European city.

If one symbol represents the city, it's the Sydney Opera House. This white-sailed construction, designed by Danish architect Jørn Utzon and caught mid-billow over the waters of Sydney Cove, is a universally recognized icon of Sydney, and the pride of the city—but there's far more on offer.

Close on its heels is the other great icon, the Sydney Harbour Bridge. You can walk across the pathway besides the trains and traffic and then catch the CityRail train back into town from the other end, while those with a daredevil spirit can venture up the catwalks and ladders to the top of the main arch.

While Sydney is one of the world's largest cities in area as well as population, (4 million people, 1,730 sq. km/668 sq. miles) most of the interesting things are in a relatively compact area around one of the finest urban harbors in the world.

It's up to you whether you explore this famous waterway by a public ferry ride from Circular Quay, take a specialized harbor tour, or simply walk along its banks, but any way you go, you'll find it's a good center point to orient yourself in this city by the sea.

As it is, there's so much to do in Sydney that you could easily spend a week here and still find yourself crashing into bed at night exhausted from trying to fit everything in.

Sydney's greatest summer experience, of course, are the beaches—with more than 20 strung along the city's oceanfront and dozens more dotted around the harbor, you'll be spoiled at the number of choices. The most famous is Bondi, a long strip of golden sand legendary for its Speedo-clad lifesavers and surfboard riders. From here a "must do" is the two-mile coastal path which leads off across the cliff tops, via cozy Tamarama beach (dubbed "Glamourama" for its chic sunworshippers), to glorious Bronte Beach, where you can cool down in the crashing waves of the Pacific.

Another beach favorite is Manly, reached by a 30-minute ferry trip from Circular Quay. In Manly, you can pick up some fish and chips

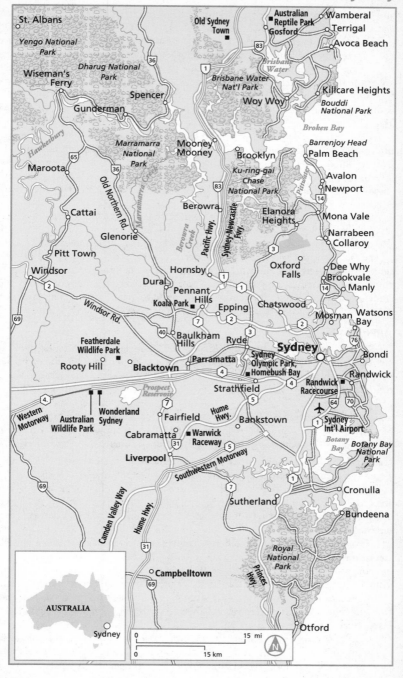

St. Albans

Yengo National Park

Wiseman's Ferry

Dharug National Park

Spencer

Gunderman

Maroota

Cattai

Glenorie

Pitt Town

Windsor

Hawkesbury

Old Northern Rd.

65

36

36

Marramarra National Park

Marramarra Creek

Mooney Mooney

Berowra Creek

Berowra

Dural

Hornsby

Koala Park

Pennant Hills

Windsor Rd.

2

69

40

7

Baulkham Hills

Featherdale Wildlife Park

Rooty Hill

Blacktown

Western Motorway

4

Australian Wildlife Park

Wonderland Sydney

Prospect Reservoir

Fairfield

Cabramatta

Warwick Raceway

Liverpool

69

31

Camden Valley Way

Hume Hwy.

31

Campbelltown

69

Old Sydney Town

Brisbane Water

83

1

Brisbane Water Nat'l Park

Woy Woy

Brooklyn

Ku-ring-gai Chase National Park

83

Elanora Heights

Sydney-Newcastle Fwy.

Pacific Hwy.

1

1

Oxford Falls

3

Epping

2

Chatswood

Ryde

3

Strathfield

5

Parramatta

4

Sydney Olympic Park; Homebush Bay

4

Bankstown

Hume Hwy.

Southwestern Motorway

5

7

Sutherland

1

Princes Hwy.

Australian Reptile Park

Gosford

Wamberal

Terrigal

Avoca Beach

Killcare Heights

Bouddi National Park

Broken Bay

Barrenjoy Head

Palm Beach

Avalon

Newport

14

Mona Vale

Narrabeen

Collaroy

Dee Why

Brookvale

14

Manly

Mosman

Watsons Bay

2

76

Sydney

Bondi

Randwick Racecourse

Randwick

64

70

Botany Bay

Sydney Int'l Airport

1

Botany Bay National Park

Cronulla

Bundeena

Royal National Park

Otford

Pittwater

AUSTRALIA

Sydney

0   15 mi

0   15 km

N

and head for the main beach, which is flanked by a row of giant Norfolk Island Pines, and enjoy the chatter of hundreds of colorful lorikeets at dusk.

The best time to return to the city is in the early evening, when the lights of the skyscrapers around Circular Quay are streaked like rainbows across the inky water of the harbor, and the sails of the Opera House and the girders of the Harbour Bridge are lit up. It's a truly magical experience.

History is also enshrined in the city's many museums and art galleries, while modern Sydney comes alive in the more recent tourist-oriented developments around Darling Harbour and the restaurant and entertainment area nearby at Cockle Bay.

It's at Darling Harbour that you'll find the Sydney Aquarium, featuring impressive underwater walkways through two enormous tanks—one teeming with fish found in Sydney Harbour, the other full of giant rays and 3-meter- (10-ft.-) long nurse sharks.

Darling Harbour is also a great starting place for your gourmet tour of Sydney's "modern Australian" cooking style, which combines the freshest ingredients with Asian spices and Mediterranean flavors.

Along with trips to the dramatic gorges and cliffs of the Blue Mountains, the wineries of Hunter Valley, and the dolphin- and whale-watching around Port Stephens—all within 2-hour drives from the city—you'll see why Sydney gets so much praise.

The frugal traveler will find that, compared to other major international destinations, Sydney offers good value for money spent. Food and public transport are quite cheap, and attractions are generally not prohibitively expensive (senior citizen and student prices are almost always available if you have identification). The price of a hotel room is far cheaper than in other big cities like New York and London.

ARRIVING

BY PLANE **Sydney International Airport** is 8 kilometers (about 5 miles) from the city center. The international and domestic terminals are separate, but linked by free shuttle buses. In both terminals, you'll find free luggage carts, wheelchairs, a post office (open Mon–Fri 9am–5pm), mailboxes, duty-free shops (including one before you go through customs on arrival), restaurants, bars, stores, showers, luggage lockers, and tourist information desks. There is also a State Transit kiosk selling bus, train, and ferry tickets; a New South Wales Travel Center desk offering cheap deals on hotels; and a Thomas Cook currency exchange. The airport is completely non-smoking.

Getting Into Town The **Sydney Airport Train Link** connects both the international and domestic airports to the City stations of Central, Museum, St. James, Circular Quay, Wynyard, and Town Hall. You'll need to change trains for all other Sydney stations. Unfortunately, the line uses existing rolling stock, has no dedicated luggage areas and as it's on a scheduled route into the city from the outer suburbs gets very crowded during rush hours (approximately 7–9am, and 4–6:30pm). If you have lots of luggage and you're going into the city then, it's probably best to take an airport bus (see below) or taxi. Otherwise, and walk to the end of the platform where there should be more room at the very front or rear of the train. There are elevators at the Airport Train Link stations, and some at the city train stations (but the crowds and lack of staff and signs mean you'll probably end up lugging it all up and down steps). The train takes 10 minutes to reach Central and then continues on to Circular Quay. Trains leave every 15 minutes or so and cost A$10 (U.S.$6.50) one-way and A$15 (U.S.$9.75) return. Special "Group Fares" are available for 2 to 4 passengers that make the train significantly cheaper than a taxi. For example: 3 or 4 people can travel to the city for A$20 (U.S.$13)—this is only $5 per person (compared with a A$30/U.S.$19.50 taxi fare). Another option is to buy a **Red TravelPass.** This includes a single journey from the airport as well as unlimited travel on trains, buses and ferries for 7 days. The TravelPass costs A$33.80 (U.S.$21.95), including a single Airport Link trip, or $39.50 (U.S.$25.70), including a return trip to the airport.

The State Transit kiosk sells the Sydney Pass, individual Airport Express tickets, and acts as a location where travel vouchers bought overseas can be exchanged for transport tickets. You can buy tickets for the various routes of the fast, comfortable green and yellow **Airport Express buses,** which travel between the city center and the terminals from 5am to 11pm. The number 300 bus runs to and from Circular Quay, The Rocks, Wynyard, and Town Hall every 15 minutes Monday to Friday and about every 30 minutes early mornings, nights, weekends, and holidays. The trip to Circular Quay takes about 45 minutes. Bus 350 runs to and from Kings Cross, Potts Point, and Elizabeth Bay every 20 minutes and takes around 30 minutes to reach Kings Cross. Both travel via Central Station (around 20 min. from the International Terminal).

Bus 351 leaves for Coogee, Bronte and Bondi beaches every 30 minutes. It takes around 55 minutes to reach Bondi Beach from the International Terminal. Bus 352 travels between Central, Chinatown, Darling Harbour, the Star City casino, the Sydney Fish Markets, and Glebe, approximately every 30 minutes. The trip time is about 30 minutes to Darling Harbour and 50 minutes to Glebe.

One-way tickets for all these buses cost A$7 (U.S.$4.55) for adults, A$4.50 (U.S.$2.90) for kids under 16, and A$15 (U.S.$9.75) for families (any number of children). A round-trip ticket costs A$10 (U.S.$6.50) for adults, A$5 (U.S.$3.25) for kids, and A$25 (U.S.$16.25) for families. You must use the return portion within two months. Buy your tickets from the Airport Express booth outside the airport terminal, or on the bus. The Airport Express buses also travel between the international and domestic terminals; an interterminal ticket costs A$2.50 (U.S.$1.60) for adults, A$1.50 (U.S.98¢) for children, and A$6.50 (U.S.$4.20) for families.

The **Kingsford Smith Airport Coach** operates to the city center from bus stops outside the terminals. This service will drop you off (and pick you up) at your hotel (pickups require at least 1 hour notice; call ☎ **02/9667 3221**). Tickets cost A$7 (U.S.$4.55) one-way and A$11 (U.S.$7.15) round-trip (the return portion can be used at any time in the future).

The **Bondi Jetbus** (☎ **0500/886 008** mobile phone; fax 02/9487 3554) will deliver you anywhere on the eastern beaches. Tickets are A$10 (U.S.$6.50) for single adult, A$8 (U.S.$5.20) each for two or more, and A$4 (U.S.$2.60) for children. Call them from the airport, and they'll pick you up in 15 minutes or less.

A **taxi** from the airport to the city center costs between A$16 (U.S$10.40) and A$20 (U.S.$13). Expect to pay around A$25 (U.S.$16.25) to Kings Cross. A new expressway, the Eastern Distributor, opened in 2000 and is a faster way to reach the city from the airport. Most taxis use this route, but it's best to ask them to take it just in case. There's a A$3.30 (U.S.$2.15) toll from the airport to the city (the taxi driver pays it and you pay at the end of the trip), but there is no toll to the airport. *Warning:* An ongoing dispute with Visa means the credit card is not accepted by taxis in Australia.

BY TRAIN   **Central Station** (☎ **13 15 00** for CityRail, and ☎ **13 22 32** for Countrylink interstate trains) is the main city and interstate train station. It's at the top of George Street in downtown Sydney. All interstate trains depart from here, and it's a major CityRail hub. Many city buses leave from neighboring Railway Square for places like Town Hall and Circular Quay.

BY BUS   The **Greyhound Pioneer Australia** terminal is at Oxford and Riley streets in Darlinghurst (☎ **13 20 30** in Australia or 02/9283 5977). **McCafferty's** (☎ **13 14 99** in Australia) operates from the **Sydney Coach Terminal** (☎ **02/9281 9366**) on the corner of Eddy Avenue and Pitt Street, bordering Central Station.

BY CRUISE SHIP   Cruise ships dock at the **Overseas Passenger Terminal** in The Rocks, just opposite the Sydney Opera House, or in Darling Harbour if The Rocks facility is already occupied by another vessel.

BY CAR   Drivers coming into Sydney from the north enter the city on the Pacific Highway, drivers from the south enter the city via the Hume and Princes highways, and those coming from the west enter the city via the Great Western Highway.

VISITOR INFORMATION

The **Sydney Visitor Centre,** 106 George St., The Rocks (☎ **02/9255 1788**), is a good place for maps, brochures, and general tourist information; it also has two floors of excellent displays on The Rocks. The office is open daily from 9am to 6pm. Also in The Rocks is the **National Parks & Wildlife Centre** (☎ **02/9247 8861**), in Cadmans Cottage, 110 George St. If you are in Circular Quay, the **CityRail Host Center** (no phone), opposite No. 5 jetty, has a wide range of brochures and a staff member on hand to help with general inquiries. It's open daily 9am to 5pm. The **Sydney Convention and Visitors Bureau** (☎ **02/9235 2424**) operates an information kiosk in Martin Place, near Castlereagh Street, Monday through Friday from 9am to 5pm. The **Manly Visitors Information Centre** (☎ **02/9977 1088**), opposite Manly beach near the Corso, offers general information, but specializes in Manly and the northern beaches. If you want to inquire about destinations and holidays within Sydney or the rest of New South Wales, call **Tourism New South Wales's** helpline at ☎ **13 20 77** in Australia.

Electronic information on cinema, theater, exhibitions, and other events can be accessed through **Talking Guides** (☎ **13 16 20** in Australia). You'll need a code number for each topic, which you can find on page 3 of the A–K section of the *Sydney Yellow Pages* phone directory. The service costs the same as a local call.

Good **websites** include **CitySearch Sydney** (www.sydney.citysearch.com.au), for events, entertainment, dining, and shopping; and **City of Sydney** (www.cityofsydney.nsw.gov.au), the official information site.

CITY LAYOUT

Sydney is one of the largest cities in the world by area, from the sea to the foothills of the Blue Mountains. It can take 2 hours' driving from the center to clear the outskirts. Thankfully, the city center is compact. The jewel in Sydney's crown is its harbor, which empties into the South Pacific though headlands known as North Head and South Head. On the southern side of the harbor are the skyscrapers of the city center; the Sydney Opera House; a string of beaches, including Bondi; and the inner-city suburbs. The Sydney Harbour Bridge and a tunnel connect the city center to the high-rises of the North Sydney business district and the northern suburbs and ocean beaches beyond.

MAIN ARTERIES & STREETS   The city's main thoroughfare, **George Street,** runs up from **Circular Quay** (pronounced key), past Wynyard CityRail station, Town Hall and to Central Station. A whole host of streets bisect the city parallel to George, including Pitt, Elizabeth, and Macquarie streets. **Macquarie Street** runs up from the Sydney Opera House, past the Royal Botanic Gardens, colonial architecture, and Hyde Park. **Martin Place** is a pedestrian thoroughfare that stretches from Macquarie to George streets. It's about halfway between Circular Quay and Town Hall—in the heart of the city center. The easy-to-spot **AMP Centrepoint Tower,** facing onto the pedestrian-only **Pitt Street Mall,** is the main city-center landmark. Next to Circular Quay and across from the Opera House is **The Rocks,** a cluster of small streets that was once city slums but is now a tourist attraction. Roads meet at Town Hall from Kings Cross in one direction and Darling Harbour in the other.

Neighborhoods in Brief

South of the Harbour

Circular Quay   This transport hub for ferries, buses, and CityRail trains is tucked between the Harbour Bridge and the Sydney Opera House. The Quay, as locals call it, is a good spot for a stroll, and its outdoor restaurants and buskers (street musicians/performers) are very popular. The Rocks, the Royal Botanic Gardens, the Contemporary Art Museum, and the start of the main shopping area (centered on Pitt and George streets) are all just a short walk away. To reach the area via public transportation, take a CityRail train, ferry, or city-bound bus to Circular Quay.

The Rocks   This small historic area, just a short stroll west of Circular Quay, is packed with colonial stone buildings, intriguing backstreets, boutiques, pubs, and top-notch restaurants and hotels. It's the city's most exclusive place to stay because of its beauty and its proximity to the Opera House and the harbor. Shops here are mostly geared toward Sydney's yuppies and wealthy Asian tourists—don't expect many bargains. On weekends, part of George Street is blocked off for The Rocks Market, with its street stalls selling tourist-oriented souvenirs and crafts. To reach the area via public transport, take any bus bound for Circular Quay or The Rocks (via George Street) or a CityRail train or ferry to Circular Quay

Town Hall   Right in the heart of the city, this area is home to the main department stores and to Sydney landmarks: the Town Hall and the Queen Victoria Building (QVB). Also look for the AMP Centrepoint Tower, and the boutique-style chain stores of Pitt Street Mall. Farther up George Street (on the same side as the Town Hall) are cinema complexes, the entrance to Sydney's Spanish district (around Liverpool Street), and the city's small Chinatown. To reach the area via public transport, take any bus from Circular Quay via George Street, or a CityRail train to the Town Hall stop.

Darling Harbour   Designed from scratch as a tourist precinct, Darling Harbour now features Sydney's main convention, exhibition, and entertainment centers; a huge waterfront promenade; the Sydney Aquarium; the giant screen Panasonic IMAX Theatre; the Sega World theme park; the Australian Maritime Museum; the Powerhouse Museum; a major food court; and plenty of shops. Star City, Sydney's casino and theater complex, opened in Darling Harbour in late 1997. Until Cockle Bay Wharf opened in early 1999 (near the Sydney Aquarium on the city side of Darling Harbour) and brought with it a few good bars and restaurants, few Sydneysiders ever visited the place. To reach the area via public transportation, take a ferry from Circular Quay (Wharf 5), the monorail from Town Hall, or the light rail (tram) from Central Station, or walk down the side road to the right of the Queen Victoria Building as you are facing it, and across the pedestrian bridge which spans the water.

Kings Cross & the Suburbs Beyond   "The Cross" is famous as the city's red-light district—though it's also home to some of the city's best known nightclubs and restaurants. It also houses plenty of backpacker hostels, a few bars, as well as some upscale hotels. The main drag, Darlinghurst Road, is short, but crammed with seedy strip joints, prostitutes, drug addicts, drunks, and down-at-heel street kids. Fortunately, there's a heavy police presence. Beyond the strip clubs and glitter, the attractive suburbs of Elizabeth Bay, Double Bay, and Rose Bay hug the waterfront. To reach the area

Sydney at a Glance

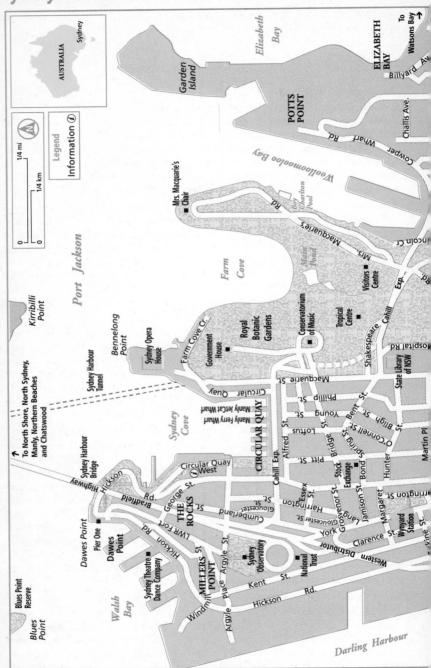

via public transportation, take bus 324, 325, or 327 from Circular Quay; bus 311 from Railway Square, Central Station; or a CityRail train to Kings Cross station.

Paddington/Oxford Street   This inner-city suburb, centered on trendy Oxford Street, is known for expensive terrace houses, off-the-wall boutiques and bookshops, popular restaurants, pubs, and nightclubs. It's the heart of Sydney's large gay community and has a liberal scattering of gay bars and dance spots. To get there via public transportation, take bus 380 or 382 from Circular Quay (via Elizabeth Street); 378 from Railway Square, Central Station; or 380 and 382 from Bondi Junction.

Darlinghurst   Wedged between grungy Kings Cross and upscale Oxford Street, this extroverted and grimy terraced suburb is home to some of the Sydney's finest cafes. It's probably not wise to walk around here at night. Take the CityRail train to Kings Cross and head right from the exit.

Central   The congested, badly polluted crossroads around Central Station, the city's main train station, has little to recommend it. Buses run from here to Circular Quay, and it's a 20-minute walk to Town Hall. The Sydney Central YHA is located here.

Newtown   This popular student area is centered around car-clogged King Street, which is lined with many alternative shops, bookstores, and cheap ethnic restaurants. People-watching is an interesting sport here—see how many belly button rings, violently colored hairdos, and Celtic arm tattoos you can spot. To reach the area via public transportation, take bus 422, 423, 426, or 428 from Circular Quay (via Castlereagh Street and City Road), or take the CityRail train to Newtown Station.

Glebe   A mecca for young professionals and students, this inner-city suburb is known for its cafes, restaurants, pubs, and shops spread out along the main thoroughfare, Glebe Point Road. This, and its location just 15 minutes from the city and 30 minutes from Circular Quay, makes it a good place to stay for budget-conscious travelers. To reach Glebe via public transportation, take bus 431, 433, or 434 from Millers Point, The Rocks (via George St.), or bus 459 from behind Town Hall.

Bondi & the Southern Beaches   Some of Sydney's most glamorous surf beaches—Bondi, Bronte, and Coogee—can be found along the South Pacific Ocean coastline southeast of the city center. Bondi is a disappointment to many tourists who are expecting more than this former working-class suburb has to offer. Bondi does have a wide sweep of beach (which is crowded in summer), some interesting eateries and drinking holes, and plenty of attitude and beautiful bodies. On weekends, it's a favorite with macho young men from the suburbs, who stand next to their souped-up cars and attempt to look cool. To reach the beaches via public transportation, take bus 380 or 382 to Bondi Beach from Circular Quay—it takes up to an hour—or, a quicker alternative is a CityRail train to Bondi Junction to connect with same buses. Bus 378 from Railway Square, Central Station (via Oxford Street) goes to Bronte, and bus 373 or 374 travels to Coogee from Circular Quay.

Watsons Bay   Watsons Bay is known for The Gap—a section of dramatic sea cliffs—as well as several good restaurants, such as Doyles on the Beach, and the popular Watsons Bay Hotel beer garden. It's a terrific spot to spend a sunny afternoon. To reach the area via public transportation, take bus 324 or 325 from Circular Quay, or a ferry from Circular Quay (Wharf 2) on Saturdays and Sundays.

North of the Harbor

North Sydney   Just across the Harbour Bridge, the high-rises of North Sydney attest to its prominence as a major business area. That said, there's little for tourists to do here, except possibly get knocked down on an extremely busy thoroughfare. Take a

CityRail train to the North Sydney stop. Chatswood (take a CityRail train from Central or Wynyard stations) has some pretty good suburban-type shopping, and Milsons Point, just across the bridge, has a decent pub called the Kirribilli Hotel and a couple of restaurants and cafes worth checking out if you've walked across the Harbour Bridge.

The North Shore   Ferries and buses provide good access to these wealthy neighborhoods across the Harbour Bridge. The gorgeous Balmoral Beach, Taronga Zoo, and upscale boutiques are the main attractions in Mosman. Take a ferry from Circular Quay (Wharf 2) to Taronga Zoo—10 minutes—and a bus from there to Balmoral Beach (another 10 min.).

Manly & The Northern Beaches   Half an hour away by ferry, or just 15 minutes by the faster JetCat, Manly is famous for its beautiful ocean beach and cheap food outlets. Farther north are gorgeous beaches popular with surfers. Unfortunately there is no CityRail train line to the northern beaches. The farthest beach from the city, Palm Beach, has magnificent surf and lagoon beaches, walking paths, and a golf course. To reach the area via public transportation, take the ferry or JetCat from Circular Quay (wharves 2 and 3) to Manly. Change at Manly for buses to the northern beaches, numbers 148 and 154 through 159. You can also take bus L90 from Wynyard Station.

West of the City Center

Balmain   Located west of the city center, a short ferry ride from Circular Quay, Balmain was once Sydney's main shipbuilding area. In the last few decades it has become trendy and expensive. The suburb has a village feel and is filled with restaurants and pubs and hosts a popular Saturday market in the grounds of the local church. Take bus 441, 442, or 432 from Town Hall or George Street, or a ferry from Circular Quay (Wharf 5), and then a bus ride up the hill to the main shopping area.

Homebush Bay   This was the main site of the Sydney 2000 Olympic Games. Here you'll find the Olympic Stadium, the Aquatic Center, and Homebush Bay Information Center, as well as parklands and a waterbird reserve. The aquatic center is open to the public, and the other venues host sporting events. To reach the area via public transportation, take a CityRail train from Circular Quay to the Olympic Park station.

2 Getting Around

BY PUBLIC TRANSPORTATION

State Transit operates the city's buses and the ferry network, CityRail runs the urban and suburban trains, and Sydney Ferries runs the public passenger ferries. Some private bus lines operate buses in the outer suburbs. In addition, a monorail connects the city center to Darling Harbour and a light rail line (called the tram) runs between Central Station and Wentworth Park in Pyrmont.

MONEY-SAVING TRANSIT PASSES   Several passes are available for visitors who will be using public transportation frequently—all work out to be much cheaper than buying individual tickets. The **SydneyPass** is a good buy if you plan to do a lot of sightseeing, but in my opinion you're better off with the flexibility offered by some of the other passes listed below.

The **SydneyPass** allows 3 days of unlimited travel in a 7-day period on buses and ferries, including the high-speed JetCat ferry to Manly, the Red Sydney Explorer Bus (see below), the Bondi and Bay Explorer Bus, the Airport Express Bus, all trains within the "Red Zone," and all harbor cruises operated by State Transit. A 3-day pass costs A$85 (U.S.$55.25) for adults, A$45 (U.S.$29.25) for children under 16, and A$215

Sydney Transportation Systems

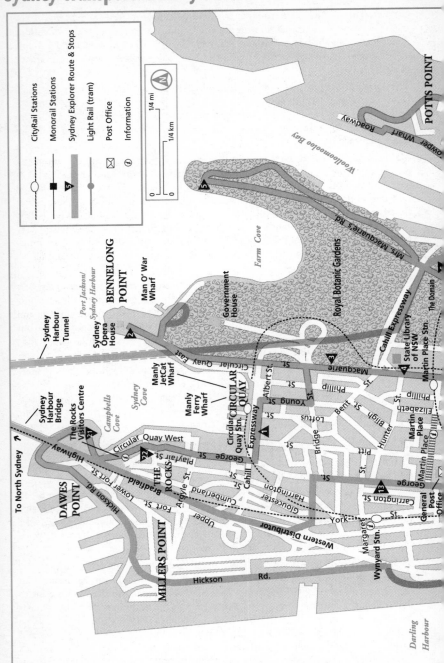

Legend

- ⬭ CityRail Stations
- ▪ Monorail Stations
- 5 Sydney Explorer Route & Stops
- ● Light Rail (tram)
- ⊠ Post Office
- ⓘ Information

N

1/4 mi
1/4 km
0

Port Jackson/
Sydney Harbour

BENNELONG
POINT

Sydney Harbour
Tunnel

Sydney
Opera House

Man O' War
Wharf

Government
House

Farm Cove

Royal Botanic Gardens

Mrs. Macquarie's Rd.

Woolloomooloo Bay

POTTS POINT

Cowper Wharf Roadway

The Domain

Cahill Expressway

State Library
of NSW

Martin Place Stn.

Macquarie St.

Albert St.

Circular Quay East

CIRCULAR
QUAY

Manly
JetCat
Wharf

Manly
Ferry Wharf

Circular
Quay Stn.

Sydney
Cove

Campbells
Cove

The Rocks
Visitors Centre

Sydney
Harbour
Bridge

DAWES
POINT

To North Sydney

Bradfield
Highway

Hickson Rd.

Lower Fort St.

THE
ROCKS

Fort St.

Upper

Argyle St.

Cumberland
St.

Gloucester
St.

Harrington

Cahill

Playfair St.

Circular Quay West

George St.

Expressway

Young St.

Loftus
St.

Bridge
St.

Phillip
St.

Bent St.

Bligh St.

Hunter
St.

Elizabeth
St.

Phillip
St.

Martin
Place

Martin Place

George
St.

General
Post
Office

Carrington St.

York
St.

Western Distributor

Margaret St.

Wynyard Stn.

MILLERS POINT

Hickson Rd.

Darling
Harbour

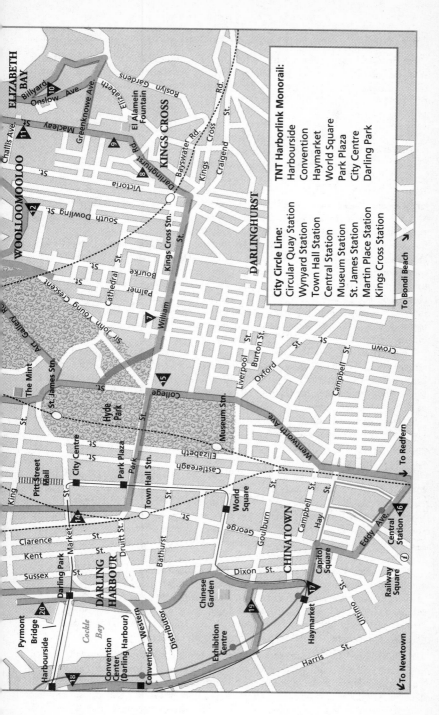

WOOLLOOMOOLOO

ELIZABETH BAY

KINGS CROSS

DARLINGHURST

DARLING HARBOUR

CHINATOWN

Billyard Ave.
Onslow Ave.
Challis Ave.
Macleay St.
Greenknowe Ave.
Elizabeth
El Alamein Fountain
Roslyn Gardens
Bayswater Rd.
Kings Cross Rd.
Craigend St.

South Dowling St.
Victoria St.
Darlinghurst Rd.
Kings Cross Stn.
Palmer St.
Bourke St.
Cathedral St.
William St.
Sir John Young Crescent
Art Gallery Rd.

The Mint
St. James Stn.
Hyde Park
College St.
Park St.
Museum Stn.
Elizabeth St.
Castlereagh St.
Liverpool St.
Burton St.
Oxford St.
Campbell St.
Crown St.
Wentworth Ave.

Pitt Street Mall
City Centre
Park Plaza
Town Hall Stn.
World Square
King St.
Market St.
Druitt St.
George St.
Goulburn St.
Hay St.
Campbell St.

Clarence St.
Kent St.
Sussex St.
Bathurst St.
Dixon St.
Capitol Square
Haymarket
Eddy Ave.

Pyrmont Bridge
Darling Park
Cockle Bay
Convention Center (Darling Harbour)
Western Distributor
Chinese Garden
Exhibition Centre
Harbourside
Convention
Harris St.
Ultimo St.
Railway Square
Central Station

To Bondi Beach
To Redfern
To Newtown

City Circle Line:
Circular Quay Station
Wynyard Station
Town Hall Station
Central Station
Museum Station
St. James Station
Martin Place Station
Kings Cross Station

TNT Harborlink Monorail:
Harbourside
Convention
Haymarket
World Square
Park Plaza
City Centre
Darling Park

81

For timetable information on buses, ferries, and trains, call the **Infoline** at ☎ **13 15 00** daily from 6am to 10pm. Pick up a **Sydney Transport Map** (a guide to train, bus, and ferry services) at any rail, bus, or ferry information office.

(U.S.$139.75) for families. A 5-day pass (5 days in a 7-day period) is A$115 (U.S.$74.75) for adults, A$60 (U.S.$39) for children, and A$290 (U.S.$188.50) for a family. There's also a seven-day pass (7 consecutive days), at A$135 (U.S.$87.75) for adults, A$70 (U.S.$45.50) for children, and A$340 (U.S.$221) for a family. Buy the SydneyPass at the airport, Countrylink offices, Public Transport ticket offices, Circular Quay ferry ticket offices, and anywhere else the SydneyPass logo is displayed.

A **Weekly Travel Pass** allows unlimited travel on buses, trains, and ferries. There are six different passes (denoted by color) depending on the distance you need to travel. The passes most used by visitors are the **Red Pass** and the **Green Pass.** The Red Pass costs A$28 (U.S.$18.20) for adults and A$14 (U.S.$9.10) for kids and covers all transportation within the city center and near surrounds. This will get you aboard inner harbor ferries, for example, but not the ferry to Manly. The Green Pass, which costs A$36 (U.S.$23.40) for adults and A$18 (U.S.$11.70) for kids, will take you to more far-flung destinations, including Manly (aboard the ferry but not the JetCat before 7pm). You can buy either pass at newsagents or bus, train, and ferry ticket outlets.

The **Day Rover** gives you unlimited bus, train, and ferry travel for one day. Tickets cost A$22 (U.S.$14.30) for adults and A$11 (U.S.$7.15) for children for travel in peak hours (before 9am), and A$17.60 (U.S.$11.44) for adults and A$8.80 (U.S.$5.72) for children for travel in off-peak hours (after 9am). The pass is available at all bus, train, and ferry ticket outlets.

A **Travelten** ticket offers 10 bus or ferry rides for a discounted price. A **blue Travelten** covers two sections on the bus route and costs A$10.40 (U.S.$6.76) for adults and A$5.20 (U.S.$3.38) for children; a **brown Travelten** covers up to nine sections and costs A$17.60 (U.S.$11.44) for adults and A$8.80 (U.S.$5.72) for children. The Travelten ferry ticket costs A$25.30 (U.S.$16.45) for adults and A$12.60 (U.S.$8.19) for kids for 10 trips within the inner harbor (excluding Manly). The Manly ferry Travelten costs A$37.40 (U.S.$24.31) for adults and A$18.70 (U.S.$12.16) for children, while the **JetCat Travelten** to Manly (before 7pm) costs A$52 (U.S.$33.80) for adults (no kid's price). Buy Travelten tickets at newsagents, bus depots, or at the Circular Quay ferry terminal. Tickets are transferable, so if two or more people are traveling together, you can all use the same ticket.

A **7-day Rail Pass** costs A$16.40 (U.S.$10.66) for adults and A$8.20 (U.S.$5.33) for children, traveling within the city center. For a full day's unlimited travel by bus, you can't go wrong with the **One Day Bus Tripper.** It costs A$9 (U.S.$5.85) for adults and A$4.50 (U.S.$2.93) for children 4 to 15, and can be bought from newsagents and at bus depots. An unlimited One-Day Bus/Ferry Tripper costs A$13 (U.S.$8.45) for adults and A$6.50 (U.S.$4.23) for children.

BY PUBLIC BUS Buses are frequent, fairly reliable and cover a wide area of metropolitan Sydney—though you might find the system a little difficult to navigate if you're visiting some of the outer suburbs. The minimum fare (which covers most short hops within the city) is A$1.40 (U.S.91¢) for adults and A70¢ (U.S.46¢)for children for a 4-kilometer (2.5-mile) "section." The farther you go, the cheaper each section is.

For example, the 44-kilometer (27-mile) trip to beautiful Palm Beach, way past Manly, costs just A$4.40 (U.S.$2.86) for adults and $2.20 (U.S.$1.43) for kids. Sections are marked on bus-stop signs).

Most buses bound for the northern suburbs, including night buses to Manly and the bus to Taronga Zoo, leave from Wynyard Park on Carrington Street, behind the main Wynyard CityRail station on George Street. Buses headed to the southern beaches, such as Bondi and Bronte, and the western and eastern suburbs leave from Circular Quay. Buses to Balmain leave from behind the Queen Victoria Building.

Call the **Transport Info Line** on ☎ **13 15 00** (www.sydneybuses.nsw.gov.au) for schedule and fares, or ask at the bus information kiosk on the corner of Alfred and Loftus streets, behind Circular Quay CityRail station (☎ **02/9219 1680**). The kiosk is open Monday through Saturday from 8am to 8pm, and Sunday from 8am to 6pm. Buses run from 4am to around midnight during the week, less frequently on weekends and holidays. Some night buses to outer suburbs run after midnight and through the night. You can purchase single tickets onboard from the driver; exact change is not required.

BY RED SYDNEY EXPLORER BUS   These bright red buses operate every day, traveling a 28 kilometer (17½ mile) circuit and stopping at 21 places of interest. These include Sydney Opera House, the Royal Botanic Gardens, the State Library, Mrs. Macquarie's Chair, the Art Gallery of New South Wales, Kings Cross, Elizabeth Bay House, Wynyard CityRail Station, Martin Place, the Queen Victoria Building, AMP Sydney Tower, the Australian Museum, Central Station, Chinatown, and Darling Harbour. Buses depart from Circular Quay at 15-minute intervals from 8:40am with the last trip departing Circular Quay at 5:25pm. This service returns to Circular Quay at 6:50pm. Board anywhere along the route where you see the distinctive red Sydney Explorer stop sign, and leave at any attraction along the way. If you want to stay on the bus from start to finish, the full circuit takes about 1½ hours. Your Sydney Explorer ticket entitles you to free travel on regular blue and white Sydney Buses services within the same zone covered by your Sydney Explorer Ticket until midnight. When planning your itinerary for the day, remember that some attractions, such as museums, close at 5pm. Tickets cost A$30 (U.S.$19.50) for adults, A$15 (U.S.$9.75) for children, and A$75 (U.S.$48.75) for a family. Buy tickets onboard the bus.

BY BONDI & BAY EXPLORER BUS   The Bondi & Bay Explorer operates every day, traveling a 30 kilometer (19 mile) circuit around the eastern harborside bays and coastal beaches and back to the city. Stops along the way include Kings Cross, Double Bay, Watsons Bay, Bondi Beach, Bronte Beach, Coogee Beach, Paddington, Oxford Street and Martin Place. The bus departs from Circular Quay at 25-minute intervals from 9:15am, with the last one departing Circular Quay at 4:20pm, returning to Circular Quay at 5:55pm. Board anywhere along the route where you see the Bondi & Bay Explorer stop sign, and leave at any attraction along the way. If you wish to stay on board from start to finish without making any stops, the entire circuit takes 1½ hours. Your ticket entitles you to free travel on regular blue and white Sydney Buses services within the same zone covered by your Bondi & Bay Explorer ticket until midnight. The one-day fare is A$30 (U.S.$19.50) for adults, A$15 (U.S.$9.75) for children under 16, and A$75 (U.S.$48.75) for families. Buy the ticket onboard.

BY FERRY & JETCAT   The best way to get a taste of a city that revolves around its harbor is to hop a ferry. The main ferry terminal is at Circular Quay. Tickets can be bought at machines at each wharf or at the main Circular Quay ticket offices just opposite Wharf 4. For **ferry** information call ☎ **13 15 00**, or visit the ferry information office opposite Wharf 4. Timetables are available for all routes.

One-way journeys in the inner harbor (virtually everywhere except Manly and Parramatta) cost A$4 (U.S.$2.60) for adults, A$2 (U.S.$1.30) for children. The ferry to Manly takes 30 minutes and costs A$5 (U.S.$3.25) for adults and A$2.50 (U.S.$1.63) for children. It leaves from Wharf 3. The JetCat (a superfast ferry) to Manly takes 15 minutes and costs A$6.30 (U.S.$4.10) for adults and children. After 7pm all trips to and from Manly are by JetCat at ferry prices. Ferries run from 6am to midnight.

BY CITYRAIL   Sydney's publicly owned train system is a cheap and efficient way to see the city. The system is limited though, with many tourist areas—including Manly, Bondi Beach, and Darling Harbour—not connected to the railway network. CityRail trains have a reputation of running late and out of timetable order. All train stations have automatic ticket machines, and most have ticket offices.

The single fare within the city center is A$2.20 (U.S.$1.43) for adults and A$1.10 (U.S.72¢) for kids. An off-peak (after 9am) return ticket costs A$2.60 (U.S.$1.69) for adults and A$2.20 (U.S.$1.43) for kids, while a peak return will cost A$4.40 (U.S.$2.86) for adults and A$2.20 (U.S.$1.43) for kids. Information is available from **InfoLine** (☎ **13 15 00;** www.staterail.nsw.gov.au) and at the **CityRail Host Centers** located opposite Wharf 4 at Circular Quay (☎ **02/9224 2649**) and at Central Station (☎ **02/9219 1977**); both centers are open daily from 9am to 5pm.

Comfortable and efficient **Countrylink** trains operating out of Central Station link the city with the far suburbs and beyond. For reservations call ☎ **13 22 32** between 6:30am and 10pm, or visit the **Countrylink Travel Center,** 11–31 York St., Wynyard (☎ **02/9224 4744**), open Monday through Friday from 8:30am to 5pm, or the Countrylink Travel Center at Circular Quay (☎ **02/9224 3400**), open Monday through Friday from 10am to 5:30pm and Saturday from 10am to 2pm.

BY MONORAIL   The metro monorail connects the central business district to Darling Harbour, and operates Monday through Wednesday from 7am to 10pm, Thursday and Friday from 7am to midnight, Saturday from 7am to midnight, and Sunday from 8am to 10pm. Tickets are A$3.50 (U.S.$2.28); children under 5 ride free. An all-day pass costs A$7 (U.S.$4.55) for adults and A$20 (U.S.$13) for a family. The trip from the city center to Darling Harbour takes around 12 minutes. Look for the gray overhead line and the plastic tubelike structures that are the stations. Call **Metro Monorail** at ☎ **02/8584 5288** (www.metrolightrail.com.au) for more information.

BY LIGHT RAIL   A system of trams opened in late 1997 with a route that traverses a 3.6 kilometer (2.2 mile) track between Central Station and Wentworth Park in Pyrmont. It provides good access to Chinatown, Paddy's Markets, Darling Harbour, the Star City casino, and the Sydney Fish Markets. The trams run every 10 minutes. The one-way fare is A$2.20 or $4.50 (U.S.$1.43 or $2.93), depending on distance. There are no child fares. A day pass for a family of five day pass costs A$20 (U.S.$13). Call **Metro Light Rail** at ☎ **02/8584 5288** (www.metrolightrail.com.au) for details.

BY TAXI

Taxis are a relatively economical way to get around Sydney. Several companies service the city center and suburbs. All journeys are metered and cost A$2.50 (U.S.$1.63) before you even go anywhere. It's another A$1.10 (U.S.72¢) if you call for a cab. You must also pay extra for waiting time, luggage over 25 kilogram (55 lb.), and if you cross either way on the Harbour Bridge or through the Harbour Tunnel (A$2.20/U.S.$1.43), and if you take the Eastern Distributor highway from the airport (A$3.30/U.S.$2.15). An extra 10% will be added to your fare if you pay by credit card. (*Note*: Visa cards are not accepted in Australian taxis due to an ongoing dispute.)

Taxis line up at ranks in the city, such as those found opposite Circular Quay and Central Station. They are also frequently found in front of hotels. A small yellow light on top of the cab means it's vacant. Cabs can be particularly hard to get on Friday and Saturday nights and between 2 and 3pm, when tired cabbies are changing shifts after 12 hours on the road. Tipping is not necessary but appreciated. Some people prefer to sit up front with the driver, but it's not considered rude if you don't. All passengers must wear seat belts by law. The **Taxi Complaints Hotline** (☎ **1800/648 478** in Australia) deals with problem taxi drivers. Taxis are licensed to carry four people.

The major outfits are **Taxis Combined Services** (☎ **02/9332 8888**); **RSL Taxis** (☎ **02/9581 1111**); **Legion Cabs** (☎ **13 14 51**); and **Premier** (☎ **13 10 17**).

BY WATER TAXI

Harbour Taxis operate 24 hours a day and are a quick and convenient way to get to waterfront restaurants, harbor attractions, and some suburbs. They can also be hired for private cruises of the harbor. A journey from Circular Quay to Watsons Bay, for example, costs about A$55 (U.S.$35.75) for two. Extra passengers cost just A$6 (U.S.$3.90) each; some taxis can hold up to 28 people. An hour's sightseeing excursion around the harbor costs A$181 (U.S. $117.65) for two. The two main operators are **Taxis Afloat** (☎ **02/9955 3222**) and **Water Taxis Combined** (☎ **02/ 9810 5010**).

BY CAR

Traffic rules, parking problems, and congestion can make getting around the city center by car a frustrating experience, but if you plan to visit some of the outer suburbs or take excursions elsewhere in New South Wales, renting a car will give you some flexibility. The **NRMA's** (National Roads and Motorists' Association—the New South Wales auto club) emergency breakdown service can be contacted at ☎ **13 11 11.**

Car rental agencies include **Avis,** 214 William St., Kings Cross (☎ **02/9357 2000**); **Budget,** 93 William St., Kings Cross (☎ **13 28 48,** or 02/9339 8888); **Dollar,** Domain Car Park, Sir John Young Car Park (☎ **02/9223 1444**); **Hertz,** corner of William and Riley streets, Kings Cross (☎ **02/9360 6621**); and **Thrifty,** 75 William St., Kings Cross (☎ **02/9380 5399**). Avis, Budget, Hertz, and Thrifty also have desks at the airport. Rates average about A$45 (U.S.$29.25) per day for weekly rentals and around A$80 (U.S.$52) for single-day rentals.

You can rent a campervan from **Campervan Rentals** (☎ **1800/246 869** in Australia or 02/9797 8027; fax 02/9716 5087) or **Britz Campervans,** 182 O'Riordan St., Mascot, NSW 2020 (☎ **1800/331 454** in Australia or 02/9667 0402). Both companies allow you to drop off your van at most state capitals, and Cairns, though Britz charges an extra A$165 (U.S.$107.25) for the convenience.

Fast Facts: Sydney

American Express   The main Amex office is at 92 Pitt St., near Martin Place (☎ **02/9239 0666**). It's open Monday through Friday from 8:30am to 5:30pm and Saturday from 9am to noon. If you lose your travelers' checks, head to the main office at 175 Liverpool St. (☎ **02/9271 1111**). It's a locked security building so you'll need to call ahead first.

Babysitters   Dial an Angel (☎ **02/9416 7511** or 02/9362 4225) offers a well-regarded baby-sitting service.

Business Hours   General office and banking hours are Monday through Friday from 9am to 5pm. Many banks, especially in the city center, open from 9:30am to 12:30pm on Saturdays. Shopping hours are usually 8:30am to 5:30pm daily

(9am–5pm on Sat), and most stores stay open until 9pm on Thursdays. Most city-center stores are open from around 10am to 4pm on Sundays.

Camera Repair The **Camera Service Centre,** 1st Floor, 203 Castlereagh St. (☎ **02/9264 7091**), is a tiny place up a flight of stairs not far from Town Hall CityRail station. It repairs many cameras on the spot, or within a couple of days if parts are needed.

Currency Exchange Most major bank branches have currency exchange services. Small foreign currency exchange offices are clustered at the airport and around Circular Quay and Kings Cross. **Thomas Cook** can be found at the airport; at 175 Pitt St. (☎ **02/9231 2877**), open Monday to Friday from 6:45am to 5:15pm and Saturday from 10am to 2pm; in the Kingsgate Shopping Center, Kings Cross (☎ **02/9356 2211**), open Monday to Friday from 9am to 5pm; and on the lower ground floor of the Queen Victoria Building (☎ **02/9264 1133**), open Monday through Saturday from 9am to 6pm (until 9pm on Fri), Sunday from 11am to 5pm.

Dentist A well-respected office in the city is **City Dental Practice,** Level 2, 229 Macquaire St. (near Martin Place) (☎ **02/9221 3300**). For dental problems after hours call **Dental Emergency Information** (☎ **02/9369 7050**).

Doctor The **Park Medical Centre,** Shop 4, 27 Park St. (☎ **02/ 9264 4488**), in the city center near Town Hall, is open Monday through Friday from 8am to 6pm; consultations cost A$40 (U.S.$26) for 15 minutes. *Note:* If you are taking a dive course during your stay, get your medical exam here. It costs A$70/U.S.$45.50, cheaper than elsewhere in Australia). The **Kings Cross Travelers' Clinic,** Suite 1, 13 Springfield Ave., Kings Cross, off Darlinghurst Road (☎ **1300/369 359** in Australia or 02/9358 3066), is a great place for travel medicines and emergency contraception pills among other things. Hotel visits in the Kings Cross area cost A$80 (U.S.$52); consultations cost A$40 (U.S.$26). The **Travelers' Medical & Vaccination Centre,** Level 7, 428 George St., in the city center (☎ **02/9221 7133**), stocks and administers all travel-related vaccinations and medications.

Embassies/Consulates All foreign embassies are based in Canberra. You'll find the following consulates in Sydney: **United States,** 19–29 Martin Place (☎ **02/ 9373 9200**); **United Kingdom,** Level 16, Gateway Building, 1 Macquarie Place, Circular Quay (☎ **02/9247 7521**); **New Zealand,** 1 Alfred St., Circular Quay (☎ **02/9247 1344**); **Canada,** Level 5, 111 Harrington St., The Rocks (☎ **02/ 9364 3000**).

Emergencies Dial ☎ **000** to call police, the fire service, or an ambulance. Call the **Emergency Prescription Service** (☎ **02/9235 0333**) for emergency drug prescriptions, and the **NRMA** for car breakdowns (☎ **13 11 11**).

Eyeglass Repair **Perfect Vision,** Shop C22A, in the Centrepoint Tower, 100 Market St. (☎ **02/9221 1010**), is open Monday through Friday from 9am to 6pm (until 9pm Thurs) and Saturday from 9am to 5pm. It's the best place to replace lost contact lenses, but bring your prescription.

Holidays See "When to Go," in chapter 2. New South Wales also observes Labour Day on the first Monday in October.

Hospitals Go to **Sydney Hospital,** on Macquarie Street, at the top of Martin Place (☎ **02/9382 7111** for emergencies). **St. Vincents Hospital** is on Victoria and Burton streets in Darlinghurst (near Kings Cross) (☎ **02/9339 1111**).

Hot Lines Contact the **Poisons Information Center** at ☎ **13 11 26;** the **Gay and Lesbian Counseling Line** (4pm to midnight) at ☎ **02/9207 2800;** the **Rape Crisis Center** at ☎ **02/9819 6565;** the **Crisis Center** at ☎ **02/9358 6577, and Alcoholics Anonymous** at ☎ **02/9663 1206.**

Internet Access Global Gossip, at 770 George St., near Central Station (☎ **02/9212 1466**), and 111 Darlinghurst Rd., Kings Cross (☎ **02/9326 9777**), offers Internet access for A$2 (U.S.$1.30) for 10 minutes or A$10 (U.S.$6.50) per hour. It's open daily from 8am to midnight. The **Surfnet Café** (☎ **02/9976 0808**), in Manly is open Monday through Saturday from 9am to 9pm and Sunday from 9am to 7pm; the **Internet Café,** Level 3, Hotel Sweeney, 236 Clarence St. (☎ **02/9261 5666**), is open Monday through Friday from 10am to 9pm and Saturday from noon to 6pm; and the **Well Connected Café,** 35 Glebe Point Rd., Glebe (☎ **02/9566 2655**), is open Monday through Thursday from 10am to 11pm, Friday and Saturday from 10am to 6pm, and Sunday from noon to 10pm.

Lost Property There is no general lost property bureau in Sydney. Contact the nearest police station if you think you've lost something. For items lost on trains, contact the **Lost Property Office,** 494 Pitt St., near Central Railway Station (☎ **02/9379 3000**), open Monday through Friday from 8:30am to 4:30pm. For items left on planes or lost at the airport, go to the Federal Airport Corporation's office on the top floor of the international terminal at Sydney International Airport (☎ **02/9667 9583**). For stuff left on buses or ferries call ☎ **02/9245 5777.** Each taxi company has its own lost property office.

Luggage Storage You can leave your bags at the International Terminal at the airport. A locker here costs A$5 (U.S.$3.25) per day, or put them in the storage room for A$7 (U.S.$4.55) per day per piece. The storage room is open from 4:30am until the last flight of the day. Call ☎ **02/9667 9848** for information. Otherwise, leave luggage at the cloakroom at Central Station, near the front of the main building off George Street (☎ **02/9219 4395**). Storage at the rail station costs A$4.50 (U.S.$2.93) per article per day. The **Travelers Contact Point,** 7th floor, 428 George St. (above the Dymocks book store) (☎ **02/9221 8744**), stores luggage for A$15 (U.S.$9.75) per piece per month. It also operates a *poste restante* service, has Internet access, a travel agency, a jobs board, and freights items back to the U.K. and Ireland.

Newspapers The *Sydney Morning Herald* is considered one of the world's best newspapers (by its management at least) and is available throughout metropolitan Sydney. The equally prestigious *Australian* is available nationwide. The metropolitan *Daily Telegraph* is a more casual read and has a couple of editions a day. The *International Herald Tribune, USA Today,* the British *Guardian Weekly* and other U.S. and U.K. newspapers can be found at Circular Quay newspaper stands and most newsagents.

Pharmacies Most suburbs have pharmacies that are open late. For after hours referral, contact the **Emergency Prescription Service** (☎ **02/9235 0333**).

Police In an emergency dial ☎ **000.** Make nonemergency police inquiries through the **Sydney Police Centre** (☎ **02/9281 0000**).

Post Office The General Post Office (GPO) is at 130 Pitt St. (☎ **13 13 17** in Australia), open Monday through Friday, 8:30am to 5:30pm, Saturday from 8am to noon. Letters can be sent c/o *Poste Restante,* GPO, Sydney, NSW 2000, Australia (☎ **02/9244 3733**), and picked up at 310 George St., on the 3rd floor of

To call Australia from the United States, dial international access code (**011**); then Australia's country code (**61**); then the area code, but be sure to drop the first zero of the area code; then the number you want to call. For example, to ring the Sydney Opera House (☎ **02/9250 7111**) from the United States, dial **011 61 2 9250 7111**.

To call the U.S. from Australia, dial international access code **0011** (note the two zeros, not one like when you call from the United States); then the country code for the United States (**1**); then the area code; then the number you want to call.

the Hunter Connection shopping center. It's open Monday through Friday from 8:15am to 5:30pm. For the nearest post office, call ☎ **1800/043 300.**

Restrooms   These can be found in the Queen Victoria Building, most department stores, Central Station and Circular Quay, near the escalators by the Sydney Aquarium, and at Harbourside Festival Marketplace in Darling Harbour.

Safety   Sydney is a safe city overall, but like anywhere else, it's good to keep your wits about you and your wallet hidden. If you wear a money belt, keep it underneath your shirt. Be wary in Kings Cross and Redfern at all hours and around Central Station and the cinema strip on George Street near Town Hall station in the evening. Other places of concern are the back lanes of Darlinghurst and along the Bondi restaurant strip when the drunks spill out after midnight. Several people have reported thieves operating at the airport on occasions. If traveling by train at night, travel in the carriages next to the guard's van, marked with a blue light on the outside.

Taxes   Beginning July 1, 2000, Australia adopted a 10% **Goods and Services Tax** (GST) on most goods and services sold in Australia. The GST applies to most travel-related goods and services, including transport, hotels, tours, and restaurants. The tax has must be included in the advertised price of the product, though it doesn't have to be displayed independently of the pre-tax price. For information about claiming tax refunds on some items, see "Fast Facts: Australia, Taxes," in chapter 2.

Telephones   Sydney's public phones take coins (A40¢ for local calls), and many also take credit cards and A$10 (U.S.$6.50) phonecards available from newsagents. **Global Gossip,** at 770 George St., near Central Station (☎ **02/9212 1466**), and 111 Darlinghurst Rd., Kings Cross (☎ **02/9326 9777**), offers cheap international telephone calls.

Transit Information   Call **InfoLine** at ☎ **13 15 00** (daily 6am–10pm).

Useful Telephone Numbers   For **news,** dial ☎ **1199;** for the **time,** ☎ **1194;** for Sydney entertainment, ☎ **11 688;** for phone directory/assistance, ☎ **12 455;** for Travelers Aid Society, ☎ **02/9211 2469.**

Weather   For the local forecast call ☎ **1196.**

3 Accommodations You Can Afford

While the 2000 Olympics have come and gone, the international exposure led to more visitors to the city and more hotels. Although it's unlikely you'll find the city's hotels completely booked if you turn up without a reservation, it's wise to reserve in advance.

Most rooms are also cheaper when bought as part of a **package** (see the section on package deals in chapter 2, "Planning an Affordable Trip to Australia").

In addition, you should always ask for "specials" when booking a hotel, especially if you are traveling in winter (June, July, and Aug) when hotels are less likely to be full. Some hotels also offer packages based on the length of time you stay, but you'll never get them if you don't ask.

Serviced apartments are well worth considering because they mean big savings on meals, and you can eat exactly what you want. Many also have free laundry facilities.

DECIDING WHERE TO STAY   The choice location for lodging in Sydney is in The Rocks and around Circular Quay, just a short stroll from the Sydney Opera House, the Harbour Bridge, the Royal Botanic Gardens, the ferry terminals, and the train station, and close to main shopping areas. Don't expect many bargains here.

Hotels around Darling Harbour are close to local attractions, including museums, the Sydney Aquarium, the Star City casino, and the IMAX Theatre. Most Darling Harbour hotels are a 15-minute walk, or a short monorail or light rail trip, from Town Hall and the central shopping district in and around Centrepoint Tower and Pitt Street Mall.

More hotels are grouped around Kings Cross, Sydney's red-light district. While some of the hotels here are among the city's best, you'll also find a range of cheaper lodgings, including several backpacker hostels. Kings Cross can be unnerving at any time, but especially so on Friday and Saturday nights when the area's strip joints and nightclubs are doing their best business. Staying here does have its advantages, though: you get a real inner-city feel and it's close to some excellent restaurants and cafes centered around the Kings Cross/Darlinghurst and Oxford Street areas. Glebe, with its many ethnic restaurants, is another inner-city suburb popular with tourists. It's well served by local bus, as well as Airport Express Bus route 352.

If you want to stay near the beach, check out the options in Manly and Bondi, though you should consider their distance from the city and the lack of CityRail trains to these areas. If you stay out after midnight, you will have to get back from the city by night bus or taxi. The latter option is expensive—a taxi to Manly from the city will cost around A$35 (U.S.$22.75), and to Bondi around A$22 (U.S.$14.30).

IN THE ROCKS

The Lord Nelson Brewery Hotel. At the corner of Kent and Argyle Sts., The Rocks, Sydney, NSW 2000. ☎ **02/9251 4044.** Fax 02/9251 1532. blair@lordnelson.com.au. 10 units, 8 with bathroom. TV TEL. A$160 (U.S.$104) double without bathroom, A$180 (U.S.$117) double with bathroom. Extra person A$15 (U.S.$9.75). Rates include continental breakfast. AE, BC, DC, MC, V. Parking not available. CityRail or ferry: Circular Quay.

Sydney's oldest pub was established in 1841, having been built in 1836 as a private residence. It's an attractive, three-story sandstone building with a pub on the ground floor, a good brasserie on the second, and rooms on the third. The "small" rooms are that, with room for not much more than a bed and a small TV. For an extra A$30

Last-Minute Room Deals

If you land without a reservation, head for the **New South Wales Travel Centre desk** (☎ 02/9667 6050) on the Arrivals Level of the airport's International Terminal. It represents every Sydney hotel (but not hostels) and offers exceptional value discounts on rooms that haven't been filled that day—you can save up to 50% on a room this way. The desk is open from 6am until the last flight of the day and also offers discounts on tours, and cheap tickets for flights within Australia.

Central Sydney Accomodations

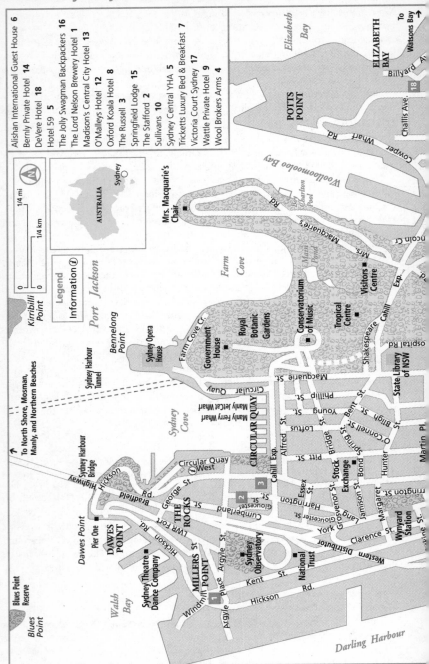

Alishan International Guest House **6**
Bernly Private Hotel **14**
DeVere Hotel **18**
Hotel 59 **5**
The Jolly Swagman Backpackers **16**
The Lord Nelson Brewery Hotel **1**
Madison's Central City Hotel **13**
O'Malleys Hotel **12**
Oxford Koala Hotel **8**
The Russell **3**
Springfield Lodge **15**
The Stafford **2**
Sullivans **10**
Sydney Central YHA **5**
Tricketts Luxury Bed & Breakfast **7**
Victoria Court Sydney **17**
Wattle Private Hotel **9**
Wool Brokers Arms **4**

Legend
Information ⓘ

AUSTRALIA

Sydney

N

0   1/4 mi
0   1/4 km

(U.S.$19.50) you get lots more space. From its creaky floorboards and bedroom walls made from convict-hewn sandstone, to the narrow corridors and the wood fire and homemade beer in the bar, the Lord Nelson positively wallows in colonial atmosphere.

✪ **The Russell.** 143A George St., The Rocks, Sydney, NSW 2000. ☎ **02/9241 3543.** Fax 02/9252 1652. www.therussell.com.au. 29 units, 19 with bathroom. TV TEL. A$110–$150 (U.S.$71.50–$97.50) double without bathroom, A$180–$229 (U.S.$117–$148.85) double with bathroom; A$230 (U.S.$149.50) suite. Extra person A$15 (U.S.$9.75). Rates include continental breakfast. AE, BC, DC, MC, V. Parking not available. CityRail or ferry: Circular Quay.

This is the coziest place to stay in The Rocks, and perhaps in all of Sydney. It's more than 100 years old, and has aged wonderfully from the creak of the floorboards to the ramshackle feel of its brightly painted corridors. Every room is different in style, size, and shape; all come with a queen-size bed and half have cable TV (you may request a TV be brought in). All rooms have immense character, including the ones added on in 1990 above the Fortune of War Hotel next door. There are no harbor views, but from some rooms you can see the tops of the ferry terminals at Circular Quay. Guests have the use of a sitting room, living room scattered with magazines and books, and a rooftop garden. Boulders restaurant serves good food on the ground floor.

WORTH A SPLURGE

✪ **The Stafford.** 75 Harrington St., The Rocks, Sydney, NSW 2000. ☎ **02/9251 6711.** Fax 02/9251 3458. staffordsydney@bigpond.com. 61 units. A/C TV TEL. A$231–$270 (U.S. $150–$175.50) studio double; A$275 (U.S. $178.75) 1-bedroom apt; A$308 (U.S. $200.20) executive 1-bedroom apt; A$292 (U.S.$189.80) terrace house; A$369 (U.S. $239.85) 1-bedroom penthouse. Extra person A$17 (U.S.$11.05). Children under 12 stay free in parents' room. Ask about weekly rates. AE, BC, DC, JCB, MC, V. Parking A$15 (U.S.$9.75). CityRail or ferry: Circular Quay.

The Stafford offers the best-located serviced apartments in Sydney, in the heart of The Rocks, close to the harbor and Circular Quay, and a short stroll from the central business district. The property consists of modern apartments in a six-story building (the best units, for their harbor and Opera House views, are on the top three floors) and 7 two-story terrace houses dating from 1870 to 1895. The Stafford is highly recommended for its location, spacious rooms, and fully equipped kitchen. There's an outdoor pool, gym, spa and sauna, and complimentary self-service laundry.

AT DARLING HARBOUR

Wool Brokers Arms. 22 Allen St., Pyrmont, NSW 2009. ☎ **02/9552 4773.** Fax 02/9552 4771. woolbrokers@ozemail.com.au. 26 units, none with bathroom. TV. A$79 (U.S.$51.35) double; A$98 (U.S.$63.70) triple; A$120 (U.S.$78) family room for four. These discounted prices are for Frommer's readers only. Rates include continental breakfast. Extra person A$20 (U.S.$13). AE, BC, MC, V. Parking A$9 (U.S.$5.85) nearby. Bus: 501 from central business district or Central Station. Light Rail: Convention Centre.

You'll find this 1886 heritage building on the far side of Darling Harbour, next to the four-star Novotel hotel and hidden behind a parking garage. It's set on a noisy road, so unless you're used to traffic, avoid the rooms at the front. Rooms are simply furnished with a double bed, a refrigerator, tea and coffee-making facilities, and a sink. Room 3 is one of the nicer ones. Family rooms have a king-size bed, a set of bunks, and two singles through an open door way. There are 19 shared bathrooms, a coin-operated laundry, and a self-service breakfast room. It's a good place for a few nights. Anywhere else around here you'll be paying at least three times as much.

IN KINGS CROSS & THE SUBURBS BEYOND

Bernly Private Hotel. 15 Springfield Ave., Potts Point, NSW 2011. ☎ **02/9358 3122.** Fax 02/9356 4405. 95 units, 12 with bathroom (shower only). TV. A$49 (U.S.$31.85) single without bathroom; $55 (U.S.$35.75) budget double without bathroom; A$82.50 (U.S.$53.63) budget double with bathroom; A$93.50 (U.S.$60.78) standard double with bathroom; A$132 (U.S.$85.80) triple with bathroom. A$20 (U.S.$13) dorm bed. Extra person A$22 (U.S.$14.30). AE, BC, DC, JCB, MC, V. On-street meter parking. CityRail: Kings Cross.

This place, tucked away just off Darlinghurst Road, is a real find. It's an ants' nest of rooms run by friendly staff, catering to everyone from short-term travelers to newly arrived immigrants. All rooms are new and clean. The more expensive rooms are superior to most others of their price in the area. Budget rooms are a bit scruffier and smaller, but perfectly livable. Some come with a microwave, and all have a small TV. Backpacker rooms have two sets of bunk beds, though just two people seem to occupy most. Some of the backpacker rooms also have a shower. There's a rooftop sundeck and a lounge with cable TV. Five family rooms come with double beds and two singles.

DeVere Hotel. 44–46 Macleay St., Potts Point, NSW 2011. ☎ **1800/818 790** in Australia, 0800/441 779 in New Zealand, or 02/9358 1211. Fax 02/9358 4685. www.devere.com.au. info@devere.com.au. 98 units. A/C TV TEL. A$107.90 (U.S.$70.14) double; superior room $A140.60 (U.S.$91.39); executive room $A162.40 (U.S.$105.56); A$206 (U.S.$133.90) suite. Extra person A$32.70 (U.S.$21.26). Children under 12 stay free in parents' room. AE, BC, DC, MC, V. Parking at nearby Landmark Hotel A$12 (U.S.$7.80) per exit. CityRail: Kings Cross. Bus: 311 from Circular Quay.

The DeVere has been recommended by several readers who comment on the friendly staff and the bargain-basement room prices when booked at the Tourism New South Wales Travel Centre. Although the rooms are modern, they are a little too standard gray corporate for my liking (though the owner says some are now yellow). Superior rooms are a bit larger, and the executive room is larger still and comes with nicer furniture. They are certainly a bargain compared to similar, but far more expensive, rooms elsewhere in Sydney. The suites have views of Elizabeth Bay, a spa bath, and a king-size bed rather than a queen. Some suites have a pretty useless kitchenette with no cooking facilities. Some standard rooms have an extra single bed. Breakfast is available from A$8 (U.S.$5.20).

✪ Hotel 59. 59 Bayswater Rd., Kings Cross, NSW 2011. ☎ **02/9360 5900.** Fax 02/9360 1828. hotel59@enternet.com.au. 8 units. A/C TV TEL. A$115 (U.S.$74.75) standard double, A$125 (U.S.$81.25) deluxe double, A$135 (U.S.$87.75) superior room. Extra person A$15 (U.S.$9.75), extra children 2–12 A$10 (U.S.$6.50). Rates include cooked breakfast. BC, MC, V. Limited parking A$5 (U.S.$3.25). CityRail: Kings Cross.

This popular and friendly B&B is well worth considering if you want to be near the Kings Cross action, but far enough away to get a decent night's sleep. Deluxe rooms have either a queen or king-size bed and a combined shower and tub, while the smaller standard rooms come with a double bed and a shower (no tub). The two large superior rooms come with two single beds and two more that can be locked together to form a king, and a separate living room. One comes with a small kitchen with a microwave and hot plates. All rooms are clean and comfortable and have private bathrooms. There is also a small guest lounge with a TV. A cooked breakfast is served up in the cafe below. There's no elevator to reach the rooms above the ground floor.

Madison's Central City Hotel. 6 Ward Ave., Elizabeth Bay, NSW 2011. ☎ **1800/060 118** in Australia, or 02/9357 1155. Fax 02/9357 1193. www.centralcityhotel.com.au. cchsydney@ one.net.au. 39 units. A/C TV TEL. A$99 (U.S.$64.35) double; A$126 (U.S.$81.90) suite. Extra person A$20 (U.S.$13). AE, BC, DC, MC, V. Free covered parking. CityRail: Kings Cross.

Madison's is about a 5-minute walk from Kings Cross CityRail station. It's modern, clean, and well priced, but a bit soulless. The standard rooms resemble motel rooms and are much smaller than the suites. Each has a combined tub and shower; the tub is quite deep, and there's no step to help you climb in. Rooms are interconnecting and thus suitable for families, though full room rates apply for each room. All come with either a queen-size bed or a set of twins. A coin-operated laundry is on the premises.

O'Malleys Hotel. 228 William St., corner of Brougham St. (P.O. Box 468), Kings Cross, NSW 2011. ☎ **02/9357 2211.** Fax 02/9357 2656. bookings@omalleyshotel.com.au. 14 units. A/C TV TEL. A$77 (U.S.$50.05) single share bathroom, A$82.50 (U.S.$53.63) single with bathroom, A$99 (U.S.$64.35) single with bathroom and harbour views; A$88 (U.S.$57.20) double share bathroom, A$93.50 (U.S.$60.78) double with bathroom, A$99 (U.S.$64.35) double with bathroom and harbour views. Rates include continental breakfast. AE, BC, MC, V. On-street parking, or parking garage available for A$8 (U.S.$5.20) overnight. CityRail: Kings Cross.

If you don't mind a short stagger up the stairs from the popular "backpackers" Irish Pub below, then you'll enjoy this place. It's a 2-minute stroll from the main Kings Cross drag and has standard size rooms. The rooms on the first floor are cheaper because they are above the bar—and the cheery hum of drinkers below could keep you awake. (The bar is open 11am–3am Mon–Sat, and noon–midnight on Sun.) Rooms on the second floor are much quieter and a good value. All are country-style with natural wood trim and a private bathroom (although bathrooms for rooms on the first floor are across the corridor).

Springfield Lodge. 9 Springfield Ave., Kings Cross, NSW 2011. ☎ **02/9358 3222.** Fax 02/9357 4742. www.wheretostay.com.au/springfieldlodge. springfield@wheretostay.com.au. 77 units, 46 with bathroom (shower only). TV. A$60 (U.S.$39) double without bathroom, A$75–$80 (U.S.$48.75–$52) double with bathroom. Extra person A$30 (U.S.$19.50); children under 12 A$10 (U.S.$6.50). BC, JCB, MC, V. 24-hr. secured parking 2 min. away for around A$12 (U.S.$7.80) a day. CityRail: Kings Cross.

The lobby of this surprising lodge just off the main Kings Cross strip doesn't inspire much confidence, but the rooms are clean and pleasant enough for a few days' stay. Standard rooms are small and dark with a small TV, a double bed, sink, and refrigerator. En suite rooms, also dark but somehow comforting, are a little larger, have both a double and a single bed and a small bathroom with shower. All rooms were repainted in 2000. The wooden floorboards in all rooms are a nice touch. You need to pay a A$10 (U.S.$6.50) deposit for your room key.

✪ **Victoria Court Sydney.** 122 Victoria St., Potts Point, NSW 2011. ☎ **1800/630 505** in Australia or 02/9357 3200. Fax 02/9357 7606. www.VictoriaCourt.com.au. info@Victoria Court.com.au . 22 units. A/C TV TEL. A$99–$115 (U.S.$64.35–$74.75) double, depending on the season; A$165 (U.S.$107.25) deluxe double with sundeck; A$250 (U.S.$162.50) honeymoon suite with balcony. Rates include buffet breakfast. Extra person A$20 (U.S.$13). AE, BC, DC, MC, V. Free parking in secured lot. CityRail: Kings Cross.

This cute little place is two 1881 terrace houses joined together; it's situated near a string of backpacker hostels and cafes in a leafy street running parallel to sleazy Darlinghurst Road. The glass-roofed breakfast room on the ground floor is a work of art decked out with hanging ferns, giant bamboo, wrought-iron tables and chairs, and a trickling fountain. Just off the breakfast room is a peaceful guest lounge stacked with books and newspapers. The very plush rooms come with either king or queen-size beds, but lack a tub in the bathroom. There's a coin-op laundry just down the road.

SUPER-CHEAP SLEEPS

The Jolly Swagman Backpackers. 27 Orwell St., Kings Cross NSW 2011. ☎ **1800/805 870** in Australia or 02/9358 6400. Fax 02/9331 0125. www.jollyswagman.com.au. stay@jollyswagman.com.au. 53 units A$16 (U.S.$10.40) dorm bed; A$22 (U.S.$14.30) per person in double. Ask about multi-day deals. MC, V. On-street metered parking. CityRail: Kings Cross.

This is one of the best backpacker hostels that dot the area between Darlinghurst Road and Victoria Street in Kings Cross. The good thing about this place is that it has two sister properties near by, so you are almost certain to get a room. The 18 dorm rooms in this property have only two bunk beds in each, which means things don't get too crowded. And couples traveling together will often find they get the room to themselves. There are also plenty of twin and double rooms, as well as two female-only dorms. The atmosphere is young and typical backpacker, with cheap meals (under A$5/U.S.$3.25) served in the ground floor cafe. There's a guest kitchen, two TV rooms, a laundry, an ironing room, bag storage, free cable movies, 24-hour Internet access, and a 24-hour travel agency. Each room is spotless and has security lockers.

IN DARLINGHURST

Oxford Koala Hotel. Corner of Oxford & Pelican sts., Darlinghurst (P.O. Box 535, Darlinghurst, NSW 2010). ☎ **1800/222 144** in Australia (outside Sydney), or 02/9269 0645. Fax 02/9283 2741. www.oxfordkoala.com.au. 330 units (including 78 apts.) A/C TV TEL. A$135–$155 (U.S. $87.75–$100.75) double; A$185–$205 (U.S. $120.25–$133.25) 1-bedroom apt. Extra person A$25 (U.S.$16.25). Children under 12 stay free in parents' room. AE, BC, DC, JCB, MC, V. Parking A$15 (U.S.$9.75) a day. Bus: 380 or any bus traveling via Taylor Square.

You won't find many three-star hotels that offer as much value for your dollar as the Oxford Koala. A popular tourist hotel, it is well placed just off trendy Oxford Street, a 5- to 10-minute bus trip from the city center and Circular Quay. There are 13 floors of rooms in this tower block; rooms on the top floor have reasonable views over the city. Superior rooms are very comfortable and more spacious than standard rooms and have better furniture. All have a shower/tub combination or just a shower. Apartments are good size, come with a full kitchen, and are serviced daily. On the premises are a swimming pool, a restaurant, and a cocktail bar.

Sullivans. 21 Oxford St., Paddington, NSW 2021. ☎ **02/9361 0211.** Fax 02/9360 3735. www.sullivans.com.au. sydney@sullivans.com.au. 64 units. A/C TV TEL. A$125 (U.S.$81.25) double. AE, BC, DC, MC, V. Limited free parking. Bus: 378, or 380 from Circular Quay.

About half of this boutique hotel's guests come from overseas, mainly from the United Kingdom and Europe, and the United States. There's also a small corporate following. Sullivans is in the heart of Sydney's most popular shopping, entertainment, restaurant, and gay pub and club areas. The hotel is popular with Americans during the Gay and Lesbian Mardi Gras in February. Rooms are cozy, with queen-size beds and a refrigerator; all have an in-suite bathroom with a shower (no tub). There's free bicycle hire, a small swimming pool, and a garden courtyard.

Wattle Private Hotel. 108 Oxford St. (at corner of Palmer St.), Darlinghurst, NSW 2010. ☎ **02/9332 4118.** Fax 02/9331 2074. wattlehotel@yahoo.com.au. 12 units. A/C MINIBAR TV TEL. A$99 (U.S.$64.35) double. Extra person A$11 (U.S.$7.15). Rates include continental breakfast. BC, MC, V. No parking. Bus: Any to Taylor Square from Circular Quay.

This attractive Edwardian-style house built between 1900 and 1910 offers homey accommodations in the fashionable inner-city suburb of Darlinghurst, known for its great cafes, nightlife, and restaurants. Rooms are found on four stories, but there's no elevator, so if you can't do stairs, try to get a room on a lower floor. Rooms are smallish but are opened up by large windows. Twin rooms have a better bathroom, with a tub. The decor is a jumble of Chinese vases, ceiling fans, and contemporary bedspreads. Laundry facilities are on the premises. The owners are very friendly.

IN GLEBE
SUPER-CHEAP SLEEPS

Alishan International Guest House. 100 Glebe Point Rd., Glebe, NSW 2037. ☎ **02/ 9566 4048.** Fax 02/9525 4686. 19 units. www.alishan.com.au. kevin@alishan.com.au. TV. A\$30 (U.S.\$19.50) dorm bed; A\$100 (U.S.\$65) double; A\$145 (U.S.\$94.25) family room. Extra person A\$15 (U.S.\$9.75). AE, BC, MC, V. Secured parking available for 6 cars, otherwise free on-street parking. Bus: 431 or 433 from George Street, or Airport Express route 352 from airport.

The Alishan is another quiet place with a real Aussie feel. It's at the city end of Glebe Point Road, just 10 minutes by bus from the shops around Town Hall. Standard dorm rooms are spotless, light and bright, and come with two sets of bunks. Doubles have a double bed, a sofa and armchair, and an en suite shower. Grab room 9 if you fancy sleeping on one of two single mattresses on the Japanese-style tatami mat floor. There's also a BBQ area, a TV room, a laundry, and internet access.

WORTH A SPLURGE

✪ **Tricketts Luxury Bed & Breakfast.** 270 Glebe Point Rd., Glebe, NSW 2037. ☎ **02/ 9552 1141.** Fax 02/9692 9462. www.citysearch.com.au/syd/trickettsbandb. 7 units. A\$154– \$176 (U.S.\$100.10–\$114.40) double; A\$198 (U.S.\$128.70) honeymoon suite. Rates include continental breakfast. No credit cards. Free parking. Bus: 431 from George Street, or Airport Express bus 352 from airport.

As soon as I walked into this atmospheric old place I wanted to ditch my modern Sydney apartment and move in. Your first impression as you enter the tessellated (stone tiled) corridor of this 1880s Victorian mansion is of an amazing jumble of plants and ornaments, high ceilings, Oriental rugs, and leaded windows. Guests play billiards over a decanter of port, or relax among magazines and wicker furniture on the balcony overlooking the fairly busy Glebe Point Road. The bedrooms are quiet and homey (no TVs). My favorites are number 2, with its wooden floorboards and king-size bed, and number 7, with its queen-size bed, extra single bed, and very large bathroom. Rooms all have showers. There's a nice courtyard out the back with a barbecue.

NEAR CENTRAL STATION

✪ **Sydney Central YHA.** 11 Rawson Place, Sydney, NSW 2000 (on the corner of Pitt St., outside Central Station). ☎ **02/9281 9111.** Fax 02/9281 9199. www.yha.com.au. sydcentral@ yhansw.org.au. 151 rooms, or 532 beds, (54 twin units). A\$24–\$29 (U.S.\$15.60–\$18.85) dorm bed; A\$72 (U.S.\$46.80) twin without bathroom, A\$80 (U.S.\$52) twin with bathroom. Non-YHA members pay A\$3 (U.S.\$1.95) extra. BC, JCB, MC, V. Parking A\$10 (U.S.\$6.50). CityRail: Central.

This award-winning youth hostel is one of the biggest and busiest in the world. With a 98% year-round occupancy rate, you'll have to book early to secure a place. Opened in 1987 in a historic nine-story building, it offers far more than standard basic accommodations. In the basement is the Scu Bar, a very popular drinking hole with pool tables and occasional entertainment. There's also a bistro selling cheap meals, a convenience store, two fully equipped kitchens, and an entertainment room with more pool tables and e-mail facilities, TV rooms on every floor, and an audiovisual room showing movies. If you want more, try the heated swimming pool and the sauna! Rooms are clean and basic. The YHA is completely accessible to travelers with disabilities. Check the YHA website for other great hostels in Sydney—including: the Glebe Point YHA in Glebe, the Sydney Beachhouse YHA in the beachside suburb of Collaroy, and Pittwater YHA in Ku-ring-gai National Park (only accessible by boat and a fabulous way to experience the "bush" around Sydney).

IN BONDI

Bondi Beach is a good place to stay to be close to the surf and sand, though if you're getting around by public transport you'll need to catch a bus to Bondi Junction, then a train to the city center (you can stay on the bus all the way, but it takes forever).

As well as the recommendations below, there's a good backpacker hostel called **Indy's** (☎ **02/9365 4900**), at 35a Hall St., offering four to eight-person dorm rooms for A$16 (U.S.$10.40) in winter and A$20 (U.S.$13) in summer, and double rooms in another site opposite North Bondi Surf Club for the same price per person.

The Hotel Bondi. 178 Campbell Parade, Bondi Beach, NSW 2026. ☎ **02/9130 3271.** Fax 02/9130 7974. 50 units, 40 with bathroom. TV. A$120 (U.S.$78) double (all with bathroom), A$150 (U.S.$97.50) double with beach view; A$160–$210 (U.S.$104–$136.50) suite. AE, BC, MC, V. Free secured parking. CityRail: Bondi Junction; then bus 380. Bus: 380 from Circular Quay or George St., or Airport Express bus 351 from airport.

This white stucco Bondi landmark is adequate for a few days' stay if you don't mind the creaks of the vintage wooden elevator and the brusque front-desk service. The corridors are in need of a lick of paint, and the rooms are slightly disheveled, but overall it retains a fairly healthy slap of 1920s grandeur. Double rooms are basic and small, with gray carpeting, a springy double bed, shower, small refrigerator, and TV. The more expensive ones have a balcony with a beach view. The six suites are nicer and have their own balconies looking out to sea. Downstairs there are seven bars, which seem to attract aggressive drunks. Given the choice (Bondi hotels are often booked far in advance) I'd stay at the friendlier Ravesi's (see below).

Ravesi's on Bondi Beach. Corner of Hall St. and Campbell Parade, Bondi Beach, NSW 2026. ☎ **02/9365 4422.** Fax 02/9365 1481. Ravesis@wheretostay.com.au. 16 units. A/C TV TEL. A$115.50 (U.S.$75.08) standard double, A$176–$181.50 (U.S.$114.40–$117.98) double with side view; A$209–$236.50 (U.S.$135.85–$153.73) split-level 1-bedroom with side view; A$209–$236.50 (U.S.$135.85–$153.73) 1-bedroom suite with ocean view. Penthouse $A324.50 (U.S.$210.93). Extra person A$20 (U.S. $13). 2 children under 12 stay free in parents' room. AE, BC, DC, MC, V. Parking at the Swiss-Grand Hotel nearby for A$5 (U.S.$3.25) for 24 hr. CityRail: Bondi Junction; then bus 380. Bus: 380 from Circular Quay.

Right on Australia's most famous golden sands, this Art Deco boutique property offers Mediterranean-influenced rooms with a beachy decor. Standard doubles are spacious, quite basic, and don't have air-conditioning—though you hardly need it with the ocean breeze. The one-bedroom suite is good for families, with two sofa beds in the living room. The split-level one-bedroom room has a bedroom upstairs and sofa bed in the living area. Rooms 5 and 6 and the split-level suite have the best views of the ocean. All rooms have Juliet balconies, and the split-level suite has its own terrace. If you're a light sleeper, request a room on the top floor because the popular Ravesi's Restaurant can cook up quite a bit of noise on busy nights.

IN MANLY

If you decide to stay at my favorite beachside suburb, then you'll need to be aware that ferries from the city stop running at midnight. If you get stranded, you'll be facing either an expensive taxi fare of around A$35 (U.S. $22.75), or you'll need to make your way to the bus stand behind Wynyard CityRail station to catch a night bus. Consider buying a Ferry Ten or JetCat Ten ticket, which will save you quite a bit of money in commuting expenses if you're staying in Manly for a few days.

As well as the recommendations below, Manly has several backpacker places worth checking out. The best include **Manly Backpackers Beachside,** 28 Ragland St., (☎ **02/9977 3411;** fax 02/9977 4379), with dorm beds for A$24 (U.S.$15.60), doubles without bathroom for A$70 (U.S.$45.50) and doubles with bathroom for A$80

(U.S.$52). There's a A$30 (U.S.$19.50) returnable key deposit. The ○ **Wharf Back-packers,** 48 East Esplanade, opposite the ferry terminal (☎ 02/9977 2800; fax: 02/9977 2820), has dorm beds for A$24 (U.S.$15.60), or A$144 (U.S.$93.60) a week.

○ **Manly Lodge.** 22 Victoria Parade, Manly, NSW 2095. ☎ **02/9977 8655.** Fax 02/9976 2090. www.manlylodge.com.au. 24 units. A/C TV. Standard double A$132–$154 (U.S.$85.80–$100.10) peak season, A$107.80–$132 (U.S.$70.07–$85.80) off-season; deluxe double A$154–$198 (U.S.$100.10–$128.70 peak season, A$132–$154 (U.S.$85.80–$100.10) off-season; family suite with spa A$264–$330 (U.S.$171.60–$214.50) peak season, A$187–$262 (U.S.$121.55–$170.30) off-season. Peak season is Christmas, Easter, and school holidays. Rates include continental breakfast. Extra person A$30 (U.S.$19.50); Extra children under 10 A$16.50 (U.S.$10.73). Ask about weekly rates; off-season specials. AE, BC, MC, V. Free parking. Ferry or JetCat: Manly.

At first sight this ramshackle building halfway between the main beach and the harbor doesn't look like much—especially the cramped hostel-like foyer bristling with tourist brochures. But don't let that put you off. Some of the rooms are lovely, and the whole place has a nice atmosphere and plenty of character. Double rooms are not exceptional and come with a double bed, stone or carpet floors, a TV and VCR, and either a spa or a tub/shower combination. Some of the standard doubles and all of the deluxe doubles have a kitchen. Family rooms have a set of bunk beds and a double in one room, and a shower. Family suites are classy; each has a small kitchen area, one double and three singles in the bedroom, and two sofa beds in the living area. The lodge also has a communal spa, sauna, gym, laundry, table tennis, and an Olympic-size trampoline.

○ **Manly Paradise Motel and Beach Plaza Apartments.** 54 North Steyne, Manly, NSW 2095. ☎ **1800/815 789** in Australia or 02/9977 5799. Fax 02/9977 6848. www.manlyparadise. com.au. enquiries@manlyparadise.com.au 40 units. A/C TV TEL. A$95–$145 (U.S.$61.75–$94.25) double motel unit; A$265 (U.S.$172.25) 2-bedroom apt. Extra person A$20 (U.S.$13). Ask about lower rates for long-term stays. AE, BC, DC, MC, V. Free secured parking. Ferry or JetCat: Manly.

I walked into this place after taking a good look around the modern Manly Waterfront Apartment Hotel next door and felt more at home here. The motel and the apartment complex are separate but share the same reception area. Though there is one motel room that goes for A$90 (U.S.$58.50), it's a bit small for my liking; the rest of the irregularly shaped rooms are big yet cozy and come with a shower (no tub) and a springy double bed. Though there is no restaurant, you can get breakfast in bed. The traffic outside can make it a little noisy during the day (but you'll probably be on the beach anyway). Some rooms have glimpses of the sea. A swimming pool (with views) on the roof is shared with the apartment complex.

The apartments are magnificent—very roomy, with thick carpets. The amenities include a private laundry, full kitchen with dishwasher, and two bathrooms (one with a tub). The sea views from the main front balcony are heart-stopping.

Periwinkle-Manly Cove Guesthouse. 18–19 E. Esplanade, Manly, NSW 2095. ☎ **02/ 9977 4668.** Fax 02/9977 6308. 18 units, 11 with bathroom. TV. A$126 (U.S.$81.90) double without bathroom, A$165 (U.S.$107.25) double with bathroom; A$148 (U.S.$96.20) triple without bathroom, A$176 (U.S.$114.40) triple with bathroom; A$160.50 (U.S.$104.33) quad without bathroom, A$192.50 (U.S.$125.13) quad with bathroom. Units with harbor views A$11 (U.S.$7.15) extra. Extra person A$33 (U.S.$21.45). Rates include continental breakfast. BC, MC, V. Free parking. Ferry or JetCat: Manly.

Nicely positioned just across the road from one of Manly's two harbor beaches, the Periwinkle is a short walk from the ferry, shops along the Corso, and the main ocean beach. Rooms are small and have a double bed, a small TV, and refrigerator. Some have a shower and toilet attached (these go for higher prices noted above), but otherwise you'll share four bathrooms (one has a tub). A full kitchen next to a pleasant-enough communal lounge means you could save money by cooking. Rooms 5 and 10 are the nicest and have screened balconies overlooking the harbor (but no bathrooms). For atmosphere I prefer the Manly Lodge (see above). No smoking inside.

WORTH A SPLURGE

✪ **Manly Pacific Parkroyal.** 55 North Steyne, Manly, NSW 2095. ☎ **800/835-7742** in the U.S. and Canada 02/9977 7666. Fax 02/9977 7822. www.parkroyal.com.au. 169 units. A/C MINIBAR TV TEL. A$283–$327 (U.S.$183.95–$212.55) double, depending on view; A$512 (U.S.$332.80) suite. Extra person A$32 (U.S.$20.80). AE, BC, DC, JCB, MC, V. Parking: $10 (U.S.$6.50). Ferry or JetCat: Manly.

If you could bottle the views from this hotel—across the sand and through the Norfolk Island Pines to the Pacific Ocean—you'd make a fortune. Standing on your private balcony in the evening with the sea breeze in your nostrils and the chirping of hundreds of lorikeets is nothing short of heaven. The Manly Pacific is the only hotel of its class in this beachside suburb. There's nothing claustrophobic here, from the broad expanse of foyer to the wide corridors and spacious rooms. Each standard room is light and modern with two double beds, a balcony, limited cable TV, and amenities from bathrobes to an iron and ironing board. Ocean views are worth the extra money. The hotel is a 10-minute stroll, or a A$4 (U.S.$2.60) taxi ride, from the Manly ferry.

Gilbert's Restaurant has fine dining and ocean views. Nell's Brasserie & Cocktail Bar serves a buffet breakfast and dinner daily. The Charlton & Star Bar and Grill has bands every evening Wednesday to Sunday and attracts a young crowd. There's also a rooftop spa, pool, gym, sauna, concierge, 24-hour room service, laundry.

IN MOSMAN

✪ **Buena Vista Hotel.** 76 Middle Head Rd., Mosman, NSW 2095. ☎ **02/9969 7022.** Fax 02/9968 2879. 14 units, (5 doubles, 6 single, 1 twin, 1 family room) none with bathroom. TV. A$82.50 (U.S.$53.63) double, A$150 (U.S.$97.50) double over Christmas and New Year's; A$99 (U.S.$64.35) family room, A$200 (U.S.$130) family room over Christmas and New Year's. Rates include continental breakfast. AE, BC, DC, MC, V. Ferry: Taronga Zoo, then a 5-min. bus ride. Bus: Taronga Zoo from Wynyard Station.

If you want to see how wealthy Sydneysiders live, then stay in this exclusive suburb just a 10-minute walk from Taronga Zoo. The rooms above this popular pub, just down the road from some of Sydney's most exclusive boutiques, are clean and comfortable, and a bargain for Sydney. Each comes with a springy queen-size bed or two singles, a small TV, and a sink; a few have balconies. All except room 13 have good city views. The best is room 1, which is larger and brighter than the rest, and comes with a large balcony with good views. Family rooms come with a double bed, a fold-out sofa bed, and a trundle bed—all in one room. All rooms share nice bathrooms. The fabulous Balmoral Beach is a 10-minute walk away, 5 minutes by bus. Ask hotel staff for ferry times and bus/ferry connection details from Taronga Zoo and Mosman wharves. Taxi from city around $22 (U.S.$14.30).

4 Great Deals on Dining

Sydney is a gourmet paradise, with an abundance of fresh seafood, a vast range of vegetables and fruit always in season, prime meats at good prices, and top-quality chefs making international names for themselves. You'll find Asian and Mediterranean cuisine have had a major influence on Australian cooking, with spices and herbs finding their way into most dishes. Immigration has brought almost every type of cuisine,

Central Sydney Dining

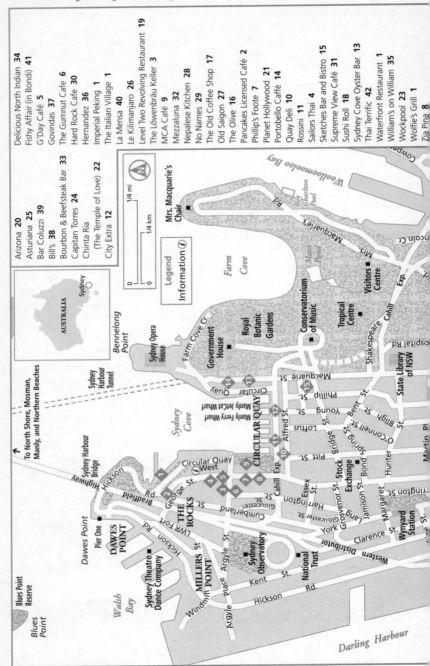

Arizona 20
Asturiana 25
Bar Coluzzi 39
Bill's 38
Bourbon & Beefsteak Bar 33
Capitan Torres 24
Chinta Ria
(The Temple of Love) 22
City Extra 12

Delicious North Indian 34
Fishy Affair (in Bondi) 41
G'Day Café 5
Govindas 37
The Gumnut Cafe 6
Hard Rock Cafe 30
Hernandez 36
Imperial Peking 1
The Italian Village 1
La Mensa 40
Le Kilimanjaro 26
Level Two Revolving Restaurant 19
The Löwenbräu Keller 3
MCA Café 9
Mezzaluna 32
Nepalese Kitchen 28
No Names 29
The Old Coffee Shop 17
Old Saigon 27
The Olive 16
Pancakes Licensed Café 2
Philip's Foote 7
Planet Hollywood 21
Portobello Caffé 14
Quay Deli 10
Rossini 11
Sailors Thai 4
Sketches Bar and Bistro 15
Supreme View Café 31
Sushi Roll 18
Sydney Cove Oyster Bar 13
Thai Terrific 42
Waterfront Restaurant 1
William's on William 35
Wockpool 23
Wolfie's Grill 1
Zia Pina 8

from African to Tibetan, from Russian to Vietnamese, with whole areas of the city dedicated to one type of food, while other areas are truly melting pots of styles.

Food is generally cheaper in Sydney and consistently of better quality, than in many other major cities of the world. Though you can certainly fill up for A$10 (U.S.$6.50) or less, or drop a cool hundred splurging at one of the city's top-class restaurants, a two-course meal in a standard restaurant will cost around A$18 to $20 (U.S.$11.70–$13) a person. Add a bottle of reasonable Australian wine, at around A$12 (U.S.$8.40), and you can eat and drink merrily for less than A$50 (U.S.$32.50) a couple.

Cheap eats in Sydney are in inner-city areas, such as along Kings Street in Newtown, Crown Street in Darlinghurst, Glebe Point Road in Glebe, and scattered among the more upscale dining spots in Kings Cross and on Oxford Street. There are some good food courts around Chinatown, including the **Sussex Street Food Court,** on Sussex Street, which offers Chinese, Malaysian, Thai, Japanese, and Vietnamese meals for A$4 to $7 (U.S.$2.60–$4.55).

Avoid the take-away booths along the ferry wharves at Circular Quay, as some of them aren't quite sanitary. The fish-and-chip shop opposite the "bottle shop" (liquor store) is an exception—it also has some of the best fries (chips) in Sydney.

Smoking is banned in Sydney restaurants, except if you're eating at sidewalk tables.

NEAR CIRCULAR QUAY

City Extra. Shop E4, Circular Quay. ☎ **02/9241 1422.** Main courses A$10.30–$17.65 (U.S.$6.70–$11.47). 10% surcharge midnight–6am, Sundays, and public holidays. Daily 24 hr. AE, BC, DC, MC, V. CityRail, bus, or ferry: Circular Quay. ITALIAN/AUSTRALIAN.

This place stays open 24 hours, so it's convenient if you get the munchies at midnight. It's also nicely placed next to the Manly ferry terminal. The plastic chairs and tables outside make it a pleasant spot to while away an inexpensive meal. All kinds of pastas are on offer, and salads, pies, steaks, ribs, fish, and Asian-influenced dishes. There's also a fat selection of desserts. That said, I agree with several of my friends who say the food is nicer and a better value next door at Rossini (see below).

Freckle Face Café. 32A Burton St., Kirribilli. ☎ **02/9957 2116.** Main courses A$7 (U.S.$4.55) eat in, A$6.50 (U.S.$4.23) takeout. No credit cards. Mon–Sat 7am–4pm. CityRail or ferry: Milsons Point. Take the left exit from the Milsons Point CityRail station, walk downhill to the traffic lights, cross the road, and it's in the street opposite. CAFE.

There's no better to place to refuel after a walk across the Harbour Bridge than this intimate cafe near the Milsons Point CityRail station on the north side of Sydney Harbour. Freckle Face specializes in sandwiches, bagels, Turkish bread, foccacia, and very good coffee. The smoked salmon, baby spinach, and cream cheese on toasted Turkish bread is one of my favorites, and the biscuits and cakes (especially the flourless orange and almond cake) are gorgeous. There are good breakfasts here for A$7.50 (U.S.$4.88), including fruit salads, muesli, fruit bread, and egg dishes. Everything is made on the premises. The staff is very friendly, so say hello to Jackie and Victoria—two freckle-faced sisters.

Portobello Caffé. No.1 Eastern Esplanade, Circular Quay East. ☎ **02/9247 8548.** Main courses A$8 (U.S. $5.20). 10% surcharge Sundays and public holidays. AE, BC, DC, JCB, MC, V. Minimum credit card purchase A$30 (U.S.$19.50). Daily 8am–11:50pm. CityRail, bus, or ferry: Circular Quay. PIZZA/SANDWICH.

Sharing the same address as the Sydney Cove Oyster Bar (and the same priceless views), the Portobello Caffé offers gourmet sandwiches on Italian wood-fired bread; small, delicious gourmet pizzas, croissants, snacks, cakes, and hot and cold drinks. Walk off with a sensational ice cream cone for around A$3 (U.S.$1.95).

✪ **Rossini.** Shop W5, Circular Quay. ☎ **02/9247 8026.** Main courses A$10–$15 (U.S.$6.50–$9.75). Cash only. Daily 7am–10pm. CityRail, bus, or ferry: Circular Quay. ITALIAN.

This cafeteria-style Italian restaurant opposite ferry Wharf 5 at Circular Quay is wonderfully positioned for people-watching. The outside tables are perfect spots for breakfast or a quick bite before a show at the Opera House. Breakfast croissants, Italian donuts, muffins, and gorgeous Danish pastries cost just A$2 (U.S. $1.30), and bacon and eggs just A$8 (U.S. $5.20). Wait to be seated for lunch or dinner, make your choice, pay your money at the counter, take a ticket, and then pick up your food. Meals, including veal parmigiana, cannelloni, ravioli, chicken crèpes, and octopus salad are often huge, and while not the best Italian you'll ever eat, they are tasty enough. Coffee fanatics I know rate the Rossini brew as only average.

Sketches Bar and Bistro. In the Hotel Inter-Continental, 117 Macquarie St. (enter from Bridge St.). ☎ **02/9240 1210.** Reservations recommended. Pasta A$10.90–$17 (U.S.$7.09–$11.05). AE, BC, DC, MC, V. Mon–Fri 5:30–9:30pm, Sat 5:30–10:30pm. CityRail, bus or ferry: Circular Quay. PASTA.

Sketches is a favorite with people going to the Opera House and those who know a good-quality cheap meal when they taste one. Here's how it works: After getting the barman's attention, point to one of three different sized plates stuck to the bar above your head—the small size is adequate if you're an average eater, the medium plate is good for filling up after a hard day of sightseeing (and no lunch), but I've yet to meet a man who can handle the large serving with its accompanying bread, pinenuts, and Parmesan cheese. Then, with ticket in hand, head toward the chefs in white hats and place your order. There are 12 pastas to choose from and several sauces, including

A Great Place for Picnic Grub

If you're looking for a sandwich or something to take on a harbor cruise or a stroll through the Royal Botanic Gardens, you can't go wrong with **Quay Deli**, E5 Alfred St. (next to the pharmacy under the Circular Quay CityRail station, facing the road; ☎ **02/9241 3571**). Everything is fresh and tasty, and there are all sorts of goodies, including gourmet sandwiches and simple take-away foods such as olives, Greek dishes, pasta, fruit salads, green salads, meat pies, and the best English-style custard tarts around. Plenty of folks buy a couple of fresh rolls and a piece of cheese, then pick up a bottle of wine from the bottle shop around the corner, and then take off somewhere for a cheerful meal. Lunch items go for A$1.80 to $4.50 (U.S.$1.17–$2.93). It's open Monday through Friday 5am to 6:45pm, Saturday 9am to 4pm. No credit cards.

The Best Places for a Picnic

A good thing about Sydney is that there are plenty of places to take a packed lunch or a take-away meal. Some of my favorite spots for a picnic are around **Circular Quay,** where you can sit on the grass outside the Museum of Contemporary Art (the huge sandstone building to the left of the ferry wharves as you face them) or on the benches provided around the waterfront itself (where you might be approached by the occasional panhandler). From Circular Quay, you could also walk toward the Sydney Opera House and make your way into the **Royal Botanic Gardens** or hop aboard a public **ferry** to, say, Darling Harbour, and eat lunch on the water. Pick up some of the best french fries in Sydney from the excellent fish and chips booth opposite the bottle shop in Circular Quay, or a bite to eat from the **Quay Deli** (see p. 103).

Another of my favorite lunch spots is **Hyde Park,** reached via Town Hall, Museum, or St. James station. The grass and benches are great for people-watching, and there are plenty of shade trees to keep you cool on a hot day. Pick up some sushi at **Sushi Roll** (see p. 108), or a gourmet Italian-style sandwich from **The Olive** (see p. 107).

You can't go wrong having lunch overlooking the waves at Bondi or Manly. At Bondi try the **North Indian Flavour** (see p. 113) for a take-away curry on the grass, and in Manly pick up a packet of fish and chips at **Manly Ocean Foods** (see p. 114).

carbonara, marinara, pesto, vegetarian, and some unusual ones to dishearten pasta purists, such as south Indian curry. Meals are cooked in front of you while you wait.

WORTH A SPLURGE

✪ **MCA Café.** Museum of Contemporary Art, Circular Quay West. ☎ **02/9241 4253.** Main courses around A$20 (U.S.$13). 10% surcharge weekends and public holidays. AE, BC, DC, MC, V. Daily noon–2:30pm. CityRail, bus, or ferry: Circular Quay. SEAFOOD.

If you find yourself at one of the 16 outside tables here, count yourself as one of the most fortunate people lunching in Sydney. The views over the ferries and the Opera House are wonderful, and you are far enough away from the crowds at Circular Quay to watch the action without feeling a spectacle yourself. Whether you sit outside or in, the food is great. Eighty percent of the dishes are seafood, but there are some pasta and meat dishes as well. The signature dishes are the trevally (an Australian gamefish) with a lemon olive and parsley salad, and the smoked salmon lasagna with eggplant caviar.

IN THE ROCKS

✪ **G'Day Café.** 83 George St., The Rocks. ☎ **02/9241 3644.** Main courses A$3–$7 (U.S.$1.95–$4.55). AE. Sun–Thurs 5am–midnight, Fri–Sat 5am–3am. CityRail, bus, or ferry: Circular Quay. CAFE.

The manager estimates that half the tourists who visit Sydney visit this little place in the heart of The Rocks. That's not surprising because it offers simple, satisfying food at around half the price you'd expect to pay in such a tourist precinct. The interior is uninspiring, but out back there's a pleasant leafy courtyard. Among the offerings are focaccia sandwiches, hearty soups, salads, burgers, lasagna, chili, and beef curry.

The Gumnut Cafe. 28 Harrington St., The Rocks. ☎ **02/9247 9591.** Main courses A$6.90–$13 (U.S.$4.49–$8.45). AE, BC, DC, MC, V. Daily 8am–5pm. CityRail, bus, or ferry: Circular Quay. MODERN AUSTRALIAN.

A hearty lunch in a courtyard shaded from the sun by giant cream-colored umbrellas—ah, heaven. With a great location in the heart of The Rocks, this restaurant also has an extensive indoor seating area, so it's a great place to take a break from all that sightseeing. The breakfast specials (A$8.50/U.S.$5.53) are popular with guests from surrounding hotels, while at lunchtime it's bustling with tourists and local office workers. Lunchtime blackboard specials cost A$11 (U.S.$7.15). More regular fare includes the disappointing Ploughman's Lunch (why spoil a traditional English meal of bread, cheese, and pickles by limiting the bread and adding unappealing vegetables and salad?), it's better to order the tasty chicken and leek pie, or pasta dishes. Filling Turkish bread sandwiches cost between A$7.70 and $9 (U.S.$5 and $5.85). The courtyard is heated in winter, making it quite cozy.

✪ **The Löwenbräu Keller.** 18 Argyle St. (at Playfair St.), The Rocks. ☎ **02/9247 7785.** Reservations recommended. Main courses A$15–$21.50 (U.S. $9.75–$13.98). AE, BC, DC, JCB, MC, V. Daily 9:30am–2am (kitchen closes at 11pm.) CityRail, bus, or ferry: Circular Quay. BAVARIAN.

Renowned for celebrating Oktoberfest every day for the past 20 years, this is the place to come to watch Aussies let their hair down. Come for lunch and munch a club sandwich or focaccia in the glassed-in atrium while observing the daytime action of The Rocks. For a livelier scene, come on Friday or Saturday night, when mass beer-sculling (chugging) and yodeling are accompanied by a brass band, and costumed waitresses ferry foaming beer steins about the atmospheric, cellarlike bowels. Hearty southern German and Austrian fare and no less than 17 German beers are served. There's a good wine list, and surprisingly, vegetarians are well catered for, too.

Pancakes Licensed Café. 10 Hickson Rd. (enter from Hickson Rd. or George St.), The Rocks. ☎ **02/9247 6371.** Reservations not accepted. Main courses A$12.95–$21.95 (U.S.$8.42–$14.27); breakfast (served 24 hr.) A$8.95–$11.95 (U.S.$5.82–$7.77). AE, BC, DC, JCB, MC, V. Daily 24 hr. CityRail, bus, or ferry: Circular Quay. AMERICAN COFFEESHOP FARE/PANCAKES.

Buttermilk and chocolate pancakes, and French crèpes filled with seafood, chicken and mushrooms, vegetables in a basil-cream sauce, or smoked ham and cheese are the most popular dishes served up in this old warehouse done up in art-deco style. The beef ribs, pastas, and pizzas are also good sellers.

ⓕ Family-Friendly Restaurants

Rossini (see above) Shop W5, Circular Quay ☎ **02/9247 8026** This indoor/outdoor dining spot next to the ferry terminals on Circular Quay offers Italian food with small pizzas and half-portion pastas perfect for children. Main courses A$7 to $14 (U.S.$4.55–$9.10). Open daily 7am to 10pm.

The Gumnut Cafe (see above) Take a break from sightseeing around The Rocks at this delightful little cafe/restaurant. Cheap lunches appealing to both adults and children are served in a leafy courtyard. Main courses A$6.90 to $13 (U.S.$4.49–$8.45). Open daily 8am to 5pm.

Level Two Revolving Restaurant (see below) This rotating eagle's-nest restaurant is located atop the impossible-to-miss Centrepoint Tower. Buffet-style meals have children's prices and a 70-minute circumnavigation of the city. Reservations recommended.

Phillip's Foote. 101 George St., The Rocks. ☎ **02/9241 1485.** Main courses A$20 (U.S.$13) weekdays, $21 (U.S.$13.65) weekends. AE, BC, JCB, MC, V. Mon–Sat noon–midnight, Sun noon–10pm. CityRail, bus, or ferry: Circular Quay. BARBECUE.

Venture behind this historic pub and you'll find a popular courtyard strung with tables and benches and large barbecues. Choose your own steak, lemon sole, trout, chicken, or pork and throw it on the "barbie." It's fun, it's filling, and you might even meet some new friends while your meal's sizzling.

✪ **Sailors Thai.** 106 George St., The Rocks. ☎ **02/9251 2466.** Reservations required in advance in restaurant; not accepted in canteen. Main courses A$14–$34 (U.S. $9.10–$22.10) in restaurant, A$11–$16 (U.S.$7.15–$10.40) in canteen. AE, BC, DC, MC, V. Restaurant Mon–Fri noon–2pm, Mon–Sat 6pm–10pm; canteen daily noon–8pm. CityRail, bus, or ferry: Circular Quay. THAI.

With a reputation as hot as the chilies in its jungle curry, Sailors Thai canteen attracts lunchtime crowds who come to eat great-tasting noodles and the likes of pork and prawn won ton soup, red curry with lychees, and Thai salads at its single, stainless steel table lined with some 40 chairs. Four other tables overlook the cruise ship terminal and the quay. Downstairs, the a la carte restaurant serves inventive food, which is a far cry from your average Thai restaurant, like sir-fried pineapple curry with chilies and cashew nuts and a wonderfully glutinous coconut ash pudding, made from the ash of burnt coconuts cooked with licorice root, coconut water, rice flower and sugar.

Zia Pina. 93 George St., The Rocks. ☎ **02/9247 2255.** Reservations recommended well in advance. Main courses A$7.80–$19 (U.S.$5.07–$12.35). AE, BC, DC, JCB, MC, V. Daily noon–3pm; Sun–Mon 5–9pm, Tues–Thurs 5–10:30pm, Fri–Sat 5–11:30pm. CityRail, bus, or ferry: Circular Quay. PIZZA/PASTA.

With 10 tables crammed downstairs and another 24 upstairs, there's not much room to breathe in this cramped traditional pizzeria and spaghetti house. But squeeze in between the close-fit brick walls and wallow in the clashes and clangs coming from the hardworking chefs in the kitchen. Pizzas come in two sizes; the larger feeds two people. Servings of delicious gelato go for a cool A$4 (U.S.$2.60).

WORTH A SPLURGE

✪ **Waterfront Restaurant.** In Campbell's Storehouse, 27 Circular Quay West, The Rocks. ☎ **02/9247 3666.** Reservations recommended. Main courses A$23.90–$42.50 (U.S.$15.54–$27.63). A$3 (U.S.$1.95) per person surcharge weekends and public holidays. AE, BC, DC, JCB, MC, V. Daily 11am–10pm. CityRail, bus, or ferry: Circular Quay.

You can't help but notice the mast, rigging, and sailing ship sails that mark this restaurant right next to the water below the main spread of The Rocks. It's popular at lunchtime when businesspeople snap up the best seats outside in the sunshine, but at night with the colors of the city washing over the harbor it can be magical. Most main courses cost a hefty A$25 (U.S.$16.25) or so, but for that you get a choice of such things as steaks, mud crab, fish fillets, prawns, or a seafood platter. The food is nice and simple, with the markup added for the glorious position and views.

In the same building, you'll find the Waterfront's sister restaurants **Wolfie's Grill** (☎ **02/9241 5577**), which serves good char-grilled beef and seafood dishes for A$22 to $26 (U.S.$14.30–$16.90), and **The Italian Village** (☎ **02/9247 6111**), which serves regional Italian cuisine for A$22 to $30 (U.S.$14.30–$19.50). The third in the line is an excellent Chinese restaurant, the ✪ **Imperial Peking** (☎ **02/9247 7073**), which serves excellent food for similar prices. All four restaurants offer fantastic water views and indoor and outdoor dining.

Happy Hour!

Head to **Arizona** (see below) for happy hour (Mon–Fri 5–8pm), when bottles of local beer, house spirits, and cheap wine go for A$2.50 (U.S.$1.62). On Friday nights and Saturdays from 6pm to 11pm cocktails are also reduced to A$3 (U.S.$1.95). A DJ spins tunes Thursday to Saturday evenings, playing dance music and classics. There's free pool on one of four tables (and free nachos) during happy hour on Thursday. If you want to grab some grub in the bar, the nachos or a burger and fries will set you back A$7.50 (U.S.$4.88).

NEAR TOWN HALL

Arizona. Corner of Pitt and Market sts. ☎ **02/9261 1077.** Main courses A$12–$18 (U.S.$7.80–$11.70). The Cowboy Bar: Mon noon–10pm, Tues noon–10:30pm, Wed noon–11pm, Thurs–Fri noon–2am, Sat noon–3:30am, Sun noon–8pm. Arizona 101 Bar & Grill: Mon–Sat noon–3pm, Mon–Wed 5–9pm, Thurs–Fri noon–10pm, Sat 5–10pm. AE, BC, DC, MC, V. CityRail, bus, or monorail: Town Hall. TEX-MEX.

Cactus-strewn frescoes, a log-cabin exterior, and Native American figurines leave no doubt about Arizona's style. Split into two separate venues, opposite each other on the second floor of a low-rise on Pitt Street (across from the Pitt Street Mall), Arizona is a fun place with good food and a youthful atmosphere, along with a couple of pool tables and a bar. Main meals include T-bone steak, char-grilled salmon steak, Cajun chicken burger, and Texas barbecued ribs and wings.

✪ **Capitan Torres.** 73 Liverpool St., (just past the cinema strip on George St., near Town Hall). ☎ **02/9264 5574.** Main courses A$16.50–$19 (U.S.$10.73–$12.35); tapas A$5.50–$9.90 (U.S.$3.58–$6.44). AE, BC, DC, JCB, MC, V. Daily noon–3pm; Mon–Sat 6–11pm, Sun 6–10pm. CityRail: Town Hall. SPANISH.

Sydney's Spanish quarter, based on Liverpool Street (a 10-min. walk from Town Hall station and past Sydney's main cinema strip) offers some great restaurants, of which Capitan Torres is my favorite. Downstairs is a tapas bar with traditional stools, Spanish serving staff, and lots of authentic dark oak. Upstairs on two floors is a fabulous restaurant with heavy wooden tables and an atmosphere thick with sangria and regional food. The garlic prawns are incredible, and the whole snapper a memorable experience. The tapas are better, though, at **Asturiana** (☎ **02/9264 1010**), another Spanish restaurant a couple of doors down on the same street.

The Olive. Shop 18, Strand Arcade. ☎ **02/9231 2962.** Main courses A$4–$6.30 (U.S.$2.60–$4.10). Cash only. Mon–Sat 6am–4pm. CityRail, bus, or monorail: Town Hall. ITALIAN/ SANDWICHES.

This tiny sandwich shop in the Strand Arcade, just off the Pitt Street Mall between Town Hall and the AMP Centrepoint Tower, is a tasty lunch option if you find yourself in the city. You can feast on Italian pastas and pizzas, focaccias, and spicy rissoles, or gourmet sandwiches filling enough to last you through an afternoon of sightseeing.

✪ **Supreme View Café.** Level 14. Law Courts Building. Queens Square. 184 Phillip St. City. ☎ 02/9230 8224. Main courses A$8–$13 (U.S.$5.20–8.45). Coffee and cake A$5 (U.S.$3.25). Open Mon–Fri 7am–5pm. Cash only. CAFE.

If you happen to be in the city center then this fabulous, largely undiscovered restaurant/ cafe is a must for the great value food and fantastic views reaching over Hyde Park and even to the harbor. It's very large inside, has panoramic windows and serves meals from the counter. Breakfasts are hearty and include bacon and eggs, omelets, and cereals. It's particularly handy if you are staying in the lower Oxford street area.

Sandwiches, Caesar salad, homemade pies, and pastas and lasagna are served all day. Even if you're not hungry it's well worth popping in for a coffee.

Sushi Roll. Sydney Central Plaza (downstairs in the food hall next to Grace Brothers dept. store on Pitt Street Mall). ☎ **02/9233 5561.** Sushi rolls A$1.70 (U.S.$1.11) each. No credit cards. Mon–Wed and Sat 8am–7pm, Thurs 8am–10pm, Sun 10am–6pm. SUSHI.

The fresh, simple food served up at this bargain-basement takeout booth is certainly a healthy alternative to the greasy edibles that many travelers end up gobbling when they're hungry. A large range of sushi and nori rolls peek out from behind the counter here, and you can eat at the tables opposite.

WORTH A SPLURGE

Level Two Revolving Restaurant. In Centrepoint Tower, Market St. (between Pitt and Castlereigh sts.). ☎ **02/9233 3722.** Reservations recommended. Lunch Mon–Sat A$34 (U.S.$22.10); lunch Sun A$37 (U.S.$24.05); early dinner A$37 (U.S.$24.05); regular dinner A$40 (U.S.$26). A$15 (U.S.$9.75) for children 3–12 at lunch and early dinner. 10% surcharge (on drinks only) weekends and public holidays. AE, BC, DC, MC, V. Daily 11:30am–2:15pm and 5–11:45pm. CityRail: St. James. Monorail: City Centre. GRILLS/ROASTS/SEAFOOD/ASIAN.

For those not scared of heights, Level Two offers an all-you-can-eat buffet—ideal for those who don't want to pay for the a la carte goodies a floor down at sister restaurant, Level One. This place is popular with tourists, who come for the great views across Sydney, on a clear day as far as the Blue Mountains. The dining area takes about an hour to rotate, but even going this slowly I find it a bit off-putting—especially when you're some 250 meters (820 ft.) up. You can heap your plate with some of 5 appetizers, then choose between 15 main courses, including steaks, roasts, pork knuckles, seafood, and Asian dishes. There are also five desserts to choose from.

AT DARLING HARBOUR

Chinta Ria (The Temple of Love). Cockle Bay Wharf Complex. ☎ **02/9264 3211.** Main courses A$12–$25 (U.S.$7.80–$16.25). AE, BC, DC, MC, V. Daily noon–2:30pm and 6–11pm. Ferry or monorail: Darling Harbour. MALAYSIAN.

Cockle Bay's star attraction for those who appreciate good food and a fun ambience without paying a fortune, Chinta Ria is on the roof terrace of the three-story Cockle Bay development. In a round building dominated by a giant golden Buddha in the center, Chinta Ria serves up good "hawker-style" (*read:* cheap, delicious) Malaysian food. The atmosphere is even more memorable. The service is slow, but who cares in such an interesting space, with plenty of nooks and crannies and society folk to look at. There are seats outside (some get the noise of the highway), but the best views unfold inside. The hot-and-sour soup makes an interesting starter, and I recommend the chili prawns and the *Hokkeien Char* (soft-cooked egg noodles with extras) as main dishes.

Planet You-Know-What

You can't miss Sydney's **Planet Hollywood,** 600 George St. (☎ **02/9267 7827**). Just look for the oversized globe opposite the cinema complexes on George Street. If you've been to a Planet Hollywood before, expect the usual Hollywood memorabilia (including the the giant stiletto shoe from *The Adventures of Priscilla, Queen of the Desert*) and plenty of burgers and the like on the menu. Two Australian touches are the grilled barramundi fish marinated in limes, and the ground Tasmanian salmon burger. It's open daily 11:30am to 1am (bar open daily 11:30am–2am). Main courses go for A$10 to $18 (U.S.$6.50–$11.70). Reservations not accepted.

Something Fishy

If you like fresh seafood at cheap prices, then saunter down to the ✪ **Sydney Fishmarket,** on the corner of Bank Street and Pyrmont Bridge Road, Pyrmont (☎ **02/9660 1611,** or call the **Fishline** at ☎ **02/9552 2180** for information on special events such as seafood cooking classes). The major fish retailers here sell sashimi at the cheapest prices in Sydney, but if you prefer your seafood cooked then don't miss out on these two fabulous outlets.

First off there's ✪ **Musumeci Seafoods,** found outside the large blue retail arcade. It's little more than a stall with a hotplate, but you won't find baby octopus cooked better in any of Sydney's glitzy restaurants. Seafood combinations are also offered, with a small plate (easily enough for one person) costing just A$5.50 (U.S.$3.58), and a large plate A$11 (U.S.$7.15). Musumeci's is open Friday and Sunday from 7am to 4pm and Saturday from 6am to 4pm.

Also mouthwatering are the stir-fries at nearby **Christies,** a seafood retailer inside the main retail building. Pick your own seafood, such as fresh calamari or mussels, and your own sauce, and they throw it straight in a wok and cook it for you on the spot. Stir-fries or great Asian-style seafood noodle dishes cost just A$5.50 (U.S.$3.58). Christies cooks are on the job daily from 7am to 7pm.

To get to the Fishmarket, take the light rail (tram) from Central Station, Chinatown, or Darling Harbour to the Fishmarket stop, or you can walk from Darling Harbour (follow the signs).

✪ **Wockpool.** In the IMAX Theatre, Southern Promenade, Darling Harbour. ☎ **02/9211 9888.** Main courses A$28–$35 (U.S.$18.20–$22.75); noodle, laksa and soups at lunchtime A$12–$14 (U.S.$7.80–$9.10). AE, BC, DC, MC, V. Daily noon–3pm, Sun–Thurs 6–10pm, Fri–Sat 6–11pm. Ferry: Darling Harbour. Monorail: Convention Center. MODERN ASIAN.

With great views of Darling Harbour, this adventuresome child of co-owners Neil Perry and chef Kylie Kwong has taken off big time. The dining room is light and spacious with glass walls opening up across the water. The essence here is Chinese with a twist, and the Sichuan duck and stir-fried spanner-crab omelet are always on the menu. Other dishes to go for are whole steamed snapper with ginger and shallot, rock lobster, and mud crab. The lunchtime noodle bar is always buzzing, with tourists, locals, and business types crunched up along the bar or around the tables, tucking into light meals such as noodles including laksas (rice noodles in curry sauce) and soups.

IN KINGS CROSS & THE SUBURBS BEYOND

Bourbon & Beefsteak Bar. 24 Darlinghurst Rd., Kings Cross. ☎ **02/9358 1144.** Reservations recommended Fri–Sun. Main courses A$8.50–$23.95 (U.S.$5.53–$15.57). A$2 (U.S.$1.30) surcharge weekends and public holidays. AE, BC, DC, MC, V. Daily 24 hr. (happy hour 4–7pm). CityRail: Kings Cross. INTERNATIONAL.

The Bourbon & Beefsteak has been a Kings Cross institution for more than 30 years and still attracts everyone from U.S. sailors and tourists to businesspeople and ravers. Since it's open 24 hours, many people like to stay awhile—occasionally you'll find someone taking a nap in the bathroom. The American-themed restaurant is busy at all hours, churning out steaks, seafood, salads, Tex-Mex, ribs, seafood specials, and pasta. Breakfast is served daily from 6 to 11am.

There's live music every night in the Piano Bar from 5 to 9pm, followed by a mixture of jazz, Top 40, and rock until 5am. A disco downstairs starts at 11pm (finishing at 6am), and a larger one takes off in The Penthouse at the Bourbon bar on Fridays and Saturdays. The music is geared toward the 18 to 25 crowd of locals and tourists.

Delicious North Indian. 62A Darlinghurst Rd., Kings Cross. ☎ **02/9357 4226.** Main courses A$4.50–$10.50 (U.S.$2.93–$6.83). AE, BC, DC, MC, V. Sun–Thurs 11:30am–11:30pm, Fri and Sat 11:30am–4am. CityRail: Kings Cross. NORTHERN INDIAN.

The bargain curries served here are worth tucking into at this Indian fast-food house located on the main Kings Cross drag. The curries aren't the best in the world, but they are spicy and filling. You can choose a mixture of any three vegetarian curries with rice for just A$4.50 (U.S.$2.93). Meat curries cost A$6.50 (U.S.$4.23). A more formal meal with just one main dish will cost a little more.

Govindas. 112 Darlinghurst Rd., Darlinghurst. ☎ **02/9380 5155.** Dinner A$13.90 (U.S.$9.04), including free movie. AE, BC, MC, V. Daily 6–11pm. CityRail: Kings Cross. VEGETARIAN.

When I think of Govindas, I can't help smiling. Perhaps it's because I'm reliving the happy vibe from the Hare Krishna center it's based in, or maybe because the food is so cheap! Or maybe it's because they even throw in a decent movie with the meal (the movie theater is on a different floor). The food is simple vegetarian, served buffet style and eaten in a basic room off black lacquer tables. Typical dishes include pastas and salads, lentil dishes, soups and casseroles. It's BYO and doctrine-free.

Hard Rock Cafe. 121–129 Crown St., Darlinghurst. ☎ **02/9331 1116.** Reservations not accepted. Main courses A$9.95–$21.95 (U.S.$6.47–$14.27). 10% surcharge weekends and public holidays. AE, BC, DC, JCB, MC, V. Daily noon–midnight. Shop daily 10am–midnight. Closed Christmas. CityRail: Museum; then walk across Hyde Park, head down the hill past the Australian Museum on William St., and turn right onto Crown St. Sydney Explorer Bus: Stop 7. AMERICAN.

The familiar half-Cadillac awning beckons you into this shrine to rock-and-roll. Items on display include costumes worn by Elvis, John Lennon, and Elton John, guitars from Sting and the Bee Gees, drums from Phil Collins and The Beatles, and one of Madonna's bras. The mainstays here are the burgers, with ribs, chicken, fish, and salads, and T-bone steaks on the menu. Most meals come with fries or baked potatoes and a salad. It's very busy on Friday and Saturday evenings from around 7:30pm to 10:30pm, when you might have to queue to get a seat.

✪ No Names. 2 Chapel St. (or 81 Stanley St.), Darlinghurst. ☎ **02/9360 4711.** Main courses A$6–$14 (U.S.$3.90–$9.10). Cash only. Daily noon–2:30pm and 6–10pm. CityRail: Kings Cross or Town Hall, then a 10-min. walk. ITALIAN.

This fabulous cafeteria-style Italian joint is the place to go in Sydney for a cheap and cheerful meal. Downstairs you can nibble on cakes or drink good coffee, but upstairs you have a choice between spaghetti and several meat or fish dishes. The servings are enormous and often far more than you can eat. You get free bread, and simple salads are cheap. Help yourself to water and cordials.

William's on William. 242 William St., Kings Cross. ☎ **02/9358 6680.** Main courses A$3.90–$11.90 (U.S.$2.54–$7.74). AE, MC, V. Daily 7:30am–11pm. CityRail: Kings Cross. CAFE/PASTA.

Just around the corner from the Kings-X Hotel, which itself is right opposite the huge Coca-Cola sign, you'll come across this scruffy little eatery. The walls need a bit of paint, the floors need to be swept, and the tacky plastic tablecloths look like they survived the last war. If you can get past this, though, you'll be very satisfied. The pastas at A$5 to $6 (U.S.$3.25–$3.90) are huge and delicious, and the all-day breakfast of bacon, egg, toast, and homemade french fries is a fantastic value at A$3.90 (U.S.$2.54). Tea and coffee are a very cheap A$1.50 (U.S.98¢).

WORTH A SPLURGE

✪ **Mezzaluna.** 123 Victoria St., Potts Point. ☎ **02/9357 1988.** www.mezzaluna.com.au. Reservations recommended. Main courses A$19.50–$31 (U.S.$12.68–$20.15). A$3 (U.S.$1.95) surcharge Sun. AE, BC, DC, MC, V. Tues–Sun noon–3pm; Tues–Sun 6pm–11pm. Closed public holidays. CityRail: Kings Cross. MODERN ITALIAN.

Exquisite food, flawless service, and an unbeatable view across the city's western skyline have helped Mezzaluna position itself among Sydney's top restaurants. A cozy, candlelit place with white walls and polished wooden floorboards, the main dining room opens up onto a huge, all-weather terrace kept warm in winter by overhead fan heaters. The restaurant's owner, Sydney culinary icon Beppi Polesi, provides an exceptional wine list to complement a menu that changes daily. There's always a fabulous risotto on the menu, while other delights may include rack of lamb roasted with olives and oregano and served with baked baby eggplant, or grilled fillet of Atlantic salmon on rocket with a borlotti bean puree. Whatever you choose, you can't go wrong. I highly recommend this place—of all Sydney's restaurants, I chose this to take my long-term girlfriend for her birthday.

IN PADDINGTON

The top end of Oxford Street, which runs from Hyde Park in central Sydney toward Bondi, has a profusion of trendy bars and cafes and a scattering of cheaper eateries among the more glamorous ones.

Laksa House. In the Windsor Castle Hotel, 72 Windsor St. (corner of Elizabeth St.). ☎ **02/9328 0741.** Reservations not accepted. Main courses A$6–$9 (U.S.$3.90–$5.85). No credit cards. Open daily noon–3pm and 6–9:30pm. Bus: Oxford St. MALAYSIAN.

The dining room here is simple but friendly, with wonderfully authentic food. The specialty is *laksa*, a spicy soup cooked with coconut milk and chicken, prawn, veggies, or tofu. Also try the peanut sauce satays, the Singapore noodles, the Indonesian rice and noodle staples of *nasi goreng* and *gado gado*, and a range of spicy curries.

La Mensa. 257 Oxford St., Paddington. ☎ **02/9332 2963.** Reservations recommended. Main courses A$10.50–$19.50 (U.S.$6.83–$12.68). AE, BC, DC, MC, V. Mon–Thurs 11am–10pm, Fri 11am–11pm, Sat 9am–11pm, Sun 9am–10pm. Bus: Oxford St. ITALIAN/MEDITERRANEAN.

Though I find clean-cut, minimal interiors like the one here to be boring, at La Mensa it has the added zest of a gourmet food and vegetable store tacked on. There's a communal table seating about 20 people, as well as smaller tables inside and out. Main courses might include a salad of salmon, asparagus and poached egg; a pumpkin, pea and leg ham risotto; grilled swordfish with chickpeas and braised tomatoes; and Tuscan-style baby chicken and potatoes.

CAFE CULTURE

Debate rages over which cafe serves the best coffee in Sydney, which has the best atmosphere, and which has the tastiest snacks. The main cafe scenes are centered around Victoria Street in Darlinghurst, Stanley Street in East Sydney, and King Street in Newtown. Other places, including Balmoral Beach on the north shore, Bondi Beach, and Paddington, all have their favored hangouts as well. A coffee or tea will range from A$2.50 to $3 (U.S.$1.63–$1.95), a muffin about the same, and a toasted sandwich from A$4 to $9 (U.S.$2.60–$5.85) depending on filling.

Note: Americans will be sorry to learn that, unlike in the States, free refills of coffee are rare in Australian restaurants and cafes. Sip slowly.

Here are a few of my favorites around town:

✪ **Balmoral Boatshed Kiosk.** 2 The Esplanade, Balmoral Beach. ☎ **02/9968 4412.** Daily 8am–7pm in summer, 8am–6pm in winter. Ferry to Taronga Zoo, then bus to Balmoral Beach.

A real find, this beautiful rustic cafe is on the water beside the dinghies and sailing craft of the wooden Balmoral Boatshed. It's a heavenly place for enjoying a breakfast muffin or a ham-and-cheese croissant while basking in the sun. This place is popular with families on weekend mornings, so if you hate kids, find another place.

Bar Coluzzi. 322 Victoria St., Darlinghurst. ☎ **02/9380 5420.** Daily 4:45am–7:30pm. CityRail: Kings Cross.

Although it may no longer serve the best coffee in Sydney, this cafe's claim to fame is that long ago it served up real espresso when the rest of the city was drinking Nescafe. People-watching is a favorite hobby at this fashionably worn-around-the edges spot in the heart of Sydney's cafe district.

✪ **Bill's.** 433 Liverpool St., Darlinghurst. ☎ **02/9360 9631.** Mon–Sat 7:30am–3pm. CityRail: Kings Cross.

The bright and airy place, strewn with flowers and magazines, serves fantastic nouveau cafe-style food. It's so popular, you might have trouble finding a seat. The signature breakfast dishes—including ricotta hot cakes with honeycomb butter and banana, and sweet corn fritters with roast tomatoes and bacon—are the stuff of legends.

✪ **Hernandez.** 60 Kings Cross Rd., Potts Point. ☎ **02/9331 2343.** Open 24 hr. CityRail: Kings Cross.

The walls of this tiny cafe are crammed with eccentric fake masterpieces, and the air is permeated with the aroma of 20 types of coffee roasted and ground on the premises. It's almost a religious experience for coffee addicts. The Spanish espresso is a treat.

✪ **The Old Coffee Shop.** Ground floor, The Strand Arcade. ☎ **02/9231 3002.** Mon–Fri 7:30am–5:30pm, Sat 8:30am–5pm, Sun 10:30am–4pm. CityRail: Town Hall.

Sydney's oldest coffee shop opened in the charming Victorian Strand Arcade in 1891. The shop may or may not serve Sydney's best java, but the Old World feel of the place and the snacks, cakes, and pastries make up for it. It's a good place to take a break from shopping and sightseeing.

IN SURRY HILLS

Nepalese Kitchen. 481 Crown St., Surry Hills. ☎ **02/9319 4264.** Main courses A$8–$12 (U.S.$5.20–$7.80); 2-course meal A$18 (U.S.$11.70). AE, BC, DC, MC, V. Daily 6pm–11pm. CityRail: Central, then a 10-min. walk up Devonshire St. NEPALESE.

Adventurous gourmands around here dig into this mildly spiced cuisine, which is like a mixture of Indian and Chinese. Steamed dumplings, called *momo*, and stuffed crispy pancakes made with black lentil flour are interesting to start with, and the goat curry is the pick of the main courses. Also popular is the char-grilled lamb or chicken marinated in roasted spices. The curries are very tasty, and there's a large selection of vegetarian dishes, including flavorsome eggplant curry. Accompany your food with *achars*, or relishes, to highlight the flavors of your dishes.

IN NEWTOWN: GREAT ETHNIC EATS

Inner-city Newtown is three stops from Central Station on CityRail, and 10 minutes by bus from central Sydney. On Newtown's main drag, King Street, many inexpensive restaurants offer food from all over the world.

Le Kilimanjaro. 280 King St., Newtown. ☎ **02/9557 4565.** Reservations not accepted. Main courses A$8.50–$9.50 (U.S.$5.53–$6.18). No credit cards. CityRail: Newtown. AFRICAN.

With so many excellent restaurants in Newtown—they close down or improve quickly if they're bad—I picked Kilimanjaro because it's the most unusual. It's a tiny place with limited seating on two floors. Basically, you enter, choose a dish off the blackboard menu and then are escorted to your seats by one of the waiters. On a recent visit I had couscous, some African bread (similar to an Indian chapatti), and the *Saussou-gor di guan* (tuna in a rich sauce). Another favorite dish is *Yassa* (chicken in a rich African sauce). All meals are served on traditional wooden plates.

✪ **Old Saigon.** 107 King St., Newtown. ☎ **02/9519 5931.** Reservations recommended. Main courses A$10–$40 (U.S.$6.50–$26). AE, BC, DC, MC, V. Wed–Fri noon–3pm; Tues–Sun 6–11pm. BYO only. CityRail: Newtown. VIETNAMESE.

Another Newtown establishment bursting with atmosphere, the Old Saigon was owned by an American war correspondent who loved Vietnam so much he ended up living there and marrying a local before coming to Australia. Just to make sure you know about it, he's put up his own photos on the walls, and strewn the place with homemade tin helicopters. His Vietnamese brother-in-law has taken over the show, but the food is still glorious, with the spicy squid dishes among my favorites. A popular pastime is grilling your own thin strips of venison, beef, wild boar, kangaroo, or crocodile over a burner at your table, then wrapping the meat up in rice paper with lettuce and mint, then dipping it in a chili sauce. I highly recommend this place for a cheap night out.

AT BONDI BEACH
The seafront drag of Campbell Parade is packed with restaurants. For a super-cheap meal at the beach, you could try the bistro at the **North Bondi R.S.L. Club,** located at 120 Ramsgate Ave., North Bondi, at the far end of Bondi Beach to your left as you look at the ocean (☎ **02/9130 3152**). Daily lunches—including fish and chips, roast meats, and schnitzel—served between noon and 2:30pm, go for just A$3 (U.S.$1.95). The dinner menu, offered from 5 to 8:30pm daily, is good value, too. Because of its special "club" status, alcohol is very cheap in the bar here.

Fishy Affair. 152–162 Campbell Parade, Bondi Beach. ☎ **02/9300 0494.** Main courses A$14.40–$21 (U.S.$9.36–$13.65). AE, BC, JCB, MC, V. Mon–Thurs noon–3pm and 6–10pm; Fri–Sat noon–3pm and 6–10:30pm; Sun noon–10pm. Bus: Bondi Beach. SEAFOOD.

Just one of many good restaurants, cafes, and takeout joints along the beach's main drag, the Fishy Affair is a standout. Sitting outside and munching on tasty fish and chips while watching the beach bums saunter past is a great way to spend an hour or so. The herb-crusted salmon steak and the smoked salmon salad are both delicious.

North Indian Flavour. 138 Campbell Parade, Bondi Beach. ☎ **02/9365 6239.** Main courses A$4.90–$7.90 (U.S.$3.19–$5.14). No credit cards. Mon–Fri noon–11pm, Sat–Sun 11:30am–11:30pm. NORTH INDIAN.

I've lost count of the times the North Indian Flavour restaurants around Sydney have satisfied a curry craving. Don't expect first-class Indian food, but it'll do if you want to fill up on something spicy. The curries and breads are displayed just inside the doorway, and you can eat on the premises or take your food down to the grassy strip in front of the beach. Most people tend to choose a selection of three curries on rice and mop it up with *naan* bread. A medium-sized serving is big enough to plug a very large appetite. Wash it down with a mango *lassi* yogurt drink for A$1.70 (U.S.$1.11). You'll find almost identical outlets on King Street in Newtown (☎ **02/ 9550 3928**), under the Grace Brothers department store on Pitt Street Mall (☎ **02/ 9221 4715**), and on Broadway opposite Central Station (☎ **02/9212 3535**).

Sydney's Best Fries

If you're looking for the best french fries in Sydney, head to **Manly Ocean Foods,** three shops down from the main beach on the Corso. Avoid the fish and chips here, though (the shark is not the best in my opinion), and spend a couple of dollars extra on barramundi, salmon, perch, or snapper.

✪ **Thai Terrific.** 147 Curlewis St., Bondi Beach. ☎ **02/9365 7794.** Reservations recommended Fri and Sat nights. Main courses A$10–$18 (U.S.$6.50–$11.70). AE, BC, DC, MC, V. Daily noon–11pm. Bus 380 to Bondi Beach. THAI.

Thai Terrific is terrific Thai. This superb place just around the corner from the Bondi Hotel is run with flair and coolly efficient service. The large back room can be very noisy, so if you prefer less din with your dinner, sit at one of the small sidewalk tables. The servings here are enormous—three people could easily fill up on just two mains. The *tom yum* soups and the prawn or seafood *laksa* noodle soups are the best I've tasted in Australia and very filling. I also highly recommend the red curries.

Equally as nice (and quieter) is the Bangkok-style ✪ **Nina's Ploy Thai Restaurant,** at 132 Wairoa Ave. (☎ **02/9365 1118**), at the corner of Warners Ave. at the end of the main Campbell Parade strip. Main courses here cost between A$8 and $12.50 (U.S.$5.60 and $8.75); cash only.

IN MANLY

Manly is 30 minutes from Circular Quay by ferry, 15 minutes by JetCat. The take-out shops lining the Corso, the pedestrian mall that runs between the ferry terminal and main beach, offer everything from Turkish kebabs to Japanese noodles.

✪ **Ashiana.** 2 Sydney Rd., Manly. ☎ **02/9977 3466.** Reservations recommended. Main courses A$9.90–$15.90 (U.S.$6.44–$10.34). AE, BC, MC, V. Daily 5:30–11pm. Ferry or JetCat: Manly. INDIAN.

You'll be hard-pressed to find a better cheap Indian restaurant in Sydney. Tucked away up a staircase next to the Steyne Hotel (just off the Corso and near the main beach), Ashiana has won prizes for its traditional spicy cooking. Portions are large and filling, and the service is friendly. The butter chicken is magnificent, while the *Malai Kofta* (cheese and potato dumplings in a mild, creamy sauce) is the best this side of Bombay. Beer is the best drink with everything. My only gripe is that it's hard to avoid cigarette smoke in such a cozy place, especially on Friday and Saturday nights when the place is packed. Clear your lungs and work off the meal with a beachside stroll afterwards. Check out the soda machine in Woolworth's just across the road for A80¢ (U.S.52¢) cold drinks—the cheapest in Sydney.

Café Tunis. 30/31 S. Steyne, Manly. ☎ **02/9976 2805.** Main courses (big enough for 2) A$17–$21 (U.S.$11.05–$13.65). AE, BC, DC, MC, V. Daily 7am–10pm. Ferry or JetCat: Manly. TUNISIAN.

Right on the beach with fabulous views across the ocean, Café Tunis dishes out huge, value-for-money portions of North African specialties. My favorite starter is the fresh tuna with vegetables and egg deep-fried in pastry. It's big enough for a main dish. Real main courses include couscous royale, with lamb, chicken, and spicy sausage, large enough for two. The grilled seafood platter is very popular and also big enough for you and a friend. Café Tunis is open for breakfast—eggs, especially the eggs Benedict, are a specialty—and for lunchtime when fish and chips is the favorite (but you can still try the authentic Tunisian desserts).

✪ **Howe's Restaurant.** 33 South Steyne, Manly. ☎ **02/9977 1877.** Reservations required Fri and Sat nights. Main courses A$6.20–$9.90 (U.S.$4.03–$6.44). AE, BC, MC, V. Tues–Sun 5–11:30pm. Closed Mondays except national holiday weekends. Ferry or JetCat: Manly. THAI/INDONESIAN/MALAYSIAN.

Mr. Howe has been phenomenally successful on the Manly food circuit with his cram 'em in and keep it cheap philosophy. The restaurant is right across from Manly's main beach (to the right as you leave the Corso), but it makes no use of its position at all. What it does do is serve excellent, simple Southeast Asian dishes, including various curries, noodles, and rice-based dishes. Mr. Howe himself is generally around offering huge smiles. Tables are lined up in long rows, so don't be surprised if you are elbow to elbow with strangers. On weekend evenings, the place is swamped with a generally young crowd. Don't leave without tasting the sticky rice with mango desert.

SUPER-CHEAP VEGETARIAN

✪ **Green's Eatery.** 1–3 Sydney Rd., Manly. ☎ **02/9977 1904.** Menu items A$2–$6.20 (U.S.$1.30–$4.03). Cash only. Daily 8am–6pm. Ferry or JetCat: Manly. VEGETARIAN.

Of the many eateries in Manly, this nice little vegetarian place, just off The Corso on the turnoff just before the Steyne Hotel, does the best lunchtime business. The food is healthy and good quality. The menu includes eleven different vegetarian burgers, curries and noodle dishes, patties and salads, soups, smoothies, and wraps. They serve some exceptionally nice cakes here, too, which despite being incredibly wholesome are still surprisingly tasty. On a nice day you can sit outside.

NORTH SYDNEY
WORTH A SPLURGE

✪ **L'Incontro Italian Restaurant.** 196 Miller St. (at McLaren St.), North Sydney. ☎ **02/9957 2274.** lincontr@sydney.net. Reservations recommended. Main courses A$19.50–$36.50 (U.S.$12.68–$23.73). AE, BC, DC, MC, V. Mon–Fri noon–3pm; Mon–Sat 6–10pm. CityRail: North Sydney. NORTHERN ITALIAN.

Less than 10 minutes by train from the city center—plus a 5-minute stroll up Miller Street (turn right up the hill as you exit the train station and take the first right)—this beauty in an easy-to-miss turn-of-the-century house is a good place for moderately priced Italian. Dishes are beautifully prepared and served in this stylish trattoria as far removed from the modern yuppie bistro as you can get. The food is exquisite. The courtyard, with its vines and ferns, is delightful in summer. Menus change regularly, so pray for the baked rainbow trout cooked with almonds and red wine butter—it's simply the best fish I've ever tasted.

4

What to See & Do
in Sydney

by Marc Llewellyn

The only problem with visiting Sydney is fitting in everything you want to do and see. A well-planned itinerary can be upset by countless other sights and experiences that suddenly become "must sees" and "must do's" once you arrive. Of course, you won't want to miss the "icon" attractions—the Opera House and the Harbour Bridge. Everyone seems to be climbing over the arch of the bridge these days, so look up for the tiny dots of people waving to the ferry passengers below.

You should also check out the native Aussie wildlife in the Taronga Zoo and the Sydney Aquarium, stroll around the "tourist" precinct of Darling Harbour and get a dose of Down Under culture at the not-too-large Australian Museum. Also try to take time out to visit one of the nearby national parks for a taste of the Australian bush, and if it's hot take your "cozzie" and towel to Bondi Beach or Manly.

Whatever you decide to do, you won't have enough time. So, don't be surprised if you find yourself planning for your next visit before your first visit is even finished.

Suggested Itineraries

If You Have 1 Day   In the morning, go down to Circular Quay to look around the Opera House and admire the Sydney Harbour Bridge. Then head over to The Rocks, stopping off at The Rocks Visitors Centre to pick up maps and information and check out the exhibits. Have lunch around Circular Quay or The Rocks, or jump on a ferry to Darling Harbour or Manly, and bring a lunch to eat on board. A guided walking tour around The Rocks should be at the top of your agenda for the afternoon. You can follow the self-guided walking tour later in this chapter, or book one of The Rocks Walking Tours (see "Harbor Cruises & Organized Tours," below). The rest of the afternoon I'd spend browsing around the stores, or head to Taronga Zoo by ferry. An option for the late afternoon, or dinner, is to take a harbor cruise.

If You Have 2 Days   On the second day, head down to Circular Quay again and take the ferry that travels beneath the Harbour Bridge and across to Darling Harbour. At Darling Harbour, visit Sydney Aquarium, for its giant sharks, seals, underwater ocean tunnels, and Barrier Reef displays. Then visit the National Maritime Museum, or

Great Deals on Sightseeing

The **Privileges Card** is a great way to save money visiting Sydney's biggest attractions. The card costs A$25 (U.S.$16.25), is good for up to 1 month, and can be used in Sydney, Canberra, and Melbourne. In Sydney, all the major attractions offer some discount if you show a Privileges Card, such as two-for-one admission or reduced-price admission if you're traveling alone, and "buy one, get one free" reductions. You'll also get discounts on harbor cruises (typically 20%), and discounts at certain restaurants (sometimes a free main course if two of you are dining, or a 20% rebate off the total bill for the cardholder and three others). To get a card, you'll need to fill out an application at www.privilegescard.com or at tourist information centers in Sydney; you'll receive a booklet with details on where you can save. Call Privileges at ☎ **1800 675 500,** or fax at 02/6254 8788. If you book in advance, the company can arrange to have the card sent to your hotel.

Another money-saving option is the **Sydney Bonus Ticket,** which includes admission to the AMP Centrepoint Tower and the Sydney Aquarium, and a morning or afternoon harbor cruise with Captain Cook Cruises. You can also use the card for discounts in the AMP Centrepoint Tower shopping complex. The card costs A$51.50 (U.S.$33.48) for adults and A$29 (U.S.$18.85) for children. Get it from any participating merchant or at the desk as you enter Centrepoint from Pitt Street Mall.

---

one of the other attractions that dot this tourist precinct. Take the monorail to Town Hall in time for sunset at the top of the AMP Centrepoint Tower.

If You Have 3 Days   If the weather's fine, head to the beach. Go to either Bondi Beach, where you can take the cliff walk to Bronte Beach and back, or take the ferry to Manly (see "Getting Around," in chapter 3) and hang out on the beach there. If you have time in the afternoon, I highly recommend visiting the Featherdale Wildlife Park—it's in the suburbs, but it's really worth the trek. Have dinner at Circular Quay with a view of the harbor and the lights of the Opera House and Harbour Bridge.

If You Have 4 Days or More   On your fourth day, get out of town. Go bushwalking in the Blue Mountains, wine tasting in the Hunter Valley, or dolphin-spotting at Port Stephens (see chapter 5 for details on all three).

1 The Opera House & Sydney Harbour

✪ **Sydney Opera House.** Bennelong Point. ☎ **02/9250 7111** for guided tours and inquiries. Fax 02/9250 7624. www.soh.nsw.gov.au. infodesk@soh.nsw.gov.au. For bookings, call ☎ **02/9250 7777;** fax 02/9251 3943; bookings@soh.nsw.gov.au. Box office open Mon–Sat 9am–8:30pm, Sun 2 hr. before performance. Tour prices A$15.40 (U.S.$10.10) for adults, A$10.60 (U.S.$6.89) for children (family prices available on application), Backstage tours cost A$25.20 (U.S.$16.38). Tours run Mon–Sun 8.30am–5pm (around every 45 min.) subject to theater availability (tour sizes are limited, so be prepared to wait). CityRail, bus, or ferry: Circular Quay. Sydney Explorer bus. Parking: Daytime A$7 (U.S.$4.55) per hr.; evening A$23 (U.S.$14.95) flat rate.

Only a handful of buildings around the world are as architecturally and culturally significant as the Sydney Opera House. But the difference between, say, the Taj Mahal, the Eiffel Tower, and the Great Pyramids of Egypt, for example, is that this great, white-sailed construction over the waters of Sydney Cove is a working building. It's a full-scale performing arts complex with five major performance spaces. The biggest

Central Sydney Attractions

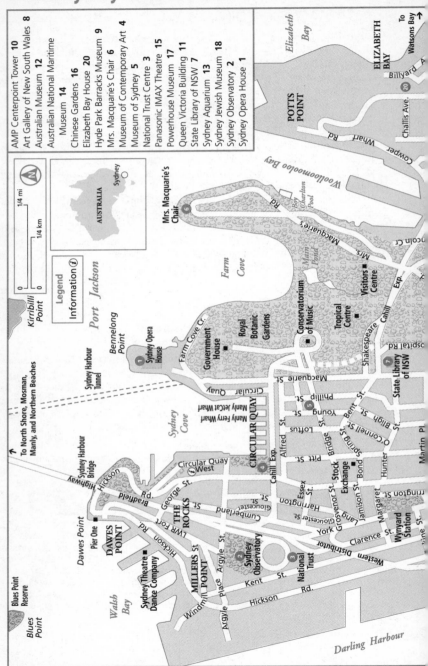

AMP Centerpoint Tower **10**
Art Gallery of New South Wales **8**
Australian Museum **12**
Australian National Maritime Museum **14**
Chinese Gardens **16**
Elizabeth Bay House **20**
Hyde Park Barracks Museum **9**
Mrs. Macquarie's Chair **6**
Museum of Contemporary Art **4**
Museum of Sydney **5**
National Trust Centre **3**
Panasonic IMAX Theatre **15**
Powerhouse Museum **17**
Queen Victoria Building **11**
State Library of NSW **7**
Sydney Aquarium **13**
Sydney Jewish Museum **18**
Sydney Observatory **2**
Sydney Opera House **1**

Legend

Information ⓘ

AUSTRALIA

Sydney

1/4 mi

1/4 km

and grandest is the 2,690-seat Concert Hall, which has about the best acoustics of any building of its type in the world. Come here to experience opera, chamber music, symphonies, dance, choral performances, and even on occasion rock and roll. The Opera Theatre is smaller, seating 1,547, and is home to operas, ballets, and dance. The Drama Theatre, seating 544, and the Playhouse, seating 398, specializes in plays and smaller-scale performances. In March 1999 the newest theater, the Boardwalk, seating 300, opened on the site of the old library. It is used for dance and experimental music.

History: The New South Wales Government raised the money for the Opera House from a public lottery. Danish Architect Jørn Utzon won a competition to design it. From the start, the project was controversial, with many Sydneysiders believing it was a monstrosity. Following a disagreement, Utzon returned home, without seeing his finished project, and the interior fell victim to a compromise design, which left too little space to perform full-scale operas. Initially the project was budgeted at A$7 million (U.S.$4.55 million), but by the time it was finished in 1973 it had cost A$102 million (U.S.$66.9 million), most raised through a series of lotteries. Since then, continual refurbishment and the major task of replacing the asbestos-infested grouting between the hundreds of thousands of white tiles that make up its shell has cost millions more.

Tours & Tickets: Guided tours of the Opera House last about an hour and are conducted daily from 9am to 4pm, except Good Friday and Christmas. Though guides try to take groups into the main theaters and around the foyers, if you don't get to see everything you want it's because the Opera House is a working venue, and there's almost always some performance, practice, or setting up to be done. Reservations are essential. Tours include approximately 200 stairs (tours for people with disabilities can be arranged). Specialized tours, focusing on the building's architectural and engineering configurations, for example, can also be arranged.

The **Tourism Services Department** at the Sydney Opera House can book packages, including dinner and a show; a tour, dinner, and a show; or a champagne interval performance. Prices vary depending on shows and dining venues. Overseas visitors can buy tickets by credit card and pick them up at the box office on arrival. Tickets for performances vary from as little as A$12 (U.S.$7.80) for children's shows to A$180 (U.S.$117) for good seats at the opera. Plays cost between A$40 and A$60 (U.S.$26–$39) on average.

Free performances ranging from musicians and performance artists, to school groups, are held outside the Opera House Sunday afternoons and during festival times.

Sydney Harbour. Officially called Port Jackson.

Sydney Harbour is the focal point of Sydney. It's entered through the Heads, two bush-topped outcrops (you'll see them if you take a ferry or JetCat to Manly), beyond which the harbor laps at 240 kilometers (149 miles) of shoreline before stretching out into the Parramatta River. Visitors are awestruck by the harbor's beauty, especially at night when the sails of the Opera House and the girders of the Harbour Bridge are lit up, and the waters swirl with the reflection of lights from the high-rises—reds, greens, blues, yellows, and oranges. During the day, it buzzes with green and yellow ferries pulling in and out of busy Circular Quay, sleek tourist craft, tall ships, giant container vessels making their way to and from the wharves of Darling Harbour, and hundreds of white-sailed yachts. The greenery along the harbor's edges is perhaps a surprising feature, and all thanks to the Sydney Harbour National Park, a haven for native trees and plants, and a feeding and breeding ground for lorikeets and nectar-eating bird life. In the center of the harbor is a series of islands, the most impressive being the tiny isle

The Harbour on the Cheap

The best way to see Sydney Harbour, of course, is from the water. Several companies operate tourist craft for fare-paying customers (see "Harbor Cruises & Organized Tours," later in this chapter), but it's easy to hop on a regular passenger ferry (see "Getting Around," in chapter 3). The best excursions are over to the beachside suburb of Manly (come back after dusk to see the lights ablaze around The Rocks and Circular Quay); to Watsons Bay, where you can have lunch and wander along the cliffs; to Darling Harbour, for all the area's entertainment and the fact that you travel right under the Harbour Bridge; and to Mosman, just for the ride and to see the grand houses that overlook exclusive harbor inlets.

---

supporting Fort Denison, which once housed convicts and acted as part of the city's defense.

✪ **Sydney Harbour Bridge.**

One thing few tourists do, but which only takes an hour or so, is to walk across the Harbour Bridge. The bridge, completed in 1932, is 1,150 meters (3,795 ft.) long and spans the 503-meter (1,600-ft.) distance from the south shore to the north. It accommodates pedestrian walkways, two railway lines, and an eight-lane road. The 30-minute stroll across offers some excellent harbor views. Once on the other side, you can take a CityRail train from Milsons Point train station back to the city (to Wynyard, Town Hall, or Central stations).

As you walk across the bridge, you should stop off at the **Pylon Lookout** (☎ 02/ **9247 3408**), located at the southeastern pylon. Admission is A$5 (U.S.$3.25) for adults, A$3 (U.S.$1.95) for children and A$12 (U.S.$7.80) for a family. From the top of this bridge support, you are 89 meters (591 ft.) above the water and get excellent views of Sydney Harbour, the ferry terminals of Circular Quay, and beyond. An interesting museum here charts the building of the bridge. Reach the pylon by walking to the far end of George Street in The Rocks toward the Harbour Bridge. Just past the Mercantile Pub on your left you'll see some stone steps that take you onto Cumberland Street. From there, it's a 2-minute walk to the steps underneath the bridge on your right. Climb four flights of stairs to reach the bridge's Western Footway, then walk along to the first pylon. *Note:* Climbing up inside the pylon involves 200 steps. The Pylon Lookout is open daily from 10am to 5pm (closed Christmas).

2 Attractions at Darling Harbour

Many head to Darling Harbour for the Harbourside Festival Marketplace, a huge structure beside the Pyrmont pedestrian and monorail bridge that's full of cheap eateries and a few interesting shops. However, Sydney's tourist precinct has more to offer.

✪ **Australian National Maritime Museum.** Darling Harbour. ☎ **02/9298 3777.** www.anmn.gov.au. A$10 (U.S.$6.50) adults, A$6 (U.S.$3.90) children, A$25 (U.S.$16.25) families (for entry without access to navy ships). A$14 (U.S.$9.10) adults, A$7 (U.S.$4.55) children, A$30 (U.S.$19.50) families (for museum entry and navy ships). Daily 9:30am–5pm (until 6:30pm in Jan). Ferry: Darling Harbour. Monorail: Harbourside. Sydney Explorer bus.

Modern Australia owes almost everything to the sea, so it's not surprising that there's a museum dedicated to the ships—from Aboriginal vessels to submarines. You'll also find ships' logs, all sorts of things to pull and tug at, and the fastest boat in the world—the *Spirit of Australia*. Docked in the harbor outside are a fully-rigged tall

A Walk on the Wild Side: Climbing the Harbour Bridge

At one time, only bridge workers had the opportunity to view Sydney from the top of the main bridge arch. But since October 1998, Sydneysiders and tourists have been able to experience the spectacular view and the exhilarating achievement of climbing to the top of one of Australia's icons. The experience takes 3 hours from check-in at the **BridgeClimb base** at 5 Cumberland St., The Rocks (☎ **02/9240 1100** or 02/8274 7777; fax 02/9240 1122; www.bridgeclimb.com; admin@bridgeclimb.com) to the completion. The office is open daily from 8am to 6pm, and climbers leave in small groups every 10 minutes or so. Climbers wear specially designed "Bridge Suits" and are harnessed to a static line. They are also breath-tested for alcohol and can't carry anything up, including cameras or video recorders. Climbs cost A$117 (U.S.$76.05) for adults and A$96 (U.S.$62.40) for children 12 to 16 on weekdays during the day; A$142 (U.S.$92.30) for adults and A$118 (U.S.$76.70) for children for night climbs Monday to Friday and weekend day climbs; and A$164 (U.S.$106.60) for adults and $140 (U.S.$91) for children on Saturday and Sunday nights. Children under 12 are not allowed to climb.

ship, an Australian Naval Destroyer, *The Vampire,* which you can clamber all over, and an Oberon Class submarine. Allow 2 hours.

Chinese Garden. Darling Harbour (adjacent to the Entertainment Centre). ☎ **02/9281 6863.** Admission A$4.50 (U.S.$2.93) adults, A$2 (U.S.1.30) children, A$10 (U.S.$6.50) families. Daily 9:30am–dusk. Ferry: Darling Harbour. Monorail: Convention. Sydney Explorer bus.

The largest Chinese garden of its type outside China offers a pleasant escape from the city concrete. It was designed by expert gardeners from China's Guangdong Province to embody principals of garden design dating back to the 5th century. Allow 30 minutes.

Powerhouse Museum. 500 Harris St., Ultimo (near Darling Harbour). ☎ **02/9217 0111.** Admission A$9 (U.S.$5.85) adults, A$2 (U.S.$1.30) children, A$20 (U.S.$13) families. Free admission 1st Sat of each month. Daily 10am–5pm. Ferry: Darling Harbour. Monorail: Harbourside. Sydney Explorer bus.

Sydney's most interactive museum is also one of the largest in the Southern Hemisphere. Inside the post-modern industrial interior you'll find all sorts of displays and gadgets relating to the sciences, transportation, human achievement, decorative art, and social history. The many hands-on exhibits make this fascinating museum worthy of a couple of hours of your time.

✪ **Sydney Aquarium.** Aquarium Pier, Darling Harbour. ☎ **02/9262 2300.** Admission A$19.50 (U.S.$12.68) adults, A$8.50 (U.S.$5.53) children, A$45 (U.S.$29.25) families. The Aquarium Link ticket, available from CityRail train stations, is a combined rail and Aquarium ticket that includes a ferry ride. Daily 9am–10pm. Seal Sanctuary closes at 7pm in summer. CityRail: Town Hall. Ferry: Darling Harbour. Sydney Explorer bus.

This is one of the world's best aquariums. The main attractions are underwater walkways through two enormous tanks: one containing an impressive collection of creatures found in Sydney Harbour, and the other full of giant rays and grey nurse sharks. Other exhibits include a giant Plexiglas room suspended inside a pool patrolled by rescued seals, and a section on the Great Barrier Reef, where thousands of colorful fish school around coral outcrops. Also on display are a couple of saltwater crocodiles and some tiny fairy penguins. Try to visit during the week when it's less crowded. Allow for around 2 hours.

3 Other Top Attractions

AMP Centrepoint Tower. Pitt and Market sts. ☎ **02/9229 7444.** Admission A$19.80 (U.S.$12.87) adults, A$12.20 (U.S.$7.93) children. Daily 9am–10:30pm. CityRail: St. James or Town Hall. Sydney Explorer bus.

The tallest building in the Southern Hemisphere is not hard to miss—it resembles a giant steel pole skewering a golden marshmallow. Standing more than 300 meters (1,860 ft.) tall, it offers stupendous 360° views across Sydney and as far as the Blue Mountains. Fortunately, an elevator rockets you to the indoor viewing platform. Unfortunately, the prices have rocketed, too. Don't be too concerned if you feel the building tremble slightly, especially in a stiff breeze—I'm told it's perfectly natural. Below the tower are three floors of stores and restaurants. Allow for 1 hour.

Hyde Park Barracks Museum. Queens Sq., Macquarie St. ☎ **02/9223 8922**. Admission A$7 (U.S.$4.55) adults, A$3 (U.S.$1.95) children, A$17 (U.S.$11.05) families. Daily 9:30am–5pm. CityRail: St. James or Martin Place. Sydney Explorer bus.

These Georgian-style barracks were designed in 1819 by the convict/architect Francis Greenway. They were built by convicts and inhabited by prisoners. These days they house relics from those early days in interesting, modern displays, including log books, early settlement artifacts, and a room full of ships' hammocks in which visitors can lie and listen to fragments of prisoner conversation. The courtyard cafe is excellent. Allow for 1 hour or more.

Museum of Contemporary Art (MCA). 140 George St., Circular Quay West. ☎ **02/9252 4033.** www.mca.com.au. Free general admission. Daily 10am–6pm (5pm in winter). CityRail, bus, ferry: Circular Quay. Sydney Explorer bus.

This imposing sandstone museum set back from the water on The Rocks-side of Circular Quay offers wacky, entertaining, inspiring, and befuddling displays of what's new (and dated) in modern art. It houses the J. W. Power Collection of more than 4,000 pieces, including works by Andy Warhol, Christo, Marcel Duchamp, and Robert Rauschenberg, as well as temporary exhibits. Guided tours are offered Monday to Saturday at noon and 2pm, and Sunday at 2pm. Worth at least an hour.

The Sydney International Aquatic and Athletic Centres. Sydney 2000 Olympic Site, Olympic Park, Homebush Bay. ☎ **02/9752 3666.** Tours A$13 (U.S.$8.45) adults, A$8.80 (U.S.$5.72) children, A$44 (U.S.$28.60) families. Explorer bus passengers pay A$8.80 (U.S.$5.72). Tours run hourly Mon–Fri between 10am–3pm and noon–2pm Sat–Sun. CityRail: Olympic Park. Explorer bus.

You can tour the best Olympic swimming complex in the world, and the athletic center where the athletes trained. Tours last 90 minutes, otherwise you can look around yourself for $2.70 (U.S.$1.75). If you fancy putting in a few laps, then be prepared to pay an additional A$5.50 (U.S.$3.58) for adults and A$4.40 (U.S.$2.86) for children.

Old Sydney Town. Pacific Hwy., Somersby. ☎ **02/4340 1104.** Admission A$22 (U.S.$14.30) adults, A$13 (U.S.$8.45) children; A$50 (U.S.$32.50) families. Wed–Sun 10am–4pm; daily during school holidays. Somersby is near the town of Gosford, 84km (52 miles) north of Sydney. To reach Gosford by car, take the Pacific Hwy. and the Sydney–Newcastle Fwy. (F3); the trip takes about an hour. CityRail trains leave from Central Station for Gosford every 30 min. From Gosford, take the bus marked Old Sydney Town (15-min. ride).

You can spend a few hours on a nice day wandering around this outdoor theme park bustling with actors dressed up like convicts, sailors, and the like. You'll see plenty of stores, buildings, and ships from the old days, and performances throughout the day. It's the Australian version of an American Wild West-theme town. Allow a half-day.

Wonderland Sydney. Wallgrove Rd., Eastern Creek. ☎ **02/9830 9100.** Admission (includes all rides and entrance to the Australian Wildlife Park) A$44 (U.S.$28.6) adults, A$29.30 (U.S.$19.05) children, family tickets only available for wildlife park. Daily 10am–6pm. CityRail: Rooty Hill (trip takes less than an hour); Wonderland buses leave from Rooty Hill station every ½-hr. on weekends, and at 8:55am, 9:32am; 10:10am, 11:35am, and 12:14pm weekdays.

If you're used to big Disneyesque extravaganzas, then this theme park (until recently called Australia's Wonderland) might be a bit of a disappointment—though I guarantee The Demon roller coaster will more than satisfy in the terror department. Other big rides are Space Probe 7, which is basically a heart-stopping drop, and a cute, rattly wooden roller coaster called the Bush Beast. Live shows and bands round out the entertainment. Admission also includes admission to a wildlife park, with all the old favorites—koalas, wombats, kangaroos, wallabies, and more. Allow a half-day.

4 Where to See Aussie Wildlife

The world-class Sydney Aquarium is discussed above in section 2, "Attractions at Darling Harbour."

Australian Reptile Park. Pacific Hwy., Somersby. ☎ **02/4340 1022.** www.reptilepark. com.au. Admission A$15.50 (U.S.$10.08) adults, A$8 (U.S.$5.20) children; A$40 (U.S.$26) families. Daily 9am–5pm. Closed Christmas. Somersby is near the town of Gosford, 84km (52 miles) north of Sydney. To reach Gosford by car, take the Pacific Hwy. and the Sydney-Newcastle Fwy. (F3); the trip takes about an hour. CityRail trains leave from Central Station for Gosford every 30 min. From Gosford, take the bus marked Australian Wildlife Park (10-min. ride).

What started off as a one-man operation supplying deadly snake antivenin in the early 1950s has ended up a nature park teeming with the slippery-looking creatures. But it's not all snakes and lizards; you'll also find saltwater crocodiles, American alligators and more cuddly creatures, such as koalas, platypus, wallabies, dingoes, and flying foxes. The park is set in beautiful bushland dissected by nature trails. A horrible fire burnt down the entire park in mid-2000, killing many of the animals. The staff was devastated, but regrouped and reopened the park in September of 2000.

✪ **Taronga Zoo.** Bradley's Head Rd., Mosman. ☎ **02/9969 2777.** Admission A$21 (U.S.$13.65) adults, A$11.50 (U.S.$7.48) children 4–15. Ask about family rates. A Zoopass (includes entry, round-trip ferry from Circular Quay, and Aerial Safari cable car ride from ferry terminal to upper entrance of zoo) is available from CityRail stations. Daily 9am–5pm (Jan 9am–9pm). Ferry: Taronga Zoo. At the Taronga Zoo wharf, a bus to the upper zoo entrance costs A$1.20 (U.S.78¢), or take a cable car to the top for A$2.50 (U.S.$1.63). The lower zoo entrance is a 2-min. walk up the hill from the wharf, but it's less tiring to explore the zoo from the top down.

Taronga has the best view of any zoo in the world. Set on a hill, it looks over Sydney Harbour, the Opera House, and the Harbour Bridge. The main attractions are the chimpanzee exhibit, the gorilla enclosure, and the Nocturnal Houses, where you can see some of Australia's many nighttime marsupials out and about, including the platypus and the cuter-than-cute bilby (the Australian Easter bunny). There's an interesting reptile display, a couple of impressive Komodo dragons, a scattering of indigenous Australian beasties—including koalas, echidnas, kangaroos, dingoes, and wombats—and more. The kangaroo and wallaby exhibit is unimaginative; you'd be better off going to Featherdale Wildlife Park (see below) for happier-looking animals. Animals are fed at various times during the day. The zoo can get very crowded on weekends, so I strongly advise visiting during the week or very early in the morning on weekends. The three sun bears near the lower ferry entrance/exit were rescued by an Australian businessman, John Stephens, from a restaurant in Cambodia, where they were to have their paws cut off and served up as an expensive soup. Allow around 2 hours.

✪ **Featherdale Wildlife Park.** 217 Kildare Rd., West Pennant Hills. ☎ **02/9622 1644.** Admission A$14 (U.S.$9.10) adults, A$7 (U.S.$4.55) children 4–14. Daily 9am–5pm. CityRail: Blacktown station, then take bus 725 to park (ask driver to tell you when to get off). By car: take the M4 motorway to Reservoir Rd., turn off, travel 4km (2½ miles), then turn left at Kildare Rd.

If you only have time to visit one wildlife park in Sydney, make it this one. The selection of native Australian animals is excellent, and, most importantly, the animals are very well cared for. You could easily spend a couple of hours here despite the park's compact size. You'll have the chance to hand-feed friendly kangaroos and wallabies, and get a photo taken next to a koala (there are many here, both the New South Wales variety and the much larger Victorian type). The park offers twice-daily bus tours, which include hotel pickup and drop-off. Allow 2 hours.

Koala Park. 84 Castle Hill Rd. West Pennant Hills. ☎ **02/9484 3141** or 02/9875 2777. Admission A$14 (U.S.$9.10) adults, A$7 (U.S.$4.55) children, A$36 (U.S.$23.40) families. Daily 9am–5pm. Closed Christmas. CityRail: Pennant Hills station via North Strathfield (45 min.), then take bus nos. 651–655 to park.

Unless you want to go all the way to Kangaroo Island in South Australia, it's unlikely you're going to spot as many koalas in the trees as you can here. There are around 55 koalas roaming within the park's leafy boundaries. Koala cuddling sessions are free, and take place at 10:20am, 11:45am, 2pm, and 3pm daily. There are also wombats, dingoes, kangaroos, wallabies, emus, and native birds here, too. You can hire a private guide to take you around for A$70 (U.S.$45.50) for a 2-hour session, or hitch onto one of the free "hostess" guides who wander around the park like Pied Pipers.

Oceanworld. West Esplanade, Manly. ☎ **02/9949 2644.** Admission A$15.90 (U.S.$10.33) adults, A$8 (U.S.$5.20) children, A$39.90 (U.S.$25.94) families. Daily 10am–5:30pm. Ferry or JetCat: Manly.

Though not as impressive as the Sydney Aquarium, Oceanworld can be combined with a visit to the wonderful Manly Beach (see below) for a nice outing. There's a good display of Barrier Reef fish, a pool of giant saltwater turtles, and yet more giant sharks.

5 Hitting the Beach

One of the big bonuses of visiting Sydney in the summer months (Dec, Jan, and Feb) is experiencing the beaches in their full glory.

Most major city beaches, such as Manly and Bondi, have lifeguards on patrol, especially during the summer months. They check the water conditions and are on the lookout for "rips"—strong ocean currents that can pull a swimmer far out to sea. Safe places to swim are marked by red and yellow flags. You must always swim between these flags, never outside them. If you are using a foam or plastic body board or "boogie board" it's also advisable to use it between the flags. Fiberglass surfboards must generally be used outside the flags. For more tips on safe swimming, see the section on "Beach Savvy for Swimmers & Surfers," in chapter 2.

Another common problem off Sydney's beaches are "blue bottles"—small blue jellyfish, often called "stingers" in Australia, and "Portuguese-Man-o'-Wars" elsewhere. You'll often find these creatures washed up along the beach; they become a hazard for

---

What About Sharks?

One of the first things visitors wonder when they hit the water in Australia is, "Are there sharks?" The answer is yes, but they are rarely spotted inshore. In reality, sharks have more reason to be scared of us than we of them, as most of them end up as the fish portion in your average packet of fish and chips (you might see shark fillets sold as "flake"). Though some beaches, such as the small beach next to the Manly ferry wharf in Manly and a section of Balmoral Beach, have permanent shark nets, most rely on portable nets that are moved from beach to beach periodically to prevent territorial sharks from setting up home alongside bathers.

---

swimmers when there's a strong breeze coming off the ocean and they're blown in to shore (watch out for warning signs on the shoreline). Minute individual stinging cells often break off the main body of the creature and can cause itching, or stinging. Other times, you can be hit by the full force of a whole blue bottle, which can wrap its tentacles around you. Blue bottles deliver a hefty punch from their many stinging cells, and you will feel a severe burning sensation almost immediately. If you are stung, ask a lifeguard for some vinegar to neutralize any stingers that haven't yet sprung into action. Otherwise, a very hot bath or shower can help relieve the pain, which can be very intense and last for up to a day.

WHICH BEACH?
SOUTH OF SYDNEY HARBOUR

Sydney's most famous beach is ✪ **Bondi.** In many ways, it's a raffish version of a California beach, with plenty of tanned skin and in-line skaters. Though the beach is nice, it's cut off from the cafe and restaurant strip that caters to beachgoers by a big ugly road that pedestrians have to funnel across in order to reach the sand. To reach Bondi Beach, take the CityRail train to Bondi Junction, transfer to bus 380 (a 15-min. bus journey). You can also catch bus 380 directly from Circular Quay (but it can take an hour or so in peak time).

If you follow the water along to your right at Bondi, you'll come across a very scenic cliff top trail that takes you to **Bronte Beach** (a 20-min. walk), via gorgeous little **Tamarama,** a boutique beach known for its dangerous rips. Bronte has better swimming than Bondi. To get to Bronte, catch bus 378 from Circular Quay, or pick up the bus at the Bondi Junction CityRail station.

Clovelly Beach, farther along the coast, is blessed with a large rock pool carved into a rock platform and sheltered from the force of the Tasman Sea. This beach is accessible for visitors in wheelchairs via a series of ramps. To reach Clovelly, take bus 339 from Circular Quay.

The cliff walk from Bondi will eventually bring you to **Coogee,** which has a pleasant strip of sand with a couple of hostels and hotels nearby. To reach Coogee, take bus 373 or 374 from Circular Quay (via Pitt, George, and Castlereagh streets, and Taylor Square on Oxford Street) or bus 314 or 315 from Bondi Junction.

NORTH OF SYDNEY HARBOUR

On the north shore you'll find ✪ **Manly,** a long curve of golden sand edged with Norfolk Island Pines (don't be fooled by the two small beaches either side of the ferry terminal). Follow the crowds shuffling through the pedestrianized **"Corso"** to the main ocean beach. You'll find one of Sydney's nicest walks here. Looking at the ocean, head right along the beachfront and follow the coastal path to the small, sheltered **Shelly Beach**—a nice area for snorkeling and swimming (there's also a small takeaway here selling drinks and snacks). Follow the paved path up the hill to the carpark. Here, a track cuts up into the bush and leads towards a firewall, which marks the entrance to **Sydney Harbour National Park.** You'll get some spectacular ocean views across to Manly and the northern beaches (the headland furthest in the distance is Palm Beach). The best way to reach Manly is on a ferry or Jetcat from Circular Quay.

Farther along the north coast are a string of ocean beaches, including the surf spots of **Curl Curl, Dee Why, Narrabeen, Mona Vale, Newport, Avalon,** and finally ✪ **Palm Beach,** a long and beautiful strip of sand, cut from the calmer waters of Pittwater by sand dunes and a golf course. Here you'll also find the **Barrenjoey Lighthouse,** which also offers fine views along the coast. Bus numbers 136 and 139 run from Manly to Curl Curl, while bus number 190 runs from Wynyard to Newport and then via the other northern beaches as far as Palm Beach.

The best harbor beach can be found at ✪ **Balmoral,** a wealthy North Shore hangout complete with its own little island and some excellent cafes and an upmarket restaurant. The beach itself is split into three separate parts. As you look towards the sea, the middle section is the most popular with sunbathers, while the wide expanse of sand to your left and the sweep of surreally beautiful sand to your right have a mere scattering. There's a caged pool area for swimming opposite the cafes if you're terrified of fish nipping at your toes). Reach Balmoral via a ferry to Taronga Zoo and then a 5-minute ride on a connecting bus from the ferry wharf (or take the special summer ferries, which also stop off at Watsons Bay and Manly).

6 Museums, Galleries, Historic Houses & More

✪ **Art Gallery of New South Wales.** Art Gallery Rd., The Domain. ☎ **02/9225 1744.** www.artgallery.nsw.gov.au. Free admission to most galleries. Special exhibitions vary, though expect to pay around A$12 (U.S.$7.80) adults, A$7 (U.S.$4.55) children. Daily 10am–5pm. Tours of general exhibits Tues–Fri 11am, noon, 1pm, and 2pm and Monday 1pm and 2pm, call for weekend times. Tours of Aboriginal galleries Tues–Fri 11am, Sat and Sun at 1pm. Free Aboriginal performance Tues–Sat at noon. CityRail: St. James. Sydney Explorer bus.

The numerous galleries here present some of the best of Australian art and many fine examples by international artists, including displays of Aboriginal and Asian art. You enter from The Domain parklands on the third floor of the museum. On the fourth floor you will find an expensive restaurant and a gallery often showing free photography displays. On the second floor is a wonderful cafe overlooking the wharves and warships of Wooloomooloo. Every January and February there is a display of the best work by students throughout the state. Allow at least 1 hour.

Grin & Bare It

If getting an all-over tan is your goal, you have a couple of options. You can head to the **nude beach** at **Lady Jane Bay,** a short walk from Camp Cove Beach (accessed from Cliff Street in Watsons Bay, reached by walking along the strip of sand—to the right as you look at the sea—at the back of the Watsons Bay Hotel). Or, you can try **Cobblers Beach,** which is accessed via a short but steep unmarked bush track that leads from the far side of the playing field oval next to the main *HMAS Penguin* naval base at the end of Bradley's Head Road in Mosman. Be prepared for a largely male scene—and the odd boatload of beer-swigging peeping toms.

Australian Museum. 6 College St. ☎ **02/9320 6000.** www.austmus.gov.au. Admission A$8 (U.S.$5.20) adults, A$3 (U.S.$1.95) children, A$19 (U.S.$12.35) families. Special exhibits cost extra. Daily 9:30am–5pm. Closed Christmas. CityRail: Museum, St. James, or Town Hall. Sydney Explorer bus.

Though nowhere near as impressive as the Natural History Museum in London or similar museums in Washington, D.C. or New York, Sydney's premier natural history museum still ranks in the top five of its kind in the world. Displays are presented thematically. The best displays are in the Aboriginal section, with its traditional clothing, weapons, and everyday implements. There are some sorry examples of stuffed Australian wildlife, too. Temporary exhibits run from time to time. Allow 1 to 2 hours.

Customs House. Alfred St., Circular Quay. ☎ **02/9320 6429.** Free general admission. Open daily 9:30am to 5pm. CityRail, bus, or ferry: Circular Quay.

This museum, in the sandstone building with the clock and flags across the large square opposite the Circular Quay CityRail station and the ferry wharves, opened in December 1998. It's worth a look inside if you're interested in architecture. You might be hooked by the series of modern art objects on the ground floor, and the traveling exhibits on the third floor—though often you won't be. Outside in the square is a cafe selling reasonably priced coffee, cakes, sandwiches, and the like. Allow 15 minutes.

St James Church. Queens Sq., Macquarie St. ☎ **02/9232 3022.** Daily 9am–5pm. Daily church services; guided tours 2 pm daily. Free admission.

Sydney's oldest surviving colonial church, begun in 1822, was designed by the Government architect Francis Greenway. At one time the church's spire served as a landmark for ships coming up the harbor, but today it looks totally lost amidst the skyscrapers. It's well worth seeking out though, especially for the plaques on the wall, which pay testament to the hard early days of the colony when people were lost at sea, "speared by blacks" and died while serving the British Empire overseas.

St Mary's Cathedral. College and Cathedral sts. ☎ **02/9230 1414.** Mon–Tues 6:30am–6:30pm, Sat 8am–7:30pm, Sun 6:30am–7:30pm.

Sydney's most impressive worship place is a giant sandstone construction between The Domain and Hyde Park. The original St Mary's was built in 1821, but the chapel was destroyed by fire. Work on the present cathedral began in 1868, but due to lack of funds remained unfinished until work began in 1999 to build the two spires (which were finished in time for the 2000 Olympics). The stained-glass windows inside are particularly impressive. St. Mary's is Roman Catholic, and was built for Sydney's large population of Irish convicts. In perhaps Sydney's worst pre-Olympic planning, the beautiful brown sandstone building was marred by a wide stretch of dark gray paving outside—now a battleground for skateboarders and city council rangers.

Elizabeth Bay House. 7 Onslow Ave., Elizabeth Bay. ☎ **02/9356 3022.** Admission A$7 (U.S.$4.55) adults, A$3 (U.S.$1.95) children, A$17 (U.S.$11.05) families. Tues–Sun 10am–4:30pm. Closed Good Friday and Christmas. Bus: 311 from Circular Quay. Sydney Explorer bus.

This magnificent example of colonial architecture was built in 1835 and was described at the time as the "finest house in the colony." Visitors can tour the whole house and get a real feeling of the history of the fledgling settlement. The house is situated on a headland and has some of the best harbor views in Sydney. Allow 1 hour.

Museum of Sydney. 37 Phillip St. ☎ **02/9251 5988.** Admission A$7 (U.S.$4.55) adults, A$3 (U.S.$1.95) children under 15. Daily 9:30am–5pm. CityRail, bus, or ferry: Circular Quay. Sydney Explorer bus.

You'll need your brain in full working order to make the most of the contents of this three-story postmodern building that encompasses the remnants of Sydney's first Government House. Far from being a conventional showcase of history, it's a minimalist collection of first-settler and Aboriginal objects and multimedia displays that invite the visitor to discover Sydney's past for him or herself. Some readers have criticized the place, saying it's not just minimalist—it's unfathomable. By the way, that forest of poles filled with hair, oyster shells, and crab claws in the courtyard adjacent to the industrial-design cafe tables is called Edge of Trees. It's a metaphor for the first contact between Aborigines and the British. There's a reasonable cafe out front. Allow an hour to a lifetime to understand.

Sydney Jewish Museum. 148 Darlinghurst Rd. (at Burton St.), Darlinghurst. ☎ **02/9360 7999.** Admission A$7 (U.S.$4.55) adults, A$4 (U.S.$2.60) children, A$16 (U.S.$10.40) families. Cash only. Mon–Thurs 10am–4pm; Fri 10am–2pm; Sun 11am–5pm. Closed Jewish holidays, Christmas, and Good Friday. CityRail: Kings Cross.

Harrowing exhibits here include documents and objects relating to the Holocaust and Jewish culture, mixed with audiovisual displays, and interactive media. There's also a museum shop, resource center, a small theater, and a kosher cafe. It's considered one of the best museums of its type in the world. Allow 1 to 2 hours.

Sydney Observatory. Observatory Hill, Watson Rd., Millers Point. ☎ **02/9217 0485.** Free admission in daytime; guided night tours (reservations essential), A$10 (U.S.$6.50) adults, A$5 (U.S.$3.25) children, and A$25 (U.S.$16.25) families. Daily 10am–5pm. CityRail, bus, or ferry: Circular Quay.

The city's only major museum of astronomy offers visitors a chance to see the southern skies through modern and historic telescopes. The best time to visit is during the night on a guided tour, when you can take a close-up look at some of the planets. Night tours are offered at 8:15pm from the end of May to the end of August and at 6:15 and 8:15pm the rest of the year; be sure to check the times when you book your tour. The planetarium and hands-on exhibits are also interesting.

State Library of NSW. Macquarie St., ☎ **02/9273 1414.** Free admission. Mon–Fri 9am–9pm; Sat, Sun, and selected holidays 11am–5pm. Closed New Year's Day, Good Friday, Christmas, and Boxing Day (Dec 26). CityRail: Martin Place. Sydney Explorer bus.

The state's main library is divided into two sections, the Mitchell and Dixon Libraries, located next to one another. A newer reference library complex nearby has two floors of reference materials, newspapers, and microfiche viewers. Leave your bags in the free lockers (you'll need a A$2/U.S.$1.30 coin, which is refundable). If you are in this area at lunchtime, I highly recommend the library's leafy Glasshouse Café, one of the best lunch spots in Sydney. The older building contains many older and more valuable books, and often hosts free art and photography displays in the upstairs galleries. A small library section in the Sydney Town Hall has international newspapers.

Vaucluse House. Wentworth Rd., Vaucluse. ☎ **02/9337 1957.** Admission A$7 (U.S.$4.55) adults, A$3 (U.S.$1.95) children. House Tues–Sun 10am–4:30pm. Grounds daily 7am–5pm. Free guided tours. Closed Good Friday and Christmas. Bus: 325 from Circular Quay.

Also looking over Sydney Harbour, this house includes lavish entertainment rooms and impressive stables and outbuildings. It was built in 1803 and was the home of Charles Wentworth, the architect of the Australian Constitution. It's set in 27 acres of gardens, bushland, and beach frontage—perfect for picnics. Allow 1 hour.

7 Parks & Gardens

IN SYDNEY

✪ **ROYAL BOTANIC GARDENS**   If you are going to spend time in one of Sydney's green spaces, then make it the Royal Botanic Gardens (☎ **02/9231 8111**), next to Sydney Opera House. The gardens were laid out in 1816 on the site of a farm that supplied food for the fledgling colony. It's informal in appearance with a scattering of duck ponds and open spaces, though there are several areas dedicated to particular plant species, such as the rose garden, the cacti and succulent display, and the central palm and the rain forest groves. **Mrs. Macquarie's Chair,** along the coast path, offers superb views of the Opera House and the Harbour Bridge (it's a favorite stop for tour buses). The giant sandstone building dominating the gardens nearest to the Opera House is **Government House,** once the official residence of the Governor of New South Wales (he moved out in 1996). The gardens are open to the public daily from 10am to 4pm, and the house is open for inspection Friday to Sunday from 10am to 3pm. Entrance to both is free. If you plan to park around here it's well to note that parking meters cost upwards of A$3 (U.S.$1.95) per hour, and you need A$1 coins.

A popular walk takes you through the Royal Botanic Gardens to the Art Gallery of New South Wales.

The botanic gardens are open daily from 7am to dusk. Admission is free.

HYDE PARK   In the center of the city is Hyde Park, a favorite with lunching business people. Of note here are the **Anzac Memorial** to Australian and New Zealand troops killed in the wars, and the **Archibald Fountain,** complete with spitting turtles and sculptures of Diana and Apollo. At night, avenues of trees are lit up with twinkling lights giving the place a magical appearance.

MORE CITY PARKS   Another Sydney favorite is the giant **Centennial Park** (☎ **02/9339 6699**), usually accessed from the top of Oxford Street. It was opened in 1888 to celebrate the centenary of European settlement, and today encompasses huge areas of lawn, several lakes, picnic areas with outdoor grills, cycling and running paths, and a cafe. It's open from sunrise to sunset. To get there, take bus 373, 374, 377, 380, 396, or 398 from the city.

A hundred years later, **Bicentennial Park,** at Australia Avenue, in Homebush Bay, came along. Forty percent of the park's total 100 hectares (247 acres) is parkland reclaimed from a dump; the rest is the largest parcel of wetlands on the Parramatta River, home to many species of local and migratory wading birds, cormorants, and pelicans. Follow park signs to the **visitor information office** (☎ **02/9763 1844**), open Monday through Friday from 10am to 4pm, and Saturday and Sunday from 9:30am to 4:30pm. To reach the park, take a CityRail train to Homebush Bay station.

BEYOND SYDNEY

SYDNEY HARBOUR NATIONAL PARK   You don't need to go far to experience Sydney's nearest national park. The Sydney Harbour National Park stretches around parts of the inner harbor and includes several small harbor islands (many first-time visitors are surprised at the amount of bushland remaining in prime real estate territory). The best walk is the **Manly to Spit Bridge Scenic Walkway** (☎ **02/9977 6522**). This 10-kilometer (6-mile) track winds its way from Manly (it starts near the Oceanarium), via Dobroyd Head to Spit Bridge (where you can catch a bus back to the city). The walk takes between 3 and 4 hours, and the views across Sydney Harbour are fabulous. Maps are available from the **Manly Visitors Information Bureau,** right opposite the main beach (☎ **02/9977 1088**).

Other access points to the park include tracks around Taronga Zoo (ask the zoo staff to point you toward the rather concealed entrances), and above tiny Shelly Beach, opposite the main beach at Manly.

Also part of the national park is the recently restored **Fort Denison,** the fortified outcrop in the middle of the harbor between Circular Quay and Manly. The fort was built during the Crimean War due to fears of a Russian invasion, and later served as a penal colony. One- to 2-hour **Heritage Tours** of the island leave from Cadmans Cottage, in The Rocks (☎ **02/9247 5033**).

Pick up maps of Sydney Harbour National Park at Cadmans Cottage.

Another great walk in Sydney can be combined with lunch or a drink at **Watsons Bay.** A 15-minute bush stroll to South Head is accessed from the small beach outside the Watsons Bay Hotel. Walk to the end of the beach (to your right as you look at the water) then up the flight of steps and bear left. There are some great views of the harbor from the lighthouse here.

MORE NATIONAL PARKS   Forming a semicircle around the city are Sydney's biggest parks of all. To the west is the **Blue Mountains National Park** (see chapter 5), to the northeast is **Ku-ring-gai Chase National Park,** and to the south is the magnificent **Royal National Park.** All three parks are home to marsupials such as echidnas and wallabies, numerous bird and reptile species, and a broad range of native plant life. Walking tracks, whether they stretch for half an hour or a few days, make each park accessible to the visitor.

Ku-ring-gai Chase National Park (☎ **02/9457 9322** or 02/ 9457 9310) is a great place to take a bushwalk through gum trees and rain forest on the lookout for wildflowers, sandstone rock formations, and Aboriginal art. There are plenty of tracks through the park, but one of my favorites is a relatively easy 2.5-kilometer (1.5-mile) tramp to **The Basin** (Track 12). The well-graded dirt path takes you down to an estuary with a beach and passes some significant Aboriginal engravings. There are also wonderful water views over Pittwater from the picnic areas at West Head. Get a free walking guide at the park entrance; gather maps and information in Sydney at the **National Parks & Wildlife Service's center** at Cadmans Cottage, 110 George St., The Rocks (☎ **02/9247 8861**). The park is open from sunrise to sunset, and admission is A$10 (U.S.$6.50) per car. You can drive to the park or catch a ferry from Palm Beach to The Basin. **Ferries** run on the hour (except at 1pm) from 9am to 5pm daily and cost A$4 (U.S.$2.60) one-way; call ☎ **02/9918 2747** for details. **Shorelink bus** 577 runs from the Turramurra CityRail station to the park entrance every hour on weekdays and every 2 hours on weekends; call ☎ **02/9457 8888** for details. There is no train service to the park. **Camping** is allowed only at The Basin (☎ **02/9457 9853**), and costs A$12 (U.S.$7.80) for two people. Book in advance.

While in the area you could visit the **Ku-ring-gai Wildflower Garden,** 420 Mona Vale Rd., St Ives (☎ **02/9440 8609**), which is essentially a huge area of natural bushland and a center for urban bushland education. There are plenty of bushwalking tracks, self-guided walks, and a number of nature-based activities. It's open daily from 8am to 4pm. Admission is A$2.50 (U.S.$1.63) for adults, A$1 (U.S.65¢) for children, and A$6 (U.S.$3.90) for families.

To the south of Sydney is the remarkable **Royal National Park,** Farrell Avenue, Sutherland (☎ **02/9542 0648**). It's the world's oldest national park, having been named as such in 1879 (Yellowstone in the United States was established in 1872 but not designated as a national park until 1883). Severe bushfires almost destroyed the whole lot in early 1994, but the trees and bush plants have recovered remarkably. There's no visitor center, but you can pick up park information at park entrances, where you'll pay a A$10 (U.S.$6.50) per car entry fee.

There are several ways to access the park, but my favorites are the little-known access points from **Bundeena** and **Otford.** To get to Bundeena, take a CityRail train from Central Station to Cronulla. Below the train station you'll find **Cronulla Wharf.** From there, hop on the delightful ferry run by **National Park Ferries** (☎ **02/9523 2990**) to Bundeena; ferries run hourly on the half hour (except 12:30pm). After you get off the ferry, the first turn on your left just up the hill will take you to Bundeena Beach. It's another 5 kilometers (3 miles) or so to the wonderfully remote Little Marley Beach, via Marley Beach (which has dangerous surf). The ferry returns to Cronulla from Bundeena hourly on the hour (except 1pm). The fare is A$3 (U.S.$1.95) each way.

An alternate way to reach the park is to take the train from Central Station to Otford, then climb the hill up to the sea cliffs. If you're driving, you might want to follow the scenic cliff-edge road down into **Wollongong.** The entrance is a little tricky to find, so you may have to ask directions. A 2-hour walk from the sea cliffs through beautiful and varying bush land and a palm forest will take you to **Burning Palms Beach.** There is no water along the route. The walk back up is steep, so only attempt this trek if you're reasonably fit. Trains to the area are irregular, and the last one departs around 4pm, so give yourself at least 2½ hours for the return trip to the train station so you don't get stranded. It's possible to walk the 26 kilometers (16 miles) from Otford to Bundeena, or vice versa, in 2 days (take all your food, water, and camping gear).

8 Especially for Kids

There are plenty of places kids can have fun in Sydney, but the recommendations below are particularly suitable for youngsters (all of the places are reviewed in full above).

Taronga Zoo (see p. 124) is an all-time favorite, where the barnyard animals, surprisingly, get as much attention as the koalas. If your kids want hands-on contact with the animals, head to **Featherdale Wildlife Park** (see p. 125), where they can get their photo taken next to a koala, and feed and stroke kangaroos and wallabies. Even more interactive are the exhibits just crying out to be touched and bashed at the **Powerhouse Museum** (see p. 122).

The sharks at **Oceanworld** (see p. 125) in Manly and the **Sydney Aquarium** (see p. 122) in Darling Harbour are big lures for kids, too, and the thrill of walking through a long plexiglass tunnel as giant manta rays perch over their heads will lead to more squeals of excitement.

Another fascinating outing for both adults and children is to crawl around inside a navy destroyer at the **National Maritime Museum** (see p. 121).

And, of course, what kid wouldn't enjoy a day at the **beach?** Sydney's got plenty to choose from, like Bondi or Manly.

9 A Stroll Through The Rocks

Sydney is a wonderful city to explore on foot. The self-guided walk outlined below, through The Rocks, is pretty much a "must-do" for any visitor to Sydney.

Walking Tour: On The Rocks

Start: The Rocks Visitor Centre and Exhibition Gallery, 106 George St.
Finish: George Street
Time: Allow around 1 hour, but longer if you stop to shop.
Best time: Any day, though Saturday brings The Rocks Market and big crowds on George Street.

The Rocks is the site of the oldest settlement in Australia. Initially, convict-built timber houses lined the rocky ridge, which gave the area its name, and dockyard buildings lined the water's edge. In the 1840s, more permanent stone buildings was erected, including most of the pubs and shops standing today. Slums grew up, too, and when the bubonic plague came to Sydney in 1900, the government demolished most of the shanty buildings. Between 1923 and 1932, many historic stone cottages were pulled down to make way for construction of the Harbour Bridge. In the 1970s the government decided to pull the lot down and replace it with giant office blocks and a hotel. Local residents protested, and following a 2-year "Green Ban" by the Builders' Labourers Federation, during which they refused to touch any historic building, the government relented.

Start your walk at:

1. **The Sydney Visitor Centre,** 106 George St., The Rocks (☎ **02/9255 1788**), open daily from 9am to 6pm. The center has plenty of information on Sydney, and a whole range of Australiana books. Upstairs is a gallery of photographs, texts, an audio-visual presentation, and objects relating to The Rocks. The building is part of the former Sydney Sailors' Home built in the 1860s.

   Outside on George Street, turn left, then turn left again at the first small avenue you come to, walking down toward the water you'll see:

2. **Cadmans Cottage,** built in 1816. This small white building was the headquarters of the government body that regulated the colony's waterways. It's named after John Cadman, a pardoned convict who became the government coxswain, and who lived here from 1827 to 1846. Before a land reclamation scheme, the water once lapped at the cottage's front door. Turn toward the water, look to the right and you'll see a row of historic buildings:

3. **The Sailors' Home,** built in 1864, is the first of them. Sydney was a rough old town, and no sooner had a sailor left his ship with his wages than he was likely to lose it in the brothels, pubs, and opium dens; gamble it away; or be mugged by gangs of "larrikins" who patrolled the back lanes. Concerned local citizens built this home to provide stricken sailors with lodging and food.

4. **The Coroners Court** (1907), next door, used to sit above the now-demolished morgue (or "Dead House"). Before the Coroners Court was built, bodies would often be dissected for autopsy on the bar of the Observer Tavern across the street. Notice the exposed original foreshore rocks displayed beneath an arch on the wall.

5. **Mariners Church,** built in 1856, is a neoclassical building mostly obscured by later buildings.

6. **Australasian Steam Navigation Company Building,** built in 1884, has a fabulous Flemish clock tower once used for spotting incoming ships. Take a look inside the Natural Australian Furniture Shop at the amazing wooden rafters. It was used as a storehouse, but before that, the location was occupied by the home of the prominent merchant Robert Campbell.

Walking Tour: On the Rocks

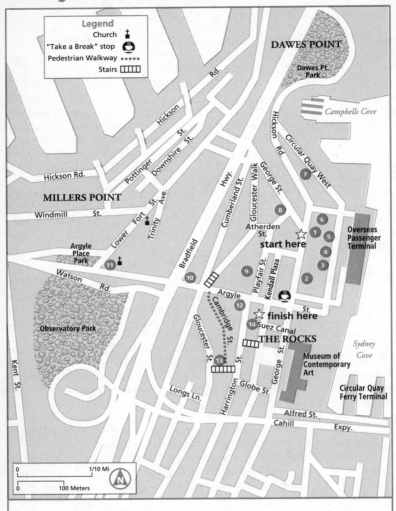

Legend
- Church ✝
- "Take a Break" stop ☕
- Pedestrian Walkway •••••
- Stairs ▭▭▭

DAWES POINT

Dawes Pt. Park

Campbells Cove

Hickson Rd.

MILLERS POINT

Windmill St.

Hickson St.

Pottinger St.

Downshire St.

Hwy.

Cumberland St.

Gloucester Walk

George St.

Circular Quay West

Atherden St.

start here ☆

Overseas Passenger Terminal

Argyle Place Park

Lower Fort St.

Trinity Ave.

Bradfield

Watson Rd.

Playfair St.

Kendall Plaza

Observatory Park

Argyle St.

Cambridge St.

finish here ☆

Suez Canal

THE ROCKS

Sydney Cove

Gloucester St.

Harrington St.

Globe St.

George St.

Museum of Contemporary Art

Kent St.

Longs Ln.

Alfred St.

Circular Quay Ferry Terminal

Cahill Expy.

0 ——— 1/10 Mi
0 ——— 100 Meters

N

The Rocks Visitor Centre and Exhibition Gallery **1**
Cadmans Cottage **2**
The Sailors Home **3**
The Coroners Court **4**
Mariners Church **5**
Australasian Steam Navigation Company Building **6**

Campbell's Storehouse **7**
Atherden Street **8**
Foundation Park **9**
The Argyle Cut **10**
Garrison Church **11**
The Clocktower Building **12**
Susannah Place **13**
The Suez Canal **14**

7. **Campbell's Storehouse** (1838 and 1890) was where Robert Campbell stored his tea, sugar, cloth, and liquor, imported from Asia. This pair of gabled buildings now houses four restaurants. From here, retrace your steps to a short flight of stairs that takes you up to Hickson Road. Turn left onto George Street, then cross the road, and turn left onto:

8. **Atherden Street,** the shortest street in Sydney; named after a local landowner. Notice the rock wall at its end that gave The Rocks its name. Turn left onto Playfair Street. Notice the markings in the rock walls where old slum dwellings used to be fixed. A little way along you'll see some steps. Follow them up to:

9. **Foundation Park,** an interesting artist's impression of what it was like inside the remaining structure of an old house in The Rocks. Follow the steps up to your right to Gloucester Walk. Follow this until you get to Argyle Street. Turn left and walk down the hill and on the corner of George Street you'll find a nice place to:

☕ **TAKE A BREAK**   The historic **Orient Hotel** has dining areas upstairs, or you could just refresh yourself with a glass of local beer from the bar (order a "schooner" if you're really thirsty, or a smaller "midi").

When you're refreshed, head back up Argyle Street, where you'll find a great archway across the road.

10. **The Argyle Cut,** was made by chain gangs chipping away at a mass of solid rock in a bid to link The Rocks to Cockle Bay (now Darling Harbour). The project was started in 1843, but 2 years later the use of convict labor for government projects was prohibited in the colony. In 1859, it was finally blasted through with explosives. At the top of the hill to your right is:

11. **Garrison Church,** built in 1839, a wonderful little Anglican church with stained-glass windows. It's engraved at the base with the names of children who died prematurely. In the early years, soldiers sat on one side of the church and free settlers sat on the other. To keep the riff-raff out, people had to pay for their pew, which was then name-tagged. Return back along Argyle Street the way you came and turn right onto Harrington Street.

12. **The Clocktower Building,** on the corner of Harrington and Argyle streets, was built on the site of demolished cottages as the government stepped up its plans to clear the area of its historic buildings. After construction, the building lay empty for 5 years as people displayed their displeasure. Ironically, perhaps, it's now the home of Tourism New South Wales, the government tourist promotion office.

Continue down Harrington Street and take a set of steep stairs to your right. At the top you'll find:

13. **Susannah Place,** 58–64 Gloucester St., a terrace of four houses built in 1844 that give visitors a glimpse into the life of working-class families of the period and later. Part of the Historic Trust of New South Wales. Guided tours are offered Saturday and Sunday from 10am to 5pm year-round and daily from 10am to 5pm in January. Tours cost A$5.50 (U.S.$3.58) for adults, and A$3.30 (U.S.$2.15) for children. Call the Historic Trust (☎ **02/9241 1893**) for details.

Go back down the stairs and backtrack on Harrington Street until you spot a thin lane to your left next to a shop selling didgeridoos. The lane is:

14. **The Suez Canal** created in the 1840s, once notorious for prostitutes and the so-called "Rocks Push"—hoodlums who dressed up as dandies in satin waist coats, tight flared pants, a bandanna around their necks, and a jaunty hat. Looking

good, they'd mug unwary sailors and citizens. The Suez Canal leads to George Street, from which you can head to the Museum of Contemporary Art or Circular Quay.

10 Harbor Cruises & Other Organized Tours

For details on the Red Sydney Explorer bus, see "Getting Around" in chapter 3, "Settling into Sydney."

HARBOR CRUISES

You shouldn't leave Sydney without taking a harbor cruise. **Sydney Ferries** (☎ **13 15 00;** or 02/9245 5600; www.sta.nsw.gov.au) offers a 1-hour morning harbor cruise with commentary departing Circular Quay, Wharf 4, daily at 10 and 11:15am. It costs A$14 (U.S.$9.10) for adults, A$9.50 (U.S.$6.18) for children under 16, and A$37.50 (U.S.$24.38) for families (any number of children under 16). A 2½-hour afternoon cruise explores more of the harbor and leaves from Wharf 4 at 1pm on weekdays and 1:30pm on weekends and public holidays. This tour costs A$21 (U.S.$13.65) for adults, A$12.50 (U.S.$8.13) for children, and A$54.50 (U.S.$35.43) for families. The highly recommended 1½-hour evening harbor tour, which takes in the city lights as far east as Double Bay and west to Goat Island, leaves Monday through Saturday at 8pm from Wharf 5. The 1½ evening tour costs A$18 (U.S.$11.70) for adults, A$11.50 (U.S.$7.48) for children, and A$47.50 (U.S.$30.88) for families.

If you are missing the Mississippi, another option is a trip on a paddle steamer. *The Sydney Showboat* (☎ 02/9552 2722; fax 02/9552 1934) departs from Campbells Cove in The Rocks. A daily lunch cruise running from 12:30 to 2pm costs A$56.20 (U.S.$36.53) for adults and A$33.50 (U.S.$21.78) for children 4 to 12; it includes a good buffet lunch, a jazz band, and commentary. Daily coffee cruises depart at 10:30am, 2:30 and 5:15pm, and cost A$20.50 ($13.33) for adults and A$12.40 (U.S.$8.06) for children. A daily dinner cruise that runs from 6:45 to 10:45pm costs A$129.80 ($84.37) for adults and A$77.80 ($50.57) for children, and a deluxe dinner cruise (more expensive food) costs A$176.20 (U.S.$114.53) for adults and a staggering A$105.90 (U.S.$68.84) for children; it includes a three-course meal, cabaret, dancers, a magician, singers, and a juggler. A Starlight dinner cruise without entertainment on the same boat costs A$85.40 (U.S.$55.51) for adults, and A$51.30 (U.S.$33.35) for children. You can buy tickets near the overseas terminal in Circular Quay.

If you're going to splurge on a cruise, the best are aboard the replica of ✪ **Captain Bligh's** *Bounty* (☎ 02/9247 1789). The boat was built for the movie *Mutiny on the Bounty,* starring Mel Gibson, Anthony Hopkins, Daniel Day-Lewis, and Liam Neeson. Standard 2-hour lunch cruises run Monday through Friday and cost A$65 (U.S.$42.25). Two-and-a-half hour dinner cruises depart daily in high season from October 1 to April 30 (Fri and Sat only from May 1–Sept 30). The cost is A$99

Harbor Cruise Tickets & Info

The one-stop shop for tickets and information on all harbor cruises is the **Australian Travel Specialists** (☎ 02/9247 5151; www.atstravel.com.au). Find outlets at jetties no. 2 and no. 6 at Circular Quay; at Manly Wharf in Manly; at the Harbourside Festival Marketplace at Darling Harbour; and inside the Oxford Koala Hotel on Oxford Street.

(U.S.$64.35) for adults. On Saturday and Sunday, a 2½-hour buffet lunch sail costs A$95 (U.S.$61.75) for adults, and a 1½-hour pre-dinner or brunch sail costs A$53 (U.S.$34.45). There's a 40% discount for children under 12 on all cruises.

Alternatively, you can cruise like a millionaire aboard the *MV Oceanos* (☎ 02/9555 4599, a 72-foot luxury motor cruiser. A 3-hour cruise, leaving Campbells Cove at 12:30pm Tuesday, Thursday, and Sunday, costs A$75 (U.S.$48.75) per person and includes a seafood lunch. Bookings are essential 2 days in advance. **Sail Venture Cruises** (☎ 02/9262 3595) has a range of cruises aboard their catamarans.

Captain Cook Cruises, departing jetty no. 6, Circular Quay, (☎ 02/9206 1122; fax 02/9251 1281; www.captcookcrus.com.au) is a major cruise company offering several harbor excursions on its sleek vessels, with commentary along the way.

The **Harbour Highlights** cruise runs at 9:30am, 11am, 12:45pm, 2:30pm and 4pm daily and takes in most of the main points of interest in 75 minutes. Cruises cost A$20 (U.S.$13) for adults and A$10 (U.S.$6.50) for children. The 1½-hour Sundowner cruise starts at 5pm daily; it costs the same as the Harbour Highlights cruise.

The **Sydney Harbour Explorer** departs at 9:30am, 11:30am, 1:30pm, and 3:30pm and combines visits to 5 major Sydney attractions with a 2-hour cruise. You can get off where you want and join the boat again later. Tickets cost A$22 (U.S.$14.30) for adults and A$15 (U.S.$9.75) for children. An **Aquarium & Zoo Cruise,** costing A$36.50 (U.S.$23.73) for adults and A$19 (U.S.$12.35) for children, includes the Sydney Harbour Explorer cruise and admission to the Sydney Aquarium or Taronga Zoo.

The company also offers a 1½-hour **Luncheon Cruise,** which leaves daily at noon. It costs A$52 (U.S.$33.80) for adults and A$39 (U.S.$25.35) for children. A **Showtime Dinner Cruise** leaves nightly at 7:30pm and includes a cabaret and dinner; it costs A$95 (U.S.$61.75) for adults and A$55 (U.S.$35.75) for children.

A nightly 1½-hour **Sunset Cruise** aboard the *John Cadman* **Cruising Restaurant boat,** departs just before sunset for A$69 (U.S.$44.85) for adults and A$35 (U.S.$22.75) for children, and includes a two-course meal and drinks. A second **Dinner Cruise** leaves at 7:30pm nightly and takes about 2½ hours around the harbor, while guests enjoy a three-course meal and bop away on the dance floor. Adults are A$95 (U.S.$61.75), and children A$55 (U.S.$35.75). Reservations are essential.

Matilda Cruises depart from Aquarium Wharf, Darling Harbour (☎ 02/9264 7377; fax 02/9261 8483; www.matilda.com.au). The modern Matilda fleet is based at Darling Harbour (but all cruises also pick up a Circular Quay) and offers 1-hour sightseeing tours, morning and afternoon coffee cruises, and daily lunch and dinner cruises. One-hour sightseeing cruises leave Darling Harbour eight times daily beginning at 9:30am (six times daily in winter beginning at 10:30am) and cost A$19.50 (U.S.$12.68) for adults and A$10 (U.S.$6.50) for children 5 to 12 and A$47.50 (U.S.$30.88) for a family. Two-hour coffee cruises leave Darling Harbour at 9:30am and 3:05pm and cost A$26 (U.S.$16.90) for adults and A$13 (U.S.$8.45) for children. Two-hour lunch cruises leave at 12:15pm daily and cost A$53.50 (U.S.$34.78) for adults and A$26.50 (U.S.$17.23) for children. Three-hour dinner cruises leave at 7pm and cost A$103 (U.S.$66.95) for adults and A$52 (U.S.$33.8) for children. All boats dock at Circular Quay's Eastern Pontoon (near The Oyster Bar, before you get to the Sydney Opera House), 20 minutes after picking up passengers at Darling Harbour.

WALKING TOURS

The center of Sydney is surprisingly compact, and you'll find you can see a lot in a day on foot. If you want to learn more about Sydney's early history, then you should book a guided tour with **The Rocks Walking Tour** (☎ 02/9247 6678), based at the Shop

K4, Kendall Lane (off Argyle Street, The Rocks). Excellent walking tours leave Monday through Friday at 10:30am, 12:30pm, and 2:30pm, and Saturday and Sunday at 11:30am and 2pm (In Jan only 10:30am–2:30pm). The 1½-hour tour costs A$14.85 (U.S.$9.65) for adults, A$9.35 (U.S.$6.08) for children 10 to 16, and A$36.85 (U.S.$23.95) for families. Accompanied children under 10 are free.

For other historical walks contact **Sydney Guided Tours** (☎ 02/9660 7157; fax 02/9660 0805). The company's owner, Maureen Fry, has been in the business for over 12 years and employs trained guides qualified in specific disciplines, such as history, architecture, and botany. She offers a range of tours including an introductory tour of Sydney, a tour of historic Macquarie Street, and many others. Walking tours cost A$17 (U.S.$11.05) for 2 hours as part of a group (call in advance to find out what's available).

A walking tour with a difference is **Unseen Sydney's History, Convicts, and Murder Most Foul** (☎ 02/9555 2700). The tour is fascinating and fun, with the guide dressed up in period gear and theatrical storytellers spinning yarns about Sydney's mysteries and intrigue. The 1½-hour tour leaves at 6:30pm sharp from Circular Quay Tuesday and Thursday through Saturday. It costs A$19.80 (U.S.$12.87) for adults and A$15.40 (U.S.$10.01) for children.

MOTORCYCLE TOURS

Blue Thunder Motorcycle Tours (☎ 02/9977 7721; or 0414/278 983) runs chauffeured Harley-Davidson tours of Sydney, the Blue Mountains, and other places around New South Wales. A 1-hour ride (you sit on the back of the bike) around the city costs A$90 (U.S.$58.50). A half-day trip to the northern beaches or down the south coast through the Royal National Park costs A$265 (U.S.$172.25) including lunch. Full day trips cost A$370 (U.S.$240.50) including lunch and snacks, and go to either the Hunter Valley, the south coast, Bathurst, or the Blue Mountains. *Helmets are mandatory for motorcyclists and their passengers.*

Another Harley-Davidson tour specialist is **Dream Legends Motor Cycle Tours** (☎ 02/9584 2451). One-hour city trips cost A$75 (U.S.$48.75), half-day jaunts go for A$225 (U.S.$146.25) and a full-day excursion "wherever you want to go" costs A$400 (U.S.$260) with lunch and drinks. A sidecar is available.

A third mean-machine operator is **Eastcoast Motorcycle Tours** (☎ 02/9247 5151). One-hour city tours cost A$99 (U.S.$65.35), and four-hour trips to the south coast, Royal national park and Pittwater cost A$270 (U.S.$175.50).

11 Staying Active

BIKING   The best place to cycle in Sydney is in Centennial Park. Rent bikes from **Centennial Park Cycles,** 50 Clovelly Rd., Randwick (☎ 02/9398 5027), 200 meters (220 yd.) from the Musgrave Avenue entrance. (The park has five main entrances). Mountain bikes cost A$9 (U.S.$5.85) for the first hour, A$13 (U.S.$8.45) for 2 hours, and A$20 (U.S.$13) for 4 hours.

Bicycles in The City, 722 George St. (near Central Station) (☎ 02/9280 2229), rents mountain bikes from A$5 (U.S.$3.25) per hour, or A$25 ($16.25) per day. You can rent in-line skates here, too, for the same daily rate with all protective clothing. *Helmets are compulsory in Australia.*

SCUBA DIVING   Plenty of people learn to dive in Sydney before taking off for the Barrier Reef. Don't expect beautiful coral reefs though. **Pro Dive** (27 Alfreda St., Coogee ☎ 02/9665 6333), offers a four-day learn-to-dive program costing $345 (U.S.$224). A day of diving for registered divers costs A$105 (U.S.$68.25).

GOLF Sydney has more than 90 golf courses and plenty of fine weather. The 18-hole championship course at **Moore Park Golf Club,** at Cleveland Street and Anzac Parade, Waterloo (☎ **02/9663 1064**), is the nearest to the city. Visitors are welcome every day except all day Friday and Sunday mornings. Green fees are A$24 (U.S.$15.60) Monday through Friday, and A$27 (U.S.$17.55) Saturday and Sunday.

One of my favorite courses is **Long Reef Golf Club,** Anzac Avenue, Colloroy (☎ **02/9982 2943**). This northern beaches course is surrounded by the Tasman Sea on three sides and has gorgeous views. Greens fees are A$25 (U.S.$16.25) midweek, and A$35 (U.S.$22.75) on weekends.

For general information on courses call the **New South Wales Golf Association** (☎ **02/9264 8433**).

FITNESS CLUBS The City Gym, 107 Crown St., East Sydney (☎ **02/9360 6247**), is a busy gym near Kings Cross. Drop-in visits are A$10 (U.S.$6.50), and it's open daily 24 hours.

IN-LINE SKATING The best places to go in-line skating are along the beachside promenades at Bondi and Manly beaches and in Centennial Park. **Manly Blades,** 49 North Steyne (☎ **02/9976 3833**), rents skates for A$12 (U.S.$7.80) for the first hour and A$6 (U.S.$3.90) for each subsequent hour, or A$25 (U.S.$16.25) per day. Lessons are A$25 (U.S.$16.25) including 1-hour skate hire and a half-hour lesson. **Bondi Boards & Blades,** 148 Curlewis St., Bondi Beach (☎ **02/9365 6555**), rents skates for A$11 (U.S.$7.15) for the first hour, A$5.50 (U.S.$3.58) for each subsequent hour, and A$20 (U.S.$13) for 24-hours. Ask about free lesson. **Total Skate,** 36 Oxford St., Paddington, near Centennial Park (☎ **02/9380 6356**), rents skates for A$10 (U.S.$6.50) for the first hour and A$5 (U.S.$3.25) for subsequent hours, and A$30 (U.S.$19.50) for 14-hours. Ask about a free lesson.

JOGGING The Royal Botanic Gardens, Centennial Park, or any beach are the best places to kick-start your body. You can also run across the Harbour Bridge, though you'll have to put up with the car fumes. Another popular spot is along the sea cliffs from Bondi Beach to Bronte Beach. The Sydney Striders running club has a list of runs, including maps, at www.sydneystriders.org.au/starguide.shtml

PARASAILING If being strapped to a harness and a parachute 100 meters (320 feet) above Sydney Harbour while being towed along by a speed boat is your idea of fun, contact **Sydney Harbour Parasailing and Scenic Tours** (☎ **02/99776781**). A regular flight will see you in the air for 8 to 10 minutes at the end of a 100-meter line. Flights cost A$55 (U.S.$35.75) per adult. Tandem rides, for children and adults, are also available. The boat departs next to the Manly ferry wharf in Manly.

SURFING **Bondi Beach** and **Tamarama** are the best surf beaches on the south side of Sydney Harbour, while **Manly, Narrabeen, Bilgola, Colloroy, Long Reef,** and **Palm** beaches are the most popular on the north side. Most beach suburbs have surf shops where you can rent a board. At Bondi Beach, the **Bondi Surf Co.,** 72Campbell Parade (☎ **02/9365 0870**), rents surfboards for A$45 (U.S.$29.25) for 4 hours or A$60 (U.S.$39) all day. Body boards cost A$20 (U.S.$13) for 2 hours and A$60 (U.S.$39) all day. In Manly, **Aloha Surf,** 44 Pittwater Rd., Manly (☎ **02/9977 3777**), also rents surfboards. Call **Manly Surf School** (☎ **0418/717 313** mobile phone) for information on surfing lessons.

SWIMMING The best place to swim indoors in Sydney is the **Sydney International Aquatic Centre,** at Olympic Park, Homebush Bay (☎ **02/9752 3666**). It's open Monday through Friday from 5am to 9:45pm, and Saturday, Sunday, and public holidays from 7am to 7pm.

Another good bet is the **North Sydney Olympic Pool,** Alfred South Street, Milsons Point (☎ **02/9955 2309**). It's just over the Harbour Bridge to your left, near the amusement park, so why not have a swim after a walk over from the city? Swimming here costs A$3.50 (U.S.$2.28) for adults and A$1.65 (U.S.$1.07) for children. More world records have been broken in this pool than in any other pool in the world.

TENNIS   There are hundreds of places around the city to play one of Australia's most popular sports. A nice spot is the **Miller's Point Tennis Court,** Kent Street, The Rocks (☎ **02/9256 2222**). It's run by the Observatory Hotel and is open daily from 7:30am to 10pm. The court costs A$25 (U.S.$16.25) per hour. The **North Sydney Tennis Centre,** 1A Little Alfred St., North Sydney (☎ **02/9371 9952**), has three courts available daily from 6am to 10pm. They cost A$16 (U.S.$10.40) until 5pm on weekdays and A$20 (U.S.$13) at other times.

WINDSURFING   My favorite spot to learn to windsurf or to set out onto the harbor is at **Balmoral Beach,** in Mosman on the North Shore. Rent boards at **Balmoral Windsurfing, Sailing and Kayaking School & Hire,** 3 The Esplanade, Balmoral Beach (☎ **02/9960 5344**). Windsurfers cost A$27 (U.S.$17.55) per hour for beginners and A$38 (U.S.$24.70) for advanced windsurfing equipment. Lessons cost A$175 (U.S.$113.75) for 5 hours teaching over a weekend for beginners, and A$195 (U.S.$126.75) for advanced lessons. This place also rents fishing boats.

YACHTING   Balmoral Boat Shed, Balmoral Beach (☎ **02/9969 6006**), rents catamarans, 12-foot aluminum run-abouts, canoes, and surf skis. The catamarans and run-abouts cost A$35 (U.S.$22.75) for the first hour (with a A$80/U.S.$52 deposit); a full day costs A$120 (U.S.$78). Other vessels, such as canoes, cost A$10 (U.S.$6.50) per hour with a A$10 (U.S.$6.50) deposit.

Sydney by Sail (☎ **02/9280 1110** or 0419/367 180 mobile phone) offers daily introductory sailing cruises on the harbor aboard 34- and 38-foot yachts. A maximum of six people sail aboard each boat, which leave from the National Maritime Museum at Darling Harbour. Ninety-minute introductory sails cost A$54 (U.S.$35.10) per person with the more popular 3 hour sail costing A$98 (U.S.$63.70). Reservations are essential.

SPECTATOR SPORTS

CRICKET   The **Sydney Cricket Ground,** at the corner of Moore Park and Driver Avenue, is famous for its 1-day and test matches, played generally from October to March. Phone the **New South Wales Cricket Association** at ☎ **02/9339 0999** for match details, and **Sportspace Tours** (☎ **02/9380 0383**) for stadium tours.

FOOTBALL   In this city, "football" means rugby league. If you want to see burly chaps pound into each other while chasing an oval ball, then be here between May and September. The biggest venue is the **Sydney Football Stadium,** which hosts "Australian Rules" football, as well as rugby and soccer, at Moore Park Road, Paddington (☎ **02/9360 6601**). Match information is available at ☎ **1900 963 133.** Buy tickets at **Ticketek** (☎ **02/9266 4800**).

HORSE RACING   Sydney has four horse racing tracks: Randwick, Canterbury, Rosehill, and Warwick Farm. The most central and most well known is **Randwick Racecourse,** Alison Street, Randwick (☎ **02/9663 8400**). The biggest race day of the week is Saturday. Entry costs A$9 (U.S.$5.85) per person. Call the **Sydney Turf Club** at ☎ **02/9930 4000** with questions about Rosehill and Canterbury, and the Randwick number above for Warwick Farm.

SURFING CARNIVALS   Every summer these uniquely Australian competitions bring large crowds to Sydney's beaches, as surf clubs compete against each other in various water sports. Contact the **Surf Lifesaving Association** (☎ **02/9597 5588** for times and locations. Other beach events include Iron Man and Iron Woman competitions, during which Australia's fittest struggle it out in combined swimming, running, and surfing events.

YACHT RACING   While sailing competitions take place on the harbor most summer weekends, the start of the **Sydney to Hobart Yacht Race** on Boxing Day (Dec 26) is not to be missed. The race starts from the harbor near the Royal Botanic Gardens. Contact **Tourism New South Wales** (☎ **02/9931 1111;** fax 02/9931 1490) or **Tourism Tasmania** (☎ **03/6230 8169;** fax 03/6230 8353) for more information.

12   Shopping

Sydney's shopping is not as good as Melbourne's, but you'll find plenty of places to keep your credit cards in action. Most shops of interest to the visitor are located in The Rocks and along George and Pitt streets (including the shops below the AMP Centrepoint Tower and along the Pitt Street Mall). Other shopping precincts worth checking out are Mosman on the North Shore and Double Bay in the eastern suburbs for boutique shopping, Chatswood for its shopping centers, the Sydney Fishmarket for the sake of it, and the various weekend markets (listed below).

You won't want to miss the **Queen Victoria Building (QVB),** on the corner of Market and George streets. This Victorian shopping arcade is one of the prettiest in the world and has some 200 boutiques—mostly men's and women's fashion—on four levels. The arcade is open 24 hours, but the shops do business Monday to Saturday from 9am to 6pm (Thurs to 9pm) and Sunday 11am to 5pm.

Several other arcades in the city center also offer good shopping potential, including the **Royal Arcade** under the Hilton Hotel; the **Imperial Arcade** near the AMP Centrepoint Tower; **Sydney Central Plaza,** beside the Grace Brothers department store on Pitt Street Mall; and the **Skygarden Arcade,** which runs from Pitt Street Mall to Castlereagh Street. The **Strand Arcade** (running between Pitt Street Mall and George Street) was built in 1892 and is interesting for its architecture and small boutiques, food stores and cafes, and the Down Town Duty Free store on the basement level.

On **Pitt Street Mall** you'll find record shops, including HMV; a branch of The Body Shop; and fashion boutiques such as Just Jeans, Jeans West, Katies, and Esprit.

SHOPPING FROM A TO Z
ABORIGINAL ARTIFACTS & CRAFTS
Coo-ee Aboriginal Art Gallery and Shop. 98 Oxford St., Paddington. ☎ **02/9332 1544.**

The proprietors of Coo-ee collect artifacts and fine art from more than 30 Aboriginal communities and dozens of individual artists. The gallery stocks the largest collection of limited-edition prints in Australia. There are plenty of hand-painted fabrics,

Shopping Hours

Regular shopping hours are generally Monday to Wednesday and Friday from 8:30 or 9am to 6pm, Thursday from 8:30 or 9am to 9pm, Saturday from 9am to 5 or 5:30pm, and Sunday from 10 or 10:30am to 5pm. Exceptions are noted in store listings below.

T-shirts, didgeridoos, boomerangs, sculpture, bark paintings, jewelry, music, and books. Don't expect bargains; you pay for the quality here. Open Monday to Saturday from 10am to 6pm and Sunday from 11am to 5pm.

Didj Beat Didjeridoo's. Shop 2, The Clock Tower Sq., Corner of Argyle and Harrington sts. ☎ **02/9251 4289.**

Here you'll find the best selection of didgeridoos in Sydney. The pieces are authentic and well priced. Open daily from 10am to 6:30pm.

Gavala. Aboriginal Art & Cultural Education Centre. Harbourside Festival Marketplace, Darling Harbour. ☎ **02/9212 7232.**

In the market for a decent boomerang or didgeridoo? Gavala is owned and operated by Aborigines, and there are plenty of authentic Aboriginal crafts for sale, including carved emu eggs, grass baskets, cards, and books. A first-rate didgeridoo will cost anywhere from A$100 to $450 (U.S.$65–$292.50). Gavala also sponsors cultural talks, didgeridoo-making lessons, and storytelling. Open daily from 10am to 9pm.

Original & Authentic Aboriginal Art. 79 George St., The Rocks. ☎ **02/9251 4222.**

Quality Aboriginal art is on offer here from some of Australia's best-known painters, including Paddy Fordham Wainburranga, whose paintings are exhibited worldwide, and Janet Forrester Nangala, whose work has been exhibited in the Australian National Gallery in Canberra. Expect to pay in the range of A$1,000 to $4,000 (U.S.$650–$2,600) for the larger paintings. There are some nice painted pots here, too, costing from A$30 to $80 (U.S.$19.50–$52). Open daily from 10am to 6.30pm.

ART PRINTS & ORIGINALS

Done Art and Design. 1 Hickson Rd., The Rocks. ☎ **02/9247 2740.**

The art is by Ken Done, who's well known for having designed his own Australian flag, which he hopes to raise over Australia should it abandon its present one following the formation of a republic. The clothing designs—which feature printed sea- and beachscapes, the odd colorful bird, and lots of pastels—are by his wife Judy. Ken Done's gallery is in Hickson Road, just off George Street, in the Rocks. Open daily from 10am to 5:30pm.

BOOKS

You'll find a selection of specialized books on Sydney and Australia at the Art Gallery of New South Wales, the Garden Shop in the Royal Botanic Gardens, the Museum of Sydney, the Australian Museum, and the State Library of New South Wales.

Discount Shopping

If you're looking for bargains, head to **Foveraux Street** between Elizabeth and Waterloo streets in Surry Hills for factory clearance shops selling end-of-the-run, last season's fashions and seconds at deep discounts. If you're really keen on bargains you might want to join **Shopping Spree Tours** (☎ **1800/625 969** in Australia, or 02/9360 6220; fax 02/9332 2641), which offers tours to factory outlets and warehouses selling everything from clothes to cookware. Full-day tours cost A$70 (U.S.$45.50) for adults and A$20 (U.S.$13) for children 3 to 12 and include pickup at your hotel, visits to 8 to 10 outlets and warehouses, and a 2-course lunch at a good restaurant. Tours depart at 8:15am daily except Sunday and public holidays.

Abbey's Bookshop. 131 York St. (behind the Queen Victoria Building). ☎ **02/9264 3111.**

This interesting, centrally located bookshop specializes in literature, history, crime, and mystery, and has a whole floor on language and education.

Angus & Robertson Bookworld. Pitt Street Mall, 168 Pitt St. ☎ **02/9235 1188.**

One of Australia's largest bookshops, with two stories of books—including a good guidebook and Australiana section—and games.

Dymocks. 424–428 George St. (just north of Market St.). ☎ **02/9235 0155.**

The largest of four book department stores in the city, Dymocks has three levels of general books and stationary. There's a reasonable travel section here with plenty of guides. Open Monday to Wednesday and Friday from 9am to 6pm, Thursday from 9am to 9pm, Saturday from 9am to 5pm, and Sunday from 10am to 5pm.

Gleebooks Bookshop. 49 Glebe Point Rd., Glebe. ☎ **02/9660 2333.**

Specializing in art, general literature, psychology, sociology, and women's studies, Gleebooks also has a secondhand store (with a large children's department) down the road at 191 Glebe Point Rd. Open daily 8am to 9pm.

Goulds Book Arcade. 32–38 King St., Newtown. ☎ **02/9519 8947.**

Located about a 10-minute walk from the Newtown CityRail station, the place is bursting at the seams with many thousands of secondhand and new books. You can browse for hours here. Open daily from 8am to midnight.

Travel Bookshop. Shop 3, 175 Liverpool St. (across from the southern end of Hyde Park, near the Museum CityRail station). ☎ **02/9261 8200.**

Hundreds of travel guides, maps, Australiana titles, coffee table books, and travel accessories line the shelves of this excellent bookshop. There's also an AMEX counter here. Open Monday to Friday from 9am to 6pm and Saturday from 10am to 5pm.

CRAFTS

Australian Craftworks. 127 George St., The Rocks. ☎ **02/9247 7156.**

This place showcases some of Australia's best arts and crafts, from some 300 Australian artists. It's displayed in a former police station built in 1882, a time of economic depression when mob riots and clashes with police were common in this area. The cells and administration areas are today used as gallery spaces. Open daily from 8:30am to 7pm.

✪ **The puppet shop at the rocks.** 77 George St., The Rocks. ☎ **02/9247 9137.** Fax 02/9418 4157.

I can't believe I kept walking past the sign outside this place for so many years without looking in. Deep in the bowels of a historic building I finally came across several cramped rooms packed with puppets, costing from a couple of dollars to a couple of hundred. The owners make their own puppets—mostly Australian in style (emus, koalas, and so on)—as well as import things from all over the world. Wooden toys abound, too. It's the best shop in Sydney! Open daily from 10am to 5:30pm.

Telopea Gallery. Shop 2 in the Metcalfe Arcade, 80–84 George St., The Rocks. ☎ **02/9241 1673.**

Run by the New South Wales Society of Arts and Crafts, the gallery exhibits works by its members, all New South Wales residents. There are wonderful glass, textile, ceramic, jewelry, fine metal, and wood-turned items for sale. Open daily from 9:30am to 5:30pm.

DEPARTMENT STORES

The two big names in Sydney shopping are David Jones and Grace Brothers. **David Jones** (☎ 02/9266 5544) is the city's largest department store, selling everything from fashion to designer furniture. You'll find the women's section on the corner of Elizabeth and Market streets, and the men's section on the corner of Castlereigh and Market streets.

   Grace Brothers (☎ 02/9238 9111) is similar to David Jones, but the building is newer and flashier. It's located on the corner of George and Market streets. Both stores are open Monday to Wednesday and Friday to Saturday from 9am to 6:00pm; Thursday from 9am to 9pm; and Sunday from 11am to 5pm.

DUTY-FREE SHOPS

Sydney has several duty-free shops selling goods at a discount. To take advantage of the bargains, you need a passport and a flight ticket, and you must export what you buy. The duty-free shop with the best buys is **Downtown Duty Free,** which has two city outlets, on the basement level of the Strand Arcade, off Pitt Street Mall (☎ 02/9233 3166) and at 105 Pitt St. (☎ 02/9221 4444). Five more stores are found at Sydney International Airport and are open from the first to the last flight of the day.

FASHION

The best places to shop for fashion are the **Queen Victoria Building** and the **Sydney Central Plaza** (on the ground floor of the mall next to the Grace Brothers department store on Pitt Street Mall). Otherwise, the major department stores and Pitt Street Mall outlets will keep you up to date.

Australian Outback Clothing

R.M. Williams. 389 George St. (between Town Hall and Central CityRail stations). ☎ 02/9262 2228.

Moleskin trousers may not be the height of fashion at the moment, but you never know! R.M. Williams boots are famous for being both tough and fashionable. You'll find Akubra hats (the classic Outback headgear), Driza-bone coats (the legendary oilskin dusters worn for generations by settlers), and kangaroo-skin belts here, too.

Thomas Cook Boot & Clothing Company. 790 George St., Haymarket. ☎ 02/9212 6616. www.thomascookclothing.com.au.

Located on George Street between Town Hall and central CityRail stations, this place specializes in Australian boots, Driza-bone coats, and Akubra hats. There's another shop at 129 Pitt St., near Martin Place (☎ 02/9232 3334).

Unisex Fashion

Country Road. 142–146 Pitt St. ☎ 02/9394 1818. www.countryroad.com.au.

This store has outlets across Australia as well as in the United States. The clothes, for men and women, are good quality but tend to be expensive (though if you suddenly need a dressy outfit and didn't pack one, this is where to find it). You'll find other branches in the Queen Victoria Building and the Skygarden Arcade, and in Bondi Junction, Darling Harbour, Double Bay, Mosman, and Chatswood.

Mostrada. Store 15G, Sydney Central Plaza, 450 George St. ☎ 02/9221 0133.

If you're looking for good-quality leather items at very reasonable prices, then this is your place. Leather jackets for men and women go for between A$199 (U.S.$129.35) and A$899 (U.S.$584.35), with an average price of around A$400 (U.S.$260). There are also bags, belts, and other leather accessories on offer.

Men's Fashion

Gowings. 45 Market St., ☎ **02/9264 6321.**

Probably the best all-round men's clothing store in Sydney, Gowings sells quality clothing on several levels. There's also an eclectic mix of gardening equipment, gourmet camping gear, odds and ends for the extrovert, a good range of Australian bush hats, and R.M. Williams boots (at around A$250/U.S.$162.5 a pair). If you want to risk it, you can even get a cheap haircut here.

There's a similar store at 319 George St., (☎ **02/9262 1281**) near Wynyard CityRail station.

Esprit Mens. Shop 10G, Sydney Central Plaza, 450 George St. ☎ **02/9233 7349.**

Not so cheap, but colorful clothes come out of this designer store where bold hues and fruity patterns are the in thing. Quality designer shirts cost around A$60 (U.S.$39).

Women's Fashion

In addition to the places listed below, head to **Oxford Street** (particularly Paddington), for more avant-garde designers.

Carla Zampatti. 143 Elizabeth St. ☎ **02/9264 3257.**

There are some thirty Carla Zampatti stores around Australia offering stylish fashions at hard-to-swallow prices. Open Monday to Saturday from 10am to 5pm.

Dorian Scott. 105 George St., The Rocks. ☎ **02/9221 8145.** Fax 02/9251 8553.

The best place to go for hand-knitted sweaters—called "jumpers"—Dorian Scott has a wide range of colorful garments from more than 200 leading Australian designers. While some items go for A$80 (U.S.$52), others will set you back a lot more. You'll also find clothing accessories for men, women, and children in this two-story emporium, including Hot Tuna surfware and Thomas Cook adventure clothing. Open Monday to Saturday from 9:30am to 7pm and Sunday from 10am to 6pm. There are also two Dorian Scott stores at Sydney International Airport (☎ **02/9667 3255**) and another at the Inter-Continental Hotel at 117 Macquarie St. (☎ **02/9247 1818**).

Food

The goodies you'll find in the downstairs food section of the **David Jones** department store on Castlereigh Street will be enough to tempt anyone off their diet. It sells the best of local and imported products to the rich and famous.

Coles. Wynyard Station, Castlereagh St., Wynyard (directly opposite the Menzies Hotel and the public bus stands). ☎ **02/9299 4769.**

One of the few supermarkets in the city center, this place is a good bet if you want to cater for yourself or are after readymade food (including tasty sandwiches) and cheap soft drinks. There's another Coles beneath the giant Coca-Cola sign on Darlinghurst Road, Kings Cross. Open daily 6am to midnight.

Darrell Lea Chocolates. At the corner of King and George sts. ☎ **02/9232 2899.**

This is the oldest location of Australia's most famous chocolate shop. Pick up some wonderful handmade chocolates as well as other unusual candies, including the best licorice this side of the Kasbah.

Sydney Fishmarket. At the corner of Bank St. and Pyrmont Bridge Rd., Pyrmont. ☎ **02/ 9660 1611.**

Finding out about what people eat can be a good introduction to a country, and in my opinion, nothing is more fascinating than a visit to the local fish market. Here you'll find seven major fish retailers selling everything from shark to Balmain bugs (a kind of squat crayfish), with hundreds of species in between. Watch out for the local pelicans being fed the fishy leftovers. There's also a Doyles restaurant and a sushi bar, a couple of cheap seafood eateries, a fruit market, and a good deli. The retail sections are open daily from 7am to 4pm. Get here by Light Rail (get off at the Fishmarket stop), or walk from Darling Harbour. Parking costs A$2 (U.S.$1.30) for the first 3 hours.

Gifts & Souvenirs

The shops at **Taronga Zoo,** the **Oceanarium** in Manly, the **Sydney Aquarium,** and the **Australian Museum** are all good sources for gifts and souvenirs. There are many shops around The Rocks worth browsing, too.

Australian Geographic. Harbourside Festival Marketplace, Darling Harbour. ☎ **02/9212 6539.**

A spinoff from the Australian version of National Geographic magazine, this store sells good quality crafts and Australiana. On offer are camping gadgets, telescopes and binoculars, garden utensils, scientific oddities, books and calendars, videos, music, toys, and lots more. There is another location in AMP Centerpoint Tower on Pitt Street (☎ **02/9231 5055**).

National Trust Gift and Bookshop. Observatory Hill, The Rocks. ☎ **02/9258 0154.**

Here you can pick up some nice souvenirs, including books, Australiana crafts, and indigenous foodstuffs. An art gallery on the premises presents changing exhibits of paintings and sculpture by Australians. There's also a cafe. Closed Monday.

The Wilderness Society Shop. AMP Centrepoint Tower, Castlereagh St. ☎ **02/9233 4674.**

Australiana is crawling out of the woodwork at this cute little craft emporium dedicated to saving the few remaining untouched forests and wilderness areas of Australia. You'll find some quality craft items, cute children's clothes, books, cards, and knick-knacks.

Markets

Balmain Market. On the grounds of St. Andrew's Church, Darling St., Balmain ☎ **02/9555 1791.**

Active from 8:30am to 4pm every Saturday, this popular market has some 140 vendors selling crafts, jewelry, and knickknacks. Take the ferry to Balmain (Darling Street); the market is a 10-minute walk up Darling Street.

Paddington Bazaar. On the grounds of St. John's Church on Oxford St., on the corner of Newcome St. (just follow the crowds). ☎ **02/9331 2646.**

At this Saturday only market you'll find everything from essential oils and designer clothes to new age jewelry and Mexican hammocks. Expect things to be busy from 10am to 4pm. Take bus 380 or 389 from Circular Quay.

Paddy's Markets. At the corner of Thomas and Hay sts., in Haymarket, near Chinatown. ☎ **1300/361 589** in Australia or 02/9325 6924.

A Sydney institution, Paddy's Markets has hundreds of stalls selling everything from cheap clothes and plants to chickens. It's open Friday to Sunday from 9am to 4:30pm. Above Paddy's Markets is **Market City** (☎ **02/9212 1388**), which has three floors of fashion stalls, food courts, and specialty shops. Of particular interest is the largest Asian-European supermarket in Australia, on level 1, and the Kam Fook yum cha Chinese restaurant on level 3, also the largest in Australia.

The Rocks Market. On George St., The Rocks.   ☎ **02/9255 1717.**

Held every Saturday and Sunday, this very touristy market has more than 100 vendors selling everything from crafts, housewares, posters, jewelry, and curios. The main street is closed to traffic from 10am to 4pm to make it easier to stroll around.

Music

Birdland. 3 Barrack St.   ☎ **02/9299 8527.** www.birdland.com.au.

This is the best store in Sydney for jazz and blues, and it stocks a sizable collection of rare items. The staff is very knowledgeable.

HMV Music Stores. Pitt Street Mall.   ☎ **02/9221 2311.**

This is one of the best music stores in Sydney. The jazz section is impressive. CDs in Australia are not cheap, with most new releases costing around A$30 to $35 (U.S.$19.50–$22.75).

Red Eye Records. Tank Stream Arcade (downstairs), at the corner of King and Pitt sts. (near Town Hall).   ☎ **02/9233 8177** (new recordings), or 02/9233 8125 (secondhand CDs). www.redeye.com.au.

These two shops, tucked away downstairs in a small arcade not far from Pitt Street Mall and the Strand Arcade, are directly across from one another. The larger store sells a wide range of modern CDs, but the smaller store sells a great collection of quality secondhand and end-of-the-line CDs for around A$20 (U.S.$13) each.

Sounds Australian. In the Argyle Stores department store, The Rocks.   ☎ **02/9247 7290.** Fax 02/9241 2873.

Anything you've ever heard that sounds Australian you can find here. From rock and pop to didgeridoo and country, it's all here. Fortunately, if you haven't a clue what's good and what's bad you can spend some time listening before you buy. The management is extremely knowledgeable.

Opals

Australian Opal Cutters. Suite 10, Level 4, National Building, 250 Pitt St.   ☎ **02/9261 2442.** www.opal.citysearch.com.au.

Learn more about opals before you buy at this shop. The staff here will give you lessons about opals to help you compare pieces.

Wine

Australian Wine Centre. 1 Alfred St., Shop 3 in Goldfields House, Circular Quay.   ☎ **02/ 9247 2755.** Fax 02/9247 2756. www.wine.ptylimited.com.

This is one of the best places in the country to pick up Australian wines by the bottle or the case. The shop stocks a wide range of wines from all over Australia, including bottles from small boutique wineries you're unlikely to find anywhere else. Individual tastings are possible at any time, though there are formal tastings every Thursday and Friday from 4 to 6pm. Wine is exported all over the world from here, so if you want to send home a crate of your favorite, you can be assured it will arrive in one piece. The center owns the wine bar and bistro next door, which is open Monday to Saturday from 6am till late. You can drink here without dining.

13 Sydney After Dark

Australians are party animals when they're in the mood: whether it's a few beers around the barbie with friends or an all-night rage at a dance club, they're always on the lookout for the next event. You'll find alcohol plays a big part in the Aussie culture.

Get hold of the "Metro" section of the Friday *Sydney Morning Herald* or the "Seven Days" pullout from the Thursday *Daily Telegraph.*

THE PERFORMING ARTS

If you have an opportunity to see a performance in the Sydney Opera House, jump at it. The "House" is actually not that impressive inside, but the walk back after the show toward the ferry terminals at Circular Quay, with the Sydney Harbour Bridge lit up to your right and the crowd all around you debating the best part of this play or who dropped a beat in that performance—well, it's like hearing Gershwin on the streets of New York—you'll want the moment to stay with you forever. For details on Sydney's famous performing arts venue, see "The Opera House & Sydney Harbour," at the beginning of this chapter.

THE OPERA, SYMPHONY & BALLET

Australian Ballet. Level 15, 115 Pitt St. ☎ **02/9223 9522.** www.australianballet.com.au.

Based in Melbourne, the Australian Ballet tours the country with its performances. The Sydney season, at the Opera House, is from mid-March until the end of April. A second Sydney season runs from November to December.

Australian Chamber Orchestra. Opera Quays, 2 East Circular Quay. ☎ **02/9357 4111;** box office ☎ 02/8274 3888. www.aco.com.au.

Based in Sydney, this well known company performs at various venues around the city, from nightclubs to specialized music venues, including the Concert Hall in the Sydney Opera House.

Opera Australia. 480 Elizabeth St., Surry Hills. ☎ **02/9699 1099;** bookings ☎ 02/9319 1088. www.opera-australia.org.au.

Opera Australia performs at the Sydney Opera House's Opera Theatre. The opera season runs January to March and June to November.

Sydney Symphony Orchestra. Level 5, 52 William St., East Sydney. ☎ **02/9334 4644;** box office 02/9334 4600. www.symphony.org.au.

The renowned Edo de Waart conducts Sydney's finest symphony orchestra, which performs throughout the year in the Opera House's Concert Hall. The main symphony season runs from March to November, and there's a summer season in February.

THEATER

Sydney's blessed with plenty of theaters, too many to list here—check the *Sydney Morning Herald,* especially the Friday edition, for information on what's in production.

Belvoir Street Theatre. 25 Belvoir St., Surry Hills. ☎ **02/9699 3444.** Tickets around A$34 (U.S.$22.10).

The hallowed boards of the Belvoir are home to Company B, which pumps out powerful local and international plays upstairs in a wonderfully moody main theater, formerly part of a tomato sauce factory. Downstairs, a smaller venue generally shows more experimental productions, such as Aboriginal performances and dance.

Capital Theatre. 13–17 Campbell St., Haymarket (near Town Hall). ☎ **02/9320 5000.** Ticket prices vary.

Sydney's grandest theater plays host to major international and local performers like, (cough), Australian singing superstar Kylie Minogue. It's also been the Sydney home of musicals such as *Miss Saigon* and *My Fair Lady.*

Her Majesty's Theatre. 107 Quay St., Haymarket (near Central Station). ☎ **02/9212 3411.** Ticket prices average A$55–$75 (U.S.$35.75–$48.75).

A quarter of a century old, this large theater is still trawling in the big musicals. Huge productions that have run here include Evita and Phantom of the Opera.

Wharf Theatre. Pier 4, Hickson Rd., The Rocks. ☎ **02/9250 1777.** www.sydneytheatre. com.au. Ticket prices vary.

This wonderful theater is on a refurbished wharf on the edge of Sydney Harbour, just beyond the Harbour Bridge. The long walk from the entrance of the pier to the theater along creaky wooden floorboards builds up excitement. The Sydney Theatre Company, a group well worth seeing whatever production is running, is based here. Dinner before the show at the Wharf's restaurant offers special views of the harbor.

THE CLUB & MUSIC SCENE
ROCK

Metro. 624 George St. ☎ **02/9264 2666.** Cover varies.

A medium-size rock venue with space for 1,000, the Metro is the best place in Sydney to see local and international acts. Tickets sell out quickly.

JAZZ, FOLK & BLUES

The Basement. 29 Reiby Place, Circular Quay. ☎ **02/9251 2797.** www.basement.com.au. Cover A$15–$20 (U.S.$9.75–$13) for local acts, A$20–$40 (U.S.$13–$26) for international performers.

Australia's hottest jazz club also manages to squeeze in plenty of blues, folk, and funk. Pick up a leaflet showing who's playing when at the door. A new Blue Note Bar specializing in jazz opened in July 1998. Acts appear every night.

The Bridge Hotel & Brasserie. 135 Victoria St., Rozelle. ☎ **02/9810 1260.** Cover A$5–$25 (U.S.$3.25–$16.25).

Come on a Sunday afternoon and you're assured of getting the blues. Friday and Saturday nights offer blues, rock, or house music depending on the whim of the management. The three-level beer garden out the back is nice on a sunny day.

It's a Festival!

If you happen to be in Australia in January, pop along to one of the many events that take place as part of the annual **Sydney Festival.** The festival kicks off just after New Year's and continues until the last week of the month, with recitals, plays, films, and performances at venues throughout the city, including Town Hall, the Royal Botanic Gardens, the Sydney Opera House, and Darling Harbour. Some of the events are free. "Jazz in The Domain" and "Symphony in The Domain" are free outdoor performances held in the Royal Botanic Gardens; each event (which generally takes place on the third and fourth weekend in January) attracts tens of thousands of Sydneysiders. For more information on the Festival, contact **Festival Ticketec** (☎ 02/9266 4111; fax 02/9267 4460). You can also buy tickets and find out about performances on the Web at www.sydneyfestival.org.au.

The Harbourside Brasserie. Pier One, Hickson Rd., Walsh Bay (behind The Rocks). ☎ **02/ 9252 3000.** www.ozemail.com.au/~harbrass. Cover A$8–$20 (U.S.$5.20–$13) depending on performer.

Eat to the beat of soul and rhythm-and-blues at this not-bad eatery. Comedy nights attract big acts. Drinks are expensive.

Soup Plus. 383 George St. (near the Queen Victoria Building). ☎ **02/9299 7728.** Cover A$6 (U.S.$3.90) Mon–Thurs; A$28 (U.S.$18.20) Fri and Sat, including 2-course meal & show.

It seemed such a pity on my last visit to this cavernous jazz bar that the cover charge forced me to eat the bistro-style food on offer, which really was poor. However, some mellow blues cheered our nonplussed group in the end.

DANCE CLUBS

Clubs come and go, and change names and music, so check the latest by planning ahead with a phone call.

Blackmarket. 111–113 Regent St., Chippendale, at the corner of Meagher St. (5-min. walk from Central Station). ☎ **02/9698 8863.** Cover A$20 (U.S.$13).

This wacky place is known for its Friday night Hellfire Club (11pm–4am every first and third Friday), where Sydneysiders of all persuasions hang out to watch "nonstop fetish performances" and live S&M shows. It's attracts a fun-loving crowd from students to office workers (about 50/50 male and female). Some people wear bondage attire. There's some good music in the dark and moody interior. Ravers continue on, or drop in after working the nightshift, at the Day Club, offering dance music from 4am to 2pm on Saturday and 4am to 6pm on Sunday.

Bourbon & Beefsteak Bar. 24 Darlinghurst Rd., Kings Cross. ☎ **02/9358 1144.** Weekend cover charge varies, but roughly A$8–$10 (U.S.$5.20–$6.50) Fri–Sat.

Right in the middle of Sydney's red-light district, this 24-hour restaurant and nightspot freaks out to dance music downstairs nightly from 11pm to 5am. It's popular with both young backpackers and the 25-to-35 crowd.

Chinese Laundry. Sussex Street (turn right as you face the bridge from Cockle Bay across to Darling Harbour and it's a 2-min. walk. Below the Slip Inn bar.). ☎ **02/9299 4777.** Fri–Sat 11pm–4am. Cover A$12 (U.S.$7.80) Fri, A$18 (U.S.$11.70) Sat.

A couple of dance floors, one with rock walls to enhance the beat of the hip-hop, trance and dance. Club wear—i.e., dress to *un*impress.

Home. Cockle Bay Wharf, Darling Harbour. ☎ **02/9266 0600.** Cover A$25 (U.S.$16.25).

Cavelike in shape and feel with a balcony to look down upon the throng, Home has a reputation for bad bouncers—like the time the *Sydney Morning Herald* newspaper had a Christmas party there and even influential journalists were abused. Still it's managed to survive—hope you can. Funk, and heavy drum & bass style music, good for the serious clubber.

Mister Goodbar. 11a Oxford St., Paddington. ☎ **02/9360 6759.** Cover A$10 (U.S.$6.50) Wed, A$5 (U.S.$3.25) Thurs, A$10 (U.S.$6.50) Fri, and A$15 (U.S.$9.75) Sat.

A young, trendy, local crowd inhabits Mister Goodbar's two good-size dance floors, which offers a range of rap, funk, and hip-hop music Wednesday to Saturday.

Riche Nightclub. In the Sydney Hilton, 259 Pitt St. ☎ **02/9266 2000.** Cover A$11 (U.S.$7.15) Fri and Sun, A$16.50 (U.S.$10.73) Sat. Free for hotel guests.

This hot spot for dancing is popular with the local over-25 club set, as well as with hotel guests wanting to shake their booties to typical "dance" music. Open only Friday and Saturday.

Tantra. 169 Oxford St., Darlinghurst. ☎ **02/9331 7729.** Cover A$15 (U.S.$9.75) Fri and Sat; A$5 (U.S.$3.25) Sun.

"Upmarket nightclubbing for models and beautiful people from the [affluent] north shore of Sydney," is how the manager described this place. The interior is pseudo-Roman with lots of pillars. The club offers hardcore club/dance music. Dress code is fashionable, with a shirt collar required for men and no sneakers. It's "70s Boogie Wonderland" night Friday; house music Saturday, and "funky" house music Sunday.

GAY & LESBIAN CLUBS

With Sydney having one of the world's largest gay communities, it's no wonder there's a happening scene here. The center of it all is Oxford Street, though Newtown has established itself as a major gay hangout, too. For information on news and events concerning gays and lesbians pick up a copy of the *Sydney Star Observer*, available at arthouse cinemas and many cafes and stores around Oxford Street.

Albury Hotel. 2–6 Oxford St. (near Barcom Ave.). ☎ **02/9361 6555.** Cover A$5 (U.S.$3.25) Fri–Sat nights.

A Sydney institution, the Albury is a *grande dame* offering drag shows nightly in the public bar, and knockout Bloody Marys in the cocktail lounge. Dancing too.

Imperial Hotel. 35–37 Erskineville Rd., Erskineville (near Union St.). ☎ **02/9519 9899.** No cover.

A couple of minutes walk from King Street in Newtown, the Imperial is a no-attitude gay venue with a pool and cocktail bar out front and a raging cabaret venue out back. Sydney's best full-production drag shows happen late on Thursday, Friday, Saturday and Sunday, with dancing in between.

Newtown Hotel. 174 King St., Newtown. ☎ **02/9557 1329.** No cover.

The octagonal bar here is the center of a casual drinking and cruising scene. The place kicks up its heels during late-night drag shows and powerfully camp discos.

Taxi Club. 40 Flinders St., Darlinghurst (near Taylor Sq., Oxford St.). ☎ **02/9331 4256.** No cover.

"Tacky Club," as it's affectionately known, is another Sydney institution old pop and new pop.

BARS

Bondi Hotel. 178 Campbell Parade, Bondi Beach. ☎ **02/9130 3271.** No cover.

This huge, whitewashed conglomerate across the road from Bondi Beach offers pool upstairs, a casual beer garden outside, and a resident DJ Thursday to Sunday from 8pm to 4am. There's also a free nightclub on Friday nights. Watch yourself, too much drink and sun turns some people nasty here.

Passing the Bar

Most of Australia's drinking holes are known as "hotels," after the tradition of providing room and board alongside a good drink in the old days. You might hear them referred to as pubs. The term "bar" is used more for upscale hotels and trendy establishments. Bars close at various times, generally from midnight to around 3am.

Cocktails with a View

There's nothing better than a fabulous view rising above the lip of a full cocktail glass. One of the best places in town to drink in the view with your libations is **Horizon,** the cocktail bar at the very top of the multi-story ANA Hotel in The Rocks (☎ **02/9250 6000**). The views of The Rocks, Circular Quay, and out across Sydney Harbour are spectacular. It's open from noon to 1am daily, except on Sunday when it closes at midnight. Go at night for the city lights.

Another good option is having a cocktail (or a bottle of champagne) in the **Bennelong Bar** in the Sydney Opera House (☎ **02/9250 7548**). Sit next to the window and you'll be treated to a very special view of the Opera House sails, the boats coming into Circular Quay, and the best view of the Harbour Bridge in the city. Cocktails here average a steep A$11 (U.S.$7.15). At press time, the bar was being refurbished, and expected to open again in November, 2001.

For more dramatic 360-degree sky high views, head to **The Summit Skylounge,** Level 47, Australia Square, 265 George St. (☎ **02/9247 9777**). It's open daily from 6pm to around midnight, and cocktails costs A$12.50 (U.S.$8.13). The place slowly revolves, which can be a bit off-putting. Don't expect plush surrounds or particularly good service here either.

The Friend in Hand. 58 Cowper St, Glebe. ☎ **02/9660 2326.**

In the same location as the fantastically cheap Caesar's No Names spaghetti house, The Friend in Hand offers cheap drinks, poetry readings on Tuesday evenings from 8:30pm, trivia night on Thursdays, and the distinctly unusual Crab Racing Party every Wednesday from around 8pm. Crab fanciers buy a crustacean for around A$4 (U.S.$2.60), give it a name, and send it off to do battle in a race against around 30 others. There are heats and finals, and victorious crustaceans win their owners prizes.

Henry the Ninth Bar. In the Sydney Hilton, 259 Pitt St. ☎ **02/9266 2000.**

This mock-Tudor drinking hole gets busy on Friday and Saturday nights. They serve up good ales in an oaky atmosphere. An Irish band whips up the patrons on Thursday and Friday nights, and a cover band does the same on Wednesday and Saturday nights. A good value happy hour brings beer prices tumbling Monday to Thursday from 5:30 to 7:30pm, Friday from 5:30 to 8:30pm, and Saturday from 8 to 10pm.

Hero of Waterloo Hotel. 81 Lower Fort St., The Rocks. ☎ **02/9252 4553.**

This sandstone landmark, built in 1845, was once allegedly the stalking ground of press gangs, who'd whack unsuspecting landlubbers on the head, push them down a trapdoor out the back, and cart them out to sea. Today, this strangely shaped sandstone drinking hole is popular with the locals, and hosts old-time jazz bands (the musicians are often in their 70s and 80s) on Saturday and Sunday afternoons from 1:30 to 6:30pm, and Irish and cover bands Friday to Sunday evenings starting at 8:30pm.

Jacksons on George. 178 George St., The Rocks. ☎ **02/9247 2727.** Cover A$10 (U.S.$6.50) for nightclub Fri–Sat after 10pm.

This place has four floors of drinking, eating, dancing, and pool playing, and is popular with tourists and after work office staff. Pool is expensive here at A$3 (U.S.$1.95) a game (you'll need to ask the rules, as Australians have their own), and drinks have a nasty habit of going up in price without warning as the evening wears on. The nightclub plays dance music, and there's a smart/casual dress code. Happy hour is Monday to Friday from 5 to 7pm, when drinks cost around one-third less than normal.

Lord Dudley Hotel. 236 Jersey Rd., Woollahra. ☎ **02/9327 5399.**

The best way to get to this great English-style pub is via the Edgecliff CityRail station (between Kings Cross and Bondi Junction). From there, bear right along the edge of the bus station, walk up the hill for 5 minutes and then take a right onto Jersey Road—ask the railway staff for the correct exit if you can find anyone working. The Lord Dudley has the best atmosphere of just about any drinking hole in Sydney, with log fires in winter, couches to relax in, three bars, and a restaurant.

Lord Nelson Hotel. At Kent and Argyle sts., The Rocks. ☎ **02/9251 4044.**

Another Sydney sandstone landmark, the Lord Nelson rivals the Hero of Waterloo for the title of "Sydney's oldest pub." A drink here is a must for any visitor. The drinks are sold English-style, in pints and half-pints, and the landlord makes his own prize-winning beers. Of these beers, Three Sheets is the most popular, but if you can handle falling over on your way home you might want to try a drop of Quail (a pale beer), Victory (based on an English bitter), and a dark beer called Admiral. You can get some good pub grub here, too. Upstairs there's a more formal brasserie.

Marble Bar. In the Sydney Hilton, 259 Pitt St. ☎ **02/9266 2000.**

Once part of a hotel demolished in the 1970s, the Marble Bar is unique in that it's the only grand cafe-style drinking hole in Australia. With oil paintings, marble columns, and brass everywhere, it's the very picture of 15th-century Italian Renaissance architecture. It's a tourist attraction in itself. Live music, generally jazz or soul, is played here Tuesday through Saturday beginning at 8:30pm. Dress smart on Friday and Saturday evenings. Drinks are normally expensive, but the happy hour (daily from 7–9pm) cuts prices down to what you'd pay for a regular drink elsewhere.

The Mercantile. 25 George St., The Rocks. ☎ **02/9247 3570.**

Sydney's original Irish bar is scruffy and loud when the music's playing in the evening, and an essential stop on any self-respecting pub crawl in The Rocks. The Guinness is some of the best you'll taste in Sydney. Irish bands kick off every night around 8pm.

Slip Inn. Sussex Street, a 2-min. walk towards the city from the Town Hall/Cockle Bay side of the pedestrian bridge across to Darling Harbour. ☎ **02/9299 4777.**

This bar and bistro is a popular city place to drink and meet. There's a garden bar downstairs set in a courtyard, along with a trattoria selling pizzas. Upstairs there's a Thai bistro open for lunch and a large square bar. It's crowded on Friday evenings, but you'll never feel like a sardine.

Watsons Bay Hotel. 1 Military Rd., Watsons Bay. ☎ **02/9337 4299.**

If it's a sunny afternoon don't waste it, get over to Watsons Bay for the best food you'll find in the sun anywhere. The beer garden serves very good seafood and BBQ meat dishes, while you sip your expensive wine or beer overlooking the harbor. Nearby are the fabulous Doyles Wharf Restaurant and Doyles at the Beach takeaway.

MOVIES

The city's major movie houses, **Hoyts** (☎ **13 27 00** in Australia), **Greater Union** (☎ **02/9267 8666**), and **Village** (☎ **02/9264 6701**), are next to each other on George Street just past Town Hall. They tend to show big budget movie releases. The best arthouse cinema is the **Hayden Orpheum Picture Palace,** 380 Military Rd.,

Cremorne (☎ **02/9908 4344**). This eight-screen Art Deco gem is an experience in itself, especially on Saturday and Sunday evenings when a Wurlitzer pops up from the center of the Cinema 2 stage, and a musician in a tux gives a stirring rendition of times gone by. Eat "Jaffas," round candy-coated chocolates, if you want to fit in. Tickets are A$14 (U.S.$9.10) adults, A$9 children; Tuesday A$7.50 (U.S.$4.88) adults, A$4.50 (U.S.$2.93) children.

THE CASINO

Star City. 80 Pyrmont St., Pyrmont (adjacent to Darling Harbour). ☎ **02/9777 9000.** No cover. Open 24 hrs. Ferry: Pyrmont (Darling Harbour). Monorail: Casino.

This huge entertainment complex has fifteen bars, twelve restaurants, two theaters—the Showroom, which presents Las Vegas-style revues, and the Lyric, Sydney's largest theater—and a huge complex of retail shops. All the usual gambling tables are here, in four main gambling areas. In all there are 2,500 slot machines to gobble your change.

New South Wales

5

by Marc Llewellyn

Mountains, forests, beaches, Outback, rivers, country, and Sydney—
these are the seven wonders of New South Wales. With so much to see,
you're not going to get to all the major attractions in one go, so you
must prioritize. If you have just a few days to spare, you should head
out to the Blue Mountains, part of the Great Dividing Range that separates the lush eastern coastal strip from the arid interior. Although
they are more hills than mountains, they are spectacular, with eucalyptus trees, deep river valleys, waterfalls, and cliffs. Another option is
to spend a day in the vineyards of the lower Hunter (the Hunter Valley). If you have a few more days, I recommend heading to Barrington
Tops National Park, north of the Hunter, for a taste of rain forest and
native animals, or down to the pristine beaches of Jervis Bay on the
south coast for gorgeous scenery and some great bushwalks.

For longer trips, you have three main touring options. You can head
north toward the Queensland border on the 964-kilometer (600-mile)
route to Brisbane. On the way you'll pass pretty seaside towns,
deserted beaches, and tropical hinterland. You can also travel along the
south coast 1,032 kilometers (640 miles) to Melbourne. Along the way
are some spectacular beaches, quaint hamlets, opportunities to spot
dolphins and whales, and national parks. If you want to experience
another side of Australia—the Outback—then head west across the
Blue Mountains. You are sure to see plenty of kangaroos, emus, reptiles, and giant wedge-tailed eagles. The main Outback destinations are
the opal mining town of Lightning Ridge, where you can meet some
of the most eccentric *fair dinkum* ("authentic" or "genuine") Aussies
anywhere.

EXPLORING THE STATE

VISITOR INFORMATION   The Sydney Visitors Centre, 106
George St., The Rocks (☎ **13 20 77** in Australia; www.tourism.nsw.
gov.au) will give you general information on what to do and where to
stay throughout the state. Otherwise, **Tourism New South Wales**
(☎ **02/9931 1111**) will direct you to the regional tourist office in the
town or area you are interested in.

GETTING AROUND   By Car   From Sydney, the **Pacific Highway**
heads along the north coast into Queensland, and the **Princes Highway** hugs the south coast and runs into Victoria. The **Sydney-
Newcastle Freeway** connects Sydney with its industrial neighbor and
the vineyards of the Hunter. **The Great Western Highway** and the

M4 Motorway head west to the Blue Mountains, while the **M5** Motorway and the **Hume Highway** are the quickest (and least interesting) ways to get to Melbourne.

The state's automobile association, the **National Roads and Motorists' Association (NRMA),** 151 Clarence St., Sydney (☎ **13 11 22** in Australia), offers free maps and touring guides to members of overseas motoring associations, including the AAA in the United States, the CAA in Canada, the AA and RAC in the United Kingdom, and the NZAA in New Zealand.

By Train   Countrylink (☎ **13 22 32** in Australia) trains go to most places of interest in the state, as far south as Melbourne in Victoria and across the border into southern Queensland. Countrylink also has special rates for car hire through Thrifty.

In 1999, one of the great trains of the world, *The Ghan,* began operating from Sydney to Alice Springs. It's high-priced considering the most expensive return flight to Alice Springs costs only marginally more than a single on *The Ghan,* but at least you get to see a slice of the NSW countryside (when you're not asleep). First-class sleepers cost A$1,199 (U.S.$779.35) for adults and A$816 ($530.40) for children one-way. Otherwise, it's A$899 (U.S.$584.35) for adults and A$540 (U.S.$351) for children in a so-called economy sleeper, and A$390 (U.S.$253.50) for adults and A$176 (U.S.$114.40) for children in an economy seat. Call **Great Southern Railways** (☎ **08/8213 4530**) for more information and bookings, or check out the timetables and fares on their website (www.gsr.com.au/fares.htm).

By Plane   Qantas (☎ **13 13 13** in Australia) and **Eastern Australia Airlines** (book through Qantas) fly to most major cities and towns within the state.

1 The Blue Mountains

Although today the ✪ **Blue Mountains** are where Sydneysiders go to escape the humidity and crowds of the city and suburbs, in the fledgling days of the colony, the mountains posed one of the most difficult barriers to early exploration. In 1813, three explorers managed to conquer the cliffs, valleys, and dense forest, and cross the mountains (which are really a series of hills covered in bush and ancient fern trees) to the plains beyond. There they found land needed for grazing and farming. The Great Western Highway and Bells Line of Road are the access roads through the region today—winding and steep in places, they are surrounded by Blue Mountains and Wollemi national parks.

The area is known for its spectacular scenery, particularly the cliff-top views into the valleys of gum trees and across to craggy outcrops that tower up from the valley floor. It's colder up here than down on the plains, and the clouds can sweep in and fill the canyons with mist in minutes, while waterfalls cascade down sheer drops, spraying the fern trees that cling to the gullies. You'll need at least a couple of days up here to get the best out of it—a single-day tour can only just scratch the surface.

The Blue Mountains area is also one of Australia's best-known adventure playgrounds. Rock climbing, caving, abseiling, bushwalking, mountain biking, horseback riding, and canoeing are all practiced here throughout the year.

Blue Haze

The Blue Mountains derive their name from the ever-present blue haze that is caused by light striking the droplets of eucalyptus oil that evaporate from the leaves of the dense surrounding forest.

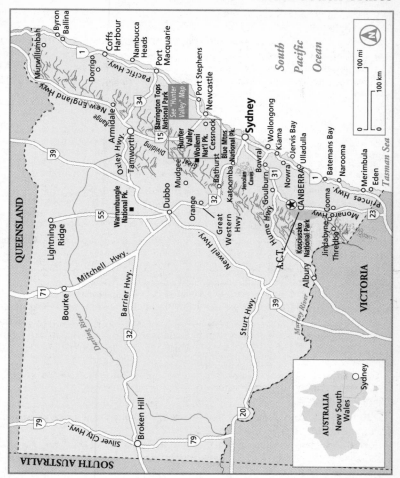

BLUE MOUNTAIN ESSENTIALS

VISITOR INFORMATION   You can pick up maps, walking guides, and other information and book accommodations at **Blue Mountains Tourism,** with locations at Echo Point Road, Katoomba, NSW 2780 (☎ **1300/653 408** in Australia or 02/4739 6266), and on the Great Western Highway at Glenbrook, a small settlement 61 kilometers (42 miles) from Sydney (same telephone number). The Katoomba information center is an attraction in itself, with giant glass windows overlooking a gum forest and cockatoos and lorikeets feeding on seed dispensers. Be sure to pick up a copy of the *Blue Mountains Pocket Guide,* a free guide to dining, accommodations, bushwalking, and entertainment in the area. Both offices are open from 9am to 5pm daily (the office at Glenbrook closes at 4:30pm on Saturday and Sunday).

The **National Park Shop,** Heritage Centre, the end of Govetts Leap Rd., Blackheath (☎ **02/4787 8877;** www.npws.nsw.gov.au), is run by the National Parks and Wildlife Service and offers detailed information about the Blue Mountains National

---
Travel Tips

If you can, try to visit the Blue Mountains on **weekdays,** when most Sydneysiders are at work and the prices are much lower. Note, too, that the colder winter months (June, July, and Aug) are the busiest time in the Blue Mountains. This period is known as **Yuletide**—the locals' version of the Christmas period, when most places offer traditional Christmas dinners and roaring log fires.

Park. The staff can also arrange personalized guided tours of the mountains. It's open daily from 9am to 4:30pm (closed Christmas).

GUIDED TOURS FROM SYDNEY   Many private bus operators offer day trips from Sydney, but it's important to shop around because some offer a guided coach tour where you just stretch your legs occasionally, while others get you out of the bus with longish bushwalks. One highly recommended operator is **Oz Trek Adventure Tours,** P.O. Box 319, Potts Point, NSW 2011 (☎ **02/9360 3444;** fax 02/9664 9134; www.oztrek.com.au; info@oztrek.com.au). Their trips include a tour of the Olympic Site, a visit to Glenbrook National Park (where you'll see kangaroos and wallabies in the wild), tours of all the major Blue Mountain sites, and a 1½-hour bushwalk. It costs just A$54 (U.S.$35.10) for adults and A$43 (U.S.$27.95) for kids.

Wonderbus (☎ **02/9555 9800;** fax 02/9555 1345; www.wonderbus.com.au; info@wonderbus.com.au) tours are good fun for all ages and include most of the major sites and a short bushwalk. Day tours leave Sydney at approximately 7:30am from The Rocks and 8:15am from Central Station (Bay 15 on Pitt Street) and return after 7pm and cost A$70 (U.S.$45.50) for adults and A$50 ($32.50) for children. Ask about discounts for two people. Overnight packages are also available.

Cox's River Escapes, P.O. Box 81, Leura, NSW 2780 (☎ **02/4784 1621** or mobile 0407 400 121; fax 02/4784 2450), offer highly recommended tours for those wanting to get off the beaten track. Half-day trips with morning or afternoon tea cost A$110 (U.S.$71.50); full-day trips with morning tea, lunch, and afternoon refreshments at entry into Jenolan Caves cost A$220 (U.S.$143).

AAT Kings, Shop 1, corner of Alfred St. and ferry wharf no. 1, Circular Quay (☎ **02/9518 6095;** fax 02/9518 6575; www.aatkings.com), operates three big bus tours of the mountains, taking in all the sights, with a couple of walks included. One includes a visit to Jenolan Caves. Tours range in cost from A$85 to $113 (U.S.$55.25–$73.45) for adults, and A$43 to $86 (U.S.$27.95–$55.90) for children. Another large operator, **Australian Pacific Tours** (☎ **1300 655 965;** fax 02/9660 5016), offers a similar trip with a visit to the Australian Wildlife Park and a quick visit to the Sydney Olympic site at Homebush Bay. This tour costs A$94 (U.S.$61.10) for adults and A$47 (U.S.$30.55) for children. If you hate big-group travel then choose another option.

BUSHWALKING & OTHER ACTIVE ENDEAVORS

Whereas almost every other activity costs money, bushwalking (hiking) is the exception to the rule that nothing in life is free. There are some 50 **walking trails** in the Blue Mountains, ranging from routes you can cover in 15 minutes to the three-day ✪ **Six Foot Track** that starts just outside Katoomba and finishes at Jenolan Caves. If you are planning to do some bushwalking, I highly recommend picking up a copy of *Sydney and Beyond—Eighty-Six Walks in NSW* by Andrew Mevissen (Macstyle Publishing). It features eight walks in the Blue Mountains, from easy 1-hour treks to 6-hour tramps. Buy it at bookshops and tourist information centers.

Great Australian Walks, 81 Elliot Street, Balmain, NSW 2041 (☎ **1300 360 499** in Australia or 02/9555 7580; fax 02/9810 6429; walkaus@nsw.bigpond.net.au), is a superb operator offering walks in the Blue Mountains. I had great fun on their three-day Six Foot Track Walk from Katoomba to Jenolan Caves. Though not a wilderness trek, it goes through rain forest and gum forests and traverses pretty farming country.

One of the best adventure operators in the area is **High 'n' Wild,** 3/5 Katoomba St., Katoomba, NSW 2780. ☎ **02/4782 6224;** fax 02/4782 6143; www.high-n-wild.com.au) offers a series of canyoning expeditions, taking in scenic rain forest gullies and caverns. Generally there's a bit of swimming and plenty of walking, wading and squeezing through tight spaces involved——and sometimes abseiling.

If you really want to test your head for heights though then try High 'n' Wild's 150-meter (480-ft.) "Mega Jump"—the highest continuous abseil in the Southern Hemisphere. This heart-pumping descent down a sheer cliff is suitable for the fearless beginner, but they assure me you soon settle in by learning the ropes on the 10-story-high junior slopes beforehand.

If that's too much to handle, you could always try a day's **rafting** on an inflatable airbed between huge towering rock walls on the Wollangambe River. There are a few minor rapids to navigate, and the bushwalk down to the river and back up again can be a little testing, but it's certainly suitable for a family outing. Abseiling costs from A$69 (U.S.$44.85) and canyoning from A$85 ($55.25). Airbed adventures cost A$169 (U.S.$109.85).

Before setting off on a bushwalk, always tell someone where you are going—plenty of people get lost every year. For other outdoor safety advice, see "Down Under Health, Safety & Outdoor Etiquette," in chapter 2.

Other excellent adventure operators are **The Blue Mountains Adventure Company,** P.O Box 242, Katoomba, NSW 2780. (☎ **02/4782 1271;** fax 02/4782 1277; www.bmac.com.au), located in Katoomba at 84a Bathurst Rd.; and the **Australian School of Mountaineering,** 166b Katoomba St., Katoomba, NSW 2780 (☎ **02/ 4782 2014;** fax 02/4782 5787). Both operators can organize rock climbing, abseiling, and canyoning expeditions, while the Blue Mountains Adventure Company also offers caving and mountain biking, and the Australian School of Mountaineering offers bushcraft and survival training. Expect to pay around A$100 (U.S.$65) for a full-day's introductory rock climbing course including abseiling, and between A$99 to $125 (U.S.$64.35–$81.25) for a day's canyoning.

If you feel like some adventure on your own, you could hire a mountain bike from ✪ **Cycletech,** 182 Katoomba St., Katoomba (☎ **02/4782 2800;** fax 02/4782 4550; cycletech@pnc.com.au). Standard mountain bikes cost A$19 (U.S.$12.35) for half a day and A$27.50 (U.S.$17.88) for a full day (superior front-suspension mountain bikes cost A$27.50 (U.S.$17.88) for a half day and A$49.50 (U.S.$32.18) for a full day).

KATOOMBA: GATEWAY TO THE BLUE MOUNTAINS
114km (71 miles) W of Sydney

Katoomba (pop. 11,200) is the largest town in the Blue Mountains and the focal point of the Blue Mountains National Park. It used to be a hard journey by horse and cart from Sydney in the 1870s, but these days it's a far easier 1½- to 2-hour trip by train, bus, or car. Today it's a low-socio-economic pocket in a very affluent region, with one of the highest unemployment rates in the State.

GETTING THERE   From Sydney travel along **Parramatta Road** and turn off onto the M4 motorway. Frequent rail services connect Sydney to Katoomba from Central Station; contact **CityRail** (☎ **13 15 00**) or **Countrylink** (☎ **13 22 32**) for details. The train trip takes 2 hours, leaving from platforms 12 and 13 of Central Station. Trains leave almost hourly, stopping at Katoomba, then at Mt. Victoria and Lithgow. An adult day-return (round-trip) ticket costs A$11.80 (U.S.$7.67) off-peak and A$20 (U.S.$13) during commuter hours. A child's day-return round-trip ticket costs A$3 (U.S.$1.95).

GETTING AROUND   If you take the train to Katoomba from Sydney, walk up the stairs from the station onto Katoomba Street; you'll see the **Savoy,** a former theatre now a restaurant. Coaches operated by **Mountain Link** (☎ **1800/801 577** in Australia or 02/4782 3333) meet most trains from Sydney outside this theater or opposite at the Carrington Hotel and take passengers to the main Blue Mountains attractions, including **Echo Point,** the **Three Sisters,** the **Skyway, Leura Village,** the **Gordon Falls,** and **Blackheath,** as well as other points. Single-ride tickets to one destination cost between A$1.40 and $6.30 (U.S.91¢–$4.10) based on distance. **The Blue Mountains Bus Company** (☎ **02/4782 4213**) also runs buses between

Katoomba, Leura, Wentworth Falls, and as far as Woodford every hour. Buses leave from either the Carrington Hotel or the Savoy. Fares are similar to Mountain Link's.

You can also connect with the **Blue Mountains Explorer Bus.** This red double-decker bus leaves from outside Katoomba train station every half hour from 9:30am. It stops at 27 major attractions and various resorts, craft galleries, and tearooms. You can get on and off as often as you want. Tickets cost A$22 (U.S.$14.30) for adults and A$11 (U.S.$7.15) for children. Weekdays you can take a 3-hour Blue Mountains Highlights Tour, which costs A$40 (U.S.$26) for adults, A$30 (U.S.$19.50) for students, and A$20 (U.S.$13) for children. Ask about family prices. Tours leave Katoomba train station Monday through Friday at 10:30am, 11:30am, and 2pm. For details contact **Fantastic Aussie Tours** (☎ **1300/300 915** in Australia, or 02/4782 1866; www.fantastic-aussie-tours.com.au).

Combined rail/bus tours from Sydney can be purchased at any **CityRail** (☎ **13 15 00** in Australia) station.

EXPLORING THE AREA

The most visited and photographed attraction in the Blue Mountains are the unusual rock formations known as the ✪ **Three Sisters.** The best place to view these astonishing-looking pinnacles is from **Echo Point Road,** right opposite the Blue Mountains Tourism office. Other good lookouts include Evans Lookout, Govetts Leap, and Hargreaves Lookout, all at Blackheath (see below).

One thing you have to do is take a ride on the ✪ **Scenic Railway,** the world's steepest. It consists of a carriage on rails that is lowered 415 meters (1,360 ft.) down into the **Jamison Valley** at a maximum incline of 52 degrees. Originally it was used to transport coal and shale from the mines below. The trip only takes a few minutes; at the bottom there are some excellent walks through forests of ancient tree ferns. Another popular attraction is the **Skyway,** a cable car that travels 300 meters (990 ft.) above the Jamison Valley. The trip takes 6 minutes round-trip. The Scenic Railway and the Skyway (☎ **02/4782 2699**) each cost A$8 (U.S.$5.20) round-trip for adults and A$3 (U.S.$1.95) for children, and operate from 9am to 5pm daily (last trip at 4:50pm). They leave from the ticket office at 1 Violet St., Katoomba (follow the signs).

Canyons, waterfalls, underground rivers—the Blue Mountains has them all, and before you experience them in person you can catch them on the screen in *The Edge* at the **MAXVISION Cinema,** 225–237 Great Western Hwy., Katoomba (☎ **02/ 4782 8900.** The special effects shown on the screen 18 meters (59 ft.) high and 24 meters (79 ft.) wide make you feel like you're part of the action. The 38-minute film is shown every 40 to 50 minutes from 10am to 5pm. Tickets are A$12.50 (U.S.$8.13) for adults, A$10.50 (U.S.$6.83) for students, and A$7.50 (U.S.$4.88) for children. The cinema is a short walk from the train station. Recent release movies are shown on

---

Seeing the Blue Mountains from the Back of a Harley

A thrilling way to see the Blue Mountains is on the back of a chauffeur-driven Harley Davidson. **Blue Thunder Bike Tours** (☎ **02/4571 1154;** fax 02/4571 2692) leave from Manly Wharf in Sydney (but they'll pick you up anywhere in the city). Rides cost A$80 (U.S.$52) for the first hour, A$130 (U.S.$84.50) for 2 hours, A$255 (U.S.$165.75) for half a day, and A$360 (U.S.$234) for a full day with lunch. The same company runs **Hot Heritage Tours,** operating out of the Blue Mountains (pickup anywhere in the Mountains), for the same prices.

part of the giant screen in the evenings. There is a restaurant and a snack bar on the premises.

WHERE TO STAY

There are plenty of places to stay throughout the Blue Mountains, including historic guest houses, B&Bs, resorts, motels, and homestays.

✪ **The Cecil.** 108 Katoomba St., Katoomba, NSW 2780. ☎ **02/4782 1411.** Fax 02/4782 5364. 23 units, 4 with bathroom. Weekend A$95–$125 (U.S.$61.75–$81.25) double; midweek A$80–$115 (U.S.$52–$74.75) double. Rates include full breakfast. Children under 15 half price. Ask about multinight midweek discounts and tour packages. AE, BC, MC, V.

Right in the center of town, this lovely old property has comfortable rooms. Rooms above the second floor (numbers 30 to 35) on the east side have great views, with room 31 offering the best views—a breathtaking vista across the mountains. Five rooms have small, attached bathrooms with showers. There's a cozy lounge area with a TV, a game room with pool and table tennis tables, a good library, and a small terraced garden out the back. Three-course dinners cost A$25 (U.S.$16.25). The breakfasts are huge enough to sustain you for a whole day's walking.

Echo Point Holiday Villas. 36 Echo Point Rd., Katoomba, NSW 2780. ☎ **02/4782 3275.** Fax 02/4782 7030. 5 villas, 2 cottages (all with shower only). TV. Fri, Sat, and public holidays A$128 (U.S.$83.20) villa; Sun–Thurs A$111 (U.S.$72.15) villa. Weekend A$220 (U.S.$143) cottage; midweek A$180 (U.S.$117) cottage. Linen A$6 (U.S.$3.90) extra per person in villas. Minimum 2-night stay required. Extra person A$12 (U.S.$7.80). AE, BC, DC, MC, V.

These are the closest self-contained accommodations to the Three Sisters Lookout. The two front-facing villas are the best because of their mountain views. Some villas have one double and two single beds, plus a foldout double bed in the lounge room. Bathrooms contain a shower, a washing machine and dryer, and a hairdryer. The villas come with full kitchens, and there are barbecue facilities in the backyard. The cottage is also self-contained and has a bathroom, central heating, and access to nice gardens.

Katoomba Mountain Lodge. 31 Lurline St., Katoomba, NSW 2780. ☎/fax **02/4782 3933.** 23 units, none with bathroom. Sun, Mon–Thurs A$58 (U.S.$37.70) double; Fri–Sat A$78 (U.S.$50.70) double. A$11–$15 (U.S.$7.15–$9.75) dorm bed. AE, BC, DC, MC, V.

This 2½-star property is quite cozy, with rooms looking out across the mountains. Dorm rooms are clean and come with 3 to 6 beds. Doubles are basic and lack a TV, but are adequate for a couple of nights. All share bathrooms. On the premises you'll find a TV lounge with a log fire, a BYO dining room, laundry, and game room. The staff can arrange tour packages. Breakfast costs an additional A$8 (U.S.$5.20) per person, dinner and breakfast costs an extra A$28 (U.S.$18.20) per person.

Katoomba YHA Hostel. 66 Waratah St. (at Lurline St.), Katoomba, NSW 2780. ☎ **02/ 4782 1416.** Fax 02/4782 6203. 80 beds in 16 rooms, most with bathroom. A$14–$19 (U.S.$9.10–$12.35) dorm bed; A$50 (U.S.$32.50) double/twin. Family rates available and guests under 18 half price. BC, MC, V.

This former guesthouse is fine for a couple of nights, if you don't mind things a little less than luxurious. It's friendly, clean, comfortable, well located, and has log fires in the living areas, a communal kitchen and dining room, and a laundry. The double rooms are simple, with either a double, twin, or bunk beds and not much else but a small bathroom. The dorms rooms accommodate from 4 to 12 people; the cheaper dorm rooms on the top floor share bathrooms.

Three Explorers Motel. 197 Lurline St., Katoomba, NSW 2780. ☎ **02/4782 1733.** Fax 02/4782 1146. 14 units. TV. Fri–Sat A$128 (U.S.$83.20) double; A$200 (U.S.$130) spa suite. Sun–Thurs A$99 (U.S.$64.35) double; A$160 (U.S.$104) spa suite. Public holidays A$132

(U.S.$85.80) double. Ask about packages and discounts for Aussie auto club members. Extra adult A$16 (U.S.$10.40) in double, A$22 (U.S.$14.30) in spa suite. Extra child under 13 A$13 (U.S.$8.45). AE, BC, DC, MC, V.

Staying in a motel isn't the ideal Blue Mountains experience, but it does offer some advantages. Rooms here vary in size, from those just large enough to fit one queen-size bed to large family units with six beds. The main selling point is that it's just a five-minute walk from Echo Point; it's also very quiet. Standard rooms are comfy and come with an attached bathroom with shower. The spa suites have a queen-size bed in the living area, a separate bedroom with a second queen-size bed, and a large bathroom. Breakfast can be served in your room, and each night there is a choice of four main courses costing around A$14 (U.S.$9.10). There's also a laundry and video rental.

Worth a Splurge

○ **Avonleigh Guest House.** 174 Lurline St., Katoomba, NSW 2780. ☎ **02/4782 1534.** Fax 02/4782 5688. 12 units. Weekend A$125–$160 (U.S.$81.25–$104) per person double including breakfast and dinner; midweek A$65 (U.S.$42.25) per person double including breakfast, A$105 (U.S.$68.25) per person double including breakfast and dinner. AE, BC, DC, MC,

This three-star 1902 property is a cozy mountain hangout with a Victorian feel. The rooms are comfortable, with antique furniture, a queen or double bed, and a nice-sized bathroom with a shower and a tub, or just a shower. The living room has high ceilings, velvet chairs, double cameo couches, and sprays of dried flowers. There's free tea and coffee in the lounge all day, and in cooler months there are open fires as well as central heating. Plenty of American and German guests stay here. Children are not encouraged, and the stairs could make it difficult for travelers with disabilities.

WHERE TO DINE

Katoomba Street has many ethnic dining choices, whether you're hungry for Greek, Chinese, or Thai. Restaurants in the Blue Mountains are generally more expensive than equivalent places in Sydney.

○ **Lindsay's.** 122 Katoomba St., Katoomba. ☎ **02/4782 2753.** Reservations recommended. Main courses A$14–$23.50 (U.S.$9.10–$15.28). AE, BC, JCB, MC, V. Open for lunch on weekends from noon–3pm; dinner daily 6pm–midnight. INTERNATIONAL.

Swiss chef Beat Ettlin has been making waves in Katoomba ever since he left some of the best European restaurants behind to try his hand at dishes such as pan-fried crocodile nibbles on pumpkin scones with a ginger dipping sauce. The food in this upscale, New York–style speakeasy is as glorious as its decor—Tiffany lamps, sketches by Australian artist Norman Lindsay, and booths lining the walls. The three-level restaurant is warmed by a cozy fire surrounded by an antique lounge stage and resounds every night to piano, classical music, or a jazz band. The menu changes every few weeks, but a recent popular dish was grilled veal medallions topped with Balmain bugs (small, saltwater crayfish), with potato and béarnaise sauce.

Paragon Café. 65 Katoomba St., Katoomba. ☎ **02/4782 2928.** Menu items vary in price. AE, MC, V. Tues–Fri 10am–3:30pm, Sat and Sun 10am–4pm. CAFE.

The Paragon has been a Blue Mountains' institution since it opened for business in 1916. Inside, it's decked out with dark wood paneling, bas-relief figures guarding the booths, and chandeliers. The homemade soups are delicious. The cafe also serves pies, pastas, grills, seafood, waffles, cakes, and a Devonshire tea of scones and cream.

The Pavilion at Echo Point. 35 Echo Point Rd., Katoomba. ☎ **02/4782 7055.** Main courses A$16 (U.S.$10.40). AE, BC, DC, MC, V. Mon–Fri 8:30am–5pm, Sat–Sun 8am–6pm. NATIVE AUSTRALIAN.

This miniature version of Sydney's Queen Victoria Building is so close to Echo Point that it looks like a shove will send it tumbling over the edge. Light fills the three-story building through a rooftop glass atrium and huge windows on the top two floors. On the ground level are a few stores; on the middle level is a food court with a burger/pie outlet, a bakery, and an ice cream counter; and on the top level is a cafe serving lots of native Australian wildlife such as kangaroo and crocodile, with a few salads thrown in for those who prefer to look at, rather than eat, the native wildlife.

TrisElies. 287 Bathurst Rd, Katoomba. ☎ **02/4782 4026.** Fax 4782 1128 Reservations recommended. Main courses A$17–$25.50. (U.S.$11.05–$16.58). Fri–Sun noon–midnight, Mon–Thurs 5pm–midnight. AE, MC, JCB, V. TRADITIONAL GREEK.

Perhaps it's the belly dancers and the plate smashing, or the smell of moussaka, but as soon as you walk into this lively eatery you feel like you've been transported to an Athenian *taverna*. The restaurant folds out onto three tiers of tables, all with a good view of the stage where every night Greek or international performances take place. The food is solid Greek fare—souvlaki, dips, fried cheese, Greek salads, casseroles like mother could have made, whitebait, and sausages in red wine—with a few Italian and Spanish extras. If it's winter, come in to warm up beside one of two log fires.

LEURA

107km (66 miles) W of Sydney; 3km W (2 miles) of Katoomba

The fashionable capital of the Blue Mountains, Leura is known for its gardens, its pretty old buildings (many of them holiday homes for Sydneysiders), and its cafes and restaurants. The National Trust has classified Leura's main street as an urban conservation area. Just outside Leura is the sublime **Point Lookout,** which has spectacular and unusual views of the Three Sisters formation in Katoomba. From the southern end of Leura Mall, a cliff drive takes you all the way back to Echo Point in Katoomba; along the way you'll get some spectacular views across the Jamison Valley.

A TEA ROOM

Bygone Beautys Tea Room. 20–22 Grose St., Leura. ☎ **02/4784 3117.** Daily 10am–5pm. Devonshire tea A$6.50 (U.S.$4.23); light meals around A$8 (U.S.$5.20), afternoon tea A$12.50 (U.S.$8.13) per person or A$22 (U.S.$14.30) for 2 people. BC, MC, V. Closed Christmas and New Year's. LIGHT MEALS/DEVONSHIRE TEA.

Everyone has to try a Devonshire tea in the Blue Mountains. It's part of the experience. This tea room is set amid the largest private antiques emporium in the Blue Mountains, yet it's still cozy in an Edwardian kind of way. As well as scones and cream, you can treat yourself to a light lunch— soup, chicken casserole, a beef curry with rice—or a traditional afternoon tea, with sandwiches, scones, homemade biscuits and cakes, all served on fine china and silver. You can browse the antiques when you finish dining.

✪ WENTWORTH FALLS

103km (62 miles) from Sydney; 7km (4 miles) from Katoomba

This pretty little town has numerous craft and antique shops, but the area is principally known for its magnificent 935-foot-high waterfall, situated in Falls Reserve. On the far side of the falls is the ✪ **National Pass Walk**—one of the best in the Blue Mountains. It's cut into a cliff face with overhanging rock faces on one side and sheer drops on the other. The views over the Jamison Valley are spectacular. The track takes you down to the base of the falls to the **Valley of the Waters.** Climbing up out of the valley is quite a bit more difficult, but just as rewarding.

WHERE TO STAY

If you want to stay in a historical cottage, then consider **Bygone Beautys Cottages,** 20-22 Grose St., Leura, NSW 2780 (☎ **02/4784 3117;** fax 02/4781 3078; www. bygonebeautys.com.au). Nine of the 17 self-contained cottages the group owns are in Wentworth Falls; the others are in Leura and Bullaburra. Prices range from A$62 to $100 (U.S.$40.30–$65) per person midweek, and A$77.50 to $130 (U.S.$50.38–$84.50) per person on weekends (with a minimum 2-night stay).

✪ Whispering Pines. The Sandpatch, and Woodlands. 178–186 Falls Rd., Wentworth Falls, NSW 2782. ☎ **02/4757 1449.** Fax 02/4757 1219. wpines@bigpond.com. 4 units in main building, 1 4-bedroom cottage at Sandpatch, 1 3-bedroom cottage at Woodlands. TV TEL. Whispering Pines: weekend A$240 (U.S.$156); midweek A$165 (U.S.$107.25). Sandpatch: A$165 (U.S.$107.25) weeknights only, extra person A$55 (U.S.$35.75). Woodlands: weekend A$220 (U.S.$143) plus A$25 (U.S.$16.25) per extra person (4 people minimum on weekends); midweek A$140 (U.S.$91) and A$25 (U.S.$16.25) per extra person. All properties require a minimum 2-night stay on weekends. Prices are per couple. AE, BC, DC, MC, V.

Whispering Pines is a grand heritage mountain guesthouse set in 4 acres of woodland gardens at the head of Wentworth Falls. Built in 1898, it continues to foster a Victorian luxury. Rooms are cozy and filled with antiques. If you want to get away from it all, then the Sandpatch property down the road is for you. It has two large bedrooms and guest living rooms with Persian rugs, polished floorboards, and all the antiques and modern luxuries you could ask for. Two people can rent the cottage, but they must pay A$50 (U.S.$32.50) on top of the price (in other words, two people have to pay for four people, even if only two stay). The cottage sleeps eight people. There's a full kitchen, a CD player, and a VCR. Woodlands is a wood cottage tucked away in the bush, with three bedrooms, a lounge room with fire, a spa bath, a laundry room, and a full kitchen.

A NICE SPOT FOR LUNCH

Conservation Hut Café. At the end of Fletcher St., Wentworth Falls. ☎ **02/4757 3827.** Menu items A$6–$15 (U.S.$3.90–$9.75). BC, MC, V. Daily 9am–5pm. CAFE.

This pleasant cafe is in the national park itself on top of a cliff overlooking the Jamison Valley. It's a good place for a bit of lunch on the balcony if you're famished after the Valley of the Waters walk, which leaves from just outside. It serves all the usual cafe fare—burgers, salads, sandwiches, and pastas. There are plenty of vegetarian options, too. There's a nice log fire inside in winter.

MEDLOW BATH

150km (90 miles) W of Sydney; 6km (3½ miles) E of Katoomba

A cozy place, with its own railway station, a secondhand bookstore, and a few properties hidden between the trees, Medlow Bath has one claim to fame—the ✪ **Hydro Majestic Hotel** (☎ **02/4788 1002**), a must for any visitor to the Blue Mountains. The historic Hydro Majestic has fabulous views over the Megalong Valley; the best time to appreciate the views is at sunset with a drink on the terrace. Otherwise it sells Devonshire Tea all day, and plenty of cakes and snacks, coffee and tea. Also drop into Medlow Bath's ✪ **Old Post Office,** now a wonderful musty secondhand bookshop and odds and ends antique store.

BLACKHEATH

114km (71 miles) W of Sydney; 14km (9 miles) W of Katoomba

Blackheath is the highest town in the Blue Mountains at 3,495 feet. **The Three Brothers** at Blackheath are not as famous as the Three Sisters in Katoomba, but you can climb two of them for fabulous views. Or try the ✪ **Cliff Walk** from Evans Lookout to Govetts Leap (named after a surveyor who mapped the region in the 1830s), where there are magnificent views over the Grose Valley and Bridal Veil Falls. The 1½-hour tramp passes through banksia, gum, and wattle forest, with spectacular views of peaks and valleys. The town has some interesting tearooms and antiques shops.

GETTING THERE The **Great Western Highway** takes motorists west from Katoomba to Blackheath. **CityRail** trains also stop at Blackheath.

VISITOR INFORMATION The **Heritage Centre** (☎ 02/4787 8877; www. npws.nsw.gov.au), operated by the National Parks and Wildlife Service, is located close to Govetts Leap Lookout on Govetts Leap Road. It has information on guided walks, camping and hiking, as well as information on local European and Aboriginal historic sites. It's open daily from 9am to 4:30pm.

EXPLORING THE AREA ON HORSEBACK

One of the nicest ways to get around is on horseback. **Werriberri Trail Rides** (☎ 02/ 4787 9171; fax 02/4787 6680), found at the base of the Blue Mountains, 10 kilometers (6 miles) from Blackheath on Megalong Road in the Megalong Valley, offers guided half-hour to 3-hour rides through the Megalong Valley. Suitable for beginners to advanced riders. Half-hour rides cost A$17 (U.S.$11.05).

WHERE TO STAY

✪ **Jemby-Rinjah Lodge.** 336 Evans Lookout Rd., Blackheath, NSW 2785. ☎ **02/4787 7622.** Fax 02/4787 6230. jembyrin@pnc.com.au. 10 cabins, 3 lodges. Cabins (occupied by up to 2 adults and 2 children): Fri–Sun and public holidays A$160–$225 (U.S.$104–$146.25); Mon–Thurs A$115–$167 (U.S.$74.75–$109.20). Extra adult A$22 (U.S.$14.30), extra child A$14 (U.S.$9.10). Linen Hire A$13.50 (U.S.$8.78) per bed. AE, BC, JCB, MC, V.

The Blue Mountains National Park is a short walk from this alternative accommodation option. There are 9 standard cabins (7 two-bedroom cabins, and 2 one-bedroom loft cabins), 1 deluxe cabin called Treetops Retreat, and 3 pole-frame lodges. The cabins are right in the bush, can sleep up to six people, and are well spaced. Each has a slow combustion heater, carpets, bathroom, a fully equipped kitchen, and a lounge and dining area. There are also automatic laundry and barbecue areas nearby. The lodges each have five bedrooms, two bathrooms, and a common lounge area with a fireplace. Composting toilets, walkways, and solar heating help protect the environment. You can rent linens, but bring your own food. Free pickup can be arranged from Blackheath train station. Treetops Retreat has a hot tub, TV and VCR, stereo, and three private balconies with bush views. It sleeps two, making it a perfect romantic getaway. The nearby walking tracks take you to the Grand Canyon; the Grose Valley Blue Gum forests; and Walls Cave, a resting place for Aborigines 10,000 years ago.

✪ JENOLAN CAVES

182km (113 miles) W of Sydney; 70 (42 miles) W of Katoomba

The winding road from Katoomba eventually takes you to a spur of the Great Dividing Range and a series of underground limestone caves considered some of the world's best. Known to the local Aborigines as "Binoomea," meaning "dark place," millions of people have come to see the amazing stalactites, stalagmites, and underground rivers and pools since the caves were opened up to the public in 1866.

GETTING THERE It's a 1½-hour drive from Katoomba to the caves. **CityRail** trains run to Katoomba and link up with daily Jenolan Caves excursions run by **Fantastic Aussie Tours** (☎ 02/4782 1866). The CityRail **Link Ticket,** which is a combination train ticket/bus tour, costs A\$60 (U.S.\$39) for adults and A\$30 (U.S.\$19.50) for children. The tour alone from Katoomba costs A\$64 (U.S.\$42) for adults and A\$32 (U.S.\$20.80) for children, so the Link Ticket is well worthwhile to buy. These prices include cave entry. You can purchase Link Tickets at any rail station.

Day trips from Sydney are operated by **AAT King's** (☎ 02/9252 2788) and **Australian Pacific Tours** (☎ 02/9252 2988; fax 02/9247 2052). Coach tours depart from the coach terminal at Circular Quay. Since you end up spending 6 hours on a coach on these day trips, I recommend staying overnight in either Jenolan Village or somewhere else in the Blue Mountains.

EXPLORING THE CAVES

There are nine caves open to the public, with guided tours conducted at the **Jenolan Caves Reserves Trust** (☎ 02/6359 3311; www.jenolancaves.org.au).

The first cave tour starts at 10am weekdays and 9:30am weekends and holidays. The final tour departs at 4.30pm (5pm in warmer months). Tours last 1 to 2 hours, and each costs between A\$12 and \$50 (U.S.\$7.80 and \$32.50) for adults, and A\$8 (U.S.\$5.20) and A\$10 (U.S.\$6.50) for children under 15. Family concessions and multiple cave packages are available. The best all-round cave is Lucas Cave; Imperial Cave is best for seniors. Adventure Cave Tours, which include canyoning, last from 3 hours to all day and cost from A\$40 to \$100 (U.S.\$26–\$65) per person.

WHERE TO STAY

The Gatehouse Jenolan. Jenolan Caves Village, NSW 2790. ☎ **02/6359 3322.** Fax 02/ 6359 3227. 13 units. Weekend rates: 4 person dorm room A\$88 (U.S.\$57.20), 6 person dorm room A\$110 (U.S.\$71.50). Weekday Rates 4 person dorm room A\$60.50 (U.S.\$39.33), 6 person dorm room A\$77 (U.S.\$50.05) with linen hire of A\$3.30 (U.S.\$2.15) per person.

The Gatehouse is a clean and cozy budget-style lodge, with a separate cottage nearby. It's located opposite the caves. The Gatehouse sleeps 66 people in seven 6-bed rooms and six 4-bed rooms in the main building. The cottage can accommodate up to four couples. There are also two common rooms, lockers, washing machines and dryers, basic kitchen facilities, and a barbecue area. There are outdoor barbecues on the premises, and apparently at least one ghost.

✪ **Jenolan Caves House.** Jenolan Caves Village, NSW 2790. ☎ **02/6359 3322.** Fax 02/ 6359 3227. www.lisp.com.au/~jenolan/. 101 units, some with bathroom. TV TEL. Weekend rates: Grand Classic A\$335.50 (U.S.\$218.08), Classic A\$265 (U.S.\$172.25), Traditional A\$165 (U.S.\$107.25), Mountain Lodge A\$209 (U.S.\$135.85). Weekday rates: Grand Classic A\$231.50 (U.S.\$150.48), Classic A\$187 (U.S.\$121.55), Traditional A\$110 (U.S.\$71.50), Mountain Lodge A\$132 (U.S.\$85.80). Family rooms also available. AE, BC, DC, MC, V.

This heritage-listed hotel was built between 1888 and 1906 and is one of the most outstanding structures in New South Wales. The main part of the enormous three-story building is constructed of sandstone and fashioned in Tudor-style black and white. Around it are several cottages and former servants quarters. Rooms vary within the main house from budget bunkrooms, to "traditional" rooms with shared bathrooms and "classic" rooms with private bathrooms. The traditional and classic rooms are both old world and cozy, with heavy furniture and views over red-tile rooftops or steep vegetated slopes. Mountain Lodge rooms are found in a separate building behind the main house and are more motel-like. The lodge's bar fills up inside and out on summer weekends; Trails Bistro sells snacks (bring your own if you're a vegetarian, though). Chisolms at Jenolan is a fine-dining restaurant serving very good Modern Australian cuisine.

2 The Hunter Valley: Wine Tasting & More

Cessnock: 190km (114 miles) N of Sydney

✪ **The Hunter Valley** (or the Hunter as it's also called) is the oldest commercial wine-producing area in Australia, and a major site for coal mining. Internationally acclaimed wines have been pouring out of here since the 1800s. Though the region falls behind the major wine-producing areas of Victoria in terms of volume, it has the advantage, from the traveler's point of view, of being just 2 hours from Sydney.

People come here to visit the vineyards' "cellar doors" for free wine tasting, to enjoy the rural scenery, to sample the area's highly regarded cuisine, or to escape from the city for a romantic weekend. The whole area is dedicated to the grape and the plate, and you'll find many superb restaurants hidden away between the vineyards and farmland.

In the **Lower Hunter**, around the towns of Cessnock and Pokolbin, you'll find over 50 wineries, including well-known producers such as Tyrell, Rothbury, Lindemans, Draytons, McGuigans, and McWilliams. Many varieties of wine are produced here, including semillon, shiraz, chardonnay, cabernet sauvignon, and pinot noir.

Farther north, the **Upper Hunter** offers the very essence of Australian rural life, with its sheep and cattle farms, historic homesteads, more wineries, and rugged bushland. The vineyards here tend to be larger than those in the south, and produce more aromatic varieties, such as traminers (a sweet white wine) and Rieslings. This being the southern hemisphere, the harvest months are February to March.

The Upper Hunter gives way to the forested heights of the nearest World Heritage-listed site to Sydney, **Barrington Tops National Park.** The park is ruggedly beautiful and is home to some of the highest Antarctic beech trees in the country. It also abounds with animals, including several marsupial species, and an abundance of bird life.

HUNTER VALLEY ESSENTIALS

GETTING THERE   To get to the wine-producing regions of the Hunter, leave Sydney via the **Harbour Bridge** or **Harbour Tunnel** and follow the signs for Newcastle. Just before Hornsby, turn off the highway and follow the signs for Cessnock. The trip will take about 2½ hours. Barrington Tops National Park is reached via the Upper Hunter town of Dungog.

Keynes Buses (☎ **1800/043 339** in Australia or 02/6543 1322) run coaches to Scone in the Hunter Valley from Sydney's Central Station. Buses depart Monday to Saturday at 3pm and arrive in Scone at 6:50pm; there's a second service on Fridays leaving at 6pm and on Sunday the bus leaves at 6:40pm. Round-trip tickets are A$74 (U.S.$48.10) for adults and A$38 (U.S.$24.70) for children.

A rental car should cost you from A$45 (U.S.$29.25) a day from Sydney, and you might put in around A$40 (U.S.$26) worth of petrol or so. In the Hunter, contact **Hertz,** 1A Aberdare Rd., Cessnock (☎ **13 30 39** in Australia, or 02/4991 2500).

ORGANIZED TRIPS FROM SYDNEY   Several companies offer day trips to the Hunter Valley from Sydney. **Wonderbus Tours** (☎ **02/9555 9800;** fax 02/9555 1345; www.wonderbus.com.au) operates a fun trip that combines wine tasting in the Hunter Valley, a visit to Oakdale Farm (a native animal reserve) near Port Stephens, and dolphin spotting at Port Stephens. The trip costs A$185 (U.S.$120.25) for adults and A$125 (U.S.$81.25) for children 5 to 12, including lunch and wine. An optional extra is a 15 minute ride on a high speed jet boat, the *Foxy*, in Port Stephens for A$33 (U.S.$21.45) for adults and A$15 (U.S.$9.75) for children.

The Hunter Valley

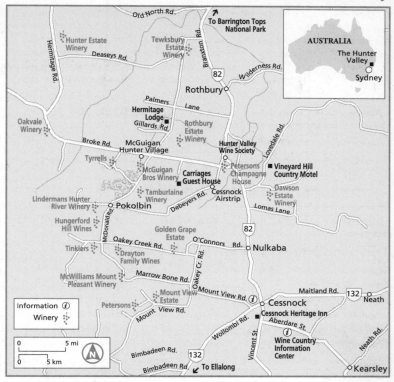

Wonderbus also offers a tour of five vineyards (instead of the three in the above trip), with lunch, costing A$140 (U.S.$91). Another option is a tour including a horse ride, lunch and afternoon wine tour by horse and carriage costing A$240 (U.S.$156).

VISITOR INFORMATION **Wine Country Visitors Information Centre,** Turner Park, Aberdare Road, Cessnock, NSW 2325 (☎ **02/4990 4477**; fax 02/4991 4518; www.winecountry.com.au), is open Monday to Friday from 9am to 5pm, Saturday from 9:30am to 5pm, and Sunday from 9:30am to 3:30pm. The staff can make accommodation bookings and answer any questions. The **Dungog Visitors Information Centre,** on Dowling Street, Dungog (☎ **02/4992 2212**), has plenty of information on the Barrington Tops area.

VISITING THE WINERIES

Many people start their journey through the Hunter at the **Hunter Valley Wine Society,** at the corner of Broke and Branxton roads in Pokolbin (☎ **02/4998 7397**). The club acts as a Hunter Valley wine clearinghouse, sending bottles and cases to members all over Australia, and some overseas. It's a good place to talk to the experts about the area's wines, and to taste a few of them. It's open daily from 9am to 5pm.

You might also like to visit the **Small Winemakers Centre,** McDonalds Road, Pokolbin (☎ **02/4998 7668**). At any one time it represents around six of the region's smaller producers.

Most wineries in the region are open for tastings, and it's acceptable to turn up, taste a couple of wines or more, then say your good-byes without buying anything (though the DUI laws would suggest that you have a designated driver). You will come across some unusual vintages, especially at the boutique wineries, but don't expect to find any bargains—city bottle shops buy in bulk and at trade price, which means you can probably get the same bottle for less in Sydney than at the cellar door in the Hunter.

Here are some of the wineries you can visit:

Drayton Family Wines. Oakey Creek Rd., Pokolbin. ☎ **02/4998 7513.** Mon–Fri 9am–5pm, Sat–Sun 10am–5pm.

Drayton's produces some spectacular shiraz.

Hunter Estate Winery. Hermitage Rd., Pokolbin. ☎ **02/4998 7777.** Daily 10am–5pm. Tours daily 11am and 2pm.

The Hunter's largest winery crushes some 6,500 tons of grapes a year. Come here for excellent semillon and shiraz.

Lindemans. McDonald Rd., Pokolbin. ☎ **02/4998 7684.** Mon–Fri 9am–4:30pm, Sat–Sun 10am–4:30pm.

This famous winery offers an interesting sparkling red shiraz.

McGuigan Brothers Winery. McDonald Rd., Pokolbin. ☎ **02/4998 7402.** Daily 9:30am–5pm. Tours daily at noon.

Another winery worth visiting in the area, McGuigan Brothers also has a cheese factory and bakery on the site.

McWilliams Mount Pleasant. Marrowbone Rd., Pokolbin. ☎ **02/4998 7505.** Daily 10am–4:30pm. Tours daily 11am.

Famous for its Elizabeth Semillon, which has won 15 trophies and 134 gold medals, and its Lovedale Semillon, which has won 24 trophies and 38 gold medals.

Mount View Estate. Mount View Rd., Mount View. ☎ **02/4990 3307.** Daily 10am–5pm.

The pioneer of Verdelho wines in Australia—a grape attributed to Portugal, but it's also grown in small quantities in Italy and France. It's a very crisp and dry white wine, which I like with seafood.

Peterson's Champagne House. At the corner of Broke and Branxton rds., Pokolbin. ☎ **02/4998 7881.** Daily 9am–5pm.

This is the only specialist champagne winery in the Hunter.

Peterson's Vineyard. Mount View Rd., Mount View. ☎ **02/4990 1704.** Mon–Sat 9am–5pm and 10am–5pm.

Peterson's produces fine chardonnay, semillon, and shiraz.

✪ **Rothbury Estate.** Broke Rd., Pokolbin. ☎ **02/4998 7555.** Daily 9:30am–4:30pm.

This very friendly winery produces the magnificent Brokenback Shiraz and the nice Mudgee Shiraz. The Rothbury Café (see "Where to Dine," below) serves meals.

A Wine-Buying Tip

The best year ever for red wines in this part of Australia was 1988, when a long, hot summer produced fewer, but more intensely flavored grapes. Stock up on anything you can find from this vintage. At the other end of the scale, 1997 was a very bad year in the Hunter, and 1996 produced an average vintage.

A Wine-Tasting Tip

Some wineries routinely offer some of their inferior wines for tastings. I've made a habit of specifically asking for a list of their premium wines available for tasting. Most wineries usually have a bottle or two of their better wines uncorked for those with a serious interest.

Tamburlaine. McDonald Rd., Pokolbin. ☎ **02/4998 7570.** Daily 9:30am–5pm.

Don't miss this boutique winery, the winner of many wine and tourism awards.

Tinklers. Pokolbin Mountains Rd., Pokolbin. ☎ **02/4998 7435.** Daily 10am–4pm.

If you want to taste the grapes in season, head to Tinklers. It sells some 30 different varieties of eating grapes between December and March, and nectarines, plums, peaches, and vegetables at other times of the year. It also offers wine tasting and free vineyard walks at 11am on Saturday and Sunday.

Tyrell's. Broke Rd., Pokolbin. ☎ **02/4993 7000.** Tours daily 1:30pm.

Tyrell's has produced some famous wines and exports all over the world.

DAY TOURS, HOT-AIR BALLOON RIDES & OTHER FUN STUFF

If you don't have a car, you'll have to get around as part of a tour, as there is no public transport running between the wineries.

Hunter Valley Day Tours, P.O. Box 59, Paterson 2421 (☎/fax **02/4938 5031,** additional fax 02/4938 5083; www.huntertourism.com/daytours) offers a wine and cheese tour with pickup from your Hunter accommodation. The tour runs from 10:15am to 3:45pm and goes to as many wineries as they can fit in. Tours costs A$80 (U.S.$52) for adults, A$30 (U.S.$19.50) for children, including lunch. A longer rain forest and winery tour includes a walk and lunch in the Watagan Mountains, followed by an afternoon of wine tasting. The tour costs A$110 (U.S.$71.50) for adults, A$30 (U.S.$19.50) for children, including morning tea and lunch.

A tranquil way to see the wineries is from above. **Balloon Aloft,** in Cessnock (☎ **1800/028 568** in Australia, or 02/4938 1955; fax 02/6344 1852), offers year-round dawn balloon flights that include a post-flight champagne and optional breakfast costing A$15 (U.S.$9.75). Flights last about an hour and cost A$205 (U.S.$133.25) for adults on weekdays and A$230 (U.S.$149.50) on weekends. Children 7 to 12 fly for A$130 (U.S.$84.50) daily.

If you like adventure, try **Grapemobile Bicycle and Walking Tours** (☎ **0500/804 039** in Australia, and tel/fax 02/4991 2339. They supply you with a mountain bike, helmet, guide, and support bus, and takes you on a meander through the wineries. Tours cost A$98 (U.S.$63.70), including a restaurant lunch. The company also runs a walking tour for A$89 (U.S.$57.85), including wine tasting and lunch.

WHERE TO STAY

The Hunter Valley is far more expensive on weekends and during public holidays, when room prices jump significantly and some properties insist on a 2-night stay. It's worthwhile checking out the information board located inside the Wine Country Visitors Information Centre (see "Visitor Information," above) for special deals, but most of the rooms tend to be in nondescript motels.

In Cessnock

Staying in Cessnock is a good idea if you don't have a car and are relying on local tour companies to pick you up and show you around the area.

Cessnock Heritage Inn. 167 Vincent St, (P.O. Box 714), Cessnock, NSW 2325. ☎ **02/ 4991 2744.** Fax 02/4991 2720. www.hunterweb.com.au/heritageinn.html. 13 units. TV TEL. Weekend A$50 (U.S.$32.50) per person with breakfast. Midweek A$55 (U.S.$35.75) double without breakfast; A$75 (U.S.$48.75) double with full breakfast. AE, BC, MC, V.

This 1920s building, built as a pub, is right in the center of Cessnock, so there's easy access to all the local pubs and restaurants. All the rooms are done in country style, with dried grasses, floral drapes, and the like. All are quite large with high ceilings but differ greatly. All have ceiling fans and free video movies.

In Ellalong

Ellalong Hotel. 80 Helena St., Ellalong, NSW 2325. ☎/fax **02/4998 1217.** 10 units, none with bathroom. Sat A$69 (U.S.$44.85); Fri A$59 (U.S.$38.35); Sun–Thurs A$55 (U.S.$35.75) per double. Rates include country breakfast. Inquire about dinner packages. No credit cards.

This 1924 pub, located only 11 kilometers (7 miles) from Cessnock, has a good Aussie country atmosphere. All rooms have a real out-in-the-country style with solid wood dressers and bouquets of dried flowers. Some have just a double bed, while others squeeze in an extra single. Rooms 1 and 2 are the best, as they've got fantastic views across to the Brokenback Ranges from their verandahs. Lunch and dinner are served in the restaurant, and counter meals are served up in the bistro.

In Pokolbin

✪ **Carriages Guest House.** Halls Rd., Pokolbin, NSW 2321. ☎ **02/4998 7591.** Fax 02/4998 7839. 10 units. A/C TV TEL. A$150 (U.S.$97.50) double, A$195–$210 (U.S.$126.75–$136.50) suite; A$245 (U.S.$159.25) spa suite. Rates include breakfast. Minimum 2-night stay on weekends. Ask about 10–20% discounts midweek. AE, BC, MC, V.

Tucked away on 36 acres, a kilometer off the main road, Carriages is a retreat in the heart of Pokolbin. The main house is a two-story double gabled building. A new two-suite cottage called the Gatehouse is on a separate part of the grounds. In the main house, downstairs rooms open onto a verandah and are furnished with antique country pine. Upstairs, the two lofty gable suites are centered around huge fireplaces. The Gatehouse suites offer five-star luxury; although new, the stained glass windows and rescued timber give them a rustic feel. Breakfast is served in your room, and Robert's

Caravan, Man

Two caravan parks in the area offer accommodation in caravans and cabins. **Cessnock Cabins and Caravan Park** (☎ **02/4990 5819;** fax 0249912944) Allandale/Branxton Road, Nulkaba (2km north of Cessnock), has 4 on-site vans for A$30 to $40 (U.S.$19.50–$26) a double and 12 cabins with shower from A$48 to $69 (U.S.$31.20–$44.85); the higher prices are for weekends. There's also camping sites here for A$14 (U.S.$9.10) and powered sites for A$16 (U.S.$10.40).

The **Valley Vineyard Tourist Park** (☎/fax **02/4990 2573**) on Mount View Road (on the way out to the vineyards) has 5 caravans for A$35 (U.S.$22.75) and 12 cabins with shower for A$55 (U.S.$35.75). Two two-bedroom units cost A$75 (U.S.$48.75). Powered sites cost A$16 to 20 (U.S.$10.40–$13) and a camping site A$12 (U.S.$7.80). There's a BYO restaurant, a camper's kitchen and a swimming pool on the site.

Something Special: A Cattle Station in the Upper Hunter

Located just off the Golden Highway, 1 hour north of Mudgee, 2½ hours west of Cessnock, and 4 hours northwest of Sydney, **Runnymeade,** Golden Highway, Runnymeade, Cassilis, NSW 2329 (☎ **02/6376 1183;** fax 02/6376 1187, a 2,000-acre sheep-and-cattle station, is a perfect place to experience Australia's agricultural side. The ranch offers farm-style lodgings in a 1930s California bungalow. Two rooms have an en suite shower, while the third shares the hosts' bathroom down the hall. The homestead offers an open fire in the living room. There are plenty of native birds in the gardens, and kangaroos are common. May is the best time to see sheep shearing, and August is best to witness lambing and calving. The hosts, Libby and David Morrow, are very good company, and guests rave about them. David offers 1-hour tours of the property for around A$30 (U.S.$19.50) per "Toyota-load," and other tours throughout the district.

Doubles go for A$80 to $90 (U.S.$52–$58.50). Rates include breakfast, but dinner is A$20 (U.S.$13) per person extra (BYO wine or beer). No credit cards.

restaurant is next door. The friendly owner, Ben Dawson, says he'll take Frommer's readers up to the top of a nearby hill where they can see plenty of wild kangaroos.

Hermitage Lodge. At Gillards and McDonalds rds., Pokolbin, NSW 2320. ☎ **02/ 4998 7639.** Fax 02/4998 7818. www.ozemail.com.au/~hlodge/. 10 units. A/C TV TEL. Weekend A$155 (U.S.$100.75) standard double; A$200 (U.S.$130) spa suites. Midweek A$95 (U.S.$61.75) standard double; A$135 (U.S.$87.75) spa suites. Rates include continental breakfast. Extra person A$15 ($9.75). Minimum 2-night stay on weekends. Ask about discounts for midweek multi-night stays. AE, BC, MC, V.

The lodge is surrounded by vineyards in the heart of wine country. Standard rooms are large and sunny and nicely decorated with queen-size beds and a double sofa bed, an iron and ironing board, a hair dryer, a fridge, and tea- and coffee-making facilities. The spa suites are larger with queen-size beds and double sofas, cathedral ceilings, spa baths, and separate showers. The more expensive suites have a separate bedroom, bathrobes, and daily newspaper. Breakfast is served in all rooms. Frommer's readers can hire bicycles for free. There's an outdoor swimming pool, and free laundry facilities. There's a great Italian restaurant, called Il Cacciatore, on the premises.

Vineyard Hill Country Motel. Lovedale Rd., Pokolbin, NSW 2321. ☎ **02/4990 4166.** Fax 02/4991 4431. 8 units. A/C MINIBAR TV TEL. Weekend A$141 (U.S.$91.65) 1-bedroom unit; A$218 (U.S.$141.70) 2-bedroom unit (for 4 people). Midweek A$97 (U.S.$63.05) 1-bedroom unit; A$165 (U.S.$107.25) 2-bedroom unit. Extra person A$16.50 (U.S.$10.73). Ask about midweek and long weekend packages. AE, BC, MC, V.

Motel is a bit of a misnomer for this place; it's more aptly described as a "fully self-contained chalet." Units are modern, with a separate bedroom, lounge and dining area, a full kitchen, and a balcony with views across a valley of vineyards to the Brokenback Ranges in the distance. It's all terrifically rural, with cows wandering about and kangaroos and possums creeping around at dusk. There's no restaurant, but there is a gourmet deli on the premises. In the garden are a large swimming pool and a spa.

IN THE UPPER HUNTER

✪ **Barrington Guest House.** Salisbury (via Dungog), NSW 2420. ☎ **02/4995 3212.** Fax 02/4995 3248. 20 rain forest cottages, 21 guesthouse units (13 with bathroom). A$145 (U.S.$94.25) per person in cottage midweek, including meals and activities; A$210 (U.S.$136.50) self-catering cottage midweek, including activities (minimum 2-night stay; second night A$190 (U.S.$123.50). A$76 (U.S.$49.40) per adult in a guesthouse room without bathroom, including meals and activities; A$116 (U.S.$75.40) per adult in a guesthouse room with bathroom, including meals and activities. Ask about packages. AE, BC, MC, V. The guesthouse is about 3½ hr. from Sydney and 1½ hr. from the main Hunter wine region. Free pickup from Dungog railway station.

Barrington Guest House is nestled in a valley just outside the Barrington Tops National Park—the nearest World Heritage site to Sydney. It retains an Old World charm and serves bacon and eggs for breakfast, scones and cream, and vegetables boiled soft enough for your dentures. The place has lace tablecloths in the dining room, a log fire beneath a brick chimney, dark mahogany walls, high ceilings, and personalized service—despite the communal mealtimes and the lack of a menu. Rooms range from the original guesthouse chambers adjoining the dining room, to new and almost luxurious two-story self-contained cottages (sleeping up to 5) that cling to a hillside. This place is popular with older travelers during the week, but attracts a range of ages on the weekends. The guesthouse grounds attract plenty of animals from the surrounding national park and act as a wildlife reserve for several rescued kangaroos. Activities include horseback riding, guided walks through the magnificent rain forest, "billy tea" tours, and night spotting for quolls (native cats) and possums, not to mention bush dancing, tennis, film evenings, and skeet shooting.

WHERE TO DINE
IN CESSNOCK

Amicos. 138 Wollombi Rd., Cessnock. ☎ **02/4991 1995.** Reservations recommended. Main courses A$11.90–$19.90 (U.S.$7.74–$12.94); pizzas A$14–$18 (U.S.$9.10–$11.70). 10% discount for take-out orders. BC, MC, V. MEXICAN/ITALIAN PIZZERIA.

You can't mistake the Mexican influence in the decor, with bunches of chili peppers, cow skulls, ponchos, masks, and frescoes, but the Mediterranean/Italian connection is more evident in the menu. Mexican dishes include the usual nachos, enchiladas, burritos, barbecued chicken, and the like, while there are a few pastas and Mediterranean dishes, such as crumbed lamb brains, too. The pizzas are pretty good, and one could just about serve four people.

IN POKOLBIN

Café Enzo. At the corner of Broke and Ekerts rds. (adjacent to Peppers Creek Antiques, near Peppers Guest House), Pokolbin. ☎ **02/4998 7233.** Main courses A$10–$18 (U.S.$6.50–$11.70). Devonshire tea A$7.50 (U.S.$4.88). AE, BC, DC, MC, V. Wed–Sun 10am–5pm (until 10pm Sat) MODERN AUSTRALIAN.

This charming little cafe offers a nice ambiance and good cuisine. Pastas, pizzettas, antipasti, and steaks dominate the menu. The pizzetta with char-grilled baby octopus, squid, and king prawns, Kalamata olives, fresh chili and onion, and freshly shaved parmigiano is particularly nice. Cakes and cheese plates are a specialty.

✪ **The Rothbury Café.** Upstairs at the Rothbury Estate, Broke Rd., Pokolbin. ☎ **02/4998 7363.** Main courses A$16–$18 (U.S.$10.40–$11.70). AE, BC, DC, MC, V. Daily noon–3pm. MODERN AUSTRALIAN.

This second-floor cafe has some of the best views across the valley; occasionally you can even spot kangaroos grazing in the fields across the way. The cafe has a Mediterranean feel, with timber tables loaded with bread and olives. Signature dishes are the chickpea-battered squid with yogurt and eggplant relish for a first course, and venison and beetroot pie or braised oxtail with orange, walnuts, olives, and polenta for main courses. Desserts include the fabulously rich chocolate-chestnut torte with berries.

Worth a Splurge

✪ **Casuarina Restaurant.** Hermitage Rd., Pokolbin. ☎ **02/4998 7888.** Reservations recommended. Main courses A$27–$34 (U.S.$17.55–$22.10). $3 (U.S.$1.95) per person surcharge weekends and public holiday. AE, DC, BC, MC, V. Daily 7pm–11pm. MODERN AUSTRALIAN.

This superb restaurant has taken a slew of awards for its cooking in recent years. The surroundings are elegant, with lots of antiques below the very high wooden ceilings. The restaurant specializes in flambés, with its signature dish being the flambé of chili lobster and prawn (for two people). Other meals to write home about are the Thai-style chicken curry and the Caesar salad.

3 Port Stephens: Dolphin & Whale-Watching

209km (130 miles) N of Sydney

✪ **Port Stephen's Bay,** just 2½ hours north of Sydney, should be at the top of any New South Wales itinerary. It's a perfect add-on to a trip to the Hunter Valley (see above). Though you can come up from Sydney for the day, I highly recommend staying in the area for at least one night. The sheltered Port Stephen's Bay itself is more than twice the size of Sydney Harbour, and clean as a newly poured bath. The sea jumps with fish, and the creamy islands and surrounding Tomaree National Park boast more species of birds than even Kakadu National Park in the Northern Territory. Two pods of bottle-nosed dolphins, around 70 in all, call the bay home, and you are almost certain to see some on a dolphin-watching cruise. Port Stephens is also a fabulous place to watch whales during their migration to the breeding grounds farther north (roughly from June 1 to mid-November—though they are less frequently seen in August). There is also a large breeding colony of koalas in Lemon Tree Passage on the south side of the Tomaree Peninsula, which makes up the southern shoreline of the bay.

The main town, Nelson Bay (pop. 7,000) is on the northern side of the peninsula. The township of Shoal Bay, farther along, and has a nice beach edged with wildflowers. Another small resort town, Anna Bay, is the largest development on the southern side of the peninsula, and has good surf beaches nearby. The Stockton Bight stretches some 35 kilometers (22 miles) from Anna Bay south to the large industrial town of Newcastle. The beach here is popular with ocean fishermen, who have the awful habit of driving their 4WDs along it. The Stockton Sand Dunes, which run behind the beach, are the longest in the Southern Hemisphere.

Opposite the Tomaree Peninsula, across the bay, are the small tourist townships of Tea Gardens and Hawks Nest, both at the mouth of the Myall River. See the Wonderbus tour of The Hunter (above) for details on a tour to Port Stephens.

ESSENTIALS

GETTING THERE   Take the Sydney-Newcastle Freeway (F3) to its end, then follow the Pacific Highway signs to Hexham and Port Stephens. **Port Stephens Coaches** (☎ **1800/045 949** in Sydney or 02/4982 2940), travel between Port Stephens and Newcastle, and to Nelson Bay from Sydney daily at 2pm. Buses leave from Eddy Avenue, near Central Station; the journey takes 3½ hours. Return tickets cost A$43 (U.S.$27.95) for adults and A$30 (U.S.$19.50) for children.

A Horse Ride Through the Dunes

You can ride a horse through the dunes with **Sahara Horse Trails** (☎ **02/4981 9077**). A 2-hour trip costs A$40 (U.S.$26), and a half-day excursion is A$60 (U.S.$39). Bookings required 1 day in advance.

VISITOR INFORMATION   The **Port Stephens Vistor Information Centre,** Victoria Parade, Nelson Bay (☎ **1800/808 900** in Australia or 02/4981 1579; fax 02/4984 1855; www.portstephens.org.au; tops@hunterlink.net.au.) is open Monday to Friday from 9am to 5pm and Saturday and Sunday from 9am to 4pm.

SEEING THE AREA

Several operators offer dolphin- and whale-watching cruises. Some of the best are aboard *Imagine* (☎ **02/4984 9000;** www.dunesnet.com/imagine/default.html), a 50-foot catamaran operated by Frank Future and Yves Papin, two real characters. They offer a daily "Island Discovery" trip that includes dolphin-watching and a trip around the offshore islands. The 4-hour cruise departs from D'Albora Marina in Nelson Bay daily at 11am and costs A$39 (U.S.$25.35) for adults, and A$19 (U.S.$12.35) for children 4 to 14, including lunch.

Four-hour whale-watching tours cost the same and leave at 11am from June 1 to November 15. You are most likely to spot humpback whales, but there's also a chance to see Minke and southern right whales.

A morning dolphin-watching cruise runs from 9am to 10:30am daily during summer and costs A$15 (U.S.$9.75) for adults, A$7 (U.S.$4.55) for children, and A$38 (U.S.$24.70) for families. If you happen to be around on the weekend nearest a full moon, ask about the company's overnight "Full Moon Tours."

Another operator, *Advance II* (☎ **02/4981 0399**), offers 2-hour dolphin cruises for A$18 (U.S.$11.70),and a 3-hour whale-watch for A$43 (U.S.$27.95). **The Port Stephens Ferry Service** (☎ **02/4981 3798** or 0419/417 689 mobile phone) operates a 2½-hour "Early Bird Dolphin Watch" daily 8:30am with a stop off at Tea Gardens. A similar 3½ cruise departs at noon (you can eat lunch at Tea Gardens), and 2-hour dolphin-watching cruise departs at 3:30pm. All cruises cost A$15 (U.S.$9.75) for adults, A$8 (U.S.$5.20) for children, and A$35 (U.S.$22.75) for families.

WHERE TO STAY

Port Stephens is very popular with Sydneysiders, especially during the Christmas holidays, the month of January, and Easter, so book well in advance for those times.

Port Stephens Motor Lodge. 44 Mangus St., Nelson Bay, NSW 2315. ☎ **02/4981 3366.** Fax 02/4984 1655. A/C TV TEL. 17. A$60–$120 (U.S.$39–$78) standard double (depending on season); A$88 (U.S.$57.20) family unit on weekdays and A$120 (U.S.$78) on weekends. Extra person A$10 (U.S.$6.50), extra person under 15 A$5 (U.S.$3.25). AE, BC, DC, MC, V.

Surrounded by tall trees and gardens, this motor lodge is a peaceful place to stay and a short stroll from the main township. The standard rooms are quite plain with raw-brick walls, a comfy double (and an extra single bed in most rooms), a private balcony, and an attached shower with hip-tub. Adjacent to the lodge is a self-contained family unit with two bedrooms, a laundry, and water views. There's a swimming pool and a barbecue area and a coin-op laundry on the grounds.

✪ **Salamanda Shores.** 147 Soldiers Point Rd., Soldiers Point, NSW 2317. ☎ **1800/655 029** in Australia or 02/4982 7210. Fax 02/4982 7890. salamanda@fastlink.com.au.

90 units. A/C TV TEL. A$160.60 (U.S.$104.39) standard double; A$229–$249 (U.S.$148.85–$161.85) family suite; A$264–$284 (U.S.$171.60–$184.60) penthouse. Extra person A$20 (U.S.$13). Ask about packages. AE, BC, DC, MC, V.

Salamanda Shores looks like a beached, ramshackle paddle steamer—it's all white-painted bricks and rails and stairs, fixed to the bay by a jetty. Set in a well-tendered, sloping garden, this five-story hotel retains a certain 1960s charm, despite undergoing selective modernization. Rooms have spas and large balconies with extensive views of the bay. When the sun rises over the water and the garden is full of lorikeets and corellas, it couldn't be more picture-book perfect.

The hotel has three bars and two restaurants, one serving simple, well-priced seafood and the other with a piano player and candles for those more intimate moments with your credit card. There's also an outdoor pool, a sauna, and a bottle shop and pub. My only complaint is that it seems a little understaffed for such a large place.

Samurai Beach Bungalows Backpackers. Frost Rd., Anna Bay, NSW 2316. ☎/fax **02/4982 1921.** 8 units, none with bathroom. A$15 (U.S.$9.75) dorm bed; A$40 (U.S.$26) standard double; A$65 (U.S.$42.25) deluxe double; A$50 (U.S.$32.50) family room for 4. BC, MC, V.

These bungalows are nicely positioned between gum trees, tree ferns, and bougainvillea. Each standard two-room bungalow shares a bathroom, and come with either bunks or double beds. Room eight gets the morning sun and rooms four, five, and six get afternoon sun. Two new deluxe rooms each have private balconies (from which you can sometimes spot koalas), an attached bathroom with shower, a TV and towels. There are communal cooking facilities in a separate covered area, a TV room, and a games room with a pool table. Guests have free use of surfboards, and can hire bikes. The staff take care of laundry for A$2 (U.S.$1.30) a load. Public buses going to Newcastle or Nelson Bay stop outside the door around every hour (there's a more restricted service on weekends). A free connecting bus meets buses from Sydney, but if you're loaded down with luggage the hostel staff will pick you up.

WHERE TO DINE

Most people head down to Nelson Bay for their meals because of the great views across the bay. You'll also find a host of cheap takeout joints here.

The Pure Pizza Cafe. D'Albora Marina. ☎ **02/4984 2800.** Main courses A$9–$16.50 (U.S.$5.85–$10.73). Daily 11am–11pm. AE, BC, DC, MC, V. PIZZA/PASTA.

Perfect for takeout, this pizza and pasta place offers pizzas for around A$10 to $24 (U.S.$6.50–$15.60), depending on toppings, pastas for between A$10 and A$15 (U.S.$6.50 and $9.75), and salads too.

Rob's on the Boardwalk. D'Albora Marina. ☎ **02/4984 4444.** Main courses A$11.50–$22.50 (U.S.$7.48–14.63). Daily 8am–until the last customer leaves. AE, BC, DC, MC, V. CAFE.

You can pick up a hearty American breakfast at this busy cafe overlooking the bay, or a snack throughout the day. The Caesar salad is popular, as are the half dozen oysters for A$12.50 (U.S.$8.13). One of the best mains is the mixed seafood bouillabaisse, while the prime scotch filet with sautéed forest mushrooms, Jerusalem artichokes, gratin potatoes, and a red wine sauce would tempt even the most committed meat-eater.

Rock Lobster. D'Albora Marina. ☎ **02/4981 1813.** Main courses A$15–$29 (U.S.$9.75–$18.85). Seafood platter for 2 A$95 (U.S.$61.75). Daily 11:30am–2:30pm and 5:30–9:00pm. AE, BC, DC, MC, V. SEAFOOD.

Eat inside or out at this peaceful yet stylish restaurant. The plump Port Stephens Oysters should be enough to tempt you to start, while main courses such as smoked salmon in layers of wonton pastry with salad and wasabi sauce, or calamari flavored with chili and coriander in breadcrumbs with spicy passion-fruit dip should fill you up. There are usually a couple of meat dishes and a vegetarian option on the menu, too.

4 North of Sydney Along the Pacific Highway: Australia's Holiday Coast

The Pacific Highway leads over the Sydney Harbour Bridge and merges into the Sydney-Newcastle Freeway. It travels on into Newcastle, an industrial seaside town, and skirts the recreational areas of Tuggerah Lake and Lake Macquarie (neither of great interest compared to what's beyond). From here, the Pacific Highway stays close to the coast until it reaches Brisbane, some 1,000 kilometers (620 miles) from Sydney.

Though the road is gradually being upgraded, the conditions vary, and the distances are long. Travelers should be aware that the route is renowned for its accidents. Though you could make it to Brisbane in a couple of days, you could also easily spend more than a week stopping off at the attractions along the way. The farther north you travel the more obviously tropical the landscape gets. By the time visitors reach the coastal resort town of Coffs Harbour, temperatures have noticeably increased and banana palms and sugar cane plantations start to appear.

Along the coast, you'll find fishing and some superb beaches, most of them virtually deserted. Inland, the Great Dividing Range, which separates the wetter eastern plains from the dry interior, throws up rain forests, extinct volcanoes, and hobby farms growing tropical fruit as you head farther north toward the Queensland border. Along the way are a series of national parks, most of them requiring detours of several kilometers. Those you shouldn't miss include the Dorrigo and Mount Warning national parks, both of which offer some of the country's best and most accessible rain forests.

PORT MACQUARIE
423km (262 miles) N of Sydney

Port Macquarie (pop. 28,000) is roughly halfway between Sydney and the Queensland border. The main attractions here are some spectacular beaches, including Flynn's, which can offer exceptional surfing. Boating and fishing are other popular pastimes.

ESSENTIALS
GETTING THERE   From Sydney, motorists follow the Pacific Highway and then the Sydney-Newcastle freeway (F3). **Eastern Australia Airways** (☎ **02/9691 2333**) flies between Sydney and Port Macquarie. The coach trip from Sydney takes about 7 hours.

VISITOR INFORMATION   The **Port Macquarie Visitor Information Centre,** at the corner of Clarence and Hay streets, under the Civic Centre (☎ **1800/025 935** in Australia, or 02/6581 8000; fax 02 6581 8010; www.portmacquarieinfo.com.au), is open Monday to Friday, 8:30am to 5pm and Saturday and Sunday from 9am to 4pm.

EXPLORING THE AREA
The Billabong Koala and Wildlife Park, 61 Billabong Dr., Port Macquarie (☎ **02/ 6585 1060**), is a family-owned nature park where you can get up close to hand-raised koalas, kangaroos, emus, wombats, many types of birds, and fish. You can pat the

koalas at 10:30am, 1:30pm, and 3:30pm. There are also barbecue facilities, picnic grounds, and a restaurant. Allow 2 hours to fully experience this recommended wildlife park. It's open daily from 9am to 5pm; admission is A$8 (U.S.$5.20) for adults and A$5 (U.S.$3.25) for children.

The 257-passenger vessel **Port Venture** (☎ 02/6583 3058) leaves from the wharf at the end of Clarence Street Tuesday, Thursday, Friday, Saturday, and Sunday at 10am and 2pm, for a 2-hour scenic cruise on the Hastings River. Cruises cost A$20 (U.S.$13) for adults, A$8 ($5.20) for children 6 to 14, and A$49 (U.S.$31.85) for families. Reservations are essential. The boat also travels up the river on a 5-hour Barbecue Cruise every Wednesday morning leaving at 10am. It docks at a private bush park along the way and passengers can tuck into a traditional Aussie barbecue of steaks, fish, and salad. You can then fish, take a bushwalk, go swimming, or take a 20-minute 4WD trip. The cruise costs A$37 (U.S.$24.05) for adults, A$18 (U.S.$11.70) for children, and A$94 (U.S.$61.10) for families. A 4-hour cruise also leaves on Monday at 10am. It costs A$35 (U.S.$22.75) for adults, A$15 (U.S.$9.75) for children, and A$88 (U.S.$57.20) for families.

WHERE TO STAY

El Paso Motor Inn. 29 Clarence St., Port Macquarie, NSW 2444. ☎ **1800/027 965** in Australia or 02/6583 1944. Fax 02/6584 1021). 55 units. A/C MINIBAR TV TEL. A$87 (U.S.$56.55) standard double; A$97 (U.S.$63.05) deluxe double; A$130 (U.S.$84.50) spa rooms; A$150 (U.S.$97.50) suite. Extra person A$10 (U.S.$6.50). A$30 (U.S.$19.50) per room surcharge Easter, Christmas, and some long weekends. BC, DC, MC, V.

Located right on the waterfront, this motel offers standard-motel type rooms; the more expensive deluxe doubles are a little larger and have newer furniture and a fresher coat of paint after being refurbished in 1998. Two rooms come with spas, and some come with kitchenettes. The third-floor three-room suite has good ocean views and a kitchenette. The motel also has a heated pool, a sauna, a spa, a recreation room, a licensed restaurant overlooking the sea, and a cocktail bar.

COFFS HARBOUR: BANANA CAPITAL OF OZ

150km (93 miles) N of Port Macquarie; 572km (355 miles) N of Sydney, 427km (265 miles) S of Brisbane

The relaxed capital of Australia's Holiday Coast, **✪ Coffs Harbour,** is bounded by rain forests, beaches, and sand. The state's "banana republic" headquarters—the area produces more bananas than anywhere else in Australia—is bordered by hillsides with neat rows of banana palms. Farther inland, the rolling hills plateau into the Dorrigo National Park, one of the best examples of accessible rain forests anywhere in the world. Also inland is the Nymboida River, known for its excellent white-water rafting.

Coffs Harbour itself is a rather disjointed place, with an old town center retail area; the Jetty Strip (with restaurants and fishing boats) near the best swimming spot, Park Beach; and a new retail area called The Plaza. Wide sweeps of suburbia separates these three areas, making it a difficult town to negotiate if you don't have a car.

ESSENTIALS

GETTING THERE It takes around 7 hours to drive from Sydney to Coffs Harbour without stops; from Brisbane it takes around 5 hours. The Pacific Highway in this region is quite dangerous: there have been many serious accidents involving drivers spending long hours behind the wheel. Ongoing road-widening projects should hopefully improve things. **Qantas** (☎ **13 13 13** in Australia) and **Eastern Australian Airlines** fly nonstop to Coffs Harbour from Sydney. Several coach companies, including

Greyhound Pioneer (☎ **13 20 30** in Australia) and **McCafferty's** (☎ **13 14 99** in Australia), make the trip from Sydney in about 9 hours. A **Countrylink** (☎ **13 22 32** in Australia) train from Sydney costs A$75 (U.S.$48.75).

VISITOR INFORMATION   The **Coffs Harbour Visitors Information Centre** (☎ **1800/025 650** in Australia, or 02/6652 1522) is just off the Pacific Highway, at the corner of Rose Avenue and Marcia Street, two blocks north of the city center. It's open daily from 9am to 5pm.

GETTING AROUND   If you don't have a car, you can get around on the **Coffs Harbour Coaches** (☎ **02/6652 2877**), which runs day trips around the area on weekdays (including a town tour on Monday, and a trip to the magnificent Dorrigo National Park on Wednesday). ✪ **Blue Tongue Transport** (☎ **1800 258 386** in Australia or 02/6651 8566, or) offers smaller tours of Dorrigo National Park daily costing $50 (U.S.$33) for adults and $40 (U.S.$26) for children; a morning city tour for $11 (U.S.$7.15); and an afternoon champagne tour of town for $22 (U.S.$14.).

CHECKING OUT THE BIG BANANA & OTHER THINGS TO DO

You can't miss the 10-meter (33-ft.) concrete banana alongside the highway at the ✪ **Big Banana Theme Park** (☎ **02/6652 4355**), 3 kilometers (2 miles) north of town. The park includes an air-conditioned, diesel-powered train that takes visitors on a 1-hour tour of the 45-acre banana plantation that contains some 18,000 trees. Along the route it passes various exhibits relating to farming, Aborigines, and local history. It stops at the property's hydroponic glasshouses and at a viewing platform and cafeteria, which serves up banana cake, banana bread, banana splits, banana shakes, and so on. The park is open daily from 9am to 4.30pm (3pm in winter). Admission is free, but the train tour costs A$10 (U.S.$6.50) for adults, A$6 (U.S.$3.90) for children, and A$25 (U.S.$16.25) for families. I had my doubts before I visited, but I must admit I ended up enthusing about it—even if it was just about the wackiness of the place.

The **Coffs Harbour Zoo** (☎ **02/6656 1330**), 10 minutes north of town on the Pacific Highway, has plenty of breeding koalas (you can pet them), as well as wombats, kangaroos, dingoes, Tasmanian Devils, water birds, and aviaries. The award-winning native gardens are full of wild birds expecting a feed. The zoo is open daily from 8:30am to 4pm. Admission is A$12 (U.S.$7.80) for adults, A$6 (U.S.$3.90) for children, and A$30 (U.S.$19.50) for families.

A free natural attraction is **Mutton Bird Island,** which you can get to via the Coffs Harbour jetty. A steep path leads up the side of the island, but the views from the top are worth it. Between September and April the island is home to thousands of shearwaters (or mutton birds), which make their nests in burrows in the ground.

If you prefer fish, try diving with gray nurse sharks, manta rays, and moray eels with **Island Snorkle and Dive** (☎ **02/6654 2860**) or **Dive Quest** (☎ **02/6654 1930**). *The Pamela Star* (☎ **02/6658 4379**) offers good-value deep-sea fishing trips including all tackle and bait, and lunch, for A$60 (U.S.$39). The boat leaves Coffs Harbour jetty at 7:30am and returns at 1:30pm daily.

For a taste of gold fever, head to **George's Gold Mine,** 40 kilometers (25 miles) west of Coffs Harbour on Bushman's Range Road (☎ **02/6654 5355** or 02/ 6654 5273). You get to go into a typical old-timer gold mine, see the "stamper battery" crushing the ore, and pan for gold. The mine is open Wednesday through Sunday (daily during school and public holidays) from 10:30am to 4pm. Admission is A$9 (U.S.$5.85) for adults, A$4.50 (U.S.$2.93) for children, A$26 (U.S.$16.90) for families.

You might also like to visit **Kiwi Down Under Farm** (☎ **02/6653 4449**), a fascinating organic farm growing kiwi fruit and macadamia nuts, among other things. No nasty sprays are used here! Free 30- to 45-minute guided tours leave at 2pm, 3pm, and 4pm on weekends and school holidays. The teashop on the premises serves amazing scones and jam for A$4.50 (U.S.$2.93) and vegetarian lunches for A$8.50 (U.S.$5.53). The farm is 14 kilometers south of Coffs Harbour; turn off at Gleniffer Road., just south of Bonville, and follow the signs for 4 kilometers (2.5 miles).

SHOPPING FOR ARTS & CRAFTS

There are several recognized "craft drives" in the area, where tourists can go in search of quality souvenirs. Pick up a free copy of *Discover the Coffs Harbour Region* from the tourist information center for more details on the dozens of craft shops in the area. One of the best is the **Australian Wild Flower Gallery** (☎ **02/6651 5763**), just of West High Street and Bennetts Road. Wolfgang Shultze carves intricate designs out of pewter, silver, and gold to make detailed animal- and plant-inspired jewelry, charms, and spoons. Pieces cost between A$5 and $36 (U.S.$3.25 and 23.40). The gallery is open daily from 9am to 5pm.

On the way to or from the Dorrigo rain forest, stop off at the township of **Bellingen,** 20 minutes south of Coffs Harbour on Waterfall Way. It's a pleasant place with several interesting craft shops. Among the best are **The Old Church** (☎ **02/6655 0438**), 8 Church St. (just off the main road), crammed full of wooden craft items, cards, furniture, wacky mobiles, incense, hats and knickknacks, and surrounded by gardens and fruit trees. It's open daily from 8:30am to 5:30pm.

EXPLORING THE RAIN FORESTS & OTHER OUTDOOR ADVENTURES

Coffs Harbour's main tourist attraction is its position as a good base for exploring the surrounding countryside. You must see the World Heritage-listed ✪ **Dorrigo National Park,** 68 kilometers (42 miles) west of Coffs Harbour, via Bellingen. Perched on the Great Dividing Range that separates the lush eastern seaboard from the arid interior, the rain forest here is one of the best I've seen in Australia (it's a pity that so much of it fell to the axes of early settlers). Entry to the rain forest is free.

The **Dorrigo Rainforest Centre** (☎ **02/6657 2309**) is the gateway to the park and has extensive information on the local rain forest. Just outside is the 21-meter-high (69-ft.-high) Skywalk, which offers a bird's-eye view of the forest canopy. There are several rain forest walks leaving either the Rainforest Centre, the Glade Picnic Area (about 1km/½-mile away), and the **Never-Never Picnic Area** (a 10km drive along Dome Road). Most tracks are suitable for wheelchairs. Bring a raincoat or an umbrella; it's not called a rain forest for nothing. The **Dorrigo Tourist Information office** (☎ **02/6657 2486**) is in the center of Dorrigo township.

One of the best tour operators in the area is the award-winning **Mountain Trails 4WD Tours** (☎ **02/6658 3333;** fax 02/6658 3299). Full-day tours that include visits to two rain forest areas and a good lunch cost A$80 (U.S.$52) for adults and A$60 (U.S.$39) for children under 16. Half-day tours of one rain forest cost A$56 (U.S.$36.40) for adults and A$40 (U.S.$26) for children.

For a bit more personal action, try horseback riding through the rain forest 23 kilometers (14 miles) southwest of Coffs Harbour with **Valery Trails** (☎ **02/6653 4301**). Two-hour rides leave at 10am and 2pm daily and cost A$35 (U.S.$22.75) per person, bookings essential.

More hectic still are ✪ **white-water rafting trips** through the wilderness on the Nymboida River with ✪ **Wow Rafting,** 1448 Coramba Rd., Coramba via Coffs Harbour, NSW 2450 (☎ **1800/640 330** in Australia or 02/6654 4066). Full-day trips, including morning tea, snack, and a barbecue meal, cost A$153 (U.S.$99.45). These adventurous trips operate year-around, depending on water levels. A 2-day trip costs A$325 (U.S.$211.25), with meals and overnight camping. If the water level in the Nymboida is low, you raft on the Goolang Creek, which offers a shorter but still exciting run. Most of the rapids are grade 3; some of them can be pretty hairy. The rafting guides are real characters; although they're safety conscious, you're sure to be dunked a few times.

Rapid Rafting 2000 (☎ **1800 629 797** in Australia, or 02/6652 1741) also run rafting trips on the Goolang River, costing $77 (U.S.$50) for a half-day trip, and A$120 (U.S.$78) for a full-day.

Looking for another adrenaline rush? Then head to the **Raleigh International Raceway** (☎ **02/6655 4017**), where you can zip around behind the wheel of your very own . . . go-kart. It's located 23 kilometers (14 miles) south of Coffs Harbour and 3 kilometers (2 miles) along Valery Road off the Pacific Highway north of Nambucca Heads. Six high-speed laps cost A$16 (U.S.$10.40), eleven cost A$23 (U.S.$14.95), and sixteen cost A$32 (U.S.$20.80). It's open daily from 9am to 5pm (6pm in summer).

The *Pacific Explorer* catamaran (☎ **0418/663 815** mobile phone, or 02/6652 7225 after working hours) operates whale-watching trips between June and October; the 2½ cruises cost A$44 (U.S.$28.60). Between November and May, they run half-day dolphin-watching cruises for the same price

WHERE TO STAY

Coffs Harbour is a popular beachside holiday spot with plenty of motels along the Pacific Highway offering standard roadside rooms from between A$35 (U.S.$22.75) to $49 (U.S.$31.85) per night. Vacancy signs are common except during Australian school holiday periods and the Christmas and Easter periods (when Coffs really fills up). A few to try are the **Caribbean Motel,** 353 High St., Coffs Harbour, NSW 2450 (☎ **02/6652 1500;** fax 02/6651 4158), with doubles ranging from A$55 to $120 (U.S.$35.75–$78) depending on the season and the view; and the **Coffs Harbour Motor Inn**, 22 Elizabeth St., Coffs Harbour, NSW 2450 (☎ **02/6652 6388;** fax 02/6652 6493), with doubles ranging from A$72 to $108 (U.S.$46.80–$70.20) depending on the season.

✪ **Pelican Beach Centre Resort.** Pacific Hwy., Coffs Harbour, NSW 2450. ☎ **1800/ 02 8882** in Australia, 800/835-7742 in the U.S. and Canada, or 02/6653 7000. Fax 02/ 6653 7066. 112 units. A/C MINIBAR TV TEL. A$98–$170 (U.S.$63.70–$110.50) standard room for 1 or 2; A$205–$265 (U.S.$133.25–$172.25) family room for up to 4; A$265–$420 (U.S.$172.25–$273) suite. Extra person A$25 (U.S.$16.25). Ask about packages and discounts. The higher rates apply Dec 26–Jan 18. AE, BC, DC, MC, V.

This Bali-style resort complex is situated 7 kilometers (4.2 miles) north of Coffs Harbour beside a long stretch of creamy sand (the beach is dangerous for swimming). Terraced over six levels, the resort's rooms all have balconies and many have ocean views. Standard rooms are light and modern, with either twin or queen beds. Family rooms have a kitchenette and dining area and one queen and two single beds divided by a half wall. Suites have a separate bedroom, kitchenette, lounge area, and spa bath. Two rooms are equipped for travelers with disabilities. Outside in the gardens are three tennis courts, a mini golf course, a volleyball court, and a lagoonlike heated pool. There are also indoor and outdoor spas, a sauna, a gym, and a barbecue area. There's also a game room and a kids club that operates on weekends and school holidays. Award-winning Shores Restaurant offers indoor and terrace dining. Taxis operate from the resort to the town center for A$3 (U.S.$1.95) each way.

Sanctuary Resort. Pacific Hwy. Coffs Harbour, NSW 2450. ☎ **02/6652 2111.** Fax 02/ 6652 4725. 37 units. A/C TV TEL. A$88 (U.S.$57.20) standard double; A$93.50 (U.S.$60.78) superior double; A$150 (U.S.$97.50) executive double. Extra person A$13.50 (U.S.$8.7800). Holiday surcharges. Ask about lower rates through Aussie auto clubs. AE, BC, DC, MC, V.

If you like animals you'll love this animal sanctuary/guest house complex 2 kilometers (1¼ miles) south of town. Wandering around are wallabies, kangaroos, peacocks, and several species of native birds. The rooms are comfortable, with the more expensive rooms being larger and more recently renovated. The executive room comes with a spa.

In Nearby Nambucca Heads

If you're really looking to get away from it all, consider the small town of Nambucca (pronounced *nam-buck-a*) Heads, 44 kilometers (27 miles) south of Coffs Harbour. They practically roll up the streets after 6pm here. The **Nambucca Valley Visitor Information Centre** (☎ **02/6568 6954;** fax 02/6568 5004; nambuct@midcoast. com.au), on the Pacific Highway on the southern entrance to town, is open daily from 9am to 5pm.

Beilby's Beach House. 1 Ocean St., Nambucca Heads, NSW 2448. ☎ **02/6568 6466.** Fax 02/6568 5822. beilbys@midcoast.com.au. 5 units, 3 with bathroom. TV. A$40–$50 (U.S.$26–$32.50) double without bathroom; A$60–$75 (U.S.$39–$48.75) double with bathroom; A$80– $100 (U.S.$52–$65) family room. Rates include breakfast. BC, MC, V.

If you're looking for a peaceful place, then come to Beilby's (named after the beach opposite). The standard rooms here are basic but comfortable and have either a queen or a double bed. Three come with an attached shower. The family room is two small rooms with an adjoining door. All rooms have a verandah overlooking a bush garden. There are polished floorboards throughout, a large swimming pool, a guest kitchen, large covered barbecue area, laundry, Internet facilities, and computer games. It's a short walk through the bird-filled bush to the beach. While a few backpackers stay here, the guests range from young couples to families and senior citizens.

Scotts Guesthouse. 4 Wellington Dr., Nambucca Heads, NSW 2448. ☎ **02/6568 6386.** Fax 02/6569 4169. 8 units. TV. A$70–$110 (U.S.$45.50–$71.50) double (depending on season). Extra person A$20 (U.S.$13). Extra child A$15 (U.S.$9.75). Rates include breakfast. AE, BC, DC, MC, V.

Scotts, a friendly B&B run by an Irish couple, offers good motel-style rooms in a modernized 1887 house not far from the beach. All rooms are spacious and very modern, and have a good-size balcony with a good view. They come with a queen-size bed, a shower, and a fridge. Family rooms have an extra double sofa bed and a single. Try to get room number 1 for the best views.

WHERE TO DINE

✪ **Seafood Mama's.** Pacific Hwy. ☎ **02/6653 6733.** Reservations recommended. Main courses A$12.50–$25 (U.S.$8.13–$16.25). AE, BC, DC, MC, V. Tues–Sat 6–10pm. ITALIAN/SEAFOOD.

This award-winning Italian restaurant packs a mean barbecue seafood dish of octopus, prawns, fish, calamari, and mussels. Also on the menu in this rustic, bottles-hanging-from-the-ceiling Italian joint are some well-regarded veal and steak dishes, and plenty of pastas, It's cheerful, friendly, and informal, and does takeout and hotel deliveries. Seafood Mama's is right on the ocean, near the Pelican Beach and the older Nautilus resorts, 7 kilometers (4.2 miles) north of Coffs Harbour.

BYRON BAY: A BEACH BOHEMIA
78km (48 miles) SE of Murwillumbah

Being the most easterly point on the Australian mainland, the sun's rays hit ✪ **Byron Bay** before anywhere else. This geographical position is good for two things: you can spot whales close to shore as they migrate north in June and July, and it's attractive to the town's "alternative" community. Painters, craftspeople, glass blowers, and poets are so plentiful they almost fall from the macadamia nut trees. The place is loaded with float tanks, "pure body products," beauty therapists, and massage centers. Though it attracts squadrons of backpackers each summer to its party scene and discos, many of the locals simply stay at home, sipping their herbal tea and preparing for the healing light of the coming dawn. Families love Byron Bay for the beautiful beaches, and surfers flock here for some of the best surfing in the world.

ESSENTIALS
GETTING THERE   If you're driving up the north coast, leave the Pacific Highway at Ballina and take the scenic coast road via Lennox Head. It's around 10 hours by car from Sydney, and 2 hours (200km/124 miles) south of Brisbane. The **Coolangatta airport** is just north of the Queensland border, 112 kilometers (69.5 miles) away. **Countrylink** (☎ **13 22 32** in Australia) runs daily trains from Sydney to Byron Bay; the one-way fare is A$92 (U.S.$59.80) one-way for adults and A$46 (U.S.$29.90) for children. **Greyhound Pioneer** (☎ **13 20 30** in Australia) buses from Sydney take around 13½ hours; the one-way coach fare is A$69 (U.S.$44.85).

ORGANIZED TOURS FROM SYDNEY   An unusual way to get to Byron is on a five-day surf safari from Sydney with **Aussie Surf Adventures,** P.O. Box 614, Toukley, NSW 2263 (☎ **1800/113 044** in Australia, or 0414/863 787 mobile; fax 02/4396 1797). The trips leave 8:30am every Monday (between Sept and May) from Sydney's Circular Quay, stopping off for surfing, body boarding, fishing, and nature walks along the way. Beginners to experienced surfers are welcomed. Included are all meals, surfing lessons, surfing equipment, accommodation and return bus to Sydney. Trips cost A$380 (U.S.$247).

A highly recommended 3-day tour is with the likeable Ivan from **Pioneering Spirit** (☎ **1800/672 422** in Australia, or 0412/048 333 mobile phone; www.users.omcs. com.au/pioneering). Suitable for adventurous travelers, the trip by minicoach leaves Sydney every Friday and stops on the way for swimming, animal spotting, a tour of the Hunter Valley and Dorrigo National Park, bushwalking. Accommodations are in basic, but interesting buildings. The trips cost A$235 (U.S.$152.75) including transport, meals (except lunch), accommodations, and entry fees.

VISITOR INFORMATION   The **Byron Visitors Centre,** 80 Jonson St., Byron Bay, NSW 2481 (☎ **02/6685 8050;** fax 02/6685 8533), is open daily from 9am to 5pm. A half hour farther south is the **Ballina Tourist Information Centre,** on the corner of Las Balsas Plaza and River Street, Ballina (☎ **02/6686 3484;** fax 02/ 6686 0136), open daily from 9am to 5pm. Two good websites on the area are www. byron-bay.com and www.byronbay-online.com.

SPECIAL EVENTS   Byron really goes to town during its Easter weekend **Blues Festival,** and on the first Sunday of every month when the extraordinary local craft market brings hippies and funky performers out from the hinterland.

HITTING THE SURF & SAND
Many accommodations in Byron Bay offer free surfboards for guests, or else head to the **Byron Bay Surf Shop,** on Lawson Street Cnr Fletcher St (☎ **02/6685 7536**),

which rents boards for A$12 (U.S.$7.80) for 4 hours and A$20 (U.S.$13) for 24 hours. The shop can also arrange surf lessons for around A$25 (U.S.$16.25) per hour.

Wategos Beach and an area off the tip of Cape Byron called **"The Pass"** are two particularly good surf spots, though since each of Byron's main beaches faces a different direction, you are bound to find the surf is up on at least one. **Main Beach,** which stretches along the front of the town (it's actually some 50km/31 miles, long), is good for swimming. West of Main Beach is **Belongil Beach,** which acts as an unofficial nudist beach when the authorities aren't cracking down on covering up. **Clarke's Beach** curves away to the east of Main Beach toward Cape Byron.

The **Cape Byron Lighthouse** on Cape Byron is one of Australia's most powerful. It's eerie to come up here at night to watch the stars and see the light reach some 40 kilometers (25 miles) out to sea. A nice walk just south of town goes through the rain forest of the **Broken Heads Nature Reserve.**

The best place to dive is at **Julian Rocks,** about 3 kilometers (2 miles) offshore. Cold currents from the south meet warmer ones from the north, which makes it a good spot to find a variety of marine sea life. **Byron Bay Dive Centre,** 111 Jonson Street (☎ **02/6685 7149**) charges A$70 (U.S.$45.50) for the first dive and A$35 (U.S.$22.75) for each subsequent dive. **Sundive,** in the Byron Hostel complex on Middleton Street (☎ **02/6685 7755**), has cheaper initial dives at A$60 (U.S.$39) each.

EXPLORING THE HILLS & RAIN FORESTS

Behind Byron you'll find hills that could make the Irish weep, as well as rain forests, waterfalls, and small holdings burgeoning with tropical fruits. A good operator taking trips inland is **Forgotten Country Ecotours** (☎ **02/6687 7843**). **Byron Bay to Bush Tours** (☎ **02/6685 6889,** or 0418/662 684 mobile; bush@mullum.com.au) operates day trips to the hippie hangout of ◐ **Nimbin** and up into the rain forest, visiting a macadamia nut farm on the way and having a barbecue on their organic farm. The trip leaves at 11am Monday to Saturday and costs A$30 (U.S.$19.50). They also operate trips to the Sunday market at Channon on the second Sunday of each month and the one at Bangalow on the fourth Sunday. These trips cost A$15 (U.S.$9.75).

WHERE TO STAY

Real estate agents **Elders R Gordon & Sons** (☎ **02/6685 6222;** eldersbb@omcs. com.au) can book rooms and cottages in Byron Bay and in the hinterland. Rates vary.

◐ **The Byron Bay Waves Motel (The Waves).** Corner of Lawson and Middleton sts. (P.O Box 647, Byron Bay 2481). ☎ **02/6685 5966.** Fax 02/6685 5977. www.byron-bay. com/waves. A/C TV TEL. 19 units. A$150–$250 (U.S.$97.50–$162.50) double depending on season; A$250–$360 (U.S.$162.50–$234) suite; A$300–$490 (U.S.$195–$318.50) penthouse. Extra person A$20 (U.S.$13), extra child under 16 A$20 (U.S.$13). AE, BC, DC, MC, V.

This exceptional motel is 60 meters (195 ft.) from Main Beach and around the corner from the town center. The rooms are very nice, and all come with a queen-size bed, a marble bathroom with shower and large tub, a safe, refrigerator, iron and ironing board, hair dryers, and tea- and coffee-making facilities. Four rooms on the ground floor have a courtyard, and one is suitable for travelers with disabilities. Toasters, in-house massage, and beauty treatments are also available. The suites have a king-size bed and a balcony. The penthouse is a plush and fully self-contained one-bedroom apartment. There are six family rooms sleeping three adults, or two adults and two children.

Byron Central Apartments. Byron St., Byron Bay, NSW 2481. ☎ **02/6685 8800.** Fax 02/6685 8802. byroncentral@one.net.au. 26 units. TV TEL. A$90–$180 (U.S.$58.50–$117) standard apt (depending on season). Higher rates apply Christmas/New Year period; low season is Apr–Sept. Ask about discounts for multiple-night stays. AE, BC, DC, MC, V.

The apartments here have ceiling fans, full kitchens, a queen-size bed and a queen-size sofa bed, and free in-house movies. Those on the first floor come with balconies. There are also a few loft-style apartments with separate dining, lounge, and sleeping areas. Units for people with disabilities are available. The landscaped, mostly concrete surrounds house a saltwater pool and a barbecue. There's also a laundry. The apartments are a 2-minute walk from the main beach and town.

✪ **Holiday Village Backpackers.** 116 Jonson St., Byron Bay, NSW 2481. ☎ **02/ 6685 8888.** Fax 02/6685 8777. 42 units, 13 with bathroom. A$55–$65 (U.S.$35.75–$42.25) double in hostel; A$70–$85 (U.S.$45.50–$55.25) self-contained double. A$21–$29 (U.S.$13.65–18.85) dorm bed. BC, DC, MC, V.

Byron Bay's original hostel is still one of the best. It's in the center of town next to Woolworth's supermarket and a few minutes' walk from the bus and train stops, the main beach, and the town center. It's a five-star backpackers, which is as good as it gets. Dorm rooms are clean, and doubles in the hostel are above average and come with a double bed, a fan, and a wardrobe. For a little more you can have a self-contained unit with a separate bedroom, lounge, and kitchen area. On the premises are a volleyball court, a spa and pool, a TV and video lounge (there's a video library), barbecues, a basketball hoop, Internet and e-mail, free surfboards, body boards, and bicycles.

✪ **Taylor's Guest House.** 160 McGettigan's Lane, Ewingsdale, Byron Bay, NSW 2481. ☎ **02/6684 7436.** Fax 02/6684 7526. 5 units, 1 cottage. TV. A$200 (U.S.$130) double; A$330 (U.S.$214.50) cottage. Rates include breakfast, cakes and biscuits, and predinner champagne cocktails. Surcharge of 20% for doubles and 50% for cottage at Christmas and Easter. AE, BC, DC, MC, V. Not suitable for children.

This beautiful guesthouse is set in five acres of gardens and rain forest. Rooms vary in price depending on whether you stay for one night or more. The guest rooms are lavishly decorated in a country style and come with either a queen- or king-size bed. The cottage is huge, has wraparound verandas and French windows, and is done up in bright Santa Fe–style colors. The cottage also comes with a laundry and the largest bed in Australia—an 8-foot by 7-foot antique English "Emperor" bed. In the garden is a very large swimming pool. A three-course dinner here costs A$50 (U.S.$32.50).

WHERE TO DINE

Beach Hotel Barbecue. In the Beach Hotel, at Bay and Johnson sts. ☎ **02/6685 6402.** Main courses A$3.90–$13.50 (U.S.$2.54–$8.78). No credit cards. Daily noon–3pm. PUB/ BARBECUE.

The outdoor meals served at this pub near the beach make it very popular with visitors and locals alike. About the cheapest thing on the menu is the burger, and the most expensive a steak. The Beach Hotel Bistro here is open from 10am to 9pm daily and serves coffee, cakes, and snacks throughout the day; a full lunch menu is served from noon to 3pm and dinner from 6 to 9pm.

Earth 'n' sea. 11 Lawson St. ☎ **02/6685 6029.** Reservations recommended. Main courses A$9.50–$23.50 (U.S.$6.18–$15.28). AE, BC, MC, V. Daily 5:30–11pm. PIZZA/PASTA.

This popular spot has been around for years and offers an extensive menu of pastas and pizzas, including some unusual combinations such as prawns, banana, and pineapple. Pizzas come in three sizes, and the small is just enough to satisfy the average appetite.

✪ **The Pass Café.** At the end of Brooke Dr., on Cape Byron Walking Track, Palm Valley. ☎ **02/6685 6074.** Main courses A$10–$25 (U.S.$6.50–$16.25). BC, MC, V. Daily 8am–3pm; Thurs–Sat until 6pm. MEDITERRANEAN.

Though not as well positioned as Rae's Restaurant and Bar (see below), the Pass Café rivals Rae's for breakfasts and lunches, and if you happen to be heading to or from the local rain forest on the Cape Byron Walking Track, you'll find this a great place to stop off. Breakfast items range from simple fresh fruit and muffins to gourmet chicken sausages. Lunch specials include Cajun chicken, octopus and calamari salad, as well as fresh fish, meat dishes, and plenty of good vegetarian options.

✪ **Raving Prawn.** Feros Arcade (between Jonson and Lawson sts.). ☎ **02/6685 6737.** Reservations recommended. Main courses A$19–$27 (U.S.$12.35–$17.55). AE, BC, DC, MC, V. Tues–Sat 6–10pm (until around 9pm in winter). Open daily during school holidays. SEAFOOD.

Fish cover the walls at this excellent place, but there's more than that on the menu. You can tuck into veal, chicken, or vegetarian dishes if you want to, but I wouldn't miss out on the fabulous signature dish, the jewfish (a kind of grouper) with a herb-mustard crust. The forest-berry tart is the best dessert on the menu.

Worth a Splurge

✪ **Rae's Restaurant and Bar.** Watago's Beach, Byron Bay. ☎ **02/6685 5366.** Reservations recommended. Dinner main courses A$37–$60 (U.S.$24.05–$39); lunch A$30–$35 (U.S.$19.50–$22.75). AE, BC, DC, MC, V. Daily 7–10pm; Sat–Sun noon–3pm. MODERN AUSTRALIAN/SEAFOOD.

You can't beat Rae's for its location or its food. It's right on the beach, about 2-minute drive from the town center, and has a secluded, privileged air about it in the nicest of ways. Inside it's Mediterranean blue and white, which complements perfectly the incoming rollers hitting the sand. The menu changes daily, but you may find grilled Atlantic salmon, red curry of roast beef filet, braised lamb shanks, and yellowfin tuna. If you have any special dietary requirements, tell the chef, and he will go out of his way to please you. Next door to the restaurant, but part of the same establishment, is Rae's on Watago's, an exclusive guesthouse offering luxury accommodations.

MURWILLUMBAH

321km (200 miles) N of Coffs Harbour; 893km (554 miles) N of Sydney; 30km (19 miles) S of Queensland border

The main town of the Tweed Valley, Murwillumbah is a good base for touring the surrounding area, which includes ✪ **Mount Warning,** picturesque country towns, and countryside dominated by sugarcane and banana.

ESSENTIALS

GETTING THERE   Murwillumbah is inland from the Pacific Highway. The nearest airport is at **Coolangatta,** 34 kilometers (21 miles) away just over the Queensland border. **Countrylink** trains (☎ **13 22 42** in Australia) link Murwillumbah with Sydney, taking 12 hours and 40 minutes. **Greyhound Pioneer** (☎ **13 20 30** in Australia) buses run from Sydney to Murwillumbah; the trip takes 14½ hours.

VISITOR INFORMATION   The **Murwillumbah Visitors Centre,** at the corner of the Pacific Highway and Alma Street, Murwillumbah, NSW 2484 (☎ **02/6672 1340**), is worth visiting before heading out to see more of the Tweed Valley or the beaches to the east. Another option is the **Tweed Heads Visitors Centre,** at the corner of Bay and Wharf streets, Tweed Heads, NSW 2485 (☎ **07/5536 4244**). Both are open Monday to Friday from 9am to 5pm, and Saturday from 9am to 1pm.

SEEING THE AREA

If you're looking for a Big Avocado to go with your Coffs Harbour Big Banana, then head for **Tropical Fruit World,** on the Pacific Highway (☎ **02/6677 7222**),

15 kilometers (9 miles) north of Murwillumbah and 15 kilometers south of Coolangatta. The Tweed Valley's top attraction grows some 400 varieties of tropical fruit, which can be discovered on an interesting 1½-hour tractor-train tour of the 200-acre tropical fruit plantation, as well as on 4WD rain forest drives and riverboat rides. It's open daily 10am to 5pm. Also on the property are a kiosk, fruit market, and gift shop. Admission to food and shopping areas is free. Guided tours cost A$22 (U.S.$14.30) for adults, A$12 (U.S.$7.80) for children 4 to 12.

The 1,154-meter (3,815-ft.) **Mount Warning** is part of the rim of an extinct volcano that formed from volcanic action some 20 to 23 million years ago. You can hike around the mountain and to the top of it on trails in the Mount Warning World Heritage Park.

WHERE TO STAY & DINE
Worth a Splurge
❂ **Crystal Creek Rainforest Retreat.** Brookers Rd., Upper Crystal Creek, Murwillumbah, NSW 2484. ☎ **02/6679 1591.** Fax 02/6679 1596). 7 cabins. TV. A$230–$245 (U.S.$149.50–$159.25). Ask about lower midweek rates and weekly specials. BC, MC, V. Pick-up service from the airport, and bus and train stations is available. Not suitable for children.

Crystal Creek is tucked away in a little valley of grazing cows just 25 minutes by car from the Pacific Highway. Self-contained cabins nestle on the edge of a rain forest bordering the Border Ranges National Park, a World Heritage Site. There are plenty of native birds, possums, echidnas, wallabies, and bandicoots around. Though the water is always cold, guests can swim in the natural pools and laze on hammocks strung up in the bush. Cabins have two comfortable rooms, a balcony, a kitchen, a barbecue, and plenty of privacy. To live up to the eco-lodge's image, everything inside is green, even the sheets. Two glass-terrace cabins overlook the rain forest and mountain and have a king-size bed and a double spa. Several tours are offered, including 4WD rain forest tours and visits to local markets and galleries. Bird-watching and canoeing are popular on the nearby lake. Guests cook their own food or eat at the casual restaurant.

AFTER DARK
The clubs up here on the border of Queensland are huge and offer cheap bistro meals as well as pricier ones in the more upscale restaurants, inexpensive drinks at the bar, entertainment, and hundreds of poker machines. The biggest in New South Wales is the **Twin Towns Services Club,** Wharf St., Tweed Heads (☎ **07/5536 2277**). Another worth checking out is **Seagulls Rugby League Club,** Gollan Drive, Tweed Heads (☎ **07/5536 3433**). Major entertainers such as Tom Jones, Joe Cocker, and Bob Hope have played here over the last few years. It's open 24 hours.

To gain admittance to these "private" clubs, you must sign the registration book just inside the door.

5 South of Sydney Along the Princes Highway

There are two main roads leading south out of Sydney: the Hume Highway and the Princes Highway. Both connect Sydney to Melbourne, but the Hume Highway is quicker. A favorite with truckies and anyone in a hurry, the Hume Highway will get you to Melbourne in about 12 hours. The Princes Highway is a scenic coastal route that can get you to Melbourne in two days, though the many attractions along the route make it well worth spending longer.

KIAMA
119km (74 miles) S of Sydney

Kiama (pop. 10,300) is famous for its **blowhole.** In fact, there are two, a large one and a smaller one, but both spurt seawater several meters into the air. The larger of the two can jet water up to 60 meters (195 ft.), but you need a large swell and strong south-easterly winds to force the sea through the rock fissure with enough force to achieve that height. The smaller of the two is more consistent, but fares better with a good northeasterly wind.

Get a map from the **Kiama Visitors Centre** (see below) to guide you around a Her-itage Walk around the historic precinct of this harborside village, including a row of National Trust workers cottages built in 1896 and open from 10am to 5pm daily. There's little reason to stay in Kiama as plenty more scenic places await further south.

ESSENTIALS
GETTING THERE   From Sydney, travel south on the Princes Highway via Wollongong. There's also a regular train service from Sydney and **Greyhound Pioneer** (☎ **13 20 30** in Australia) coach service. The trip by coach takes about 2 hours.

VISITOR INFORMATION   The **Kiama Visitors Centre** at Blowhole Point, Kiama (☎ **02/4232 3322;** fax 02/4226 3260; www.kiama.net/tourism.htm; kiama tourism@ozemail.com.au.), is open daily from 9am to 5pm.

JERVIS BAY: OFF-THE-BEATEN-TRACK GEM
182km (113 miles S of Sydney)

Bouderee National Park at ✪ **Jervis Bay** is nothing short of spectacular. You should make a trip here even if you have to miss out on some of Sydney's treasures. How does this grab you: miles of deserted beaches, the whitest sand in the world, kangaroos you can stroke, lorikeets who mob you for food during the day time and possums who do the same at night, pods of dolphins, some great walks through gorgeous bushland, and a real Aboriginal spirituality-of-place? I could go on, but it's best you see it for yourself.

ESSENTIALS
GETTING THERE   It's best to reach Jervis Bay via Huskisson, 24 kilometers (15 miles) southeast of Nowra on the Princes Highway. Approximately 16 kilometers (10 miles) south of Nowra, turn left onto the Jervis Bay Road to Huskisson. The entrance to Bouderee National Park is just after Huskisson. It's about a 3-hour drive from Sydney.

Australian Pacific Tours (☎ **02/9247 7222;** fax 02/9247 2052; www.aptours. com.au) runs a dolphin-watching cruise from Sydney every day from early October to mid-April, and Monday and Thursday in winter. The 12-hour trip—7 of which are on the coach—includes a visit to the Kiama blowhole, a 3-hour luncheon cruise for bottlenose dolphins, and a stop at Fitzroy Falls in the Southern Highlands. The trip costs A$116.50 (U.S.$75.73) for adults, and A$108.50 (U.S.$70.53) for children.

VISITOR INFORMATION   For information on the area, contact the **Shoalhaven Visitors Centre,** at the corner of Princes Hwy & Pleasant Way, Nowra (☎ **1800/ 024 261** in Australia, or 02/4421 0778; www.shoalhaven.nsw.gov.au). Pick up maps and book camping sites at the **Bouderee National Park** office (☎ **02/4443 0977**), located just beyond Huskisson; it's open daily from 9am to 4pm. Hyams Beach Store (☎ **02/4443 0242**) has an accommodation guide listing 34 rental properties from A$100 (U.S.$65) a weekend.

SEEING THE AREA

If you want to see the best spots, you'll need to pay the park entrance fee of A$7.50 (U.S.$4.88). The entrance sticker lasts seven days. Some places you can visit include ✪ **Hyams Beach,** reputed to have the whitest sand in the world. Notice how it squeaks when you walk on it. Wear sunscreen! The reflection off the beach can burn your skin in minutes. **Hole in the Wall Beach** has interesting rock formations and a smell of natural sulfur. Summer Cloud Bay is secluded and offers excellent fishing.

Dolphin Watch Cruises, 74 Owen St., Huskisson (☎ **1800/246 010** in Australia or 02/4441 6311,) runs a hardy vessel out of Huskisson on the lookout for the resident pod of bottlenose dolphins—and says you have "more than a 95% chance of seeing them." Lunch cruises run daily at 1pm, and a coffee cruise runs at 10am on Saturdays and Sundays and holidays. The 2½-hour lunch cruise costs A$35 (U.S.$22.75) for adults and A$19.50 (U.S.$12.68) for children including lunch. The 2-hour coffee cruise costs A$20 (U.S.$13) for adults and A$10 (U.S.$6.50) for children. It's possible to see humpback and southern right whales in June, July, September, and October.

WHERE TO STAY & DINE

If you have a tent and camping gear, all the better. ✪ **Caves Beach** is a quiet spot (except when the birds chorus at dawn) located just a stroll away from a good beach; it's home to resident Eastern Grey kangaroos. A campsite here costs A$8 (U.S.$5.20) per tent in winter and A$10 (U.S.$6.50) in summer and on public holidays. It's about a 250 meter (¼ mile) walk from the car park to the campground. **Greenpatch** is more dirt than grass, but you get your own area and it's suitable for campervans. It's infested with over-friendly possums around dusk. A camp spot here costs A$13 (U.S.$8.45) in winter and A$16 (U.S.$10.40) in summer.

For supplies, head to the area's main towns, **Huskisson** (pop. 930) and **Vincentia** (pop. 2,350). The **Huskisson RSL Club,** overlooking the wharf area on Owen Street (☎ **02/4441 5282**), has a good cheap bistro and a bar. You'll have to sign in just inside the main entrance door.

Huskisson Beach Tourist Resort. Beach St., Huskisson, Jervis Bay, NSW 2540. ☎ /fax **02/ 4441 5142.** 38 units. TV. Fri–Sat A$75–$105 (U.S.$48.75–68.25) cabin, Sun–Thurs A$60–$95 (U.S.$39–$61.75) cabin. BC, DC, MC, V.

This resort is the very pinnacle of cabin accommodation on this part of the east coast. Cabins vary in price depending on size, but even the smallest has room enough for a double bed, triple bunks, and a small kitchen with microwave. Larger cabins have two separate bedrooms. There's a swimming pool, a game room, a full-size tennis court, and barbecue facilities on the grounds.

✪ **Jervis Bay Guest House.** 1 Beach St., Huskisson, NSW 2540 ☎ **02/4441 7658.** Fax 02/4441 7659. www.oztourism.com.au/jervisbay/index.html. 4 units. A$120–$220 (U.S.$78–$143) double depending on season. Rates include breakfast. BC, DC, MC, V. After the Jervis Bay Hotel, take the second road to the left and follow it to the end. Children under 16 not allowed.

This new guesthouse has four distinctly different rooms, all with private bathroom. One room has a Jacuzzi and two rooms face the water. All rooms have plush robes and hair dryers. Breakfast is a hearty affair and could include emu sausages, and thick slabs of bacon followed by a tropical fruit platter.

Jervis Bay Hotel. Owen St., Huskisson, NSW 2540. ☎ **02/4441 5001.** 7 units, none with bathroom. A$55 (U.S.$35.75) double; A$80–$100 (U.S.$52–$65) family room. AE, BC, DC, MC, V.

Rooms at the "Huskie Pub," as it's known, are clean and simple, with not much more than a double bed and coffee- and tea-making facilities. One family room has two small rooms, with a double in one and a set of bunks in the other. Rooms share bathrooms down the hall. There's also a little common room and ironing facilities. The pub below is popular with locals and the odd tourist who comes to eat pretty reasonable bistro food, play pool, and listen to bands on the weekends. The bar closes around 10pm during the week and no later than 11:45pm on Friday and Saturday nights. The Thai restaurant across the road is pretty good.

BATEMANS BAY

275km (171 miles) S of Sydney

This laid-back holiday town offers good surfing, arts and crafts galleries, boat trips up the Clyde River, good game fishing, and bushwalks in Morton and Deua national parks.

ESSENTIALS

GETTING THERE   Batemans Bay is about a 5½- to 6-hour drive from Sydney. **Premier Motor Service** (☎ **1300/368 100** in Australia, or 02/4423 5233) runs coaches to Batemans Bay from Sydney's Central Station.

VISITOR INFORMATION   **Batemans Bay Visitor Information Centre,** at the corner of Princes Highway and Beach Road (☎ **1800/802 528** in Australia or 02/ 4472 6800), is open daily from 9am to 5pm.

Game Fishing & a River Cruise

If you fancy some serious fishing contact **OB1 Charters,** Marina, Beach Road, Batemans Bay (☎ **1800/641 065** in Australia, or tel/fax 02/4472 3944). The company runs full-day game fishing trips and morning snapper fishing trips (afternoon snapper trips in summer, too). Expect to encounter black marlin, blue marlin, giant king fish, mako sharks, albacore tuna, yellowfin tuna, and blue tuna in winter. The trip includes tackle and bait, afternoon and morning teas but must provide your own lunch. It costs A$150 (U.S.$97.50) per person. Snapper (a nice-tasting fish) trips include all gear and bait, and morning or afternoon tea for A$80 (U.S.$52).

A river cruise on the **MV Merinda,** Innes Boatshed, Orient St., Batemans Bay (☎ **02/4472 4052;** fax 02/4472 4754), is pleasant. The 3-hour cruise leaves at 11:30am daily and travels inland past townships, forests, and farmland. It costs A$22 (U.S.$14.30) for adults, A$11 ($7.15) for children and A$50 (U.S.$32.50) for families; a fish-and-chip lunch is A$6 (U.S.$3.90) extra and a seafood basket for two is A$12 (U.S.$7.80).

A Nice Place to Stay

✪ **The Esplanade.** 23 Beach Rd. (P.O. Box 202), Batemans Bay, NSW 2536. ☎ **1800/659 884** in Australia or 02/4472 0200. Fax 02/4472 0277. 23 units. A/C TV TEL. A$104.50–$176 (U.S.$67.93–$114.40) double, depending on season; A$176–$203.50 (U.S.$114.40–$132.28) suite. Extra person A$11.50 (U.S.$7.48). Children under 18 stay free in parents' room. AE, BC, DC, MC, V.

This four-star hotel is right on the Batemans Bay river estuary and close to the town center. Rooms are light and well furnished, and all have kitchenettes and balconies (some with good water views). Some doubles and suites have spas; they cost the same as non-spa rooms, so specify if you want one when booking. Eat at the hotel's a la carte restaurant or at the Batemans Bay Soldiers' Club just opposite, which has a restaurant, a bistro, cheap drinks, and a free evening kids club.

NAROOMA

345km (214 miles) from Sydney

○ **Narooma** is a pleasant seaside town with beautiful deserted beaches, an interesting golf course right on a headland, a natural rock formation in the shape of Australia (popular with camera-wielding tourists), and excellent fishing. However, its major attraction is ○ **Montague Island,** the breeding colony for thousands of shearwaters (or mutton birds, as they're also called) and a hangout for juvenile seals.

Just 18 kilometers (11 miles) farther south is ○ **Central Tilba,** one of the prettiest towns in Australia and the headquarters of the boutique **ABC Cheese Factory.** Don't miss this charming historical township (pop. 35; 1 million visitors annually).

ESSENTIALS

GETTING THERE   Narooma is a 7-hour drive from Sydney down the Princes Highway. **Premier Motor Service** (☎ **1300/368 100** in Australia or 02/4423 5233) runs coaches to Narooma from Sydney's Central Station.

VISITOR INFORMATION   The **Narooma Visitors Centre,** Princes Highway, Narooma (☎ **1800/240 003** or 02/4476 2881; fax 02/4476 1690; www.naturecoast-tourism.com.au), is open daily from 9am to 5pm.

WHAT TO SEE & DO: WHALES, GOLF & MORE

A must if you're visiting the area is a boat tour with ○ **Narooma Charters** (☎ **02/ 4476 2240**). It offers spectacular tours of the coast on the lookout for dolphins, seal colonies, and little penguins, and also includes a tour of ○ **Montague Island.** Morning and afternoon tours take 3½ hours and cost A$66 (U.S.$42.90) for adults, A$49.50 (U.S.$32.18) for children and A$198 (U.S.$128.70) for families. A 4½-hour tour includes some of the world's best whale-watching (between mid-September and early December) and costs A$88 (U.S.$57.20) for adults, A$71.50 (U.S.$46.48) for children and A$297 (U.S.$193.05) for families. The last time I went on this trip we saw eight humpback whales, some of them mothers with calves. The company also offers game fishing from February to the end of June and scuba diving in the seal colonies from August to the end of December. Dives cost A$66 (U.S.$42.90) for a double dive, plus approximately A$33 (U.S.$21.45) for gear rental.

Narooma Golf Club, Narooma (☎ **02/4476 2522**), has one of the most challenging coastal courses in Australia. A round will cost you A$25 (U.S.$16.25).

While in the area I recommend stopping off at the ○ **Umbarra Aboriginal Cultural Centre,** Wallaga Lake, just off the Princes Highway on Bermagui Road (☎ **02/4473 7232**). The center offers activities such as boomerang and spear throwing, and painting with natural ochres for A$6.25 (U.S.$4.06) per person, or A$20 (U.S.$13) for a family. There are also discussions, Aboriginal archival displays, and a retail store. It's open Monday to Friday from 9am to 5pm and Saturday and Sunday from 9am to 4pm (closed Sundays in winter). The center's guides also offer 2- to 4-hour 4WD/walking trips of nearby ○ **Mount Dromedary** and **Mumbulla Mountain,** taking in sacred sites. The tours cost A$45 (U.S.$29.25) per person. Reservations are essential.

If you want to attempt Mount Dromedary without a guide, ask for directions in Narooma. The hike to the top takes around 3 hours.

AN AFFORDABLE PLACE TO STAY

✪ **Whale Motor Inn.** Princes Hwy., Narooma, NSW 2546. ☎ **02/4476 2411.** Fax 02/ 4476 1995. 17 units. A/C TV TEL. A$70–$125 (U.S.$45.50–$81.25) double; A$80–$125 (U.S.$52–$81.25) suite. Extra person A$10 (U.S.$6.50). AE, BC, DC, MC, V.

This nice, quiet motor inn has the best ocean views on the south coast and the largest rooms in town. Standard rooms have a queen-size and a single-person sofa bed. The standard suites have a separate bedroom, two additional sofa beds, and a kitchenette. Executive and spa suites are spacious, better furnished, and have a kitchenette and a large balcony or patio. The restaurant, Harpoons, specializes in local seafood. There's also a swimming pool.

MERIMBULA

480km (385 miles) S of Sydney; 580km (464 miles) NE of Melbourne

This seaside resort (pop. approx. 7,000) is the last place of interest before the Princes Highway crosses into Victoria. Merimbula is a good center from which to discover the surrounding Ben Boyd National Park and Mimosa Rocks National Park, both of which offer bushwalking. Another park, Bournda National Park, is situated around a lake and encompasses good walking trails and a surf beach.

Golf is the game of choice in Merimbula, and the area's most popular venue is the **Pambula-Merimbula Golf Club** (☎ 02/6495 6154), where you can spot kangaroos on the fairways of the 27-hole course. It cost A$14 (U.S.$9.10) for nine holes, or A$25 (U.S.$16.25) for the day. Another favorite is **Tura Beach Country Club** (☎ **02/6495 9002**), known for its coastal views. A round of 18 holes costs A$20 (U.S.$13).

Eden, 20 kilometers (12.4 miles) south of Merimbula, was once a major whaling port. The gruesome **Eden Killer Whale Museum,** on Imlay Street in Eden (☎ 02/ **6496 2094**), is the only reason to stop here. It has a dubious array of relics, including boats, axes, and remnants of the last of the area's killer whales, called Old Tom. The museum is open Monday to Saturday from 9:15am to 3:45pm Sunday from 11:15am to 3:45pm. In January it's open from 9:15am to 4:45pm daily. Admission is A$5.50 (U.S.$3.58) for adults and A$1.50 (U.S.98¢) for children. Thankfully you can still see a scattering of whales off the coast in October and November.

ESSENTIALS

GETTING THERE   The drive from either Sydney or Melbourne takes about 7 hours. The **Greyhound Pioneer** (☎ **13 20 30** in Australia) bus trip from Sydney takes more than 8 hours.

VISITOR INFORMATION   The **Merimbula Tourist Information Centre,** at Beach Street, Merimbula (☎ **1800/150 457** in Australia or 02/6495 1129; fax 02/6495 1250), is open daily from 9am to 5pm (10am–4pm in winter).

SPECIAL EVENTS   Jazz fans should head for the **Merimbula Jazz Festival** held over the long Queens Birthday weekend, the second weekend in June. A country music festival takes place the last weekend in October.

WHERE TO STAY

Ocean View Motor Inn. Merimbula Dr. and View St., Merimbula, NSW 2548. ☎ **02/ 6495 2300.** Fax 02/6495 3443. oceanview@asitis.net.au. 20 units. A/C TV TEL. A$60–$120 (U.S.$39–$78) double (depending on season). Extra person A$10 (U.S.$6.50). BC, MC, V.

This pleasant motel has good water views from 12 of its rooms (the best are numbers 9, 10, and 11), which are spacious and modern, with brick walls, patterned carpets, and one long balcony serving the top six rooms. Fourteen rooms have kitchenettes. All have showers. It's a friendly place, with an outdoor saltwater pool and a Laundromat on the premises. Breakfast is served to your room for A$7 (U.S.$4.55) extra.

6 The Snowy Mountains: Australia's Ski Country

Thredbo: 519km (322 miles) SW of Sydney; 208km (129 miles) SW of Canberra; 543km (331 miles) NE of Melbourne

Made famous by Banjo Patterson's 1890 poem the "Man from Snowy River," ✪ **the Snowy Mountains** are most commonly used for what you'd least expect in Australia—skiing. It starts to snow around June and carries on until September, and hundreds of thousands of people flock here to ski at the major ski resorts—Thredbo and Perisher Blue, and to a lesser extent Charlotte Pass and Mount Selwyn. It's certainly different skiing, with ghostly white gums as obstacles instead of pine trees.

The whole region is part of the **Kosciuszko** (pronounced *ko-zi-os-co*) **National Park,** the largest alpine area in Australia. During the summer months the park is a beautiful place for walking, and in spring the profusion of wildflowers is exquisite. A series of lakes in the area, including the one in the resort town of Jindabyne, are favorites with trout fishermen.

Visitors either stay at **Jindabyne,** 62 kilometers (39 miles) south of Cooma, or **Thredbo Village,** 36 kilometers (20 miles) southwest of Jindabyne. Jindabyne is a pretty bleak-looking resort town on the banks of the man-made Lake Jindabyne, which was born when the Snowy River was damned to provide hydroelectric power.

Thredbo Village is set in a valley of Mount Crackenback and resembles European-style resorts. From here, the **Crackenback Chairlift** provides easy access to the top of Mount Kosciuszko, which at 2,228 meters (7,352 ft.) is Australia's highest peak. The mountain has stunning views and some good walks. Thredbo was the scene of a 1997 disaster that gripped the nation. At 11:40pm on a dark wintry night of July 30, a freak landslide smashed into two ski lodges. Twenty people were buried under the wreckage, and for days rescuers tried to shore up the hill and slowly pick through the rubble, all the while aware it could all shift again at any moment and bury them, too. Ultimately there was only one survivor, a ski instructor who had managed to make it through freezing conditions for more than 36 hours.

SNOWY MOUNTAIN ESSENTIALS

GETTING THERE   From Sydney, the Parramatta Road runs into the Hume Highway in the suburb of Ashfield. Follow the Hume Highway south to Goulburn, where you turn onto the Federal Highway toward Canberra. From there take the Monaro Highway to Cooma, then follow the Alpine Way through Jindabyne and on to Thredbo. Chains may have to be used on the slopes in winter and can be rented from local service stations. The trip takes around 7 hours from Sydney with short breaks.

Qantaslink (☎ **13 13 13**) has a twice daily service to the Snowy Mountains Airport in Cooma from Sydney. In the winter months frequency increases to up to ten

Ski Condition Updates

For up-to-date ski conditions call: Perisher Blue, ☎ **02/6459 4485;** Thredbo, ☎ **02/6459 4100;** Charlotte Pass, ☎ **02/6457 5247;** or Mount Selwyn, ☎ **02/ 6454 9488.**

flights daily. Several operators offer transfer services from the airport into the mountains and transfers from Canberra airport can also be arranged. Car rental is available at Cooma Airport, in Cooma and at Canberra Airport.

In winter (from around June–Oct), **Greyhound Pioneer** (☎ **13 20 30** in Australia) operates daily buses between Sydney and Cooma, via Canberra. The journey takes around 7 hours from Sydney and 3 hours from Canberra. A one-way ticket costs A$50 (U.S.$32.50).

VISITOR INFORMATION   Pick up information about the ski fields and accommodations either at the **Cooma Visitors Centre,** 119 Sharp St., Cooma, NSW 2630 (☎ **02/6450 1740;** fax 02/6450 1798), or at the **Snowy Region Visitor Centre,** Kosciuszko Rd., Jindabyne, NSW 2627 (☎ **02/6450 5600;** fax 02/6456 1249).

HITTING THE SLOPES & OTHER ADVENTURES

Skiing is the most popular activity around here. More than 50 ski lifts serve the combined fields of ✪ **Perisher Valley, Mount Blue Cow, Smiggins Holes,** and **Guthega.** Perisher Valley offers the best overall slopes; Mount Blue Cow is generally very crowded; Smiggins Holes offer good slopes for beginners; and Guthega has nice light, powdery snow and less-crowded conditions. ✪ **Thredbo** has some challenging runs and the longest downhill runs, but I still prefer Perisher for atmosphere. A day's ski pass costs around A$62 (U.S.$40.30) for adults, and A$36 (U.S.$23.40) for children.

A **ski-tube train** between Jindabyne and Thredbo on the Alpine Way travels through the mountains to Perisher Valley and then to Blue Cow. It costs A$10 (U.S.$6.50) a day for adult skiers and A$6 (U.S.$3.90) for child skiers; A$22 (U.S.$14.30) for non-skiing adults and A$11 (U.S.$7.15) for non-skiing children. Prices are cheaper in summer. Ski gear can be rented at numerous places in Jindabyne and Thredbo.

In the summer, the region is popular for hiking, canoeing, fishing, and golf. Thredbo Village has tennis courts, a nine-hole golf course, and mountain-bike trails.

WHERE TO STAY

You'll have to book months ahead to find a place to stay during the ski season (especially on weekends), and don't expect to find a lot of bargains. The **Kosciuszko Accommodation Centre,** Nuggets Crossing, Jindabyne, NSW 2627 (☎ **1800/ 026 354** in Australia, or 02/6456 2022; fax 02/6456 2945), can help find and book accommodations in the area. Other private agents who can help find you a spot for the night include The **Snowy Mountains Reservation Centre** (☎ **02/6456 2633**), and the **Thredbo Resort Centre** (☎ **1800/020 622** in Australia).

In Thredbo

Thredbo Alpine Apartments. Thredbo, NSW 2628. ☎ **1800/026 333** in Australia or 02/ 6459 4299. Fax 02/6459 4195. 35 units. TV TEL. Winter weekends A$210–$441 (U.S.$136.50–$286.65) 1-bedroom apt; A$289–$628 (U.S.$187.85–$408.20) 2-bedroom apt; A$394–$770 (U.S.$256.10–$500.50) 3-bedroom apt; midweek rates approximately 20% cheaper. Higher rates apply July 30–Sept 2. Summer A$127–$164 (U.S.$82.55–$106.60) 1-bedroom apt; A$159–$190 (U.S.$103.35–$123.50) 2-bedroom apt; A$180–$210 (U.S.$117–$136.50) 3-bedroom apt. Ask about weekly rates. AE, BC, DC, MC, V. Undercover parking.

These apartments are very similar to the Riverside Cabins (see above) and are managed by the same people. All have balconies with mountain views. Some have queen-size beds. There's a limited daily maid service and in-house movies.

Following in the Footsteps of the Man from Snowy River

✪ **Horseback riding** is a popular activity for those wanting to ride like the "Man from Snowy River." **Reynella Kosciusko Rides,** located in Adamanaby, 44 kilometers (27 miles) northwest of Cooma (☎ **1800/029 909** in Australia, 02/6454 2386; fax 02/6454 2530; reynellarides.com.au), offers excursions through the Kosciuszko National Park from October to April. Three-day/four-night rides costs A$799 (U.S.$519.35), and the five-day/six-night ride A$1,207 (U.S.$784.55). Transfers from Cooma cost A$33 (U.S.$21.45) each way. The trips are all-inclusive with camping and homestead accommodations. Shorter rides are offered by **Jindabyne Trail Rides** (☎ **02/6456 2421;** fax 02/6456 1254). Gentle, 90 minute rides cost A$25 (U.S.$16.25) per person.

Thredbo Alpine Hotel. Thredbo, (P.O Box 80) Thredbo NSW 2625. ☎ **02/6459 4200.** Fax 02/6459 4201. www.thredbo.com.au. reception@thredbo.com.au. 65 units. MINIBAR TV TEL. Winter A$220–$478 (U.S.$143–$310.70) double. Summer A$147–$180 (U.S.$95.55–$117) double. Ask about weekly rates and packages. Rates include breakfast. AE, BC, DC, MC, V.

The center of activity in Thredbo after the skiing is finished for the day is this large resort-style lodge. Rooms vary; those on the top floor of the three-story hotel were refurbished in 1998 and have a king-size bed instead of a standard queen. The rooms are all wood paneled. Thredbo's only nightclub is here. There's also a swimming pool, a sauna, and a spa.

Riverside Cabins. Thredbo, NSW 2625. ☎ **1800/026 333** in Australia or 02/6459 4299. Fax 02/6459 4195. 36 units. TV TEL. Winter A$160–$516 (U.S.$104–$335.40) double. Summer A$117–$164 (U.S.$76.05–$106.60) double. Ask about weekly rates. AE, BC, DC, MC, V.

These studio and one-bedroom cabins are above the Thredbo River and overlook the Crackenback Range. They're also a short walk from the Thredbo Alpine Hotel and local shops. Most rooms have balconies.

7 Outback New South Wales

The Outback is a powerful Australian image. Though it's hot and dusty, and prone to flies, it can also be a romantic place where wedge-tailed eagles float in the shimmering heat and where you can spin around in a circle and follow the unbroken horizon. If you drive out here, be on the lookout for emus, large flightless birds that dart across roads. It's so quiet you can hear the scales of a sleepy lizard as long as your forearm, scraping the rumpled track as it turns to taste the air with its long, blue tongue.

The scenery is like a huge canvas with a restricted palette of paint: blood red for the dirt, straw yellow for the blotches of Mitchell grass, a searing blue for the surreally large sky. There is room to be yourself in the Outback, and you'll find out that personalities can roam toward the eccentric side. It's a hard-working place, too, where miners, sheep and cattle farmers, and others eke out a living in Australia's hard center.

BROKEN HILL

1,157km (717 miles) W of Sydney; 508km (315 miles) NE of Adelaide

At heart, ✪ **Broken Hill**—or "Silver City"—is still a hard-working, hard-drinking mining town. Its beginnings can be traced back to 1883 when a boundary rider named

Charles Rasp noticed something odd about the craggy rock outcrops at a place called the Broken Hill. Today, the city's main drag, Argent Street, bristles with finely crafted colonial mansions, heritage homes, hotels, and public buildings. Look deeper and you see the town's quirkiness. Around one corner you'll find the radio station built to resemble a giant wireless set with round knobs for windows, and around another the headquarters of the Housewives Association, which ruled the town with an iron apron for generations. Then there's the Palace Hotel—made famous in the movie *The Adventures of Priscilla, Queen of the Desert*—with its high painted walls and a mural of Botticelli's *Birth of Venus* on the ceiling two flights up.

Traditionally a hard-drinking, but religious town, Broken Hill has 23 pubs (down from 73 in its heyday around the turn of the last century) and plenty of churches, as well as a Catholic cathedral, a synagogue, and a mosque to serve its 24,500 inhabitants.

ESSENTIALS

GETTING THERE By Car, take the Great Western Highway from Sydney to Dubbo, then the Mitchell Highway to the Barrier Highway, which will take you to Broken Hill. **Southern Australian Airlines** (book through Qantas, ☎ 13 13 13 in Australia) also connects Broken Hill to Adelaide, Melbourne, and Mildura.

The *Indian Pacific* train stops here on its way to Perth. It departs Sydney for Broken Hill at 2:55pm on Monday and Thursday and arrives at Broken Hill at 9am the next morning. The fare is A$395 (U.S.$256.75) for adults and A$265 (U.S.$172.25) for children in a first-class sleeper, A$272 (U.S.$176.80) for adults and A$182 (U.S.$118.30) for children in an economy sleeper, and A$117 (U.S.$76.05) for adults and A$59 (U.S.$38.35) for children in an economy seat. The train also runs between Sydney and Adelaide via Broken Hill. Call **Great Southern Railways** (☎ 08/8213 4530) for more information, or check out the timetables and fares at www.gsr.com.au/fares.htm.

Greyhound Pioneer (☎ 13 20 30 in Australia) runs buses from Adelaide for A$69.30 (U.S.$45.05); the trip takes 7 hours. The 16-hour trip from Sydney costs A$111.10 (U.S.$72.22).

VISITOR INFORMATION The Broken Hill Tourist and Travelers Centre, at Blende and Bromide streets, Broken Hill, NSW 2880 (☎ 08/8087 6077; fax 08/8088 5209; www.murrayoutback.org.au), is open daily from 8:30am to 5pm. The **National Parks & Wildlife Service (NPWS)** office is at 183 Argent St. (☎ 08/8088 5933), and the **Royal Automobile Association of South Australia,** which offers reciprocal services to other national and international auto-club members, is at 261 Argent St. (☎ 08/8088 4999).

Note: The area code in Broken Hill is 08, the same as the South Australia code, not 02, the New South Wales code.

Outback Driving Tips

To find the **Nahiku Coffee Shop, Smoked Fish Stand,** and **Ti Gallery,** watch for mile marker 28 on the Hana Highway (no phone). Pick up locally made baked goods at the small coffee shop, then move on to the main attraction: the cast-iron smoker, which puts out smoked and grilled chicken, beef, and fresh local fish. The teriyaki-based marinade, made by the owner, adds a special touch to the fish (ono, ahi, marlin) and meats, sold for $3 a skewer.

Does Anybody Really Know What Time it Is? _____

Broken Hill runs its clocks to **central standard time,** to correspond with South Australia. The surrounding country, however, runs half an hour faster at eastern standard time.

GETTING AROUND   Silver City Tours, 380 Argent St. (☎ **08/8087 3144**), conducts tours of the city and surrounding Outback. City tours take around 4 hours and cost A$32 (U.S.$20.80) for adults and A$10 (U.S.$6.50) for children. They also offer a range of other tours of the area. **Broken Hill Outback Tours,** 160-170 Crystal St. (P. O. Box 199) Broken Hill, NSW 2880 (☎ **1800/670 120** in Australia, or 08/8087 7800; fax 08/8088 3813) conducts 3- to 6-day tours of the area.

Hertz (☎ **08/8087 2719;** fax 08/8087 4838) rents 4WD vehicles suitable for exploring the area.

EXPLORING THE TOWN: ART GALLERIES, A MINE TOUR & THE WORLD'S LARGEST SCHOOLROOM

With the largest regional gallery in New South Wales and 27 private galleries, Broken Hill has more places per capita to see art than anywhere else in Australia. The **Broken Hill City Art Gallery,** Chloride St., between Blende and Beryl streets (☎ **08/8088 5491**) houses an extensive collection of Australian colonial and impressionist works. Of particular interest is the **Silver Tree,** a sculpture wrought from pure silver mined from beneath Broken Hill. This is also a good place to see works by the "Brushmen of the Bush," a well-known group of artists, including Pro Hart, Jack Absalom, Eric Minchin, and Hugh Schultz, who spent many days sitting around campfires in the bush trying to capture its essence in paint. The gallery is open Monday to Friday from 10am to 5pm, and Saturday and Sunday from 1pm to 5pm. Admission is A$3 (U.S.$1.95) adults, A$2 (U.S.$1.30) for children, and A$6 (U.S.$3.90) for families.

Other galleries worth visiting include **Absalom's Gallery,** 638 Chapple St. (☎ **08/ 8087 5881**), and the **Pro Hart Gallery,** 108 Wyman St. (☎ **08/8087 2441**). All are open daily. Pro Hart's gallery is worth a look. Apart from his own works—including some based on incidents and scenes relating to Broken Hill—the gallery is crammed with everything from a bas-relief of Salvador Dalí to a landscape by Claude Monet.

To get a real taste of mining in Broken Hill, take an underground tour at **Delprat's Mine** (☎ **08/8088 1604**). Visitors go 120 meters (396 ft.) below the surface. Children under 6 are not allowed. Tours run Monday to Friday at 10:30am and Saturday at 2pm. The 2-hour tour costs A$23 (U.S.$14.95) for adults and A$18 (U.S.$11.70) for children.

Don't miss the **School of the Air** and the **Royal Flying Doctor Service base,** both of which help show the enormity of the Australian interior. The School of the Air— the largest school room in the world, with students scattered over 800,000 square kilometers (312,000 sq. miles)—conducts lessons via two-way radios. Visitors can listen in on part of the day's first teaching session Monday through Friday at 8:30am (except public holidays). Bookings are essential and must be made through the Broken Hill Tourist and Travelers Centre (see "Visitor Information," above). Tours costs A$2 (U.S.$1.30) per person. The Royal Flying Doctor Service base is at the Broken Hill Airport (☎ **08/8080 1777**). The service maintains communication with more than 400 outback stations, ready to fly in case of an emergency. The base at Broken Hill covers 25% of New South Wales, as well as parts of Queensland and South Australia.

Continuous explanatory lessons are held at the base Monday to Friday from 9am to noon and 1 to 5pm; Saturday and Sunday from 10am to 4pm. Admission is A$3 (U.S.$1.95) for adults; free for children.

WHAT TO SEE & DO NEARBY

VISITING A GHOST TOWN   At least 44 movies have been filmed in the Wild West town of ✪ **Silverton** (pop. 50), 23 kilometers (14 miles) northwest of Broken Hill. It's the Wild West Australian-style, with camels instead of horses sometimes placed in front of the Silverton Pub, which is well worth a visit for its kitschy Australian appeal. Silverton once had a population of 3,000 following the discovery of silver here in 1882, but within 7 years almost everyone had left. There are some good art galleries here, as well as a restored jail and hotel.

DISCOVERING ABORIGINAL HANDPRINTS   ✪ **Mootwingee National Park,** 130 kilometers (80 miles) northeast of Broken Hill, was one of the most important spiritual meeting places for Aborigines on the continent. Groups came from all over the country to peck out abstract engravings on the rocks with sharpened quartz tools and to sign their handprints to show they belonged to the place. The ancient, weathered fireplaces are still here, laid out like a giant map to show where each visiting group came from. Hundreds of ochre outlines of hands and animal paws, some up to 30,000 years old, are stenciled on rock overhangs. The fabulous 2-hour Outback trip from Broken Hill to Mootwingee is along red-dirt tracks not really suitable for 2WD and should not be attempted after a heavy rain.

  Mootwingee National Park (☎ **08/8088 5933**) or book through **Mootwingee Heritage Tours** ☎ **08/8088 7000** organizes tours of the sites every Wednesday and Saturday morning at 10:30am Broken Hill time (11am Mootwingee, or Eastern Standard, time). The tours may be canceled in very hot weather. The **NPWS** office in Broken Hill (☎ **08/8088 5933**) also has details. You can camp at the Homestead Creek campground for A$11 (U.S.$7.15) a night. It has its own water supply.

EXPLORING WHITE CLIFFS   ✪ **White Cliffs,** 290 kilometers (180 miles) east of Broken Hill, is an opal-mining town bigger than it looks. Unlike Lightning Ridge (below), which produces mainly black opals, White Cliffs is known for its less valuable white opals (as is Coober Pedy in South Australia). To escape the summer heat, most houses are built underground in mine shafts, where the temperature is a constant 23°C (73°F). Prospecting started here in 1889, when kangaroo shooters found the colorful stones scattered on the ground. A year later, the rush was on and by the turn of the century about 4,000 people were digging and sifting in a lawless, waterless hell of a place. White Cliffs is smaller than Coober Pedy and less touristy—which is its great charm. You also have a lot more freedom to wander around the old opal tailings here, whereas in Coober Pedy they discourage it. However, given the hard choice between White Cliffs and Lightning Ridge (see below), I'd have to plump for the latter (though if you have time you certainly should see both).

A Fabulous Place to Enjoy the Sunset

Just outside Broken Hill in the ✪ **Living Desert Nature Park** is the best collection of sculptures this side of Stonehenge. Twelve sandstone obelisks, up to 3 meters (10 ft.) high and carved totem-like by artists from as far away as Georgia, Syria, Mexico, and the Tiwi Islands, make up the Sculpture Symposium. Surrounding them on all sides is brooding mulga scrub. It's fantastic at sunset.

A Little Night Putting

If you fancy an after-hours round of golf in the dirt (and who doesn't?), contact the secretary of the **White Cliffs Golf Club,** John Painter (☎ **08/8091 6715** after hours). He'll be happy to supply you with a golf club or two and a couple of balls for A$2 (U.S.$1.30). Otherwise, put A$2 (U.S.$1.30) in the black box at the first tee if you have your own clubs—but be warned, bush playing can damage your clubs, and crows often make off with the balls. Visitors can play daily day or night, but if you want some company, then turn up on Sunday when club members shoot it out.

Today, the country looks like an inverted moonscape, pimpled with bone-white heaps of gritty clay dug from the 50,000 mine shafts that surround the town. These days, White Cliffs is more renowned for its eccentricity. Take **Jock's Place,** an old underground museum full to the beams with junk pulled from old mine shafts. Then there's a house made of beer flagons and a nine-hole ✪ **dirt golf course** where the locals play at night with fluorescent green golf balls.

WHERE TO STAY: ABOVE GROUND & BELOW

One option is to rent a local cottage from **Broken Hill Historic Cottages** (☎ **08/8087 9966** for A$80 (U.S.$52) a night, or **Sue Spicer's Holiday Cottages** (☎ **08/8087 8488**), who rents fully equipped cottages for A$65 (U.S.$42.25) per night and up.

Broken Hill Overlander Motor Inn. 142 Iodide St., Broken Hill, NSW 2880. ☎ **08/8088 2566.** Fax 08/8088 4377. Reservations can be made through Best Western (☎ **800/780-7234** in the U.S. and Canada, 0800/39 3130 in the U.K., 0800/237 893 in New Zealand, or 13 17 79 in Australia). 15 units. A/C TV TEL. A$82–$105 (U.S.$53.30–$68.25) double; A$130 (U.S.$84.50) 2 bed unit. Extra person A$10 (U.S.$6.50). AE, BC, DC, JCB, MC, V.

This is my favorite place to stay in Broken Hill, although admittedly that's not saying much in this Outback town. It's set back from the road, has nice green areas with a pool and barbecue facilities, and is very quiet. There is also a spa and sauna. The more expensive four-star rated rooms are much nicer and larger than the cheaper variants,. Two family rooms sleep up to six in a combination of single and queen-size beds.

Mario the Palace Hotel. 227 Argent St., Broken Hill, NSW 2880. ☎ **08/8088 1699.** Fax 08/8087 6240. 51 units, 10 with bathroom. A/C TV TEL. A$44 (U.S.$28.60) double without bathroom; A$53–$65 (U.S.$34.45–$42.25) double with bathroom. AE, BC, DC, MC, V.

With its high painted walls, a mural of Botticelli's *Birth of Venus* on the ceiling two flights up, and an office crammed with stuffed animal heads and crabs, the Palace Hotel is an intriguing sanctuary for the night. The owners have put a lot of work into restoring the place. The more expensive doubles are larger and come with a small lounge area, but all are comfortable and cool. Ten double rooms come with an attached shower. Mario has owned the place for "donkey's years" as he says, but he has plans to sell it.

✪ **Underground Motel.** Smiths Hill (P.O. Box 427), White Cliffs, NSW 2836. ☎ **1800/021 154** in Australia or 08/8091 6677. Fax 08/8091 6654. 30 units, none with bathroom. A$79 (U.S.$51.35) double. Extra person A$24 (U.S.$15.60). BC, MC, V.

I love this place; it's worth making the trip out to White Cliffs to stay here for the night. All but two of the rooms are underground; they're reached by a maze of spacious tunnels dug out of the rock and sealed with epoxy-resin to keep out the damp and dust. The temperature below ground is a constant 22°C (71°F), which is decidedly cooler than a summer day outside. Rooms are comfortable though basic, and toilets and showers are shared. Turn the light off and it's dark as a cave. Upstairs is a bar and a dining room, where at dinner guests sit around large round tables and dig into the roast of the day (vegetarians are catered to, also). There's also a pool on the premises.

WHERE TO DINE

The best place for a meal Aussie-style is at one of the local clubs. You'll find one of the best bistros at the **Barrier Social & Democratic Club,** at 218 Argent St. (☎ **08/ 8088 4477**). It serves breakfast, lunch, and dinner. There's also a whole host of Chinese restaurants around town, including the **Oceania Chinese Restaurant** on Argent Street (☎ **08/8087 3695**), which has a A$7 (U.S.$4.55) lunch special.

LIGHTNING RIDGE: OPALS GALORE

765km (474 miles) NW of Sydney; 572km (355 miles) SW of Brisbane

✪ **Lightning Ridge,** or "The Ridge" as the locals call it, is perhaps the most fascinating place to visit in all of New South Wales. It's a hard-working opal-mining town in the arid northern reaches of New South Wales—where summer temperatures regularly hover around the 45°C (113°F) mark. Lightning Ridge thrives off the largest deposit of black opal in the world. Good quality opals from here can fetch a miner around A$8,000 (U.S.$5,200) per carat, and stones worth upwards of A$500,000 (U.S.$325,000) each are not unheard of. Tourists come here to get a taste of life in Australia's "Wild West". A popular tourist activity in the opal fields is to pick over the old white heaps of mine tailings. Stories (perhaps tall tales) abound of tourists finding overlooked opals worth thousands of dollars.

I strongly recommend you visit the ✪ **Grawin** and **Glengarry opal fields**, about an hour from Lightning Ridge on a dirt track barely suitable for 2WD cars (check with locals before you go). These full-on frontier townships are bristling with drills and hoists pulling out loads of dirt and buzzing with news of the latest opal rush. If you can convince a local to take you there, all the better, as the tracks can be misleading.

ESSENTIALS

GETTING THERE From Sydney it takes about 9 hours to drive to Lightning Ridge, via Bathurst, Dubbo, and the fascinating town of Walgett. **Countrylink Holidays** (☎ **13 28 29** in Australia) offer a 3-night/4-day Lightning Ridge tour from Sydney for A$373 (U.S.$242.45) for adults, and A$187 (U.S.$121.55) for children, including accommodation, some meals, and entrance fees, train fare is additional, ask about specials.

VISITOR INFORMATION The **Lightning Ridge Tourist Information Centre** on Morilla Street, P.O. Box 1779, Lightning Ridge, NSW 2834 (☎ **02/6829 0565;** fax 02/6829 0565), is open Monday to Friday from 8:30am to 4pm.

SPECIAL EVENTS If you're in Australia around Easter, make sure you come to Lightning Ridge for the **Great Goat Race** and the rodeo.

SEEING THE TOWN

Any visit to Lightning Ridge should start with an orientation trip with **Black Opal Tours** (☎ **02/6829 0368;** fax 02/6829 1206). The company offers a 5-hour tour of the opal fields for A$65 (U.S.$42.25) per person. Also ask about their shorter tours as well as their 2- and 3-day tours of the area.

Among the many points of interest is the 15-meter-tall (50 ft.) ✪ **Amigo's Castle,** which dominates the worked-out opal fields surrounding the modern township of Lightning Ridge. Complete with turrets, battlements, dungeons, and a wishing well, the castle has been rising out of these arid lands for 17 years, with every rock scavenged from the surrounding area and lugged in a wheelbarrow or in a rucksack on Amigo's back. The wonderful Amigo hasn't taken out insurance on the property, so there are no official tours, though if he feels like a bit of company he'll show you around.

The ✪ **Artesian Bore Baths,** 2 kilometers (1 mile) from the post office on Pandora Street are free of charge, open 24 hours a day, and said to have therapeutic value. The water temperature hovers between 40°C and 50°C (104°F to 122°F). It's an amazing place to visit at night when the stars are out above.

The **Bevan's Black Opal & Cactus Nursery** (☎ 02/6829 0429) contains more than 2,000 species of cactus and succulent plants, with many rare specimens. Betty Bevan cuts her own opals, and many are on display. Admission is A$4 (U.S.$2.60).

There are plenty of opal shops, galleries, walk-in mines, and other unique things to see in Lightning Ridge. You might want to take a look at **Gemopal Pottery** (☎ 02/6829 0375), on the road to the Bore Baths. The resident potter makes some nice pots out of clay mine tailings and lives in one of his five old Sydney railway carriages.

WHERE TO STAY & DINE

The Wallangulla Motel. Morilla St. (at Agate St.), Lightning Ridge, NSW 2834. ☎ **02/6829 0542.** Fax 02/6829 0070. 43 units. A/C TV TEL. A$55–$83 (U.S.$35.75–$53.95) double; A$77–$94 (U.S.$50.05–$61.10) triple; A$108–$121 (U.S.$70.20–$78.65) family room with spa. AE, BC, DC, MC, V.

The best motel in town offers two standards of rooms, the cheaper rooms being in an older section of the property. Newer rooms are well-furnished and generally nicer; they're worth the extra money. Two large family rooms have two bedrooms and a living room; one has a spa bath. Guests can use the barbecue facilities, and there is a special arrangement with the bowling club over the road for meals there to be charged to your room. The Bowling Club has a restaurant with pretty good food and a very cheap bistro.

Brisbane 6

by Lee Mylne

Queensland's capital is relaxed and laid-back, set along the banks of the wide brown Brisbane River. The city has grown up in recent years, assured of its attractions and confident of its appeal. It's one of those places that people don't always appreciate until they spend some time there, but which gives a welcome as warm as the weather. Green and leafy, it has huge Moreton Bay fig trees to give shade, and in the summer the purple haze of jacarandas competes with the blaze of poinciana trees in bloom. Palm trees sway and a mango tree in the backyard is almost *de rigeur*.

For major commercial tourist attractions, head south of the city to the theme parks which line the Brisbane–Gold Coast corridor. Brisbane folk don't see that as a drawback. They'll urge you to discover the delights of a city rich in history and character and get to know the locals . . . it's easy, as Queenslanders will strike up a conversation with just about anyone.

Brisbane (pronounced *Briz*-bun) is renowned for its timber "Queenslander" cottages and houses, set high on stumps to catch the breeze, with wide shady verandahs. In some inner city suburbs, Queenslanders have been converted to trendy cafes and restaurants, or into shops.

In the city center, gracious colonial sandstone buildings stand next to modern glass towers. Wander in the city botanic gardens, in-line skate or bike along the riverfront, have a cool drink in a pub beergarden, or get out on the river on a CityCat high speed ferry. There are several bridges across the river, the most famous and attractive being the Story Bridge. On a weekend, browse in the handcrafts markets, listen to the buskers and people-watch. You can even cool off at a manmade beach. There's a lot of free entertainment, and plenty to keep you busy. Getting around is cheap, good food—including fantastic seafood—is abundant, and accommodations are affordable, especially in some comfortable and elegant bed-and-breakfasts.

Brisbane is on the southern coast of the state, with the Sunshine Coast less than 2 hour drive to the north, and the Gold Coast an hour to the south. The Brisbane River flows into Moreton Bay, which is dotted with islands that offer their own delights.

1 Orientation

ARRIVING

BY PLANE More than 30 airlines fly into **Brisbane International Airport** from Europe, Asia, and New Zealand, including Qantas, Air New Zealand, Singapore Airlines, and Cathay Pacific. From North America you will most likely fly to Sydney and connect, or fly direct from Auckland, in New Zealand. Qantas operates flights throughout the day from state capitals, Cairns, and several other regional towns. Newcomer **Virgin Blue,** (☎ **13 67 89** in Australia) offers considerably cheaper fares and flies between Sydney, Brisbane, Melbourne and Adelaide. Regional Queensland airline **Flight West** (☎ **13 00 92** in Australia) serves the city from other towns within the state.

Brisbane International Airport is 16 kilometers (10 miles) from the city, and the domestic terminal is 2 kilometers (1¼ miles) farther away. The Arrivals Floor, on Level 2, has an information desk open to meet all flights, help with flight inquiries, dispense tourist information, and make hotel bookings. It also has lockers that cost A$5 to $10 (U.S.$3.25–$6.50) for 24 hours, and a check-in counter for passengers transferring to domestic flights. Travelex currency-exchange bureaus are located on both the departures and arrivals floors. **Avis** (☎ **07/3860 4200**), **Budget** (☎ **07/3860 4466**), **Hertz** (☎ **07/3860 4522**), and **Thrifty** (☎ **07/3860 4588**) have desks on Level 2; in the airport there is also a free callboard connecting you to smaller local car rental companies that may offer better rates. Showers and baby change rooms are located on levels 2, 3, and 4; Level 4 has an ATM.

The domestic terminal has lockers, A$6 (U.S.$3.90) for 24 hours, currency exchange, showers, and the big four car-rental desks (telephone numbers above). An inter-terminal shuttle runs every 15 minutes and costs A$2.50 (U.S.$1.63).

Skytrans (☎ **07/3236 1000**) runs a shuttle bus from the airport to Roma Street Transit Centre every 30 minutes from 5am to 2pm and every 45 minutes from 2pm to 8:45pm. It costs A$9 (U.S.$5.85) per person, A$15 (U.S.$9.75) for two and A$20 (U.S.$13) for three to Roma St Transit Centre, or $11 (U.S. $7.15) for hotel dropoff. Kids 4 to 14 pay A$5 (U.S.$3.25). Return fare is A$15 (U.S.$9.75), or same day return fare is A$12 (U.S.$7.80). The trip takes 40 minutes, no reservations required. No public buses serve the airport. A taxi to the city costs around A$20 (U.S.$13) from the international terminal and A$24 (U.S.$15.60) from the domestic terminal.

BY TRAIN **Queensland Rail** (☎ **13 22 32** in Queensland, or 07/3235 1122) operates several long-distance trains most days of the week to Brisbane from Cairns. The 32-hour trip from Cairns costs A$155.10 (U.S.$100.82) for a sitting berth, and A$193.60 (U.S.$125.84) for an economy-class sleeper. **Countrylink** (☎ **13 22 32** in New South Wales, or 02/9379 1298) runs daily service to Brisbane from Sydney. The 13½-hour trip costs A$110 to $154 (U.S.$71.50–$100.10) in a sitting berth, and

The Train from the Plane

Airtrain, (☎ **1800 155 194** in Australia, or 07/3211 2855; www.airtrain.com.au) an elevated rail link from Brisbane's airport terminals to the city and the Gold Coast, was rolled out with great fanfare in May, 2001. It runs every 15 minutes from 5:30am to 11:30pm, with a fare from Central Station to the airport costing A$9 (U.S.$5.85) and taking about 22 minutes. It also links the airport with the Gold Coast twice an hour, a 92-minute trip that costs A$20 (U.S.$13).

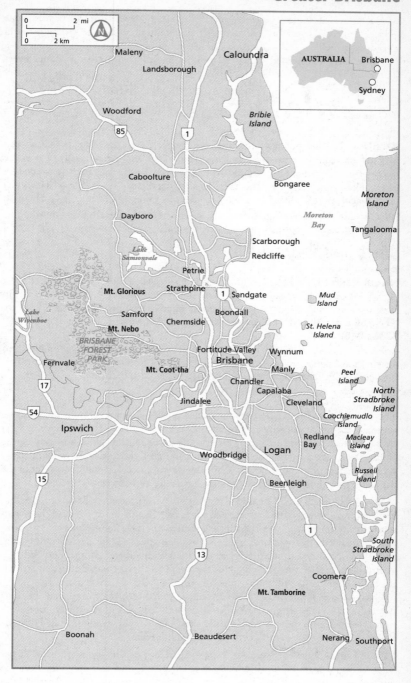

Greater Brisbane

Maleny
Landsborough
Caloundra

AUSTRALIA
Brisbane
Sydney

Woodford
85
1

Bribie
Island

Caboolture

Bongaree

Moreton
Island

Dayboro

Moreton
Bay

Tangalooma

Lake
Samsonvale

Scarborough
Redcliffe

Petrie

Mt. Glorious
Strathpine
1
Sandgate

Lake
Wivenhoe

Samford
Mt. Nebo
Chermside
Boondall

Mud
Island

BRISBANE
FOREST
PARK

Fortitude Valley
Brisbane
Wynnum

St. Helena
Island

Fernvale

Mt. Coot-tha
Chandler
Manly

Peel
Island

17

Jindalee
Capalaba

North
Stradbroke
Island

54

Cleveland

Coochiemudlo
Island

Ipswich

Woodbridge

Logan

Redland
Bay

Macleay
Island

15

Beenleigh

Russell
Island

1

South
Stradbroke
Island

13

Coomera

Mt. Tamborine

Boonah
Beaudesert
Nerang
Southport

A$231 (U.S.$150.15) for a sleeper. Make sure you book the through-service; some services transfer to coach in Murwillumbah, just south of the border, tacking an extra 2¼ hours to the trip. This train/coach service has no sleepers.

All intercity and interstate trains pull into **Brisbane Transit Centre at Roma Street** (in the city center), often called the Roma Street Transit Centre. From here, most city and Spring Hill hotels are a few blocks' walk or a quick cab ride away. The Transit Centre has food outlets, showers, tourist information, and lockers.

Queensland Rail CityTrain (☎ **07/3235 5555**) provides daily train service from the Sunshine Coast, and plentiful services from the Gold Coast.

BY BUS   Coaches pull into the Brisbane Transit Centre (see "By Train," above). **McCafferty's** and **Greyhound Pioneer** serve the city several times daily. A one-way Cairns–Brisbane ticket costs around A$156 (U.S.$101.40), and the trip takes 28½ hours. The Sydney–Brisbane trip takes 18 hours and costs A$77 (U.S.$50.05) one-way. **Coachtrans** (☎ **07/5588 8777**) provides plentiful service from the Gold Coast.

BY CAR   The Bruce Highway from Cairns enters the city from the north. The Pacific Highway enters Brisbane from Sydney in the south.

VISITOR INFORMATION

Brisbane Tourism, P.O. Box 12260, Elizabeth St., Brisbane, QLD 4002 (☎ **07/ 3221 8411;** fax 07/3229 5126), has a booth in the Queen Street Mall at Albert Street (☎ **07/3229 5918**). It's open from 9am to 5:30pm Monday through Thursday, to 7pm or later Friday, and to 4pm Saturday; Sunday it's open from 10am to 4pm. **The Roma Street Transit Centre** is another source of tourist information (☎ **07/ 3236 2020**).

The free weekly *Brisbane News,* available in newsstands, cafes, hotel lobbies, and information booths, is a great source of information on dining, entertainment, performing arts, galleries, shopping, and Brisbane's laid-back lifestyle.

CITY LAYOUT

The city center's glass office towers shimmer in the sun on a curve of the Brisbane River. In the tip of the curve are the Brisbane City Gardens. The 30-meter (98-ft.) cliffs of Kangaroo Point rise on the eastern side of the south bank; to the west are the South Bank Parklands and the Queensland Cultural Centre, known as South Bank. Five kilometers (3 miles) west, Mt. Coot-tha (pronounced *Coo*-tha) looms out of the flat plain, providing a great vantage point for gazing over the city.

MAIN ARTERIES & STREETS   It's easy to navigate central Brisbane once you know all the east-west streets are named for female British royalty, and all the north-south streets are named after their male counterparts. The "female" streets start with Ann in the north, followed by Adelaide, Queen, Elizabeth, Charlotte, Mary, Margaret, and Alice. From east to west, the streets are Edward, Albert, George, and William. William becomes North Quay, flanking the river's northeast bank. Brunswick Street is the main thoroughfare running through Fortitude Valley and New Farm.

Queen Street is the main thoroughfare; it becomes a pedestrian mall between Edward and George streets. Roma Street exits the city diagonally to the northwest. Ann Street leads all the way east into Fortitude Valley. The main street in Fortitude Valley is Brunswick St., which runs right into New Farm.

STREET MAPS   *The Brisbane Map,* free from Brisbane Tourism (see "Visitor Information, above") or your concierge, is a lightweight map that shows the river and outlying suburbs, as well as the city. It's great for drivers because it shows parking lots and one-way traffic directions on the confusing city-center grid. Rental cars usually come with street directories. Newsagents and some bookstores sell it, and the state auto club, the **R.A.C.Q.,** in the General Post Office, 261 Queen St. (☎ **13 19 05**) is also a source.

Neighborhoods in Brief

City Center The vibrant city center is where a lot of eating, shopping, and socializing gets done. Queen Street Mall, in the heart of town, is popular with shopaholics and cinemagoers, especially on weekends and Fridays (when stores stay open until 9pm). The Eagle Street financial/legal district houses some great restaurants with river views, and on Sundays there are fashionable markets by the Riverside office tower. Much of Brisbane's elegant colonial architecture is in the city center, too. Strollers, bike riders, and in-line skaters shake the summer heat in the green haven of the Brisbane City Gardens at the central business district's southern end.

South Bank A 7-minute walk across Victoria Bridge at the western end of Queen Street takes you to South Bank, a peaceful public playground that includes the Queensland Cultural Centre and the parks, rain-forest walks, bars, and restaurants of South Bank Parklands. This is where people come to see a play, meet for dinner, shop in weekend markets, or just relax on the riverbank.

Fortitude Valley Ten years ago, this suburb of derelict warehouses just east of the city center was one of the sleazier parts of town. Today "the Valley," as the locals call it, is a stomping-ground for smart young folk who meet in restored pubs and eat in cool cafes. The lanterns, food stores, and shopping mall of Chinatown are here, too. Take Turbot Street from the city to the Valley's main drag, Brunswick Street.

New Farm Always a nice residential suburb, New Farm is fast becoming the city's "in" destination for cafe-hopping, shopping, and cinema-going. Merthyr Street is where the action is, especially on Friday and Saturday nights. From the intersection of Wickham and Brunswick streets, follow Brunswick southeast for 13 blocks to Merthyr.

Paddington If you think this hilltop suburb northwest of the city is the prettiest in Brisbane, many will agree. Brightly painted Queenslander cottages line the main street, Latrobe Terrace, as it winds west along a ridge top. Many houses have been turned into shops and cafes, and the street is never empty of people browsing for antiques, enjoying coffee and cake, or just moseying around to admire the charming architecture.

Park Road, Milton A street rather than a neighborhood, this is Brisbane's answer to Rome. Italian restaurants line the street, buzzing with white collar office workers who down cappuccinos at alfresco restaurants, scout interior design stores for a new *objet* to grace the living room, and stock up on European designer rags.

West End This small inner-city enclave is alive with ethnic restaurants, cafes, and the odd interesting housewares or fashion store. Most action is at the intersection of Vulture and Boundary streets, where Asian grocers and delis abound.

Bulimba An emerging fashionable suburb, Bulimba has a long connection with the river through the boat-building industry, and one of the nicest ways to get there is by CityCat. Oxford St. emulates Park Road lately, with lots of cafes and trendy shops.

2 Getting Around

BY PUBLIC TRANSPORTATION

Bus, train, and ferry service is coordinated by Brisbane Transport. For timetable and route inquiries, call **Transinfo** ☎ **13 12 30.** Convenient places to buy transit passes and pick up timetables and route maps are the Brisbane Transport outlets on the Elizabeth Street-level of the Myer Centre, which fronts Queen Street Mall; Brisbane Transport's Brisbane Administration Centre, 69 Ann Street; the Roma Street Transit Centre; or Brisbane Tourism's information kiosk in Queen Street Mall. You can buy passes on the bus, at the train station (if the pass has a train component), or on the ferry. Any news agency displaying a yellow-and-white *Bus & Ferry Tickets Sold Here* banner sells bus/ferry passes, but not train passes, special tour tickets, or family passes.

A single zone on the bus, train, or ferry costs A$1.40 (U.S.91¢). Kids under 5 travel free, kids ages 5 to 15 pay half fare; seniors except Queensland residents and all students pay full fare. If you plan on doing lots of bussing and ferrying around, **weekly passes** and **Ten Trip Saver** tickets are available from the outlets described above.

The Brisbane Mobility Map, produced by the Brisbane City Council, outlines wheelchair access to buildings in the city center, as well as a detailed guide to the Queen St Mall and a map of the Brisbane Botanic Gardens at Mt. Coot-tha. The council's disability services unit also has a range of other publications including a Braille Trail and an access guide to parks.

These can be obtained from council customer service centers (☎ 07/3403 4268).

MONEY-SAVING PASSES   The **Rover Link pass** is good for one day of travel on most trains, ferries, and buses. The pass cannot be used on weekday trains before 9am, and there are limits to how far you can go on the trains, but the pass will get you as far as the Australian Woolshed, which is probably as far as you will be traveling anyhow. The Rover Link costs A$9 (U.S.$5.85).

It's possible you won't use trains to get around Brisbane, as most attractions are on the bus and ferry networks. In that case, get a **Day Rover** pass, which allows unlimited travel on buses and ferries for A$8 (U.S.$5.20).

On weekends and holidays, it's cheaper to buy an **Off-Peak Saver** pass, which lets you travel on buses and ferries all day for A$5 (U.S.$3.25) for adults. The Off-Peak Saver is available on weekdays, but it is not convenient for sightseeing because it does not cover the cost of travel before 9am and between 3:30pm and 7pm.

Note that passes can't be used on the City Circle bus line (see "By Bus," below) on tour buses like City Sights (see "River Cruises & Other Organized Tours").

If you see peak-hour buses displaying a full fare only sign, that does not mean you cannot travel on them with a discounted ticket or pass. It just means you will have to purchase your full-fare ticket or pass from a ticket agent before boarding the bus.

The excellent ✪ **City Sights bus tour** entitles you to unlimited travel on buses, ferries, and CityCats for the day, and at the same time gets you around to 19 points of interest (see "River Cruises & Other Organized Tours," later in this chapter for details.)

BY BUS   Buses operate from around 5am to 11pm weekdays, with fewer services on weekends. On Sunday many routes stop around 5pm. Midweek, the smart way to get around the city center is aboard City Circle bus no. 333, which does a loop every 10 to 15 minutes around Eagle, Alice, George, Roma, and Albert streets as far north as Wickham Terrace, then up Ann Street and down Adelaide Street. It's wheelchair-accessible. Look for the blue-and-white stops. A ticket anywhere on the route costs A80¢ (U.S.50¢). It runs Monday through Friday from 7am to 5:40pm. Most buses depart from City Hall at King George Square, from Adelaide or Ann Streets.

BY FERRY   Ferries run from around 6am to 10:30pm daily. The fast **CityCat** ferries run to many places of interest, including South Bank and the Queensland Cultural Centre; the restaurants and Sunday markets at the Riverside Centre; and New Farm Park, not far from the cafes of Merthyr Street. They run every half hour between Queensland University, approximately 9 kilometers (5½ miles) along the river to the south, and Brett's Wharf, about 9 kilometers (5½ miles) to the north. Slower but more frequent Inner City and Cross-River ferries stop at a few more points, including the south end of South Bank Parklands, Kangaroo Point, and Edward Street right outside the City Botanic Gardens.

Even with a transit pass, you can't travel on ferries for more than 2 consecutive hours at a time. You are free to do another 2 hours later in the day if you wish. Two hours on the CityCat takes you the entire length of its run.

BY TRAIN   Brisbane's suburban rail network is fast, quiet, safe, and clean. Trains run from around 5am to midnight, stopping at about 11pm on Sundays. All trains leave Central Station, between Turbot and Ann streets at Edward Street.

BY TAXI   Call **Yellow Cabs** (☎ **13 19 24** in Australia) and **Black and White Taxis** (☎ **13 10 08** in Australia). There are major taxi ranks at each end of the Queen Street Mall, on Edward Street and George Street (outside the Treasury Casino).

BY CAR   Brisbane's grid of one-way streets can be confusing, so plan your route before you set off. Brisbane's biggest car park is at the **Myer Centre** (enter from Elizabeth Street) and is open 24 hours (☎ **07/3221 4199**). Most hotels and motels have free parking for guests.

Avis (☎ **07/3221 2900**), **Budget** (☎ **07/3220 0699**), and **Hertz** (☎ **07/3221 6166**) all have outlets in the city center. **Thrifty** (☎ **07/3252 5994**) is on the edge of the city center at 325 Wickham St., Fortitude Valley. Local company **Shoe Strings Car Rental** (☎ **07/3268 3334**), located near the airport, seems to have good rates and delivers cars to the airport for free.

Fast Facts: Brisbane

American Express   The office at 131 Elizabeth St. (☎ **07/3229 2729**) cashes traveler's checks, exchanges currency, and refunds lost traveler's checks.

Business Hours   Banks are open Monday through Thursday from 9:30am to 4pm, and until 5pm on Fridays. See "Shopping," for store hours. Some restaurants close Monday and/or Tuesday nights, and bars are generally open from 10am or 11am until midnight.

Currency Exchange   Travelex, Lennons Plaza, Queen Street Mall between Albert and George streets (☎ **07/3229 8610**), is open Monday through Friday from 9am to 6pm, Saturday from 9am to 5pm, Sunday from 10:30am to 4:30pm.

Dentist   The **Adelaide and Albert Street Dental Centre,** located at the Travellers Medical Service (see "Doctor," below) is open Monday through Friday from 8am to 6pm and Saturday from 9am to 1pm; the dental surgery is on call 24 hours. Call ☎ **07/3229 4121.**

Doctor   City Mall 24 Hour Medical Service is located upstairs at 245 Albert St. at Adelaide Street, diagonally opposite City Hall (☎ **07/3211 3611**). It's open Monday through Friday from 7:30am to 7pm, Saturday from 9am to 5pm, and Sunday from 10am to 4pm; doctors are on call for home visits 24 hours.

Brisbane

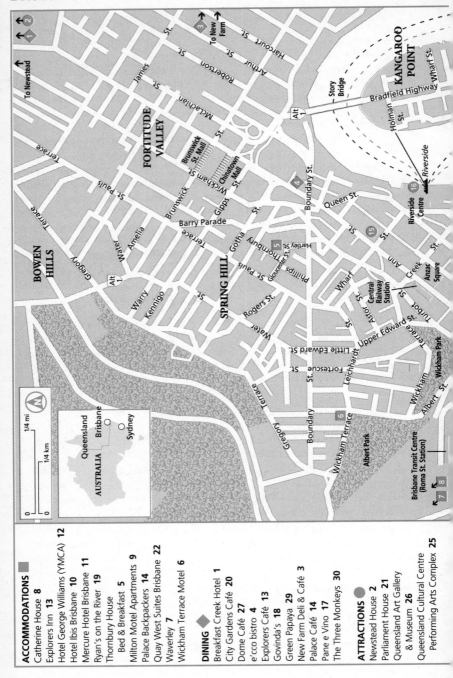

ACCOMMODATIONS ■
Catherine House **8**
Explorers Inn **13**
Hotel George Williams (YMCA) **12**
Hotel Ibis Brisbane **10**
Mercure Hotel Brisbane **11**
Ryan's on the River **19**
Thornbury House
    Bed & Breakfast **5**
Milton Motel Apartments **9**
Palace Backpackers **14**
Quay West Suites Brisbane **22**
Waverley **7**
Wickham Terrace Motel **6**

DINING ◆
Breakfast Creek Hotel **1**
City Gardens Café **20**
Dome Café **27**
e'cco bistro **4**
Explorers Café **13**
Govinda's **18**
Green Papaya **29**
New Farm Deli & Café **3**
Palace Café **14**
Pane e Vino **17**
The Three Monkeys **30**

ATTRACTIONS ●
Newstead House **2**
Parliament House **21**
Queensland Art Gallery
    & Museum **26**
Queensland Cultural Centre
Performing Arts Complex **25**

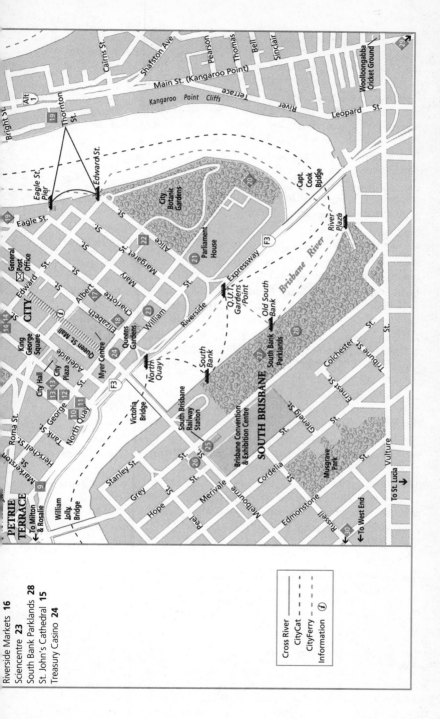

Riverside Markets **16**
Sciencentre **23**
South Bank Parklands **28**
St. John's Cathedral **15**
Treasury Casino **24**

Cross River ———
CityCat – – –
CityFerry – – –
Information (i)

Drugstores (Chemist Shops)   The T&G Corner Day & Night Pharmacy, 141 Queen Street Mall (☎ **07/3221 4585**) is open Monday through Friday from 7:30am to 9pm, Saturday from 8am to 9pm, and Sunday from 9:30am to 5:30pm. There is also a pharmacy under the City Mall

Embassies/Consulates   The United States, Canada and New Zealand have no representation in Brisbane; see chapter 3, "Settling into Sydney," for those countries' nearest offices. **The British Consul General** is at Level 26, Waterfront Place, 1 Eagle St. (☎ **07/3223 3200**).

Emergencies   Dial ☎ **000** for fire, ambulance, or police help in an emergency. This is a free call from a private or public telephone.

Eyeglass Repair   **OPSM** in the Wintergarden, 171–209 Queen Street Mall (☎ **07/3221 1158**), and in the Myer Centre, 91 Queen Street Mall (☎ **07/3229 2913**), is a reputable chain retailer and repairer of eyeglasses.

Hospitals   The nearest casualty ward is at **Royal Brisbane Hospital,** about a 15-minute drive from the city at Herston Road, Herston (☎ **07/3636 8111**).

Hot Lines   Lifeline (☎ **13 11 14**) is a 24-hour emotional crisis counseling service. **Alcoholics Anonymous** (☎ **07/3255 9162**).

Internet Access   The **Global Gossip** chain of Internet cafes' Brisbane outlet is at 288 Edward St. (☎ **07/3229 4033**) and **The Hub Internet Cafe** is at 125 Margaret St (☎ **03/3229 1119**).

Lost Property   For lost property on **trains,** call ☎ **07/3235 1859,** 10:15am to 2:15pm Monday through Friday; on ferries and buses, call the **Brisbane City Council** (☎ **07/3403 8888**). Call police headquarters (☎ **07/3364 6464**) for the telephone number of the station closest to where the item was lost.

Luggage Storage/Lockers   Lockers are located on Level A (use the Albert Street entrance) in the **Myer Centre,** Queen Street Mall (☎ **07/3221 4199**). The **Brisbane Transit Centre** on Roma Street also has baggage lockers.

Newspapers/Magazines   *The Courier-Mail* (Mon–Sat) and the *Sunday Mail* are Brisbane's daily newspapers. The free color weekly *Brisbane News* provides a good guide to dining, entertainment, and shopping.

Police   Dial ☎ **000** in an emergency, or ☎ **07/3364 6464** for police headquarters. Police are stationed 24 hours a day beside the Brisbane Tourism information booth on Queen Street Mall at Albert Street (☎ **07/3220 0752**).

Safety   Brisbane is relatively crime free, but as in any large city, personal safety should be considered especially when out at night. Stick to well-lit streets and busy precincts.

Time Zone   Brisbane is GMT plus 10 hours. It does not observe daylight saving time, which means it's on the same time as Sydney and Melbourne in winter, and 1 hour behind those cities from October to March, when they go to daylight saving. For the exact local time, call ☎ **1194.**

Weather   Call ☎ **1196** for the southeast Queensland weather forecast.

3 Accommodations You Can Afford

Accommodations in Brisbane are generally cheaper than in Sydney. Brisbane has many clean motels, nifty little budget places, and B&Bs in stylish homes close to the city or right in the heart of town. Spring Hill is just a few blocks (uphill) from the city center. For Kangaroo Point you need to drive or bus over the Story Bridge, or take one of the ferries (trip time: 3 min.) that depart every 10 minutes from 5:30am to midnight.

✪ **Catherine House.** 151 Kelvin Grove Rd., Kelvin Grove, Brisbane, QLD 4059. ☎ **07/ 3839 6988.** Fax 07/3236 9093. www.babs.com.au/catherine/index.htm. 2 double units, 1 family room (sleeps 4) and 1 self-contained flat (sleeps 5), all with private bathrooms. A/C. A$77 (U.S.$50.05) single; A$105 (U.S.$68.25) double; self-contained flat A$420 (U.S.$273) per week. Extra persons A$25 (U.S.$16.25). Rates include full breakfast. Ask about packages. AE, BC, DC, MC, V. Free parking. Free pickup from Roma St. Transit Centre on request.

Hostess Joy Harman used to be the chef at one of Brisbane's leading restaurants, so be prepared for gastronomic treats at her large, pretty two-story 1881 house. The rooms are all done up differently in Victorian style; each has hair dryers, tea and coffee-making facilities, and a television. The guest lounge is cozy, with an open fireplace for winter, but on a hot Queensland evening most guests retreat to the cool rear deck looking onto the large fenced swimming pool and palm-filled gardens. Joy will cook and serve gourmet dinners on request—an offer you would be wise to take! There is also a guest laundry. No smoking indoors.

✪ **Explorers Inn.** 63 Turbot St. (near George St.), Brisbane, QLD 4000. ☎ **1800/623 288** in Australia, or 07/3211 3488. Fax 07/3211 3499. www.powerup.com.au/~explorer. 58 units (all with shower only). A/C TV TEL. A$75–$97 (U.S.$48.75–$63.05) double. No charge for third person. AE, BC, DC, MC, V. No parking; car park opposite charges A$6 (U.S.$3.90) per day weekends/public holidays and weekdays a maximum of about A$16 (U.S.$10.40) per day. Train: Roma St. Bus:City Circle 333.

You will be knocked over when you see such style and value in one place—and in the heart of town! The tiny, ship-shape rooms were designed by the architect/owners to fill all your needs. Each has a narrow, curving slip of desk; a minifridge; a clock-radio; individually controlled air-conditioning; and a tiny private bathroom only minutely bigger than the shower cubicle it holds (the front desk lends hair dryers). The friendly staff is will help with tour bookings. The river is a block away, and it's two blocks to the Roma Street Transit Centre. Downstairs is the equally good-value Explorers Café restaurant and bar (see "Great Deals on Dining," below).

✪ **Hotel George Williams (YMCA).** 317–325 George St. (between Turbot and Ann sts.), Brisbane, QLD 4000. ☎ **1800/064 858** or 07/3308 0700. Fax 07/3308 0733. 42 units (all private bathrooms, some with shower only). A/C TV TEL. Rack rate A$104 (U.S.$67.60) double; standby doubles from A$81 (U.S.$52.65). Extra person A$17 (U.S.$11.05). Children 4 and under free in parents' room. Ask about packages. AE, BC, DC, MC, V. Free parking. Train: Roma St. Bus: City Circle 333.

This groovy joint is a Y? Your room looks like it belongs in a design magazine, with its colorful bedcovers, chrome chairs, and artsy bedside lamps on curly chrome stands. The very small rooms can accommodate up to four adults. Each has a tiny private bathroom, a wardrobe, a full-length mirror, self-serve tea and coffee, a minifridge, and individually controlled air-conditioning. Three rooms are set up for guests with disabilities. Among the facilities and services are 24-hour reception, laundry and dry cleaning services, safe deposit boxes, free baby baths if you're with an infant, hair dryers, and free access to the YMCA gym downstairs. The hip licensed cafe serves breakfast and operates as an all-day bistro, with dining inside or out on the sunny terrace. The Y is close to the river and Roma Street Transit Centre.

Hotel Ibis Brisbane. 27–35 Turbot St. (between North Quay and George St.), Brisbane, QLD 4000. ☎ **1800/221-4542** in the U.S. and Canada, 1300/65 6565 in Australia , 0181/ 283 4500 in the U.K., 0800/44 4422 in New Zealand, or 07/3237 2333. Fax 07/3237 2444. 218 units. A/C TV TEL. A$109 (U.S.$70.85) double. Extra person A$22 (U.S.$14.30). Children

16 and under stay free in parents' room if they use existing bedding. Ask about weekend packages. AE, BC, DC, JCB, MC, V. Discounted parking approx. A$10 (U.S.$6.50) in nearby parking lots. Train: Roma St. Bus: City Circle 333.

Rooms at this sister property to the nearby Mercure (see below) are bigger than the Mercure's, and a good value if you don't mind doing without a few of the frills of its slightly ritzier sibling: no river views, no in-room iron and board, no minibar, no pool. The hotel was rebuilt inside a gutted building in 1998 with simple, smartly furnished rooms, and have small but nice bathrooms with hair dryers. Three rooms are designed for guests with disabilities. There is 11am to 11pm room service, laundry and dry cleaning service, and a tour desk. The Ibis shares the Mercure's restaurant and bar.

Milton Motel Apartments. 19 Sheehan St., Milton, Brisbane, QLD 4064. ☎ **07/3876 2360.** Fax 07/3876 2359. www.milton-motel.com.au. 36 units. A/C TV TEL. From A$70 (U.S.$45.50) studio double; A$100 (U.S.$65) family apt. to sleep 4. Weekly and monthly rates available. AE, BC, MC, V. Free parking. Train: Milton.

A short train ride from downtown, close to the restaurant strip of Park Road, this two-story Tuscan-style complex has accommodation options including studio and two-bedroom apartments. It's just a stroll to the river; and a half-hour walk on the bike path to the city center. The apartments are modern, light, and compact but well designed. There are kitchen and laundry facilities in all units. All units have a balcony and cable TV. They are serviced three times a week. There's a pool, too. No smoking indoors.

Mercure Hotel Brisbane. 85–87 North Quay, Brisbane, QLD 4000. ☎ **1800/221 4542** in the U.S. and Canada, 1300/65 6565 in Australia, 0181/283 4500 in the U.K., 0800/44 4422 in New Zealand, or 07/3236 3300. Fax 07/3236 1035. 191 units. A/C MINIBAR TV TEL. A$160 (U.S.$104) double; A$195 (U.S.$126.75) studio suite; A$210 (U.S.$136.50) executive suite. Extra person A$22 (U.S.$14.30). Children under 16 free in parents' room with existing bedding. Ask about weekend packages. AE, BC, DC, JCB, MC, V. Discounted parking A$10 (U.S.$6.50) in adjacent parking lot. Train: Roma St. Bus: City Circle 333.

You'll get fantastic views from the riverside rooms of this bright 14-story hotel across the water from South Bank. The compact rooms have comfortable furniture and a small, modern bathroom with hair dryer. Business travelers like it, so look forward to corporate-class treats such as complimentary newspapers, 24-hour room service, and a cocktail bar. There's a pool, sauna, and Jacuzzi, and the YMCA gym is nearby. The rooms are a little conservative compared to the ultrasleek Art Deco lobby and restaurant, but the river panorama more than compensates! Half the rooms have water views; the others have city outlooks.

✪ Ryan's on the River. 269 Main St. (at Scott St.), Kangaroo Point, Brisbane, QLD 4169. ☎ **07/3391 1011.** Fax 07/3391 1824. www.ryans.com.au. 23 units (all with shower only). A/C TV TEL. A$129–$159 (U.S.$83.85–$103.35) double. Extra person A$10 (U.S.$6.50). Ask about packages. AE, BC, DC, MC, V. Free secured parking. Ferry: Thornton St. from Edward St. or Eagle St. Pier (Cross River Ferry).

River and city views from every room, friendly staff, and large, airy rooms make this one of Brisbane's best moderately priced hotels. The city ferry stop is a 2-minute walk across a strip of parkland, where a riverside walk/bike path leads to a playground, the Kangaroo Point cliffs, and all the way to South Bank. Out under a pergola by the salt-water pool and lounge chairs by the river, you can cook up a barbecue dinner provided by the hotel for just A$10 (U.S.$6.50). Breakfast is served out here, too. The rooms all have irons and boards, hair dryers, and balconies. Rooms on the south side have partial views of the river, those on the north are quieter and have great city and Story Bridge views (the bridge lights up at night), and rooms on the west side get a superb river-and-city vista that's the envy of every five-star hotel in Brisbane.

⭘ **Thornbury House Bed & Breakfast.** 1 Thornbury St., Spring Hill, Brisbane, QLD 4000. ☎ **07/3832 5985.** Fax 07/3832 7255. 5 units, all with private bathrooms, and 1 self-contained unit. TV. A$77 (U.S.$50.05) single; A$99–$110 (U.S.$64.35–$71.50) double. Self-contained unit A$420 (U.S.$273) per week. Rates include full breakfast. AE, BC, MC, V. Metered on-street parking. Airport shuttle.

Michelle Bugler has turned her 1886 cottage into a retreat from the city. Every room is individually decorated with Oriental rugs, comfy beds, high-quality bathrobes, and old furniture and knickknacks. The bathrooms are impeccably clean and hair dryers are in all rooms. One room is air-conditioned; the others have fans. Downstairs is a self-contained apartment with modern decor. Michelle serves a scrumptious breakfast in the courtyard, where you can have tea, coffee, cookies, and the newspaper all day. A short walk from this quiet street brings you to the city center. Guests may use Michelle's microwave and laundry, and there's a pay phone in the hall. No smoking indoors.

⭘ **Waverley.** 5 Latrobe Terrace at Cochrane St., Paddington, Brisbane, QLD 4064. ☎ **07/ 3369 8973,** or 0419/741 282 mobile phone. Fax 07/3876 6655. 2 units and 2 self-contained apts. (all with en suite). TV. A$77 (U.S.$50.05) single; A$99–$105 (U.S.$64.35–$68.25) double; self-contained apt. A$425 (U.S.$276.25) per week. Extra person A$25 (U.S.$16.25). Rates include full breakfast. AE, BC, DC, MC, V. Free parking. Pickup available on request from transit center.

On the main shopping strip in trendy Paddington, this lovely three-story 1888 residence retains most of its original features such as tongue-in-groove walls, soaring ceilings, and polished timber floors. The two air-conditioned front rooms are spacious and individually furnished with orthopedic mattresses, comfy sofas, and attractive bathrooms. You can also stay in two self-contained apartments (with fans) downstairs. Your hostess, Annette Henry, cooks a hearty breakfast (her fresh muffins are very popular). There's also a lounge, and a rear deck on both levels. Facilities include a laundry, pay phone, and hair dryers in each room. No smoking indoors.

Wickham Terrace Motel. 491 Wickham Terrace, Spring Hill, Brisbane, QLD 4000. ☎ **1800/ 773 069** in Australia, or 07/3839 9611. Fax 07/3832 5348. 47 units (some with shower only). A/C TV TEL. A$97–$103 (U.S.$63.05–$66.95) single; A$104–A$109 (U.S.$67.60–$70.85) double. Extra person A$11 (U.S.$7.15); children under 14 A$6 (U.S.$3.90) each. Discounts apply for direct bookings. AE, BC, DC, JCB, MC, V. Free parking. Train: Roma St. Bus: City Circle 333.

It's a 10-minute walk to the city from this modest, respectable Best Western motel overlooking leafy Albert Park. While the public areas may be somewhat dated, the rooms are a good size, neat and airy with firm mattresses, desks, and iron and board. Some have furnished balconies. There's a small pool, Jacuzzi, sundeck, and barbecue out back, and a cocktail bar. The restaurant serves breakfast and dinner.

SUPER-CHEAP SLEEPS

Palace Backpackers. Corner of Ann and Edward sts., Brisbane, QLD 4000. ☎ **1800/ 676 340** in Australia, or 07/3211 2433. Fax 07/3211 2466. 120 units (350 beds), none with bathroom. A$33 (U.S.$21.45) single; A$45 (U.S.$29.25) double; A$17–$20 (U.S.$11.05–$13) dorm bed. 4 night and weekly rates available. BC, MC, V. Train: Central. Bus: City Circle 333. Courtesy shuttle to and from Roma St. Transit Center 7:45am–7pm.

Once a temperance hall, this lovely Heritage-listed five-story building with wrought-iron lace verandahs now plays host to less than temperate backpackers. Don't avoid it on that account; the place is well run, and a beautiful restoration has provided simple, pleasant private rooms with iron beds, proper mattresses and crisp linen, lockers, and either air-conditioning or fans. Only someone literally carrying a backpack is entitled to a dorm bed. The spick-and-span renovated bathrooms are cleaned twice a day. There are rooms and bathrooms for travelers with disabilities. There's a rooftop sundeck with a barbecue, TV lounges with Internet access, a tour desk, a communal kitchen, and an excellent cafe (see "Great Deals on Dining," below). No smoking in rooms.

WORTH A SPLURGE

✪ **Quay West Suites Brisbane.** 132 Alice St. (between Albert and George sts.), Brisbane, QLD 4000. ☎ **1800/672 726** in Australia, or 07/3853 6000. Fax 07/3853 6060. 95 apts. A/C MINIBAR TV TEL. A$290–$310 (U.S.$188.50–$201.50) 1-bedroom apt; A$340–$450 (U.S.$221–$292.50) 2-bedroom apt. Extra person A$30 (U.S.$19.50). Bed & Breakfast weekend pkg., including breakfast, A$195 (U.S.$126.75) 1-bedroom apt. Ask about other special packages. AE, BC, DC, JCB, MC, V. Valet and self-parking A$8 (U.S.$5.20). Bus: City Circle 333. Ferry: Edward St. (Inner City and Cross River Ferry); or Riverside (CityCat), then a 10-min. stroll.

When the business folk go home on Fridays, they leave this glamorous all-suite hotel, just 4 blocks from Queen Street Mall, available, with excellent package deals. A one-bedroom suite will sleep four with the sofa bed. The suites have all the amenities of a five-star hotel—daily servicing, 24-hour room service, concierge, a bar and restaurant with a lovely outdoor terrace—and the their own laundry, dining area, separate bedroom, and fully equipped kitchen. Pamper yourself in the plunge pool or Jacuzzi; then back in your room, gaze over the Botanic Gardens, read the free newspaper, turn up your stereo, or watch TV (both of them).

4 Great Deals on Dining

There are plenty of places to eat well at a reasonable price in Brisbane. For cheap meals, head to the stylish Merthyr Street bistro strip in New Farm, the cafes of Given Terrace and Latrobe Terrace in Paddington, the Asian restaurants around the intersection of Vulture and Boundary Streets in West End, and the cheap and cheerful cafes huddling shoulder to shoulder in Brunswick Street Mall in Fortitude Valley. Fortitude Valley is also where you'll find Brisbane's Chinatown. There are also loads of moderately priced restaurants on Park Road in Milton, though few of these are BYO. In the city center you'll find cheap, lively sidewalk cafes along Albert Street.

A cluster of fabulously affordable good restaurants has mushroomed recently in the unlikely location of Baroona Road and Nash Street in Rosalie, an otherwise sleepy suburb next to Paddington. Rosalie is about a A$8 (U.S.$5.20) cab ride from the city.

IN THE CITY CENTER

✪ **Explorers Café.** 63 Turbot St. (near corner of George St.) ☎ **07/3211 3488.** Reservations recommended at lunch. Main courses A$9–$15.90 (U.S.$5.85–$10.34) dinner, A$5.50–$13.90 (U.S.$3.58–$9.04) lunch, A$5–$9.90 (U.S.$3.25–$6.44) breakfast. AE, BC, DC, MC, V. Daily 7–9:30am, noon–2pm, 6–8:30pm; open for coffee all day. Happy hour Mon–Fri 5–6pm. Train: Roma St. Bus: City Circle 333. INTERNATIONAL.

What a find, you think, as you stumble on this pleasant restaurant under the Explorers Inn (see "Accommodations You Can Afford," above). Decent-sized lunches like chicken satay on rice cost a reasonable A$8.50 (U.S.$5.53), a seafood salad is A$6 (U.S.$3.90), and a generous club sandwich is A$8.50 (U.S.$5.53). City office workers think the place is a find, too, so you'll have to reserve a table in the morning to get ahead of them for lunch. The ambience is warm and dignified for such an inexpensive joint, with brick walls, potted palms, matting, and a corrugated iron bar. At night the crowd switches to guests from the hotel and the meals get a bit beefier—lamb curry, rib fillet, and so on. A small pasta makes a generous dinner for A$9 (U.S.$5.85).

Pane e Vino. Albert St. at Charlotte St. ☎ **07/3220 0044.** Reservations recommended at lunch. Main courses A$11.90–$19.90 (U.S.$7.74–$12.94); foccacias and panini A$7–$8.50 (U.S.$4.55–$5.53); breakfast A$1.50–$8.90 (U.S.98¢–$5.79). AE, BC, DC, MC, V. Sun–Thurs 7:30am–10pm, Fri–Sat 7:30am–11:30pm. Bus: City Circle 333. MODERN ITALIAN/CAFE FARE.

A laid-back attitude attracts a mixed lunch set to this contemporary open-sided cafe on a busy street corner. Sit inside in the modish decor of polished concrete floors and sleek timber, or choose a sidewalk table. The simple but sophisticated all-day menu boasts things like grilled King snapper on creamed zucchini with tomato, olive, and basil butter sauce. There's also a wide variety of lighter risottos and pastas, huge focaccias and tasty panini (say, prosciutto, mushroom, onion, and provolone).

SUPER-CHEAP EATS

Govinda's. 199 Elizabeth St. (opposite Myer Centre), 2nd fl. ☎ **07/3210 0255.** A$6 (U.S.$3.90) all-you-can-eat; A$5 (U.S.$3.25) students and seniors. No credit cards. Mon–Sat 11:30am–2:30pm, Fri 5:30–8:30pm. Sunday Feast 5:30–8:30pm A$3 (U.S.$1.95) all-you-can-eat, with lectures and dancing. Bus: City Circle 333. VEGETARIAN.

If you're a seasoned vegetarian traveler in Oz, you already know to seek out the Hare Krishnas' chain of Govinda restaurants. This one serves vegetable casserole, dahl, samosas, deep-fried kofta balls, and other tasty stuff. The atmosphere is pretty spartan, but who cares when the food is so satisfying? This is a stimulant-free zone, so don't come expecting alcohol, tea, or coffee. They do takeout.

Palace Café. In the Palace Backpackers, corner of Ann and Edward sts. ☎ **07/3211 2433.** Breakfast, A$3–$7.50 (U.S.$1.95–$4.88). Lunch, A$7–$11 (U.S.$4.55–$7.15). No credit cards. Daily 7.30am–2pm, for breakfast and lunch. Train: Central. Bus: City Circle 333. CAFE FARE.

It's designed for the backpackers upstairs (see "Accommodations You Can Afford," above), but you don't have to sleep here to dine at this airy, colorful cafe. Start the day with a "big breakfast" of toast, bacon, egg, sausage, tomato, hash browns, or the all-you-can-eat continental breakfast. There's an a la carte menu for lunch. A TV, magazines, and two computers with Internet access make the place feel homey.

IN NEW FARM

New Farm Deli & Café. Merthyr St. at Brunswick St. ☎ **07/3358 2634.** Reservations recommended at dinner. Main courses A$3.50–$12.50 (U.S.$2.28–$8.13). AE, BC, DC, MC, V. Mon–Sat 7am–6pm, Fri–Sat 6pm–late, Sun 7am–5pm. Closed public holidays. Bus: 167, 168, 178. CAFE FARE.

Well-heeled locals and the corporate crowd pack this cheery deli located at the rear of a shopping complex. Try to get a seat outside. Loads of inventive pastas, filling focaccia sandwiches, and gourmet burgers stack the menu, and there are blackboard specials such as hot pancetta, and tomato and mushroom risotto. Service is fast and pleasant.

IN MILTON

Arrivederci Pizza Al Metro. 1 Park Rd. ☎ **07/3369 8500.** Reservations recommended Fri and Sat dinner. Pizzas for 2 A$9.50–14.50 (U.S.$6.18–$9.43); pizzas for 4 A$9.50–$26 (U.S.$6.18–$16.90). AE, BC, DC, MC, V. Daily 10am–late. Train: Milton. Bus: 410. PIZZA.

Cheapest of the bunch along the Park Road restaurant strip is this pizzeria with airy indoor seating and some alfresco tables. They offer 21 toppings, mostly the basic but tasty kinds like salami, peppers, cheese, and mushrooms. It's just a humble joint, but it's a nice night out if you bring a bottle of red, dine outside, and then stroll up the street to people-watch and windowshop.

IN MT. COOT-THA

The Summit. At the Mt. Coot-tha Lookout, Sir Samuel Griffith Dr., Mt. Coot-tha. ☎ **07/ 3369 9922.** Reservations recommended Fri and Sat nights. Main courses A$19.90–$22.90 (U.S.$12.94–$14.89). Prix-fixe 3-course menu A$38.50 (U.S.$25.03). Sun brunch A$11.90 (U.S.$7.74) adults, A$6.90 (U.S.$4.49) child under 12. 3-course early-bird menu A$19.90 (U.S.$12.94) available from 3pm if you finish by 7pm. AE, BC, DC, JCB, MC, V. Daily 11:30am–midnight; Sun brunch from 8am. Bus: 471. From Roma Street Transit Centre, take Upper Roma St. and Milton Rd. 3.5km (2 miles) west to the Western Freeway roundabout at Toowong Cemetery, veer slightly right into Sir Samuel Griffith Dr., and go approx. 3km (2 miles). MODERN AUSTRALIAN.

It's hard to find a nicer setting than this mountaintop Queenslander. Part 19th century, part period-style addition, the restaurant is wrapped by covered decks with a super city view. A changing menu features Queensland produce, each dish teamed with an award-winning Queensland wine. Try grilled barramundi fillet, or grilled kangaroo loin and spicy kangaroo sausage on sweet potato mash. When you've finished, head for the observation deck, with views of Moreton Bay by day, and the city lights by night.

IN EAST BRISBANE

✪ **Green Papaya.** 898 Stanley St East (at Potts St.), East Brisbane. ☎ **07/3217 3599.** Reservations recommended. Main courses A$12–$28 (U.S.$7.80–$18.20); entrees A$10–$16 (U.S.$6.50–$10.40); noodles A$17 (U.S.$11.05); soups A$12–$15 (U.S.$7.80–$9.75). Banquet menus (for minimum of 4 people) A$30–$35 (U.S.$19.50–$22.75). AE, BC, DC, MC, V. Tues–Sun 6–10pm. Closed Christmas to early Jan. Located a 10-min. drive from town and 1 block from the Wolloongabba Cricket Ground. NORTH VIETNAMESE.

Clean, fresh, and simple are the key words to describe owner/chef Lien Yeoman's approach to her native cuisine. Two cheerful rooms painted yellow and blue are usually crowded with a faithful clientele. If you don't know your *Bo Cay Ngot* (spicy beef) from your *Nom Du Du* (green papaya salad), the staff gives advice. They're licensed but you can bring your own wine only (no beer or spirits), with corkage of A$3 (U.S.$1.95) per person is charged. Cooking classes are also offered from time to time, so call for the current schedule.

IN WEST END

The Three Monkeys. 58 Mollison St. (just off Boundary St.) ☎ **07/3844 6045.** Main courses A$4.50–$7.90 (U.S.$2.93–$5.14). AE, BC, MC, V. Mon–Thurs 9am–midnight, Fri–Sat 9am–1am, Sun 10am–late. Bus: 167, 177. CAFE FARE.

Locals make a beeline for this hippie-chic cafe after a show at the Queensland Performing Arts Complex a few blocks away. What draws them? Huge plates of hearty homemade stuff like lasagna, moussaka, and vegetarian courgette bake, with fresh side salads, at absurdly low prices. The dark rooms are bedecked with so many Moroccan fabrics, Asian wooden gewgaws, and wind chimes you fear you might never emerge; but eventually you get to a palmy courtyard in back. The sinful cakes are a must.

IN ALBION

Breakfast Creek Hotel. 2 Kingsford Smith Drive (at Breakfast Creek Rd.), Albion. ☎ **07/ 3262 5988.** Main courses A$13.50–$19.90 (U.S.$8.78–$12.94). AE, BC, DC, MC, V. Meals daily noon–2:30pm; Mon–Fri 5:30–9:30pm, Sat 5–9:30pm, Sun 5–8:30pm. Pub: Sun–Thurs 10am–10pm, Fri–Sat 10am–11pm. Bus: 300, 322. Wickham St. becomes Breakfast Creek Rd; the hotel is just off the route to the airport. STEAK.

Listed by the National Trust, the Breakfast Creek Hotel has been treasured by Brisbane people since 1889. Known fondly as "the Brekky Creek," or simply "The Creek," it is quintessentially Queensland. With a view over the Brisbane River, "The Creek" is

① Family-Friendly Restaurants

City Gardens Cafe, Brisbane City Gardens, Alice St in the city. ☎ **07/3229 1554.** Fax 07/3210 0780. Daily 9am to 4pm daily. All major credit cards. Special kids' menu, colored pencils, balloons and lollipops keep the young ones happy here. There's ramp access for strollers, and kids can play in the park while you watch from the outside tables on the vine-covered verandah. On the kids' menu are such treats as mini-Hawaiian pizza, toasted fingers (toast strips with melted cheese or other topping), potato skins and a Fire Engine mocktail (raspberry lemonade). Food is A$4.95 (U.S.$3.22), drinks A$2.50 (U.S.$1.63).

Summit Restaurant, Sir Samuel Griffith Drive, Mt. Coot-tha. ☎ **07/3369 9922.** Fax 07/3369 8937. Daily 11:30am to late, from 8am on Sundays. All major credit cards. Children's menu features chicken fingers with honey dipping sauce (A$8.70/U.S.$5.66), sirloin steak burger with fried onions (A$9.80/$6.37), and an old-fashioned banana split (A$4.70/U.S.$3.06). On Sundays there's a live band.

Morgan's Seafood Restaurant, Bird o' Passage Parade, Scarborough. ☎ **07/ 3203 5744.** Fax 07/3880 1844. Daily for lunch and dinner. All major credit cards. A Brisbane institution, Morgan's offers great views across to Moreton Island and is paradise for parents and kids. The restaurant has its own fleet of trawlers which dock nearby to disgorge mussels, mud crabs, prawns, oysters, and the freshest reef fish. Classic seafood platters and Asian style dishes are available, and kids can choose anything they like for a "pint-sized" special price of A$9.90 (U.S.$6.44). Even the Teppanyaki grill has a kids' menu which includes yakitori, fish furai, and chicken kara age (A$9.60–$10.50/U.S.$6.24–$6.83). All children's meals include steamed rice, and ice cream for dessert.

famed for its gigantic steaks, all served with mushroom, chili or pepper sauce. Order a XXXX (Fourex) beer "off the wood" (from the keg), sit in the beer garden under umbrellas, and check out the blackboard menu. There are five bars, including the Spanish Steakhouse. If steak's not your meat, there are fish and chicken, too—but the steak is what people come for. Every meal is served with an Idaho potato with bacon sauce, coleslaw, and tomato. On footy nights (Aussie Rules Football, Rugby League, or Rugby Union) be prepared for crowds. There's a band on Sunday afternoons.

WORTH A SPLURGE

✪ **e'cco bistro.** 100 Boundary St. (at Adelaide St.). ☎ **07/3831 8344.** Reservations required. Main courses A$23.50–$24.50 (U.S.$15.28–$15.93). AE, BC, DC, MC, V. Tues–Fri noon–2:30pm; Tues–Sat 6–10:30pm. Also open Mon Nov–Christmas. Closed Christmas until 2nd week of Jan. MODERN AUSTRALIAN.

Located in a renovated former tea warehouse on the city fringe, this multi-award-winning bistro counts the title of Australia's top restaurant award (the Remy Martin Cognac/Gourmet Traveller Restaurant of the Year) among its claims to fame. It's well-known for doing simple food exceptionally well. Large windows, bold colors, and modern furniture make it a pleasant setting in what is becoming a small but popular restaurant enclave in this part of town. It is licensed but you can BYO wine for a corkage fee. Reservations are a must, as it can be difficult to get a table.

5 Exploring Brisbane

WHERE TO CUDDLE A KOALA & OTHER TOP ATTRACTIONS

Lone Pine Koala Sanctuary. Jesmond Rd., Fig Tree Pocket. ☎ **07/3378 1366.** Fax 07/ 3878 1770. www.koala.net. Admission A$14.30 (U.S.$9.30) adults; A$9.35 (U.S.$6.08) children 3–13; family pass A$35 (U.S.$22.75); A$11.55 (U.S.$7.51) seniors, backpackers and students with ID, A$8.80 (U.S.$5.72) pensioners. Daily including Christmas 7:30am–5pm, 1.30–5pm on Anzac Day (Apr 25).

Lone Pine is one of the few places where koala cuddling is still allowed in Australia. Banned in New South Wales and Victoria, Queensland allows you to cuddle a koala under strict rules which ensure each animal is handled for less than 30 minutes a day—and they get every third day off! When it opened in 1927, Lone Pine had only two koalas, Jack and Jill, but is now home to more than 130 of the furry marsupials. You can cuddle them any time of the day for free, and have your photo taken holding one for A$12.60 (U.S.$8.19); once you have purchased one photograph, your companions can take photos of you with their own cameras. Koalas sleep about 18 hours a day, which has led to a myth that they get "stoned" on the eucalyptus oil in the leaves they eat. That's just a rumor. They move slowly because the leaves aren't a high-energy food, and with a diet consisting mostly of eucalyptus, the koalas need their rest!

You can also hand-feed kangaroos and wallabies (A50¢/U.S.35¢ for a bag of food), and get up close with emus, parrots, wombats, Tasmanian devils, skinks, lace monitors, frogs, bats, turtles, possums, and other Aussie wildlife. There is a restaurant and cafe, and free picnic and barbecue facilities overlooking the river. There is also a currency-exchange and a gift shop.

Getting There: The scenic route to Lone Pine is a cruise down the Brisbane River on the *M.V. Miramar* (☎ **07/3221 0300**). The boat departs North Quay at the top end of Queen Street Mall, beside the casino next to Victoria Bridge, at 10am and makes the 19-kilometer (12-mile) trip upriver to Lone Pine in 90 minutes, cruising past Queenslander homes and native bush, all with a commentary from the captain. You have 2 hours to explore Lone Pine before arriving back in the city at 2:45pm. The fare is A$33 (U.S.$21.45) for adults and A$19 (U.S.$12.35) for children ages 3 to 13, including a map, transfers from city hotels when available, and discounted entry to Lone Pine. Cruises are every day except Christmas and Anzac Day (Apr 25).

By car, take Milton Road to the roundabout at Toowong cemetery, and then take the Great Western Freeway toward Ipswich. Signs will direct you to Fig Tree Pocket and Lone Pine. The sanctuary is 20 minutes from the city center by car. Bus 430 goes to the Sanctuary from the Koala platform "N" at the Myer Centre, Queen St Mall, and leaves hourly from 8:45am to 3:45pm weekdays; 8:30am to 4:30pm weekends and public holidays. Bus fare is A$2.80 (U.S.$1.82) adults and A$1.40 (U.S.91¢) children.

South Bank Parklands. At South Bank across Victoria Bridge at western end of Queen St. ☎ **07/3867 2051** for Visitor Information Centre or 07/3867 2020 for recorded entertainment information. Free admission. Park: daily 24 hr.; Visitor Information Centre: Sun–Thurs 8am–6pm, Fri 8am–10pm, Sat 8am–8pm. Train: South Brisbane. Ferry: South Bank (CityCat) and Old South Bank (Inner City Ferry). Bus: Many bus routes depart Adelaide St. near Albert St., cross the Victoria Bridge, and stop at the Queensland Cultural Centre; walk through the Centre to South Bank Parklands. Underground parking in Queensland Cultural Centre. The Parklands are a 7-min. walk from town.

When you don't feel like splurging, follow the locals to this 40-acre complex of parks, restaurants, souvenir shops, playgrounds, street theater, weekend markets, and a man-made beach lined with palm trees, with waves and sand, where you can swim. You can also stroll the meandering pathways, or cycle through the park; meet friends over a latte; enjoy the city views. From the parklands it's an easy wander to the museum, art gallery, and other buildings of the adjacent Queensland Cultural Centre (see below).

Queensland Cultural Centre. At South Bank across Victoria Bridge at western end of Queen St. ☎ **07/3840 7595.** Train: South Brisbane. Ferry: South Bank (CityCat) and Old South Bank (Inner City Ferry). Bus: Countless bus routes depart Adelaide St. near Albert St., cross the Victoria Bridge, and stop outside. Plentiful underground parking. The Centre is a 7-min. walk from town.

Adjacent to South Bank Parklands (see above), this complex of buildings stretching along the south bank of the Brisbane River houses many of the city's performing arts venues as well as the state art gallery, museum, and library in a series of interlinked buildings. Thanks to plenty of open plazas and fountains, it is a pleasing place to wander or to just sit and watch the river and the city skyline.

The **Queensland Performing Arts Complex** (☎ 07/3840 7444 administration or 07/3840 7431 backstage tours) houses the 2,000-seat Lyric Theatre for musicals, ballet, and opera; the 1,800-seat Concert Hall for orchestral performances; the 850-seat Optus Playhouse Theatre for plays; and the 315-seat Cremorne Theatre for theater-in-the-round, cabaret, and experimental works. The complex has a restaurant and a cafe. Free short front-of-house tours leave from the ticket sales foyer at noon Monday through Friday; no bookings are needed. Backstage tours must be booked and cost A$5.50 (U.S.$3.58) adults, A$2.75 (U.S.$1.79) children, concessions and students.

The **Queensland Art Gallery** (☎ 07/3840 7303) not only attracts major exhibitions, such as works by Renoir and Van Gogh, it showcases modern Australian painters, sculptors, and other artists. Indoor/outdoor light-filled spaces and water features give it an uplifting feel. Admission is free. Free guided tours run Monday through Friday at 11am, 1pm, and 2pm; Saturdays at 11am, 2pm, and 3pm; Sundays at 11am, 1pm, and 3pm. There is a gift shop and bistro. The gallery is open daily from 10am to 5pm; closed Good Friday, Christmas, and until noon on Anzac Day (Apr 25).

The **Queensland Museum** on the corner of Grey and Melbourne streets (☎ 07/ 3840 7555) displays an eclectic collection ranging from natural history specimens and fossils to a World War I German tank. Kids like the blue whale model suspended from the entrance. There's a cafe and gift shop. Admission is free, except to traveling exhibitions, and open daily from 9:30am to 5pm; closed Christmas and Good Friday.

MORE ATTRACTIONS

Australian Woolshed. 148 Samford Rd., Ferny Hills. ☎ **07/3872 1100.** Admission to ram show A$15 (U.S.$9.75) adults, A$11 (U.S.$7.15) seniors and students, A$10 (U.S.$6.50) children 3–14, A$42.50 (U.S.$27.63) family. Waterslide A$5.50 (U.S.$3.58) for 1 hr.; A$7.50 (U.S.$4.88) for 4 hr. Unlimited minigolf A$5 (U.S.$3.25). Package of A$22 (U.S.$14.30) includes unlimited waterslide use, 9 holes of minigolf, ram show, dog show and animal farm. Daily 7:30am–4pm (Ram show 8am, 9:30am, 11am, 1pm, and 2:30pm) except Christmas Day and Anzac Day (Apr 25) morning. Train: Ferny Grove (station is 800m/½ mile) from the Woolshed). Kelvin Grove Rd. from the city becomes Enoggera Rd., then Samford Rd.; the trip is 14km (8½ miles).

A trip to this Australian sheep farm/theme park is the next best thing to actually visiting a sheep station. The ram show features eight trained rams that answer to their names and walk through the audience to their named spots on the stage. There's also sheep-shearing, wool-spinning, and sheepdog demonstrations, and you can get your hands dirty classing wool, milking cows, bottle-feeding baby farm animals, feeding kangaroos, and cuddling koalas. The gift shop has won awards for its Australian-made

Cheap Thrills: What to See & Do for Free (or Almost) in Brisbane

- **Free shows at South Bank Parklands.** On weekends and holidays, there is almost always free entertainment at South Bank Parklands, such as street theater, live bands, movies under the stars, or concerts. Even when there's nothing going on, it's a great place to hang out, picnic by the river, and people-watch. Call the entertainment line (☎ **07/3867 2020**) to see what's on.

- **Attend a lecture, film, or gallery talk at the Queensland Art Gallery or Queensland Museum Theater.** Free lectures and gallery talks on a topical artist or issue are held the first Wednesday of the month at the Gallery, and most Wednesdays and some Saturdays at the Museum. A free "Sunday at the Gallery" program features a talk, film, or musical performance and kids' activities. Book a seat for Wednesdays and Fridays; just show up on Sundays. Call ☎ **07/3840 7303** for details.

- **Watch the Queensland Parliament in action.** If Parliament is sitting (in session), the best show in town can sometimes be in the Green Chamber at Parliament House (see "More Attractions," above). Aussie politicians drop decorum in Parliament for no-holds-barred trading of taunts and insults that are sometimes banal, sometimes shocking, often funny. The free 10:30am tour at Question Time is the juiciest, when each party tries to goad the other.

- **Climb to the top of the City Hall clock tower.** For a fabulous view of the city, take the elevator from the ground floor, and then from the third floor. The clock tower elevator lets you out into the glassed-in observation. The lift to the top of the clock tower operates Monday through Saturday 10am to 4pm. If you're there on the quarter hour you'll get a close-up view of the chimes. Try not to be there at midday, when the clock chimes 12—it's deafening!

- **"Walking the walk" on the Mangrove Boardwalk.** The Mangrove Boardwalk extends 400 meters (¼ mile) out over the Brisbane River in the Brisbane City Gardens, along Alice Street. It's open and lit up until midnight. Free guided tours of the gardens are run at 11am and 1pm Monday throught Saturday (except public holidays).

- **Check out the stunning St John's Anglican Cathedral.** At 373 Ann St, you can watch stonemasons work on the West End of the building, nearing completion after almost a century. Free guided tours of the cathedral are offered at 10am and 2pm Monday through Saturday, at 2pm on Sunday.

quality souvenirs. A rustic restaurant serves Aussie specialties, including billy tea and damper. On some Friday and Saturday nights the Woolshed hosts a traditional bush dance and dinner, with country dancing, spoon-playing, sing-a-longs, a live bush band, and three-course dinner. Tickets are A$38.50 (U.S.$25.03) per person. The fun starts at 7pm and goes until midnight. Reservations required, over-18 only.

Brisbane Botanic Gardens at Mt. Coot-tha. Mt. Coot-tha Rd., Toowong, 7km (4 miles) from the city. ☎ **07/3403 2533.** Free admission to Botanic Gardens. Planetarium Sky Theatre A$10 (U.S.$6.50) adults, A$8.50 (U.S.$5.53) for seniors and students, A$6 (U.S.$3.90) children under 15 (not recommended for children under 6), A$28 (U.S.$18.20) family. Gardens open daily 8am–5pm (5:30pm in summer). Planetarium Sky Theatre Wed–Fri 3:30 and

7:30pm; Sat 1:30, 3:30, and 7:30pm; Sun 1:30 and 3:30pm. Reservations suggested; call ☎ **07/3403 2578** Wed–Sun noon–7pm. Bus: 471. See "River Cruises & Other Organized Tours," for details on Brisbane Transport's daily bus tour.

A 15-minute drive or bus ride takes you to these 130-acre gardens at the base of Mt. Coot-tha. They feature Aussie natives and exotics, including an arid zone, a glass Tropical Dome conservatory housing rain forest plants, a cactus house, fragrant plants, a Japanese garden, African and American plants, wetlands, pine forests, and a bamboo grove. There are lakes and walking trails, usually a horticultural show or arts-and-crafts display in the auditorium on weekends, and a cafe. Free 1-hour guided tours leave the kiosk at 11am and 1pm Monday through Saturday (except public holidays).

While you're here, don't miss the Sir Thomas Brisbane Planetarium, where a fascinating 45-minute astronomical show explores the Brisbane night sky.

Newstead House. Newstead Park, Breakfast Creek Rd., Newstead. ☎ **07/3216 1846.** Admission A$4.40 (U.S.$2.86) adults, A$3.30 (U.S.$2.15) seniors and students, A$2.20 (U.S.$1.43) children 6–16, and A$11 (U.S.$7.15) for a family pass. Mon–Fri 10am–4pm, Sun and most public holidays 2–5pm. Closed Christmas, Boxing Day (Dec 26), Good Friday, and Anzac Day (Apr 25). Bus: 300, 306, 322.

Brisbane's oldest surviving home sits in late Victorian splendor in a peaceful park overlooking the Brisbane River. Wander the rooms, admire the gracious exterior dating from 1846, and on Sundays and public holidays between March and November, take Devonshire tea. The U.S. Army occupied the house during World War II, and the first American war memorial built in Australia stands on Newstead Point on the grounds.

Parliament House. George St. at Alice St. ☎ **07/3406 7562.** Free admission, tours. Tours Mon–Fri at 9:30am, 10:30am, 11:15am, 2:30pm, 3:15pm, 4:15pm; Sun 10am–2pm when Parliament is not in session. Mon–Fri 10:30am, 2:30pm when Parliament is in session. Bus: City Circle 333. Ferry: Queensland University of Technology (QUT) Gardens Point (CityCat and Inner City Ferry).

Queensland's seat of government was built in 1868 in an odd but happy mix of French Renaissance and tropical colonial styles. It's impressive from the outside, and guided 20-minute tours show off its ornate interior of Waterford chandeliers, Colebrookdale balustrades, and the gold-leaf ceilings in the Council Chamber. When Parliament is in session, the tour is restricted, but you can see Parliament in action. The House is on Brisbane's Heritage Trail (see "City Strolls," below) and the City Sights tour bus.

✪ **Sciencentre.** 110 George St. between Mary and Charlotte sts. ☎ **07/3220 0166.** Admission A$8 (U.S.$5.20) adults, A$6 (U.S.$3.90) seniors, students, and children 5–15, A$2 (U.S.$1.30) children 3–4, and A$28 (U.S.$18.20) for a family pass. Open daily 10am–5pm. Closed Good Friday and Christmas, and until 1pm Anzac Day (Apr 25). Bus: City Circle 333. Ferry: Queensland University of Technology (QUT) Gardens Point (CityCat and Inner City Ferry).

Adults love this hands-on science museum as much as the kids 12 and younger for whom it was designed. Become part of a battery, see walls expand before your eyes, watch shadows float in space, carry a briefcase with a mind of its own—these and other amazing feats demonstrating the principles of science cover three fascinating floors. Twenty-minute interactive shows run throughout the day.

CITY STROLLS

Because Brisbane is leafy, warm, and full of colonial-era Queenslander architecture, it is a great city for a stroll. Pick up a free Heritage Trail Map from the Brisbane Tourism information booths (see "Visitor Information," above) and explore on your own. The guides have a history of the area, and excellent detailed information and illustrations of historic buildings and other sights along the way. Free guided walks of the **Brisbane**

City Gardens (☎ 07/3403 7913) at Alice Street leave from the rotunda at the Albert Street entrance Tuesday through Sunday at 11am and 1pm (except public holidays). Rain forest, camellias, lily ponds, palm groves, and formal flowerbeds offer a blissfully cool reprieve on a summer's day. The Gardens are free and open 24 hours.

For organized walking tours, see below.

6 River Cruises & Other Organized Tours

RIVER CRUISES   Cruises along the Brisbane River aboard the **Club Crocodile River Queen paddle wheeler** (☎ 07/3221 1300) are a good way to take in the Queenslander homes, historic buildings, and tropical foliage—especially in October and November when the jacaranda trees bloom. The boat departs from the Eagle Street Pier at 12:15am (boarding at 11:45am) and returns at 1:45pm. The cheapest option is the A$22 (U.S.$14.30) "coffee, tea and cookies" fare, which provides a snack (you can also get a meal). Children pay half price; seniors get a 15% discount.

BUS TOURS   Brisbane Transport (☎ 13 12 30 in Australia) runs two bus tours that are a much better value than commercial tours, especially as tour tickets entitle you to unlimited access to buses, ferries, and CityCats for the day. The ✪ **City Sights** bus tour stops at 19 points of interest in a continuous loop around the city center, South Bank, and Fortitude Valley, including Chinatown, South Bank Parklands, the Queensland Cultural Centre, Sciencentre, the Riverside Centre (where markets are held Sundays), the City Botanic Gardens, the casino, and various historical buildings. The driver of the blue and yellow bus gives a commentary, and you can hop on and off at any stop. The bus departs every 45 minutes from 9am to 4:15pm daily except Christmas, Good Friday and Anzac Day (Apr 25). The whole trip, without stopping, takes 80 minutes. Tickets cost A$18 (U.S.$11.70) for adults, A$12 (U.S.$7.80) for children ages 5 to 15. Buy your ticket on board. You can join anywhere along the route, but the most central stop is City Hall, Stop 2 on Adelaide Street at Albert Street. Daily except Christmas, Good Friday, and Anzac Day.

The **City Nights** tour shows you the city lights from Mt. Coot-tha, the Brisbane River at South Bank, the illuminated cliffs at Kangaroo Point, New Farm Park, and Fortitude Valley. It departs City Hall, Stop 2 on Adelaide Street, at 6pm daily (Mar–Oct) and 6:30pm (Nov–Feb) and takes about 2½ hours. Daily except Christmas, New Year's Eve, Good Friday, and Anzac Day. Tickets are A$18 (U.S.$11.70) for adults, A$12 (U.S.$7.80) for kids ages 5 to 15. The trip also includes a sector by City-Cat from South Bank to New Farm Park, where the bus is waiting to pick you up again.

WALKING TOURS   The Brisbane City Council sponsors **Walking for Pleasure** (☎ 07/3403 8888): Most days a free guided walk departs from somewhere in the city or suburbs, exploring all kinds of territory from bushland to heritage buildings to

River Cruises on the Cheap

One of the cheapest tours in town is cruising the river on the fast ✪ **CityCat** ferries. Board at North Quay, QUT Gardens Point, or Riverside and head downstream under the Story Bridge to New Farm Park, past Newstead House to the restaurant row at Brett's Wharves; glide upriver past the city and South Bank to the University of Queensland's lovely campus (take a peek at its impressive Great Court). This trip will set you back a whopping A$3.20 (U.S.$2.08)!

riverscapes to cemeteries. The walks are aimed at locals, not tourists, so you get to explore Brisbane side-by-side with the townsfolk. Every walk has a flexible distance option and usually lasts about 2 hours. Most are easy, but some are more demanding. Most start and finish near public transport and end near a food outlet of some kind.

Historical Walking Tours are run by local historian Brian Ogden (☎ **07/3217 3673**), who leads visitors on a journey into Brisbane's past, telling tales dating from convict settlement through the present day. Three different routes are taken and tours depart Monday at 9:30am, Wednesday at 7pm and Saturday at 8:30am and 1:30pm.

You may encounter things that go bump in the night on **Brisbane Ghost Tours** (☎ **07/3272 6234**), when you relive the city's gruesome past with guide Jack Sim. City walking tours run every Friday night and other haunted activities include **Boggo Road Gaol** ghost tours, sleepovers and haunted film nights.

Read and walk the **Albert Street Literary Trail,** the best way to experience the city from a writer's view! Pick up a map from any Brisbane City Council Service Centre, ward office or library (☎ **07/3403 8888**).

Chinatown Tours, run by Barbara Harman (☎ **07/3289 1919**), explore the spice of Asian food and crafts in Fortitude Valley, finishing with a delicious Yum Cha lunch.

Great Brisbane Walks, an inexpensive guide to more than 40 of Brisbane's best walks, is available from Brisbane City Council (☎ **07/3403 8888**). Another good book for those intending to explore Brisbane by foot is *Walking Brisbane,* a guide to 30 walks in and around the city, available from most bookshops.

7 Outdoor Pursuits in Brisbane

ACTIVITIES

ABSEILING & ROCK CLIMBING   The **Kangaroo Point** cliffs south of the Story Bridge are a breeze for first-time abseilers—so they say. **Outdoor Pursuits** (☎ **07/ 3397 7779**) stages rock climbs up the cliffs every second Sunday from 8:30am. The experience lasts 3½ hours and costs A$33 (U.S.$21.45) per person. At 1pm you can abseil back during a 4-hour session for A$38.50 (U.S.$25.03) per person. You will fit in four or five abseils in an afternoon. If you want to climb in the morning and abseil in the afternoon, you can buy both experiences as a package for A$60.50 (U.S.$39.33).

BIKING   Bike tracks stretch for 400 kilometers (219 miles) around Brisbane. You often share them with pedestrians and in-line skaters. One great scenic route starts just west of the Story Bridge, sweeps through the City Botanic Gardens, and follows the river all the way to the University of Queensland campus at St Lucia; it's about 9 kilometers (5½ miles), all up. **Brisbane Bicycle Sales and Hire,** 87 Albert St. (☎ **07/3229 2433**), will rent you a bike and give you the Brisbane City Council's free detailed bike maps. Rentals start at A$9 (U.S.$5.85) for 1 hour and go up to A$20 (U.S.$13) for the day; overnight and weekly rentals are available. The price includes helmets, which are compulsory in Australia. **Hotel Cycle Hire** (☎ **04/0800 3198** mobile phone) rents bikes, helmets and maps for A$30 (U.S.$19.50) for a half day, A$40 (U.S.$26) full day, A$70 (U.S.$45.50) for 2 days. The fee includes a Day Rover ticket, so you can take your bike on the CityCat to places like the University of Queensland or Bretts Wharf, great places to ride. The company also operates an easy escorted tour each afternoon for about 3 hours, leaving from the Brisbane City Gardens. **The Brisbane City Council** at City Hall (☎ **07/3403 8888**) and Brisbane Tourism's information booths (see "Visitor Information," above) also give out bike maps.

BUSHWALKING   Brisbane Forest Park, a 71,250-acre expanse of bush land, waterfalls, and rain forest a 20-minute drive north of the city, has many hiking trails from just a few hundred meters long up to 8 kilometers (5 miles). Some tracks have themes—one highlights the native mammals in the park. Another hike, the 1.8-kilometer (just over 1-mile) Mt. Coot-tha Aboriginal Art Trail, showcases contemporary Aboriginal art with tree carvings, rock paintings, etchings, and a dance pit. Most walks depart from one of seven regional centers that are up to a 20-minute drive from headquarters, so you will need a car. Make a day of it and pack a picnic. **Park Headquarters** (☎ 07/3300 4855) is at 60 Mt. Nebo Rd., The Gap, where there's a wildlife display, restaurant, crafts shop, and information center.

IN-LINE SKATING   In-line skaters can use the network of bike/pedestrian paths. See "Biking," for where to find a map or just head down to the **City Botanic Gardens** at Alice Street and find your own way out along the river. **SkateBiz,** 101 Albert St. (☎ 07/3220 0157), rents blades and protective gear for A$10/U.S.$6.50 (the price goes up to A$12/U.S.$7.80 on Sunday) for 2 hours. All-day rental is A$25 (U.S.$16.25). Take photo ID. The store is open daily.

JOGGING   Take any pedestrian/bike path (see "Biking," for information about where to find a bike map) or head to the City Botanic Gardens and out along the river.

SPECTATOR SPORTS

Aussie Rules football and cricket are played at "The Gabba," as Aussies call **Brisbane Cricket Ground,** 411 Vulture St. at Stanley Street, Woolloongabba, a 5-minute drive south of the city. Among the many buses to the Gabba are 165, 169, 185, 189, and 195.

AUSTRALIAN RULES FOOTBALL (AFL)   The Brisbane Lions are the local heroes in this uniquely Aussie sport. Tickets are about A$30 (U.S.$19.50); book through **TicketMaster** (☎ 13 61 22 in Australia). The season begins in late March and ends in late August. Most games are played on Saturday night.

CRICKET   Boring to some, fascinating to others, cricket is big business in Australia, and some of the most important national and international matches are played in Brisbane in the season from October to late February. Most matches are played midweek and weekends during the day; a few are played at night. Most tickets cost between A$22 (U.S.$14.30) and A$65 (U.S.$42.25). Book through **TicketMaster** (☎ 13 61 22 in Australia, or 07/3404 6644 in Brisbane or on www.ticketmaster.com.au).

8 The Shopping Scene

Brisbane's best shopping is centered on **Queen Street Mall.** Fronting the mall at 171–209 Queen Street, under the Hilton, is the three-level **Wintergarden** complex (☎ 07/3229 9755), housing upscale jewelers and Aussie fashion designers. Farther up the mall at 91 Queen St. at Albert Street is the **Myer Centre** (☎ 07/3221 4199), which has Brisbane's biggest department store and five levels of moderately priced stores, mostly clothing. The historic **Brisbane Arcade,** 160 Queen Street Mall, (☎ 07/3221 5977) is lined with the boutiques of highly regarded local Queensland designers. Just down the mall you'll find the **Broadway on the Mall** arcade (☎ 07/3229 5233), which stocks affordable fashion, gifts, and accessories on two levels.

The trendy suburb of ✪ **Paddington,** a couple of miles from the city by cab (or take the bus no. 144 to Bardon), is where to go for antiques, books, art, crafts, one-of-a-kind clothing, and gifts. The shops—cute, colorfully painted Queenslander cottages—line the main street, Given Terrace, which becomes Latrobe Terrace. Don't miss the second wave of shops around the bend from the first lot.

You will find some elegant houseware and fashion boutiques, galleries, one or two antique shops, and cafes and restaurants on **Park Road,** linking Coronation Drive and Milton Road in Milton. Parking is difficult, so take the Ipswich train from Central or Roma Street station to Milton station. Park Road is around the corner from the station.

SHOPPING HOURS   Shops are open from 8:30am to 5:30pm Monday through Friday, 8:30am to 5pm on Saturday, and 10:30am to 4pm on Sunday. They stay open until 9pm Friday in the city, when the Queen Street Mall is abuzz with cinemagoers and revelers, and Thursday in Paddington. In the suburbs, stores often close Sunday.

MARKETS   Authentic retro '50s and '60s fashion, offbeat stuff like old LPs, second-hand crafts, and all kinds of junk and treasure are up for sale at Brisbane's only alternative markets, **Brunswick Street Markets,** Brunswick Street next to Chinatown Mall, in Fortitude Valley (☎ **0418/886 400** mobile phone). Hang around in one of the many coffee shops and listen to live folk bands. It's held Saturday from 7am to 4pm.

Friday night is a fun time to visit the **South Bank Craft and Lantern Markets,** Stanley Street Plaza, South Bank Parklands (☎ **07/3870 2807**), because the buzzing, outdoor, handcrafts market is lit by lanterns. The market is held Friday from 5pm to 10pm, Saturday from 11am to 5pm, and Sunday from 9am to 5pm.

Brisbane's glamour set likes trawling the **Riverside Markets** at the Riverside Centre, 123 Eagle St. (☎ **07/3289 7077,** or 0414/888 041 mobile phone), to buy attractive housewares, colorful pottery, wooden blanket chests, handmade toys, painted flowerpots, and other stylish items. It's held Sunday from 8am to 4pm.

9 Brisbane After Dark

You can find out about festivals, concerts, and performing arts events, and book tickets through **Ticketek** (☎ **13 19 31** in Queensland, 07/3404 6700 outside Queensland; www.ticketek.com.au. You can book in person at Ticketek agencies, the most convenient of which are on Level E at the Myer Centre at 91 Queen Street Mall, in the Roma Street Transit Centre, and in the Visitor Information Centre at South Bank Parklands. Or try **TicketMaster,** (☎ **13 16 00** or www.ticketmaster.com.au).

QTIX (☎ **13 62 46** in Australia) is a major booking agent for performing arts and classical music, including events at the Queensland Performing Arts Complex (QPAC). There is a A$6.60 (U.S.$4.29) fee per booking, not per ticket. You can also inquire and book in person at the box office at QPAC between 9am and 9pm Monday through Saturday, and at its outlet at the South Bank Parklands Visitor Information Centre.

The free weekly newspaper *Brisbane News* lists performing arts; jazz and classical music performances; art exhibitions; rock concerts; and public events. The free weekly *TimeOff,* which comes out Wednesdays and can be found in bars and cafes, is a good guide to live music, as is the *Courier-Mail* newspaper on Thursday.

THE PERFORMING ARTS

Most of Brisbane's performing arts happen at the Queensland Performing Arts Complex (QPAC) at Queensland Cultural Centre (see "Exploring Brisbane," earlier in this chapter). For information and tickets, call QTIX (see above) or www.qtix.com.au.

THEATER

Brisbane Powerhouse—Centre for the Live Arts. 119 Lamington St, New Farm, (☎ **07/3254 4518.** Tickets A$20–$32 (U.S.$13–$20.80) "All Ages" shows for under-26.

A former electric power station, this massive brick building at New Farm has been transformed into a dynamic art space for exhibitions, performance and live art. Despite its new life, the building retains its unique character, emphasized by a mix of industrial metal, glass, and stark surfaces etched with 20 years of graffiti. It is a short walk from the New Farm ferry terminal along the riverfront through New Farm Park.

La Boite Theatre. Performing at La Boite Theatre, 57 Hale St., Petrie Terrace. ☎ **07/ 3369 1622.** Tickets A$27 (U.S.$17.55); previews A$15 (U.S.$9.75).

This innovative company performs contemporary Australian plays in a tiny theater-in-the-round on the edge of the city center.

qtc (Queensland Theatre Company). Performing at Optus Playhouse and Cremorne Theatres at the Queensland Performing Arts Complex (QPAC), South Bank. ☎ **07/3840 7000** administration. Tickets A$27–$45 (U.S.$17.55–$29.25); student rush tickets available 1 hr. before performance A$18 (U.S.$11.70).

Queensland's state theater company's seven or so productions a year run the gamut from Shakespeare to premiere Australian works.

CLASSICAL MUSIC

The Brisbane City Council (☎ **07/3403 8888)** sponsors free lunchtime concerts in City Hall most Thursdays, and sometimes on other days, too, usually from 12:30 to 1:30pm. Performers range from classical to percussion/folk fusion to military bands.

Queensland Orchestra. Performing at the Concert Hall in the Queensland Performing Arts Complex (QPAC), City Hall, and intimate works at its studios at 53 Ferry Rd., West End. ☎ **07/3377 5000** for administration. Tickets A$32–$42 (U.S.$20.80–$27.30); student rush tickets available 30 min. before start of performance A$10 (U.S.$6.50).

The state's leading orchestra plays a mix of classical and contemporary orchestral and chamber music. They also make the odd foray into fun material, such as Cole Porter and gospel. Free talks are given in the foyer 1 hour before all major performances. Their occasional "Tea and Symphony" concerts at City Hall include tea and coffee.

OPERA

Opera Queensland. Performing in the Lyric Theatre at the Queensland Performing Arts Complex (QPAC). ☎ **07/3875 3030** for administration. Tickets A$30–$105 (U.S.$19.50–$68.25).

This state company performs a lively repertoire of works, such as Bizet's *The Pearl Fishers*, Mozart's *The Magic Flute*, and Gilbert & Sullivan's *The Mikado*, as well as modern works, musicals and choral concerts. Free talks on the opera you are about to see start in the foyer 45 minutes before every performance, and free close-up tours of the set are held after every performance (except the final night).

THE CLUB & MUSIC SCENE
NIGHTCLUBS

Downunder Bar. Palace Backpackers, corner Ann and Edward sts. ☎ **07/3211 2433.** No cover. Mon–Fri noon to 3am, Sat–Sun 5pm–3am.

In the basement of the Palace Backpackers, this is Brisbane's only dedicated back-packer and university student party bar open every night, so it's packed every night. There are nightly specials and giveaways, (everyone who wears a dress during the Monday night viewings of "Friends" gets free drinks) and the emphasis is on fun.

Empire Hotel. 339 Brunswick St. at Ann St., New Farm. ☎ **07/3852 1216.** Cover Fri–Sat A$6 (U.S.$3.90). Fri–Sat 9pm–5am.

Super-cool young groovers dance to an all-night beat upstairs in one of Brisbane's most historic hotels.

Fridays. Upstairs in Riverside Centre, 123 Eagle St. ☎ **07/3832 2122.** Cover A$5–$7 (U.S.$3.25–$4.55).

This indoor/outdoor bar, restaurant, and club complex overlooking the Brisbane River is a haunt for professionals in their 20s and for university students. Every night sees some kind of unbeatable happy-hour deal, cocktail club, or drinks special, and the dance action starts around 11pm. Every second Wednesday from 6pm the Wine Club welcomes over-30s with all the wine, champagne, spirits, beer, food, and live bands they can take for A$25 (U.S.$16.25). Live music plays on the impressive riverfront terrace from 3:30pm or so on Sunday. As the name implies, Friday is the big night.

Margaux's. 5th fl. of the Brisbane Hilton, 190 Elizabeth St. ☎ **07/3234 2000.** Cover A$5 (U.S.$3.25) on Saturday night. Fri–Sat 9:30–3am. Happy hour 9:30–10:30pm.

A smart mid-30s to mid-40s crowd gathers to dance and chat over cocktails and supper at this clubby joint.

COOL SPOTS FOR JAZZ & BLUES

Brisbane Jazz Club. 1 Annie St, Kangaroo Point. ☎ **07/3391 2006.** Sat 8pm–11.30pm, Sun 7.30pm–11pm. Cover A$8 (U.S.$5.20), or A$12 (U.S.$7.80) Sun afternoon. CityCat to Holman St.

On the riverfront under the Story Bridge, the club features traditional and mainstream jazz Saturday nights and big band dance music Sunday nights. About once a month on Friday nights, Queensland Conservatorium students play modern jazz, and once a month on Sunday afternoons, special events such as a jazz brunch on the deck are held.

Centra Brisbane Jazz-n-Blues Bar. Ground fl. of the Centra hotel, next to Roma Street Transit Centre, Roma St. ☎ **07/3238 2222.** Cover A$5 (U.S.$3.25), and varying cover charges for major visiting acts. No cover Tues.

One of Brisbane's leading live jazz venues is in the unlikely setting of this busy hotel. A mixed crowd in their 20s to 40s listens to jazz on Tuesday, a lucky dip of styles on Wednesday, blues on Thursday, and funk on Friday and Saturday.

PUBS & BARS

City Rowers Tavern. Eagle St. Pier, 1 Eagle St. ☎ **07/3221 2888.** Cover varies.

Downstairs is a modern tavern with great river views from the terrace, pool tables, a big sports screen, and sometimes live bands; upstairs is a nightclub playing the latest disco hits. Waterfront workers (the kind that wear Italian suits, not the sort that shift cargo) drink up big at the 5 to 9pm happy hour.

Empire Hotel. 339 Brunswick St. at Ann St., New Farm. ☎ **07/3852 1216.**

Friday and Saturday nights find this heritage-listed pub packed with the Hip, the Young, and the Beautiful. Don't come here in a suit, and forget about it if you're over 35—you're not welcome. Most nights a DJ plays in the downstairs Art Nouveau bar. By day, the place is more like a friendly country pub.

Hotel Wickham. 308 Wickham St., Fortitude Valley. ☎ **07/3852 1301.** No cover.

Drag shows entertain a mixed girl/guy crowd every night here at the city's premier gay venue. By day it's a pub, by night it's a club with DJs. Tuesday is boys' night,

Wednesday is karaoke night. When the action gets too much, chill out at the pool tables, in the video poker lounge, or in the cafe.

Jameson's Restaurant & Bar. 475 Adelaide St. ☎ **07/3831 7633.**

This wine bar leads a chameleon-like existence—it might host a literary event with a novelist one night, comedy cabaret the next, a Great Debate on a topic like "Better: Sex or Horseracing?" the following, live jazz the night after, and '80s dance tunes to finish the week. No matter what's going on, the mood is always friendly and stylish.

Plough Inn. South Bank Parklands. ☎ **07/3844 7777.**

Kick back on the wide wooden verandah or lounge in the beer garden at this authentic recreation of an Aussie country pub. There are live bands Friday and Saturday nights and Sunday afternoon. The steak bar is open for lunch and dinner daily.

THE CASINO

Treasury Casino. On Queen St. between George and William sts. ☎ **07/3306 8888.** Must be 18 to enter; neat casual attire required (no beachwear or thongs). Open 24 hr. Closed Christmas, Good Friday, and until 1pm Anzac Day (Apr 25).

A modern casino is housed in this gorgeous 1886 building, which once was, ironically enough, the state's Treasury offices. Three levels of 100 gaming tables offer roulette, blackjack, baccarat, craps, sic-bo, and traditional Aussie two-up. There are more than 1,000 slot machines. Of the several eateries, go for lunch or dinner at Pastano, where nothing is over A$10 (U.S.$6.50). Free live bands appear nightly in the Livewire Bar. Ask about Ride and Dine deals where your bus, train, ferry, or taxi fare entitles you to buy a package of cheap gaming chips and a meal.

10 Moreton Bay & Islands

The Brisbane River runs into beautiful Moreton Bay, studded with hundreds of small islands—and a few large ones. Some, such as the former quarantine station and leper colony of Peel Island and Bird and Goat islands, can only be reached by private vessel. Others are national parks, and some are accessible either by tour boat or public ferry.

NORTH STRADBROKE ISLAND

A popular holiday spot for Brisbane families is **North Stradbroke Island,** one of the world's largest sand islands, with long white beaches fringing the east coast and fishing towns strung along the sheltered western side of the island.

GETTING THERE & GETTING AROUND   Stradbroke Ferries (☎ 07/3286 2666), operates a water taxi service from Toondah Harbour, Middle St, Cleveland to **Dunwich,** one of North Stradbroke's main townships. The trip takes about 30 minutes and costs A$10.50 (U.S.$6.83) round-trip for adults. The vehicle barge takes walk-on passengers for A$8.50 (U.S.$5.53) round-trip (this takes about an hour). A bus service meets almost every water taxi or ferry, and operates between the three main settlements, Dunwich, Amity and Point Lookout. The trip takes about 30 minutes to either place and costs A$8.60 (U.S.$5.59) for adults.

VISITOR INFORMATION   The North Stradbroke Visitor Information Centre (☎ 07/4309 9555), in Junner St, Dunwich (about 200m from the ferry terminal) is open weekdays from 8:30am to 5pm and weekends 9am to 3pm.

WHAT TO SEE & DO   North Stradbroke Island, "Straddie" to the locals, was once home to a large Aboriginal population and still retains much of their history. The

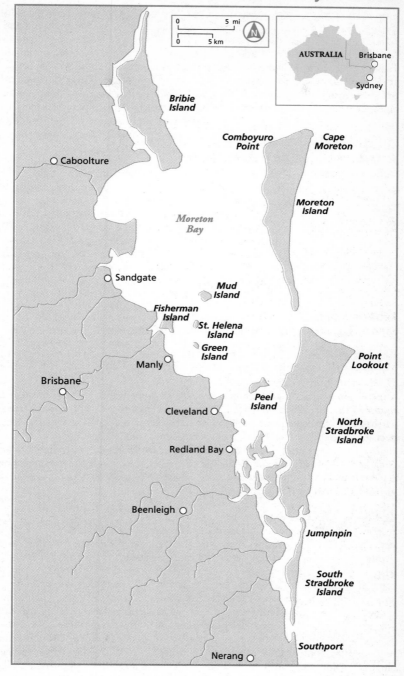

Moreton Bay & Islands

0 5 mi
0 5 km

N

AUSTRALIA
Brisbane
Sydney

Bribie
Island

Comboyuro
Point

Cape
Moreton

O Caboolture

Moreton
Bay

Moreton
Island

O Sandgate

Mud
Island

Fisherman
Island

St. Helena
Island

Green
Island

Point
Lookout

Manly O

Brisbane
O

Cleveland O

Peel
Island

North
Stradbroke
Island

Redland Bay O

Beenleigh O

Jumpinpin

South
Stradbroke
Island

Southport

Nerang O

main town, where the ferry or water taxi will drop you, is **Dunwich.** Over the years the town has been a convict outstation, a Catholic mission, quarantine station and benevolent institution. The local museum is open Wednesday and Saturday 10am to 2pm and displays historic photographs, items salvaged from shipwrecks, and information about the early settlement of the island. A self-guided historical walk begins at the information center, where you can pick up a free map. **Point Lookout,** at the northern tip of the island, is Queensland's most easterly point. A "must" for all visitors is the **North Gorge Headlands Walk,** for breathtaking views and for spotting turtles, dolphins, and whales. There are plenty of places to stay on the island, at motels, low-key resorts, caravan parks, and camping grounds.

SOUTH STRADBROKE ISLAND

South Stradbroke is accessible from Runaway Bay near Southport, at the Gold Coast—about 45 minutes drive south of Brisbane city. There are three resorts on the island and three camping grounds. The resorts run boats for guests only, so the only other way to get to the island is by water taxi. **Gold Coast water taxi** (☎ 07/ 0418 759 789) takes groups to the camping grounds and resorts for about A$10 (U.S.$6.50) per person (minimum of six people plus camping gear, if necessary). **Couran Cove Resort** runs day tours for A$50.45 (U.S.$32.79) per person which includes return transfers from Runaway Bay, morning tea, guided rain forest tour, lunch, and use of resort facilities for the rest of the afternoon. Fastcat leaves Runaway Bay at 10am, and you can return on either the 3 or 5pm boat.

WORTH A SPLURGE

✪ **Couran Cove Resort.** South Stradbroke Island. ☎ **1800 632 211** or 07/5597 9000. Fax 07/5597 9090. www.couran-cove.com.au. 357 units including hotel rooms and eco-cabins. Nature cabins (sleep from 3–8) from A$157 (U.S.$102.05) per night with a minimum 3 nights stay. Waterfront from A$205 (U.S.$133.25) per night (no minimum stay). 10% discount for 7 nights or more. AE, BC, DC, MC, V.

This is a luxury island resort, unique for its range of more than 30 recreational and sporting activities, such as a 9-meter (30-ft.) rock climbing wall, 3 lane sprint track, baseball and softball pitching cage, beach volleyball court, bocce and lawn bowls, shuffleboard, surfing, fishing, a star gazing observatory, and a High Ropes Challenge course. Developed under the guidance of Australian Olympic runner Ron Clarke (who lit the flame at the 1956 Melbourne Olympics), the resort is also committed to environmentally-friendly practices. Guests can rent bicycles, with bike paths extending to the fantastic surf beach.

✪ MORETON ISLAND

At more than 200 square kilometers in area, Moreton is the second-largest sand mass in the world (after Queensland's Fraser Island) and has the world's largest sandhill, **Mt. Tempest.** There are three settlements and the **Tangalooma Wild Dolphin Resort,** where guests and visitors can take part in hand-feeding a pod of wild dolphins, which come in to the jetty each evening. It's an experience for which they line up in great anticipation, but be warned—it is highly regulated, you can't touch the dolphins and it's over in a few seconds! Moreton has some other claims to fame: you can visit the 102 acre "desert" and toboggan down the sand dunes. Or you can snorkel around the 12 wrecks just north of the resort, and visit historic points of interest including the sandstone lighthouse at **Cape Moreton,** built in 1857. A 4WD is essential for getting around, but tours are run from the resort. Permits for access and camping are available from National Park rangers and ferry operators.

GETTING THERE   The *Tangalooma Flyer* ferry leaves Brisbane's Pinkenba wharf twice a day, at 10am and 5pm (10am and 2pm on Sun) for the 75 minute trip. Coaches leave from Roma Street Transit Center at 9am daily to connect with the *Flyer* and pick up from city and Spring Hill hotels on request. Return trips leave Tangalooma at 3:30pm daily except Saturday, when they leave at noon and 4:30pm. The one-way fare is A$26 (U.S.$16.90) adults and A$13 (U.S.$8.45) children aged 3 to 14. The *Combie Trader* vehicular and passenger ferry (☎ 07/3203 6399, www. moreton-island.com), departs from Scarborough on the Redcliffe Peninsula in Brisbane's northern suburbs for Bulwer, on Moreton's northwest coast daily except Tuesday. The 2-hour trip costs A$11.50 (U.S.$7.15) for adults, A$10 (U.S.$6.50) for students 16 and over, and A$6 (U.S.$3.90) for children 5 to 15 years each way for walk-on passengers. The timetables do change, so confirm ahead of time.

WHERE TO STAY

Tangalooma Wild Dolphin Resort. PO Box 1102, Eagle Farm, QLD 4009; ☎ **1300 652 250** or 07/3268 6333. www.tangalooma.com. 170 units, including 36 modern 2-story family villas. A$78–$105 (U.S.$50.70–$68.25) per person. TV TEL. Ask about packages. AE, BC, DC, JCB, MC, V.

The villas are pricier and are a little further from the resort facilities. Once the southern hemisphere's largest whaling station, Tangalooma is the only resort on the island. It's seen better days, but the big attraction is the dolphins and guests are guaranteed one chance during their visit to feed the wild pod that comes into the jetty each evening. Tangalooma is a good base for exploring the rest of the island, and a variety of good tours are available, including whale-watching cruises (June–Oct). There is also a dolphin research center. Other facilities include two swimming pools, a cafe, a restaurant, a bistro, water sports equipment for hire, a food and souvenir shop, and sports including archery, tennis, golf and squash. Meal packages are also available. Units in the main resort area each sleep 4 to 5 people. Each has balcony, limited cooking facilities (including microwave), fans, private bathrooms (shower only), phone and refrigerator.

OTHER MORETON BAY ISLANDS

THE BAY ISLANDS   Four small islands in Moreton Bay are known collectively as "the Bay Islands." They are Russell, Lamb, Macleay and Karragarra islands, clustered in the calm passage between the mainland and North Stradbroke at the southern end of Moreton Bay. They are perfect for day-tripping, and the **Bay Islands water taxi service** (☎ 07/3409 1145) from Redland Bay takes 10 to 20 minutes. It's A$9.10 (U.S.$5.92) round-trip for adults, and A$1.20 (U.S.78¢) to island-hop between each.

✪ **ST. HELENA ISLAND**   For 65 years, from 1867 to 1932, St. Helena was a prison island, known as "the hellhole of the Pacific" to the nearly 4,000 souls incarcerated there. Today, the prison ruins are a tourist attraction, with a small museum in the restored and reconstructed Deputy Superintendent's Cottage. Entry to the island—now a National Park—is by guided tour only. Excellent tours, most involving a re-enactment of life on the island jail, are run by **AB Sea Cruises** (☎ 07/3396 3994 7am–7pm daily; tour bookings 07/3893 1240; fax 07/3393 3726; www.abseacruises. com.au), leaving from Manly Boat Harbour. Tours cost A$55 (U.S.$35.75) for adults, A$48 (U.S.$31.20) concessions, A$27 (U.S.$17.55) for children, and A$119 (U.S.$77.35) for a family of four. The tour leaves at 9:30am weekdays, returning at 2:30pm, and 11am to 4pm on weekends and public holidays and includes a box lunch.

Eco-tours, run in conjunction with the Wildlife Preservation Society of Queensland and the Queensland National Parks and Wildlife Service, take visitors to parts of the island not seen on the historical tours. The same departure times and prices apply. **St. Helena By Night Ghost Tours** (take a flashlight!) on the aptly named launch *Cat-o-Nine Tails* include onboard entertainment, buffet dinner with licensed bar, spooky "ghost train" ride and a dramatized version of life in the prison. Night tours—usually on Friday and Saturday nights—cost A\$67 (U.S.\$43.55) for adults, A\$35 (U.S.\$22.75) for children, or A\$139 (U.S.\$90.35) for a family of four.

COOCHIEMUDLO ISLAND   British explorer Matthew Flinders landed here in 1799, and this event is re-enacted each July. "Coochie" is small enough to walk or cycle around, and is a great place for water sports along the 3.5 kilometer (2.1 miles) of beaches—windsurfing, sailing, swimming and paddle-skiing are available. There is a 9-hole golf course, a tennis court, licensed cafe, galleries, and accommodations. Camping is not allowed. **The Bay Islands taxi service** (☎ **07/3409 1145**) leaves from the Victoria Point jetty (Colburn Ave) and Cleveland. The trip takes about 5 minutes from Victoria Point and costs A\$2 (U.S.\$1.30) each way. From Cleveland, it takes about 20 minutes and costs A\$9 (U.S.\$5.85) round-trip.

Queensland & the Great Barrier Reef

7

by Lee Mylne

With a landscape three times the size of Texas and a population that hugs the coast but embraces the Outback, Queensland is a treasure trove of stunning scenery, fantastic yarns and eccentric personalities. Its most famous attraction is the Great Barrier Reef . . . hardly the only thing worth seeing. Great beaches, tropical weather, and the mystique of the outback make "where to go" one of the most difficult decisions for visitors.

White sandy beaches grace almost the entire coast, and just offshore are a string of the beautiful islands and coral atolls. At the southern end, just north of the New South Wales border, the travelers head for the Gold Coast beaches and theme parks. In the north, from Townsville to Cape York, the rainforest teems with unique flora and fauna.

The fertile coastal fringe and tropical climate is perfect for cultivating such fruits as bananas and pineapples and the warm, wet coastline hosts enough sugar cane fields that the area produces a significant amount of the world's sugar.

Brisbane is the state's amenable capital (see chapter 6). Less than an hour's drive south is the Gold Coast "glitter strip," with its 35 kilometers (22 miles) of surf and sandy beaches. To the north of Brisbane lies the Sunshine Coast—more white beaches, crystal-clear waters, and rolling green mountains dotted with villages.

Further north is the Fraser Coast and South Burnett. Maryborough will fascinate history buffs, with its original Queenslander homes and reminders of yesteryear. The majestic pines of the Bunya Mountains provide a lush backdrop for the South Burnett Valley, an area rich in history, agriculture, wineries and country towns.

No one should miss the stunning wild beauty of the largest sand island in the world, World Heritage–listed Fraser Island. Each year from August to October, humpback whales come to frolic in the sheltered waters between Fraser Island and Hervey Bay.

Inland, the gold, peanut, beef, wine and emu country offers another insight into Queensland country life. Inland are rich farming areas and the gemfield towns of Sapphire, Emerald, Rubyvale, and Anakie, which still attract modern day miners keen to seek their fortune where beautiful gems can still be unearthed by lucky fossickers.

The Town of 1770 marks the spot where Captain James Cook and his crew came ashore from the *Endeavour* in 1770. The clear waters and pristine coastline have changed little since then. Nearby Gladstone

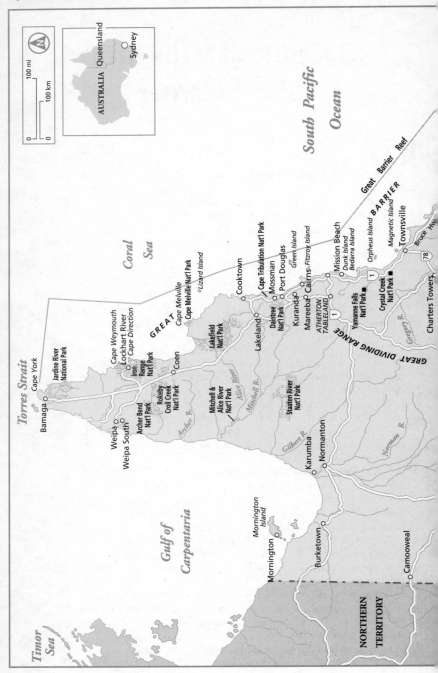

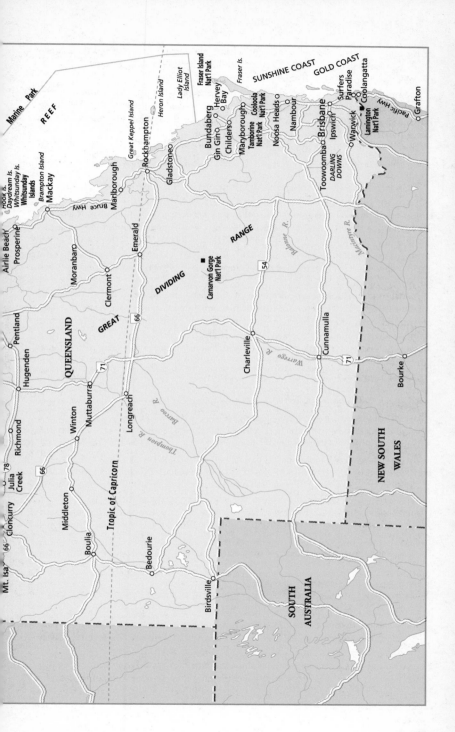

boasts many industries as well as a large yachting marina and good seafood restaurants. Gladstone is the gateway to Heron Island, an idyllic coral cay, where you'll find a turtle rookery and other wildlife.

Around Rockhampton, the beef capital of Australia, more than three million cattle roam among the gum trees, and at local pubs, steak sandwiches and barbecued *snags* (sausages) are always on the *plat du jour*. Throughout the region, the wonders of the Great Barrier Reef are within easy reach.

Travelling north along the coast, you will be drawn along by one tropical island after another until you get to the 74 islands of the Whitsunday and Cumberland groups.

Then you will enter a land where tropical islands, lush rainforest, rugged mountains and romantic rivers unite. Green sugar cane fields are everywhere—Mackay is the largest sugar-producing region in Australia. This attractive city has its own beach, and the harbor is a departure point for cruises to the Great Barrier Reef and the Whitsunday islands. The Whitsundays region is on the same latitude as Tahiti, and for my money is equally lovely. The idyllic island playground is laced with coral reefs rising out of calm, blue waters teeming with colorful coral and fish, and it's warm enough for swimming all year round.

North of the Whitsundays is popular Dunk Island and the rainforest settlement of Mission Beach. The delights of the tropics are apparent everywhere in this area of Tropical North Queensland. From islands dotted with palm trees to Wet Tropics Rainforest, the region is populated with friendly, laid-back people. The port city of Townsville boasts 320 days of sunshine per year, and marks the start of the Great Green Way—an area of great natural beauty leading to Cairns. The trip could take anywhere from four hours to 14 days depending on how many detours you wish to make.

Further north, you come to Cairns, with rainforest hills and villages to explore and a harbor full of cruise and dive boats waiting to take you to the Reef. Cairns is fine as a base, but many savvy travelers head an hour north to the village of Port Douglas preferring its peaceful rural atmosphere, uncrowded beach, and less developed environs

A visit to Queensland would not be complete without at least one trip into the Outback. You can head west from Rockhampton, to discover the heart of Queensland at Longreach, Barcaldine and Winton, or from Townsville to the mining town of Mt. Isa. From Cairns, the Gulf Savannah region is rich in welcoming small towns.

It's possible to spend a small fortune on water sports, sailing trips, cruises, game-fishing excursions, and rain-forest 4WD tours in Queensland, but this chapter will help you scout out the best deals. Cheap accommodations and food are generally plentiful, and the sunshine and beaches are always free.

Queensland in 3 Days

If you have only 3 days in Queensland, you could happily spend them all on Heron Island, in my opinion, the most stunning Great Barrier Reef coral cay. Or you could spend all your time on a 3-day, 2-night sailing trip around the Whitsunday Islands. From here, you can head to the outer Great Barrier Reef for a day.

If you go to Cairns, spend the first day taking the Skyrail Rainforest Cableway—the longest cableway in the world—over the rain forest to the mountaintop rain forest village of Kuranda. The next day take a day trip to the Great Barrier Reef, perhaps aboard Quicksilver's *Wavepiercer* catamaran. The next day explore the World Heritage–listed Daintree Rain Forest on a 4WD day safari.

Cheap Thrills: What to See & Do for Free (or Almost) in Queensland

- **Breathing in the sea air on a stroll along The Esplanade in Cairns.** Watch the cruise boats pull in during the late afternoon, and at night join the throngs of people enjoying a cheap feed at the hordes of fish-and-chips shops, hamburger joints, and pizzerias lining the strip.
- **Strolling the Flecker Botanic Gardens.** Located 3 kilometers (1.8 miles) northwest of Cairns, the walking tracks, gardens, ferns, wetlands, and orchids are blissful in the summer heat and relaxing anytime.
- **Exploring the Wet Tropics rain forests at Mission Beach.** The Daintree Rain Forest north of Cairns is best explored on a commercial 4WD safari, but the even denser Wet Tropics rain forests at Mission Beach, a 90-minute drive south of Cairns, can be explored on foot for nothing. You may even spot a cassowary, a giant ostrich-like bird with blue horny head like a dinosaur!
- **Hitting the beach!** Beaches are always free in Oz, and Queensland has hundreds of them. Park your towel on any of Cairns's pretty palm-lined crescents, such as Palm Cove or Trinity Beach, or head south to the almost deserted, incandescently beautiful Mission Beach, which is bordered by thick jungle and has magical views across to Dunk Island.
- **Joining a free ranger-guided walk at Kingfisher Bay Resort on Fraser Island.** Learn how Aboriginals used native plants for food, spot dolphins and dugongs (manatees) from the headland, or look for native dingoes. The walks take place every day.
- **Checking out a koala colony.** You don't have to pay admission to a wildlife park to see koalas. Likely spots to find them in the wild include Noosa National Park, just a stroll from the main shopping strip on Hastings Street in Noosa Heads. Say hello to the koalas, then carry on around the headland along the park's network of trails. Park entry is free.
- **Feeding the birds at O'Reilly's Rainforest Guesthouse in the Gold Coast hinterland.** Brilliant black and gold Regent bowerbirds, crimson and cobalt rosellas, and a flurry of other wild birds wait to be fed every morning. You will gasp with delight when they land on your hands to eat.

EXPLORING THE QUEENSLAND COAST

Without a doubt your itinerary will include at least one trip to the Great Barrier Reef. The Reef starts around Bundaberg and runs up the Queensland coast to New Guinea, so you have lots of departure points from which to explore. Don't think you have to go through Cairns or Port Douglas; the reef is as accessible and magnificent from the Whitsundays, Townsville, Gladstone and Bundaberg. Cairns has the advantage of good flight connections from Melbourne, Sydney, and Brisbane.

VISITOR INFORMATION   The Queensland Travel Centre is a great resource on touring the entire state, including the Great Barrier Reef. For information visit the Destination Queensland website at www.queensland-holidays.com.au or call ☎ **13 18 01. Tourism Queensland** has offices in the United States and the United Kingdom—see "Visitor Information" in chapter 2.

Life's a Beach

Which Queensland beach is right for you? Surfers will head to the Gold Coast or Sunshine Coast close to Brisbane; divers to the Great Barrier Reef. North of Gladstone, deadly box jellyfish, known as "stingers," put a stop to all swimming on the mainland (but not the islands) from October to May.

Never swim in unprotected seas at that time. Many popular beaches have small net enclosures for safe swimming, but it can be a drag having to stay within those. If you love swimming and you're visiting this part of Queensland in stinger season, head to an island or choose a hotel with a good pool!

You will also find excellent information on the **Great Barrier Reef Visitors Bureau's** website, www.great-barrier-reef.com. This is not an official tourist site but is owned by **Travel Online,** PO Box 1792, Milton, QLD 4064 (☎ **07/3876 4644;** fax 07/3876 4645), which offers itinerary planning and booking services for a wide range of accommodations and tours throughout north Queensland.

For information on B&Bs and farmstays in Cairns, Port Douglas, Mission Beach, and Townsville, contact the **Bed & Breakfast and Farmstay Association of Tropical North Queensland Inc.,** c/o Lilybank Bed & Breakfast, 75 Kamerunga Rd., Stratford, Cairns, QLD 4870 (☎ **07/4058 1227;** fax 07/4058 1990; www.bnbnq.com.au).

WHEN TO GO   Australia's winter (June–Aug) is high season in Queensland as shivering southerners from Sydney and Melbourne head north to the sun. Summer is hot and sticky across most of the state and in Brisbane. From the Whitsundays northward, winter almost doesn't exist. See "When to Go" in chapter 2 for average temperatures and days of rainfall in Brisbane and Cairns. North Queensland, from around Cairns northward, gets a monsoonal Wet Season from December to March or April, with heavy rains and cyclones. You can visit the Great Barrier Reef during the Wet without a problem, but swollen creeks and floodwaters sometimes cut off parts of the Daintree Rainforest. If you want to visit north Queensland between January and April, try heading a little farther south to the beautiful Whitsundays, which are generally beyond the reach of the rains (although not beyond the reach of cyclones).

GETTING AROUND   **By Car**   The Bruce Highway runs along the coast from Brisbane to Cairns. It is mostly a two-lane highway, and the scenery is pretty much eucalyptus bush land, but from Mackay north you will pass through sugar canefields.

Tourism Queensland publishes regional motoring guides. All you are likely to need, however, is a state map from the **Royal Automobile Club of Queensland** (RACQ), 300 St. Pauls Terrace, Fortitude Valley, Brisbane, QLD 4006 (☎ **13 19 05** in Australia, or 07/3361 2444). In Brisbane, you can get maps and advice from the RACQ office in the General Post Office (GPO) at 261 Queen Street. For road condition reports, call ☎ **07/3219 0900.** The state's **Department of Natural Resources** (☎ **07/3896 3216**) publishes an excellent range of "Sunmap" maps that highlight tourist attractions, national parks, and the like, although they are of limited use as road maps. You can pick these up at newsagents and gas stations throughout the state.

By Bus   McCafferty's (☎ **13 14 99** in Australia) and **Greyhound Pioneer** (☎ **13 20 30** in Australia) make the trip from Brisbane to Cairns in about 28 hours, stopping at most towns along the route. Both have good-value passes. Another option is the cheap, fun "alternative" buses, beloved of students and backpackers, which ply the Queensland coast. See chapter 2 for more details on getting around by bus.

By Train **Queensland Rail** (☎ **13 22 32** in Queensland, or 07/3235 1122) operates several long-distance trains of varying degrees of luxury along the Brisbane–Cairns route, a 32-hour trip. See the "Getting Around" section in chapter 2 for more details.

By Plane It isn't the cheapest, but it is the fastest way to eat miles in such a big state. Beware the "milk run" flights that stop at every tiny town en route, as these can eat valuable vacation time. **Qantas** and its subsudiary airline **Sunstate** (book through Qantas) serve most coastal towns from Brisbane, but only a few from Cairns.

1 Exploring the Great Barrier Reef

It's the only living structure on Earth visible from the moon; at 348,700 square kilometers (238,899 sq. miles), it's bigger than many countries; it's over 2,000 kilometers (1,250 miles) long, stretching from Lady Elliot Island off Bundaberg to just south of Papua New Guinea; it's home to over a thousand species of fish, hundreds of varieties of corals, thousands of kinds of shellfish, and uncountable sponges, worms, starfish, and sea urchins; in short, the Great Barrier Reef is the Eighth Wonder of the World. The Great Barrier Reef is a World Heritage Site and is the biggest Marine Park in the world.

INTRODUCING THE GREAT BARRIER REEF

The Reef is not a plant, but a conglomeration of tiny animals called coral polyps. They coat themselves in limestone to keep safe, and as they die, the limestone bodies cement into a reef on which more living coral grows. And so it goes, the endless building of a megametropolis of coral polyp skyscrapers just under the surface of the water.

You will see three kinds of reef on the Great Barrier Reef—fringing, ribbon, and platform. *Fringe reef* is the stuff just off the shore of islands and along the mainland. *Ribbon reefs* create "streamers" of thin long reef along the outer edge of the Reef, and are found north of Cairns. *Platform,* or *patch reefs,* are splotches of coral emerging from the continental shelf along the Queensland coast. Platform reefs are the most common, and what most people think of when they refer to the Great Barrier Reef. Island resorts in the Great Barrier Reef Marine Park are either "continental," meaning they are essentially part of the Australian landmass, or "cays," crushed dead coral and sand amassed over time by water action. Dazzling coral and fish life surround cays. Continental islands may have terrific coral, some coral, or none at all.

Along with dazzling fish, the Reef is home to large numbers of green and loggerhead turtles, one of the biggest dugong (manatee) populations in the world, sharks, giant manta rays, and sea snakes. In winter (July–Sept) humpback whales gather in the warm waters around the Hervey Bay and the Whitsunday islands to calve.

You can snorkel, dive, fish (recreational fishing is permitted in most zones of the Reef), or fly over the Reef. The "Outer Reef," the network of platform and ribbon reefs that lies an average of 65 kilometers (41 miles) off the coast (about 1 hr. to 90 min. by boat from the mainland) is what most people are referring to when they talk

When to Visit the Reef

April to November is the best time to visit. December to March can be uncomfortably hot and humid, particularly as far north as the Whitsundays, Cairns, and Port Douglas. In the winter months (June–Aug), the water can be a touch chilly (Aussies think so, anyway), but it rarely drops below 22° C (72° F).

Reef Tax

Every passenger over 4 years old must pay a A$4 (U.S.$2.60) Environmental Management Charge (EMC), commonly called "reef tax," on every visit to the Great Barrier Reef. This money goes towards the management and conservation of the Reef. Your tour operator collects it when you pay for your trip.

about the Great Barrier Reef. You should get out and see that, but there is plenty of fringing reef to explore around the islands closer to the mainland.

Learning about the Reef before you get there will enhance your visit. ✪ **Reef Teach** (☎ 07/4031 7794) is an evening slide show and talk by Paddy Colwell, a marine biologist and diver. He shares much valuable information and history about the Reef: how it was formed; how coral grows; what dangerous creatures to avoid; how to take successful underwater photos. It's offered throughout the year at 14 Spence St., Cairns, Monday through Saturday at 6:15pm, and costs A$13 (U.S.$8.45) per person.

Townsville is the headquarters of the **Great Barrier Reef Marine Park Authority,** and a visit to its showcase, ✪ **Reef HQ** (see "The North Coast: Mission Beach, Townsville & the Islands," below) is a superb introduction. The star attraction at the aquarium is a living reef ecosystem in a massive viewing tank. For more information, write the Authority at P.O. Box 1379, Townsville, QLD 4810 (☎ **07/ 4750 0700;** fax 07/4772 6093; www.gbrmpa.gov.au or www.reefHQ.org.au).

EXPLORING THE REEF

✪ **Snorkeling** the Reef can be a wondrous experience. Green and purple clams, pink sponges, red starfish and purple sea urchins, and fish from electric blue to neon yellow to lime are a truly magical sight. Coral's rich colors only survive with lots of light, so the nearer the surface the brighter and richer the marine life. That means snorkelers bobbing about on top of the Reef are in a prime position to see it at its best.

If your Reef cruise offers a **guided snorkel tour,** often called a "snorkel safari," take it. They are worth the extra cost of A$25 (U.S.$16.25) or so. Most safaris are suitable for both beginners and advanced snorkelers, and are led by marine biologists. They will tell you heaps about the fascinating sea creatures before you. Snorkeling is easy to master, and the crew on cruise boats is always happy to tutor you.

A day trip to the Reef also offers you a great opportunity to go diving—even if you have never dived before. Every major cruise boat listed in "Day Trips to the Reef," and many dedicated dive boats listed in "Diving the Reef" (see below) offer introductory dives that allow you to dive without certification to a depth of 6 meters (20 ft.) in the company of an instructor. You will need to complete a medical questionnaire on board and then undergo a 30-minute briefing session on the boat. Intro dives are also referred to as "resort dives" because many resorts offer something similar, giving you one or two hours' instruction in their pools before taking you to a nearby reef to dive.

CHOOSING A GATEWAY TO THE REEF

Travelers' lore has it that Cairns and Port Douglas are the best places from which to access the Reef. They are both great jumping off points, but the quality of the coral is just as good off any town along the coast between Gladstone and Cairns. The Reef is pretty much equidistant from any point on the coast—about 90 minutes away by high-speed catamaran. An exception is Townsville, where the Reef is about 2½ hours away. Think carefully about where you would like to base yourself.

The main gateways, north to south, are **Port Douglas, Cairns, Mission Beach, Townsville,** the **Whitsunday islands, Gladstone** (for Heron Island) and **Bundaberg.**

The Great Barrier Reef

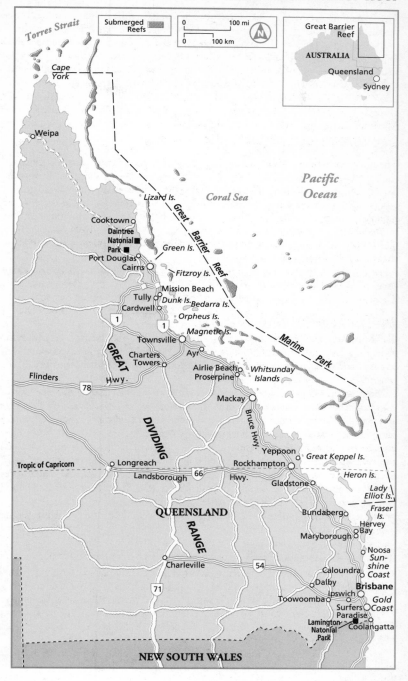

Torres Strait

Submerged Reefs

0   100 mi
0   100 km

Great Barrier Reef

AUSTRALIA

Queensland

Sydney

Cape York

Weipa

Pacific Ocean

Coral Sea

Lizard Is.

Great Barrier Reef

Cooktown

Daintree Natoinal Park

Green Is.

Port Douglas

Cairns

Fitzroy Is.

Mission Beach

Tully

Dunk Is.

Bedarra Is.

Cardwell

Orpheus Is.

Magnetic Is.

Townsville

Charters Towers

Ayr

Marine   Park

Flinders

78

Hwy.

GREAT

Airlie Beach

Proserpine

Whitsunday Islands

Mackay

DIVIDING

Bruce Hwy.

Yeppoon

Tropic of Capricorn

Longreach

Landsborough

66

Hwy.

Rockhampton

Great Keppel Is.

Heron Is.

Gladstone

Lady Elliot Is.

QUEENSLAND

RANGE

Bundaberg

Fraser Is.

Maryborough

Hervey Bay

Noosa

Sun-shine Coast

Charleville

54

Caloundra

Dalby

Brisbane

Toowoomba

Ipswich

Gold Coast

71

Surfers Paradise

Lamington Natoinal Park

Coolangatta

NEW SOUTH WALES

The Whitsundays have the added attractions of being dazzling islands (and the chance to sail around them); resorts offering water sports and other activities; and a large array of diving, fishing, and day cruises. You can snorkel every day off your island or join a sailing or cruise day trip to a number of magnificent inner reefs much nearer than the main Outer Reef. Many people stay in Cairns because of easy airport access.

If you are a nonswimmer, choose a Reef cruise that visits a coral cay, because a cay slopes gradually into shallow water and the surrounding coral. The Low Isles at Port Douglas; Green Island, Michaelmas Cay, or Upolu Cay off Cairns; Beaver Cay off Mission Beach and Heron Island are all good locations.

DAY TRIPS TO THE REEF

The most common way to get to the Reef is on one of the big motorized catamarans that carry up to 300 passengers and depart from Cairns, Port Douglas, Townsville, Mission Beach, and the Whitsunday mainland and islands. The boats are air-conditioned and have a bar, videos, and educational material on board, as well as a biologist who gives a talk on the Reef's ecology. The boats tie up at their own private pontoons anchored to a platform reef. The pontoons have glass-bottom boats for folks who don't want to get wet, dry underwater viewing platforms, usually a bar, sundecks, shaded seats, and often showers.

An alternative to traveling on a big tour boat is to go on one of the multitude of smaller boats. These typically visit two or three Reef sites rather than just one. There are usually no more than 20 passengers, so the crew offers you personal atten-tion, and you and the other passengers can have a fun, friendly time. Another bonus of going in a small boat is that you will have the coral pretty much all to yourself. The drawbacks are that you have only the cramped deck to sit on when you get out of the water, and your traveling time to the Reef may be longer. If you're a nervous snorkeler, you may feel safer going in a big boat, and surrounded by 300 other passengers in the water.

Most day-trip fares include snorkel gear—fins, mask, and snorkel, and wet suits in winter, although you rarely need them—free use of the underwater viewing chambers and glass-bottomboat rides, a buffet or barbecue lunch, and morning and afternoon refreshments. Most of the big boat operators and many of the smaller boats offer introductory dives for novices, and regular dives for certified divers. Diving is optional and costs extra. The big boats post snorkeling scouts to keep a lookout for anyone in trouble and to count heads. If you wear glasses, check whether your boat offers pre-scription masks as this could make a big difference to the quality of your experience! You can also travel as a snorkel-only passenger on most dive boats, too.

The major launching points for day trips to the Reef follow, listed north to south.

Reef Safety Warnings

Coral is very sharp and coral cuts get infected quickly. If you cut yourself, ask cruise boat staff for antiseptic cream and apply it right away.

The sun and reflected light off the water will burn you fast. Put sunscreen on your back and the back of your legs, especially around your knees and the back of your neck, even behind your ears, places that will be exposed as you swim face down. Apply more when you leave the water.

The Great Barrier Reef is a Marine Park. Removing coral (living or dead), shells, or any other natural item is an offense, not to mention offensive!

Feeling Green?

If you are inclined to be seasick, come prepared with medication. Some boats sell a ginger-based natural antiseasickness pill, but it doesn't always work!

FROM PORT DOUGLAS

The most glamorous large vessels visiting the Outer Reef are the ✪ **Quicksilver** *Wavepiercers* (☎ 07/4099 5500) based in Port Douglas. These ultra-sleek high-speed, air-conditioned 37-meter (121-ft.) and 45.5-meter (149-ft.) catamarans carry 300 or 440 passengers to Agincourt Reef, a ribbon reef 39 nautical miles (72km/43 miles) from shore on the very outer edge of the Reef. After the 90-minute trip to the Reef you tie up at a two-story pontoon, where you spend 3½ hours on the Reef.

Quicksilver departs Marina Mirage at 10am daily except Christmas. The cost for the day is A$150 (U.S.$97.50) for adults, half price for kids 4 to 14. Coach transfers from Port Douglas hotels are A$5 (U.S.$3.25) for adults, A$2.50 (U.S.$1.63) for children. Cairns and northern beaches passengers can join the boat, too (see "From Cairns," below). Guided snorkel safaris cost A$31 (U.S.$20.15) per person, and introductory dives cost A$107 (U.S.$69.55) per person. Qualified divers take a dive-tender boat to make two dives for A$104 (U.S.$67.60) per person, gear included. Because Quicksilver is so popular, do book snorkel safaris and dives in advance.

The dive boat *Poseidon* (see "Diving the Reef," below) welcomes snorkelers. There's a Reef ecology talk en route and a guided snorkel safari. Lunch and transfers from Port Douglas hotels are included in Poseidon's price of A$125 (U.S.$81.25) for adults and A$90 (U.S.$58.50) for children ages 3 to 12. Round-trip transfers from Cairns and the northern beaches are A$12 (U.S.$7.80) adults, half price for kids.

Port Douglas also offers easy day-trip access to the Low Isles, two pretty coral-wrapped cays close to shore on the Inner Reef. See the "Port Douglas, Daintree & the Cape Tribulation Area" section in this chapter.

FROM CAIRNS

Cairns passengers can board the **Quicksilver** *Wavepiercer* (see above, "From Port Douglas") in Cairns at the Marlin Marina at 8am and at Palm Cove Jetty on Cairns' northern beaches at 8:30am. It arrives at Port Douglas at 9:30am and leaves for the Reef at 10am. Trips run daily except Christmas. The fare for the whole day for Cairns and Palm Cove passengers is A$160 (U.S.$104) for adults, A$82.50 (U.S.$53.62) for kids 4 to 14. A free pickup from your hotel is included in the price.

If you prefer to visit the Reef direct from Cairns, large-scale operator **Great Adventures** (☎ 07/4044 9944) does daily cruises in fast, air-conditioned catamarans to a three-level pontoon on the Outer Reef. The pontoon has a children's swimming area, a semisubmersible boat, and an underwater observatory. You get at least 3 hours on the Reef. The cost for the day is A$139 (U.S.$90.35) for adults, A$69.50 (U.S.$45.18) for children 4 to 14, and A$347.50 (U.S.$225.88) for a family of four. Hotel transfers are available from Cairns and the northern beaches for an extra cost. The boat departs the Great Adventures terminal at Trinity Wharf near the Hilton.

Guided snorkel tours are A$15 (U.S.$9.75) per person extra. Introductory dives cost A$88 (U.S.$57.20) per person extra, while certified divers pay A$60 (U.S.$39) for one dive, A$88 (U.S.$57.20) for two dives, or A$175 (U.S.$113.75) for the whole day—cruise, lunch, snorkeling, and two dives with all gear.

You can also depart Cairns with Great Adventures at 8:30am and spend 2 hours on Green Island en route. This gives you time to walk nature trails, rent snorkel gear and water sports equipment, or laze on the beach before continuing to the Outer Reef. This cruise costs A$155 (U.S.$100.75) per adult and A$85.50 (U.S.$55.58) per child, or A$387.50 (U.S.$251.88) per family. Guests staying on Green Island can join the cruise for A$110 (U.S.$71.50) adults.

Sunlover Cruises (☎ **1800/810 512** in Australia, or 07/4050 1333) has a choice of two Outer Reef trips aboard its large, fast catamarans. The first stops at Fitzroy Island for a guided rain-forest walk before heading to Moore Reef on the Outer Reef. Transfers from city and northern beaches hotels are included. The day costs A$142 (U.S.$92.30) adults, A$71 (U.S.$46.15) for children 4 to 14, and A$335 (U.S.$217.75) for a family of four. This trip consists of 1 hour on Fitzroy and about 3 on the Reef. Note that a free, guided snorkel safari is included in the price—that's good value.

Sunlover's second trip departs Cairns and picks up passengers at Palm Cove then heads to Arlington Reef. You spend about 4 hours total on the Reef. The price is A$126 (U.S.$81.90) for adults, A$63 (U.S.$40.95) for kids, and A$315 (U.S.$204.75) for a family.

Introductory dives on both trips cost A$93 (U.S.$60.45), certified divers pay A$83 (U.S.$53.95), including all gear. Both cruises include lunch and transfers from Cairns and northern beaches hotels. Both depart Trinity Wharf in Cairns at 9:30am daily.

An alternative to motoring to the Reef is to sail to it. **Ocean Spirit Cruises** (☎ **1800/644 227** in Australia, or 07/4031 2920) operates two sailing catamarans that take 100 to 150 passengers to Michaelmas Cay or Upolu Cay, lovely white sand cays on the Outer Reef surrounded by rich reefs. This trip is a good value, since it includes a pleasant 2 hours sailing to either cay, a guided snorkeling safari, guided beach walk, and a free glass of bubbly and live music on the way home—in addition to the usual reef ecology talks, semisubmersible rides, lunch, and transfers from your Cairns or northern beaches hotel. Another plus is that you spend your out-of-water time on a beautiful beach, not on a pontoon or boat deck. You get about 4 hours on the Reef.

The day trip to Michaelmas Cay is A$150 (U.S.$97.50) for adults, A$75 (U.S.$48.75) for children ages 4 to 14, and A$415 (U.S.$269.75) for a family of two adults and two kids. The day trip to Upolu Cay costs A$122 (U.S.$79.30) for adults, A$61 (U.S.$39.65) for kids, and A$330 (U.S.$214.50) for a family. Transfers from Cairns and the northern beaches are free, but cost extra from Port Douglas. Introductory dives cost A$85 (U.S.$55.25), certified divers pay A$53 (U.S.$34.45) for one or A$85 (U.S.$55.25) for two, gear included. An introductory dive/sail package to Upolu costs A$180 (U.S.$117) per person. The boats depart Marlin Marina at 8:30am daily.

FROM MISSION BEACH

Mission Beach is the closest point on the mainland to the Reef, 1 hour by the high-speed *Quick Cat* catamaran (☎ 1800/654 242 in Australia, or 07/4068 7289). The trip starts with an hour at Dunk Island 20 minutes offshore, where you can walk rain forest trails, play on the beach, parasail or jet ski for an extra fee. Then it's a 1-hour trip to sandy Beaver Cay on the Outer Reef, where you have 3 hours to snorkel or check out the coral from a semi-submersible or glass-bottom boat. There's no shade on the cay, so a hat and sunscreen are musts. The trip departs Clump Point Jetty at 10am; it departs daily in high season between July 1 and October 31, and every day except Sunday the rest of the year. It costs A$134 (U.S.$87.10) for adults and A$67 (U.S.$43.55) for children 4 to 14. An introductory scuba dive costs A$77 (U.S.$50.05) for the first dive and A$33 (U.S.$21.45) for the second. Prebook your introductory scuba dive. Qualified divers pay A$55 (U.S.$35.75) for the first dive,

A\$33 (U.S.\$21.45) for the second, all gear included. Free pickups from Mission Beach are included. You can also join this trip from Cairns; coach connections from your Cairns hotel cost an extra A\$15 (U.S.\$9.75) for adults and A\$7.50 (U.S.\$4.88) for children. Ask about Sunday specials during high season.

FROM TOWNSVILLE

The only Reef cruise operator to offer fishing as well as snorkeling and diving is **Pure Pleasure Cruises** (☎ **07/4721 3555**), which operates the large *Wavepiercer 2001* catamaran to a pontoon on Kelso Reef, where you will find 350 types of hard and soft corals and 1,500 fish species. A marine biologist gives talks en route. The cruise costs A\$122 (U.S.\$79.30) for adults, A\$111 (U.S.\$72.15) seniors and students, A\$61

Budget Snorkeling & Diving

As well as the "big guys" listed here, many smaller operators run cruises to the Reef from Cairns that are usually more affordable. **Down Under Dive** (☎ **1800/ 079 099** in Australia, or 07/4052 8300; fax 07/4031 1373; reservations@down underdive.com.au) offers trips aboard its catamaran, Supercat, departing from Marlin Marina at 8:30am daily. Although its capacity is 200 passengers, the boat carries a maximum of 80. The day trip is just A\$75 (U.S.\$48.75) for snorkelers or A\$125 (U.S.\$81.25) for certified divers (includes two dives and all gear) including a guided snorkel safari and visits to two sites. Introductory dives cost A\$130 (U.S.\$84.50) for the first one and A\$30 (U.S.\$19.50) for a second. A family pass for two adults and two children 4 to 14 is A\$260 (U.S.\$169). Hotel pickups are A\$6 (U.S.\$3.90) from the city or A\$12 (U.S.\$7.80) from the northern beaches.

Seahorse (☎ **07/4041 1919**), a 20-passenger 15.2-meter (50-ft.) sailing schooner, visits Upolu Cay daily for just A\$60 (U.S.\$39) per adult and A\$35 (U.S.\$22.75) children 3 to 13. Like the big guys, it has an onboard marine naturalist; unlike the big guys, its guided snorkel safari is free. You can even lend a hand sailing if you like. Introductory dives are A\$45 (U.S.\$29.25), and a certified dive is just A\$25 (U.S.\$16.25) with all gear supplied.

Reef Magic (☎ **07/4031 1588**) is a 22-meter (72-ft.) air-conditioned catamaran that runs from Marlin Marina in Cairns daily at 9am to one of 10 Outer Reef locations, where the Reef is yours for 5 hours. The boat holds 140 people, but usually carries between 50 and 80. The price of A\$99 (U.S.\$64.35) for adults, A\$59 (U.S.\$38.35) for children 4 to 14, and A\$286 (U.S.\$185.90) for a family of four includes a glass-bottom boat trip. Transfers from Cairns and northern beaches hotels are available for an extra A\$6 (U.S.\$3.90) per person or A\$24 (U.S.\$15.60) per family. A guided snorkel tour is A\$22 (U.S.\$14.30). Introductory divers pay A\$55 (U.S.\$35.75) for the first dive and A\$27 (U.S.\$17.55) for a second; certified divers pay A\$33 (U.S.\$21.45) for one, A\$25 (U.S.\$16.25) for the second. Wet suits are A\$6 (U.S.\$3.90) for snorkelers.

Don't overlook ✪ **Green Island,** a stunning coral cay on the Inner Reef 50 minutes east of Cairns, as a Reef destination. It's closer to the mainland, and the snorkeling and diving are every bit as good as on the Outer Reef. Unlike the Outer Reef, where you will most likely be stuck on a pontoon or a boat when you are not in the water, Green Island has beautiful white coral sand beaches to lie on and lush rain forest to stroll in. See the "Cairns" section in this chapter.

(U.S.$39.65) for children 4 to 15. The family price is A$305 (U.S.$198.25) for two adults and three children. Glass-bottom boat trips are free, and guided snorkeling tours are A$23 (U.S.$14.95). Introductory dives are an extra A$66 (U.S.$42.90), and qualified divers can make two dives for A$55 (U.S.$35.75). If you would rather catch fish than look at them, you can head to deeper water to cast a line for sweetlip, coral trout, and other reef beauties. The staff will clean and wrap your catch, and your hotel chef should be happy to cook it for you. Fishing is included in the cruise price. Cruises depart from Reef HQ every day except Monday and Thursday at 9am and from Picnic Bay Jetty on Magnetic Island at 9:15am. Hotel pick up can be arranged at a cost of A$5 (U.S.$3.25) round-trip. The boat takes 186 passengers, is air-conditioned, and has a video and bar. The trip takes 2½ hours each way, which gives you 3½ to 4 hours on the Reef.

FROM THE WHITSUNDAYS

FantaSea Cruises (☎ **07/4946 5111**) makes a daily trip to Hardy Reef from Shute Harbour, near Airlie Beach, in a high-speed, air-conditioned catamaran. The boat has a bar, and a biologist gives a marine ecology talk en route. You anchor at the FantaSea Reefworld pontoon, and spend up to 3½ hours on the Reef. The day trip costs A$145 (U.S.$94.25) for adults, A$120 (U.S.$78) for seniors and students, A$75 (U.S.$48.75) for children 4 to 14, and A$336 (U.S.$218.40) for a family of four. Guided snorkel safaris cost A$22 (U.S.$14.30) extra. Cruise/dive packages are available for A$45 (U.S.$29.25) extra for both introductory and certified dives. Wet suit hire is A$7 (U.S.$4.55). Cruises departs at 8:15am, 8:30am or 8:45am and pick up passengers at South Molle, Hamilton, Long and Lindeman island resorts. If you're staying at Airlie Beach, the company provides free coach transfers to Shute Harbour.

A fun alternative to a day trip is FantaSea's **Reef Sleep,** where you spend the night on the pontoon. It's fabulous chance to snorkel at night when the coral is luminescent and nocturnal sea creatures get busy. The trip costs A$305 (U.S.$198.25) per person and includes a marine biologist's slide presentation, two scuba dives, plenty of night snorkeling, two buffet lunches, dinner under the stars with wine, breakfast and more snorkeling on the second day. Accommodations are clean, comfortable bunkhouses. There's a limit of eight guests per night, so you have the Reef all to yourself.

MULTIDAY CRUISES ALONG THE REEF

Down Under Dive (☎ **1800/079 099** in Australia, or 07/4052 8300; fax 07/4031 1373; www.downunderdive.com.au) in Cairns offers an affordable chance to "sleep on the Reef" aboard a 42.6-meter (140-ft.) 1890s-style brigantine, the S.V. *Atlantic Clipper*. She's a sleek, romantic ship with towering masts, a roomy Jacuzzi on the foredeck, a bar, comfortable dining room, and single, double, triple or quad-share airconditioned cabins. A motorized launch takes you from Cairns to the ship's reef mooring; from there you sail to up to the four popular reef complexes of Norman, Hastings, and Saxon reefs, and Michaelmas Cay. The emphasis is on fun and relaxation, with lots of snorkeling and diving. Trips range from a 2-day, 1-night stay in a two, three or four berth cabin for A$210 (U.S.$136.50) for snorkelers or A$290 (U.S.$188.50) for divers, to a 4-day, 3-night journey for A$420 (U.S.$273) for snorkelers or A$550 (U.S.$357.50) for divers. Add a surcharge of A$20 (U.S.$13) per person per night for a double cabin and A$30 (U.S.$19.50) for a double cabin with shower. The allinclusive prices include dive and snorkel gear (including prescription masks), meals, and pickups from your Cairns city accommodation. Transfers from Port Douglas available for an extra A$12 (U.S.$7.80). Reef tax of A$4 (U.S.$2.60) per person per day (to a maximum of A$12/U.S.$7.80) applies.

If you don't have time for a full day on the Outer Reef, don't forget that you can dive the coral cay of **Green Island,** just 27 kilometers (16 miles) off Cairns, in half a day (see "Exploring the Islands & Beaches" in the Cairns section in this chapter). Just remember you can't fly for 24 hours after a dive.

DIVING THE REEF

Divers have a big choice of dive boats that make 1-day runs to the Outer Reef and live-aboard dive boats making excursions that last up to a week. As a general rule, on a typical 5-hour day trip to the Reef, you will fit in about two dives.

The outfits listed below will give you an idea of the diving trips available and general costs. This is by no means a complete list of operators on the Reef—there are far too many to include here. "The Active-Vacation Planner" in chapter 2 has more pointers for locating a dive operator. The prices quoted include full gear rental; knock off about A$20 (U.S.$13) if you have your own gear.

FROM CAIRNS   Tusa Dive (☎ 07/4031 1248; www.tusadive.com) runs two 20-meter (65-ft.) dive boats daily to two dive sites from a choice of 21 locations on the Outer Reef. A day's diving costs A$175 (U.S.$113.75) with wet suits, guided snorkel tours, lunch, and transfers from Cairns or northern beaches hotels. For an extra A$65 (U.S.$42.25) you can get a video of the day's dive. If you want to be shown the best spots under the water, you can take a guided dive for an extra A$15 (U.S.$9.75). Day trips for introductory divers cost A$175 (U.S.$113.75) for one dive or A$205 (U.S.$133.25) for two. There's a maximum of 25 per group, so you get personal attention. The company is the Nitrox and Rebreather facility for north Queensland, and certified divers can take two introductory dives on Nitrox/Safe Air in one day for A$175 (U.S.$113.75).

Deep Sea Divers Den (☎ 07/4031 2223; www.divers-den.com) does day trips to the Outer Reef. The cost is A$70 (U.S.$45.50) for snorkelers. Divers pay A$120 (U.S.$78), which covers two dives, all dive gear, wet suit, reef tax, snorkel gear, and lunch. A day trip with an introductory dive is A$115 (U.S.$74.75), or A$145 (U.S.$94.25) with two intro dives. Hotel pickups are free in Cairns. The boat departs daily at 7:30am.

TAKA II (☎ 07/4051 8722; fax 07/4031 2739; www.taka.com.au) is a solid 22-meter (72-ft.) live-aboard vessel that makes a 3-night trip to the ribbon reefs Cod Hole, Clam Garden, Agincourt Reef, and Opal Reefs. The boat carries a maximum of 26 people in air-conditioned deluxe double or single cabins, standard double cabins, or quad-share cabins. The trip costs from A$765 to 985 (U.S.$497.25–$640.25) from January to June, depending on your choice of cabin, and includes 10 dives, hotel pickups, and all meals. Dive gear rental is A$66 (U.S.$42.90) extra. From July to December add about A$155 (U.S.$100.75) per person to the price. An alternative 4-night journey to the Coral Sea is A$875 to $1,095 (U.S.$568.75–$711.75) per person, including 14 dives. Add about A$170 (U.S.$110.50) per person to the price from July to December. Gear rental is A$88 (U.S.$57.20) extra on this trip. TAKA runs underwater photography courses in conjunction with its trips for A$165 (U.S.$107.25) plus camera hire of A$75 (U.S.$48.75). Add reef tax of A$12 (U.S.$7.80) per person to prices. Snorkelers can deduct about A$100 (U.S.$65) from the prices.

FROM PORT DOUGLAS The waters off Port Douglas are home to coral spires and swim-throughs at the Cathedrals; giant clams and pelagics at Barracuda Pass; a village of parrot fish, anemone fish, unicorn fish, and two Moray eels at the pinnacle of Nursery Bommie; fan corals at Split-Bommie; and many other wonderful sites.

Poseidon (☎ **07/4099 4772**) is a fast 18-meter (58-ft.) vessel that visits three Outer Reef sites. The day-trip price of A$125 (U.S.$81.25) for adults, A$90 (U.S.$58.50) for kids 3 to 12 includes snorkel gear, a marine biology talk, snorkel safaris, lunch, and pickups from Port Douglas hotels. Certified divers pay A$22 (U.S.$14.30) extra per dive, plus A$30 (U.S.$19.50) gear rental. Guides will accompany you, free of charge, to show you great locations. Introductory divers pay A$70 (U.S.$45.50) for one dive, and A$40 (U.S.$26) each for the second and third. The vessel carries no more than 48 passengers, and gets you to the Reef in just over an hour, which gives you 5 hours on the coral. The boat departs Marina Mirage daily at 8:30am.

The Quicksilver Wavepiercers (see "Day Trips to the Reef," earlier in this section) runs dive-tender boats from their pontoon.

FROM MISSION BEACH **Quick Cat Dive Adventures** (see "Day Trips to the Reef," above) takes divers on its day cruises to the Reef.

FROM TOWNSVILLE Off Townsville, you can dive not only the Reef but also a wreck, the ✪ *Yongala,* which lies off the coast in 30 meters (98 ft.) of water with good visibility. A cyclone sent the *Yongala* with 49 passengers and 72 crewmembers to the bottom of the sea in a cyclone in 1911. Today it's surrounded by a mass of coral and rich marine life, including barracuda, grouper, rays, and turtles. **Diving Dreams** (☎ **07/4721 2500;** fax 07/4721 2549; www.divingdreams.com; info@divingdreams. com) runs 2 or 3-day trips, which include dives at the *Yongala,* with prices starting at around A$290 (U.S.$188.50).

FROM THE WHITSUNDAYS In and around the Whitsunday Islands, you can visit the Outer Reef and explore the many excellent Reef dive sites close to shore. Two of the more established companies are **Reef Dive** (☎ **1800/075 120** in Australia, or 07/4946 6508) and **Kelly Dive** (☎ **1800/063 454** in Australia, or 07/4946 6122). A day trip with scuba and snorkel gear, two dives, lunch, and a pickup from your Airlie Beach accommodations costs around A$135 (U.S.$87.75) per person.

DIVE COURSES Many companies in Queensland offer dive courses, from open-water certification up to dive master, rescue diver, and instructor level. To take a course, you will need a medical exam by a Queensland doctor (your dive school will arrange it). You will also need two passport photos for your certificate, and you must be able to swim! Some courses take as few as 3 days, but 5 days is generally regarded as the best. Open-water certification usually requires 2 days of theory in a pool, followed by 2 or 3 days out on the Reef, where you make between four and nine dives.

> ### Money-Saving Tip
>
> Dive-course prices drop if you travel to the Reef each day for your practical sessions, instead of living aboard the company's boat. Of course, then you have to pay for your meals and accommodations on land, so tally up the cost for both before you commit to either.
>
> If time is short, a PADI referral course might suit you. You can do your pool and theory work at home and spend 2 or 3 days on the Reef doing your qualifying dives.

Deep Sea Divers Den (☎ 07/4031 2223; fax 07/4031 1210) claims to have certified about 55,000 divers since 1974. The 5-day open-water course involves 2 days of theory in the pool in Cairns, and 3 days and 2 nights on a live-aboard boat. The course costs A$545 (U.S.$354.25) per person, including all meals on the boat, nine dives (including a guided night dive), all gear and a wet suit, and transfers from your city hotel. The same course over 4 nights, with 1 night on the boat and 4 dives, costs A$435 (U.S.$282.75). New courses begin every day of the week.

Quicksilver Dive (☎ 07/4038 1500; www.quicksilverdive.com.au) has a 2-day referral course starting every Thursday, for A$380 (U.S.$247) including equipment, transfers and lunch.

Other dive-course operators in Cairns include **Pro Dive** (☎ 07/4031 5255; fax 07/4051 9955), **Down Under Dive** (see above), **Rum Runner** (☎ 07/4052 1388; fax 07/4052 1488), **TAKA Dive** (see above), and **Tusa Dive** (☎ 07/4031 1248; fax 07/4031 5221). **Great Adventures** (☎ 07/4051 0455; fax 07/4051 7556) runs courses on Fitzroy Island off Cairns. In Port Douglas, **Quicksilver Dive** (☎ 07/4099 5050; fax 07/4099 4065), the same company that operates the Quicksilver catamaran to the Reef, offers reasonably priced courses. In Townsville, **Diving Dreams** (see above) and **The Dive Bell** (☎ 07/4721 1155; fax 07/4772 3119; enq@divebell. com.au) run courses for all levels of diver. In the Whitsundays, contact **Reef Dive** (☎ 07/4946 6508; fax 07/4946 5007) or **Kelly Dive** (☎ 07/4946 6122; fax 07/4946 4368). In Bundaberg, contact **Salty's Dive Centre** (☎ 07/4151 6422; fax 07/4151 4938).

2 Cairns

346km (207½ miles) N of Townsville; 1,807km (1,084 miles) N of Brisbane

The Great Barrier Reef and the Wet Tropics Rain forest, both two World Heritage attractions, are just a short hop from each other, offering glimpses of two completely different environments. In parts of the far north, the rainforest touches the reef. Cairns is the gateway to these natural attractions, and to manmade attractions such as the Skyrail Rainforest Cableway. It's also a stepping-stone to islands of the Great Barrier Reef and the grasslands of the Gulf Savannah.

When international tourism to the Great Barrier Reef boomed a decade or two ago, Cairns boomed with it. What was once a small farming town boasts five-star hotels, island resorts, big Reef-cruise catamarans in the harbor, and too many souvenir shops.

The 110-million-year-old rain forest, the **Daintree,** where plants that are fossils elsewhere in the world exist in living color, is just a couple of hours north of Cairns. The Daintree is part of the Wet Tropics, a World Heritage–listed area that stretches from north of Townsville to south of Cooktown, beyond Cairns, and houses half of Australia's animal and plant species.

If you are spending more than a day or two in the area, consider basing yourself on the city's pretty northern beaches, in Kuranda, or in Port Douglas (see "Port Douglas, Daintree & the Cape Tribulation Area" later in this chapter). Although prices will be higher in the peak season, which is the Australian winter and early spring from July to October, the town has affordable accommodations year-round.

ESSENTIALS
GETTING THERE By Plane Qantas (☎ 13 13 13 in Australia) has direct flights throughout the day to Cairns from Sydney and Brisbane, and at least one flight a day from Alice Springs and Darwin. Qantas also flies direct from Ayers Rock once or twice a day. From Melbourne you can fly direct some days, but most flights

connect through Sydney or Brisbane. **Flight West Airlines** (☎ **13 00 92** in Australia) has daily services from Darwin and Alice Springs as well as Mackay and Townsville. **Sunstate Airlines** (book through Qantas) also flies several times a day from Townsville, and **Airlink** (book through Qantas) has flights from Alice Springs and Ayers Rock. Several international carriers fly to Cairns from Asia and New Zealand.

   Cairns Airport is 8 kilometers (5 miles) north of downtown, and a 5-minute walk or a A$2 (U.S.$1.30) shuttle ride separates the domestic and international terminals. The cheapest ride to your hotel is the **Australia Coach** (☎ **07/4031 3555**) shuttle, which costs A$4.50 (U.S.$2.93), A$3 (U.S.$1.95) children 2 to 12 years. It meets major flights at both terminals for transfers to city hotels. Bookings are not needed. **Coral Coaches** (☎ **07/4031 7577**) meets most flights between 6am and 8:15pm and does frequent dropoffs and pickups at city, northern beaches and Port Douglas accommodations. Some trips require reservations; others are first-come, first-served, but booking is a good idea. The adult one-way fare is A$7.40 (U.S.$4.81) to the city, A$11.40 (U.S.$7.41) to Trinity Beach, A$14.80 (U.S.$9.62) to Palm Cove. Children 4 to 14 pay half-price, seniors get a 40% discount.

   A taxi from the airport costs around $10.50 (U.S.$6.83) to the city, A$26 (U.S.$16.90) to Trinity Beach, and A$34 (U.S.$22.10) to Palm Cove. Call **Black & White Taxis** (☎ **13 10 08**, or 07/4051 5333 in Cairns).

   Avis, Budget, Hertz, and Thrifty all have **car rental** offices at the domestic and international terminals (see "Getting Around," below).

By Train   Long-distance trains operate from Brisbane several times a week, calling at most towns and cities along the way on a route that is loosely parallel to the Bruce Highway. Trains arrive at **Cairns Central terminal** (☎ **13 22 32** in Australia for reservations or inquiries 24 hours, or 07/4052 6297 for the terminal from 8am to 6pm, 07/4052 6203 after hours) on Bunda Street in the center of town. There are no showers, lockers, or currency exchange; there are 24-hour ATMs outside the Cairns Central shopping mall, right above the terminal. The trip from Brisbane takes around 30 hours. An upright seat on the *Sunlander* or *Spirit of the Tropics* costs A$155 (U.S.$100.75). Sleeping berths, available only on the *Sunlander,* cost A$193 (U.S.$125.45) for a shared three-berth cabin and A$288 (U.S.$187.20) for a private cabin.

   For more details on Queensland's long-haul trains, see chapter 2.

By Bus   **McCafferty's** (☎ **13 14 99** or 07/4051 5899 for Cairns terminal) and **Greyhound Pioneer** (☎ **13 20 30** or 07/4051 3388 for Cairns terminal) buses pull into Trinity Wharf Centre on Wharf Street in the center of town. Buses travel from the south via all towns and cities on the Bruce Highway, and from the west from Alice Springs and Darwin via Tennant Creek on the Stuart Highway and the Outback mining town of Mt. Isa to Townsville, where they join the Bruce Highway and head north.

   The 46-hour Sydney–Cairns trip costs A$249.70 (U.S.$162.31), the 28½-hour trip from Brisbane is A$167.20 (U.S.$109.68), and from Darwin, the journey takes 41 hours and costs A$335.50 (U.S.$218.08).

By Car   From Brisbane and all major towns in the south, you'll enter Cairns on the Bruce Highway. To reach the northern beaches or Port Douglas from Cairns, take Sheridan Street in the city center, which becomes the Captain Cook Highway.

VISITOR INFORMATION   **Tourism Tropical North Queensland** is located at 51 The Esplanade, Cairns, QLD 4870 (☎ **07/4051 3588;** fax 07/4051 0127; www.tnq.org.au). Its Visitor Information Centre has information on Cairns and its environs as well as on Mission Beach, Port Douglas and the Daintree rain forest, Cape

Cairns

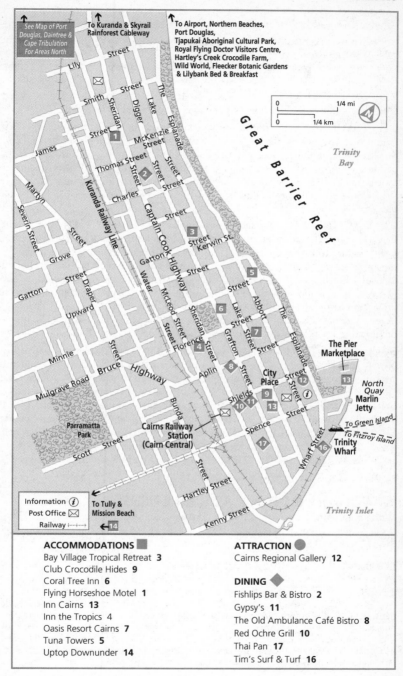

See Map of Port Douglas, Daintree & Cape Tribulation For Areas North

↑ To Kuranda & Skyrail Rainforest Cableway

↑ To Airport, Northern Beaches, Port Douglas, Tjapukai Aboriginal Cultural Park, Royal Flying Doctor Visitors Centre, Hartley's Creek Crocodile Farm, Wild World, Fleecker Botanic Gardens & Lilybank Bed & Breakfast

Lily Street
Smith Street
Sheridan Street
Digger Street
McKenzie Street
Thomas Street
Charles Street
James
Martyn
Severin Street
Grove Street
Gatton Street
Draper Street
Upward Street
Minnie Street
Bruce Highway
Mulgrave Road
Parramatta Park
Scott Street
Bunda Street
Cairns Railway Station (Cairn Central)
Shields Street
Spence Street
Hartley Street
Kenny Street
The Esplanade
Lake Street
Kerwin St.
Abbott Street
Grafton Street
Florence Street
Aplin Street
City Place
Wharf Street
The Pier Marketplace
North Quay
Marlin Jetty
Trinity Wharf
To Green Island
To Fitzroy Island
Trinity Inlet
Trinity Bay

Great Barrier Reef

Kuranda Railway Line
Captain Cook Highway
Gatton Highway
Water Street
McLeod Street
Sheridan Street

0   1/4 mi
0   1/4 km

To Tully & Mission Beach

Information ⓘ
Post Office ✉
Railway ⊢—⊢—⊣

1 **2** **3** **4** **5** **6** **7** **8** **9** **10** **11** **12** **13** **14** **16** **17**

ACCOMMODATIONS
Bay Village Tropical Retreat **3**
Club Crocodile Hides **9**
Coral Tree Inn **6**
Flying Horseshoe Motel **1**
Inn Cairns **13**
Inn the Tropics **4**
Oasis Resort Cairns **7**
Tuna Towers **5**
Uptop Downunder **14**

ATTRACTION
Cairns Regional Gallery **12**

DINING
Fishlips Bar & Bistro **2**
Gypsy's **11**
The Old Ambulance Café Bistro **8**
Red Ochre Grill **10**
Thai Pan **17**
Tim's Surf & Turf **16**

Croc Alert!

Dangerous crocodiles inhabit Cairns waterways. Do not swim in, or stand on the bank of, any river or stream.

York, and Outback Queensland. It's open daily from 8:30am to 5:30pm, closed Christmas and Boxing Day (Dec 26) and after 1pm on public holidays.

CITY LAYOUT Cairns's downtown precinct is laid out on a grid five blocks deep bounded in the east by the **Esplanade** on the water, and in the west by **McLeod Street,** where the train station and the Cairns Central shopping mall are located. In between are shops, offices, and restaurants. Cruises to the Great Barrier Reef and other tour boats leave from the edge of this 5-block area, either from **Trinity Wharf** on Wharf Street, beside the Hilton, or from the adjacent **Marlin Marina** beside the Pier Mall.

GETTING AROUND **By Bus** **Local Sunbus** (☎ 07/4057 7411) buses depart City Place at the intersection of Lake and Shields streets. Buy tickets and passes on board, and try to have correct change. You can hail buses anywhere it's convenient for the driver to stop. Buses 1, 1A, and 2X (a seasonal June-to-Nov. express service) travel to Trinity Beach; and 1, 1B, 1X (weekend express), and 2X travel to Palm Cove. The "N" route runs along the highway from the city to Palm Cove all night until dawn on Friday and Saturday nights, stopping at all beaches in between. Most other buses run from early morning until almost midnight. A "Beaches" pass allowing 24 hours' unlimited travel as far as the northern beaches is A$8.95 (U.S.$5.82).

By Car **Avis** (☎ 07/4051 5911), **Budget** (☎ 07/4051 9222), **Hertz** (☎ 07/4051 6399), and **Thrifty** (☎ 07/4051 8099) all have office in Cairns city and at the airport. One long-established local outfit, **Sugarland Car Rentals,** has reasonable rates and offices in Cairns (☎ 07/4052 1300) and Palm Cove (☎ 07/4059 1087). **Britz Australia** (☎ 1800/33 1454 in Australia), **Budget Campervan Rentals** (☎ 07/ 4032 2065), **Koala Campervan Rentals** (☎ 07/4053 6740), and **Maui Rentals** (☎ 07/4051 3010) rent motorhomes. Britz and most major rental car companies rent 4WDs. If you're in the market for one of these, compare the big guys' prices with those at **Cairns 4WD Hire** (☎ 07/4051 0822). This local outfit also rents camping gear.

By Taxi Call **Black & White Taxis** at ☎ **13 10 08.**

WHAT TO SEE & DO IN & AROUND CAIRNS

Without a doubt, the top attraction in Cairns—apart from the Great Barrier Reef— is the Tjapukai Aboriginal Cultural Park (see below) For details on visiting the Reef from Cairns, see "Exploring the Great Barrier Reef," earlier in this chapter.

LEARNING ABOUT ABORIGINAL CULTURE

✪ **Tjapukai Aboriginal Cultural Park.** Off the Capt. Cook Hwy. (beside the Skyrail terminal), Smithfield. ☎ **07/4042 9900.** Admission A$27 (U.S.$17.55) adults, A$13.50 (U.S.$8.88) children 4–14, A$67.50 (U.S.$43.88) family of 4. Ask about packages that include transfers, lunch and guided Magic Space tour, or Skyrail and/or Scenic Rail travel to and from Kuranda. Daily 9am–5pm. Closed Christmas and New Year's Day. Bus: 1C, 1E, 1G, 1H. Book shuttle transfers from Cairns and northern beaches hotels (A$14/U.S.$9.10 adults and A$7/U.S.$4.55 children) through the park. Park is 15 min. north of Cairns and 15 min. south of Palm Cove along the Captain Cook Hwy.

The Tjapukai (pronounced *Jab-oo-gai*) cultural center was founded in 1987 by theater director and accountant Don and his French-Canadian show dancer wife, Judy. The

Freemans worked closely with local Aborigines, including acclaimed dancer and song-writer David Hudson, to establish a dance theater in Kuranda, which has evolved into the multi-award winning cultural park you see today. Don and Judy are still involved, but the park is 51 percent owned by the Aboriginal people who work in it.

Housed in a striking modern building incorporating Aboriginal themes and colors, the Tjapukai experience is not to be missed. Allow at least 2 to 3 hours to see everything, and you will leave with an insight into the history and culture of the traditional people of the Kuranda region.

The Creation Theatre is a mix of culture and technology, where the latest in illusion, theatrics and technology are used to tell the story of the creation of the world according to the spiritual beliefs of Tjapukai people. Actors interact with spectacular special effects and large holographic images, to illustrate the legends. The production is performed in the Tjapukai language, translated through headsets. Move on through the **Magic Space** museum and gallery to the **History Theatre,** where a 20-minute film relates the history of the Tjapukai people since the coming of white settlers.

Outside, a suspension bridge links the main building with a cultural village where you can try boomerang and spear throwing, fire-making and didgeridoo playing, and learn about bush foods and medicines. In the open-sided Dance Theatre, Aboriginal men and women perform dances incorporating ancient and new steps.

Shows and demonstrations are planned so visitors can move from one to another easily. The complex also includes a restaurant and coffee shop, and an art and crafts gallery and shop featuring the work of local Aboriginal artists and crafts workers.

MORE ATTRACTIONS

Three kilometers (1.8 miles) northwest of Cairns in Edge Hill, are the **Flecker Botanic Gardens,** 94 Collins Ave., (☎ **07/4044 3398**). You can see the wetlands, which include beautiful ferns and orchids, by following the park's many walking trails, and also inspect gardens illustrating Aboriginal plant use. Recently added is Australia's Gondwana Inheritance garden, devoted to the history of plant evolution. Free guided walks are at 1pm Monday to Friday. There is a licensed cafe and a nice book/gift shop. The gardens are open Monday to Friday 7:30am to 5:30pm, and from 8:30am weekends. The gardens are a 10-minute drive from the city, or take bus 1B.

In Cairns

Cairns Regional Gallery. Shields St. at Abbott St. ☎ **07/4031 6865.** Admission A$6 (U.S.$3.90) adults, A$3 (U.S.$1.95) seniors, students, and children 10–17; free admission on Fri. Daily 10am–6pm. Closed Good Friday and Christmas.

Modern paintings, sculpture, computer installations, and other works by a changing array of Australian and international artists are on show at Cairns' premier gallery, including pieces by Aboriginals and Torres Strait Islanders from Australia's far north. Make time to enjoy a cup of coffee on the alfresco terrace cafe.

Royal Flying Doctor Visitors Centre. 1 Junction St., Edge Hill. ☎ **07/4053 5687.** Admission A$5 (U.S.$3.25) adults, A$2.50 (U.S.$1.63) children, A$15 (U.S.$9.75) family pass for 2 adults and unlimited kids. Mon–Sat 9am–5pm. Closed Good Friday and Christmas. Bus: 6, 6A.

Travel Tip

If you stay in Cairns, check out what there is to see and do in and around Port Douglas (see "Port Douglas, Daintree & the Cape Tribulation Area," this chapter). Many tour operators in Port Douglas offer free or inexpensive transfers from Cairns.

The Royal Flying Doctor Service (RFDS), the free aeromedical service that provides a "mantle of safety" for Outback Australians, has a base in Cairns. You can watch a film and attend a talk on how the service began, browse through memorabilia, and board a former RFDS plane.

Hartley's Creek Crocodile Farm. Capt. Cook Hwy. (40km/24 miles N of Cairns, 25km/ 15 miles S of Port Douglas). ☎ **07/4055 3576.** Admission A$16 (U.S.$10.40) adults, A$14 (U.S.$9.10) students, A$8 (U.S.$5.20) children 4–14, A$40 (U.S.$26) family pass for 2 adults and unlimited kids. Daily 8:30am–5pm. Closed Christmas. Transfers available through Coral Coaches (☎ **07/ 4031 7577**).

This crocodile farm may be only a humble attraction in the rain forest, but many visitors find the sinister fascination of its huge crocs makes up for the modest scale. At 11am you can see these monsters get hand-fed or hear a talk on the less aggressive freshwater crocodiles. At 3pm you can witness the infamous saltwater crocodile "death roll" during the 45-minute croc attack show. Kids will enjoy patting koalas and learning about dingoes and other Aussie animals at the 30-minute mammal talk at 1pm; at 2pm there is a snake show; and at 4pm it's koala-feeding time. This attraction makes a good stop en route to Port Douglas, and is also the place to ensure you get to see a cassowary. Crocodiles don't move much except when they eat, so go at show time to see them in action. The same advice applies to visiting Wild World (see below).

Wild World. Captain Cook Hwy. (22km/13 miles N of Cairns), Palm Cove ☎ **07/4055 3669.** Admission A$20 (U.S.$13) adults, A$10 (U.S.$6.50) children 4–15. Daily 8:30am–5pm. Closed Christmas. Bus: 1B. Transfers available through Coral Coaches (☎ **07/4031 7577**).

Get a dose of your favorite Aussie wildlife here—some kind of talk or show takes place just about every 15 or 30 minutes throughout the day, including koala cuddling and talks (have your photo taken cuddling one for A$8/U.S.$5.20), saltwater croc feeding and talks, lorikeet feeding, cane toad racing, and snake talks. Lots of other animals are here, too: kangaroos (which you can feed), emus, cassowaries, dingoes, and native birds in a walk-through aviary. An Aboriginal culture show runs several times during the day. The park also runs a nocturnal tour, in which you can see many of the more elusive creatures. To take the park's **Cairns Night Zoo tour,** book by 4pm that day, earlier if you want transfers. The evening includes a wildlife-spotlighting walk where you can pat a koala and a possum and feed kangaroos, a BBQ dinner with beer and wine, billy tea and damper, supper, and dancing to a live Aussie bush band.

EXPLORING THE ISLANDS & BEACHES

You don't have to go all the way to the Outer Great Barrier Reef to snorkel and get a taste of island living off Cairns. Green and Fitzroy Islands offer reef, rain-forest tours, beaches, and water sports less than an hour from the city wharf. See "Where to Stay" later in this section for details of the resort on Fitzroy Island.

✪ **GREEN ISLAND** Fifty minutes and 27 kilometers (16 miles) east of Cairns by motorized catamaran is 37-acre Green Island, a beautiful Great Barrier Reef coral cay surrounded by dazzling reefs and marine life. The island is home to an expensive eco-resort, but anyone can visit for the day. You can snorkel over reefs (ask staff to point out the easiest-to-get-to snorkeling spots) or glide over the coral in a glass-bottom boat, rent water-sports equipment, go parasailing, take an introductory or certified dive, walk through rain and vine forest, swim in a pool, or laze on the white coral sand beach. If you don't snorkel, take a look at the display of clown fish, potato cod, anemones, and other fishy things at the little underwater observatory on the jetty.

The island has a small private attraction called **Marineland Melanesia,** where you can see old nautical artifacts; primitive art; a turtle and reef aquarium; and live crocodiles, including Cassius, at 5.5 meters (18 ft.) claimed to be the biggest saltwater croc in captivity. Admission is A$8.50 (U.S.$5.53) adults and A$4 (U.S.$2.60) kids, with croc shows at 10:30am and 1:45pm.

Great Adventures (☎ 07/4044 9944) and **Big Cat Green Island Reef Cruises** (☎ 07/4051 0444) make half- and full-day trips to Green Island from Cairns. Expect to pay around A$50 (U.S.$32.50) for a half-day trip with snorkel gear or a glass-bottom boat cruise. A full-day trip can be as much as A$90 (U.S.$58.50), but Big Cat makes a day trip for as little as A$49 (U.S.$31.85). Big Cat's boat is slower, but you still get 5½ hours on the island. Both pick up from hotels in Cairns, the northern beaches, and Port Douglas for a little extra; Big Cat runs to the island direct from Palm Cove also. Boat transfers alone with the island's ferry operator, Great Adventures, are A$44 (U.S.$28.60) adults, A$22 (U.S.$14.30) kids 4 to 14, round-trip.

You can stay for dinner at Green Island Resort's restaurant, Emerald's, and return on Great Adventures' 10:30pm staff run. Bookings are essential; the 10:30pm boat runs only Tuesday, Wednesday, Friday, and Sunday.

FITZROY ISLAND   Scenic Fitzroy Island is a rain-forested national park 45 minutes from Cairns, offering good diving. You can rent windsurfers, catamarans, and canoes; hike to the mountaintop lighthouse; view coral from a glass-bottom boat or take a short boat trip from the island to snorkel it; take a beginners' or certified dive; and swim in the pool. A day trip is the price of the ferry fare at A$36 (U.S.$23.40) round-trip, A$18 (U.S.$11.70) for kids 4 to 14, or A$90 (U.S.$58.50) for a family of 4. There are four departures a day. Book through **Raging Thunder Adventures** (☎ 07/4030 7990). Raging Thunder also runs guided sea-kayak expeditions around Fitzroy Island. The trips include transfers from your Cairns hotel and a boat transfer to the island, 3 hours of kayaking, snorkeling gear, lunch on a deserted beach, and a rain-forest walk to the lighthouse. The full-day trip costs A$110 (U.S.$71.50). You can also stay on the island for as little as A$31 (U.S.$20.15) per person per night in multi-share bunkhouse accommodation (see "Where to Stay," later in this chapter).

A SIDE TRIP TO KURANDA

Few travelers visit Cairns without making a day trip to the mountain village of **Kuranda,** 34 kilometers (20½ miles) west of Cairns near the Barron Gorge National Park. Although it's undeniably touristy, the cool mountain air and mist-wrapped rain forest refuse to be spoiled. The shopping in Kuranda—for leather, Australian wool sweaters, opals, crafts, and more—is a little more individual and unusual than in Cairns, and the cafes and restaurants are more atmospheric. The town is easily negotiated on foot, so pick up a visitors' guide and map at the Skyrail gondola station or train station (see below for how to get there) when you arrive.

GETTING THERE   Getting to Kuranda is part of the fun. Some people drive the winding 25-kilometer (15-mile) mountain road, but the most popular routes are to chuff up the mountainside in a scenic train, or to glide silently over the rain forest canopy in the world's longest gondola cableway, the ✪ **Skyrail Rainforest Cableway.**

The most popular way to get there is to go one-way on the Skyrail (mornings are best for photography) and the other way on the train.

By Skyrail   The Skyrail Rainforest Cableway (☎ 07/4038 1555) is a magnificent feat of engineering and one of Australia's best tourism attractions. Six-person gondolas leave every few seconds from the terminal in the northern Cairns suburb of Smithfield for the 7.5 kilometer (4½ mile) journey. The view of the coast as you ascend is wonderful. As you rise over the foothills of the coastal range, watch the lush green of the rain forest take over beneath you. Looking back, there are panoramic views over Cairns and north towards Trinity Bay. On a clear day, you can see Green Island. There are two stops along the 7.5 kilometers (4.6 miles) journey to Kuranda—at Red Peak and Barron Falls—and about 90 minutes is needed to do it properly. After about 10 minutes, you reach Red Peak. You are now 545 meters (179 ft.) above sea level, and massive kauri pines dominate the view. You must change gondolas at each station, so stroll around the boardwalks for the ground view of the rainforest. Guided walks are run every 20 minutes. Then it's on to Barron Falls station. A rain forest information center has been established here and there are boardwalks to the lookouts for views of the Barron Gorge and Falls. From Barron Falls station, the gondola travels over the thickly rainforested range, and it's easy to spot ferns and orchids and the blue butterflies of the region. As you reach the end of the trip, the gondola passes over the Barron River and across the Kuranda railway line.

A one-way ticket is A$30 (U.S.$19.50) for adults and A$15 (U.S.$9.75) for children 4 to 14 (hotel transfers are not available); a round-trip ticket, including transfers from your Cairns or northern beaches hotel, is A$59 (U.S.$38.35) for adults, A$29.50 (U.S.$19.18) for children, or A$147.50 (U.S.$95.55) family, and A$73 (U.S.$47.45) for adults, A$36.50 (U.S.$23.73) for children or A$182.50 (U.S.$118.63) from Port Douglas. You must make a reservation to travel within a 15-minute segment. Don't worry if it rains—one of the best trips I've made on Skyrail was in a misty rain which added a new dimension to the rainforest. The cableway operates from 8am to 5pm, with last boarding at the Cairns end at 3:45pm. The Skyrail terminal is on the Captain Cook Highway at Kamerunga Road, Caravonica Lakes, 15 kilometers (9 miles) north of Cairns's city center.

By Scenic Railway The 34-kilometer (20½-mile) **Kuranda Scenic Railway** (☎ **1800/620 324** in Australia, or 07/4031 3636) is rated as one of the top five scenic rail journeys in the world. The train snakes through the magnificent vistas of the Barron Gorge National Park, past gorges and waterfalls on the 90-minute trip from Cairns to Kuranda. It rises 328 meters (1,076 ft.) and goes through 15 tunnels before emerging at the Kuranda station, which sits amidst an abundance of ferns. Built by hand over five years in the late 1880s, the railway track is a monument to the 1,500 men who toiled to link the two towns, and the ride on the steam train adds to the atmosphere. It departs Cairns Central at 8:30am and 9:30am Sunday through Friday every day except Christmas and leaves Kuranda at 2pm and 3:30pm Sunday through Friday. (Sat departure from Cairns Central is at 8:30am only, with return trip at 3:30pm only.) The fare is A$29.60 (U.S.$19.24) one-way for adults, A$19.50 (U.S.$12.68) for Australian seniors and students, and A$15 (U.S.$9.75) for children 4 to 14. A pass for a family of four (available Mon and Thurs–Sat) is A$74 (U.S.$48.10) one-way.

Skyrail/Train Combination Tickets In most cases, these packages represent convenience rather than savings. A package combining one-way travel on the Skyrail and a trip back on the Scenic Railway is A$59.60 (U.S.$38.74) for adults and A$30 (U.S.$19.50) for children; A$66.60 (U.S.$43.29) for adults and A$33.50 (U.S.$21.78) for kids with round-trip transfers from Cairns or the northern beaches. A shuttle bus operates between the Skyrail terminal and the nearest train station at Freshwater, 7 kilometers (4 miles) away, for A$4 (U.S.$2.60) adults, A$2 (U.S.$1.30) kids one-way. A three-way package including the Skyrail, the Scenic Railway, and entry to the Tjapukai Aboriginal Cultural Park (see above) is A$86.60 (U.S.$56.29) for adults and A$43.50 (U.S.$28.28) for kids, or A$100 (U.S.$65) for adults and A$50.50 (U.S.$32.83) for kids including transfers from Cairns/northern beaches. Book packages through Skyrail, Queensland Rail, or the Tjapukai Aboriginal Cultural Park.

By Bus   The cheapest way to reach Kuranda is by bus. **White Car Coaches** (☎ 07/ **4091 1855**) operates daily bus service to Kuranda from 48 Spence St., Cairns. The fare is A$7 (U.S.$4.55) for adults, A$3.50 (U.S.$2.28) for children 4 to 12.

BROWSING KURANDA'S MARKETS

Kuranda is known for its markets that sell locally made arts and crafts, fresh produce, boomerangs, T-shirts, and jewelry. There are two markets—the small "original" markets behind **Kuranda Market Arcade** (open Wed–Fri and Sun, ☎ **07/4093 8060**), which mainly sell cheap imports; and the 90-stall **Heritage markets** (open daily 9am– 3pm), which offer better quality and a wider variety of goods. Try to visit Kuranda Wednesday through Friday or Sunday when both markets are open.

Even the Heritage markets are being invaded by commercial imported products, and in response, a group of about 50 local artisans sell their work in the ✪ **Kuranda Arts Co-operative,** 20 Coondoo St. (☎ **07/4093 9026**), open from 10am to 4pm daily. You will find quality furniture crafted from recycled Australian hardwoods, jewelry, handcrafts, and all kinds of stuff here.

SOAKING UP THE RAIN-FOREST SCENERY

You can explore the rain forest, the river esplanade, or Barron Falls along a number of easy walking tracks. If you want to learn about the rain forest, explore it with Brian Clarke of ✪ **Kuranda Rainforest Tours** (☎ **07/4093 7476**) who runs informative 45-minute river cruises. The cruises depart regularly from 10:15am to 2:30pm from the riverside landing across the railway footbridge near the train station. He also runs a daily walk through the rain forest, leaving at 11:45am and returning at 12:45pm. Brian is a former professional crocodile hunter and has lived in the rain forest for more than 30 years. The cruise or the walk costs A$12.50 (U.S.$8.13) for adults, A$6 (U.S.$3.90) for children 5 to 15, and A$30 (U.S.$19.50) for families. Buy your tickets on board.

KURANDA'S NATURE PARKS & OTHER ATTRACTIONS

Of Kuranda's two walk-through aviaries, ✪ **Birdworld** (☎ 07/4093 9188), behind the Heritage Markets off Rob Veivers Drive, is probably the most interesting, as it has eye-catching macaws and a cassowary. The ✪ **Aviary,** 8 Thongon St. (☎ **07/ 4093 7411**), is good if you want to see a bigger range of Australian species. Birdworld is open daily from 9am to 4pm; admission is A$10 (U.S.$6.50) for adults, A$9 (U.S.$5.85) for seniors, and A$3 (U.S.$1.95) for school-age children. The Aviary is open 10am to 4pm; admission is A$10 (U.S.$6.50) for adults, A$9 (U.S.$5.85) for seniors and students, A$4.50 (U.S.$2.93) for children ages 4 to 16, and A$25 (U.S.$16.25) for a family of four. Both are closed Christmas.

Rainforestation Nature Park. On the Kennedy Hwy., a 5-min. drive from the center of Kuranda. ☎ **07/4093 9033.** Daily 9am–4pm. Closed Christmas. Shuttle from outside Skyrail/train terminal 9:45–11am and the Australian Butterfly Sanctuary 10am–2:45pm; A$6 (U.S.$3.90) adults, A$3 (U.S.$1.95) children, and A$13.75 (U.S.$8.94) family, round-trip.

At this 100-acre nature and cultural complex, you can take a 45-minute ride into the rain forest in a World War II amphibious Army Duck. You'll hear commentary on orchids and other rain forest wildlife along the way. You can also see a performance by Aboriginal dancers, learn Aboriginal legends and throw a boomerang on the Dreamtime Walk; or have your photo taken cuddling a koala in the wildlife park. You can do any of these activities separately, or do them all (except cuddle a koala) in a package that costs A$32.50 (U.S.$21.13) for adults, A$16.25 (U.S.$10.57) for kids 4 to 14, or A$81.25 (U.S.$52.82) for a family of five. Koala photos are A$11.50 (U.S.$7.48). The Army Duck runs on the hour beginning at 10am; Aboriginal dancers perform at 11:30am and 2pm; and the 30-minute Dreamtime Walk leaves at 11am, noon, 1:30pm, and 2:30pm.

✪ **Australian Butterfly Sanctuary.** 8 Rob Veivers Dr. ☎ **07/4093 7575.** Admission A$11.50 (U.S.$7.48) adults, A$10.50 (U.S.$6.83) seniors, A$5 (U.S.$3.25) children 5–16; family pass A$28 (U.S.$18.20) for 2 adults and 2 kids; extra child A$4 (U.S.$2.90). Daily 9:45am–4pm. Free guided tours every 15 min.; last tour departs 3:15pm. Closed Christmas.

A rainbow-hued array of 1,500 tropical butterflies—including the electric blue "Ulysses" and Australia's largest, the Cairns birdwing—are housed in a lush walk-through enclosure. Take the free tour and learn about the butterfly's fascinating life cycle. The butterflies will land on you if you wear pink, red, and other bright colors.

EXPLORING THE WET TROPICS

The 110-million-year-old World Heritage–listed Daintree Rain Forest, 2 hours north of Cairns, gets most of the attention (and is covered later this chapter), but tracts of rain forest closer to Cairns are just as pristine. These are all part of the **Wet Tropics** that stretch from Cape Tribulation to Townsville. This dense, lush environment has remained unchanged by Ice Ages and other geological events, and the plants and animals here retain primitive characteristics. Within the tract's mangroves, eucalyptus, and tropical rain forest are 65% of Australia's bird species, 60% of its butterfly species, and many of its frogs, reptiles, bats, marsupials, and orchids.

Because so much wildlife is nocturnal and difficult to spot, consider taking a **Wait-A-While Environmental Tour** (☎ 07/4033 1153). Their naturalist guides take you into the forest to spot a range of wildlife: musky-rat kangaroos, platypus, ringtail possums, cassowaries, amethystine pythons, birds, and tree frogs. They use only low-watt bulbs and quiet 4WD or off-road vehicles. Tours, which go to the Atherton Tableland or the Daintree wilderness, depart Cairns daily at 2pm and return around midnight or 1am. The cost, A$132 (U.S.$85.80) for adults and A$97 (U.S.$63.05) for children under 15, includes binoculars, flashlights, reference books, National Park permits, dinner in a country restaurant or a picnic dinner, and candlelit supper in the rain forest. Tour groups include no more than eight people. The Atherton trip is best for viewing wildlife; the Daintree trip is more about getting back to a true wilderness.

Just over 50 kilometers (30 miles) southwest of Cairns in the Wooroonooran National Park are the rain-forested slopes of **Mt. Bartle Frere,** at 1,622 meters (5,320 ft.) the highest peak in Queensland. **The Adventure Company** (☎ 800/388-7333 in the United States, or 07/ 4051 4777) runs 2- and 4-day hikes on the mountain, camping out in hammocks.

WHITE-WATER RAFTING & OTHER OUTDOOR ACTIVITIES

The Adventure Company (see above) offers a wide range of outdoor adventures, from hiking or biking through the rain forest to kayaking in the Great Barrier Reef Marine

---

Wildlife-Viewing Tip

If you want to spot wildlife, be careful which rain-forest tour you pick. To avoid contact with humans, animals are increasingly retreating to higher altitudes; but most tour operators to the Daintree and Cape Tribulation National Parks stick to the lowlands. Many people on those tours end up asking "Where are all the animals?" The afternoon-into-night trips offered by **Wait-a-While Environmental Tours** offer the most wildlife-viewing for your buck.

The Secret of the Seasons

High season in Cairns runs from early July to early October; 2-week school vacations around Easter, mid-July, and in late September; also the Christmas holiday through January. Hotel occupancy is high in those periods, so book ahead. During the low season, from November to June, ask about discounted rates. Many hotels will be willing to negotiate. Standby rates are usually easy to come by then, too.

Park. It also offers white-water rafting, bungee jumping, hot-air ballooning, four-wheel driving, skydiving, and other high-octane thrills.

RnR Rafting (☎ 07/4051 7777) and **Raging Thunder Adventures** (☎ 07/4030 7990) serve as one-stop booking shops for a plethora of action pursuits in and around Cairns, such as hot-air ballooning, skydiving, jet boating, riding, ATV safaris, parasailing, and rafting. Ask them about multipursuit packages.

BIKING   Cairns hosted the 1996 World Mountain Bike Championships. Bike trails crisscross the hills behind the city. **Dan's Mountain Biking** (☎ 07/4033 0128) runs a wide range of full and half day guided tours in small groups from A$65 to $125 (U.S.$42.25–$81.25) per person.

BUNGEE JUMPING   Contact **A. J. Hackett Bungy** (☎ 07/4057 7188). The cost is A$99 (U.S.$64.35) per person. Free transport is provided to the site, which is 20 minutes north of town on McGregor Road.

FISHING   Cairns is the world's giant black marlin capital. Catches of over 1,000 pounds aren't unusual around here. The game-fishing season is September to December, with November the biggest month. Book early, as game boats are reserved months in advance. Game fishers can also battle Pacific sailfish, dogtooth and yellowfin tuna, Spanish mackerel, wahoo, dolphinfish, barracuda, and tiger shark. Reef anglers can expect to land coral trout, red emperor (sea perch), and sweetlip. Mangrove jack, barramundi, and tarpon lurk in the estuaries. Call **Destination Cairns Marketing,** Shop 5 in the Hilton Hotel complex, Wharf Street (☎ 1800/807 730 in Australia, or 07/4051 4107), to book a charter. Expect to pay around A$400 (U.S.$260) per person per day for heavy-tackle game fishing, A$190 to $250 (U.S.$123.50–$162.50) for light tackle stuff, A$100 to $145 (U.S.$65–$94.25) for reef fishing, and A$120 (U.S.$78) for a day or A$60 (U.S.$39) for a half day in the Cairns Inlet estuary.

GOLF   Greens fees at the lush 9-hole course at **Novotel Palm Cove Resort,** Coral Coast Drive, Palm Cove (☎ 07/4059 1234) are just A$15 (U.S.$9.75); clubs are an additional A$15 (U.S.$9.75) and a cart is A$15 (U.S.$9.75).

WATER SPORTS   **Cairns Parasail & Watersport Adventures** (☎ 07/4031 7888) offers parasailing, jet-boat rides, jet ski rental, and "chariot" rides (in an inflatable two-seat contraption pulled by a speedboat) in Trinity Harbour. The chariot ride costs A$25 (U.S.$16.25) and each other activity costs A$65 (U.S.$42.25); prices include pickup from your Cairns city hotel. They also offer packages combining these with bungee jumping, white-water rafting, fishing, skydiving, 4WD safaris, horseback riding, and trips to Green Island or the Great Barrier Reef. The company is on the ground floor, marina-side, in The Pier Marketplace on the Esplanade.

WHITE-WATER RAFTING   Several outfits offer white-water rafting trips from Cairns on the Grade 3 to 4 ✪ **Tully River,** 90 minutes south of Cairns near Mission Beach; the Grade 3 **Barron River** in the hills behind the city; and the Grade 4 to five 5 of the inland **Johnstone River.** One of the best is ✪ **RnR Rafting** (☎ 07/4051 7777), or book through The Adventure Company, above.

Where's the Beach?

Swaying palms and sandy white beaches—the stuff of postcards—are only a few minutes' drive north of Cairns. This is the Marlin Coast, which runs between the Captain Cook Highway and the Coral Sea. Heading north from Cairns, the beaches are Machans Beach, Holloway's Beach, Yorkey's Knob, Trinity Beach, Kewarra Beach, Clifton Beach, Palm Cove, and Ellis Beach, in that order.

The locals have kept quiet about these beautiful spots for years. At Machans Beach, about 10 kilometers (6 miles) north of Cairns airport, the esplanade is lined with private homes. The closest commercial beachfront accommodation north of Cairns is at Holloways Beach.

Holloways, like most of the beaches along the Marlin Coast, is patrolled and has a swimming enclosure for use during stinger season (Oct–May). There's playground equipment for the kids in the beachfront park, while parents can watch from the shady deck at the beachfront cafe.

At **Yorkeys Knob,** new apartment blocks line Sims Esplanade, across the road from beachside picnic shelters and the lifeguard post. Yorkeys Knob also has a golf course and marina. **The Half Moon Bay Country Club Golf Course** is off Wattle St, and is well signposted from the main road into town.

Trinity Beach, one of the most popular of the northern beaches, is a 1.5-kilometer (just under 1 mile) stretch of sand, complete with swaying coconut palms. **Vasey Esplanade** is a colorful, bustling mix of apartments, restaurants, shops and holidaymakers. On the beach, you can rent a jet ski, catamaran, paddle-ski, windsurfer or boogie board, or join an impromptu game of beach volleyball. At the southern end of the beach, take the **Ron McKauge Walk** for 350 meters (1150 ft.) along the beach and around the point for spectacular views north over Trinity Beach and south to Yorkeys Knob marina. On the hill above Trinity Beach is the old pub, with million dollar views of the beach and Coral Sea.

Next is **Kewarra Beach,** home to a budget-busting luxury resort well hidden from the beach itself. From Kewarra Beach you can see all the way to Palm Cove. To walk there along the beach would take you past Clifton Beach.

Palm Cove has a long jetty for fishing or boarding one of the day-tripper boats that pull in. Melaleuca trees line **Williams Esplanade,** softening the row of hotels and apartments. Here, nothing can be built higher than the trees.

Absolute beachfront means just that at **Ellis Beach,** the most northerly, just 30 minutes from Cairns. This is one of the most unspoiled stretches of the coast, a 5-kilometer (3.1-mile) beach, fringed by 150 palms and dotted with mango trees.

One-day trips on the Tully are suitable for all ages and abilities and are quite popular (see the description in "The North Coast: Mission Beach, Townsville & the Islands" section later in this chapter). The trip costs A$128 (U.S.$83.20) from Cairns, or A$138 (U.S.$89.70) from Port Douglas, including transfers.

Closer to Cairns, the gentler Barron River is good choice for the timid. The half-day trip with RnR Rafting costs about A$79 (U.S.$51.35) from Cairns or A$90 (U.S.$58.50) from Port Douglas, including pickup and 2-hours' rafting.

WHERE TO STAY

Cairns has a good supply of affordable accommodations, both in the heart of the city and along the northern beaches. You can also stay in the peaceful village of Kuranda, or get away from it all at an island resort.

IN CAIRNS

Unless noted otherwise, shops, restaurants, cinemas, the casino, bus terminals, the train station, and the Marlin Marina and Trinity Wharf departure terminals for Great Barrier Reef cruises are all within walking distance of the following accommodations.

✪ Bay Village Tropical Retreat. Corner Lake and Gatton sts., Cairns, QLD 4870. ☎ **07/ 4051 4622.** Fax 07/4051 4057. www.bayvillage.com.au. reservations@bayvillage.com.au. 63 units (most with shower only). A/C TV TEL. A$123.30 (U.S.$80.15) double; A$137.50 (U.S.$89.38) studio; A$192.50 (U.S.$125.13) 2-bedroom apt. Extra person A$22 (U.S.$14.30). Children under 15 stay free in parents' room. Crib A$5.50 (U.S.$3.58). AE, BC, DC, MC, V. Limited free parking; ample on-street parking. Free city center and airport shuttle.

A swimming pool tucked in a lush garden courtyard adds to the charm at this two-story hotel a half-mile from the city center. All accommodations are smartly decorated and a decent size, but the studio apartments with kitchenettes are especially roomy; a few even have decadent double showers. The bathrooms are compact but fine; all have hair dryers. Helpful staff members are always around. Facilities include a free barbecue; room service; and a rustic, European-style restaurant.

Cairns Bed & Breakfast. 48 Russell St., Edge Hill, Cairns, QLD 4870. ☎ **07/4032 4121** or 0413 274 612 mobile phone. Fax 07/4053 6557. www.cairnsbnb.com.au. cairnsbnb@ internetnorth.com.au. 3 units (all with shower only). A/C TV. A$75 (U.S.$48.75) single; A$95 (U.S.$61.75) double. Rates include full breakfast. No credit cards. Free on-street parking. Free transfers from airport, trains and coach terminals (arrange when booking).

Norah and Bernie Hollis's B&B is 5 kilometers (3 miles) away from the airport or city in a pleasant suburb close to good restaurants, the bus, and on the edge of a conservation wetlands area popular with bird-watchers. Guests share the house with Bill the dog, Martin the cat, and dozens of Norah's teddy bears. Each cool, tile-floored room has its own entrance; all are furnished in Laura Ashley, with throw rugs, embroidered towels, and framed prints. Hair dryers are available. Breakfast is served by the pool. Your hosts are a good source for advice on tours (Bernie is a tour guide), which mostly pick up from the door. No smoking.

Club Crocodile Hides Hotel. 87 Lake St., Cairns, QLD 4870. ☎ **1800/079 266** in Australia, or 07/4051 1266. Fax 07/4031 2276. www.flagchoice.com.au. 107 units, 70 with bathroom (68 with shower only). AC TV TEL. A$75 (U.S.$48.75) double without bathroom; A$95 (U.S.$61.75) double with bathroom. Rates include continental breakfast. Ask about packages. AE, BC, DC, MC, V. Free parking. Airport shuttle.

Time has left this colonial three-story hotel overlooking a pedestrian plaza in the center of town a little worse for the wear, but it does have redeeming features, such as the high ceilings with ornate plasterwork, new carpets, and fresh paint in all the rooms. Choose from smallish rooms in the original 1885 building, or larger, lighter tile-floored rooms in the 1960s wing. The bathrooms in the new wing are a vivid contrast to the dated shower units in the old building. Most rooms have no views, but a few open onto a huge verandah that overlooks the busy streets. This is a great spot to eat your basic breakfast, but it gets very noisy on Friday and Saturday nights when the public bar below starts to roar. The hotel belongs to the Flag chain.

✪ **Coral Tree Inn.** 166–172 Grafton St., Cairns, QLD 4870. ☎ **07/4031 3744.** Fax 07/4031 3064. www.coraltreeinn.com.au. reservations@coraltreeinn.com.au. 58 units (some with shower only). A/C TV TEL. A$106 (U.S.$68.90) double; A$136 (U.S.$88.40) suite. Extra person A$10 (U.S.$6.50). AE, BC, DC, MC, V. Limited free parking; ample on-street parking. Airport shuttle.

The focal point of this airy, resort-style motel a 5-minute walk from the city center is the friendly communal kitchen that overlooks the small palm-lined pool and sundeck. It's a great spot to cook up a steak or reef fish fillet on the free barbie and join other guests at the big tables. Local restaurants deliver, free fresh-roasted coffee is on all day, and a vending machine sells wine and beer. The smallish, basic but neat motel rooms have white painted brick walls, terra-cotta tile or freshly carpeted floors, and clean new bathrooms sporting marble-look laminate countertops (ask for a hair dryer at reception). The suites on the top (third) floor are huge and stylish enough for any corporate traveler. They are some of the best-value accommodations in town. All rooms have a private balcony or patio; some look out onto the drab commercial buildings next door, but most look out over the pool. A tour desk takes care of your tour and rental car bookings. Ask about packages, which include cruises and other tours.

Flying Horseshoe Motel. 281–289 Sheridan St., Cairns, QLD 4870. ☎ **07/4051 3022.** Fax 07/4031 2761. flying-horseshoe@bestwestern.com.au. 51 units (shower only). A/C MINIBAR TV TEL. A$85–$95 (U.S.$55.25–$61.75) single; A$95–$105 (U.S.$61.75–$68) double; A$105 (U.S.$68.25) single studio apt, A$115 (U.S.$75.75) double studio apt. Extra person A$10 (U.S.$6.50); children under 15 A$5 (U.S.$3.25). AE, BC, DC, JCB, MC, V. Free parking. Free pickup from airport, train or bus station.

You will find clean rooms and a warm welcome from your hosts at this pleasant spot halfway between the airport and the city center. It is a A$3 (U.S.$1.95) bus ride, A$9 (U.S.$5.85) taxi ride or a pleasant 30-minute walk along the Esplanade to the city. Here you can breathe in the balmy evening air from your balcony, gather round the pool for a buffet, or soak in the Jacuzzi in the courtyard. Every room is freshly decorated and spacious, with hair dryer in the bathroom; business rooms are slightly bigger. The apartments are by a main road, so expect some traffic noise. There is 24-hour reception and helpful staff run a tour- and car-rental desk and can arrange dry cleaning. There's free newspaper delivery, in-room massages, babysitting, and secretarial services. The bus to the city stops just across the road.

✪ **Lilybank Bed & Breakfast.** 75 Kamerunga Rd., Stratford, Cairns, QLD 4870. ☎ **07/4055 1123.** Fax 07/4058 1990. www.lilybank.com.au. hosts@lilybank.com.au. 6 units (4 with shower only). A/C. A$61 (U.S.$39.65) single; A$75–$97 (U.S.$48.75–$63.05) double. Additional person A$25 (U.S.$16.25). Rates include full breakfast. AE, BC, MC, V. Free parking. Bus: 1E, 1F. Taxi from airport approx. A$11 (U.S.$7.15). Children not permitted.

This lovely 1870s Queenslander homestead, originally the mayor's residence, is located in a leafy suburb 6 kilometers (3¾ miles) from the airport and a 10-minute drive from the city. Guests sleep in large, attractive rooms, all individually decorated with such features as wrought-iron beds and patchwork quilts. Each bathroom is different, but all are comfortable and a good size (hair dryers are available). The largest room has French doors opening onto a "sleep-out," an enclosed verandah with two

---

Travel Tip

Almost all tour companies and Great Barrier Reef cruise operators will pick you up and drop you off whether you're staying in Cairns, on the northern beaches, or even as far afield as Port Douglas.

extra beds. You can also stay in the gardener's cottage with slate floors, stained-glass windows, a king-size bed, and a bar. The house is set in gardens with a rock-lined salt-water pool. Breakfast is served in the garden room by the fishpond. Your engaging hosts are Mike and Pat Woolford, and you share the house with three poodles, an irrepressible galah, and a giant green tree frog. There's a guest TV lounge, a guest kitchen, and phone, fax and e-mail access. Many tours pick up at the door, and several good restaurants are a stroll away, so you don't need a car to stay here. No smoking indoors.

Super-Cheap Sleeps

✪ **Inn the Tropics.** 141 Sheridan St., Cairns, QLD 4870. ☎ **1800/807 055** in Australia, or 07/4031 1088. Fax 07/4051 7110. www.cairns.net.au/~innthetropics. innthetropics@ cairns.net.au. 51 units, 6 with bathroom (shower only). A$33 (U.S.$21.45) single without bathroom, A$44 (U.S.$28.06) single with bathroom; A$44 (U.S.$28.60) double without bathroom, A$55 (U.S.$35.75) double with bathroom. AE, BC, DC, MC, V. Limited free parking. Airport shuttle.

A cut above a backpacker hostel, this cheerful, well-run lodge in the city center has small, simple but appealing private rooms with a minifridge and sink, tea- and coffee-making facilities, well-lit clean private bathrooms with plenty of counter space, and freshly painted concrete brick walls. Some even have TVs. Homey touches abound, from the framed Monet prints to the ornamental seahorses on the doors. The shared bathrooms are very clean. Air-conditioning is A$1 (U.S.65¢) for 3 hours. Out in the courtyard is a pretty pool and a barbecue where guests can cook their own dinner. The management rents bikes, runs an extensive tour desk, and provides currency exchange.

Uptop Downunder. 164 Spence St., Cairns, QLD 4870. ☎ **1800/243 944** in Australia, or 07/4051 3636. Fax 07/4052 1211. www.uptopdownunder.com. uptop@uptodownunder. com.au. 45 units (none with bathroom). A$32 (U.S.$20.80) single; A$38 (U.S.$25.70) double. A$18 (U.S.$11.70) dorm bed. AE, BC, MC, V. Free parking for 15 cars. Free transfer from airport, train, or coach terminal (book in advance, or call when you arrive). Lodge runs free shuttle to town throughout the day.

After a hard day's sightseeing, it's a pleasure to return to the lounge chairs around the palm-lined pool at this cheerful backpacker lodge set amid an acre of tropical gardens. The dorm rooms are clean; the private rooms are simple but airy and clean, with a double and a single bed and minifridge. Some are air-conditioned (a must Nov–Mar), others have fans. Don't fuss about sharing the showers—the communal bathroom block and laundry are superclean. The staff is friendly; amenities include a communal kitchen and dining area, a barbecue, free tea and coffee, a basic grocery store and snack bar, a TV lounge, bikes for rent, telephones, e-mail access, safes, and a tour desk.

Worth a Splurge

✪ **Inn Cairns.** 71 Lake St., Cairns, QLD 4870. ☎ **07/4041 2350.** Fax 07/4041 2420. www.inncairns.com.au. bookings@inncairns.com.au. 38 units. A/C TV TEL. A$159 (U.S.$103.35) double. Extra person A$17 (U.S.$11.05). Children under 5 free in parents' room. AE, BC, DC, MC, V. Free parking. Airport shuttle.

If you want stylish surroundings, you'll like these spacious new one-bedroom apartments in the town center. They feature terra-cotta floors, wrought-iron and rattan furniture, and timber-louvered blinds. The roomy bathrooms are equally smart, with thick white towels. Guests can enjoy the sun on the rooftop deck, which has palms and views to the sea, or around the small but elegant pool and barbecue gazebo. Each apartment has a VCR, intercom, and laundry; hair dryers are available at reception. Stock up on supplies at the supermarket across the road, or dine at the bistro downstairs. You're three blocks from where the Great Barrier Reef cruises depart.

Oasis Resort Cairns. 122 Lake St., Cairns, QLD 4870. ☎ **1300/656565** in Australia, 800/221–4542 in the U.S. and Canada, 020/8283 4500 in the U.K., 0800/44 4422 in New

Zealand, or 07/4080 1888. Fax 07/4080 1889. www.oasis-cairns.com.au. info@oasis-cairns.com.au. 314 units. A/C MINIBAR TV TEL. A$197–$219 (U.S.$128.05–$142.35) double; A$328 (U.S.$213.20) suite. Extra person A$32.50 (U.S.$21.13). 2 children under 17 stay free in parents' room if they use existing bedding; free cribs. Ask about packages. AE, BC, DC, JCB, MC, V. Free parking. Airport shuttle.

So what if downtown Cairns doesn't have a beach? You've got a neat little sandy one right here—and a swim-up bar—at the big swimming pool in the expansive courtyard at this six-story resort in the heart of town. The rooms are not the biggest you've seen in an upscale hotel, but they are neat and colorful. All have balconies, views into tropical gardens or over the pool/sundeck/bar area, and good bathrooms with hair dryers. The roomy suites have a TV in the bedroom and a large Jacuzzi bath, arguably the best-value suites in town. Other amenities include a gym, kiddie pool, a concierge and tour desk, room service, and a free newspaper delivered to your door.

Tuna Towers. 145 The Esplanade at Minnie St., Cairns, QLD 4870. ☎ **07/4051 4688.** Fax 07/4051 8129. www.tunatowers.com.au/. res@tunatowers.com.au. 60 units. A/C MINIBAR TV TEL. A$124 (U.S.$80.60) double; A$140 (U.S.$91) studio apt. double; A$167 (U.S.$108.55) suite. Extra person A$10 (U.S.$6.50). AE, BC, DC, JCB, MC, V. Limited free parking. Airport shuttle.

You get wonderful views of Trinity Bay or nice views of the city and mountains from the balcony of every room at this multistory motel and apartment complex. From outside, the building is attractive and modern; inside, the accommodations are light, spacious, and airy with up-to-date decor. Every bathroom is modern and is equipped with a hair dryer. There's a small pool and Jacuzzi out front, and a pleasant restaurant and cocktail bar. It's just a couple of blocks to the center of town.

ON THE NORTHERN BEACHES

Beaches at Holloways. 2 Marietta St., Holloways Beach, Cairns, QLD 4870. ☎ **07/4055 9972.** Fax 07/4055 9886. www.beaches-at-holloways.com.au. bookings@beaches-at-holloways.com.au. 3 units (2 with shower only). A/C. A$50–$75 (U.S.$32.50–$48.75) single; A$70–$80 (U.S.$45.50–$52) double. Extra person A$20 (U.S.$13). Rates include full breakfast. BC, MC, V. Free on-street parking. Bus: 1C, 1H, N.

Relaxed owners David and Josephine Hopkins have given over the upstairs of their light-filled home opposite Holloways Beach to guests. Rooms are fresh and comfortable; bathrooms pretty, practical, and come with hair dryers and bathrobes. Two front rooms open onto a lovely bougainvillea-clad verandah overlooking the sea. There's a pool in the garden, and a guest TV lounge. Several inexpensive restaurants, including a good alfresco Italian BYO, are just down the road. No smoking indoors.

✪ **Ellis Beach Oceanfront Bungalows.** Captain Cook Highway, Ellis Beach, QLD 4879. ☎ **07/4055 3538.** Fax 07/4055 3077, 1800 637 036 in Australia. www.ellisbeachbungalows.com.au. bill@ellisbeachbungalows.com.au. 1-and 2-bedroom bungalows, all with private bathrooms. A/C. A$140 (U.S.$91) double. Extra person A$15 (U.S.$9.75). Children under 3 free in parents' room. Cribs A$5 (U.S.$3.25). Full breakfast available for A$11 (U.S.$7.15) adult or A$8 (U.S.$5.20) children 3–14. AE, BC, MC, V.

Set on arguably the loveliest of the northern beaches, these bungalows reside under waving palm trees between the Coral Sea and a backdrop of mountainous rain forest. Lifeguards patrol the beach, and there are stinger nets in season as well as a shady swimming pool and toddlers' wading pool. There's plenty of privacy and the bungalows are basic but pleasant. Sit on the verandah and gaze at the ocean (keep an eye out for dolphins). Each bungalow has a full kitchen and there are also coin-operated barbecues, a tour desk and car rental, phone and fax facilities and a restaurant if you don't want to cook every night. Next door is a caravan park.

Safe Swimming

Northern beaches have small, netted enclosures for swimming from October to May,because ocean swimming off the Queensland beaches becomes quite dangerous when the poisonous marine stingers (jellyfish) are present.

○ **The Reef Retreat.** 10–14 Harpa St., Palm Cove, Cairns, QLD 4879. ☎ **07/4059 1744.** Fax 07/4059 1745. www.reefretreat.com.au. sales@reefretreat.com.au. 36 units (17 with shower only, 13 with shower and Jacuzzi). A/C TV TEL. A $130 (U.S.$85) studio double; A$140–$160 (U.S.$91–$104) suite; A$250 (U.S.$162.50) 2-bedroom apt. (sleeps 4). Extra person A$22 (U.S.$14.30). Children under 3 stay free in parents' room if they use existing bedding; crib A$22 (U.S.$14.30). AE, BC, DC, MC, V. Free parking. Bus: 1, 1B 1X, 2X, N. Airport shuttle.

Tucked back one row of buildings from the beach is this little gem—a low-rise collection of studios and suites built around a swimming pool in a peaceful grove of palms and silver paperbarks. All rooms in the newer or renovated wings have cool tile floors and teak and cane furniture. The studios are a terrific value, much larger than the average hotel room. In some, you can see the sea from your bed. The extra-private honeymoon suites have a Jacuzzi and a kitchenette on the balcony, enclosed by blinds. Every room has a kitchenette; the apartment and one suite have a full kitchen. There's a free barbecue, and a Jacuzzi. There is an iron and ironing board in the laundry, and hair dryers are free from reception. There's no elevator. Serviced twice weekly; one free service for stays of 5 days or longer. Extra services A$16 (U.S.$10.40).

Tropical Holiday Units. 63–73 Moore St. (at Trinity Beach Rd.), Trinity Beach, Cairns, QLD 4879. ☎ **07/4057 6699.** Fax 07/4057 6565. www.ozemail.com.au/~trophol/. trophol@ozemail.com.au. 43 units (with shower only). A/C TV TEL. A$96–$128 (U.S.$62.40–$83.20) 1-bedroom apt, A$120–$160 (U.S.$78–$104) 2-bedroom apt. Extra person A$18 (U.S.$11.70). Children under 4 stay free. Weekly rates available. AE, BC, DC, MC, V. Free parking. Bus: 1, 1A, 3X, N. Airport shuttle. Free airport transfers for guests staying 5 nights or more.

You're a block from Trinity Beach at these roomy, well-equipped apartments. The furnishings are rather dated, but each has everything a family or couple could want for a penny-wise vacation—a kitchen, comfy living and dining area, large bedrooms, laundry, balcony, and the luxury of space. Servicing is weekly. There are three salt-water pools and Jacuzzis and a barbecue. The friendly managers book your rental cars and tours. A general store, a pub, and inexpensive eateries are just down the road.

IN KURANDA

A 30-minute winding mountain drive, a 90-minute train trip, or a 40-minute Skyrail gondola ride over the treetops brings you to this pretty village in the hills behind Cairns. A local bus travels from two to five times a day from Cairns city for A$7 (U.S.$4.55) one-way. Kuranda is cool, rain-foresty, and blissfully peaceful, despite the daily influx of tourists from the city. There are a handful of good restaurants and quite a lot to see and do. One drawback is that not many tours pick up here. Guests at Kuranda Rain-forest Resort can take a free shuttle into Cairns to meet most tours.

Kuranda Rainforest Park. Kuranda Heights Rd., Kuranda, QLD 4872. ☎/fax **07/4093 7316.** www.kurandatouristpark.com. kur.vanp@internetnorth.com.au. 11 units (with private bathroom, shower only); 8 backpacker rooms. TV. Family cottages A$88 (U.S.$57.20) double; extra adult A$11 (U.S.$7.15); each child A$5.50 (U.S.$3.58). A$66 (U.S.$42.90) double for cottages for couples, park cabins or poolside cabins. A$30 (U.S.$19.50) double for backpacker twin rooms (1 group room sleeps 6 for A$15/U.S.$9.75 per person). A$15 (U.S.$9.75) double for unpowered camp sites and A$17 (U.S.$11.05) for powered sites. AE, BC, MC, V.

The rainforest and exotic, colorful parklike gardens are the setting for this combination of cabins, backpacker rooms and campsites. Annette and Hans Christensen have established their getaway on 10 acres just 10 minute walk from Kuranda's amenities. You can take a canoe on the nearby Barron River or go spotlighting on the grounds at night to see some of the local wildlife. A large freeform saltwater pool is ideal for a relaxing swim. There's also a public phone/fax, Internet access, tour desk and store.

Kuranda Rainforest Resort. Kennedy Hwy. at Greenhills Rd., Kuranda, QLD 4872. ☎ **1800/806 996** in Australia or 07/4093 7555. Fax 07/4093 7567. 70 units (all with shower only). TV TEL. A$85 (U.S.$55.25) double; A$170 (U.S.$110.50) split-level pole cabin. BC, MC, V. Airport transfers A$10 (U.S.$6.50) per person.

A 2-minute drive from the center of Kuranda village, this retreat consists of rustic cedar cabins nestled into dense rain forest. Whether you opt for a standard cabin, or the larger split-level pole variety with cooking facilities, a bed downstairs, and three or four single beds or bunks on the mezzanine level (reached by a ladder), you will feel delightfully snug in the interiors. The bathrooms are small but neatly tiled. Enjoy a rain-forest-wrapped swimming pool, Jacuzzi, and children's pool that look as though they were carved from natural rock (check out the honeymoon cave behind the pool's waterfall), and the open-air poolside restaurant where bandicoots and birds are regular visitors. Reception runs a tour desk; there's also a tennis court and a gym. You can hand-feed wallabies in the on-site sanctuary. A shuttle runs into Kuranda and Cairns.

ON AN ISLAND

Of several island resorts off Cairns, the Fitzroy Island Resort is the most affordable. It is idyllic, but every time you want to join a tour or go shopping on the mainland, you must pay for a transfer—about A$30 (U.S.$19.50) round-trip.

Fitzroy Island. 35km/22 miles SE of Cairns. P.O. Box 1109, Cairns, QLD 4870. ☎ **07/4051 9588.** Fax 07/4052 1335. www.fitzroyislandresort.com.au. info@fitzroyislandresort.com.au. 8 cabins (all with shower only); 32 bunkhouses (none with private bathroom). Cabins A$220 (U.S.$143) double. Extra person A$35 (U.S.$22.75). Bunkhouses A$31 (U.S.$20.15) per person per bed (sharing with up to 3 other people); A$116 (U.S.$75.40) double (sole use); A$150 (U.S.$97.50) family bunkhouse. AE, BC, DC, JCB, MC, V. Round-trip transfers 3–4 times daily from Cairns (approx. 45 min.) cost A$36 (U.S.$23.40) adults, A$18 (U.S.$11.70) children 4–14.

This is probably the most affordable island resort on the Great Barrier Reef. It's targeted at a young crowd looking for action and eco-fun in a beautiful location. It's no glamour-puss palace, but it was revamped in 2000 in a low-key way, with a new restaurant, spruced-up linens and upholstery, and a makeover around the pool area. Fitzroy is a continental island offering little in the way of fringing coral and only a few narrow strips of coral sand. What it does have are catamarans, outrigger canoes, and surf skis; glass-bottomboat rides; and hiking trails through dense national-park forest to a lighthouse. Divers can make drift dives over the reefs dotted around the island to see manta rays, reef sharks, turtles, and plenty of coral. There is good snorkeling at two points around the island that you can reach twice a day on the dive boat, at an extra fee. You can also catch the **Sunlover Cruises** day trip to the outer Great Barrier Reef.

Each of the modestly comfortable beach cabins has a queen-size bed in front and two bunks in the back, fans, a TV, a minifridge, an iron, and a hair dryer, and a large balcony with views through the trees to the sea. The bunkhouse accommodations are basic fan-cooled carpeted rooms with bunks and/or beds. Bunkhouse guests can use the communal kitchen if they BYO supplies from the mainland.

Dining/Diversions: The restaurant is moderately priced, a kiosk sells cheap takeout food, and a poolside grill and bar does casual meals. The Raging Thunder Beach Bar, "the only nightclub on the Reef," gets going Friday and Saturday nights.

Amenities: A dive shop, offering introductory and certified dives and certification courses, other water sports, a small swimming pool, volleyball, tour desk, boutique.

WHERE TO DINE
In Cairns

Cairns is not known for its restaurants. Many of them are fairly ordinary, but it's possible to find good food at good prices. Many listed below are popular local hangouts. The Esplanade along the seafront is always good for a cost-conscious feed, as it's packed with cheap cafes, pizzerias, fish-and-chips places, and ice-cream parlors. The Pier Marketplace on the waterfront beside Marlin Marina has a food court with water views, but you will find better quality at the food court in the Cairns Central Mall (☎ **07/4041 4111**) over the railway station on McLeod Street. All but a few food outlets in the mall close at night.

Gypsy's Restaurant. 41A Shields St., Cairns. ☎ **07/4051 5530.** Reservations recommended. Main courses A$16–$22 (U.S.$10.40–$14.30); pasta specials A$12 (U.S.$7.80). Daily 11am–midnight. AE, BC, DC, MC, V. MODERN AUSTRALIAN.

Part restaurant, part bar, part club—no one seems to know just what Gypsy's is, but they love it just the same.You can sit outside or in the recently renovated cavernous interior. The menu has choices for vegetarians, some pastas, and a range of main courses, such as kangaroo fillet on warm Asian greens with coriander-peanut pesto. After 10pm Wednesday to Saturday, a live band strikes up anything from soft melodies to top 40. Licensed and BYO wine only (no BYO beer or spirits).

Mediterraneo. 74 Shields St. ☎ **07/4051 4335.** Reservations recommended on weekends. Main courses A$17.50–$21.80 (U.S.$11.33–$14.17); pasta A$12.50–$15.50 (U.S.$8.13–$10.08). BC, MC, V. Tues–Sun 6pm–late. ITALIAN.

Friendly, professional service and talented chefs keep the locals coming back for more. Many of the menu's classic dishes come with a modern twist, such as the fettucine portofino with prawns, shallots, cream, and an untraditional hint of curry. And don't overlook the traditional favorites, such as like a mixed seafood casserole; beef with white wine and mushrooms; and veal topped with Parma ham, provolone, and tomato sauce. Such dishes might raise a yawn from trendy diners, but here they are cooked with aplomb. The decor is trendy but not showy, just a polished concrete floor, framed sketches on the wall, and timber tables. There's also a courtyard out the back. BYO.

The Old Ambulance Café Bistro. 135 Grafton St., Cairns. ☎ **07/4051 0511.** Main courses A$9.80–$14.50 (U.S.$6.37–$9.43). Mon 7am–6pm, Tues–Thurs 7am–10:30pm, Fri–Sat 7am–11:30pm. AE, BC, DC, MC, V. LIGHT FARE.

Drop in for a coffee, a slice of cake, a toasted foccacia sandwich, a baked potato with special toppings, or a light but filling meal of eggplant parmigiana, prawn and chicken risotto, or chicken breast with Heike's famous curry vinaigrette. The small menu is supplemented by blackboard specials each day, and the food is nicely prepared. This trendy little place used to be an ambulance station, but young corporate types and moms with prams have replaced the wailing sirens. BYO.

✪ **Red Ochre Grill.** 43 Shields St. ☎ **07/4051 0100.** Reservations recommended. Main courses A$8.50–$18 (U.S.$5.53–$11.70) lunch, A$17.50–A$25 (U.S.$11.3340–$16.25) dinner. Australian game platter A$32 (U.S.$20.80) per person, seafood platter A$42 (U.S.$27.30) per person. AE, BC, DC, JCB, MC, V. Mon–Sat noon–3pm, daily 6pm–late. GOURMET BUSH TUCKER.

You could accuse this restaurant/bar of using weird and wonderful Aussie ingredients as a gimmick to pull in crowds, but the folks who flock here are anything but gullible—they know good food. Daily specials are big on fresh local seafood, such as tempura bugs (a delectable crustacean) on lemongrass skewers. On the regular menu is emu pate with bush tomato chili jam and fresh damper, and wallaby topside done over a mallee-fired grill (mallee is a timber) with sweet potato mash. You can even eat the Aussie coat of arms by ordering a game platter of kangaroo and emu served with native warrigal spinach and yam gratin. Although the place is slick enough for a night out, it is also informal enough for a casual meal.

Thai Pan. 43–45 Grafton St. ☎ **07/4052 1708.** Reservations recommended. Main courses A$15.70–$A19.50 (U.S.$10.21–$12.68). AE, BC, DC, MC, V. Daily 5:30pm–10:30pm. LAO/THAI.

Delicately fragrant curries and carefully prepared stir-fries and soups are served in this humble brick restaurant. Thai food is always a sure bet in Australia, and this place is no exception. Try the pad gratium (tender beef fried in a complex garlic sauce with crisp vegetables); one of the many seafood dishes, such as the mixed seafood cooked in basil and a hint of chili; or one of the plentiful vegetarian choices. As with many Asian restaurants, the wine list is unremarkable, so bring your own. Licensed and BYO.

✪ **Tim's Surf & Turf.** Upstairs, Trinity Wharf 28–34 Wharf St (end of Abbott St.). ☎ **07/4031 6866.** Reservations accepted only for groups of 8 more. Main courses A$7.15–$20.90 (U.S.$4.65–$13.59); many dishes under A$13 (U.S.$8.45); kids menu A$3.50–$4.50 (U.S.$2.28–$2.93). No credit cards. Daily noon–2:30pm and 5:30–9:30pm. STEAK/SEAFOOD.

For huge hearty meals at unbeatable prices, you can't go wrong at this cheerful chain outlet overlooking Trinity Inlet. The seafood platters, oysters, thick grain-fed steaks, pastas, roasts, quiche, and other simple fare are all cooked with skill.

Worth a Splurge
✪ **Fishlips Bar & Bistro.** 228 Sheridan St. (between Charles and McKenzie sts.) ☎ **07/4041 1700.** Reservations recommended. Main courses A$17.50–$31 (U.S.$11.38–$20.15); most dishes less than A$22 (U.S.$14.30). AE, BC, DC, JCB, MC, V. Fri noon–2:30pm; daily 6pm–late. MOD OZ SEAFOOD.

Ask locals where they go for seafood—as opposed to where they send tourists—and they direct you to this 1920s bluebird-blue shack about 2 kilometers (1¼ miles) from town. Chef Ian Candy is renowned for thinking up new ways to present seafood and cooking it with flair. Appetizers might be a salad of reef fish, squid, mussels, and prawns wok-tossed on greens with cracked bugs (a kind of lobster, not an insect). The popular local barramundi, or "barra," usually shows up in two incarnations, maybe simply beer-battered with rough-cut chips (fries) and fresh tartar sauce, or dressed up tandoori-style with cucumber, yogurt, and tomato risotto. There are non-seafood options as well, such as wok-tossed crocodile with pumpkin seed salsa. There's a vegetarian choice on every menu, too. How nice to see that 30-odd wines on the wine list come by the glass. Dine in the pretty blue-and-yellow interior, complete with portholes, or on the deck out front decorated with bright blue pots and palm trees. It's licensed Sunday through Thursday, and BYO wine only (no BYO beer or spirits).

On the Northern Beaches
Colonies. Upstairs in Paradise Village shopping center, Williams Esplanade, Palm Cove. ☎ **07/4055 3058.** Reservations recommended at dinner. Main courses A$18.50–$23.90 (U.S.$12.03–$15.54). Daily 7:30am–10:30pm. Closed part of February and/or March. AE, BC, DC, MC, V. Bus: 1, 1B, 1X, 2X, N. MOD OZ.

It may not have the ocean frontage of the grander restaurants along Williams Esplanade, but you are within earshot of the waves on the verandah of this cheery aerie upstairs behind a seafront building. The atmosphere is simple enough for a morning coffee, and special enough at night for a full-fledged dinner of mussels sautéed in

R.S.L. (Returned Services League) Clubs are great places for a cheap feed. Almost all Queensland towns have an R.S.L. Club and they all have restaurants with main courses usually priced at under A$15 (U.S.$9.75). The food is pretty basic—roasts, pastas and so on—and the decor usually modest. And if you fancy a flutter after your meal, most of them also have gaming machines and Keno. As they're clubs, you have to sign in at the door, but visitors are welcome.

white wine, followed by peppered lamb fillet in red wine and herbs with a port mint glaze. The long menu includes loads of inexpensive choices at lunch and dinner: pastas, vegetable soups, green chicken curry, and hot scones with bacon and melted cheese. The extra-yummy desserts include banana splits and "spacacamino," vanilla ice cream dressed with Scotch whisky and freshly ground coffee beans. Licensed and BYO.

Mezza Luna Trattoria. 77 Vasey Esplanade, Trinity Beach. ☎ **07/4055 6958.** Pizzas A$12.50–$18.50 (U.S.$8.13–$12.03). Main courses A$15.50–$19.50 (U.S.$10.08–$12.68). AE, BC, DC, MC, V. Daily 11am–10pm. PIZZA.

It's no surprise that this place has been voted the best pizza joint in Queensland. Now the humble pizza place has been joined by a full-blown trattoria with a range of other dishes, but the pizzas are still as good. Try the Mezza Luna (tomato, mozzarella, Italian ham, mushroom, marinated artichoke, olives and oregano) or the Gamberi (local prawns, mozzarella, onion and fresh basil on a mango base). There are also more traditional toppings, as well as linguini, spaghetti and lamb, chicken and fish dishes. BYO (corkage A$1.50/U.S.98¢ per person).

Worth a Splurge

Far Horizons. At the Angsana resort, 1 Veivers Rd. (southern end of Williams Esplanade), Palm Cove. ☎ **07/4055 3000.** Reservations recommended. Main courses A$20.50–$28.50 (U.S.$13.33–$18.53). AE, BC, DC, JCB, MC, V. Daily 6:30–midnight (last orders at 9:30pm). Bus: 1, 1B, 1X, 2X, N. MOD OZ.

You are just yards from the beach at this pleasant restaurant within the resort. The laid-back fine-dining fare includes plenty of fresh seafood. One of the favorites is bug-tails panfried with steamed bok choy and sweet soya beurre blanc. The restaurant sometimes sets up dining on the lawn among the palm trees beside the beach. The service is relaxed and friendly and the crowd is a mix of hotel guests from this and other nearby resorts. On Friday and Saturday nights, a guitarist plays in the cocktail bar.

3 Port Douglas, Daintree & the Cape Tribulation Area

Port Douglas 67km (40 miles) N of Cairns; Mossman 19km (11½ miles) N of Port Douglas; Daintree 49km (29½ miles) N of Port Douglas; Cape Tribulation 34km (20½ miles) N of Daintree

The tiny fishing village of ✪ **Port Douglas** is where "the rainforest meets the reef." The Daintree Rain Forest and the Great Barrier Reef, two great wonders of the natural world, are right next to each other. Just over an hour's drive from Cairns, through rain forest and along the sea, Port Douglas may be a one-horse town, but its main street is lined with stylish shops and trendy restaurants, and its beautiful ✪ **Four Mile Beach** is not to be missed.

Folks often base themselves in "Port," as the locals call it, because they like the peaceful rural surroundings, the uncrowded beach, and the charmed absence of tacky development (so far, anyway). Don't think you will be isolated if you stay here—many reef and rain-forest tours originate in Port Douglas and many of the tours discussed in the Cairns section earlier in this chapter pick up from Port Douglas.

Daintree National Park lies just north of Port Douglas; just north of that is Cape Tribulation National Park, another wild rain forest with hilly headlands down to the sea. Exploring these national parks is easy on a 4WD day safari from Port Douglas.

ESSENTIALS

GETTING THERE Port Douglas is a scenic 65-minute drive from Cairns, in part along a narrow twisty road that skirts the coast. Take Sheridan Street north out of the city as it becomes the Captain Cook Highway; stay on the highway and follow the signs to Mossman and Mareeba until you reach the Port Douglas turnoff on your right.

The cheapest way to get to Port Douglas is also the most glamorous, on the giant **Quicksilver *Wavepiercer*** (☎ 07/4099 5500) catamarans along the green hilly coastline. They depart Marlin Marina in Cairns at 8am, Palm Cove jetty at 8:30am, and arrive in Port Douglas at 9:30am. You can stay onboard and go straight to the Great Barrier Reef for the day if you like. Transfers from Cairns are A$22 (U.S.$14.30) one-way, A$32 (U.S.$20.80) round-trip, half price for kids ages 4 to 14.

A one-way ticket aboard **Coral Coaches** (☎ 07/4031 7577) to Port Douglas hotels is A$20.50 (U.S.$13.33) from Cairns city hotels, or A$25 (U.S.$16.25) from the Cairns airport. Fares for children 14 and under are half price. The coaches meet all major flights between 6am and 8:15pm. It's not strictly necessary, but it's a good idea to book; five buses per day are reservations only.

VISITOR INFORMATION Write to the **Port Douglas Daintree Tourism Association,** PO Box 511, Port Douglas, QLD 4871 (☎ 07/4099 4588;). They don't have an office in Port Douglas. Instead, visitors should visit one of several private tour information and booking centers in town. One of the biggest and most centrally located is the **Port Douglas Tourist Information Centre,** 23 Macrossan St. (☎ 07/4099 5599), open from 7:30am to 6pm or later daily.

GETTING AROUND Of the major rental car companies, only **Budget** (☎ 07/4099 4690) and **Avis** (☎ 07/4099 4331) have offices in Port Douglas. Check out the good deals from the local companies, including **Port Douglas Car Rental** (☎ 07/4098 5898) and **Crocodile Car Rentals** (☎ 07/4099 5555). All rent 4WDs as well as regular vehicles, and these are needed if you plan to drive to Cape Tribulation.

Local bus company **Coral Coaches** (☎ 07/4099 5351) makes a circuit of town that stops at most places you will want to visit, such as the Rainforest Habitat, Four Mile Beach, and Marina Mirage. Fares range from A$1.30 to $3.20 (U.S.85¢–$2.08). The bus starts at 7:30am and runs hourly until 9am, then half hourly until midnight.

Safety Tips

The **tap water** is *not* safe for drinking in Port Douglas. Most hotels provide free bottled water.

Deadly marine stingers (jellyfish) infest the water from October to May; swim only in areas partitioned off by stinger nets during those months.

Port Douglas, Daintree & Cape Tribulation

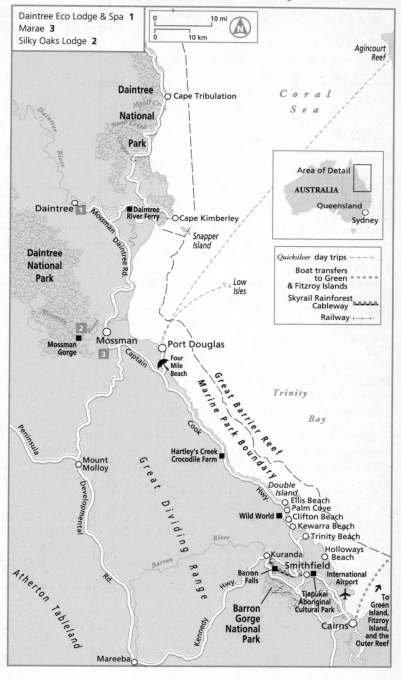

Daintree Eco Lodge & Spa **1**
Marae **3**
Silky Oaks Lodge **2**

0 _____ 10 mi
0 _____ 10 km

Coral Sea

Daintree

Cape Tribulation

National

Myall Cr.

Noah Creek

Park

Area of Detail

AUSTRALIA

Queensland

Sydney

Daintree **1**

Daintree River Ferry

Cape Kimberley

Mossman Daintree Rd.

Daintree River

Snapper Island

Daintree National Park

Quicksilver day trips - - -

Boat transfers to Green & Fitzroy Islands

Skyrail Rainforest Cableway

Railway

Low Isles

Mossman River

2

Mossman

3

Mossman Gorge

Port Douglas

Four Mile Beach

Captain

Great Barrier Reef

Marine Park Boundary

Trinity Bay

Cook

Peninsula

Mount Molloy

Hartley's Creek Crocodile Farm

Double Island

Developmental

Great Dividing Range

Ellis Beach
Palm Cove
Clifton Beach
Wild World
Kewarra Beach
Trinity Beach

River

Barron River

Holloways Beach

Kuranda

Smithfield

Hwy.

Barron Falls

International Airport

Atherton Tableland

Rd.

Kennedy Hwy.

Tjapukai Aboriginal Cultural Park

Barron Gorge National Park

Cairns

To Green Island, Fitzroy Island, and the Outer Reef

Mareeba

A good way to get around the town's flat streets is by **bike. Port Douglas Bike Hire** (☎ **07/4099 5799**) at 40–42 Macrossan Street (opposite Westpac Bank) rents bikes for A$14 (U.S.$9.10) for 24 hours. The shop is open 9am to 5pm.

If you need a taxi, call **Port Douglas Taxis** (☎ **07/4099 5345**).

WHAT TO SEE & DO

EXPLORING THE GREAT BARRIER REEF   For details on diving and snorkeling the outer Great Barrier Reef from Port Douglas, see the "Exploring the Great Barrier Reef" section earlier in this chapter.

Another way to spend a pleasant day on the Great Barrier Reef, closer to shore, is to visit the **Low Isles** 15 kilometers (9 miles) northeast of Port Douglas. There is nothing to the isles—just 3.75-acre coral cay specks of lush vegetation surrounded by white sand and 55 acres of coral—which is what makes them so appealing.

The trip aboard the 30-meter (98-ft.) luxury sailing catamaran *Wavedancer* (☎ **07/4099 5500**), is A $100 (U.S.$65) per adult, kids 4 to 14 half price, and families A$250 (U.S.$162.50) You can make an introductory scuba dive for an extra A$87 (U.S.$56.55) per person. The *Wavepiercer* departs Marlin Marina in Cairns at 8am and Palm Cove Jetty on the northern beaches at 8:30am to connect with *Wavedancer* departures from Port Douglas. The company picks you up free from your hotel.

Snorkeling boat *Wavelength* (☎ **07/4099 5031**) does a half-day trip to the Low Isles for just A$83 (U.S.$53.95) for adults, A$60 (U.S.$39) for children 2 to 12, or A$223 (U.S.$144.95) for a family. The trip incorporates a guided beach walk and a snorkeling tour with a marine biologist and includes snorkel gear and transfers from your hotel. Both beginners and experienced snorkelers will like this trip. It departs Wednesday and Saturday from the Wavelength jetty in Wharf Street at 8:30am and returns at 1pm.

EXPLORING DAINTREE & CAPE TRIBULATION   Almost everyone who comes to Port Douglas takes a guided 4WD day trip into the Daintree and Cape Tribulation rain forests. Although they are referred to as two separate national parks, the forests that cover them merge into one.

You can rent a 4WD and explore on your own (that is the cheapest option if you're traveling in a group of two or more), but you won't understand much about what you are seeing unless you have a guide to interpret it for you. Most companies basically cover the same territory and sights, including a one-hour Daintree River cruise to spot crocs, a visit to the lovely **Marrdja Botanical Walk,** a stroll along an isolated beach, lunch at a pretty spot somewhere in the forest, and a visit to Mossman Gorge. Some tours also go to the picturesque **Bloomfield Falls** in Cape Tribulation National Park. Expect to pay about A$110 (U.S.$71.50) per adult and about A$75 (U.S.$48.75) per child. Trips that include Bloomfield Falls are about A$30 (U.S.$19.50) more. A plethora of tour operators offers such trips. Among the more established are **Trek North Safaris** (☎ 07/4051 4328), **BTS Tours** (☎ **07/4099 5665**), and **De Luxe Safaris** (☎ **07/4098 2097**). Some tour operators pay tour desks a commission to recommend their tours, but those tours may not necessarily be the best for your needs. Take tour desks' recommendations with a grain of salt, and try to get a recommendation from other travelers. You may not see too much wildlife, as rain forest animals are either shy, camouflaged, nocturnal, or all three! Most 4WD tours will pick you up in Port Douglas at no charge (from Cairns and the northern beaches you usually have to pay a small fee). Floods and swollen creeks can quash your plans to explore the Daintree in the Wet Season (Dec–Mar or Apr), so keep your plans flexible then.

The Land that Time Forgot

The World Heritage–listed Daintree Rainforest has remained largely unchanged over the past 110 million years. It is home to rare plants that provide key links in the evolution story. In the 140,000-acre **Daintree National Park** you will find cycads, dinosaur trees, fan palms, giant strangler figs, and epiphytes like the basket fern, staghorn, and elkhorn. Nighttime croc-spotting tours on the Daintree River vie for popularity with early morning cruises to see the rich bird life. Pythons, lizards, frogs, and electric blue Ulysses butterflies attract photographers, and sport fishermen come here to do battle with the big barramundi.

If your chosen safari does not visit **Mossman Gorge,** 21 kilometers (12½ miles) northwest of Port Douglas near the sugar town of Mossman, try to get there on your own. The gushing river tumbling over boulders, and the short forest walks are magical. (Don't climb on the rocks or enter the river, as strong currents are dangerous and have claimed at least one life in recent years). **Coral Coaches** (☎ 07/ 4099 5351) makes runs to the gorge from Port Douglas about 10 times a day for A$22 (U.S.$14.30) round-trip. Pack a picnic and make a pleasant couple of hours of it.

Most 4WD Daintree tours include a 1-hour cruise on the ✪ **Daintree River,** but if yours doesn't, or you want more time on the river, cruises are available on a variety of boats, from open-sided "river trains" to small fishing boats. One of the best is offered by Dan Irby's **Mangrove Adventures** (☎ 07/4090 7017), whose small open boat can get up side creeks the bigger boats can't. Dan is a wildlife artist and photographer; he takes no more than 10 people at a time on 2-, 3- and 4-hour cruises. Chances are you will spot lots of fascinating wildlife on his 2-hour night cruise. A 2-hour trip costs A$38.50 (U.S.$25.03). Night trips depart from the **Daintree Eco Lodge,** 20 Mossman Daintree Rd., 4 kilometers (2½ miles) south of Daintree village; day trips leave from the Daintree River ferry crossing. Take the Captain Cook Highway north to Mossman, where it becomes the Mossman Daintree Road, and follow it for 24 kilometers (15½ miles) to the posted turnoff for the ferry on your right. The ferry is 5 kilometers (3 miles) from there. You will need a car to get there.

Bird-watchers love the Wet Tropics rain forests of which the Daintree and Cape Tribulation national parks are part. More than half of Australia's bird species have been recorded within 200 kilometers (120 miles) of this area. **Fine Feather Tours** (☎ 07/ 4094 1199) offers a full-day bird-watching safari from the Wet Tropics to the Outback for A$145 (U.S.$94.25), and a cruise on the Daintree River for A$90 (U.S.$58.50).

✪ **Rainforest Habitat wildlife sanctuary** (☎ 07/4099 3235) is a great place to see the animals too shy to be spotted in the wild. Here, 150 species from the Wet Tropics are gathered in one place. You can see saltwater and freshwater crocodiles, feed kangaroos, and have your photo taken beside (but not holding) a koala (from 10 to 11am and 3 to 4pm, for a donation). The highlight is the walk-through aviary, which houses 70 Wet Tropics bird species. You'll get the most out of your visit if you take one of the excellent free guided tours that leave every hour on the hour between 9am and 3pm. Rainforest Habitat is located on Port Douglas Road at the turnoff from the Captain Cook Highway. It's open daily from 8am to 5:30pm (last entry at 4:30pm); admission is A$18 (U.S.$11.70) for adults, A$16.20 (U.S.$10.53) seniors and students, A$9 (U.S.$5.85) for kids 4 to 14. Second child admitted free with a family. Between 8am and 11am, the park serves a champagne buffet breakfast for A$34 (U.S.$22.10) for adults and A$17 (U.S.$11.05) for kids, including admission. Allow 2 hours here.

One company that shows you plenty of rainforest creatures in the wild is **Wait-A-While Environmental Tours** (☎ 07/4033 1153) whose rainforest wildlife-spotting walks are described in "Exploring the Wet Tropics," in the Cairns section earlier in this chapter. Port Douglas visitors can join their Daintree tour, which departs at 3pm Monday, Wednesday, and Thursday, and gets back around midnight or 1am; the tour costs A$121 (U.S.$78.65) for adults, A$88 (U.S.$57.20) for kids under 15.

DISCOVERING ABORIGINAL CULTURE In addition to **Native Guide Safari Tours** (see "Exploring the Daintree & Cape Tribulation," above), the native KuKu-Yalanji tribe will teach you about bush medicines and foods, Dreamtime legends, and the sacred sites their families have called home for tens of thousands of years. ✪ **KuKu-Yalanji Dreamtime Tours** (☎ 07/4098 1305) offers a 1-hour guided walk through the forest to see cave paintings and sites sacred to the tribe; the tour is followed by a Dreamtime story over billy tea and damper in a bark warun (a kind of shelter). You can buy artifacts from the tribe's information center, gift shop, and art gallery. The tours depart Monday through Friday at 10am, 11:30am, 1pm, and 2:30pm from the Kuku-Yalangi community on the road to Mossman Gorge (1km/½ mile before you reach the Gorge parking lot). Tours cost A$15 (U.S.$9.75) for adults, A$12 (U.S.$7.80) for seniors and A$7.50 (U.S.$4.88) for children.

Hazel Douglas of ✪ **Native Guide Safari Tours** (☎ 07/4098 2206; www.native guidesafaritours.com.au) runs an 4WD tour of the rain forest from an Aboriginal perspective. Hazel is an Aboriginal who grew up in a tribal lifestyle in the Daintree. She imparts her knowledge of the plants, animals, Dreamtime myths, and Aboriginal history on a full-day tour departing at 9:15am from your Port Douglas hotel. Passengers from Cairns transfer up on the Quicksilver catamaran and return either by coach (northern beaches) or catamaran (Cairns city). The trip costs A$120 (U.S.$78) for adults and A$80 (U.S.$52) for children ages 3 to 14 from Port Douglas, and A$10 (U.S.$6.50) extra from Cairns or the northern beaches.

OUTDOOR ACTIVITIES

Some companies in Cairns that offer outdoor activities will provide inexpensive or free pick-ups from Port Douglas hotels. See "White-Water Rafting & Other Outdoor Activities" in the Cairns section above for details.

The cheapest and best outdoor activity in Port Douglas, however, is to do absolutely nothing but laze on spectacular ✪ **Four Mile Beach.** From May to September the water is stinger-free. From October to April, you should swim only in the area enclosed by the stinger safety net. **Get High Parafly** (☎ 07/4099 6366) offers parasailing, jet skiing, inflatable tube rides, waterskiing, and other water sports on the beach. Expect to pay around A$30 to $60 (U.S.$19.50–$39) for each activity. A boat runs every hour on the hour between 9am and 5pm from the booking office at Berth C4 at Marina Mirage to the company's beach location at Four Mile Beach.

Visitor greens fees at the championship **Sheraton Mirage golf course** on Port Douglas Road are a steep A$135 (U.S.$87.50) for 18 holes. Whacking a ball on the hotel's aquatic driving range is a more manageable A$6 (U.S.$3.90) for a small bucket of balls, A$12 (U.S.$7.80) for a big one, plus A$2 (U.S.$1.30) for club rental. Contact the Pro Shop (☎ 07/4099 5537). An 18-hole round on the humbler but equally

---

> **The Secret of the Seasons**
>
> High season in Port Douglas is generally from June 1 through October 31.

picturesque 72 par public course at the **Mossman Golf Club,** Newell Beach Road, Mossman (☎ **07/ 4098 2089)** is A$25 (U.S.$16.25), or A$15 (U.S.$9.75) for nine holes.

Mowbray Valley Trail Rides (☎ **07/4099 3268),** located 13 kilometers (8 miles) inland, offers half-day rides through rain forest and sugarcane fields to Collards Falls, or to a swimming hole in the Hidden Valley, for A$60 (U.S.$39). It also runs full-day trips along the Bump Track, followed by a dip in a rain-forest pool and barbecue at Mowbray Falls. Transfers from Port Douglas hotels are included. Transfers from Cairns are A$15 (U.S.$9.75) per person. **Wonga Beach Trail Rides** (☎ **07/4098 7583)** does 3-hour rides through the rain forest and along Wonga Beach, 35 minutes north of Port Douglas, for A$65 (U.S.$42.25), including transfers from Port Douglas.

Bike 'n' Hike (☎ **07/4099 4650** for the booking agent) takes small groups biking, hiking, and swimming in lagoons in the Hidden Valley in the rain forest near Port Douglas. You don't need to be a strong cyclist to take part. Half-day tours cost A$60 (U.S.$39). Full-day tours cost A$82 (U.S.$53). Pickups from Port Douglas hotels, a mountain bike, snack, drinks (lunch on the full-day trip) are included. Transfers from Cairns and Palm Cove are extra. Experienced mountain bikers can descend the steep 14-kilometer (8½-mile) Bump Track through dense rain forest from the top of the Great Dividing Range on a half-day trip designed for a maximum of four riders.

WHERE TO STAY

Although there are plenty of ritzy hotels and resorts in Port Douglas, you can find good, inexpensive places. Many of the value-for-money choices are holiday apartments with kitchens (you can save money on meals). Booking agent **Port Douglas Accommodation** (☎ **1800/645 566** in Australia, or 07/4099 4488; fax 07/4099 4455; www.portdouglasaccom.com.au) represents several affordable apartments.

✪ **Archipelago Studio Apartments.** 72 Macrossan St., Port Douglas, QLD 4871. ☎ **07/ 4099 5387.** Fax 07/4099 4847. www.archipelago.com.au/. archipelago@portdouglas.tnq. com.au. 21 units (with shower only). A/C TV TEL. High season A$109–$164 (U.S.$70.85–$106.60) double; low season A$87–$135 (U.S.$56.55–$87.75) double. Extra person A$15 (U.S.$9.75). BC, MC, V. Free parking. No children allowed.

You won't find a friendlier or more convenient place in Port Douglas than these apartments 10 seconds from the beach and a 10-minute walk from town. The apartments are on the small side (most suit only three people, max), but are well cared for with neatly painted walls, cane furniture, and bright bedcovers. All have a kitchenette and compact, tiled bathrooms. You can opt for a tiny Garden apartment with a patio; or upgrade to a Balcony or Seaview apartment, a bit larger, with private balconies. Seaview apartments are roomy and have side-on views along Four Mile Beach. Towels are changed daily and linen weekly, but general servicing will cost you A$20 (U.S.$13) extra. There's a saltwater pool with a Jacuzzi, sundeck, and barbecue; a laundry with iron and ironing board; and hair dryers at the front desk. The hospitable proprietor, Wolfgang Klein, will advise you on the best tours and make your bookings.

Pelican Inn. 123 Davidson St., Port Douglas, QLD 4871. ☎ **07/4099 5266.** Fax 07/4099 5821. www.pelican-inn.com.au. reservations@pelican-inn.com.au. 17 units. A/C MINIBAR TV TEL. High season A$110 (U.S.$71.50) double; low season A$99 (U.S.$64.35) double. Extra person A$15 (U.S.$9.75); children 3–12 A$5 (U.S.$3.25). Cribs A$5 (U.S.$3.25). AE, BC, DC, MC, V.

This neatly maintained little Flag motel is just a 10-minute stroll from town. Each good-sized, spick-and-span room has freshly painted walls, a microwave, toaster, and a sink. The bathrooms are a little old but have plenty of counter space and nice thick towels. Hair dryers are available from the front desk, and an iron and ironing board are in the laundry. The motel's spacious and hip Mediterranean restaurant is popular with locals. The pool is lovely, but not very private. Four Mile Beach a short stroll away (in stinger season, it's about a 20-minute walk to the stinger net).

Port Douglas Terrace. 17 The Esplanade, Port Douglas, QLD 4871. ☎ **1800/621 195** in Australia, or 07/4099 5397. Fax 07/4099 5206. www.portdouglasbeachfront.com.au. beaches@portdouglasterrace.com.au.17 units (some with shower only). A/C TV TEL. High season A$195 (U.S.$126.75) 1-bedroom beachfront apt; A$160 (U.S.$104) 1-bedroom garden apt; A$230 (U.S.$149.50) 2-bedroom beachfront apt; A$160 (U.S.$104) 2-bedroom garden apt; A$240 (U.S.$156) 2-bedroom penthouse. Low season A$145 (U.S.$94.45) 1-bedroom beachfront apt; A$165 (U.S.$107.25) 2-bedroom beachfront apt; A$120 (U.S.$78) 2-bedroom garden apt; A$175 (U.S.$113.75) 2-bedroom penthouse. Extra person A$25 (U.S.$16.25). A$6 (U.S.$3.90) crib. AE, BC, DC, JCB, MC, V. Free parking. Transfers from Cairns airport are A$25 (U.S.$16.25) each way.

The best-value beachfront accommodations in town, especially in low season, are these clean, quiet units in this low-rise complex on Four Mile Beach, a short walk from town. The apartments are airy and respectably furnished with an open-plan kitchen (some with dishwashers), tiny but up-to-date bathrooms with hair dryers, laundry facilities, cool tile floors, balconies, and VCRs. All are serviced weekly. Room 4 has a garden patio as well as sea views. The roomier penthouses (rooms 11 and 14) have rooftop living areas overlooking the sea and larger bathrooms. If you don't mind missing out on a view, the two-bedroom units in the gardens at the rear are a little darker but also cheaper and nice enough with cane furniture and a garden patio. A lovely saltwater pool is tucked among the palms, and there's a tennis court.

✪ **Port O'Call Lodge.** Port St. at Craven Close, Port Douglas, QLD 4871. ☎ **1800/ 892 800** in Australia or 07/4099 5422. Fax 07/4099 5495. 28 units (all with shower only). High season (June–Sept) A$85–$95 (U.S.$55.25–$61.75) double; low season (Nov–April) A$65–$75 (U.S.$42.25–$48.75) double. Additional person A$11 (U.S.$7.15). A$21 (U.S.$13.65) dorm bed (A$18/U.S.$11.70 for YHA/Hostelling International members). Children under 3 free in parents' room. BC, MC, V. Free minibus to and from Cairns Mon, Wed, and Sat. Free parking.

There's a communal feeling to this modest motel, on a suburban street a 10-minute walk from town. Backpackers, families, and anyone on a budget seems to treat it like a second home, swapping travel stories as they cook up a meal in the group kitchen and dining room. The rooms are light and fresh with tile floors, loads of luggage and bench space, air-conditioning, and small patios. The compact bathrooms are efficiently laid out with old but neat fixtures (BYO hair dryer). The deluxe rooms have a TV, clock radio, tea and coffee facilities, and a minifridge. The dorm rooms have private bathrooms and no more than five beds and/or bunks. At night the poolside bistro is the place to be (see "Where to Dine," below). Other facilities include board games, pay phone, Internet access, guest safe, and a kiosk. The friendly desk staff is happy to make tour recommendations and bookings.

Money-Saving Tip

Another accommodation option is camping. You will find both campsites and air-conditioned self-contained park cabins at many prime locations around the state. Check the **Q-Parks website** (www.qparks.asn.au) for a full list of accredited parks which can offer big savings.

Worth a Splurge:
Restaurants in the Rain Forest

Dining in the rain forest, surrounded by ferns, burbling brooks, and birdsong, is a great experience. At **Baaru House restaurant,** at the luxury Daintree Eco Lodge, 20 Mossman Daintree Rd. (☎ **07/4098 6100**), 4 kilometers (2½ miles) south of Daintree village, which is 49 kilometers (30 miles) north of Port Douglas, you dine in an airy timber pole house surrounded by the sounds of crickets, frogs, birds, and rushing water. Hearty and delicious, main courses cost up to A$30 (U.S.$19.50). It's open daily 7 to 10am, noon to 2pm, and 6pm to 9pm.

At the ✪ **Tree House Restaurant** at Silky Oaks Lodge (☎ **07/4098 1666**), 7 kilometers (4 miles) west of Mossman, which is 19 kilometers (11½ miles) north of Port Douglas, you dine on upscale modern Australian fare at polished timber tables on a verandah above the Mossman River. It's open all day, serving meals from 7 to 10am, noon to 2:30pm, and 6 to 9pm. Breakfasts are A$15 (U.S.$9.75) continental or A$25 (U.S.$16.25) full. Main courses are A$16.50 to $19.50 (U.S.$10.73–$12.68) at lunch, A$19.50 to $25 (U.S.$12.68–$16.25) at dinner. Tea is served from 2:30 to 5pm. Bring your swimsuit and take a dip in the river beforehand. Take the Captain Cook Highway about 3 kilometers (2 miles) past Mossman and turn left into Finlayvale Road at the small Silky Oaks Lodge sign. Take care, as the road is a narrow country lane.

You don't have to leave Port Douglas to eat in the trees. **Treetops** at the Radisson Treetops Resort, Port Douglas Road (☎ **07/4030 4333**), has five open-sided tree houses high in the rain forest canopy overlooking the pool. Each has about four tables. The atmosphere is magical as the sophisticated dishes, including a fair nod to seafood, are cooked in front of your eyes over an open flame. Expect to pay about A$60 (U.S.$39) per person for a three-course *table d'haute* menu. Hours are seasonal, so check ahead. It is usually open for dinner only.

A LUXURY B&B HIDEAWAY IN THE COUNTRY

✪ **Marae.** Lot 1, Ponzo Rd., Shannonvale (P.O. Box 133, Port Douglas, QLD 4871). ☎ **07/4098 4900.** Fax 07/4098 4099. www.marae.com.au. marae@internetnorth.com.au,. 3 bedrooms (2 with shower only). A/C, TV. A$100 (U.S.$65) double. Minimum 2-night stay. Rates include full breakfast. BC, MC, V. From Port Douglas take Captain Cook Hwy. toward Mossman for 10km (6 miles), turn left onto Mt. Molloy turnoff for 1km (½ mile), then turn right onto Ponzo Rd. for 2km (1¼ mile); Marae's driveway is on your left. You need your own transport. No children under 13 allowed.

Your hostess Andy Morris has turned her stunning timber home on a rural hillside 15 kilometers (9 miles) from Port Douglas, into a soothing retreat. The rustic-meets-sleek contemporary bedrooms have white mosquito nets and smart linens on timber beds, and elegant bathrooms with hair dryers. The downstairs room opens onto a plunge pool overlooking the valley. Wallabies and bandicoots feed in the garden, kingfishers and honey eaters use the pool, and butterflies are everywhere. You can laze on the two decks, or wander the rain-forest trails of Mossman Gorge just a few miles away.

WHERE TO DINE IN PORT DOUGLAS

A good place to chill out by the water over an inexpensive meal is the **Port Douglas & District Combined Club,** 7 Ashford St. (☎ **07/4099 5553**). It's a humble corrugated iron shed with pool tables and slot machines, but the food is remarkably good, and it's got the same water views of Dickson Inlet as the pricier On the Inlet down the road (see below). It's open 10am to 10pm daily, for meals 12:30 to 2pm and 5:30 to 8:30pm.

Court House Hotel. Macrossan St. at Wharf St. ☎ **07/4099 5181.** Daily 11:30am–2pm and 5:30–9pm. PUB GRUB.

You won't find a cooler or more relaxing spot to enjoy a meal than under the giant mango tree in the courtyard of this 120-year old pub. Order at the counter, buy your drinks inside at the bar, and collect your meal when your number is called. Toasted sandwiches, porterhouse steaks with red wine butter, fish burgers, and Thai red chicken curry is what you can expect, cooked well and in big servings, too. They do kids' meals too. The ambience is unpretentious, and the place is famed for its live entertainment. If you happen to be here on July 4, you'll see why the American Independence Day party is one of the highlights of the social calendar in "Port" year after year.

On the Inlet. 3 Inlet St. ☎ **07/4099 5255.** Reservations recommended in high season. Main courses A$16–$25 (U.S.$10.40–$16.25). AE, BC, DC, JCB, MC, V. Daily noon–3:30pm; 5:30pm–late Happy hour with snacks 4–6pm. SEAFOOD.

No-nonsense seafood and a no-fuss atmosphere make this waterside venue popular with the locals; just plastic chairs on a shady deck with nice views. Kick back over a long lunch, which might include fried calamari, followed by a stack of chilled Moreton Bay bugs. Or try the sizzling garlic prawns for an appetizer and a seafood plate of fried fish, calamari, prawns, scallops, and fries for a main course. From the Sunset Bar you can watch stingrays and groupers feed below. A take-out section up front serves fish-and-chips. The restaurant doubles as a seafood wholesaler, so you know it's fresh.

Port O' Call Bistro. Port St. at Craven Close. ☎ **07/4099 5422.** Main courses A$8.50–$11.50 (U.S.$5.53–$7.48). Open 6–9pm. Happy hour 5–7pm. Bar opens 4pm. BC, MC, V.

Locals patronize this casual poolside bistro and bar at the Port O' Call Lodge (see "Where to Stay" above) almost as often as guests do, because it offers good food in hearty portions at painless prices. In the glow of the torches around the pool, the atmosphere is fun and friendly. Tuesday night is the popular curry night with little over A$10 (U.S.$6.50), and Sunday is roast night.

✪ **Salsa Bar & Grill.** 38 Macrossan St. ☎ **07/4099 4922.** Reservations recommended. Main courses A$19–$22.50 (U.S.$12.35–$14.63). AE, BC, DC, JCB, MC, V. Mon–Sat noon–late; Sun 7:30am–late. MOD OZ/CALIFORNIAN.

First the buzzing crowds dining on the street catch your eye. Then the prices grab you. Then you taste the terrific food, and know why locals dig this groovy trendsetter. Try the bacon and beef burger with tomato chili jam, or the grilled barramundi with citrus beurre blanc. By day the tablecloths are brown paper; at night the white cloths

Port Douglas After Dark

Locals meet at the 120-year-old **Court House Hotel** (☎ 07/ 4099 5181) at the west end of Macrossan Street at Wharf Street. It might appear a bit dodgy, but you will find the natives friendly. Live bands play Monday, Friday, and Saturday nights and Sunday afternoon. The pub is open daily 10am until midnight (until 9pm Sunday).

come out. There's always lounge music playing, and the contemporary bar next door is a good place for a pre- or post-dinner cocktail.

WORTH A SPLURGE

✪ **Nautilus.** 17 Murphy St. (entry also from Macrossan St.), Port Douglas. ☎ **07/4099 5330.** Reservations recommended. Main courses A$25.90–$36 (U.S.$16.85–$23). AE, BC, DC, JCB, MC, V. Daily 6:30pm–late. TROPICAL/SEAFOOD.

The Clintons (Bill and Hillary) dined here in 1996 and by all accounts loved it. The restaurant, keeping the locals happy since 1953, is extremely popular, with an appealing outdoor setting where you can dine under palm trees and stars and a reputation for cleverly cooked seafood. Melbourne-trained chef Gregory Bull makes the most of local produce and seafood, serving up delights like the grilled yellowfin tuna on salt-cod mash and drizzled with green olive tapenade. Or you may prefer to go for the fresh mud crab, barramundi, or the barbecue tiger prawns. There are plenty of choices for non-seafood eaters, too. If you want a meal fit for a president, you can order what he ordered-a fresh seafood tapas plate, followed by deep-fried coral trout with sweet chili sauce and Asian spices, and rounded off with a hot mango soufflé.

4 The North Coast: Mission Beach, Townsville & the Islands

For years the lovely town of ✪ **Mission Beach** was a well-kept secret. Farmers retired here; then those who liked to drop out and chill out discovered it; today, it's a petite, prosperous, and stunningly pretty rain forest town. The beach is one of the most gorgeous in Australia, a long white strip fringed with dense tangled vine forests, the only surviving lowlands rain forest in the Australian tropics. It is also one of the least crowded and least spoiled.

The nearby **Tully River** is the white-water rafting capital of Australia (although the folks on the Nymboida River in New South Wales might argue about that). Thrill-seekers can also bungee jump and tandem skydive when they're not rushing down the rapids between lush rain-forest banks.

From Mission Beach it's a matter of minutes in a ferry to **Dunk Island,** a resort island that welcomes day-trippers. You can even kayak there from the mainland. Mission Beach is closer to the Great Barrier Reef than any other point on the coast: just an hour; and cruise boats depart daily from the jetty, stopping en route at Dunk Island.

A few hours' drive south brings you to Townsville, also a gateway to the Great Barrier Reef, but more important to visitors, a gateway to **Magnetic Island,** a picturesque, laid-back haven for the flip-flop and water sports crowd.

MISSION BEACH: THE CASSOWARY COAST

140km (84 miles) S of Cairns; 240km (144 miles) N of Townsville

Tucked off the Bruce Highway, the exquisite township of Mission Beach has managed to duck the tourist hordes. It's a conglomeration of four beachfront towns: South Mission Beach, Wongaling Beach, Mission Beach proper, and Bingil Bay. Most commercial activity revolves around the small nucleus of shops and businesses at Mission Beach proper. It's so isolated that signs on the way into town warn you to watch out for cassowaries crossing the road. A dense rain forest hides the town from view until you come around the corner to Mission Beach proper to find tidy villages of appealing hotels, neat shops, and smart restaurants. Just through the trees is the fabulous beach. A mile or so north of the main settlement is Clump Point Jetty.

Wildlife Safety Tips

Endangered cassowaries (ostrich-like birds with a blue bony crown on their head) can kill with their enormous claws, so never approach one. If you disturb one, back off slowly and hide behind a tree.

Dangerous crocodiles inhabit the local waterways. Do not swim in, or stand on the bank of, any river or stream.

You will spend plenty of time lazing and strolling the area's 14 kilometers (8½ miles) of gorgeous beaches, but be careful about where you swim. Deadly marine stingers inhabit the sea from October through April; in these times swim only within the stinger nets at the north and south ends of Mission Beach.

ESSENTIALS

GETTING THERE   By Car   From Cairns, follow the Bruce Highway south. The Mission Beach turn-off is at the tiny town of El Arish, about 15 kilometers (9 miles) north of Tully. Mission Beach is 25 kilometers (15 miles) off the highway. It's a 90-minute trip from Cairns. If you're coming from Townsville, there is an earlier turnoff just north of Tully that leads 18 kilometers (11 miles) to South Mission Beach.

By Bus   Mission Beach Bus & Coach (☎ 07/4068 7400) operates four door-to-door shuttles a day from Cairns for A$28 (U.S.$18.20) per person, and from the Cairns airport for A$33 (U.S.$21.45) per person. One service a day runs from the northern beaches at A$38 (U.S.$24.70) per person. **McCafferty's** (☎ 13 14 99 in Australia) and **Greyhound Pioneer** (☎ 13 20 30 in Australia) coaches both stop in Mission Beach proper (not South Mission Beach) several times daily on their Cairns–Brisbane–Cairns runs. Trip time from Brisbane is over 26 hours.

By Train   Four trains a week on the Cairns–Brisbane–Cairns route call at the nearest train station, Tully, about 20 kilometers (13 miles) away. The one-way fare is A$24.20 (U.S.$15.73) from Cairns for the 3¼-hour trip; from Brisbane it is A$150.70 (U.S.$97.95), or A$189.20 (U.S.$122.85) in an economy-class sleeper. Call Queensland Rail's long-distance division, **Traveltrain** (☎ 1800/806 468 in Australia, or 07/3235 1122). A **taxi** from Tully to Mission Beach with **Tully Taxis & Buses** (☎ 07/4068 3937) is about A$40 (U.S.$26).

A bus transfer from Tully to Mission Beach with **Mission Beach Bus & Coach** (☎ 07/4068 7400) is A$5 (U.S.$3.25).

VISITOR INFORMATION   The Mission Beach Visitor Centre, Porters Promenade, Mission Beach, QLD 4852 (☎ 07/4068 7099; fax 07/4068 7066; www.missionbch.com), is located at the northern end of town. It's open Monday through Saturday 9am to 5pm, and Sunday 9am to 4pm.

GETTING AROUND   The local **bus** (☎ 07/4068 7400, or call the bus driver while he's driving at 0419/745 875 mobile phone) travels day and night between the communities, stopping outside all the accommodations listed below, at Clump Point Jetty, and at Wongaling Beach near the water taxi to Dunk Island. **Sugarland Car Rentals** (☎ 07/4068 8272) is the only rental car company in town. **Mission Beach Taxis** are on ☎ 07/4068 8155.

WHAT TO SEE & DO IN THE AREA

EXPLORING THE REEF   The Quick Cat runs snorkel and dive trips from Mission Beach to Beaver Cay on the outer Great Barrier Reef. See "Exploring the Great Barrier Reef" section earlier in this chapter for details.

WHITE-WATER RAFTING ON THE TULLY   A day's rafting through the rain forest on the Grade 3 to 4 Tully River is a memorable. In raft-speak, Grade 4 means "exciting rafting on moderate rapids with a continuous need to maneuver rafts." On the Tully, that translates to hair-raising but manageable rapids punctuated by calming stretches. You don't need experience, just a decent level of agility and an enthusiastic attitude. ✪ **RnR Rafting** (☎ 07/4051 7777) runs a trip that includes 5 hours on the river with fun-loving and expert guides, a barbecue lunch in the rain forest, and a video screening of your adventure. With transfers, the day costs A$128 (U.S.$83.20) from Mission Beach, A$138 (U.S.$89.70) from Cairns or the northern beaches, and A$149 (U.S.$96.85) from Port Douglas. The trip runs daily, and you must be 13 years or older.

EXPLORING THE RAIN FOREST & COAST   Walking, wildlife spotting, canoeing in the forest, and kayaking along the pristine coast are all well worth doing. Hiking trails abound through national-park rain forest, fan palm groves, and along the beach. The 8-kilometer (5-mile) **Licuala Fan Palm track** starts at the parking lot on the Mission Beach-Tully Road about 1.5 kilometers (1 mile) west of the turnoff to South Mission Beach. It leads through dense forest, over creeks, and comes out on the El Arish-Mission Beach Road about 7 kilometers (4 miles) north of the post office. When you come out, you can cross the road and keep going on the 1.2-kilometer (less than 1-mile) **Lacey Creek loop** in the Tam O'Shanter State Forest. A shorter **Rainforest Circuit** option leads from the parking lot at the start of the Licuala Fan Palm track and makes a 1.2-kilometer (less than a mile) loop incorporating a fan palm boardwalk. There's also a 10-minute "follow the cassowary footprints to the nest" children's walk leading from the parking lot.

If you would rather see the sea than rain forest, take the 7-kilometer (4-mile) **Edmund Kennedy track,** which starts below the Horizon resort at the southern end of the Kennedy Esplanade in South Mission Beach. You get alternating views of the ocean and the rain forest on this trail. The Mission Beach Visitor Centre has free trail maps.

Ingrid Marker of **Sunbird Adventures** (☎ 07/4068 8229) offers a range of sea-kayaking and trekking expeditions that interpret the rich environment around you. Groups are limited to eight, so you get personal attention and time to ask questions. Her half-day sea kayak expedition (A$48/U.S.$31.20 per person) journeys around Bingil Bay. Her full-day rain-forest trek visits the Liverpool/Nyleta Creek area, and includes a dip in a natural swimming hole (A$59/U.S.$38.35 per person). Her night walks are held on Bicton Hill and are great for kids because they spot glow-in-the-dark fungi, and frogs and shrimps in the streams (A$25/U.S.$16.25 per person). The sea kayaks and full-day treks depart at 8am; the night walks depart at 7pm, returning around 9:30pm. Ingrid picks you up from your accommodation for free. All food on the trip is locally grown organic produce. Not all tours depart every day, so check her schedule.

HITTING THE BEACH   Of course, lazing on the uncrowded beach is what everyone comes to Mission Beach to do. From June to September you can swim anywhere, and the water is still warm; from October to May stick to the stinger safety nets at Mission Beach proper (behind Castaways resort) and South Mission Beach.

Travel Tip

There is no bank in Mission Beach, and the only ATM is at Mission Beach Resort, Wongaling Beach, so come with enough cash, traveler's checks, and/or a credit card.

A DAY TRIP TO DUNK ISLAND If you're a beachcomber at heart, Dunk will fulfill your dreams. Just 5 kilometers (3 miles) offshore from Mission Beach, Dunk was the inspiration for E.J. Banfield's book *Confessions of a Beachcomber.* Banfield moved to Dunk in the early 1900s to live out what he thought would be a short life. He lived for another 23 years, which must say something about the restorative powers of a piece of paradise. Ed and wife Bertha Banfield's graves are along the track to Mt. Kootaloo.

Thick bush land and rain forest cover much of the island's 12 square kilometers (5 square miles), most of which is a national park. The island is renowned for its myriad birds and electric-blue Ulysses butterflies.

Staying at the upscale Dunk Island Resort is a budget-busting experience, but you can pop over for the day to snorkel, hike in the forest, or do water sports. **Dunk Island Ferry & Cruises** (☎ 07/4068 7211; or 07/4065 6333 after hours) runs round-trip cruises for A$26 (U.S.$16.90) for adults and A$11 (U.S.$7.15) for kids 10 to 14 (free for younger kids). This cruise costs the same as the regular water taxi fare (see below) and includes free snorkeling gear (with a A$20/U.S.$13 refundable deposit). There are daily departures from Clump Point Jetty. You can also get to Dunk by the **water taxi** (☎ 07/4068 8310), which runs six times a day from Wongaling Beach. The round-trip fare is A$22 (U.S.$14.30) for adults and A$11 (U.S.$7.15) for kids 4 to 14, but does not include snorkel gear, which costs A$10 (U.S.$6.50) extra per person. Ask at your accommodation about transfers between Clump Point and South Mission Beach.

Once on Dunk, you pay as you go for activities and equipment rental on the island. Everything from waterskiing to catamaran sailing is available, but Dunk has such nice beaches and rain forest walking trails (half a dozen, ranging in duration from 15 minutes to 4 hours), that you won't need to shell out a chunk of change for water sports to enjoy the day. On Monday and Thursday mornings, you can visit an artist's gallery reached via a 40-minute trail through the rain forest; admission is A$4 (U.S.$2.60).

Ingrid Marker of **Sunbird Adventures** (see above) runs unusual full-day guided ✪ **sea-kayak expeditions** to Dunk Island. Ingrid says if you can pedal a bike for an hour, you can sea kayak for the hour it takes to get to the island. You glide over reefs, looking for sea turtles; spend the morning snorkeling in Coconut Bay; have a picnic lunch of oysters, mussels, and fresh produce (all organic) in Hidden Palm Valley; then hike the rain forest. At morning and afternoon tea you get a choice of no less than nine organic teas and coffees. The trip costs A$80 (U.S.$52) per person.

WHERE TO STAY

✪ **Beachcomber Coconut Caravan Village.** Kennedy Esplanade, South Mission Beach, QLD 4854. ☎ **07/4068 8129.** Fax 07/4068 8671. www.big4.com.au. big4bccv@bigpond. com.au. 27 cabins, 15 with bathroom (shower only), 4 with spa baths; 80 powered sites, approx. 20 tent sites. Unpowered campsite A$15.50 (U.S.$10.08) single, A$17.50 (U.S.$11.33) double; powered campsite A$20 (U.S.$13) double. Cabins A$45–$68 (U.S.$29.25–$44.20) double. 2-bedroom villas A$90 (U.S.$58.50); spa villas A$105 (U.S.$68.25). Extra person A$6 (U.S.$3.90) in campsite, children 2–14 A$3 (U.S.$1.95); extra person A$12 (U.S.$7.80) in cabin, children A$6 (U.S.$3.90). Linen and towel hire A$7 (U.S.$4.55), A$4 (U.S.$2.60) blanket in regular cabins (free in deluxe cabins). BC, MC, V.

This caravan park, across the road from the beach (and, more important in summer, the stinger net), wins the local garden award every year. Its neat lawns and abundant palms are lovely, as are the new, smartly painted deluxe cabins, which are almost as roomy and as well appointed as an apartment. Villas have en suite bathrooms with a hair dryer and fluffy white towels, a separate living and dining area, a good-size kitchen, a master bedroom, bunkroom for the kids, and a Jacuzzi! The regular cabins have older decor and less room, but they're fine enough. Campers have a communal kitchen, a fridge, and barbecues. Pitch your tent at the jungle's edge, and keep an eye out for the cassowaries that stroll in now and then. There's a tour desk, a pool with lounge chairs, free Ping-Pong, half-court tennis, a TV and game room, playground, basketball hoop, a take-out shop which also sells basic groceries.

Mackays. 7 Porter Promenade, Mission Beach, QLD 4852. ☎ **07/4068 7212.** Fax 07/4068 7095. 22 units (some with shower only). TEL,TV. A$77–A$99 (U.S.$50.05–$64) double; A$99 (U.S.$64.35) double 1-bedroom apt. Higher rates apply at Easter. Extra person A$16.50 (U.S.$10.73), children under 14 A$6.60 (U.S.$4.29). Crib A$6.60 (U.S.$4.29). Ask about special packages. BC, MC, V.

This delightfully well-kept motel is one of the best-value places to stay in town. It's 80 meters (260 ft.) from the beach and 400 meters (¼ mile) from the heart of Mission Beach. The friendly Mackay family repaints the rooms annually, so the place always looks brand new. All the rooms are pleasant and spacious with tiled floors, cane sofas, and very clean bathrooms (BYO hair dryer). Those in the newer section are air-conditioned, and some have views of the granite-lined pool and gardens. Rooms in the older painted-brick wing have garden views from a communal patio and no air-conditioning. Be sure to ask about the packages, they can be very good deals.

Mission Beach Eco Village. Clump Point Rd., Mission Beach. QLD 4852. ☎ **07/4068 7534.** Fax 07/4068 7538. www.ecovillage.com.au. ecovilla@znet.net.au. 17 bungalows (all with shower; 6 with spa bath). A/C TV TEL. A$130 (U.S.$84.50) double; A$141 (U.S.$91.65) family or spa bungalow. Lower rates for singles in Feb, Mar (except Easter), and Nov. Minimum 2-night stay. Additional person A$11 (U.S.$7.15). AE, BC, DC, MC, V.

This lodge occupies a magical site in the rain forest on Clump Point, surrounded on three sides by water. You don't see the sea from your room, but it's a step away to the sandy beach where you can swim and snorkel in a picture-perfect lagoon. The owner is planning to provide stinger suits so guests can participate in water activities year-round. Stay in simple, roomy bungalows under the trees. Each has pine paneling, tile floor, a very clean bathroom, and a deck. Some have a kitchenette and a dining area, some have Jacuzzis; family bungalows have three bunks for the kids. An iron and ironing board and a hair dryer are either in your room or available at the front desk or in the laundry. Breakfast is served on your balcony, and dinner is among the trees in an open-sided Malaysian longhouse-style restaurant and bar. The natural-looking pool is lined with rocks and trees, and there's a Jacuzzi, barbecue area and a small playground.

Worth a Splurge

✪ **The Horizon.** Explorer Dr., South Mission Beach, QLD 4852. ☎ **1800/079 090** in Australia, or 07/4068 8154. Fax 07/4068 8596. www.thehorizon.com.au. info@thehorizon.com.au. 55 units (all with bathroom). A/C MINIBAR TV TEL. A$195–$230 (U.S.$126.75–$149.50) double. Extra person A$30 (U.S.$19.50). AE, BC, DC, MC, V.

With its beguiling views across the pool to Dunk Island, its rain forest setting, and its impressive rooms, this resort perched on a steep hillside is one of the most comfortable and beautiful you will find Down Under. Even the least expensive rooms are spacious and have luxurious bathrooms fitted with hair dryers. All but a handful of rooms have some kind of sea view; a half dozen retain the older-style bathrooms from a previous resort development, but the sea views from these rooms are the best. It's just a minute or two down the rain forest track to the beach, there is a day/night tennis court, and the tour desk will book you on day trips if you ever decide to leave the sundeck.

WHERE TO DINE

Having a picnic on the beach or in one of the many small rain forest parks and barbecue areas that dot the beachfront is the obvious way to enjoy a meal in Mission Beach. The **Mission Beach Gourmet Delicatessen**, (☎ 07/ 4068 7660) is the place to stock up on cheap, tasty outdoor fare. Most restaurants and cafes are in Mission Beach proper, but you will find a couple more in South Mission Beach. For tasty, cheap meals, try **That'll Do** (☎ 07/4068 7300); it's next to the supermarket on Porter's Promenade in Mission Beach. The burgers, fish and chips, chili, and ice cream rarely cost more than A$4 (U.S.$2.60). Take your food to go, or eat at one of the plastic tables. You can even BYO. It's open 11am to 8pm; closed Thursday.

Friends. Porters Promenade (opposite Campbell St.), Mission Beach. ☎ **07/4068 7107,** or 07/4068 7440 (9am–5pm). Reservations recommended. Main courses A$12.50–$22 (U.S.$8.13–$14.30). AE, BC, MC, V. Mon–Sat 6:30pm–late. Open Sun on long weekends. Closed for 1 month during Feb–Mar. HOME COOKING.

The cozy interior and a hearty menu favoring local seafood make this place a long-standing favorite with locals. Appetizers include mussels Normandy, oysters done three ways, and garlic prawns; main courses feature lamb shanks; eye fillet steak with Diane, mushroom, or green peppercorn sauce; and chicken hotpot. Settle in with a homemade dessert and liqueur coffee after dinner. Licensed and BYO.

TOWNSVILLE & MAGNETIC ISLAND

346km (207½ miles) S of Cairns; 1,371km (822½ miles) N of Brisbane

With a population of 140,000, Townsville claims to be Australia's largest tropical city. Because of its size, and economy based on mining, manufacturing, education and tourism, it is sometimes unjustly overlooked as a holiday destination. The people are friendly; the city pleasant, and there's plenty to do. The town is nestled by the sea below the pink face of **Castle Rock,** which looms 300 meters (about 1,000 ft.) above, and the beachfront has recently undergone a A$29 million (U.S.$18½ million) revamp.

Townsville's major attraction is the world-class **Museum of Tropical Queensland,** where a full-size replica of the HMS *Pandora* is the stunning centerpiece. The museum is next to one of the city's most enduring attractions, the ReefHQ aquarium.

Remnants of bygone times are still apparent in surrounding towns like **Charters Towers** and **Ravenswood,** which offer splendid examples of colonial architecture, historic hotels, museums and displays of old gold mining machinery and cottages.

Cruises depart from the harbour for the Great Barrier Reef, about 2½ hours away, and just 5 miles offshore is Magnetic Island—"Maggie" to the locals—a popular place for water sports, hiking, and spotting koalas in the wild.

ESSENTIALS

GETTING THERE Townsville is on the Bruce Highway, a 3-hour drive north of Airlie Beach and 4½ hours south of Cairns. The Bruce Highway breaks temporarily in the city. From the south, take Bruce Highway Alt. 1 route into the city. From the north, the highway leads into the city as Ingham Road.

Qantas (☎ 13 13 13 in Australia), and subsidiary **Sunstate Airlines** (book through Qantas) have many flights a day from Cairns, and several from Brisbane. Sunstate flies from Proserpine and Hamilton Island airports in the Whitsundays.

Airport Transfers & Tours (☎ 07/4775 5544) runs a door-to-door airport shuttle. It meets only flights from Brisbane, not from Cairns or elsewhere. A trip into town is A$6 (U.S.$3.90) one-way or A$10 (U.S.$6.50) return, less if there are two of you. Reservations are not needed.

Several **Queensland Rail** (☎ 13 22 32 in Queensland, or 07/3235 1122) long-distance trains stop at Townsville each week. The trip from Cairns is 5½ hours and costs A$47.30 (U.S.$30.75). From Brisbane the journey takes just over 20 hours; fares range from A$135.30 (U.S.$87.75) for a sitting berth to A$173.80 (U.S.$112.97) for an economy-class sleeper.

Greyhound Pioneer (☎ 13 20 30 in Australia) and **McCafferty's** (☎ 13 14 99 in Australia) buses stop at Townsville regularly on their Cairns–Brisbane–Cairns routes. The fare from Cairns is about A$44 (U.S.$28.60); trip time is 6 hours. The fare from Brisbane is about A$130 (U.S.$84.50); trip time is 22½ hours.

VISITOR INFORMATION   For an information packet, contact **Townsville Enterprise Limited,** P.O. Box 1043, Townsville, QLD 4810 (☎ 07/4726 2728; www.townsvilleonline.com.au). It has two Information Centres. One is in the heart of town on Flinders Mall (☎ 1800/801 902 in Australia, or 07/4721 3660); it's open Monday through Friday from 9am to 5pm, and weekends from 9am to 1pm. The other is on the Bruce Highway 10 kilometers (6 miles) south of the city (☎ 07/4778 3555); it is open daily from 9am to 5pm. Townsville Enterprise supplies information on Magnetic Island, but also check the island's website at www.magnetic-island.com.au.

GETTING AROUND   Local **Sunbus** (☎ 07/4725 8482) buses depart Flinders Street Mall. Car-rental chains include **Avis** (☎ 07/4721 2688), **Budget** (☎ 07/4725 2344), **Hertz** (☎ 07/4775 5950), and **Thrifty** (☎ 07/4725 4600).

Detours Coaches (☎ 07/4721 5977) runs tours to most attractions in Townsville.

THE TOP ATTRACTIONS

For details on visiting the Great Barrier Reef from Townsville, see "Exploring the Great Barrier Reef" earlier in this chapter.

✪ **Reef HQ.** 2–68 Flinders St. ☎ **07/4750 0800.** Admission A$16 (U.S.$10.40) adults, A$13.80 (U.S.$8.97) seniors and students, A$7 (U.S.$4.55) children 4–14, A$38 (U.S.$25) family pass. Daily 9am–5pm. Closed Christmas.

Reef HQ is the reef education center for the Great Barrier Reef Marine Park Authority's headquarters and has the largest living coral reef aquarium in the world. The highlight is walking through a 20 meter-long (66 ft.) see-through tunnel, gazing right into a giant predator tank where sharks cruise. The wreck of the *SS Yongala* provides an eerie backdrop for blacktip and whitetip reef sharks, leopard sharks and nurse sharks, sharing their watery home with stingrays, giant trevally and a green turtle. Watching them feed is quite a spectacle. The tunnel also reveals the 2.5 million liter (650,000 gal.) coral reef exhibit, with its hard and soft corals providing a home for thousands of colorful fish, giant clams, sea cucumbers, sea stars and other creatures. There's a scuba dive show where the divers speak to you via intercom while they feed the fish. Other highlights include a marine creature touch-tank, a wild sea-turtle rehabilitation center plus great interactive activities for children. Reef HQ is an easy walk from the city center.

Museum of Tropical Queensland. 78–102 Flinders St (next to Reef HQ). ☎ **07/4726 0600.** Admission A$9 (U.S.$5.85) adults, A$5 (U.S.$3.25) children 4–16, A$6.50 (U.S.$4.23) seniors and students, A$24 (U.S.$15.60) family of 4. Daily 9am–5pm. Closed Christmas, Good Friday and Anzac Day morning (April 25).

A stunning addition to Townsville's skyline is this new A$22 million (U.S.$14.3 million) museum, with its curved roof reminiscent of a ship in full sail. In pride of place is the exhibition of relics salvaged from the wreck of HMS *Pandora,* which lies 33 meters (106 ft.) under water on the edge of the Great Barrier Reef, 120 kilometers (75 miles) east of Cape York. The *Pandora* exhibit includes a replica of a section of the ship's bow and its foremast. Standing three stories high, the replica and its copper-clad keel were crafted by local shipwrights for the museum. *Pandora* sank in 1791 and the wreck was discovered in 1977. The exhibition traces the ship's voyage and the retrieval of the sunken treasure. The museum has six galleries, including a hands-on science centre, and a natural history display which looks at life in tropical Queensland—above and below the water. Another is dedicated to north Queensland's indigenous heritage, with items from Torres Strait and the South Sea Islands as well as stories from people of different cultures about the settlement and labour of north Queensland.

OTHER THINGS TO SEE & DO

The Strand is a 2.5 kilometers (1.5 miles) strip with safe swimming beaches, a fitness circuit, a waterpark for the kids, and plenty of covered picnic areas and free gas barbecues. Stroll along the promenade or relax at one of many cafes, restaurants and bars while you gaze across the Coral Sea to Magnetic Island. For the more active, there are areas to in-line skate, bicycle, walk, or fish, and a basketball half-court. Four rocky headlands and a picturesque jetty adjacent to Strand Park provide good fishing, and two surf lifesaving clubs service the three swimming areas along The Strand. With 300 days of sunshine each year, Townsville is a place where you'll enjoy cooling off—in either the Olympic-sized **Tobruk Pool,** the seawater **Rockpool,** or at the beach itself. During summer (Nov–Mar), three safe swimming enclosures operate to keep swimmers safe from marine stingers, and if water sports are on your agenda try a jet ski, hire a canoe or take to the latest in pedal skis. A state-of-the-art waterpark has waterfalls, hydrants, waterslides and water cannons, plus a huge bucket of water which continually fills until it overturns and dumps water on those below.

Don't miss the views of Cleveland Bay and Magnetic Island from Castle Hill; it's a 2.5-kilometer (1½-mile) drive or a shorter, but steep, walk up from town. To drive to the top, follow Stanley Street west from Flinders Mall to Castle Hill Drive; the walking trails up are posted en route.

Cotters Market, held every Sunday in Flinders Mall from 8:30am to 1pm, has 200 stalls featuring works by local and regional artists. There's everything from pottery and lead-lighting to homemade chocolates and orchids on sale. Townsville's three major suburban shopping complexes, containing major department stores and speciality shops, are Stockland in Aitkenvale, Castletown in Pimlico and Willows in Kirwan.

At the **Billabong Sanctuary** (☎ **07/4778 8344**) on the Bruce Highway 17 kilometers (11 miles) south of town, you can see a range of Aussie wildlife in a natural setting, hold a koala, a (baby) crocodile, python, wombat or fruit bat, and hand-feed kangaroos (free with admission). There are talks and shows continuously from 10am; one of the most popular is the saltwater crocodile feeding at noon and 2:30pm. There are also Aboriginal cultural talks. Admission is A$19.80 (U.S.$12.87) for adults, A$15.40 (U.S.$10.01) for students and seniors, A$9.90 (U.S.$6.44) for kids 3 to 16, and A$47.30 (U.S.$30.88) for a family of five. The sanctuary is open every day except Christmas from 8am to 5pm. Take your swimsuit as there is a pool. To save money on cafe food, pack a picnic or barbecue supplies and eat in the pleasant grounds.

WHERE TO STAY

Aquarius on the Beach. 75 The Strand, Townsville, QLD 4810. ☎ **1800/62 2474** in Australia; or 07/4772 4255. Fax 07/4721 1316. www.aquarius-townsville.com.au. 100 units. A/C TV TEL. A$115.50–$126.50 (U.S.$75.08–$82.23) double. Extra person A$22 (U.S.$14.30). AE, BC, DC, MC, V. Airport shuttle.

You get nice views of the bay and Magnetic Island from every room at this slightly older-style 14-story waterfront hotel. It's popular with business travelers who like the location and the practical amenities: room service, car rental desk, an excellent top-floor restaurant (see "Where to Dine," below), a palm-lined swimming pool and children's pool, free in-room movies, and a free taxi phone in the lobby. With a kitchenette, sofa, desk, and a small dining table with two chairs squeezed into every room, there's not much space left over, but the accommodations are comfortable. If space is important to you, ask for a corner room, as they are slightly larger. The nice bathrooms come with hair dryers. Parts of the decor are a little faded and worse for wear, but the views and facilities make this a good value. The Strand beach is across the road; the center of town and the island ferry terminals are a 15-minute walk away.

Seagulls Resort. 74 The Esplanade, Belgian Gardens, QLD 4810. ☎ **1800/079 929** in Australia, or 07/4721 3111. Fax 07/4721 3133. www.seagulls.com.au. resort@seagulls.com.au. 70 units (with shower only). A/C TV TEL. A$99–$110 (U.S.$64.35–$71.50) double; A$139 (U.S.$90.35) 2-bedroom apt. Extra person A$15 (U.S.$9.75); children under 14 A$9 (U.S.$5.85). AE, BC, DC, MC, V. Airport shuttle. Bus: 4, 5, 5A, 7.

This popular low-key resort, a 5-minute drive from the city, is built around an inviting freeform saltwater pool in 3 acres of dense tropical gardens. Despite its Esplanade location, the rooms do not boast waterfront views, but they are comfortable and a good size. The larger Reef suites have painted brick walls, a sofa, dining furniture, and a kitchen sink. Apartments have a main bedroom and a bunk bedroom, a kitchenette, dining furniture, and roomy balcony. The fittings are modest but in good condition. Every room has a hair dryer. The whole resort is wheelchair-friendly, with bathroom facilities for people with disabilities. The accommodation wings are centered on the pool and its pretty open-sided restaurant, which is popular with locals. There's a tour desk, gift shop, room service at dinner, a pool bar (daily happy hour from 5–6pm), free in-room movies, a small tennis court, barbecue, and playground for the kids. It's not within walking distance of town, but the resort makes free transfers to the city and Magnetic Island ferry terminals. Most tour companies pick up at the door.

A B&B with Victorian Charm
✪ **The Rocks.** 20 Cleveland Terrace, Townsville, QLD 4810. ☎ **07/4771 5700,** or 0416/044 409 mobile phone. Fax 07/4771 5711. www.therocksguesthouse.com. therocks@therocksguesthouse.com. 8 units, 1 with private bathroom (shower only). A$97–$107 (U.S.$63.05–$69.55) double. Rates include continental breakfast. AE, BC, DC, MC, V. Airport shuttle.

If you have a weakness for Victoriana, you will swoon when you enter this exquisitely renovated Queenslander home. The owners have fitted it with genuine 19th-century antiques, from the crimson velvet settee to the grandfather clock in the drawing room. Even your meals are served on period dinnerware. Every room is decorated with lovely linens, old trunks, and in a few, even original washbasins tastefully wrapped in muslin "gowns." One of the rooms served as an operating theater when U.S. forces occupied the house during World War II. Five rooms are air-conditioned. One has an en suite bathroom; the others share a historically decorated bathroom with a cast-iron clawfoot bath. Complimentary sherry is served at 6pm on the wide verandah, where you have lovely views of Magnetic Island and Cleveland Bay. Despite the old-world ambience, the house has telephone, fax, Internet, and e-mail access for guests (although not in your room). Free tea and coffee are available. There's also an outdoor Jacuzzi, a billiards table (antique, of course) and guest laundry. The Strand is a minute's stroll away, and you are a 10 to 15-minute walk from town and the Magnetic Island ferries.

WHERE TO DINE
Apart from the suggestions below, you will find more restaurants and cafes on Palmer Street, an easy stroll across the river from Flinders Mall.

Michel's Cafe and Bar. 7 Palmer St. ☎ **07/4724 1460.** Reservations recommended. Main courses A$10.90–$23 (U.S.$7.09–$14.95). AE, BC, DC, MC, V. Tues–Fri 11:30am–2pm, Tues–Sun 5:30pm–10pm. MOD OZ.

This big contemporary space is popular with Townsville's "in" crowd. Owner/chef Michel Flores works in the open kitchen where he can keep an eye on the excellent service. You might choose a Louisiana blackened rib fillet, or kangaroo. There are also plenty of casual choices like the stylish pizzas or warm salads.

Worth a Splurge

✪ **Zouí Alto.** On 14th fl. at Aquarius on the Beach, 75 The Strand. ☎ **07/4721 4700.** Reservations recommended. Main courses A$17.50–$22 (U.S.$11.330–$14.30). AE, BC, MC, V. Daily 7–9:30am; Fri noon–3pm; Mon–Sat 6:30–9:30pm. Bus: 1B. MOD OZ.

This is not just one of the best restaurants in Townsville, it's one of the best in the country. Chef Mark Edwards turns out terrific food, while his effusive wife Eleni runs the front of the house, which is idiosyncratically decked out in primary splashes and Greek urns. Main courses include ravioli with fillings ranging from pumpkin and blue cheese, sweet potato and ginger, or sun-dried tomato and goat's cheese when I visited, and blue-eye cod coated in chili and tomato jam on a mound of champ with coriander and peanut pesto. Go for breakfast, or arrive before sunset, to make the most of the spectacular views of Castle Hill on one side and the bay on the other.

TOWNSVILLE AFTER DARK

Not much happens until Friday and Saturday night in Townsville. **The Bank Niteclub,** 169 Flinders St. East (☎ 07/4771 6148) gets a young crowd who party, dance, and pick each other up. Less frenetic social animals prefer the city's lovely historical pubs edged with wrought-iron lace verandahs. The most popular is the ✪ **Exchange,** 151 Flinders St. East (☎ 07/4771 3335)—choose your poison from the hip wine bar downstairs or the Western bourbon and cigar saloon upstairs; ask the bar staff to tell you about the resident ghost. Errol Flynn used to like staying at **The Australian Hotel,** 11 Palmer St. (☎ 07/4771 4339); no doubt he knocked back a beer or two on the wide upstairs verandah, and you can, too.

The Quarterdeck (☎ 07/4722 2333), by the water, belongs to the Jupiters Hotel & Casino at the Breakwater marina on Sir Leslie Thiess Drive, and has dinner music Thursday evening, live bands Friday and Saturday night from 9pm, and live jazz on Sunday winter afternoons and summer evenings. A grill is open for steaks, seafood, and light meals from 11:30am to 9pm daily. You may want to combine a meal here with a visit to the casino off the hotel lobby.

A SIDE TRIP TO MAGNETIC ISLAND

8km (5 miles) E of Townsville

"Maggie" is a delightful 51-square-kilometer (20-sq.-mile) national park island 20 minutes from Townsville by ferry. Only 2,500 locals live here, but it's also popular with mainlanders who love its holiday atmosphere. If you want an island interlude during your Aussie vacation but don't want to pay through the nose at the ritzy island resorts, Maggie is an ideal alternative. It is a busy little place as visitors and locals zip about between the small settlements dotted around its coast, but peace-seeking visitors will find plenty of unspoiled nature to restore their souls. Most people come for the 20 or so pristine (and amazingly uncrowded) bays and white beaches that rim the island, but hikers, botanists, and bird-watchers may want to explore the eucalyptus woods, patches of gully rain forest, and granite tors. (The island got its name when Captain Cook thought the "magnetic" rocks were interfering with his compass readings.) The place is famous for wild koalas easily spotted up in the gum trees by the side

Magnetic Island Travel Tips

If you're going over to Magnetic Island for the day, pick up a copy of the free *Magnetic Island Guide* from any tourist information center or hotel lobby or at the ferry terminal in Townsville before you go. Because there are so many choices of activities, it will help if you plan your day before you arrive.

There is no bank on the island, so carry cash (not every place will cash traveler's checks) and a credit card.

Be warned: Marine stingers make swimming and snorkeling a bad idea from October to May except at the safe swimming enclosure at Picnic Bay. You can do water sports on top of the water, if you wear a lycra stinger-suit, but they are quite uncomfortable in the intensely sticky summer heat from November to March.

---

of the road; ask a local to point you to the nearest colony. Rock wallabies are often spotted in the early morning. Maggie is off the international tourist trail by and large, and it's definitely a casual kind of place, so leave your Prada stilettos in your suitcase.

GETTING THERE & GETTING AROUND   You can take your own car across on the ferry, but most people get around by renting a fun open-sided minimoke (a small jeep-like vehicle) from the oodles of moke rental outfits on the island. Minimokes are unlikely to send your speedometer much over 60 kilometers per hour (36 mph). **Holiday Moke Hire** (☎ **07/4778 5703**) near the jetty rents them for around A$35 (U.S.$22.75) a day, plus A30¢ (U.S.19¢) per kilometer. Even cheaper is the frequent bus service (that comes with a free commentary from the driver). You can purchase a single fare, but the all-day pass at A$11 (U.S.$7.15) for adults, A$5.50 (U.S.$3.58) for kids, or A$27.50 (U.S.$17.88) for a family of 4 can be a good value.

Sunferries (☎ **07/4771 3855** Flinders Street terminal, or 07/4721 4798 Breakwater terminal) runs services from the 168–192 Flinders Street terminal and the Breakwater terminal on Sir Leslie Thiess Drive throughout the day. The company has a courtesy coach that will pick you up from your hotel for the 10:30am ferry. Roundtrip tickets are A$14 (U.S.$9.10) for adults, A$12 (U.S.$7.80) for students, A$6.70 (U.S.$4.36) for seniors and children ages 5 to 15, and A$29 (U.S.$18.859) for a family of 5. Combination tickets combining the ferry with an all-day Magnetic Island bus pass or minimoke rental can save you a couple of dollars.

Out & About on the Island

There is no end to the things you can do on Maggie—snorkeling, swimming in one of a dozen or more bays, catamaran sailing, waterskiing, paraflying, horseback riding on the beach, biking, tennis or golf, scuba diving, sea kayaking, sailing or cruising around the island, taking a Harley Davidson tour, fishing, and more. Equipment for all these activities is for rent on the island at reasonably moderate prices.

Most activities are spread out around **Picnic Bay** (where the ferry pulls in) and the island's three settlements: **Arcadia, Nelly Bay,** and **Horseshoe Bay.**

The island is not on the Great Barrier Reef, but its waters are part of the Great Barrier Reef Marine Park. There's good reef snorkeling at Florence Bay on the southern edge, Arthur Bay on the northern edge, and Geoffrey Bay, where you can reef-walk at low tide (wear sturdy shoes and do not walk directly on coral to avoid damaging it). First-time snorkelers will have an easy time in Maggie's weak currents and softly sloping beaches. Outside stinger season there is good swimming at many secluded bays found all around the island. Alma Bay is a good choice for families as it is reef free and has shady lawns and a playground; Rocky Bay is a petite, secluded cove.

One of the best, and most popular, of the island's 20 kilometers (12 miles) of hiking trails is the Nelly Bay to Arcadia trail, a one-way journey of 5 kilometers (3 miles) that takes 2½ hours. The first 45 minutes, starting in rain forest and climbing gradually to a saddle between Nelly Bay and Horseshoe, are the most interesting. Another excellent walk is the 2-kilometer (1¼-mile) trail to the Forts, remnants of World War II defenses, which, not surprisingly, have great 360° sea views. The best koala spotting is on the track up to the Forts off Horseshoe Bay Road. Carry water wherever you go on the island, as some bays and hiking trails are not near shops.

If you feel like splurging, consider the jet ski circumnavigation of the island offered by **Adrenalin Jet Ski Tours & Hire** (☎ 07/4778 5533). The 3-hour tour is conducted on 2-seat jet skis and costs A$99 (U.S.$64.35), which includes your wet suit, life jacket and stinger suits in season. Tours depart from Horseshoe Bay morning and afternoon. Keep your eyes peeled for dolphins, dugongs (manatees), and sea turtles.

Where to Stay & Dine

Magnetic Island has plenty of affordable accommodations; from motels and apartments to A-frame chalets and permanent tents. To book a room, call **Magnetic Island Holidays** (☎ 07/4778 5155; magneticislandholidays@ultra.net.au). In the peak season (June–Sept), some apartments are available on a weekly basis only. Maggie is littered with inexpensive restaurants, laid-back cafes, and take-out joints. Popular with locals is **Andy's Chinese Restaurant** in Picnic Bay (☎ 07/ 4778 5706), which offers decent meals for under A$15 (U.S.$9.75) per person. It's BYOB.

Dandaloo Gardens. 40–42 Hayles Ave., Arcadia, Magnetic Island, QLD 4819. ☎ **07/4778 5174.** Fax 07/4778 5185. www.dandaloogardens.com.au. pennyandphil@dandaloo gardens.com.au. 8 units (with shower only). A/C TV. A$71.50–$82.50 (U.S.$46.48–$53.63) apt. (sleeps 5 or 6). Weekly and standby rates available. AE, BC, DC, MC, V.

Tucked under rainforest trees and crimson bougainvillea, these airy free-standing cabin-style apartments are ideal for families. Each has a roomy living area and a kitchen, and there's playground equipment on the grounds. The interiors are simple but appealing, with polished timber floors and freshly painted walls. The four cabins in the back are a little older. Four units have VCRs, and each has a deck or patio. The bathrooms are short on space for families, but are smart looking and clean. The grounds are lovely and quiet (except for the voluble birds); there's a pool, lounge chairs, and a barbecue.

Maggie's Beach House. Pacific Drive, Horseshoe Bay, Magnetic Island, QLD 4819. ☎ **1800/001 544** in Australia or 07/4778 5144. Fax 07/4778 5198. www.maggiesbeach house.com.au. info@maggiesbeachhouse.com.au. 35 units, 14 with ensuite bathroom (with shower only). A/C. A$21 (U.S.$13.65) dorm beds; A$55 (U.S.$35.75) single/double with VIP/YHA card, A$75 (U.S.$48.75) without. BC, MC, V. Free pickup from all daytime ferries.

Just a 30-second walk to the beach and calm sheltered waters of Horseshoe Bay, Maggie's Beach House was purpose-built for backpackers and opened in September 2000. You can laze in a hammock under the trees, or join a guided walk to spot koalas and enjoy spectacular 360° views of the island at sunset. Maggie's is fast gaining a reputation for its great budget meals (A$6–$14/U.S.$3.90–$9.10) which include burgers, steaks, fish and salads. Each night there are three specials, including kangaroo fillets, barramundi and other Australian fare. If you prefer to cook for yourself, there's a common kitchen and barbecues. Other facilities include three guest laundries, an Internet cafe, swimming pool, and a tour desk, which can organize anything from fishing charters to Harley Davidson tours, water sports, or sky-diving.

5   The Whitsunday Coast & Islands

A day's drive, or a 1-hour flight south of Cairns brings you to the collection of 74 islands known as the Whitsundays. No more than three nautical miles separates most of them, and they contain countless bays, beaches, coral reefs, and fishing spots. On the same latitude as Hawaii, the water is at least 22°C (72°F) year-round, the sun shines most of the year, and winter requires only a light jacket at night.

The islands are composed of densely forested national parkland, mostly uninhabited, and the surrounding waters belong to the Great Barrier Reef Marine Park. Don't expect palm trees and coconuts, these islands are covered with dry-looking pine and eucalyptus forests full of dense undergrowth, and rocky coral coves far outnumber the few sandy beaches. More than half a dozen islands have resorts that offer many outdoor activities: snorkeling, scuba diving, sailing trips, reef fishing, waterskiing, jet skiing, parasailing, sea kayaking, hiking, rides over the coral in semi-submersibles, fish feeding, putt-putting around in dinghies to secluded beaches, tennis, squash, and aqua-aerobics classes. Accommodations range from small, low-key wilderness retreats to midrange family havens to Australia's most luxurious resort, Hayman.

The village of **Airlie Beach** is the center of the action on the mainland. The Whitsundays are just as good a stepping stone to the outer Great Barrier Reef as Cairns—some people think it is better because you don't have to make the 90-minute trip to the Reef before you hit coral. Just about any Whitsunday island has fringing reef around its shores, and there are good snorkeling reefs between the islands, a quick boat ride away from your island or mainland accommodations.

ESSENTIALS

GETTING THERE   By Car   The Bruce Highway leads south from Cairns or north from Brisbane to Proserpine, 26 kilometers (16 miles) inland from Airlie Beach. Take the "Whitsunday" turnoff to reach Airlie Beach and Shute Harbour. Allow a good 8 hours to drive from Cairns. There are several car-storage facilities at Shute Harbour. Sandra and Roger Boynton of **Whitsunday Car Security** (☎ **07/4946 9955** or 0419/729 605) collect your car anywhere in the Whitsunday area and store it in locked undercover parking for A$13.50 (U.S.$8.88) per 24 hours.

By Plane   There are two air routes to the Whitsundays: **Hamilton Island airport,** and **Proserpine airport** on the mainland. **Qantas** (☎ **13 13 13** in Australia) flies direct to Hamilton Island from Sydney. **Airlink** (book through Qantas) flies daily from Brisbane. **Sunstate Airlines** (book through Qantas) flies daily from Cairns. Airlink and Sunstate fly to Proserpine from Brisbane, and from Cairns via Townsville.

If you stay on an island, the resort may book your launch transfers automatically. These may appear on your airline ticket, in which case your luggage will be checked through to the island.

Money-Saving Tips

Does all this fun in the Whitsunday Islands come cheap? If you stay in a hotel on the mainland, yes. If you stay on an island, no. On any trip to the Whitsundays, you'll usually spend money on water sports, sailing, diving expeditions, and the like—all potential budget–busters. But standby and package deals on activities and accommodations abound most of the year, even at the most luxurious resorts.

Safety Tips

Although they have not been sighted at Airlie Beach for 5 years, deadly marine stingers may inhabit the shoreline from October to April. The best place to swim during these months is in the brand new Airlie Beach lagoon.

The rivers here are home to dangerous saltwater crocodiles (which actully live in fresh water), so no swimming in streams, rivers, and water holes.

By Train Several **Queensland Rail** (☎ **13 22 32** in Queensland, or 07/3235 1122) long-distance trains stop at Proserpine every week. The one-way fare is A$73.70 (U.S.$47.91) from Cairns. From Brisbane fares range from A$119.90 (U.S.$77.94) for a sitting berth to A$158.40 (U.S.$102.96) for an economy-class sleeper.

By Bus **Greyhound Pioneer** (☎ **13 20 30** in Australia) and **McCafferty's** (☎ 13 14 99 in Australia) operate plentiful daily services to Airlie Beach from Brisbane (trip time: around 18 hr.) and Cairns (trip time: 9–10½ hr.). The fare is A$124.30 (U.S.$80.99) from Brisbane and A$71.50 (U.S.$46.48) from Cairns.

Whitsunday Transit (☎ **1300/655 449** or 07/4945 4011) meets all flights and trains at Proserpine to provide door-to-door transfers to Airlie Beach hotels, or to Shute Harbour. The fare is A$12 (U.S.$7.80), half price for kids 4 to 14.

VISITOR INFORMATION Before you travel, contact **Tourism Whitsundays,** P.O. Box 83, Whitsunday, QLD 4802 (☎ **07/4946 6673;** fax 07/4946 7387; www.whitsundayinformation.com.au). Another website is www.whitsunday.net.au. Tourism Whitsundays' information center (☎ **1800/801 252** in Australia, or 07/4945 3711) is in Proserpine, on the Bruce Highway in the town's south. It's open Monday to Saturday from 8:30am to 5:30pm, Sunday from 10am to 5pm.

If you're staying in Airlie Beach, it's easier to pick up information from the private booking agents lining the main street, which all stock a vast range of cruise, tour, and hotel information, and make bookings free of charge. They all have much the same stuff; but because some manifest certain boats exclusively, and prices can vary a little from one to the next, shop around.

GETTING AROUND Island ferries and Great Barrier Reef cruises leave from **Shute Harbour,** a 10-minute drive south of Airlie Beach on Shute Harbour Road. Most other tour-boat operators and bareboat charters anchor at **Abel Point Marina,** a 15-minute walk west from Airlie Beach.

Avis (☎ **07/4946 6318**), **Hertz** (☎ **07/4946 4687**), and **Thrifty** (☎ **07/4946 7727**) have outlets in Airlie Beach and Proserpine Airport (telephone numbers serve both locations). Budget has no Whitsundays office.

Local bus company **Whitsunday Transit** (☎ **1300/65 5449** or 07/4945 4011) runs a half-hourly service between Airlie Beach and Shute Harbour to meet all ferries. The fare is A$3.60 (U.S.$2.34).

Most tour-boat operators pick up guests free from Airlie Beach hotels and call at some or all island resorts.

Whitsunday All Over (☎ **1300/366 494** in Australia, or 07/4946 9499), **Whitsunday Island Adventure Cruises** (☎ **07/4946 5255** for the booking agent), and **FantaSea Cruises** (☎ **1800/650 851** in Australia, or 07/4946 5111) make ferry transfers from Shute Harbour to the islands and between the islands. One-way trips cost from A$8 (U.S.$5.20) for the short hop from Daydream Island to South Molle Island, to A$24 (U.S.$15.60) from Hamilton Island to the mainland. Children 4 to

The Whitsunday Islands

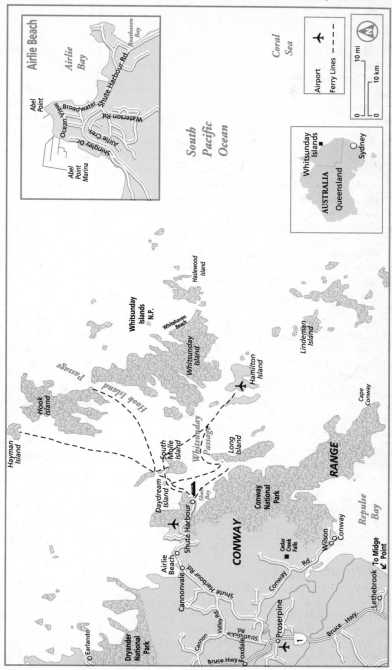

Come Sail with Me

"Bareboating" isn't an aquatic form of nudism; it simply means that you are sailing the boat yourself. And if that seems pretty daunting, rest assured that thousands of people do it safely every year, with a little tuition before they set out. Most of the many bareboat yacht charter companies in the islands will want one person on the boat to have a little experience at the helm of a vessel, but don't worry if you don't know one end of a boat from another. You do not need a license, and sailing is surprisingly easy in these uncrowded waters, where the channels are deep and hazard-free and the seas are protected from big swells by the Great Barrier Reef farther out. The 74 islands are so close to each other that land is always in sight, and safe anchorages are everywhere. If you have absolutely no boating experience, the company may require you to take a skipper along for the first day at a typical extra cost of A$140 (U.S.$91) a day. If you think you know what you're doing but want that extra reassurance, you can choose to have a skipper accompany you for an extra fee for the first couple of hours, or even overnight, to help you get the hang of things. In any case, most companies mail you a preparation kit before you leave, and you get a thorough 2- to 3-hour briefing before departure and are given easy-to-read maps marking channels, anchorage points, and the very few dangerous reefs. Your charter company will radio in once or twice a day to check that you're still afloat, and you can contact them any time for advice.

Most yachts are fitted for two to eight passengers. Try to get a boat with two berths more than you need if you can afford it, as space is always tight. The boats usually have a galley kitchen, a barbecue mounted to the stern, hot showers, toilet, linen, a radio and/or stereo, a motorized dinghy, and snorkeling equipment. Sleeping quarters are usually not that luxurious and include a mix of single galley berths and one or two compact private cabins. You can buy your own provisions or have the charter company stock the boat for you for about A$30 (U.S.$19.50) per person per day. Most operators will load a windsurfer, fishing tackle, and scuba diving equipment on request for an extra fee, if they are not standard.

In peak season (see below) you may have to charter the boat for a week. At other times, most companies have a minimum of 5 days, but many will rent for

14 pay about half price. It's not necessary to book, but do book your arrival and departure ferry so you don't miss your connections. Don't assume a boat leaves every 10 minutes; most islands receive a boat only every 2 to 4 hours, some only once or twice a day.

CHOOSING A BASE

Many people like to combine a stay at Airlie Beach with a few days on an island. The advantages of staying on the mainland are cheaper accommodations, a choice of restaurants, and freedom to visit a different island each day. There is jet skiing, kayaking, parasailing, catamaran hire and wind surfing on the mainland.

The main advantage of staying on an island is that swimming, snorkeling, bushwalking, and water sports, many of them free, are right outside your door. The deadly stingers that can infest Airlie's shores do not make it to the islands, so swimming is safe

3 nights if you ask, rather than let a vessel sit idle. Five nights is a good length of time allowing you to get familiar with the boat, then relax and enjoy yourself.

For a 5-night rental in peak season, expect to pay around A$350 to $600 (U.S.$227.50–$390) for a four- to six-berth yacht, per boat, per night. Rates in the off-season, and even in the Whitsundays' busiest time from June to August, will be anywhere from A$30 to $70 (U.S.$19.50–$45.50) less. If you are prepared to book within 14 days of when you want to sail, the deals can be even better; you should usually be able to find a boat at such late notice in the off-season. You will be asked for a credit card deposit of around A$750 (U.S.$487.50). Mooring fees of A$20 to $65 (U.S.$13–$42.25) per boat per night apply if you want to dock in one of the half-dozen island resorts.

A number of bareboat charter companies offer "sail 'n stay" packages that combine a few days sailing with a few days at an island resort.

Most bareboat charter companies will make complete holiday arrangements for you in the islands, including accommodations, transfers, tours, and sporting activities. Most operate out of Airlie Beach or Hamilton Island, or both. Some of the better–known bareboat charter companies include **Australian Bareboat Charters** (☎ **1800/075 000** in Australia, or 07/4946 9381; fax 07/4946 9220; www.ozemail.com.au/~bareboat), **Queensland Yacht Charters** (☎ **1800/075 013** in Australia, or 07/4946 7400; fax 07/4946 7698; www.yachtcharters.com.au), **Sail Whitsunday** (☎ **1800/075 045** in Australia, or 07/4946 7070; fax 07/4946 7044;) www.whitsunday.net.au/bareboat/sailwhit.htm, **The Moorings** (☎ **888/952-8420** in the U.S.; www.moorings.com; in Australia contact the company's booking agents **Club Seafarer** ☎ **1300/656 484**, or 02/9389 5856; fax 02/9389 9341; www.seafarer.com.au) **Whitsunday Rent-A-Yacht** (☎ **1800/075 111** in Australia, or 07/4946 9232; fax 07/4946 9512; www.rentayacht.com.au). Tourism Whitsundays (see "Visitor Information," above) can furnish you with a complete list of operators.

If you don't want to sail yourself, there are countless skippered sailing trips through the islands (see the "Sailing & Snorkeling Trips" section for details).

year-round. You won't be isolated if you stay on an island, as most reef cruise boats, "sail & snorkel" yacht excursions, Whitehaven Beach cruises, dive boats, fishing vessels, and so on stop at the island resorts on a frequent basis. Be warned, however, that once you're "captive" on an island, you may be slugged with high food and drink prices. Bear in mind, too, that although most island resorts offer non-motorized water sports, such as windsurfing and catamarans, for free, you will pay for activities that use fuel, such as parasailing, waterskiing, and dinghy rental.

In some places in the islands, extreme low tides may reveal rocky mud flats below the sand line. Water sports can be limited at low tide because of the low water level.

EXPLORING THE ISLANDS
SAILING & SNORKELING TRIPS A cheaper alternative to skippering your own yacht around the Whitsundays is to join one of the numerous yachts offering three-day, two-night sailing adventures around the islands. You can get involved with

sailing the boat as much or as little as you want, snorkel over one dazzling reef after another, beachcomb, explore national park trails, learn to sail if you want, call in secluded bays, swim, sunbathe, and generally have a laid-back good time. A few companies offer introductory and qualified scuba diving for an extra cost per dive. Most boats carry a maximum of 12 passengers, so the atmosphere is always friendly and fun. The food is generally good, the showers are usually hot, and you sleep in comfortable but small berths off the galley. Some have petite private twin or double cabins.

In peak season, expect to pay A$300 to $360 (U.S.$195–$234) per person. Prices usually include all meals, Marine Park entrance fees, snorkel gear, and courtesy transfers to the departure point (Abel Point Marina or Shute Harbour). In the off-season, the boats compete hard for passengers; you'll see signboards on the main street in Airlie Beach advertising standby deals for A$250 (U.S.$162.50) or even as low as A$200 (U.S.$130). Among the better-known operators are *Ragamuffin II* (☎ **07/4946 7777**), a 55-foot ocean-going yacht; and **Prosail** (☎ **07/4946 5433**), which runs trips on a fleet of 19 yachts. Prosail offers day trips as well as multi-day sailing, specializing in 3-day, 2-night guided sailing trips through the Marine Park and Great Barrier Reef Marine Park. All trips include sailing, snorkeling, scuba diving, and bush walking and you can sail on world famous maxi-yachts such as *Matador, Condor, Apollo,* and *Hammer.* They also offer 2- and 5-day packages. Prices start at A$265 (U.S.$172.25) for a 2-day, 1-night trip, including meals and snorkeling equipment. You can bring your own alcohol if you wish. Contact the Tourism Whitsundays (see "Visitor Information," above) for details on other charters.

ISLAND HOPPING   Day-trippers to Hamilton, Daydream, South Molle, Club Crocodile Long Island, and Hook Island resorts can rent the hotels' water sports equipment, laze by the beaches and pools, scuba dive, join the resorts' activities programs, hike their trails, and eat at some or all of their restaurants. See "The Whitsunday Island Resorts," later in this chapter, for details on Hamilton, South Molle, and Hook islands. **Club Crocodile Long Island** is a rather noisy, unpretentious resort that has plentiful water sports, picturesque hiking trails, wild wallabies, and a large beach-cum-tidal flat where you can laze on lounges. At press time, **Daydream Island** was closed for a major renovation. It was scheduled to re-open in June or July of 2001. For information /updates, call ☎ **07/4948 8701.**

You can get to the islands on your own by ferry (see "Getting Around," above), or take an organized day trip that visits one, two, or even three islands in a day. **FantaSea Cruises** (☎ **1800/650 851** in Australia, or 07/4946 5111), **Whitsunday All Over** (☎ **1300/366 494** in Australia, or 07/4946 6900), and **Whitsunday Island Adventure Cruises** (☎ **07/4946 5255** for the booking agent) all offer them, as do several yachts. Whitsunday All Over also does a day trip to ✪ **Bali Hai,** an uninhabited isle where you can snorkel, dive, view the coral from a large submersible, or laze on the sand. Rates for day trips range from A$36.50 to $75 (U.S.$23.73–$48.75). Whitsunday All Over's "Action Pack" trips are a good value.

How to Get the Best Deal

High season in the Whitsundays is during school vacations: mid-April, late June to early July, late September to early October, late December, and all of January. The Aussie winter from June to August is tight, too. You have to book months ahead to get high-season accommodations, but any other time you can get very good deals indeed. Specials on accommodations, sailing trips, day cruises, and diving excursions leap off the blackboards outside the tour-booking agents in Airlie Beach.

Hitting the Sand at Whitehaven Beach

The 6-kilometer (3¾-mile) stretch of pure white silica sand on ✪ **Whitehaven Beach** will leave you in rapture. The beach, on an uninhabited Whitsunday Island, does not boast much coral, but swimming is good, and the forested shore is beautiful for walks. Take a book and chill out. Some sailboat day trips visit, and several motorized vessel operators, including **Lindeman Pacific** (☎ **07/4946 6922,** or 07/4946 5580 after hours) and **Fantasea Cruises** (☎ **07/4946 5111**). Expect to pay around A$65 (U.S.$42.25) per person for the day, with lunch.

Hamilton Island, (see "Where to Stay") 16 kilometers (9½ miles) southeast of Shute Harbour, is one of the most developed islands, and its resort has the widest range of activities, including coral snorkeling (at low tide), parasailing, waterskiing, windsurfing, speedboat rides, sailing and fishing trips to nearby islets, tennis and squash, go-karts, a shooting range, minigolf, and an aquatic driving range. There are hiking trails, including a challenging trek up Passage Peak for panoramic views; a 1-hour bus tour that includes a stop at the island's small fauna park, which has koalas and other Aussie wildlife; and a lovely freeform pool with lots of lounge chairs. Because the resort is spread out and divided by a steep hill, you will probably want to use the minibus taxi service which costs A$2 (U.S.$1.30) per person one-way anywhere on the island. Renting a golf cart not cheap: A$15 (U.S.$9.75) per hour or A$55 (U.S.$35.75) per day. There's a bakery, deli, and some cheap pizza/cafe/burger-style options among the resort's 10 restaurants, and a couple of pleasant bars.

South Molle Island, (see "Where to Stay"), 7 kilometers (4¼ miles) from Shute Harbour, is an unpretentious but pretty island covered with rain forests and open grassland. Visitors can golf on the 9-hole course; use the catamarans, windsurfers, and paddle skis; go parasailing, waterskiing, or jet skiing; laze on the palm-lined beach or by the pool and Jacuzzi; or hike 16 kilometers (9½ miles) of national park walking trails, including a steep climb to Spion Kop peak for fabulous 360°_views of the Whitsundays. Free fish-feeding takes place on the jetty at 10am and rainbow lorikeet-feeding is at 3pm. You can take a speedboat to nearby reefs for a guided snorkel safari, or rent a dinghy to putt-putt around the shore to a secluded snorkeling or fishing spot. The coffee shop serves inexpensive meals, and there's a bar.

Daydream Island, 8 kilometers (5 miles) from Shute Harbour, is a popular day-trip choice because it has a good patch of coral reef just offshore. At press time the resort was closed to undergo a A$20 million (U.S.$13 million) refurbishment.

Day-trippers to **Club Crocodile Long Island Resort** on Long Island (see "Where to Stay"), 10 kilometers (6 miles) from Shute Harbour, can rent water-sports equipment and use the resort's beach, Jacuzzi, gym and sauna, volleyball court, basketball court, table tennis tables, and tennis courts. You can hike 20 kilometers (12 miles) of rain-forest trails, swim in two pools, and snorkel among the modest coral in the bay. A 20-minute walk from Club Crocodile takes you to quiet little Palm Bay Hideaway, where you can swim, order meals, and chill out on a tiny pretty bay.

Hook Island (see "Where to Stay"), 40 kilometers (24 miles) from Shute Harbour, is the best day-trip destination for snorkelers. Gear costs A$5 (U.S.$3.25) per person per day to rent; you can also rent canoes, visit the underwater observatory for A$7 (U.S.$4.55) adults and A$4 (U.S.$2.60) kids, go diving, and walk bushland trails. The cafe and licensed bar sell meals.

Getting There   You can get to the islands by taking one of the scheduled boats (see "Getting Around," above), or join one of the many organized day trips. The major

Humpback whales migrate to the Whitsundays every July to September to calve. These leviathans come right up to the boat. **Fantasea Cruises** (☎ **07/4946 5111**) runs whale-watching cruises in season; trips feature an onboard whale talk and videos. The cost is about A$95 (U.S.$61.75) per adult, and if you don't see any whales, you can go again another day for free, or choose another of Fantasea's cruises.

day-trip operators are **FantaSea Cruises** (☎ **07/4946 5111**), **Whitsunday All Over** (☎ **1300/366 494** or 07/4946 6900) and **Seatrek Cruises** (☎ **07/4946 5255** for the booking agent). Several yachts also offer day trips.

MORE OUTDOOR ACTIVITIES

FISHING   Reef fishing is superb throughout the islands; red emperor, coral trout, sweetlip, and snapper are common catches. A popular charter vessel is the 54-foot timber cruiser *Moruya* (☎ **07/4946 6665,** or 07/4946 7127 after hours). Day trips depart Shute Harbour daily at 9:45am and return at 5:45pm. They include lunch, bait, and hand reels. Fishing rods can be hired for A$15 (U.S.$9.75) for the day, or bring your own. The crew will even clean your catch. Adults pay A$75 (U.S.$48.75), seniors A$70 (U.S.$45.50), children 4 to 14 A$37 (U.S.$24.05) and a family of 4 A$185 (U.S.$120.25).

The 40-foot *Marlin Blue* (☎ **07/4948 0999** for bookings) takes reef and game anglers from Abel Point Marina and South Molle Island Resort for A$245 (U.S.$159.25) per person for a full day, on a shared charter. That includes lunch, bait, and tackle; drinks are extra. The boat departs the mainland at 7am and returns around 5:30pm.

If you want to undertake your own fishing expedition, several outfitters rent boats. **Harbourside Boat Hire** (☎ **07/4946 9330**) in Shute Harbour rents motorized dinghies for A$50 (U.S.$32.50) for a half day or A$70 (U.S.$45.50) for a full day. Half-cabin cruisers cost A$70 (U.S.$45.50) for a half day or A$120 (U.S.$78) for a full day. They also sell tackle, bait, ice and all your fishing needs.

ECO TOURS   Visitors to the Whitsundays can get up-close-and-personal with crocodiles in their natural habitat on tours run by Proserpine resident Steve Watson. **Proserpine River Eco Tours** (☎ **0408 071 544** mobile phone) combines an open-air wagon ride through pristine wetlands and a boat trip on the river to learn more about one of Queensland's major crocodile-breeding grounds. This is the only place to see crocs in safety in the wild south of the Daintree. Bus pickups run from Airlie Beach, Cannonvale and Proserpine for morning and afternoon tours, which each run for about four hours, depending on tides, and costs A$48 (U.S.$31.20) per person.

HIKING & 4WD SAFARIS   The hills behind Airlie Beach stretch into nearby Conway State Forest and are rich in giant strangler figs, ferns, and palms. If you're lucky you'll spot a blue Ulysses butterfly. Several companies offer half-day 4WD safaris. Hiking trails ranging in length from 1 kilometer (just over half a mile) to 5.4 kilometer (3¼ miles) lead through the forest or down to the beach in Conway National Park, which spans Shute Harbour Road between Airlie Beach and Shute Harbour. One trail has signboards explaining the Aboriginal uses of the plants you are passing; several trails offer impressive views of the islands. The trails depart from one of three parking lots along Shute Harbour Road. **The Queensland Parks and Wildlife Service information center** (☎ **07/4946 7022**) on Shute Harbour Road at

Mandalay Road, 2.5 kilometers (1½ miles) northeast of Airlie Beach has maps and self-guiding brochures; it's open Monday through Friday from 8am to 5pm and most, but not all, Saturdays from 9am to 1pm.

SEA KAYAKING   If you have strong arms, sea kayaking is a wonderful way to enjoy the islands. Daydream Island and the beaches and bays of the North, Mid, and South Molle are all within paddling distance of the mainland. It's common to see dolphins, turtles, and sharks. One of the area's established operators is **Salty Dog Sea Kayaking** (☎ **07/4946 1388** or 0419 544 841 mobile phone; www.saltydog.com.au; saltydog@ mackay.net.au), which takes escorted day trips through the islands on Monday, Thursday, and Friday, departing at 8:30am, returning at 5pm. The trips usually depart from Shute Harbour, but run from the island resorts on request. Two-day expeditions depart Tuesday and Saturday. A day trip is A$80 (U.S.$52) per person, 2-day trips are A$235 (U.S.$152.75); rates include snorkel gear, meals, pickup, and on overnight trips, camping gear. They also deliver sea kayaks anywhere in the Whitsundays. A full day's rental is from A$40 (U.S.$26) for a single kayak, A$70 (U.S.$45.50) for a double, including delivery and pickup and safety equipment.

WATER SPORTS   Airlie Beach is not great for swimming or snorkeling, but you can rent jet skis, WaveRunners, windsurfers, aquabikes, pedal cats, catamarans, and paddle skis to use on the bay. Choose from the several rental outfits along the beach.

AIRLIE BEACH
640km (384 miles) S of Cairns; 1,146km (687½ miles) N of Brisbane

The town of Airlie Beach, only a few blocks long, is the focal point of activity on the Whitsunday mainland. It has some decent accommodations, a small selection of good restaurants and bars, a boutique or two, and facilities such as banks and a supermarket. Cruises and yachts depart from either Shute Harbour, a 10-minute drive south on Shute Harbour Road, or Abel Point Marina, a 10-minute walk west along the shore or a quick drive over the hill on Shute Harbour Road.

Airlie Beach has a new A$8 million (U.S.$5.2 million) artificial lagoon, offset by sandy beaches and landscaped parkland, which resolves the problem of where to swim in stinger season. The lagoon is the size of about six full-size Olympic swimming pools, set in 10 acres of botanic gardens, with a children's pool, plenty of shade, barbecues, picnic shelters, toilets and showers, and parking.

Perched on the edge of the Coral Sea, with views across Pioneer Bay and the Whitsunday Passage, Airlie Beach has a village atmosphere where life revolves around the beach and the marina by day, and the bars and restaurants by night.

The spit of land between Airlie Bay and Boathaven Bay is home to the **Airlie Beach Sailing Club.** Shute Harbour, 11 kilometers (7 miles) from Airlie Beach, is one of Queensland's busiest ports, filled with yachts, cruisers, water taxis, ferries and fishermen. For a bird's-eye view, head to the **Lions Lookout.**

WHERE TO STAY

Airlie Beach Hotel. 16 The Esplanade (foot entrance on Shute Harbour Rd.), Airlie Beach, QLD 4802. ☎ **07/4946 6233.** Fax 07/4946 7476. www.airliebeachhotel.com.au. 56 hotel units, 4 suites, 20 motel–style units. A/C TV TEL. A$83 (U.S.$53.95) double for motel units; A$132–$154 (U.S.$85.80–$100.10) double for hotel units; A$198 (U.S.$128.70) double for suites. AE, BC, DC, MC, V. Free secure parking.

Extensively refurbished in mid-2000, the hotel is in the middle of town, next to the beach. The original 20 motel units have been totally refurbished, and 60 new beachfront units have been added, including 4 suites. New facilities include a swimming pool, tour desk, and guest laundry. The original Mangrove Jack's restaurant (see Where to Dine, below) remains intact, and is joined by a second bar and grill restaurant, Capers, which has tables overlooking the beach and which turns into a late night dance bar after 10pm.

Boathaven Lodge. 440 Shute Harbour Rd., Airlie Beach, QLD 4802. ☎ **07/4946 6421.** Fax 07/4946 4808. www.boathavenresort.com. boathaven@whitsunday.net.au. 12 units (with shower only). A/C TV. A$95 (U.S.$61.75) double, studio; A$120 (U.S.$78) 1-bedroom apt; A$145 (U.S.$94.25) 2-bedroom apt. Extra adult A$20 (U.S.$13); child under 15 A$10 (U.S.$6.50). Studios, apts, and penthouses A$120–$250 (U.S.$78–$162.50). AE, BC, DC, MC, V.

Friendly hosts Jan and Peter Cox run these well-maintained studio and one- and two-bedroom apartments, 400 meters (¼-mile) from town among lovely gardens. All have views over Boathaven Bay, as does the pool and Jacuzzi. The simple, attractive one-bedroom apartments are new and airy, with big living areas, kitchenettes, modern bathrooms (borrow a hair dryer at reception), indoor palms, and large timber decks. Jan and Peter also advise on tours and make bookings. In recent renovations, a second pool and waterfall have replaced the smaller, older studios near the road.

Whitsunday Terraces Resort. Golden Orchid Dr. (off Shute Harbour Rd.), Airlie Beach, QLD 4802. ☎ **1800/075 062** in Australia, or 07/4946 6788. Fax 07/4946 7128. www.whit sunday.net.au/terraces.htm. terraces@whitsunday.net.au. 65 units. A/C TV TEL. A$138 (U.S.$89.70) studio, A$149 (U.S.$96.85) 1-bedroom apartment. Extra person A$15 (U.S.$9.75). Rates lower for stays of 3 nights or more. AE, BC, DC, MC, V.

These studio and one-bedroom apartments on a hillside a steep 2-minute walk above Airlie Beach are my pick for the "value with a view" prize. The one-bedroom apartments have especially roomy, light-filled living rooms, and every apartment has a big balcony. All are furnished differently, but to a high standard, and serviced daily. The front desk lends hair dryers. Guests gather around the swimming pool/sundeck/restaurant/cocktail bar, which, like the rooms, has sweeping views over the town to the bay and Twin Cone Island. The friendly managers run a tour desk.

Whitsunday Wanderers Resort. Shute Harbour Rd., Airlie Beach, QLD 4802. ☎ **1800/ 075 069** in Australia, or 07/4946 6446. Fax 07/4946 6761. 104 units (with shower only). A/C TV TEL. A$120 (U.S.$78) double. Ask about off-season discounts, overnight and honeymoon packages, and packages that include meals. AE, BC, MC, V. Free parking.

Set in 18 acres of tropical gardens on the main street of Airlie Beach, this resort fits right in with the laid-back Airlie lifestyle. Accommodations are scattered around the grounds in blocks of four- to eight-rooms with open-air parking. The decor is old-fashioned, but you get plenty of space, a kitchenette, a decent-sized bathroom, and a big balcony or patio. Hair dryers are on loan at reception, and irons and ironing boards in the communal laundry. This is a good choice for families as there is plenty of room for the kids to run around, five half- and full-size tennis courts, an 18-hole minigolf course, archery, table tennis, volleyball, several pools, a Jacuzzi, a gym, and a kids' playground. All except the tennis courts are free of charge. There's also a free kids club during vacations. There's a restaurant, a bar, barbecues, and comprehensive tour desk.

WHERE TO DINE

Mamma's Boys International Food Court & the Boardwalk Bar. In and next to Magnum's Backpacker's & Bar, Shute Harbour Rd. ☎ **07/4946 6266.** Menu items A$2.50–$15 (U.S.$1.63–$9.75); many meals under A$10 (U.S.$6.50). AE, BC, DC, MC, V. Daily 11am–late. STEAK/INTERNATIONAL FOOD COURT.

Eating in Airlie is all about being casual, and you won't find a nicer place to hang out than under the old tree in this atmospheric streetside courtyard. Fetch a big, tasty meal from the food court next door, and eat at one of the timber tables under the tree. Go for Thai, Chinese, or Malaysian noodles; barbecued prime ribs from Butcher Bob's Grill; a beef kabob with spicy peanut sauce from Ahmed's Kebabs; a chargrilled seafood pizza from Mamma's Boys; catch of the day battered or crumbed from Old Salty's . . . you get the picture. A band plays most nights. The food court also does takeout.

✪ **Mangrove Jack's.** In the Airlie Beach Hotel, 16 The Esplanade (enter via Shute Harbour Rd.). ☎ **07/4946 6233.** Reservations recommended. Main courses A$7.90–$19.90 (U.S.$5.14–$12.94). AE, BC, DC, MC, V. Daily 10am–midnight. WOOD-FIRED PIZZA/CAFE FARE.

Bareboat sailors, sugar farmers, Sydney yuppies, and European backpackers all flock to this open-fronted sports bar/restaurant. The mood is upbeat but casual, the surrounds are spick-and-span, and the food passes muster. Wood-fired pizza with trendy toppings is the specialty. There is no table service; just place your order at the bar and collect your food when your number is called. More than 50 wines come by the glass.

THE WHITSUNDAY ISLAND RESORTS

Almost no island resort in the Whitsundays comes cheap. There are about 10 resorts of varying degrees of splendor; accommodations range from positively glitzy to comfortably midrange to downright old-fashioned.

Of the full-service resorts, **Club Crocodile Long Island** and **South Molle Island Resort** represent the best value, as the rates at each include all meals. Both islands' rates also include a lot of activities. As a general rule, non-motorized activities and water sports such as catamarans, windsurfers, and paddle skis are free, while you pay extra for activities that use fuel, such as parasailing or waterskiing. Of the two resorts, South Molle is prettier and a tad more upscale than Club Crocodile Long Island. It also has faster and more frequent connections to the mainland and other islands.

If you're looking for an alternative to these "big" island resorts, consider the quiet, low-key affairs tucked away under the palms, often with few facilities to speak of. **Hook Island Wilderness Resort** and **Whitsunday Wilderness Lodge** fall into this category. Unlike South Molle Island Resort and Club Crocodile, these resorts usually don't offer day trips to the Great Barrier Reef, fishing expeditions, dive excursions, and sail-and-snorkel trips, but that suits their quiet, nature-loving guests just fine.

Club Crocodile Long Island. Long Island, Whitsunday Islands (Private Mail Bag 26, Mackay, QLD 4740). ☎ **1800/075 125** in Australia, or 07/4946 9400 (or book through Flag International). Fax 07/4946 9555. www.clubcroc.com.au. clubcroc@powerup.com.au. 156 units, 140 with bathroom (shower only). Beachfront & Garden units A$281–$318 (U.S.$182.65–$201.50) single, A$360–$410 (U.S.$234–$266.50) double; children 3–17 A$55 (U.S.$35.75). Lodge rooms A$141 (U.S.$91.65) single, A$220 (U.S.$143) double. Rates include all meals. Lower rates in off-season. Ask about standby, honeymoon, overnight, and longer-stay packages. AE, BC, DC, JCB, MC, V. Whitsunday All Over (☎ **07/4946 6900**) provides 30-min. launch transfers from Shute Harbour for A$36.50 (U.S.$23.73) adults, A$15.50 (U.S.$10.08) children or A$89 (U.S.$57.85) family round-trip.

Club Croc is probably the most unpretentious of all the Whitsunday resorts, and its package deals make it popular with families and young couples. It faces a wide, curving bay that has good reef snorkeling. Lots of beachfront water sports await: catamaran sailing, windsurfing, surf skiing, jet skiing, waterskiing, scuba diving, and more. You can join organized activities, like jet ski races, or do your own thing. Entertainment can be anything from a raging disco to casino games, live bands, karaoke, talent shows, or cane toad races. Other free activities include aerobics, beach and pool volleyball, basketball, table tennis, and tennis. There are also 20 kilometers (12 miles) of national park trails, where you often see wallabies; two swimming pools; a gym, Jacuzzi, and sauna; and a kids' playground. A free Kids' Club provides activities for 4- to 12-year-olds, and babysitting can be arranged for a fee. The resort has a beauty salon and boutique.

The beachfront rooms have a Mediterranean look, with glass-louver windows and a view of the sea through the trees. Garden rooms, located behind the beachfront rooms, are a little older and darker with painted brick walls and carpeted floors. Both types have air-conditioning, minifridges, TVs, telephones, and patios or balconies. Your best value, however, are the appealing Lodge rooms, which have polished timber floors, freshly painted walls, and a fan (but no bathroom, telephone, or view). They're compact but nice if you just want a bed and don't mind shared bathroom facilities. They have no air-conditioning, so take them only from April to October. Hair dryers are available at reception, and there is a laundromat. There's nothing fancy about the food in the seafront buffet restaurant, so you may want to buy a barbecue-it-yourself meat pack from the little cafe. Casual is the byword here; pack your old surf shorts.

Hook Island Wilderness Resort. Hook Island (40km/25 miles NE of Shute Harbour), Whitsunday Islands. (Postal address: P.M.B. 23, Mackay, QLD 4741.) ☎ **07/4946 9380.** Fax 07/4946 9470. www.hookis.com. enquiries@hookis.com. 20 tent sites; 2 10-bed dormitories; 10 cabins, 4 with bathroom (shower only). A/C. A$66 (U.S.$42.90) cabin without bathroom double; extra adult A$22 (U.S.$14.30), extra child 4–14 A$16.50 (U.S.$10.73). A$104.50 (U.S.$67.93) cabin with bathroom double; extra adult A$27.50 (U.S.$17.88), extra child A$22 (U.S.$14.30). Tent site A$14.30 (U.S.$9.30) adult, A$7.70 (U.S.$5.01) child 4–14. Dorm bed A$22 (U.S.$14.30) adult, A$16.50 (U.S.$10.73) child (linen supplied). Ask about packages. BC, MC, V. **Whitsunday Island Adventure Cruises** (☎ 07/4946 5255 for the booking agent) provides transfers from the mainland (Shute Harbour) at A$35 (U.S.$22.75) per person, round-trip (trip time: 1–1½ hr.).

This humble collection of cabins and campsites on a white sandy beach is one of the few really affordable island resorts on the Great Barrier Reef. It's popular with backpackers and anybody who just wants to dive, rent canoes, play beach volleyball, visit the underwater observatory, hike, fish, laze in the pool and Jacuzzi, and chill out. Good snorkeling is footsteps from shore, and the resort's dive center conducts first-time and regular dives. Hook is a national park and the second-largest Whitsunday island.

You need to be able to get along without room service, in-room telephones, and smart accommodations; the cabins are just basic huts with beds or bunks sleeping six or eight. All accommodations come with fresh bed linen (BYO bath towels), tea- and coffee-making facilities, and a minifridge. Bring your own hair dryer. There is a casual cafe and bar. A store sells essentials, but try to come with everything you need. Snorkel gear costs A$10 (U.S.$6.50) for the duration of your stay. The staff will drop you off at a deserted beach for A$10 (U.S.$6.50) per person or take you to coral gardens for A$20 (U.S.$13) per person. Apart from Whitsunday Island Adventure Cruises' once-daily launch, and daily day trips to Whitehaven Beach and the outer Reef, almost no sailboats, fishing boats, or other tours call here.

Money-Saving Tips

You will probably have to pay the "rack" rates quoted below during school vacations. Other times, you can usually get a package deal that's a much better value. Qantas offers airfare-inclusive packages from most Australian state-capital cities and Cairns. If you show up in the Whitsundays in the off-season without a reservation, you can sometimes snare an excellent standby deal. It never hurts to ask.

South Molle Island Resort. South Molle Island (7km/4 miles E of Shute Harbour), Whitsunday Islands. (Postal address: P.M.B. 21, Mackay, QLD 4741). ☎ **1800/075 080** in Australia, or 07/4946 9433. Fax 07/4946 9580. www.southmolleisland.com.au. info@southmolleisland.com.au. 200 units (some with shower only, some with Jacuzzi). AC TV TEL. A$342–$474 (U.S.$222.30–$308.10) double. Extra adult A$171–$237 (U.S.$111.15–$154.05); extra child 3–14 A$55 (U.S.$35.75). Family rates available in some rooms. Rates include all meals. Ask about packages. AE, BC, DC, MC, V. **FantaSea Cruises** (☎ **1800/650 851** in Australia, or 07/4946 5111) and **Whitsunday All Over** (☎ **1300/366 494** in Australia, or 07/4946 9499) provides launch transfers from Shute Harbour and most other islands.

South Molle is a good-value island choice. It's not glamorous but it's pretty, with many free activities, and all meals included in the rates. The complex, built around a curving white sand bay, is getting on in years, so expect a nicely maintained but modest collection of accommodations nestled in tropical gardens or along a hillside. Each unit has sea, garden, or golf course views. Following a 1998 to 1999 refurbishing, some beachfront units, especially those with Jacuzzis, are looking positively trendy. The front desk lends hair dryers, and there is a laundromat.

The 1,000-acre island is a hilly National Park of grasslands, rain forest, and eucalypts with 16 kilometers (10 miles) of walking trails, including a steep climb to Mt. Jeffreys for fabulous 360° views. As well as a basic but pretty 9-hole golf course (small charge for balls), there are catamarans, windsurfers, and paddle-skis (all free), jet skis, water skis, a gym, a Jacuzzi and sauna, archery, table tennis, a toddler's pool, a volleyball net, two day/night tennis courts, and fishing tackle and snorkel gear to rent, plus a beauty salon and boutique. The swimming pool is a big rectangle, but it is lined with welcoming lounge chairs under palms, as is the beach. A packed daily activities program offers everything from parasailing to coconut-throwing competitions. The dive shop makes dive and snorkel day trips, takes first-timers diving in the bay, and runs courses. The island is rimmed with inlets accessible by hiking or rented dinghy. On some days, snorkeling safaris are run to better reefs than those around the island. Rainbow lorikeets are everywhere, even on your shoulder stealing food at fish feeding time. A free kids' club for 5-and-unders operates every day, and during Aussie school vacations a free club runs for 6- to 12-year-olds.

Although the dining room lacks sea views, the buffet food is fine; good meals are available at extra cost in Coral's restaurant some nights, and a cafe sells light meals. There's live entertainment every night in the bar, from a staff song-and-dance show to cane toad racing to the Friday-night "Flames of Polynesia" dinner show.

Palm Terrace. Hamilton Island Resort, Hamilton Island (16km/10 miles SE of Shute Harbour), Whitsunday Islands, QLD 4803. ☎ **1800/075 110** in Australia, or 02/8353 8444 (reservations office in Sydney), or 07/4946 9999 (the island). Fax 02/8353 8499 (reservations office in Sydney) or 07/4946 8888 (the island). www.hamiltonisland.com.au. vacation@hamiltonisland.com.au. 60 units, all with bathroom (shower only). A/C, MINIBAR, TV, TEL. A$250 (U.S.$162.50) per room per night (all units sleep 4). AE, BC, DC, MC, V, JCB. Ask about packages. Airlines fly into Hamilton Island Airport. Free airport-resort transfers for all guests. FantaSea Cruises (☎ **1800/650 851** in Australia, or 07/4946 5111) provides the cheapest transfers from the mainland (Shute Harbour) and most other islands

More than A$2.3 million (U.S.$1.5 million) was spent converting an existing lodge into this budget hotel on ritzy Hamilton Island. The hotel, which opened in January 2001, is set in quiet gardens near Catseye Beach and resort. About a third of the rooms have uninterrupted ocean and beach views. The island has four other hotels, ranging from private bungalows to a five-star luxury Beach Club as well as a choice of privately-owned luxury apartments and villas. The rooms in Palm Terrace are large and have big balconies. Each sleeps a maximum of 4 and has a king-size bed as well as a choice of double sofa bed or a single bed with a trundle. Guests have free use of non-motorized watercraft. Families staying in the Palm Terrace can take advantage of the Kids Stay, Play and Eat for Free program which includes free accommodation for children (using existing bedding), free admission to the Clownfish Club and free meals in a selection of the island's restaurants when dining with their parents.

✪ **Whitsunday Wilderness Lodge.** Long Island (16km/10 miles SE of Shute Harbour), Whitsunday Islands. (Postal address: c/o 30 Swan Terrace, Windsor, Brisbane, QLD 4030.) ☎ /fax **07/3357 3843** (Brisbane reservations office) or 07/4946 9787 (the island; all bookings and enquiries to Brisbane office). www.southlongisland.com. info@ecoventure.com.au. 10 units (with shower only). A$1,782 (U.S.$1,158.30) double for 3 nights. Rates include all meals, helicopter transfers from Hamilton Island Airport, daily excursions, and equipment. 3-night minimum stay required. Rates decrease with longer stays. 1 night free with 4-night stay over Beachcomber Day (first Tues of every month). BC, MC, V. No children under 15.

This resort was designed to show off the Whitsundays' natural beauty. Tucked in a cove under hoop pines and palms, this environmentally friendly lodge on a National Park island is for people who want to explore the wilderness in basic comfort, without the crowds, activities, or artificial atmosphere of a resort. It's also a great place to meet other travelers. A maximum 20 guests stay in simple, smart cabins facing the sea; each has a double and single bed, modern bathroom, and private deck with sea view. The lodge is solar-powered, so hair dryers and irons are a no-no. There is no TV or radio, only one public phone, and breezes replace air-conditioning. Social life centers on an open-sided gazebo by the beach, equipped with a natural-history library and CDs, where everyone dines together under the Milky Way on fabulous buffet-style campfire meals. Access is by a short but stunning helicopter flight from Hamilton Island.

Every morning (except Sun), the resort managers decide what the day's excursion will be, usually aboard the lodge's gleaming 34-foot catamaran. You might sail to tidal flats to look for red and purple rhinoceros starfish, sea kayak the mangroves to spot giant green sea turtles (common around the lodge), sail to South Molle Island to hike, snorkel the fringing reef on uninhabited islands, or bushwalk to a magical milkwood grove. You don't have to join in, you can laze in the hammocks, or head off with a free sea kayak and snorkel gear. The beach is more tidal flat than sand, but clean and firm enough for sunbathing. Wildlife abounds, including Myrtle, the lodge's pet kangaroo. Guests here consider it a plus that no ferries or cruise boats call and that the lodge is inaccessible to day-trippers or hikers from other resorts. The only available commercial tour (at a fee) is a seaplane flight to snorkel the outer Great Barrier Reef. On Beachcomber Days, guests are asked to help clear debris from the islands' shores in the course of the day's fun. It's easy and a small effort to keep the island pristine.

CAMPING ON THE ISLANDS

Despite the fact that camping facilities are almost nonexistent, camping on uninhabited islands in the Whitsundays is delightful. There are no showers, and few spots have toilets or even shelters, so be prepared to really rough it. Campfires are not permitted on the islands, so you will need a gas stove. **Island Camping Connection** (☎ 07/4946 5255) arranges camping on several deserted islands. The company provides transfers to any island for A$45 (U.S.$29.25) per person (two-person minimum) round-trip (price includes water containers). They also rent camping kits with tent, bedroll, gas stove, mess kit, cutlery, cooler and torch for A$40 (U.S.$26) for two people for the first day, A$15 (U.S.$9.75) every day thereafter. You need to bring other necessities such as toilet paper, linen, insect repellent and washing-up gear. They also rent snorkel gear for A$11 (U.S.$7.15) per person for the duration of your camp. You bring your own food, a sense of adventure, and a **permit** from the Queensland Parks and Wildlife Service. Permits are A$3.85 (U.S.$2.50) per person, per night for any-one over 5 years old; you can pick them up from the **QPWS office** on Shute Harbour Road at Mandalay Road, in Airlie Beach (☎ **07/4946 7022**). The office is open Monday through Friday from 8am to 5pm, and most but not all Saturdays from 9am to 1pm. You must organize your boat transport before you go for your permit—consider a sea kayak! Although there are loads of sites, book ahead to secure a spot during school vacations.

6 The Capricorn Coast & the Southern Reef Islands

South of the Whitsundays, the Bruce Highway travels through rural country until it hits the beaches of the Sunshine Coast north of Brisbane. It may not be the tourism heartland of the state, but there's plenty to discover. The most spectacular Great Barrier Reef island, **Heron Island,** is off the coast from Gladstone. Heron's reefs offer much to tantalize beneath the ocean's surface, its waters boasting 21 great dive sites. In summer, giant turtles nest on its beaches and in winter humpback whales cruise by.

North of Gladstone is **Rockhampton** and the pretty Capricorn Coast, named after the Tropic of Capricorn that runs through it. Rockhampton is also a stepping-stone to **Great Keppel Island,** a resort island popular with happy-go-lucky travelers and young Aussies on holiday. To the south, off the town of Bundaberg, lies another tiny coral cay, **Lady Elliot Island,** which is a nesting site for tens of thousands of sea birds, and has a first-rate fringing reef. Two little-known attractions in Bundaberg are its good shore scuba diving and a loggerhead turtle rookery that operates in summer on the beach. Farther south is the world's largest sand island: the World Heritage listed **Fraser Island,** which can be negotiated only on foot or by 4WD.

ROCKHAMPTON: THE BEEF CAPITAL
1,055km (633 miles) S of Cairns; 638km (383 miles) N of Brisbane

"Rocky" is the unofficial capital of the sprawling beef-cattle country inland, and the gateway to Great Keppel Island, which boasts some of the few inexpensive island retreats in Queensland. Heritage buildings line the Fitzroy River, where barramundi await keen fishermen. Every Friday night at the **Great Western Hotel,** bullriding cowboys take to the rodeo ring to test their skills against local Brahman bulls.

ESSENTIALS
GETTING THERE   By Car   Rockhampton is on the Bruce Highway, a 3½-hour drive south of Mackay, and almost 2 hours north of Gladstone.

By Plane   Sunstate Airlines and **Airlink** (book through Qantas at ☎ **13 13 13** in Australia) have flights from Brisbane, and from Cairns via Townsville and Mackay. Sunstate flies from Bundaberg and Gladstone.

By Train   Several **Queensland Rail** (☎ **13 22 32** in Queensland, or 07/3235 1122) **trains** call into Rockhampton weekly or daily on the Brisbane–Cairns route. The trip from Brisbane takes 7 hours on the high-speed Tilt train; the fare is A$77 (U.S.$50.05) economy class and A$166.10 (U.S. $107.97) business class. From Cairns the train takes 19½ hours and costs A$199.90 (U.S.$129.94) for a sitting berth, A$158.40 (U.S.$102.96) for an economy-class sleeper.

By Bus   McCafferty's (☎ **13 14 99** in Australia) and **Greyhound Pioneer** (☎ **13 20 30** in Australia) call at Rockhampton on their many daily coach services between Brisbane and Cairns. The fare is A$66 (U.S.$42.90) from Brisbane (trip time: just over 11 hr.) and A$103 (U.S.$66.95) from Cairns (trip time: about 16½ hr.).

VISITOR INFORMATION   Drop by the **Capricorn Tourism bureau,** whose information center is at the city's southern entrance on Gladstone Road (at the Capricorn Spire; ☎ **07/4927 2055**). It's open daily 9am to 5pm.

GETTING AROUND   Avis (☎ **07/4927 3344**), **Budget** (☎ **07/4926 4888**), **Hertz** (☎ **07/4922 2721**), and **Thrifty** (☎ **07/4927 8755**) have offices in Rockhampton.

EXPLORING THE AREA: CAVERNS, ABORIGINAL CULTURE & MORE

✪ Olsen's Capricorn Caverns (☎ **07/ 4934 2883**) 23 kilometers (13 miles) north of Rockhampton at Olsen's Caves Road, off the Bruce Highway, have been a popular attraction in these parts ever since Norwegian pioneer John Olsen stumbled upon them in 1882. The limestone caves have origins in an ancient coral reef (380 million years old) and are a maze of small tunnels and larger chambers. The one-hour tour which winds through large caverns with stalactite and stalagmite formations before entering the 20 meter (64 ft.) high Cathedral Cave is A$11 (U.S.$7.15) for adults, A$10 (U.S.$6.50) for seniors and students, and A$5.50 (U.S.$3.58) for children ages 5 to 15; it departs daily on the hour from 9am to 4pm (closing time is 5pm). Spelunkers (over 16 years) can squeeze through tunnels and chimneys and rock-climb on a 4-hour adventure tour that costs A$45 (U.S.$29.25); book 24 hours ahead. Plan enough time here to walk the 30-minute dry rain-forest trail, watch the video on bats in the interpretive center, and feed the wild kangaroos. From December 1 to January 10, you can catch the Summer Solstice light cave on a tour departing every morning at 11am. On the longest day of the year a ray of pure light pours through a hole in the limestone caves. It's known as the **Summer Solstice** phenomena and is the only time of year when the sun is directly over the Tropic of Capricorn. The caves are also home to thousands of small insectivorous bats, which leave the cave at sunset to feed. Three resident flying foxes housed near the kiosk also provide much interest for visitors of all ages. You can buy sandwiches from the kiosk, take a dip in the pool, and camp for A$10 (U.S.$6.50) double for a tent site or A$16 (U.S.$10.40) for a powered site. **Rothery's Coaches** (☎ **07/4922 4320**) provide transfers from town.

Another great place to go "batty" is at **Mt. Etna Caves National Park,** not far from Olsen's Capricorn Caverns. Tens of thousands of female bent wing bats pour from a small shaft atop a limestone cavern to feed in the evening. After gorging on insects, they return to **Bat Cleft** limestone caves, one of only five Little Bent Wing Bat maternity sites in the world. Guided tours are run in January and February by the Rockhampton's Department of Environment. Book tours through the **Department of Environment** (☎ **07/4936 0511**) or **Capricorn Tourism** (☎ **07/4927 2055**).

Also on Olsen's Caves Road, 2 kilometers (1¼ miles) off the highway, are the **Cammoo Caves** (☎ **07/4934 2774**), where you can guide yourself on a 45-minute walk. Admission is A$7 (U.S.$4.55) for adults, A$6 (U.S.$3.90) for students and seniors, and A$3 (U.S.$1.95) for children 5 to 15; the caves are open daily from 8:30am to 4:30pm. Closed Christmas and Good Friday.

The **Dreamtime Cultural Centre** (☎ **07/4936 1655**) located on the Bruce Highway opposite the Yeppoon turnoff, 6 kilometers (3¾ miles) north of town, showcases Aboriginal culture. Ninety-minute tours of burial sites and rock art, with didgeridoo demonstrations and boomerang-throwing classes, run daily at 10:30am and 1pm. There's also a sandstone cave replica, a display on the dugong (manatee) culture of the Torres Strait Islanders, and an Aboriginal crafts shop. The center is open daily 10am to 3:30pm. Closed Anzac Day, Christmas, and New Year's Day. Admission, including the tour, is A$12.10 (U.S.$7.87) for adults and A$5.50 (U.S.$3.58) for kids.

Rockhampton has two free public gardens, nice for a stroll and a barbecue. **The Kershaw Gardens,** which display Aussie rain forest, wetland, and fragrant plants from north of the 30th parallel, also have a monorail and a pioneer-style slab hut where Devonshire teas are served. Enter off Charles Street. Admission is free to the small zoo in the **Rockhampton Botanic Gardens** (☎ **07/4922 1654**), which features chimps, crocs, 'roos, koalas, monkeys, flying foxes, lorikeets, and other creatures. It's open 6am to 6pm daily. Enter off Ann Street or Spencer Street.

WHERE TO STAY

Southside Holiday Village. Lower Dawson Rd. (south side of town), Rockhampton, QLD 4700. ☎ **1800/075 911** in Australia, or 07/4927 3013. Fax 07/4927 7750. 20 tent sites; 37 powered campsites, 6 with bathroom (shower only); 26 cabins and villas, 20 with bathroom (shower only). Tent site A$15 (U.S.$9.75) single or double; extra person A$5 (U.S.$3.25), children A$4 (U.S.$2.60). Powered campsite A$20 (U.S.$13) single or double. Caravan A$32 (U.S.$20.80) single, A$35 (U.S.$22.75) double; extra person A$6 (U.S.$3.90). Cabins and villas A$36–$56 (U.S.$23.40–$36.40) single, A$39–$59 (U.S.$25.35–$38.35) double; additional person A$6–$8 (U.S.$3.90–$5.20). Linen in caravans and cabins A$6 (U.S.$3.90) per set per night or A$15 (U.S.$9.75) per week. A$6 (U.S.$3.90) surcharge applies on cabins and villas on long weekends and public holidays. BC, MC, V.

Set in landscaped grounds near the tourist bureau, this well-run park of villas, cabins, and campgrounds is as pleasant a place to stay as you could ask for. The kids will like the playground, the half tennis court, and the water slide in the pool, you will like the spick-and-span air-conditioned villas with separate bedrooms, bunk beds, tiny but neat bathrooms with fresh towels and hair dryers, cooking facilities, iron and board, TV, and latticed patios. Ask for a villa away from the main road. Three times a day, Monday to Saturday, the park runs a courtesy coach into town and the Botanic Gardens.

WHERE TO DINE

Rockhampton R.S.L. Club. Cambridge St. ☎ **07/4927 1737.** Reservations recommended on weekends. Smart dress required. Main courses A$8–$13.50 (U.S.$5.20–$8.88). No credit cards. Mon–Sat noon–2pm, 6–8pm. Club open 10am–midnight. TRADITIONAL AUSTRALIAN.

How can you beat the roast of the day when it includes three huge slices of pork with generous servings of hot vegetables and potatoes smothered in gravy, for under A$12 (U.S.$7.80)? By ordering the half-serve, that's how, because that's still enough to fill you up. Australia's Returned Services League (R.S.L.) clubs are renowned for big meals at small prices. The wine is a great value, too. Sign in at the door.

GREAT KEPPEL ISLAND
15km (9 miles) E off Rockhampton

This 3,635-acre island is home to **Great Keppel Island Resort** (☎ **07/4939 5044**), renowned among Australians for its water sports and activities. Room rates at the resort are budget-busting, but anyone can take a day trip from the mainland. Day-trippers can pay to use much of the resort's water sports equipment, swim for free in one of its pools, patronize the store, eat at the inexpensive cafe or moderately priced Anchorage Char Grill, and drink at the Wreck Bar. Seventeen beaches on the island are accessible by walking trails or dinghy (which you can rent). Stop by the information center near the Wreck Bar to book activities and pick up walking trail maps. The shallow waters and fringing reef make the island a good choice for beginner divers; experienced divers will see corals, sea snakes, turtles, and rays. Book your diving excursions at the Beach Hut at Keppel Haven (see "Where to Stay"). If you stay overnight, you will likely see one of the island's spectacular sunsets.

Boom in the Net

A water activity invented in Oz is "boom netting," in which a large net is thrown off the back of a boat, and participants hang off it (and hang onto their bathing suits, as they sometimes lose tops or bottoms) and are towed across the waves.

GETTING THERE　A launch operated by **Keppel Tourist Services** (☎ **07/4933 6744**) makes the 30-minute crossing from Rosslyn Bay Harbour, approximately 55 kilometers (33 miles) east of Rockhampton, daily at 7:30am, 9:15am, 11:30am, and 3:30pm. It leaves the island at 8:15am, 2pm, and 4:30pm. An extra 6pm service runs Fridays, returning at 6:40pm. A\$30 (U.S.\$19.50) adults, A\$22 (U.S.\$14.30) seniors, A\$15 (U.S.\$9.75) children 5 to 14, and A\$70 (U.S.\$45.50) family of 4.

From Rockhampton, take the Capricorn Coast scenic drive route "10" to Emu Park and follow the signs to Rosslyn Bay Harbour. If you're coming from the north, the scenic drive turnoff is north of the city, and then it's 46 kilometers (27½ miles) to the harbor. You can leave your car in undercover storage at **Great Keppel Island Security Car Park** (☎ **07/4933 6670**) at 422 Scenic Highway, near the harbor.

Rothery's Coaches (☎ **07/4922 4320**) runs a daily service from Kern Arcade on Bolsover Street in Rockhampton to Rosslyn Bay Harbour and back, three times a day. You can request a free pickup from the airport, train station, or your hotel. Round-trip fares from town are A\$15.40 (U.S.\$10.01) for adults, A\$12 (U.S.\$7.80) for seniors and students, A\$7.70 (U.S.\$5.01) for children 5 to 14, and A\$38.50 (U.S.\$25.03) for a family of 4. The round-trip fare to/from the airport is A\$27.50 (U.S.\$17.88) for adults, A\$22 (U.S.\$14.30) for seniors and students, A\$13.75 (U.S.\$8.94) for children, and A\$68.75 (U.S.\$44.69) for families.

The cheapest way to visit is to go on the ferry and plan your own day. Your second choice is to book a day-trip with Keppel Tourist Services that includes lunch at Keppel Haven (see below) and free use of snorkeling gear. This costs A\$75 (U.S.\$48.75) for adults, A\$46 (U.S.\$39.90) for children 5 to 14, and A\$193 (U.S.\$125.45) for families of 4.

The company also runs a morning half-day tour which includes a visit to the Middle Island underwater observatory and a glass-bottomboat ride. The cost is A\$44 (U.S.\$28.60) adults, A\$22 (U.S.\$14.30) children, and A\$110 (U.S.\$71.50) for a family. Boom-netting trips from the island also run at 2:30pm for the same price.

VISITOR INFORMATION　The **Great Keppel Island Information Centre** at the ferry terminal at Rosslyn Bay Harbour (☎ **1800/77 4488** in Australia) dispenses information about the island's activities and accommodations.

WHERE TO STAY

Keppel Haven. Great Keppel Island via Rockhampton, QLD 4700. ☎ **1800/35 6744** in Australia, or 07/4933 6744. Fax 07/4933 6429. ktsgki@networx.com.au. 40 permanent tents, none with bathroom; 6 family tents (double bed and 3 single beds); 12 cabins (each sleeps 6), all with bathroom (shower only). 12 bunkhouses (with 1 bathroom per 2 rooms). Tent A\$17.50 (U.S.\$11.33) per person triple or quad-share, A\$20 (U.S.\$13) per person twin/double, A\$27.50 (U.S.\$17.88) single. Cabins A\$120 (U.S.\$78) twin or double; extra person A\$20 (U.S.\$13). Bunkhouses A\$80 (U.S.\$52) double/twin; A\$25 (U.S.\$16.25) quad share. Family tents A\$20 (U.S.\$13) per adult and A\$12 (U.S.\$7.80) children 5–14 years. Children under 5 free. A\$5 (U.S.\$3.25) per person linen for duration of stay for tents. Cabins and bunkhouses have linen supplied. Ask about 3-day, 2-night packages with Keppel Tourist Services that include ferry transfers and a half day snorkeling or boom-netting cruise. BC, MC, V.

Not far from the ferry dropoff point at the beach is this enclave of humble but pretty cabins and tents. Renovated in 1998, the cabins have terra cotta-look floors, bright new kitchenettes, small double bedrooms, four bunks in the living/dining area, fans, and a porch. The permanent tents are bigger than those at Keppel Kampout (see below) and come with twin or double beds, four bunks separated by a canvas partition, and have electricity. Catamarans, windsurfers, fishing tackle, snorkel gear, and dinghies are available on a pay-as-you-go basis. There's a restaurant, general store selling basic groceries, and three communal kitchens and barbecues. The front desk has hair dryers; BYO towels or hire them (towels in cabins.)

No matter where you stay on the island, you can eat at the casual but fine bistro at Keppel Haven (such a good value it attracts guests from the main resort), at the island's pizza joint, and at the cafe or Anchorage Grill at Great Keppel Island Resort.

Keppel Kampout. Great Keppel Island via Rockhampton, QLD 4700. ☎ **1800/35 6744** in Australia, or 07/4933 6744. Fax 07/4933 6429. ktsgki@networx.com.au. 23 permanent tents (none with bathroom). A$66 (U.S.$42.90) per person, shared accommodation. Standby rate A$60 (U.S.$39) per person. Rates include 3 meals a day, water sports, and snorkeling and boom-netting tours. Ask about 2 night packages for added savings. BC, MC, V.

The tents here are closer to permanent rooms: they have raised floors, little verandahs, twin beds, cupboards and linen, and electricity. They're on a landscaped patch next door to Keppel Haven and a short walk from Great Keppel Island Resort and the beach. Catamarans, windsurfers, fishing tackle, snorkeling trips, and boom netting cruises are all free and all your meals (even wine at dinner) are included in the one low price! All that is asked is that you wash your own dishes. BYO towels; they provide hair dryers.

YHA Backpackers Village. Great Keppel Island, P.O. Box 571, Yeppoon, QLD 4703. ☎ **07/4933 6416** (7am–5pm). ktsgki@networx.com.au. 30 permanent tents (none with bathroom). 8 rooms are quad share, 20 are doubles and 2 are family rooms. A$17.60 (U.S.$11.44) adults and A$11 (U.S.$7.15) children 5 to 14 year for shared rooms, A$28 (U.S.$18.20) per person single, A$20 (U.S.$13) per person double/twin, A$60 (U.S.$39) per family room. BC, MC, V.

This self-contained permanent safari village adjoins Keppel Haven Resort, and if you stay here, you have access to all the resort's facilities and budget meal packages, a bar, barbecue, boat/canoes, cafe, general store, Internet and e-mail access, and a tour desk which provides information on activities including hiking, diving, fishing, snorkeling, and windsurfing. The village also offers a package which includes one night's accomodation in Rockhampton, return bus and boat transfers, and 2 nights on the island for A$91 (U.S.$59.15) per person quad share or A$99 (U.S.$64.35) per person double for YHA members or A$96 (U.S.$62.40) per person quad share and A$106 (U.S.$68.90) per person double for non-members.

GLADSTONE: GATEWAY TO HERON ISLAND
550km (330 miles) N of Brisbane; 1,162 (697½ miles) S of Cairns

The industrial port town of Gladstone is the departure point for beautiful Heron Island. It is also home to the delectable mud-crab, best savored over a glass of wine at

---

Money-Saving Tip

Keppel Tourist Services provides discounted round-trip transfers from the mainland for A$30 (U.S.$19.50) per adult for guests of YHA Backpackers Village, Keppel Kampout and Keppel Haven.

the award-winning **Flinders Seafood Restaurant.** About 25 kilometers (16 miles) south of the town are the beach towns of **Boyne Island** and **Tannum Sands,** worth a detour.

ESSENTIALS

GETTING THERE & GETTING AROUND　By Car　Gladstone is on the coast 21 kilometers (12½ miles) off the Bruce Highway.

By Plane　Sunstate Airlines (book through Qantas) has many flights a day from Brisbane (trip time: 85 min.) and one direct flight a day from Rockhampton. From Cairns Sunstate operates a "milk run" via Townsville, Mackay, and Rockhampton.

By Train　Queensland Rail (☎ **13 22 32** in Queensland, or 07/3235 1122) operates trains most days to Gladstone from Brisbane and Cairns. The fare from Brisbane (6 hr. on the high-speed Tilt train) is A$69.30 (U.S.$45.05); fares from Cairns (20 hr.) range from A$124.30 (U.S.$80.80) for a sitting berth to A$162.80 (U.S.$105.82) for an economy-class sleeper.

By Bus　McCafferty's and **Greyhound Pioneer** stop daily in Gladstone on their Brisbane–Cairns runs. The fare is A$57 (U.S.$37.05) from Brisbane (10½ hr.) and A$105 (U.S.$68.25) from Cairns (17½ hr.).

　Avis (☎ **07/4978 2633**), **Budget** (☎ **07/4972 8488**), **Hertz** (☎ **07/4978 6899**) and **Thrifty** (☎ **07/4972 5999**) all have offices in Gladstone.

VISITOR INFORMATION　The Gladstone Area Promotion & Development Bureau's Information Centre is located in the ferry terminal at Gladstone Marina, Bryan Jordan Drive, Gladstone, QLD 4680 (☎ **07/4972 9922;** fax 07/4972 5006). It's open 8:30am to 5pm Monday through Friday, and 9am to 5pm Saturday and Sunday.

WHERE TO STAY

Country Plaza International. 100 Goondoon St., Gladstone, QLD 4680. ☎ **07/4972 4499.** Fax 07/ 4972 4921. 72 units. A/C MINIBAR TV TEL. A$128 (U.S.$83.20) double. AE, BC, DC, MC, V. Free parking. Free shuttle from airport, coach terminal, marina, and train station.

This four-level hotel in the center of town runs a free shuttle to the wharf for guests bound for Heron Island. Gladstone's best hotel, it caters primarily to business travelers, so it has ample facilities—spacious rooms with a sofa, modern bathrooms with hair dryers, in-room irons and ironing boards, fax/modem outlets, an upscale seafood restaurant, room service, complimentary tea and coffee in the lobby, and an outdoor swimming pool and sundeck. Most rooms have views over the port or the city.

HERON ISLAND: JEWEL OF THE REEF

72km (43¼ miles) NE of Gladstone

The difference between Heron and other islands is that once there, you have no need to travel further to the reef. Step off the beach, and you enter magnificent fields of coral that seem to stretch for miles. The myriad life forms which abound are accessible to everyone through diving, snorkeling, reef walks at low tide or aboard a semi-submersible vessel which allows you to view the ocean floor without getting wet. When geologist Joseph Bette Jukes named this piece of paradise in 1843, he overlooked the turtles for which it is now famous and commemorated the reef herons that abounded on the island. There has been a resort here since 1932, and in 1943, the island was made a National Park. It is a haven for wildlife and people, and an experience of a lifetime is guaranteed at almost any time of year. Heron is a rookery for giant green and loggerhead turtles. Resort guests gather on the beach from late November to February to watch the turtles lay eggs, and from February to mid-April see the hatched babies scuttle down to the water. Humpback whales pass through from June to September.

Three days on Heron gives plenty of time to see everything. The island is so small you can walk around it at a leisurely pace in about half an hour. One of the first things to do is to take advantage of the organized activities which operate several times a day and are designed so guests can plan their own days. Snorkeling and reef walking are major occupations for visitors—if they're not diving, that is, for the island is home to 21 of the world's most stunning dive sites.

Guided island walks are another way to explore the island. Walks include a visit to the research station based on the island. As for the reef walk, just borrow a pair of sandshoes, a balance pole and a viewing bucket and head off with a guide at low tide. The walk can take up to 90 minutes, but there's no compulsion to stay; if it gets too hot you can head back for the sanctuary of your room or the shady bar area.

A fishing trip should also be on the agenda, even for non-anglers. The reef fish seem to jump onto the hook and the resort chef is happy to cook it for you for dinner!

GETTING THERE   A courtesy coach meets flights at 10:30am to take guests to Gladstone Marina for the 2-hour launch transfer to the island; it departs 11am daily (except Christmas). Round-trip boat transfer costs A$160 (U.S.$104) for adults, half price for children 3 to 14. Take seasick medication with you, especially on the out-bound trip. It is often rough, though for some reason, the return journey is not as bad.

WHERE TO STAY & DINE: WORTH A SPLURGE

✪ Heron Island Resort. Via Gladstone, QLD 4680 (P&O Resorts, GPO Box 5287, Sydney, NSW 2001). ☎ **1800 737 678** in Australia, 800/225 9849 in the U.S. and Canada, 020 7805 3875 in the U.K., 02/9257 5050 or fax 02/9299 2477 (Sydney reservations office), or 07/4972 9055 (the island). www.poresorts.com.au. resorts-reservations@poaustralia.com. 117 units, 87 with bathroom (86 with shower only). Cabins A$182 (U.S.$118.30) per person, or A$140 (U.S.$91) per person quad-share. A$266 (U.S.$172.90) per person Reef suite, A$310 (U.S.$202) per person Heron suite; A$510 (U.S.$331.50) single or A$420 (U.S.$273) per person double Beach House or Point Suite. Children 3–14 A$80 (U.S.$52). No children allowed in Point suites or Beach House. Free crib. Rates include all meals. Ask about special packages. AE, BC, DC, JCB, MC, V.

Comfortable rather than glamorous is the best way to describe the resort. As one guest told me: "This is not a place where you have to dress up to walk across the lobby." The Reef Suites are standard motel-style rooms; Heron Suites near the beach have screened-off sleeping quarters; and Point Suites, which have great views, are actually one big room with a king-size bed and a sitting area. There's also a beach house, which has a separate bedroom. All are pleasant and come with hair dryers. The cheapest option is to stay in one of the 30 clean Turtle Cabins, which come with double and/or single bunks and shared bathroom facilities. You may end up sharing the cabin with a stranger. None of the rooms are air-conditioned, but all have fans. If you want to stay in touch with the world you will have to use the public telephone and TV.

Dining/Diversions: The maitre d' assigns your table in the restaurant on the first night, similar to a cruise. Breakfast and lunch are fabulous buffets, and dinner is usually an excellent four-course menu. The Saturday night seafood buffet is excellent. Beware while eating in the restaurant—your table is likely to be raided by friendly rails or other small birds. Coffee and snacks are available between meals at the Pandanus Lounge bar overlooking the reef. There is some kind of entertainment nightly, be it a band, a bush dance, games, dancing, or movies.

Up Close & Personal with a Turtle

The egg in my hand is warm, soft and about the size of a ping pong ball. At our feet, a giant green turtle sighs deeply as she lays a clutch of about 120 eggs in a pear-shaped chamber dug from the sand. A tear rolls from her eye. In the distance the wedgetail shearwaters call to each other over the sound of the waves.

Our guide has retrieved the turtle egg from the egg chamber, and we pass it around in silence. It is just one of the amazing experiences a few days on Heron Island can bring. The egg-laying ritual of the turtles is central to a trip to Heron Island in the summer, when they make their annual visit to the sandy shores of the atoll. At night and in the early morning, small groups of people gather on the beaches to witness the turtles lumber up the beach, dig a hole and lay their eggs.

Every night during the season, volunteer guides from the University of Queensland research station based on the island are on hand to give an added dimension to the experience. You can watch and ask questions as the researchers tag and measure the turtles before they return to the water.

Or get up early in the morning and head to the beach. In a few minutes, I had found turtle tracks and followed them up the beach to find a nesting female. Nearby, another two turtles had attracted small clusters of spectators. The turtles are not easily disturbed and you can get very close.

The laying season is from December to February, with the hatchlings scrambling down the beach from January to May. Only one in 5,000 hatchlings will live to return in about 50 years to lay their own eggs.

Another good place to watch the turtles nesting is at **Mon Repos Beach** outside Bundaberg. Mon Repos Conservation Park is one of the largest loggerhead turtle rookeries in the South Pacific. The visitor center by the beach has a great on the turtle life cycle and shows films at approximately 7:30pm each night in summer. Visitors can turn up anytime from 7pm on; the action goes on through the night, sometimes as late as 6am. Nesting happens around high tide; hatching usually occurs between 8pm and midnight. Get there early to join the first group of 70 people, the maximum allowed at one laying or hatching. Crowds can be up to 500 strong in mid-December and January. You may have to wait around for quite a while, and in fact, on our visit here with two young children we gave up when our turn had not come by about midnight. Take a flashlight if you can.

The **Mon Repos Turtle Rookery** (☎ **07/4159 1652** for the visitor center) is 14 kilometers (8½ miles) east of Bundaberg's town center. Follow Bourbong Street out of town toward Burnett Heads as it becomes Bundaberg–Bargara Road. Take the Port Road to the left and look for the Mon Repos signs to the right. Admission is A$4 (U.S.$2.60) for adults, A$2 (U.S.$1.30) for seniors and children ages 5 to 15, and A$10 (U.S.$6.50) for a family.

Amenities: There's a swimming pool, pavement chess, free day/night tennis court, game room, boutique/shop, free childcare for 5- to 10-year-olds during school vacations, babysitting (must be prebooked). Snorkel gear can be hired for A$10 (U.S.$6.50) per day. You can join a guided snorkel safari from the beach, or take a 5-minute boat trip to snorkel the reef edge. If you do not snorkel, you can see the coral from the windows of a semi-submersible boat. A National Parks interpretive center has reference material on the local plants and animals. There are barbecue cruises to nearby Wilson Island and sunset cruises, a beachside pool and lovely beaches. The resort runs two dive trips a day, plus adventure and night dives as well as introductory dives for first-timers. Dive packages for up to 10 days are available.

BUNDABERG: GATEWAY TO LADY ELLIOT ISLAND
384km (230½ miles) N of Brisbane; 1,439km (863½ miles) S of Cairns

The small sugar town of Bundaberg is the closest to the southernmost point of the Great Barrier Reef. If you visit the area between November and March, allow an evening to visit the Mon Repos turtle rookery. Divers may want to take in some of Australia's best shore diving right off Bundaberg's beaches.

GETTING THERE & GETTING AROUND **By Car** Bundaberg is on the Isis Highway, about 50 kilometers (31 miles) off the Bruce Highway from Gin Gin in the north and 53 kilometers (33 miles) off the Bruce Highway from just north of Childers in the south.

By Plane **Sunstate Airlines** (book through Qantas at ☎ **13 13 13** in Australia) flies from Brisbane. Sunstate also flies from Cairns via Townsville, Mackay, and Rockhampton, and direct from Gladstone.

By Train **Queensland Rail** (☎ **13 22 32** in Queensland, or 07/3235 1122) trains stop in Bundaberg most days en route between Brisbane and Cairns. The fare is A$49.50 (U.S.$32.18) from Brisbane; fares range from A$135.30 (U.S.$87.75) for a sitting berth to A$257.40 (U.S.$167.05) for a first-class berth from Cairns.

By Bus **McCafferty's** (☎ **13 14 99** in Australia) and **Greyhound Pioneer** (☎ **13 20 30** in Australia) call many times a day on their coach runs between Brisbane and Cairns. The 7-hour trip from Brisbane costs around A$46 (U.S.$29.90). From Cairns it is a 22-hour trip, for which the fare is A$125 (U.S.$81.25).

Avis (☎ **07/4152 1877**), **Budget** (☎ **07/4153 1600**), **Hertz** (☎ **07/4155 2403**), and **Thrifty** (☎ **07/4151 6222**) all have offices in Bundaberg.

VISITOR INFORMATION The **Bundaberg District Tourism and Development Board Information Center** is at 271 Bourbong St. at Mulgrave Street, Bundaberg, QLD 4670 (☎ **1800/060 499** in Australia, or 07/4152 2333; www.tour groups.net). It's open daily from 9am to 5pm.

WHAT TO SEE & DO
The best shore diving in Queensland is in Bundaberg's **Woongarra Marine Park.** It has soft and hard corals, urchins, rays, sea snakes, and 60 fish species, plus a World War II Beaufort bomber wreck. There are several scuba operators. **Salty's Dive Centre** (☎ **1800/ 625 476** in Australia, or 07/4151 6422; fax 07/4151 4938; www.saltys.net; dive@saltys.net) rents dive gear for A$45 (U.S.$29.25). They also run 4-day learn-to-dive courses from A$169 (U.S.$109.85) per person, and a 3 day/3 night southern Great Barrier Reef dive cruise for A$495 (U.S.$321.75). A 5-day diving course is A$580 (U.S.$377), including the 3 day/night cruise.

Money-Saving Tip

Heron Island's only resort isn't cheap, but we mention it because it's a good value. You can't make a daytrip to Heron Island, so if you want to visit, you have to stay overnight. Meals are included in the tariff, and a number of activities, so factor that into your decision on whether to visit.

Travel Tip _____

When you land on the grass airstrip at Lady Elliot Island, you'll think you're on the set of Hitchcock's "The Birds." The air is thick with tens of thousands of swirling noddy terns and bridal terns that nest in every available branch. They leave their mark on every surface, including you (so bring a big cheap hat for protection).

WHERE TO STAY

Acacia Motor Inn. 248 Bourbong St., Bundaberg, QLD 4670. ☎ **1800/35 1375** in Australia, or 07/4152 3411. Fax 07/4152 2387. 26 units. A/C TV TEL. A$60 (U.S.$39) single; A$70 (U.S.$45.50) double. Extra person A$10 (U.S.$6.50) adults, A$6 (U.S.$3.90) children under 12. A$5 (U.S.$3.25) crib. AE, BC, DC, MC, V.

This tidy motel is a short stroll from the town center. It offers dated but clean, well-kept rooms and extra-large family rooms at a decent price. Some rooms have hair dryers. Local restaurants provide room service, and many are walking distance. There's a pool.

LADY ELLIOT ISLAND

80km (48 miles) NE of Bundaberg

The southernmost Great Barrier Reef island, Lady Elliot is a 105-acre coral cay ringed by a wide shallow lagoon filled with dazzling coral life.

Reef walking, snorkeling, and diving are why people come to this coral cay that's so small you can walk across it in 15 minutes. You may snorkel and reef-walk during the 2 to 3 hours before and after high tide, so plan your schedule accordingly. You will see dazzling corals and brilliantly colored fish, clams, sponges, urchins, and anemones. Divers will see a range of marine life, including green and loggerhead turtles (which nest on the beach from November to March). Whales pass by from June to September.

Lady Elliot is a sparse, grassy island rookery, not a lush tropical paradise, so you won't find white sand and palm trees. Some folks find it too spartan; others relish the beautiful, peaceful location with reef all around. Just be prepared for the musty smell and constant noise of those birds.

GETTING THERE You reach the island via a 25-minute flight from Bundaberg. Connections are available from Hervey Bay and Maroochydore. Book your air travel along with your accommodation. Round-trip fares are A$159 (U.S.$103.35) for adults and A$80 (U.S.$52) for children 3 to 14.

WHERE TO STAY

Lady Elliot Island Resort. Great Barrier Reef via Bundaberg. (P.O. Box 206, Torquay, QLD 4655). ☎ **1800/072 200** in Australia, or 07/4125 5344. Fax 07/4125 5778. 40 units, 20 with bathroom (shower only). A$138 (U.S.$89.70) for tent cabins; A$176 (U.S.$114.40) for Reef units; A$198 (U.S.$128.70) for Island Suites. Ask about multi-night packages, and dive packages. AE, BC, DC, MC, V.

Lady Elliot's accommodation is fairly basic, but visitors come here for the reef. Reef units have a double bed (some also have two bunks), a chair or two, wardrobe space, and a deck with views through the trees to the sea. Island suites are more luxurious and have a kitchenette, a small living/dining area, one or two separate bedrooms, and great sea views from the deck. Both have modern bathrooms, a fridge, and tea and coffee. The lodge rooms contain a bed or bunks and a small wardrobe. The permanent tents have electric lighting and a wooden floor, and are spacious and cool. Lodges and tents share the public toilets and showers. All accommodations have fans. There are few resort facilities, other than a boutique, a swimming pool, a casual bar and snack area, and an education center. There is no air-conditioning, no keys (secure storage is at front desk), no TVs, no radio, and one public telephone. The food is basic. The low-key activities program includes bush tucker tours, fish feeding, guided snorkeling, badminton, and movie screenings, most of which are free. The island accommodates no more than 140 guests at any one time, so you pretty much get the reef to yourself.

7 Fraser Island: Eco–Adventures & 4WD Fun

1,547 (928¼ miles) S of Cairns; 260km (156 miles) N of Brisbane; 15km (9 miles) E of Hervey Bay

The biggest sand island in the world, this 405,000-acre World Heritage–listed island off the central Queensland coast attracts a mix of sensitive eco-tourists and Aussie fishermen. Fraser is almost untouched, with eucalyptus woodlands, soaring dunes, clear creeks, ancient rain forest, blue lakes, ochre-colored sand cliffs, and a stunning 75-mile-long beach. For 4WD fans though, Fraser's beauty lies in its complete absence of paved roads. On weekends when the fish are running, it's nothing to see 100 4WDs lining **75-Mile Beach,** which is a gazetted road. Pedestrians should beware!

ESSENTIALS

GETTING THERE   By Car   Hervey (pronounced *Harvey*) Bay is the main gateway to the island. Take the Bruce Highway to Maryborough, then the 34-kilometer (21-mile) road to Hervey Bay. If approaching from the north, turn off the highway at Torbanlea, north of Maryborough, and cut across to Hervey Bay. Allow 3 hours from the Sunshine Coast, a good 5 from Brisbane.

Guests at **Kingfisher Bay Resort** (see below) can get to the resort aboard the **Kingfisher Bay Fastcat,** which departs Urangan Boat Harbour at Hervey Bay six times a day between 8:30am and 6:30pm. Round-trip fare for the 40-minute crossing is A$35 (U.S.$22.75) adults and A$18 (U.S.$11.70) kids 4 to 14. The resort runs a courtesy shuttle from Hervey Bay's airport and coach terminal to the harbor. You can park free in the open at the Fastcat terminal; **Fraser Coast Secure Vehicle Storage,** at 629 The Esplanade (☎ **07/4125 2783**), a 5-minute walk from the terminal, gives covered parking for A$7.70 to $9.90 (U.S.$5.01–$6.44) per 24 hours.

By Bus   Both **Greyhound Pioneer** and **McCafferty's** coaches stop several times a day in Hervey Bay on their Brisbane–Cairns–Brisbane routes. The 6-hour trip from Brisbane costs around A$37.40 (U.S.$24.31). From Cairns, the fare is A$152.90 (U.S.$99.39) for a 23-hour trip.

By Train   The nearest train station is in **Maryborough West,** 34 kilometers (20¼ miles) from Hervey Bay. Passengers on the high-speed Tilt train (Sun–Fri) and the *Spirit of Capricorn* (Sat) can book a connecting bus service to Urangan Boat Harbour via **Queensland Rail** (☎ **13 22 32** in Queensland, or 07/3235 1122). The fare from Brisbane for the 2½-hour Tilt train trip or the 4½-hour *Spirit of Capricorn* trip is A$42.90 (U.S.$27.89), plus A$4.40 (U.S.$2.86) for the bus. Fares are A$144.10 (U.S.$93.67) in a sitting berth and A$182.60 (U.S.$118.69) in an economy-class sleeper from Cairns (trip time: just under 27 hr.). Train passengers from the north must take a courtesy shuttle to Maryborough Central, then take the next available local bus to Urangan Boat Harbour.

By Plane   **Sunstate Airlines** (book through Qantas) has 1 or 2 direct daily flights from Brisbane to Hervey Bay.

GETTING THERE & AROUND BY 4WD   Four-wheel drive is the only permissible mode of vehicle transport on the island. Many 4WD rental outfits are based in Hervey Bay. You'll pay between about A$100 (U.S.$65) and A$160 (U.S.$104) a day, plus around A$20 to $35 (U.S.$13–$22.75) per day to reduce the deductible, which is usually A$4,000 (U.S.$2,600), plus a deposit (typically A$500/U.S.$325). You must also buy a **Vehicle Access Permit,** which costs A$30 (U.S.$19.50) from your rental car company or Urangan Boat Harbour or the Mary River Heads boat ramp, or A$40 (U.S.$26) from a Queensland Parks and Wildlife Service office on the island. Both **Bay 4WD Centre** (☎ **07/4128 2981;** www.bay4wd.com.au) and **Ausbay 4WD Rentals** (☎ **1800/679 479** in Australia, or 07/4124 6177;) rent 4WDs, offer camping and accommodated 4WD packages; rent camping gear; get your Vehicle Access Permits, barge bookings, camping permits, and secure storage for your own car; and pick you up free from the airport, bus station, or your hotel. Ausbay allows 1-day rental (at a slightly higher price); Bay 4WD demands a minimum 2.

Four-wheel drives transfer by **Fraser Venture barge** (☎ **07/4125 4444**), which runs at least three times a day from Mary River Heads, 17 kilometers (11 miles) south of Urangan Boat Harbour. The round-trip fare for vehicle and driver is A$77 (U.S.$50.06), plus A$5.50 (U.S.$3.58) per extra passenger. It is a good idea to book a place for the 10-minute crossing.

Kingfisher Bay 4WD Hire (☎ **07/4120 3366**) in Kingfisher Bay Resort (see below) rents 4WDs for A$195 (U.S.$126.75) a day, plus a A$500 (U.S.$325) bond and a A$2,000 (U.S.$1,300) deductible. They allow 1-day rentals. Book in advance.

Fraser Island Taxi Service (☎ **07/4127 9188**) will take you anywhere on the island—in a 4WD, of course. It's based at Eurong on the island's eastern side. A typical fare, from Kingfisher Bay Resort across the island to go fishing on 75 Mile Beach, say, is A$50 (U.S.$32.50). The taxi seats five.

VISITOR INFORMATION   Contact the **Hervey Bay Tourism & Development Bureau,** 10 Bideford St., Hervey Bay, QLD 4655 (☎ **1800/811 728 in Australia,** or 07/4124 9609; www.herveybaytourism.com.au). A better site is . **The Marina Kiosk** (☎ **07/4128 9800**) at Urangan Boat Harbour is a one-stop booking and information agency for all Fraser-related travel. Several Queensland Parks and Wildlife Service information offices are on the island.

There are no towns and very few facilities, food stores, or services on the island, so if you're camping, take all supplies with you.

4WD Fundamentals

Driving a 4WD is great fun and not hard for a beginner, but if you've never driven one, get a good briefing from your rental company before you head out. Fraser's loose sand tracks can be tricky, and getting bogged is common. The beach can be dangerous for the novice—if you travel too high up, you can get trapped in soft sand; if you travel too low, a wave can bog your vehicle in soft sand under the water (and rust your car). Car rental companies don't like that, and they can smell salt on an axle a mile away! Stick to the firmest tracks, know the tides, and ask for advice. You'll have to drive a lot slower on a 4WD trail than you would on a conventional road; take that into account when you plan your day. For example, it takes a full day to get to Indian Head and back, and then only when the tide is favorable. Look out for light planes landing on the beach (which is a runway as well as a road).

ECO-EXPLORING THE ISLAND

Fraser's gem-like turquoise lakes and tea-colored "perched" lakes in the dunes are among the island's biggest attractions. The brilliant blue ✪ **Lake McKenzie** is absolutely beautiful; a swim here may be the highlight of your visit. **Lake Birrabeen** is another popular swimming spot. Don't miss a refreshing swim in the fast-flowing clear shallows of ✪ **Eli Creek.** Wade up the creek for a mile or two and let the current carry you back down. You should also take the boardwalk through a verdant forest of palms and ferns along the banks of **Wanggoolba Creek.**

Don't swim at **75 Mile Beach,** which hugs the eastern edge of the island—there are dangerously strong currents and a healthy shark population to contend with. Instead, swim in the ✪ **Champagne Pools** (also called the Aquarium)—pockets of soft sand protected from the worst of the waves by rocks. The bubbling seawater turns the pools into miniature spas. The pools are just north of **Indian Head**, a 60-meter (197-ft.) rocky outcrop at the northern end of the beach.

View the island's famous colored sand in its natural setting—the 70-meter (230-ft.) cliffs called the **Cathedrals,** which stretch for miles north of the settlement of Happy Valley on the eastern side of the Island.

Some of Queensland's best fishing is on Fraser Island. Anglers can throw a line in the surf gutters off the beach (freshwater fishing is not allowed). Bream, whiting, flathead, and swallowtail are the beach catches. Indian Head is good for rock species and tailor, and the waters east off Waddy Point yield northern and southern reef fish. Kingfisher Bay Resort (see "Where to Stay & Dine: Worth a Splurge," below) offers free fish clinics, rents tackle, and organizes half-day fishing jaunts.

From August through October, tour boats crowd the straits to see humpback whales returning to Antarctica with calves in tow. Kingfisher Bay Resort runs a ✪ **whale-watching cruise** from Urangan Harbour.

WHERE TO STAY

✪ **Fraser Island Retreat.** Happy Valley, Fraser Island, QLD 4650. ☎ **1800/446 655** in Australia, or 07/4127 9144. Fax 07/4127 9131. retreat@fraserislandaccommodation.com. 9 units. TV. A$83 (U.S.$53.95) per person. AE, BC, MC, V. Ask about package deals.

This is the wild side of Fraser Island, just minutes from 75 Mile Beach. Don't come expecting a luxury resort, but one that has comfortable timber cottages and all the amenities you need. There's a small swimming pool, surrounded by a timber deck and deck chairs, and each cottage has a small verandah. The rooms all have fans, cooking facilities, a small fridge, television, and VCR (you can rent videos). The Satinay bar and bistro is open for all meals, but be warned that it is used by day tour buses as their lunch stop, so can be crowded at those times. If you want to cook for yourself, there's a general store that sells food and take-out liquor. It also sells fuel, ice and gas for campers. You can also hire a 4WD from the resort. The only access is by plane (**Air Fraser Island** ☎ 07/4125 3600) or bus. **Fraser Island Top Tours** (☎ 1800/063 933 or 07/4125 3933) will transfer guests to the resort from Hervey Bay and also runs day tours of the island for A$82 (U.S.$53.30) adults and A$49 (U.S.$31.85) children.

WORTH A SPLURGE

✪ **Kingfisher Bay Resort.** Fraser Island (PMB 1, Urangan, QLD 4655). ☎ **1800/072 555** in Australia, or 07/4120 3333. Fax 07/4120 3326. www.kingfisherbay.com. reservations@ kingfisherbay.com. 252 units. TV TEL. A$250 (U.S.$162.50) double or triple. A$825 (U.S.$536.25) 3 nights in 2-bedroom villa (sleeps 5), A$1,275 (U.S.$828.75) 3 nights in 3-bedroom villa (sleeps 6); minimum 3-night stay in villas. Extra person A$22 (U.S.$14.30). Free crib. Ask about package deals. AE, BC, DC, MC, V.

Organized Tours & Package Deals on Fraser Island

If staying at the Kingfisher Bay Resort is beyond your budget, consider a **day trip** or booking a package. Kingfisher Bay Resort offers a range of packages. Its 3-day, 2-night package, including Fastcat transfers from Hervey Bay, tours of the island, and quad-share accommodations in the Wilderness Lodge (see "Worth a Splurge" above), is A$270 (U.S.$175.50) per person, including most meals. The resort also offers a day trip from Hervey Bay with touring and lunch for A$99 (U.S.$64.35) per person.

This sleek, environment-friendly eco-resort lies low along Fraser's west coast. The air-conditioned rooms are smart and contemporary, with a Japanese screen opening onto a balcony looking into the bush. The 2- and 3-bedroom villas have kitchens. Travelers on package tours (see "Organized Tours & Package Deals on Fraser Island" above) stay in the rustic Wilderness Lodge, which is actually eight lodges, each with four double, twin, or four-bunk rooms; simple but atmospheric shared living quarters; shared bathrooms; and a deck. They are not air-conditioned but have fans. Guests who aren't on a package tour have access only to the Sandbar restaurant and pool, but that's a fun place to be, and you are still free to join in all the daily activities.

The resort's impressive lineup of eco-educational activities includes daily 4WD tours with a ranger to points of interest, free guided walks daily, and an excellent free Junior Eco-Ranger program on weekends and school vacations. You can also join bird-watching tours, fly- and reef fishing trips, guided canoe trips, sunset champagne sails, and dugong (manatee) spotting cruises. Wildlife videos play continuously in the lobby, and the on-site ranger office lists the animals and plants you are most likely to spot.

Other facilities include two swimming pools, Jacuzzi, sundeck, water sports equipment and fishing tackle for rent, day/night tennis courts, volleyball, game room, tour desk, babysitting, and (for a fee) a kids' club.

CAMPING

Fraser has eight camping areas, most with showers and toilets. Camping permits, which you can buy at the various **Queensland Parks & Wildlife Service** offices on the island (☎ **07/4127 9128**), are A$3.85 (U.S.$2.50) per person per night.

8 The Sunshine Coast

Warm sunshine, beaches upon beaches, trendy restaurants and a relaxed lifestyle attract Aussies to the Sunshine Coast in droves. Despite some unsightly commercial development in recent years, the Sunshine Coast is still a great spot if you like lazing on sandy beaches and enjoying a good meal.

The Sunshine Coast starts at **Caloundra,** 83 kilometers (50 miles) north of Brisbane and runs all the way to **Rainbow Beach,** 40 kilometers (24 miles) north of **Noosa Heads,** where the fashionable crowd goes. There are plenty of inexpensive motels and holiday apartments to rent. Noosa's restaurants are great, and while none are super- expensive, few are cheap—so be prepared to spend a little if you want to eat out.

Most of the Noosa's sunbathing, dining, shopping, and socializing takes place on trendy Hastings Street, Noosa Heads, and the adjacent Main Beach. The commercial strip of Noosa Junction is a 1-minute drive; a 3-minute drive west along the river takes

The Sunshine Coast

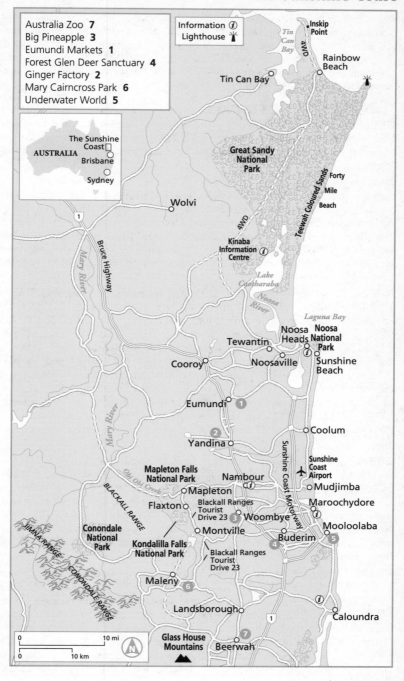

Australia Zoo **7**
Big Pineapple **3**
Eumundi Markets **1**
Forest Glen Deer Sanctuary **4**
Ginger Factory **2**
Mary Cairncross Park **6**
Underwater World **5**

Information ⓘ
Lighthouse 🛱

AUSTRALIA
The Sunshine Coast
Brisbane
Sydney

Inskip Point
Tin Can Bay
Rainbow Beach
Tin Can Bay

Great Sandy National Park

Wolvi

Teewah Coloured Sands
Forty Mile Beach

Kinaba Information Centre ⓘ

Lake Cootharaba
Noosa River

Laguna Bay

Noosa Heads
Noosa National Park
Tewantin
Cooroy
Noosaville
Sunshine Beach

Eumundi ①

Coolum

Yandina ②

Mapleton Falls National Park
Nambour
Mapleton
Flaxton
Blackall Ranges Tourist Drive 23
Woombye ③
Montville
Conondale National Park
Kondalilla Falls National Park
Blackall Ranges Tourist Drive 23
Buderim ④

Sunshine Coast Motorway
Sunshine Coast Airport
Mudjimba
Maroochydore
Mooloolaba ⑤

BLACKALL RANGE
JIMNA RANGE
CONONDALE RANGE
Obi Obi Creek
Mary River
Bruce Highway
Mary River

Maleny ⑥

Landsborough

Glass House Mountains
Beerwah ⑦

Caloundra

0   10 mi
0   10 km

you to low-key **Noosaville,** where Australian families rent holiday apartments. Giving Noosa a run for its money is the newly spruced up **Mooloolaba,** about 30 kilometers (18 miles) south, which has a better beach and about 90 great restaurants.

A short drive away, in the hinterland, mountain towns like Maleny, Montville and Mapleton lead the way to the stunning beauty of the Glass House Mountains, a dramatic series of 13 volcanic plugs.

SUNSHINE COAST ESSENTIALS

GETTING THERE   By Car   If you're driving from Brisbane, take the Bruce Highway north to Aussie World theme park at Palmview, then exit onto the Sunshine Motorway to Mooloolaba, Maroochydore or Noosa Heads. The trip takes about 2 hours.

By Plane   **Sunstate Airlines** (book through **Qantas**) has many flights daily, a 30-minute trip from Brisbane to the **Sunshine Coast Airport** in Maroochydore, 42 kilometers (25¼ miles) south of Noosa Heads. Qantas flies from Sydney several times a day and has direct flights from Sydney and Melbourne on weekends. From Cairns, you will need to fly to Brisbane and back to Maroochydore. **Henry's Airport Bus Service** (☎ **07/5474 0199**) meets all flights; door-to-door transfers to Noosa Heads are A$14 (U.S.$9.10) for adults and A$7 (U.S.$4.55) for kids ages 4 to 14, one-way. Bookings are not necessary.

By Train   The nearest station to Noosa Heads is in **Cooroy,** 25 kilometers (15 miles) away, to which **Queensland Rail** (☎ **13 22 32** in Queensland, or 07/3235 1122) operates two daily services from Brisbane on its suburban **CityTrain** (☎ **07/3235 5555**) network. The trip takes about 2 hours and 20 minutes and the fare is A$14.40 (U.S.$9.36). Queensland Rail's long-distance trains departing Brisbane pick up but do not drop off passengers in Cooroy, with the exception of the high-speed Tilt train (which runs Sun–Fri) and the *Spirit of Capricorn* (which runs Sat). The fare on both trains is A$24.20 (U.S.$15.73). Several Queensland Rail trains make the 29½-hour trip from Cairns each week; the fare is A$150.70 (U.S.$97.96) for a sitting berth, A$189.20 (U.S.$122.98) for an economy-class sleeper. Local bus company **Sunbus** (☎ **131 230** or 07/5492 8700) meets most trains at Cooroy station and travels to Noosa Heads; take bus no. 12.

By Bus   Several companies have service to Noosa Heads from Brisbane, including **Sun-air** (☎ **1800/804 340** in Australia, or 07/5478 2811) and **Suncoast Pacific** (☎ **07/5443 1011** on the Sunshine Coast, 07/3236 1901 in Brisbane) which also runs from Hervey Bay. **McCafferty's** and **Greyhound Pioneer** run daily from all major towns along the Bruce Highway between Brisbane and Cairns. The trip to Noosa Heads takes 2 hours, 20 minutes from Brisbane, and just under 26 hours from Cairns. It's A$16 (U.S.$10.40) one-way from Brisbane and A$152 (U.S.$98.80) from Cairns.

VISITOR INFORMATION   Write for information to **Tourism Sunshine Coast Ltd.,** P.O. Box 264, Mooloolaba, QLD 4557 (☎ **07/5477 7311;** fax 07/5477 7322; www.sunshinecoast.org). In Noosa, visit the **Tourism Noosa Information Centre** (☎ **07/5447 4988;** fax 07/5474 9494) at the eastern roundabout on Hastings Street where it intersects Noosa Drive. It's open daily from 9am to 5pm. Other tourist information centres are: **Nambour Information Centre,** Currie St, Nambour (☎ **07/ 5476 0199**); **Maroochy Tourism,** Sixth Avenue and Aerodrome Rd, Maroochydore, (☎ **07/5479 1566**); **Caloundra City Information Centre,** 7 Caloundra Rd, Caloundra (☎ **07/5491 0202**).

GETTING AROUND Major car rental agencies on the Sunshine Coast are **Avis** (☎ **07/5443 5055** Sunshine Coast Airport, 07/5447 4933 Noosa Heads), **Budget** (☎ **07/5448 7455** airport, 07/5474 2820 Noosa), **Hertz** (**07/5448 9731** airport, 07/5447 2253 Noosa Heads), and **Thrifty** (☎ **07/5443 1733** airport, 07/5447 2299 Noosa Heads). Many local outfits rent cars and 4WDs, including **Trusty** (☎ **07/5447 4777**).

The local bus company is **Sunbus** (☎ **13 12 30** in Australia, or 07/5492 8700).

EXPLORING THE AREA

HITTING THE BEACH & OTHER OUTDOOR FUN Main Beach, Noosa Heads, is the place to swim, surf, and sunbathe. If the bikini-clad supermodel looka-likes are too much, head to Sunshine Beach, just behind Noosa Junction off the David Low Way, about 2 kilometers (1¼ miles) from Noosa Heads. It's just as beautiful. Both beaches are patrolled 365 days a year.

Learn to **surf** with two-time Australian and World Pro–Am champ **Merrick Davis** (☎ **0418/787 577** mobile phone or info@learntosurf.com.au), who's lived in Noosa for the past 6 years. Merrick runs 2-hour lessons on Main Beach daily for A$35 (U.S.$22.75), 3-day certificate courses for A$95 (U.S.$61.75) and 5 day courses for A$125 (U.S.$81.25). He will pick you up and drop you off at your lodging, and also rents surfboards and body boards.

If you want to rent a windsurfer, canoe, kayak, surf ski, catamaran, jet ski, or canopied fishing boat that you can play with on the Noosa River, or take upriver into **Great Sandy National Park** (see below), check out the dozens of outfits along Gympie Terrace between James Street and Robert Street in Noosaville.

The **Aussie Sea Kayak Company** (☎ **07/5477 5335** or 0407/049 747 mobile phone; rod&nat@ausseakayak.com.au), at The Wharf, Mooloolaba runs a 2-hour sun-set paddle on the Maroochy River every day for A$40 (U.S.$26), including a glass of champagne on your return as reward for all the hard work! Owner/operators Natalie Stephenson and Rod Withyman are qualified kayak guides and instructors who worked for various companies in the U.S., Canada and Mexico before returning to Australia to set up their tours. Half-day tours run every day for 3 to 4 hours at Mooloolaba (A$60/U.S.$39), day tours for 6 hours, Tuesday, Friday, and Saturday at Noosa (A$105/U.S.$68.25). The company also runs overnight adventures to Moreton and North Stradbroke Islands, and to Fraser Island and the Whitsundays for up to 6 days.

EXPLORING NOOSA NATIONAL PARK A 10-minute stroll from Hastings Street brings you to the 1,080-acre Noosa National Park. Anywhere you see a crowd looking up, you're sure to spot a koala. They're often seen in the unlikely venue of the parking lot at the park entrance. A network of well-posted walking trails leads through the bush. The most scenic is the 2.7 kilometer (1½ mile) coastal trail. The shortest is the 1 kilometer (half-mile) Palm Grove circuit; the longest is the 4.7 kilometer (3 mile) Tanglewood trail inland to Hell's Gates, definitely worth the effort.

NORTH OF NOOSA: GREAT SANDY NATIONAL PARK Stretching north of Noosa along the coast is the 140,000-acre Great Sandy National Park (often called Cooloola National Park), home to forests, beach, and freshwater lakes, including the state's largest, Lake Cootharaba. A popular thing to do is cruise the silent Everglades formed by the Noosa River and tributary creeks. The park's information office, the **Kinaba Information Center** (☎ **07/5449 7364**), is on the western shore of Lake Cootharaba, about 30 kilometers (18 miles) from Noosaville. It has a display on the area's geography and a mangrove boardwalk; it's accessible only by boat, which you can rent from the numerous outfits in Noosaville. Several operators run half-day cruises into the Everglades, and guided kayak tours explore the park's lower reaches.

The other option is to take a 4WD along 40-Mile Beach, a designated highway with traffic laws, for a close-up view of the Teewah colored sand cliffs. This is a great place to get away from the crowds and enjoy nature's wonders. Lifeguards are not on duty, so do not swim alone, and take care. Tours are available, or you can rent a 4WD and explore on your own. To reach the beach, cross Noosa River on the ferry at Tewantin, then take Maximilian Drive for 4 kilometers (2½ miles) to the beach. Stock up on water, food, and gas in Tewantin. The **ferry** (☎ 07/5449 8013) costs A$8 (U.S.$5.20) per vehicle round-trip; it operates from 6am to 10pm Sunday through Thursday, and 6am to midnight Friday and Saturday.

WILDLIFE PARKS & THEME PARKS   Small theme parks seem to thrive on the Sunshine Coast. Don't expect thrill rides, but you might find some of them a pleasant way to spend a few hours.

A transparent tunnel with an 80-meter (256-ft.) moving walkway takes you through a tank filled with sharks, stingrays, groupers, eels, and coral, one highlight at **Underwater World** (☎ 07/5444 8488), at The Wharf, Mooloolaba. Kids can pick up starfish and sea cucumbers in the touch pool, and there are static displays on whales and sharks, shark-breeding and freshwater crocodile talks, an otter enclosure, and a 30-minute seal show. You can also swim with the seals (A$65/U.S.$42.25), dive with the sharks (A$94/U.S.$61.10, for certified divers, including gear, or A$110/U.S.$71.50 for non-divers) or get up close to a seal over Sunday breakfast for A$27 (U.S.$17.55) adults, A$21 (U.S.$13.65) children 3 to 15, A$25 (U.S.$16.25) seniors and students, or A$99 (U.S.$64.35) family of 5. Breakfast with a seal prices include entry to Underwater World. It's open daily from 9am to 6pm (last entry at 5pm). Closed Christmas. Admission is A$21.50 (U.S.$13.98) for adults, A$14 (U.S.$9.10) for seniors and students, A$11 (U.S.$7.15) for children 3 to 15, and A$55 (U.S.$35.75) for a family of 5. Allow 2 hours to see everything, more if you want to attend all the talks.

At the **Ginger Factory,** Pioneer Road, Yandina (☎ 07/5446 7096), you can watch the works of a ginger-processing plant that supplies most of the world's sugar-cured ginger. You can also shop for ginger plants and a huge range of ginger products, and browse a handful of gift shops. Entry is free. The park is open from 9am to 5pm daily; closed Christmas. (The factory is closed some weekends and around Christmas; you should call first, to make sure it's open.)

Look for the **Big Pineapple** (☎ 07/5442 1333; www.bigpineapple.com.au), 6 kilometers (3½ miles) south of Nambour on the Nambour Connection Road in Woombye. You can tell it's the Big Pineapple because it's 16-meters- (52½-ft.-) tall! You can take a train ride through a pineapple plantation, ride through a rain forest and a macadamia farm in a macadamia-shaped carriage, and take a boat ride through a hydroponics greenhouse. The park also has a baby animal farm, kangaroos, koalas, a rain-forest walk, a small but excellent nocturnal exhibit called Creatures of the Night, and a gift shop. It's open 365 days a year from 9am to 5pm; (opens later on Christmas and ANZAC Day; call for times). Entry is free; the plantation train, animal nursery and macadamia tour each cost A$8.80 (U.S.$5.72) adults and A$7.70 (U.S.$5.01) children 4 to 14; the hydroponics boat ride costs A$7.70 (U.S.$5.01) adults and A$6.60 (U.S.$4.29) children, entry to **Creatures of the Night** costs A$5.50 (U.S.$3.58) adults and A$3.30 (U.S.$2.15) children. A family pass to all tours is A$62.70 (U.S.$40.76) for 2 adults and up to 4 children. Allow half a day if you do everything.

Forest Glen Deer Sanctuary, Tanawha Tourist Drive, Forest Glen (☎ 07/5445 1274), has over 200 deer, kangaroos, wallabies, koalas, wombats, possums, sugar gliders, emus and more. You can drive through the Sanctuary and feed the animals from your vehicle, while a ranger escorts a Safari Trolley Tour. There's a restaurant, gift shop, and playground onsite. Admission is A$10 (U.S.$6.50) and A$5 (U.S.$3.25) for children 5 to 15. The sanctuary is open 9am to 5pm daily, except Christmas.

A **"Funshine" pass** gives discounted entry to the Australia Zoo, Underwater World and Forest Glen Deer Sanctuary. It's available from travel agents and automobile associations (in Queensland that's the **RACQ, ☎ 3361 24060**) for A$49.40 (U.S.$32.11) adults, A$25.50 (U.S.$16.38) children 3 to 15, and A$132.80 (U.S.$86.32) family of 5.

A SCENIC MOUNTAINTOP DRIVE THROUGH THE SUNSHINE COAST HINTERLAND

A leisurely drive along the lush ridgetop of the ✪ **Blackall Ranges** behind Noosa is a popular half- or full-day excursion. Cute mountain villages full of crafts shops and cafes, and terrific views of the coast are the main attractions. Macadamia nuts, peaches, and other homegrown produce is often for sale by the road at dirt-cheap prices.

On Wednesdays and Saturdays, start at the colorful outdoor ✪ **Eumundi Markets** in the historical village of Eumundi, 13 kilometers (8 miles) west of Noosa along the Eumundi Road. Locals and visitors wander under the huge shady trees among dozens of stalls selling locally grown organic lemonade, fruit, groovy hats, teddy bears, antique linen, homemade soaps, handcrafted hardwood furniture—even live emu chicks! Get your face painted, your palm read or your feet massaged. Listen to some didgeridoo music or bush poetry. When shopping's done, everyone pops into the trendy cafes on Eumundi's main street. The market runs from 6:30am to 2pm both days.

From Eumundi, take the Bruce Highway to **Nambour** and turn right onto the Nambour-Mapleton road. (The turnoff is just before you enter Nambour, so if you hit the town, you've gone too far.) A winding 12-kilometer (7¼-mile) climb up the range between rolling farmland and forest brings you to **Mapleton.** Stop at the pub for some

---

Crocodile Hunter, Live!

Farther south on the Glass House Mountains Tourist Drive 24 at Beerwah, off the Bruce Highway, is **Australia Zoo** (☎ 07/5494 1134; www.crocodilehunter.com), which showcases Australian animals in interactive demonstrations with their keepers. The zoo's owners, Steve and Terri Irwin, are renowned for manhandling dangerous saltwater crocs and are familiar to U.S. audiences from their show "Animal Planet's Crocodile Hunter," and other TV appearances.

There's otter feeding at 10:30am; a snake show at 11am; Galapagos tortoise feeding at 11:30am; an American alligator show at noon; at 12:30pm check out the foxes and camels; otter feeding again at 1pm; pat a koala at 2:30pm; hold a python at 2:45pm; a birds-of-prey demonstration at 3pm; and otters again at 3:30pm. The highlight is the saltwater croc show at 1:30pm. You can also hand-feed 'roos, watch venomous snakes and pythons, and see wild birds on the grounds. Irwin is not always on the premises, but we're told he tries to be there during school holidays. Admission is A$16.50 (U.S.$10.73) for adults, A$13.50 (U.S.$8.88) for seniors and students, A$8.50 (U.S.$5.53) for kids ages 3 to 14, and A$39.90 (U.S.$25.94) for a family of 5. AE, BC, MC, V. The park is open daily 8:30am to 4pm. Closed Christmas.

spectacular views from the verandah. From here, detour almost 4 kilometers (2½ miles) to see the 120-meter (393½-ft.) **Mapleton Falls.** A 200-meter (656-ft.) bushwalk departs from the picnic grounds and ends with great views over the Obi Obi Valley. There is also a 1.3 kilometer (¾ mile) circuit.

Back on the Mapleton–Maleny Road, head south 3.5 kilometers (2 miles) through lush forest and farms to **Flaxton Gardens.** Perched on the cliff with breathtaking coast views is a wine cellar offering tastings and sales, a pottery, a cafe, and gift shop. A bit farther south you can detour right and walk the 4.6 kilometers (2¾ miles) round-trip trail to the base of the 80-meter (262-ft.) **Kondalilla Falls.** You can swim here. It's a slippery downhill walk, and the climb back up can be tough.

Take the main road south for 5.5 kilometers (3½ miles) to **Montville.** This English-style village has become such a tourist stop that it has lost some of its character and lots of people decry its touristy facade. But everyone still ends up strolling the tree-lined streets and browsing the gift shops and galleries.

About 13 kilometers (8 miles) down the road, is **Maleny,** more modern and less commercialized than Montville. Be sure to follow the signs around to **Mary Cairncross Park** for spectacular views of the ✪ **Glass House Mountains,** 11 volcanic plugs protruding out of the plains. The park has a kiosk, a playground, free wood barbecues, and a rain forest information center; a 1.7-kilometer (1 mile) walking trail loops through the rain forest past some giant strangler figs.

You can return to Noosa the way you came or, if you're in a hurry, you can drive down to Landsborough and rejoin the Bruce Highway.

WHERE TO STAY

✪ **Halse Lodge.** 2 Halse Lane, off Noosa Dr. at Noosa Parade, Noosa Heads, QLD 4567. ☎ **1800/242 567** in Australia, or 07/5447 3377. Fax 07/5447 2929. www.halselodge. com.au. backpacker@halselodge.com.au. 26 units (all with shared bathroom). 5 double rooms, 3 twin rooms, 1 twin bunk room, 1 twin/triple room, 6 share dorms (sleep 6) and 10 share dorms (sleep 4). A$47 (U.S.$30.55) double for YHA/Hostelling International members or A$52 (U.S.$33.80) non-members twin/double; A$75–$80 (U.S.$48.75–$52) 3-share; A$21–$23 (U.S.$13.65–$14.95) dorms. BC, MC, V.

It's a backpackers' hostel, but don't let that put you off staying here. The gracious National Trust-listed Queenslander house is set in two acres of rain forest on a hill overlooking the town and the sea, and just 100 meters (110 yds.) from Noosa's Main Beach. It's almost as cozy and welcoming as a B&B, and it's kept extra-clean by on-the-ball managers. There's a kitchen, but smart guests order breakfasts (prices start at A$2.50 (U.S.$1.63). Dinner in the bistro is an equally good deal, with main courses starting at A$7.50 (U.S.$4.88). Smoking is not permitted in rooms, but there are areas on the verandah where you can indulge.

Jacaranda. 12 Hastings St. ☎ **07/5447 4011** via Holiday Noosa. Fax 07/5447 3410. www. holidaynoosa.com.au. holnoosa@holidaynoosa.com.au. 28 units (with shower only). A/C TV TEL. High season A$145 (U.S.$94.25) studio, A$220 (U.S.$143) suite; low season A$95 (U.S.$61.75) studio, A$135 (U.S.$87.75) suite. BC, MC, V.

These units are not as fancy as the swank apartment blocks up on the hill, but if you don't mind views of the river instead of the ocean, this neat block set back off the road in the thick of the Hastings Street action will do fine. Most of the one-bedroom apartments face the Noosa River; a few look onto the parking lot and the small, shady swimming pool. The decor is fine—stone-look tile floors, painted brick walls, and lime-washed furniture—although the kitchens are a little old. The studios are small, dark, and lack views, and have only a toaster and crockery, not a kitchen. Bring your own hair dryer. The beach is just down the alleyway across the road.

Room rates on the Sunshine Coast are mostly moderate, but they spike in the Christmas period from December 26 to January 26, during school holidays, and the week after Easter. Book well ahead at these times. Weekends are often busy, too.

✪ **Noosa Village Motel.** 10 Hastings St., Noosa Heads, QLD 4567. ☎ **07/5447 5800.** Fax 07/5474 9282. 11 units (with shower only). TV. High season A$155 (U.S.$100.75) double, A$190 (U.S.$123.50) family room; low season A$95 (U.S.$61.75) double, A$135 (U.S.$87.75) family room. Extra person A$11–$15 (U.S.$7.15–$9.75). BC, MC, V.

All the letters from satisfied guests pinned up on the wall here convinced us that this clean, bright little motel in the heart of Hastings Street was worth recommending—and that's before we saw the pleasant rooms. Each one is spacious and freshly painted with a toaster and crockery, a refrigerator, a small but spotless shower, and a ceiling fan. Better than the rooms, though, is the cheerful atmosphere. Proprietors John and Mary Skelton are continually sprucing up the place.

IN THE HINTERLAND

✪ **Avocado Grove Bed & Breakfast.** 10 Carramar Ct., Flaxton, QLD 4560. ☎/fax **07/ 5445 7585.** www.babs.com.au/avocado. 4 units, 3 with bathroom (shower only), 1 with private adjacent bathroom. A$105 (U.S.$68.25) double; A$120 (U.S.$78) suite. Rates include full breakfast. Ask about weekend and midweek packages. BC, MC, V. Turn right off ridge-top road onto Ensbey Rd.; Carramar Ct. is the first left.

Noela and Ray Troyahn's modern Queenslander home is in a peaceful setting in the middle of an avocado grove just off the ridgetop road. The cozy, comfortable rooms have country-style furniture, full-length windows opening onto private verandahs, fans, and oil heaters for cool mountain nights. Hair dryers are supplied. The big suite downstairs has a TV and a fridge. Colorful parrots and other birds are a common sight. Guests are welcome to picnic on the sloping lawns that have wonderful views west to Obi Obi Gorge in the Connondale Ranges. Noela prepares a big country-style breakfast, and provides tea and coffee any time. No smoking indoors.

Worth a Splurge

✪ **Zanzibar.** 47–51 The Esplanade (entry from First Avenue), Mooloolaba, QLD 4557. ☎ **1800 199 487** in Australia or 07/5444 5633. Fax 07/5444 5733. www.zanzibarresort. com.au. info@zanzibarresort.com.au. A/C, TV, TEL. A$168 (U.S. $109.20) 1-bedroom apt; A$190 (U.S.$123.50) 2-bedroom apt; A$234 (U.S.$152.10) 3-bedroom apt low season. Minimum 7 night stay applies in high season, but specials are sometimes available.

These luxury apartments all have ocean views, and are just across the road from Mooloolaba beach. There's a spa bath in every apartment and generous balconies where you can sit and watch the action on the beach and the esplanade. The decor is African-inspired, as you'd expect from the name, and it's not too overwhelming. There's plenty of space and full cooking facilities. Courtyard apartments (which are more expensive) have an outside spa and barbecue area. The pool is heated, there's a gym if you feel the urge to exercise, and security car parking.

WHERE TO DINE

Noosa's Hastings Street comes alive at night with vacationers wining and dining at restaurants as sophisticated as those in Sydney and Melbourne. For a great breakfast try **Café Le Monde** at the southern end of Hastings St (opposite the back of the Surf Club), or **Bistro C,** one of the few restaurants that still has beachfront dining. **Noosa Junction** is a better, if less attractive, bet for cheap eats and there are about 90 restaurants at

Mooloolaba to choose from. Noosa National Park has barbecues and tables at the entrance and many quiet spots with great ocean views.

Noosa Yacht and Rowing Club. Chaplin Park, Gympie Terrace, Noosaville, QLD 4566. ☎ **07/5449 8602.** Bookings not required. Main courses under A$15 (U.S.$9.75). No credit cards. Daily noon–2:15pm, 5:30pm–8:15pm, Sun 8am–10:30am.

Value-for-money food and a great location on the Noosa River make this a popular venue for locals and visitors. Sit out on the deck and enjoy the cruising boats or a stunning sunset. It's basic roasts, seafood and steak, and there are daily specials. The A$5 (U.S.$3.25) lunch deal is a great bargain. It can get crowded so get there early.

✪ **Season.** 25 Hastings St, Noosa Heads, QLD 4567. ☎ **07/5447 3747.** Reservations accepted only on the day you dine. Light meals and main courses A$16–$30 (U.S.$10.40–$19.95). AE, BC, DC, MC, V. Daily 5:30–10pm. MOD OZ.

Ever since chef Gary Skelton opened this casual place, it has been full of vacationing Sydney-siders who used to patronize his groovy Sydney pizza joint. Choose from a sliding scale of dish sizes, ranging from the salmon fish cakes with an avocado, asparagus, and rocket salad, to the chargrilled beef with blue cheese souffle. The menu is seasonal, but seafood always gets a good run. BYO. Smoking is not permitted.

Wok In Noosa. 77 Noosa Drive (at the roundabout at Sunshine Beach Rd), Noosa Junction. ☎ **07/5448 0372.** Main courses A$7.50–$13 (U.S.$4.88–$8.45). BC, MC, V. Daily noon–9pm. ASIAN NOODLES.

Locals flock to this clean, cheery joint for tasty meals that are usually under about A$15 (U.S.$9.75). Most get their food to go, but some eat in the colorful dining room, where you help yourself to cutlery, a bottle opener, and wine glasses. Don't overlook the big range of laksas, a tummy-filler that comes in a bowl the size of a baby's bathtub. They deliver—minimum order is A$15 (U.S.$9.75), plus A$2.50 (U.S.$1.63) delivery charge. Kids' meals are A$5.50 (U.S.$3.58), plus a free popsicle. BYO.

WORTH A SPLURGE

Ricky Ricardo's. 2/2 Quamby Place (inside the shopping center), Noosa Sound, QLD 4567. ☎ **07/5447 2455.** Reservations recommended. Main courses A$19.50–$25.40 (U.S.$12.68–$16.51). AE, BC, DC, MC, V. Daily noon to midnight. MOD OZ.

Owners Leonie Palmer and Steven Fisher have been on the Noosa restaurant scene for years, and their latest restaurant is as popular as its predecessors. I'd choose it for lunch over dinner simply because of the fantastic setting; the food is sensational at any time. You can sit over a long lunch drinking in the view across the Noosa River while nibbling from an innovative tapas menu or something more substantial. The menu is Mediterranean style, with fresh seafood and regional produce used throughout.

9 The Gold Coast

Love it or hate it, the Gold Coast is an Australian icon. Bronzed lifesavers, bikini-clad meter maids, tanned tourists draped with gold jewellery, high-rise apartment towers that cast long shadows over parts of the beach . . . but the glitz, the glitter and the overdevelopment pales into insignificance as soon as you hit the beach. The white sands stretch uninterrupted for 70 kilometers (18 miles), making up for the long strips of neon-lit motels, and cheap souvenir shops. Since the '50s, Australians have been flocking to this strip of coastline and that hasn't changed. Today, they're queuing up with tourists from all around the world to get into the theme parks but everyone can still find a quiet spot on the beach and the sun shines on.

The Gold Coast

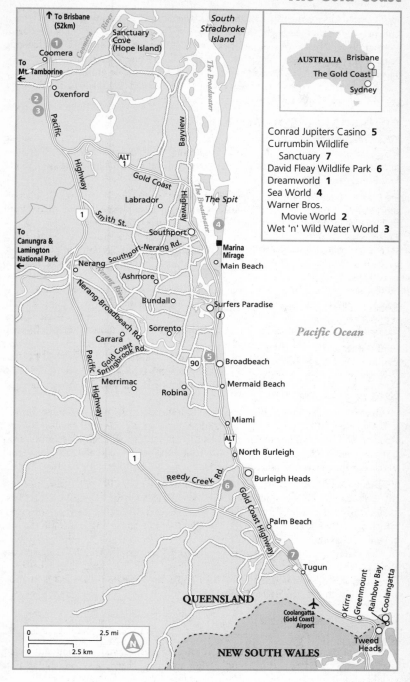

To Brisbane (52km)

Coomera River

Sanctuary Cove (Hope Island)

South Stradbroke Island

To Mt. Tamborine

Coomera ①

Oxenford ②
③

The Broadwater

AUSTRALIA Brisbane
The Gold Coast
Sydney

Conrad Jupiters Casino **5**
Currumbin Wildlife
    Sanctuary **7**
David Fleay Wildlife Park **6**
Dreamworld **1**
Sea World **4**
Warner Bros.
    Movie World **2**
Wet 'n' Wild Water World **3**

Pacific Highway

Bayview

Gold Coast Highway

Labrador

The Spit

ALT 1

Southport ④
1

Smith St.

Marina Mirage
Main Beach

To Canungra & Lamington National Park

Nerang
Southport-Nerang Rd.
Ashmore

Nerang River

Bundall

Surfers Paradise ⓘ

Pacific Ocean

Nerang-Broadbeach Rd.

Sorrento

Carrara

Gold Coast Springbrook Rd.

Merrimac

90 ⑤ Broadbeach

Robina

Mermaid Beach

Pacific Highway

Miami

ALT 1

1

North Burleigh

Reedy Creek Rd.

⑥ Burleigh Heads

Gold Coast Highway

Palm Beach

QUEENSLAND

⑦ Tugun

Kirra
Greenmount
Rainbow Bay
Coolangatta

Coolangatta (Gold Coast) Airport

Tweed Heads

0   2.5 mi
0   2.5 km

NEW SOUTH WALES

329

The Gold Coast's theme parks are not as large or as sophisticated as Disney World, but they're exciting enough. Apart from the three major parks—**Dreamworld, Warner Bros. Movie World,** and **Sea World**—there are of plenty of smaller-scale ones. If theme parks aren't your thing, there are also 40 golf courses, dinner cruises, and loads of adrenaline-based outdoor activities, from bungee jumping to jet skiing. The best activity on the Gold Coast, though, is the natural kind, and it doesn't cost a cent—hitting the surf and lazing on the beach.

GOLD COAST ESSENTIALS

GETTING THERE   By Car   Access to the Gold Coast Highway, which runs the length of the Coast, is off the Pacific Highway from Sydney or Brisbane. The drive takes about 80 minutes from Brisbane. From Sydney it's an 11-hour trip, sometimes longer, on the crowded, rundown Pacific Highway.

By Plane   Domestic flights land at **Gold Coast Airport** at Coolangatta, 25 kilometers (15 miles) south of Surfers Paradise. **Qantas** operates plenty of direct flights from Sydney, Melbourne, and Brisbane. **Coachtrans** airport shuttles (☎ **13 12 30** in Queensland, or 07/5588 8747) meet every flight; the fare to Surfers Paradise is A$11 (U.S.$7.15) one-way and A$16.50 (U.S.$10.73) round-trip. A taxi from the airport to Surfers Paradise is about A$30 (U.S.$19.50), depending on traffic, which can be heavy.

The nearest international gateway is Brisbane International Airport. The **Coachtrans Airporter** bus meets most flights and makes about 20 trips a day from the domestic and international terminals at **Brisbane Airport** to Gold Coast accommodations for A$35 (U.S.$22.75) adults, A$18 (U.S.$11.70) children 4 to 14. The trip takes about 90 minutes to Surfers Paradise. No need to book in advance unless you are on an evening flight. **The Gold Coast Tourist Shuttle** (☎ **07/5574 5111**) also runs transfers from Brisbane Airport, for A$27.50 (U.S.$17.88) adults, A$14.50 (U.S.$9.43) children 4- to 14 or A$69.50 (U.S.$45.18) family of 4. You must book this service.

Airtrain services linking Brisbane Airport and the Gold Coast beginning May 7, 2001 will cost A$17.75 (U.S.$11.48) adults. Direct services between Brisbane's international and domestic terminals and Gold Coast stations will run twice an hour in both directions. The trip from the airport to Robina on the southern end of the Gold Coast is expected to take about 90 minutes.

By Bus   Coachtrans (☎ **13 12 30** in Queensland, or 07/5588 8777) also runs regular public buses daily between Brisbane and the Gold Coast, leaving from the **Brisbane Transit Centre** on Roma Street. Every second service on average is express, which takes 1 hour, 20 minutes to Surfers Paradise. The fare is A$13 (U.S.$8.45) one-way. Bookings are not necessary.

McCafferty's (☎ **13 14 99**) and **Greyhound Pioneer** (☎ **13 20 30**) make daily stops at Surfers Paradise from Sydney and Brisbane. The trip from Sydney takes 15 to 16 hours, and the fare is A$82.50 (U.S.$53.63). Trip time from Brisbane is 90 minutes, and the fare is A$15.40 (U.S.$10.01).

Money-Saving Tips

Discount coupons and special deals on tours, cruises, car rental, restaurants, nightclubs, etc, are advertised in countless free weekly pocket guides available in hotel lobbies and shops everywhere. Grab a handful and make the most of them!

The Secret of the Seasons

School holidays, especially the Christmas vacation from mid-December to the end of January, are peak season on the Gold Coast. Accommodations are booked months in advance at these times. The rest of the year, occupancy levels plummet and so do rates! Packages and deals abound in the off-season, and perfectly adequate motel rooms can go for as little as A$50 (U.S.$32.50) double on standby.

By Train   Suburban trains (call **Queensland Rail Citytrain** at ☎ **07/3235 5555**) depart Brisbane Central and Roma Street stations every 30 minutes for the 80-minute trip to the Gold Coast suburb of Robina. The fare is A$9.10 (U.S.$5.91) adults, A$4.60 (U.S.$2.99) children ages 5 to 15. Numerous local buses meet the trains to take passengers to Surfers Paradise.

If you come by train to Surfers Paradise from Sydney or other southern cities (call **Countrylink** at ☎ **13 22 32** in Australia, or 07/9379 1298), you will need to transfer to a connecting coach in Casino or Murwillumbah, which are just south of the Queensland border. The trip from Sydney takes 14 to 15 hours and the fare is A$98 (U.S.$63.70) for a sitting berth, and A$227 (U.S.$147.55) for a sleeper.

VISITOR INFORMATION   The Gold Coast Tourism Bureau has an information kiosk on Cavill Avenue in Surfers Paradise (☎ **07/5538 4419**). It is stacked with brochures on things to see and do, and they will book tours and arrange accommodations for you. The kiosk is open Monday through Friday from 8:30am to 5:30pm, Saturdays and public holidays from 9am to 5:30pm, and Sundays from 9am to 3:30pm. A second information booth is at the corner of Griffith & Warner streets, Coolangatta (☎ **07/5536 7765**). It is open 8am to 4pm weekdays, 8am to 3pm Saturdays, 8am to 1pm public holidays, closed Sundays.

To get material in advance, write the bureau at P.O. Box 7091, Gold Coast Mail Centre, QLD 9726 (☎ **07/5592 2699;** fax 07/5570 3144; www.goldcoast tourism.com.au).

ORIENTATION   The heart of the Gold Coast is ✪ **Surfers Paradise** ("Surfers" to the locals), a high-rise forest of apartment towers, shops, cheap eateries, taverns, and amusement parlors. The pedestrian-only **Cavill Mall** in the center of town connects the Gold Coast Highway to **The Esplanade,** which runs along the beach.

The **Gold Coast Highway** is the main artery that connects the beachside suburbs lining the coast. Just north of Surfers is ✪ **Main Beach,** where Tedder Avenue is lined with shops, restaurants, and cafes. Heading south from Surfers, the main beach centres are **Broadbeach,** where retail complexes and restaurants are mushrooming; family-oriented **Burleigh Heads;** and the twin towns of **Coolangatta** in Queensland and **Tweed Heads** just over the border in New South Wales. Coolangatta still has the small-town feel ideal for families, despite some major development in the past few years. Gold Coast Airport is the other side of the highway from Coolangatta township.

West of Surfers Paradise and Broadbeach are the affluent suburbs of Ashmore and Nerang, where luxury residential estates and many of the region's championship golf courses have sprung up.

GETTING AROUND   You don't really need a car to get around. The hotels listed below are within walking distance of the beach, shops, and restaurants, and many tour companies pick up at hotels. You can reach the theme parks by bus. A car is handy for a day trip to the hinterland, and to get around to restaurants and golf courses. Parking is cheap and plentiful in numerous parking lots and on the side streets between the Gold Coast Highway and The Esplanade.

Avis (☎ 07/5539 9388), **Budget** (☎ 97/5538 1344), **Hertz** (☎ 07/5538 5366), and **Thrifty** (☎ 07/5538 6511) have outlets in Surfers Paradise and at Gold Coast Airport. Many local outfits rent cars at cheap rates.

Surfside Buslines (☎ 13 12 30 in Queensland) is the local bus company. Its best deal is a Gold Pass that allows you to hop on and off the buses anytime you like. It costs A$15 (U.S.$9.75) adults and A$8 (U.S.$5.20) children and seniors for 24 hours and A$25 to $13 (U.S.$16.25–$8.45) for 3 days; 5-, 7-, 10- and 14-day passes are also available. This is a particularly good deal if you're planning to visit the theme parks, as the company's **Gold Coast Tourist Shuttle** operates door to door transfers 4 times every morning from anywhere on the coastal strip. You must book for this, but if you are staying in Surfers Paradise or Broadbeach you can just hop on the Surfside Theme Park Express which leaves every 15 minutes from 8:30am to 11am from Pacific Fair shopping center at Broadbeach and picks up at bus stops along the way.

WHAT TO SEE & DO ON THE COAST
HITTING THE BEACHES

Needless to say, the wide white sandy beaches are the number one attraction on the Gold Coast—and best of all, they're free! No fewer than 35 patrolled beaches stretch almost uninterrupted from the Spit north of Surfers Paradise to Rainbow Bay, south of Coolangatta. In fact, the Gold Coast is really just one long fabulous beach—all you need do is step onto it at any point and you will spot the nearest set of red and yellow flags that signal safe swimming. The most popular beaches are ✪ **Main Beach**, **Surfers North, Elkhorn Avenue, Surfers Paradise, Mermaid Beach, Burleigh Heads, Coolangatta**, and **Greenmount.** All are patrolled 365 days a year.

Surfers will find a decent wave most places they put in their board, but the best breaks are at Burleigh Heads, Duranbah and Kirra. **Surfers Beach Club** (☎ 07/5526 7077), on The Esplanade in front of the Paradise Centre (opposite McDonald's on Cavill Mall), rents surfboards, body boards, inline skates and bikes for A$20 to $25 (U.S.$13–$16.25) per 24 hours.

Cavill Mall is a good place for people-watching. Here you will find a **Ripley's Believe It or Not Museum,** souvenir stores, and loads of cheap restaurants. In the **Paradise Centre** on the mall's southern side are more shops, shooting galleries, a bowling alley, electronic video games, bumper cars, and an 18-hole minigolf course.

DOING THE THEME PARKS

The big three are Dreamworld, Sea World, and Warner Bros. Movie World. Right next door to Movie World is **Wet 'n' Wild Water World.**

Sea World is the only major theme park in the center of town. The others are in northern bushland on the Pacific Highway, about a 15 to 20 minutes drive from Surfers Paradise. You can ride free to the theme parks and get a free Gold Pass for unlimited bus travel for 24 hours if you buy your park entry ticket aboard a Surfside Buslines (☎ 13 12 30 in Queensland) bus. Park tickets bought on the bus cost the same as they do at the gates, but you avoid the entry queues. Take bus 1A or 3 to Movie World and Wet 'n' Wild; bus 1A or 10 to Dreamworld; and bus 2 or 9 to Sea World.

Coachtrans (☎ 1800 426 224 in Australia or 07/5592 3488) does daily door-to-door transfers to the big three parks, and Wet 'n' Wild, and Currumbin Bird Sanctuary. Round-trip fare is A$15 (U.S.$9.75) for adults, A$9 (U.S.$5.85) for kids, or

A$39 (U.S.$25.35) for a family of 4. The company also does round-trip transfers to Sea World for A$9 (U.S.$5.85) for adults, A$5 (U.S.$3.25) for children, and A$23 (U.S.$14.95) for a family. Book a day ahead, especially in peak season.

You can also hail the regular Coachtrans buses that run daily every 30 to 45 minutes between the Gold Coast and Brisbane. They will be marked Brisbane, and you will find them on the Gold Coast Highway.

Dreamworld. Pacific Hwy. (25km/15 miles north of Surfers Paradise), Coomera. ☎ **1800/ 073 300** in Australia, 07/5588 1111, or 07/5588 1122 (24-hr info line). Admission (all-inclusive except skill games, souvenir photos, and helicopter rides) A$52 (U.S.$33.80) adults, A$32 (U.S.$208.80) children 6–13. Daily 10am–5pm; Main St., Plaza Restaurant, and Koala Country open at 9am. Closed Christmas and until 1:30pm Anzac Day (Apr 25). Extended hours during Dec and Jan.

Adrenaline-crazed thrillseekers will love the action rides, such as the aptly-named Giant Drop in which you freefall 39 stories in 5 seconds or the Tower of Terror which propels you forwards and upwards at 4.5G before falling backwards 38 stories in 7 seconds. They'll also get a kick out of the Thunderbolt, Australia's fastest double-loop roller coaster; Wipeout, which spins, twists, and tumbles you upside down in a random sequence (but exerts only a sissy 2.5G of pressure); and Enterprise, which loops the loop at 60 kilometers per hour (36 mph). These high-octane rides make the park's other offerings look tame. Dreamworld is laid out Disney-style—except that here giant koalas Kenny and Belinda roam the streets instead of Disney characters. Other offerings include an Imax theater, an Aussie wildlife park where you can cuddle a koala and feed kangaroos, river cruises livened up by a bushranger shootout on the banks, a magic show, skills games, and a carousel and other rides for young kids. A big highlight is to watch trainers swim, wrestle, and play with Bengal tigers on Tiger Island. Naturally, souvenir stores, restaurants, cafes, and ice-cream shops abound. There's a waterslide park, too, so bring your swimsuit.

Sea World. Sea World Dr. (3km/2 miles north of Surfers Paradise), The Spit, Main Beach. ☎ **07/5588 2222**, or 07/5588 2205 for recorded show times. Admission (all-inclusive except dolphin experiences, helicopter rides, and powered water sports) A$52 (U.S.$33.80) adults, A$33 (U.S.$21.45) seniors (Australian and NZ residents only) and children 4–13. Daily 9:30am–5pm; Anzac Day (Apr 25) 1:30pm–6:30pm. Closed Christmas.

It's not as sophisticated as similar parks in the U.S., but people still flock to see performing dolphins and sea lions, ski shows, an aquarium, shark feeding, and an array of rides. A monorail gets you around the grounds, and there's a free waterslide playground. Waterskiing, parasailing, WaveRunners, and banana rides are available for an extra fee. Adults (14 and over) can snorkel with dolphins, seals or sharks for A$80 to $105 (U.S.$52–$68.25) including a souvenir photo. Kids can attend a 30-minute dolphin talk, pat one, and have their photo taken with it for A$40 (U.S.$26). One of the most popular attractions is Polar Bear Shores, in which Ping Ping and Kanook frolic and dive in a large, deep pool and hunt for fish. Visitors can watch through large underwater viewing windows.

Money-Saving Tip

Sea World, Warner Bros. Movie World, and Wet 'n' Wild sell a **3 Park Super Pass** that gets you a full-day's entry to each park plus a free return visit to the one you like best. It costs A$135 (U.S.$87.75) for adults and A$86 (U.S.$55.90) for kids 4 to 13. You can only buy it from a travel agency.

Warner Bros. Movie World. Pacific Hwy. (21km/12½ miles north of Surfers Paradise), Oxenford. ☎ **07/5573 3999,** or 07/5573 8485 for recorded information. Admission (all-inclusive) A$52 (U.S.$33.80) adults, A$33 (U.S.$21.45) seniors (Australian and NZ residents only) and children 4–13. Daily 9:30am–5:30pm; rides and attractions operate 10am–5pm. Closed Christmas. Extended hours during Dec and Jan.

Australia's answer to Universal Studios just about matches its U.S. counterpart for thrills and spills. The park is based around working studios where *The Phantom,* starring Billy Zane; *20,000 Leagues Under the Sea,* with Michael Caine; and *Streetfighter,* with Jean-Claude Van Damme were filmed. If you already know how Superman flies across skyscrapers and you've heard a Foley sound studio in action before, the train ride around the sets might not interest you, but it's a great introduction to cinema tricks for first-timers. It features a stage show in the Riddler's Lair set from *Batman Forever.* Movie World has a couple of tummy-turning rides as well, including the Lethal Weapon roller coaster and Batman—The Ride, a simulated high-speed chase in the Batmobile. Don't miss the hilarious Police Academy Stunt Show. Other attractions include an illusion show, a bloopers cinema, and a Wild West flume ride. Young kids can take rides and see stage shows with Australia's own Looney Tune, Taz, and Porky Pig in the Looney Tunes Village, and there's a Looney Tunes Parade through the streets each day. If you can stomach Daffy Duck and Wonder Woman first thing in the morning, join them and other characters for "Breakfast with the Stars," at 9:50am. Most parades and shows take place between 11am and 4pm.

Wet 'n' Wild. Pacific Hwy. (next to Warner Bros. Movie World), Oxenford. ☎ **07/5573 6233,** or 07/5573 2255 for recorded information. Admission A$31 (U.S.$20.15) adults, A$20 (U.S.$13) children 4–13. Daily Jan 10am–9pm, Feb 10am–5pm, Mar–Apr 10am–4:30pm, May–Aug 10am–4pm, Sep–Oct 10am–4:30pm, Nov–Dec 10am–5pm. Open to 9pm on Dive-In Movie nights. Closed Christmas and open from 1:30pm Anzac Day (Apr 25).

Hurtling down a seven-story flume of fiberglass at 70 kilometers per hour (44 mph) is just one of many waterslide options at this aquatic park. The rides have names like Double Screamer, Mammoth Falls, The Twister, Terror Canyon and White Water Mountain. That just about says it all. Scaredy-cats can stick to the four regular white-water flumes, float gently past palm-studded "islands" in the Calypso Beach section, or swim in the artificial breakers in the Wave Pool or the regular pool. There's also a water playground for young kids. Every night in January, and Saturday night from September to April, is Dive-In Movie night, during which film fans can recline on a rubber tube in the pool while watching the flick on a giant screen. A stunt show plays at 2:30pm (5pm on movie nights). The water is heated to 26°C (79°F) for year-round swimming.

EXPLORING THE WILDLIFE & AUSTRALIAN PARKS

✪ **Currumbin Wildlife Sanctuary.** 28 Tomewin St, Currumbin (18km/11 miles south of Surfers Paradise). ☎ **07/5534 1266.** Admission A$18.40 (U.S.$11.96) adults, A$10.40 (U.S.$6.76) seniors and children 4–15, A$46.20 (U.S.$30.03) family of 4. Daily 8am–5pm. Closed Christmas and until 1pm Anzac Day (Apr 25).

Currumbin used to be called a bird sanctuary, and it is almost synonymous with the wild rainbow lorikeets that flock here by the hundreds twice a day for feeding. It's quite amazing, as flocks of chattering birds descend onto visitors holding trays of food for them. These beautiful birds have a vivid green back, blue head, and red and yellow chest. Lorikeet feeding is at 8am and 4pm. Don't miss it. You can also have your photo taken cuddling a koala, feed kangaroos, stroll or take a free miniature steam train ride through the park, and attend animal talks and feeding demonstrations. An Aboriginal song and dance show takes place daily. The park's 67 acres are home to

1,400 native birds and animals, and lots of native birds are also drawn to the sanctuary's wetlands. In 2001, the park introduced behind-the-scenes tours which visit the animal hospital and endangered species breeding area, and a birds of prey display. Allow several hours to see everything.

✪ **David Fleay Wildlife Park.** West Burleigh Rd. (17km/10¼ miles south of Surfers Paradise), West Burleigh. ☎ **07/5576 2411.** Admission A$13 (U.S.$8.45) adults, A$8.50 (U.S.$5.53) seniors and students, A$6.50 (U.S.$4.23) children 4–17, or A$33 (U.S.$21.45) for a family of 6. Free re-entry if rained out. Daily 9am–5pm. Closed Christmas Day and until 1pm Anzac Day (Apr 25).

Established in 1952 by Australian naturalist David Fleay, this is one of Australia's premier wildlife parks. You'll see a platypus, saltwater and freshwater crocodiles, wallabies, kangaroos, glider possums, dingoes, wombats, the rare Lumholtz's tree kangaroo, and a range of Australian birds, including emus, cassowaries, wedge-tail eagles, black swans, and lorikeets. You walk on a series of boardwalks through picturesque mangrove, rain forest, and eucalyptus habitats, where most of the animals roam free. The nocturnal house is open 11am to 5pm daily, and this is where you'll see many of the most elusive animals including Australia's answer to the Easter bunny, the bilby. A program of talks and demonstrations throughout the day includes a reptile show and saltwater croc feeding—usually only from October to April, when the crocs are hungry. Aboriginal rangers from the Gomberriberri and Bundjalung communities give talks about weaponry, bush medicine and their links with the region. Volunteers give free, guided tours throughout the day. The Queensland National Parks and Wildlife Service have run the park since 1983, but David Fleay lived here until his death in 1993. Because the QNPWS frowns on handling animals, you can't cuddle a koala or hand-feed kangaroos here. There's a cafe, a gift shop, and picnic tables.

CRUISING THE COAST

The Gold Coast is overrun with all kinds of cruise boats and sailing vessels clamoring to take you out for a morning or a day on **The Broadwater,** a calm strip of water between the mainland and The Spit, north of Surfers Paradise and Main Beach. Wander down to Marina Mirage, off Sea World Drive, in Main Beach, and take your pick from the many boats based there.

Two of the biggest companies are **Shangri-La Cruises** (☎ 07/5557 8888) and **Island Queen Showboat Cruises** (☎ 07/5557 8800). Both run a similar range of cruises, including morning shopping forays to Sanctuary Cove Marine Village, seafood buffet luncheon trips to Stradbroke Island, canal cruises to spy on the luxury homes in the waterway estates, Polynesian or Vegas-theme dinner cruises, and transfers to the theme parks. The boats have air-conditioned covered spaces, bars, and an open-top deck. Expect to pay A$36.30 (U.S.$23.60) for a 2-hour shopping cruise, and A$71.50 (U.S.$46.48) for a dinner cruise. Senior, children's and family rates are also available.

GETTING ACTIVE

Surfers Beach Club (☎ 07/5526 7077), on The Esplanade in front of the Paradise Centre (opposite McDonald's on Cavill Mall), rents surfboards and other sports gear, including in-line skates for A$15 (U.S.$9.75) for 3 hours. For high-powered water sports, contact one of the many operators on The Broadwater at Sea World Drive, such as **Aussie Bob's** (☎ 07/5591 7577), located at Berth 14D at Marina Mirage.

Follow the screams to **Banzai Bungey** (☎ 07/5526 7611), on the corner of the Gold Coast Highway and Palm Ave., Surfers Paradise where you can bungee jump for A$75 (U.S.$48.75). For an extra A$15 (U.S.$9.75) they will also throw in a video for

Golf on the Cheap

Hitting the links on the Gold Coast doesn't have to cost you an arm and a leg. At the cheap and cheerful end of the spectrum is **Emerald Lakes Golf Course** on Nerang-Broadbeach Road at Alabaster Drive, Carrara (☎ **07/5594 4400**). The course welcomes all comers for just A$18 (U.S.$11.70) for nine championship holes on a par-70 course. The course is 10 minutes inland from Surfers Paradise.

you to show your friends, a certificate, and a bungee cord sample. And all this plus a T-shirt will cost you a total of A$105 (U.S.$68.25). It is open daily 10am to 10pm, and there are also the bungee rocket (where you start on the ground and are flung skywards) and fly-coaster rides if the jump didn't give you a big enough adrenaline rush.

The Gold Coast boasts more than 40 golf courses. Nine holes generally cost A$35 (U.S.$22.75), including a cart, with additional charges of around A$12.50 (U.S.$8.13) for clubs and A$10 (U.S.$6.50) for shoes. Grandest is the **Hope Island Golf Club,** Oxenford-Southport Road, Hope Island, 25 minutes north of Surfers Paradise (☎ **07/5530 8988**), designed by the Thomson–Wolveridge team. A 9-hole round is A$55 (U.S.$35.75), but few golfers can resist going the whole 18 for A$99 (U.S.$64.35), including cart rental. Other championship fairways can be found at **The Palms** at the Hyatt Regency Sanctuary Cove Resort, Casey Road, Sanctuary Cove on Hope Island (☎ **07/5577 6031**); **Lakelands,** Gooding Drive, Merrimac (☎ **07/5579 8700**), designed by Jack Nicklaus; and the two 18-hole courses at **Royal Pines Resort,** Ross Street, Ashmore (☎ **07/5592 9173**).

WHERE TO STAY

Ashmore Palms Holiday Village. 71 Hinde St., Ashmore, QLD 4214. ☎ **07/5539 3222.** Fax 07/5597 1576. www.ashmorepalms.com.au. sales@ashmorepalms.com.au. 85 units (with shower only). A/C. A$82–$102 (U.S.$53.30–$66.30) double Melanesian cabins; A$88–$108 (U.S.$57.20–$70.20) double holiday villas; A$95–$115 (U.S.$61.75–$74.75) hibiscus chalets; A$100–$120 double (U.S.$65–$78) family villa; A$100–$210 (U.S.$65–$136.50) double palm cottage. Extra adult A$10 (U.S.$6.50); extra child 3–13 A$6 (U.S.$3.90). 2 night minimum stay applies in low season, and 7-night minimum at Easter and Christmas holidays. Linen hire is A$8–$12 (U.S.$5.20–$7.80) per stay. Crib A$2 (U.S.$1.30) per night or A$10 (U.S.$6.50) per week.

A rare collection of 22 colorful South American macaws is a major attraction at this award-winning budget tourist park. The former caravan park has grown and developed as the Illich family has transformed it into a lush tropical garden of 14.5 acres complete with swimming lagoon and waterfall, heated pool with fountains, full size tennis courts, barbecues, laundries, a general store, playgrounds and a 1 kilometer (.6 miles) rain forest walk through thousands of palm trees. Most of the cabins have a private balcony overlooking the gardens. The new deluxe Mediterranean-style Macaw Mansions are the first two-story cabins in Queensland. Ashmore Palms has twice won the Australian Tourism Award (1999 and 2000) for best budget accommodation, and although it is located in the Gold Coast suburbs, it is still less than a 10-minute drive to Surfers Paradise. It also has the advantage of being less than 15 minutes from the theme parks.

✪ **Mercure Resort Surfers Paradise.** 122 Ferny Ave., Surfers Paradise, QLD 4217. ☎ **1800/074 111** in Australia, 1800/221 4542 in the U.S. and Canada, 0181/283 4500 in the U.K., 0800/44 4422 in New Zealand, or 07/5579 4444. Fax 07/5579 4492. www. mercuresurfers.com.au. bookatmrsp@oze-mail.com.au. 405 units. A/C TV TEL. A$170–$190

(U.S.$110.50–$123.50) double; A$230–$190 (U.S.$149.50–$123.50) family room. Extra person, children under 16 if they use existing bedding A$22 (U.S.$14.30). Free crib. Ask about special packages. AE, BC, DC, JCB, MC, V.

If you're a parent and your idea of a holiday is to not even see your kids for most of the day, this place is for you. The resort has a licensed childcare center for little ones as young as 6 weeks up to 4 years old. For 5- to 12-year-olds, there's the Gecko Club, complete with pedal minicars, the Leonardo de Gecko painting room, and an underwater themed pirate adventure world. You can sip cocktails around the leafy pool complex and watch the kids play on the water slide. The childcare center charges a moderate fee, but the Gecko Club is free; both operate daily year-round. The low-rise building is comfortable, not grand; rooms have views of the pool or the tropical gardens. All rooms were refurbished in 2000 and have hair dryers, irons, and ironing boards. Family quarters sleep up to five in two separate rooms, and some have kitchenettes. Features like a daily activity program, outdoor climbing wall, two restaurants and a bar, karaoke nights, a sauna, Jacuzzi, tennis courts, a basketball court, and a tour desk make this hotel good value for the money. The center of Surfers Paradise and the patrolled beach are a few blocks across the highway. Some rooms are near the highway, so ask for a quiet spot.

Pink Poodle. 2903 Gold Coast Hwy. (at Fern St.), Surfers Paradise, QLD 4217. ☎ **131 779** or 07/5539 9211. Fax 07/5539 9136. www.bestwestern.com.au/pinkpoodle. pinkpoodle@bestwestern.com.au. 20 units (with shower only, 1 with Jacuzzi). A/C TV TEL. A$68–$99 (U.S.$44.20–$64.35) single; A$78–$99 (U.S.$50.70–$64.35) double. A$30 (U.S.$19.50) surcharge from mid-Dec to mid-Jan. Extra person, children under 12, A$10 (U.S.$6.50). Crib A$10 (U.S.$6.50). AE, BC, DC, MC, V.

You can't miss the pink neon poodle, which has been a Gold Coast landmark for decades. Once an institution with Australian honeymooners, the Pink Poodle has recently been renovated and is now part of the Best Western chain. It's an easy 1.2-kilometer (¾-mile) walk south of Surfers Paradise's shopping and restaurant area, and there's a patrolled beach at the end of the street. There are hair dryers, irons and ironing boards in the rooms, and most have balconies or patios. Even in the room closest to the highway, the traffic noise is muted; it's the rainbow lorikeets in the trees outside that will wake you up. A nice garden pool and a Jacuzzi face a suburban street. The restaurant has room service and the front desk runs a tour desk.

GOOD-VALUE VACATION APARTMENTS

Apartments make good sense for families and for any traveler who is prepared to self-cater to save money. Because the Gold Coast has a dramatic oversupply of apartments that stand empty except during school vacations, you can get a spacious modern unit with ocean views for the cost of a low-priced midrange hotel. The three complexes listed below are particularly good values. Apartment block developers got in quick to snag the best beachfront spots when the Gold Coast boomed in the 1970s, so it's apartment complexes, not hotels, that have the best ocean views.

Accommodations Tip

Most accommodations will require a 1-week minimum stay during school holiday periods, and a 4-day minimum stay at Easter and during the Indy car race carnival in October; book well ahead for those times.

Indy Madness

When the **Gold Coast Indy car race** takes over the town for 4 days in October, hotel rates skyrocket and most hostelries demand a minimum stay of 3 or 4 nights. Don't leave accommodation bookings to the last minute! Contact the **Gold Coast Tourism Bureau** (☎ **07/5538 4419**, fax 07/5570 3259) to find out the exact dates.

○ **Bahia Beachfront Apartments.** 154 The Esplanade, Surfers Paradise, QLD 4217. ☎ **07/5538 3322.** Fax 07/5592 0318. www.bahia.com.au. info@bahia.com.au. 30 units. TV TEL. High season A$127 (U.S.$82.55) double 1-bedroom apt, A$172 (U.S.$111.80) double 2-bedroom apt; low season A$98 (U.S.$63.70) 1-bedroom apt, A$135 (U.S.$87.75) 2-bedroom apt. Extra person A$15 (U.S.$9.75). Weekly rates available. AE, BC, DC, JCB,MC, V.

You get champagne views at a beer prices at this apartment complex 800 meters (½ mile) north of the town center. Rising 14 floors, the building offers units that are big and airy, simply but neatly furnished, with a big modern kitchen, and combined bathroom/laundry. Front-facing units have a mirrored rear wall to reflect the ocean. Like many apartments on the Gold Coast, these are not air-conditioned, but the sea breeze is a good substitute on all but the hottest days. Corner apartments have two balconies, and only units in the southwest corner of the building and on the first two floors miss out on the sea view. Unlike most Coast apartments, these are serviced daily. There's a tour desk, heated pool, child's pool, gym equipment, sauna, and Jacuzzi. A patrolled beach is across the road.

○ **Calypso Plaza.** 87–105 Griffith St., Coolangatta, QLD 4225. ☎ **1800/062 189** in Australia or 07/5599 0000. Fax 07/5599 0099. www.mirvachotels.com.au. reservationcalypso plaza@mirvachotels.com.au. 155 units all with private bathroom. A/C TV TEL. A$130–$250 (U.S.$84.50–$162.50) double. AE, BC, DC, JCB, MC, V Free undercover parking.

Just 10 minutes from Gold Coast Airport, this is one of Coolangatta's new developments but it somehow manages not to spoil the feel of the town. It is just across the road from the beach, but boasts its own huge freeform lagoon, complete with waterslides that the kids will love. There's also a separate swimming pool for smaller kids. The one- and two-bedroom apartments have sweeping views across the beach and ocean, and all have balconies with outdoor furniture, from which to enjoy them. All two-bedroom apartments have two bathrooms, and there's also a laundry in each apartment. Other facilities include a tour desk, room service, babysitting, currency exchange, and a shuttle bus to local golf, tennis and service clubs.

○ **Trickett Gardens Holiday Inn.** 24–30 Trickett St., Surfers Paradise, QLD 4217. ☎ **1800/074 290** in Australia, or 07/5539 0988. Fax 07/5592 0791. www.about-australia. com/trickett/index.htm. bobmille@fan.net.au. 33 units (with shower only). A/C TV TEL. High season (Dec 26 to mid-Jan) A$132 (U.S.$85.80) double 1-bedroom apt, A$160 (U.S.$104) double 2-bedroom apt; low season A$100 (U.S.$65) double 1-bedroom apt, A$108 (U.S.$70.20) double 2-bedroom apt. Extra person A$20 (U.S.$13), A$6 (U.S.$3.90) for children under 3 with extra bedding. AE, BC, DC, JCB, MC, V. Free parking.

This well-maintained three-story apartment block 100 meters (a few hundred ft.) from the beach and 2 blocks from Cavill Mall is not one of the Holiday Inn chain, but a family-run affair. It's hard to beat for location, price, and comfort. The one- and two-bedroom painted brick apartments have simple, neat furnishings, spacious airy living area, kitchen, safes, and a small combined bathroom and laundry with a hair dryer. Each has a balcony overlooking the pool (which is heated in winter), Jacuzzi, and barbecue under the bougainvillea and palms. There's room service at breakfast and dinner, tour desk, and free newspaper delivery daily. No smoking indoors.

WHERE TO DINE

The Gold Coast is full to the rafters with cheap restaurants, especially in and around Cavill Mall. Look for discount coupons in the free tourist guides available in hotel lobbies and information booths. Many stylish restaurants and cafes, most reasonably priced, are springing up around Surf Parade and Victoria Avenue at Broadbeach, as well as in the nearby Oasis shopping mall. A coffee and an Italian-style gourmet sandwich by the water won't cost the earth at the stylish Marina Mirage shopping center opposite the Sheraton on Sea World Drive at Main Beach, nor at one of the hip Tedder Avenue cafes in Main Beach.

Billy T. Bones On the Beachfront Café Bar Grill. Under the Iluka Beach Resort Hotel, The Esplanade at Hanlan St., Surfers Paradise. ☎ **07/5526 7913.** Main courses A$6.90–$17.95 (U.S.$4.49–$11.67). AE, BC, DC, JCB, MC, V. Mon–Fri 11am–10pm; weekends 6:30am–10pm. STEAK/PASTA/SEAFOOD.

Write down your order at one of the timber dining tables, hand it to the waitress, and sit back to enjoy the sea views from this casual spot across the road from the beach. They do big cooked breakfasts for A$6.90 (U.S.$4.49), with thick toast and decent coffee. The long list of lunch and dinner options includes pastas, burgers, honey tempura prawns on rice, or southern fried chicken. Grain-fed steaks, hard to find Down Under, come with a baked potato with bacon bits and sour cream, coleslaw, and a choice of mushroom, pepper, or chili sauce. Look for the good-value blackboard specials.

✪ **Eazy Peazy Thai and Japanezy.** Tedder Ave. at Peak Ave., Main Beach. ☎ **07/5591 9000.** Main courses A$9.90–$19.90 (U.S.$6.44–$12.94). AE, BC, DC, MC, V. Tues–Sun noon–3pm and daily 6–10pm, Sat–Sun noon–10pm. THAI AND JAPANESE.

You can have a quick feed of tempura at the noodle bar or make a night of it at the relaxed tables and chairs set up alfresco on the corner of happening Tedder Avenue. Everything on the lengthy menu is light and tasty, from the sushi to the Thai chili beef salad to the marinated fried chicken on light Japanese veggies. The soups are good fillers for around A$8 (U.S.$5.20).

WORTH A SPLURGE

✪ **RPR's.** 21st fl., Royal Pines Resort, Ross St., Ashmore. ☎ **07/5597 1111.** Reservations recommended. Main courses A$28.50–$32.50 (U.S.$18.53–$21.13); Sunset Dining special A$43.50 (U.S.$28.28) for 2 courses and glass of champagne if you are seated by 5:30pm and leave by 7pm. AE, BC, DC, JCB, MC, V. Mon–Sat 6pm–9:30pm. MOD OZ.

Chef Michael Mayne turns out some of the slickest dishes on the Gold Coast in this atmospheric aerie with views of the city lights from every table. Meat dishes like grain-fed Mandalong lamb with roast garlic and olive oil mash sit alongside a range of fish and chicken offerings. Fresh reef fish on eggplant caponatta with baby spinach and salsa verde is just one of the tempting array. Save room for dessert, which might be the pistachio sable with carmelised mission figs, pure cream and vanilla syrup.

THE GOLD COAST AFTER DARK

The jeans and T-shirt set love the laid-back **Billy's Beach House** on The Esplanade at Hanlan Street, Surfers Paradise (☎ **07/5531 5666**) for its drinks specials. There's always a live band Sunday nights. At night a dress code of long pants and enclosed shoes (that is, no thongs or sandals) applies. All ages and types frequent **Melba's,** 46 Cavill Ave., Surfers Paradise (☎ **07/5538 7411**), a popular neon-lit dance club. Tuesday and Thursday are ladies' nights (with male strippers on Thursdays), and cocktails are A$4 (U.S.$2.60) all night. Cover is A$8 (U.S.$5.20).

A genuine Rolls Royce parked in the corner at **Rolls** nightclub at the Sheraton Mirage, Sea World Drive, Main Beach (☎ 07/5591 1488) can be reserved as your booth for the night. A mixed-age crowd of sophisticated locals rubs shoulders with hotel guests. There is a A$5 (U.S.$3.25) cover; the club opens Friday and Saturday night. At 10:30pm they push back the tables at **Saks,** Marina Mirage, Sea World Drive, Main Beach (☎ 07/5591 2755) and the elegant cafe/wine bar becomes a dance floor for fashionable 20- and 30-somethings. Friday, Saturday, and Sunday are the coolest nights to turn up, there's a live band Sundays, no cover.

Revelers 20 to 35 years old go to **Shooters Saloon Bar,** in the Mark shopping complex, Orchid Avenue, Surfers Paradise (☎ 07/5592 1144) for a fun, hip, but not slavishly trendy night of dancing. There's usually some kind of competition going on, from Bachelor of the Year awards to swimwear parades. Cover is A$5 (U.S.$3.25) after 10pm. It's open daily from 11am to 5am.

It's not as big some Vegas casinos, but **Conrad Jupiters Casino,** Gold Coast Highway, Broadbeach (☎ 07/5592 1133), has plenty to keep the gambler amused—88 gaming tables and 1,100-plus slot machines with roulette, blackjack, Caribbean stud poker, baccarat and minibaccarat, craps, Pai Gow and Sic Bo, as well as the classic Aussie two-up. Downstairs the 1,100-seat **Jupiter's Theatre** stages floor shows and live music; there are nine bars, including an English-style pub. Of the six restaurants, the good-value Food Fantasy buffet is outrageously popular, so be prepared to wait. The casino is open 24 hours. You must be 18 to enter, and smart, casual dress is required.

Many head for the **Twin Towns Services Club,** Pacific Highway at Marine Parade, Tweed Heads (☎ 1800/014 014 in Australia, or 07/5536 1977 for bookings, and 07/5536 2277 for administration) for the 400 slot machines, Keno, and Club Tab for sports betting, but you can also catch popular acts like Petula Clark, Charlie Pride, Glen Campbell, Don McLean, and Gene Pitney in the Auditorium (tickets for performances A$20 to $35/U.S.$13–$22.75). Live music plays every afternoon and evening. Just to make sure nothing comes between you and the one-armed bandits (slot machines), there's a supervised children's lounge (entry A$4.40/U.S.$2.86 per child) open every evening until 10pm Sunday to Thursday and until midnight Friday and Saturday. Although the club is over the state border by a matter of meters (yards), it ignores NSW daylight saving and runs on Queensland time all year round. Admission is free.

10 The Gold Coast Hinterland: Back to Nature

The cool, green Gold Coast hinterland— is only a half-hour drive from the Coast, but is a world away from the neon lights, theme parks and crowds. Up here, at an altitude of 500 to 1,000 meters (about 1,500–3,500 ft.), the tree ferns drip moisture, the air is crisp, and there's no pressure to do anything too quickly.

Mt. Tamborine shelters several villages known for their craft shops, galleries, cafes, and lovely B&Bs. Easy walking trails wander from the streets through rain forest and eucalyptus woodland, and as you drive you will discover magnificent views.

The impressive 50,500-acre ✪ **Lamington National Park** lies to the south of Mt. Tamborine. The park, at around 1,000 meters (3,328 ft.) above sea level, is a refreshing eucalyptus and rain forest wilderness criss-crossed with walking trails. It's famous for its rich, colorful bird life, wallabies, possums, and other wildlife. The road to the park is full of twists and turns, and as you wind higher and higher, gnarled tangled vines and dense eucalyptus and ferns make a canopy across the road so dark you need your car headlights on. The park is about 90 minutes from the coast—but once you're ensconced in your mountain retreat, the world will seem remote.

The hinterland is close enough to the Gold Coast and Brisbane to make a pleasant day trip, but you will almost certainly want to stay overnight, or longer, once you breathe that restorative mountain air.

MT. TAMBORINE

40km (24 miles) NW of Surfers Paradise; 70km (42 miles) S of Brisbane

Craft shops, teahouses, and idyllic mountain vistas bring visitors to Mt. Tamborine. The mountaintop is more a plateau than a peak, and it's home to a string of villages, all a mile or so apart—Eagle Heights, North Tamborine, and Mt. Tamborine proper. Many of the shops and cafes are only open Thursday, Friday, and weekends.

ESSENTIALS

GETTING THERE   From the Gold Coast, head to Nerang and follow the signs that say Beaudesert. The Mt. Tamborine turnoff is off this road. Alternatively, head up the Pacific Highway to Oxenford and take the Mt. Tamborine turnoff, the first exit after Warner Bros. Movie World. Many tour operators run minibus and 4WD day trips from the Gold Coast, and some also run tours from Brisbane.

VISITOR INFORMATION   Stop at the **Gold Coast Tourism Bureau** (see "Visitor Information" for the Gold Coast, above) for information and tourist maps before you head out. Brisbane Tourism outlets (See "Visitor Information" in chapter 6) also have information. Once you arrive, the **Tamborine Mountain Information Centre** is in Doughety Park, where Geissmann Drive becomes Main Western Road in North Tamborine (☎ **07/5545 3200**). It's open daily from 10:30am to 3:30pm.

EXPLORING THE MOUNTAIN

With a map in hand, you are well equipped to drive around Mt. Tamborine's roads to admire the wonderful views over the valleys and to poke around in the shops. New Age candles, homemade soaps, maple pecan fudge, framed tropical watercolors, German cuckoo clocks, and Aussie antiques are some of the things you can buy in the mountain's crafty stores. The best place to shop is the quaint strip of galleries, cafes, and shops known as Gallery Walk on Long Road, between North Tamborine and Eagle Heights. Eagle Heights has few shops but great views back toward the coast. North Tamborine is mainly a commercial center where you still find the odd nice gallery or two. Mt. Tamborine itself is mainly residential.

The cool air has lent itself to winemaking, still in its infancy in this neck of the woods, but **Mount Tamborine Vineyard and Winery,** 32 Hartley Rd. (☎ **07/5545 3506**), northwest of North Tamborine off the Main Western Road, has offerings including shiraz, merlot, grenache merlot, sauvignon blanc, chardonnay, and muscat. The cellar door is open for free tastings from 10am to 4pm daily.

Allow time to walk some of the trails that wind through forest throughout the villages. Most are reasonably short and easy. The Mt. Tamborine Information Center has maps marking them.

WHERE TO STAY: A RAIN FOREST B&B

✪ **Tamborine Mountain Bed & Breakfast.** 19–23 Witherby Crescent, Eagle Heights, QLD 4721. ☎ **07/5545 3595.** Fax 07/5545 3322. 4 units (1 with bathtub, others shower only). A/C TV. A$80–$110 (U.S.$52–$71.50) double; A$135–$160 (U.S.$87.75–$104) double on Sat nights. Rates include full breakfast. AE, BC, MC, V. No children allowed.

Elizabeth Finneymore's restful timber home has stunning 180° views to the ocean from the breakfast balcony. Laze by the open fire in the timber-lined living room, or out on the verandah where rainbow lorikeets, kookaburras, and crimson rosellas flit around the bird feeders. The ferny gardens have four rustic timber rooms, each individually decorated in Edwardian/cottage style, equipped with a VCR and small refrigerator. Elizabeth will lend hair dryers. The rooms are heated in winter. The Queensland Automobile Association, the RACQ, awards the place five stars. No smoking indoors.

LAMINGTON NATIONAL PARK
70km (42 miles) W of Gold Coast; 115km (69 miles) S of Brisbane

Subtropical rain forest, 2,000-year-old, moss-covered Antarctic beech trees, giant strangler figs, and misty mountain air characterize Lamington's suddenly ascending peaks and plunging valleys. It's one of the most important subtropical parks in southeast Queensland, and one of the loveliest. The park has 160 kilometers (96 miles) of walking trails that track through thick forest, past ferny waterfalls, and along mountain ridges with soaring views across green valleys. The trails vary in difficulty and length, from 1-kilometer (½-mile) strolls up to 23-kilometer (14-mile) treks. The park is a haven for bird lovers who come to see and photograph the rosellas, bowerbirds, and other species that live here, but that's not the only wildlife you will see. Groups of small wallabies, called pademelons, graze outside your room. In summer you may see giant carpet pythons curled up in a tree or large goannas sunning themselves on rock ledges. Near streams a hissing Lamington Spiny Crayfish, an aggressive little monster 6 inches long, patterned in royal blue and white, may challenge you. The park comes alive with owls, possums, and sugar gliders at night.

Most visitors are fascinated by the park's Antarctic beech trees, which begin to appear above the 1,000-meter (3,330-ft.) line. Like something from a medieval fairy tale, these mossy monarchs of the forest stand 20 meters (66 ft.) tall and measure up to 8 meters (26 ft.) in girth. They are survivors of a time when Australia and Antarctica belonged to the super-continent, Gondwana, when it was covered by wet, tropical rain forest. The species survived the last Ice Age, and the trees at Lamington are about 2,000 years old, suckered off root systems about 8,000 years old. The trees are a 2½ hour walk from O'Reilly's Rainforest Guesthouse (see below).

ESSENTIALS
GETTING THERE   By Car   O'Reilly's is 37 kilometers (22¼ miles) from the town of Canungra. The road is very twisty, so take it slowly, allow yourself an hour

---

Tips for Exploring Lamington National Park

The easiest way to explore the park is to base yourself at **O'Reilly's Rainforest Guesthouse** in the Green Mountains section of the park, or at **Binnaburra Mountain Lodge** in the Binnaburra section (see "Where to Stay & Dine: Worth a Splurge," below). Most of the trails lead from one or the other of these resorts, and a 23-kilometer (14-mile) Border Trail connects them; it follows the New South Wales-Queensland border for much of the way, and can be walked by most reasonably fit folk in a day. Guided walks and activities at both resorts are for houseguests only; however, both properties welcome day visitors who just want to walk the trails for free. Both have inexpensive cafes for day-trippers.

It's a good idea to bring a torch (flashlight) and maybe binoculars for wildlife spotting. The temperature is often 4°C to 5°C (10°F to 20°F) cooler than on the Gold Coast, so bring a sweater in summer and bundle up in winter when nights get close to freezing. September to October is orchid season, and the frogs come out in noisy abundance in February and March.

from Canungra to reach O'Reilly's, and plan to arrive before dark. Binnaburra is 35 kilometers (21 miles) from Nerang via Beechmont, or 26 kilometers (15½ miles) from Canungra, on a similarly winding mountain road. From the Gold Coast go west to Nerang, where you can turn off to Binnaburra via Beechmont, or go on to Canungra where you will see the O'Reilly's and Binnaburra turnoffs. From Brisbane, follow the Pacific Highway south and take the Beenleigh/Mt. Tamborine exit to Mt. Tamborine. From there follow the signs to Canungra. Allow a good 2½ hours to get to either resort from Brisbane, and 90 minutes from the Gold Coast. Binnaburra sells unleaded fuel; O'Reilly's has emergency supplies only.

By Coach   The Mountain Coach Company (☎ 07/5524 4249) does daily transfers to O'Reilly's from the Gold Coast, leaving the airport at 8am, picking up at hotels on the way, and arriving at O'Reilly's at 12:30pm. The fare is A$44 (U.S.$28.60) adults round-trip. The return trip leaves O'Reilly's at 2:30pm, arriving at the airport by 5:30pm. **Allstate Scenic Tours** (☎ 07/3003 0700) makes a run from outside the Roma Street Transit Centre in Brisbane every day except Saturday at 9:30am, arriving at O'Reilly's at 12:30pm. It costs A$44 (U.S.$28.60) adults round-trip.

The Binnaburra resort runs a shuttle from the Gold Coast that costs A$22 (U.S.$14.30) per adult, half price for kids 5 to 14, each way. It runs on demand, and should be booked when making accommodation bookings.

DAY TRIPS   Companies running day tours from both Brisbane and the Gold Coast include **Coachtrans** (☎ 1300/36 1788, or 07/3236 4165), and **Backtracks 4WD Safaris** (☎ 1800/356 693 in Australia, or 07/5573 5693). The Gold Coast Tourism Bureau can get you in touch with other operators; see "Visitor Information" in the "Gold Coast" section.

VISITOR INFORMATION   The best sources of hiking information are O'Reilly's Rainforest Guesthouse and Binnaburra Mountain Lodge (see "Where to Stay," below for both); ask them to send you copies of their walking maps. There is a national parks information office at both properties. For detailed information on hiking and camping in the park, contact the **ranger** at Lamington National Park, Green Mountains section (which is at O'Reilly's), via Canungra, QLD 4211 (☎ 07/5544 0634).

WHERE TO STAY & DINE: WORTH A SPLURGE

The rates at these two mountaintop retreats include all activities, morning and afternoon tea, and supper; those at Binnaburra include three meals a day. There is little difference in the quality of each. The rooms are cozier at Binnaburra, and its lounge and dining room are more modern and attractive; the family-owned O'Reilly's is a little homier and more welcoming. Both offer ample walking trails of similar type and distance; guided walks and nighttime wildlife-spotting trips; hearty food; and a restful, enjoyable experience. Inquire about special-interest workshops both run throughout the year, ranging from gourmet weekends to mountain-jogging programs.

✪ **Binnaburra Mountain Lodge.** Beechmont via Canungra, QLD 4211. ☎ **1800/074 260** in Australia, or 07/5533 3622. Fax 07/5533 3747. www.binnaburralodge.com.au. info@binnaburralodge.com.au. 40 cabins, 22 with bathroom (shower only). MINIBAR. A$250–378 (U.S.$162.50–$245.70) double. Single supplement A$22 (U.S.$14.30) per night for 1–2 nights, A$11 (U.S.$7.15) for 3 or more nights; A$55 (U.S.$35.75) children 5–16. No sole use at Christmas and Easter holidays. Rates decrease with every night you stay. Rates include all meals and activities. Ask about multi-night packages. Minimum 2-night stay weekends, 3-night stay public holidays. AE, BC, DC, MC, V.

Binnaburra is every bit the postcard-perfect mountain lodge: picturesque chalets nestled in the forest, a fire roaring in the lounge, and birds twittering in the trees.

The original cabins, built in 1935, are still in use today; they've been outfitted with modern comforts, but not 20th-century "inconveniences," such as telephones, radios, or clocks. Of the 21 trails leading from the lodge, 9 are short walks of less than 6 kilometers (3½ miles). The 12 longer trails range from a 9-kilometer (5½-mile) walk through "dry" rain forest to the 23-kilometer (14-mile) Border Trail to O'Reilly's. On Tuesday the resort buses hikers to O'Reilly's so they can spend the day walking back to Binnaburra. The lodge also conducts abseiling at least twice a week for anyone from beginners to advanced adventurers. Evening diversions might consist of parlor games, a weekly bush dance, or slide presentations on local natural history. Kids can entertain themselves in the excellent playground; special activities for kids are offered on Saturdays and during school holidays.

All the accommodations have pine-paneled walls, floral bedcovers, heaters and electric blankets. The most attractive and spacious are the mud-brick and weatherboard Acacia cabins, which have private bathrooms and the best views over the Numinbah Valley. There are two kinds of less-expensive Casuarina cabins—the nicest are the small and very cozy huts with a pitched ceiling, a washbasin, and a nice aspect into the forest and over the valley. Less atmospheric are the bunkroom-style rooms that sleep four to six people—good for families and groups of friends. Guests in Casuarina cabins share bathroom facilities, which include a Jacuzzi. Meals are served in the lovely stone-and-timber dining room. Seating is communal, so you get to meet other travelers. Free tea and coffee are on the boil all day. There is also a craft shop, a natural history library, a laundromat, and conference rooms.

✪ **O'Reilly's Rainforest Guesthouse.** Via Canungra, Lamington National Park Rd., Lamington National Park, QLD 4275. ☎ **1800/688 722** in Australia, or 07/5544 0644. Fax 07/5544 0638. www.oreillys.com.au. reservations@oreillys.com.au. 52 units. A$108–$137 (U.S.$70.20–89.05) single; A$177–$274 (U.S.$115.05–$178.10) double. Canopy Suites A$191 (U.S.$124.15) per person. Extra person A$22 (U.S.$14.30); children 17 and under free in parents' room if they use existing bedding. Free crib. Rates include all activities. Rates decrease with every night you stay. Minimum 2-night stay weekends, 3-night stay long weekends, 4-night stay Easter and Christmas. Ask about packages for stays of 2 nights or more. Meal plans A$69 (U.S.$45.85) adults, A$34 (U.S.$22.10) children 10–17, A$17 (U.S.$11.05) children 4–9 for 3 meals per day; 2-meal packages available. AE, BC, DC, MC, V.

Highlights of your stay will be the chance to hand-feed brilliantly colored rain forest birds every morning and the fact that the staff will unfailingly remember you by name for your entire stay. Nestled high on a cleared plateau, the buildings are closed in on three sides by dense tangled rain forest and open to picturesque mountain views to the west. The rain forest begins right at the parking lot, from which 19 trails fan out through the bush. For those who don't want to venture too far, the Treetop Walk is just a few meters (yards) from the resort. You can walk the 15-meter (50-ft.) high suspension bridge through the forest canopy, and climb to the two treetop observation decks 30 meters (100 ft.) above ground for unbelievable views. One of the nicest trails is the 7.6-kilometer (4½-mile) round-trip to Elabana Falls, which takes about half a day. The staff run half-day and full-day guided walks, and half-day 4WD bus trips. Every night there is a slide show on the area's wildlife or history. Don't miss the remarkable story of Bernard O'Reilly's one-man search for a crashed aircraft on the mountain. You may also enjoy spot-lighting walks to see possums, glowworms, and, in season, luminous fungi. Sometimes in summer there are cliff-top campfire nights with steaks cooked over the fire. On weekends and school holidays there is a "Scrub Club" for kids over age 5.

The timber resort complex is inviting rather than grand, but new suites and the refurbishment of older rooms have added a touch of luxury in the past year. The comfortable guest lounge has an open fire and is scattered with old-fashioned sofas, chairs, and an upright piano. The six rooms in the Tooloona block, which dates from the 1930s, have communal bathrooms and basic furniture. The motel-style Elabana rooms have en suite bathrooms. The 37 Bithongabel rooms have the best views and also have en suite bathrooms. Six family rooms in this block have bunks for kids, and two rooms are wheelchair accessible. The newest, and most expensive, rooms are the Canopy Suites, twice as large as any of the other rooms, with luxuries like a king-size four-poster bed, fireplace, spa, library, audio system and bar. At meals, the maitre d' assigns you to a table in the dining room, so you get to meet other guests. If you don't buy a meal package, buffet breakfast costs A$22 (U.S.$14.30), lunch costs A$26 (U.S.$16.90), and a three-course dinner is A$37 (U.S.$24.05). Before dinner, guests head to the hexagonal timber bar, perched up high for great sunset views and half-price cocktails (5–6:30pm). Other facilities include a cafe and gift shop, swimming pool, sauna and spa, day/night tennis court, basketball court, game room, laundromat, babysitting, and free tea, coffee, and cookies all day.

CAMPING

✪ **Binnaburra Campsite.** Beechmont via Canungra, QLD 4211. ☎ **1800/074 260** in Australia, or 07/5533 3622. Fax 07/5533 3747. www.binnaburralodge.com.au. info@binnaburralodge.com.au. 6 powered campsites, 12 unpowered tent sites; 17 permanent tents (none with bathroom). Tent sites A$10 (U.S.$6.50) adult, A$7 (U.S.$4.55) seniors and students, A$30 (U.S.$19.50) family of 4; powered site A$3.50 (U.S.$2.28) extra per person per night. Permanent tents A$40 (U.S.$26) for a 2-bed tent, A$60 (U.S.$39) for a 4-bed tent. Children 5–15 half price. BYO linen. Ask about weekly discounts and midweek specials. AE, BC, DC, MC, V.

Binnaburra Mountain Lodge's campsite is perched on the hill a few hundred meters/yards from the main building. Permanent tents have screened windows, pine beds and mattresses, table settings and electric light. They have great valley views from a private verandah. Campers may pay to take part in the lodge activities and take meals in the dining room if it's not full. The onsite store sells basic take-out food and groceries that you can cook on the coin-operated gas barbecues (bring your own cutlery and crockery). You share shower blocks, and there's a coin-op laundromat and a public payphone. If you want to light a campfire, buy wood before you arrive.

11 Outback Queensland

Spread over 3,000 kilometers (1,875 miles), the Outback is a heartstopping land of clear blue skies, burnished sunsets, rolling plains, rugged ranges and endless vistas. Populated with colorful characters that could have walked off a movie set, the Outback is the heart and soul of Queensland. This is where the Aussie tradition of mateship was born, as pioneering cattlemen and their families battled the elements to make a go of it. The Queensland Outback is the birthplace of Australian legends like Waltzing Matilda. History comes alive when you get to places like the Burke River at Boulia, where explorers Burke and Wills filled their waterbags and modern-day travellers are invited to do the same, or at Lark Quarry, where dinosaurs once roamed.

The main centers of Queensland outback life are the towns of Charleville, Barcaldine, Longreach and Winton, and the mining town of Mt. Isa. They may be small, but they offer a completely different view of this vast state to that which you will get on the coast, and they are definitely worth the effort it takes to get to them.

Can You be a *Survivor?*

If you've always wanted to be a contestant on the hit TV show *Survivor,* here's your chance to prove yourself (if only to yourself), in the Queensland outback where *Survivor 2—The Australian Outback* took place.

There is a tour that will take you to the exact location, on Goshen Station, about three hours southwest of Cairns, where the tribes competed. Officially sanctioned by the producers of *Survivor* and the owners of Goshen Station, the tour visits the sites used by the Kucha and Ogakor tribes and explores the harsh but beautiful countryside made famous in the series.

The tour is run by the Cairns-based **Adventure Company Australia** (☎ **07/ 4051 4777;** fax 07/4051 4888; www.adventures.com.au).

For eight days, participants pit their mental and physical skills against the outback in an adventure tour that includes biking, canoeing and hiking the savannah lands surrounding the Herbert River of North Queensland. On the eighth day, tour members vote for the "most likely survivor" among the group—but without the million-dollar prize!

The tour is designed to include many of the challenges faced by *Survivor* contestants, as well as including time to explore, relax and enjoy the environment. Tour guides have an in-depth knowledge of the region, the history and culture of the traditional Aboriginal owners and the struggles of the first European settlers.

Activities include mountain biking to Blencoe Falls, canoeing the Herbert River, visits to the two tribal campsites, night spotlighting for native flora and fauna, camping close to the Tribal Council rock (and holding your own Tribal Council), exploring remnant rainforest 300 million years old, fishing for barramundi, and experiencing life on an Australian cattle station (ranch).

Tours depart Cairns every Sunday from May to November, and are likely to run under the "Survivor" banner for at least the next two years. The cost is A$1,590 (U.S.$1,033.50) for adults and A$1,390 (U.S.$903.50) for children 8 to 13. The last Sunday departure in any month is available for families with children as young as 8 years. The minimum age on all other tours is 14 years. Cost includes all meals, basic accommodation and camping, all equipment for listed activities including camping gear, safety equipment, team bandana and water bottle, and transfers.

LONGREACH
700km (437 miles) W of Rockhampton; 1,286km (804 miles) NW of Brisbane.

With a population of about 4,500, Longreach is the largest town in Queensland's Central West. One of the biggest surprises for first-time visitors to Longreach is that the town is set on the banks of a wide brown river, the Thomson. And after a hard day's travelling or sightseeing around Longreach, there's nothing more relaxing than a sunset cruise on river or a campfire on its banks. This is bush ranger country, and wherever you go in this area, you'll hear the story of Captain Starlight, the cattle rustler who's become part of local folklore . . . it's one of those stories which gets better with each telling, and which has been immortalized in the classic Australian novel *Robbery Under Arms* by Rolfe Boldrewood. There's plenty to do in Longreach, and tour operators are on hand to take the difficulty out of the distances involved.

GETTING THERE **By Car** From Brisbane, Longreach is 1,286 kilometers (804 miles) northwest. Take the Warrego Highway west through Toowoomba and Roma, heading toward Charleville. About 90 kilometers (56 miles) before Charleville, head north to Augathella and join the Matilda Highway. From there it is about 320 kilometer (200 miles) to Barcaldine, and from there head west another 108 kilometers (67 miles) to Longreach. From Rockhampton, the Capricorn Highway heads almost directly west through Emerald and Alpha for about 590 kilometers (369 miles) before joining the Matilda Highway.

By Plane Qantas (☎ 13 13 13 in Australia), flies into historic Longreach Airport from several destinations in Australia.

By Train **Queensland Rail Traveltrain** (☎ 13 22 32) runs the train *Spirit of the Outback* from Brisbane to Longreach via Rockhampton every Tuesday and Friday, returning on Thursday and Sunday. It's A$135.50 (U.S.$88.08) for a seat from Brisbane or A$173.80 to $257.40 (U.S.$113.97–$167.31) (for a sleeper. Alternatively, you can join the train at Rockhampton at 4:30am on Wednesday or Saturday. The trip takes about 24½ hours from Brisbane, or 13½ hours from Rockhampton.

By Bus **McCafferty's Coaches** (☎ 13 14 99) runs between Brisbane and Longreach daily. The trip takes 18 hours and costs A$92 (U.S.$59.80). There is a service from Rockhampton to Longreach on Thursday and Sunday, taking 10½ hours and costing A$59 (U.S.$38.35).

VISITOR INFORMATION The **Longreach Visitor Information Centre** is at Qantas Park (☎ **07/4658 3555;** fax 07/4658 3733). Another good source of information is the **Outback Queensland Tourism Authority** (☎ 1800 247 966).

GETTING AROUND Rental car companies **Budget** ☎ **07/4658 2322** and **Avis** ☎ **07/13 63 33** or 07/4658 1799 both have agents in Longreach. Several tour companies offer tours in and around Longreach and to attractions in other outback towns in the Central West.

One of the best is Alan Smith's ✪ **Outback Aussie Tours** (☎ **1300 787 890**), which runs trips taking in Longreach, Ilfracombe, Winton and Barcaldine, as well as the Lark Quarry dinosaur site. **Longreach Outback Travel Centre** (☎ **07/4658 1776**) has information on a variety of tours.

THE TOP ATTRACTIONS

✪ **Australian Stockman's Hall of Fame and Outback Heritage Centre.** Ilfracombe Rd, Longreach. (☎ **07/4658 2166.** Fax 07/4658 2495. www.outbackheritage.com.au. museum@outbackheritage.com.au. Daily 9am–5pm except Christmas. A$17 (U.S.$11.05) adults, A$14 (U.S.$9.10) seniors, A$8 (U.S.$5.20) children.

This should be the first stop on any visit to Longreach. I could spend all day at the Hall of Fame, try to allow at least four hours. A tribute to the pioneers who developed the Outback, the center honors explorers, stockmen, poets and artists. Part museum, part memorial, part interactive display, this world-class attraction is educational, entertaining and quite amazing. Exhibits are updated regularly and give a fascinating insight into the Aboriginal and European history of Australia, blending modern technology with artefacts and relics of a bygone age.

School of Distance Education. Ilfracombe Rd, Longreach. ☎ **07/4658 4222.** A$3 (U.S.$1.95) adults, A$1 (U.S.65¢) seniors and children. Guided tours at 9am and 10am on school days only.

Giving you insight into the isolation of outback families are the tours of this unique school system. You can watch a teacher conducting on-air lessons via two-way radio to students on far-flung stations. Hundreds of children in western Queensland take advantage of this form of education.

Qantas Founders Outback Museum. Qantas hangar, Longreach Airport. ☎ **07/4658 3737.** qfom@tpgi.com.au. Daily 9am–5pm except Christmas. A$7 (U.S. $4.55) adults, A$5 (U.S. $3.25) seniors, A$3 (U.S. $1.95) children.

Anyone who's ever flown on Australia's first airline will be interested in this tribute to pioneer aviators. Longreach is the original home of Qantas, as the airline's operational base from 1922 to 1934, when Australia's first six aircraft were built here. During World War II, Longreach was used as a base by U.S. Flying Fortress bombers for their Pacific operations. The hangar now houses the first stage of the museum. The main exhibit is a full-size replica of an AVRO 504K, the first type of aircraft operated by Qantas.

OTHER THINGS TO SEE & DO

Thomson River cruises are run by two local companies, **Billabong Boat Cruises** (☎ 07/4658 1776) and **Yellowbelly Express Cruises** (☎ 07/4658 2360). Lunchtime and evening cruises are run. A 3-hour evening cruise with ✪ **Yellowbelly Express** includes pickup from Longreach accommodations and dinner, and costs A$34 (U.S.$22.10) adults, A$31 (U.S.$20.15) children aged 15 to 18, A$18 (U.S.$11.70) children 4 to 14, or A$86 (U.S.$55.90) for a family. At the end of the night, you'll be entertained by some of the local talent, which could be bush poetry or a singalong.

Take a half-day tour to Oakley Station to experience life on a cattle and sheep property. The station is a 15 minute drive from town, so you won't be spending a lot of time getting there. Four generations of the Forrest family have farmed this land, with Brahmin cattle and merino sheep. The 3-hour tour includes morning tea with the Forrests, and costs A$31 (U.S.$20.15) adults, A$21 (U.S.$13.65) children 4 to 14 and can be booked through any of the tour companies or **Longreach Outback Travel Centre** (☎ 07/4658 1776).

A 30-minute drive from Longreach is the small town of **Ilfracombe.** Attractions include the folk museum which has a large collection of old vehicles, including a horse-drawn wool wagon, sulkies, cart and farm machinery. The museum also has a turn-of-the-century police cell and a collection of Aboriginal artifacts, historic photographs and early pioneering silver and china.

Stop at the historic Wellshot Hotel in Ilfracombe for a cool drink. Named for the largest sheep station in the world in its heyday, the pub is a popular local watering hole.

WHERE TO STAY

Albert Park Motel. Sir Hudson Fysh Drive, Longreach, Qld 4730. ☎ **07/4658 2411.** fax 07/4658 3181. 56 units (with shower only). A/C TEL TV. Rates A$68.20 (U.S.$44.33) single, A$79.20 (U.S.$51.48) double. Some units sleep up to 6 people. AE, BC, DC, MC, V.

The Albert Park is conveniently located just 200 meters (660 ft.) from the airport (and Qantas Founders Museum) and 500 meters (1600 ft.) from the Australian Stockmen's Hall of Fame. It's about 1.5 kilometers (just under a mile) to the center of town. Each room has VCR, small fridge and tea/coffee making facilities. The Oasis restaurant is open for dinner 7 days, and is usually open for breakfast in high season (Easter–Oct). The a la carte dinner menu offers large meals at reasonable prices. There's also an undercover, heated, saltwater swimming pool and a spa.

WINTON

175km (109 miles) NW of Longreach; 1500km (94 miles) NW of Brisbane; 470km (294 miles) E of Mt Isa

Winton is best known as the place where Banjo Paterson wrote "Waltzing Matilda" in 1885, for which the nearby Combo Waterhole was the inspiration. The town has a population of 1,200 and most of its major attractions are linked to the song.

GETTING THERE & AROUND   The nearest car hire is in Longreach. Roads are all sealed between Winton, Longreach and Mt Isa. **McCafferty's** (☎ **13 14 99**) has daily coach services between Longreach and Mt. Isa, stopping at Winton. Coach connections from Longreach to Winton are also available to passengers on the *Spirit of the Outback* train (**Queensland Rail Traveltrain** ☎ **13 22 32**). **Qantas** (☎ **13 13 13** in Australia) has daily flights from several Australian cities.

VISITOR INFORMATION   **Waltzing Matilda Centre,** Elderslie St, Winton ☎ **07/4657 1466;** fax 07/4567 1886. www.matildacentre.com.au; matilda@the hub.com.au). Or try the **Outback Queensland Tourism Authority** (☎ **1800 247 966**) for information before you arrive.

THE TOP ATTRACTIONS

Waltzing Matilda Centre. Elderslie St, Winton. ☎ **07/4657 1466.** Fax 07/4567 1886. matilda@thehub.com.au. Daily except Christmas and New Year's Day. A$14 (U.S.$9.10) adults, A$12 (U.S.$7.80) seniors and children, A$30 (U.S.$19.50) family.

This 2-year-old center is dedicated to Australia's most famous song, written by the Banjo Paterson in 1898 at Dagworth Station, near Winton. The center uses modern technology and interactive displays to celebrate the writer's life and times and the role his song has played in Australia's psyche. There's also an art gallery, local history museum, restaurant and gift shop.

   Combo Waterhole Conservation Park, believed to be the inspiration for Waltzing Matilda, is a short drive off the Matilda Highway, about 150 kilometers (94 miles) north of Winton. For more information call Queensland National Parks and Wildlife Service in Winton ☎ **07/4657 1192** or in Longreach 07/4652 7333.

   Lark Quarry Conservation Park (☎ **07/4658 1761** between 8:30am and 5pm weekdays only) is where dinosaurs once prowled. Hundreds of fossilized dinosaur footprints are preserved in rock that was once the muddy shore of a prehistoric lake. Lark Quarry is 110 kilometers (69 miles) southwest of Winton, and it is a dirt (unsealed) road all the way from Winton, about a 2-hour drive. Before setting out, check road conditions and directions with **Winton Shire Council** (☎ **07/4657 1188.** The best way to get to the site is by guided tour. **Diamantina Outback Tours** in Winton (☎ **07/4657 1514;** fax 07/4657 1722) and **Outback Aussie Tours** in Longreach (☎ **1300 787 890**) both run tours to the quarry. Outback Aussie Tours runs a 12-hour day tour to Winton for A$122 (U.S.$79.30) adults, A$87 (U.S.$56.55) children 3 to 17, which includes Lark Quarry (Apr–Oct only).

WHERE TO STAY

Pelican Waters Motel. 16 Elderslie St., Winton. ☎ **07/4657 1211.** Fax 07/4657 1331. www.jasons.com.au. 26 units (with shower only). A/C TV TEL. A$75 (U.S.$48.75) single; A$86 (U.S.$55.90) double; 2-bedroom unit A$135 (U.S.$87.75). AE, BC, DC, MC, V.

This is one of Winton's newest motels, which opened in 2000. All rooms have a Queen size and a single bed, a minifridge, tea/coffee making facilities and a computer/fax modem. Two rooms are specially designed for people with disabilities. The licensed restaurant, Mulga Bill's, has an outback theme, complete with corrugated iron and offers a full a la carte menu featuring seafood and steaks. It is open daily for break-fast and dinner and does room service in the evenings. Other facilities include under-cover parking, a swimming pool, barbecue and free shuttle from the airport. It's only 500 meters (1,600 ft) from the Waltzing Matilda Centre.

MT. ISA
893km (558 miles)W of Townsville; 633km (395 miles) NW of Longreach

Mt. Isa is Queensland's largest provincial city west of the Great Dividing Range. The town was built around mining, and the population of 22,000 reflects that in the 50 different nationalities represented. The huge Mt. Isa Mine dominates the town. It is the world's largest single producer of copper, silver, lead and zinc. There's not much here in the way of culture, but you might find it interesting anyway. A social highlight of the year is the annual **Mt. Isa Rodeo** (☎ 07/4743 2706), held every August.

GETTING THERE By Car Mt Isa is 893 kilometers (558 miles) west of Townsville on the Flinders Highway. From Longreach, take the Landsborough High-way northwest through Winton and on to Cloncurry. Mt Isa is about 120 kilometers (75 miles) west of Cloncurry on the Barkly Highway. The total trip from Longreach is 633 kilometers (395 miles). Motorists should check all road conditions with local authorities before setting out.

By Train Queensland Rail Traveltrain (☎ 13 22 32) operates the *Inlander* train from Townsville to Mt. Isa every Sunday and Wednesday, returning on Monday and Friday. The 977 kilometers (610 miles) journey takes 20½ hours and costs A$91.30 (U.S. $59.35) adult for a seat or A$129.80 to $191.40 (U.S.$84.37–$124.41) for a sleeper.

By Bus McCafferty's (☎ 13 14 99) and **Greyhound Pioneer** (☎ 13 20 30 or 07/3258 1800) both service Mt. Isa from Townsville. The trip takes about 12 hours and costs A$93 (U.S.$60.45) one-way.

By Plane Macair (book through Qantas) serves Mt. Isa from Brisbane and Townsville.

VISITOR INFORMATION Riversleigh Fossil Museum and Tourist Informa-tion Centre, Marian St, Mt. Isa. Call (☎ **1300 659 660** in Australia or 07/4749 1555, fax 07/4743 6296. riversleigh@tpgi.com.au.

GETTING AROUND Avis (☎ 07/4743 3733) is the only car hire company in town.

THE TOP ATTRACTIONS
Lawn Hill National Park. About 500km (312 miles) NW of Mt Isa.

Sheer red cliff walls, deep flowing green water, walking tracks and Aboriginal sites are the features of this outback oasis. World Heritage–listed Riversleigh is part of Lawn Hill's fossil section. **Campbells Tours and Safaris** (☎ 07/4743 2006) has a 3-day tour from Mt. Isa for A$451 (U.S.$293.15) adult, A$275 (U.S.$178.75) children 3 to 14. You stay at a permanent camp under the paperbark trees at Gregory River with hot and cold showers and a great swimming and recreation area equipped with canoes. The guided tour takes you to Riversleigh's fossil fields the first day, followed by a full day in the national park bushwalking, visiting Aboriginal rock art, canoeing Lawn Hill Creek and swimming in the natural spa. On the third day there's a visit to the limestone grottos and time for swimming, canoeing or fishing before heading back to Mt. Isa.

Mt. Isa Mine Tours. ☎ **1300 659 660** in Australia or 07/47459 1555. A$40 (U.S. $26) adults. Bookings essential and should be made as far in advance as possible.

If you are over 16 you can tour the underground workings of Queensland's largest mine and see the operations 1.6 kilometers (1 mile) below ground, exploring some of the 600 kilometers (375 miles) of tunnels that make up the mine. Full safety gear is provided and the tour varies daily depending on the work being carried out at the mine. Mt. Isa Tours also runs a 2-hour surface tour of the mine, which takes in open cut mines, shafts, smelters and workshops. You don't get off the bus but it is quite interesting anyway. The cost is A$16 (U.S.$10.40) adults and half price for children.

Riversleigh Fossil Centre. ☎ **07/4749 1555.** Fax 07/4743 6296. riversleigh@tpgi. com.au. A$5 (U.S.$3.25) adults, A$3 (U.S.$1.95) seniors and children.

This interpretive center gives insight into life in the Riversleigh region some 25 million years ago. The fossil fields have given up some of their secrets and dioramas recreate some of the ancient animal life, such as an Obdurodon, an ancestral platypus.

Royal Flying Doctor Base. 11 Barkley Highway, Mt. Isa. ☎ **07/4743 2800.** A$4 (U.S.$2.60). www.flyingdoctorqueensland.net. Mon–Fri. 9am–5 pm. A$2.50 (U.S.$1.63) adults, A.50¢ (U.S.33¢) children.

A 25-minute movie shows the history of the Royal Flying Doctor Service and gives an understanding of the lifestyle of Outback people. There's also a souvenir shop. Picnic and barbecue facilities are available in shaded gardens.

WHERE TO STAY & DINE

Mt. Isa has plenty of accommodation, from backpacker hostels and caravan parks to host farms and four-star hotels. Make sure your lodgings are air-conditioned because you'll need it.

Mercure Inn Burke & Wills. Grace and Camooweal sts., Mt Isa, QLD 4825. ☎ **1800/ 679 178** in Australia or 07/4743 8000. Fax 07/4743 8424. A$137–$182 (U.S.$89.05– $118.30) single or double per night. Free cribs. AE, BC, D, MC, V. 56 units (all with bathroom, 9 with shower only). A/C, TV, TEL. Free parking.

This is Mt. Isa's best hotel and it's right in the heart of town, just a A$11 (U.S.$7.15) taxi ride from the airport or A$6 (U.S.$3.90) from the bus or train station. In this heat, you don't want to be far from anything, especially if you're walking. The hotel has a pool and spa, a guest laundry and tour desk. Every room has an iron and ironing board as well as tea and coffee making facilities. Hair dryers are available from reception. There's also room service, but the hotel's Explorer's restaurant is among the best in town, and the adjoining cocktail bar is a pleasant place for a pre-dinner drink. The restaurant is open every day for breakfast, and for dinner Monday to Saturday.

8

The Red Centre

by Marc Llewellyn

Wide open spaces, fiery red sand as far as the eye can see, mysterious monoliths, cloudless sky, harsh sunlight, and kangaroos at dusk: The Red Centre is the iconic, ancient, "Down Under" Australia. It's home to ancient mountain ranges; "living fossil" palm trees that survived the Ice Age; the powerful Finke River, thought to be the world's first moving body of water; and of course, Ayers Rock, which the Aborigines call Uluru. Aboriginal people have lived here for thousands of years, long before the Pyramids were a twinkle in a Pharaoh's eye. The Centre is still largely unexplored by white Australians. A single highway cuts through it from Adelaide in the south to Darwin in the north; a few 4WD tracks make a lonely spider web across it; but there are many areas where non-Aborigines have never set foot.

Alice Springs is the unofficial capital of Central Australia. First off, let's get one thing straight—Alice Springs and Uluru are not side-by-side. Never a day goes by that a tourist does not wander into the Alice Springs visitor center after lunch and say he or she wants to "go and see the Rock this afternoon." The Rock is 462 kilometers (272 miles) away—or about 3½ hours by car, or 5 hours by slower tourist coaches. You can see it in a day from Alice, but it takes a Herculean effort.

The Red Centre is far more than the Rock. Allow yourself a few days to experience all there is to see and do in this iconic heart of Australia—such as visiting the impressive Olgas monoliths near Ayers Rock, stark Kings Canyon, or the School of the Air in Alice Springs; taking an Aboriginal bush tucker walk; or staying at an Outback homestead where you can hike, ride horses, or learn to throw a boomerang. If you base yourself at Alice Springs, it's easy to radiate out to lesser known but beautiful attractions like Palm Valley, Glen Helen Gorge, and Standley Chasm. Too many international visitors (and Australians, too) fly in, snap a photo of the Rock, and head home, only to miss the real essence of the desert.

Is the Centre expensive? If you camp, join a safari, or stay in bunkhouse accommodations with shared bathrooms, no. You will have no trouble finding a nice hotel room, cabin, or the like with a private bathroom in Alice Springs for less than A$100 (U.S.$65). However, Kings Canyon Resort and Ayers Rock Resort, the other two main accommodation centers, can be pricey. This chapter's "Kings Canyon" and "Uluru-Kata Tjuta National Park" sections contain advice on how to enjoy these places and preserve your budget.

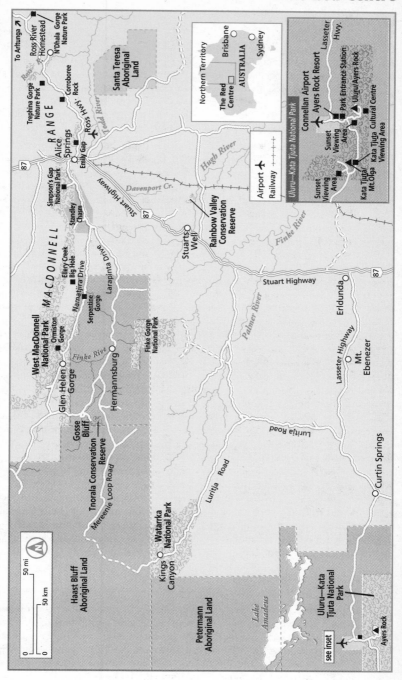

Inset (Uluru–Kata Tjuta National Park):
Lasseter Hwy.
Connellan Airport
Ayers Rock Resort
Park Entrance Station
Uluru/Ayers Rock
Sunset Viewing Area
Kata Tjuta Cultural Centre
Kata Tjuta/Mt. Olga
Kata Tjuta Viewing Area
Sunset Viewing Area

Uluru–Kata Tjuta National Park

Airport
Railway

Locator map:
Northern Territory
The Red Centre
AUSTRALIA
Brisbane
Sydney

Main map labels:
To Arltunga
Ross River Homestead
N'Dhala Gorge Nature Park
Santa Teresa Aboriginal Land
Trephina Gorge Nature Park
Corroboree Rock
Ross River
Ross Hwy.
RANGE
Alice Springs
Emily Gap
Simpson's Gap National Park
Standley Chasm
Ellery Creek Big Hole
Namatjira Drive
Serpentine Gorge
Larapinta Drive
Stuart Highway
Davenport Cr.
Hugh River
Stuarts Well
Rainbow Valley Conservation Reserve
Finke River
Erldunda
Stuart Highway
Palmer River
MACDONNELL
West MacDonnell National Park
Ormiston Gorge
Glen Helen Gorge
Finke River
Hermannsburg
Finke Gorge National Park
Gosse Bluff
Tnorala Conservation Reserve
Mereenie Loop Road
Lasseter Highway
Mt. Ebenezer
Luritja Road
Haast Bluff Aboriginal Land
Watarrka National Park
Kings Canyon
Luritja Road
Curtin Springs
Petermann Aboriginal Land
Lake Amadeus
Uluru–Kata Tjuta National Park
see inset
Ayers Rock

50 mi
50 km
0
0

EXPLORING THE RED CENTRE

VISITOR INFORMATION   The **Northern Territory Tourist Commission (NTTC)** is located at Tourism House, 43 Mitchell St., Darwin, NT 0800 (☎ **08/8999 3900**; www.nttc.com.au—click on the "U.S." tab for information tailored to American travelers). The Commission publishes a good annual guide to Central Australia that details hotels, tour operators, car-rental companies, airlines, and attractions. A free guide to Alice Springs, Ayers Rock, and Tennant Creek, called "Welcome to Central Australia" (www.welcometocentralaustralia.com.au) is a similar offering and is available at airports, car-rental offices and hotels in the region.

DRIVING TIPS   The **Automobile Association of the Northern Territory (AANT),** 79–81 Smith St., Darwin, NT 0800 (☎ **08/8981 3837**) offers reciprocal emergency breakdown service to members of overseas automobile associations, as well as motoring maps, accommodation guides, and advice from its Darwin office. It has no office in the Red Centre. For 24-hour **emergency roadside service** call ☎ **08/8952 1087.** If you do break down in a remote area don't leave your car—it can be far easier to spot, especially from the air, than a tiny, sweating figure. For road conditions call ☎ **1800/246 199** in Australia for a 24-hour recorded report.

The few sealed (paved) roads in the Northern Territory are the highways and a few arterial roads. A conventional 2WD car will get you to 95% of everything you'll want to see, but consider renting a 4WD for complete freedom. Be warned though, car hire and insurance is pretty expensive, petrol is usually around 25% more expensive than in the big cities, and distances can be huge. That said, traveling by car can be a far more comfortable way of exploring than tourist coach.

Outside settled areas, the Northern Territory has no speed limit, but before you hit the gas pedal, consider the risk of hitting wild camels, kangaroos, cattle, and wildlife such as lizards and birds. Nocturnal animals such as kangaroos can be common at dusk and in the early morning, so avoid traveling at these times. A white road sign bearing a black circle outline crossed by a diagonal black line indicates the point when speed restrictions no longer apply.

Road trains—heavy trucks with several wagons behind—drunk drivers, and fatigue are two other major threats. Stop and rest every 2 hours. Seat belts are mandatory in the Northern Territory (and everywhere else in Australia). The driver is responsible for passengers wearing seatbelts and will incur heavy fines if spotted by marked and unmarked police cars. For details on safe driving, review the tips in the "By Car" section of "Getting Around Australia" in chapter 2.

If you plan to "go bush" in remote regions not covered by this guide, you may need a permit to cross Aboriginal land from the relevant Aboriginal Lands Council. This can be a drawn-out bureaucratic affair that can take weeks, so plan ahead. The Northern Territory Tourist Commission (see above) can put you in touch with the appropriate council. All good road maps mark Aboriginal land clearly.

Red Centre Travel Tips

Uluru is notorious for its plagues of flies in summer. Don't be embarrassed to cover your hat and head with the fly-nets sold in souvenir stores—you'll look like the Beekeeper from Outer Space, but there will be "no flies on you, mate"—an Aussie way of saying you are doing the right thing. Insect repellent is also handy—even if it's just to drive off the mosquitos, which feast after dusk. Wear a broadbrimmed hat, and high-SPF sunscreen. In winter, temperatures drop below freezing at night in the Alice and Uluru, and the wind can be sharp, so bring plenty of warm clothing.

Tips for Campers

If you will be camping in a national park, know that not all permit fires, and those that do permit them only in designated fireplaces—you must collect firewood outside the park. Camping is usually permitted only at designated campgrounds.

Always carry plenty more drinking water than you think you'll need in your car and when you hike. Before setting off from major settlements, fill your tank with petrol—it may seem obvious, but getting stranded in the desert is no fun at all.

TOUR OPERATORS   There is no end of coach, minicoach, and 4WD operators with itineraries taking in some or all the highlights of the region. They depart either from Alice Springs or Ayers Rock, and usually offer accommodations ranging from comfortable motels and basic cabins, to shared bunkhouses, tents, or *swags* (sleeping bags) under the stars. Most pack a lot into a 2- or 3-day trip, though you can find more leisurely trips that run for 6 days or more.

AAT Kings (☎ **03/9274 7422** is the Melbourne-based central reservations office; www.aatkings.com.au), specializes in mainstream coach tours but also has 4WD camping itineraries; **Wayoutback Desert Safaris** (☎ **08/8952 4324** or 1800 224 324 in Australia; www.wayoutback.com.au) offers a good 3-day camping safari to Ayers Rock, the Olgas and Kings Canyon, leaving Alice Springs daily. The tour costs A$375 (U.S.$243.75) inclusive and uses 9- to 13-seat Toyota 4WDs. Another recommended operator, aimed at 18 to 35 year olds, is **Quick Route** (☎ **08/8952 7788,** 1800 018 035 in Australia; www.quickroute.com.au), which runs a 2-day camping safari out of Alice Springs in a 22-seater minicoach, again to Ayers Rock, the Olgas and Kings Canyon. This tour costs A$265 (U.S.$172.25) but be prepared for a 5:30am start. Also popular are **Adventure Tours** (☎ **08/8936 1311,** or 1300 654 604 in Australia; www.adventuretours.com.au) which a 2-day small-group tour to Kings Canyon, Ayers Rock and the Olgas from Alice Springs with a choice of camping or accommodations at Ayers Rock Resort. The tour costs A$270 (U.S.$175.50), with accommodation options extra. The company also offers a daytrip from Alice Springs to other Outback attractions, such as Simpsons Gap and Ormiston Gorge for A$75 (U.S.$48.75); a 3-day camping safari to Ayers Rock, the Olgas and Kings Canyon for A$375 (U.S.$243.75); and a 5-day off-road camping safari to the big three sights as well as other fascinating areas, for A$585 (U.S.$380.25). Adventure Tours also offers a "Desert Venturer" tour between Alice Springs and Cairns, via Ayers Rock. The 7-day trip involves camping and costs A$765 (U.S.$497.25). Other options are a 6-day Alice Springs to Darwin, or vice versa, for A$595 (U.S.$386.75); a 10-day Darwin to Alice Springs trip for A$1,075 (U.S.$698.75); and a 5-day Adelaide to Alice Springs tour for A$245 (U.S.$159.25).

1 Alice Springs

462km (277 miles) NE of Ayers Rock; 1,491km (894½ miles) S of Darwin; 1,544km (932½ miles) N of Adelaide; 2,954km (1,772½ miles) NW of Sydney

"The Alice" as Australians fondly dub it, is the unofficial capital of Outback Australia. In the early 1870s, a handful of telegraph-station workers struggled nearly 1000 miles north from Adelaide through uncompromising desert to settle by a spring in what must truly have seemed like the end of the earth. Alice Springs, as the little settlement was called, was nothing but a few huts built around a repeater station on the ambitious telegraph line that eventually linked Adelaide with Darwin and the rest of the world.

Today, Alice Springs is a sprawling, awkward-looking, but quite friendly city of 27,000. This is the heart of the Aboriginal "Arrernte" tribe's country, and Alice is a rich source of tours, shops, and galleries for anyone with an interest in Aboriginal culture, art, or souvenirs. You'll see plenty of Aboriginal people around—and it's obvious that quite a few of them are living on the fringes of Western society. Some are "drift-ins" from far-flung communities elsewhere, having been thrown out of their local communities for causing too much trouble. Unfortunately, crime—especially car theft, and the occasional muggings of unwary backpackers—is a fact of life.

The building of an airstrip at Ayers Rock means many tourists avoid Alice Springs these days, but if you do end up here you'll see that it still has a certain charm. The striking red folds of the ✪ **MacDonnell Ranges,** which surround Alice Springs, hide shady gorges with picnic grounds, and picturesque spring-fed swimming holes. Around and about are old gold-rush towns, quirky museums, and a couple of cattle stations that welcome visitors. One of the world's top 10 desert golf courses abuts the ranges.

Despite the isolation, Alice Springs is not an expensive town to visit. Accommodations, restaurants, and attractions are, for the most part, modestly priced.

ESSENTIALS

GETTING THERE   **Qantas** (☎ 13 13 13 in Australia) flies direct once a day from Sydney, Adelaide and Darwin; and its subsidiary, **Airlink** (book through Qantas) flies from Perth, from Darwin, between 2 and 5 times a day from Ayers Rock, and once or twice a day from Cairns. **Airnorth** (☎ 1800 627 474 in Australia) does a "Centre Run" from Darwin via Katherine and Tennant Creek every day except Sunday. Flight time to Alice is 3½ hours from Sydney and Perth, and 2½ hours from Cairns.

The **Alice Springs Airport Shuttle** (☎ 1800/621 188 in the Northern Territory, or 08/8953 0310) meets all major flights (but not flights from smaller regional areas like Tennant Creek), and costs A$9.90 (U.S.$6.44) one-way or A$15.50 (U.S.$10.08) round-trip per person. It stops off and picks up from Alice Spring hotels and hostels. A taxi from the airport to town, about 15 kilometers (9 miles), costs A$22.50 (U.S.$14.63).

By Train   The *Ghan* **train,** named after Afghani camel-train drivers who carried supplies in the Red Centre in the 1800s, makes the 45-hour trip from Sydney via Broken Hill and Adelaide to Alice every week. It also does a weekly 35-hour trip from Melbourne via Adelaide. The twice-weekly 19-hour Adelaide-Alice stretch is treeless and empty, if fascinatingly so, so don't be concerned that you'll miss it by overnighting on the train. For fares and schedules call **Great Southern Railway** (☎ 13 21 47 in Australia, or 08/8213 4696; www.gsr.com.au).

By Bus   **Greyhound-Pioneer** (☎ 13 20 30 in Australia) runs daily from Adelaide and Darwin. **McCafferty's** (☎ 13 14 99 in Australia) operates four times a week from Adelaide, daily from Darwin. The trip is around 21 hours from Darwin and costs about A$157 (U.S.$102.05) one-way. Greyhound does a daily run from Ayers Rock; McCafferty's runs on Sunday, Tuesday, Thursday, and Friday. The trip takes 5¾ with Greyhound, 7 with McCafferty's. The fare is around A$62 (U.S.$40.30).

By Car   Alice Springs is on the **Stuart Highway** linking Adelaide and Darwin. Allow a very long 2 days, or a more comfortable 3 days to drive from Adelaide; the same goes from Darwin. From Sydney, connect to the Stuart Highway via Broken Hill and Port Augusta north of Adelaide; from Cairns join the Stuart Highway at Tennant Creek. Both routes are long and dull, and best avoided. From Perth it is a longer, duller drive across the Nullarbor Plain to connect with the Stuart Highway at Port Augusta.

Alice Springs

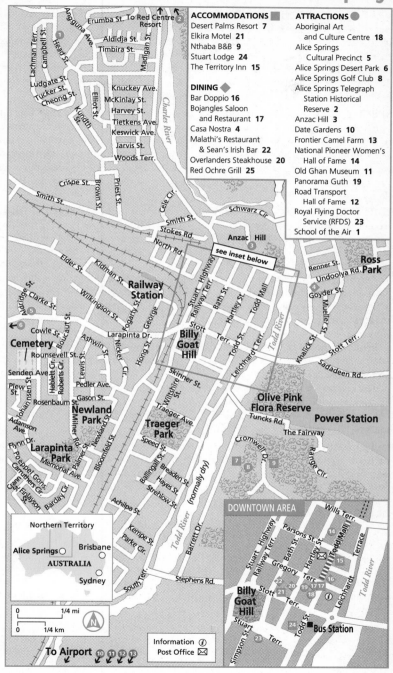

ACCOMMODATIONS ■
Desert Palms Resort **7**
Elkira Motel **21**
Nthaba B&B **9**
Stuart Lodge **24**
The Territory Inn **15**

DINING ◆
Bar Doppio **16**
Bojangles Saloon
  and Restaurant **17**
Casa Nostra **4**
Malathi's Restaurant
  & Sean's Irish Bar **22**
Overlanders Steakhouse **20**
Red Ochre Grill **25**

ATTRACTIONS ●
Aboriginal Art
  and Culture Centre **18**
Alice Springs
  Cultural Precinct **5**
Alice Springs Desert Park **6**
Alice Springs Golf Club **8**
Alice Springs Telegraph
  Station Historical
  Reserve **2**
Anzac Hill **3**
Date Gardens **10**
Frontier Camel Farm **13**
National Pioneer Women's
  Hall of Fame **14**
Old Ghan Museum **11**
Panorama Guth **19**
Road Transport
  Hall of Fame **12**
Royal Flying Doctor
  Service (RFDS) **23**
School of the Air **1**

VISITOR INFORMATION   The Central Australian Tourism Industry Association (CATIA) Visitor Information Centre, 60 Gregory Terrace, Alice Springs, NT 0870 (☎ **1800/645 1299** in Australia, or 08/8952 5800; www.centralaustralian tourism.com), is the official one-stop shop for bookings and touring information for the entire Red Centre. It has a Parks and Wildlife Commission of the Northern Territory desk with National Parks notes. It's open Monday through Friday from 8:30am to 5:30pm, and from 9am to 4pm weekends and public holidays.

SPECIAL EVENTS   The town hosts a couple of bizarre events. **The Camel Cup** (an actual camel race) is on the second Saturday in July. On a Saturday in late September or early October, folks from hundreds of miles around turn out for a day of fun and celebration at the **Henley-on-Todd Regatta.** Crowds cheer as the proud owners of gaudy homemade bottomless "boats" race them on foot or on 4WD chassis down the dry Todd River bed, which runs through the center of town. Well, what else do you do on a river that only flows 3 days a year? See chapter 2 for more details.

GETTING AROUND   Avis (☎ **08/8953 5533**), **Budget** (☎ **08/8952 8899**), **Boomerang Rentals** (☎ **08/8955 5171**); **Hertz** (☎ **08/8952 2644**), and **Territory Thrifty Car Rental** (☎ **08/8952 9999**) all rent conventional and 4WD vehicles. As a price guide, a new Toyota Sedan hired from Hertz at Alice Springs airport, for 4 days with unlimited mileage, costs A$705 (U.S.$458.25), including taxes. A 10-year-old Toyota hired from Boomerang Rentals at their office in Alice Springs, for 4 days with 500 kilometers free mileage a day, costs A$352 (U.S.$228.80) inclusive. Petrol is extra.

Territory Thrifty Car Rental rents complete camping kits with tents, sleeping bags, cooking utensils, and a gas stove for A$25 (U.S.$16.25) per day to camp. Book in advance.

Britz Australia (☎ **08/8952 8814**), **Budget Campervan Rentals** (☎ **08/8952 8049**), **Hertz Campervans** (☎ **08/8953 5333**), and **Maui Rentals** (☎ **08/8952 5353**) rent campervans.

The best way get around in town is aboard the Alice Wanderer bus (see "Organized Tours, below, for details). Taxis fares are exorbitant, presumably because there is only one outfit in town, **Alice Springs Taxis** (☎ **131 008** or 08/8952 1877). Virtually all tours pick up from hotels and hostels.

CITY LAYOUT   Todd Mall is the heart of town. Most shops, businesses and restaurants are here or within a few blocks. Some of the larger hotels, the casino, the golf course, and many attractions are a few miles outside of town, a bit too far to reach on foot. The dry Todd River "flows" through the city east of Todd Mall.

SEEING THE SIGHTS IN ALICE

○ Aboriginal Art and Culture Centre. 86 Todd St. ☎ **08/8952 3408.** Admission A$2 (U.S.$1.30). Daily 8am–6pm. Closed Christmas and Good Friday.

Set up by the local Arrernte tribe of Aboriginal people, this small, interesting museum has exhibits on Aboriginal foods and music, and a timeline of Aboriginal history since "contact," as the arrival of Europeans is called. A limited range of artifacts is for sale downstairs, and a huge art gallery of works is for sale upstairs. Allow anywhere from 15 minutes to 2 hours.

Alice Springs Cultural Precinct. Larapinta Drive at Memorial Ave., 2km (1¼ miles) south of town. ☎ **08/8952 1411.** Incorporating the Museum of Central Australia (☎ **08/8951 1122**); Central Australian Aviation Museum, Territory Craft, and the Memorial Cemetary. Admission A$7 (U.S.$4.55) adults; A$4 (U.S.$2.60) children 5–16, seniors and students; A$18 (U.S.$11.70) family. Daily 10am–5pm. Closed Christmas, New Year's Day and Good Friday. Take a cab or the Alice Wanderer bus (see "Organized Tours," below).

A Degree from Didgeridoo University

Think with a bit of practice you could be the Wynton Marsalis of central Australia? Then there's only one place for you to hone your talents—✪ **Didgeridoo University,** at the Aboriginal Art & Culture Centre (see above).

Paul Ah Chee-Ngala has set up the "campus" to satisfy an ever-growing demand from travelers to master the apparently simple but evocative rhythms of the didgeridoo. The university is an alcove in the culture center, and the degree takes just 1 hour. Classes begin every day at 1pm and cost A$11.50 (U.S.$7.48) for adults, A$5.50 (U.S.$3.58) for children (or are free as part of the Centre's half-day tour described in "Organized Tours," below.) Paul guarantees you will be able to make kangaroo hop sounds on the thing by the end of the hour—unless you are one of the one in 30 people who cannot blow through their lips! The trick is to breathe in and blow out at the same time, a technique known as circular breathing.

When buying a didgeridoo, keep in mind there is no such thing as a "good" or "bad" one. Look for one that is resonant and has a sound you like. The diameter, the wood used, and the unique surface of the wood inside the instrument are what make each didgeridoo unique. Traditionally, didgeridoos were never painted, so don't worry about selecting an "authentic" design on yours. The pitch of the instrument can vary from a high wail on G to a deep and somber A that was mostly used only in ceremonies. The shorter the didgeridoo, the higher the pitch.

If you can't take a "degree" at the Aboriginal Art and Culture Centre, you can learn to play this ancient instrument in your living room via an audio lesson on the center's website, www.aboriginalart.com.au. The site sells didgeridoos, too.

Several attractions cluster within walking distance of each other here. Along with fossils, natural history displays and meteorites, the Museum of Central Australia houses the Strehlow exhibition, an absorbing display of research into Aboriginal language and customs. The Araluen Centre for Arts & Entertainment has three art galleries of Aboriginal and contemporary Aussie artists; check out the "Honey Ant Dreaming" stained glass window in its foyer. The Aviation Museum, small but interesting, preserves the Territory's aerial history with old radios, engines, several aircraft, and wreckage. You can buy craft works, and maybe catch the artists at work, in the Territory Craft gallery. The cemetery contains the graves of local key figures, including famous Aussie artist Albert Namitjira, and a number of "Afghani" (Pakistani) camel herders buried facing Mecca. Count on up to 3 hours to see the lot.

✪ **Alice Springs Desert Park.** Larapinta Dr., 6km (3¾ miles) north of town. ☎ **08/8951 8788.** Admission A$18 (U.S.$11.70) adults; A$9 (U.S.$5.85) seniors, students, and children 5–16; A$40 (U.S.$26) family of 6. Daily 7:30am–6pm (last entry 5pm). Closed Christmas. Desert Park Transfers (☎ **08/8952 4667**) gets you and from the park from your hotel for A$25 (U.S.$16.25) for adults, A$16 (U.S.$10.40) for seniors, students, and children 5–16. Price includes park admission.

By means of a 1.6 kilometers (1 mile) trail through three reconstructed Central Australian habitats, this wildlife and flora park shows you 120 or so animal species that live in the desert around Alice, but are hard to spot in the wild. These include a collection of 25 centimeter (10 in.) giant stick insects, speedy bush mice called dunnarts, the big-eared bilby, and striped raccoon-like numbats. Don't miss the exciting Birds of

Prey show at 10am and 3:30pm. A short film, shown hourly, on Australia's geological past, has a surprise at the end—see for yourself! Guides do free talks throughout the day. Allow 3 hours.

Frontier Camel Farm. On the Ross Hwy (4km/2½ miles from town). ☎ **1800/806 499** in Australia, or 08/8953 0444. Free Admission to shop. Admission to display room A$6 (U.S.$3.90) adults, A$3 (U.S.$1.95) children 5–12, A$12 (U.S.$7.80) family. Admission to display room and short camel ride A$10 (U.S.$6.50) adults, A$9 (U.S.$5.85) seniors and students, A$6 (U.S.$3.90) children, A$25 (U.S.$16.25) family. Daily 1am–5pm; camel rides 10:30am–noon daily, also 1–2:30pm Apr–Oct. Closed Christmas, New Year's Day, and Camel Cup Day (2nd Sat. in July). Take a cab or the Alice Wanderer bus (see "Organized Tours," below).

Camels might not be the first animals that come to mind when you think of Australia, but their ability to get by without water was key to opening up the arid inland parts of the country to European settlement in the 1800s. With the advent of cars, many were set loose, and today there are 200,000 of them roaming the Central Australian deserts. Australia even exports them to the Middle East! Here you can take a short camel ride and browse through a display of photos, videos, and camel memorabilia. A shop sells camel leather, camel wool, camel cosmetics—even camel guano for your garden.

National Pioneer Women's Hall of Fame. The Old Courthouse, 27 Hartley St. ☎ **08/8952 9006.** Admission A$2 (U.S.$1.30). Daily 10am–5pm. Closed mid-Dec to early Feb.

With a collection of photographs, domestic artifacts and other memorabilia, this museum remembers over 100 ordinary Aussie women who were pioneers in their fields, ranging from farmers, and governesses to pilots.

✪ **Alice Springs Telegraph Station Historical Reserve.** On the Stuart Hwy. 4km (2.5 miles) north of town. ☎ **08/8952 3993.** Free admission to picnic grounds and trails; station A$6 (U.S.$3.90) adults, A$4.50 (U.S.$2.93) seniors and students, A$3 (U.S.$1.95) children 5–15. Daily 8am–5pm (picnic grounds and trails open until 9pm).Sattion closed Christmas; pictic grounds open 365 days a year. Take a cab or the Alice Wanderer bus (see "Organized Tours," below), or the 4km (2.5 mile) riverside walking/bike track that starts near the corner of Wills Terrace and Undoolya Rd.

Alice Springs began life as this charming telegraph repeater station in 1871. Today the old station is set by a pretty water hole amid red bouldered hills, sprawling gum trees full of parrots, and green lawns. You wander around the old station master's residence; the telegraph office, with its Morse code machine tap-tapping away; the shoeing yard packed with blacksmith's equipment; and the stables, housing vintage buggies and saddlery. A printed guide is available from the staff. From May to October, "kitchen maids" in period dress serve scones and *damper* (bread) straight from the original wood-fired ovens. Allow a good hour to see everything, more to walk one of the several hiking trails leading from the grounds. This is a lovely picnic spot.

Royal Flying Doctor Service (RFDS). 8–10 Stuart Terrace (at the end of Hartley St). ☎ **08/8952 1129.** Admission A$5.25 (U.S.$3.42) adults, A$2.50 (U.S.$1.63) children 6–15. Mon–Sat 9am–4pm (last tour departs 4pm), Sun and public holidays 1–4pm. Closed Christmas and New Year's Day.

Alice Springs is a major base for this airborne medical service that treats people living in remote Outback areas. See the radio operations in action here as they handle the odd emergency and, more commonly, routine clinic and diagnosis calls. Half-hour tours of the base and museum begin every 30 minutes and include an interesting short video.

○ **School of the Air.** 80 Head St. ☎ **08/8951 6834.** Admission A$3.50 (U.S.$2.38) adults, A$2.50 (U.S.$1.63) seniors and children 5–16, A$12 (U.S.$7.80) family. Mon–Sat and public holidays 8:30am–4:30pm, Sun 1:30–4:30pm. Closed Christmas, Boxing Day (Dec 26), New Year's Day; sometimes also closed Good Friday. Bus: 3.

Sitting in on school lessons may not be your idea of a vacation, but this school is different—it broadcasts by radio to a 1,300,000 square kilometers (501,800 sq. mile) "schoolroom" of children on remote Outback stations. That's a classroom the size of Germany, Great Britain, Ireland, New Zealand, and Japan combined—or twice the size of Texas. You can listen in live when classes are in session, and also hear taped classes, watch a video, and browse kids' artwork, old radios and photos.

ORGANIZED TOURS
AROUND TOWN & OUT IN THE DESERT

The ○ **Alice Wanderer** bus (☎ **1800/669 111** in Australia, or 08/8952 2111) makes a running loop of town attractions every 70 minutes from 9am; with the last departure at 4pm. Hop on and off as you please, and enjoy the commentary from the driver. It departs daily from the southern end of Todd Mall. Tickets are sold onboard and cost A$22 (U.S.$14.30) for adults, A$20 (U.S.$13) for seniors, and A$13 (U.S.$8.45) for students and children 4 to 14. Call for a free pickup from your hotel.

The bus calls at most major attractions listed above, plus ANZAC Hill, for a two-minute photo stop; the **Road Transport Hall of Fame;** the **Old** *Ghan* **Museum,** housing the original *Ghan* train that plied the Adelaide-Alice Springs line from 1929 to 1980; the **Date Gardens;** and **Panorama Guth,** an art gallery housing a 360 degree painting by artist Henk Guth.

Many Alice-based companies do guided day trips and extended tours of Alice and also of the East and West Macs, Hermannsburg, the Mereenie Loop Road, and Finke Gorge National Park. See "Exploring the Red Centre" at the beginning of this chapter.

ABORIGINAL TOURS

The ○ **Half-Day Aboriginal Tour** offered by the Aboriginal Art and Culture Centre, features an explanation of the Dreamtime creation era, a gentle bush tucker walk; and a chance to throw a boomerang and a traditional spear, learn about tools and weapons. Hear about Aboriginal culture, beliefs, and relationships over billy tea and damper, and see a dance performance. The tour ends with a 1-hour didgeridoo lesson at 1 pm. The trip departs daily at 8:30am and returns at 11:30am. The price, which includes hotel pickup, is A$79 (U.S.$51.35) for adults, half-price for children 3 to 14; or A$59 (U.S.$38.35) for adults if you drive yourself to the community 15 kilometers (9 miles) south of Alice.

At the Walpiri Community on an ○ **Aboriginal Dreamtime & Bushtucker Tour** with Rod Steinert Tours (☎ **08/8955 5095**), you meet Aboriginal elders who still observe many ancient ways, carrying on traditions dating back thousands of years. Speak to them about their religious beliefs, hunting skills and daily life, try throwing a boomerang or spear, watch half a dozen men and women perform an Aboriginal dance (a "corroboree"), sample witchetty grubs, and if you wish, buy crafts and artwork. The trip departs daily at 8:30am and returns at 11:30am. The price, which includes hotel pickup, is A$79 (U.S.$51.35) for adults, half-price for kids 3 to 14; or A$59 (U.S.$38.35) adults if you drive yourself to the community 15 kilometers (9 miles) south of Alice.

ACTIVE PURSUITS

CAMEL SAFARIS　Riding a camel down the dry Todd River is a great way to get a feel for the landscape. **Frontier Camel Farm** (☎ **1800/806 499** in Australia, or 08/8953 0444) runs a 1-hour ✪ **Camel Ramble** down the riverbed, a browse through the Frontier Camel Farm's camel display. With transfers from your hotel it costs A$49 (U.S.$31.85) for adults and A$27 (U.S.$17.55) for kids ages 6 to 12. Rides depart daily at 8:30am and 1:30pm April through October, and 8:30am and 3pm November through March. Kids under 6 can ride if the cameleer on duty agrees.

HOT-AIR BALLOON FLIGHTS　Floating above the desert at dawn as kangaroos bound away beneath is a popular experience in Central Australia. There's a price to pay though—you have to get up 90 minutes before dawn. Expect to pay upwards of A$210 (U.S.$136.50), around 30% less for children, for a 1-hour flight followed by champagne breakfast in the bush. Children under 6 are discouraged, because they cannot see over the basket. Contact **Spinifex Ballooning** (☎ **1800/677 893** in Australia, or 08/8953 4800) and **Outback Ballooning** (☎ **1800/809 790** in Australia, or 08/8952 8723). The jaunt takes most of the morning by the time you take your flight, have breakfast, and get back to town.

BUSHWALKING　The rugged country around Alice Springs is made for hiking, as long as you carry plenty of water, tell someone where you are going, and avoid walking in the heat of the day. One of Australia's newest long distance hiking trails, the 250-kilometer (156-mile) ✪ **Larapinta Trail** winds west from Alice Springs through the sparse red ranges, striking gorges, picturesque semi-desert scenery, and rich bird life of the West MacDonnell National Park. Hikes on the trail range in difficulty from easy to hard, but all have been designed with ordinary people in mind who are fit enough to trek with a backpack. While some of its 13 sections aren't yet complete, sections 1 to 3 and 8 to 12 are ready now. Sections vary in distance from an 8-kilometers (5-miles) to several 23- to 29-kilometer (14- to 17½-mile) stretches that take at least 2 days each. The Parks & Wildlife Commission desk at the CATIA Visitor Information Centre in Alice Springs (see "Visitor Information," above) sells trail maps for A$3.30 (U.S.$2.15) per section, maintains a voluntary walker registration system, and provides information on trail conditions and campsites. Camping facilities will be simple at best on the popular routes; nonexistent on less-traveled sections, which means you pitch your tent wherever looks good. Walking any section in the summer heat—from November until March—is foolish, and can lead to your untimely demise.

　Alice Wanderer Sightseeing Tours (☎ **1800/669 111** in Australia, or 08/8952 2111) runs transfers to access points on the trail, where you can pick up a choice of 1-, 2-, or 3-day hikes. **Trek Larapinta** (☎ **08/8953 2933;** www.treklarapinta.com. au) leads guided hikes of one or more days between April and October.

BIKING　A gentle undulating 17-kilometer (11-mile) bike trail leads from John Flynn's Grave on Larapinta Drive 7 kilometers (4 miles) from town through bushland and desert to Simpson's Gap (see "West MacDonnell National Park," below). John Flynn, of course, invented the two-way radio. **Centre Cycles** (☎ **08/8953 2966**) on Lindsay Avenue at Undoolya Road, rents bikes for A$15 (U.S.$9.75) per day. *Note:* Carry water, as the two taps en route are far apart. Bike during cooler months only.

GOLF　The **Alice Springs Golf Club** (☎ **08/8952 5440**), 1 kilometer (half a mile) from town on Cromwell Drive, boasts a Thomson-Wolveridge golf course rated one of the top 10 desert courses in the world by the pros. It's open daily from 7am to 6pm in winter, from 6am to 6:30pm in summer. Nine holes are A$17.50 (U.S.$11.38), plus A$10 (U.S.$6.50) for clubs, and A$15 (U.S.$9.75) for a cart.

SHOPPING AT THE SOURCE FOR ABORIGINAL ART

Top of the shopping list for most travelers to Alice is Aboriginal art and crafts. You will find no shortage of stuff: linen and canvas paintings, didgeridoos, spears, clapping sticks, *coolamons* (a dish used by women to carry anything from water to babies), animal carvings, baskets, and bead jewelry, books and CDs. Prices can soar into the thousands of dollars for large canvases by world-renowned painters, but you will find plenty of small works for under A$200 (U.S.$130). Major artworks sell unmounted for ease of shipment, which most galleries arrange on your behalf. Store hours we quote below can vary with the seasons and the crowds, so confirm them ahead of time.

A good place to start is the biggest gallery in town, upstairs at the **Aboriginal Art and Culture Centre** (see "Seeing the Sights in Alice," above). The Centre is open daily 8am to 6pm; or you can order its art, didgeridoos, artifacts, and books over the Internet at www.aboriginalart.com.au.

See artists at work when you drop by **Jukurrpa Artists,** on Stott Terrace between Gap Road and Leichhardt Terrace (☎ **08/8953 1052**). This Aboriginal women's co-operative studio/gallery sells the "pattern and dot" paintings in the Western Desert style, plus carvings, craft items, weapons, tools, and seed jewelry. It's open Monday through Friday from 9am to 3pm. Order from their website at www.ozemail.com.au/~jukurrpa.

You can make your own didgeridoo if you have half a day at **Dust Storm Didgeridoos,** 45 Gap Rd. (☎ **08/8952 2739**). They offer custom-designed and off-the-shelf didges, boomerangs and other artifacts. Open Monday through Friday from noon to 6pm, and Saturday from 10am to 6pm. This is a private home, so call first.

Aboriginal-owned **Warumpi Arts,** 105 Gregory Terrace (☎ **08/8952 9066**) sells wooden artifacts, seed necklaces and canvas and board paintings in the dramatic, earth-hued designs of the Papunya people, who live 250 kilometers (156 miles) west of Alice. Another Aboriginal-owned gallery, **Papunya Tula Artists,** 78 Todd St. (☎ **08/8952 4731**) sells paintings from Papunya and other artists living in the desert as far as 700 kilometers (438 miles) west of Alice Springs. Both are open Monday through Friday from 9am to 5pm, and Saturday and sometimes Sunday in high season.

Several stores on Todd Mall sell affordable Aboriginal art and souvenirs. The oldest and biggest, the **Original Dreamtime Gallery,** 63 Todd Mall (☎ **08/8952 8861**) stocks a huge selection and packs, mails, and insures your purchases free of charge anywhere in the world. It also shows visiting exhibitions of Aboriginal art. It's open Monday to Saturday from 9am to 6pm, and Sunday from 10am to 2pm.

Arunta Art Gallery & Bookshop, 72 Todd St. (☎ **08/8952 1544**) stocks some Aboriginal and European artworks, Aboriginal artifacts, and a range of books on Aboriginal art, language, and archaeology as well as Australian history, geology, wildlife, and biographies. It's open Monday through Saturday from 10am to 5:30pm.

Serious collectors should head for **Gallery Gondwana,** 43 Todd Mall (☎ **08/8953 1577**). Since 1990, owner Roslyn Premont has written about and presented desert art, and currently works with a small group of gifted artists. The gallery is open Monday through Friday 9:30am to 6pm, and Saturday from 10am to 5pm, or by appointment. Today's Aboriginal bands mix ancient and hip new rhythms to create some wonderful sounds. For the country's biggest range of indigenous music, head to the **CAAMA** (Central Australian Aboriginal Media Association) store at 101 Todd St. (☎ **08/8952 9207**), inside the association's studios. It also stocks books on Aboriginal art and issues, children's books with Aboriginal story lines, a line of Aboriginal fabrics and cushions, and Yamba the Honey Ant dolls, modeled after a kids' character on the local Aboriginal television station, Imparja. It's open Monday through Friday from 9am to 5pm, sometimes Saturday from 10am to 2pm in high season.

WHERE TO STAY

As well as the more upmarket properties listed below, there are several backpacker resorts offering dorm rooms and doubles. Among them is **Melanka Backpacker Resort** (☎ **1800/815 066** in Australia; www.melanka.com.au), which offers dorm beds for A$15 (U.S.$9.75); "deluxe" four-bed rooms for A$18 (U.S.$11.70); and doubles for A$38 (U.S.$24.70). It has two pools, a tour desk, and a disco. Suited for travelers wanting parties and company, it's rather Spartan and worn around the edges.

✪ Desert Palms Resort. 74 Barrett Drive (1km/half a mile from town), Alice Springs, NT 0870. ☎ **1800/678 037** in Australia, or 08/8952 5977. Fax 08/8953 4176. www.sahara tours.com.au/despalms.htm. 80 units (with shower only). A/C TV TEL. A$92 (U.S.$59.80) double. Extra person A$10 (U.S.$6.50). AE, BC, DC, MC, V. Free coach station/train station/airport shuttle twice daily; free resort-to-town shuttle 4 times daily.

Right next to Lasseter's Casino (where the food can be awful) and the Alice Springs Golf Club (to which guests enjoy honorary social membership), these cabins set behind manicured palms and pink bougainvillea are one of the cheeriest places to stay in Alice. Don't be deterred by their poky prefab appearance; inside they are surprisingly large, well kept, and inviting, with a pine-pitched ceiling, a minikitchen, a sliver of bathroom sporting new white tiles and fittings, and a pert little furnished front deck. A pretty sundeck and pool with its own little island is out front; there's also a tennis court. The pleasant staff at front desk loan hair dryers, process your film, do laundry service, sell basic grocery and liquor supplies, and book your tours.

Elkira Motel. 65 Bath St., Alice Springs, NT 0870. ☎ **1800/809 252** in Australia, or 08/8952 1222. Fax 08/8953 1370. www.bestwestern.com.au/elkira. 56 units (some with shower only). A/C TV TEL. A$70–$85 (U.S.$45.50–$55.25) budget doubles (depending on season); A$110 (U.S.$71.50) standard double; A$120 (U.S.$78) deluxe double. Family rooms are same price, though extra person costs A$10 (U.S.$6.50); extra child under 3 A$5 (U.S.$3.25). AE, BC, DC, MC, V. Free parking. Airport shuttle.

The cheapest rooms in the heart of town—that are still decent, that is—are at this unpretentious, clean Best Western motel. Standard rooms are dated, with lots of wood and tile floors. They each have a fridge and shower. Two standard family rooms come with a double bed and three singles. The 42 deluxe rooms have a little more space than the standard rooms, and 9 have microwaves and some have queen-size beds. Nine deluxe family rooms are nicer still, and come with a kitchenette—and as they cost the same as normal deluxe room are well worth asking for even if you're traveling as a couple. All deluxe family rooms and a few deluxe doubles have bathrooms. Ask for a room away from the road, as the traffic is noisy during the day. The 7 budget rooms are also a little dated, but though small, are comfortable, and quiet. They come with a double bed, a TV, shower, fridge, and hair dryer. On the property are a modest pool, a barbecue area under trees, a couple of courtyards, a tour desk, a laundry, a reasonabl priced restaurant, a breakfast room—and a friendly Doberman called Charlie.

✪ Nthaba B&B. 83 Cromwell Dr., Alice Springs, NT 0870. ☎ **08/8952 9003.** Fax 08/8953 3295. nthaba@ozemail.com.au. 1 freestanding cottage (shower only). A/C TV. A$90 (U.S.$58.50) single; A$120 (U.S.$78) double. Weekly rates available. Rates include full breakfast. BC, MC, V.

Your hostess Anne Cormack has created a delightful oasis of green terraced lawns and garden blooms in the red dust of central Australia at her home, about 1.5 kilometers (1 mile) from the town center. You stay in a charming slate-floored brick cottage with its own entrance, a petite sitting room, separate twin or double bedroom (the twin beds zip together to form a comfortable king size), and your own bathroom with a hair dryer. You can prepare light meals in the kitchenette. The cottage is beautifully furnished with classic and antique pieces. There's no private phone, but you are welcome to use Anne's. The Alice Springs Golf Club is a short walk away. No smoking.

Red Centre Resort. Stuart Hwy. (north of town), Alice Springs, NT 0870. ☎ **1800/089 616** in Australia, or 08/8950 5555. Fax 08/8952 8300. www.aurora-resorts.com.au. 127 units, 99 with bathroom (shower only). TV TEL. A$113 (U.S.$73.45) double motel room; A$123 (U.S.$79.95) double apt. Additional person A$15 (U.S.$9.75) extra. A$15 (U.S.$9.75) per person in quad-share bunkhouse (supply your own linen). All rates include 5% tax. Children 14 and under free in parents' room if they use existing bedding. AE, BC, DC, MC, V. Free airport shuttle.

Although it's 4.5 kilometers (3 miles) from the center of town, this laid-back 7-hectare (18-acre) complex of motel rooms, studio apartments with kitchenettes, and bunkhouse rooms, has such a friendly ambience you won't mind making the trip. A free shuttle runs into town throughout the day, so you won't be stranded. The heart of the place is the pool and the poolside bistro, where everyone gathers to swap tour notes or enjoy the live entertainment that plays most nights in the cooler months. You get lots for your money—a tour desk, an a la carte restaurant and casual bistro, a day/night tennis court, a volleyball court, a game room with pool tables and Ping-Pong, a pool for the kids, babysitting, dry cleaning, room service, Internet access, and a free temporary e-mail address. Management will supply free utensils if you want to cook up a storm on the barbecue. The spick-and-span motel rooms and apartments are air-conditioned and have exposed brick walls, fashionable whitewashed furniture, and ample space. Iron and boards and hair dryers are available at reception. The motel rooms are serviced daily, and the apartments weekly.

The Territory Inn. Leichhardt Terrace (backing on to Todd Mall), Alice Springs, NT 0870. ☎ **1800/089 644** in Australia, or 08/8950 6666. Fax 08/8952 7829. www.aurora-resorts.com.au. 108 units (all with shower only, 1 suite with Jacuzzi). A/C MINIBAR TV TEL. A$140–$150 (U.S.$91–$97.50) double, A$210 (U.S.$136.50) suite. Extra person A$15 (U.S.$9.75). Children under 14 free in parents' room if they use existing bedding. AE, BC, DC, JCB, MC, V. Free parking.

This pleasant hotel is bang in the center of town. Rooms in the newer wing are your standard modern variety, clean, biggish, and decorated nicely enough. Those in the original wing are small and a little dark, but have a pretty heritage theme with floral bedcovers and lace curtains. All have iron and board and free movies. The courtyard has a barbecue and covered dining area, and there is a tour desk, hair dryers for loan, and a post-checkout shower room. The tiny heated pool and Jacuzzi are in a utilitarian corner, so this is not the place for chilling out poolside; stay here for the walking distance to shops and restaurants. Room service is from the marvelous Red Ochre Grill (see "Where to Dine," below).

SUPER-CHEAP SLEEPS

Stuart Lodge. Stuart Terrace (between Hartley and Todd sts.), Alice Springs, NT 0870. ☎ **1800/249 124** in Australia (YWCA central reservations), or 08/8952 1894. Fax 08/8952 2449. stuart.lodge@ywca.org.au. 31 units, 1 with bathroom (tub/shower). A/C. A$38.50 (U.S.$25.03) single; A$49.50 (U.S.$32.18) double; A$60 (U.S.$39) triple. 10% discount YWCA members. Free crib. Weekly rates available. BC, MC, V.

Two blocks from Todd Mall and close to the long distance coach terminals, this YWCA-owned hostel is quieter and less rowdy than the average backpacker lodge, so it is popular with solo travelers, seniors, and anyone wanting party-free privacy. It offers diminutive but neatly painted single, double, and triple rooms that are serviced daily; a robe, a writing desk, and self-serve tea and coffee are standard. By the time you read this, all rooms should have minifridges, too. Every two rooms share one (old but clean) bathroom; the front desk lends hair dryers. The furnishings are pretty humble, but there's a small pool, a communal kitchen, and free barbecues, a tour desk, Internet access, a pay phone, TV lounges, and a laundry. The continental breakfast is a bargain at A$4.50 (U.S.$2.93). The friendly managers are very helpful. No smoking.

WHERE TO DINE

Alice Springs doesn't overflow with restaurants, but it does have a few worth checking out, and most of them are affordable. See the "Dinner in the Desert" box for where to find ripper Aussie bush dinners, Outback-style.

✪ **Bar Doppio.** 2 & 3 Fan Arcade (off the southern end of Todd Mall). ☎ **08/8952 6525.** Reservations not accepted. Main courses A$7–$11 (U.S.$4.55–$7.15) lunch, A$7–$16 (U.S.$4.55–$10.40) dinner; sandwiches average A$6 (U.S.$3.90). No credit cards. Mon–Sat 7:30am–9pm, Sun 10am–4pm. Closed public holidays; may close Christmas–New Year. EAST-MEETS-WEST CAFE FARE.

If you're in need of a dose of cool—style, as well as air-conditioning—this laid-back arcade cafe is the place to chill over good coffee and feast on cheap, wholesome food. Sacks of coffee beans are stacked all over, gypsy music plays, no tables and chairs match, there are world magazines to read, and the staff doesn't care if you sit here all day. It's largely vegetarian, but fish and meat figure on the blackboard menu. Try lamb chermoula cutlets on Gabriella potatoes with rocket, red onion and tomato salad, chicken laksa, Turkish bread sandwiches, or spuds with hot toppings. Hot and cold breakfast choices stay on the menu until 11am. They do takeout. BYO.

✪ **Bojangles Saloon and Restaurant.** 80 Todd St. ☎ **08/8952 2873.** Reservations not needed. Main courses A$7–$18 (U.S.$4.55–$11.70) front bar; A$12–$25 (U.S.$7.80–$16.25) restaurant. AE, BC, DC, MC, V. Lunch: noon–3pm daily; dinner 6–10pm daily. TEX-MEX/MIXED.

Swing open the saloon doors and enter a world of cowhide seats, thick wooden tables, assorted Western-style knickknacks, original American Civil War guns, and so on. The front bar is friendly and serves up good beers by the bottle or schooner, and reasonable food such as burgers, nachos, salads, and fish and chips. The restaurant out back has more gourmet offerings, but either way it's a great atmosphere. Aussie-style country and folk singers strum away in the evenings, and the bar staff are terrific.

✪ **Casa Nostra.** Corner of Undoolya Rd. and Sturt Terrace. ☎ **08/8952 6749.** Reservations strongly recommended. Main courses A$10–$19 (U.S.$6.50–$12.35); average A$13 (U.S.$8.45). BC, MC, V. Mon–Sat 5pm–late. Closed Christmas–end of January. ITALIAN.

The only difference between this cheery homespun Italian family eatery and every other Italian restaurant in the world is that this one has autographed photos of Tom Selleck pinned to the wall. Judging by his scrawled praise, Tom loved eating here (on location in Alice filming *Quigley Down Under*) as much as the locals do. You have seen the red-checked tablecloths and the basket-clad Chianti bottles before; the food may surprise you for being so darn good. A long list of pastas (like the masterful carbonara), traditional pizzas, and chicken and veal dishes are the main offerings. It's BYO.

Malathi's Restaurant & Sean's Irish Bar. 51 Bath St. (opposite Kmart) ☎ **08/8952 1858.** Reservations recommended. Main courses A$13.20–$26 (U.S.$8.58–$16.90); many dishes under A$20 (U.S.$13). AE, BC, DC, MC, V. Restaurant: Mon–Sat 5:30pm–late. Bar: daily 3:30pm–late. ASIAN/WESTERN.

Located in an unprepossessing building a couple of blocks from Todd Mall, Malathi's serves up an eclectic assortment of Asian dishes plus a few true blue Aussie choices,

Dinner in the Desert

Why sit in a perfectly good restaurant when you can eat outside in the dust? Because you came to the Outback to be outside, that's why. Your feet might get dirty, but your tastebuds, eyes and ears will like the experience.

Ayers Rock Resort's ✪ **Sounds of Silence** dinner is a must. In an outdoor clearing, sip champagne and nibble canapés as the sun sets over the Rock to the strains of a lone didgeridoo—played by a white man (the excuse is that didgeridoos don't come from this part of the world, but from Arnhem Land—though there seem to be plenty of local Aboriginals who play) then sit at white-clothed, candlelit tables to a serve-yourself meal of kangaroo, barramundi, and emu. Last time I was here they served pretty poor pumpkin soup to begin, the main courses were varied from bland to nice, and the Aussie wines were bad examples indeed. However, after dinner, the lanterns fade, and you are left with stillness (apart from an occasional roaming dingo looking for scraps). It is the first time some city folk have ever heard silence. Next, an astronomer points out the constellations of the Southern Hemisphere, and you have a chance to see the stars through powerful telescopes. Sounds of Silence is held nightly, weather permitting, and costs A$105 (U.S.$68.25) for adults and A$53 (U.S.$34.45) for children 5 to 16, including transfers from Ayers Rock Resort. It's mighty popular, so book 3 months ahead in peak season. Book through the Ayers Rock Resort office in Sydney (☎ **02/9339 1040** or 1300/139 889; www.ayersrockresort.com.au).

A 1-hour sunset saunter on camelback down the dry Todd River is part of the ✪ **Take a Camel Out to Dinner** nights offered by **Frontier Camel Tours** (☎ **1800/806 499** in Australia, or 08/8953 0444) in Alice Springs. Setting off from the Mecca Date Gardens, it's a journey past river red gums while black cockatoos whirl overhead. At the **Frontier Camel Farm** (see "Seeing the Sights in Alice"), you dine on a three-course meal of kangaroo sausages, barramundi or steak, with wattleseed bread, wine and beer. The meal is served inside, not out in the sand. The cost of A$95 (U.S.$61.75) for adults and A$70 (U.S.$45.50) for children 6 to 12 includes pickup from your hotel. The rides run nightly year-round, departing at 4pm April through October, and at 5pm November through March.

At **Camp Oven Kitchen's** bush dinners, you sit down at white-clothed, lamp-lit tables in a fire-lit clearing to soup and damper, kangaroo kebabs, roast beef and vegetables, golden syrup dumplings with ice cream, and billy tea. After, there's a night sky talk and bush ballads. The meal, including transfers from your hotel but not including drinks, costs A$76 (U.S.$49.40) for adults and A$61 (U.S.$39.65) for kids under 12. It departs 5:30pm May to September, 6pm in October to April. Call **Alice Springs Holidays** (☎ **08/8953 1411**; www.alice springsholidays.com.au).

such as King Island steak. Don't be put off by the pink walls, old carpet, and Asian print tablecloths: the food is outstanding. I can recommend the lamb korma (a kind of mild curry). You might want to try the Lakshmi King prawns cooked in Indian flavors or the Thai coconut curry. They do takeout, too. Buy wine at the restaurant or bring your own (but don't BYO beer or spirits). The Irish bar serves cheap stews and Guinness, and occasionally there's a live band.

○ **Red Ochre Grill.** Todd Mall. ☎ **08/8952 9614.** Reservations recommended at dinner. Main courses A$7.50–$21.50 (U.S.$4.88–$13.98) lunch; A$15–$22.50 (U.S.$9.75–$14.63) dinner; buffet breakfast A$10.50–$15 (U.S.$6.83–$9.75). AE, BC, DC, MC, V. Daily 6:30am–10pm. GOURMET BUSH TUCKER.

If you have never tried wallaby mignons on a bed of native pasta and polenta cake with a native berry and red wine cream sauce, or barramundi baked in paperbark with wild lime and coriander butter, now's your chance. The chef at this upscale chain fuses Aussie bush ingredients with dishes from around the world; although the results might sound strange, they are mouthwatering. Opt for the contemporary interior fronting Todd Mall, or outside in the attractive courtyard.

WORTH A SPLURGE

○ **Overlanders Steakhouse.** 72 Hartley St. ☎ **08/8952 2159.** Reservations essential in peak season. Main courses A$17.50–$25 (U.S.$11.38–$16.25); Drover's Blowout A$41.25 (U.S.$26.83). Ask about meal packages with drinks and transfers. AE, BC, DC, JCB, MC, V. Daily 6pm–late. STEAK/AUSSIE TUCKER.

This landmark on the Alice dining scene is famous for its "Drover's Blowout" menu, which assaults the mega-hungry with soup and damper; then a platter of crocodile vol-au-vents, camel and kangaroo filet, and emu medallions—these are just the appetizers—followed by Scotch fillet steak in red wine and mushroom sauce, or barramundi, with potatoes and vegetables, followed by dessert. There's a regular menu with 700 gram (1 lb. 10 oz.) grain fed steak, plus lots of lighter fare. The barn-like interior is Outback all through, from the rustic bar to the saddlebags hanging from the roof beams. An "Overlanders' Table" seats solo diners together.

2 Road Trips from Alice Springs

THE WEST MACDONNELL RANGES

WEST MACDONNELL NATIONAL PARK The approximately 300-kilometer (188-mile) round-trip drive west from Alice Springs into West MacDonnell National Park is a stark but picturesque trip to a series of red gorges, semi-desert country, and peaceful swimming holes. You may not stop at every gorge en route; most folks call at two or three and enjoy a picnic lunch at one.

From Alice, take Larapinta Drive west for 18 kilometers (11 miles) to the 8-kilometer (5-mile) turn-off to **Simpson's Gap,** a shady water hole between steep ridges lined with ghost gums. Black-footed rock wallabies hop out on the cliffs in the late afternoon (so you may want to time a visit here on your way back to Alice). There are a couple of short trails, including a 500-meter (⅓ mile) Ghost Gum circuit, and a 17-kilometer (11 mile) round-trip trail to **Bond Gap.** Swimming is not permitted. The place has an information center/ranger station and free barbecues.

Twenty-three kilometers (14 miles) down Larapinta Road and 9 kilometers (5½ miles) down a turnoff, is **Standley Chasm** (☎ 08/8956 7440). This naturally-hewn cleft in the rock is only a few meters wide but 80 meters (262 ft.) high, reached by a 10-minute creek-side trail. Aim to be here at midday, when the walls glow orange in the overhead sun. You may escape the crowds if you walk through the chasm to the upper ramparts. A kiosk sells snacks and drinks. Admission is A$5.50 (U.S.$3.58) for adults and A$4 (U.S.$2.60) for seniors and children 5 to 14. The Chasm opens 8am to 6pm daily, with last entry at 5pm (closed Christmas).

Six kilometers (3¾ miles) past Standley Chasm, you can branch right onto Namatjira Drive and head 42 kilometers (26 miles) to picturesque **Ellery Creek Big Hole.** The water is so nippy the tourism authority warns swimmers to take a flotation device as a defense against cramp. A 3-kilometer (2-mile) walking trail explains the area's geological history.

Eleven kilometers (7 miles) farther along Namatjira Drive is **Serpentine Gorge,** where a trail leads up to a lookout for a lovely view of the ranges through the gorge walls. Another 12 kilometers (7.5 miles) on are **ochre pits,** which Aboriginal people quarried for body paint and for decorating objects used in ceremonial performances. A 3-hour bushwalk on the Larapinta Trail leads from here to Inarlanga Pass in the Heavitree ranges. Twenty-six kilometers (16 miles) farther west, 8 kilometers (5 miles) from the main road, is **Ormiston Gorge and Pound** (☎ **08/8956 7799** for the ranger station/visitor center). This is a good spot to picnic, swim in the wide deep pool below red cliffs, and walk a choice of trails, such as the 30-minute Ghost Gum Lookout trail or the easy and picturesque 7-kilometer (4-mile) loop through the pound (allow 3–4 hr.). Because the waterhole is wide, the water is good swimming temperature in summer. You can camp here for A$5 (U.S.$3.25) per adult, and A$2 (U.S.$1.30) per child 5 to 15. The campground has hot showers and free gas barbecues.

A couple of miles on is **Glen Helen Gorge** where the Finke River cuts through the ranges, with more gorge swimming, and helicopter flights. **Glen Helen Resort** (☎ **1800/896 110** in Australia, or 08/8956 7489; fax 08/8956 7495; www.melanka. com.au) has 25 motel rooms, quad-share bunkhouses, a campground, a restaurant serving three meals a day, a bar, and free barbecues for which they sell meat. Motel rooms are A$116 (U.S.$75.40) double, bunkhouses are A$64 (U.S.$41.60) per room, a tent site is A$8 (U.S.$5.20) per person, and a powered campsite is A$20 (U.S.$13) double.

ROAD-TRIP TIPS FOR THE EAST & WEST MACS

Come prepared with food (a picnic perhaps, or meat to barbecue), drinking water, and a full gas tank, as facilities are scarce. Bring your own food if camping. Leaded, unleaded and diesel fuel is sold at Glen Helen Lodge, Hermannsburg, and Ross River Homestead. Wear walking shoes.

Because the waterholes in the East and West Macs are mostly spring-fed, the water can be intensely cold. Take only short dips to avoid cramp and hypothermia, don't swim alone, and be careful of underwater snags. Some holes dry up with no rain. Don't wear sunscreen if you swim, as it pollutes a source of drinking water for native animals.

Two-wheel drive rental cars will not be insured on unsealed (unpaved) roads—that means the last few miles into Trephina Gorge Nature Park, the 11-kilometer (7 mile) road into N'Dhala Gorge Nature Park, and the 36-kilometer (22½-mile) road to Arl-tunga Historical Reserve, all in the East Macs. Some unsealed access roads can be impassable after heavy rain. The West MacDonnell road is sealed to Glen Helen Gorge; a few points of interest may require driving for short lengths on unpaved road.

Before setting off, drop into the **Parks and Wildlife Commission of the Northern Territory** desk at the CATIA Visitor Information Centre (see "Visitor Information," above). It can fill you in on road conditions, and on the free ranger talks, walks, and slide shows taking place at some points of interest in the West and East Macs from April to October. Entry to all parks and reserves is free, except for Standley Chasm.

ORGANIZED TOURS   See "Organized Tours" earlier in the Alice Springs section for companies that run coach or 4WD tours of a half-day, full day or longer to the West and East Macs. Expect to pay about A$100 (U.S.$65) for a full-day trip.

Tips for Driving the Mereenie Loop Road

Despite what some sources say, this road is too rough for a 2WD car, and anyhow, rental companies will not rent you a one for this trip. Drive your 4WD at a sensible pace to avoid rolling it. The road crosses Aboriginal land, for which you will need a A$2 (U.S.$1.30) per vehicle permit from the **CATIA Visitor Information Centre** in Alice Springs, the gas station in Hermannsburg, or **Kings Canyon Resort.** It comes with a color guide and mud-map, and grants you entry to the Tnorala crater.

Camping and turning off is not permitted anywhere along the road. Take food and plenty of water, and keep the gas tank full.

TRAVELING THE MEREENIE LOOP ROAD If you have a 4WD, you can carry on 17 kilometers (11 miles) west past Glen Helen Gorge, and link back south and east 99 kilometers (62 miles) to **Hermannsburg** (described below), then go on 267 kilometers (167 miles) to **Kings Canyon** (see below). This route follows a rough, unsealed road generally referred to as the Mereenie Loop Road, although technically the Mereenie Loop begins at Katapata Pass, some 70 kilometers (44 miles) west of Hermannsburg. There's not much to see, but the desert, low mountain scenery and wide open spaces really tell you you're in the Outback, mate! (You can shave 44 kilometers (28 miles) off by not going all the way into Hermannsburg from Glen Helen Gorge, as you have to double back 22 kilometers (14 miles) to re-join the Loop.) About 55 kilometers (34 miles) from either Glen Helen or Hermannsburg, you can visit ✪ **Tnorala (Gosse Bluff) Conservation Reserve,** a spectacular 5-kilometer (3-mile) crater left by a meteorite that smashed to earth 142 million years ago. A 4WD track leads to a picnic area inside the crater.

Allowing a long half-day to drive from Alice to Kings Canyon via the Mereenie Loop, plus sightseeing time.

Hermannsburg Historical Precinct An alternative to visiting the West Mac gorges is to take Larapinta Drive 128 kilometers (80 miles) from Alice Springs to the old Lutheran Mission at the Hermannsburg Historical Precinct (☎ **08/8956 7402**). Some maps will show this route as unsealed, but it is now paved. Settled by German missionaries in the 1870s, the town has pretty farmhouse-style mission buildings, which have been restored. There is a museum, a gallery housing works by famous Aussie artist Albert Namatjira, and tearooms serving a fabulous apple strudel from a recipe imported from Germany in 1898. The Mission is open daily 9am to 4pm March through November, and daily 10am to 4pm December through February. Admission to the precinct with tea or coffee is A$4.50 (U.S.$2.93) for adults, A$3 (U.S.$1.95) for school age kids, or A$12 (U.S.$7.80) for a family, plus A$3.50 (U.S.$2.28) per person, or A$12 (U.S.$7.80) per family, for a guided gallery tour, which departs every hour. The precinct is closed from December 24 through January 2 or 3, and on Good Friday.

From Hermannsburg you can join up with the Mereenie Loop Road (see above) to Kings Canyon.

✪ **FINKE GORGE NATIONAL PARK** West of Hermannsburg is the turn-off to the 46,000-hectare (113,620-acre) Finke Gorge National Park, 16 kilometers (10 miles) to the south on an unpaved road. The park is famous for **Palm Valley,** where groves of *Livistona mariae* cabbage palms have grown since the area was a prehistoric jungle. You will need a 4WD to explore this park. Four walking trails between 1.5 kilometers (1 mile) and 5 kilometers (3 miles) take you among the palms to a lookout over cliffs; one is a signposted trail exploring Aboriginal culture. There is a campsite about 4 kilometers (2½ miles) from the palms; it has showers, toilets, and free barbecues. Collect your firewood outside the park. Camping is A$5 (U.S.$3.25) for adults, A$2 (U.S.$1.30) for children 5 to 15. For information, call into the **CATIA Visitor Information Centre in Alice Springs** before you leave; there is no visitor center in the park. The ranger station (☎ **08/8956 7401**) is for emergencies only.

THE EAST MACDONNELL RANGES

Not as many tourists tread the path on the Ross Highway into the East Macs, but if you do, you'll be rewarded with lush walking trails, fewer crowds, and traces of Aboriginal history. We even spotted wild camels. At the end of the drive, 86 kilometers (54 miles) from Alice, is the *dinky-di* (that's Australian for "authentic"—as is "fair dinkum") **Ross River Homestead** (see "Where to Stay," below). Day trippers are welcome. As the homestead stages a whipcracking and billy tea experience from 10am to noon daily, consider heading there first, then dropping in on the attractions below as you return.

The first points of interest are **Emily Gap,** 10 kilometers (6 miles) from Alice, and **Jessie Gap,** 7 kilometers (4 miles). Jessie is the prettiest picnic spot. You can cool off in Emily Gap swimming hole if there is any water. Don't miss the "Caterpillar Dreaming" Aboriginal art on the wall, on your right as you walk through. Because the painting is archaeologically important, and this is an Aboriginal sacred site, visitors are asked not to touch it.

At **Corroboree Rock,** 37 kilometers (23 miles) on, you can make a short climb up this rocky outcrop that was important to local Aborigines. The highly polished rock "seat" at the hole high up in it means Aboriginal people have used this rock for eons.

Twenty-two kilometers (13¾ miles) on is the turn-off to **Trephina Gorge Nature Park,** an 18 square kilometer (7 square mile) beauty spot with peaceful walking trails ranging from 45 minutes to 4½ hours. An easy amble between the brick red walls of the gorge to a water hole only takes a few minutes. The last 5 kilometers (3 miles) of the 9-kilometer (5.5-mile) access road into the park are unsealed, but you can make it in a conventional car.

Not far past the Trephina Gorge Nature Park exit is the turnoff to the goldrush ghost town of **Arltunga Historical Reserve** (☎ **08/8956 9770** for the visitor center and ranger station), 36 kilometers (23 miles) off the highway on the unsealed Arltunga Road. Gold was found here in 1887 and mined until 1913. You can wander through the ruined miners' stone houses with a self-guiding brochure; explore the underground mines (take a flashlight); visit the restored police station and jail; and *fossick* (rummage) for riches. A month's fossicking permit for a family is A$5 (U.S.$3.25) from the Arltunga Bush Hotel (see below). The visitor center is open from 8am to 5pm and has a slideshow on the early settlers. Close by the Reserve is the **Arltunga Bush Hotel** (☎ **08/8956 9797**), a pub with cold beer, hot meals all day, basic rooms without bathroom for A$38.50 (U.S.$25.03) double, and campsites with hot showers for A$5.50 (U.S.$3.58) per person. Hotel guests share the campground bathrooms. Bring cash, as the hotel doesn't take credit cards.

N'Dhala Gorge Nature Park, 10 kilometers (6 miles) past Trephina Gorge Nature Park, just before you reach Ross River Homestead, houses an "open air art gallery" of rock carvings, or petroglyphs, left by the Eastern Arrernte Aboriginal people. There are thought to be some 6,000 rock carvings, hundreds or thousands of years old, in this eerily quiet gorge, along with rock paintings. A 1.5-kilometer (1-mile) signposted trail leads you past some carvings and explains their Dreamtime meanings. A 4WD vehicle is a must to traverse the 11-kilometer (7-mile) access road.

The Ross Highway is sealed all the way to Ross River Homestead. Basic **camping** facilities with pit toilets and barbecues, but no showers, or even drinking water in N'Dhala's case, are available at Trephina and N'Dhala. The camping fee is A$2.50 (U.S.$1.63) for adults and A$1 (U.S.65¢) for children.

WHERE TO STAY

Ross River Homestead. Ross Hwy., 86km (54 miles) east of Alice Springs (P.O. Box 3271, Alice Springs, NT 0871). ☎ **1800/241 711** in Australia, or 08/8956 9711. Fax 08/8956 9823. http://rossriver.goau.net. 48 units, 30 with bathroom (shower only); A/C. Cabin A$79 (U.S.$51.35) double. Extra person A$17 (U.S.$11.05). Bunkhouse quad-share A$20 (U.S.$13) per person with linen. Unpowered campsite A$6 (U.S.$3.90) per adult; powered campsite A$9 (U.S.$5.85) per adult. Lower rates for kids in bunkhouses and campgrounds. AE, BC, DC, MC, V. Coach transfers from Alice Springs A$25 (U.S.$16.25) per person, round-trip.

This fair dinkum ("genuine") 100-year-old station offers day visitors and overnight guests a condensed taste of Outback life. Entry to the homestead, its restaurant and bar, the barbecue, four scenic bushwalking trails, and kangaroo enclosure is free (get feed for them from the stables); so are the pool and Jacuzzi if you patronize the bar or restaurant. A 1-hour horse or camel ride is A$33 (U.S.$21.45)—half- and full-day rides are available, a 30-minute wagon ride is A$8 (U.S.$5.20), and whipcracking and boomerang throwing lessons over billy tea and damper, offered from 10am to noon, cost A$5.50 (U.S.$3.58). A 4WD half-day safari at A$55 (U.S.$35.75) should be on offer this year. All activity prices are lower for kids under 12. It's best to book activities ahead. Overnight accommodations are roomy log cabins; there are also basic quad-share bunkhouses, with shared bathrooms, and campgrounds with a general store. The whitewashed original homestead has been converted to a restaurant with Edwardian furniture, open for breakfast, lunch, and dinner at moderate prices. If enough folk are interested, the homestead does cookouts under the stars, sometimes combined with overnight horse and camel camping safaris. Call to check if any are scheduled.

3 Kings Canyon

Anyone who saw the film *The Adventures of Priscilla, Queen of the Desert* will remember the stony plateau the transvestites climb to gaze over the plain below. You can stand on that same spot (sequined underpants optional) at ✪ **Kings Canyon** in **Watarrka National Park** (☎ **08/8956 7460** for park headquarters), 320 kilometers (200 miles) southwest of Alice Springs as the crow flies. The red walls of the canyon drop 100 meters (about 330 ft.) to glass-clear rock pools and centuries-old gum trees.

The way to explore is on the 6-kilometer (3¾-mile) walk up the side (short but steep!) and around the rim. Even for the fit, it's a strenuous 3- to 4-hour hike, but worth the effort. It leads through a range of sandstone mounds called the **Lost City,** across a bridge to the Garden of Eden, a pocket of waterholes surrounded by ferns about half way along, then back along the other side of the canyon through more sandstone rocks to the starting point. There are lookout points en route. If you visit after the odd occasion when rain falls, the canyon will teem with waterfalls. In winter, don't set off too early, as sunlight does not light up the canyon walls until mid-morning.

If you are not up to the rim walk, you can still hike along the shady 2.6 kilometers (1.7 miles) round-trip trail along the mostly dry **Kings Creek bed** on the canyon floor. The trail goes to a lookout point and comes back the same way; it takes an hour. Wear sturdy boots, as the ground can be very rocky. This walk is good for very young kids and travelers in wheelchairs for the first 700 meters (half a mile).

Both walks are well sign-posted. Avoid the rim walk in the middle of the day between September and May; it's too hot.

Apart from campgrounds, the only place to stay in Watarrka National Park is at **Kings Canyon Resort** (see "Where to Stay & Dine," below). **AAT Kings** provides a coach to and from the resort to the start of the walks for A$38 (U.S.$24.70) per adult, A$19 (U.S.$12.35) children under 15, roundtrip. It departs daily at 6am in summer, 7am in winter (rim walk) and 7am in summer, 8am in winter (creekbed walk). It's best to book a seat; through Kings Canyon Resort.

You can also explore the park from an Aboriginal viewpoint with ✪ **Lilla Aboriginal Tours** (book through Kings Canyon Resort). Aboriginal guides take you on an easy 1 kilometer (0.6 mile) walk to sacred caves and rock painting sites. You learn about the artworks, hear the Dreamtime events that created the land around you, discover plant medicines and food, and have a go at throwing a spear and a boomerang. The tour lasts 1½ to 2 hours and departs at 9am, 11am, and 4pm daily (closed mid-Dec to mid-Jan) from the Lilla community, 14 kilometers (9 miles) from Kings Canyon Resort. The resort does transfers for A$20 (U.S.$13) per person, round-trip, or A$30 (U.S.$19.50) for two of you. The tour costs A$29.70 (U.S.$19.31) for adults, A$24.20 (U.S.$15.73) for seniors and students, and is free for kids under 15.

Professional Helicopter Services (☎ **08/8956 7873;** www.phs.com.au) makes 12- to 15-minute scenic flights over the canyon for A$90 (U.S.$58.50) per adult, and usually half-price for children under 13 (depending on their weight, not their age).

ESSENTIALS

GETTING THERE   By Plane   Murray Cosson's Australian Outback Flights (☎/fax **08/8952 4625;** www.octa4.net.au/mcosson) offers chartered aerial day trips from Alice Springs. An 8-hour day with Murray Cosson including a flight over the West MacDonnell Ranges and Gosse Bluff meteorite crater, rim walk and lunch is around A$410 (U.S.$266.50) per person (based on a minimum two passengers).

By Car Four-wheel-drive fans can drive themselves to Kings Canyon from Alice Springs on the unpaved Mereenie Loop Road (see "Road Trips from Alice Springs," above).

The route is the 480-kilometer (300-mile) trip from Alice Springs south via the Stuart Highway, then west onto the Lasseter Highway, then north and west on the Luritja Road. All three roads are sealed. Uluru (Ayers Rock) is 306 kilometers (191 miles) to the south on a sealed road; from Yulara, take the Lasseter Highway east for 125 kilometers (78 miles), then turn left onto Luritja Road for 168 kilometers (118 miles) to Kings Canyon Resort.

Kings Canyon Resort sells leaded and unleaded petrol and diesel.

By Organized Tour Numerous coach and 4WD tour outfits call at Kings Canyon, with time allowed for the rim walk. See "Exploring the Red Centre" at the start of this chapter for recommended companies.

Uluru Motorcycle Tours (☎ **08/8956 2019;** members.ozemail.com.au/~uluruharleys) takes you on a 1-day tour by Harley Davidson from Ayers Rock Resort for A$550 (U.S.$357.50) per person (as a passenger) or A$580 (U.S.$377) per person (you drive). Time is allowed to walk the rim.

WHERE TO STAY & DINE

Kings Canyon Resort. Luritja Rd., Watarrka National Park, NT 0872. ☎ **1800/817 622** in Australia, or 08/8956 7442. Fax 08/8956 7410. www.ayersrockresort.com.au. 164 units (128 with bathroom, of which 32 have Jacuzzis); 66 powered campsites and tent sites. A/C TV. High season (July 1–Nov 30) A$305–$370 (U.S.$198.25–$240.50) double. Low season (Dec 1–Jun 30) A$256–$321 (U.S.$166.40–$208.65) double. Extra adult A$22 (U.S.$14.30). Children under 16 free in parents' room with existing bedding. High season A$92 (U.S.$59.80) double lodge room, A$171 (U.S.$111.15) family lodge room (sleeps 5), A$155 (U.S.$100.75) quad-share lodge room or A$40 (U.S.$26) per bed in quad-share lodge room (sharing with strangers). Low season A$90 (U.S.$58.50) double lodge room, A$165 (U.S.$107.25) family lodge room (sleeps 5), A$150 (U.S.$97.50) quad-share lodge room or A$40 (U.S.$26) per bed in quad-share lodge room (sharing with strangers). No children in lodge rooms unless room is booked for sole use. Tent sites A$11 (U.S.$7.15) per person; powered sites A$26 (U.S.$16.90) double. Additional person A$10 (U.S.$6.50) adults, A$5 (U.S.$3.25) children 6–15 in powered campsite. Children under 16 dine free at breakfast and dinner buffets with adult at Carmichael's. Ask about packages in conjunction with Ayers Rock Resort and Alice Springs Resort. AE, BC, DC, JCB, MC, V.

This attractive, low-slung complex 7 kilometers (4 miles) from Kings Canyon blends into its surroundings. The nicely decorated rooms have telephones, hair dryers, free movies, and range views from the balcony. All but four of the deluxe rooms are new as of 1999 and have desert views from the glass-enclosed Jacuzzi. The double, twin, quad, and family lodge rooms are a good budget choice, with neatly painted concrete brick walls, tiled floors, heating and air-conditioning, minifridge, a dining setting for four, and a communal kitchen and bathroom facilities. The quad-shares have lockers (should you opt to share with a stranger). Dine in the cafe, in Carmichael's restaurant, or cook up a steak at the free barbecue area. There is a well-stocked mini-mart, two bars, two swimming pools, tour desk, tennis court, gift shop, room service, babysitting, secretarial services, conference facilities for 30, and a sunset viewing platform.

4 Uluru-Kata Tjuta National Park (Ayers Rock/The Olgas)

462km (289 miles) SW of Alice Springs; 1,934km (1,202 miles) S of Darwin; 1,571km (976 miles) N of Adelaide; 2,841km (1,765 miles) NW of Sydney

Ayers Rock is the Australia tourism industry's icon, a glamorous red stone that has been splashed on more posters than Cindy Crawford has been on magazine covers. Just why do people trek from all over the world to gawk at it? Is it its size? Hardly, for nearby Mt. Conner is three times as big. Is it the shape? How so, when most folks agree the neighboring Olgas are prettier? You can only put its popularity down to the faint shiver up the spine and the indescribable sense of place it evokes in anyone who looks at it. Even taciturn Aussie bushmen reckon it's "got somethin' spiritual about it."

✪ **Ayers Rock** is commonly known by its Aboriginal name, Uluru. In 1985 the ✪ **Uluru-Kata Tjuta National Park** was returned to its Aboriginal owners, the Pitjantjatjara and Yankunytjatjara people, together known as the Anangu, who manage the property jointly with the Australian government. People used to speculate that the Rock was a meteorite, but we now know it was formed by conglomerate sediments laid down 600 to 700 million years ago in an ancient inland sea and thrust up above

The Rock in a Day?

You *can* visit Ayers Rock in a day from Alice, but it's a looong day. Most coach tours pack a Rock base walk or climb, a visit to the Olgas, a visit to the Uluru-Kata Tjuta Cultural Centre, and champagne sunset at the Rock into a day trip that leaves Alice around 5:30am in winter or 6am in summer, and gets back very late.

Only consider a day trip in the cooler months between May and September. In summer, it is too hot to do much at the Rock from early morning to late afternoon.

ground 348 meters (1,141 ft.) by geological forces. With a circumference of 9.4 kilometers (6 miles) the Rock is no pebble, especially as two-thirds of it is thought to be underground. On photos it looks like a big smooth blob. In the flesh, it's more interesting—dappled with holes and overhangs, its sides are draped with curtains of stone, creating little coves hiding waterholes and Aboriginal rock art.

Don't think a visit to Uluru is just about snapping a few photos and going home. You can walk around the Rock, climb it (although the owners prefer you don't), fly over it, ride a camel to it, motorcycle around it on a Harley-Davidson, trek through the Olgas, eat in an outdoor restaurant, tour the night sky, and join Aboriginal people on some rather special walks. Give yourself at least a couple of days in this area.

Isolation (and a lack of competition?) makes most things expensive at Ayers Rock, from accommodations to meals to transfers. An organized coach tour or 4WD camping safari is often the cheapest way to see the place. The "Exploring the Red Centre" section at the start of this chapter lists some recommended tour companies.

JUST THE FACTS

GETTING THERE   By Plane   Qantas (☎ 13 13 13 in Australia) flies direct from Sydney daily, and **Airlink** (book through Qantas) flies from Alice Springs two or three times a day, daily from Perth and twice daily from Cairns. All airlines' flights from most other ports around Australia go via Alice Springs. Book flights at least 21 days in advance, as prices become increasingly more expensive towards the date of flight. The airport is 6 kilometers (3¾ miles) from Ayers Rock Resort. A free shuttle ferries all resort guests, including campers, to their door.

Murray Cosson's Australian Outback Flights (☎/fax **08/8952 4625;** www.aus tralianoutbackflights.com.au) does an aerial day trip from Alice Springs that includes scenic flights over the West MacDonnell Ranges, Kings Canyon, Gosse Bluff meteorite crater, and Lake Amadeus; a rental car at Ayers Rock; National Park entry fee; and lunch. Expect to pay around A$520 (U.S.$338) per person (based on a minimum two passengers).

By Bus   Greyhound Pioneer (☎ 13 20 30 in Australia) makes a daily trip from Alice Springs. **McCafferty's** (☎ 13 14 99 in Australia) serves the Rock from Alice on Sunday, Tuesday, Thursday, and Friday. The trip takes about 5½ hours, and the 1-way fare is around A$62 (U.S.$40.30). Both companies drop you at Ayers Rock Resort.

Greyhound Pioneer also does a 2-day tour of Ayers Rock from Alice Springs, looping back to Alice via Kings Canyon on an optional third day.

By Car   Take the Stuart Highway south from Alice Springs for 199 kilometers (124 miles), and turn right onto the Lasseter Highway for 244 kilometers (153 miles) to Ayers Rock Resort. The Rock itself is 18 kilometers (11 miles) further on. (Everyone mistakes the mesa they first see along the way for Ayers Rock; it's Mt. Conner).

If you want to rent a car in Alice Springs and drop it at Ayers Rock, brace yourself for a 1-way penalty. Territory Thrifty Car Rental charges a 1-way fee of A$80 (U.S.$52) for bookings under 3 days; Hertz charges A$125 (U.S.$81.25) for bookings under 7 days; and Avis charges A$125 (U.S.$81.25) for bookings of 2 days or less. As we wrote, Budget did not allow one-way Alice-Ayers Rock rentals. See "Getting Around" in the Alice Springs section for car-rental companies.

VISITOR INFORMATION   For information before you leave home, contact the **Central Australian Tourism Industry Association (CATIA)** in Alice (see "Visitor Information" in Alice Springs section, above). Uluru-Kata Tjuta National Park's official website is www.ea.gov.au/parks/uluru/index.html. Also try Ayers Rock Resort's website: www.ayersrockresort.com.au; click on "Activities".

The **Ayers Rock Resort Visitor Centre**, next to the Desert Gardens Hotel (☎ **08/8957 7377;** fax 08/8956 2403) has displays on the area's geology, wildlife, and Aboriginal heritage, plus a souvenir store selling books and videos. It's open daily from 8:30am to 7:30pm. You can book tours at the tour desk within every hostelry at Ayers Rock Resort, or visit the **Ayers Rock Resort Tour & Information Centre** (☎ **08/8956 2240**) at the shopping center in the resort complex. It dispenses information on tours as far afield as Kings Canyon and Alice Springs. It's open daily from 8:30am to 8:30pm. Ayers Rock Resort stages a nightly **slide show** as an introduction to the Red Centre's wildlife, geology and Aboriginal culture.

One kilometer (half a mile) from the base of the Rock is the ✪ **Cultural Centre** (☎ **08/8956 3138**), owned and run by the Anangu, the Aboriginal owners of Uluru. It uses eyecatching wall displays, frescoes, interactive recordings, and videos to tell about Aboriginal Dreamtime myths and laws. It's worth spending some time here to understand a little about Aboriginal culture. A National Park desk here has information on ranger-guided activities, park notes, animal, plant, and bird-watching checklists, a cafe, the Maruku Arts and Crafts gallery selling Aboriginal wares, and a European-style crafts gallery. Open daily from 7am to 5:30pm.

PARK ENTRANCE FEES   Entry to the Uluru-Kata Tjuta National Park is A$16.25 (U.S.$10.56) per adult; free for children under 16. The pass is valid for 3 days. The cost of the pass is included in many organized tours, but always check.

RULES & REGULATIONS   You wouldn't like folks photographing your face, church or backyard without permission, and for the same reason the Anangu ask you not to photograph sacred sites or Aboriginal people without permission. They ask that you approach sacred sites quietly and respectfully.

GETTING AROUND

Every time you want to get from point A to point B at Ayers Rock, it costs. **Ayers Rock Resort** runs a free shuttle every 15 minutes or so around the resort complex between 10:30am and 6pm and 6:30pm and 12:30am (that is, after midnight), but to get to the Rock itself or to the Olgas, you will need to take transfers, join a tour, or have your own wheels.

BY SHUTTLE   The easiest and cheapest way to get around is with **Uluru Express** (☎ **08/8956 2152**). This company provides minibus transport from Ayers Rock Resort to and from the Rock every 45 minutes, and four times a day to the Olgas. Sunrise trips to Ayers Rock, with a guided walk, cost A$35 (U.S.$22.75) for adults, and A$20 (U.S.$13) for children; a transfer to the Rock and back costs A$30 (U.S.$19.50) for adults, and A$15 (U.S.$9.75) for children.

BY CAR   If there are two of you, it might be cheaper to rent a car than pay for transfers. All roads in the area are sealed, so a 4WD is unnecessary. Expect to pay around A$75 to $90 (U.S.$48.75–$58.50) per day for a medium-sized car. Rates drop somewhat in low season. Most car-rental companies will give you the first 100 kilometers (63 miles) free, then charge A25¢ (U.S.16¢) per kilometer after that, or A28¢ per kilometer in a 4WD. Take this into account, as the round-trip from the resort to the Olgas is more than 100 kilometers (63 miles), and that's without driving to the Rock. Only **Avis** (☎ **08/8956 2266**), **Hertz** (☎ **08/8956 2244**), and **Territory Thrifty Car**

Rental (☎ **08/8956 2030;** book 4WDs through its Darwin office 08/8924 0000) have outlets at Ayers Rock. All rent regular cars and 4WDs. Booking agent **The Outback Travel Shop** (☎ **08/8955 5288;** www.outbacktravelshop.com.au) in Alice Springs will do you a better deal with Territory Thrifty than you'll get going direct.

BY ORGANIZED TOUR   Several tour companies run daily sunrise and sunset viewings, circumnavigations of the Rock by coach or on foot, guided walks at the Rock or the Olgas, camel rides, observatory evenings, visits to the Uluru-Kata Tjuta Cultural Centre, and combinations of all these. Some do "passes" containing the most popular activities. Virtually every company picks you up at your accommodation door. Among the companies are **Uluru Experience** (☎ **1800/803 174** in Australia, or 08/8956 2563; www.ecotours.com.au), which specializes in eco-tours for small groups; large coach operator **AAT Kings** (☎ **08/8956 2171** is the Ayers Rock office; www.aatkings.com.au); and luxury chauffeured car/mini-coach/4WD operators **Tailormade Tours (08/8952 1731;** www.ozemail.com.au/~tmade/) and **VIP Travel Australia** (☎ **1800/806 412** in Australia, or 08/8956 2388; www.vipaustralia.com.au), which do personalized tours and upscale treats like private desert barbecues and champagne tailgate dinners overlooking the Rock or the Olgas.

ABORIGINAL TOURS   Because ✪ **Anangu Tours** (☎ **08/8956 2123**) is owned and run by the Rock's Aboriginal owners, its tours give you a firsthand insight into Aboriginal culture. Tours are in the Anangu language, translated to English by an interpreter. On the 2-hour, 2-kilometer (1¼-mile) Liru Walk tour leading from the Cultural Centre to the Rock, you hear Dreamtime stories, discover bush tucker, have a go at throwing a spear, and the like. The walk is named after the ancestral army of poisonous snake men whose battles left scars on the face of the Rock. It departs daily at 8:30am April to September, 8am in March and October, and 7:30am November to February, and costs A$47 (U.S.$30.55) for adults, A$24 (U.S.$15.60) for children 5 to 15. This doesn't include hotel pickup; if you want that, you will have to join the **Aboriginal Uluru Tour,** which includes sunrise at the Rock and continental breakfast at the Cultural Centre cafe overlooking Uluru, as well as the Liru Walk, for a hefty A$98 (U.S.$63.70) for adults (or A$79/U.S.$51.35 without breakfast) and A$69 (U.S.$44.85) for children (or A$54/U.S.$35.10 without breakfast). It departs an hour before sunrise and takes 4½ to 5½ hours.

The company also does a **Kuniya walk,** where you visit the Kata Tjuta Cultural Centre, the Mutitjulu waterhole at the base of the Rock, learn about bush foods, and see rock paintings, before watching the sunset over Uluru. It departs at 2:30pm April through September, 3:30pm October through March and costs A$79 (U.S.$51.35) for adults and A$54 (U.S.$35.10) for children with transfers, or A$47 (U.S.$30.55) for adults and A$24 (U.S.$15.60) for children without transfers.

Ask about family discounts, and slightly cheaper rates for doing more than one tour.

DISCOVERING AYERS ROCK

AT SUNRISE & SUNSET   Sunset is the peak time to catch the Rock's beauty, when fiery oranges, peaches, pinks, reds, and then indigo and deep violet creep across its face as if it were a giant opal. The sunset viewing car parks are free (as long as you have bought your National Park entry pass). Several companies offer sunset tours from the resort; a coach tour with **AAT Kings** (☎ **08/8956 2171**) departs 90 minutes before sunset, includes a free glass of wine with which to watch the "show," and returns 20 minutes after sundown; the cost is A$28 (U.S.$18.20) for adults, A$25 (U.S.$16.25) seniors and students, and half-price for children 4 to 14.

At sunrise the colors are less dramatic, but the spectacle of the Rock being unveiled by the dawn to birdsong is quite moving. You'll need an early start—most tours leave about 75 minutes before the sun comes up.

CLIMBING IT   Aborigines refer to tourists as "minga"—little ants—because that's what we look like as we crawl up Uluru. Climbing this thing is no picnic—there's sometimes a strong wind that can blow you right off, the walls are almost vertical in places so you have to hold on to a chain, and it can be freezing cold or insanely hot. People have died climbing the rock from heart attacks, heat stress, exposure, or simply falling off, so if you are unfit, have breathing difficulties, heart trouble, high or low blood pressure, or are just plain scared of heights, don't do it. The Rock is closed to climbers when temperatures exceed 36°C (97°F)—which they often do between November and March—and when wind speed exceeds 25 knots (28.77 mph), so plan the climb for the stillness of early morning. Wherever you go at Uluru and the Olgas, bring drinking water with you from the resort. There are no kiosks and few water tanks at either monolith. Bring drinking water from the resort.

If all that does not put you off, you will be rewarded with 360° views of the plain below, the Olgas, and Mt. Conner. The surface is rutted with ravines about 2.5 meters (8 ft.) deep, so be prepared for scrambling. The climb takes about at least 1 hour up for the fit, and 1 hour down. Less sure-footed types should allow 3 to 4 hours all told.

The Anangu do not like people climbing Uluru because the climb follows the trail their ancestral Dreamtime Mala men took when they first came to Uluru. They allow people to climb, but prefer that they don't.

WALKING, DRIVING, OR BUSING AROUND IT   The easy 9.4 kilometer (6 mile) **Base Walk** circumnavigating Uluru takes about 2 hours, but allow time to linger around the water holes, caves, folds, and overhangs that make up its walls. A shorter walk is the easy 1 kilometer (0.6 mile) round-trip trail from the Mutitjulu parking lot to the pretty water hole near the Rock's base, where there is some rock art. The **Liru Track** is another easy trail; it runs 2 kilometers (1¼ miles) from the Cultural Centre to Uluru, where it links with the Base Walk.

Make time for the free daily 2-kilometer (1¼-mile) ✪ **Mala Walk,** where the ranger, who is often an Aborigine, explains the Dreamtime myths behind Uluru, talks about traditional Aboriginal lifestyles and hunting techniques, and explains the significance of the rock art and other sites along the way. It leaves the Mala Walk sign at the base of the Uluru climb at 10am May through September, and at a cooler 8am October through April. Allow 1 or 2 hours.

Before setting off, arm yourself with the self-guided walking notes available for A$1 (U.S.65¢) from the Cultural Centre (see "Visitor Information," above).

A sealed road runs around the Rock.

Uluru Experience (see earlier in this chapter) conducts two guided Base tours, which give you an insight into natural history, rock art, and Dreamtime beliefs. Both arrive in time for sunrise: one is a 5-hour walk, the other is a 4-hour tour in a vehicle that incorporates short walks to the Rock base and a stop at the Uluru-Kata Tjuta Cultural Centre. Both include breakfast and cost A$98 (U.S.$63.70) for adults and A$65

Green Thumbs in the Red Centre

To explore **Ayers Rock Resort's** native gardens, join the gardener for a free 1-hour walk, Monday through Friday (except public holidays), departing from the Sails in the Desert lobby, usually at 7:30am. Check the exact departure time with the hotel.

Most tourists do Uluru in the mornings and the Olgas in the afternoon. Beat the crowds by reversing the order and walk the Valley of the Winds in the morning and visit Uluru in the afternoon. That way you will find both more silent and spiritual.

(U.S.$42.25) for children 6 to 15. Kids under 6 are free but their meals are not included. The 5-hour walk is not suited to kids under 10.

FLYING OVER IT Ayers Rock Scenic Flights (☎ 08/8956 2345) does a 110-minute Uluru/Olgas/Lake Amadeus/Kings Canyon "joyflight" for A$275 (U.S.$178.75) adults, A$235 (U.S.$152.75) kids 3 to 12. They also do an aerial day trip from Ayers Rock Resort that incorporates a guided canyon walk for A$425 (U.S.$276.25) per adult, A$390 (U.S.$253.50) per child 3 to 12.

Murray Cosson's Australian Outback Flights (☎ 08/8952 4625; www.australianoutbackflights.com.au) and **Wright's Air** (☎ 08/8955 5670) both offer aerial day trips on a charter basis from Alice Springs. An 8-hour day with Murray Cosson including a flight over Gosse Bluff meteorite crater, the rim walk, and lunch is A$407 (U.S.$264.55) per person (based on a minimum two passengers).

MOTORCYCLING AROUND IT A blast out to the Rock at sunset with ✪ **Uluru Motorcycle Tours** (☎ 08/8956 2019; members.ozemail.com.au/~uluruharleys) will set you back A$120 (U.S.$78), or A$180 (U.S.$117) to the Olgas. They drive the bike, you sit behind, hang on, and make like Dennis Hopper in *Easy Rider.* They do sunrise rides, laps of the Rock, and Rock and/or Olgas tours with walks, also. Self-ride tours are available, at a hefty price.

VIEWING IT ON CAMELBACK Frontier Camel Tours (☎ 1800/806 499 in Australia, or 08/8956 2444) makes daily forays aboard "ships of the desert" to view Uluru at sunrise and sunset. Amble through red sand dunes with great views of the Rock, dismount to watch the sun rise or sink over it, and ride back to the depot for billy tea and yummy beer bread in the morning, or champagne in the evening. They say a soul travels at the same pace as a camel; it's certainly a peaceful way to see the Rock. The 2-hour rides depart Ayers Rock Resort 1 hour before sunrise, or 1½ hours before sunset, and cost A$76 (U.S.$49.40) per person, including transfers from your hotel. Some connect to coach Base Tours of the Rock. Each day between 10:30am and midday you can visit the depot's camels and display free of charge, and take a short camel ride for A$10 (U.S.$6.50) for adults, or A$6 (U.S.$3.90) for children 5 to 12.

EXPLORING THE OLGAS

Although not everyone has heard of massive ✪ **Mt. Olga** (or "the Olgas"), a sister monolith 50 kilometers (31 miles) west of Uluru, many folks prefer her looks and ambience. Known to the Aborigines as Kata Tjuta or "many heads," the Olgas' 36 momentous red domes bulge out of the earth like turned clay on a potter's wheel. The tallest dome is actually 200 meters (656 ft.) higher than Ayers Rock. The Olgas are more important in Aboriginal Dreamtime legend than Uluru.

Two walking trails take you in among the domes, the 7.4-kilometer (4½-mile) Valley of the Winds walk, which is challenging and takes 3 to 5 hours, and the 2.6-kilometer (1½-mile) Gorge walk, which is easy and takes about an hour. The Valley of the Winds trail is the more rewarding in terms of scenery. Both have lookout points and shady stretches. The Valley of the Winds trail is closed when temperatures rise above 36°C (97°F).

WHERE TO STAY & DINE

Ayers Rock Resort is not only *in* the township of Yulara—it *is* the township. This is the only place to stay at or near Uluru. It is about 16 kilometers (10 miles) from the Rock, outside the national park boundary. Because everyone is either a tourist or lives and works here, the resort has a village atmosphere—with a supermarket, a bank, a post office, babysitting services, medical center, beauty salon, gift, clothing and souvenir shops, a cinema (both indoor and outdoor), and conference facilities.

You have a choice of six self-contained places to stay, from hotel rooms and apartment buildings to bunkhouses and campsites. All guests may use all the pools, restaurants, and other facilities of every hostelry, except the Sails in the Desert pool, which is reserved for Sails guests. You can book accommodations through the resort's central reservations office in Sydney (☎ **1300/139 889** in Australia, or 02/9339 1040, fax 02/9332 4555, www.ayersrockresort.com.au). You can also book Kings Canyon Resort and Alice Springs Resort accommodations through this office. High season is July 1 to November 30. Book well ahead in this period.

Ayers Rock Campground. Yulara Dr., Yulara, NT 0872. ☎ **08/8956 2055.** Fax 08/8956 2260. 220 tent sites, 198 powered sites, 14 cabins (none with bathroom). A$132 (U.S.$85.80) cabin for up to 6 people. A$13 (U.S.$8.45) per person tent site; A$29 (U.S.$18.85) double powered site. Additional person A$11 (U.S.$7.15) adults, A$5 (U.S.$3.25) children 6–15 in powered site. AE, BC, DC, JCB, MC, V. Free airport shuttle.

Instead of red dust you get blissfully green lawns at this campground, which has its own pool, barbecues, clean communal bathrooms, telephones, laundromat, and even its own tour desk. If you don't want to camp but you want to travel cheap, consider the cabins. They're clean, modern, and a great value with a kitchenette, petite dining furniture, a double bed, and four bunks. They share bathroom facilities. Territory Thrifty Car Rental (see "Getting Around," earlier in this chapter) rents camping gear to its customers for A$25 (U.S.$16.25) per day; you must book it ahead.

Outback Pioneer Hotel and Lodge. Yulara Dr., Yulara, NT 0872. ☎ **08/8957 7888.** Fax 08/8957 7615. 125 units, all with bathroom; 12 cabins, none with bathroom; 36 quad-share bunkrooms and 4 20-bed single-sex dorms, none with bathroom. A/C MINIBAR TV TEL. High season A$331 (U.S.$215.15) double, A$147 (U.S.$95.55) cabin. Low season A$303 (U.S.$196.95) double, A$138 (U.S.$89.70) cabin. Extra person A$22 (U.S.$14.30). Bunkroom bed A$38 (U.S.$24.70), dorm bed A$30 (U.S.$19.50), year-round. No children under 16 in bunkhouses unless room is booked for sole use. AE, BC, DC, JCB, MC, V. Free airport shuttle.

A happy, all-ages crowd congregates at this collection of hotel rooms, cabins, bunkrooms and dorms. The decent-size hotel rooms got a refurb in 1999; each has an uncramped bathroom, pay-per-view movies, and hair dryer. Some also have a sink and a microwave. The cabins have a double bed and a bunk bed, shared bathroom facilities and shared kitchen, but are comfortably decked out with self-serve tea and coffee, and a minirefrigerator. Out by the nice pool there are plenty of sundeck lounges. The Bough House Restaurant and Bar does a-la-carte lunch and buffet dinners, and there is a dirt-cheap kiosk, but just about the entire resort gathers nightly at the ✪ **Pioneer**

A Money-Saving Tip

Ayers Rock Resort, Alice Springs Resort, and Kings Canyon Resort are operated by the same company, and packages for stays at one, two, or all three resorts are sometimes available. Some include airfares from Australian state capitals, tours, and 4WD safaris. Ask when making your reservation.

When You See the Southern Cross for the Very First Time . . .

Little light pollution means the night sky in the Red Centre is a dazzler. At the **Ayers Rock Observatory,** you can check out your zodiac constellation and take a 1-hour tour of the Southern Hemisphere heavens (they're different from the Northern Hemisphere stars).

To visit the observatory, you must join a tour with **Uluru Experience** (☎ **1800/ 803 174** in Australia, or 08/8956 2563), who provide hotel pickup and a tour. Tours depart twice a night; times vary. It costs A$30 (U.S.$19.50) for adults, A$22 (U.S.$14.30) for children 6 to 15, and A$63 (U.S.$40.95) for a family.

Barbeque and Bar. This rustic barn with big tables, lots of beer, and live music is the place to join the throngs throwing a steak on the communal cook-it-yourself barbie.

Spinifex Lodge. Yulara Dr., Yulara, NT 0872. ☎ **08/8957 7888.** Fax 08/8957 7755. 34 units and 34 quad-share bunkhouses, none with bathroom. A/C TV TEL. High season A$145 (U.S.$94.25) double or bunkhouse. Low season A$135 (U.S.$87.75) double or bunkhouse. Extra person A$22 (U.S.$14.30). AE, BC, DC, JCB, MC, V. Free airport shuttle.

If you don't mind shared bathrooms, your best budget bet outside camping are these clean, cool, smartly furnished rooms. Both the twin/double rooms and the bunkrooms have a kitchenette, and pay-per-view movies. There's no pool, but you can walk a few hundred yards and use the one at Desert Gardens. There's no restaurant either, but a few eateries and the supermarket are next door.

5 En Route to Darwin from Alice Springs

Alice Springs-Darwin: 1,489km (931 miles)

If you're driving the Stuart Highway from Alice Springs to Darwin, or vice versa, settle in for a long trip, because there's not a lot to see, apart from great sunsets. The terrain is flat and monotonous most of the way. From **Elliott** north, war buffs can stop at numerous **World War II sites;** mostly things like stores, depots, and overgrown U.S. airfields. White-on-brown tourist road signs mark their locations. Allow at least two very long days to reach Darwin; 3 days to do it comfortably, spending the night at Tennant Creek and Katherine; 4 or more days to see and do stuff en route. Fuel is cheapest at Katherine and Tennant Creek. The Darwin Region Tourism Association (see Darwin, "Visitor Information," in chapter 9) sells listen-as-you-drive cassette tapes about the Stuart Highway's history, which may lighten up the trip a little. *Note:* Review the driving precautions discussed at the beginning of this chapter.

The first sight from Alice Springs is the ✪ **Devil's Marbles Conservation Reserve,** by the highway 393 kilometers (246 miles) north of Alice, just beyond Wauchope. These are hundreds of granite boulders, some the size of houses, that have balanced perilously on top of one another for thousands of years. To you and me, they are rocks but to the Aborigines, they are Karlu Karlu, the eggs of the Rainbow Serpent, the Dreamtime Creator. Entry is free. Don't confuse them with the much less impressive Devil's Pebbles near Tennant Creek.

You will likely spend the night in **Tennant Creek** (pop. 3,670), 114 kilometers (71 miles) north of the Devil's Marbles. Its down-at-heel appearance belies the fact that it is the third biggest gold-producing town in Australia. Assorted gold-related attractions await you here, including a mine, a working battery stamp, and a museum. All are located, along with the Tennant Creek Regional Tourist Association information center, in the **Battery Hill Regional Centre,** 1.5 kilometers (1 mile) east of the town center on Peko Rd., Tennant Creek, NT 0860 (☎ **08/8962 3388;** fax 08/8962 2509; tcrta@topend.com.au; see the Northern Territory Tourist Commission website at www.nttc.com.au). The somewhat dated **Bluestone Motor Inn,** 1 Paterson St. (the same street as the Stuart Highway), Tennant Creek, NT 0860 (☎ **08/8962 2617;** fax 08/8962 2883) provides the best digs in town.

At **Renner Springs** (pop. 18) roadhouse, 161 kilometers (101 miles) up the road stop for a "coldie" (cold beer) with the "truckies" (truck drivers) at the rough-and-ready Desert Hotel. At Elliott (pop. 450), 91 kilometers (57 miles) on, you're halfway to Darwin. Detour a few miles west off the highway for a beer at the wonderful **Outback pub at Daly Waters** (☎ **08/8975 9927**), 152 kilometers (95 miles) past Elliott. Its walls are festooned with rusty tools, antique bottles, and every memento imaginable from visitors who have stopped by since 1938. It sells meals and fuel. Next to the pub is a World War II aerodrome with the wreckage of a B-25 Mitchell bomber and a DC-3. Entry to the 1930s hangar housing wartime memorabilia is A$2 (U.S.$1.30).

A dip in the thermal pools at **Mataranka,** 165 kilometers (103 miles) up the highway, is a soothing antidote to driving (see "Katherine" in chapter 9 for details). Katherine and Nitmiluk National Park (see chapter 9) are 110 kilometers (69 miles) farther on. Ninety-one kilometers (57 miles) past Katherine is the goldrush town of **Pine Creek.** Just north of here you can swing right onto the sealed (paved) Kakadu Highway and head to Darwin via Kakadu National Park (a total 455 kilometers/ 284 miles), or stick to the Stuart Highway (225km/141 miles). At the end of the Stuart Highway in Darwin, the road turns back on itself and heads south to Adelaide.

The Top End 9

by Natalie Kruger and Marc Llewellyn

The "Top End" is the term Aussies use to refer to the vast sweep of barely inhabited country from Broome on the west coast of Western Australia to Arnhemland in the Northern Territory and eastern Queensland. It is the place Mick "Crocodile" Dundee called home, a genuine last frontier, a place of wild beauty and, sometimes, hardship.

The rugged northwest portion of Western Australia is known as the Kimberley, where cattle farming, pearl farming, and tourism thrive in a moonscape of red cliffs, waterfalls, rivers, sparse gums, and wetland lagoons. You can visit a million-acre cattle station rich in ancient Aboriginal rock art sites, tour the world's largest diamond mine, cruise the Ord River to see hundreds of native birds, ride a camel on the beach, hike ancient gorges, visit a pearl farm, and shop for the world's biggest South Sea pearls.

The northern reaches of the Northern Territory are slightly more populated than the Kimberley, but only just. Darwin, the capital, is a smallish city, rich, modern, and tropical. Katherine to its south is a farming town famous for a beautiful river gorge. Here you can drop by on an Aboriginal community, explore vast cattle stations, canoe jungly rivers, and soak in natural thermal pools. To the east of Darwin and Katherine is World Heritage—listed Kakadu National Park, home to wetlands, crocodiles, and millions of birds—one-third of the country's bird species, in fact. Farther east still is Arnhemland, a seemingly endless stretch of rocky ridges and flooding rivers owned by Aboriginal people. Few white folk ever penetrate here, and those that do need a permit.

Life is different in the Top End from elsewhere in Australia, especially in the Northern Territory. It has a slightly lawless image that I suspect Territorians enjoy cultivating among tenderfoot Aussies from south of the border. The isolation, the intense humidity in the Wet Season, monsoonal floods, human-eating crocodiles, and other dangers breed a tough kind of person. Mick "Crocodile" Dundee may only be a movie character, but the writers didn't exaggerate entirely when they invented him.

EXPLORING THE TOP END

Read "Exploring the Red Centre" at the start of chapter 8; it contains information on traveling the entire Northern Territory.

VISITOR INFORMATION The **Northern Territory Tourist Commission (NTTC), of Top End Tourism** as it now prefers to be called, (see "Exploring the Red Centre" in chapter 8) can supply you with information on traveling Darwin, Litchfield National Park, Kakadu National Park, Katherine, and other destinations in the Territory. The Darwin Region Tourism Association and the Katherine Region Tourist Association (listed in the "Darwin" and "Katherine" sections of this chapter) can also supply information about the entire Top End and the Kimberley.

Your best source of information on the Kimberley region is the **Broome Tourist Bureau** or the **Kununurra Tourist Bureau** (listed under "The Kimberley: A Far-Flung Wilderness" in this chapter). You can also contact the **Western Australian Tourism Commission (WATC),** 16 St. Georges Terrace, Perth, WA 6000 (☎ **08/9220 1700;** fax 08/9220 1702; www.westernaustralia.net).

WHEN TO GO   The sanest time to visit the Top End is in the winter Dry Season ("the Dry"). Not a cloud will grace the sky, and temperatures will be comfortable, even hot in the middle of the day. The Dry runs roughly from late April to the end of October. It is high season, so book every tour, hotel, or campsite in advance. The Wet Season ("the Wet") runs from November (sometimes as early as October) to March or April, sometimes a few weeks longer in the Kimberley. While it does not rain 24 hours a day during the Wet, it comes down in buckets, usually for an hour or two each day, mainly in the late afternoon or overnight. The land floods as far as the eye can see, the humidity is murderous and the temperatures hit the high 30s°C (86°F). The floods cut off many attractions, sometimes suddenly, and some tour companies shut up shop for the season. Cyclones may hit the coast during the Wet, with the same savagery as hurricanes hit Florida. Many people find the "build-up" to the Wet in October and November, when clouds gather but do not break, the toughest time to be there.

Having said all that, the Wet is a wonderful time to travel. Waterfalls become massive torrents, lightning storms crackle across the afternoon sky, the land turns green, cloud cover keeps the worst of the sun off, and crowds vanish. Keep your plans flexible to account for floods, take it real slow in the heat, and carry loads of drinking water, and you should be OK. Even if you normally camp, sleep in air-conditioned accommodations now. Book tours ahead, as most will operate on a reduced schedule.

GETTING AROUND   The Automobile Association of the Northern Territory (AANT) and the Royal Automobile Club of Western Australia (RACWA) (see "Getting Around Australia," in chapter 2) are a good source of maps and road advice.

Go-it-alone travelers will like the **Blue Banana** (☎ **08/8945 6800;** fax 08/8927 5808; www.octa4.net.au/banana), a minibus that does a running loop between Darwin, Kakadu National Park, Katherine, and Litchfield National Park. Jump on and off at any of the 26 stops, pick up the bus on its next trip through (it runs 4 days a week), and get treated to a guided commentary and photo stops en route. The only real rule is that you must book your next leg 24 hours in advance. The whole loop is A$170 (U.S.$110.50), or you can buy a single leg. You're responsible for your own meals, accommodations, and activities. The company rents camping gear.

TRAVELING IN THE WET   Some roads will be underwater throughout the Wet, while others can flood unexpectedly, leaving you cut off for hours, days, or even months. Flash floods pose dangers to unwary motorists. Don't cross a flooded road unless you know the water is shallow, the current gentle, and the road intact. Never wade into the water, as crocodiles may be present. If you're cut off, the only thing to do is wait, so travel with food and drinking water in remote parts. Check road conditions every day by calling the **Northern Territory Department of Transport & Works'** 24-hour recorded report on road conditions (☎ **1800/246 199** in Australia); dropping into or calling the AANT (see above) in Darwin during office hours;

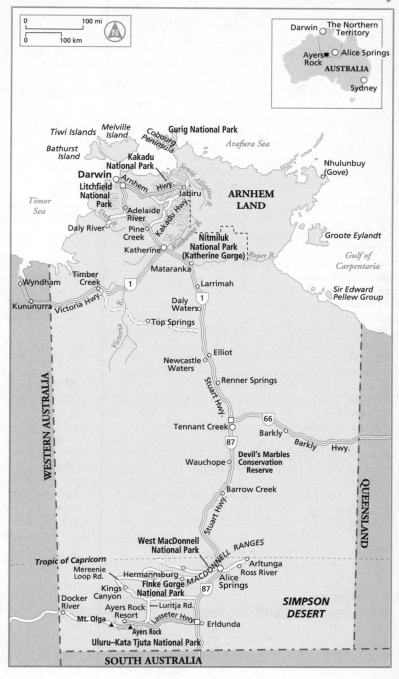

The Northern Territory

0 100 mi
0 100 km

N

Darwin · The Northern Territory
Ayers Rock ■ ○ Alice Springs
AUSTRALIA
Sydney ○

Tiwi Islands
Melville Island
Bathurst Island

Cobourg Peninsula
Gurig National Park
Arafura Sea

Kakadu National Park

Darwin □
Litchfield National Park
Adelaide River
Daly River
Pine Creek
Katherine
Mataranka

Arnhem Hwy.
Jabiru
Kakadu Hwy.

South Alligator R.
Katherine R.

ARNHEM LAND

Nhulunbuy (Gove)

Nitmiluk National Park (Katherine Gorge)
Roper R.

Groote Eylandt

Gulf of Carpentaria

Timor Sea

Daly R.

Victoria R.

Larrimah

Wyndham
Timber Creek
Kununurra

1

Victoria Hwy.

Daly Waters

Top Springs

Sir Edward Pellew Group

Newcastle Waters
Elliot

Renner Springs

Stuart Hwy.

Tennant Creek
66
Barkly
Barkly Hwy.

87

Devil's Marbles Conservation Reserve
Wauchope

Barrow Creek

Stuart Hwy.

WESTERN AUSTRALIA

QUEENSLAND

West MacDonnell National Park

MACDONNELL RANGES

Tropic of Capricorn
Mereenie Loop Rd.
Hermannsburg
Finke Gorge National Park
Kings Canyon
Docker River
Ayers Rock Resort
Mt. Olga
Ayers Rock
Uluru–Kata Tjuta National Park

Arltunga
Ross River
Alice Springs
87
Luritja Rd.
Lasseter Hwy.
Erldunda

SIMPSON DESERT

SOUTH AUSTRALIA

Croc Alert! (& Other Safety Tips)

Saltwater **crocodiles** are a serious threat in the sea, estuaries, lakes, wetlands, waterfall pools, and rivers of the Top End—even hundreds of kilometers inland. They may be called "saltwater" crocs, but they live in fresh water. Never jump in the water or stand on the bank unless you want to be lunch.

Always carry 4 liters (a gallon) of **drinking water** per person a day when walking (increase to 1 liter/ a quarter gallon per person per hour in summer). Wear a broad-brimmed hat, high-factor sunscreen lotion, and insect repellent containing DEET (Aerogard and RID brands both contain it) to protect against the dangerous Ross River Fever virus carried by mosquitoes.

Deadly **marine stingers** (see "Dangerous Aussie Wildlife" in chapter 2) put a stop to ocean swimming in the Top End from October to April.

---

or tuning into the local radio stations as you drive. Local tour companies, tourist bureaus and police stations should also be able to help. In the Kimberley, call the **Main Roads Western Australia** department (☎ **1800/013 314** in Australia) for a 24-hour recorded report.

TOUR OPERATORS   Taking an organized tour can solve the hassles posed by distance, isolation, and Wet floods in the Top End, and it will show you things you might not discover on your own. There is no shortage of companies running coach, mini-bus, and 4WD tours from Broome, Kununurra, Darwin and even Alice Springs. A loop through Darwin, Litchfield National Park, Kakadu National Park, and Katherine is a popular triangle that shows you a lot in a short time.

Reputable companies include: **AAT Kings** (☎ **1800/334 009** in Australia, or 03/9274 7422, fax 03/9274 7400, www.aatkings.com.au); **Sahara Outback Tours** (☎ **1800/806 240** in Australia, or 08/8953 0881; fax 08/8953 2414; www.saharatours.com.au); **Northern Territory Adventure Tours** (☎ **08/8936 1300;** fax 08/8981 4317; www.adventuretours.com.au); and **Billy Can Tours** (☎ **1800/813 484** in Australia, or 08/8981 9813; fax 08/8941 0803; www.billycan.com.au).

Katherine-based **Far Out Adventures** (☎ **08/8972 2552;** fax 08/8972 2228; www.farout.com.au) does 4WD small-group camping adventures into Kakadu, Darwin, Arnhemland, Litchfield National Park, Katherine, the Kimberley and more remote regions across the Top End. Join an organized tour, or have proprietor/guide Mike Keighley tailor a private adventure for you. Mike is one of a select group of operators with Australia's Advanced Eco Tour Accreditation and Savannah Guide status, and has a tremendous knowledge of the Top End's geography, Aboriginal culture and ecology. Fun and personal, accompanied by "bush gourmet" meals, his trips are ideal for nature-lovers; many incorporate canoeing wilderness rivers with affiliate eco-tour operator, Gecko Canoeing.

For details of tour operators running from Darwin to Broome, see "The Kimberley" section in this chapter.

1 Darwin

1,489km (930 miles) N of Alice Springs

Named after the founder of evolution himself, Australia's northernmost capital (pop. 97,750) has proud white civic buildings, pink bougainvillea, and a touch of Asian exoticism. It's a modern tropical capital—extremely modern, actually, as most of it was rebuilt after Cyclone Tracy wiped out the city on Christmas Eve 1974. Don't fuss

Darwin

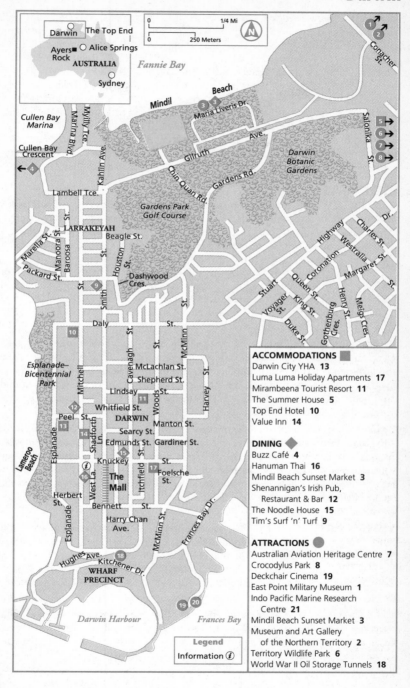

Darwin · The Top End

Ayers Rock · Alice Springs

AUSTRALIA

Sydney

Fannie Bay

Cullen Bay Marina

Cullen Bay Crescent

Mindil · **Beach**

Maria Liveris Dr.

Darwin Botanic Gardens

Gliruth Ave.

Gardens Rd.

Chin Quan Rd.

Lambell Tce.

LARRAKEYAH

Beagle St.

Gardens Park Golf Course

Marella St.

Manoora St.

Baroosa

Packard St.

Houston St.

Dashwood Cres.

Smith St.

Daly St.

McLachlan St.

Shepherd St.

Lindsay St.

Whitfield St.

DARWIN

Manton St.

Searcy St.

Edmunds St. Gardiner St.

Knuckey St.

The Mall

Foelsche St.

Herbert St.

Bennett St.

Harry Chan Ave.

Hughes Ave.

Kitchener Dr.

WHARF PRECINCT

Esplanade–Bicentennial Park

Mitchell St.

Cavenagh St.

Peel St.

Shadforth Ln.

West La.

Esplanade

Lameroo Beach

McMinn St.

Harvey St.

Woods St.

Itchfield St.

Frances Bay Dr.

Highway

Charles St.

Westralia St.

Coronation Dr.

Margaret St.

Stuart Highway

Queen St.

King St.

Voyager St.

Duke St.

Gothenburg Cres.

Henry St.

Melgs Cres.

Salonika St.

Conacher St.

Darwin Harbour

Frances Bay

ACCOMMODATIONS
Darwin City YHA **13**
Luma Luma Holiday Apartments **17**
Mirambeena Tourist Resort **11**
The Summer House **5**
Top End Hotel **10**
Value Inn **14**

DINING ◆
Buzz Café **4**
Hanuman Thai **16**
Mindil Beach Sunset Market **3**
Shenannigan's Irish Pub, Restaurant & Bar **12**
The Noodle House **15**
Tim's Surf 'n' Turf **9**

ATTRACTIONS ●
Australian Aviation Heritage Centre **7**
Crocodylus Park **8**
Deckchair Cinema **19**
East Point Military Museum **1**
Indo Pacific Marine Research Centre **21**
Mindil Beach Sunset Market **3**
Museum and Art Gallery of the Northern Territory **2**
Territory Wildlife Park **6**
World War II Oil Storage Tunnels **18**

Legend

Information ⓘ

about unpacking your jacket and tie here. Shorts and rubber thongs (flip-flops) will get you most places—even the official state invitations stipulate dress as "Territory Rig," meaning long pants and a short-sleeved open-necked shirt for men.

The city is most commonly used as a stepping-off point to Kakadu National Park, Katherine Gorge, and the Kimberley. Australians look at you askance when you say you're visiting this place—"What the heck are you going to do in Darwin?" they ask in amazement—but I like its mix of frontier rawness, scenic beauty and sophisticated food. Give yourself at least a day to wander the streets and parklands, visit the wildlife attractions, and maybe explore the city's World War II history (the harbor contains an official U.S. war grave). The wetland's fishing is excellent by boat or helicopter, as is the shopping for Aboriginal art and the Top End's South Sea pearls. An easy day trip away is the beautiful Litchfield National Park, one of the Territory's best-kept secrets.

ESSENTIALS

GETTING THERE   By Plane   Qantas (☎ **13 13 13** in Australia) serves Darwin daily from most state capitals; flights are either direct or connect in Alice Springs. Qantas flies direct from Cairns daily, and **Airlink** (book through Qantas) makes a Broome-Darwin flight twice a week. It also operates an extra service most days from Katherine. There are also direct international flights to Darwin from Asia.

Darwin Airport Shuttle Services (☎ **1800/358 945** in the Northern Territory, or 08/8981 5066) meets every flight and delivers to city hotels for A$7.50 (U.S.$4.88) one-way or A$13 (U.S.$8.45) round-trip. Children under teen age travel free. You don't need to book a seat. A cab to the city is around A$15 (U.S.$9.75), or A$17 (U.S.$11.05) at night, on Sundays and public holidays.

By Bus   Greyhound Pioneer (☎ **13 20 30** in Australia) and **McCafferty's** (☎ **13 14 99** in Australia) each make a daily coach run to Darwin from Alice Springs. The trip takes around 18½ hours, and the fare is A$165 (U.S.$107.25). Greyhound also has daily service from Broome via Kununurra and Katherine; this trip takes around 26½ hours and costs A$230 (U.S.$149.50). Both companies run from Cairns via Townsville and Tennant Creek.

By Car   Darwin is at the end of the **Stuart Highway.** Allow at least 2 very long days, 3 to be comfortable, to drive from Alice Springs (see "En Route to Darwin from Alice Springs," in chapter 8. The nearest road route from the east is the Barkly Highway which connects with the Stuart Highway at Tennant Creek, 922 kilometers (576 miles) south. The nearest road from the west is the Victoria Highway which joins the Stuart Highway at Katherine, 314 kilometers (196 miles) to the south.

There is no train service to Darwin.

VISITOR INFORMATION   The Darwin Region Tourism Association (☎ **08/ 8981 4300;** fax 08/8981 0653; drtainfo@ozemail.com.au) at Beagle House, Knuckey St. at Mitchell St., Darwin, NT 0800, is the place to go for maps, bookings and information. It's open Monday through Friday 8:30am to 5:45pm, Saturday 9am to 2:45pm, and Sunday and public holidays 10am to 1:45pm. It stocks official guides to all the Top End's national parks, too.

CITY LAYOUT   The heart of the city is the **Smith Street pedestrian mall. One street over is the lively **Mitchell Street Tourist Precinct,** full of backpacker lodges, cheap eateries, and souvenir stores. Two streets past that is the harborfront **Esplanade.** In the Old Wharf precinct, near town, are a couple of tourist attractions, a jetty popular with local fishermen, and a working dock. Cullen Bay Marina is a "millionaire's row" of restaurants, cafes, and expensive boats; it's about a 25-minute walk northwest of town. A couple of miles northwest of the town center is Fannie Bay, where you'll find the Botanic Gardens, sailing club, golf course, museum and art gallery, and casino.

GETTING AROUND   For car and 4WD rentals, call **Avis** (☎ **08/8981 9922**), **Budget** (☎ **08/8981 9800**), **Hertz** (☎ **08/8941 0944**), or **Territory Thrifty Car Rental** (☎ **08/8924 0000**).

Darwinbus (☎ **08/8924 7666**) is the local bus company. The city terminus is on Harry Chan Avenue (behind the Commonwealth Bank and Qantas buildings). Get timetables there, or from the Darwin Region Tourism Association (see "Visitor Information," above).

The Tour Tub bus (☎ **1800/63 2225** in Australia, or 08/8981 5233) does a loop of most city attractions and major hotels between 9am and 4pm daily. Hop on and off as often as you like all day for A$22 (U.S.$14.30) for adults and A$13.20 (U.S.$8.58) for children 4 to 12. It departs the Knuckey Street end of Smith Street Mall. **Darwin Day Tours** (☎ **08/8981 8696**) has a range of sightseeing tours.

Call **Darwin Radio Taxis** (☎ **131 008**) for a cab. The taxi stand is at the Knuckey Street end of Smith Street Mall.

WHAT TO SEE & DO: CITY STROLLS, WORLD WAR II HISTORY, FISHING & MORE

Darwin's ample parks, stunning harbor, and tropical clime make it a lovely city for strolling during the Dry. The Darwin Region Tourism Association (see "Visitor Information," above) has free maps of a Historical Stroll which takes you to 17 points of interest around town; the Esplanade makes a pleasantly short and shady saunter; and the **Darwin Botanic Gardens** (☎ **08/8981 1958**), on Gardens Road 1.5 kilometers (1 mile) from town, have paths through palms, orchids, and lawns, and an Aboriginal plant use trail. Entry is free daily. Take bus 4 or 6.

The long but pleasant 5-kilometer (3-mile) trail along **Fannie Bay** from the MGM Grand hotel to the **East Point Military Museum** is worth doing. Keep a lookout for the 2,000 wild wallabies on the east side of Alec Fong Lim Drive near the museum.

Darwin has two wildlife parks worth visiting. At the **Territory Wildlife Park** (☎ **08/8988 7200**), 61 kilometers (38 miles) south of Darwin you can take a free shuttle or walk 6 kilometers (3¾ miles) of bush trails to see native Northern Territory wildlife in 12 natural habitats, such as bats, bilbies, birds in a walk-through aviary, sawfish and stingrays in a walk-through aquarium, spiders, crocs, and kangaroos (but not koalas, as they don't live in the Territory). Go first thing to see the animals at their liveliest. Take the Stuart Highway for 50 kilometers (31 miles) and turn right onto the Cox Peninsula Road for another 11 kilometers (7 miles). Allow 4 hours to see everything, plus traveling time. It is open daily 8:30am to 6pm (last entry at 4pm), and closed Christmas. Admission is A$18 (U.S.$11.70) for adults, A$9 (U.S.$5.85) for seniors and students and children 5 to 16, and A$40 (U.S.$26) for a family of 6.

In addition to housing a fascinating crocodile museum, **Crocodylus Park** (☎ **08/ 8922 4500**), a 15-minute drive from town at the end of McMillan's Road in Berrimah, holds exciting croc-feeding sessions and free guided tours at 10am, noon, and 2pm. It is open daily 9am to 5pm (closed Christmas). Admission is A$19.50 (U.S.$12.68) for adults, A$16 (U.S.$10.40) for seniors, and A$10 (U.S.$6.50) for children 5 to 15. The park is 5 minutes from Darwin Airport; take bus no. 5 (Mon–Fri only).

The **Museum and Art Gallery of the Northern Territory,** Conacher Street, Fannie Bay (☎ **08/8999 8201**), also holds an attraction for crocodile fans—the preserved body of Sweetheart, a 5.1-meter (17-ft.) woman-eating saltwater croc captured in Kakadu National Park. The museum and gallery have good sections on Aboriginal,

Southeast Asian and Pacific art and culture. Both gallery and museum are open Monday through Friday from 9am to 5pm, and 10am to 5pm weekends and public holidays (closed Christmas and Good Friday). The cafe has lovely bay views. Admission is free to permanent exhibits. Take bus no. 4 or 6.

Darwin was an Allied supply base during World War II. The **East Point Military Museum,** East Point Road, East Point (☎ **08/8981 9702**), housed in a WWII gun command post, plays a video of the 1943 Japanese bombing of Darwin and has fine displays of photos, memorabilia, artillery, armored vehicles, and weaponry. It is open daily 9:30am to 5pm (closed Christmas and Good Friday). Admission is A$9 (U.S.$5.85) for adults, A$8 (U.S.$5.20) for seniors, A$4.50 (U.S.$2.93) for children under 15, and A$25 (U.S.$16.25) for a family.

Military or aircraft buffs should not miss the ✪ **Australian Aviation Heritage Centre,** 557 Stuart Hwy., Winnellie (☎ **08/8947 2145**). A B-52 bomber on loan from the United States is the prized exhibit, but the center also boasts a B-25 Mitchell bomber, Mirage and Sabre fighter jets, Japanese Zero fighter wreckage, and displays on World War II and Vietnam. It is open daily 9am to 5pm. Admission is A$11 (U.S.$7.15) for adults, A$7.50 (U.S.$4.88) for seniors and students, A$6 (U.S.$3.90) for children 6 to 12, and A$28 (U.S.$18.20) for a family. It is 10 minutes from town; take the no. 5 or 8 bus. On Kitchener Drive in the Old Wharf precinct, you can walk through the **World War II oil storage tunnels** (☎ **1800/63 2225** in Australia, or 08/8981 5233), which contain a collection of black and white photographs of the war in Darwin, each one hauntingly lit in the dark. Admission is A$4 (U.S.$2.60). The tunnels are usually closed December 10-27, and all February, and its hours are restricted during the Wet. On the Esplanade stands a monument to the destroyer **U.S.S. Robert E. Peary** which went down in Darwin Harbour taking 88 lives.

At the **Indo Pacific Marine Research Centre** at Stokes Hill Wharf (☎ **08/8981 1294**), you watch a brief film before taking a guided tour of living coral reefs in tanks. The 3½ hour night show at 7pm (Wed, Fri and Sun only) is especially good as coral is luminous in the dark; it's combined with seafood dinner for A$69.50 adults (U.S.$45.18), A$32.45 (U.S.$21.09) kids under 14. The 1-hour day tour is A$15.50 (U.S.$10.08), and A$5.50 (U.S.$3.58) for kids. The centre opens daily from 9am to 5pm, only to 1pm in the Wet. Between May and October the Centre does 6-hour guided eco-explorations of the city's mangroves and rock pools for A$82.50 (U.S.$53.63) or A$64.90 (U.S.$42.19) for children.

The Top End's vast wetlands and warm oceans are close to fishing heaven. The big prey is barramundi, but the other catches include tarpon, salmon, and marlin. Loads of charter boats conduct jaunts from a morning to up to 10 days in the rivers and wetlands around Darwin, Kakadu National Park, and remote Arnhemland. If you just want to cast a line in Darwin Harbour, **Tour Tub Fishing Charters** (☎ **1800/63 2225** in Australia, or 08/8981 5233) will take you out for A$75 (U.S.$48.75) for a

---

The Darwin Shopping Scene

Darwin's best buys are Aboriginal art and crafts, pearls, opals, and diamonds. For a great range of artworks and artifacts, check out **Raintree Aboriginal Fine Arts,** 20 Knuckey St. (☎ **08/8941 9933**). The world's best South Sea pearls are farmed in Top End seas. Buy, or just drool in the window, at **Paspaley Pearls,** off Smith St. Mall in Bennett St. (☎ **08/8981 9332**). **The World of Opal,** 44 Smith St. Mall (☎ **08/8981 8981**), has a recreation of an opal mine in their showroom.

It makes you sigh, especially on Darwin's lovely hot days, but crocodiles render Darwin's lovely turquoise seas a no-swim zone all year round. Locals sunbathe on **Casuarina Beach,** and swim within view of the sea in **Lake Alexander** on Alec Fong Lim Drive in East Point Reserve. It's that, or hit the hotel pool!

half-day, or A\$135 (U.S.\$87.75) for a full day. On the inland wetlands, one of the most experienced operators is **Land-A-Barra** Tours (☎ **08/8932 2543**), which takes a maximum three anglers on day trips for A\$264 (U.S.\$171.60) per person, or extended fishing safaris with meals and basic accommodation for A\$407 (U.S.\$264.55) per person, per day. Prices are cheaper for three people, pricier for a single traveler.

WHERE TO STAY

Darwin's remoteness means accommodation is not all that cheap, especially from April to October, the peak travel Dry Season. From November to March, the Wet Season, hotels usually drop their rates.

Luma Luma Holiday Apartments. Knuckey St. at Woods St., Darwin, NT 0800. ☎ **1800/656 988** in Australia or 08/8981 1899. Fax 08/8981 1882. 64 units (all with shower only). A/C TV TEL. Dry Season A\$146 (U.S.\$94.90) studio, A\$168 (U.S.\$109.20) 1-bedroom apt (sleeps 4), A\$242 (U.S.\$157.30) 2-bedroom apt (sleeps 6). Wet Season A\$85 (U.S.\$55.25) studio, A\$110 (U.S.\$71.50) 1-bedroom apt. A\$162 (U.S.\$105.30) 2-bedroom apt. Extra bed A\$15 (U.S.\$9.75). Free crib. AE, BC, DC, JCB, MC, V. Free parking.

These nicely decorated, good-size serviced apartments built in the city center in 1997 are perfect for families. Even the one-bedroom apartment sleeps four comfortably; take a two-bedroom apartment and the kids get their own bathroom en suite and their own TV in the bedroom. The studios have a kitchenette, whereas apartments come with full kitchens. Bathrooms are big enough for everyone to spread out all their gear; the front desk lends hair dryers. The complex has a nice big swimming pool, an important consideration in Darwin's heat. Apartments from the third to the top (seventh) floor have views over the city. Smith Street Mall is just 2 blocks away. No smoking.

Mirambeena Tourist Resort. 64 Cavenagh St., Darwin, NT 0800. ☎ **1800/891 100** in Australia or 08/8946 0111. Fax 08/8981 5116. www.mirambeena.com.au. 225 units (all with shower only). A/C TV TEL. A\$147–\$185 (U.S.\$95.55–\$120.25) double, A\$225 (U.S.\$146.25) town house (sleeps 4). Extra person A\$25 (U.S.\$16.25). Children under 3 stay free in parents' room. Ask about lower rates Oct–April. AE, BC, DC, MC, V. Free parking (limited), plus on-street parking. Bus: 4, 5, 6, 8, 10.

You're just a stone's throw from the city center at this modern hotel complex, where the tempting saltwater swimming pools, Jacuzzis, and the treetop restaurant, all shaded by the leaves of a sprawling strangler fig, have a castaway island feel. All rooms were refurbished in 1998 to a high standard; each is a decent size and has a hair dryer, iron and board, free in-room movies, and some kind of garden or pool view. Townhouses with kitchenettes are good for families, if you can handle sharing the compact bathroom with your kids. The place also has a pool bar and cafe, minibar on request, dry-cleaning service, room service, a gym, a game room, minigolf, bike rental, a children's pool, babysitting, a tour desk, conference facilities, secretarial service, and a lobby shop.

Top End Hotel. Mitchell St. at Daly St., Darwin, NT 0801. ☎ **1800/626 151** in Australia or 08/8981 6511. Fax 08/8941 1253. www.bestwestern.com.au. topendhotelaccommodation@tmgroup.com.au. 40 units (all with shower only). A/C TV TEL. Dry Season A$132 (U.S.$85.80) double, A$144 (U.S.$93.60) triple. Wet Season A$115 (U.S.$74.75) double, A$126 (U.S.$81.90) triple. Extra person A$20 (U.S.$13) adult, A$16 (U.S.$10.40) child under 12. AE, BC, DC, JCB, MC, V. Free parking. Bus: 4, 5, 6, 8, 10.

This two-story Best Western hotel has a quiet ambience, despite the trendy complex of bars, restaurants, sports-betting outlets, slot machines, and a liquor store on one side. Most of the rooms face a saltwater swimming pool surrounded by lawn, lounge chairs, tall palms and BBQs rather than the bar complex. Front desk sells meat packs for you to cook up on the barbie. Rooms were renovated at the end of 1998, and each is a good size with quality fittings, free in-room movies, and a furnished patio or balcony. You're just across the road from fish feeding and the Esplanade, close to restaurants and a 1 kilometer stroll (half a mile) from Smith Street Mall.

✪ **The Summer House.** 3 Quarry Crescent, Stuart Park (PO Box 104, Parap, NT 0820). ☎ **08/8981 9992.** Fax 08/8981 0009. www.bed-and-breakfast.au.com/SummerHouse BandB.htm. shbb@octa4.net.au. 3 units (all with shower only). A/C TV. A$120 (U.S.$78) double, A$200 (U.S.$130) for 2-bedroom apt (sleeps 4). Rates include continental breakfast. Rates A$10 (U.S.$6.50) lower without breakfast. AE, BC, MC, V. Free parking. Bus: 5, 6, 8, 10 only. From the airport, take the Stuart Highway 5km (3 miles) to Stuart Park; turn left onto Woolner Rd., immediately right onto Iliffe St., right onto Armidale St., and left onto Quarry Crescent.

Jill Farrand has created a tropical hideaway in her converted apartment block. Two rooms sport white walls, polished concrete floors and wrought iron furniture (one with Balinese bamboo armchairs and 10-foot high exotic flower arrangements), while a third has a retro look. All have louver windows to encourage a breeze, mosaic bathrooms (with hair dryer), and one or two bedrooms, a living area, and a kitchenette. Jill delivers a continental breakfast in the morning. The place is in a leafy suburb 3 kilometers (2 miles) from town and 5 kilometers (3 miles) from the airport, on the local bus route. A Jacuzzi in the jungly garden is great for cooling off on hot nights. No smoking indoors.

Value Inn. 50 Mitchell St., Darwin, NT 0800. ☎ **08/8981 4733.** Fax 08/8981 4730. www. valueinn.com.au. reservations@valueinn.com.au. 93 units (with shower only). A/C TV. Dry Season A$77 (U.S.$50.05) double. Wet Season A$59 (U.S.$38.35) double. No charge for extra person. AE, BC, MC, V. Free parking for approx. 40 cars.

The cheerful rooms at this neat little hotel in the Mitchell Street Tourist Precinct are compact but tidy, and have colorful modern fittings. Each room is just big enough to hold a queen-size and a single bed, a mini-refrigerator, and a writing table. The views aren't much, but you'll probably spend your time in the cafes along the street. Smith Street Mall and the Esplanade walking path are two blocks away. There's a public pay phone and a coffee vending machine on each floor, and a teensy garden swimming pool off the carpark.

SUPER-CHEAP SLEEPS

Darwin City YHA. 69 Mitchell St., Darwin, NT 0800. ☎ **08/8981 3995.** Fax 08/8981 6674. yhant@ozemail.com.au. 130 units, 2 with bathroom (shower only). A/C A$40 (U.S.$26) double without bathroom; A$54 (U.S.$35.10) double with bathroom. A$15–$17 (U.S.$9.75–$11.05) dorm bed. Extra A$3.50 (U.S.$2.28) per person for non-YHA/HI members. Linen A$2 (U.S.$1.30) for length of stay. BC, MC, V. Ample on-street parking. Bus: 4 or 5 (6 or 10 citybound only). Free airport shuttle.

The single and double rooms at this upbeat backpacker hostel in the Mitchell Street Tourist Precinct are basic, but the mattresses are firm, and the communal bathrooms are clean. Well-behaved guests laze elbow-to-elbow around the pool; a second lofty sundeck and an open-air kitchen and dining area overlook the pool. The hostel also has TV rooms, and bikes for rent. A major tour desk in the lobby offers an array of sensibly priced trips and activities. Reception is open 24 hours and has safes. Shenanigan's Irish pub (see "Where to Dine," below) is in the complex, and coach terminals, cheap cafes, the Smith Street Mall, and the Esplanade are steps away. The air-conditioning is noisy and is turned on only between 7pm and 9am, so think twice about staying here in Darwin's horrifically hot summer.

WHERE TO DINE

Cullen Bay Marina, a 25-minute walk from town or a short cab ride, is packed with cool restaurants and cafes. If it's Thursday, don't even think about eating anywhere other than the **Mindil Beach Markets** (see below). The cool crowd hangs at **Roma Bar,** 30 Cavenagh St. (☎ **08/8981 6729**) for good coffee and cheap nosh; it's open Monday through Friday 7am to 5pm, Saturday and Sunday 8am to 2pm.

Hanuman Thai. 28 Mitchell St. ☎ **08/8941 3500.** Reservations recommended. Main courses A$8.50–$20.50 (U.S.$5.53–$13.33). AE, BC, DC, JCB, MC, V. Mon–Fri noon–2:30pm; daily 6:30pm–late. CONTEMPORARY THAI/NONYA/TANDOORI.

This elegant restaurant is a business lunch venue by day and as a rendezvous for couples, families, and more business folk by night. It serves up sophisticated dishes cooked with skill, such as marinated chicken wrapped in *pandan* leaves with a mild chili and malt sugar sauce, and grilled local Gulf prawns with a sauce of crushed coriander and coconut milk sprinkled with *kaffir* lime leaf julienne. Desserts are a Thai take on French classics, such as black rice brûlée and *lychee bavarois.*

Shenannigan's Irish Pub, Restaurant & Bar. 69 Mitchell St. at Peel St. ☎ **08/8981 2100.** Reservations recommended. Daily specials approx. A$9.50–$14 (U.S.$6.18–$9.10). Main courses A$9–$18. (U.S.$5.85–$11.70). AE, BC, DC, MC, V. Meals daily noon–2:30pm, 6–9pm (snack menu 3–5:30pm); bar daily 11am–2am. IRISH PUB FARE.

Hearty Irish stews and braised beef and Guinness pies (plus the odd pint of Guinness itself) gets everyone in the mood for eating, talking, and dancing at this convivial bar/restaurant. Like Irish pubs all over the world, this one draws a friendly mix of solo travelers, families, seniors, and backpackers, who eat and drink in wooden booths, standing up at bar tables, or by the fire. As well as meat dishes, there is a snack menu with lighter stuff like toasted sandwiches, and good-value nightly specials, such as chicken and chili pasta or barramundi in white wine sauce with fries and salad. There's live entertainment here every night ranging from karaoke, to trivia quizzes and bands.

The Noodle House. 33 Knuckey St. ☎ **08/8941 1742.** Main courses A$6–$22 (U.S.$3.90–$14.30). AE, BC, MC, V. Mon–Fri 11am–2pm; daily 6–10pm. CHINESE.

Cheap Eats & More!

If it's Thursday, join the entire city (well, 8,000 locals) at the ✪ **Mindil Beach Sunset Market** to feast at the 60 terrific and cheap Asian food stalls, listen to live bands, wander 200 art and crafts stalls, and mingle with the masseurs, tarot card readers, and street performers. The action runs from 5pm to 10pm in the Dry (May–Oct). A smaller market runs Sunday between June and September from 4pm to 9pm. The beach is a A$6 (U.S.$3.90) cab ride from town, and the Tour Tub does A$4 (U.S.$2.60) transfers between 5pm and 9:30pm Thursday from major city hotels and the Knuckey Street end of Smith Street Mall. Or take bus 4.

Twenty bucks will buy you a huge feed at this unpretentious eatery just around the corner from Smith Street Mall. Tummy-fillers like pineapple and chicken fried rice or beef fried rice are especially cheap. The menu lists many meat dishes, such as Szechuan beef or chicken and roast duck, and there are the usual Chinese soup suspects. The brown tiled floor, pink vinyl tablecloths, and plastic flowers are not exactly the stuff romantic dinners for two are made of, but the place has a friendly atmosphere. BYO.

✪ **Tim's Surf 'n' Turf.** In the Asti Motel, Smith St. at Packard Place ☎ **08/8981 9979.** Main courses A$7.90–$16 (U.S.$5.14–$10.40). Many dishes around A$10/U.S.$6.50; seafood platter for 2 A$28.50 (U.S.$18.53). BC, MC, V. Mon–Fri noon–2pm; daily 5:30–9:30pm. STEAK/SEAFOOD.

Locals fairly bash the door down to get into this restaurant housed under a cheap motel on the city fringe. The modest surroundings are not the attraction, so what is? Hearty, no-nonsense food cooked well in portions big enough to feed an army. Tim's steaks are monsters up to 800 grams (25½-oz., over an inch thick and grain-fed, a boon in Australia where the beef is mostly grass-fed and hence a little chewy. Garlic prawns, crocodile schnitzel, lasagna, oysters, quiche, and roast of the day are typical menu items. There are meals for kids, too.

WORTH A SPLURGE

✪ **Buzz Café.** At the Cullen Bay Marina. ☎ **08/8941 1141.** Reservations recommended in the Dry. Main courses A$16.50–$25 (U.S.$10.73–$16.25). AE, BC, DC, MC, V. Mon–Fri noon–2am, Sat 10am–2am (including brunch), Sun 9am–2am. MODERN AUSTRALIAN.

Local movers and shakers come to this busy outdoor venue to move, shake, and enjoy the views over the marina from the deck. There are more terrific views from inside the men's bathroom and I don't mean views of the guys—girls, get a male to take you in there and show you what I mean! The food is fresh, flavorsome East-meets-West fare like jungle curry of chicken with snake beans and green peppercorns, or pan-fried barramundi on potato mash in a lemon butter sauce. Lots of folk wash the meal down with a cocktail—try the mango daiquiris—from the bar.

DARWIN AFTER DARK

If it's Thursday, you are mad to be anywhere except the Mindil Beach Markets (described earlier). Ditto if it's Sunday evening and you're not at the free **Sunset Jazz** on the lawns at the MGM Grand Casino once a month from May to October. A good spot to catch Darwin's movie-set sunsets any night is the super-casual **Darwin Sailing Club,** Atkins Drive on Fannie Bay (☎ **08/8981 1700**). Ask the manager to sign you in. A bistro serves affordable meals from noon to 2pm and from 6 to 9pm daily, and the bar is open from 10am until midnight, and until 2am Friday and Saturday.

Lie back at the **Deckchair Cinema** (☎ **08/8981 0700**) to watch Aussie hits, foreign films, and cult classics under the stars. Movies are screened Wednesday through Sunday in the Dry (Apr or May–Oct or Nov) with late sessions Friday and Saturday nights. At press time, the cinema was looking for a new location; it is currently located off Mavie Street behind Old Stokes Hill Power Station near the Wharf (a 20-minute walk from the center of town). Tickets are A$11 (U.S.$7.15).

Darwin Entertainment Centre, 93 Mitchell St. (☎ **08/8981 9022** administration, 08/8981 1222 box office) is the city's main performing arts venue.

The gaming tables at the **MGM Grand Casino,** Gilruth Avenue, Mindil Beach (☎ **08/8943 8888**), are in play from noon until 4am, and until 6am Saturday and Sundays. Slot machines are in play 24 hours. The dress regulation is neat, but casual.

PUBS, CLUBS & LIVE MUSIC

The cafes and restaurants of Cullen Bay Marina are a good place to be, day or night, but especially for Dry season sunsets. On most nights, **Shenannigan's Irish Pub,** 69 Mitchell St. at Peel St. (☎ **08/8981 2100**) has that wonderful mix of live Irish music, dancing, blarney, and laughter called "craik," oiled by ample Guinness. When the U.S. Marines are in town, they head to **Rorke's Drift,** 46 Mitchell St.(☎ **08/8941 7171**), an English-style pub and cafe, which offers dance nights on Friday and Saturday, live music on at least one night a week and "male and female entertainers" (*read:* strippers) on Monday and Tuesday. **Sweetheart's** in the MGM Grand Casino (see above) is a popular nightclub for 18s to 45s. Live jazz, blues, and classic rock and soul play nightly at **Nirvana Restaurant,** 130 Smith St. (☎ **08/8981 2025**), a 1970s relic renowned for good Indian, Malay, and Thai food. **Tracy's Bar** in the Central Darwin Hotel, 122 The Esplanade (☎ **08/8981 5388**), is a pleasant after work watering hole. The stylish complex of pool bar, DJ, beer garden, grill, sports bar and upscale restaurant that is the **Top End Hotel,** Mitchell Street at Daly Street (☎ **08/8981 6511**) has something to suit just about everyone.

A SIDE TRIP TO LITCHFIELD NATIONAL PARK

120km (75 miles) S of Darwin

A 90-minute drive south of Darwin is a miniature Garden of Eden full of monsoonal forests, waterfalls, rocky sandstone escarpments, natural swimming holes, and prehistoric cycads that look like they walked off the set of Jurassic Park. ✪ **Litchfield National Park** is much smaller (a mere 146,000 hectares/360,620 acres) and less famous than Kakadu, yet most folks would say it is prettier.

Its main attractions are the spring-fed swimming holes, like the magical plunge pool at **Florence Falls,** 27 kilometers (17 miles) from the eastern park entrance, surrounded by high sandstone cliffs and monsoon rain forest. It's quite a hike down to the water, so the easily accessible pool at **Wangi Falls,** 49 kilometers (31 miles) from the eastern entrance, actually gets more crowds. Surrounded by cliffs and forests and a pretty outlook from the top, it has beauty enough of its own. More idyllic swimming grottos are to be had a couple of miles away at **Buley Rockhole,** a series of cute birdbath-like rockholes and waterfalls. There are a number of manageably short walking trails through the park, too, and by the time you arrive, a mooted 70-kilometer (44-mile) hiking circuit around the top of the **Tabletop Range** may be in place. It will link many waterfalls not currently seen by visitors to the park. If you have a 4WD vehicle, you can swim at **Sandy Creek Falls,** just under 50 kilometers (31 miles) from the eastern entrance, or visit the **"Lost City,"** a group of sandstone rock formations. All these water holes are regarded as crocodile-free; the same is not true of the Finniss and Reynolds rivers in the park, so no leaping into those! The park is also home to thousands of termite mounds up to 2 meters (6.5 ft.) high.

ESSENTIALS

GETTING THERE   From Darwin, head south for just over 86 kilometers (54 miles) on the Stuart Highway and follow the park turnoff on the right through the town of Batchelor for 34 kilometers (21 miles).

Northern Territory Adventure Tours (☎ **1300/654 604** in Australia, or 08/8936 1300) makes day trips from Darwin.

VISITOR INFORMATION   The Parks & Wildlife Commission district office in Batchelor on the corner of Nurdina Street and Pinaroo Crescent (☎ **08/8976 0282**) has maps and information; most locations of interest have signboards. Entry is free.

GETTING AROUND   Roads to most water holes in the park are paved, although a few areas are only accessible by 4WD. In the Wet Season (approximately November to April), some roads in the park may be closed, usually the 4WD ones, and the Wangi water hole may be off limits due to turbulence and strong currents. Check with the Parks & Wildlife Commission office before you leave Darwin during this time.

CAMPING   There are basic campsites with toilets, showers, and wood-fired barbecues at Florence Falls and Wangi Falls, plus several other sites with fewer facilities throughout the park. You may collect firewood in the park, but not around the campgrounds. The camping fee is A$6.60 (U.S.$4.29) for adults, A$3.30 (U.S.$2.15) for kids under 16, and A$15.40 (U.S.$10.01) for families. A kiosk at Wangi Falls sells basic supplies, but stock up on fuel and alcohol in Batchelor.

2 Kakadu National Park

257km (161 miles) E of Darwin

✪ **Kakadu National Park,** a World Heritage area, is Australia's largest national park at a mere 1,755,200 hectares (4,335,344 acres).

Cruising the lily-clad wetlands to spot crocodiles, swimming in exquisite natural water holes, hiking through spear grass and cycads, fishing for barramundi, soaring in a light aircraft over torrential waterfalls during the Wet, photographing the millions of birds and thousands of saltwater crocodiles that live here, flying over the somehow eerie red sandstone escarpment that juts 200 meters (650 ft.) above the floodplain, and admiring Aboriginal rock art sites—these activities are what draw people to Kakadu. Some 275 species of birds and 75 species of reptiles inhabit the park, making it one of the richest wildlife habitats in the country.

The name "Kakadu" comes from "Gagudju," the group of languages spoken in the northern part of the park. It is thought that Aboriginal people have lived in this part of the world for 50,000 years. Today, Aborigines manage the park as its owners in conjunction with the Australian government. This is one of the few places in Australia where some Aborigines stick to a traditional lifestyle of hunting and living off the land. They keep away from prying eyes, but their culture is on display at a cultural center and at rock art sites. Kakadu and the vast wilds of Arnhemland to the east are the birthplace of the "x-ray" style of art for which Aboriginal artists are famous.

To nature-loving Aussies, Kakadu is a true ecological jewel. They're right, but be aware that the hefty distances between points of interest, and that sameness that infects so much Australian landscape, can detract from Kakadu's appeal for some folk.

Moves are under way to class the park as "threatened" under World Heritage listing, partly due to uranium mining within its boundaries. Don't think the mine will impact on your experience of the place. It is a pinprick on the Kakadu's sweeping landscape.

JUST THE FACTS

VISITOR INFORMATION   Both of the park's entry stations—the northern one on the Arnhem Highway used by visitors from Darwin and the southern on the Kakadu Highway for visitors from Katherine—hand out free visitor guides with maps, and in the Dry they issue a timetable of free guided ranger walks, talks, and slide shows taking place that week. Park headquarters is at the **Bowali Visitor Centre** (☎ **08/ 8938 1120**) on the Kakadu Highway, 5 kilometers (3 miles) from Jabiru, 100 kilometers (63 miles) from the northern entry station and 131 kilometers (82 miles) from the southern entry station. This attractive, environmentally friendly Outback-style center shows videos every 30 or 60 minutes on the park's natural history and Aboriginal culture, stocks maps and free park notes, has a library and displays, and information officers are on hand. There is a gift shop and a café, open daily from 8am to 5pm.

You can also book tours and get information at the **Jabiru Travel Centre,** Shop 6, Tasman Plaza, Jabiru, NT 0886 (☎ **08/8979 2548;** fax 08/8979 2482; wendymchugh@ bigpond.com.au).

Before you arrive, you can find information on Kakadu, and book tours to it, at the **Darwin Region Tourism Association visitor center** (see "Visitor Information" in the Darwin section, earlier in this chapter). You can also contact the rangers at **Kakadu National Park,** P.O. Box 71, Jabiru, NT 0886 (☎ **08/8938 1120;** fax 08/8938 1123, KakaduNationalPark@ea.gov.au). The best website on Kakadu is the Northern Territory Tourist Commission's site at www.nttc.com.au.

WHEN TO GO   Kakadu has two distinct seasons—Wet and Dry. The Dry Season from May to October is overwhelmingly the best time to go, thanks to equable temperatures around 30°C (86°F) and sunny days. Many tours, park hotels, and even campsites are booked a year in advance; so don't travel without reservations. In the Wet Season, from November through April, floodwaters cover much of the park, some attractions are cut off unexpectedly, and the heat and humidity are extreme. Some tour companies do not run during the Wet, and ranger talks, walks, and slide shows are not offered. The upside of visiting during the Wet is that the crowds vanish, the brownish vegetation bursts into green, waterfalls swell from a trickle to a roar, and lightning storms are spectacular, especially in the very hot "build-up" to the season in October and November. The landscape can change dramatically from one day to the next as floodwaters rise and fall, so be prepared for surprises, both nice ones—like giant flocks of geese that are here today, gone tomorrow—and unwelcome ones, like blocked roads. Although it pours down all day, it is more common for the rain to fall in late afternoon storms and at night. Take it easy in the humidity and don't even think about camping in this heat—stay in air-conditioned accommodations.

GETTING THERE   Follow the Stuart Highway 34 kilometers (21 miles) south of Darwin, and turn left onto the Arnhem Highway all the way to the park's northern entrance station. The trip takes 2½ to 3 hours. If you're coming from the south, turn off the Stuart Highway at Pine Creek onto the Kakadu Highway and follow the Kakadu Highway for 79 kilometers (49 miles) to the park's southern entrance station. **Greyhound Pioneer** (☎ **13 20 30** in Australia) makes a daily run from Darwin for A$40 (U.S.$26), leaving at 6:30am. The Blue Banana bus (see "Exploring the Top End" at the start of this chapter) visits the park from Darwin.

FEES & REGULATIONS   The park entry fee of A$16.30 (U.S.$10.60) per adult is valid for 14 days. Children 15 and under are free.

TIPS FOR EXPLORING   Kakadu is a big place—about 200 kilometers (125 miles) long by 100 kilometers (63 miles) wide—so plan to spend a couple of nights here. It is really too far and too big to see much in a day from Darwin.

Most attractions are accessible in a conventional vehicle on sealed (paved) roads, but a 4WD vehicle allows you to get to more falls, water holes, and campsites. **Territory Thrifty** (☎ **08/8979 2552**) rents cars at the Gagudju Crocodile Hotel, otherwise rent a car in Darwin. If you 4WD it, always check road the conditions at the **Bowali Visitor Centre** (☎ **08/8938 1120**). In the Wet Season (late Nov–Apr), call daily to check floodwater levels on all roads, paved and unpaved. The Bowali Visitor Centre, main attractions such as Nourlangie and Yellow Water Billabong, and the towns of Jabiru and Cooinda stay above the floodwaters year-round.

Never Smile at a You-Know-What

The Aboriginal Gagudju people of the Top End have long worshipped a giant crocodile called Ginga, but the way white Australians go on about these reptilian relics of a primeval age, you'd think they worshipped 'em, too. There is scarcely a soul in the Northern Territory who will not earbash you with his or her particular croc story, and each one you hear will be weirder and taller than the last.

Aussies may be good at pulling your leg, but when they warn you not to swim in crocodile country, they're not kidding. Crocodiles are good at pulling your leg, too—literally. To be sure you don't end up as lunch, here are some tips:

1. There are two kinds of crocs in Australia, the highly dangerous and enormously powerful saltwater or "estuarine" kind, and the "harmless" freshwater kind, which will only attack if threatened or accidentally stood on. Saltwater crocs can and do swim in the ocean, but they live in fresh water.

2. Don't swim in any waterway, swimming hole, or waterfall unless someone authoritative like a recognized tour operator or a park ranger has specifically told you that it is safe. You can never be sure where these critters lurk from year to year because, every Wet Season, crocs head upriver to breed and spread out over a wide flooded area. As the floodwaters subside in the Dry, they are trapped in whatever waterway they happen to be in at the time—so what was a safe swimming hole last Dry Season might not be croc-free this year.

3. Never stand on or walk along a riverbank, stand well back when fishing. A 20-foot croc can be 1 inch under the surface of that muddy water, yet remain invisible. They move so fast you won't see them until you're in their jaws.

4. Make camp and clean fish at least 25 meters (82 ft.) back from the bank.

And what if you come face-to-face with a crocodile? Everyone has different advice, but it all boils down to two things. Make your peace with God, or run!

Facilities are limited in Kakadu. The only town of any size is **Jabiru** (pop. 1,455), a mining community where you can find a bank. The only other real settlements are accommodation houses (see "Where to Stay & Dine," below).

A big range of coach, minibus and 4WD tours and camping safaris taking an average of one to 3 days depart from Darwin every day. These are a good idea, because many of Kakadu's geological, ecological, and Aboriginal attractions only come to life with a guide, and the best water holes, lookouts, and wildlife viewing spots change dramatically from month to month, or even from day to day.

SEEING THE HIGHLIGHTS
En Route to Kakadu

En route to the park, stop in at the **Fogg Dam Conservation Reserve** (☎ **08/8988 8009** is the ranger), 25 kilometers (15½ miles) down the Arnhem Highway plus 10 kilometers (6 miles) off the highway. Here you'll get a close-up look at geese, egrets, ibis, brolgas, and other wetland birds from boardwalks leading through monsoon forests to raised lookouts. Entry is free every day of the year.

Four kilometers (2½ miles) down the Arnhem Highway at Beatrice Hill, you may want to call in on the **Window on the Wetlands Visitor Centre** (☎ **08/8988 8188**), a hilltop center with views across the Adelaide River floodplain and touchscreen information on the wetlands' ecology. It's free and open daily from 7:30am to 7:30pm.

Just past Beatrice Hill on the highway at the Adelaide River (you can't miss the statue of a grinning croc), you can join the **Original Jumping Crocodiles** cruise (☎ **08/8988 8144**) aboard the *Adelaide River Queen* to watch wild crocodiles leap out of the water for hunks of meat dangled over the edge by the boat crew. The 90-minute cruise departs 9am, 11am, 1pm and 3pm from May to August, and 9am, 11am and 2:30pm September to April (closed Dec 24–25). It costs A$31 (U.S.$20.15) for adults, A$27 (U.S.$17.55) for seniors, and A$18 (U.S.$11.70) for children 5 to 15. Farther down the track at Annaburroo, you can stop for a drink at the **Bark Hut Inn** on your left (☎ **08/8978 8988**). Well, pretend you want a drink; you're actually here for an eyeful of the colorfully tough Territory truckies and station hands who often prop up the bar, looking like extras from Crocodile Dundee.

TOP PARK ATTRACTIONS

WETLANDS CRUISES One of the biggest attractions in the park is **Yellow Water Billabong,** a lush lake 50 kilometers (31 miles) south of the Bowali Visitor Centre at Cooinda (pop. 20). It's rich with freshwater mangroves, paperbarks, pandanus palms, water lilies, and marvelous swathes of thousands of birds gathering here to drink—sea eagles, honking magpie geese, kites, china blue kingfishers, and jacanas, called "Jesus birds" because they seem to walk on water as they step nimbly across the lily pads. This is also one of the best places to spot saltwater crocs. Cruises in canopied boats with a running commentary depart near Gagudju Lodge Cooinda six times a day from 6:45am in the Dry (May–Nov) and 7am in the Wet (Dec–Apr). A 90-minute cruise costs A$33 (U.S.$21.45) for adults and A$15 (U.S.$9.75) for children 2 to 14, and a 2-hour cruise costs A$38.50 (U.S.$25.03) for adults and A$16.50 (U.S.$10.73) for children (in dry only). Book through **Gagudju Lodge Cooinda** (see "Where to Stay & Dine," below). Even though it means spending the night in the park and getting up before dawn, the sunrise cruise is especially good, when the dawn silence is broken by an overture that builds to a full-blown orchestral performance, courtesy of the birds. In the Wet, when the billabong floods to join up with Jim Jim Creek and the South Alligator River, the bird life spreads far and wide and the crocs head upriver to breed, so don't expect wildlife viewing to be that spectacular.

Another excellent cruise is the **Guluyambi Aboriginal Culture Tour** (☎ **1800/ 089 113** in Australia or 08/8979 2411 for booking agent—Kakadu Tours) on the East Alligator River, which forms the border between Kakadu and Arnhemland. Unlike the Yellow Water journey, which focuses on crocs, birds, and plants, this cruise tells you about Aboriginal myths, bush tucker, and hunting techniques. The cruise is limited to 25 passengers. Cruise last 1 hour and 45 minutes and leaves at 9am, 11am, 1pm, and 3pm daily from May to October; the schedule shifts to a half-day cruise on the Magela Creek system in the Wet, with a climb of Ubirr Rock. Transportation to the boat in

Glowing Attraction?

Not all of Kakadu's attractions are natural. Tours of the **Ranger Uranium Mine,** 13 kilometers (8 miles) east of the Bowali Visitor Centre, reveal how this extremely controversial material is extracted from a large open-cut mine and turned into yellowcake to fire nuclear power plants around the world. 90-minute tours depart daily May through October at 10:30am and 1:30pm (and at 8:30am and 3pm when demand is high) and cost A$17 (U.S.$11.05) adults, A$10 (U.S.$6.50) kids ages 4 to 14. The tours depart by bus from Jabiru Airport, which is near the mine. Book through **Kakadu Tours** (☎ **1800/089 113** in Australia, or 08/8979 2411).

Croc Alert!

Though folk do swim at Jim Jim, Twin Falls, and other water holes, such as Gubara, Maguk, and Koolpin Gorge, do so at your own risk. Saltwater crocodiles have been known to slip through the traps rangers set alongside popular swimming holes. *NEVER swim without checking with a ranger that the water hole is croc-free;* if you are unsure, the only place rangers recommend you swim is the hotel pool.

---

the Dry season is not included, so you will need to get yourself to the departure point at the Upstream Boat Ramp, 44 kilometers (28 miles) east of the Bowali Visitor Centre. A free bus runs to the ramp from Merl campground or the Border Store. In the Wet, the trip picks up from the Gagudju Crocodile Hotel at 10am. The cruise costs A$30 (U.S.$19.50) for adults and A$15 (U.S.$9.75) for children 4 to 14.

ABORIGINAL ART & CULTURE   There are as many as 5,000 art sites throughout the park, of which the Aboriginal owners make a few accessible to visitors. The two best are **Nourlangie Rock** and **Ubirr Rock.** Nourlangie, 31 kilometers (19 miles) southeast of the Bowali Visitor Centre, features "x-ray" style paintings of animals and a vivid striped Dreamtime figure of Namarrgon, the "Lightning Man," alongside modern depictions of a white man in cowboy boots, a rifle, and a sailing ship. Rangers have told me that Nourlangie is a "tourist" art site and that there is "much better" stuff hidden elsewhere in the park, but this one is pretty impressive! You'll also find rock paintings at Nanguluwur, near Nourlangie, and at Ubirr Rock, which is worth the 250m (800 ft.) steep climb for the great views of the floodplain at sunset. Access to Ubirr can be limited in the Wet, but the views of afternoon fork lightning storms up here at that time are breathtaking. Unlike most sites in Kakadu, Ubirr is not open 24 hours—it opens at 8:30am from May to November and at 2pm from December to April, and closes every day at sunset. There is a 1.5-kilometer (1-mile) signposted trail around Nourlangie's paintings, a 3.4-kilometer (2-mile) trail at Nanguluwur, and a 1-kilometer (0.6-mile) track at Ubirr. Access to all of these sites is free.

You can see sisplays and videos of the bush tucker, Dreamtime creation myths and lifestyles of the Bininj Aboriginal people at the **Warradjan Aboriginal Cultural Centre** (☎ **08/8979 0051**) at Cooinda. This circular building was built in the shape of a pignose turtle at the direction of the Aboriginal owners. There's also a gift shop selling didgeridoos, bark paintings by local artists, and baskets woven from pandanus fronds. The center is open from 9am to 5pm daily, and admission is free. It is connected to Gagudju Lodge Cooinda and the Yellow Water Billabong by a 1-kilometer (half a mile) walk trail.

SWIMMING, FISHING & BUSHWALKING

In the eastern section of the park rises a massive red sandstone escarpment that sets the stage for two magnificent waterfalls, ✪ **Jim Jim Falls** and ✪ **Twin Falls.** In the Dry, the volume of water may not be all that impressive, but their settings are magical. Both are accessible by 4WD only, and neither is open in the Wet. A 1-kilometer (half a mile) walk over rocks and through rain forest leads to a deep green plunge pool at Jim Jim Falls, 103 kilometers (64 miles) from the Bowali Visitor Centre. The water is wrapped by an almost perfectly circular 150 meters (490-ft.) cliff. The road may be upgraded by the time you read this, but if not, allow 2 hours to drive the final 60 unpaved kilometers (37½ miles) off the highway. Due to floodwaters, Jim Jim Falls may not open until as late as June.

Paddling past the odd "harmless" freshwater crocodile at nearby Twin Falls is great, too. The falls descend into a natural pool edged by a sandy beach and surrounded by bush and high cliffs. John and Bronwen Malligan of **Kakadu Gorge and Waterfall Tours** (☎ **08/8979 0111,** or 08/8979 2025 after hours) run an excellent small group day trip to the falls for active people. You bushwalk into Jim Jim Falls for morning tea, 4WD through the bush, then paddle in a tandem canoe to Twin Falls for lunch. Tours depart daily from Jabiru and Cooinda from May to November and cost A$130 (U.S.$84.50) for adults, A$110 (U.S.$71.50) for kids 4 to 14 (no kids under 4 allowed). Book in advance for July, the busiest month.

Remember the idyllic pool that Paul Hogan and Linda Koslowski plunged into in the movie "Crocodile Dundee?" That was **Gunlom Falls,** about 170 kilometers (106 miles) south of the Bowali Visitor Centre. A climb to the top of the falls rewards you with great views of southern Kakadu. Access is by 4WD and can be cut off in the Wet.

Kakadu's wetlands are brimful of barramundi, and there is nothing Territorians like more than to hop in a tin dinghy barely big enough to resist a croc attack and go looking for them. John and Bronwen Malligan, also run **Kakadu Fishing Tours** (☎ **08/8979 0111,** or 08/8979 2025 after hours) in a 4.75 meter sportfishing boat. They depart from Jabiru, 5 kilometers (3 miles) east of the Bowali Visitor Centre, and cost A$120 (U.S.$78) per person for a half day (A$190/U.S.$123.50 if there is only one of you) and A$240 (U.S.$156) per person for a full day. They also do fly-fishing.

A wide-ranging collection of bush and wetlands trails lead throughout the park, including many short strolls and six half- to full-day treks. Typical trails include a 600m (less than ½ mile) amble through the Manngarre Monsoon Forest near Ubirr Rock; an easy 3.8-kilometer (2-mile) circular walk at the Iligadjar Wetlands near the Bowali Visitor Centre; or a tough 12-kilometer (7.5-mile) trek through rugged sandstone country at Nourlangie Rock.

One of the best wetlands walks is at **Mamukala wetlands,** 29 kilometers (18 miles) from Jabiru. Countless thousands of magpie geese feed here, especially in the late Dry Season around October. An observation platform gives you a good view of them, and a sign explains the dramatic seasonal changes the wetlands undergo. Choose from a 1-kilometer (half a mile) or 3-kilometer (2-mile) meander. The Bowali Visitor Centre sells hiking trail maps. There are also some challenging unmarked trails along creeks and gorges, for which you will need good navigational skills.

CAMPING

There are more than 20 campsites, many with few facilities, all mostly near popular billabongs and wetlands.

The best-equipped campsites are at **Gagudju Lodge Cooinda** (see "Where to Stay & Dine," below). Campers are free to use all of the facilities here, although in extremely busy times, the pool may be available only to bungalow guests.

Tent site-only campgrounds with hot showers and toilets are at **Gunlom, Mardugal Billabong, Muirella Park** near Nourlangie Rock, and **Merl** in the northeast. A ranger visits campgrounds daily to collect a nightly fee of A$5 (U.S.$3.25) per person.

Bushwalking Tips

Try to plan your walk in the early morning or late afternoon, especially in the Wet, as the heat can dehydrate you quickly. If you want to camp at an undesignated campsite on an overnight walk, you will need a camping permit from the rangers at the Bowali Visitor Centre, which can take a week to arrange.

Fewer crowds, no camping fees, and the peace of the bush are the payoffs for going without showers and having only basic toilets, or none, at the free "bush camps" throughout the park. Inquire at the park entry stations or at the Bowali Visitor Centre for a map marking them.

Some campsites need a 4WD to reach them, and most are be closed in the Wet. Gagudju Lodge Cooinda opens year-round.

If you want to camp in the wild rather than a designated campground, you will need a permit from the Bowali Visitor Centre. These can take a week to process, so plan ahead. Bring a mosquito net, as mosquitoes here carry the potentially dangerous Ross River virus. RID and Aerogard are two brands that help protect against it.

WHERE TO STAY & DINE

There are few options to stay in Kakadu, and prices aren't cheap, especially in the high season (usually Apr 1–Nov 30).

Aurora Kakadu Lodge & Caravan Park. Jabiru Dr., Kakadu National Park, NT 0886. ☎ **1800/811 154** in Australia, or 08/8979 2422. Fax 08/8979 2254. www.aurora-resorts. com.au. 24 triple- or quad-share bunkrooms, none with bathroom, 186 powered and 100 unpowered campsites. High season A$121 (U.S.$78.65) bunkroom (sleeps up to 4 people). Low season A$115 (U.S.$74.75) bunkroom. A$20 (U.S.$13) double, unpowered campsite; A$25 (U.S.$16.25) double, powered campsite. AE, BC, DC, MC, V.

Located within walking distance of Jabiru and 2 kilometers (1¼ mile) from the Bowali Visitor Centre, this van park offers simple air-conditioned bunk rooms with one double bed and a single bed, or four bunks, plus a minifridge and self-serve tea and coffee. Bunkroom guests use communal bathroom and kitchen facilities. The nice gardens are home to a swimming pool, Jacuzzi, and barbecues; and there's a bar, bistro, and laundry. No smoking in bunkrooms.

Gagudju Lodge Cooinda. Kakadu Hwy. (50km/31 miles south of Bowali Visitor Centre), Jim Jim, NT 0886. ☎ **1800/500 401** in Australia, 800/835-7742 in the U.S. and Canada, 0345/58 1666 in the U.K. or 020/8335 1304 in London, 0800/801 111 in New Zealand, or 08/8979 0145. Fax 08/8979 0148. www.sphc.com.au. COOINDA1@bigpond.com. A/C. 48 bungalows (all with shower only), 34 budget rooms (none with bathroom), 57 powered and 310 unpowered campsites. Bungalow A$198 (U.S.$128.70) double. Extra person A$27.50 (U.S.$17.88); children under 13 free in parents' room. Budget room A$30.80 (U.S.$20.02) per bed, or A$25 (U.S.$16.25) per bed for YHA/HI members. A$13.50 (U.S.$8.78) per adult powered campsite; A$10.50 (U.S.$6.83) per adult, unpowered campsite. Children 2-12 free in campsite. Expect lower rates in bungalows and budget rooms in the Wet. AE, BC, DC, JCB, MC, V.

This pleasantly modest lodge is situated at the departure point for Yellow Water Billabong cruises. The bungalows are simply furnished, but big and comfortable; they come with a telephone. Hair dryers and babysitters are available on request. The budget rooms are bunk beds (four have double beds) in a corrugated iron demountable (portable cabin) with shared bathrooms. They rent on a per bed basis, so you may find yourself sharing with a stranger. Tropical gardens keep the place cool, and there is a small shady pool. The lodge is something of a town center, so there is a general store, a gift shop, a tour desk, currency exchange, a post office, fuel, and other useful facilities. Cook up a 'roo steak in the nightly do-it-yourself barbecue in the satisfyingly rustic and ultra-casual **Barra Bar & Bistro**, or go for the excellent bush tucker a la carte meals at lunch or dinner in Mimi's, which has a really nice "bush sophisticated" ambience. The Barra Bistro does full buffet breakfast and an all-day snack menu, and has live entertainment in the Dry Season most nights. Scenic flights take off from the lodge's airstrip, and the Warradjan Aboriginal Cultural Centre is a 15-minute walk.

Kakaku Resort. Arnhem Hwy. (41km/24½ miles west of Bowali Visitor Centre), Kakadu National Park, NT 0886. ☎ **1800/818 845** in Australia, or 08/8979 0166. Fax 08/8979 0147. www.aurora-resorts.com.au. 138 units, 60 unpowered campsites. A/C TV TEL. High season A$185 (U.S.$120.25) double; low season A$138 (U.S.$89.70) double. Additional person A$33 (U.S.$21.45) extra. Children 5–14 50% discount. A$10 (U.S.$6.50) double. Additional person in campsite A$5 (U.S.$3.25) extra. AE, BC, DC, MC, V.

This property is near the northern entrance to the park. The downside is that it is the farthest accommodation from major attractions like Yellow Waters and Nourlangie, although many tour operators pick up here. The upside is that the resort's green lawns and tropical gardens adorned with wandering peacocks and chattering native birds are a wonderfully restful haven from the harsh surrounds of Kakadu outside. All but the end rooms of the neatly decorated motel-style accommodations have pitched timber ceilings, and all have restful green views from a balcony or patio. Hair dryers are free at reception. There's a buffet restaurant, a cafe and bar, a day/night tennis court, a shady swimming pool, a Jacuzzi, and a good tour desk. Don't yield to the temptation to dive into the lily-filled lagoon down the back—like every other waterway in Kakadu, it is home to saltwater crocs! A 3.6-kilometer (2-mile) nature trail winds from the hotel through monsoon forest and past a billabong. Keep an eye out for standby specials—when I visited at the start of the Wet in late October a double room and breakfast, booked within 72 hours, was going for A$90 (U.S.$58.50).

3 Katherine

314km (196 miles) S of Darwin; 512km (320 miles) E of Kununurra; 1,177 (736 miles) N of Alice Springs

The local townsfolk in Katherine (pop. 9,450) are proud that more people cruise Katherine Gorge every year than visit Ayers Rock. Dramatic orange walls dropping to a blue-green tranquil river make the gorge a powerful drawing card, all the more so because it is an unexpected delight in the middle of the dry Arnhemland plateau.

The gorge and its surrounding river ecosystem are located in the 292,008-hectare (721,269-acre) **Nitmiluk National Park.** In the Dry, the gorge is a haven not just for cruisers but for canoeists who must dodge the odd freshwater crocodile (the "friendly" kind) as they paddle up between its walls. In the Wet, the gorge can become a foaming torrent at times, and jet boating is sometimes the only way to tackle it. Hikers will find nice trails any time of year. Farther afield from Katherine are hot springs to soak in, water holes to swim in, uncrowded rivers to canoe, caves to explore, and Aboriginal communities who show visitors how to make dot paintings and find bush tucker.

ESSENTIALS

GETTING THERE   Airnorth (☎ **1800/627 474** in Australia, or 08/8945 2866,) flies daily from Darwin, and every day except Saturday from Alice Springs via Tennant Creek. It's a 50-minute trip from Darwin and a 3-hour flight from Alice.

McCafferty's (☎ **13 14 99** in Australia) and **Greyhound Pioneer** (☎ **13 20 30** in Australia) stop in Katherine on their Darwin-Alice Springs and Alice Springs-Darwin routes, which both companies run daily. Greyhound also calls daily from Broome via Kununurra. It's a 4-hour trip from Darwin costing A$44 (U.S.$28.60) twice daily; from Alice it's a 14-hour journey for which the fare is A$144 (U.S.$93.60); and the 22-hour trip from Broome costs A$204 (U.S.$132.60).

Katherine is on the Stuart Highway, which links Darwin and Alice Springs. From Alice Springs, allow a good 2 days to make the drive—see "En Route to Darwin from Alice Springs" in chapter 8, "The Red Centre." The Victoria Highway begins in Katherine and heads west to Kununurra. There is no direct route from the east.

VISITOR INFORMATION The **Katherine Region Tourist Association,** Stuart Hwy., at Lindsay St., Katherine, NT 0850 (☎ **08/8972 2650;** fax 08/8972 2969; krta@nt-tech.com.au) has information on things to see—not only around Katherine, but as far afield as Kakadu and the Kimberley. It's open Monday through Friday 9am to 5pm and, in the Dry Season only, weekends 10am to 3pm.

The **Nitmiluk Visitor Centre** (☎ **08/8972 1886**) on the Gorge Road, 32 kilometers (20 miles) from town, dispenses information on the Nitmiluk National Park and sells tickets for gorge cruises, which depart right outside. The ranger station is here also. The Centre has maps, displays on the park's plant life, birds, geology and Aboriginal history, a gift shop, and a cafe. It's open daily 7am to 7pm, sometimes closing a little earlier in the Wet. Entry to the Park is free.

GETTING AROUND **Avis** (☎ **08/8971 0520**), **Budget** (☎ **08/8971 1333**), **Hertz** (☎ **08/8971 1111**) and **Territory Thrifty Car Rental** (☎ **08/8972 3183**) have outlets in Katherine.

Travel North (☎ **1800/089 103** in Australia or 08/8972 1044) makes transfers from Katherine hotels to the cruise, canoe, and helicopter departure points at the Nitmiluk Visitor Centre. Roundtrip fares are A$17.50 (U.S.$11.38) for adults and A$8.50 (U.S.$5.53) for kids 5 to 15. The company also runs local tours and activities such as horse-riding dinners on cattle stations, visits to an old homestead, and transfers to as far away as Mataranka Thermal Pools (see below). For personalized tours both off-the-beaten path and around town, contact **Far Out Adventures** (☎ **08/8972 2552**).

EXPLORING KATHERINE GORGE (NITMILUK NATIONAL PARK)

Cruising the gorge in an open-sided boat is the most popular way to appreciate its beauty. Katherine Gorge is actually a series of 13 gorges, but most cruises only ply the first two, as the second gorge is the most photogenic. All cruises are operated by **Travel North** (☎ **1800/089 103** in Australia, or 08/8972 1044). Most folks take the 2-hour cruise, which depart four times a day and cost A$34 (U.S.$22.10) for adults and A$13.50 (U.S.$8.78) for children 5 to 15. There is also a daily 4-hour cruise for A$49 (U.S.$31.85) for adults and A$22 (U.S.$14.30) for kids, although you will probably be satisfied with 2 hours. If you want to spend the whole day outdoors, take the 8-hour safari to the fifth gorge (available Apr–Oct only). In addition to cruising, you get to swim, hike for 5 kilometers (3 miles) over sometimes-rough terrain, and have a barbecue lunch. All-day trips cost A$85 (U.S.$55.25) per person, adult or child. Because each gorge is cut off from the next by rapids, all cruises involve some walking along the bank to transfer to a boat in the next gorge, so wear sturdy shoes.

In the Wet season, the cruises may not operate on days when the floodwaters really start to swirl. Instead, Travel North runs a jet boat those days as far as the third gorge. This 45-minute adventure costs A$39 (U.S.$25.35) for adults and A$29 (U.S.$18.85) for kids five to 15. Departure times vary from day to day.

Cruising is nice, but in a canoe you can discover sandy banks and waterfalls, and get up close to the gorge walls, the birds, and those crocs (don't worry, they're the freshwater kind). The gorges are separated by rocks, so be prepared to carry your canoe quite often. Half-day canoe rental from Travel North is A$28 (U.S.$18.20) for a single canoe and A$42 (U.S.$27.30) for a double, and full-day rental is A$39 (U.S.$25.35) for a single canoe and A$58 (U.S.$37.70) for a double. There is a A$20 (U.S.$13) refundable deposit, and A$60 (U.S.$39) if you want to camp out on the river bank overnight. Once the river gets too high for go-it-alone canoeing during the Wet, Travel North runs guided canoeing adventures instead. These last 5½ hours and cost $41 (U.S.$27) per person. In fact, guided paddles are a good idea any time of year as you will learn and see more. The most knowledgeable such company is ✪ **Gecko Canoeing** (☎ **1800/634 319** in Australia, or 08/8972 2224), whose tours are accredited for their eco-tourism content. Gecko's owner/guide, Martin Wohling, has attained Australia's elite "Savannah Guide" eco-tour guide status. They will pick you up from your accommodation for an all-day escorted canoe safari at a cost of A$125 (U.S.$81.25) per person. In the Dry, the company also runs canoeing and camping safaris (with any other activities you like thrown in such as mountain biking, rock climbing, wildlife photography, hiking or fishing) of up to 12 days in little-explored wildernesses nearby, such as the Flora and Daly River systems.

Some 100 kilometers (63 miles) of hiking trails crisscross Nitmiluk National Park, ranging in duration from 1 hour to the lookout to 5 days to Edith Falls (see below). Trails—through rocky sandstone-conglomerate terrain and forests, past water holes and along the gorge—depart the Nitmiluk National Park ranger station, located in the **Nitmiluk Visitor Centre** (☎ **08/8972 1886**), where you can pick up trail maps. Overnight walks require a deposit of between A$20 (U.S.$13) and A$50 (U.S.$32.50) per person, payable at the Nitmiluk Visitor Centre.

One of the nicest spots in the Park is actually 42 kilometers (26 miles) north of Katherine, 20 kilometers (12½ miles) off the Stuart Highway. ✪ **Edith Falls** is a real Eden of natural (croc-free) swimming holes bordered by red cliffs, monsoonal forest, and pandanus trees. A 2.6-kilometer (1½-mile) round-trip bushwalk from the Falls, which takes about 2 hours, incorporates a dip at the upper pool en route.

More than the gorge itself, the aerial views of the ravine-ridden **Arnhem Plateau,** which stretches uninhabited to the horizon, are arresting. **North Australian Helicopters** (☎ **08/8972 1666**) does 12- and 24-minute flights over the gorge for A$75 (U.S.$48.75) and A$125 (U.S.$81.25). It also does longer flights on to Kakadu National Park.

ABORIGINAL CULTURE TOURS, HOT SPRINGS & MORE

On a one-day visit to the ✪ **Manyallaluk Aboriginal community,** a 90-minute drive southeast from Katherine, you chat with Aboriginal people about how they splice traditional ways with twentieth century living; take a guided bushwalk to look for native medicines and bush tucker like green ants (they're refreshing!); try lighting a fire with two sticks, weaving baskets, throwing spears, painting on bark, and playing a didgeridoo; take a dip in a natural water hole; and buy locally-made Aboriginal art and artifacts at better prices than you may find elsewhere. Lunch is a terrific barbecue featuring stuff like high-grade kangaroo fillet, kangaroo tail, Scotch filet steak, or barramundi cooked in paperbark on hot coals. Some visitors rush into these tours and expect the community to be a kind of Aboriginal Culture World theme park with a new attraction every 10 minutes, but that's not how it is. It's an unstructured experience (this is the community's home), so it's up to you to take part. A 1-day tour from Katherine costs A$132 (U.S.$85.80) for adults and A$71.50 (U.S.$46.48) for children 6 to 15, or A$99 (U.S.$64.35) adults and A$60.50 (U.S.$39.33) for children if you drive yourself. The last 35 kilometers (22 miles) of road is unsealed (unpaved), for which rental cars will be insured only if they are 4WD. The tour runs Monday through Friday from April to September; check to see what is happening in the Wet. You can camp overnight for A$5 (U.S.$3.25) adults, A$3 (U.S.$1.95) children, or A$15 (U.S.$9.75) double for a powered site. Call **Manyallaluk: The Dreaming Place** (☎ **08/8975 4727**).

The Manyallaluk community also does a 2-day experience on request, for small groups, subject to availability. Spend the first day doing the activities above, camp overnight, and the next day exploring areas by 4WD rarely seen by white folk, visiting ancient rock art sites and swimming at a remote waterfall. The price is negotiable, but you're looking at a lead-in of A$400 (U.S.$260) per person. Book ahead.

In the 500 million-year-old **Cutta Cutta Caves** (☎ **08/8972 1940**), 29 kilometers (18 miles) south of Katherine off the Stuart Highway, you will see limestone stalagmites and stalactites and maybe glimpse the resident Orange Horseshoe and Ghost bats. You must take a 1-hour tour to see the caves; they depart six times a day from 9am and cost A$9.50 (U.S.$6.18) for adults, A$4.50 (U.S.$2.93) for children 5 to 15.

One hundred and ten kilometers (69 miles) south of Katherine on the Stuart Highway is the town of **Mataranka** (pop. 665), where you can soak at the ✪ **Mataranka Thermal Pools.** These manmade pools are fed by 34°C (93°F) spring water, which bubbles up from the earth at a rate of 16,495 liters (4123¾ gallons) per minute! It's a little paradise, surrounded by palms, pandanus, and a colony of flying foxes. The pools are open 24 hours, and admission is free. They are 7 kilometers (4 miles) along Homestead Road, which is off the highway 1½ kilometers (1 mile) south of Mataranka township. The pools are within the grounds of **Mataranka Homestead Tourist Resort** (☎ **08/8975 4544**), less a resort than a low-key collection of motel rooms, cabins, campgrounds, a restaurant or two, and a très casual bar. While you're here, inspect some re-created Aboriginal "gunyahs," or bark shelters, and a replica of the slab-hut Elsey Homestead (see below). From May to September a free homestead tour operates daily at 11am. The homestead and pools lie within the 13,840-hectare (34,185-acre) **Elsey National Park.** A sealed road winds from the homestead along the banks of the Roper River, where there are swimming holes and walking trails, including a shaded 4-kilometer (2½ miles) trail into **Mataranka Falls.** *Note:* Ask the homestead to direct you to croc-free swimming areas. The homestead sells handlines to fish for barramundi and rents canoes.

Back in town, you can soak your cares away at the pleasantly warm **Katherine Hot Springs,** under shady trees 3 kilometers (2 miles) from town on Riverbank Drive. Entry is free. At the **School of the Air,** Giles Street (☎ **08/8972 1833**), you can sit in on an 800,000-square-kilometer (262,400-sq.-mile) "classroom" as children from the Outback do their lessons by radio. Forty-five minute tours begin on the hour from 9am up to and including 2pm (there's no tour at noon). Tours also run during school holidays and public holidays minus the on-air classes. The school is open Monday through Friday 9am to 3pm from mid-March until mid-December. Admission is A$5 (U.S.$3.25) for adults and A$2 (U.S.$1.30) for school-age kids.

Mike Keighley of **Far Out Adventures** (☎ **08/8972 2552**) runs numerous eco- and cultural-tours around Katherine. One of his best is his "Never Never" tour, an all-day chill-out on a beautiful patch of the 5,000 square kilometer (1,930 sq. mile) ✪ **Elsey Station,** 140 kilometers (88 miles) southeast of Katherine, made famous as the setting of the Aussie book and film *We of the Never Never.* Meet children of the Mangarrayi Aboriginal people, sample bush tucker, learn a little bush medicine, and swim in a vine-clad natural "spa-pool" in the Roper River. The day costs A$200 (U.S.$130) adults, A$150 (U.S.$97.50) children 5 to 15. Mike has been accepted as an honorary family member of the Mangarrayi people and is a mine of information about Aboriginal culture and the bush. He can extend this trip into an overnight camp/canoe safari to Elsey Falls and the water lilies on Red Lily Lagoon.

Mike also runs croc-spotting campfire cruises on the Katherine River Monday, Wednesday, and Friday through Sunday nights from April to October. They cost A$45 (U.S.$29.25) per adult and A$20 (U.S.$13) for kids, departing at 6pm from your hotel.

WHERE TO STAY & DINE

The Nitmiluk National Park ranger station in the Nitmiluk Visitor Centre has maps of available "bush campsites" throughout the park. These are very basic sites—no showers, no soaps or shampoos allowed because they pollute the river system, and simple pit toilets or none at all. Most are beside natural swimming holes. You must stop for a camping permit from the ranger station beforehand; the camping fee is A$3 (U.S.$1.95) per person per night.

Travel North (see above) runs the **Gorge Caravan Park** next to the Nitmiluk Visitor Centre. Wallabies sometimes hop into the shady grounds here. Fees are A$7 (U.S.$4.55) per adult, A$4.50 (U.S.$2.93) per child for a tent site, and A$19 (U.S.$12.35) double for a powered site.

Knotts Crossing Resort. Corner Giles and Cameron sts., Katherine, NT 0850. ☎ **08/8972 2511.** Fax 08/8972 2628. www.knottscrossing.com.au. 123 units (some with shower only; cabins have adjacent private bathroom), 41 powered and unpowered campsites. A/C TV. A$75 (U.S.$48.75) double cabin; A$85 (U.S.$55.25) double "village" room; A$110–$120 (U.S.$71.50–$78) double motel room. Extra person A$10 (U.S.$6.50) adult and A$5 (U.S.$3.25) child under 16, cabin or village room; A$11–$16.50 (U.S.$7.15–$10.73) per person extra, motel room. AE, BC, DC, MC, V.

You have a choice of huge, well-furnished motel rooms, some with kitchenettes, minibars, and in-room faxes; cabins with their own private bathrooms just outside the door; or campgrounds, all located among the tropical landscaping at this low-key resort. You can also opt for "village" rooms, built in 1998 and furnished with a double bed and bunks, bathroom, kitchenette, TV, telephone and a joint verandah facing a small private garden pool with a barbecue. The cabins have no telephone but offer a little more privacy, with a kitchenette and TV. Locals meet at the casual bar beside the large pool and Jacuzzi, and Katie's Bistro is one of the smartest places to eat in town. A small sundries store doubles as a tour and car rental desk.

4 The Kimberley: A Far-Flung Wilderness

Most Aussies would be hard put to name a settlement, river, or mountain within the ✪ **Kimberley,** so rarely visited and sparsely inhabited is this wilderness. This is an old, old land of rocky plateaus stretching for thousands of square miles, jungly ravines, endless bush, crocodile-infested wetlands, boab trees with trunks shaped like bottles, lily-filled rockpools, island-strewn coastline, droughts in winter, and massive floods in summer. The dry, spreading scenery reminds me a little of Africa or India. In the Dry, the area's biggest river, the Fitzroy, is just that—bone dry—but in the Wet, its swollen banks are second only to the Amazon in the volume of water that surges to the sea. Aqua and scarlet are two colors that will hit you in the eye; a luminous aqua for the sea and the fiery scarlet of the fine soil hereabouts called "pindan". The area is famous for Wandjina-style Aboriginal rock art depicting people with circular hair-dos that look more than a little like beings from outer space. It is also known for another kind of rock art known as "Bradshaw figures," stick-like representations of human forms, which may be the oldest art on earth. Only 25,000 people live in the Kimberley's 420,000 square kilometers. That's three times the size of England.

The unofficial capital of the East Kimberley is **Kununurra.** It's a small agricultural town that serves as the gateway to wildlife river cruises; the Bungle Bungles, a massive labyrinth of beehive-shaped rock formations; and a million-acre cattle station where you can hike, fish, and cruise palm-filled gorges by day and sleep in comfy permanent safari tents or homestead rooms by night. The main town in the West Kimberley is the Outback port of **Broome,** whose waters give up the world's biggest and best South

Sea pearls. Linking Kununurra and Derby, near Broome, is the **Gibb River Road,** an isolated 4WD track through cattle station country that is becoming popular with adventure travelers. The region is home to some of Australia's best national parks, containing rock formations like the Bungle Bungles, and ancient fossilized coral reefs.

Off the West Kimberley coast is a jigsaw puzzle of 10,000 or more barely inhabited islands, the **Bonaparte** and **Buccaneer Archipelagos,** the last named in honor of the pirate's pirate, William Dampier, who sailed here in 1688. In fact, much of the appeal of the Kimberley coastline lies in the knowledge that few Westerners have clapped eyes on it since the first explorers of the 17th century.

EXPLORING THE KIMBERLEY

The Kimberley lies within Western Australia, so see "Exploring the State" at the start of chapter 10 for general tips on getting around in the state.

VISITOR INFORMATION   The **Kimberley Tourism Association**, PO BOX 554, Broome, WA 6725 (☎ **08/9193 6660;** fax 08/9193 6662; www.ebroome.com/kimberley) supplies information on the entire region. The **Kununurra Tourist Bureau** and the **Broome Tourist Bureau** (contact info listed later in this chapter) also handle enquiries on things to see and do across the entire Kimberley, and you can drop into their information offices once you arrive.

GETTING AROUND   Enormous distances, high petrol costs (often A$1 per liter or more, equivalent to U.S.$2.45 per U.S. gallon), Wet Season floods, and very limited roads and other facilities can make traveling the Kimberley expensive and time-consuming. The place has lots of attractions that are so remote that only aerial tours or charter boats can reach them. Many more sights are accessible only on unpaved roads, for which your 2WD rental car is not insured and probably can't handle, so if you do not want to rely on tours, rent a 4WD. Allow for an average speed of 60 kilometers-per-hour (37.5 mph.) on the area's rough unsealed roads, and never exceed 80 kilometers-per-hour (50 mph), as unexpected dips and smooth patches can take drivers by surprise. Most rental outfits will allow one-way rentals between Broome and Kununurra, or vice versa, at a ball-park surcharge of A$350 to $500 (U.S.$227.50–$325). Review the "Driving Safety," "What to Do if Your Vehicle Breaks Down," and "Tips for Four-Wheel Drivers" sections in chapter 2 before setting off. **Kimberley Caravan & Outback Supplies,** 65 Frederick Street, Broome (☎ **1800/645 909** in Australia, or 08/9193 5909; fax 08/9193 6878) sells and rents every piece of camping equipment you need, from tents and *mozzie* (mosquito) nets to cooking utensils. A complete set is around A$48 (U.S.$31.20) per day for two people; weekly rates are available.

Taking a guided 4WD camping or accommodated safari is a neat way to sidestep the challenges of Kimberley travel. Safaris depart Broome, Kununurra, or Darwin, and last between 2 days and 2 weeks. A popular route is the cross-Kimberley journey between Broome and Kununurra, or vice versa. If you opt for this route, look for tours that traverse the adventurous **Gibb River Road,** rather than the less interesting highway via Halls Creek and Fitzroy Crossing. Most safaris only run in the Dry Season from April/May to October/November. Respected operators include **East Kimberley Tours** (☎ **1800/682 213** in Australia or 08/9168 2213; fax 08/9168 2544; www.comswest.net.au/~ektoursb); **Kimberley Wilderness Adventures** (☎ **08/9192 5741;** fax 08/9192 5761; www.kimberleywilderness.com.au/Generalinfo.htm); **Northern Territory Adventure Tours** (☎ **08/8936 1300;** fax 08/8981 4317; www.adventuretours.com.au); and **Safari Treks** (☎ **08/9271 1271;** fax 08/9271 9901; www.safaritreks.com.au).

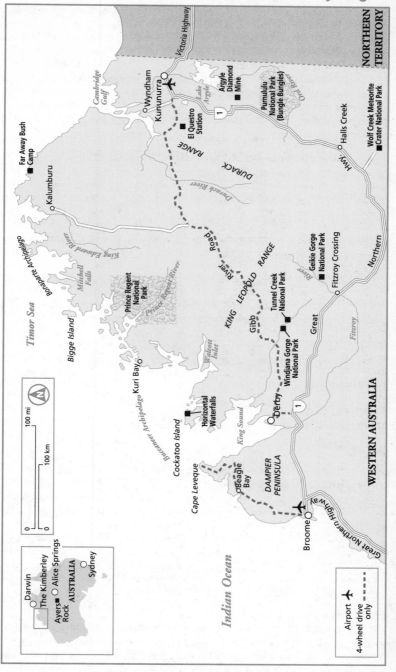

Far Away Bush Camp

Kalumburu

Kununurra

Wyndham

Victoria Highway

Argyle Diamond Mine

Purnululu National Park (Bungle Bungles)

Ord River

Lake Argyle

El Questro Station

Halls Creek

Wolf Creek Meteorite Crater National Park

Cambridge Gulf

DURACK RANGE

Durack River

Bonaparte Archipelago

King Edward River

Mitchell Falls

Prince Regent National Park

Prince Regent River

Gibb River Road

KING LEOPOLD RANGE

Tunnel Creek National Park

Windjana Gorge National Park

Geikie Gorge National Park

Fitzroy Crossing

Northern Hwy

Bigge Island

Timor Sea

Walcott Inlet

Great River

Fitzroy

WESTERN AUSTRALIA

Buccaneer Archipelago

Kuri Bay

Cockatoo Island

Horizontal Waterfalls

King Sound

Derby

Cape Leveque

Beagle Bay

DAMPIER PENINSULA

Broome

Great Northern Highway

Indian Ocean

100 mi

100 km

Darwin

The Kimberley

Alice Springs

Ayers Rock

AUSTRALIA

Sydney

Airport

4-wheel drive only

Broome Aviation (☎ **08/9192 1369;** fax 08/9192 2476; www.broomeaviation. com) and **King Leopold Air** (☎ **1800/637 155** in Australia, or 08/9193 7155; fax 08/9192 2484; www.kingleopoldair.com.au)—based in Broome—and **Alligator Airways** (☎ **08/9168 1333;** fax 08/9168 2704; www.alligatorairways.com.au) and **Slingair Heliwork** (☎ **1800/095 500** in Australia or 08/9169 1300; fax 08/9168 1129; www.slingair.com.au)—based in Kununurra—run a range of flight-seeing tours all over the Kimberley, lasting from a couple of hours to several days. Some flights incorporate sight-seeing on the ground, hiking in national parks, 4WD trips, overnights at fishing camps, or calls into vast cattle stations. Slingair offers a Kimberley Airpass.

BIRD-WATCHING & BUSHWALKING WITH CAMELS

More than one-third of Australia's bird species live in the Kimberley. The blue, green, yellow and violet Gouldian finch, Nankeen night heron, tawny frogmouth, and hundreds more get "twitchers," as locals affectionately dub bird-watchers, excited. The **Broome Bird Observatory** research station (☎ **08/9193 5600;** fax 08/9192 3364), 25 kilometers (16 miles) out of town on Roebuck Bay, monitors the thousands of migratory wetlands birds that gather here from Siberia. It offers 2-hour tours from Broome of shorebird, mangrove, and bush species, and has basic accommodations and camping facilities for real enthusiasts.

In the cooler Dry Season, bushwalking in this unspoiled environment is delightful. **Kimberley Bushwalks** (☎/fax **08/9192 7077;** www.bushwalks.com) has hit on the neat idea of using camels to carry your gear (or you can ride them). It visits places inaccessible by car or boat from Broome, such as forested parts of the Fitzroy River, into the Great Sandy Desert sandhills, through ancient springs and billabongs, and to the Ngyginah Aboriginal people in the purple Mt. Anderson ranges. Some walks are themed around stuff like learning to make didgeridoos, stargazing, or meditation and yoga. Prices start at A$120 (U.S.$78) per person for 1-day walks; treks go up to 10 days or more.

KUNUNURRA

827km (517 miles) SW of Darwin; 1,032km (645 miles) E of Broome

Given the arid conditions in the Kimberley, it's quite a surprise to swoop over a field of sugar cane as you come in to land at Kununurra. This little town (pop. 5,000) is an agricultural center created by the damming of the Ord River to form Lake Argyle.

Kununurra itself (the name is Aboriginal for "Meeting of Big Waters") has little to spark your interest, but it is the gateway to several outstanding attractions. A cruise down the Ord River to see wild birds, dramatic cliffs, and crocs is a must. So is a flight over or a hike into the Bungle Bungles (Purnululu National Park), monumental orange domes of rock that look like giant beehives. The world's biggest diamond mine is not in South Africa but out in the rugged Kimberley wilds near Kununurra, and can be visited by air every day. The town is also a gateway to El Questro, a 1 million-acre cattle station where you can hike magnificent gorges, fish, cruise rivers, ride horses, and see some of Australia's most breathtaking Aboriginal art.

ESSENTIALS

GETTING THERE **Airnorth** (☎ **08/8945 2999;** www.airnorth.com.au) flies to Kununurra from Darwin from 2 to 3 times a day and from Broome once a day.

There is no train to Kununurra. **Greyhound Pioneer** (☎ **13 20 30** in Australia) serves the town daily from Broome and daily from Darwin via Katherine. From

Broome the trip takes about 13½ hours, and the one-way fare is A$158.40 (U.S.$102.96); from Darwin, the trip time is around 9 hours, and the fare is A$118.80 (U.S.$77.22).

Kununurra is 512 kilometers (320 miles) west of Katherine on the Victoria Highway. The Great Northern Highway from Broome connects with the Victoria Highway 45 kilometers (28 miles) west of Kununurra. The Gibb River Road is an alternate 4WD scenic route from Derby near Broome (see later in this chapter); it connects with the Great Northern Highway 53 kilometers (33 miles) west of town.

VISITOR INFORMATION   The **Kununurra Tourist Bureau** is at Coolibah Drive, Kununurra, WA 6743 (☎ **08/9168 1177;** fax 08/9168 2598). Its hours change with the crowds and the season, but it usually opens from 8am to 5pm daily in the Dry. In the Wet it may operate reduced hours weekdays and may even close weekends.

GETTING AROUND   Avis (☎ **08/9169 1258**), **Budget** (☎ **08/9168 2033**), **Hertz** (☎ **08/9169 1424**), and **Territory Thrifty** (☎ **08/9169 1911**) all rent 4WD vehicles, as does local company **Handy Rentals** (☎ **08/9169 1188**). At the time of writing, no company in Kununurra rented camping gear or campervans.

WHAT TO SEE & DO

ON THE ORD RIVER   Cruise outfits will offer you the option of cruising the Ord River or Lake Argyle, a massive manmade blue inland sea ringed by stony red cliffs that could hold 19 Sydney Harbours, but go for the Ord. The Ord River is one of the most picturesque waterways in Australia, lined by bulbous red cliffs in parts, and teeming with all kinds of wetland birds and freshwater crocodiles. Jeff Haley of **Triple J. Tours** (☎ **1800/242 682** in Australia, or 08/9168 2682) runs excellent cruises along it. There are several different itineraries, but the most popular starts with a 70-kilometer (44-mile) coach ride and commentary to Lake Argyle, a wander through a historic homestead, then the 55-kilometer (34-mile) cruise back to Kununurra. The boat travels fast and is a bit noisy, but Jeff pulls in at numerous tranquil spots and does a great picnic lunch on the bank. This costs A$92 (U.S.$59.80) for adults and A$50 (U.S.$32.50) for children 4 to 15, including pickup from your hotel. Recommended.

Big Waters Kimberley Canoe Safaris (☎ **1800/641 998** in Australia, or 08/9169 1998) offers a 3-day self-guided canoeing/camping safari down the Grade 1 (that means "gentle") Ord River. The company provides transfers from Kununurra to the river, in two-person Canadian canoes, camping and cooking gear, watertight barrels, and plastic cooler boxes (called an esky in Australia); you provide the food and the sense of adventure. It costs A$135 (U.S.$87.75) per person. The company also runs an afternoon guided canoe trip for A$45 (U.S.$29.25) per person.

A day on the river to fish for barramundi with Greg Harman's **Ultimate Adventures** (☎ **08/9168 2310**) costs A$230 (U.S.$149.50) per person, if there are two of you. Greg also does trips of up to 10 days to remote fishing camps.

DIAMONDS IN THE ROUGH   Turning out 34 million carats a year—that's about eight tons of pure diamond, or one-third of total world output—the **Argyle Diamond Mine** is the only mine in the world to produce the rare pink diamond in commercial quantities, as well as champagne, cognac, yellow, green, and white rocks. During a 3½ to 4 hour visit, you will see rough and polished gems in the viewing room, see gems get extracted from the huge open-cut mine as long as safety conditions permit that day, and, if you like, buy some. For security reasons, you must join an organized aerial tour with either **Belray Diamond Tours,** and its affiliate, Alligator Airways (☎ **1800/632 533** in Australia, or 08/9168 1014) or **Slingair Heliwork**

(☎ **1800/095 500** in Australia, or 08/9169 1300). I'd recommend you opt for a flight that covers the nearby Purnululu National Park (Bungle Bungles) and Lake Argyle as well, which both companies offer for around A$325 (U.S.$211.25). Belray Diamond Tours does a coach trip Thursdays from June to September, but it's a 2½ hour drive each way. The company also does a three-day aerial/4WD trip incorporating the mine tour and camping and hiking in Purnululu National Park. Kids under 12 are not permitted on mine tours. A couple of jewelry stores in Kununurra sell Argyle diamonds.

SPENDING THE DAY AT EL QUESTRO STATION   You do not have to stay at ✪ **El Questro** (see "Where to Stay," below) to enjoy the wonderful facilities. When Englishman Will Burrell bought this one million-acre cattle station in 1991, he turned it into a kind of Outback holiday camp where anyone from the jet set to humble 4WD enthusiasts could revel in its rugged beauty. Although it's a working cattle station, guests do not really get involved in the cow side of things. Instead, they go barramundi fishing and heli-fishing in wetlands and rivers, soak under palm trees in the thermal waters of Zebedee Springs, hike the rainforest of Pentecost Gorge, take half-day 4WD fishing safaris, cruise tranquil Chamberlain Gorge, ride horses across stony plains, photograph towering red rocky ranges, join rangers on bird-watching tours, or explore a rich lode of Aboriginal rock paintings. It's an unspoiled, primeval place.

Day-trippers are welcome for A$12.50 (U.S.$8.13), plus the regular fees charged for all activities. Children 3 to 12 are half-price. The staff at El Questro's office in Kununurra, on Banksia Street, will give you a map and point out all there is to see and do, and you will find the rangers friendly and knowledgeable. Pay there or at the station store near the campground (see "Where to Stay," below), where you can buy basic supplies and fuel and rent 4WDs and camping gear. Most activities depart here. The station does organized day trips from Kununurra for A$135 (U.S.$87.75) per person. Ask staff to identify which swimming spots are croc-free, and don't swim anywhere else!

You pay for most activities—between A$12.50 (U.S.$8.13) (the park entrance fee) to walk Emma Gorge and A$395 (U.S.$256.75) for a half-day's heli-fishing. A typical price is A$37 (U.S.$24.05) for a gorge cruise. Guests at Emma Gorge will usually pay A$12 (U.S.$7.80) roundtrip to transfer to join tours and activities departing the station store. The tour desk also arranges such off-station activities as day trips on the Ord River, to the Argyle diamond mine and the Bungle Bungles, and extended tours throughout the Kimberley as far afield as Broome.

WHERE TO STAY
At El Questro
✪ **El Questro.** Gibb River Rd., 100 (63 miles) southwest of Kununurra (P.O. Box 909, Kununurra, WA 6743). ☎ **08/9169 1777.** Fax 08/9169 1383. www.elquestro.com.au. sales@elquestro.com.au. See below for lodging options. AE, BC, DC, MC, V. 4WD transfers from Kununurra cost A$90–$100 (U.S.$58.50–$65) per adult round-trip; children 3–12 half-price. Take the Great Northern Highway 58km (36 miles) toward Wyndham, then the (unsealed) Gibb River Road 26km (16 miles) to Emma Gorge Resort, or a further 23km (14 miles) to the station store.

Apart from the prohibitively expensive upscale homestead, there are other accommodation options at the station, as described below.

El Questro Bungalows. See contact details above. 12 bungalows, all with bathroom (shower only). A/C. A$170 (U.S.$110.50) double. Extra person A$32–33 (U.S.$20.80–$21.45). The Bungalows are 90 min. by road from Kununurra.

These basic but comfortable rooms located by the store at the heart of the station operations are good for families, or anyone without their own transport. Some have single beds and bunks, while 8 new ones are quite spiffy with stylish queen-size beds and balconies overlooking the Pentecost River. The Steakhouse restaurant and bar serves three meals a day, such as "barra burgers." A swimming hole is nearby.

Black Cockatoo Riverside Camping: Forty-five riverside camp locations near the station store are available for a nightly charge of A$16.50 (U.S.$10.73) per adult (less in the Wet season), and free for children under 12. Campers share shower facilities and use the bungalows' restaurant. More secluded riverside campsites are a 10-minute drive.

Emma Gorge Resort. See contact details above. 35 tent cabins (17 with bathroom). A$133–$198 (U.S.$86.45–$128.70) double, A$30 (U.S.$19.50) children 3–12, A$192.50 (U.S.$124.80) family tent with 1 double and 2 single beds. Emma Gorge is 1 hr. by road from Kununurra.

This neatly kept oasis of permanent tents around lush lawns under pandanus palms at the foot of the soaring red Cockburn Range is a great way to "camp" in the wilderness without sacrificing comfort. Although they are "only" tents, the accommodations are very comfortable, for they have a wooden floor, electric lights, a standing fan, insect screens, nice firm twin beds, a bedside table, and a torch (flashlight) for getting around at night. Those without bathrooms share clean and modern facilities. Reception stocks sundries and souvenirs and lends hair dryers. The bush verandah restaurant and bar serves up gourmet bush tucker meals that would put many big city restaurants to shame. There's a manmade swimming pool, but most folks walk the 1.6-kilometer (1-mile) trail along lush Emma Gorge to the natural swimming hole and trickling waterfall enclosed by 46-meter (150-ft.) cliffs. This walk is free to guests.

In Kununurra

Country Club Hotel. 47 Coolibah Drive, Kununurra, WA 6743. ☎ **08/9168 1024.** Fax 08/9168 1189. www.countryclubhotel.com.au. 88 units, all with bathroom (8 with tub). A/C TV TEL. Dry Season A$154 (U.S.$100.10) double, A$203.50 (U.S.$132.23) apt. Wet Season A$132 (U.S.$85.80) double, A$170.50 (U.S.$110.83) apt. Extra person A$22 (U.S.$14.30). Children under 17 stay free in parents' room. AE, BC, DC, MC, V.

Located just down the road from the tourist bureau, this lowrise Flag motel is the best equipped of Kununurra's modest inventory. Nestled among tropical gardens, it has a lovely shaded pool with loungechairs and poolside dining, a Chinese restaurant, an all-day grill restaurant, and a couple of bars. The rooms are neat, clean and modern, with plenty of space. Front desk acts as a tour desk, and loans hair dryers.

PURNULULU (BUNGLE BUNGLES) NATIONAL PARK

Rising out of the landscape 250 kilometers (156 miles) south of Kununurra are thousands of enormous sandstone domes 200 to 300 meters (656–984 ft.) high called the ✪ **Bungle Bungles.** Thought to be named either after "bundle bundle" grass or the bungle beetle, the Bungle Bungles get their distinctive orange and gray stripes from algae found in the permeable layers and mineral graining in non-permeable layers. The formations are 360 million years old.

The domes look spectacular from the air—and that's the only way to see them in the Wet, as the park is closed to ground traffic January 1 through March 31. As the waters subside (sometimes not until early June, and they may swell again in late October), the soaring gorges and forested creeks at the base of the Bungle Bungles are accessible on foot. Highlights are the beehive-shaped walls of **Cathedral Gorge,** the rock pool at **Frog Hole Gorge,** and palm-filled **Echidna Chasm.** Keep an eye peeled for rainbow bee-eaters, flocks of budgerigars, rare nailtail wallabies, and euros, a kind of kangaroo.

There are several campgrounds with pit toilets, wood barbecues, and water (boil before drinking) but no showers and no telephones. The camping fee is A$7 (U.S.$4.55) for adults, A$1 (U.S.65¢) for kids under 16. Bring food and fuel with you. For information call the state **Department of Conservation and Land Management (CALM)** (☎ 08/9168 0200) in Kununurra; there is a ranger station in the park during the season.

GETTING THERE & GETTING AROUND   Most folks take a scenic flight over the park in a light aircraft or helicopter from Kununurra for about A$200 (U.S.$130). The flight takes about 2 hours. Contact **Slingair Heliwork** (☎ **1800/095 500** in Australia, or 08/9169 1300) or **Alligator Airways** (☎ **1800/632 533** in Australia, or 08/9168 1333). Both also do a combined air/hiking day trip. Alligator Airways does a 3-day aerial/hiking/camping trip incorporating the Argyle diamond mine tour.

Road access is 4WD only. To explore by car, you will need at least one night to explore Purnululu's 3,000 square kilometers (1,158 sq. miles); entry is A$8 (U.S.$5.20) per vehicle. Take the Victoria Highway 45 kilometers (28 miles) west of Kununurra, turn left onto the Great Northern Highway for 201 kilometers (126 miles) to the park turnoff, and allow 2 hours to cover the final tough 53 kilometers (33 miles) from the highway to the park entrance. Turkey Creek, 53 kilometers (33 miles) north of the turnoff, is the nearest place for supplies.

Several companies offer 4WD hiking/camping safaris from Kununurra lasting 2 to 4 days. A 2-day adventure with **Bungle Bungles Adventure Tours** (☎ **1800/641 998** in Australia, or 08/9169; fax 08/9168 3998) costs A$260 (U.S.$169).

DRIVING THE GIBB RIVER ROAD

If you really want to discover the Outback, mate, the Gibb River Road is for you. Traversing this sandy, rocky, unpaved 660-kilometer (413-mile) 4WD track that links the east and west Kimberley is fast becoming a "must-do" for seasoned adventure travelers. Populated only by stark red ranges, rivers that flood to the horizon in the Wet and vanish to dustbowls in the Dry, fern-fringed swimming holes and waterfalls, and huge cattle stations, it is a road for self-reliant folk who seek wilderness and know how to change a tire. Homesteads along the way offer activities such as barramundi fishing in lilyclad water holes, hikes through gorges, and aerial tours to remote Prince Regent Nature Reserve, King's Cascade, Mitchell Falls, the Horizontal Waterfalls, and other spots on the north Kimberley Coast. Some serve meals and have basic accommodations, ranging from campsites with hot showers to rooms at the homestead. They ain't the lap of luxury, but neither is the road. Expect ribbed "corrugation" on the gravel, soft patches, and bumpy rocks that will limit your speed to 60 kilometers per hour (37.5 mph) or slower much of the way. It's possible to drive the road in 2 days or even one, but give yourself 3 to 5 days to do some sightseeing. *Note:* you can only count on the road being passable from May to October; much of it is under water in the Wet.

The road starts on the Great Northern Highway, 53 kilometers (33 miles) west of Kununurra. **El Questro Station** (see "Where to Stay" in the Kununurra section above) is the first stop, 33 kilometers (21 miles) along. It finishes in **Derby**, a small coastal town 221 kilometers (138 miles) northeast of Broome. The Great Northern Highway connects Derby with Broome. **Windjana Gorge** and **Tunnel Creek National Parks** (described in this chapter) are accessed off the road.

To drive the road in a rented 4WD, you will need written permission from your rental car company. Carry cash (forget about ATMs out here, and travelers' checks are not always accepted), spare fuel, enough drinking water and food to last three or four days longer than you think you'll need, a tool kit, a tire puncture repair kit and a high lift jack, a spare tire, radiator hoses, a spare fan belt, and a first aid kit. Your rental car company should provide all of this, except your supplies. If you want to stay in rooms rather than in the campground, book ahead. Even so, carry camping gear in case tire punctures, swollen creeks, or some other circumstance holds you up between homesteads. Some homesteads are private farms not open to the public, and their owners take a dim view of poorly prepared tourists begging them for water, fuel, or food. Swim only where the locals tell you, on account of crocodiles.

Before setting off, obtain a copy of the A$3 (U.S.$1.95) *Gibb River And Kalumburu Road Travellers Guide,* published by the Derby Tourist Bureau and updated every year, that lists accommodations, the very few fuel stops, and other facilities along the way. It is available from the tourist bureaus in Kununurra and Broome, or you can order it in advance from the bureau (☎ **91/911 426;** derbytb@comswest.net.au).

Plenty of 4WD safari tours operate on the road between Broome and Kununurra, and even from Darwin, taking between 5 and 10 days. See "Exploring the Kimberley" on p. 408 for companies to contact.

TUNNEL CREEK & WINDJANA GORGE NATIONAL PARKS

Windjana Gorge National Park is 240 kilometers (150 miles) east of Broome, 21 kilometers (13 miles) off the Gibb River Road. The 350 million-year-old walls of the gorge, which shoot straight up as high as 100 meters (328 ft.) above the sandy desert floor, are an old limestone barrier reef. A picturesque 7-kilometer (4-mile) round-trip trail winds through the gorge, revealing fossilized marine creatures from the Devonian period. This reef is part of a much larger barrier reef—comprising hundreds of coral patches, some a couple of miles across, other hundreds of miles wide—created when this part of Australia was an ocean floor. As the ocean subsided, those coral-building creatures kept on building their reefs higher. When the ocean floor pushed up above sea level, the reefs were left high and dry and became the **Napier Ranges.** The **Lennard River,** which carved Windjana Gorge, only flows in the Wet, but freshwater crocodiles, fruit bats, and birds are common year-round in and around the residual pools.

Thirty kilometers (19 miles) southeast of Windjana Gorge is **Tunnel Creek National Park,** where you can explore a cave tunneled by the river through the ancient limestone reef system. To reach it, you wade through the creek for 750 meters (about half a mile) in the dark. Before you leave Broome, ask your hotel to lend you a torch (flashlight) to reveal the tunnel's stalactites, fish, five bat species including rare ghost bats, and even the odd freshwater croc (the "friendly" sort). Wear shoes you can get wet, and expect the water to be cold!

GETTING THERE & GETTING AROUND   You can include Windjana and Tunnel Creek on a Gibb River Road safari, or visit from Broome. Take the Great Northern Highway east for 187 kilometers (117 miles), take a left onto the Derby Highway for 43 kilometers (27 miles) to Derby, then head east along the Gibb River Road. Note: The last 70 kilometers (44 miles) to Windjana, and from there to Tunnel Creek, is unpaved, so you will need a 4WD. Both parks are usually closed in the Wet from November or December to mid-April.

Camping at Windjana Gorge costs A$7 (U.S.$4.55) for adults, A$1 (U.S.65¢) for kids under 16. The campground has cold showers, toilets, barbecues and wood, and a public telephone, but no food or fuel. There is no camping, food, water, or ranger station in Tunnel Creek National Park. Neither park has an entry fee. Coach and 4WD day tours run from Broome.

For park information, and to check accessibility and road conditions outside June to September, call the state **Department of Conservation and Land Management (CALM)** in Broome (☎ **08/9192 1036**).

GEIKIE GORGE NATIONAL PARK

Freshwater versions of saltwater beasties such as sharks, sawfish, and stingrays lurk in the Fitzroy River, which flows through Geikie Gorge (pronounced *Geekie*). Although strictly speaking, the gorge is part of an ancient Devonian reef, like Windjana Gorge and Tunnel Creek, its gold and grey 30-meter (98-ft.) walls were built not by coral but by algae. Like Windjana Gorge, its walls show primitive life forms that inhabited a time before reptiles and mammals were around. Today, pandanus palms, wild passion fruit, mangroves, and river gums line the banks, and freshwater crocodiles and all kinds of birds can be seen, especially in the Dry. If you spot a stream of water arching out of the river, that's an archer fish targeting an insect by spitting at it. There are moves afoot to dam the mighty Fitzroy, which makes sense to some farmers, but will wreak havoc on the ecology of fish and rare birds and flood Aboriginal cultural sites.

The most popular way to experience the park is on a wildlife and geology cruise with the park rangers. They conduct four 1-hour cruises each day, fewer in the seasonal cusp around April/May and September/October. Cruises cost A$17.50 (U.S.$11.38) for adults, and just A$2 (U.S.$1.30) for school-age kids. Bookings are not needed. There are also two walking trails to explore, a 1-hour round-trip "reef" trail along the base of the gorge wall, and a 20-minute walk along the river bank to a fishing and swimming hole.

Cruises run April to November; the gorge is open but may be cut off by floods December to March. There are picnic facilities (buy food in Fitzroy Crossing), but no camping.

For inquiries on the cruise schedule and any other matters, call the **Department of Conservation and Land Management (CALM)** in Fitzroy Crossing (☎ **08/9191 5121**) or in the Dry season at the gorge (☎ **08/9191 5112**).

GETTING THERE & GETTING AROUND Entry to the park is free. The gorge is 418 kilometers (261 miles) east of Broome, so be prepared for a long day. The road is paved all the way. Take care with the water level on the several concrete fords. The nearest town is **Fitzroy Crossing,** 18 kilometers (11 miles) before the entrance (☎ **08/9191 5355** is the Fitzroy Crossing Tourist Bureau). No rangers are based in the park during the Wet. Coach and 4WD day tours are available from Broome.

BROOME

2,250 kilometers (1,406 miles) N of Perth; 1,859 kilometers (1,161 miles) SW of Darwin

Part rough Outback town, part glam seaside resort, the pearling port of ✪ **Broome** (pop. 11,000) is a fascinating mixture of Australia and Asia. Chinese and Japanese pearl divers used to work the pearling luggers in this isolated little town in the old days, and as the Chinese settled here they affixed their architecture to typical Australian buildings. The result is a main street so cute it could be a movie set, with rows of Australian corrugated iron stores wrapped by verandahs and trimmed with Chinese peaked roofs. The people are a unique mixture, too, as Anglo-Saxon/Irish Aussies and Chinese, Filipino and Malayan pearl workers often married Aboriginal women. The Japanese tended to return home rather than settle here, but not all of them made it. Cyclones, the "bends," sharks, and crocodiles all took their toll. The Japanese legacy in the town is a rather eerie **divers' cemetery** with Asian inscriptions on 900 rough-hewn headstones, incongruously surrounded by the Aussie bush.

For such a small and remote place, Broome is surprisingly sophisticated. Walk the streets of Chinatown and you will rub shoulders with Aussie tourists, itinerant workers, Asian food store proprietors, tough-as-nails cattle hands, and well-heeled visitors from Europe and America downing good coffee at the couple of trendy cafes. Broome's world-renowned South Sea pearls are still its bread and butter, but the old timber pearling luggers have been replaced with gleaming high-tech vessels equipped with helipads and stainless steel security doors.

To be honest, it's hard to explain Broome's appeal. There is not all that much to do here really, but it is somehow just a nice place to be. You can shop for pearls, of course, and it's a good base for exploring the wider Kimberley, but most people come to laze by the jade-green Indian Ocean on Cable Beach, ride camels along the sand as the sun plops into the sea, fish the unplundered seas, and soak up the gorgeous reds, blues and greens of the Kimberley coast.

ESSENTIALS

GETTING THERE   **Airlink** (book through Qantas) flies from Perth 6 times a week, and has a couple of flights a week from both Alice Springs and Darwin. The trip to Broome from Sydney and other state capitals is a lengthy affair via Perth, or via Alice Springs and Darwin. **Airnorth** (☎ **08/8945 2999**; www.airnorth.com.au) flies to Bromme from Darwin once or twice daily, and from Kununurra.

Greyhound Pioneer (☎ **13 20 30** in Australia) has a daily service from Perth that takes around 32 hours and extra express services some days that take around 27 hours. The fare is A$266 (U.S.$172.90). Greyhound's daily service from Darwin via Katherine and Kununurra takes around 24 hours; the one-way fare is A$230 (U.S.$149.50).

There is no train service to Broome.

Broome is 34 kilometers (21 miles) off the Great Northern Highway, which leads from Perth in the south, Kununurra to the east. The Gibb River Road is an alternate 4WD scenic route from Kununurra (see "Driving the Gibb River Road," above).

VISITOR INFORMATION   **The Broome Tourist Bureau** is on the Great Northern Highway (locals call it the Broome Highway) at Bagot Street, Broome, WA 6725 (☎ **08/9192 2222;** fax 08/9192 2063; www.ebroome.com/tourism). In the Dry, it's open Monday through Friday 8am to 5pm, and Saturday and Sunday 9am to 4pm; in the Wet, it's open Monday through Friday 9am to 5pm, Saturday, Sunday and public holidays 9am to 1pm.

Book accommodation and tours well ahead in the peak June to August season.

GETTING AROUND   **ATC Rent A Car** (☎ 08/9193 7788); **Avis** (☎ 08/9193 5980), **Broome Car Rentals** (☎ 1800/676 725 in Australia, or 08/9192 2210), **Budget** (☎ 08/9193 5355), **Hertz** (☎ 08/9192 1428), and **Thrifty** (☎ 08/9193 6787) all rent cars and 4WDs. For campervans or 4WD campers, contact ATC Rent A Car (above; fax 08/9193 6693); or **THL Rentals** (☎ 08/9192 2647; fax 08/9192 2648) who are agents for Britz, Koala and Maui campervans.

The **Town Bus** (☎ **08/9193 6000**) does an hourly loop of most attractions from 7.20am to 6:15pm daily, more often in the middle of the day in the Dry. A single fare is A$2.50 (U.S.$1.65), and a day pass is A$8 (U.S.$5.20).

Broome Taxis (☎ **08/9192 1133**) operates the airport shuttle to your hotel door. For a cab call **Roebuck Taxis** (☎ **1800/880 330**).

Broome Day Tours (☎ **1800/801 068** in Australia or 08/9192 1068) runs tours of the town and further afield to gorges and other natural attractions. **Over the Top Adventure Tours** (☎ **08/9192 3977**) runs 1- and 2-day 4WD tours to hard-to-get-to wilderness spots like the Dampier Peninsula.

WHAT TO SEE & DO: PEARLS, CAMEL RIDES, OUTDOOR MOVIES & MORE

When you arrive, head to Chinatown in the town center on Carnarvon Street and Dampier Terrace to get a feel for the town. It's not all that Chinese anymore, but most shops, cafes, and galleries are here. The Broome Tourist Bureau gives out maps to a 2-kilometer (1¼ mile) trail taking in the town's historic buildings.

Probably the most popular Dry Season "activity" is lazing on the 22 glorious white sandy kilometers (14 miles) of ✪ **Cable Beach.** The beach is 6 kilometers (3¾ miles) out of town; the town bus runs there regularly. A beach hut near **Cable Beach Inter-Continental Resort** rents beach and watersports equipment in the Dry. From November to April the water is off-limits due to marine stingers. Crocodiles, on the other hand, do not like surf so you should be safe swimming here. Make a point of being at the beach for at least one of the magnificently rosy sunsets in the Dry. A novel way to experience the beach is on camelback. A 1-hour ride with **Red Sun Camel Safaris** (☎ **08/9193 7423,** or 0419/954 996) costs A$33 (U.S.$21.45) adults, A$22 (U.S.$14.30) kids 11 to 15 and A$11 (U.S.$7.15) for kids 5 to 10. Reigning four-time state surf champ **Josh Parmateer** (☎ **0418/958 264**) gives 2-hour surf lessons on the beach from July to September for A$80 (U.S.$52) per person, or A$30 (U.S.$19.50) per person for 2 hours if there are two of you. He supplies the boards, wetsuits and a guarantee you'll be standing by the end of the lesson!

Definitely drop by the **Pearl Luggers,** 44 Dampier Terrace (☎ **08/9192 2059**). A 75-minute session here includes a look over two restored Broome pearling luggers, a browse through a small well-equipped pearling museum, and a riveting and hilarious talk about pearl diving as it used to be by former First Divers, Richard "Salty" Baillieu or Steve "Zimmo" Zimmerle. Don't miss it. Admission is A$15 (U.S.$9.75) adults, A$13.50 (U.S.$8.78) seniors and students, A$9 (U.S.$5.85) for children 8 to 17. The attraction opens 9am to 5pm May to October, 10am to about 2:30pm November to April; tours run 9:30am, 11am, 1pm and 3pm in the Dry, and 11am and 1pm in the Wet. Closed Christmas.

A dinosaur footprint 120 million years old is on show at very low tide on the cliff at **Gantheaume Point,** 6 kilometers (3¾ miles) from town. The town authorities have set a plaster cast of it higher up on the rocks, so you can see it anytime. Take a picture of the point's palette of glowing red cliffs, white beach and turquoise water.

You should also take a peek at the haunting **Japanese pearl divers' cemetery** on Port Drive. Entry is free.

During a tour of the **Willie Creek Pearl Farm** (☎ **08/9193 6000**), 38 kilometers (24 miles) north of town, you will see the delicate process of an oyster getting "seeded" with a nucleus to form a pearl, and learn about pearl farming firsthand from the managers. The tour costs A$25 (U.S.$16.25) adults, A$12 (U.S.$7.80) children 5 to 15.

Stairway to the Moon

You've heard of a stairway to heaven? Well, Broome has a stairway to the moon. On the happy coincidence of a full moon and a low 10-meter tide (which happens about 3 consecutive nights a month from March to October), nature treats the town to a special show as the light of the rising moon falls on the rippled sand and mudflats in Roebuck Bay, looking for all the world like a "staircase to the moon." The best place to see it is from the cliff-top restaurant at the Mangrove Hotel (see "Where to Stay & Dine", below), or from the food and craft markets held at Town Beach most staircase nights.

Book first. The road to the farm is 4WD-only and tides can cut it off; coach tours operate here costing A$55 (U.S.$35.75) for adults and A$27.50 (U.S.$17.88) for kids.

The daily croc-feeding session is the best time to visit the **Malcolm Douglas Broome Crocodile Park,** next to Cable Beach Inter-Continental Resort, Cable Beach Rd. (☎ **08/9192 1489**).

Several art galleries sell vivid oil and watercolor Kimberley landscapes and a small range of Aboriginal art. **Matso's,** 60 Hamersley St. (☎ **08/9193 5811**), stocks the biggest range of European and Aboriginal paintings, sculpture, pottery, carvings and books in an historic pearling master's house, and has a lovely verandah cafe and boutique brewery turning out unusual recipes like chili beer. It opens daily from 10am to 5pm, meals from 8am.

On Saturday from 8am to 1pm, browse the **markets** in the gardens of the colonial Courthouse at the corner of Frederick and Hamersley Streets. It used to be the official station for the cable from Broome to Java. Don't bet the ranch on this tale being gospel, but locals like to tell you that when the British authorities packed up the building materials for the courthouse in Britain and addressed it to "The Kimberley," they meant them to end up in the Kimberley, South Africa. Instead, the stuff arrived in the Kimberley, Australia. The town kept the building, and so can proudly lay claim to having Australia's only Zulu-proof courthouse.

A number of boats run sunset cruises on Roebuck Bay or off Cable Beach. Fishing for trevally, Spanish mackerel, barracuda, barramundi, queenfish, tuna, shark, sailfish, marlin, salmon (May–Aug), and reef fish is excellent around Broome; fly and sport fishing is also worth a try. Rent tackle and try your luck from the deep-water jetty near **Town Beach** 2 kilometers (1¼ miles) south of town, or join one of charter boats running day trips. **FAD Game Fishing Charters** (☎ **08/9192 3998**) and **Lucky Strike Charters** (☎ **08/9193 7375**) are two of the respected ones. Cyclones, rain, high winds, and strong tides can restrict fishing from December to March.

Australia's First Family of pearling, the Paspaleys, sell their wonderfully elegant jewelry at **Paspaley Pearls,** Carnarvon Street at Short Street (☎ **08/9192 2203**). **Linney's** and **Broome Pearls** are two other reputable jewelers nearby.

Don't leave without taking in a recent-release movie at the adorable **Sun Pictures** outdoor cinema, Carnarvon Street near Short Street (☎ **08/9192 1077**). Built in 1916, these are the oldest "picture gardens" in the world, where the audience sits in (saggy) canvas deckchairs. Films are even screened through the rain in the Wet. Tickets are A$11 (U.S.$7.15). Open nightly except Christmas.

WHERE TO STAY & DINE

As well as in-hotel dining, head over to the **Cable Beach Inter-Continental Resort,** Cable Beach Road (☎ **1800/095 508** in Australia) for Broome's greatest range of menus. There's Pandanus for elegant dinners in a pond-side setting; Sketches pasta bar; all-day dining inside or on the terrace at the casual colonial-style Lord Mac's; the Kimberley Grill for steaks and stuff; and the Walking Wok for Mongolian stir-fries. The last two both close in the Wet.

✪ **The Kimberley Club.** 62 Frederick St., Broome, WA 6725. ☎ **08/9192 3233.** Fax 08/9192 3530. 50 quad-share dorm beds, 24 private units. A$17–$19 (U.S.$11.05–$12.35) dorm bed; A$65 (U.S.$42.25) double. AE, BC, DC, MC, V. Free pickup from Greyhound Pioneer terminal.

This stylish new Outback-style lodge within walking distance of town might be aimed at the backpacker market, but travelers of all persuasions will like its clean private rooms furnished simply with a double or twin beds and two bunks. You share the clean new shower/toilet facilities, and can rent towels for A$2 (U.S.$1.30) for the duration of your stay. The air-conditioning is coin-operated at A$1 (U.S.65¢) for 4 hours, although you are unlikely to need it in the Dry, thanks to some clever airflow work by the architects. The rooms are spartan (no TV, no tea and coffee, no fridge, no sink), but you will spend most of your time around the rock-lined pool and the large, rustic open-sided dining area. The crowd is always friendly, so this is a great spot to socialize and meet other travelers. There's a TV lounge, Internet access, a small volleyball court, pool tables, Ping-Pong, a communal kitchen, and a tour desk with an emphasis on fun, cheap, and exciting activities. The Fat Time Bar serves hearty meals like Thai green chicken curry or lasagna for A$8 (U.S.$5.20). You need to like loud music to stay here, but it's lights-out at 11pm, so everyone gets some sleep. Excellent value for the money.

Mangrove Hotel. 120 Carnarvon St., Broome, WA 6725. ☎ **1800/094 818** in Australia or 08/9192 1303. Fax 08/9193 5169. www.mangrovehotel.com.au. mangrovehotel@bigpond. com. 67 units, all with bathroom (2 with Jacuzzi, one with tub). A/C TV TEL. High season (Apr–Oct) A$143–$165 (U.S.$92.95–$107.25) double, A$220 (U.S.$143) suite, A$264 (U.S.$171.60) 2-bedroom apt (sleeps 4). Low season (Nov–March) A$121–$143 (U.S.$78.65–$9.95) double, A$198 (U.S.$128.70) suite, A$242 (U.S.$157.30) 2-bedroom apt (sleeps 4). Extra person A$33 (U.S.$21.45). Children under 3 stay free in parents' room. Ask about packages in the Wet season. AE, BC, DC, MC, V. Free airport shuttle.

The best views in Broome are across Roebuck Bay from this clifftop hotel is a 5-minute walk from town. It's worth hightailing it back from sightseeing just to watch dusk fall over the bay from the lovely Tides Garden outdoor restaurant, where tables and chairs are set out on the lawns under the palms and along the cliff edge. Tides Garden is popular with locals for good, affordable food, and Charter's restaurant inside is one of Broome's best. There's no faulting the clean, well-kept standard rooms, the ultra-roomy deluxe rooms with sea views (a good value), the two suites that have a Jacuzzi, and the two-bedroom apartment. All have hair dryers and iron and board. Two swimming pools and two Jacuzzis set in the lawns overlooking the bay, room service, and a tour desk are among the amenities. The town bus stop is across the road.

Perth & Western Australia

by Natalie Kruger and Marc Llewellyn

Many international visitors—heck, many Australians!—never make the trek to Western Australia. It's too far away, expensive to fly to, too big when you get there, they say. That is all true, especially the bit about it being big (it's 2.5 million sq. km, or 965,000 sq. miles) but don't dismiss a trip out of hand. Flights need not be expensive (if you're an international traveler flying on air pass coupons—see chapter 2), and some of Australia's best snorkeling and diving, cutest historic towns, most splendid scenery, and fantastic wine regions are here. Every spring (Sept–Nov Down Under) the state offers an unbelievable profusion of wildflowers almost everywhere. The capital, Perth, has great food, a fabulous outdoor life of biking and beaches, plenty of museums that are well worth a look, and a beautiful historic port called Fremantle.

The Southwest "hook" of the state, below Perth, is thought by many to be the loveliest part of Western Australia, and also the easiest region to visit outside Perth. Massive stands of karri and jarrah trees stretch to the sky, the surf is world-class, and the coastline wave-smashed and rugged. If you think trees, surf, and cliffs are a tad ho-hum, you can tour the area's wineries. The Southwest's Margaret River region is responsible for turning out some of Australia's finest reds and whites.

Head east 400 miles inland from Perth and you strike what, in the 1890s, was the richest square mile of gold-bearing earth ever found in the world. The mining town of Kalgoorlie, Australia's biggest gold producer, fuses ornate 19th-century architecture with a zeal for pumping out near 2,000 ounces of gold a day in the twenty-first century. If Australia has an iconic country town then Kalgoorlie is it.

Once you drive north of Perth past Geraldton on the Midwest coast, you know you're in the Outback. Orange sand, scrubby trees, and spiky grass called spinifex are all you see for hundreds of miles. About 850 kilometers (531 miles) north of Perth is a special phenomenon: daily visits by wild dolphins to the shores of Monkey Mia. Another 872 kilometers (545 miles) on is one of Australia's best-kept secrets, a 260-kilometer (163-mile) coral reef called Ningaloo, stretching along the isolated Outback shore. It's a second Great Barrier Reef, barely discovered by world travelers or Aussies themselves. The reef is making a name for itself as a whale shark habitat, where you can swim with these mysterious 12-meter (40-ft.) fish-monsters every Aussie fall.

EXPLORING THE STATE

VISITOR INFORMATION The Western Australian Tourism Commission (WATC) is the official source of information on touring the state. Its website (www. westernaustralia.net) provides an overview but not a thorough rundown on what to see and do. It may be better to go to or write to the WATC's **Western Australian Tourist Centre,** Albert Facey House, 469 Wellington St., on the corner of Forrest Place (☎ **1300/361 351** in Australia, or 08/9483 1111; fax 08/9481 0190). They can send you maps and brochures, give advice, and make bookings. It's open Monday through Thursday 8:30am to 6pm (5pm in winter), Friday 8:30am to 7pm (6pm in winter), Saturday 8:30am to 5pm, and Sunday from 10am to 5pm (3pm in winter).

A good source of ideas for nature-based activities and attractions in the state's national and marine parks is the **"W.A. Naturally" centre,** 47 Henry St., Fremantle, WA 6160 (☎ **08/9430 8600;** fax 08/9430 8699), run by the state Department of Conservation and Land Management (CALM)—check out their website at www.calm.wa.gov.au. Drop by or write for information. The center is open every day except Tuesday from 10am to 5:30pm.

WHEN TO GO Perth is blessed with long, dry summers and mild wet winters. You will want warm gear in the Southwest winters, but temperatures rarely hit the freezing point.

Much north of Perth, summer is hell, when temperatures soar well into the 40s°C (over 104°F to 120°F). Avoid these parts from December to March; February is worst. Winter (June–Aug) in the mid-, northern and inland reaches of the state is pleasantly cool, sometimes even hot.

GETTING AROUND Before you plan a motoring tour of this state three times as big as Texas, consider the distance, and the mostly arid, flat, and monotonous countryside. The Southwest makes pretty motoring; elsewhere, fly, unless you want to count sheep in all those vast brown paddocks you will be whizzing through if you drive.

If you do hit the road, remember that Western Australia is largely devoid of people, gas stations (so keep the gas tank full), and emergency help. Road trains and wildlife pose a road threat more so here than in any other state, so avoid driving at night, dusk, and dawn—all prime animal feeding times. Read the "Driving Safety" section in chapter 2 before setting off.

The Royal Automobile Club of Western Australia (RACWA) (see section 13, "Getting Around Australia" in chapter 2) is a good source of maps and motoring advice. For a recorded road condition report, call the state **Main Roads Department** (☎ **1800/013 314** in Australia).

Airlink (☎ **08/9225 8383;** or book through Qantas) is a major regional airline. **Greyhound Pioneer** (☎ **13 20 30** in Australia) is the only interstate coach company serving Western Australia. It travels the highway from Adelaide over to Perth, then up the coast to Broome and across to Darwin.

The only train to Western Australia from outside the state is the *Indian Pacific* from Adelaide to Perth (see "Getting Around Australia" in chapter 2). Inside the state, long-distance trains only run in the southern third of the state. They are operated by **Westrail** (☎ **13 10 53** in Western Australia, or 08/9326 2222; fax 08/9326 2619) from Perth to Bunbury south of Perth, Northam eastwards in the Avon Valley, and Kalgoorlie. Westrail also runs connecting coach services to the Southwest and the southern coast, and as far north as Kalbarri (but not Monkey Mia) on the Midwest coast.

Western Australia

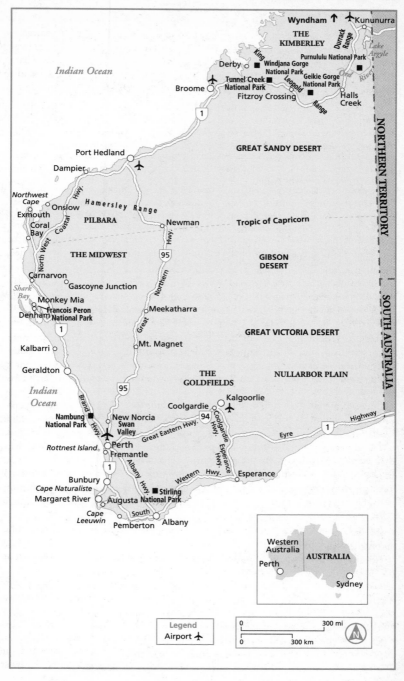

Indian Ocean

Wyndham ↑ ✈ Kununurra

**THE
KIMBERLEY**

Durrack Range

Lake Argyle

Derby ■ Windjana Gorge
National Park

Purnululu National Park ■

King

Leopold

Ord River

Tunnel Creek
National Park ■

Geikie Gorge
National Park ■

Broome ✈ ○

Fitzroy Crossing

Halls
Creek

Range

1

Port Hedland ✈

GREAT SANDY DESERT

Dampier ○

Northwest
Cape

○ Onslow

Hamersley Range

North West Coastal Hwy.

Exmouth ○
Coral Bay ○

PILBARA

Newman ○

Tropic of Capricorn

THE MIDWEST

95

**GIBSON
DESERT**

Carnarvon ○

Shark Bay

Gascoyne Junction ○

Monkey Mia ○
Francois Peron National Park ■
Denham ○

Great Northern Hwy.

Meekatharra ○

GREAT VICTORIA DESERT

1

Kalbarri ○

Mt. Magnet ○

Geraldton ○

**THE
GOLDFIELDS**

NULLARBOR PLAIN

Indian
Ocean

95

Coolgardie ○

■ Kalgoorlie ✈

Nambung
National Park ■

New Norcia
Swan
Valley

94

Coolgardie Hwy.

Great Eastern Hwy.

Eyre

Highway

1

Rottnest Island ○

✈ Perth
Fremantle ○

Albany Hwy.

Esperance Hwy.

Western Hwy.

Esperance ○

1

Bunbury ○

Cape Naturaliste ○

Stirling ■
National Park

Margaret River ○
Augusta ○

Cape
Leeuwin ○

South

Pemberton ○ Albany ○

NORTHERN TERRITORY

SOUTH AUSTRALIA

Western
Australia

AUSTRALIA

Perth ○

Sydney ○

Legend
Airport ✈

0   300 mi
0   300 km

N

423

Tip-Toeing Through the Wildflowers

Every year from August to mid-November, Mother Nature blesses just about the entire state of Western Australia with a carpet of 12,000 species of white, yellow, mauve, pink, red, and blue ✪ **wildflowers.**

This annual burgeoning is matched by an explosion of wildflower shows and festivals in country towns throughout the state, and coach and rail tour companies go into overdrive ferrying petal enthusiasts from all around Australia and the globe on wildflower tours. Conveniently, the blossoms cluster in the cooler southern half of the state, where you can easily explore them on day trips from Perth, or on longer jaunts of up to 5 days or so. September and October are usually the best months.

Motorhomes are not necessary as motels are plentiful, but they make good sense if you plan a long-distance state tour. Australia's biggest motorhome outfit, **Britz Campervan Rentals & Tours,** has an office in Perth (☎ **08/9478 3488**).

The most popular route is what the tourism authority calls the **Everlasting Trail** running through sparsely populated country north of Perth. It follows the Great Northern Highway to Wubin, 272 kilometers (170 miles) north of Perth, and on to the country town of Mullewa (another 222 kilometers/139 miles north), which puts on one of the state's best wildflower shows for a week every August. From here, head west 98 kilometers (61 miles) to Geraldton and 424 kilometers (265 miles) back to Perth down the Brand Highway for more floral sensations. This route has little of interest except flowers; instead, I would combine my wildflower-watching with wine tasting on a jaunt to the much prettier, less isolated Southwest (see "Margaret River & the Southwest," later in the chapter). If time is short, don't despair. You can see ample blossoms right in Perth at Kings Park & Botanic Garden, which conducts free guided walks through its 200 species during its 10-day Wildflower Festival every September or October.

Because Australian flora is adapted to desert conditions, it tends to sprout on dry, sunny days following a rain shower. For this reason, the Western Australia Tourist Centre (see "Visitor Information" in "Exploring the State" above) runs a Wildflower Desk during the season to keep you up on whatever hot spot is blooming brightest that week, and book you on one of the many coach, rail, or 4WD wildflower tours. Interstate buses and trains and hotels fill up in wildflower season, so book ahead.

TOUR OPERATORS   **Australian Pinnacle Tours** (☎ **1800/999 304** in Australia, or 08/9221 5411; fax 08/9221 5477; www.pinnacletours.com.au) specializes in coach tours around Perth and throughout the state. **Overland 4WD Safaris** (☎ **08/9524 7122;** fax 08/9524 8044; www.overland.com.au) runs 4WD safaris from Perth with an off-the-beaten-track bent.

Aerial tours make sense in W.A. Contact **Complete Aviation Services** (☎ **1800/ 632 221** in Australia, or 08/9478 2749; fax 08/9478 2759; www.casair.com.au) or **Kookaburra Air** (☎ **08/9354 1158;** fax 08/9354 5898; www.kookaburra.iinet. net.au). Both do tours departing Perth throughout Western Australia, including the Kimberley (see chapter 9) and the Red Centre (see chapter 8). Both offer custom-tailored itineraries as well as pre-set tours.

✪ **Landscope Expeditions** is an excellent nature-lovers' tour program run by the state **Conservation and Land Management Department (CALM)** (☎ **08/9380 2433** is the University of Western Australia which handles bookings, or fax 08/9380 1066 for a schedule, or check it out at www.calm.wa.gov.au). You might assist CALM scientists on research projects, such as reintroducing native species to the Shark Bay

World Heritage region, observing eclipses from a boat in the remote Houtman Abrolhos Islands, or learning about 17th-century Dutch shipwrecks on the Zuytdorp Cliffs.

1 Perth

4,405km (2,753 miles) W of Sydney; 2,557km (1,598 miles) S of Broome

If you like Sydney, you'll probably like Perth. It has the same skyscrapers glinting in the sun, a remarkably blue sky, the same outdoorsy vibrancy, and like Sydney, the ocean and glorious white beaches are just a bus ride from downtown. Perth likes to boast it gets more sunshine than any other city in Australia, some 300 days a year.

You probably know the city and its port town of Fremantle best as the site of Australia's defense of the America's Cup yachting trophy in 1987. On that occasion the Cup returned to American shores where it had lived for so long, but the enthusiasm the event whipped up in Perth lives on. Far from being one of those drab, anonymous capitals, Perth has lots of fun stuff to do. Wander through the impressively restored historic warehouses, museums, and working docks of bustling Fremantle; stock up at the plentiful Aboriginal art and souvenir stores; eat at some of the country's best restaurants (no, they're not all in Sydney and Melbourne); go snorkeling and sea kayaking with wild sea lions; bushwalk through a 1,000-acre park in the middle of the city; and pedal your bike to a great snorkeling spot on ✪ **Rottnest Island,** a miniature reef resort 19 kilometers (12 miles) offshore.

Perth also gives you several good choices of side trips: Wander the streets of historical York, drop in on the Benedictine monks in the Spanish Renaissance town of New Norcia, nip out to the Swan Valley vineyards 20 minutes from town, or spend a few days in Margaret River country, one of Australia's most revered wine regions.

PERTH ORIENTATION

ARRIVING   By Plane   Qantas (☎ **13 13 13** in Australia) flies at least once a day, if not more often, from all mainland state capitals, either direct or with mostly only one stop. **Airlink** (☎ **08/9225 8383,** or book through Qantas) flies direct from Alice Springs daily, and once a day from Cairns via Ayers Rock.

Perth International Airport is 20 kilometers (12.5 miles) northeast of the city, and the domestic terminal is 8 kilometers (5 miles) closer. Both offer currency exchange, ATMs, showers, baby change rooms, lockers, Internet access, direct-dial accommodation boards, mailboxes (the newsstand sells stamps), and a limited range of tourist information. Mobile (cell) telephones can be rented at the international terminal. **Avis** (☎ **08/9277 1177** domestic terminal, 08/9477 1302 international terminal), **Budget** (☎ **08/9277 9277**), **Hertz** (☎ **08/9479 4788**), and **Thrifty** (☎ **08/9464 7333**) all have desks at both terminals.

Feature Tours runs the airport-city shuttle (☎ **08/9479 4131**), which meets all international and interstate flights. It does not meet specifically meet intrastate flights. There is no need to book. Transfers to the city from the international terminal cost A$11 (U.S.$7.15) for adults, A$7 (U.S.$4.55) for children 2 to 15. Domestic terminal-city transfers are A$9 (U.S.$5.85) for adults and A$5.50 (U.S.$3.58) for kids. Transfers between the domestic and international terminals are A$8 (U.S.$5.20) for adults, and A$6 (U.S.$3.90) for kids. Qantas runs a free bus between terminals for its passengers. The private **Fremantle Airport Shuttle** (☎ **08/9383 4115**) operates eight services a day between the airport and Fremantle hotels on demand, so you must book in advance. The fare is A$15 (U.S.$9.75), or A$12 (U.S.$7.80) per person for two or more people traveling together, and A$28 (U.S.$18.20) for a family. Public buses 200, 201, 202, 208, and 209 run to the city from the domestic terminal only. A taxi to the city is about A$25 (U.S.$16.25) from the international terminal and A$20 (U.S.$13) from the domestic terminal.

By Train The 3-day journey to Perth from Sydney via Broken Hill, Adelaide, and Kalgoorlie aboard the ✪ *Indian Pacific* is an experience in itself. The train runs twice a week in each direction. The one-way fare ranges from A$1,499 (U.S.$974.35) in first class with meals and en suite bathroom, to A$1199 (U.S.$779.77) in comfy second class (meals extra, and shared bathrooms), down to A$459 (U.S.$298.35) for the sit-up-all-the-way coach class (not a good idea). Connections are available from Melbourne on *The Overland* train. Fares will be higher—A$1,717 (U.S.$1,116.05) in first class—during Western Australia's wildflower season from September through mid-November. See "Getting around Australia" in chapter 2 for contact details. For information, schedules, and reservations on the *Prospector* from Kalgoorlie, call **Great Southern Railways** (☎ **13 21 47**). The trip takes 7¾ hours. All long-distance trains pull into the **East Perth Terminal,** Summers Street off Lord Street, East Perth. A taxi to the city center costs about A$8 (U.S.$5.20).

By Bus **Greyhound Pioneer** (☎ **13 20 30** in Australia) runs daily coach services from Sydney, via Canberra and Adelaide (trip time: 54 hr. from Sydney, almost 35 hr. from Adelaide). It also has service daily from Darwin via Kununurra and Broome (trip time: 56 hours). Traveling from Alice Springs requires a connection in Adelaide. The Sydney-Perth fare is A$335 (U.S.$217.75) and Darwin-Perth is A$496 (U.S.$322.40).

By Car There are only two road routes from interstate. The 2,423-kilometer (1,514-mile) route from Broome in the north follows the Great Northern Highway (not so great for road quality), the North West Coastal Highway (a decent enough two-lane affair) and the **Brand Highway** (pretty good). The 2,708-kilometer (1,693-mile) route from Adelaide includes hundreds of miles along some of the world's straightest road on the treeless Nullarbor Plain. Arm yourself with an up-to-date road map before setting off on this route, and carry spare gas. It's not a bad idea to contact the South Australian or Western Australian state auto clubs (listed under "Getting Around Australia" in chapter 2) for more advice on crossing the Nullarbor. Both routes cross mostly featureless and lonely semi-desert, sheep ranches or wheat-fields most of the way, with very few towns en route. For that reason, I don't recommend either!

VISITOR INFORMATION The Western Australian Tourism Commission's **Western Australian Tourist Centre,** Albert Facey House, 469 Wellington St. at Forrest Place (☎ **1300/361 351** in Australia, or 08/9483 1111; fax 08/9483 0190; www.westernaustralia.net), is the official visitor information source. It's open Monday through Thursday 8:30am to 6pm (5pm in winter), Friday 8:30am to 7pm (6pm in winter), Saturday 8:30am to 5pm, and Sunday from 10am to 5pm (3pm in winter). Another source of free information and booking is the **Perth Tourist Lounge,** Level 2, Carillon City Arcade, off 680 Hay Street Mall (☎ **08/9229 2238;** fax 08/9229 2220). It's open Monday through Saturday 9am to 5:30pm and Sunday noon to 4pm.

For an un-touristy lowdown on the city's restaurants, cultural life, shops, bars, festivals, and concerts, buy the local quarterly magazine *Scoop* (A$7.95/U.S.$5.17; www.scoop.com.au) or pick up the free color newspaper, *Perth Weekly.* Both are readily available around town in newsagents, cafes, tour desks and such places.

CITY LAYOUT The city center is 19 kilometers (12 miles) upriver from the Indian Ocean, on the north bank of the Swan River. **Hay Street** and **Murray Street** are the two major thoroughfares, 1 block apart; both are bisected by pedestrian malls between William and Barrack streets. It helps to know that Adelaide Terrace and St. Georges Terrace are the same street. The name change occurs at Victoria Avenue.

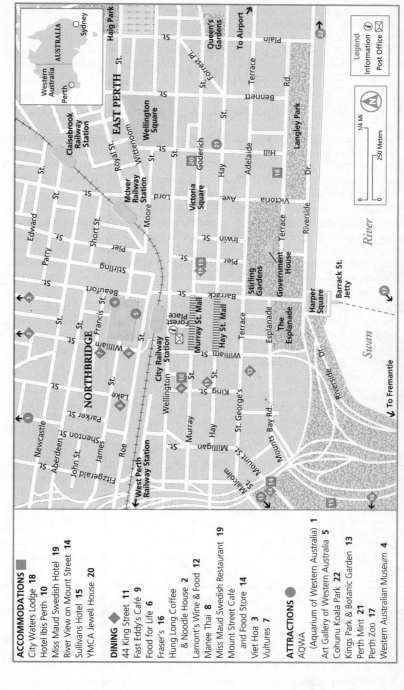

Perth

Western Australia

Perth

AUSTRALIA

Sydney

Haig Park

EAST PERTH

NORTHBRIDGE

Claisebrook Railway Station

McIver Railway Station

Wellington Square

Queen's Gardens

To Airport

Victoria Square

City Railway Station

West Perth Railway Station

Forrest Place

Murray St. Mall

Hay St. Mall

Stirling Gardens

Government House

The Esplanade

Harper Square

Barrack St. Jetty

Langley Park

Swan

River

To Fremantle

Legend
- ⓘ Information
- ✉ Post Office

N

¼ Mi

250 Meters

ACCOMMODATIONS ■
City Waters Lodge **18**
Hotel Ibis Perth **10**
Miss Maud Swedish Hotel **19**
River View on Mount Street **14**
Sullivans Hotel **15**
YMCA Jewell House **20**

DINING ◆
44 King Street **11**
Fast Eddy's Café **9**
Food for Life **6**
Fraser's **16**
Hung Long Coffee
   & Noodle House **2**
Lamont's Wine & Food **12**
Manee Thai **8**
Miss Maud Swedish Restaurant **19**
Mount Street Café
   and Food Store **14**
Viet Hoa **3**
Vultures **7**

ATTRACTIONS ●
AQWA
   (Aquarium of Western Australia) **1**
Art Gallery of Western Australia **5**
Cohunu Koala Park **22**
Kings Park & Botanic Garden **13**
Perth Mint **21**
Perth Zoo **17**
Western Australian Museum **4**

427

MAPS Of the many free pocket guides to Perth at tour desks and in hotel lobbies, *Your Guide to Perth & Fremantle* has the best street map, because it shows one-way streets, public toilets and telephones, taxi stands, post offices, police stations, and street numbers as well as most attractions and hotels. The **Royal Automobile Club of Western Australia** (see "Exploring the State" at the beginning of this chapter) is a good source of maps to the entire state.

Neighborhoods in Brief

City Center The central business district (called the **CBD**) is home to shops and department stores connected by a honeycomb of shopping arcades. A good introduction to Perth's charms is to take in the views from the pedestrian/bike path that skirts the river along Riverside Drive. Within walking distance on the western edge of town is Kings Park & Botanic Garden.

Northbridge Just about all of Perth's nightclubs, and a good many of its cool restaurants, bars, and cafes are in this 5-block precinct just north of the railway line, within easy walking distance of the city center. James, Beaufort, Aberdeen, and Lake streets roughly bound it. What locals call the Cultural Centre—an umbrella term that means the Western Australian Museum, the Art Gallery of Western Australia, the State Library, and the Perth Institute of Contemporary Arts—is here too. The free Blue CAT buses deliver you right into the heart of this buzzing precinct.

Subiaco This well-heeled suburb is on the other side of Kings Park from the city. Saturday morning wouldn't be Saturday morning for Perth's see-and-be-seen crowd without a stroll through "Subi's" cafes, markets, upscale boutiques, antique shops, and art galleries. Intersecting Hay Street and Rokeby (pronounced *Rockerby*) Road are the main promenades. Take the train to Subiaco station.

Fremantle Not only is this Perth's working port, "Freo" is Perth's second city heart, and locals' favorite weekend spot to relax, eat, shop, and sail. A careful 1980s restoration of its Victorian warehouses saw it emerge as a marvelous living example of a 19th-century seaport—kind of like Fisherman's Wharf in San Francisco without the stale commercial taint. Fremantle is 19 kilometers (12 miles) downriver on the mouth of the Swan. See "A Day Out in Fremantle" later in this chapter.

Scarborough Beach This is one of Perth's prize beaches, 12 kilometers (7½ miles) north of the city center. The district is a little tatty with that oversupply of cheap take-out food outlets that plague Aussie beaches, but if you like sun, sand, and surf, this is the place to be. You will find supermarkets, bars, restaurants, shops, and surf gear rental stores here. Allow 15 to 20 minutes to get there by car, 35 minutes on the bus.

GETTING AROUND

BY PUBLIC TRANSPORTATION **Transperth** runs Perth's buses, trains, and ferries. For route and timetable information, call ☎ **13 62 13** in Western Australia, or drop into the **Transperth InfoCentres** at the Plaza Arcade off Hay Street Mall, the Perth Railway Station, the Wellington Street bus station, or the **City Bus Port** on Mounts Bay Road. You can transfer from bus to ferry to train on one ticket within its expiry time. Travel costs A$1.70 (U.S.$1.11) in one zone (to Subiaco, for instance), and A$2.50 (U.S.$1.63) in two, which gets you most places, including Fremantle. Non-Australian seniors and students don't qualify for discounted fares; kids ages 5 to 14 do.

MultiRider passes give you 10 trips at a savings of 15%; they come in a range of prices good for various numbers of zones. A **DayRider** pass allows 1 day's unlimited

A Free Ride

A welcome freebie in Perth is the **Free Transit Zone (FTZ).** You can travel free on trains and buses within this zone any hour, day and night. It is bounded by Kings Park Road, Fraser Avenue, Thomas Street and Loftus Street in the west; Newcastle Street in the north; and the river in the south and east. Basically, this means you can travel to Kings Park, Northbridge, east to major sporting grounds, and anywhere in the city center for free. Signs mark the boundaries; ask the driver if you're unsure.

---

travel after 9am on weekdays and all day on weekends and public holidays, and costs A$6.50 (U.S.$4.23). If you're a family, it may be worth getting a **MaxiRider,** valid for one day's unlimited travel for a group of seven people with a maximum of two adults. MaxiRiders are aimed at Perth families, so are only valid weekends, public holidays, after 9am during Western Australian school holidays, after 6pm year-round Monday to Thursday, and after 3pm Friday. They cost A$6.50 (U.S.$4.23). Passes, collectively known as **FastCards,** are sold at **Newspower** newsagents and at Transperth InfoCentres. To use the passes, validate them in the machines located on board in the case of buses, and on the platform or wharf in the case of trains and ferries.

Buses and trains run from about 5:30am until about 11:30pm.

By Bus   The **Wellington Street Bus Station,** located next to Perth Railway Station at Forrest Place, and the **City Bus Port** on the western edge of the city on Mounts Bay Road, are the two main depots. The vast majority of buses travel along St. Georges Terrace. Drivers do not always stop unless you hail. Buy tickets from the driver. By far the best way to get around town is on the silver, free **CAT** (Central Area Transit) **buses** that run a continual loop of the city and Northbridge. The **Red CAT** runs east-west every 5 minutes, Monday through Friday 6:50am to 6:20pm, and once every hour from 10am to 6pm weekends. The **Blue CAT** runs north-south as far north as Northbridge and south to Barrack Street Jetty every 8 minutes from 6:50am. The last Blue Cat service is at 6:20pm Monday through Thursday, and on Friday it continues every 15 minutes from 6:20pm through until 1:05am Saturday morning. It also runs Saturdays from 8:30am to 1am (Sunday morning) every 12 minutes, and Sundays every 15 minutes from 10am to 5pm. Look for the silver CAT bus stops. Transperth InfoCentres (see above) dispense free route maps.

The **Perth Tram Co.** tours (see "Whale-Watching Cruises, Tram Trips & Other Tours" later in this chapter) are a good way to get around, too.

By Train   Trains in Perth are fast, clean, and safe. They start from about 5:30am and run every 15 minutes so more often during the day, and every half-hour at night until midnight. **NightRider** trains depart Perth at midnight, 1am, and 2am Friday and Saturday night, and 3am from December to March, stopping at all stations on all lines. All trains leave from **Perth Railway Station** opposite Forrest Place on Wellington Street. Buy your ticket before you board, at the vending machines on the platform.

By Ferry   You will probably only use ferries to visit Perth Zoo. They run every half-hour or so, more often in peak hour, from 6:50am weekdays and 7:50am weekends, until 7:15pm (9:15pm Fri–Sat in summer Sept–Apr) from the **Barrack Street Jetty** to **Mends Street** in South Perth. Buy tickets before you board from the machine on the wharf. The trip takes 7 minutes.

BY TAXI   Perth's two taxi companies are **Swan Taxis** (☎ **13 1330**) and **Black & White Taxis** (☎ **08/9333 3333**). Ranks are located at Perth Railway Station, and at both ends of Hay Street Mall.

BY CAR Perth's signposting is notorious for telling you where you have been, not where you are going—for example, some interstate highways are announced with insignificant signs more suited to a side street.

CarePark, 152-158 St. Georges Terrace between William and King Street (☎ **08/ 9321 0667**) charges A$2.20 (U.S.$1.43) per hour, and is open Monday to Friday 6:30am to 8pm (until midnight Fri), Saturday from 8am to 6:30pm, and Sunday from 8:30am to 6:30pm. The charge is A$3 (U.S.$1.95) between 5pm and midnight Friday, all day Saturday or Sunday. There is no charge for leaving your car overnight.

The major car-rental companies are **Avis** (☎ **08/9325 7677**), **Budget** (☎ **08/ 9322 1100**), **Hertz** (☎ **08/9321 7777**), and **Thrifty** (☎ **08/9464 7444**). All have both city and Fremantle outlets. **ATC Rent-A-Car** (☎ **1800/999 888** in Australia but outside Western Australia, or 08/9325 1833) is a locally owned outfit with offices in Monkey Mia and Broome; it also rents camping kits. **Hawk Rent-A-Car** (☎ **08/ 9221 9688**) is another local operator worth a try.

Fast Facts: Perth

American Express The bureau, located at 645 Hay Street Mall (☎ **08/9261 2711**), is open Monday through Friday 9am to 5pm and Saturday 9am to noon.

Business Hours Banks open Monday through Thursday 9:30am to 4pm and until 5pm Friday. Shopping hours are usually 9am to 5:30pm Monday through Friday (until 9pm on Thurs in the suburbs and Fremantle, and until 9pm Fri in the city), and 9am to 5pm on Saturday. On Sunday most major stores (but not all) open noon to 4pm or later in the city, and from 10am to 6pm in Fremantle.

Currency Exchange Go to the American Express office (see above) or **Interforex,** Shop 24, London Court off Hay Street Mall (☎ **08/9325 7418**), open daily 9am to 5:30pm, and until 9pm Friday. Interforex has a Fremantle bureau at the corner of William and Adelaide streets (☎ **08/9431 7022**) open daily from 8am to 8pm.

Dentist Forrest Chase Dental Centre (☎ **08/9221 4749**) is on the Upper Walkway Level, Forrest Chase shopping complex, 425 Wellington St. opposite Perth Railway Station. Open daily 8am to 8pm, it can be reached after hours on ☎ **08/9383 1620.**

Doctor Central City Medical Centre is on the Perth Railway Station concourse, 420 Wellington St. (☎ **08/9221 4747;** this number diverts to an on-call doctor after hours). It is open daily from 7am to 7pm.

Drugstores Forrest Chase Pharmacy (☎ **08/9221 1691**), on the upper level of the Forrest Chase shopping center on Wellington Street (near the dental surgery listed above) is open Monday to Saturday 8:30am to 7pm (and until 9pm Fri), and Sunday 10am to 6pm. **Shenton Pharmacy,** 214 Nicholson Rd., Subiaco (☎ **08/9381 1358** business and after hours), will deliver across Perth.

Embassies/Consulates The **United States Consulate-General** is at 16 St. Georges Terrace (☎ **08/9231 9400**). The **Canadian Consulate** is at 267 St. Georges Terrace (☎ **08/9322 7930**). The **British Consulate-General** is at 77 St. Georges Terrace (☎ **08/9221 5400**). The **Irish Consulate** is at 10 Lilika Rd., City Beach (☎ **08/9385 8247**).

Emergencies Dial ☎ **000** for fire, ambulance, or police in an emergency. This is a free call, and no coins are needed from a public phone.

Hospitals Royal Perth Hospital in the city center has a public casualty ward (☎ **08/9224 2244**). Enter from Victoria Square, accessed from Murray Street.

Lost Property For lost property on public transport, call **Transperth** administration at ☎ **08/9320 9320.** Check with the local police station closest to where the item was lost (central police operations ☎ 13 14 44 can give you the nearest station's telephone number).

Luggage Storage/Lockers The Perth Tourist Lounge, Level 2, Carillon City Arcade, 680 Hay Street Mall (☎ **08/9229 2238**), rents lockers and stores baggage for A$1 (U.S.65¢) for small bags, A$3 (U.S.$1.95) for large ones, during its hours: Monday through Saturday from 9am to 5:30pm, and Sunday noon to 4pm. There are baggage lockers at both terminals at the airport.

Police Dial ☎ **000** in an emergency. City Police Station, 1 Hay St., East Perth (☎ **08/9222 1048**), the City Watch police bureau at Perth Railway Station, and Fremantle Police Station, 45 Henderson St. (☎ **08/9430 5244**), are open 24 hours. For general police inquiries call ☎ **13 14 44.**

Post Office The General Post Office on Forrest Place (☎ **13 13 18**) is open Monday through Friday 8am to 5:30pm, Saturday 9am to 12:30pm, and Sunday noon to 4pm. There are also post offices at 26 and 66 St. Georges Terrace, at Cloisters Square at 863 Hay St., and in just about every suburb. Most post offices open Monday to Friday 9am to 5pm; some also open Saturday mornings.

Safety Perth is safe, but steer clear of the back streets of Northbridge at night, as groups of teenage boys have been known to pick fights.

Time Zone Western Australian time (WST) is GMT plus 8 hours, and has no daylight saving. This means it is normally 2 hours behind Sydney and Melbourne, 3 from October to March when New South Wales and Victoria go to daylight saving. Call ☎ **1194** for the exact local time.

Weather Call ☎ **1196** for a recorded local weather forecast.

WHERE TO STAY

Perth has a surfeit of upscale hotels in the city center, so it's possible to get a good deal in an expensive lodging when the business travelers go home. Definitely ask about weekend deals. If you're not afraid to negotiate, you can strike a good deal on weeknights too, if business is slow across town.

IN THE CITY CENTER

City Waters Lodge. 118 Terrace Rd. (between Victoria Ave. and Hill St.), Perth, WA 6000. ☎ **1800/999 030** in Australia or 08/9325 1566. Fax 08/9221 2794. www.citywaters. com.au. 72 units. A/C TV TEL. A$78 (U.S.$50.70) double, A$83 (U.S.$53.95) triple or family apt (sleeps 4), A$118 (U.S.$76.70) 2-bedroom apt (sleeps 5). Weekly rates available. BC, MC, V. Free parking. Blue CAT Stop 19 "Barrack Square." Airport shuttle.

Try to get an apartment on the end of this old, neatly maintained three-story block by the river, as they have parkland views. The fixtures in these one- and two-bedroom apartments are aged, especially in the kitchen and bathroom, but you get plenty of space, daily servicing, and the same brand of mattresses used by the city's five-star hotels. Two-bedroom have two TV's and two phones. All rooms received new beds, paint, and carpets in 1999. The hosts carry your luggage, order in continental breakfast from a nearby deli, and run a tour/car-rental desk. City buses run along St. Georges Terrace a block away, and you're a 5-block walk from Hay Street Mall.

Hotel Ibis Perth. 334 Murray St. (between William and King Sts.), Perth, WA 6000. ☎ **1800/221-4542** in the U.S. and Canada, 1300/65 6565 in Australia, 020/8283 4500 in the U.K., 0800/44 4422 in New Zealand, or 08/9322 2844. Fax 08/9321 6314. www.hotel web.fr. 174 units (all with shower only). A/C MINIBAR TV TEL. A$140.80 (U.S.$91.52) double, A$206.80 (U.S.$134.42) suite. Extra person A$30 (U.S.$19.50). Children 12 and under stay free in parents' room if they use existing bedding. Ask about weekend packages. AE, BC, DC, JCB, MC, V. Discounted self-parking A$8 (U.S.$5.20) at the nearby Queen Street Carpark. Bus: Red CAT Stop 15 "Murray St. Mall West," or Blue CAT Stop 17 "Hay Street Mall West." Airport shuttle.

Ibis is one of those reputable chain brands of the "four-star facilities at a three-star price" variety. You may find the modern, neat, and comfortable rooms a bit on the small side, but families will like the separate bedroom for Mum and Dad, and business travelers will like the express checkout and business center. Rooms have pay-per-view movies, hair dryers and iron and board. You get plenty for the price, including a free drink on arrival, room service, dry cleaning service, a car-rental and tour desk, and discounted rates at a nearby gym. Downstairs is a convivial street-front bistro and bar popular with locals. Shops, cinemas, and malls are just a block or two along the street.

○ Miss Maud Swedish Hotel. 97 Murray St. (at Pier St.), Perth, WA 6000. ☎ **1800/998 022** in Australia, or 08/9325 3900. Fax 08/9221 3225. www.missmaud.com.au. 51 units (41 with shower only). A/C MINIBAR TV TEL. A$115–$125 (U.S.$74.75–$81.25) double. Extra person A$10 (U.S.$6.50). Rates include full smorgasbord breakfast. AE, BC, DC, JCB, MC, V. Discounted parking A$7.50 (U.S.$4.88) at the Kings Hotel carpark 1 block away on Hay St. between Pier and Irwin sts. Bus: Red CAT Stop 1 "Pier St."; Blue and Weekend CAT Stop 5 "Murray St. Mall East." Airport shuttle.

Staying at this adorable hotel in the heart of town is like staying at grandma's. Never mind that the bedspread clashes with the carpet and the paint's peeling off the door— the rooms are getting refurbished, anyhow. You're here for the homey ambience, the cozy rooms sporting wall-sized murals of Scandinavian pine forests, and a staff that's more polite and on the ball than those in most five-star hotels. You also get limited room service, a 24-hour front desk, hair dryers, laundry/dry cleaning service, a private sundeck tucked away as a little surprise up among the rooftops, and a tour desk. The real Miss Maud, Maud Edmiston wants guests to feel they are in a European family hotel like in her Swedish homeland, and she succeeds. A fabulous full buffet breakfast is included at Miss Maud Swedish Restaurant downstairs (see "Great Deals on Dining," below).

River View on Mount Street. 42 Mount St., Perth, WA 6000. ☎ **08/9321 8963.** Fax 08/9322 5956. www.riverview.au.com. 50 units (all with shower only). A/C TV TEL. A$82.50 (U.S.$53.63) apt (sleeps 3). AE, BC, DC, MC, V. Limited free parking. Bus: Red CAT Stop 18 "QVI" (located over the freeway footbridge accessed from the corner of St. Georges Terrace and Milligan St.). Airport shuttle.

In a quiet leafy street a short walk from the center of town and Kings Park, these roomy studio apartments in an older-style 1960's block were all refurbished in 1999 with new kitchens, smart bathrooms, and fresh carpets, curtains, and fittings. The result is great style at a great price. Some have views of the river, and all have a data-port for laptops. Servicing is done weekly. The helpful managers run a tour/car rental desk, loan hair dryers, and get your dry cleaning done. You will probably breakfast at the excellent Mount Street Café and Food Store downstairs (see "Great Deals on Dining," below), which also sells prepared curries and deli items. Be prepared to hike three stories as there is no elevator. No smoking.

Sullivans Hotel. 166 Mounts Bay Rd., Perth, WA 6000. ☎ **1800/99 9294** in Australia or 08/9321 8022. Fax 08/9481 6762. www.sullivans.com.au. 68 units (66 with shower only). A/C TV TEL. A$110–$130 (U.S.$71.50–$84.50) up to 4 people in room, A$150–$175

(U.S.$97.50–$113.75) 1- and 2-bedroom apt. Ask about packages. Weekly rates available. AE, BC, DC, MC, V. Free parking. Bus: 72, 201 (the hotel is within the Free Transit Zone). Airport shuttle.

This family-owned hotel about 1.5 kilometers (1 mile) from town is popular with Europeans for its small-scale ambience. Despite being on the main road into the city, none of the rooms are noisy. They are simply furnished with laminate fittings, not glamorous but clean and large, with hair dryers. Larger Deluxe rooms come with desks, safes and balconies with views over parkland and freeway to the river. There are also two apartments with kitchenettes. Out back is a pleasant and private swimming pool with a sundeck and BBQ. Bikes are free for guests, and there is a tour/car rental desk, free movies, room service (no delivery charge), 24-hour front desk, and an affordable restaurant. The Swan River is a stroll away, and Kings Park is a steep walk up the hill.

Super-Cheap Sleeps

YMCA Jewell House. 180 Goderich St., Perth, WA 6000. ☎ **1800/998 212** in Australia, or 08/9325 8488. Fax 08/9221 4694. jewellhouse@bigpond.com. 250 units, none with bathroom. A$44–$48.40 (U.S.$28.60–$31.46) double, A$71.80 (U.S.$46.67) family room (sleeps 5). AE, BC, DC, JCB, MC, V. Free off-street parking for 16 cars. Bus: Red CAT Stop 4 "Bennett Street." Airport shuttle.

You may not like the dingy carpets and pre-loved furniture in this 11-story one-time nurses' quarters, but you will love the prices and the river panorama from the south rooms. Bathrooms are communal but clean and should be refurbished by the time you get here. Rooms contain beds, a fan, self-serve tea and coffee, and linen and towels, but heck, splash out the extra A$4.80 (U.S.$3.12) on "deluxe" quarters with a TV and minifridge. BYO hair dryer. Maid service is daily. There is 24-hour reception, currency exchange, TV lounges, a wonderfully affordable dining room, and a helpful staff. The Perth Mint is a block away, and Hay Street Mall is a 5-block stroll.

In Fremantle

There's a perpetual holiday atmosphere in this picturesque port city. Although you are 19 kilometers (12 miles) from Perth's city center, public transport connections are good, so you can happily explore all of Perth from here—and most of top attractions are in Freo anyhow. There are good restaurants and a happening nightlife, too.

✪ **Danum House.** 6 Fothergill St. (at Bellevue Terrace), Fremantle, WA 6160. ☎ **08/9336 3735.** Fax 08/9335 3414. www.staywa.net.au/ads/danum. Danum@iinet.net.au. 2 units (both with shower only). TV. A$90–$110 (U.S.$58.50–$71.50) double. Minimum 2-night stay. Rates include full breakfast. BC, MC, V. Ample on-street parking. Train: Fremantle. Fremantle airport shuttle. Children not permitted.

Cheerful hostess Christine Sherwin has created a welcoming haven in her beautiful Federation (ca. 1909) home within walking distance of town. One room, decked out in bold reds and greens, opens onto a cottage garden. The other large room has an ornate mantle, floral wallpaper, long drapes, and a daybed, as well as a real bed for sleeping. Both sport antiques, ornate ceiling roses and cornices, fireplaces, very high ceilings, and fans. Even the bathrooms (one en suite, one with private access) share the colonial decor. Guests have separate access to the house. Christine serves a hearty cooked breakfast with plunger coffee, and you can wind down after a hard day's sightseeing in the comfy lounge over books, CDs, free tea and coffee, and complimentary port and chocolates. Hair dryers and iron and board are available. No smoking.

Fremantle Colonial Accommodation. 215 High St., Fremantle, WA 6160. ☎ **08/9430 6568.** Fax 08/9430 6405. 6 units in guest house, 2 with bathroom (shower only). 3 cottages, all with bathroom (1 with shower only). TV. Guest house A$70–$90 (U.S.$45.50–$58.50) single; A$75–$100 (U.S.$48.75–$65) double. Additional person A$10–$15 (U.S.$6.50–$9.75) extra. Rates in guest house include continental breakfast. Cottages A$130 (U.S.$84.50) double. Additional person A$20 (U.S.$13) extra (maximum total A$170/U.S.$110.50 for 5 people). BC, MC, V. Free parking. Train: Fremantle. Fremantle airport shuttle.

A stroll in any direction from this historical terrace house on Freo's main street brings you to a museum, a harbor, shops, or other attractions. All the rooms are decorated in colonial style—one has a blue-and-yellow liberty-print quilt and an ornate plaster ceiling rose, another has lace curtains and a fireplace. The clean bathrooms are tiled in dark green or maroon and white. All rooms are air-conditioned. They vary in size but all have a table with cereals, tea and coffee, a kettle, a toaster, and a minifridge. Your hostess, Val Wieland, delivers juice, milk, yogurt, fruit, and bread for toasting to your room by 6pm the night before, so you eat when you like. Every room is supplied with bathrobes. This is more a guesthouse where people come and go, than a personal B&B where you get to know your host. The in-room dining tables are quite small, as are the TVs, so this place is more for folks who just want somewhere to lay their heads at night, rather than a comfortable establishment in which to hang around for half the day.

For better value, try one of Val's three limestone cottages. Perched on a hill overlooking the town, 1 block behind the guesthouse, they were built in the 19th century as prison guards' and nurses' quarters. Val has restored the interiors to their original colors. Each has two pretty bedrooms with patchwork quilts, complimentary toiletries, fireplaces, antique furniture, and rag dolls or teddy bears in the corner. Each also has a large eat-in kitchen with a modern stove alongside the original wood-fired one, a sunroom, laundry facilities, a cute wooden porch out front, and a lovely stone courtyard out back with outdoor dining furniture. They have fans, and may be air-conditioned by the time you stay. One is fitted for travelers with disabilities.

GREAT DEALS ON DINING

Perth's restaurant scene bubbles over with terrific ethnic places that are kind to your wallet and a treat for your tastebuds. If you can't find the kind of cuisine you want in Northbridge, it probably doesn't exist, for this restaurant mecca has Thai, Greek, Vietnamese, Malaysian, Italian, Chinese, and about every other kind of food you can think of. Don't forget that going BYO (Bring Your Own wine or beer) lessens the pain in your wallet. Some restaurants charge corkage fees, usually A$1 or $2 (U.S.65¢–$1.30) per person, but sometimes as much as A$4 (U.S.$2.60) per person.

For inexpensive pasta, a Turkish bread sandwich, or excellent coffee and cake, you can't beat Perth's homegrown **DOME** chain of cafes. You will spot their dark green logo at Trinity Arcade between Hay St. Mall and St. Georges Terrace (☎ **08/9226 0210**); 149 James St., Northbridge (☎ **08/9328 8094**); 13 South Terrace, Fremantle (☎ **08/9336 3040**); 19 Napoleon St., Cottesloe (☎ **08/9383 1071**); 26 Rokeby Rd., Subiaco (☎ **08/9381 5664**); and on Rottnest Island (☎ **08/9292 5026**).

Western Australian law bans smoking in enclosed public spaces like restaurants.

IN THE CITY CENTER

Fast Eddy's Café. 454 Murray St. (at Milligan St.). ☎ **08/9321 2552.** Main courses A$5–$15 (U.S.$3.25–$9.75); average A$10 (U.S.$6.50). BC, MC, V. Daily 24 hr., 365 days. Red CAT Stop 27 "Milligan St.". FAST FOOD.

A hefty menu of good hearty food from burgers to pancakes to milk shakes, and full fry-up brekkies are served all hours at this popular local chain. The fun interior is decked out with 1930's soap powder posters and Coca-Cola advertisements. One side is table service; the same food will cost you about a third of the already low prices, at the Victorian era-meets-1950s diner on the other side.

✪ **Fraser's.** Fraser Ave. (next to the Visitor Information Centre), Kings Park. ☎ **08/9481 7100.** Reservations essential. Main courses A$22–$45 (U.S.$14.30–$29.25); average A$26 (U.S.$16.70). AE, BC, DC, MC, V. Mon–Fri 7–10:30am, Sat–Sun 7:30–11am; Mon–Fri noon–3pm, Sat–Sun 12:30–3:30pm; daily 6–10:30pm; supper daily 10pm–late. Closed Good Friday. Bus: 33 stops outside the Visitor Centre; 103, 104, 200, 202, 208, and 209 stop outside the park gates. Red CAT Stop 25 "Havelock Street" is 1 block to the north of the gates. MODERN AUSTRALIAN/SEAFOOD.

What a sensational view from this hilltop restaurant—the city skyscrapers and Swan River are so close you could almost reach out and touch them—even better, the victuals matches the vista. Executive chef Chris Taylor's dab hand with seafood, which comprises about 70 percent of the menu, has made the place a finalist in national "restaurant of the year" awards more than once. Seared Atlantic salmon with oyster mushrooms and bok choy is typical, and so is wok-fried baby octopus with chili jam and bean sprouts. The duck is also legendary. The spiced beef chunks with eggplant pahie (curry) and lentil dahl accompanied by chutney and yogurt salsa was possibly the best meal I've ever had. To maximize the view, ask for a seat on the terrace.

✪ **44 King Street.** 44 King St. ☎ **08/9321 4476.** Reservations not accepted. Grazing menu A$3.20–$11.50 (U.S.$2.08–$7.48) breakfast, A$9.50–$24 (U.S.$6.18–$15.60) lunch and dinner. AE, BC, DC, MC, V. Daily 7am–late. Bus: Red CAT Stop 28 "King Street," Blue CAT Stop 1 "Cloisters." MODERN AUSTRALIAN.

Socialites and hip corporate types adorn this sophisticated hangout, whose interior is a mix of industrial design and European cafe with dark timber tables, exposed air ducts, and windows onto the street. Thai spiced roast blue eye trevally with green papaya salad and crispy squid is a typical lunch or dinner choice; lemon curd crepe stack with berry compote is on the breakfast menu. Not only does the menu helpfully list two wine suggestions for each dish, it does taster-size glasses from around A$3 to $7.50 (U.S.$1.95–$4.88) from a long wine list, even of top-notch wines like a A$85 (U.S.$55.25) Mountadam merlot. Lots of folk drop in just for coffee, roasted on site, and the famous cakes. All meals are available as takeout.

✪ **Mount Street Café and Food Store.** Under the "River View on Mount Street" apartments, 42 Mount St. ☎ **08/9485 1411.** Reservations recommended Thurs–Sun. Main courses A$5.50–$24.50 (U.S.$3.58–$15.93); many meals under A$15 (U.S.$9.75) at breakfast and lunch. BC, MC, V. Summer: daily 7:30am–5pm, except Friday 7.30–11pm. Winter: daily 7:30am–5pm. Bus: Red CAT Stop 18 "QVI" (located over the freeway footbridge accessed from corner of St. Georges Terrace and Milligan St.). MODERN AUSTRALIAN.

Chef Toby Uhlrich was executive chef at the Hilton before making the move to this charming alfresco cafe on the edge of the central business district. Come for dinners like milk-fed veal with blackcurrant glaze on spinach fettuccini, lunches like lemon pepper chicken breast with bacon, salad, and mayo on dark rye with julienne vegetables, and good value breakfasts like eggs Benedict in huge portions, beautifully presented on dark rye with the freshest asparagus I dare say you ever had. Dine inside at a few tables, or out on the shaded stone terrace which holds contemporary timber tables and magazine stands. Drop by anytime for cakes and good coffee, but be prepared to fight the regulars for a table. BYO.

A Swedish Smorgasbord

Miss Maud Swedish Restaurant. 97 Murray St. at Pier St. (below Miss Maud Swedish Hotel). ☎ **08/9325 3900.** Reservations recommended. Smorgasbord breakfast A$15.95 (U.S.$10.37) Mon–Fri, A$16.95 (U.S.$11.02) Sat–Sun and public holidays; lunch A$23.95 (U.S.$15.57) Mon–Fri, A$26.95 (U.S.$16.87) Sat–Sun and public holidays; dinner A$29.65 (U.S.$19.27) Sun–Thurs, A$32.95 (U.S.$21.42) Fri–Sat. Cheaper smorgasbord prices for children 4–13. A la carte main courses, sandwiches, and light meals A$8–$20 (U.S.$5.20–$13).

Great Takeout

It's a takeout, not a restaurant, but some of the tastiest dishes in Perth are at
✪ **Lamont's Wine & Food,** 125 St. Georges Terrace (☎ **08/9321 9907**). Grab
some veal ravioli with goat's cheese, roast capsicum and eggplant; or chicken with
chermoula, couscous, pumpkin, and parsley and find a shady tree to eat under. Main
courses cost A$7 to $13 (U.S.$4.55–$8.45), while sandwiches cost between A$5
(U.S.$3.25) and A$6.50 (U.S.$4.23). Desserts, such as macadamia tarts and blue-
berry trifle, are all under A$6 (U.S.$3.90). They also sell their own label of wine.
You can eat more of chef Kate Lamont's scrummy food at her eponymous restaurants at 11 Brown Street, East Perth (☎ **08/9202 1566**), and in the Swan Valley
(see "Side Trips from Perth," later in this chapter).

Dine and leave by 7:15pm Mon–Sat for a A$5 (U.S.$3.25) discount. AE, BC, DC, JCB, MC, V.
Open all day for coffee and cake. Meals: daily 6:45–10am, noon–3pm, and 5:30–11pm.
Open 365 days. Bus: Red CAT Stop 1 "Pier St.," Blue CAT Stop 5 "Murray St. Mall East."
INTERNATIONAL.

"Good food and plenty of it" is the motto at Miss Maud (Edmiston's) homey establishment, and the crowds packing the place prove it works. Most diners skip the long
a la carte menu and go straight for the smorgasbord. At breakfast, that means 50 dishes
including pancakes cooked before your eyes. At lunch and dinner you can tuck into
soup, 10 salads, a big range of seafood (including oysters at dinner), cold meats, roasts,
hot vegetables, pasta, cheeses, European-style breads, half a dozen tortes, fruit, and ice
cream—65 dishes in all. Service is fast and polite.

IN NORTHBRIDGE

Hung Long Coffee & Noodle House. 344 William St. ☎ **08/9227 9541.** Main courses
A$5.50–$7.50 (U.S.$3.58–$4.88). AE, BC, MC, V. Thurs–Tues 10am–3pm, 5–10:30pm. Train:
Perth. Bus: Blue and Weekend CAT Stop 10 "Aberdeen Street." VIETNAMESE.

How would you know to walk a couple of blocks up William Street to this ultra-clean,
humble diner unless locals (or Frommer's), tipped you off? It's just laminate tables in
a bare room, but who cares when the ingredients are fresh, the service friendly, and the
food cheap. The most expensive thing on the long menu is "Vietnamese beef stew egg
noodle soup cooked slowly with Chinese herbs, cinnamon, lemon grass, ginger, and
tomato and served with French bread." How's that for A$7.50 (U.S.$4.88)? BYO.

Manee Thai. 19 Lake St. ☎ **08/9228 1991.** Reservations recommended Fri and Sat night.
Main courses A$11.80–$15.50 (U.S.$7.67–$10.08); buffet A$19.95 (U.S.$12.97). AE, BC, DC,
MC, V. Tues–Sun 6:30–10:30pm. Train: Perth. Bus: Blue and Weekend CAT Stop 14 "James
Street." THAI.

Gold-framed mirrors, rosewood chairs, and a hushed ambience make this a good
choice for a not-too-expensive night out. This is upscale, authentic Thai, focused
almost entirely on chicken, duck, and fish. Unusually for a Thai menu, there is little
for vegetarians. I couldn't complain about the tasty *toong tong*, wrapped parcels of pork
with chili dipping sauce, nor about the hearty chicken *mussaman* curry. If you want to
try a little of everything, always fun with Thai food, opt for the buffet. Service is atten-
tive. The wine list prices are OK, but beware the BYO corkage fee of A$4 (U.S.$2.60)
per person! Licensed and BYO.

Viet Hoa. 349 William St. ☎ **08/9328 2127.** Reservations recommended on Fri and Sat
night. Most main courses A$5–$14 (U.S.$3.25–$9.10). AE, BC, MC, V. Daily 10am–10pm.
Train: Perth. Bus: Blue and Weekend CAT Stop 10 "Aberdeen Street." VIETNAMESE.

With its tablecloths, fake plants, and airy dimensions, the Viet Hoa is a little more upscale than the Hung Long Coffee & Noodle House (see above) across the road, but the prices are just a few dollars higher. The cold Vietnamese spring rolls remind you what fresh food is supposed to taste like. The stir-fries, satays, and sweet-and-sour dishes are huge, so don't over-order! BYO.

Vultures. Francis St. at William St., Northbridge. ☎ **08/9227 9087.** Reservations recommended for dinner Fri–Sat. Main courses A$13.80–$25.50 (U.S.$8.97–$16.58); dine-in or takeout sandwiches at lunch Mon–Fri A$6–$9 (U.S.$3.90–$5.85). AE, BC, DC, MC, V. Sun–Thurs noon–11pm, Fri–Sat noon–2am. Open 365 days a year. Bus: Blue CAT Stop 9 "TAFE." MODERN AUSTRALIAN.

This large, relaxed, and groovy coffee lounge-cum-restaurant suits all occasions and all types, from couples doing dinner *a deux* in the streetside courtyard, to teen nightclubbers hanging out after a big night. You can even lie down in Balinese four-poster wedding beds instead of sitting at tables, with cushions to sit on and a low coffee table inside. The food is surprisingly good, from lightish stuff—gourmet sandwiches (Monday to Friday), roast chicken nachos, curry laksa—to stylish mains like veal ribs on parsnip and potato mash with snow peas and a Dijon cream jus. Rainbow-colored cocktails are a specialty.

ON THE BEACH

The Blue Duck. 151 Marine Parade, North Cottesloe. ☎ **08/9385 2499.** Reservations recommended, especially on weekends. Main courses A$2.90–$13.50 (U.S.$1.89–$8.78) breakfast, A$11.50–$26.50 (U.S.$7.48–$17.23) all day menu (many meals under $20/U.S$13). Buffet breakfast Sat–Sun and public holidays only A$13–$19 (U.S.$8.45–$12.35). Kids' menu A$6.50–$8.50 (U.S.$4.23–$5.53). AE, BC, DC, MC, V. Daily 6am–late (from 6:30am in winter). Bus: 71, 72, 73. MODERN AUSTRALIAN.

For ocean views it's hard to beat this casual restaurant right over the sand. Although the interior lacks the balcony's panoramic position, it has an upbeat seaside ambience and is as packed as the porch. The long all-day menu has lots of light choices like chicken Caesar salad, as well as steaks, grilled fish, gourmet burgers, and wood-fired pizzas with such toppings as roast pumpkin with sweet onion jam, gorgonzola, and rocket (arugula). Licensed and BYO (bottled wine only: That means no BYO beer or spirits).

✪ **Indiana Tea House.** 99 Marine Parade (on Cottesloe Beach opposite Forrest St.), Cottesloe. ☎ **08/9385 5005.** Reservations recommended. Grazing menu A$10.50–$35 (U.S.$6.83–$22.75); most meals under A$30 (U.S.$19.50). AE, BC, DC, MC, V. Weekdays 11am–late, weekends 8am–late. Bus: 71, 72, 73. MODERN AUSTRALIAN.

The colonial Asian trappings at this delightful turn-of-the-century bathhouse-turned-restaurant on Cottesloe Beach—the bamboo birdcages, plaster lions, and palms—make me want to head straight for the tropical timber bar and order a Singapore Sling. Actually, the stucco building with bay windows and wooden floors is new—it just looks old. The Spice Islands-meets-Down Under food is up to date, a grazing menu of light to full-on dishes, such as Goan spiced mussels with cucumber, chili and mint raita and garlic naan bread; or char-grilled yellow fin tuna on sesame-crushed potatoes

Super-Cheap Eats in Northbridge

Bless the Hare Krishnas for their wonderful cheap restaurants dispensing delicious vegetarian nourishment. **"Food for Life"** at 200 William St., Northbridge (☎ **08/ 9227 1684**) serves an all-you-can-eat buffet for just A$5 (U.S.$3.25) (A$4/ U.S.$2.60 for seniors and students) Monday to Friday from noon to 2:30pm.

Java Joints

Don't leave Freo without a "short black" (that's an espresso) or a "flat white" (coffee with milk) at the port's "cappuccino strip" on South Terrace. On weekends this street bursts at the seams with locals flocking to alfresco Italian-style cafes serving good java and excellent foccacia, pasta, and pizza. **DOME, Old Papa's,** and **Gino's Trattoria & Cafe** are three to look for.

---

with mango salsa. Seafood is a big item. The place is just as popular with business folk cutting deals as it is with arty types browsing the papers over their caffe latte. Go in the daytime to make the most of those ocean views, or at sunset.

IN FREMANTLE

There's a Fremantle branch of **Fast Eddy's** (see above) at 13 Essex St. (☎ **08/9336 1671**) and another **Miss Maud Swedish Restaurant** (see above) at 33 South Terrace (☎ **08/9336 1599**)—the breakfast buffet is only available weekends, though.

Gino's Pizzeria. 95 Market St. (behind Gino's Trattoria & Café on South Terrace). ☎ **08/ 9430 6126.** Reservations recommended on weekends; some tables always kept unreserved. Pizzas A$8.25–$17.60. (U.S.$5.36–$11.44). Main courses A$12.65–$18.65 (U.S.$8.22–$12.12). AE, BC, DC, JCB, MC, V. Daily 6pm–late, Fri–Sun from noon. Train: Fremantle. WOOD-FIRED PIZZA/ITALIAN.

All the traditional favorites get served up alongside the tastiest wood-fired pizzas in Perth. Servings are huge—one pizza is enough for two. The pizza base is high, airy, and crispy, and the toppings are innovative, like blue castello cheese, leek and parsley, or roast lamb with pesto salsa and pine nuts. Traditional main courses such as pasta and veal parmagiana share the menu with trendier offerings such as chargrilled swordfish in balsamic vinaigrette. The decor is upbeat with terrazzo tables, a concrete and timber floor, and stainless-steel bar. Licensed and BYO (BYO spirits not permitted).

WHAT TO SEE & DO IN PERTH

Art Gallery of Western Australia. 47 James St. (enter near the walkway opposite Perth Railway Station), Northbridge. ☎ **08/9492 6600** administration, 08/9492 6622 recorded information line. Free admission. Entry fee may apply to special exhibits. Daily 10am–5pm; from 1pm Anzac Day (April 25). Closed Christmas, New Year's Day and Good Friday. Train: Perth. Bus: Blue CAT Stop 7 "Culture Centre."

Outstanding among this state gallery's international and Australian paintings, prints, sculpture, craft, and drawings is the Aboriginal art collection, the finest in Australia. A free guided tour of a particular collection runs once a day, most days; call for times.

Cohunu Koala Park. Off Mills Rd. E., Gosnells (or located in the suburb of Martin on some maps). ☎ **08/9390 6090.** Admission A$17 (U.S.$11.05) adults, A$8 (U.S.$5.20) children 3–13. Animal feed A40¢ (U.S.26¢). Daily 10am–5pm; weekends 10am–5.30pm, koala photo sessions 10am–4pm. Closed Christmas. Train: Gosnells on Armadale line plus A$10 (U.S.$6.50) cab. By car: Take Riverside Dr. across Swan River onto Albany Hwy., follow for approx. 25km (16 miles) to Gosnells, turn left onto Tonkin Hwy. and right half a mile later onto Mills Rd. E. (approx. 35-min. drive from city). A cab from the city is approx. A$30 (U.S.$19.50).

This wildlife park is your big chance to have your photo taken cuddling a koala (for A$25/U.S.$16.25, or A$12/U.S.$7.80 if you take it yourself). You can also feed 100 kangaroos, wallabies and emus wandering in natural enclosures, see wombats, dingoes and llamas, and walk through an aviary housing Aussie native birds. Wild water birds collect on the ponds in the park's 18 hectares (45 acres). A small train will ferry you around part of the grounds for an extra A$2 (U.S.$1.30).

Kings Park & Botanic Garden. Fraser Ave. off Kings Park Rd. ☎ **08/9480 3600.** Free admission. Daily 24 hr., 365 days. The Visitor Information Centre on Fraser Ave. inside the park is open daily 9:30am–4pm (closed Christmas and Good Friday). Bus: 33 stops outside the Visitor Centre and extends into the park on Sat afternoon, and much of the day Sunday and public holidays; 103, 104, 200, 202, 208, and 209 stop outside the gates. Red CAT Stop 25 "Havelock Street" is 1 block to the north of the gates.

On the edge of the city center is Perth's pride and joy, a 400-hectare (988-acre) park of botanic gardens and uncultivated bushland. Here you can inspect weird and wonderful Western Australian flora, get to know the solitude of the Australian bush, and bike, hike, or drive an extensive network of roads and trails. Visiting the wildflower displays from August to October is a highlight on many Perth residents' calendars. Aboriginal art is on show in the gallery under the city lookout on Fraser Avenue. There are BBQ and picnic facilities, several extensive playgrounds, bikes for rent (behind the Visitor Information Centre), tearooms and the incomparable Fraser's (see "Dining," above).

Pick up self-guiding maps from the Visitor Information Centre, or join one of the daily free-guided walks departing from the giant Karri Log outside it. Walks usually depart 10am and 2pm (but check before you show up) and take 1½ hours, or up to 3 hours on bushwalks. The **Perth Tram Co.** (☎ **08/9322 2006**) runs 1-hour tours of the park and neighboring University of Western Australia in replica 1899 wooden trams. Tours depart daily from outside the Visitor Information Centre on Fraser Avenue at 11am, 12:15pm, 1:15pm, and 2:15pm (and occasionally at 3:15pm on Sunday subject to demand; check with the driver). Tickets cost A$10 (U.S.$6.50) for adults, A$8 (U.S.$5.20) for seniors, A$5 (U.S.$3.25) for children 4 to 14, and A$25 (U.S.$16.25) families. Buy tickets on board.

Perth Mint. 310 Hay St. at Hill St., East Perth. ☎ **08/9421 7425.** Admission A$6.60 (U.S.$4.29) adults, A$5.50 (U.S.$3.58) seniors and students, A$3.30 (U.S.$2.15) school-age children, A$16.50 (U.S.$10.73) families; free admission to the shop. Daily 9am–4pm. Closed Christmas, New Year's Day, Anzac Day (Apr 25) and Good Friday.

During the 1890s gold rush, a monthly escort brought gold to this infant mint from Kalgoorlie to be made into coins for Great Britain, Australia, and other countries. Bullion is still traded in this lovely late-Victorian building today, so if you stumble across a gold nugget on your travels through Western Australia, you know where to bring it! You can mint your own medallion for an extra A$15 (U.S.$9.75), handle a A$200,000 (U.S.$130,000) 400-ounce gold bar, see coins being minted, ogle a sizable collection of nuggets, and watch a gold pour on the hour from 10am weekdays, and from 10am to noon inclusive on weekends. A 30-minute free-guided tour departs half an hour before every pour. The shop sells gold coins and nugget jewelry.

Perth Zoo. 20 Labouchere Rd., South Perth. ☎ **08/9474 3551** for recorded information, 08/9367 7988 administration. Admission A$11 (U.S.$7.15) adults, A$5.50 (U.S.$3.58) children 4–15, A$30 (U.S.$19.50) family of 4. Daily 9am–5pm (open 365 days a year). Ferry: Barrack St. Jetty to Mends St. Jetty, South Perth. Bus: 108 or 110 from stand 42, St. Georges Terrace at William St.

Picture Perfect

For the only photo of Perth you'll need, snap the view over the city and river from the War Memorial in Kings Park—it's superb day or night

This is a good place to see numbats, wombats, Tasmanian devils, echidnas (the Aussie answer to the porcupine), dingoes, kangaroos, koalas, crocodiles, black swans, and just about every other kind of Aussie wildlife in natural habitats. Notable exotic animals include orangutans, Rothschild's giraffes, Asian elephants, and Sumatran tigers. Feeding demonstrations and talks run throughout the day. There are picnic facilities.

Aqua. Sorrento Quay at Hillarys Boat Harbour, 91 Southside Dr., Hillarys. ☎ **08/9447 7500.** Admission A$18 (U.S.$11.70) adults, A$9 (U.S.$5.85) children 3–14, A$13.50 (U.S.$8.78) seniors and students, A$49 (U.S.$31.85) family of 4 plus A$5 (U.S.$3.25) per extra child. Daily 9am–5pm. Closed Christmas. Train and bus: Take Joondalup train line (also called the Currambine line) to Warwick, transfer to bus 423 (*Note:* only 3 bus services run Sunday). By car, take Mitchell Hwy. 23km (14 miles) north, turn left into Hepburn Ave., and follow signs to the "Oceanarium."

You won't catch performing dolphins a la Sea World, but there's plenty for kids to see here, including a moving 40-meter (128 ft.) walkway through an underwater tunnel of sharks, rays, and turtles; a touch pool which even has a (small!) shark; and lots of aquaria that showcase the marine life of the Western Australian coast, including leafy sea dragons, coral reefs, jelly fish, crocodiles, and dangerous sea critters. Keepers feed sharks and the touchpool creatures daily. For A$75 (U.S.$48.75), qualified divers can dive with sharks, and for the same fee anyone over 12 can swim with fur seals on weekends, Wednesdays and Fridays. Book both experiences well in advance.

Western Australian Museum. Francis St. at Beaufort St. (or enter off James Street Mall), Northbridge. ☎ **08/9427 2700.** Free admission (donation requested). Admission fee may apply to special exhibitions. Daily 9:30am–5pm; Anzac Day (Apr 25) and Boxing Day (Dec 26) 1–5pm. Closed Christmas and Good Friday. Train: Perth. Bus: Blue CAT Stop 8 "Museum."

Kids will like the dinosaur gallery, the drawers full of insects in the lobby, the mammal and blue whale skeletons on the well-stocked aquatic zoology floor, the butterfly gallery, and the bizarre "megamouth" shark preserved in a tank set in the ground in the courtyard. The main attraction for grownups is one of the best collections of Aboriginal artifacts and rare photographs in the country.

HITTING THE BEACHES

Perth shares Sydney's good luck in having beaches in the metropolitan area—19 of them, in fact, along the 35-kilometer (22-mile) Sunset Coast from Cottesloe in the south to Quinns Rocks in the north. Mornings are best as a strong afternoon wind, known as the "Fremantle Doctor," can be unpleasant, especially in summer. Always swim between the red and yellow flags, which denote a "safe swimming" zone.

A walk/cycle path runs along 15 beaches from Sorrento Beach in the north down to Port Beach on Fremantle's outskirts in the south. It veers inland for a few miles at Swanbourne, where it also cuts out for a few blocks; you should easily pick it up again.

On weekends and public holidays from the last Saturday in September to the last Sunday in April, the **Sunset Coaster** bus 928 stops hourly during the day at most beaches on its way from Fremantle to Hillarys and beyond. It also operates in the reverse direction. You can take a surfboard under 2 meters on the 928.

All beaches have ample parking. The three most popular are:

COTTESLOE This pretty crescent, graced by the Edwardian-style Indiana Tea House restaurant (see "Dining," above), is Perth's most fashionable beach. It has safe swimming, a small surf break, and a kiosk. There are a couple of cafes nearby. Train: Cottesloe, then a walk of several hundred meters. Bus direct to the beach: 71, 72, or 73.

SCARBOROUGH Biggest of them all, Scarborough's white sands stretch for miles from the base of the Hotel Rendezvous Observation City Perth. Swimming is generally safe, and surfers are always guaranteed a wave, although inexperienced swimmers should take a rain check when the surf is rough. The busy shopping precinct across the road means there's always somewhere to buy lunch and drinks. Bus: 400.

TRIGG   Surfers like Trigg best for its consistent swells. It has a kiosk. Bus: 400 to Scarborough, then a 10-minute walk north.

A DAY OUT IN FREMANTLE

The heritage port precinct of ✪ **Fremantle,** 19 kilometers (12 miles) from downtown Perth on the mouth of the Swan River, is probably best known outside Australia as the site of the 1987 America's Cup challenge. Just before that event, the city embarked on a major restoration of its gracious but rundown warehouses and derelict Victorian buildings. The Cup may be gone, but today "Freo" is a bustling district of 150 National Trust buildings, alfresco cafes, museums, galleries, pubs, markets, and shops in a well-preserved historical atmosphere. It's still a working port so you will see fishing boats unloading, and yachts gliding in and out of the harbor. The ambience is so authentic that locals make a beeline for the place every weekend, resulting in a hubbub of buzzing shoppers, market stallholders, java drinkers, yachties, tourists, and fishermen. Allow a full day to take in even half the sights—and don't forget to knock back an ale or two on the verandahs of one of the gorgeous old pubs.

ESSENTIALS

GETTING THERE   Parking is plentiful, but driving can be a pain, as many of the streets are one-way. Most attractions are within walking distance, so take the train to Fremantle station and explore on foot.

A nice way to get to the port and see Perth's suburbs at the same time is on cruises run by several companies once or twice a day from Barrack Street Jetty. See "Whale-Watching Cruises, Tram Trips & Other Tours" later in this chapter for cruise operators.

GETTING AROUND   The easiest way to explore is on foot. Elaine Berry, of the Western Australian Maritime Museum (see below), leads a 90-minute **walking tour** for A$10 (U.S.$6.50) for adults, A$7.50 (U.S.$4.88) for seniors, and A$3 (U.S.$1.95) for school-age kids; you must book by calling the museum ☎ **08/9431 8455,** or Elaine at home (☎ **08/9336 1906**) on weekends. She schedules the tours on a day and time to suit you. Check with the **Fremantle Tourist Bureau** if the free **Clipper** bus makes a running loop of local attractions; at press time this service had ceased but plans were under way to revive it. **Fremantle Trams** (☎ **08/9339 8719**)— an old tram carriage now on wheels, not tram tracks—conducts various tour routes of 45 or 90 minutes, departing eight times a day from **Fremantle Town Hall** from 10am, with the last tour at 4pm. Tickets cost A$8 to $12 (U.S.$5.20–$7.80) adults, A$7 to $10 (U.S.$4.55–$6.50) seniors, A$3 to $5 (U.S.$1.95–$3.25) for children 15 and under, and A$15 to $20 (U.S.$9.75–$13) for families. Buy tickets on board. **Fremantle Ghost Walks** (☎ **0401 588187** for bookings; 08/9336 1916 for enquiries) leads 1-hour spook saunters Monday at 8pm; tickets are A$15 (U.S.$9.75) adults, A$10 (U.S.$6.50) seniors and students, and A$8 (U.S.$5.20) kids aged 6 to 15, plus a BOCS telephone booking fee of A$6 (U.S.$3.90) per booking.

VISITOR INFORMATION   The **Fremantle Tourist Bureau** is located in Town Hall, Kings Square at High Street, Fremantle, WA 6160 (☎ **08/9431 7878;** fax 08/9431 7755; www.fremantle.wa.gov.au). It's open Monday through Saturday 9am to 5pm and Sunday 12:30 to 4:30pm. Seeing the Sights in Fremantle

You will want to explore some of Freo's excellent museums and other attractions below, but take time to stroll the streets and admire the 19th-century offices and warehouses, many now painted in rich historically accurate colors. As soon as you arrive, wander down to the docks—either **Victoria Quay,** where sailing craft come and go, or **Fishing Boat Harbour** off Mews Road, where the boats bring in their catches—to get a breath of salt air.

Freo's best shopping is arts and crafts, from handblown glass to Aboriginal art to alpaca wool clothing. Worth a look are the assorted art, craft, and souvenir stores on **High Street** west of the mall; the **E Shed markets** on Victoria Quay (Fri–Sun only, 9am–6pm); and **Bannister Street CraftWorks,** an arts cooperative where you often spy the artists at work (11am–5:30pm; closed Mon). The **Fremantle Markets,** 74 South Terrace at Henderson Street (☎ **08/9335 2515**), mostly sell cheap imported handicrafts, jewelry, housewares, and clothing, as well as inexpensive food. They open Friday 9am to 9pm, Saturday 9am to 5pm, and Sunday and any public holidays that fall on a Monday, 10am to 5pm.

The most popular watering holes are the **Sail & Anchor,** 64 South Terrace (☎ **08/ 9335 8433**), which brews its own Brass Monkey Stout; the **Norfolk,** 47 South Terrace at Norfolk Street (☎ **08/9335 5405**); and the beautifully restored front bar and garden courtyard at **Phillimore's Café & Bar** at His Majesty's Hotel, on Phillimore Street at Mouat Street (☎ **08/9335 9596**). The happening "cappuccino strip" on **South Terrace** is good for people-watching.

Fremantle Arts Centre. 1 Finnerty St. ☎ **08/9432 9555.** Free admission. Daily 10am–5pm. Closed Christmas and Good Friday, Boxing Day (Dec 26) and New Year's Day.

Housed in a neo-Gothic 1860s building built by convicts, this center contains excellent contemporary arts and crafts galleries with a constantly changing array of works. There is a shop selling high-quality Western Australian crafts, a bookshop with Australian literature and art books, and a courtyard cafe. Free musical concerts play on the lawn every Sunday between September and April or May from 2 to 4pm.

Fremantle History Museum. 1 Finnerty St. at Ord St. (part of the Fremantle Arts Centre, see above). ☎ **08/9430 7966.** Free admission. Sun–Fri 10:30am–4:30pm, Sat and public holidays 1–5pm. Closed Christmas, Boxing Day (Dec 26), and Good Friday.

Housed in a convict-built former lunatic asylum next to the Fremantle Arts Centre, this small but packed museum uses lots of old photographs and personal possessions to paint a realistic picture of what life was like for Fremantle's first settlers, the Aboriginal people they displaced, and later generations up to the present day.

Fremantle Prison. 1 The Terrace. ☎ **08/9430 7177.** Free admission to courtyard. Tours A$12 (U.S.$7.80) adults, A$4.80 (U.S.$3.12) children 6–15; candlelight tours Wed and Fri. A$14.40 (U.S.$9.36) adults, A$7.20 (U.S.$4.68) children. A$2 (U.S.$1.30) discount on admission to Fremantle Trams passengers (see "Getting Around," below). Daily 10am–5pm (5pm tour excludes women's prison tour), Wed and Fri from 7pm. Closed Christmas and Good Friday.

Even jails sported attractive architecture back in the 1850s. This picturesque limestone jail, built by convicts who no doubt ended up inside it, was a maximum-security prison until 1991. You can enter the courtyard free, but to see bushranger (highwayman) Joe Moondyne's cell, the gallows, and cells walls featuring some wonderful artwork by the former inmates, you need to take the 75-minute tour, which runs every half hour throughout the day. It is followed by a 45-minute tour of the women's cells. You must book for the Wednesday and Friday night candlelight tours, which take 90 minutes.

The Roundhouse. 10 Arthur Head (entry over the railway line from High St.) ☎ **08/9335 1881.** Admission by donation. Daily 10.30am–3pm. Closed Good Friday and Christmas.

A peep at this 12-sided jail, the state's oldest public building (ca. 1830), will only take a minute. There are no displays or memorabilia, but it's worth a look for itself and for the sea views on the other side. Whaling took place from the beach below the jail last century, and the time cannon just to its west, a replica of a gun salvaged from an 1878 wreck, is fired daily and a time ball dropped at 1pm, just as it was in the 1800s.

✪ **Western Australian Maritime Museum.** Cliff St. ☎ **08/9431 8444.** Free admission (donation requested). Daily 9:30am–5pm, Anzac Day (April 25), and Boxing Day (Dec 26) 1–5pm. Free guided 30-min tours daily 11am and 2pm. Closed Christmas and Good Friday.

Fascinating archaeological displays of shipwrecks and treasure recovered off the treacherous Western Australian coast are well worth a visit here, housed over two floors in a historic stone warehouse. Displays date from the 1600s, when Dutch explorers became the first Europeans to encounter Australia, and promptly abandoned its harsh shores as being useless.

WHALE-WATCHING CRUISES, TRAM TRIPS & OTHER TOURS

Boat Torque (☎ 1300/368 686 in Australia, or 08/9221 5844), **Golden Sun** (☎ 08/9325 1616), and **Oceanic Cruises** (☎ 08/9325 1191) run an assortment of cruises on the Swan River, some as far as Fremantle, and to historic homes and vineyards in the Swan Valley. **Captain Cook Cruises** (☎ 08/9325 3341) cruises on the Perth-Fremantle route only. From September through November, Perth's waters are alive with southern right whales and humpback whales returning from the north with their calves. To join a 2- or 3-hour jaunt to watch them, contact Boat Torque, Oceanic Cruises, or the **Rottnest Express ferry** (☎ 08/9335 6406), which does whale-watch trips between ferry runs. Departure days and times vary from year to year with every cruise operator, so check ahead. The average price is around A$25 (U.S.$16.25), about half-price for kids. Most depart Fremantle; Boat Torque also does them from Hillarys Boat Harbour. The company provides coach connections to Hillarys from Perth. The **Perth Tram Co.** (☎ 08/9322 2006) makes a daily-guided loop of city attractions, the casino and Kings Park in replica 1899 wooden trams; hop on and off as often as you wish. Tickets, which you buy on board, cost A$15 (U.S.$9.75) for adults, A$13 (U.S.$8.45) for seniors, A$7 (U.S.$4.55) for children 4 to 14, and A$37 (U.S.$24.05) families. City-casino, city-Kings Park and casino-Kings Park legs are also available. Join anywhere; the tram starts at 565 Hay Street at 9:40am and makes six 90-minute loops a day.

Feature Tours (☎ 1800/999 819 in Australia, or 08/9479 4131; fax 08/9479 4130; www.ft.com.au) runs half- and full-day coach tours to attractions in and around Perth.

OUTDOOR ACTIVITIES & SPECTATOR SPORTS

BIKING   Bike tracks run along the Swan River, through Kings Park, down to the beaches. There is a great 9.5-kilometer (6-mile) track around Perth Water, the broad expanse of river in front of the CBD, that starts at the Swan River on Riverside Drive in the city and goes over the Causeway bridge, back along the other bank and over the bridge at the Narrows back to the city. The state Department of Transport's cycling division, **Bikewest,** publishes bike route maps to the city. They are available in bike shops, and also at newsagents.

An hour's rental with **Koala Bike Hire,** in the car park behind Fraser's restaurant in Kings Park (☎ 08/9321 3061) is A$4 (U.S.$2.60), or A$15 (U.S.$9.75) for the day, which includes a helmet (required by law in W.A.), lock, and maps of Kings Park.

CANOEING, KAYAKING & WHITE-WATER RAFTING   Rivergods (☎ 08/9259 0749) runs canoeing, sea kayaking, and whitewater rafting adventures on the Swan and other rivers near Perth. The company's one-day sea kayak trip to snorkel and swim with wild sea lions in the Shoalwater Islands Marine Park, just south of Perth, gets rave reviews. You also paddle see penguins being fed on Penguin Island. On the return journey you tie your kayaks together, raise a kite and kayak-sail home! The cost for the day is A$105 (U.S.$68.25). Pickup from your hotel is an extra A$10 (U.S.$6.50). This trip runs daily from September or October to June.

FISHING   Dhufish, pink snapper, cod, marlin, shark, tuna and mahi-mahi are running in the ocean off Perth. **Mill's Charters** at Hillarys Boat Harbour, approximately 25 kilometers (15½ miles) north of the city center (☎ **08/9246 5334,** or 08/9401 0833 after hours) runs full-day deep sea trips aboard 60-foot and 70-foot cruisers for A$90 (U.S.$58.50) weekdays and A$99 (U.S.$64.35) on weekends and public holidays. That includes tackle and bait; BYO lunch and drinks. The company also runs game fishing day trips, for which you're looking at A$250 (U.S.$162.50) per person. Another great fishing spot is Rottnest Island (see "Side Trips From Perth," below). **Rottnest Malibu Diving** (☎ **08/9292 5111**) rents tackle for beach and jetty fishing, and does fishing tours to the pick of the island's bays in winter months.

GOLF   Convenient to the city is **Burswood Park Golf Course,** part of the Burswood International Resort Casino complex, across the Swan River from town on the Great Eastern Highway, Burswood (☎ **08/9362 7576** for the pro shop). Great city views, and wild black swans and pelicans make this a pretty course. A 9-hole round is just A$12 (U.S.$7.80) weekdays and A$15 (U.S.$9.75) weekends. A cart for 9 holes is A$20 (U.S.$13), and club rental is A$15 (U.S.$9.75). Even more scenic are the 27 championship fairways designed by Robert Trent Jones, Jr., at **Joondalup Resort,** Country Club Boulevard, Connolly, 25-kilometers (15½-miles) north of Perth (☎ **08/9400 8811** is the pro shop); and **The Vines Resort** in the Swan Valley (☎ **08/9297 0222** is the pro shop, which has two 18-hole bushland courses. It was ranked No. 1 Golf Resort in Australia by *Golf Australia* magazine in 2000. Kangaroos often come onto the course at Joondalup and The Vines. Expect to pay around A$60 to $80 (U.S.$39–$52) for 9 holes at either. **Koala Golf** (☎ **08/9221 2688**) runs day trips to various courses.

SAILING   The tallest Tall Ship in Australia, the lovely three-masted barquentine *STS Leeuwin II* (☎ **08/9430 4105**), sails from B Shed at Victoria Quay, Fremantle, when she is not out on charter. Leisurely day trips from 10am to 3pm are A$99 (U.S.$64.35) for adults and A$50 (U.S.$32.50) for children under 13. The ship sometimes does 3-hour sails at twilight costing A$55 (U.S.$35.75) for adults and A$30 (U.S.$19.50) for children. Experienced sailors can sail on Wednesday and Saturday afternoons in summer with members of the **Royal Perth Yacht Club,** Australia II Drive, Crawley (☎ **08/9389 1555;** ask for the sailing administrator) if there is a place free aboard. All-white dress standards apply.

SCUBA DIVING & SNORKELING   Rottnest Island's corals, reef fish, and limestone caverns, in 18- to 35-meter (59- to 128-ft.) visibility, are a gift from heaven to Perth divers and snorkelers. Contact **Rottnest Malibu Diving** (☎ **08/9292 5111**) on Rottnest Island (see "Side Trips From Perth," below) to rent gear or join a dive trip. **Diving Ventures,** at 37 Barrack St. in Perth (☎ **08/9421 1052**), conducts dive day trips from Perth to Rottnest Island, and also to the wreck of the *HMAS Swan* off Dunsborough in the state's Southwest, a 250-ft long destroyer which was scuttled for divers' pleasure a couple of years ago. A day trip to either spot costs A$135 (U.S.$87.75) with two dives, including lunch and all gear. The company also rents scuba gear. It has an outlet at 384 South Terrace, Fremantle, too.

SURFING   You will find good surfing at many beaches, Scarborough and Trigg in particular. See the "Hitting the Beaches" section earlier in this chapter. Rottnest Island (see "Side Trips from Perth," below) also has good breaks. **Murray Smith Surf Centre,** Shop 14, Luna Maxi Mart, Scarborough (☎ **08/9245 2988**), rents long boards for A$20 (U.S.$13) for half a day or A$30 (U.S.$19.50) for the day, plus a A$100 (U.S.$65) refundable deposit. They also rent body boards. **Surfing WA** (☎ **08/9448 0004**) runs hour-long surfing classes for A$40 (U.S.$26) per person, or A$35 (U.S.$22.75) per person for two people. Boards, wetsuits and sunscreen are provided. Lessons run daily at any beach where there are waves. That usually turns out to be Trigg or Scarborough.

SPECTATOR SPORTS

AUSTRALIAN RULES FOOTBALL (AFL)   Perth's Aussie Rules team, the **West Coast Eagles,** is based at Subiaco Oval, 171 Subiaco Road, Subiaco (☎ **08/9381 1111**). Book tickets through **TicketMaster 7** (☎ **13 61 22** for bookings; 1902/29 1502 is a toll line for recorded events information). Three matches a year take place at the WACA cricket ground (see below). The season runs from March to August; most games play Friday and Saturday nights and Sunday afternoons.

CRICKET   The Western Australian Cricket Association grounds, **Nelson Crescent,** East Perth (☎ **08/9265 7222**), whose acronym WACA is pronounced "Whacker" by loving fans, is host to major matches over the November to March season. Games range from an afternoon to 5 days, and are played mostly by day, occasionally at night. Tickets cost as little as A$6 (U.S.$3.90) for many lesser matches and go up to about A$45 (U.S.$29.25) for the big matches. Book seats to international matches through **TicketMaster 7** (☎ **13 61 22;** 1902/29 1502 is a toll line for recorded events information); tickets to national matches are only available at the gate.

THE SHOPPING SCENE

Perth's city center is a major retail precinct. Most shops are located on the parallel Hay Street and Murray Street malls, located 1 block apart, and in the network of arcades running off them such as the Plaza, City and Carillon City arcades. **London Court** off Hay Street Mall is a recreated Tudor street lined with one-off fashion, gift, and jewelry shops. Off Murray Street Mall on Forrest Place is the **Forrest Chase shopping center** housing the Myer department store and boutiques on two gallery levels. Add to your collection of international designer brands on posh **King Street.**

If you want to avoid the chains, skip the city center and spend half a day in **Subiaco** or "Subi," where Hay Street and Rokeby Road are lined with smart boutiques, home accessories shops, art galleries, cafes, antique shops and markets. The Colonnade shopping center at 388 Hay Street showcases groovy young Aussie fashion designers in its Studio 388 section. Fremantle's shopping is mostly limited to a good selection of crafts, markets, and Aboriginal souvenirs.

Shops are open until 9pm on Friday in the city, and until 9pm on Thursday in Subiaco and Fremantle.

ABORIGINAL ART & CRAFTS

Creative Native, 32 King St. (☎ **08/9322 3398**), stocks Perth's widest range of Aboriginal art and crafts, including carvings, boomerangs, bowls, carved emu eggs, a huge range of didgeridoos, and Aboriginal-print merchandise from men's ties to potholders. Upstairs is a gallery selling original works by some renowned Aboriginal artists. There's another branch at 65 High St., Fremantle (☎ **08/9335 6995**).

The **Mossenson Gallery,** 115 Hay St., Subiaco (☎ **08/9388 2899**) and 82 High St., Fremantle (☎ **08/9335 2911**), stocks works on canvas, paper, and bark, as well as artifacts, textiles, pottery, didgeridoos, boomerangs, and sculpture by famous and emerging Aboriginal artists. Serious collectors should find something they like here.

Desert Designs

Aboriginal artist Jimmy Pike grew up in Western Australia's Sandy Desert and began transferring his Dreamtime art and designs to fabrics in 1981. Today his highly successful range of merchandise includes clothing. The children's gear is especially cute. The **Japingka Gallery,** 47 High St., Fremantle (☎ **08/9335 8265**), stocks original paintings and limited edition prints by Jimmy, his artistic partner, Doris Gingingara, and many other Aboriginal artists. It also stocks authentic didgeridoos, artifacts, and stunning high-quality hand-tufted woolen floor rugs in Aboriginal designs. For clothing and accessories featuring designs by Jimmy, Doris and other leading Aboriginal artists, visit the **Desert Designs** boutique at 114 High Street Mall, Fremantle (☎ **08/9430 4101**).

JEWELRY

Western Australia is renowned for farming the world's best South Sea pearls off Broome, for Argyle diamonds mined in the Kimberley, and for being one of the world's biggest gold producers. Most shops give tax-free prices to international travelers who present their airline ticket and passport; how much that tax amounts to was not clear when we went to print, due to a re-shuffling of Australia's tax rates. **Artisans of the Sea,** corner of Marine Terrace and Collie Street, Fremantle (☎ **08/9336 3633**), is owned by the Kailis family, which runs one of the world's biggest pearling operations. This store sells South Sea pearl strands and gold jewelry.

Family-owned sister stores, **Costello's,** Shop 5–6, London Court (☎ **08/9325 8588**), and **Swan Diamonds,** Shop 4, London Court (☎ **08/9325 8166**), have tasteful, understated jewelry. The designers at **Linneys Jewellers,** 37 Rokeby Rd., Subiaco (☎ **08/9382 4077**), turn out sleekly artistic one-of-a-kind pieces. Costello's, Swan Diamonds and Linneys all use opals, Argyle diamonds, and Broome pearls.

For opals to suit all budgets, head to **Quilpie Opals,** Shop 6, Piccadilly Arcade off Hay Street Mall (☎ **08/9321 8687**).

PERTH AFTER DARK

Scoop and the *Perth Weekly* (see "Perth Orientation," earlier in this chapter) are good sources of information on festivals and concerts, performing arts, classical music, exhibitions, and the like. Your best guide to dance clubs, concerts, gig listings, art house cinemas, and galleries is the *X-press* newspaper, free every Thursday at pubs, cafes, and live-music venues across town. *The West Australian* and *Sunday Times* newspapers publish some entertainment information, including cinema guides.

Two major booking agents handle bookings to most of the city's major performing arts, entertainment and sporting events: **BOCS** (☎ **08/9484 1133** for bookings; **Yellow Pages Talking Guide** ☎ **13 16 20** in Perth for recorded event listings) and **Ticketmaster 7** (☎ **13 61 22** for sporting events or 13 61 00 for all other events, or ☎ **1902/29 1502,** a pay-by-the-minute line for recorded events information).

THE PERFORMING ARTS   The West Australian Opera Company and **West Australian Ballet** usually perform at His Majesty's Theatre, 825 Hay St., a restored "grande-dame" venue from the early 1900's. Perth's leading theatrical company, the **Black Swan Theatre Company,** mostly plays at the Subiaco Theatre Centre, 180 Hamersley Rd., Subiaco. The **West Australian Symphony Orchestra** (☎ **08/9326 0000** for bookings, or call BOCS) usually performs at the Perth Concert Hall, 5 St. Georges Terrace next to the Duxton Hotel. Blessed with the best acoustics of any such venue in Australia, it has housed performances by the international orchestras, comedian Billy Connolly, and musician B.B. King. You can book opera, ballet, and the Black Swan Theatre Company tickets through BOCS.

The month-long **Perth International Arts Festival** (books through BOCS) showcases contemporary performing and visual arts every January, February or March, many events taking place outdoors. In summer, look for outdoor concerts at Perth Zoo (☎ **08/9474 3551** for recorded information, 08/9367 7988 administration) and outdoor concerts, plays, and movies, in Kings Park (☎ **08/9480 3600**).

PUBS & DANCE CLUBS   Northbridge houses most of city's lively pubs and dance clubs. Don't forget Freo has good pubs, too (we recommend three in "A Day Out in Fremantle," earlier in this chapter). For a trendy take on the traditional corner pub, head to **The Brass Monkey,** 209 William St. at James Street, Northbridge (☎ **08/ 9227 9596**). Downstairs are several bars and a beer garden; upstairs is the Monkey Bar cocktail bar (open Fri–Sat nights only, when a DJ plays) and a nice verandah brasserie. Stand-up comedy plays Wednesday night in the Monkey Bar for a A$10 (U.S.$6.50) cover. In Subiaco, "suits" flock to the "**Subi**," also known as the Subiaco Hotel, 465 Hay St. at Rokeby Road, Subiaco (☎ **08/9381 1028**), a popular historical pub with a stylish cafe. It's big on Friday night.

Metropolis, 146 Roe St., Northbridge (☎ **08/9228 0500**) is a huge complex of dance floors and bars over several levels, where Aussie and touring bands play. If your dancing 'til 6am days are over but you want to get down, hit it at **Margeaux's,** a nightclub popular with 30-, 40- and 50-somethings, in the Perth Parmelia Hilton, 14 Mill St. (☎ **08/9215 2000**). It opens Wednesday, Friday and Saturday nights.

THE CASINO   A 2000-seat showroom that hosts a variety of major acts is located in the **Burswood International Resort Casino,** on the Great Eastern Highway just over the river from the city (☎ **08/9362 7646** for guest information; for show bookings call 08/9484 7000 for the box office or call BOCS-see above). Free live bands, discos or karaoke play nightly in the Cabaret Lounge, and there are nine restaurants and five bars in the resort/casino complex. On the gaming floor are 126 tables, 1,160 video gaming machines, a VIP players' room, and a Keno Lounge. Except for Christmas Day, Good Friday, and Anzac Day, the casino is open 24 hours. Dress standards are smart casual—no jeans or T-shirts at night, for example. It's about a A$10 (U.S.$6.50) cab ride from the city, or take a train to Burswood station.

2 Side Trips from Perth

ROTTNEST ISLAND: GETTING FACE-TO-FACE WITH THE FISHES
19km (12 miles) W of Perth

The delightful wildlife reserve of ✪ **Rottnest Island** just off the Perth coast is like the city's own Great Barrier Reef in miniature. Its jewel-bright turquoise waters, warm currents, rocky coves, and many sheltered beaches harbor coral reefs and 360 kinds of fish that make for fabulous snorkeling. You may spot humpback whales from September to December, and dolphins surfing the waves anytime. The island is also home to 10,000 quokkas, cute otter-like marsupials that reach up to your knees. A wonderful thing about Rottnest is that it's car-free. Everyone gets around by bike (or bus, if you tire of pedaling). The island is 11 kilometers (7 miles) long and 4.5 kilometers (3 miles) across at its widest point. Essentials

GETTING THERE   Boat Torque (☎ **1300/368 686** or 08/9221 5844) and **Oceanic Cruises** (☎ **08/9325 1191**) each operate services at least twice a day from

Perth (trip time: approx. 1 hr., 45 min.), and as many as four times a day from Fremantle (trip time: approx. 25 min.). The **Rottnest Express ferry** (☎ **08/9335 6406**) runs four or five times a day from Fremantle only. Typical roundtrip fares from Perth are A$53 (U.S.$34.45); or A$38 (U.S.$24.70) roundtrip from Fremantle. This includes a free pickup from your Perth hotel for Perth departures. You pay about A$5 (U.S.$3.25) more if you return on a later day. Most boat operators offer day-trip and accommodation packages.

Kookaburra Air (☎ **08/9354 1158**) does half-day, full-day and two-day trips, either on a fly/fly or fly/cruise basis, departing Jandakot Airport, a 20-minute drive from downtown Perth. Return pickups from your hotel are included, but tours are not; you spend your time on the island however you wish. A full-day fly/fly trip costs A$150 (U.S.$97.50) per adult, and A$75 (U.S.$48.75) per child ages 3 to 12.

VISITOR INFORMATION For information before you arrive, write to the **Rottnest Island Authority,** E Shed, Victoria Quay, Fremantle, WA 6160 (☎ **08/ 9432 9300;** fax 08/9432 9339; www.rottnest.wa.gov.au). The **Rottnest Island Visitor Centre** (☎ **08/9372 9752**) is right at the end of the jetty.

GETTING AROUND Ferries pull into the jetty in the main town, called "Settlement" at Thomson Bay. **Bell-A-Bike Rottnest** (☎ **08/9292 5105**), next to the Rottnest Hotel near the jetty, rents bikes in every size, speed, and type imaginable, as well as holders for everything from surfboards to babies. An 18-speed bike is A$20 (U.S.$13) for a 9-hour day (plus a A$25/U.S.$16.25 refundable deposit), including a helmet (compulsory in Oz) and lock. There is no need to book a bike. The yellow **Bayseeker** bus does regular circumnavigations calling at all the best bays. An all-day ticket costs A$5.50 (U.S.$3.58) for adults, A$3 (U.S.$1.95) for seniors and students, A$2.20 (U.S.$1.43) children 4 to 12, and A$12 (U.S.$7.80) for families of four. Buy tickets on board.

A free bus runs between the airport and the five communities around the island.

Snorkeling, Diving, Surfing & Fishing

Most people come to Rottnest to snorkel, swim, surf, dive, or fish. As soon as you arrive, rent a bike and your preferred aquatic gear and pedal around the coast until you come to a beach that suits you. (Don't forget to carry drinking water and food, as the only shops are at Settlement). **The Basin, Little Parakeet Bay,** and **Little Salmon Bay** are good snorkel spots. The Visitor Centre sells A$5 (U.S.$3.25) maps to suggested snorkel trails in 20 bays. Surfers should try **Cathedral Rocks** or **Strickland Bay.** Fishermen will catch squid, salmon, and tailor as well as all kinds of reef fish. **Rottnest Malibu Diving** (☎ **08/9292 5111**), near the jetty, rents snorkel gear, dive gear, wetsuits, surfboards, body boards, aquabikes, and fishing tackle. The company conducts trips to some of the 100-plus dive sites around Rottnest. Some feature

Island Orientation Tours

Many first-time visitors take the 2-hour **Island Bus Tour** because it is a good introduction to the bays and the island's cultural and natural history—and because it includes a stop to pat the quokkas. It costs A$13.20 (U.S.$8.58) for adults, A$9.90 (U.S.$6.44) for seniors and students, A$6.60 (U.S.$4.29) for kids 4 to 12, and A$32 (U.S.$20.80) families of four. Departure times vary, but expect them to run twice a day, usually around 10:30am and 1:30pm. Buy tickets from the Visitor Centre.

limestone caverns and some of the island's 14 shipwrecks. A shore or boat dive with all gear included is A$60. (U.S.$39). If you have never dived before but want to try, a 1- to 2-hour theory lesson followed by a boat dive is A$135 (U.S.$87.75).

FOR HISTORY BUFFS

Rottnest has quite a bit to offer history buffs, who may want to walk (45-minute trip), cycle, or take the train to the **Oliver Hill** 1930's gun emplacements, which has intact 9.2 inch guns and battery tunnels housing an engine room, plotting room, and observation posts. You can explore the 1.5-kilometer (1-mile) heritage trail on your own (buy a map from the Visitor Centre for a dollar or so), or take a guided 1-hour tour on the hour between 11am and 2pm inclusive. The train fare, which includes the tour except for the last trip of the day, costs A$9.90 (U.S.$6.44) for adults, A$6.60 (U.S.$4.29) for seniors and students, and children 4 to 12, and A$24 (U.S.$15.60) for families of four. It departs from the station near the Visitor Centre hourly from 10:30am to 2:30pm inclusive.

Volunteer guides run free 1-hour historical walking tours of architectural points of interest around **Thomson Bay,** many of them built last century, like the Governor's residence, the chapel, the octagonal prison, the small museum (open daily 11am–4pm), and the former Boys' Reformatory. They depart from the Environment Office at 11:30am and 2:30pm daily. Another 1-hour heritage trail takes you to the memorial marking de Vlamingh, the Dutch explorer who named the island Rott Enest (Rat Nest) in 1696 when he mistook quokkas for varmints. Self-guiding maps to both these trails are sold at the Visitor Centre for a dollar or two.

WHERE TO STAY & DINE

Call the **Rottnest Island Authority's accommodation booking service** (☎ 08/9432 9111; fax 08/9432 9315) to book one of the island's 250-plus holiday homes, apartments, cabins, historic cottages, or the campground. Don't expect anything too new or upscale. Water and electricity restrictions mean no accommodation is air-conditioned. You should book well in advance all through summer.

Allison Camping Area and Caroline Thomson Camping Area. c/o Rottnest Island Authority, E Shed, Victoria Quay, Fremantle, WA 6160. ☎ **08/9432 9111.** Fax 08/9372 9715. www.rottnest.wa.gov.au. 52 cabins, 30 with bathroom. 50 tent sites. Summer A$24.20–$37.40 (U.S.$15.73–$24.31) cabin without bathroom; A$63.80 (U.S.$41.47) cabin with bathroom. Winter A$19.80–$28.60 (U.S.$12.87–$18.59) cabin without bathroom; A$59.40 (U.S.$38.61) cabin with bathroom. Tent site A$5.50 (U.S.$3.58) adults, A$2.75 (U.S.$1.79) children under 12, year-round. Minimum 2-night stay weekends. BC, MC, V.

Of the island's two camping areas, both located at Thomson Bay, the Allison Camping Area is the larger, with tent sites and two-, four- and six-berth cabins with a fridge and cooktop but no running water or bathroom. The Caroline Thomson Camping Area has canvas cabins with private bathrooms and kitchenettes. Both campgrounds have a shower and toilet block, and gas barbecues. Alcohol is not permitted, and a quiet time rule applies between 11pm and 7am.

Rottnest Hotel. Rottnest Island, WA 6161. ☎ **08/9292 5011.** Fax 08/9292 5188. 18 units (all with shower only). TV. Summer A$165–$185 (U.S.$107.25–$120.25) double; shoulder A$120–$140 (U.S.$78–$91) double; winter A$100–$120 (U.S.$65–$78) double. Rates include continental breakfast. Extra person A$40 (U.S.$26). AE, BC, DC, MC, V.

This appealing 1864 building near the jetty, once the state governor's summer residence, is now the local pub where daytrippers gather in the sports bar, the upscale restaurant, or the large open air beer garden to admire the ocean views over an ale or two. The building contains pleasant, modern motel-style rooms renovated four years ago, some with a small patio and sea views. The rooms here are the pick of the places to stay on the island.

Rottnest Youth Hostel. Kingstown Barracks, c/o Post Office, Rottnest Island, WA 6161. ☎ **08/9372 9780.** Fax 08/9292 5141. 9 units, none with bathroom. A$48.40 (U.S.$31.46) double, or A$41.80 (U.S.$27.17) double for YHA/HI members. Additional person A$10 (U.S.$6.50). A$20.90 (U.S.$13.59) dorm bed, or A$17.60 (U.S.$11.44) for YHA/Hostelling International members. BC, MC, V.

As well as dorm rooms, this YHA/Hostelling International-property has private family rooms furnished simply with a double bed and double bunks. Located in Kingstown, 1.2 kilometers (less than a mile) from Thomson Bay, it is housed in 1936 barracks that were used by the Australian Army until 1984. It serves cheap meals, provides a barbecue, and has a TV room.

Apart from the good restaurants at the hotels listed below and a couple of lackluster takeout joints, your only other dining option is the excellent **DOME cafe** at the jetty.

Shoulder season is usually April to May, and again from September to November or December. Winter is June to August.

IN PURSUIT OF THE GRAPE IN THE SWAN VALLEY
20km (13 miles) NE of Perth

Twenty minutes from the city center of Perth is the Swan Valley, home to two of Australia's best wine labels. In all there are 30 or so wineries along with wildlife parks, antique shops, a few art and craft galleries, several good restaurants, and Australia's best golf resort. Some restaurants and wineries close Monday and Tuesday.

Lord Street from the Perth city center becomes Guildford Road and takes you to Guildford at the start of the Swan Valley. The **Swan Valley Visitor Information Centre** is in the Guildford Village Potters Studio at 22 Meadow St., Guildford (☎ **08/ 9279 9859;** fax 08/9279 2931; www.swanvalley-holiday.com.au). It's open Monday through Friday 9:30am to 3pm, and Saturday and Sunday 9:30am to 4pm. Several companies (see "Whale-Watching Cruises, Tram Trips & Other Tours," above) run day cruises from Perth.

TOURING THE WINERIES & OTHER THINGS TO DO
Most Swan wineries are small family-run affairs, but an exception is **Houghton's,** Dale Road, Middle Swan (☎ **08/9274 5100**). This is Western Australia's oldest, biggest and most venerable winery. The big-beamed timber cellar has old winemaking machinery on show, and there are beautiful picnic grounds (especially nice in November when mauve jacaranda trees blossom), a cafe, and an art gallery selling works by local artists. The other big-name winery is **Sandalford,** 3210 West Swan Rd., Caversham (☎ **08/9274 5922**). It has a gift shop and pleasant vine-covered cafe; by the time you read this it may be conducting tours at a fee. Both wineries' cellar doors are open daily for free tastings from 10am to 5pm.

If you have kids, call at the **Caversham Wildlife Park,** Arthur Street, West Swan (☎ **08/9274 2202**). You can stroke koalas (but not hold them, as the owner believes it stresses them), feed kangaroos, pat farm animals, take a camel ride for A$4.50 (U.S.$2.93), and gawk at 200 species of mostly Western Australian wildlife. It's open daily 9am to 5pm. Admission is A$10 (U.S.$6.50) for adults, A$8 (U.S.$5.20) for seniors and students, and A$4.50 (U.S.$2.93) for children 2 to 14.

Shoppers should browse the junk-shop strip on **James Street,** in Guildford (most shops are open daily), or visit **Woodbridge,** a beautifully restored 1883 manor house at Ford Street, in West Midland (☎ **08/9274 2432**). The house is open Monday through Saturday (closed Wed) 1 to 4pm, and Sunday and public holidays 11am to 5pm; closed July for restorative maintenance, and Christmas, Boxing Day (Dec 26) and Good Friday. Admission is A$3.50 (U.S.$2.28) for adults, A$1.50 (U.S.98¢) for seniors and school-age children, and A$8 (U.S.$5.20) for a family. Its tearoom opens at noon.

WHERE TO STAY

The Swan is too close to Perth to require an overnight stay, but you may want to treat yourself at one of these properties.

Worth a Splurge

✪ **Hansons Swan Valley.** 60 Forest Rd., Henley Brook, WA 6055. ☎ **08/9296 3366.** Fax 08/9296 3332. members.iinet.net.au/~hansons. hansons@iinet.net.au. 10 units (6 with Jacuzzis and shower, 4 with shower only). A/C MINIBAR TV TEL. A$155–$220 (U.S.$100.75–$143) double. Rates include full breakfast. AE, BC, DC, MC, V. Take West Swan Rd. to Henley Brook, turn right at Little River Winery into Forrest St. Hansons is on the left at end of the road. Children under 15 not permitted.

At last, some of you will cry as you step into the sleek entry hall, a B&B that's not hokey or drowning in chintz. Instead, these rooms have stark white walls and groovy furniture a la Philippe Starck. All rooms have bathrobes, VCRs, and minibars stocked with cheeses, chocolates, and other goodies. Former ad execs Jon and Selina Hanson built their house to create a slick B&B of the kind they would like to stay in themselves, and it works. The house is set on a 10-hectare (25-acre) farm and has a small swimming pool. It also has great breakfasts and dinners. No smoking indoors.

WHERE TO DINE

✪ **Lamont Winery, Gallery & Restaurant.** 85 Bisdee Rd., Millendon near Upper Swan. ☎ **08/9296 4485.** Reservations recommended, especially for dinner. Main courses A$24.75–$28.95 (U.S.$16.09–$18.82). AE, BC, DC, MC, V. Wed–Sun 10am–5pm, Sat 6:30pm–late. Closed for 2 weeks from Dec. 24. Take the Great Northern Hwy. to Baskerville near Upper Swan, take a right on to Haddrill Rd. for 1.6km (1 mile), right on to Moore Rd. for 1km (just over half a mile), and right on to Bisdee Rd. MODERN AUSTRALIAN.

This highly regarded restaurant is housed in a rustic timber building at Lamont Winery. Full-flavored main courses such as roast lamb filet with a mustard crust in a spinach and sweet potato salad with honey vinaigrette, and gutsy desserts such as warm chocolate pudding with chocolate sauce and vanilla ice cream, ensure lots of regulars make the drive from Perth. Marron, a local crustacean, is a specialty. A gallery on the grounds shows Western Australian art and crafts.

YORK: TAKING A STEP BACK IN HISTORY
97km (60 miles) E of Perth

The state's first inland settlement, this peaceful National Trust-classified village on the Avon River oozes charm from an unspoiled Victorian streetscape. There are lovely B&Bs, historic buildings of stone wrapped by wrought iron lace verandahs, art galleries, a rose garden, a medley of museums including one housing a A$30-million (U.S.$19½-million) display of vintage cars, and one of the state's finest jarrah furniture shops. The rolling green hills (well, green for hot, dry Australia) around are lovely. Bring a picnic and enjoy it on the shady grass by the river.

GETTING THERE From downtown Perth, take Lord Street, which becomes Guildford Road to Midland, where it becomes the Great Eastern Highway. Follow this for a further 32 kilometers (20 miles) to The Lakes, then take the York turnoff right onto the Great Southern Highway for 47 kilometers (29 miles). The drive takes about

75 minutes. **Westrail** (☎ **13 10 53** in Western Australia, 1800/099 150 from inter-state, or 08/9326 2222) runs a daily coach service from Perth for A$10.35 (U.S.$6.73) adults, A$5.15 (U.S.$3.35) children under 16, one-way. Check ahead if you plan to travel on a public holiday or during Western Australian school vacations, as schedules sometimes change then. The **York Tourist Bureau** is within the Town Hall, Avon Terrace at Joaquina Street, York, WA 6302 (☎ **08/9641 1301;** fax 08/ 9641 1787; www.yorkwa.com.au). It's open daily 9am to 5pm. Exploring the Town

Wandering the streets is the best way to soak up the charm of York's old buildings, like the restored railway station, the Town Hall built in 1911, the library, the convent, old pubs like the York and the Castle, St. Patrick's church, the Uniting Church, the Holy Trinity Church with its stained glass windows, the fire station, and the old hospital. Among the sights worth seeing is the **Old Gaol and Court House,** 132 Avon Terrace (☎ **08/9641 2072**) housing a colonial-era courtroom still in use, cells, stables, and a trooper's cottage. It's open Monday to Friday 11am to 4pm, weekends and holidays from 10am to 4pm, although times can vary as the staff is volunteers; closed Christmas and Good Friday. Admission is A$3 (U.S.$1.95) for adults, A$1.50 (U.S.98¢) for seniors and children under 14, and A$7.50 (U.S.$4.88) for families.

The short walk out of town to the excellent **Residency Museum,** Brook Street (☎ **08/9641 1751**), is well worth it for its displays of everything from prayer books, children's toys, needlework and old kitchenware to antique furniture, farm tools, and other memorabilia of life in York in days gone by. It's open Tuesday to Thursday and public holidays from 1 to 3pm, Saturday and Sunday from noon to 4pm, and also Monday to Friday from 1pm to 3pm in school vacations (times vary as the staff are volunteers; closed Christmas and Good Friday). Admission is A$2 (U.S.$1.30) for adults and A$1.50 (U.S.98¢) for children aged 5 to 16.

If you visit on a Friday, Saturday, Sunday, or Monday (10am to 4:30pm) in autumn or spring (usually the end of September to early December, and late March to early June), you can explore the evolution of the rose at the **Avon Valley Historical Rose Garden** (☎ **08/9641 1469**), 2 kilometers (1¼ miles) out of town on Osnaburg Road. Admission is A$4 (U.S.$2.60) adults; free for children under 15. Of the several special-interest museums in York, the ✪ **York Motor Museum,** 116-124 Avon Terrace (☎ **08/9641 1288**), is the most spectacular. Among the 150 or so veteran, vintage, classic, and racing vehicles and motorcycles on display are the world's first car (an 1886 Benz), a 1904 Napier, and the Williams Formula 1 car in which Aussie Alan Jones won the world championship in 1980. The museum is open daily from 9:30am to 4pm. Admission is A$6 (U.S.$3.90) for adults, A$5 (U.S.$3.25) for seniors, and A$3 (U.S.$1.95) for children under 12.

Take a peek at the superb craftsmanship at ✪ **Jah-Roc Furniture** (☎ **08/9641 2522**) in the wonderful Old Flour Mill on Broome Street, even if you can't afford tens of thousands of dollars for a dining table handcrafted from a single slab of recycled jarrah. The showroom is open daily from 10am to 5pm.

WHERE TO STAY

✪ **Hillside Country Retreat.** Forrest St., York, WA 6302. ☎ **08/9641 1065.** Fax 08/9641 2417. hillside@avon.net.au. 6 units (all with shower only). A/C TV. A$130 (U.S.$84.50) double. Rates include full breakfast. No credit cards.

When a U.S. diplomat stayed at this adorable historical homestead a few years ago, he said he'd never seen so much stuff in one place. He was referring to the old pogo sticks, farm machinery, wooden ice skates, original radios, old road signs, the 1910 washing machine, and countless other relics of a bygone era that grace every spare inch of wall and floor space. So intrigued are guests by all this history that the owners conduct free tours after breakfast of the grand front rooms, likewise stocked with old books, precious china, and much besides. Each individually furnished room has a potbelly stove, VCR, hair dryer, and minifridge, and you get treated to fresh flowers in your room, complimentary port, sherry, chocolates, plunger coffee, and a daily newspaper. Whether you stay in the homestead or in the rustic mud-brick servants' quarters, your room has pretty antique furnishings. There is a tennis court and a small private pool. Breakfast is served in the garden from a deliciously quaint pagoda called the Morris Edwards Tea and Ginger Beer House. Smoking is prohibited indoors.

NEW NORCIA: A TOUCH OF EUROPE IN AUSTRALIA
132km (83 miles) N of Perth

It's the last thing you expect to see in the Australian bush—a Benedictine monastery town with European architecture, a fine museum, and a collection of Renaissance art—but New Norcia is no mirage. Boasting a population of 55 (when everyone's at home, that is), this pretty town and the surrounding 8,000-hectare (19,760-acre) farm were established in 1846 by Spanish Benedictine missionaries. Visitors can tour beautifully frescoed chapels, marvel at one of the finest religious art collections in Australia, stock up on famous New Norcia nutcake straight from the monastery's 120-year-old wood-fired ovens, and attend prayers with the 18 monks who live here.

GETTING THERE   New Norcia is an easy 2-hour drive from Perth. From downtown, take Lord Street, which becomes Guildford Road to Midland; here join the Great Northern Highway to New Norcia. **Westrail** (☎ **13 10 53** in Western Australia, 1800/099 150 from interstate, or 08/9326 2222) runs a coach service Sunday, Tuesday, Thursday and Friday from Perth for A$13.85 (U.S.$9) one-way. Check ahead if you plan to travel on a public holiday or during Western Australian school vacations, as schedules sometimes change then. **Greyhound Pioneer** (☎ **13 20 30** in Australia) coaches run from Perth Friday and Sunday, arriving at 5:20pm though. The fare is A$37.40 (U.S.$24.31). Day tours from Perth are available. There is no train.

Conference groups can book the town solid, so reserve accommodation and tours in advance, especially in wildflower season from August to October. Write for information and book town tours at the **New Norcia Tourist Information Centre,** New Norcia, WA 6509 (☎ **08/9654 8056;** fax 08/9654 8124; www.newnorcia.wa.edu.au), in the Museum and Art Gallery, just off the highway behind St. Joseph's, beside the Trading Post and Roadhouse. Its hours are those of the museum and gallery (see below).

EXPLORING THE TOWN & MONASTERY
The New Norcia Tourist Information Centre's 2-hour ✪ **walking tours** are a must. Tickets cost A$10 (U.S.$6.50) for adults and A$5 (U.S.$3.25) for children 12 to 17; free for younger children. Tours depart daily except Christmas at 11am and 1:30pm, and allow time for you to attend prayers with the monks if you wish. The guide covers some of the town's 27 National Trust-classified buildings and gives an insight into the monks' lifestyle. You will also see the frescoes in the old monastery chapel and in St. Ildephonsus' and St. Gertrude's colleges. Much of the monastery is closed to visitors, but the tour does show you the fruit gardens and a glimpse of the men-only courtyard. Heritage walking trail maps sold for A$3 (U.S.$1.95) at the Tourist Information Centre include more buildings not visited on the tour, such as the octagonal apiary.

The ✪ **museum and art gallery** are full of relics from the monks' past—old mechanical and musical instruments, artifacts from the days when New Norcia was an Aboriginal mission, gifts to the monks from the Queen of Spain, and an astounding collection of paintings by Spanish and Italian artists. The oldest I saw was dated 1492. Give yourself at least an hour here, easily more. The museum and gallery are open daily 9:30am to 5pm August through October, and 10am to 4:30pm November through July (closed Christmas). Admission is A$4 (U.S.$2.60) for adults, A$3 (U.S.$1.95) for seniors and students, and A$1 (U.S.65¢) for children 6 to 12.

Apart from joining the monks for 15-minute prayers in the monastery five times a day (midday and 2:30pm are most convenient for day visitors), you can join them for Mass in the Holy Trinity Abbey Church Monday through Saturday at 7:30am and on Sunday at 9am.

WHERE TO STAY

New Norcia Hotel. Great Northern Hwy., New Norcia, WA 6509. ☎ **08/9654 8034.** Fax 08/9654 8011. 17 units (1 only with bathroom). A$65 (U.S.$42.25) double without bathroom; A$90 (U.S.$58.50) double with bathroom. Extra person A$10 (U.S.$6.50). AE, BC, MC, V.

When they thought a Spanish Royal visit to New Norcia was imminent in 1926, the monks built this grandiose white hotel fit for, well, a king. Sadly, the Royals never materialized, and the building fell into disrepair. Only the grand central staircase, soaring pressed metal ceilings and imposing Iberian facade hint at the splendor that was. Two years ago new carpets, curtains, beds, and hair dryers were put in, but be prepared for rather grim rooms. Only one has an en suite bathroom, air-con and a TV. Still, it's nice to eat a meal at the rather dated bar (or take your plate into the charmingly faded Dining Room), and to sit on the football-sized front verandah upstairs. The bar gets jumping on Friday and Saturday nights when local farmers come to town. This is the only place to stay in town.

3 Margaret River & the Southwest: Wine Tasting & Underground Wonders

Margaret River 290km (181 miles) S of Perth

Say "Margaret River" to Australians and they reply "great wine!" with their eyes all lit up. The area's 38 wineries nestle among statuesque forests of karri, one of the world's tallest trees. The wineries contribute only around 1% to Australia's wine output, yet they turn out 10% of the country's top-notch "premium" wines. Not even most Aussies know about the Southwest's other drawing cards, though—like the spectacular surf breaks on the 130-kilometer (81-mile) coast from Cape Naturaliste in the north to Cape Leeuwin on the southwest tip of Australia; the coastal cliffs perfect for abseiling and rock-climbing; and the honeycomb of limestone caves filled with stalagmites and stalactites. Whales pass by from June through December, wildflowers line the roads August through October, and wild birds, kangaroos, and cute shingleback lizards are everywhere. If you like hiking, pack your boots, because there are plenty of trails from a 15-minute stroll around Margaret River township, to a ✪ 6-day Cape-to-Cape trek along the sea cliffs. The Southwest is truly one of Australia's last great wildernesses, and one of my favorite parts of the country.

Like wine regions the world over, the Southwest has its fair share of cozy B&Bs, art and craft galleries, and some super restaurants. Plan to stay at least 2 days.

ESSENTIALS

GETTING THERE It's a 3½-hour drive to Margaret River from Perth; take the inland South Western Highway (the quickest route) or the tad more scenic Old Coast Road to Bunbury, where you pick up the Bussell Highway to Margaret River.

Leeuwin Estate winery (book through its Fremantle office ☎ 08/9430 4099; fax 08/9430 5687) does "Flying Visit" day and overnight trips from Perth. A day trip including return flights, three-course a-la-carte lunch at its restaurant (wine costs extra), winery tour and tasting, and a district tour costs A$297 (U.S.$193.05) per person.

Southwest Coachlines (☎ 08/9324 2333) runs a daily service, and two on weekends, to Margaret River from Perth for A$24.70 (U.S.$16.06). Westrail (☎ 13 10 53 in Western Australia, 1800/099 150 in Australia from interstate, or 08/9326 2222) runs a daily train from Perth to Bunbury with coach connections to Margaret River (taking just over 4½ hr.), and a separate all-coach service from Perth, once or twice a day every day except Saturday. Westrail's coach service takes over 5 hours, and you transfer by local bus (which does not run Sundays or public holidays) to a different coach in Bunbury. Fares are A$26.15 (U.S.$17) with either mode. Westrail schedules can differ on a public holiday or during Western Australian school vacations.

VISITOR INFORMATION   You will pass many wineries before you get to Margaret River township, but it's worth heading first to the Augusta Margaret River Tourism Association information center to pick up a winery guide. It is on the Bussell Highway at Tunbridge Street, Margaret River, WA 6285 (☎ 08/9757 2911; fax 08/9757 3287; www.margaretriverwa.com). It is open daily 9am to 5pm.

GETTING AROUND   Nine kilometers (5.5 miles) past Busselton, which marks the start of the Southwest, the Bussell Highway makes a left and heads south among the wineries through Vasse, 25 kilometers (15½ miles) on through the village of Cowaramup, 11 kilometers (7 miles) farther through Margaret River proper, and 43 kilometers (27 miles) on to windswept Cape Leeuwin and the fishing port of Augusta.

A car is close to essential. Avis (☎ 1800/679 880 within Australia for reservations in the Southwest, or 08/9757 3686 for the Margaret River office) has offices in Bunbury, Busselton, and Margaret River.

Margaret River Tour Company (☎ 0419/91 7166) and Milesaway Tours (☎ 1800/818 102 in Australia or 08/9754 2929) run sightseeing, adventure, and winery tours from Margaret River.

TOURING THE WINERIES

Fans of premium wines will have a field day in the Southwest. Cabernet sauvignon and merlot are the star reds, while Chardonnay, semillon, and sauvignon blanc are the pick among whites. Most wineries offer free tastings from 10am to 4:30pm daily.

The "big three" are Cape Mentelle, 4 kilometers (2.5 miles) west of Margaret River on Wallcliffe Road (☎ 08/9757 3266); ✪ Leeuwin Estate, Stevens Road, Margaret River (☎ 08/9757 6253); and Vasse Felix, Caves Road at Harman's Road South, Cowaramup (☎ 08/9755 5242). Leeuwin Estate has a towering reputation, especially for Chardonnay. It does winery tours three times a day. A relative newcomer,

---

Special Events in the Southwest

Every February or March, Leeuwin Estate Winery (☎ 08/9757 6253; fax 08/9757 6364; www.leeuwinestate.com.au) stages a spectacular ✪ outdoor concert starring some leading showbiz lights (Shirley Bassey, Julio Iglesias, or Diana Ross are past performers), attended by 6,000 picnicking guests. Tickets are A$104.50 (U.S.$68.93). This is a BIG local event, so book months ahead.

The Margaret River Wine Region Festival runs over a week in November.

A Wine-Buying Tip

The place to buy wine if you want to take it out of Australia is the **Margaret River Regional Wine Centre,** 9 Bussell Hwy., Cowaramup (☎ **08/9755 5501**), as most wineries don't deliver internationally. It stocks every local wine, does daily tastings of select vintages, sells maps and winery guides, and has an expert staff to help you purchase wisely, and even tailor your day's foray. It is open Monday through Saturday 10am to 8pm, and Sunday noon to 6pm (closed Christmas and Good Friday). Order off its website at www.mrwines.com.

Voyager Estate, Stevens Road, Margaret River (☎ **08/9757 6358**), has exquisite rose gardens around a South African Cape Dutch-style cellar, and does a highly drinkable shiraz grenache. Other good labels to look for are Arlewood Estate, Cullen Willyabrup Wines, Evans & Tate, Fermoy Estate, Lenton Brae, and Sandalford Wines.

WHAT ELSE: CAVES, BUSH TUCKER & MORE

Five of the Southwest's 350 or so limestone caves are open to the public, done up by Nature with elaborate stalactite formations. Before or after you visit one, call at the excellent **CaveWorks eco-interpretive center** at Lake Cave, Caves Road, 15 kilometers (9 miles) south of Wallcliffe Road (☎ **08/9757 7411**), open daily except Christmas from 9am to 5pm. Entry is free if you tour Lake, Jewel, Mammoth, or Moondyne caves, or A$5 (U.S.$3.25) for adults and A$3 (U.S.$1.95) for children 4 to 16. Lake Cave, right outside CaveWorks and 300 steps down an ancient sinkhole, contains a pond in which exquisite stalactites are reflected. A few minutes north along Caves Road is **Mammoth Cave,** where you can inspect the fossilized jaw of a baby zygotaurus trilobus, an extinct giant wombat. **Jewel Cave,** 8 kilometers (5 miles) north of Augusta on Caves Road, is the prettiest. Tours of Lake and Jewel and self-guided tours of Mammoth cost A$13 (U.S.$8.45) each for adults, A$5 (U.S.$3.25) for children 4 to 16. A 7-day **Grand Pass** to all three plus CaveWorks saves you money. Mammoth is open from 9am to 5pm (last tour at 4pm); tours of Lake and Jewel run hourly from 9:30am to the last tour at 3:30pm. Sometimes extra tours are scheduled in school vacations. The caves open every day except Christmas. Book tours through CaveWorks.

Just next to Jewel Cave is **Moondyne Cave,** an "adventure cave" where you get down and dirty crawling on your hands and knees, in the protective clothing supplied. This 2-hour experience costs A$25 (U.S.$16.25) for adults and A$18 (U.S.$11.70) for kids 10 to 16 (kids under 10 are not permitted, and an adult must accompany kids). Tours depart daily at 2pm; book 24 hours ahead. Book through CaveWorks. A similar adventure tour taking about 3 hours (sometimes more, sometimes less) is offered at **Ngilgi Cave,** Caves Road, Yallingup (☎ **08/9755 2152**), for A$35 (U.S.$22.75) for anyone over 14. It departs daily at 9:30am; book 24 hours ahead. Ngilgi's main chamber has beautiful translucent stalactite "shawls," which anyone can explore on a semi-guided tour. This costs A$12 (U.S.$7.80) for adults and A$5 (U.S.$3.25) children 5 to 17, and run half-hourly from 9:30am. The cave is open daily from 9:30am with the last tour at 3:30pm (4pm in school vacations, 4:30pm in Christmas school vacations).

You can pick your own kiwifruit, raspberries, and other fruit at **The Berry Farm,** 222 Bessell Rd. outside Margaret River (☎ **08/9757 5054**), or buy attractively packaged sparkling, dessert, and port wines; jams; and vinegars. The farm is open daily 10am to 4:30pm (closed Christmas, Boxing Day, New Year's Day and Good Friday).

Greg Miller of **Adventure Plus** (☎ 0419/961 716) arranges all kinds of outdoor adventures from abseiling and rock climbing coastal cliffs, to caving, canoeing, hiking, and camping. He welcomes beginners. Prices very with the activity; expect to pay around A$100 (U.S.$65) for a day's action. Plenty of hiking trails are suited to an afternoon's ramble. The tourist information center in Margaret River (see "Visitor Information") sells trail maps for a few dollars each, including to all the sections of the Cape-to-Cape cliff-edge walk from Cape Naturaliste to Cape Leeuwin.

Try to make time for one of two tours offered by ✪ **"Bushtucker Woman" Helen Lee** (☎ 0419/91 1971, or 9757 9084). On one tour, she has you canoeing up the river, exploring a cave, and eating smoked emu, grub pate (I'm not kidding) and other Aboriginal delicacies on a river island. It runs from 10am to 2pm, and costs A$33 (U.S.$21.45) for adults and A$16.50 (U.S.$10.73) for children. Highly recommended! Her winery tour has an alternative bent incorporating short karri-forest walks, insights into organic wine-making, tastings at several wineries, a visit to Leeuwin Estate's herb garden, and a picnic lunch of bush tucker and local cheeses, hams, and dips. Just one of the things she teaches you is how vaporized peppermint oil from the native trees condenses on the grapes to create the distinctive flavor of Margaret River whites. The 5-hour tour departs noon and costs A$44 (U.S.$28.60).

Surfing lessons from four-time Western Australian professional surfing champion ✪ **Josh Parmateer** (☎ 08/9757 3850 or 0418/958 264) are a must—take it from this surf virgin! Two-hour lessons in the waist-deep surf at Prevelly Park Beach, 9 kilometers (5½ miles) west of Margaret River, run daily and cost A$80 (U.S.$52) per person, or A$30 (U.S.$19.50) per person if there are two of you. Josh supplies the boards and wetsuits and pick-up from your hotel. Lessons run October to June. If you are already a Master of the Surf Universe, try the legendary **Smiths Beach** or the **Three Bears** (Mama, Papa, and Baby) break at Yallingup, the double-barreled North Point at Gracetown, or the plentiful breaks at Prevelly Park. **Beach Life,** 117 Bussell Hwy., Margaret River (☎ 08/9757 2888), rents boards for A$40 (U.S.$26) for 24 hours.

From June to December whales play just offshore along the coast. There is a **whale lookout** near the Cape Naturaliste lighthouse. Daily 3-hour whale-watching cruises with ✪ **Naturaliste Charters** (☎ 08/9755 2276) depart June to September from Augusta. September to December, departures switch to Dunsborough, where humpbacks rest their calves. Expect to pay around A$45 (U.S.$29.25) for adults and around A$30 (U.S.$19.50) for children 4 to 14. Children under 4 are free.

Art & craft galleries are thick on the ground in the Southwest. One of the most upscale is **Gunyulgup Galleries,** Gunyulgup Valley Drive near Yallingup (☎ 08/9755 2177), which has top-of-the-line jewelry, glass, ceramics, and artworks.

Scenic Drives & a Spectacular View

The picturesque 106-kilometer (66-mile) north-south drive along Caves Road, the length of the Southwest from Busselton in the north, to Augusta on Cape Leeuwin in the south, is worth doing. Don't miss ✪ **Boranup Drive,** a scenic detour off Caves Road through towering karris—although your rental car is not insured on its unpaved surface! It departs Caves Road 6 kilometers (3¾ miles) south of Mammoth Cave and rejoins it after a 14-kilometer (8¾-mile) meander. Near Augusta, a sweeping ocean view—and sometimes even of seals, whales, and dolphins—awaits those who climb to the top of Cape Leeuwin lighthouse. It is open every day except Christmas 9am to 4pm (the stairs close 3:45pm). Entry is A$4 (U.S.$2.60) for adults and A$2 (U.S.$1.30) for children under 16.

WHERE TO STAY

It's not the prettiest village in the Southwest, but Margaret River has necessities like banks, a supermarket, a few restaurants and shops. The blink-and-you-miss-it hamlet of Cowaramup is closer to more wineries, and has a general store, a restaurant, and one or two interesting craft shops. Vasse is a tiny settlement at the northern edge of the Southwest. Some places may demand a minimum 2-night stay on weekends.

IN MARGARET RIVER

Rosewood Cottage. 54 Wallcliffe Rd., Margaret River, WA 6285. ☎ **08/9757 2845.** Fax 08/9757 3509. rosewood@swisp.net.au. 4 units (3 with shower only). A$93.50–$99 (U.S.$61.78–$64.35) double with continental breakfast; A$99 (U.S.$64.35) double apt with continental breakfast. Extra person A$27.50 (U.S.$17.88) in apt. AE, BC, MC, V.

This cozy B&B accommodates guests in English-style rooms with exposed roof beams, soft floral decor, ceiling fans. The new two-bedroom apartment has a living area and kitchenette, set up for travelers with disabilities. Guests can rest up in winter by the fire in the sitting room equipped with CDs, a TV, and books, or out on the verandah overlooking the lovely garden in summer. Rosewood is famous for its homemade waffles and jams at breakfast, served in the country-style dining room. It is an easy stroll to the Margaret River main street from the house. No smoking indoors.

IN COWARAMUP

The Noble Grape. Lot 18, Bussell Hwy., Cowaramup, WA 6284. ☎/fax **08/9755 5538.** www.babs.com.au/noblegrape. noblegrape@netserv.net.au. 6 units (all with shower only). TV. A$99–$110 (U.S.$64.35–$71.50) double. Additional person A$22 (U.S.$14.30). Rates include continental breakfast. AE, BC, DC, MC, V.

English cottage gardens surround Louise and Chris Stokes' colonial-style B&B. Each well-maintained room is adorned with antiques and has a modern bathroom, heating and ceiling fans, a sitting area, and a small rear patio opening onto bird-filled trees. One caters to travelers with disabilities. Louise fixes a buffet of homemade muffins, jams, muesli, yogurts, and plunger coffee every morning, and serves a cooked breakfast for an extra A$7 (U.S.$4.55). An inexpensive room service menu is a welcome sight if you don't feel like dining out. Hair dryers are at reception. No smoking indoors.

IN VASSE

Newtown House. Bussell Hwy. (9km/5½ miles past Busselton), Vasse, WA 6280. ☎/fax **08/ 9755 4485.** 4 units (all with shower only). MINIBAR TV. A$140 (U.S.$91) double. Rates include continental breakfast. AE, BC, DC, MC, V. The property is on the right just after the Bussell Hwy. turns left (south).

Set in lavender and rose gardens, this National Trust-listed 1851 homestead has four rooms with "contemporary country" decor, furnished with wrought-iron table and chairs, pine furniture, and touches like potpourri "dream sacks" on your pillow. The fixings for a gourmet continental breakfast are sent up to your room the night before. Wander out back to chat with the resident painter in the barn-cum-studio, and eat in the unbeatably excellent restaurant (see "Where to Dine," below). Smoking is prohibited.

WHERE TO DINE

Many wineries also serve light meals, which can be accompanied by some of what you've sampled. Good restaurants attached to wineries include those at Vasse Felix, Amberley Estate, Driftwood Estate, and Brookland Valley Vineyard. Of these, Leeuwin Estate, Stevens Road, **Margaret River** (☎ **08/9757 6253**), is probably the best. You can stock up for a picnic at the supermarket in Margaret River. Cape Mentelle and Vasse Felix both have green shady picnic areas beside a brook.

WORTH A SPLURGE

✪ **Newtown House.** Bussell Hwy. (9km/5½ miles past Busselton), Vasse. ☎ **08/9755 4485.** Reservations recommended. Main courses A$9.50–$18 (U.S.$6.18–$11.70) at lunch, A$22.50–$26 (U.S.$14.63–$16.90) at dinner. AE, BC, DC, MC, V. Tues–Sat 10am–4:30pm, 6pm–late. MODERN FRENCH/AUSTRALIAN.

The Southwest boasts some of the best restaurants in Australia, and this is one of 'em. Folks come from far and wide to savor chef Stephen Reagan's skill in preparing such dishes as rare local venison with roast pears, beetroot, and red wine glaze. Desserts are no letdown, either—caramel soufflé with lavender ice cream and hot caramel sauce is typical. Located in a historic homestead, the restaurant consists of two simple, intimate rooms with sisal matting and contemporary, boldly colored walls. See "Where to Stay," above, for details on accommodations here. Even better, it's BYO.

The Valley Café. Carters Rd. (near Caves Rd.), Margaret River. ☎ **08/9757 3225.** Reservations recommended. Main courses A$16–$22.50 (U.S.$10.40–$14.63). Seafood at market price. AE, BC, DC, MC, V. Daily 8:30am–4pm; Fri–Sat (and Sun on 3-day weekends) 6–10pm. MODERN AUSTRALIAN.

Voted most popular South West Cafe in 1999, this pleasant establishment serves up stylish breakfasts, lunches and dinners with views over the surrounding countryside. Lunch might be crispy squid salad, or risotto with Augusta smoked chicken, sun-dried capsicum (bell pepper), and shaved Parmesan. Dinner might be cured Atlantic salmon with polenta, asparagus and caramelized balsamic vinegar. BYO.

4 The Goldfields

595km (372 miles) E of Perth

After Paddy Hannan struck gold in 1893, the wheatbelt town of Kalgoorlie found itself sitting on the "Golden Mile," the richest square mile of gold-bearing earth in the world, at the time. Today Kalgoorlie (pop. 33,000) is still an Outback boomtown, a mixture of yesteryear charm and 21st century gold fever. The town is literally perched on the edge of the **Super Pit,** the world's biggest open-cut gold mine, currently 4.5 kilometers (3 miles) long, 1.5 kilometers (1 mile) wide, and 290 meters (951 ft.) deep. It yields around 680,000 ounces of the yellow stuff every year—a mere 1,863 ounces a day. An estimated 30 million ounces is still in the ground. Hardly surprisingly, Kalgoorlie Consolidated Gold Mines, which operates the pit, is Australia's biggest gold producer.

Walking down the streets fronted with wrought-iron lace verandahs is like stumbling onto a Western movie set. Countless bars still do the roaring trade they notched up in the 1890s, only now they serve gold mining executives from Adelaide and Perth.

Life on the Golden Mile is not so lively for everyone, however. Just down the road 39 kilometers (24 miles) is **Coolgardie** (pop. 1,400), another 1890s gold rush boomtown where the gold ran out in 1963. The town's semi-abandoned air is a sad foil to Kalgoorlie's brash energy, but much of her lovely architecture remains. The thing to do here is just wandering the gracious streets for a pleasant nostalgia buzz.

ESSENTIALS

GETTING THERE Airlink (book through **Qantas** at ☎ **13 13 13** in Australia) flies to Kalgoorlie from Perth. Airlink also flies direct from Adelaide daily.

Greyhound Pioneer (☎ **13 20 30** in Australia) makes the 8-hour trip daily from Perth for A$103.40 (U.S.$67.21). Greyhound's daily service from Adelaide takes around 24½ hours and costs A$229.90 (U.S.$149.44). **Goldrush Tours** (☎ **1800/ 62 0440** in Australia or 08/9021 2954) runs an express coach service from Perth five times a week for $65.

Kalgoorlie is a stop on the 3-day *Indian-Pacific* train service, which runs between Sydney and Perth through Adelaide twice a week. See Section 11, "Getting Around Australia" in chapter 2 for details. *The Prospector* train makes 11 trips a week from Perth to Kalgoorlie for A$49.30 (U.S.$32.05). Call Westrail (☎ **13 10 53** in Western Australia, 1800/099 150 in Australia from interstate, or 08/9326 2222).

From Perth, take the Great Eastern Highway. If you want to make the 2,182-kilometer (1,364-mile) journey on the Eyre Highway from Adelaide, which features the longest straight stretch of highway in the world on the mind-numbingly empty Nullarbor Plain, contact the South Australian or Western Australian state auto clubs listed under "Getting Around Australia" in chapter 2 for advice. There are only a handful of small towns and gas stops en route. I don't recommend it as it's boring landscape most of the way!

VISITOR INFORMATION   The **Kalgoorlie-Boulder Tourist Centre,** 250 Hannan St., Kalgoorlie, WA 6430 (☎ **08/9021 1966;** fax 08/9021 2180; www.kalgoorlieandwagoldfields.com.au), dispenses information on Kalgoorlie, Coolgardie, and outlying regions. Boulder is a suburb of Kalgoorlie. The centre's walking trail map to the town's architecture, which sells for a few dollars, is worth buying. The center is open Monday through Friday 8:30am to 5pm; Saturday, Sunday and holidays 9am to 5pm. The **Coolgardie Tourist Bureau,** 62 Bayley St., Coolgardie, WA 6429 (☎ **08/ 9026 6090;** fax 08/9026 6008), is open daily 9am to 5pm.

GETTING AROUND   **Avis** (☎ **08/9021 1722**), **Budget** (☎ **08/9093 2300**), **Hertz** (☎ **08/9093 2211**), and **Osborne Thrifty** (☎ 08/9021 4722) have offices in Kalgoorlie.

Kalgoorlie Adventure Bus runs a daily service to Hannans North Historic Mining Reserve and the Super Pit for A$5.50 (U.S.$3.58) per person per attraction, roundtrip. It also runs to other attractions around town every second day. Buy tickets at the Tourist Centre, above. The Tourist Centre also sells an exclusive A$16 (U.S.$10.40) round-trip taxi fare to Hannans North Historic Mining Reserve.

As well as coach, 4WD and guided self-drive 2WD and 4WD bush tours of Kalgoorlie, Coolgardie and outlying ghost towns, local tour operators will take you gold prospecting in outlying regions from half a day for up to several days.

TOURING A GOLD MINE & OTHER ADVENTURES

As you might guess, gold is a common thread running through many of the town's attractions. The best is ✪ **Hannans North Historic Mining Reserve,** Broad Arrow Road, 6 kilometers (3¾ miles) north of the Tourist Centre on the Goldfields Highway (☎ **08/9091 4074**), where you can venture underground to see what was once a working gold mine, pan for gold, watch a gold pour, watch the interesting video in a

---

Streets of Gold

In Kalgoorlie's young days, its streets were paved with a blackish spoil from the mining process called "tellurides." When someone realized tellurides contain up to 40% gold and 10% silver, those streets were ripped up in one big hurry. The city fathers had paved the streets with gold and didn't even know it!

recreated miner's tent, and pore over an extensive collection of mining memorabilia, old shaft heads, machinery, and huts in a recreated miners' village. The exhibits are well done, I think. Underground tours, pouring, and panning each take place three times a day, one after the other. The admission fee, which includes all activities, is A$16.50 (U.S.$10.73) for adults, A$12 (U.S.$7.80) for seniors and students, A$8.50 (U.S.$5.53) for school-age kids, and A$42 (U.S.$27.30) for a family. It is open daily 9am to 4:30pm (closed Christmas). Wear enclosed shoes, and allow 3 to 4 hours to see the lot. In late 2001 the reserve will expand to include a new **Australian Prospectors and Miners Hall of Fame,** focusing on prospecting, the business of mining, minerals, and mining's role in the economy.

The **Museum of the Goldfields,** 17 Hannan St. (☎ **08/9021 8533**), contains the first 400 ounce gold bar minted in town, the Western Australian State Gold Collection, and some historical displays on the region. The museum is open daily from 10am to 4:30pm, closed Christmas and Good Friday. Admission is by donation. Allow an hour.

Don't leave town without seeing the **Super Pit open-cut mine.** There is a lookout platform at Outram Street in Boulder, off the Goldfields Highway (called the Eastern Bypass Road on some maps). It is open daily from 6am to 7pm except when blasting closes it temporarily (check with the tourist center). Entry is free.

When they're not digging money out of the ground, hard-bitten locals gamble for it at the **Bush Two-Up School,** a rusty and roofless corrugated iron ring among the eucalypts, 7 kilometers (4 miles) north of town on the Goldfields Highway. The game is a simple bet on the fifty-fifty chance of a penny landing heads or tails. The ring opens daily around 5pm to dusk, or later if the crowds are big (closed Christmas and Good Friday). Admission is free. Kids under 18 are not permitted.

The **Royal Flying Doctor Service (RFDS)** (☎ **08/9093 7500**) base at Kalgoorlie-Boulder Airport is open for visitors to browse artifacts, see a video, and inspect a plane if one is in. It is open Monday to Friday from 11am to 3pm. Admission is by donation.

Full-blood Aboriginal Geoffrey Stokes of ✪ **Yamatji Bitja Aboriginal Bush Tours** (☎ **08/9093 3745** or 0407/378 602) grew up the Aboriginal way in the bush. On his full-day 4WD tours you do stuff like forage for bush tucker, eat witchetty grubs (if you're game!), cook kangaroo over a fire, track emus, and learn Aboriginal bushcraft. Tours cost A$80 (U.S.$52.05), half-price for kids 4 to 12; he picks you up from your hotel. Geoff also does twilight campfire evenings costing A$35 (U.S.$22.75), and overnight tours costing A$170 (U.S.$110.50).

EXPLORING COOLGARDIE

Wandering Coolgardie's quiet streets graced with historical facades is a pleasant stroll back in time. Signboards erected around the place, many with photos, detail what each site was like in the town's heyday at the turn of the last century. The **Goldfields Exhibition,** 62 Bayley St. (☎ **08/9026 6090**), tells the town's story in an 1898 building once used as the mining warden's courthouse (the Tourist Bureau is also here). It has a huge bottle collection, too. Admission is A$3.30 (U.S.$2.15) for adults, A$2.75 (U.S.$1.79) for seniors, A$1.10 (U.S.72¢) for children under 16, or A$7.70 (U.S.$5.01) for a family. It's open daily except Christmas from 9am to 5pm. The **Railway Station Museum** (☎ **08/9026 6388**) in Woodward Street, houses gold rush and transport memorabilia in the original 1896 station building and the engine, two carriages, and the guard's van of a turn-of-the-century steam train. It's open daily 9am to 4pm (closed Christmas, Boxing Day and Good Friday). Admission is by donation.

If you like period architecture and interiors, browse the restored National Trust-owned **Warden Finnerty's Residence** (☎ **08/9026 6028**) on McKenzie Street off Hunt Street. It was built in 1895 for the mining warden. It is open daily from 9am to 4pm; admission is A$2 (U.S.$1.30) adults, A$1 (U.S.65¢) seniors and school-age kids, A$4 (U.S.$2.60) for a family.

The **Coolgardie Camel Farm,** 4 kilometers (2½ miles) west of Coolgardie on the Great Eastern Highway (☎ **08/9026 6159**) leads rides through the bush on the mode of transport they used in the goldfields in the old days - camels.

WHERE TO STAY

Mercure Inn. Overland Kalgoorlie. Lower Hannan St., Kalgoorlie, WA 6430. ☎ **800/ 221-4542** in the U.S. and Canada 1300/66 6565 in Australia, 020/8283 4500 in the U.K., 0800/44 4422 in New Zealand, or 08/9021 1433. Fax 08/9021 1121. www.hotelweb.fr. mercureoverland@bigpond.com.au. 87 units (with shower only). A/C MINIBAR TV TEL. A$110 (U.S.$71.50) double, A$152 (U.S.$98.80) family. Extra person A$22 (U.S.$14.30). Children under 17 stay free in parents's room if they use existing bedding. AE, BC, DC, MC, V.

This serviceable motel is on the highway (but quiet) about 2 kilometers (1¼ miles) from town, so you will need your own wheels or take a cab to go exploring. Tours pick up from the door. The rooms are modern, clean, and a good size; family rooms have an extra bedroom and kitchenettes. There's a nice restaurant and cocktail bar, room service at dinner, free movies, a swimming pool, and a tour and car rental desk.

WHERE TO DINE

Akudjura. 418 Hannan St. (next to Hannan's View Motel). ☎ **08/9091 3311.** Reservations recommended. Main courses A$11.95–$24 (U.S.$7.77–$15.60); seafood platter A$60 (U.S.$39); lunch from A$7.50 (U.S.$4.88). AE, BC, DC, MC, V. Daily 10:30am–late (Note: kitchen closes at 8:30pm). MODERN AUSTRALIAN.

The Italianate outdoor terrace under sailcloth and the timber floors, curved silver bar, and blondwood furniture make this Kalgoorlie's first groovy restaurant. Bright young waitstaff provide snappy service from a long and stylish menu of salads like chicken Caesar, pastas like smoked salmon fettuccine, steaks including a kangaroo version, and seafood dishes (yep, even in the desert) like Tasmanian salmon in a citrus and corian-der dressing. Lighter fare is available outside meal hours.

5 The Midwest & the Northwest: Where the Outback Meets the Sea

The Midwest and Northwest coasts of Western Australia are treeless, riverless semi-desert, occupied by sheep stations and a handful of people. Temperatures soar into the 40s°C (over 115°F) in summer, and the sand burns bright orange in the blazing sun. But it's not the land you come here for—it's what's in the sea that you're interested in. Since the 1960s, a pod of bottle-nosed dolphins has been coming in to shallow water at ✪ **Monkey Mia** in the World Heritage-listed Shark Bay Marine Park to greet delighted humans. Their magical presence has generated worldwide publicity and drawn people from every corner of the globe. So popular are the dolphins that a resort has been built on the lonely shore just to accommodate the crowds.

Another 872 kilometers (545 miles) by road north on the Northwest Cape, adven-ture seekers from around the world come to snorkel with awesome whale sharks—measuring up to 18 meters (59 ft.) long—every fall (Mar–early June). The Cape's parched shore and green waters hide an even more dazzling secret though—a second barrier reef 260 kilometers (163 miles) long and 2 kilometers (1¼ miles) wide called Ningaloo Marine Park. It protects 250 species of coral and 450 kinds of fish, dolphins, mantas, whales, and turtles in its 5,000 square kilometers (1,640 square miles). Even the Great Barrier Reef can't beat ⊙ **Ningaloo Reef's** proximity to shore—just a step or two off the beach delivers you into a magical underwater garden. What is so amazing about the reef is not that it is here, but that so few people know about it—a mere 8,000 tourists a year. To you, that means beaches pretty much to yourself, seas boiling with marine life humans haven't scared away, unspoiled scenery, and a genuine sense of the frontier.

The Midwest and Northwest are lonely, remote, and really too hot to visit between November and March, when some tour operators close down on account of the heat. The best time to visit is April to October, when it is still warm enough to swim, though snorkelers might want a wetsuit from June through August. Both regions are too far south to get the Top End's Wet Season, so humidity is always low. Facilities are scarce and distances are immense in this neck of the woods, so be prepared for that.

SHARK BAY (MONKEY MIA)
853km (533 miles) N of Perth; 1,867km (1,167 miles) S of Broome

Monkey Mia's famous dolphins aren't part of a theme park attraction, but wild creatures that come and go as they will. That said, they rarely miss a day. Apart from these delightful mammals, Shark Bay's waters heave with fish, turtles, the world's biggest population of dugongs, also known as manatees (10,000 at last count), manta rays, sea snakes, and June through October, whales. On the tip of the Peron Peninsula, which juts out like the middle prong of a "W" into the Shark Bay Marine Park, is Francois Peron National Park, home to many endangered species, white beaches comprised entirely of shells, and "living fossils"—rock-like structures on the shore called stromatolites. The bay's only town is the one-time pearling town of Denham (pop. 500), 129 kilometers (81 miles) from the highway, which has a hotel or two, a restaurant or two, a couple of shops, and several fishing charter operators. There is no settlement, only a pleasant but basic resort (see below), at Monkey Mia.

ESSENTIALS
GETTING THERE   Western Airlines (☎ **1800/998 097** in Australia, or 08/9277 4022) both flies two or three times a week from Perth **to Shark Bay Airport** (also called Monkey Mia Airport), 18 kilometers (11 miles) from Monkey Mia Dolphin Resort. The one-way fare with Western Airlines is A$299 (U.S.$194.35). No airline operates from towns other than Perth. The **Shark Bay Airport Bus** (☎ **08/9948 1358**) meets every flight and transfers you to Monkey Mia Dolphin Resort (see "Where to Stay & Dine," below) for A$7.70 (U.S.$5.01) per person one-way. There is no train to Shark Bay. **Greyhound Pioneer** (☎ **13 20 30** in Australia) travels once or twice a day from Perth, daily from Broome, and three times a week from Exmouth via Coral Bay, to the Overlander Roadhouse at the Shark Bay turnoff on the North West Coastal Highway. These services connect with a coach service to Monkey Mia Dolphin Resort coach service. The 9-hour trip from Perth costs A$155.10 (U.S.$100.82). From Exmouth, it's a 7-hour trip, and from Broome, 22½ hours through featureless landscape—*not* recommended!

The 9- to 10-hour drive from Perth is uninteresting and lonely. Beware wildlife on the road and keep the gas tank full. Take the Brand Highway to Geraldton, 424 kilometers (265 miles) north of Perth, then the North West Coastal Highway for 280 kilometers (175 miles) to the Overlander Roadhouse. Turn left onto the Denham-Hamelin Road. Monkey Mia is 152 kilometers (95 miles) from the turnoff, 27 kilometers (17 miles) past Denham. If you want to break the journey, the **Mercure Inn Geraldton,** Brand Highway, Geraldton, WA 6530 (☎ **08/9921 2455;** fax

08/9921 5830), has smart, clean motel rooms. Rates are A$127 (U.S.$82.55) double; specials are available most nights. In spring, consider the **Everlasting Trail** wildflower route to Geraldton, described in the introduction to this chapter.

Numerous coach and 4WD tours run from Perth. Feature Tours does 24-hour "express" overnight coach tours from Perth. **Kookaburra Air and Complete Aviation Services** do aerial day trips and multi-day tours from Perth. These companies' contact details appear in "Exploring the State" at the start of this chapter.

VISITOR INFORMATION   Wide-ranging information on Shark Bay's natural history and local tours is available at the **Dolphin Visitor's Centre** (☎ **08/9948 1366**) within Monkey Mia Dolphin Resort (see "Where to Stay & Dine," below). Videos run throughout the day, and researchers (mostly from American universities) give free talks and slide shows some nights. The official Visitor Information outlet is the **Shark Bay Tourist Association's Centre** at Knight Terrace, Denham, WA 6537 (☎/fax **08/9948 1253;** www.sharkbay.asn.au), open daily 8am to 6:30pm. The state Department of Conservation and Land Management is a good source of information on Shark Bay Marine Park, Francois Peron National Park, and Hamelin Pool Marine Nature Reserve; it has an office in Denham, or contact its "WA Naturally" information center in Perth (see "Exploring the State," earlier this chapter). Admission to the Monkey Mia Reserve, in which Monkey Mia Dolphin Resort is located, is A$6 (U.S.$3.90) per adult, A$2 (U.S.$1.30) per child 7 to 16, and A$12 (U.S.$7.80) for a family and is valid for two consecutive days.

ATMs and banks are nonexistent. Banking agencies are located within the tourist association center and the newsagent in Denham.

GETTING AROUND   **Shark Bay Car Hire** (☎ **08/9948 1247**) delivers cars and 4WDs to the airport and the resort from its Denham office. Several companies offer tours to all the main attractions.

MEETING THE DOLPHINS

At 7am guests at Monkey Mia Dolphin Resort are already gathering on the beach in quiet anticipation of the dolphins' arrival. By 8am three or more dolphins usually show, and they come and go until the early afternoon. Because of the crowds the dolphins attract (about 40 people a session in low season, busloads in high season), a park ranger instructs everyone to line up knee-deep in the water as the playful swimmers cruise by your legs. You may not approach them or reach out to pat them (research shows dolphins veer away from people trying to pat them, anyhow) but they do come up to touch people of their accord sometimes. Sometimes the dolphins even offer you a fish as a present! Feeding times are different each day so the dolphins won't become dependent on the food. Once the crowd disperses, savvy swimmers dive into the water just up the beach outside the no-swimmers-allowed Dolphin Interaction Area, because the dolphins may head there after the "show." Apart from the Monkey Mia Reserve entry fee, there is no charge to see the creatures.

A GREAT SEA-LIFE CRUISE, LIVING "FOSSILS" & MORE

Don't do what so many visitors do—come to Monkey Mia, see the dolphins, then shoot back to Perth. I found my cruise to see Shark Bay's incredible marine life on the sailing catamaran ✪ *Shotover* (☎ **1800/24 1481** in Australia, or 08/9948 1481) to be even better than the dolphins! During a 2½-hour dugong (manatee) cruise we saw a hammerhead shark, a baby great white, two very large sea snakes that we hauled out of the water for a closer look, three turtles, oodles of dolphins that came up to the boat, and a baby dugong riding on its mum's back. Every passenger is given Polaroid sunglasses, which help you spot underwater animals. Sometimes you see dozens of dugong; note they leave the area mid-May to August, though. The dugong cruise departs 1pm daily from Monkey Mia Dolphin Resort and costs A$44 (U.S.$28.60). The Shotover also does a daily 2-hour dolphin cruise at 10:30am (A$38.50/ U.S.$25.03), a sunset cruise, and September through March, a nightly "Astronomy Under Sail" cruise. Children 7 to 16 are half-price on all cruises, free for younger kids.

On your way in or out of Monkey Mia, stop by the **Hamelin Pool Historic Telegraph Station** (☎ **08/9942 5905**), 41 kilometers (25½ miles) from the highway turnoff. A small museum houses old equipment, farming tools, and historical odds and sods from the 19th-century days when Monkey Mia was a repeater station on a telegraph line. Entry to the museum includes an explanation of the local stromatolites, rocky formations about a foot high created by the planet's first oxygen-breathing cells—Earth's first life, in other words. From the station, you can wander down to **Shell Beach** at Hamelin Pool and have a look at them. You may find them something of an anticlimax, but following the signposted boardwalk over their tidal zone proves more interesting. The "sand" on the beach is zillions of teensy white shells, which were quarried as bricks to build some of the local buildings. The museum tour costs A$4.40 (U.S.$2.86) for adults, A$2.20 (U.S.$1.43) for kids under 16, and A$12.10 (U.S.$7.87) for families, and runs about every half hour daily. There's a cafe and gift store, too.

You can explore the saltpans, dunes, coastal cliffs, walking trails and old homestead in the nearby 52,500-hectare (129,675-acre) **Francois Peron National Park,** either alone (you will need a 4WD) or on a half- or full-day tour—although not everyone will appreciate the park's harsh scenery. You should easily spot wallabies, birds and emus, and turtles, dolphins, rays, dugongs and, in season, whales from the cliffs. Other activities in the region include half- and full-day sport fishing trips from Denham and a couple of pearl farm tours.

WHERE TO STAY & DINE

Monkey Mia Dolphin Resort. Monkey Mia Rd., Shark Bay (P.O. Box 119, Denham, WA 6537). ☎ **1800/653 611** in Australia, or 08/9948 1320. Fax 08/9948 1034. www. monkeymia.com.au. Tent sites; 58 powered sites; 10 onsite caravans; 6 "canvas condo" permanent tents to sleep 6, all with bathroom (shower only); 13 park homes to sleep 6, none with bathroom; 60 motel rooms, all with bathroom (shower only). A$35.20–$79.20 (U.S.$22.88–$51.48) up to 3 or 4 people sharing caravan rented from resort plus A$2 (U.S.$1.30) per night for power hookup; A$79.20 (U.S.$51.78) up to 4 people in canvas condo; A$90.20 (U.S.$58.63) up to 4 people in park home; A$157.30–$179.30 (U.S.$102.25–$116.55) double or triple, motel room. Extra person A$11 (U.S.$7.15). Linen A$11 (U.S.$7.15) per person in park homes, canvas condos, and caravans for duration of stay. Lower rates Feb 1–Mar 31 (excluding Easter) and May 1–Jun 30. Weekly rates available. AE, BC, DC, MC, V.

Set right on the beach the dolphins visit, this oasis of green lawns and palms doubles as a town settlement. Most comfortable are the spacious air-conditioned motel rooms (the Deluxe kind look right on to the beach and have their own barbecues); safari tent "canvas condos" with carpeted floors, electricity, a fridge, and a separate kitchen/dining area from the bedroom (but no air-conditioning); and air-conditioned demountable "park homes" with cooking facilities. The resort has a tour desk, well-stocked minimarket, two tennis courts, a volleyball court, a pool and Jacuzzi fed by naturally warm underground water, a cafe for takeout, and the pleasant Bough Shed Restaurant overlooking the sea. Most tours in the area depart from the resort.

THE NORTHWEST CAPE

1,272km (795 miles) N of Perth; 1,567km (979 miles) S of Broome

Driving along the only road on the **☉ Northwest Cape** is like driving on the moon. Hundreds of tall red anthills march to the horizon, sheep and 'roos threaten to get under the wheels, and the sun beats down from a harsh sky. On the Cape's western shore is **Coral Bay,** a tiny cluster of dive shops, backpacker lodges, a low-key resort and charter boats nestled on sand so white, water so blue, and ochre dust so orange you think the townsfolk computer-enhanced it. Stretching north of town are deserted sandy beaches edged by coral. On the Cape's east coast is **Exmouth** (pop. 3,500), born in 1967 as a support town to the nearby Harold E. Holt Naval Communications Station, a joint Australian/United States center. Apart from whale shark diving, scuba diving and snorkeling in Ningaloo Marine Park are the big activities, along with 4WD trips over the arid Cape Range National Park and surrounding sheep stations.

Exmouth and Coral Bay are 150 kilometers (94 miles) apart. Coral Bay is several degrees cooler than Exmouth and has divine diving, swimming, and snorkeling; a restaurant and takeout or two, and a bar; a small supermarket; and little else. Exmouth is hot, dusty, and charmless, but has more facilities, including a supermarket, an ATM and an outdoor cinema. Most tours not having to do with the reef, such as 4WD safaris, leave from Exmouth. Both places have plenty of dive and snorkel companies. Wherever you stay, book ahead in whale shark season (Mar–early June).

ESSENTIALS

GETTING THERE   Skywest Airlines (☎ **13 13 00** in Australia; www.Skywest. com.au) flies to **Learmonth Airport,** 35 kilometers (22 miles) from Exmonth. A shuttle bus meets every flight and takes you to your Exmouth hotel for A$15 (U.S.$9.75) one-way. It does not take bookings. **Coral Bay Adventures** (☎ **08/9942 5955**) makes transfers, on demand, from Learmonth to Coral Bay, approximately 120 kilometers (75 miles) away, for A$85 (U.S.$55.25) per person one-way.

Greyhound Pioneer operates three services a week from Perth to Coral Bay and Exmouth. The trip is close to 17 hours and costs A$180 (U.S.$110.70) to Coral Bay and A$200 (U.S.$130) to Exmouth. Greyhound's daily Perth-Broome and Broome-Perth services connect with a local bus service to Exmouth at the turn-off on the highway at Giralia. The change happens in the wee hours of the morning. There is no train to the Northwest Cape.

The 14-hour drive from Perth (plus rest stops) is through lonely country on a two-lane highway. Check your contract allows you to drive your rental car this far north of Perth. Wildlife will be thick on the ground, and gas stations thin. Take the Brand Highway to Geraldton, 424 kilometers (265 miles) north of Perth, then the North West Coastal Highway for 623 kilometers (389 miles) to Minilya gas station; the Exmouth turn-off is 7 kilometers (4 miles) north of here. Exmouth is a further 225 kilometers (141 miles) from the turnoff. Overnight at the Mercure Inn Geraldton, listed in "Getting There" under "Shark Bay (Monkey Mia)," above, or in Carnarvon, which is the only town between Geraldton and Exmouth. Everything else that looks like a town on your map is just a gas station.

VISITOR INFORMATION The **Exmouth Tourist Bureau,** Murat Road, Exmouth, WA 6707 (☎ **08/9949 1176;** fax 08/9949 1441; www.exmouth-australia.com), is open daily 8:30am to 5pm. The **Milyering Visitors Centre,** 52 kilometers (32½ miles) northwest of Exmouth, is the Cape Range National Park's information center, run by the Department of Conservation and Land Management

(CALM). The **Coral Bay Supermarket,** Coral Bay Arcade, Robinson Street, Coral Bay, WA 6701 (☎/fax **08/9942 5988**) doubles as the tourist information center there. There is only one ATM cash machine on the Cape, in Exmouth.

GETTING AROUND   Many tours and dive operators pick up from either Exmouth or Coral Bay accommodations, but not usually both. The roads along the cape to Exmouth and around the tip as far down as Turquoise Bay are paved, as is the road across the cape to Coral Bay. To explore more widely, rent a 4WD, available only from Avis and Budget. **Avis** (☎ **08/9949 2492**), **Budget** (☎ **08/9949 1534**), **Hertz** (☎ **08/9144 1221**) and local operator **Allen's Car Hire** (☎ **08/9949 2403**) have offices in Exmouth; there is no car rental in Coral Bay.

Ningaloo Reef Bus (☎ **08/9949 1776**) runs from Exmouth accommodations around the cape as far as Turquoise Bay, stopping at the Milyering Visitors Centre. It departs at 9am and gets back around 3:30pm, running every day except Thursday from April to September, and four days a week from October to May. The round-trip fare to Turquoise Bay is A$20 (U.S.$13). Ask about the sea kayak-and-snorkeling day trip, or the overnight safari camp-out, offered by the bus's operator, Ningaloo Reef Retreat.

DIVING WITH WHALE SHARKS

"Diving" is not really a correct term for this activity, because it's by snorkeling that you get close to these leviathans. Whale sharks are sharks, not whales, and they are the world's biggest fish, reaching 12 to 18 meters (39–59 ft.) in length. Terrified? Don't be. Their gigantic size belies a gentle nature and slow swimming speed, and despite having a mouth big enough to swallow a boatload of snorkelers, they eat plankton (which cannot possibly be confused with humans by the fish). Several boat operators take people out to swim alongside the fish when they appear March through early June. A trip with **Exmouth Diving Centre** (☎ **1800/655 156** in Australia or 08/9949 1201; fax 08/9949 1680; www.exmouthdiving.com.au) or its Coral Bay sister company, **Ningaloo Reef Diving Centre** (☎ **08/9942 5824;** fax 08/9942 5836; www.exmouthdiving.com.au) costs A$250 (U.S.$162.50), and takes a day. Shark protection regulations limit your boat to 10 snorkelers and a maximum 90 minutes with any one fish; your boat is free to search for several fish in one day. Most boats stop at reefs for more snorkeling, and some incorporate optional scuba dives.

DIVING, SNORKELING, FISHING & FOUR-WHEEL-DRIVING

Scuba dive the unspoiled waters of the Cape and you will see marvelous reef formations, grouper, manta rays, angel fish, octopus, morays, potato cod, which you can hand feed, and other underwater marvels. Divers often spot humpback and false killer whales, large sharks, dolphins, and turtles. Loads of dive companies in Exmouth and Coral Bay rent gear and run daily dive trips and learn-to-dive courses, including the two listed in "Diving with Whale Sharks," above. A two-dive day trip costs around A$110 (U.S.$71.50) with all gear supplied. Live-aboard trips also run. Three great snorkeling spots are right off the shore at Coral Bay; **Bundegi Beach,** a short drive north of Exmouth; and at beautiful ✪ **Turquoise Bay** approximately 60 kilometers (37½ miles) from Exmouth on the cape's western coast. Walk up the beach, wade in, and let the bay's gentle current carry you back over the fish. In deeper offshore waters off Coral Bay you can snorkel with manta rays with a "wingspan" up to 7 meters (23 ft.). They are least common in August and September. Ningaloo Reef Diving Centre (see above) runs a manta snorkel tour for A$85 (U.S.$55.25), or A$150 (U.S.$97.50) if you want to dive with the creatures. Snorkel gear from the numerous dive operators in either town rents for about A$12 (U.S.$7.80) per day, and Ningaloo Reef Bus passengers use it for free on the day of travel! Tour companies run snorkel tours or glass-bottom boat rides from either town.

Reef fish, tuna and Spanish mackerel are common catches in these waters, and black, blue, and striped marlin run outside the reef from September to January. Up to a dozen boats operate reef and game fishing day trips out of Exmouth and Coral Bay, and tackle and tin fishing dinghies are easily rented in either town.

Green and loggerhead turtles nest at night from November through February or March on the Cape's beaches. Take a flashlight and look for them, or join one of turtle watch tours. From August to November, boats run cruises from either town to spot humpback whales. Dugongs are a common sight for snorkelers and divers, too.

Because the Cape has few roads, which don't show you many sights anyhow, touring is best done on a "Top of the Range" off-road 240-kilometer (150-mile) 4WD escapade with ✪ Neil McLeod's **Ningaloo Safari Tours** (☎ **08/9949 1550**). Neil takes you over the arid limestone ridges of the 50,581-hectare (124,935-acre) Cape Range National Park, down to dazzling Turquoise Bay for snorkeling, climbing up an old lighthouse, cruising orange-walled Yardie Creek Gorge to spot rock wallabies, and scarfing his Mum's fruitcake. I have never seen so many 'roos in one place, including big reds. He knows heaps about the area's geology, wildlife, history and Aboriginal culture, too. This full-day trip departs your Exmouth hotel at 7:30am, and costs A$135 (U.S.$87.75) for adults and A$95 (U.S.$61.75) for children under 12. Highly recommended.

WHERE TO STAY & DINE
In Exmouth
Potshot Hotel Resort. Murat Rd., Exmouth, WA 6707. ☎ **08/9949 1200.** Fax 08/9949 1486. 97 units (all with shower only). A/C TV. A$85–$89 (U.S.$55.25–$57.85) homestead room, A$118–$126 (U.S.$76.70–$81.90) for 3 people in room, A$137 (U.S.$89.05) for 4 people in 2-bedroom apt, A$198 (U.S.$128.70) for 4 people in 3-bedroom apt. Extra person A$10 (U.S.$6.50). AE, BC, DC, JCB, MC, V.

The grounds here are hot and dusty, but the hotel is a bright, modern complex right in town, with a Jacuzzi, swimming pool, tennis courts, and minigolf. The cocktail bar around the pool is the only shady place in town to enjoy a drink, which explains its popularity with locals. The restaurant is devoid of atmosphere but has a long menu, good food, and a nice wine list. The brick motel rooms are cool and spacious; the homestead rooms are smaller, and more basic; there are two-bedroom apartments; and across the road are new three-bedroom apartments. Most rooms have telephones.

In Coral Bay
Ningaloo Reef Resort. At the end of Robinson St., Coral Bay, WA 6701. ☎ **08/9942 5934.** Fax 08/9942 5953. www.coralbay.org. WHALESHARK@Bigpond.com. 34 units, all with bathroom (shower only). A$126.50–$132 (U.S.$82.23–$85.80) double, A$159.50–$275 (U.S.$103.68–$178.75) apt. Extra person A$11 (U.S.$7.15) adults. Ask about weekly rates. BC, MC, V.

This low-rise complex of motel rooms, studios, and apartments stands out as the best place to stay among Coral Bay's profusion of backpacker hostels. Located on a blissfully green lawn with a swimming pool overlooking the bay, the rooms are not fancy, but they're clean, with aspects towards the bay and the pool. Hair dryers are available. The place has a restaurant and a nice communal air, thanks to the bar doubling as the local pub.

Adelaide & South Australia

11

by Marc Llewellyn

Adelaide has a major advantage over the other Australian state capitals in that it has Outback, vineyards, major wetlands, animal sanctuaries, a major river, and mountain ranges virtually on its doorstep. Meals and lodgings are also cheaper than in Sydney or Melbourne, and it has the small-town advantage of being easy to get around. If you plan to travel outside the city, then a trip to one of the wine-growing areas has to be on your itinerary, since Australian wines have been taking home many international wine prizes in the last few years. Of all the wine areas, the ✪ **Barossa Valley** is the nearest to Adelaide and the most interesting. Centered on Tanunda, the Barossa is well known for its German architecture, including its 19th-century Lutheran churches, as well as its dozens of pretty hamlets, fine restaurants, and vineyards offering cellar-door tastings.

If you want to see animals instead of, or in addition to, grapes, you're in luck. You're likely to come across the odd kangaroo or wallaby near the main settlements, especially at dusk, or you could visit one of the area's many wildlife reserves. Otherwise head out into the Outback where animals abound, or over to Kangaroo Island, which is without a doubt, the best place in Australia to see many types of native animals in the wild without having to travel enormous distances.

Another place worth visiting is the craggy Flinders Ranges, some 460 kilometers (285 miles) north of Adelaide. Though the scenery along the way is mostly unattractive grazing properties devoid of trees, the Flinders Ranges offer an incredible landscape of multicolored rocks, rough-and-ready characters, and even camel treks though the semi-desert. On the other side of the mountain ranges the real Outback starts.

The South Australian Outback is serenely beautiful, with giant skies, wildflowers after the rains, red earth, and little water. Out here you'll find bizarre opal-mining towns, such as Coober Pedy, where summer temperatures can reach 50°C (122°F) and where most people live underground to escape the heat.

If you prefer your landscape with a little more moisture, head to the Coorong, a water-bird sanctuary rivaled only by Kakadu National Park in the Northern Territory (see chapter 9).

EXPLORING THE STATE

VISITOR INFORMATION The **South Australia Travel Centre,** 18 King William Street (☎ **1300 655 276** in Australia, or 08/8303 2033; fax 08/8303 2249; www.visit-southaustralia.com.au; sthaustour@tourism.sa.gov.au) is the best place to collect information on Adelaide and South Australia. It's open weekdays from 8:30am to 5pm and weekends from 9am to 2pm.

For general information about the South Australia's national parks contact the **Department of Environment and Natural Resources Information Centre,** Australis House, 77 Grenfell St., Adelaide 5000 (☎ **08/8204 1910;** fax 08/8204 1919). It's open Monday to Friday from 9am to 5pm.

GETTING AROUND South Australia, at four times the size of the United Kingdom, has a lot of empty space between places of interest. The best way to see it is by car, though a limited rail service connects Adelaide with some areas. The **Stuart Highway** bisects the state from south to north; it runs from Adelaide through industrial Port Augusta (gateway to the Flinders Ranges), and through Coober Pedy to Alice Springs in the Red Centre. The **Eyre Highway** travels westward along the coastline and into Western Australia, while the **Barrier Highway** enters New South Wales just before the mining city of Broken Hill (see chapter 6). The **Princes Highway** takes you east to Melbourne. You should seek travel advice from the **Royal Automobile Association of South Australia (RAA),** 41 Hindmarsh Square, Adelaide, SA 5000 (☎ **13 11 11** in South Australia only, or 08/8202 4500; fax 08/8202 4520; www.raa.net), if you are planning to drive into the Outback regions. The RAA provides route maps and emergency breakdown service.

Qantas (☎ **13 13 13** in Australia) and **Ansett** (☎ **13 13 00** in Australia) fly to Adelaide from the major state capitals.

Both **Greyhound Pioneer** (☎ **13 20 30** in Australia) and **McCafferty's** (☎ **13 14 99** in Australia) service South Australia. Within the state the largest operator is **Stateliner** (☎ **08/8415 5555**).

1 Adelaide

Adelaide, "The City of Churches," has a reputation as a sleepy place, full of parkland and surrounded by vineyards. It is in many ways a throwback to the lifestyle of 1950s Australia—a lifestyle that the more progressive state capitals have left behind.

Numerous parks and gardens, wide tree-lined streets, the River Torrens running through its center, sidewalk cafes, colonial architecture, and, of course, the churches help make it a pleasant, open city, perfect for strolling or bicycling.

Though the immigrant population has added a cosmopolitan flair to the restaurant scene, Adelaide still has a rather English feeling about it. That's not surprising when you learn that Adelaide was the only capital settled entirely by English free settlers rather than convicts, and that it attracted more after World War II, when Brits flocked here to work in the city's car parts and domestic appliance industries.

But it was earlier immigrants, from Germany, who gave Adelaide and the surrounding area a romantic twist. Arriving as religious refugees in the 1830s, German immigrants brought with them their winemaking skills, and established wineries. Today, more than one-third of all Australian wine—including some of the world's best—comes from areas mostly within an hour's drive from Adelaide. As a result, Adelaidians of all socio-economic groups are more versed in wine than even the French and regularly compare vintages, wine-growing regions, and winemaking trends.

Any time of the year is a good time to visit Adelaide, though May to August can be chilly and December and January hot.

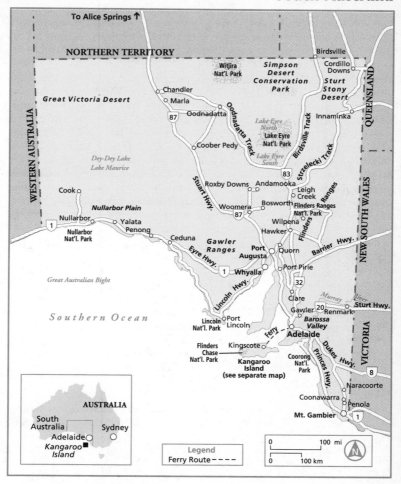

ORIENTATION

ARRIVING   By Plane   Adelaide International Airport is 5 kilometers (3 miles) west of the city center. Major car-rental companies (Avis, Budget, Hertz, and Thrifty) have desks in the international and domestic terminals. You can pick up a few tourist brochures here, but there is no official tourist desk. Lockers are available, but you'll need exact change when you retrieve your luggage. In the domestic terminal there's a bank and a post office. There is a stamp machine in the international terminal. Both terminals have showers, currency-exchange desks, shops, and places to eat.

The Transit Bus (☎ **08/8381 5311;** www.transitregency.com.au) links the airport with major city hotels and the rail and bus stations. On weekdays, buses leave the terminals at 30-minute intervals from 5:00am to 9:30pm, and on weekends and public holidays hourly (on the half-hour). Adult tickets are A$6.60 (U.S.$4.29) one-way and A$11 (U.S.$7.15) round-trip. Child tickets cost A$2.20 (U.S.$1.43) each way.

A taxi to the city will cost around A$17 (U.S.$11.05).

The Adelaide Festival
& Other Special Events

Adelaide is home to Australia's largest performing arts festival, the **Adelaide Festival,** held in March during even-numbered years (the dates are Mar 1–10 in 2002). The festival includes literary and visual arts as well as dance, opera, classical music, jazz, cabaret and comedy. The festival encompasses Writers' Week and a fringe comedy festival. For more information, contact **Adelaide Festival,** P.O. Box 8116, Station Arcade, Adelaide, SA 5000 (☎ **08/8216 4444;** fax 08/ 8216 4455; www.adelaidefestival.org.au.

In February and March of odd-numbered years, the 3-day **Womadelaide Festival** of world music takes place. Crowds of 60,000 or more watch Australian and international artists. E-mail Womadelaide at apadmin@artsprojects.com.au).

By Train   One of the great trains of Australia, *The Indian Pacific,* transports passengers from Sydney to Adelaide (trip time: 28 hr.) and from Adelaide to Perth (trip time: 36 hr.) twice a week on Monday and Thursday. Tickets from Sydney to Adelaide are A$521 (U.S.$338.65) for adults and A$349 (U.S.$226.85) for children in first class, A$376 (U.S.$244.40) for adults and A$252 (U.S.$163.80) for children in an holiday class, and A$176 (U.S.$114.40) for adults and A$88 (U.S.$57.20) for children in an coach class. *The Indian Pacific* then continues on to Perth.

The other legendary Australian train is *The Ghan,* which runs from Melbourne to Adelaide and then up to Alice Springs weekly from November to April and twice a week from May to October; trip time from Adelaide to Alice Springs is 20 hours. *The Ghan* also runs a service from Alice Springs to Sydney. Tickets from Melbourne to Adelaide are A$346 (U.S.$224.90) for adults and A$232 (U.S.$150.80) for children in first class, A$221 (U.S.$143.65) for adults and A$148 (U.S.$96.20) for children in holiday class, and A$57 (U.S.$37.05) for adults and A$33 (U.S.$21.45) for children in an economy seat.

The Overlander provides service between Adelaide and Melbourne (trip time: 12 hr.). Tickets are A$156 (U.S.$101.40) for adults and A$105 (U.S.$68.25) for children in first class, and A$57 (U.S.$37.05) for adults and A$33 (U.S.$21.45) for children in economy. Round-trip fares for all these trains work out much cheaper than the single fare doubled.

Call **Great Southern Railways** (☎ **08/8213 4530**) for more information and bookings, or check out the timetables and fares on their website (www.gsr.com. au/fares.htm).

The **Keswick Interstate Rail Passenger Terminal,** located 2 kilometers (1¼ miles) west of the city center, is Adelaide's main railway station.

By Bus   Intercity coaches terminate at the central bus station, 101 Franklin St. (☎ **08/8415 5533**), near Morphett Street in the city center.

Adventurous types should consider traveling to Adelaide from Melbourne (or vice versa) on the ✪ **Wayward Bus,** operated by the **Wayward Bus Touring Company,** P.O. Box 7076, Adelaide, SA 5000 (☎ **1800/882 823** in Australia, or 08/8232 6646; fax 08/8232 1455; www.waywardbus.com.au).These 21-seat buses make the trip in 3½ days via the Great Ocean Road; the fare is A$265 (U.S.$172.25) with backpacker's accommodation and A$370 (U.S.$240.50) with motel accommodation. You spend around 3 hours a day on the bus, and the driver acts as your guide. A picnic or cafe lunch each day and entry to national parks are included in the fare. You can leave the trip and rejoin another later. Reservations are essential.

VISITOR INFORMATION   Head to the **South Australia Travel Centre,** 18 King William Street (☎ **1300 655 276** in Australia or 08/8303 2033; fax 08/8303 2249; www.visit-southaustralia.com.au), for maps and travel advice. It's open weekdays from 9am to 5pm and weekends from 9am to 2pm. There's also an information booth on Rundle Mall open daily from 10am to 5pm.

CITY LAYOUT   Adelaide is a simple city to navigate because of its gridlike pattern, which was planned down to each wide street and airy square by Colonel William Light in 1836. The city's official center is Victoria Square, where you'll find the Town Hall. Bisecting the city from south to north is the city's main thoroughfare, **King William Street.** Streets running perpendicular to King William Street change their names on either side, so that Franklin Street, for example, changes into Flinders Street. Of these cross streets, the most interesting to the visitor are the restaurant strips of Gouger Street and Rundle Street, the latter running into the pedestrian shopping precinct of Rundle Mall. Another is Hindley Street, with its inexpensive restaurants and nightlife. On the banks of the River Torrens north of the city center you'll find **Adelaide Plaza,** home of the Festival Centre, the Convention Centre, and the Adelaide Casino. Bordering the city center on the north and south are **North Terrace,** lined with galleries and museums, which leads to the Botanic Gardens, and **South Terrace.**

Follow King William Street south and you'll be chasing the tram to the beachside suburb of **Glenelg,** follow it north and it crosses the River Torrens and flows into sophisticated **North Adelaide,** an area crammed with Victorian and Edwardian architecture. The main avenues in North Adelaide, O'Connell and Melbourne streets, are lined with restaurants, cafes, and bistros that offer the tastes of a multicultural city.

To the northwest of the city center is **Port Adelaide,** a seaport and the historic maritime heart of South Australia and the home to some of the finest colonial buildings in the state, as well as good pubs and restaurants.

GETTING AROUND

BY PUBLIC TRANSPORTATION   By Bus   Adelaide's public bus network is divided into three zones, and fares are calculated according to the number of zones traveled. The city center is classed as Zone 1. The fare in Zone 1 is A$1.60 (U.S.$1.04) from 9am to 3pm on weekdays and A$2.80 (U.S.$1.82) most other times. You can buy tickets on board the bus or at newsagents around the city. You can pick up a free metro information guide and get timetable and destination information over the phone, or in person at the **Passenger Transport Board Information Centre** (☎ **08/8210 1000**), on the corner of Currie and King William streets. It's open Monday to Saturday from 8am to 6pm and Sunday from 10:30am to 5.30pm.

The **CityFree bus** operates free bus service every 15 minutes (Mon–Thurs 8:30am–6pm, Fri to 9pm, and Sat to 5pm) around the city center along North Terrace, East Terrace, Grenfell Street, Pulteney Street, Wakefield Street, Grote Street, Morphett Street, Light Square, Hindley Street, and West Terrace. Another free bus, the **Bee Line,** runs along North Terrace, down King William Street to Victoria Street. Routes are well signposted. All CityFree buses are wheelchair-accessible.

Bus numbers 181, and 182 run from the city to North Adelaide.

The **Adelaide Explorer** bus (☎ **08/8364 1933**) stops at 10 sights around town and costs A$39 (U.S.$25.35) for adults, A$18 (U.S.$11.70) for children, and A$65 (U.S.$42.25) for families of four. The bus stops at each destination every 1½ hours in

A Money-Saving Transit Pass

If you plan to get around the city via public transit, it's a good idea to purchase a **Daytrip** ticket, which covers unlimited travel on buses, trams, and city trains within the metro area for one day. The pass costs A$5.40 (U.S.$3.51) for adults and A$2.70 (U.S.$1.76) for children 5 to 15 and are available at most train stations, newsagents, and the **Passenger Transport Board Information Centre** (☎ **08/8210 1000**).

summer and every 3 hours in winter. The full loop takes a leisurely 2¾ hours, with commentary. Buy tickets on the bus.

By Tram The **Glenelg Tram** runs between Victoria Square and the beach suburb of Glenelg. Tickets are valid for 2 hours and cost A$1.60 (U.S.$1.04) for adults and A80¢(U.S.52¢) for children 5 to 14 from 9am to 3pm, and A$2.80 (U.S.$1.82) for adults and A$1 (U.S.65¢) for children at other times. The journey takes 29 minutes.

BY TAXI & CAR The major cab companies are **Yellow Cabs** (☎ **13 22 27** in South Australia only), **Suburban** (☎ **08/8211 8888**), and **Amalgamated** (☎ **08/8223 3333**). **Access Cabs** (☎ **1300/360 940** in South Australia only) offers wheelchair taxis. The base fare is A$2 (U.S.$1.30) Monday through Friday from 6am to 7pm and Saturday from 6am to 7pm; A$2.90 (U.S.$1.89) Monday through Friday from 7pm to 6am, Saturday after 7pm, and all day Sunday.

Major car-rental companies in the area are **Avis,** 136 North Terrace (☎ **08/8410 5727**); **Budget,** 274 North Terrace (☎ **08/8223 1400**); **Hertz,** 233 Morphett St. (☎ **08/8231 2856**); and **Thrifty,** 296 Hindley St. (☎ **08/8211 8788**).

The **Royal Automobile Association of South Australia (RAA),** 41 Hindmarsh Sq. (☎ **13 11 11** in South Australia or 08/8202 4500; fax 08/8202 4520; www.raa.net), has route maps and provides emergency breakdown services.

Fast Facts: Adelaide

American Express The Amex office, at 13 Grenfell St. (☎ **08/8202 1400**), is open during normal business hours.

Business Hours Generally, banks are open Monday to Thursday from 9:30am to 4pm and Friday from 9:30am to 5pm. Stores are generally open Monday to Thursday from 9am to 5:30pm, Friday from 9am to 9pm, Saturday from 9am to 5pm, and Sunday from 11am to 5pm.

Currency Exchange Banks and hotels, the casino, and the Myer department store in Rundle Mall all cash traveler's checks. The **Thomas Cook** office is at 45 Grenfell St. (☎ **08/8212 3354**).

Dentist Contact the **Australian Dental Association Emergency Information Service** (☎ **08/8272 8111**), open nightly 5pm to 9pm, and Saturday and Sunday 9am to 9pm. It will put you in touch with a dentist. You can also contact the office of **Dr. Brook,** 231 North Terrace (☎ **08/8223 6988**), open during normal business hours.

Doctor Contact the **Royal Adelaide Hospital,** on North Terrace (☎ **08/8222 4000**). The **Travellers' Medical & Vaccination Centre,** 29 Gilbert Place (☎ **08/8212 7522**), offers vaccinations and other travel-related medicines.

Emergencies Dial ☎ **000** to call an ambulance, the fire department, or the police in a emergency.

Adelaide Accommodations, Dining & Attractions

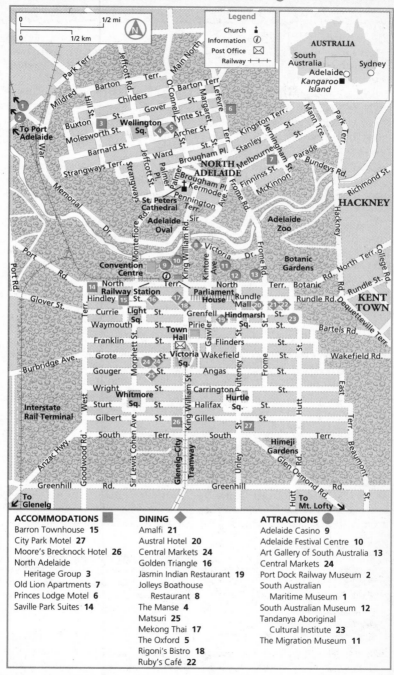

ACCOMMODATIONS ■
Barron Townhouse **15**
City Park Motel **27**
Moore's Brecknock Hotel **26**
North Adelaide
 Heritage Group **3**
Old Lion Apartments **7**
Princes Lodge Motel **6**
Saville Park Suites **14**

DINING ◆
Amalfi **21**
Austral Hotel **20**
Central Markets **24**
Golden Triangle **16**
Jasmin Indian Restaurant **19**
Jolleys Boathouse
 Restaurant **8**
The Manse **4**
Matsuri **25**
Mekong Thai **17**
The Oxford **5**
Rigoni's Bistro **18**
Ruby's Café **22**

ATTRACTIONS ●
Adelaide Casino **9**
Adelaide Festival Centre **10**
Art Gallery of South Australia **13**
Central Markets **24**
Port Dock Railway Museum **2**
South Australian
 Maritime Museum **1**
South Australian Museum **12**
Tandanya Aboriginal
 Cultural Institute **23**
The Migration Museum **11**

Hospitals   The **Royal Adelaide Hospital,** North Terrace (☎ **08/8222 4000**), is located in the city center.

Hot Lines   Call the **Crisis Care Centre** at ☎ **13 16 11;** the **Royal Automobile Association** of South Australia (RAA) at ☎ **08/8202 4500;** the **Disability Information and Resource Centre** at ☎ **08/8223 7522.**

Internet Access   The **Ngapartji Multimedia Centre,** 211 Rundle St., (☎ **08/8232 0839**), has e-mail and Internet access Monday through Thursday 8:30am to 9pm, Friday and Saturday 9am through 10pm, Sunday noon through 7pm. The **Blah Blah Internet Café,** 255 Waymouth St., next to Adelaide Backpackers Hostel, (☎ **08/8221 5299**), offers access for A$5 (U.S.$3.25) an hour.

Lost Property   If you've lost something on the street, contact the nearest police station. For items left on public transport contact the **Lost Property Office,** on the main concourse of the Adelaide Railway Station on North Terrace (☎ **08/8218 2552**); it's open Monday through Friday from 9am to 5pm.

Luggage Storage/Lockers   There are luggage lockers at **Adelaide Airport** in the domestic terminal for A$1 (U.S.65¢) per hour to a maximum of A$7 (U.S.$4.55) for 24 hours. You need exact change. At the **Central Bus Station** on Franklin Street (☎ **08/8415 5533**) lockers cost A$2 (U.S.$1.30) for 24 hours.

Pharmacies   Called "chemists." **Burden Chemists,** Shop 11, Southern Cross Arcade, King William St. (☎ **08/8231 4701**), is open Monday through Thursday from 8am to 6pm, Friday from 8am to 8pm, and Saturday from 9am to 1pm.

Post Office   The **General Post Office (GPO),** 141 King William St., Adelaide, SA 5000 (☎ **08/8216 2222**), is open Monday through Friday from 8am to 6pm, Saturday 8:30am to noon. General delivery (*poste restante*) can be picked up Monday through Friday from 7am to 5:30pm; 9am to 1pm on Sunday.

Restrooms   Public restrooms can be found at the **Central Market Arcade,** between Grote and Gouger streets, in both **Hindmarsh** and **Victoria** squares, and at **James Place** (off Rundle Mall).

Safety   Adelaide is a very safe city, though it's wise to avoid walking along the River Torrens and through side streets near Hindley Street after dark.

WHERE TO STAY

The **South Australia Travel Centre** (see "Visitor Information," above) can supply information on B&Bs and homestays around the state. Satellite or cable TV are rare in South Australian hotels, though some provide pay-per-view movies.

IN THE CITY CENTER

Barron Townhouse. 164 Hindley St., Adelaide, SA 5000. ☎ **1800/888 241** in Australia, 800/624-3524 in the U.S. and Canada, 0800/892 407 in the U.K., 0800/803 524 in New Zealand, or 08/8211 8255. Fax 08/8231 1179. www.barrontownhouse.com.au. 68 units. A/C MINIBAR TV TEL. A$132 (U.S.$85.80) standard double, A$176 (U.S.$114.40) deluxe double;

A Travel Tip

If you plan to be in town during the Adelaide Festival, make sure you book your accommodations well in advance. Accommodations can also get pretty scarce during the Christmas and New Year's period, so it's wise to book well in advance then, too

A$186 (U.S.$120.90) executive room; A$140 (U.S.$91) family. Extra person A$18 (U.S$11.70). Children under 12 stay free in parents' room. Lower rates in off-season and weekends. Ask about package deals. AE, BC, DC, JCB, MC, V. Free parking.

Friendly staff and garish china flamingos welcome you to this four-star concrete block. It's a 10- to 15-minute walk from the center of town, 5 minutes from the casino, and not far from the nightclub and red-light district. Rooms are spacious and comfortable enough, with everything including a hair dryer. There's a very nice pool and sauna on the rooftop. Downstairs is the informal Flamingos bistro. The cocktail lounge is more of the same, but with a better view of the traffic lights on the busy road outside.

City Park Motel. 471 Pulteney St., Adelaide, SA 5000. ☎ **08/8223 1444.** Fax 08/8223 1133. 18 units, 14 with bathroom (shower only). A/C TV TEL. A$55 (U.S.$35.75) double without bathroom; A$75 (U.S.$48.75) double with bathroom. Extra person A$10 (U.S.$6.50). AE, BC, DC, MC, V. Free parking. The tram to Glenelg stops around the corner, and 3 streets up is a bus stop for the free City Loop bus.

The rooms in this first-floor motel just outside the city center have modern furnishings and nice bathrooms with a shower. Some rooms have private balconies. Also on the premises is a separate bathroom with a tub. The best room is number 45. Downstairs there's a new cocktail bar, nightclub, and bistro.

Moore's Brecknock Hotel. 401 King William St., Adelaide, SA 5000. ☎ **08/8231 5467.** Fax 08/8410 1968. 10 units, none with bathroom. A/C. A$55 (U.S.$35.75) double; A$75 (U.S.$48.75) triple. Rates include continental breakfast. AE, BC, DC, MC, V. Free parking. The tram to Glenelg stops in front of the hotel.

Adelaide's original Irish pub, built in 1851, still attracts a lot of Irish who come here for the great selection of beer and reasonably priced home-style cooking—it reputedly serves Adelaide's best hamburgers. It's also very popular with American guests who use the hotel accommodation upstairs as a base from which to discover Kangaroo Island and other parts of the state. The Brecknock is about 4 blocks from Victoria Square and is run by Kerry Moore and his Canadian wife Tricia. There are live bands downstairs on Friday, Saturday, and Sunday evenings, but the music finishes at 1am on Friday and Saturday, and 10pm on Sunday, so you shouldn't have too much trouble sleeping. Rooms are large and pleasantly done out in old-world style. Each has a double and a single bed, and a sink, with the bathrooms down the hall.

✪ **Saville Park Suites Adelaide.** 255 Hindley St., Adelaide SA 5000. ☎ **1800/882 601** in Australia or 08/8231 8333. Fax 08/8217 2519. 144 units. AC MINIBAR TV TEL. A$138 (U.S.$89.70) 1-bedroom studio; A$182 (U.S.$118.30) 2-bedroom executive; A$198 (U.S.$128.70) 2-bedroom premium. Up to 2 people in studio and 4 in other units. AE, BC, CB, DC, MC, V. Parking A$5 (U.S.$3.25).

You can't miss this conglomerate of russet-red bricks just on the outskirts of the city center (about a 10-min. walk). Rooms are nice and spacious, if a bit formal, which is not surprising since the place is popular with business travelers. Each room has a fully equipped kitchen and laundry and a private balcony. Everything you'd expect to find in a four-star hotel you'll find here. On the premises is the Zipp Restaurant and Wine Bar, where Tommy Chang serves up an innovative menu.

IN NORTH ADELAIDE

This suburb across the river is an interesting place to stay because of its nice architecture and good restaurants. It's about a 10-minute bus ride from the city center.

✪ **Old Lion Apartments.** 9 Jerningham St., North Adelaide, SA 5006. ☎ **08/8223 0500.** Fax 08/8223 0588. reservations@majesticapartments.com.au. 57 units. A/C TV TEL. A$148 (U.S.$96.20) 1-bedroom apt; A$164.50 (U.S.$106.93) 2-bedroom apt; A$203 (U.S.$131.95)

3-bedroom apt. Extra adult A$16.50 (U.S.$10.73), extra child 3–12 A$5.50 (U.S.$3.58). AE, BC, CB, DC, MC, V. Parking A$5 (U.S.$3.25). Bus: 184, 224, 226, 228, or 229.

These pleasant apartments are inside a renovated brewery. The complex is about a 15-minute walk from the city center and is on a direct bus route. Rooms are spacious, with high ceilings, and come with a kitchenette, a living room, French doors separating bedrooms from living quarters, a shower and tub, and a balcony. All apartments also have use of a washing machine and dryer. VCRs and videos are available for rent at the front desk. Continental breakfast costs A$8.50 (U.S.$5.53) extra.

Princes Lodge Motel. 73 Lefevre Terrace, North Adelaide 5006. ☎ **08/8267 5566.** Fax 08/8239 0787. princeslodge@senet.com.au. 21 units. A/C TV TEL. A$55 (U.S$35.75) double with separate private bathroom; A$66 (U.S$42.90) with attached bathroom. Rates include continental breakfast. AE, BC, DC, MC, V. Bus: 222 from Victoria Square (with pickups along King William St.).

One of the best motels in Adelaide, the Princes Lodge looks more like a private home than your typical brick roadside structure. Rooms are nicely decorated and have the usual motel appliances, and generally come with a double and a single bed. There are three family rooms, one of which has a double and three singles; another has six beds in one room. The motel is within walking distance of the restaurants on O'Connell Street, and a A$5 (U.S.$3.25) taxi ride from the city center. There's a laundry on the premises.

Worth a Splurge

❍ North Adelaide Heritage Group. Office: 109 Glen Osmond Rd., Eastwood, SA 5063. ☎ **08/8272 1355** or 0418/289 494 (mobile phone). Fax 08/8272 1355. www.adelaide heritage.com. reservations@adelaideheritage.com. 19 apts, cottages, and suites. TV TEL. Prices A$145–$330 (U.S.$94.25–$214.50) double, depending on accommodation. Extra person A$60–$85 (U.S.$39–$55.25). Children under 12 A$30 (U.S.$19.50). AE, BC, DC, JCB, MC, V.

It's worth coming to Adelaide just to stay in one of these out-of-this-world apartments, cottages, and suites. Each of the 18 properties in North Adelaide and Eastwood are fabulous. I recommend the former Friendly Meeting Chapel Hall, which was once the headquarters of the "Albert Lodge No. 6 of the Independent Order of Oddfellows, Manchester Unity Friendly Society and the Court Huntsman's Pride No. 2478 of the Ancient Order of Foresters Friendly Society." The structure is a small, simple gabled hall of bluestone rubble trimmed with brick and resembles a small church. Built in 1878, it's stocked with period pieces and antiques and rounded off with a modern, fully stocked kitchen; a huge spa bath; a queen-size bed; and a CD player and TV.

Another standout place is George Lowe Esquire unit. This 19th-century apartment is also stocked with antiques, has a huge four-poster bed, a separate bathroom, a lounge, and a full kitchen. Guests also have use of nice gardens. Owners Rodney and Regina Twiss have added all those little touches that make you feel like home, from magazines liberally piled up everywhere to bacon and eggs in the fridge. All properties are within easy walking distance of the main attractions in the area. The company has just bought the old North Adelaide Fire Station and has renovated it into three separate apartments.

In Glenelg

I'd recommend anyone, without hesitation, to stay in Glenelg rather than in the city center. The journey to the city center by car or tram takes less than 30 minutes, and the airport is less than 10 minutes away. Add to this the sea, the lovely beach, the fun fair, the great shops, the good pub, and the nice accommodations and you have a perfect place to ease up on your holiday.

Atlantic Tower Motor Inn. 760 Anzac Hwy., Glenelg, SA 5045. ☎ **08/8294 1011.** Fax 08/8376 0964. atlantic@senet.com.au. 27 units (20 with shower only). A/C TV TEL. A$77 (U.S.$50.05) double; A$99 (U.S.$64.35) deluxe double; A$145 (U.S.$94.25) suite. Extra person A$12 (U.S.$7.80). Children under 15 stay free in parents' room. Free parking. Hotel is 1 block from the tram stop.

If you're looking for relatively inexpensive accommodations near the beach, this is your place. You can't miss this tubular building not far from the sea, with its slowly revolving restaurant on the 12th floor. Rooms are simple, but very bright, and have nice park views through large windows. Each room has a double and a single bed—and even toaster. The Deluxe rooms are a bit nicer and come with baths rather than just showers. Suites have two rooms and excellent views; the most expensive have a spa. The gently turning Rock Lobster Cafe upstairs is open for lunch on Thursday, Friday, and Sunday (no lunch on Saturday) and dinner every evening.

WHERE TO DINE

With more than 600 restaurants, pubs, and cafes, Adelaide boasts more dining spots per capita than anywhere else in Australia. Many of them are clustered in particular areas, such as Rundle Street in the city and Gouger Street and North Adelaide—where you'll find almost every style of cuisine you can imagine. For cheap noodles, laksas, sushi, and cakes head to Adelaide's popular **Central Markets** (☎ **08/8203 7494**), behind the Adelaide Hilton Hotel between Gouger and Grote streets.

Because of South Australia's healthy wine industry, you'll find that many of the more expensive restaurants have extensive wine lists—though with spicier foods it's probably wiser to stick with beer, or a fruity white in a pinch. Many Adelaide restaurants allow diners to bring their own wine (BYO), but most charge a steep corkage fee to open your bottle—A$6 (U.S.$3.90) or so is not uncommon.

IN THE CITY CENTRE

Amalfi. 29 Frome St. (just off Rundle St.). ☎ **08/8223 1948.** Reservations recommended. Main courses A$13.50–$16.50 (U.S$8.78–$10.73). AE, BC, DC, MC, V. Mon–Thurs 11:30am–3pm and 5:30–11pm (until midnight Fri), Sat 5:30pm–midnight. ITALIAN.

Come here for good Italian cooking at reasonable prices served up in a lively atmosphere. The pizzas are the best in Adelaide—though a little expensive—and consistently good veal and pasta dishes are always on the menu. Be sure to check out the daily specials board, where you can pick out a very good fish dish or two.

Austral Hotel. 205 Rundle St. ☎ **08/8223 4660.** Reservations recommended. Main courses A$6.50–$13.50 (U.S.$4.23–$8.78) in bistro and A$14.90–$22 (U.S.$9.69–$14.30) in restaurant. AE, BC, MC, V. Mon–Thurs 12am–3pm and 5:30pm–9:30pm, Fri–Sun 12pm–10:00pm. MODERN AUSTRALIAN.

This large pub, with its dark timber and forest-colored wallpaper, is a pleasant place for a good-value pub meal. You can either eat at the bar, outside on the street, or in the dining room. The bistro serves burgers, fish and chips, pastas, laksas, and Thai curries. The restaurant is a bit more upscale, and offers risotto, hand-made crab ravioli, beef fillets, chicken dishes, venison, paella, and baby octopus.

Golden Triangle. 106a Hindley St. ☎ **08/8211 8222.** Reservations recommended. Main courses A$9.50–$15 (U.S.$6.18–$9.75). AE, BC, DC, MC, V. Daily noon–2:30pm; 5pm–until last customer. THAI/LAOS/BURMESE.

From Thai chicken laksa and Burmese beef curry to tom-yum soup and Indonesian Nasee Goreng, the Golden Triangle serves the lot. This grotto-like joint is dark, cramped, and badly furnished—with sea-green walls, a Buddha in the corner, and just 10 tables—but all this only serves to emphasize the wonderfully authentic food that will blow your socks off. Dinner specials—including a starter and main course (except seafood); a glass of wine, fruit juice, or coffee; and a ticket thrown for the nearby movie complex—cost just A$22.50 (U.S.$14.63).

Jasmin Indian Restaurant. 31 Hindmarsh Square. ☎ **08/8223 7837.** Reservations recommended. Main courses A$16.90–$18.90 (U.S.$10.99–12.29). Lunch banquet A$27 (U.S.$17.55), dinner banquet A$33 (U.S.$21.45). AE, BC, DC, JCB, MC, V. Tues–Fri noon–3pm; Tues–Sat 5:30–10pm. NORTH INDIAN.

Prices have crept up as this place has gotten more popular, but this family-run Adelaide institution a block south of Rundle Mall is still a good value. Indian artifacts and signed cricket bats from Indian teams decorate the walls. The atmosphere is comfortable yet busy, and the service is professional. The house special is the very hot beef vindaloo, but all the old favorites, such as tandoori chicken, butter chicken (a big seller here), lamb korma, and malabari beef with coconut cream, ginger and garlic, are here, too. Mop it all up with naan bread, and cool your palate with a side dish of raita. The suji halwa, a semolina pudding with nuts, is the best I've tasted. Smoking is not permitted.

✪ **Jolleys Boathouse Restaurant.** Jolleys Lane. ☎ **08/8223 2891.** Reservations recommended. Main courses A$20–$24.50 (U.S.$13–$15.93). Lunch A$22 (U.S.$14.30) for 1 course, A$34.50 (U.S.$22.43) for 2 courses, and A$42.50 (U.S.$27.63) for 3 courses. AE, BC, DC, MC, V. Daily noon–2:30pm; Mon–Sat 6:30–9.30pm. MODERN AUSTRALIAN.

Jolleys is situated on the banks of the River Torrens, with views of boats, ducks, and black swans. Business people and ladies-who-lunch rush for the three outside tables for alfresco dining, but if you miss out, the bright and airy interior, with its cream-colored tablecloths and director's chairs, isn't too much of a letdown. You might start with the intriguing goat's curd ravioli with red pesto and chives. Moving on, you could tuck into the roasted duck with hazelnut risotto (close your eyes to the peaceful quacking out on the river if you can). The banana and cardomon soufflé for dessert is wicked.

✪ **Matsuri.** 167 Gouger St. ☎ **08/8231 3494.** Reservations recommended. Main courses A$8.60–$23 (U.S.$5.59–$14.95). AE, BC, DC, MC, V. Fri noon–2pm; Wed–Mon 5:30–10pm. JAPANESE.

I really like the atmosphere in this very good Japanese restaurant on the popular Gouger Street restaurant strip. The food is prepared by Takaomi Kitamura, world-famous ice sculptor and sushi master. The sushi and sashimi dishes are some of the best in Australia. Monday night is "sushi festival night," when sushi is half price. During happy hour Wednesday to Sunday, sushi is 30% off if you place your order before 7pm (you can pre-order over the phone and eat later). Other popular dishes include vegetarian and seafood tempura, *yose nobe* (a hot pot of vegetables, seafood, and chicken), and *chawan mushi* (a steamed custard dish). The service is friendly and considerate. Corkage fee is a steep A$4.50 (U.S.$2.93) a bottle.

Mekong Thai. 68 Hindley St. ☎ **08/8231 2914.** Main courses A$10.90–$12.90 (U.S.$7.09–$8.39). AE, BC, DC, MC, V. Daily 5:15pm–late. THAI/MALAYSIAN/HALAL.

Though this place is not much to look at—with simple tables and chairs, some outside in a portico—it has a fiery reputation for good food among in-the-know locals. The food is spicy and authentic, and the portions are filling. It's also a vegetarian's paradise, with at least 16 meat-free mains on the ethnically varied menu. It's Adelaide's only fully *halal* (suitable for Muslims) restaurant.

Rigoni's Bistro. 27 Leigh St. ☎ **08/8231 5160.** Reservations recommended. Main courses A$14.50–$22 (U.S.$9.43–$14.30); antipasto bar (lunch only) A$11.50–$13.75 (U.S.$7.48–$8.94). AE, BC, DC, JCB, MC, V. Mon–Fri noon–2:30pm and 6:30–10pm, Sat 6:30–10pm. ITALIAN.

Located on a narrow lane west of King William Street, this traditional Italian trattoria is often packed at lunch, though less frantic in the evening. It's big and bright with high ceilings and russet quarry tiles. A long bar runs through the middle of the dining room; brass plates mark the stools of regular diners. The food is very traditional and quite good. The chalkboard menu often changes, but you are quite likely to find lasagna, veal in white wine, marinated fish, and various pasta dishes. There's also an extensive salad bar with a variety of antipasto. An outside dining area was added last year.

✪ **Ruby's Café.** 255b Rundle St. ☎ **08/8224 0365.** Main courses A$7.70–$15.20 (U.S.$5.01–$9.88). AE, BC, MC, V. Sun 9am–5pm and 6:30–11.30pm; daily 6:30–11:30pm. MODERN AUSTRALIAN.

Situated in suitably unpretentious surroundings for a former market cafe catering to the local workers, Ruby's is an Adelaide institution. It still has its laminated tables and the "no spitting, no coarse language" sign behind the bar, despite being far more up-market than that. Basically, you get a very good restaurant meal in an old cafe atmosphere at very good prices. Served up are filling curries and fancier pasta dishes, hearty meals such as lamb shanks, and quite a few vegetarian options. For dessert I recommend the toffee pudding with toffee sauce. The menu changes every 6 weeks.

Something Different—Dining Tours. ☎ **08/8336 8333** or 0412/842 242 (mobile). Fax/message 08/8336 4075. www.food-fun-wine.com.au. graeme@food-fun-wine.com.au.

If you like good food and wine, but can't decide on just one restaurant, try one of Graeme Andrews's tours. He offers eight food and wine tours showcasing the Central Market, Chinatown and Gouger Street restaurant precincts. Call or e-mail for times and prices, which start from A$28 (U.S$18.20). Private tours are also available on request.

IN NORTH ADELAIDE

✪ **The Manse.** 142 Tynte St., North Adelaide. ☎ **08/8267 4636.** Reservations recommended. A$30 (U.S.$19.50) for 2 courses. Tues–Fri noon–3pm; Mon–Sat 6:30–10pm. AE, BC, DC, MC, V. Bus: 182, 224, 226, 228, or 229. SEAFOOD.

Swiss chef Bernhard Oehrli has a fine touch when it comes to seafood, and I recommend this place wholeheartedly. The surroundings are neat and gracious, with a log fire inside to keep you warm in winter and room to dine outside on the sidewalk on sunnier days. As for the food, the scallops here are almost fresh enough to waddle off the warmed cucumber base and head for sea, while the rare tuna in Japanese-style tempura is so delicate it literally melts in your mouth. If you want something other than seafood, then you can't go wrong with the duck or veal dishes. For dessert try the warm chocolate gâteau or the rhubarb gratin with ice cream.

✪ **The Oxford.** 101 O'Connell St., North Adelaide. ☎ **08/8267 2652.** Reservations recommended, especially for lunch and dinner Fri and dinner Sat. Main courses A$14.50–$20.50 (U.S.$9.43–$13.33). AE, BC, DC, MC, V. Mon–Fri noon–3pm; Mon–Sat 6–10pm or later. Bus: 182, 22, 224, 226, 228, or 229. MODERN AUSTRALIAN.

This restaurant has won nearly twice as many gold medals for cooking as Mark Spitz won for swimming (seven golds in the 1972 Olympic Games). The Oxford is highly praised for its creative, contemporary food in a range of mixed-up styles. It's big and busy and housed in a renovated, character-filled 1870s building. Inside you'll find crisp white tablecloths, a single page menu, and a stainless steel kitchen whipping up steam. The signature dishes are the red-roasted spatchcock (a small chicken) with water chestnut, chicken-and-cashew-nut spring roll, black-bean mayonnaise, and coconut broth; and the wonderful Caesar salad. Other favorites include satay fried chicken; jellyfish with Moroccan-spiced salsa; and poached prawns with natural oysters, served with wasabi, nori rolls, and soy dressing. The wine list is extensive.

SEEING THE SIGHTS

Adelaide is a very laid-back city. It's not jam-packed with tourist-oriented attractions like some of the larger state capitals, though **The Migration Museum** (see below) is easily one of the best museums in Australia. The best way to enjoy this pleasant city is to take things nice and easy. Take a walk beside the River Torrens, take the tram to the beachside suburb of Glenelg, and spend the evenings sipping wine and sampling some of the country's best alfresco dining.

THE TOP ATTRACTIONS

✪ **Art Gallery of South Australia.** North Terrace. ☎ **08/8207 7000.** Free admission. Daily 10am–5pm. Guided tours Mon–Fri 11am and 2pm, Sat–Sun 11am and 3pm. Closed Christmas Day.

Adelaide's premier public art gallery has a good range of local and overseas works and a fine Asian ceramics collection. Of particular interest are Charles Hall's *Proclamation of South Australia 1836,* Nicholas Chevalier's painting of the departure of explorers Burke and Wills from Melbourne; several examples of works by Australian painters Sidney Nolan, Albert Tucker and Arthur Boyd, and some excellent contemporary art. The bookshop has an extensive collection of art publications. Allow 1 to 2 hours.

✪ **The Migration Museum.** 82 Kintore Ave. ☎ **08/8207 7580.** Admission by donation. Mon–Fri 10am–5pm, Sat–Sun and public holidays 1–5pm. Closed Good Friday and Christmas. Bus: Any to North Terrace.

This tiny museum, dedicated to immigration and multiculturalism, is one of the most important and fascinating in Australia. With touching, personal displays, it tells the story of the waves of immigrants who have helped shape this multicultural society, from the boatloads of convicts who came here in 1788 to the ethnic groups who have been trickling in over the past 2 centuries. Allow 1 hour.

South Australian Maritime Museum. 126 Lipson St., Port Adelaide. ☎ **08/8207 6255.** Admission A$8.50 (U.S.$5.53) adults, A$3.50 (U.S.$2.28) children, A$22 (U.S.$14.30) families. Daily 10am–5pm. Closed Christmas. Bus 151 or 153 from North Terrace in the city (opposite Parliament House) to Stop 40 (Port Adelaide). Train: Port Adelaide.

Over 150 years of maritime history are commemorated in this museum. Most of the exhibits can be found in the 1850s Bond Store, but the museum also incorporates an 1863 lighthouse and three vessels moored alongside Wharf No. 1, just a short walk away. The fully rigged replica of the 54-foot ketch *Active II* is very impressive. Allow 1½ hours. Port Adelaide is approximately 30 minutes from the city center by bus.

✪ **South Australian Museum.** On North Terrace between the State Library and the Art Gallery. ☎ **08/8207 7500.** Free admission. Daily 10am–5pm. Closed Good Friday and Christmas.

The star attraction of this interesting museum is the new Australian Aboriginal Cultures Gallery that opened in March 2000. On display is an extensive collection of utensils, spears, tools, bush medicine, food samples, photographs and the like. Also within the museum is a sorry-looking collection of stuffed native animals (sadly also including a few extinct marsupials, including the Tasmanian Tiger); a good collection of Papua New Guinea artifacts; and excellent mineral and butterfly collections.

If you're interested in learning even more about the exhibits, take one of the **Behind-the-Scenes Tours.** The tours are conducted after museum hours and cost A$12 (U.S.$7.80) for adults. Allow 2 hours.

Tandanya Aboriginal Cultural Institute. 253 Grenfell St. ☎ **08/8223 2467.** Admission A$4 (U.S.$2.60) adults, A$3 (U.S.$1.95) children 13 and under, A$10 (U.S.$6.50) families. Daily 10am–5pm.

This place offers a great opportunity to experience Aboriginal life through Aboriginal eyes. Exhibits change regularly, but all give insight into Aboriginal art and cultural activities. At noon every day there's a didgeridoo performance. A shop sells Aboriginal art and books on Aboriginal culture, while a cafe on the premises serves up several bush tucker (native food) items. Allow 1 hour.

THE FLORA & THE FAUNA

Adelaide Zoo. Frome Rd. ☎ **08/8267 3255.** Admission A$12 (U.S.$7.80) adults, A$7 (U.S.$4.55) children. Daily 9:30am–5pm. Bus 272 or 273 from Currie Street to bus stop 2 (approx. 5 min.).

If you've already experienced the wonderful Melbourne Zoo, or even Taronga Zoo in Sydney, it's probably not worth coming here. But if this is going to be your only chance to see a kangaroo in captivity, then definitely stop by. Of course, other Australian animals live at the zoo, too, and the nicely landscaped gardens and lack of crowds make it a pleasant place for an entertaining stroll. The zoo houses the only Pygmy blue-tongue lizard in captivity in Australia, a species thought to be extinct since the 1940s, until a specimen was discovered inside the belly of a dead snake. Allow 1 hour.

Botanic Gardens. North Terrace. ☎ **08/8228 2311.** Free admission. Mon–Fri 8am–sunset, Sat–Sun 9am–sunset.

You'll feel like you're at the true heart of the city when you stroll among the office workers having lunch on the lawns here. Park highlights include a broad avenue of shady Moreton Bay figs, duck ponds, water lilies, an Italianate garden, a palm house, and the Bicentennial Conservatory—a large glass dome full of rain-forest species. You might want to have lunch in the **Botanic Gardens Restaurant** (☎ 08/8223 3526) surrounded by bird song and lush vegetation; it's open daily from 10am to 5pm.

FOR TRAIN BUFFS

Port Dock Railway Museum. Lipton St., North Adelaide. ☎ **08/8341 1690.** Admission A$9 (U.S.$5.85) adults, A$3.50 (U.S.$2.28) children, and A$20 (U.S.$13) families. Daily 10am–5pm. Bus 151 or 153 from North terrace, opposite Parliament House, to stop 40 (approx. 30 min.)

This former railway yard houses Australia's largest and finest collection of locomotives engines and rolling stock—with around 104 items on display including some 30 engines. Among the most impressive trains on show are the gigantic "Mountain" class engines, and so-called "Tea and Sugar" trains that once ran between railway camps in remote parts of the desert. Entrance includes a train ride. Allow 1½ hours.

ORGANIZED TOURS

Festival Tours (☎ **1300 858 687** in Australia, or 08/8374 1270) offers sightseeing tours for A$35 (U.S.$22.75) for adults, A$24 (U.S.$15.60) for children. Tours operate from 9:30am to noon every day except Sunday. The bus can pick you up at your hotel.

The **Adelaide Explorer** (☎ **08/8364 1933**) is a replica tram that circles the city stopping off at a number of attractions along the way, including Glenelg. The full route takes 2¾ hours to complete, you can get on or off along the route and rejoin another tram later on. Buses depart from 38 King William St. daily at 9am, 10:20am, 12:10pm, 1:30pm and 3pm. Tickets are A$29 (U.S.$18.85) for adults and A$17.50 (U.S.$11.38) for children 6 to 14. Ask about family discounts.

A Trip to the Seaside

If you need a beach fix in Adelaide, head to **Glenelg,** just a 30-minute tram ride from the city center. Glenelg has much more to offer than just the beach, the ocean, and a classic pier. It's also where you catch the ferry to **Kangaroo Island** and is home to some interesting attractions. For maps and brochures, head to the **Glenelg Tourist Information Centre** (☎ 08/8294 5833), in the Foreshore Building near the seafront. It's open daily from 9am to 5pm.

You can see pieces of *HMS Buffalo,* Adelphi Terrace, Patawalonga Boat Haven, Glenelg (☎ 08/8294 7000), a full-scale replica of the ship that brought the first settlers to South Australia, if you dine at the seafood restaurant here. Main courses cost between A$19 and A$25 (U.S.$12.35 and $16.25)

The carousel and giant gray hillock you can see from the seafront are part of the **Magic Mountain amusement park,** Colley Reserve, Glenelg (☎ 08/8294 8199). You can keep the kiddies happy for hours here on the waterslides, bumper boats, miniature golf, shooting galleries, and video games. Waterslides cost A$13 (U.S.$8.45) for an hour and A$7.50 (U.S.$4.88) for 30 minutes. A 3-hour lock-in on Saturday mornings and school holidays from 9am to noon, with unlimited use of supervised water slides and most other attractions, costs A$16 (U.S.$10.40).

Want to get fact-to-face with one of South Australia's famous great white sharks (and live to tell the story)? **The Shark Museum,** The Glenelg Town Hall, Mosely Square., (☎ 08/8376 3373), has full-size models of the terrors of the sea, as well as filming cages, shark jaws, photos, and fossils. Admission is A$6.60 (U.S.$4.29) for adults and A$4.40 (U.S.$2.86) for children and A$16.50 (U.S.$10.73) for a family. It's open from 10am to 5pm Monday to Saturday and 11am to 5pm on Sunday.

History buffs will want to visit the **Old Gum Tree.** It was under this tree that Governor Hindmarsh read the 1836 proclamation making South Australia a colony; it's on MacFarlane Street.

The tram to Glenelg leaves Victoria Square in the city.

ENJOYING THE GREAT OUTDOORS

Biking   Adelaide's parks and riverbanks are very popular with cyclists. Rent your bicycle from **Linear Park Hire** (☎ 018/844 588 mobile phone). The going rate is A$15 to 20 (U.S$9.75–$13) for 24-hours, including helmet, lock, and baby-seat (if needed). **Recreation SA** (☎ 08/8226 7301) publishes a brochure showing Adelaide's bike routes. Pick one up at the South Australia Travel Centre (see "Visitor Information," earlier in chapter). **The Map Shop,** 6 Peel St. (☎ 08/8231 2033), is also a good source for maps.

HIKING & JOGGING   The banks of the River Torrens are a good place for a jog. The truly fit and/or adventurous, might want to tackle the **Heysen Trail,** a spectacular 1,600-kilometer (992-mile) walk through bush, farmland, and rugged hill country that starts 80 kilometer (50 miles) south of Adelaide and goes to the Flinders Ranges by way of the Adelaide Hills and the Barossa Valley. For more information on the trail, visit the South Australia Travel Centre (see "Visitor Information," earlier in chapter).

GOLF   The **City of Adelaide Golf Course** (☎ 08/8267 2171) is close to town and has two short 18-hole courses and a full-size championship course. Greens fees are

A$14 to $16.80 (U.S.$9.10–$10.92) weekdays and A$16.20 to $19 (U.S.$10.53–$12.35) weekends, depending on the course, Monday through Friday, plus A$3 (U.S.$1.95) extra on weekends. Club rental is available. Prices are lower after 4pm.

TAKING IN AN AUSSIE RULES GAME & OTHER SPECTATOR SPORTS

CRICKET The **Adelaide Oval** (☎ **08/8300 3800**), on the corner of War Memorial Drive and King William Street, is the venue for matches during the summer.

FOOTBALL Unlike New South Wales, where Rugby League is the most popular winter sport, here in Adelaide you'll find plenty of Australian Rules fanatics. Games are usually played on a Saturday either at the Adelaide Oval (see above) or at **Football Park** (☎ **08/8268 2088**), on Turner Drive, West Lakes. The home teams are the Adelaide Crows and the Port Adelaide Power. Games are played February to October, with the finals held in September and October. Tickets must be purchased well in advance from **BASS** (☎ **13 12 46** in South Australia, or 08/8400 2205).

THE SHOPPING SCENE

Rundle Mall (between King Williams and Pulteney streets) is Adelaide's main shopping street. This pedestrian-only street is home to all the big names in fashion.

Adelaide's **Central Markets** (☎ **08/8203 7494**), behind the Adelaide Hilton Hotel between Gouger and Grote streets, make up the largest produce market in the Southern Hemisphere. They're a good place to shop for vegetables, fruit, meat, fish, and the like, although the markets are worth seeing even if you're not looking for picnic fixings. The markets, held in a huge warehouse-like structure, are open Tuesday from 7am to 5:30pm, Thursday from 11am to 5:30pm, Friday from 7am to 9pm, and Saturday from 7am to 3pm. **Market Adventures** (☎ **08/8336 8333,** or mobile 0412/842 242; fax/message 08/8336 4075) runs behind-the-scenes tours every Tuesday and Thursday at 10:30am and 1:30pm, Friday at 10am and 2pm, and Saturday at 8:30am. Tours cost A$28 (U.S.$18.20) for adults and A$15 (U.S.$9.75) for children 3 to 11. Phone for directions. The company also runs a **Dawn Market Tour** of the markets at 7:15am four days a week for A$49 (U.S.$31.85) including breakfast.

The six-story **Myer Centre,** next door to the Myer department store, 22–38 Rundle Mall, has a Body Shop (on the ground floor), for beauty products; an Australian Geographic shop (on level 3), for top-quality Australiana; and Exotica (on level 2), where you can find unusual futuristic gifts.

Just off Rundle Mall, at Shop 6 in the City Cross Arcade, is **L'Unique** (☎ **08/8231 0030**), a good craft shop selling South Australian pottery, jewelry, woodcraft, handblown glass, and original paintings.

The renowned **Jam Factory Craft and Design Centre,** in the Lions Art Centre, 19 Morphett St. (☎ **08/8410 0727**), sells an excellent range of locally made ceramics, glass, furniture, and metal items. You can also watch the craftspeople at work.

Shopping for Opals

South Australia is home to the world's largest sources of white opals (the more expensive black opals come from Lightning Ridge in New South Wales). There are plenty of places to buy around town, **but Opal Field Gems,** 33 King William St. (☎ **08/8212 5300**) is one of the best. As a rule, you're not going to find any bargains, so just buy what you like (and can afford—good opals cost a lot!)

For the best **boots** in Australia, head to the **R.M. Williams shop** on Gawler Place (☎ **08/8232 3611**) for the best simple boots you're likely to find, as well as other Aussie fashion icons, including Akubra hats, moleskin pants, and Driza-bone coats.

ADELAIDE AFTER DARK

The *Adelaide Advertiser* lists all performances and exhibitions in its entertainment pages. The free tourist guide *Today in Adelaide*, available in most hotels, also has information. Tickets for theater and other entertainment events in Adelaide can be purchased from **BASS** ticket outlets at the following locations: Festival Theatre, Adelaide Festival Centre, King William Road; Centre Pharmacy, 19 Central Market Arcade; Verandah Music, 182 Rundle St.; and on the 5th floor of the Myer department store, Rundle Mall. Call BASS at ☎ **13 12 46** in South Australia or 08/8400 2205.

THE PERFORMING ARTS

The major concert hall is **the Adelaide Festival Centre,** King William Road (☎ **08/ 8216 8600** for general inquiries; 08/8400 2205 for box office). The Festival Centre encompasses three auditoriums: the 1,978-seat Festival Theatre, the 612-seat Playhouse, and the 350-seat Space Centre. This is the place to see opera, ballet, drama, orchestral concerts, the Adelaide Symphony Orchestra, plays, and experimental drama.

The complex also includes an outdoor amphitheater used for jazz, rock and roll, and country music concerts; an art gallery; a bistro; a piano bar; and the Silver Jubilee Organ, the world's largest transportable concert-hall organ (built in Austria to commemorate Queen Elizabeth II's Silver Jubilee).

The **Adelaide Repertory Festival** presents a season of five productions, ranging from drama to comedy, at **the Arts Theatre,** 53 Angus St. (☎ **08/8221 5644**). Playwrights Alan Ayckbourne and Terrence Rattigan are among the many who have had plays performed here. The theatre, which is just a short walk away from many hotels and restaurants, is also the home of the **Metropolitan Musical Theatre Company,** which presents two musical comedy productions a year. Tickets cost around A$16 (U.S.$10.40) for adults and A$11 (U.S.$7.15) for children.

Her Majesty's Theatre, 58 Grote St. (☎ **08/8216 8600**), is a 1,000-seat venue opposite Central Markets that presents drama, comedy, smaller musicals, dance, opera, and recitals. Tickets are generally A$30 to $55 (U.S.$19.50–$35.75).

THE BAR & CLUB SCENE

Adelaide's nightlife ranges from twiddling your thumbs to nude lap dancers. For adult entertainment (strip clubs), head to Hindley Street—there are a few pubs there, too, but I wouldn't recommend them. For information on gay and lesbian options, pick up a copy of the *Adelaide Gay Times.*

As for all-age pubs, the locals will point you toward **The Austral,** 205 Rundle Street (☎ **08/8223 4660**); **The Lion,** at the corner of Melbourne and Jerningham streets (☎ **08/8367 0222**); and the **British Hotel,** 58 Finniss St. (☎ **08/8267 2188**), in North Adelaide, where you can cook your own steak on the courtyard barbecue. Also popular with both visitors and locals alike is the **Earl of Aberdeen,** 316 Pulteney St., at Carrington Street (☎ **08/8223 6433**), a colonial-style pub popular for after-work drinks. **The Port Dock,** 10 Todd St., Port Adelaide (☎ **08/8240 0187**), was licensed as a pub in 1864; it brews four of its own beers and pumps them directly to its three bars with old English beer engines. Most pubs are open from 11am to midnight.

TRYING YOUR LUCK AT THE CASINO

Next to the Adelaide Hyatt, and dwarfed by the old railway station it's situated in, is the **Adelaide Casino,** North Terrace (☎ **1800/888 711** in Australia, or 08/ 8212 2811). The casino has two floors of gaming tables and slot machines, as well as four bars and several dining options, including fast-food station and buffet. The casino is open Sunday to Thursday from 10am to 4am and Friday and Saturday from 10am to 6am.

2 Side Trips from Adelaide

THE BAROSSA: ON THE TRAIL OF THE GRAPE

More than a quarter of Australia's wines, and a disproportionate number of top labels, originate in ✪ **the Barossa** and Eden valleys—collectively known as the Barossa. Beginning just 45 kilometers (28 miles) northeast of Adelaide and easily accessible, the area has had an enormous influence on the city's culture. In fact, Adelaidians of all socioeconomic levels partake in more wine talk than the French. German settlers from Silesia, who came to escape religious persecution, first settled the area. They brought with them their particular brand of culture, their food, and their vines. They also built the Lutheran churches that dominate the Barossa's skyline. With the help of wealthy English aristocrats, the wine industry went from strength to strength. Today, there are more than 50 wineries in an area that still retains its German flavor.

The focal points of the areas are **Angaston,** the farthest away from Adelaide; **Nuri- ootpa,** the center of the rural services industry; and **Tanunda,** the nearest town to the city. Each has interesting architecture, craft and antique shops, and specialty food out- lets. If you are adventurous, you might want to hire a bike in Adelaide and take it on the train to **Gawler,** and cycle through the Barossa. Other options are exploring the are by hot-air balloon, Harley-Davidson motorcycle, or limousine.

ESSENTIALS

WHEN TO GO   The best times to visit are in the spring (Sept and Oct), when it's not too hot and there are flowering trees and shrubs, and in the fall (Apr and May), when the leaves turn red. The wine harvest is late summer/early autumn (Feb and Mar). The least crowded time is winter (June, July, and Aug).

GETTING THERE   If you have a car (by far the most flexible way to visit the Barossa), I recommend taking the scenic route from Adelaide (the route doesn't have a specific name, but it's obvious on any map). It takes about half an hour longer than the Main North Road through Gawler, but the trip is well worthwhile. Follow the signs to Birdwood, Springton, Mount Pleasant, and Angaston.

So Much Wine, So Little Time

If you have the choice of exploring either the Barossa or the Hunter Valley in New South Wales (see chapter 5), I recommend the Barossa, which despite being a little more touristy, has more to offer in terms of history and architecture.

Another famous wine-producing region is the **Coonawarra,** 381 kilometers (236 miles) southeast of Adelaide, near the border with Victoria; it's convenient if you're driving from Melbourne. The area is just 12 kilometers (7 miles) long and 2 kilometers (just over 1 mile wide), but the countryside is crammed with historical villages and 16 wineries. **The Clare Valley,** 135 kilometers (84 miles) north of Ade- laide, is another pretty area; it produces some outstanding cool-climate wines.

Drinking & Driving—Don't Do It!

If you'll be chasing the grape around the Barossa, choose a designated driver or take a guided tour. Australia's drunk-driving laws are strict and rigidly enforced.

Public buses run infrequently to the major centers from Adelaide. There are no buses between wineries.

ORGANIZED TOURS FROM ADELAIDE Various companies run sightseeing tours. One of the best, **Festival Tours** (☎ 08/8374 1270), offers a day trip visiting three wineries and other attractions. It costs A$62 (U.S$40.30) for adults, A$48 (U.S$31.20) for children, including a restaurant lunch. The tour departs daily at the corner of Rundle Mall and King William Street at 9:20am and picks up at hotels beforehand.

VISITOR INFORMATION The excellent **Barossa Wine and Visitor Centre,** 66–68 Murray St., Tanunda, SA 5352 (☎ 08/8563 0600; www.barossa-region.org; bwta@dove.net.au), is open Monday to Friday from 9am to 5pm, and Saturday and Sunday from 10am to 4pm. It's worth popping into the center's small audiovisual display for an introduction to the world of wine; entry is A$2 (U.S.$1.30) for adults; children are free. You'll need a least an hour to look around.

Wines are often cheaper at the ✪ **Tanunda Cellars "bottleshop,"** or retail outlet, located at 14 Murray Street, Tanunda (☎ 08/8563 3544; tanundacellars@dove.com.au) than at the winery door. This historic 1858 stone bottleshop also houses one of Australia's finest collections of vintage wines.

TOURING THE WINERIES

With some 48 wineries offering free cellar-door tastings and/or daily tours charting the winemaking process, you won't be stuck for places to visit. All wineries are well posted. Below are a few of my favorites, but don't be shy about just stopping whenever you find a winery that takes your fancy. A tip: try a sparkling red. It may turn up noses elsewhere, and it takes getting used to, but with the popularity of Australian wine, it may well be the great tipple of the future.

Orlando. Barossa Hwy., Rowland Flat. ☎ **08/8521 3140.** Mon–Fri 10am–5pm, Sat–Sun and public holidays 10am–4pm.

This large winery was established in 1847 and is today the home of many award-winning brands. Its big seller is the well-known Jacobs Creek brand, now sold worldwide. Premium wines include the Lawson Shiraz and the Jacaranda Ridge Cabernet, and new vintages of either will set you back at least A$45 (U.S.$29.25) a bottle. There is an opal shop, a craft shop, and a picnic area with BBQs.

Penfolds. Nuriootpa. ☎ **08/8301 5400.** Mon–Sun 10am–4.30pm.

Australia's biggest wine producer churns out some 22.5 million liters (5.8 million U.S. gallons) from this one winery every year. Penfolds also owns other wineries all over the country. It all started when Dr. Christopher Rawson planted a few vines in 1844 to make wine for his patients. The winery now houses the largest oak barrel maturation cellars in the Southern Hemisphere.

Rockford. Krondorf Rd., Tanunda. ☎ **08/8563 2720.** Mon–Sat 11am–5pm.

Most of the buildings here were constructed in 1984 out of recycled local materials, but you'd never know. The wine is pressed between mid-March and the end of April, in the traditional way with machinery from the turn of the century. It's a fascinating sight. Demand for Rockford wines, especially the Basket Pressed Shiraz, far exceeds supply.

Seppelts. Seppeltsfield. **08/8562 8028.** Mon–Fri 10am–5pm, Sat–Sun 11:00am–5:00pm. Tours hourly Mon–Fri 11am–3pm; Sat–Sun 11:30am, 1:30pm, and 2:30pm. Adults A$5 (U.S.$3.25), children A$2 (U.S.$1.30).

Joseph Seppelt, an immigrant from Silesia, founded this National Trust-listed property in 1857. The wine tour around the gardens and bluestone buildings is considered one of the best in the world. Check out the family's Romanesque mausoleum on a nearby slope skirted by palms planted during the 1930s recession to keep winery workers employed.

Wolf Blass. Strut Hwy., Nuriootpa. ☎ **08/8562 1955.** Mon–Fri 9:00am–5.00pm, Sat–Sun 10am–5.00pm.

This winery's Germanic-style black-label vintages have an excellent international reputation, while its cheaper yellow-label vintages are the toast of many a Sydney dinner party. The small Wolf Blass museum is worth a peek.

Yalumba. Eden Valley Rd., Angaston. ☎ **08/8561 3200.** www.yalumba.com.au. Mon–Fri 8.30am–5pm, Sat 10.00am–5pm, Sun nooon–5pm.

This winery was built in 1849, making it the oldest family-owned wine-making business in Australia. It's also huge. Look out for the sad-looking Himalayan bear in the corner of the large tasting room, following a run-in with a hunting rifle; it's been Yalumba's advertising gimmick. The winery's Signature Red Cabernet-Shiraz is among the best you'll ever taste.

WHERE TO STAY

There are plenty of standard motels and lots of interesting B&Bs throughout the Barossa, some with rooms for as little as A$60 (U.S.$39). Weekends often find rooms are often booked out and prices higher than weekdays. The *Barossa Wine & Visitor Centre* (see "Visitor Information," above) can provide information on additional accommodation choices and off-season deals.

Barossa Park Motel. Barossa Valley Hwy., Lyndoch (P.O. Box 370, Lyndoch, SA 5351). ☎ **08/8524 4268.** Fax 08/8524 4725. 34 units. A/C MINIBAR TV TEL. A$90 (U.S.$58.50) double, A$100 (U.S.$65) executive double; A$146 (U.S.$94.90) including dinner. Extra adult A$13 (U.S.$8.45), extra child under 12 A$8 (U.S.$5.20). Ask about packages. AE, BC, DC, MC, V.

Unlike your average motor inn, this one is set well back from the road within its own large grounds. The rooms are quite large, and some interconnect, which can be handy if you are traveling with a family. All rooms are comfortable and clean, and have a queen-size bed and at least another single. All have connecting bathrooms with a shower. Executive doubles are slightly plusher. There's a fully licensed restaurant, an outdoor pool and spa, and a game room on the premises.

Barossa Valley (SA) Tourist Park. Penrice Rd., Nuriootpa 5355. ☎ **08/8562 1404.** Fax 08 85622 615. barpark@dove.net.au. 27 cabins, 19 with bathroom. A/C TV. A$30 (U.S.$19.50) double without bathroom; A$45–$60 (U.S.$29.25–$39) double with bathroom. Extra adult A$5 (U.S.$3.25), extra child 3–15 A$3 (U.S.$1.95). AE, BC, DC, MC, V.

This very peaceful place is set way back from the road and abuts a nature lake and wildlife reserve. The cabins are simple but come with just about everything you'll need for a pleasant-enough stay. Cabins have a combination of doubles, singles, and bunk beds. All units have a small kitchenette, although only the more expensive cabins have a microwave. There's a swimming pool just down the road, and a laundry, a barbecue, and tennis courts on the property. If you don't have your own linen you'll be charged A$5 (U.S.$3.25) per single bed and A$10 (U.S.$6.50) per double.

◯ **Collingrove Homestead.** Eden Valley Rd., Angaston, SA 5351. ☎ **08/8564 2061.** Fax 08/8564 3600. 5 units, 3 with bathroom. A$150 (U.S.$97.50) double without bathroom; A$180 (U.S.$117) double with bathroom. Rates include full breakfast. AE, BC, DC, MC, V.

In my opinion, Collingrove is not just the best country-house experience in the area but, I daresay, anywhere in Australia. It was originally the home of John Howard Angas, one of the first settlers of South Australia. The homestead was originally built in 1856, and additions were made as Angas's successful sheep business prospered. The hallway is festooned with spears, artillery shells, rifles, oil portraits, and the mounted heads of various stags and tigers. English oak paneling and creaky floorboards add a certain nuance, and the cedar kitchen, library, glorious dining room, and various other places are all bursting with antiques and knickknacks. What the quaint, individually decorated guest rooms lack in modern amenities—no phones or TVs—they make up for in charm. The modern communal spa is set in the old stables, with its flagstone floors and old horse harnesses; there's also a flagstone-floored tennis court. Even if you don't stay here, visitors can indulge in Devonshire tea on the terrace daily for A$5 (U.S.$3.25) and can tour the property Monday through Friday from 1pm to 4:30pm and Saturday and Sunday from 11am to 4:30pm. The tour costs A$4 (U.S.$2.60) for adults and A$1.50 (U.S.98¢) for children. Sunday brunch is also popular.

◯ **The Hermitage of Marananga.** Corner of Seppeltsfield and Stonewell rds., Marananga, SA 5351. ☎ **08/8562 2722.** Fax 08/8562 3133. thehermitage@dove.net.au. 11 units, including 1 apt. A/C MINIBAR TV TEL. A$190 (U.S.$123.50) double; A$230 (U.S.$149.50) spa room; $230 (U.S.$149.50) apt. Rates include cooked breakfast. AE, BC, DC, MC, V.

This is far and away the best of the area's motels. The rooms are awkwardly shaped but have been recently renovated. Each has a small balcony, a fridge, and tea- and coffee-making facilities. The main building is old-fashioned and bursting with character. It's also cool in the heat of summer. Outside are a swimming pool and spa, and fantastic views over the valley and to the ranges beyond. A four-course, country-style dinner in the restaurant costs around A$45 (U.S.$29.25). There are good walks around the property and at dusk plenty of kangaroos in the surrounding fields. The new apartment has a private balcony overlooking the vineyards, a separate bedroom, and a double sleeper sofa in the living room.

◯ **Marble Lodge.** 21 Dean St., Angaston, SA 5351. ☎ **08/8564 2478.** Fax 08/8564 2941. www.marblelodge.com.au Reservations recommended. 2 units. A/C TV TEL. A$165 (U.S.$107.25) suite. Rate includes breakfast, bottle of champagne, and minibar drinks. AE, BC, DC, MC, V.

Wake up and smell the roses—there are plenty in the beautiful gardens surrounding this romantic historic property (as well as a tennis court, and several deer and kangaroos). Away from the main house is a lodge made of local marble that's divided into two suites. The larger suite has two rooms and an open fireplace. The second is basically a large bed/sitting room, with an open fireplace. Both have access to the shared spa bath and are furnished in antiques. There's always fresh fruit, homemade biscuits, and chocolates in the room, and it's a 5-minute walk to three local restaurants. A double room, with shared bathroom, is sometimes available in the homestead itself.

WHERE TO DINE

The Barossa prides itself on its cuisine as well as its wine, so you'll find plenty of places of note to eat, many serving traditional German foods. Put the **1918 Bistro & Grill,**

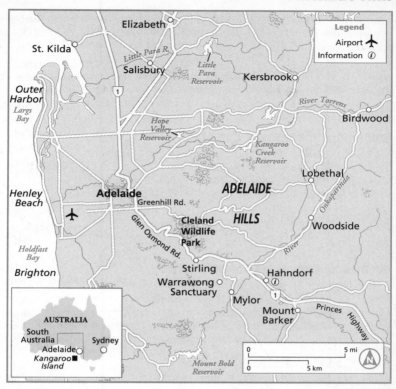

94 Murray St., Tanunda (☎ **08/8563 0405**) on top of your list. Appetizers, ranging in price from A$8.90 to $13 (U.S.$5.78–$8.45), are enough to fill you up. I recommend the baked mushrooms. Another hot spot, for lunch or dinner, is **Vintner's Bar & Grill,** Nuriootpa Road, Angaston (☎ **08/8564 2488**); the wine list here is six pages long! Main courses cost A$15 to $19 (U.S.$9.75–$12.35). Both restaurants serve essentially Modern Australian cuisine. You'll find perhaps the valley's best German-style bakery in Lyndoch, the **Lyndoch Bakery,** on the Barossa Highway (☎ **08/8524 4422**). In Angaston you must stop off at the **Angas Park Hotel,** 28 Murray St. (☎ **08/8562 1050**), which serves up home-cooked meals.

THE ADELAIDE HILLS

Only a 25-minute drive from Adelaide and visible even from the main shopping street, you'll find the tree-lined slopes and valleys, orchards, vineyards, winding roads, and historic townships of the Adelaide Hills. You might want to walk part of the **Heysen Trail** (see "Enjoying the Great Outdoors" in the Adelaide section earlier in this chapter), browse the shops in Hahndorf, stop in Melba's Chocolate Factory in Woodside, or visit Cleland Wildlife Park or Warrawong Sanctuary. Should you decide to stay overnight, the area offers lots of cozy B&Bs.

ESSENTIALS

GETTING THERE The Adelaide Hills are just 25 minutes from Adelaide by car via **Greenhill** and **Glen Osmond** roads. **Adelaide Sightseeing** (☎ **08/8231 4144**) runs outings to the gorgeous little town of Hahndorf (see below) as well as to Cleland Wildlife Park. An afternoon excursion to Hahndorf costs A$30 (U.S.$19.50) for adults and A$20 (U.S.$13) for children; the tour to Cleland costs A$26 (U.S.$16.90) for adults and A$20 (U.S.$13) for children, including park entry.

VISITOR INFORMATION Visitor information and bookings are available through the **Adelaide Hills Tourist Information Centre,** 41 Main St., Hahndorf (☎ **08/8388 1185**). It's open Monday to Friday from 9am to 4pm. Otherwise, detailed maps are available at the South Australia Travel Centre in Adelaide.

BIRDWOOD: FOR VINTAGE CAR FANS

Birdwood, located 46 kilometers (28 miles) east and slightly north of Adelaide, is best known for the restored 1852 flour mill that now contains the ✪ **National Motor Museum** (☎ **08/8568 5006**). Here you'll find the best collection of vintage cars anywhere in Australia. Among them is the first vehicle to cross Australia (in 1908). The complex also includes tearooms and a gift shop, and you can picnic along banks of the upper reaches of the River Torrens. The museum is open daily from 9am to 5pm (closed Christmas). Admission is A$9 (U.S.$5.85) for adults, A$4 (U.S.$2.60) for children 5 to 15, and A$24 (U.S.$15.60) for a family of four.

WOODSIDE: CHOCOLATE LOVERS UNITE!

Visitors come here for **Melba's Chocolate Factory,** Henry Street (☎ **08/8389 7868**), where chocoholics will find a huge range of handmade chocolates. Melba's is part of **Heritage Park,** a complex that includes a wood turner, a cheese maker, ceramics studio, leather maker, and a craft shop. It's open Monday to Friday from 10am to 4pm; and Saturday, Sunday, and public holidays from noon to 5pm.

MYLOR: GETTING BACK TO NATURE

Mylor is located 25 kilometers (15 miles) southeast of Adelaide, and 10 kilometers (6 miles) south of Mt. Lofty via the town of Crafters. Here you'll find the **Warrawong Sanctuary,** Stock Road, Mylor (P.O. Box 1135, Stirling, SA 5152; ☎ **08/8370 9197;** fax 08/8370 8332). Unlike many other wildlife parks, the animals here are not kept in enclosed runs. Instead, park founder Dr. John Wamsley took a 35-acre tract of former farming land, replanted it with natural bush, fenced it off, and went around shooting the introduced rabbits, cats, dogs, and foxes that plague much of Australia. Then the good doctor took to reintroducing animals native to the site—such as kangaroos, various types of wallabies, bandicoots, beetongs, platypuses, possums, frogs, birds, and reptiles. They are all thriving, not only because he eliminated their unnatural predators, but also because he recreated waterways, rain forests, and black-water ponds. The animals roam free, and you're guided through on 1½-hour dawn or sunset walks that costs A$18 (U.S.$11.70) for adults and A$12 (U.S.$7.80) for children. There's a restaurant on the premises, and you can even stay overnight in large cabins with bathrooms, wall-to-wall carpeting, and air-conditioning. The cabins cost A$125 (U.S.$81.25) per person with both dawn and dusk tours, a 2-course dinner and breakfast.

Compared to **Cleland Wildlife Park** (see below), there is less of a variety of animals here (you won't find any koalas for example), but it's more educational and you get the feeling that you're in the wild rather than in a zoo.

HAHNDORF: GERMAN HERITAGE, CRAFTS & MORE

✪ **Hahndorf,** a historic German-style village is one of South Australia's most popular tourist destinations. Founded in 1839 by Lutherans fleeing religious persecution in their homeland of eastern Prussia, the town is located 29 kilometers (18 miles) southeast of Adelaide. They brought with them their winemaking skills, foods, and architectural inheritance. Hahndorf still resembles a small German town in appearance and atmosphere, and is included on the World Heritage List as a Historical German Settlement. Walking around you'll notice St. Paul's Lutheran Church, erected in 1890. The **Wool Factory**, **L'Unique Fine Arts & Craft,** and **Bamfurlong Fine Crafts** are all worth checking out and are all within walking distance of Main Street.

Busway Travel (☎ **08/8410 6888;** fax 08/8410 3833) operates half-day tours to Hahndorf, including a German lunch, and a visit to **Mt. Lofty Summit** (see below) Tours cost A$28 (U.S.$18.20) for adults and A$19 (U.S.$12.35) for children. Tours leave from the Busway Travel offices on Bank Street, off North Terrace, in Adelaide.

Where to Stay

✪ **The Hahndorf Resort.** 145A Main St., Hahndorf, SA 5245. ☎ **08/8388 7921.** Fax 08/8388 7282. 60 units. A/C TV TEL. A$60.50 (U.S.$39.33) cabin; A$86.90 (U.S.$56.23) motel room; $97.90–$165 (U.S.$63.70–$107.25) chalet. A$11 (U.S.$7.15) extra adult; A$5.50 (U.S.$3.58) extra child. AE, BC, DC, MC, V.

This large resort has a variety of accommodations, as well as approximately 80 caravan and tent sites. The self-contained, air-conditioned cabins come with a bathroom, a small kitchen area, a TV, and linen. Motel rooms are typical and come with queen-size beds (some have an extra single) and a shower. The chalets look like they're straight out of Bavaria; each can accommodate from two to five people in one or two bedrooms. All have a full kitchen and an attached bathroom with shower. Some overlook a small lake. The spa chalets are larger and, of course, come with a spa bath. There's a restaurant with main courses averaging around A$15 (U.S.$9.75), a swimming pool, a small gym, a couple of putting greens, a canoe lake, a half-size tennis court, a laundry, and a few emus, kangaroos and horses running around in an animal sanctuary. Bicycles are available for rent.

Where to Dine

✪ **Karl's German Coffee Shop.** 17 Main St., Hahndorf. ☎ **08/8388 7171.** Main courses A$3.90–$10.50 (U.S.$2.54–$6.83) at lunch; A$8.90–$13.90 (U.S.$5.79–$9.04) at dinner. AE, BC, DC, MC, V. Wed–Sun 11am–10pm and public holidays. GERMAN.

Pop into this Bavarian beer-cellar-style eatery at anytime of day for good homemade cakes and coffee. At lunch, the ploughman's lunch goes down well, as do the German sausages with sauerkraut. Dinner favorites include seafood, steaks, and chicken dishes.

OAKBANK: A DAY AT THE RACES

This is the spot for the Adelaide hills' biggest event, the Easter **Oakbank Racing Carnival,** part of the Australia-wide "picnic races" that take place in small towns throughout the nation. The Oakbank horse races attract crowds in excess of 70,000 a day over the long Easter weekend. General admission is A$9 (U.S.$5.85), plus another A$5 (U.S.$3.25) for admission to the grandstand. The **Oakbank Racing Club** (☎ **08/8212 6279**), is just off the main road, you can't miss it.

Where to Stay

✪ **Adelaide Hills Country Cottages.** P.O. Box 100, Oakbank, SA 5243. ☎ **08/8388 4193.** Fax 08/8388 4733. www.ahcc.com.au. 5 cottages. A/C TV. A$145–$230 (U.S.$94.25–$149.50). Extra person A$55 (U.S.$35.75). Rates include provisions for full-cooked breakfast. A 1-night rate will include a surcharge of A$30 (U.S.$19.50). Ask about lower weekly rates. BC, MC, V. Oakbank is 35 min. from Adelaide, 7 min. from Hahndorf, and less than an hr. from the Barossa Valley.

These three self-contained cottages have won several tourism awards, including the 1998 Australian Tourist Commission award for hosted accommodation in Australia—which is a big deal. They are 1 kilometer (0.6 miles) apart and are surrounded by 150 acres of countryside. The Apple Tree cottage, circa 1860, sleeps up to five, has a spa bath and antiques, and overlooks an orchard and a lake; the Gum Tree Cottage sleeps four and has wonderful views; and the Lavender Fields Cottage also sleeps up to four and overlooks a lily-fringed duck pond. All of the cottages have open fireplaces and fully equipped kitchens. This is a great place to relax and a good base for exploring the area. You'll get a couple of free drinks and a fruit basket upon arrival.

MT. LOFTY: VIEWS & 'ROOS

Visitors make the pilgrimage to the top of the 2,300-foot Mt. Lofty, 16 kilometers (10 miles) southeast of Adelaide, for the panoramic views over Adelaide, the surrounding Adelaide plains, and the Mt. Lofty Ranges. There are several nice bush walks from the top. You can find the **Summit Restaurant** (☎ **08/8339 2600**) up here, too; it's open for lunch daily and dinner Wednesday through Sunday. Main courses cost between A$13.90 and A$19.90 (U.S.$9.04 and $12.94) and include roasted field mushrooms on polenta, roast duck breast with black rice, and veal porterhouse. In the same building is the **Summit Café,** selling good sandwiches and cakes, and Devonshire tea for A$6 (U.S.$3.90). The restaurant runs a limo service to Adelaide and back for up to four people for A$80 (U.S.$52) round-trip.

Almost at the top of Mt. Lofty, off Summit Road, is the **Cleland Wildlife Park** (☎ **08/8339 2444**). Here you'll find all the usual Australian animals on offer—including the largest male red kangaroo I've ever seen. Though the park is not near as good as similar wildlife parks elsewhere in Australia, it does have a very good wetlands aviary. One of the drawbacks of Cleland is that it's got some unimaginative enclosures, most notably the one for the Tasmanian devils. The park is open daily from 9:30am to 4:30pm. Visitors can meet at the Tasmanian devil enclosure at 2pm and join the animal feed run by following a tractor around the park as it drops off food.

Admission to Cleland is A$9.50 (U.S.$6.18) for adults, A$5.50 (U.S.$3.58) for children 3 to 14, and A$23.50 (U.S.$15.28) for families. Koala holding is allowed during the photo sessions daily from 2 to 4pm daily (but not on very hot summer days); on Sundays and holidays there's an additional session from 10am to noon. The privilege will cost you A$10 (U.S.$6.50) per photo. A kiosk and restaurant are on the premises.

It's a bit of a hassle getting to either place by public transport. To get to the Mount Lofty Lookout take bus 163 Monday to Friday, and number 165 on weekends from Currie Street in the city. Ask the driver to drop you off at "Crafters." The trip takes 30 minutes. From there you'll need to take a short taxi ride to the top, so pre-arrange pick up with **Tony's Taxis** on ☎ **08/8388 5988.**

To get to Cleland take bus 822 from Currie Street and get off at bus stop 19b. There are only two services daily, at 10 and noon, Monday to Friday. Take the 10am bus and ask the bus driver for the exact return time. The trip to Cleland takes 40 minutes.

3 Kangaroo Island

110km (68 miles) South of Adelaide

There is nowhere better than Kangaroo Island to see Australian marsupials in the wild. Period. Spend a couple of days on the island with the right guide and you can walk along a beach past a colony of sea lions; spot hundreds of New Zealand fur seals playing together in foreshore rock pools; creep through the bush on the trail of wallabies; stroke semi-tame kangaroos; spot sea eagles, black swans, sacred ibis, pelicans, fairy penguins, galahs, crimson rosellas, the rare glossy cockatoo, and the endangered stone curlew; come across goannas and the island's lone emu; pick out bunches of koalas hanging sleepily in the trees above your head; and, if you're lucky, see platypus, echidna, bandicoots, reclusive pygmy possums, and lots, lots more.

The secrets to Kangaroo Island's success are its perfect conditions; the most important of which is the fact that there are no introduced foxes or rabbits to take their toll on the native inhabitants or their environment. The island was also never colonized by the dingo—Australia's "native" dog—which was believed to have been introduced from Asia some 4,000 years ago. About one-third of the island is unspoiled national park, and there are plenty of wildlife corridors to give the animals a chance to move about the island, thus lessening the problems of inbreeding.

While the animals are what most people come to see, no one goes away without also being impressed by the scenery. Kangaroo Island has low mallee scrubland, dense eucalyptus forests, rugged coastal scenery, gorgeous beaches, caves, lagoons, and black-water swamps. The effect of 150 years of European colonization has taken its toll, though. In South Australia as a whole, some 27 mammal, 5 bird, 1 reptile, and 30 plant species have become extinct since the state was discovered by the English seafarer Matthew Flinders in 1802.

The island's history is a rugged one. Aboriginal people inhabited the island as early as 10,000 years ago, but abandoned it for unexplained reasons. In the 19th century, it was settled by pirates, mutineers, cutthroats, deserters from English, French, and American ships, and escaped convicts from the eastern colonies. Sealers also arrived and took a heavy toll on the local seal and sea lion population—in just 1 year, 1803–04, they managed to kill more than 20,000 of these animals. Between 1802 and 1836, Aboriginal women from both the mainland and Tasmania were kidnapped, brought to Kangaroo Island, and forced to work catching and skinning seals, kangaroos, and wallabies, and lugging salt from the salt mines

In 1836, Kangaroo Island became the first place in South Australia to be officially settled. The state's capital was Kingscote, until it was abandoned a couple of years later in favor of Adelaide. In spite of its early settlement, Kangaroo Island had very few residents until after World War II, when returned soldiers set up farms here. Today, more than a million sheep are raised on the island. The island also acts as an official bee sanctuary to protect the genetic purity of the Lugurian bee, introduced in 1881 and believed to be the only place in the world where this strain of bee survives.

ISLAND ESSENTIALS

WHEN TO GO   The best time to visit Kangaroo Island is between November and March (though you'll have difficulty finding accommodations over the Christmas school holiday period). July and August tend to be rainy, and winter can be cold (though often milder than on the mainland around Adelaide). Many companies offer 1-day trips to Kangaroo Island from Adelaide, but I would strongly advise you to tailor your holiday to spend at least 2 days here, though 3 or even 5 would be even better. There really is a lot to see, and you won't regret spending the extra time.

A Travel Tip

I'd advise buying an **NPWS Island Pass** if you'll be exploring the island on your own. It costs A\$28 (U.S.\$18.20) for adults, A\$22 (U.S.\$14.30) for children, and A\$77 (U.S.\$50.05) for families and includes guided tours of Seal Bay, Kelly Hill Caves, Cape Borda, and Cape Willoughby; also included is access to Flinders Chase National Park, where a A\$13 (U.S.\$8.45) charge per vehicle is usually levied. The pass doesn't cover penguin tours, or camping fees.

Kangaroo Island

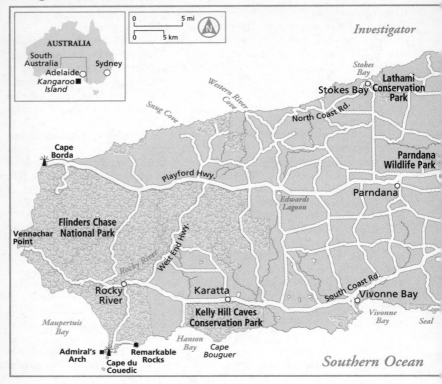

GETTING THERE   You can fly to Kangaroo Island on **Emu Airways** (☎ 08/8234 3711; emuair@dove.net.au), or **Kendell Airlines** (☎ 13 13 00; in Australia; www. kendell.com.au) both of which offer daily service from Adelaide.

If you prefer to go there by sea, **Kangaroo Island SeaLink** (☎ 13 13 01 in Australia, or 08/8202 8688; www.sealink.com.au; kiexpert@sealink.com.au) operates two oceangoing vehicle and passenger ferries four times daily (up to ten times a day during peak periods) from Cape Jervis on the tip of the mainland to Penneshaw on Kangaroo Island. The trip takes 40 minutes and costs A$64 (U.S.$41.60) round-trip for adults, A$32 (U.S.$20.80) for children 3 to 14, and A$138 (U.S.$89.70) for cars. Connecting bus service from Adelaide to Cape Jervis is provided at an extra A$32 (U.S.$20.80) for adults round-trip, and A$16 (U.S.$10.40) for children. Count on 3 hours for the whole trip from Adelaide if you take the connecting bus. Sealink also runs a range of island tours, including the 2-day/1-night "Ultimate Touring Adventure" which costs from $249 (U.S.$161.85) per person twin share.

VISITOR INFORMATION   **Tourism Kangaroo Island,** The Gateway Information Centre, Howard Drive, Penneshaw (P.O. Box 336, Penneshaw, Kangaroo Island, SA 5222; ☎ 08/8553 1185; fax 08/8553 1255; www.tourkangarooisland.com.au; tourki@kin.on.net), has plenty of maps and information and can book accommodations and island tours. For more information on the island's national parks contact the **National Parks and Wildlife Service (NPWS)** office, 39 Dauncey St. (P.O. Box 39,

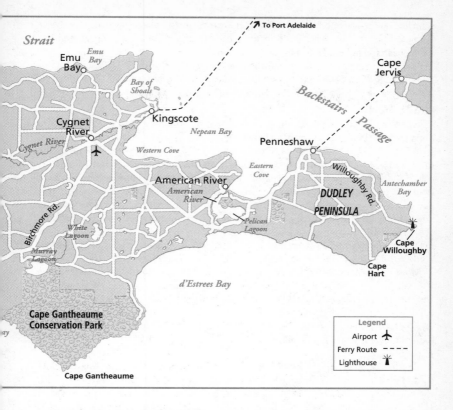

Kingscote, SA 5223; ☎ **08/8553 2381;** fax 08/8553 2531), open Monday to Friday from 9am to 5pm.

In addition, hotel and motel staff generally carry a stack of tourist brochures and can point you in the right direction as far as where to go and what to see.

ISLAND LAYOUT Kangaroo Island is Australia's third largest island, at 156 kilometers (97 miles) long and 57 kilometers (35 miles) wide at its widest point. The distance across the narrowest point is only 2 kilometers (1.25 miles). About 3,900 people live on the island. More than half of them live on the northeast coast in one of the three main towns: **Kingscote** (pop. 1,800), **Penneshaw** (pop. 250), and **American River** (pop. 200). The island's major attractions, however, are located farther from the mainland; Flinders Chase National Park is in the far west, Lathami Conservation Park is on the north coast, and Seal Bay and Kelly's Caves are on the south coast.

GETTING AROUND Apart from a bus service which connects Kingscote, Penneshawa nd American River, there is no public transport on the island. An **Airport Shuttle Service** (☎ **08/8553 2390**) can transport you from Kingscote Airport to your Kingscote accommodation. The 15-minute trip costs A$11 (U.S.$7.15) for adults and A$6 (U.S.$3.90) for children. The shuttle meets all Kendell flights. Major roads between Penneshaw, American River, Kingscote, and Parndana are paved, as is the road to Seal Bay. Most other roads are made of ironstone gravel, and can be very slippery if corners are approached too quickly. All roads are accessible by 2WD vehicles, but if you're bringing over a rental car from the mainland make sure your policy allows you to drive on Kangaroo Island's roads. Avoid driving at night—animals rarely fare best in a collision with a car.

Cars rental agencies on the island include **Budget** (☎ **08/8553 3133,** or 08/8553 1034; fax 08/8553 2888), **Hertz & Kangaroo Island Rental Cars** (☎ **1800 088 296** in Australia, or 08/8553 2390; fax 08/8553 2878). You can pick up cars at the airport or ferry terminals.

ORGANIZED TOURS ✪ Budget travelers can't go wrong with one of the tours organized by **Penneshaw Youth Hostel,** 43 North Terrace, Penneshaw, Kangaroo Island, SA 5222 (☎ **08/8553 1284;** fax 08/8553 1295; advhost@kin.on.net). The most popular includes an afternoon pickup from the main bus station in Adelaide, coach and ferry to the island, a penguin tour that evening and dorm accommodation (you can pay a little extra to upgrade to a double room, but book ahead). The next day involves a 10 hour touring, taking in most of the main attractions. That evening you return to Adelaide. The tour—called "the Sunset Tour"—costs A$176 (U.S.$114.40).

Another interesting tour arranged by these guys includes a dive (novices should contact the hostel to find about basic training. This costs A$265 (U.S.$172.25).

More expensive options include a tour by **Kangaroo Island Wilderness Tours** (☎ **08/8559 2220;** fax 08/8559 2288), which operates several 4WD vehicles (maximum six people) and takes visitors around the islands on 1-day trips costing A$205 (U.S.$133.25) per person, including transfers, an excellent lunch with wine, and park entry fees. Two, three-, and four-day trips, including meals and accommodation, cost A$513 (U.S.$333.45), A$821 (U.S.$533.65), and A$1,129 (U.S.$733.85) respectively.

Another excellent operator is ✪ **Adventure Charters of Kangaroo Island,** Playford Highway, Cygnet River, SA 5223 (☎ **08/8553 9119;** fax 08/8553 9122), with the knowledgeable and gregarious Craig Wickham at the helm (day trips cost A$225 (U.S.$146.25) a day with a big lunch, or A$402 (U.S.$261.30) for a 1-day safari including Kendell flights from and to Adelaide).

Kangaroo Island Odysseys, P.O. Box 494, Penneshaw, SA 5222 (☎ **08/8553 1311;** fax 08/8553 1294) offers a similar day trip in small vehicles for A$215 (U.S.$139.75) per person, including lunch.

EXPLORING THE ISLAND

The island is much bigger than you might think, and you can spend a fair bit of time just getting from one place of interest to the next. Of the many places to see, ✪ **Flinders Chase National Park** is one of the most important. It took 30 years of lobbying until politicians agreed to preserve this unique western region of the island in 1919. Today, it makes up around 17% of the island and is home to true wilderness, some beautiful coastal scenery, two old lighthouses, and plenty of animals. Birdwatchers have recorded at least 243 species of birds here. Koalas are so common that they're almost falling out of the trees. Platypus have been seen, but you'll probably need to make a special effort and sit next to a stream in the dark for a few hours to have any chance of spotting one. In the works are plans to develop a series of

---

Please Don't Feed the Animals

Kangaroos and wallabies might beg for food, but they are lactose-intolerant and can go blind, or catch disease, from human food.

Culling Koalas on Kangaroo Island—
A National Dilemma

Koalas are cute. They're fluffy, they're sleepy, and they're cuddly. And they eat an awful lot. In the early 1920s, 18 koalas were introduced to Kangaroo Island for the first time. Over the years, without predators and disease, and an abundant supply of eucalyptus trees, they have prospered. By 1996, there were some 4,000 koalas on the island, and their favorite trees were looking ragged. Some koalas were already suffering; some people even claimed the animals were starving.

Rather than waiting to see if the lack of adequate food and the koalas' natural territorial nature would stabilize the population, the South Australian Government decided the only option was to shoot Australia's ambassador to the world. The public outcry was enormous, with the Japanese even threatening to advise their citizens to boycott Down Under. Obviously, another solution was needed. Some scientists maintained that the koalas could not be relocated to the mainland because there were few places left to put them, with so much of their preferable habitat having already fallen to the chainsaw. Conservationists blamed Kangaroo Island's farmers for depleting the island of more than 50% of its vegetation. The koala is endangered, the conservationists reminded the politicians; the smaller northern variety is threatened with extinction in New South Wales due to deforestation, encounters with dogs and cars, and disease. The larger sub-species in Victoria, which includes the Kangaroo Island koalas, are also threatened. In the end a compromise was met. The koalas are to be trapped and neutered, a couple of thousand a year, until their numbers are stable. A few conscientious farmers will plant more trees. Other farmers will, no doubt, continue to see the koalas as pests.

When European settlers came to Australia, there were countless millions of koalas. In modern times, most Australians will never see one in the wild.

walking trails, boardwalks, and platypus observation hides at the Rocky River Waterhole, which should greatly increase visitors' chances of viewing the elusive critters. Kangaroos, wallabies, and brush-tailed possums, on the other hand, are so tame and numerous that the authorities were forced to erect a barrier around the Rocky River Campground to stop them from bounding up and carrying away picnickers' sandwiches!

The most impressive coastal scenery can be found at **Cape du Couedic** at the southern tip of the park, where millions of years of crashing ocean have created curious structures—like the hollowed-out limestone promontory called **Admiral's Arch** and the aptly named **Remarkable Rocks,** where you'll see huge boulders balancing on top of a massive granite dome. At Admiral's Arch there is a colony of some 4,000 New Zealand fur seals that are easily spotted playing in the rock pools and resting on the rocks. During rough weather this place can be spectacular. Recently, the road from Rocky River Park Headquarters to Admiral's Arch and Remarkable Rocks was paved to within 4 kilometers of Rocky River. A new parking lot and loop trail also has been developed at Remarkable Rocks. There's also a new road, parking lot, and trail system around the Cape du Couedic heritage lighthouse district.

Elsewhere on the island, you shouldn't miss out on the unforgettable experience of walking through a colony of **Australian sea lions** at Seal Bay. The Seal Bay

Conservation Park was declared in 1972, and these days some 100,000 people visit it each year. Boardwalks have been built through the dunes to the beach to reduce the impact of so many feet. The colony consists of about 500 animals, but at any one time you might see up to 100 basking with their pups here. The rangers who supervise the area lead guided trips throughout the day, every 15 to 30 minutes from 9am to 4:15pm. If you come here without a group, you must join a tour. Tours cost A$7.50 (U.S.$4.88) for an adult, A$5 (U.S.$3.25) for a child, and A$15 (U.S.$9.75) for a family.

Lathami Conservation Park, just to the east of Stokes Bay, is a wonderful place to see wallabies in the wild. Just dip in under the low canopy of casuarina pines and walk silently, keeping your eyes peeled, and you're almost certain to spot them. If you're fortunate you may even come across a very rare glossy cockatoo—it's big and black and feeds mainly on casuarina nuts.

Another interesting spot, especially for bird-watchers, is Murray Lagoon, on the northern edge of Cape Gantheaume Conservation Park. It's the largest lagoon on the island and an important habitat for thousands of water birds. Contact the NPWS (see "Visitor Information," above) for information on a ranger-guided Wetland Wade.

If you want to see **fairy penguins**—tiny animals that stand just 33 centimeters (13 in.) tall—forget the touristy show at Phillip Island near Melbourne. On Kangaroo Island you get to see them in a totally natural environment. Tours are conducted nightly by the NPWS (see "Visitor Information," above) and cost A$7 (U.S.$4.55) for adults, A$5.50 (U.S.$3.58) for children, and A$20 (U.S.$13) for families. Times of tours change seasonally, so call NPWS to confirm. Tours of a colony near **Penneshaw** gather at the Interpretive Centre adjacent to the penguins, and tours of the **Kingscote** colony meet at the reception desk of the Ozone Hotel.

For a fabulous day boat fishing for everything from King George Whiting, trevally and snapper to mullet and mackerel contact with **Kangaroo Island Fishing Charters** (☎ 08/8553 5247). A day out costs $110 (U.S.$71.50) including lunch.

Finally, Kangaroo Island is renowned for its fresh food and across the island you'll see signs beckoning to you to come and have a taste of cheese, honey, wine, or such like. One place worth stopping off at is **Clifford's Honey Farm** (☎ 08/8553 8295), which is open daily from 9am to 5pm.

WHERE TO STAY

There are more than 40 places to choose from on the island, from cozy B&Bs to campgrounds. If you feel like sleeping out in 1 of 40 self-contained cottages or coastal lodgings, then contact **Kangaroo Island Remote and Coastal Farm Accommodation** (☎ 08/8553 1233; fax 08/8553 1190; www.ki-ferryconnections.com). Standards vary and prices range from A$65 to $100 (U.S.$42.25–$65) for each property. The staff can also arrange lodgings in local farms, homes, and B&Bs for A$60 (U.S.$39) to $110 (U.S.$71.50) for a double with breakfast.

The **NPWS** (see "Visitor Information," above) also offers basic but comfortable lodgings for rent, including relatively isolated ✪ **lighthouse cottages** at Cape Willoughby, Cape Borda, and Cape du Couedic, from A$21 to $36.50 (U.S.$13.65–$23.73) per adult per night (though the minimum charge per stay is between A$49 and A$110/U.S.$31.85 and $71.50 for a cottage).

If you're on a super-tight budget, head to the **Penneshaw Youth Hostel,** 43 North Terrace, Penneshaw, Kangaroo Island, SA 5222 (☎ 08/8553 1284; fax 08/8553 1295), with dorm beds for A$16 (U.S.$10.40) and doubles for A$38 (U.S.$24.70). It costs A$1 (U.S.65¢) less for YHA members.

Camping is allowed only at designated sites for a minimal fee, the main place being at Rocky River in Flinders Chase National Park.

IN & NEAR KINGSCOTE

Ozone Hotel. The Foreshore (P.O. Box 145), Kingscote, SA 5223. ☎ **08/8553 2011.** Fax 08/8553 2249. 37 units. A/C TV TEL. A$91–$112.50 (U.S.$59.15–$73.13) double; A$102–$123 (U.S.$66.30–$79.95) triple. Extra person A$11 (U.S.$7.15). AE, BC, DC, JCB, MC, V.

The best known of Kangaroo Island's lodging alternatives, the Ozone gets its name from the aroma from the sea—which virtually laps at its door. It's a nice, centrally located choice, with a restaurant, a casual bistro serving good meals, a couple of bars, a game room, a pool and sauna, and a laundry. Rooms are comfortable with plenty of space; the majority of the more expensive ones have water views of Nepean Bay. Family rooms have a double bed and two single beds.

✪ **Wisteria Lodge.** 7 Cygnet Rd. Kingscote, SA 5223. Reservations can be made through Flag Inns (☎ **800/624 3524** in the U.S. and Canada, 0800/892 407 in the U.K., 0800/803 524 in New Zealand, 13 24 00 in Australia). Fax 08/8553 2200. 20 units. A/C MINIBAR TV TEL. A$130 (U.S.$84.50) double. Spa room A$165 (U.S.$107.25) double. Extra adult A$18–$20 (U.S.$11.70–$13); extra child 3–12 A$14–$17 (U.S.$9.10–$11.05). Breakfast A$11.50 (U.S.$7.48) extra. Ask about packages including transport to the island, transfers, meals, and day tours). AE, BC, DC, MC, V.

All rooms at the modern, and definitely unglamorous-looking, Wisteria Lodge are standard motel-type, boosted by ocean views over Nepean Bay. Deluxe rooms offer a spa and queen-size beds. There's a pool, a spa, a playground, and half-size tennis court here, too. Simple meals, such as pastas, steak, apricot chicken, and fish, are served in the Beachcomber restaurant. Reservations are essential for the restaurant.

IN AMERICAN RIVER

Popular with fishermen and located 37 kilometers (23 miles) from Kingscote, American River lacks a beach, but offers black swans on Pelican Lagoon instead. Wild wallabies abound, and egrets, magpies, and cockatoos offer early morning wakeup calls.

Casuarina Holiday Units. 9 Ryberg Rd., American River, SA 5221. TV. ☎ /fax **08/8553 7020.** 6 units. TV. A$50 (U.S.$32.50) double. BC, V.

These simple, country-style units are a good value. Each comes with a double bed, two singles, a fan, a heater, a TV, and an attached shower. There's a laundry, a barbecue, a children's playground, and fish-cleaning facilities if you manage to catch anything.

✪ **Kangaroo Island Lodge.** Scenic Road, American River, SA 5221. ☎ **08/8553 7053.** Fax 08/8553 7030. www.kangarooislandlodge.com.au. 38 units. $142 (U.S.$92.30) waterview doubles; $115 (U.S.$74.75) poolside double. Extra person $17 (U.S.$11). AE, BC, DC, MC, V.

Though Kangaroo Island Lodge was originally built in 1801, renovations in late 1999 have so completely overhauled the place that you would be hard pressed to find anything rustic remaining. What you have though is a very nicely appointed property with pleasant, quiet motel-style rooms, a good swimming pool, spa and sauna and a nice restaurant and bar (mains average A$17.50/U.S$11.38). The lodge looks over Pelican Lagoon (rightly famous for its pelicans), but it's a little too far away from it to make the water view double rooms really worth the extra cost.

Wanderers Rest. Bayview Road (P.O. Box 34), American River, SA 5221. ☎ **08/8553 7140.** Fax 08/8553 7282. www.wanderersrest.com.au. wanderers@kin.on.net. 9 units. MINIBAR TV. A$174 (U.S.$113.10) double; A$224 (U.S.$145.60) triple. Rates include full breakfast. Ask about value packages and ferry transport deals. AE, BC, DC, MC, V. Children under 12 not accepted

This pleasant guesthouse is set on a hillside with panoramic views across the sea to the mainland. It has large, comfortable rooms with balconies. All rooms come with king-size beds that convert to twins. You get a shower, but no tub. There's a pool and spa in the garden and a game room. Breakfasts are hearty, packed lunches are available, and dinnertime can be a hoot, with guests sipping beers and wine around the dining room table and tucking into King George whiting caught that day. There are other meals available, such as steak, lamb chops, local oysters, and a vegetarian stir-fry. Main course cost $19 (U.S$12.35). The restaurant is fully licensed. Smoking is not permitted.

In Parndana

Developed by soldier-settlers after World War II, Parndana today is a rural service center situated a 25-minute drive from Seal Bay and Stokes Bay, and just around the corner from **Parndana Wildlife Park,** which has more than 50 aviaries with collections of native and other birds, some of them rare and protected.

✪ **The Open House.** 70 Smith St., Parndana, SA 5221. ☎ **08/8559 6113.** Fax 08/8559 6088. 4 units. A$123 (U.S.$79.95) per person with dinner and breakfast included; A$93 (U.S.$60.45) per person with just breakfast included. A$93 (U.S.$60.45) per child under 14 with dinner and breakfast included; A$77 (U.S.$50.05) per child with just breakfast included. BC, MC, V.

The best thing about the Open House is mealtimes, when the guests get together around a communal table and tuck into delicious home-cooked meals. The rooms—two with double beds, one with a queen size bed, one with two singles, and a family room sleeping up to four—are comfortable and homey and come with a private bathroom with shower. The very friendly owner, Sarah Wall, took over the house in June 1998, soon after she moved here, but she can already offer excellent advice on what to do around the island, and whips up a mean packed lunch for A$22 (U.S.$14.30).

Other Places

✪ **Hanson Bay Cabins.** Hanson Bay Company, PO Box 614, Kingscote, SA 5225. ☎ **08/8853 2603.** Fax 08/8853 2673. 6 cabins. A$110–$120 (U.S.$71.50–$78) cabin for 2. Extra adult A$17 (U.S.$11.05). Extra child A$11 (U.S.$7.15). There's a A$17 (U.S.$11.05) surcharge for staying only 1 night. AE, BC, DC, MC, V.

Located on the southwest coast of the island on the South Coast Road, Hanson Bay Cabins are a row of four comfortable log cabins perched above a fabulous beach. The cabins each have a large picture window facing the southern ocean, and come with a full kitchen, a bathroom, two bedrooms (including a double bed and three singles in all), and a wood stove. Bring your own food and supplies from Kingscote, American River or Penneshaw. The ocean can get really wild and dramatic around here with strong offshore winds wiping-up the sand and spray. The cottages are near to most of the major attractions so make a good base. Salmon are often caught off the beach.

WHERE TO DINE

You'll find that most accommodation places on Kangaroo Island provide meals for guests (at an additional cost, usually). Most day tours around the island include lunch. You'll find a few cheap take-out booths around the island at the popular tourist spots. For lunch you could get sandwiches at the deli on Dauncey Street, behind the Ozone Hotel, in Kingscote.

In Penneshaw

✪ **Cape Willoughby Café.** Cape Willoughby. ☎ **08/8553 1333.** Main courses A$12–$17 (U.S.$7.80–$11.05). AE, BC, DC, MC, V. Ring ahead for opening times and bookings. LOCAL PRODUCE.

This fabulous restaurant is perched on a cliff top on the far eastern tip of the island, right next to **Cape Willoughby Lighthouse** (an attraction in itself). One wall is all glass, and there's a verandah outside with ocean views. King George Whiting is a specialty, as are the desserts (the sticky date pudding is great!). The restaurant changed hands in late 2000, so anything can happen. 45-minute tours of the lighthouse leave from the office at 10am, 11am, 12.30pm, and 2pm daily. They cost A$6 (U.S.$3.90) for adults, A$4.50 (U.S.$2.93) for children and A$16.50 (U.S.$10.73) a family.

Dolphin Rock Café. 43 North Terrace (next to the YHA). ☎ **08/8553 1284.** Main courses A$3– $9.50 (U.S.$1.95–$6.18). AE, BC, MC, V . Winter Wed–Mon 7:30am–7:30pm; summer daily 7am–8:30pm. FAST FOOD.

Plastic tables and chairs and budget meals are what's offered here. Very popular with backpackers are the budget meals including individual pizzas, and French fries and gravy. Also on offer are fish and chips, hamburgers, and roasted chicken. Across the road, the fairy penguins come in at dusk.

4 Outback South Australia

South Australia is the driest state in Australia. You can see this when you leave the parklands of Adelaide for the interior. The Outback is as harsh as it is beautiful. Much of it is made up of stony desert, saltpans, and sand hills, roamed by kangaroos and wild goats. After spring rains, though, the area can burst alive with wildflowers.

It was always difficult to travel through these parts, and even today there are only four main routes that traverse it. One of them, the **Birdsville Track,** is famed in Outback history as the trail along which stockman once drove their herds of cattle south from Queensland. Another, the **Strzelecki Track,** runs through remote sand dune country to Innaminka and on to Coopers Creek. Both of these tracks cut through the "dog fence"—a 5,600-kilometer (3,500-mile) long barrier designed to keep dingoes out of the pastoral lands to the south.

If you follow the Stuart Highway, or the **Oodnadatta Track,** you'll pass the mining towns of Coober Pedy, Andamooka, and Mintabie, where people from all over the world have been turned loose in the maddening search for opal. Out here, too, are national parks, such as the daunting Simpson Desert Conservation Park, with its seemingly endless blood-red sand dunes and spinifex plains; and **Lake Eyre National Park,** with its dried-up salt pan that, during the rare event of a flood, is a temporary home to thousands of water birds.

THE FLINDERS RANGES NATIONAL PARK
460km (285 miles) N of Adelaide

The dramatic craggy peaks and ridges that make up the ✪ **Flinders Ranges** rise out of the South Australian desert country. The colors of the rock vary from deep red to orange, with sedimentary lines visible as they run down the sides of cliffs. Much of the greenery is stunted arid land vegetation. Ever since the introduction of a devastating rabbit virus in 1996, and with the continued culling of hundreds of thousands of wild

An Outback Travel Warning

If you intend to drive through the Outback, take care. Distances between points of interest can be huge, and water supplies, petrol, food, and accommodations are far apart. Always travel with a good map and plenty of expert advice. If you plan to travel off-road, a 4WD vehicle is a must.

A Spectacular Bushwalk

The **Heysen Trail,** named after the painter Sir Hans Heysen, is a 2,000-kilometer (1,200-mile) track that starts in the northern Flinders Ranges, traverses the Flinders and the Lofty ranges, and ends up at the coast at Cape Jervis. The most interesting section of the trail is through the Flinders Ranges, where the dramatic reds of the Outback contrast at times with waterholes and tree-lined creeks.

Ecotrek (☎ **08/8383 7198;** fax 08/8383 7377; ecotrek@ozemail.com.au) runs 7-day walking tours of the Flinders Ranges part of the Heysen Trail, with overnight stays at sheep stations. It's a real Aussie adventure. Each day consists of 5 hours of walking, but you only carry a daypack, and the going is fairly easy. Treks cost A$890 (U.S.$578.50) including guide, accommodation, food, and transfers to and from Adelaide.

---

goats, shoots and saplings that for decades were nibbled away have started to turn what was once bare land back into bush. The most remarkable attraction is **Wilpena Pound,** a natural circle of cliff faces that form a huge depression on top of a mountainous ledge. The wind whipping over the cliff edges can produce some white-knuckle turbulence if you fly over it in a light aircraft. Kangaroos and emus can sometimes be seen wandering around the park, but outside the park kangaroos are heavily culled.

ESSENTIALS

GETTING THERE   By car, take either **Highway 1** out of Adelaide to Port Augusta (3½ hr.), then head east on **Route 47** via Quorn and Hawker (another 45 min.). It's another hour to Wilpena Pound. Alternatively, take the **scenic route** (it doesn't have a specific name) through the Clare Valley (around 5 hr.): From Adelaide head to Gawler and then through the Clare Valley; follow signs to Gladstone, Melrose, Wilmington, and Quorn.

Premier Stateliner (☎ **08/8415 5555**) runs five buses every day from Adelaide to Port Augusta for A$31.20 (U.S.$20.28) one-way. The company also runs buses to Wilpena Pound via Hawker and Quorn, leaving Adelaide at 8:30am on Wednesday and 11am on Friday. Fares each way are A$39.90 (U.S.$25.94) to Quorn, A$52.30 (U.S.$34) to Hawker, and A$56.30 (U.S.$36.60) to Wilpena Pound. Buses return to Adelaide from Wilpena Pound at 11am on Thursday, 7:15pm on Friday (arriving in Adelaide at 5am), and 3:05pm on Sunday.

The best tour operator to the national park from Adelaide is **Wallaby Tracks Adventure Tours** (☎ 1800/639 933 or 08/8648 6655; fax 08/8648 6898; http://headbush.mtx.net; headbush@dove.net.au). The company's 3-night mountain safari, including camping, costs A$279 (U.S.$181.35), while a 2-night Weekend Escape package departing Adelaide every Friday afternoon and returning Sunday night costs A$199 (U.S.$129.35). It also runs trips to the Flinders from Port Augusta and Quorn, as well as a 10-day Australian bush expedition from Adelaide to Alice Springs called ✪ Heading Bush Adventures. On this tour you get to experience the Flinders Ranges, the Oodnatta Track, Coober Pedy, the Simpson Desert, Ayres Rock, the Olgas, Kings Canyon, and Aboriginal communities. This remarkable trip costs A$750 (U.S.$487.50), including meals and bush camping, and focuses on Aboriginal culture.

VISITOR INFORMATION   Before setting off, contact the **Flinders Ranges and Outback of South Australia Regional Tourism Association (FROSATA)** at PO Box

2083, Port Augusta (☎ **1800/633 060** in Australia), for advice on roads and conditions. I strongly recommend a visit to the **Wadlata Outback Centre** at 41 Flinders Terrace, Port Augusta (☎ **08/8642 4511**), an excellent, award-winning interactive museum and information center. The museum costs A$7 (U.S.$4.55) for adults and A$4.50 (U.S.$2.93) for children and is open Monday to Friday from 9am to 5:30pm, and Saturday and Sunday from 10am to 4pm.

In Hawker, the Mobil service station and the post office act as information outlets.

The park entrance fee is A$7.50 (U.S.$4.88) per vehicle payable at the National Parks and Wildlife Service office near the Wilpena Pound Resort, or by exchanging cash for a ticket at unmanned ticket booths around the park.

GETTING AROUND Kev's Kamel Kapers (☎ **0419/839 288** mobile phone) offers remarkable 2-hour sunset camel safaris for A$25 (U.S$16.25); half-day excursions for A$50 (U.S.$32.50); and full-day safaris including a champagne lunch for A$80 (U.S.$52) for adults and A$60 (U.S.$39) for children under 16. Overnight camel treks are available, and on weekends and public holidays 15-minute rides cost just A$5 (U.S.$3.25). The tours only run from March to the end of October and leave from Hawker (call beforehand for exact pick-up spot). Kev is often unreachable, so check with the tourist association for his whereabouts.

WHERE TO STAY

✪ Andu Lodge. 12 First St., Quorn, SA 5043. ☎ **1800/639 933** in Australia or 08/8648 6655. Fax 08/8648 6898. headbush@dove.net.au. 64 beds. A$46 (U.S.$29.90) double; A$82 (U.S.$53.30) family room (sleeps 4). A$18–$22 (U.S.$11.70–$14.30) dorm bed. AE, BC, DC, MC, V.

This fabulous backpackers' lodge is one of the best in Australia. Situated in Quorn, in the central Flinders Ranges (42 kilometers/26 miles from Port Augusta), this upscale former hotel is air-conditioned in summer, heated in winter, and has nice clean rooms (dorms sleep six). There's also a TV room, a laundry, a computer for e-mailing, and a kitchen area. The hostel offers transfers from Port Augusta for A$6 (U.S.$3.90) each way and runs a range of trips with an emphasis on Aboriginal culture and eco-tourism. Guests can also rent mountain bikes. Quorn (pop. 1,300) was where the old *Ghan* railway used to start and finish from, and where part of the movie *Gallipoli* was filmed. The town has four friendly pubs, all serving meals for A$5 (U.S.$3.25).

✪ Prairie Hotel. Corner of High St. and West Terrace, Parachilna, SA 5730. ☎ **08/8648 4844.** Fax 08/8648 4606. www.prairiehotel.com.au. 12 units. A/C MINIBAR. A$105–$145 (U.S.$68.25–$94.25) double; A$195 (U.S.$126.75) double with spa. Extra person A$35 (U.S.$22.75). Rates include light breakfast. AE, BC, DC, MC, V.

If you are going to stay anywhere near the Flinders Ranges stay here. This tiny, tin-roofed, stone-walled pub offers a memorable experience and is well worth the dusty 89-kilometer (55-mile) drive north alongside the Ranges from Hawker on the A83. A new addition to the pub contains nice rooms, each with a queen-size bed and a shower. The older-style rooms are smaller and quaint. Three units have spa tubs. The bar out front is a great place to meet the locals and other travelers (who all shake their heads in wonder that this magnificent place is still so undiscovered). Meals here, prepared by "Flinders Feral Food," are top-notch—very nearly the best I've had in Australia. Among their specialties are so-called "feral" foods, such as kangaroo tail soup to start and a mixed grill of emu sausages, camel steak, and kangaroo as a main course. The owner's brother runs remarkable scenic flights over Wilpena Pound and out to the salt lakes. From here you could head to the township of William Creek for a sidetrip to see the giant salt-lake, Lake Eyre, and then onwards west to Coober Pedy.

Wilpena Pound Resort. Wilpena Pound, SA 5434. ☎ **1800/805 802** in Australia or 08/8648 0004. Fax 08/8648 0028. 60 units. A/C TV. A$95–$135 (U.S.$61.75–$87.75) double; A$145 (U.S.$94.25) self-contained units. Extra adult A$10 (U.S.$6.50). Extra child 2–14 A$5 (U.S.$3.25). AE, BC, DC, MC, V.

The nearest place to the Wilpena Pound, this partly refurbished resort almost monopolizes the overnight tourist market around here. Standard rooms are adequate and offer respite from the summer heat. The self-contained units come with a stovetop, a microwave, a basin, and cooking utensils. There is also a rather tacky dining room and bar, a general store, and a pool. The resort also operates a campground. Campsites cost A$17 (U.S.$11.05) per night for two people with power and A$11 (U.S.$7.15) per night for two people without power, and A$3 (U.S.$1.95) for each extra person. There are some good walks around the area. The resort also offers half-hour scenic flights over the Ranges for A$125 (U.S.$81.25) for one person, A$75 (U.S.$48.75) per person for two, or A$65 (U.S.$42.25) per person for three or more. They also operate 4WD tours with lunch for A$80 (U.S.$52) for a full day and A$65 (U.S.$42.25) for a half day.

WHERE TO DINE

The **Old Ghan Restaurant** on Leigh Creek Road, Hawker (☎ **08/8648 4176**), is open for lunch and dinner Wednesday through Sunday; the restaurant used to be a railway station on the Ghan railway line to Alice Springs before the line was shifted sideways due to flooding. The food here is unexciting, but the homemade pies have a following. If you find yourself in Port Augusta, the area's main town, head to the **Standpipe Motor Inn** (☎ **08/8642 4033**) for excellent Indian food. The rooms here are nice enough, and quiet, and cost A$80 (U.S.$52) for a double.

COOBER PEDY   *opalcapitaloftheworld.com.au*

854km (529 miles) NW of Adelaide; 689km (427 miles) S of Alice Springs

Tourists come to the Outback opal-mining town of ✪ **Coober Pedy** for one thing: the people. More than 3,500 people, from 44 nations, work and sleep mainly underground here—the majority suffering from the so-called opal fever, which keeps you digging and digging on the trail of the elusive shimmering rocks. Though some residents are secretive and like to keep themselves to themselves, many others are colorful characters all ready to stop for a chat and spin a few yarns.

Historically, Coober Pedy was a rough place, and it still has a certain Wild West air about it. The first **opal** was found here in 1915, but it wasn't until 1917 when the Trans Continental Railway was completed, that people began seriously digging for opal. Since then, they have mainly lived underground—not surprising when you encounter the heat, the dust, and the flies for yourself.

The town got its name from the Aboriginal words "kupa piti," commonly thought to mean "white man in a hole." Remnants of the holes left by early miners are everywhere, mostly in the form of bleached-white hills of waste called "mullock heaps." Tourists are discouraged from wandering around the old tailing sites because the locals get fed up when visitors fall down the mine shafts.

As for the town itself, there isn't that much to look at, except a couple of underground churches, some casual restaurants, a handful of opal stores, and the necessary service-type businesses. These places are all within stumbling distance of each other on the main highway.

ESSENTIALS

GETTING THERE   **Greyhound Pioneer** (☎ **13 20 30** in Australia) runs from Adelaide to Coober Pedy for A$76 (U.S.$49.40) for adults and A$61 (U.S.$39.65) for children one-way. The trip takes about 12 hours. The bus from Alice Springs to Coober Pedy costs A$75 (U.S.$48.75) for adults, A$60 (U.S.$39) for children. Passengers bound for Ayers Rock transfer at Erldunda. If you drive from Adelaide it takes about 9 hours to reach Coober Pedy on the Stuart Highway. It's another 7 hours to Alice Springs, 700 kilometers (437 miles) away. **Kendell Airlines** (☎ **13 13 00** in Australia; www.kendell.com.au) flies to Coober Pedy from Adelaide.

VISITOR INFORMATION   The **Coober Pedy Tourist Information Centre,** Hutchinson St. Coober Pedy (☎ **1800/637 076** in Australia, or 08/8672 5298) is open Monday to Friday from 8.30am to 5pm (closed public holidays).

SEEING THE TOWN

Desert Cave Hotel (☎ **08/8672 5688**) run tours of the opal fields and township for guests and non-guests. Tours include visits to an underground mine, a home, and potteries, and a tour of the underground Serbian Church. You also see an opal-cutting demonstration and "noodle" through mullock heaps. The 4-hour tour costs A$39 (U.S.$25.35) for adults, A$19.50 (U.S.$12.68) for children, A$95 (U.S.$61.75) for families.

If you want to see parts of Australia that most Australians never see, join a ✪ **Mail Run** for a 12-hour journey into the bush. Tours leave every Monday and Thursday from **Underground Books** (☎ **08/8672 5558**) in Coober Pedy (yep, it's a bookshop underground) and travel 600 kilometers (372 miles) of dirt roads to Oodnatta and William Creek cattle station, stopping at different stations along the route. It can get hot and dusty outside, but it's relatively comfortable inside the air-conditioned 4WD. Bring your own lunch, or buy it along the way. Tours cost A$75 (U.S.$48.75) for adults and A$55 (U.S$35.75) for children under 12, though kids might find the trip difficult. This could be one of the most memorable experiences you have in Australia.

WHERE TO STAY

✪ **The Backpacker's Inn at Radeka's Downunder Motel.** 1 Oliver St., Coober Pedy, SA 5723. ☎ **08/8672 5223.** Fax 08/86725821. 150 beds, including 6 twins; 9 motel rooms. Dorm beds A$17 (U.S.$11.05); motel rooms A$88 (U.S.$57.20) double. Extra person A$11.99 (U.S.$7.79). AE, BC, MC, V. Free parking. *radekadownunder.com.au*

Whereas all other "underground" rooms in Coober Pedy are actually built into the side of a hill, the centrally-located hostel here is actually underground—some 6½ meters directly below the top-side building that is. This makes for comfortable temperatures all year round. Odd-looking dorms have no doors and are scooped out of the rock. They contain just four beds, though there are two large dorms sleeping up to 20 people. The twin rooms are simply furnished but pleasant. Guests have the use of a TV and video room, a pool table, new kitchen and dining room and a bar. The motel rooms are comfortable, and come with attached bathrooms with a shower. Some have a kitchenette. Room 9 is huge with a double and two sets of bunk beds. All motel rooms are dug out of the side of a hill. Radeka's also runs a good opal tour.

The Desert Cave Hotel. Hutchison St., Coober Pedy (P.O. Box 223, Coober Pedy, SA 5723). ☎ **08/8672 5688.** Fax 08/8672 5198. 50 units, 19 underground. A/C MINIBAR TV TEL. A$168 (U.S.$109.20) double; A$185 (U.S.$120.25) family room (sleeps 5). Extra person A$16.60 (U.S.$10.79). AE, BC, DC, MC, V. Free parking.

opalcave cooperpedy.com.au
backpacker $15+

A Fabulous Four-Wheel-Drive Adventure

With a hired vehicle from Adelaide, it's a day's drive north through the Clare Valley wine region (stop off for a traditional Aussie lunch at ✪ **Bluey Blundstone's Café** at Melrose ☎ **08/8666 2173**) to the Prairie Hotel (see above). The next day it's a 3- to 4-hour drive to **William Creek,** an unusual Outback town with a takeaway and pub/hotel. Just 20 kilometer (12 miles) before you reach town is a turn-off to Lake Eyre, a giant salt lake which flooded in 2000 and should hold water for a couple more years (**Wrightsair** offers 1-hour flights over Lake Eyre for $110 (U.S.$71.50) per person. ☎ /mobile **0418 336 748**). Camping beside the lake is a magical experience. The next day it's a 166 kilometer (103 miles) drive to Coober Pedy (see above), and from there its a 9-hour drive back to Adelaide.

Though not the only underground hotel in the world (there's another wonderful one in White Cliffs in New South Wales), this is the only one with a pool and spa. Personally, I find the place to be a little soulless and in need of refurbishment. The bar's "pokie" machines are noisy, and you can hear your neighbors in the next room (heaven help you if the TVs turned up loud enough for you to hear, because it can send next door into curses). A winding staircase is well worth clambering up for the specialty char-grilled dishes served at the far from atmospheric Umbertos restaurant. A cafe offers lighter meals for lunch, and there's a game room, a pool, and a spa.

WHERE TO DINE
The Opal Inn (☎ **08/8672 5054**) offers good-value counter meals off the typical pub-grub variety. For something a bit different, head to **Traces** (☎ **08/8672 5147**), the township's favorite Greek restaurant.

5 The Coorong

Few places in the world attract as much wildfowl as the Coorong, one of Australia's most precious sanctuaries. The Coorong is made up of an area that includes the mouth of the Murray River, the huge Lake Alexandrina, the smaller Lake Albert, and a long, thin sand spit called the Younghusband Peninsula. A small, but by far the most scenic, part of this area is encompassed in the Coorong National Park. The area is under constant environmental threat due to pollutants coming south via the Murray River from the farmlands to the north. It still manages to play host to large colonies of native and visiting birds, such as the Australian pelican, black swans, royal spoonbills, greenshank, and the extremely rare hooded plover.

If it were possible to count all the birds here you'd probably run out of steam after some 45,000 ducks, 5,000 black swans, 2,000 Cape Barren Geese, and 122,000 waders. This last figure is even more significant when you consider it corresponds to a total South Australian population of waders standing at 200,000, and an overall Australian population of some 403,000.

Add to these figures the thousands of pelicans—with around 3,000 birds nesting here annually it's the largest permanent breeding colony in Australia, and countless gulls, terns and cormorants and you'll soon realize why the Coorong and the adjoining Lower Murray Lakes form one of the most important waterbird habitats in Australia

The national park, which stands out starkly against the degraded farmland surrounding it, is also home to several species of marsupials, including wombats.

The best time to visit the Coorong is in December and January, when the lakes are full of migratory birds from overseas. However, plenty of birds can be spotted year-round. Note: binoculars and patience are highly recommended.

ESSENTIALS

GETTING THERE   The best way to visit the Coorong is by car, though a guided tour of the area is highly recommended once you arrive at either the main settlement of **Goolwa** on the western fringe of the waterways, or at **Meninge,** on the eastern boundary. From Adelaide follow the **Princes Highway** along the coast.

VISITOR INFORMATION   The **Goolwa Tourist Information Centre,** BF Lawrie Lane, Goolwa (☎ **08/8555 1144**), has information on the area and can book accommodations.

GETTING AROUND   The best operator in the area is **Coorong Nature Tours** (☎ **08/8574 0037,** or 0428 714 793 mobile phone; www.lm.net.au/~coorongnat/; coorongnat@lm.net.au), based in Narrung. The tours are run by David Dadd, a delightful, unassuming Cockney who fell in love with the Coorong when he arrived at the age of 11. He offers memorable 1, 2 and 3-day tours of the area, with pickup in Meningie or Adelaide. Full-day tours cost A$132 (U.S.$85.80) per person from Meningie or A$185 (U.S.$120.25) per person from Adelaide. Reservations are essential.

WHERE TO STAY

There are plenty of hotels, B&Bs, campgrounds, and caravan parks in Goolwa and along the main road that runs parallel to the national park. One I prefer is the **Goolwa Camping and Tourist Park,** 40 Castle Rd, Goolwa, SA 5214 (☎ **08/8555 2144**). It has 70 caravans and a large area for tents. A two-berth van costs A$25 (U.S.$16.25) a night, and a six-berth A$35 (U.S.$22.75) for the first two people and A$5 (U.S.$3.25) an adult (A$3/U.S.$1.95 for a child) extra. Bring your own bedding.

Grahams Castle Resort. Crn of Castle and Bradford sts, Goolwa, SA 5214. ☎ **08/8555 3300,** or 1800 243 303 in Australia. Fax 08/8555 3828. 22 units. A$15 (U.S.$9.75) per person. AE, BC, DC, MC, V.

This former conference center is classified as a three-star backpackers accommodation, and comes with a swimming pool, tennis court, cafe, and laundry. Rooms are very basic with two single beds, heating, and a shower shared between two rooms. It's very popular with budget groups, so it could get noisy.

✪ **Poltalloch.** P.M.B.3, Narrung via Tailem Bend, SA 5260. ☎ **08/8574 0088.** Fax 08/8574 0065. 3 units. TV. A$95–$165 (U.S.$61.75–$107.25) per cottage. Extra person A$25 (U.S.$16.25). BC, MC, V.

Located in the middle of nowhere on the eastern edge of the Coorong, Poltalloch is a working farm—with plenty of cows, ducks, chickens, and dogs wandering about—that seems more like a village. The whole place is classified by the National Trust of South Australia, and history is evident everywhere, from the cottages once used by farm hands to the giant wooden shearing shed and other outbuildings.

You can stay in a choice of five cottages scattered across the property. **The Shearer's Hut** is a stone cottage that sleeps up to nine people; the **Overseers** stone cottage sleeps up to eight people; the **Boundary Rider's Cottage** is built of timber, iron, and stone, and sleeps five; and the **Station Hand's Cottage** sleeps four. The **Shearer's Quarters** is mainly for large groups and sleeps 12. All of the units are modern and comfortable inside and have their own kitchen facilities and barbecues. I stayed in the Station Hand's Cottage, once the home of Aboriginal workers. I loved the mix of rural feeling and modern conveniences.

There's a private beach on the property if you want to swim in the lake, and guests have the use of a dingy, a canoe, a tennis court, and a Ping-Pong table. Fascinating historical tours of the property cost A$9 (U.S$5.85) for adults, and A$4.50 (U.S$2.93) for children with a minimum charge of A$27 (U.S$17.55). Reservations are essential. Breakfast provisions are available for A$13 (U.S$8.45) per person. Coorong Nature Tours will pick you up from here for no extra charge. There's plenty of birdlife on and around the property.

Melbourne 12

by Marc Llewellyn

Melbourne, the capital of Victoria and Australia's second-largest city, with a population well over 3 million, is a melting pot of cultures. For a start, there are more people of Greek descent living here than in any other city in the world, except Athens. Then there are the Chinese, the Italians, the Vietnamese, and the Lebanese—they've all added something. In fact, almost one-third of Melburnians were born overseas or have parents who were born overseas. With such a diverse population, and with trams rattling through the streets and a host of stately European architecture surrounding you, you could easily forget you're in Australia at all (except for the glorious palm trees standing incongruously along the avenues, particularly at the beach). Melbourne (pronounced *Mel*-bun) is a restless, image-conscious city that's always exciting and always changing, depending what street or suburb you find yourself exploring.

Throughout Australia, Melbourne has a reputation of being at the head of the pack when it comes to shopping, restaurants, fashion, music, nightlife and cafe culture. Time after time, it's beat out other state capitals in bids for major international concerts, plays, exhibitions, and sporting events, such as the Formula One Grand Prix, and was the first Australian city to host the Olympics in 1956.

The city also revels in its healthy rivalry with northern neighbor, Sydney, but Melbournians almost all adore their city—often described as the "most livable" in the world—whereas Sydneysiders are more half-hearted in praise for their abode.

Melbourne's roots go back to the 1850s, when gold was found in the surrounding hills. British settlers flocked here and their descendents have made it a point of pride that their city was freely settled, rather than having its original inhabitants forced there in convict chains. The city grew wealthy and remained largely a conservative bastion until World War II, when another wave of immigration, this time mainly from southern Europe, made it a more relaxed place. As further waves of migrants arrived, Melbourne evolved into the exciting, cosmopolitan city it is today.

Frugal travelers will be happy to hear that the public transport system is a great cheap way to explore the city and hotel prices are slightly lower than in Sydney. You can save a lot of money on food if you stick to the cheap-eat zones, such as Chinatown, and pick up lunchtime snacks around the city in places like the Queen Victoria Market.

1 Orientation

ARRIVING

BY PLANE   Melbourne's main international and domestic airport is **Tullamarine Airport,** located 22 kilometers (14 miles) northwest of the city center. If you're traveling from Sydney, the flight will take you around 1 hour 20 minutes. It's a five-minute walk between the international and domestic terminals. If you are flying within Australia with Virgin Blue, you'll find they depart from the international terminal rather than the domestic terminal (but you can't buy duty-free goods if you're flying on this airline). Travelers' information desks are open on both levels of the international terminal building from 6am until the last flight. There are snack bars, a restaurant, currency exchange facilities, and duty-free shops in the international terminal. There's also a post office, open daily from 9am to 5pm, but stamps are available from vending machines after hours, as well as mail boxes. ATM cash machines are available at both terminals. Showers are also available on the first floor of the international area. Baggage trolleys are free in the international baggage claim hall, but cost A$2 (U.S.$1.30) if hired in the car park, departure lounge, or the domestic terminal. Baggage lockers cost A$4 (U.S.$2.60) per day, depending on size.

Thrifty (☎ **03/9330 1522,** or 1800 652 008 in Australia), **Budget** (☎ **13 27 27** in Australia), **Avis** (☎ **03/9338 1800,** or 1800 225 533 in Australia), and **Hertz** (☎ **03/9379 9955,** or 13 30 39 in Australia), all have rental desks at the airport.

Getting into Town   Skybus (☎ **03/9662 9275**) picks up passengers in front of the baggage claim area every 30 minutes from 6:40am to 11:40pm, and hourly 11:40pm to 6:40am. The trip into the center takes around 35 minutes and costs A$10 (U.S.$6.50) one way for adults and A$4.50 (U.S.$2.93) for children under 15. The service travels direct to Spencer Street Railway Station, where free shuttle buses transfer you to city hotels. When you want to return to the airport, book the Skybus service a few hours in advance and allow at least 40 minutes for traveling time. Buy tickets onboard, or from Skybus desks outside the baggage claim areas.

A taxi to the city center takes about 30 minutes and costs around A$35 (U.S.$22.75).

Many of the hostels and backpackers, and some hotels and motels offer free airport pickups and drop-offs. Phone or e-mail ahead for this service.

BY TRAIN   Interstate trains arrive at Spencer Street Railway Station, at Spencer and Little Collins Streets (5 blocks from Swanston Street in the city center). Taxis and buses connect with the city. The Sydney-Melbourne XPT travels between Australia's two largest cities daily; trip time is 10½ hours. The full fare (booked on the day of travel) is A$110 (U.S.$71.50) in economy, or A$77 (U.S.$50.05) (booked 2 days in advance), A$66 (U.S.$42.90) (booked a week in advance), and A$55 (U.S.$35.75) (booked 2 weeks in advance). The first class fare is A$154 (U.S.$100.10) on day of travel, A$107.80 (U.S.$70.07) (2 days in advance), A$92.40 (U.S.$60.06) (a week in advance), and A$77 (U.S.$50.05) (2 weeks in advance). A first class sleeper costs A$231 (U.S.$150.15) (booked on day of travel), A$184.80 (U.S.$120.12) (2 days in advance), A$169.40 (U.S.$110.11) (a week in advance), and A$154 (U.S.$100.10) (2 weeks in advance). Students presenting an ISIC international student card travel at 'a week in advance price' in all categories, even if booked on the day. Call **Countrylink** on ☎ **13 22 32,** or access their website at www.countrylink.nsw.gov.au.

The *Overlander* provides daily service to and from Melbourne and Adelaide (trip time: 12 hr.). Fares are A$57 (U.S.$37.05) in economy and A$105 (U.S.$68.25) for a first-class sleeper. You can take a car onto the Overlander for A$110 (U.S.$71.50).

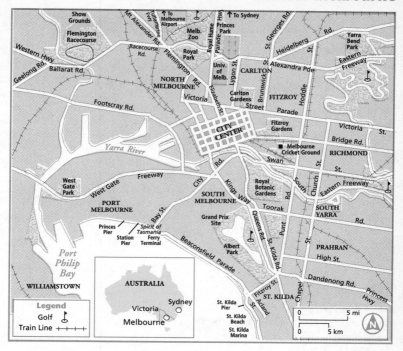

Call **Great Southern Railway** on ☎ **132 147**, or check their website at: www. gsr.com.au.

Daylink services also connect Melbourne with Adelaide. This trip is by train from Melbourne to Bendigo, and bus from Bendigo to Adelaide. Total trip time is 11 hours, and the fare is A$52 (U.S.$33.80) in economy and A$60.50 (U.S.$39.33) in first class.

The Canberra Link connects Melbourne with the nation's capital, and consists of a train journey from Melbourne to Wadonga, and bus from there to Canberra. The journey takes around 11 hours and costs A$50 (U.S.$32.50) in economy, and A$65.80 (U.S.$42.77) in first class.

For train information and reservations for the daylink services to Adelaide and Canberra call **V/Line** (☎ **136 196** in Australia, or 03/9619 5000), or visit their website on: www.vlinepassenger.com.au.

BY BUS   Several bus companies connect Melbourne with other state capitals and regional areas of Victoria. Among the biggest operators are **Greyhound Pioneer** (☎ **13 20 30** in Australia, or 03/9600 1687) and **McCafferty's** (☎ **13 14 99** in Australia, or 03/9670 2533). Greyhound Pioneer buses depart and arrive at Melbourne's **Transit Centre,** at 58 Franklin St. McCafferty's coaches depart and arrive from the Spencer Street Bus Terminal at 205 Spencer Street, on the western side of the city, just north of the Spencer Street Railway Station. New arrivals can take a tram or taxi from the station to their hotel. **V/Line buses** (☎ **13 22 32** in Australia), which travel all over Victoria, also depart from the Spencer Street Bus Terminal.

BY CAR   You can drive from Sydney to Melbourne along the Hume Highway, though a much nicer route is via the coastal Princes Highway, for which you will need a minimum of 2 days, with stops. For information on all aspects of road travel in Victoria, contact the **Royal Automotive Club** of Victoria (☎ **03/9790 3333**).

VISITOR INFORMATION

Your first stop should be the **Victorian Visitors Information Center,** Melbourne Town Hall, Swanston Street, at the corner of Little Collins Street (☎ **13 28 42** in Australia; www.tourism.vic.gov.au). You'll find everything you need here, and the staff can make reservations for accommodations and tours. The center is open Monday to Friday from 9am to 6pm and Saturday and Sunday from 9am to 5pm. **Tourism Victoria's** official website is www.visitvictoria.com. The **Melbourne Greeter Service** operates from the Town Hall, too. They connect visitors to local volunteers who offer free one-on-one orientation tours of the city. Book at least three days in advance on ☎ **03/9658 9524;** fax 03/9654 1054), and make sure you state your interests.

You'll find some information services at **The National Trust Shop,** Shop 21, Block Arcade, 282 Collins St. (☎ **03/9654 7448**), and at **Information Victoria,** 356 Collins St. (☎ **1300/366 356**). Staffed information booths are also found in Bourke Street Mall, Flinders Street Station (on the corner of Flinders Street and Swanston Walk), and at the Queen Victoria Markets (on the corner of Therry and Queen streets).

Good websites on the city include CitySearch Melbourne, www. melbourne.city search.com.au and www.melbourne.org.

CITY LAYOUT

Melbourne is situated on the Yarra River and stretches inland from Port Phillip Bay, which lies to its south. Look at a map, and you'll see a distinct central oblong area bordered by Flinders Street to the south, Latrobe Street to the north, Spring Street to the east, and Spencer Street to the west. Cutting north-to-south through its center are the two main shopping thoroughfares: Swanston Street and Elizabeth Street. A series of cross streets, including Bourke Street Mall, a pedestrian-only shopping thoroughfare, runs between the major thoroughfares. If you continue south along Swanston Street, and over the river, it turns into St. Kilda Road, which runs to the coast. Melbourne's urban "villages," including South Yarra, Richmond, Carlton, and Fitzroy, surround the center. The suburb of St. Kilda has a rather scruffy beach. If you've visited Sydney, you'll find Melbourne's city center to be smaller and less congested with people and cars.

Neighborhoods in Brief

Melbourne is huge. At more than 6,110 square kilometers (9,776 sq. miles), it's one of the biggest cities in the world. Below are the areas of most interest to visitors:

City Center   Made up of a grid of streets north of the Yarra River, the city center is bordered to the south by Flinders Street and to the north by Latrobe Street. The eastern and western borders are Spring Street and Spencer Street, respectively. There's some good shopping around here, good cafes, and in recent years an active nightlife has sprung up with the opening of a swath of good bars. The gateway to the city is the imposing Flinders Street Station, with its dome and clock tower, from which more than 100,000 commuters emerge for work on weekdays.

Chinatown   This colorful section of the city center is centered on Little Bourke Street between Swanston and Exhibition streets. The area marks Australia's oldest permanent Chinese settlement, dating from the 1850s, when a few boarding houses here catered for Chinese prospectors lured by the state's gold rushes. Plenty of cheap restaurants are strung around its narrow alleyways. Tram: Any to the city.

Carlton   North of the city center, Carlton is a tourist mecca famous for the Italian restaurants strung along Lygon Street with outdoor seating—though the quality of the food served up here is very variable. There is nothing glamorous about this rambling inner-city suburb with its distinct Italian flair. It's the home of the University of Melbourne, so there's a healthy student scene. From Bourke Street Mall, count on a 15-minute walk to reach the restaurant strip. Tram: 1 or 22 from Swanston St.

Fitzroy   A ruggedly bohemian place, 2 kilometers (1¼ miles) north of the city center, Fitzroy is raw and funky, filled with students and artists and popular for people watching. Fitzroy revolves around Brunswick Street, with its cheap restaurant scene, busy cafes, late night bookshops, art galleries, and pubs (often featuring live music). Around the corner, on Johnston Street, are tapas bars, Flamenco restaurants and Spanish clubs. Tram: 11 from Collins Street.

Richmond   One of Melbourne's earliest settlements is a multicultural quarter based around historic streets and back lanes. Victoria Street is reminiscent of Ho Chi Minh City, with Vietnamese sights, sounds, aromas, and restaurants. Bridge Road is a fashion precinct. Tram: 48 or 75 from Flinders Street to Bridge Road; 70 from Batmans Avenue at Princes Bridge to Swan Street; 109 from Bourke Street to Victoria Street.

Southgate   This entertainment district on the banks of the Yarra River opposite Flinders Street Station (linked by a pedestrian bridge) is the site of the Crown casino—Australia's largest—which also offers restaurants, bars, cafes, nightclubs, cinemas and designer shops. On the city side of the river is the Melbourne Aquarium. All are an easy stroll from Flinders Street Station. Tram: 8 from Swanston Street.

St. Kilda   Very hip and bohemian in a shabby sort of way, this seaside suburb (6km/4 miles south of the city center) has Melbourne's highest concentration of dining spots, ranging from glitzy to cheap, and some superb cake shops and delis. The Esplanade, which hugs the unremarkable beach with its brown waters, is the scene of a lively Sunday market filled with arts and crafts stalls. Ackland Street houses many of St Kilda's restaurants, ranging from Chinese to Jewish. Brush up on your in-line skating skills and wear your RayBans. Tram: 10 or 12 from Collins Street; 15 or 16 from Swanston Street; 96 from Bourke Street.

South Yarra/Prahan   This posh part of town is crammed with boutiques, cinemas, nightclubs, and galleries. Chapel Street is famous for its well-heeled eateries and fashion houses, while Commercial Road is popular with the gay and lesbian community. Just off Chapel Street in Prahan is Greville Street, a bohemian enclave featuring retro boutiques and music outlets. Every Sunday the Greville Street Market offers arts, crafts, secondhand clothes and jewelry from noon to 5pm. Tram: 8, or 72 from Swanston Street.

South Melbourne   One of the oldest working-class districts of the city, South Melbourne is known for its historic buildings, old-fashioned pubs and hotels, and its markets. Tram: 12 from Collins Street; 1 from Swanston Street.

The River District   The muddy Yarra River runs southeast beside the fabulous Botanic Gardens and near other attractions such as The Victorian Arts Centre, the National Gallery of Australia, the Sydney Myer Music Bowl and the Melbourne Cricket Ground (MCG).

Williamstown   A lack of extensive development has left this outer waterfront suburb with a rich architectural heritage centered on Ferguson Street and Nelson Place—both

A City Center Walk

A good place to start any stroll in Melbourne is from Southgate on the south side of the Yarra River. You could pop into the Victorian Arts Centre while you're in the vicinity. Cross the Princes Bridge and you enter the city center. At the corner of Flinders Street and Swanston Street to your right is Flinders Street Station, the Edwardian hub of Melbourne's rail network and a popular meeting point for Melburnians. Walk up the pedestrian-only Swanston Street (avoiding the trams) and you pass St. Paul's Cathedral on your right followed by City Square. The square, which was redeveloped in 1998-99 incorporates a series of modernist bronze statues of tall, thin men striding amongst the crowds, as well as a statues of Robert Burke and William Wills, the first settlers to cross Australia from south to north in 1860–61. Turn left into Collins Street and you come to the Block Arcade with its boutique shops and cafes. Walk north to Little Collins Street, where to your left is the Royal Arcade, guarded by the mythical giants Gog and Magog on either side of Gaunte's Clock (which tolls on the hour). Running between Swanston and Elizabeth Streets is Bourke Street Mall, a pedestrian precinct crammed with shops and musicians. Again, watch out for the trams.

Bourke Street runs off eastwards and ends at Spring Street, next to the Windsor Hotel—a great place for an upmarket lunch or tea. Opposite The Windsor on the other side of the road are the State Houses of Parliament, which are worth popping into for a tour, or to sit up in the gallery if Parliament is in session. Walk down Spring Street and you come to the Old Treasury Building, which houses some interesting exhibitions that cover Melbourne's gold-rush history. The Treasury Gardens and the Fitzroy Gardens (look out for Cook's Cottage) further east make for a break from the city. From here you can head up Landsdown Street and turn left into Cathedral Place for a visit to St. Patrick's Cathedral.

The walking tour should take an hour or so nonstop, but you'll find you need a full day or more to really appreciate all the sights.

reminiscent of old England. On the Strand, overlooking the sea, are a line of bistros and restaurants, and a World War II warship museum. Ferry: from Southgate, the World Trade Center, or St. Kilda Pier.

2 Getting Around

BY PUBLIC TRANSPORTATION
The Met operates trams, trains, and buses. Generally, tourists and locals travel around the city and to the outlying suburbs by tram.

BY TRAM Melbourne has the oldest tram network in the world. Trams are an essential part of the city, as well as being a cultural icon. There are some 700 mostly green and yellow trams running over 325 kilometers (200 miles) of track. Instead of phasing out this non-smoggy method of transport, Melbourne is expanding the network.

Tram travel within the city and to all suburbs mentioned in this chapter costs A$1.50 (U.S.98¢) for adults, A80¢ (U.S.52¢) for children for a single journey. Or you can buy a 2-Hour **Metcard** good for unlimited transport on buses or trains for up to two hours. Metcards cost A$2.40 (U.S.$1.56) for adults and A$1.35 (U.S.88¢) for children. If you plan to pack an awful lot in, then try the Zone 1 Metcard Daily ticket, which allows travel on all transport within the city center and surrounding suburbs mentioned in this chapter from 5:30am to midnight (when transportation stops) and costs A$4.60 (U.S.$2.99) for adults and A$2.40 (U.S.$1.56) for children. Metcard Weekly tickets cost A$20 (U.S.$13) for adults and A$9.95 (U.S.$6.47) for children.

Buy single-trip and 2-hour tram tickets at ticket machines on trams, special ticket offices (such as at the tram terminal on Elizabeth Street, near the corner of Flinders Street), at most newsagents, and at Metcard vending machines at many railway stations. A Metcard needs to be validated by the Metcard Validator machine on the tram, station platforms, or onboard buses before each journey, except for the two-hour Metcard ticket purchased from a vending machine on a tram, which is automatically validated for that journey only. Vending machines on trams only accept coins—so make sure you have enough change when you get on. Larger vending machines at train stations will give change and you can purchase tickets with bills up to A$10 (U.S.$6.50).

You can pick up a free route map from the **Victorian Visitors Information Center,** in the Town Hall on Swanston Street., or at the **Met Information Centre,** 103 Elizabeth St., at the corner of Collins Street (☎ **13 16 38** in Australia; www.victrip.com.au). The latter is open Monday to Friday from 8:30am to 4:30pm, and Saturday from 9am to 1pm.

MONEY-SAVING TRANSIT PASS

The **Getabout Travelcard,** which can be used by two adults and up to four children, is good 1 day of travel on Saturdays and Sundays only. It costs A$9.50 (U.S.$6.18). Buy it at newsagents.

The **City Circle Tram** is the best way to get around the center of Melbourne-and it's free. You can pick up a free map of the downtown area on the tram, and a staff member is on board to do a little commentary and answer tourist questions. These burgundy and cream trams travel a circular route between all the major central attractions, and past shopping malls and arcades. The trams run, in both directions, every 10 minutes between 10am to 3pm weekdays, and 10am to 6pm weekends, except Good Friday and Christmas Day. City Circle Tram stops are marked with a burgundy sign.

Regular trams can be hailed at green and gold tram stops. To signal you want to get off, press the red button near the handrails, or pull the cord above your head.

BY EXPLORER BUS

City Explorer (☎ **03/9650 7000**) operates double-decker London-style buses that pick up and drop off at 21 stops around the city, including the Melbourne Aquarium, Crown Casino, Queen Victoria Markets, Crown Casino, Captain Cook's Cottage, Chinatown, the Melbourne Zoo, and the Botanic Gardens, among others. There's full commentary on board. You can hop on and off as often as you want during the day. A bus returns to each stop half-hourly. The first bus leaves Town Hall on Swanston Street at 9:30am and the last leaves at 2:30pm. Tickets cost A$30 (U.S.$19.50) for adults, A$25 (U.S.$16.25) for students and YHA members, A$15 (U.S.$9.75) for children under 14, and A$75 (U.S.$48.75) for a family of five. Buy them from the driver or at the booth outside the Visitor Information Centre near Melbourne Town Hall.

BY TAXI

Cabs are plentiful in the city, but may be difficult to hail in the city center late Friday and Saturday nights. Taxi companies include **Silver Top** (☎ **13 10 08,** or 03/9345 3455), **Embassy** (☎ **13 17 55,** or 03/9277 3444), and **Black Cabs Combined**

(☎ **13 22 27**). An illuminated rooftop light shows a cab is free. For wheelchair accessible cabs call the **Central Booking Office** (☎ **1300/ 364 050**) at least a day in advance.

BY CAR

Driving in Melbourne is not fun. Roads can be confusing, there are trams and aggressive drivers everywhere, and there is a strange rule about turning right from the left lane at major intersections (which leaves the left lane free for oncoming trams and free for through traffic). Here, you must wait for the lights to turn amber before turning. Also, you must always stop behind a tram if it stops, as passengers usually step directly into the road. Add to this the general lack of parking spaces and expensive hotel valet parking charges, and you'll know why it's better to get on a tram instead. For road rules pick up a copy of the **Victorian Road Traffic** handbook from bookshops, or a Vic Roads office (☎ **13 11 71** in Australia for the nearest office).

Major car rental companies include **Avis,** 400 Elizabeth St. (☎ **03/9663 6366**); **Budget,** 398 Elizabeth St. (☎ **03/9203 4844**); **Hertz,** 97 Franklin St. (☎ **03/9698 2555**); **Delta,** 110 A'beckett St, (☎ **03/9600 9025**); and **Thrifty,** 390 Elizabeth St. (☎ **03/9663 5200**). Expect to pay from A\$30 (U.S.\$19.50) a day for a small car.

Fast Facts: Melbourne

American Express   The main Amex office is at 233 Collins St. (☎ **03/9633 6333**). It's open Monday to Friday from 9am to 5:30pm, and Saturday from 9am to noon.

Business Hours   In general, stores are open Monday to Thursday, Friday from 9am to 9pm, Saturday from 9am to 5:30pm, and Sunday from 10am to 5pm. The larger department stores stay open on Thursday evening until 9pm. Banks are open Monday to Thursday from 9:30am to 4pm, and Friday from 9:30am to 5pm.

Camera Repair   **Vintech Camera Repairs,** 5th Floor, 358 Lonsdale St. (☎ **03/9602 1820**) or mobile 0418 515 662, is well regarded.

Dentist   Call the **Dental Emergency Service** (☎ **03/9341 0222**) for emergency referral to a local dentist.

Doctor   The casualty department (emergency room) at the **Royal Melbourne Hospital,** Grattan Street, Parkville (☎ **03/9342 7000**) responds to emergencies. **The Traveller's Medical & Vaccination Centre,** 2nd Floor, 393 Little Bourke St. (☎ **03/9602 5788**), offers full vaccination and travel medical services.

Consulates   The following English-speaking countries have consulates in Melbourne: **United States,** level 6, 553 St. Kilda Rd. (☎ **03/9526 5900**); **United Kingdom,** Level 17, 90 Collins St. (☎ **03/9650 4155**); and **Canada,** 1st Floor, 123 Camberwell Rd., Hawthorn (☎ **03/9811 9999**).

Emergencies   In an emergency, call ☎ **000** for police, ambulance, or the fire department.

Hotlines   **Care Ring—Your Crisis Line,** call ☎ **13 61 69; Alcoholics Anonymous** ☎ **03/9429 1833.**

Internet Access   **Melbourne Central Internet,** Level 2, Melbourne Central, at the corner of Elizabeth and Latrobe streets (☎ **03/9663 8410**) is open Monday to Thursday from 10am to 6pm Friday from 10am to 7pm, Saturday from 10am to 5:30pm and on Sunday from 11am to 5pm. Another option is **Global Gossip,** 440 Elizabeth St., (☎ **03/9663 0511**), open daily from 8am to 1am.

Lost Property   Contact your nearest police station, or call in at the **Melbourne Town Hall,** Swanston Street, City (☎ **03/9658 9774**).

Pharmacies   **The McGibbony & Beaumont Pharmacy** is in the Grand Hyatt hotel complex, 123 Collins St. (☎ **03/9650 1823**). It's open Monday to Thursday from 8am to 6:30pm, Friday from 8am to 7pm, Saturday from 9:30am to 2:30pm, and Sunday from 9:30am to noon.

Post Office   The **General Post Office (GPO)** is at the corner of Bourke Street Mall and Elizabeth Street (☎ **03/9203 3042**). It's open Monday to Friday from 8:15am to 5:30pm, Saturday from 10am to 3pm. *Poste restante* hours are the same.

Safety   St. Kilda might be coming up in the world, but it's still wise not to walk around there late at night. Parks and gardens can also be risky at night, as can the area around the King Street nightclubs.

Taxes   Sales taxes, where it exists, is included in the price, as is the 10% Goods and Services Tax (GST) . There is no hotel tax as yet in Melbourne.

Telephones   For **Directory Assistance** call ☎ **1223;** for **International Directory Assistance** call ☎ **1225.**

Weather   Call ☎ **1196** for recorded weather information.

3 Accommodations You Can Afford

Getting a room is generally easy enough on weekends, when business travelers have gone home. You need to book well in advance, however, during the city's big events (the weekend before the Melbourne Cup, during the Grand Prix and the Ford Australia Open). Hostels in the St. Kilda area tend to fill up quickly in December and January.

Once considered dead after working hours, the city center has been rejuvenated in recent years, and you'll feel right in the heart of the action if you stay here. Otherwise, the suburbs are all exciting satellites, with good street life, restaurants, and pubs—all just a quick tram ride from the city center. (Transportation from the airport to the suburbs is a little more expensive and complicated than to the city center, however.)

If you arrive without accommodation, go to the travelers' information desks (☎ **03/9297 1814**), located on both floors of the international terminal at Tullarmine, open daily from 6am to last flight. They, and the Victorian Visitor Information Centre in the Melbourne Town Hall (☎ **03/9650 7721**), offer last-minute bookings without a fee.

IN THE CITY CENTER

✪ **Ibis Melbourne.** 15–21 Therry St., Melbourne, VIC 3000. ☎ **03/9639 2399,** or 1300/ 65 65 65 in Australia, 800/221-4542 in the U.S. and Canada, 0800/44 4422 in New Zealand. Fax 03/9639 1988. www.accorhotel.com. reservations@ibismelbourne.com.au. 250 units (some with shower only). AC TV TEL. A$109–$114 (U.S.$70.85–$74.10) double (depending on high/low season); A$139–$145 (U.S.$90.35–$94.25) 1-bedroom apt; A$186–$198 (U.S.$120.90–$128.70) 2-bedroom apt. Additional person A$27 (U.S.$17.55). Children under 12 free in parents' room. Ask about package deals. AE, BC, DC, MC, V. Parking A$8 (U.S.$5.20).

The good-value Ibis is right next door to the bus station and a short walk from the central shopping areas. The four-star rooms are spacious, immaculate, and bright, and have an attached shower. Apartments come with kitchenettes and a tub. All guests have free use of the swimming pool, sauna, and spa just up the road at the Melbourne City Baths. There's a restaurant, a bar, and a business center on the premises.

Hotel Y. YWCA Melbourne, 489 Elizabeth St., Melbourne, VIC 3000. ☎ **1800/249 124** in Australia or 03/9329 5188. Fax 03/9329 1469. melb@ywca.org.au. or hotely@ywca.net. 60 units. A$93–$115 (U.S.$60.45–$74.75) double; A$104–$126 triple (U.S.$67.60–$81.90); A$170 (U.S.$110.5) apt (for 2 people). Extra person A$16.50 (U.S.$10.73). No parking. AE, BC, DC, MC, V.

All rooms at the Y are sparsely furnished and not overly large, and as such do not represent such great value. The most expensive doubles and triples have been refurbished recently and have a TV, a refrigerator, and air-conditioning. The one-bedroom apartment has a queen-size bed with an en suite bathroom, and the lounge has a double pullout bed and a small kitchenette. A cafe on the premises serves breakfast, lunch and light snacks. The Y welcomes both women and men. The hotel is situated right near the Queen Victoria Market and is a short tram ride down Elizabeth Street or a 10-minute walk from the city center.

Kingsgate Hotel. 131 King St., Melbourne, VIC 3000. ☎ **03/9629 4171** or 1300 73 41 71. Fax 03/9629 7110. www.kingsgatehotel.com.au. info@kingsgatehotel.com.au. 225 units (104 with bathroom). A$69–$99 (U.S.$44.85–$64.35) double; A$89–$119 (U.S.$57.85–$77.35) triple; A$139 (U.S.$90.35) deluxe quad. AE, BC, DC, MC, V. Parking A$5.50 (U.S.$3.58) a day at Crown Casino, a 5-min. walk away.

Melbourne's only city-based 2½-star hotel is a 10-minute walk from the city center. It's an interesting place, which feels like a very basic B&B, though a major refurbishment was done last year—to attract airline staff. From the outside, the hotel resembles a terrace building, but inside it's a maze of corridors and rooms. The staff is very friendly. The "economy" rooms are for backpackers only. They're dark and have two single beds and a hand basin; there's barely enough room to swing a backpack. Pricier "executive" rooms, are light, spacious, and have a bouncy double bed (or two twins), a TV, and an en suite bathroom. A cooked breakfast costs A$7 (U.S.$4.55) extra. The 15 or so deluxe quad rooms have a double bed and two singles.

SUPER-CHEAP SLEEPS

✪ **Flinders Station Hotel Backpackers.** 35 Elizabeth St., Melbourne, VIC 3000. ☎ **03/9620 5100.** Fax 03/9620 5101. www.flindersbackpackers.com.au. Around 250 beds in 40 units, 6 units with bathrooms. A$56 (U.S.$36.40) double without bathroom; A$72 (U.S.$46.80) double with bathroom. A$16–$25 (U.S.$10.40–$16.25) dorm bed (depending on size of dorm). Prices less in winter. BC, MC, V. No parking.

This centrally located budget hotel occupies five floors and is so large that no one on staff seems to know exactly how many rooms there are. Standard rooms are basic, but modern and clean. There are 10 communal showers and restrooms per floor. There's a coin-op laundry, a full kitchen, a TV room, a bar, and a bottle shop. The place has been so popular since in opening in 1998 that plans are afoot to open another hostel—called Melbourne International Backpackers—on the corner of Franklin and Elizabeth streets, in the city, in mid-2001.

✪ **Toad Hall.** 441 Elizabeth St., Melbourne, VIC 3000. ☎ **03/9600 9010.** Fax 03/9600 9013. www.users.bigpond.com/toadhall.hotel/. toadhall.hotel@bigpond.com. 85 dorm beds in 16 rooms; 8 doubles, 4 with bathroom; 12 twin rooms, 2 with bathroom. A$60 (U.S.$39) double/twin without bathroom; A$90 (U.S.$58.50) double/twin with bathroom. A$25 (U.S.$16.25) dorm bed (A$1/U.S.65¢ discount per dorm, and $2/U.S.$1.30 per double/twin for YHA members). BC, MC, V. Parking A$6 (U.S.$3.90).

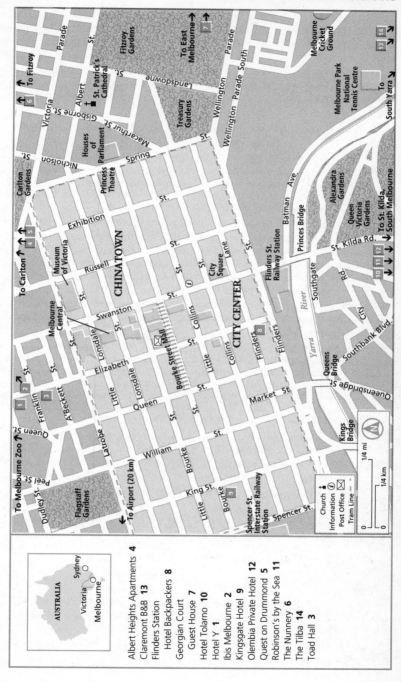

Albert Heights Apartments **4**
Claremont B&B **13**
Flinders Station
Hotel Backpackers **8**
Georgian Court
  Guest House **7**
Hotel Tolarno **10**
Hotel Y **1**
Ibis Melbourne **2**
Kingsgate Hotel **9**
Olembia Private Hotel **12**
Quest on Drummond **5**
Robinson's by the Sea **11**
The Nunnery **6**
The Tilba **14**
Toad Hall **3**

"It's one of the best in Australia" is what one well-traveled guest said of Toad Hall. I agree; this 1858 mansion is an excellent value. It's just down the road from Queen Victoria Market and a few minutes walk to the main shopping areas. Dorms are segregated by sex, with four to six bunk beds in each. Doubles and twins are small, but like the dorms, are clean and quite comfortable, with springy beds. Each room has tea- and coffee-making facilities. I really liked the large communal kitchen, dining room, and outdoor courtyard. There are three TV lounges with satellite TV, a laundry, and a tour-booking service.

IN CARLTON

✪ **Albert Heights Apartments.** 83 Albert St., East Melbourne, VIC 3002. ☎ **1800/800 117** in Australia, or 03/9419 0955. Fax 03/9419 9517. www.albertheights.com.au. enq@ albertheights.com.au. 34 units. A/C TV TEL. A$152 (U.S.$98.80) double; A$122 (U.S.$79.30) for members of any international auto club with identification. Additional person A$25 (U.S.$16.25) adults; A$20 (U.S.$13.50) children under 15. Ask about special deals. AE, BC, DC, MC, V. Free parking. Tram: 42 or 109; or a 10-min. walk to city.

For good, moderately priced accommodations with cooking facilities, so you can cut down on meal costs, you can't go wrong with the Albert Heights, a favorite of American travelers. It's in a very nice area of Melbourne a few minutes' walk from the city center. There are parks at each end of the street. Each unit in this neat brick building is large, clean, and attractive. If you want your own space, or are traveling with your family, you can use the sofa bed in the living room. Each unit comes with a full kitchen with a microwave (no conventional oven), a dining area, a large bathroom, a VCR, and two phones. A very popular Jacuzzi and a laundry are on the premises.

Georgian Court Guest House. 21 George St., East Melbourne, VIC 3002. ☎ **03/9419 6353.** Fax 03/9416 0895. www.georgiancourt.aunz.com. georgian@dataline.net.au. 31 units, 21 with bathroom. TV. A$84.70 (U.S.$55.06) double without bathroom; A$106.70 (U.S.$69.36) double with bathroom. A$10–$20 (U.S.$6.50–$13) surcharge during busy periods, such as the Melbourne Grand Prix and other major sporting events. Additional adult A$22 (U.S.$14.30), children under 15 A$11 (U.S.$7.15). Rates include buffet breakfast. AE, BC, DC, MC, V. Free parking. Tram: 78 from Flinders Street, or 48 from Spencer Street. Georgian Court is behind the Hilton, a 15-min. walk from the city center.

The Georgian Court's appearance hasn't changed much since it was built in 1910—and it still fits like a favorite shirt. The sitting and dining rooms have high ceilings, and offer a bit of old world atmosphere. The bedrooms are nice, though furnished with little more than plain pine furniture and a double bed. Upstairs rooms with bathrooms have air-conditioning and other rooms have fans. Most rooms were renovated in 2000.

Quest on Drummond. 371 Drummond St., Carlton, VIC 3053. ☎ **03/9486 1777.** Fax 03/ 9482 2649. www.questapartments.com.au. questdrummond@questapartments.com.au. 10 units. TV TEL. A$98.80 (U.S.$64.22) studio apt; A$107.80 (U.S.$70.07) 1-bedroom apt. AE, BC, DC, MC, V. Off-street parking. Tram: 1 or 22 from Swanston St.

Very nice and functional three-star self-catering apartments at a decent price are what you'll find at this good, semi-budget option. All apartments are modern and clean, and come with a full kitchen. One-bedroom apartments also have a sofa bed and all those little extras like a hair dryer and an iron and ironing board. There's a communal laundry, and breakfast packs are available on request, but no reception on the premises (though the management is only a phone call and a two-minute walk away). It's within walking distance of the city center.

IN FITZROY

✪ **The Nunnery.** 116 Nicholson St., Fitzroy, Melbourne, VIC 3065. ☎ **1800 032 635** in Australia or 03/9419 8637. Fax 03/9417 7736. www.bakpakgroup.com/nunnery/. 30 units, none with bathroom. A$45 (U.S.$29.25) single; A$55–$65 (U.S.$35.75–$42.25) double; A$80 (U.S.$52) triple. A$19–$25 (U.S.$12.35–$16.25) dorm bed. BC, MC, V. Off-street parking. Tram: 96 from the city to East Brunswick (stop 13).

This former convent is an exceptional budget accommodation. Set in a terrace on the city's edge, the Nunnery is perfectly situated near the restaurant and nightlife on Lygon Street and Brunswick Street in nearby Carlton. Rooms vary in size from three-bed dorms to singles in former nun's cells. Twin rooms come with either two singles or a set of bunks. All have basic furnishings and share bathrooms. Some second floor rooms have good views over the neighboring Royal Exhibition Buildings and the city skyline. There's a large guest kitchen, a small courtyard where you can eat breakfast, Internet access, and a large sitting room filled with couches, a fireplace, and a TV. A new boutique wing opened in November 2000 and has two doubles for A$85 (U.S.$55.25), five family rooms, and a single for A$65 (U.S.$42.25). These rooms are a little nicer than those in main section, but still have shared facilities. The staff here is very friendly.

IN ST. KILDA

✪ **Hotel Tolarno.** 42 Fitzroy St., St. Kilda, Melbourne, VIC 3182. ☎ **03/9537 0200.** Fax 03/9534 7800. www.hoteltolarno.com.au. mail@hoteltolarno.com.au. 34 units. AC TV TEL. A$110 (U.S.$71.50) standard doubles; A$135–$260 (U.S.$87.75–$169) balcony double; A$180–$260 (U.S.$117–$169) suite (sleeps up to 4). Additional person A$20 (U.S.$13). AE, BC, DC, MC, V. On-street parking. Tram: 16 from Swanston St.; 96 from Flinders St. (about a 15-min. ride).

The quirky Hotel Tolarno is in the middle of St. Kilda's cafe and restaurant strip, and a long stone's throw away from the beach. The place was renovated and expanded in 1998 and has a new foyer and breakfast room and lounge. Rich red carpets bedeck the corridors throughout this 1950s and 60s retro-style building. Rooms vary, but all are modern and nice. Some of the most popular rooms are in the front of the building and have balconies overlooking the main street. The more expensive of those come with a separate kitchen and lounge. Suites vary from one and two bedroom, and don't have balconies, though some have Jacuzzis. Breakfast is A$8 (U.S.$5.20) per person extra. There's a restaurant and bar on the property.

Olembia Private Hotel. 96 Barkly St., St. Kilda, Melbourne, VIC 3182. ☎ **03/9537 1412.** Fax 03/9537 1600. www.olembia.com.au. stay@olembia.com.au. 23 units, none with bathroom. A$44 (U.S.$28.60) single; A$64 (U.S.$41.60) double. A$21 (U.S.$13.65) dorm bed. AE, BC, MC, V. Free parking. Tram: 96 from Bourke Street to stop 138.

This sprawling Edwardian house, built in 1922, is set back from a busy St. Kilda street behind a leafy courtyard. It's popular with tourists, business travelers, and young families; and everyone gets together for the frequent video nights, wine and cheese parties, and barbecues. The clean bedrooms are simply furnished, with little more than a double bed, or two singles, a desk, a hand basin, and a wardrobe. Rooms have been recently repainted and upgraded. Guests share six bathrooms. There's a guest kitchen, a dining room, a very comfortable sitting room, and a courtyard area with barbecues. The Olembia is near St. Kilda beach and the host of restaurants lining Acland Street.

✪ **Robinson's by the Sea.** 335 Beaconsfield Parade, St. Kilda, Melbourne, VIC 3182. ☎ **03/9534 2683.** Fax 03/9534 2683. www.robinsonsbythesea.com.au. wendyr@alphalink. com.au. 5 units, none with bathroom. A$165 (U.S.$107.25) double. Rates include cooked breakfast. AE, BC, DC, MC, V. Free parking. Tram: 12 to Cowderoy St., St. Kilda.

If you want something very special, Robinson's by the Sea fits the bill. The management (and pet dog) at this 1870s heritage B&B just across the road from the beach are incredibly friendly. They encourage an evening social scene, and downstairs you'll find a comfortable, antique-filled living room and a dining room. Four of the five bedrooms are located upstairs. Each unit is unique. For example, the Eastern Room has a four-poster queen-size bed and Indian and Chinese furniture, whereas the Rose Room is decorated with patterned flowers and pastel colors. The units all share three communal bathrooms, one with a tub and shower, a second with a shower, and the third with a Jacuzzi tub and shower. There are wood floorboards and fireplaces throughout.

IN SOUTH YARRA

Claremont B&B. 189 Toorak Rd., South Yarra, VIC 3141. ☎ **03/9826 8000,** or 03/9286 8222. Fax 03/9827 8652. www.melbaccom.com.au. claremont189@bigpond.com. 80 units, none with bathroom. TV. A$56 (U.S.$36.40) single; A$68 (U.S.$44.20) double. Additional person A$10 (U.S.$6.50). Children stay free in parents' room. Rates include continental breakfast. AE, BC, DC, MC, V.

The high ceilings and the mosaic tiles in the lobby welcome visitors into this old world hotel, which reopened in 1995 after a complete overhaul. It's an attractive place, though sparsely furnished. The two-star rated rooms are comfortable enough, and each come with a double or a single bed, a TV, and a refrigerator. On the premises you'll find a coin-op laundry and 24-hour tea and coffee. There is no elevator in this three-story building with 72 stairs, so it could be a bad choice for travelers with disabilities.

WORTH A SPLURGE

✪ **The Tilba.** 30 W. Toorak Rd. (at Domain St.), South Yarra, VIC 3141. ☎ **03/9867 8844.** Fax 03/9867 6567. 15 units, 1 cottage. TV TEL. A$140–$195 (U.S.$91–$126.75) double. Rates include breakfast. AE, BC, DC, MC, V. Closed the first week of Jan, Easter week, and the last week of Dec. Free parking. Tram: 6, 8, or 72 from Swanston St. No children under 12.

With its turreted facade, antique furniture, and leaded windows, the Tilba is the city's most elegant and romantic small hotel. Built in 1907, the Tilba started life as a private mansion and was used as an army hostel during World War II; it has been an exclusive hotel since the early '90s. The tranquil mansion overlooking Faulkner Park, attracts mostly business travelers, who appreciate the homelike atmosphere. The bedrooms, some of which were former stables or lofts, are unique in size, design, and color. The sitting and breakfast rooms are decorated with antiques and have open fireplaces.

4 Great Deals on Dining

Melbourne's ethnically diverse population ensures a healthy selection of international cooking styles. Chinatown, in the city center, is a fabulous hunting ground for authentic Chinese, Malaysian, Thai, Indonesian, Japanese, and Vietnamese fare, often at bargain prices. Carlton has plenty of Italian cuisine, but generally the outdoor restaurants on Lygon Street are aimed at unsuspecting tourists, and are frequently overpriced and disappointing, so avoid them; Richmond is crammed with Greek and Vietnamese restaurants; and Fitzroy has cheap Asian, Turkish, Mediterranean, and vegetarian food. To see and be seen, head to Chapel Street or Toorak Road in South Yarra, or to St. Kilda to take in the sea breeze and join the throng of Melburnites dining out along Fitzroy and Ackland streets. Most of the cheaper places in Melbourne are strictly BYO (bring-your-own wine or beer). Smoking is currently possible in cafes and restaurants, but check before lighting up, as moves are being made to ban it.

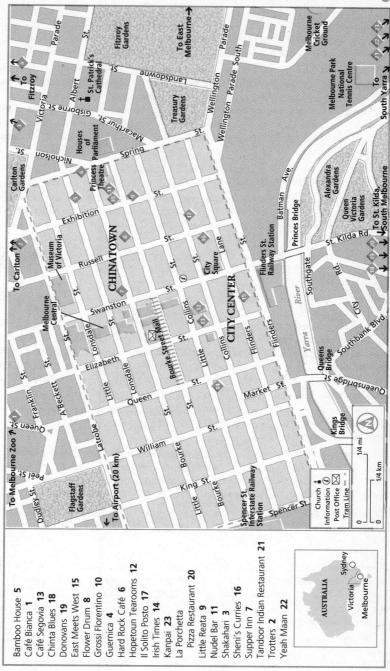

IN THE CITY CENTER

⭐ **Bamboo House.** 47 Little Burke St. ☎ **03/9662 1565.** Reservations recommended. Main courses A$17–$24 (U.S.$11.05–$15.60). AE, BC, DC, MC, V. Mon–Fri noon–3pm; Mon–Sat 5:30–11pm, Sun 5:30–10pm. NORTHERN REGIONAL CHINESE/CANTONESE.

If Flower Drum (see "Worth a Splurge," below) is full (or breaks your budget), try this place, which is esteemed by both the Chinese community and local business big shots. The service here really is a pleasure, and the food (especially the delicious chicken with shallot sauce) is worth writing home about. The waiters are all eager to help you construct a feast from the myriad Cantonese and northern Chinese dishes. (Don't leave without a taste of the duck in plum sauce!) Other popular dishes include pan-fried dumplings, spring onion pancakes, and the signature dish, Sichuan smoked duck.

⭐ **Café Segovia.** 33 Block Arcade. ☎ **03/9650 2373.** Main courses A$8–$13 (U.S.$5.20–$8.45). Mon–Fri 7:30am–11pm, Sat 8am–6pm, Sun 9am–5pm. AE, BC, DC, MC, V. CAFE.

Café Segovia is one of the most atmospheric cafes in Australia, with a smoky, sensual interior reminiscent of Spain. Seating is also available outside in the arcade itself, but you'll have to come early at lunchtime to nab a chair. Typical cafe food is on offer, such as focaccias, cakes, and light meals.

Grossi Florentino. 80 Bourke St. ☎ **03/9662 1811.** Reservations recommended. Main courses $16–$35 (U.S.$10.40–$22.75). AE, BC, DC, MC, V. Mon–Fri noon–3pm; Mon–Sat 6–11pm. ITALIAN.

Under the management of the Grossi family, the restaurant formerly known as Florentinos has perked up to become probably the best Italian restaurant in Melbourne. It's split into three sections, with a casual bistro downstairs, next to the Cellar bar (where you can pick up a bowl of pasta for around A$10/U.S.$6.50). Upstairs, you can find the fine dining restaurant with its chandeliers and murals reflecting the Florentine way of life. On the menu here you could find veal shanks braised with tomato and red wine on a bed of saffron, as well as typical Italian risotto, seafood, and steak dishes.

Hard Rock Cafe. 1 Bourke St. (next to The Windsor Hotel). ☎ **03/9633 6193.** Reservations recommended. Main course A$9.75–$19.95 (U.S.$6.34–$12.97). AE, BC, DC, MC, V. Daily noon–midnight. AMERICAN.

You know the drill. The ubiquitous Hard Rock serves up large portions of typical theme-restaurant fare—nachos, T-bone steaks, chicken, salads, and burgers—in a rock and roll atmosphere. Bottomless soft drinks are served, but there are no free refills for coffee. The music can get overpoweringly loud.j

⭐ **Hopetoun Tearooms.** Shops 1 and 2, Block Arcade. ☎ **03/9650 2777.** Main courses A$4.50–$8.50 (U.S.$2.93–$5.53) (minimum charge A$5/U.S.$3.25 per person noon–2pm). Mon–Thurs 8:30am–5pm, Fri 8:30am–6pm, Sat 10am–3:30pm. Closed Sun. AE, BC, DC, MC, V. CAFE.

The first cup of coffee served in this Melbourne institution left the pot in 1891. It's all very civilized here, with green and white Regency wallpaper and marble tables. The cakes are very good; the sandwiches go for A$4.50 to $6.50 (U.S.$2.93–$4.23) and the focaccias for A$7 to $8.50 (U.S.$4.55–$5.53). Scones, croissants, and grilled food are also available.

Il Solito Posto. Basement of 113 Collins St. (enter via George Parade). ☎ **03/9654 4466.** Reservations recommended. Main courses A$8.50–$13 (U.S.$5.53–$8.45) in bistro, A$18.50–$27.50 (U.S.$12.03–$17.88) in trattoria. AE, BC, DC, MC, V. Mon–Sat 7:30am–1am. NORTHERN ITALIAN.

This sunken restaurant is split into two parts. The casual bistro has a blackboard menu offering good pastas, soups, and salads. Then there's the sharper and more upmarket trattoria, with its a la carte menu offering the likes of steak, fish, and veal dishes. The coffee is good, too.

Irish Times. 427 Little Collins St. ☎ **03/9642 1699.** Reservations advisable. Main courses A$8.50–$18 (U.S.$5.53–$11.70). AE, BC, DC, MC, V. Sun–Tues 11am–midnight; Wed–Sat 11am–3am. Not BYO. IRISH/MODERN AUSTRALIAN.

An Irish bar more authentic than most, the Irish Times is a character-filled eating and drinking escape from the rush of the city outside which serves up generous portions and Guinness on tap. Popular dishes include the warm chicken salad, mussels in a creamy broth, Caesar salad, and Irish dishes such as *boxty* (patties of mashed potato, leek and onion) with an accompanying tomato relish. There's a live band on Thursday and Friday evenings from 9.30pm and on Saturday from 10.30pm.

Little Reata. 68 Little Collins St. ☎ **03/9654 5917.** Reservations recommended. Main courses A$10.50–$16 (U.S.$6.83–$10.40). AE, BC, DC, MC, V. Daily 5:30pm–7am (limited menu 11pm–5am); Tues–Fri noon–2:30pm. TEX-MEX.

Typical Tex-Mex cooking is served up inside the blood red walls of this dimly lit restaurant. The house specialty is the chicken fajitas (chicken marinated in tequila and lime with tortillas, salad, salsa, and sour cream). There's an interesting cocktail selection available for A$6 to $8.50 (U.S.$3.90–$5.53).

Nudel Bar. 76 Bourke St. ☎ **03/9662 9100.** Reservations advisable Fri and Sat evenings. Main courses A$12.50–$14.50 (U.S.$8.13–$9.43). AE, BC, DC, MC, V. Sun–Thurs 11am–11pm, Fri–Sat 11am–midnight. Not BYO. NOODLES.

A favorite with city slickers, the Nudel Bar serves up a variety of noodle dishes to the crowded tables and bar. Examples of what you might find here are cold spicy green tea noodles, *mee goreng* and sticky rice pudding is a favorite for dessert.

Supper Inn. 15 Celestial Ave. ☎ **03/9663 4759.** Reservations recommended. Main courses A$9–$12 (U.S.$5.85–$7.80). AE, BC, DC, MC, V. Daily 5:30pm–2:30am. CANTONESE.

Head here if you get the Chinese food munchies late at night. It's a friendly place with a mixed crowd of locals and tourists chowing down on such dishes as steaming bowls of congee (a rice-based porridge), barbecued suckling pig, mud crab, or stuffed scallops. Everything's authentic, not like some of the Westernized slop you often get served.

SUPER-CHEAP EATS

✪ **Café Bianca.** Store 97–98, Queen Victoria Market. No phone. Main courses A$2.60–$3.80 (U.S.$1.69–$2.47). Market hours. No credit cards. PIZZA.

Inside the main market building, past the meat and fish sellers, and farther on past a range of cake and deli stalls is the best little pizza takeout in Australia. It's tiny, and there's nowhere to sit, but who has time to hang around with so much to see anyway? All the pizzas, including such gourmet concoctions as chicken tandoori pizza, fresh asparagus pizza, and potato and herb pizza, are homemade. Don't be fooled by the pretenders to the pizza crown that can be found nearby.

East Meets West. 271 Flinders Lane. ☎ **03/9650 8877.** Main courses A$5.50–$7 (U.S.$3.58–$4.55). AE, BC, DC, MC, V. Mon–Fri 10am–6:30pm, Sat 10:30am–2:30pm. ASIAN/FAST FOOD.

This little place is great for a quick Indian curry, a plate of noodles, some spring rolls, or fish and chips. It's simple and cheap, with a few small tables. The curries are delicious and come in medium and large portions.

Sheni's Curries. Shop 16, 161 Collins St. (on the corner of Flinders Lane and Russell St., opposite the entrance to the Grand Hyatt). ☎ **03/9654 3535.** Lunch specials A$4.50–$7 (U.S.$2.93–$4.55). No credit cards. Mon–Fri 11am–4pm. SRI LANKAN.

This tiny, busy place (it seats 30) offers a small range of excellent value, authentic Sri Lankan curries. You can dine here or take your lunch special to go. Choose between three vegetable dishes and a choice of meat and seafood dishes. All meals come with rice, three types of chutney, and a papadam. You can also buy extra items such as samosas and roti.

WORTH A SPLURGE
⭐ **Flower Drum.** 17 Market Lane. ☎ **03/9662 3655.** Reservations required. Main courses A$25–$30 (U.S.$16.25–$19.50). Mon–Sat noon–3pm and 6–11pm, Sun 6–10:30pm. AE, BC, DC, MC, V. CANTONESE.

Praise pours in from all sides for this upscale choice just off Little Bourke Street, Chinatown's main drag. Take a slow elevator up to the restaurant, which has widely spaced tables (perfect for politicians and business people to clinch deals). Take note of the specials—the chefs are creative and utilize the best ingredients they find in the markets each day. The signature dish here is the Peking duck, although the buttered garfish is my favorite main course. The king crab dumplings in soup are a great starter. You can also prearrange a banquet for two or more diners; you'll be served more unusual dishes (such as abalone). One- or 2-day advance notice is required.

CARLTON
⭐ **Trotters.** 400 Lygon St, Carlton. ☎ **03/9347 5657.** Main courses A$4.50–$8 (U.S.$2.93–$5.20). AE, BC, DC, MC, V. Mon–Fri 7:30am–10pm, Sat 8am–10pm, Sun 9:30am–10pm. Tram: Any tram going north along Swanston St. toward Melbourne University. CAFE

If you want a great breakfast and you're staying in Carlton, then Trotters is easily the best place you'll come across. All the classics: bacon and eggs, homemade cakes and croissants, as well as good coffee. Seating is both indoors and out.

VEGETARIAN DELIGHTS IN CARLTON
Shakahari. 201–203 Faraday St., Carlton. ☎ **03/9347 3848.** Main courses A$12.50 (U.S.$8.13). AE, BC, DC, MC, V. Mon–Sat noon–3:30pm, Sun–Thurs 6–9:30pm, Fri–Sat 6–10:30pm. Tram: Any tram going north along Swanston St. toward Melbourne University. VEGETARIAN.

Good vegetarian food isn't just a meal without meat; it's a creation in its own right. At Shakahari you are assured of a creative meal that's not at all bland. The large restaurant is quite low key, but the service can be a bit inconsistent. The Sate Samsara (skewered, lightly fried vegetables and tofu pieces with a peanut dip) is a winner, as is the couscous, served in a vast earthenware pot. Also served up are curries, croquettes, tempura avocado, and veggie burgers (on a plate with salad, not in a bun).

WORTH A SPLURGE IN FITZROY
⭐ **Guernica.** 257 Brunswick St., Fitzroy. ☎ **03/9416 0969.** Reservations recommended. Main courses A$17.90–$22.90 (U.S.$11.64–$14.89). AE, BC, DC, MC, V. Sun–Fri noon–3pm; daily 6–10:30pm. Tram: 11 from Collins St., or 86 from Bourke St. MODERN AUSTRALIAN.

Dimly lit and featuring a giant print of Picasso's famous painting, this restaurant serves up some exciting dishes, many jazzed up with a healthy tingle of spice or pepper. Choices range from the coconut-fried garfish with Vietnamese fried noodles to the spiced lamb cutlets with creamed feta cheese, roasted eggplant, and lemon and pomegranate molasses. The desserts are some of the best in town and include the marvelous palm sugar caramelized rice pudding with toasted coconut ice cream. Check out the blackboard selections of good Australian wines by the glass. The restaurant is non-smoking in the evenings until 10pm.

SEASIDE DINING IN ST. KILDA

Chinta Blues. 6 Acland St., St. Kilda. ☎ **03/9534 9233.** Reservations recommended. Main courses A$7.50–$16 (U.S.$4.88–$10.40). AE, BC, MC, V. Mon–Wed noon–2:30pm and 6–10pm, Thurs–Sat noon–2:30pm and 6–10:45pm, Sun noon–9:45pm. Tram: 16 from Swanston St. or 96 from Bourke St. MALAYSIAN.

If you're looking for simple, satisfying food with a healthy touch of spice, head to this popular eatery. Favorites are the laksa, the Mei Goreng, the chicken curry, the sambal spinach, and a chicken dish called *ayam blues*. It's very busy, especially at lunch.

La Porchetta Pizza Restaurant. 80 Acland St., St. Kilda. ☎ **03/9534 1888.** Main courses A$5–$13.50 (U.S.$3.20–$8.78). Sun–Thurs 11am–midnight, Fri–Sat 11am–2am. Tram: 16 from Swanston St. or 96 from Bourke St. PIZZA.

This very busy, quite large, and noisy pizza joint is a very good value. There are some 22 different pizzas to choose from, with the largest (ranging in price from A$6 to $7.80 (U.S.$3.90–$5.07) being just large enough to fill two. A range of pasta dishes cost from A$6 to $9 (U.S.$3.90–5.85). Chicken, seafood, veal, and steaks are also on the menu. The heart-pounding pace here means it's not for the faint-hearted.

WORTH A SPLURGE

✪ **Donovans.** 40 Jacka Blvd., St. Kilda. ☎ **03/9534 8221.** Reservations recommended. Main courses A$23–$32 (U.S.$14.95–$20.80). Daily noon–10:30pm. AE, BC, DC, MC, V. Tram: 12 from Collins St., 16 from Swanston St., 94 or 96 from Bourke St. MODERN MEDITERRANEAN.

Donovans is so near the sea that you expect the fish to jump through the door and onto the plate—and indeed, you do get extremely fresh seafood. The restaurant is all higgledy-piggledy and charming, with lots of cushions, a log fire, and the sound of jazz and breakers on the beach. The menu includes a mind-boggling 53 dishes, so you are sure to find something you like. Try the swordfish fillet with warm onion relish, or the homestyle fish stew, big enough for two, with lots of prawns, clams, mussels, and fish. If you're not a big fish eater, then choose from several pasta and meat dishes.

MORE ETHNIC EATS IN SOUTH YARRA

Kanpai. 569 Chapel St., South Yarra. ☎ **03/9827 4379.** Reservations recommended. Main courses A$12–$34 (U.S.$7.80–$22.10). (average price A$12.50/U.S.$8.13). AE, BC, DC, MC, V. Daily noon–11pm. Tram: 6, 8, or 72 from Swanston St. JAPANESE.

You have to book early in the day to get a seat at this popular restaurant on the Chapel Street restaurant strip. The sushi and sashimi dishes are very fresh, and the miso soup is well worth plundering with your chopsticks. There's a good vegetarian selection, too.

Tandoor Indian Restaurant. 517 Chapel St., South Yarra. ☎ **03/9827 8247.** Reservations recommended Fri and Sat night. Main courses A$9–$17 (U.S.$5.85–$11.05). AE, BC, DC, MC, V. Tues–Fri noon–2:30pm; daily 6–11pm. Tram: 6, 8, or 72 from Swanston St. INDIAN.

This basic Indian restaurant was far less crowded than many of the others on the Chapel Street strip when I last visited—all I can say is that the "in" crowd didn't know what it was missing. The curries here are rich and spicy, with the vegetarian paneer butter masala and the cheese kofta being some of the best I've tasted in Australia. Some dishes, such as the crab masala curry, are truly inspirational. The main courses are quite large, so you'll probably not need a first course, but I highly recommend side dishes of *naan* bread (one per person) and a cucumber raita to cool the palate.

⊙ **Yeah Maan.** 340 Punt Rd. (at Fawkner St.), South Yarra. ☎ **03/9820 2707.** Reservations not accepted. Main courses A$8.60–$13 (U.S.$5.59–$8.45). AE, BC, DC, MC, V. Tues–Sat 6–10:30pm, Sun 5–9:30pm. Tram: 6, 8, or 72 from Swanston St. CARIBBEAN.

Is this the coolest restaurant in Australia or what? Calypso music wafts amid the home-made triangle-backed chairs, diners wait for a table in the lounge, palm trees sway—and the food! Wow! The whole place is rockin', mon, with the 75 seats almost continually occupied. The authentic Trinidadian goat curry is a must, as is the Barbados burrito. The Jamaican KFC (chicken marinated for 2 days in approximately 30 spices and then smoked), and the Jumbo-Jumbie cassava shoestring fries (cassava is similar to a potato), are very, very popular. The staff is ultrafriendly.

5 Seeing the Sights

Melbourne may not have as many major attractions as Sydney, but visitors come here to experience the contrasts of old world architecture and the exciting feel of a truly multicultural city.

If you'd like to see the city aboard a leisurely cruise, call **Melbourne River Cruises** (☎ **03/9614 1215** Mon to Fri or 03/9650 2055 on weekends). This company offers a 2½-hour round-trip cruise on the Yarra River costing A$16.50 (U.S.$10.73) for adults, A$8.80 (U.S.$5.72) for children ages 3 to 12, A$13.20 (U.S.$8.58) concession, and A$41.80 (U.S.$27.17) for a family.

SIGHTSEEING SUGGESTIONS FOR FIRST-TIME VISITORS

If you have time to see only one major attraction in Melbourne, then by all means make it the **Melbourne Zoo.** If you have the luxury to follow a more leisurely itinerary, here are my suggestions:

If You Have 1 Day Take a trip up to the top of the **Rialto Towers Observation Deck** to get your bearings, then visit the **National Gallery of Victoria,** walk through the **Botanic Gardens,** and stroll around the city streets. If you have time, head to **Phillip Island** to see the fairy penguins.

If You Have 2 Days Visit the **Queen Victoria Market** and take a tram to the **Melbourne Zoo.** You might head out to **St. Kilda** in the evening, for a great choice of restaurants.

If You Have 3 Days Rent a car or take a bus trip to explore the environs of Melbourne. I'd suggest either touring the **Yarra Valley wineries** and the **Healesville Sanctuary,** or going to the **Mornington Peninsula** and staying overnight in Portsea. Another option is a two-day excursion down the **Great Ocean Road** (see chapter 13).

If You Have 4 Days Head out to the **Dandenong Ranges** or the gold-field town of **Ballarat** (see chapter 13).

THE TOP ATTRACTIONS

⊙ **Melbourne Zoo.** Elliot Ave., Parkville. ☎ **03/9285 9300** or 03/9347 9530. www.zoo.org.au. Admission A$16.40 (U.S.$10.66) adults, A$8.10 (U.S.$5.27) children under 14, and A$44.30 (U.S.$28.80) family. Daily 9am–5pm. Free guided tours Mon–Fri 10am–3pm, Sat–Sun 11am–4pm (go to the Friends of the Zoo Office to arrange tours). Tram: 55 or 56 going north on William St. to stop 25; 18, 19, 20 from Elizabeth St. to Stop 16 (then it's a short walk to your left following signposts). Train: Royal Park Station. Bus: City Explorer.

This place is a must see. Built in 1862, it's the oldest zoo in the world, and still among the best. There are some 3,000 animals here, including the ever-popular kangaroos, wallabies, echidnas, koalas, wombats, and platypus. Rather than being locked up in cages, most animals are set in almost natural surroundings or well-tended gardens.

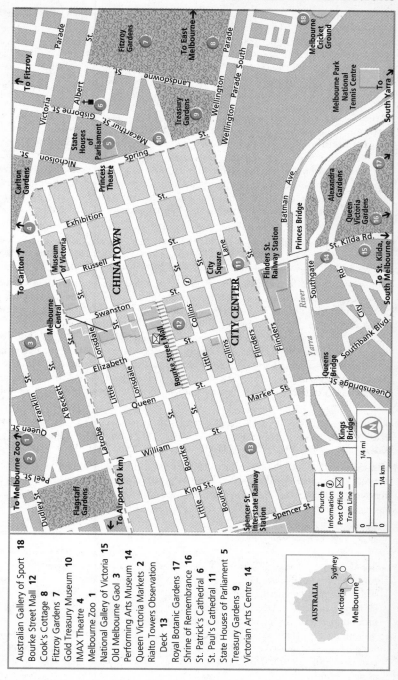

Australian Gallery of Sport **18**
Bourke Street Mall **12**
Cook's Cottage **8**
Fitzroy Gardens **7**
Gold Treasury Museum **10**
IMAX Theatre **4**
Melbourne Zoo **1**
National Gallery of Victoria **15**
Old Melbourne Gaol **3**
Performing Arts Museum **14**
Queen Victoria Markets **2**
Rialto Towers Observation
   Deck **13**
Royal Botanic Gardens **17**
Shrine of Remembrance **16**
St. Patrick's Cathedral **6**
St. Paul's Cathedral **11**
State Houses of Parliament **5**
Treasury Gardens **9**
Victorian Arts Centre **14**

Don't miss the butterfly house, with its thousands of colorful Australian butterflies flying around; the enormous free-flight aviary; the lowland gorilla exhibit; and the treetop monkey displays. Allow at least one hour if you just want to see the Australian natives and around 2½ hours for the whole zoo.

✪ **National Gallery of Victoria.** 285–321 Russell St. ☎ **03/9208 0203.** www.ngv.vic. gov.au Free general admission; call about special exhibits. Daily 10am–5pm. Closed Good Friday and Christmas. Tram: any southbound tram on Swanston St.

This is the best place in Victoria to view Aboriginal art, as well as colonial Australian, Asian, and European works. Look for works by artists such as Sidney Nolan, Russell Drysdale, and Tom Roberts; there are also a few works by Rembrandt, Picasso, Manet, and Turner. A free Aboriginal arts tour starts at 2pm every Thursday. There is a cafe and a restaurant on the premises. Currently involved in a major expansion and redevelopment, the museum moved its Australian collection to a new building in Federation Square, on the corner of Flinders and Swanston in May 2001, and the whole gallery will be packed up and moved to its original home at 180 St. Kilda Road in November 2002. Allow one hour.

✪ **Old Melbourne Gaol.** Russell St. ☎ **03/9663 7228.** www.vicnet.net.au/~omgaol. Admission A$9 (U.S.$5.85) adults, A$6 (U.S.$3.90) children, A$26 (U.S.$16.90) families. Daily 9:30am–4:30pm. Tram: City Circle tram to corner of Russell and Latrobe sts.

I love this cramped former prison with its tiny cells and spooky collection of death masks and artifacts relating to 19th-century prison life. Some 135 hangings took place here, including that of the notorious bandit (and Australian hero) Ned Kelly, in 1880. The scaffold where he was hung is still in place, and his gun, as well asand a suit of armor used by a member of his gang are on display. The jail closed in 1929. The display profiles of former prisoners give a fabulous perspective of what it was like to be locked up here. Chilling night tours run every Sunday and Wednesday (call ahead and check the schedule); they cost A$18 (U.S.$11.70) for adults and A$10 (U.S.$6.50) for children (though the tour is not recommended for children under 12). Allow 1 hour or more.

Melbourne Aquarium. Corner of King and Flinders St, opposite Crown Casino. ☎ **03/ 9620 0999.** www.melbourneaquarium.com.au. Daily 9am–6pm. Admission A$19 (U.S.$12.35) adults, A$9 (U.S.$5.85) children under 16, A$49 (U.S.$31.85) family of 5.

Opened in early 2000, the Melbourne Aquarium is a much smaller version of the one in Sydney. Stretched over three levels, it features a large Barrier Reef-type exhibit, some interesting jellyfish displays, and an enormous walkthrough tank filled with larger fish,

Penguins in the City

If you can't make it down to Phillip Island, you can see wild penguins without leaving Melbourne. **Penguin Waters** (☎ **03/9645 0533;** www.penguinwaters.com.au) runs boat trips daily (weather permitting) into the harbor looking for fairy penguins, which live along the jetties built for the '56 Olympics. You can see them swimming alongside the boat and the crew shines lights onto the coastline from the shallows to pick out penguins drying off on the rocks. Two-hour trips leave from Southgate, and 90-minute trips from St. Kilda. Both offer a BBQ onboard, included in the price. Ring in advance to book and get directions to the wharves. Two-hour dinner cruises cost A$45 (U.S.$29.25) for adults, 50% off for children under 12. Lunchtime cruises are offered for A$25 (U.S.$16.25).

sharks and rays. Altogether though, it was pretty disappointing and didn't live up to the hype. Allow 30 minutes.

✪ **Queen Victoria Markets.** Between Peel, Victoria, Elizabeth, and Therry sts. on the northern edge of the city center. ☎ **03/9269 5822.** www.qvm.com.au. Tues–Thurs 6am–2pm, Fri 6am–6pm, Sat 6am–3pm, Sun 9am–4pm. Tram: any tram traveling north along William St. or Elizabeth St.

The Queen Vic is a Melbourne institution covering several blocks. There are hundreds of indoor and outdoor stalls, where you can find virtually anything from live rabbits to bargain basement clothes. The markets can get cramped, and there's a lot of junk to sort through, but you'll get a real taste of Melbourne and its ethnic mix here. Look for the interesting delicatessen section, and cheap eateries. Allow at least an hour.

Two organized 2-hour tours of the market take in its food and heritage. The **Foodies Dream Tour** departs every Tuesday, Thursday, Friday, and Saturday at 10am and costs A$22 (U.S.$14.30) and A$15 (U.S.$9.75) for children under 15, including sampling. The Heritage Market Tour departs on the same days but at 10:30am and includes morning tea. It costs A$16.50 (U.S.$10.73) for adults, and "would most likely bore children to death," according to the guide. Call ☎ **03/9320 5822** for reservations.

Rialto Towers Observation Desk. Rialto Building, 55th Floor, Collins St. (between William and King sts.). ☎ **03/9629 8222.** Admission A$9.90 (U.S.$6.44) adults, A$5.50 (U.S.$3.58) children, A$27.50 (U.S.$17.88) families. Sun–Thurs 10am–10pm, Fri–Sat 10am–11pm. Tram: Any tram on Collins St.

From the observation deck near the top of the tallest building in the Southern Hemisphere, you get magnificent 360° views of Melbourne and beyond. See if you can spot the Melbourne Cricket Ground (MCG) and the new Crown Casino. A 20-minute film costing A$2 (U.S.$1.30) shows you what you're looking at, but you might as well just take a map up with you and figure it out for yourself. Of interest are the displays telling about life in Melbourne, past and present. There's a licensed cafe here, too. Allow one hour.

St. Pauls Cathedral. Flinders and Swanston sts. ☎ **03/9650 3791.** www.iaccess.com.au/stpauls/main.html. Daily 7:30am–6pm.

Built in the 1880s (with spires added in 1926) from the designs of William Butterfield, a famous English Gothic revival architect, the Anglican St. Pauls Cathedral is noteworthy for its highly decorative interior and English organ built by T.C. Lewis. Gold mosaics cover the walls, Victorian tiles the floors, there are intricate wood carvings, wonderful stained glass windows, and the cathedral sports the second highest spire, at 98 meters (107 ft.) in the Anglican Communion. (The tallest spire is on top of Salisbury Cathedral in England. It's 123m/134 ft.) A boy's choir sings at 5:10pm Monday to Friday during school times, and twice on Sunday at 10:30am and 6pm. Outside is a statue of Matthew Flinders, who became the first sailor to navigate the Australian mainland between 1801 and 1803 in the *Tom Thumb*. Allow 15 minutes.

St Patrick's Cathedral. Cathedral Place. ☎ **03/9662 2233.** Mon–Fri 6:30am–6pm; Sat–Sun 7:15am–7:30pm.

Though lacking the intricacy of design of St. Pauls, the Roman Catholic St. Patrick's is an interesting Gothic Revival construction with exceptional stained glass windows. Built between 1858 and 1940 (consecrated in 1897), St. Patrick's was closely associated with immigrants from Ireland escaping the potato famine. In the courtyard out front is a statue of the Irish patriot Daniel O'Connell. Allow 15 minutes.

State Houses of Parliament. Spring St. ☎ **03/9651 8911.** Free admission. Mon–Fri 9am–4pm. Guided tours 10am, 11am, noon, 2pm, 3pm, and 3:45 on weekdays when parliament is not in session. Bookings advisable.

Now the home of the Victorian Parliament, this monument to Victorian (as in Queen Victoria) architecture at the top of a run of sandstone steps was built in 1856. During the Australian Federation from 1900 to 1927, it was used as the National Parliament. When the State Government is in session—generally on Tuesday afternoon and all day Wednesday and Thursday between March and July, and again between August and November—you can view the proceedings from the public gallery. Do call ahead as sitting times vary. During non-sitting times both the extremely opulent Upper House and the less ornate Lower House chambers are open to the public. Allow 30 minutes.

✪ **Gold Treasury Museum.** Old Treasury Building. Spring St. (top of Collins St.) ☎ **03/9651 2233.** www.oldtreasurymuseum.org.au. A$7 (U.S.$4.55) adults, $3.50 (U.S.$2.28) children, A$18 (U.S.$11.70) family. Mon–Fri 9am–5pm, weekends and public holidays 10am–4pm.

Designed by the architect J.J. Clarke (when he was only 19) and built in 1857, The Old Treasury Building is an imposing neoclassical sandstone building, which once housed precious metal from the Ballarat and Bendigo gold rushes. The gold was stored in eight thick-walled vaults underground and protected by iron bars. The "Built on Gold" Exhibition within the vaults themselves is a high tech multimedia show featuring videos and displays showing how the gold was dug up, sold, transported and housed. In the basement are the restored living quarters of a caretaker who lived there from 1916–28. The ground floor is taken up by a display showing how Melbourne was built using the profits from the gold rushes. A temporary exhibition gallery on the premises can feature anything from prints to gold thread embroidery. Allow 1 hour.

Rippon Lea House Museum & Historic Garden. 192 Hotham St., Elsternwick. ☎ **03/9523 6095.** Admission A$9 (U.S.$5.85) adults, A$5 (U.S.$3.25) children 5–16, A$20 (U.S.$13) families of up to six. Open daily 10am–5pm (house closes at 4:45pm). Daily guided tours of house every half-hour 10:30am–4pm and tour of estate at 2pm. Closed Good Friday and Christmas Day. Tram: 67 to Stop 40, then walk up Hotham St. Bus: 216/219 from Bourke and Queen sts. in the city to Stop 4. Train: Sandringham Line from Flinders Street Station to Rippon Lea Station.

This grand Victorian house, 8 kilometers (5 miles) from the city center, is worth a visit to get a feel for old money Melbourne. Boasting dozens of rooms, Rippon Lea House was built by socialite Sir Frederick Thomas Sargood between 1868 and 1903; a pool and ballroom were added in the 1930s. Though the Romanesque architecture is interesting (note the stained glass and polychrome brickwork), the real attraction is the surrounding 5.3 hectares (13 acres) of gorgeous gardens, which include a conservatory, a lake, a lookout tower, an orchard, and extensive flowerbeds and ornate shrubbery. If you're here on a weekend, a public holiday, or during school vacations, you might like to drop into the tearoom, which is open from 11am to 4pm. Allow 2 hours.

PARKS & GARDENS

The ✪ **Royal Botanic Gardens,** 2 kilometers (1¼ miles) south of the city on Birdwood Avenue, off St. Kilda Road (☎ **03/9252 2300;** www.rbgmelb.org.au), are the best of their type in Australia and well worth a few hours. More than 100 acres of gardens are lush and blooming with more than 12,000 plant species from all over the world. Don't miss a visit to the oldest part of the garden, the Tennyson Lawn, with its 120-year-old English elm trees. Other special corners include a fern gully, camellia gardens, herb garden, rain forests packed with fruit bats (whose presence is now threatening the survival of some of the trees), and ponds full of ducks and black swans.

You can discover the gardens by wandering at your own pace (most plant species are labeled), or you can take one of the free guided walks that leave the national Herbarium Building, F Gate, Sunday to Friday at 11am and noon. Bring snacks and your picnic blanket to **Shakespeare in the Park,** a popular summer event in the gardens. Performances occur in January and February, and tickets cost around A$30 (U.S.$19.50). Call ☎ **03/9252 2300** for details. The gardens are open November to March from 7:30am to 8:30pm, in April from 7:30am to 6pm, May to Aug 7:30am to 5.30pm, Sept and Oct 7:30am to 6.00pm. Admission is free. To get there, catch the tram on route 8, traveling south on St. Kilda Rd., and get off at Stop 21. Allow 2 to 4 hours.

Nearby, in King's Domain, take a look at Victoria's first Government House, **Latrobe's Cottage** (☎ **03/9654 5528**). It was built in England and transported to Australia brick by brick in 1836. Admission is A$2 (U.S.$1.30) per person. The cottage is open from 11am to 4pm every Monday, Wednesday, Saturday and Sunday. On the other side of Birdwood Avenue is the Shrine of Remembrance, a memorial to the servicemen lost in Australia's wars. It's designed so that at 11am on Remembrance Day (Nov 11), a beam of sunlight hits the Stone of Remembrance in the Inner Shrine. Note the eternal flame in the forecourt. King's Domain is Stop 12 on the route 15 tram traveling south along St. Kilda Road.

In Fitzroy Gardens, off Wellington Parade, is **Cook's Cottage** (☎ **03/9419 4677**), which was moved to Melbourne from Great Ayton, in Yorkshire, England, in 1934 to mark Victoria's centenary. It's claimed (with some debate) that Captain Cook lived here between his long voyages. Inside, it's spartan and cramped, not unlike a ship's cabin. Admission is A$3 (U.S.$1.95) for adults, A$1.50 (U.S.98¢) for children 5 to 15, and A$7.50 (U.S.$4.88) for families of up to six. It's open daily from 9am to 5pm. Also east of the central business district are the Treasury Gardens. Look out for the memorial to John F. Kennedy near the lake. Treasury Gardens and Fitzroy Gardens can be reached on Tram 75 which travels east along Flinders Street. Get off at Stop 14 for Treasury Gardens and Stop 14A for Fitzroy Gardens.

6 Enjoying the Great Outdoors or Catching an Aussie Rules Football Match

OUTDOOR ACTIVITIES

BALLOONING   Melbourne by Balloon, Balloon Sunrise Office, 41 Dover St., Richmond (☎ **03/9427 7596;** fax 03/9427 7597), offers flights over the city plus a champagne breakfast after you land. Dawn flights cost A$225 (U.S.$146.25) for adults, and A$155 (U.S.$100.75) for children under 12 (but if they're under 4 feet tall they won't be able to see over the basket). Advance reservations are essential.

BIKING   Extensive bicycle paths wind through the city and suburbs. For details on the 20 most popular routes, pick up a copy of **Melbourne Bike Tours,** published by Bicycle Victoria (☎ **03/9328 3000;** fax 03/9328 2288; www.bv.com.au), available at most bookshops. Bicycle Victoria also runs several major cycling tours throughout the state every year.

Bike Now, 320 Toorak Rd., South Yarra (☎ **03/9826 6870**), rents bicycles for A$15 (U.S.$9.75) for 2 hours, A$20 (U.S.$13) for 4 hours, A$30 (U.S.$19.50) for a full day, and A$70 (U.S.$45.50) for a week. The shop is open weekdays from 9am to 7pm, Saturday from 9am to 5pm, and Sunday from 11am to 5pm. Take tram 8 to Toorak Road.

You can also rent a bike from **Hire a Bike** at St. Kilda Pier (☎ **03/9531 7403,** Non-Australians must show their passports.

GOLF One of the best public golf courses in Australia is **Yarra Bend,** Yarra Bend Road, Fairfield (☎ **03/9481 3729**). Greens fees are about A$15 (U.S.$9.75), and club rental is A$10 (U.S.$6.50) more for a half set and A$25 (U.S.$16.25) for a full set.

The **Royal Melbourne Golf Club,** in the suburb of Black Rock, 24km (15 miles) from the city center, is rated as one of the world's 10 best golf courses. It's open to members only, but if you belong to a topnotch golf club at home, you might be able to wheedle your way in.

For more information on golf in Victoria, contact the **Victorian Golf Association,** 15 Bardolph St., Burwood (☎ **03/9889 6731**).

IN-LINE SKATING The promenade in St. Kilda is a popular place to strap on a pair of skates. You can rent them at **Rock'n'n'Roll'n,** 11a Fitzroy St., St. Kilda (☎ **03/ 9525 3434**). The first hour is A$8 (U.S.$5.20). Successive hours are less expensive.

TENNIS The venue for the Australian Open, is the **Melbourne Park National Tennis Centre,** on Batman Avenue (☎ **03/9286 1244;** www.melbournepark.com. au). When tournaments are not scheduled, its 22 outdoor courts and 4 indoor courts are open to the public. You can rent courts Monday to Friday from 7am to 11pm, and Saturday and Sunday from 9am to 6pm. Charges range from A$14 (U.S.$9.10) to $30 (U.S.$19.50) per hour, depending on the court and time of day (outdoor courts are cheapest). Show courts 1, 2, and 3 are also for hire at the same prices. Racquets are also available for A$3 (U.S.$1.95).

SPECTATOR SPORTS

CAR RACING The annual **Australian Formula One Grand Prix** takes place in early March. Call Ticketmaster (☎ **13 61 22** in Australia), or the Grand Prix Hotline (☎ **13 16 41** in Australia, or 03/9258 7100) for information. Also check out the Grand Prix's website at www.grandprix.com.au.

CRICKET From October to March, cricket's the name of the game in Melbourne. The **Melbourne Cricket Ground (MCG),** Brunton Avenue, Yarra Park, Jolimont (☎ **03/9657 8879**), once the main stadium for the 1956 Melbourne Olympic Games, is perhaps Australia's most hallowed cricket field. The stadium can accommodate 97,500 people. For the uninitiated, "one day" games are the ones to look out for; "Test" games take several days to complete. Buy tickets at the gate or in advance from **TicketMaster** (☎ **13 61 22** in Australia; www.ticketmaster.com.au).

Tours of the MCG and its museum leave every half hour daily from 10am to 3pm. The Australian Gallery of Sport and the Olympic Museum are also at the MCG. The Olympic Museum traces the development of the modern Olympics with individual display sections for each city.

FOOTBALL Melbourne's number one sport is **Australian Rules Football**—or simply, "the footy"—a skillful, but often violent, game the likes of which you've never seen (unless you have ESPN). Melbourne sports ten of the 16 Australian Football League (AFL) teams, with the others coming from Adelaide, Perth, Sydney and Brisbane. The season starts the third weekend in March and ends with the Grand Final on the last Saturday in September. The most accessible grounds are at The Melbourne Cricket Ground (MCG)—take tram 75 along Wellington Parade, and the Optus Oval at Carlton (tram 19 from Elizabeth Street). Tickets cost around A$12 (U.S.$7.80) per person, or A$30 (U.S.$19.50) for a family of four. For game information, call **AFL Headquarters** at ☎ **03/9643 1999.** Buy tickets at TicketMaster (☎ **13 61 22** in Australia; www.ticketmaster.com.au).

HORSE RACING   The Melbourne Cup, run on the first Tuesday in November, has been fought for by the best of Australia's thoroughbreds (and a few from overseas) since 1861. Melbourne society puts on a show when they all dress up for the occasion, and it seems that the entire nation stops in its tracks to at least tune in on TV.

The city has four race tracks: **Flemington** (which holds the Melbourne Cup), on Epson Road in Flemington (☎ **03/9371 7171**); **Moonee Valley,** on McPherson Street in Mooney Ponds (☎ **03/9373 2222**); **Caulfield,** on Station Street in Caulfield (☎ **03/9257 7200**); and **Sandown,** on Racecourse Drive in Springvale (☎ **03/9518 1300**). If you're staying in the city center, Flemington and Moonee Valley tracks are the easiest to get to. Take tram 57 from Flinders Street to reach the Flemington race-track, and catch tram 59 from Elizabeth Street to travel to Moonee Valley.

TENNIS   The Australian Open, one of the world's four Grand Slam events, is played during the last two weeks of January every year at the Melbourne Park National Tennis Center, on Batman Avenue (☎ **03/9286 1234**). Tickets for the Australian Open go on sale in mid-October and are available through Ticketek (☎ **03/9299 9079**) and also on the Open's website, www.ausopen.org. Guided tours of the center are offered from April to October, Wednesday to Friday, when events aren't scheduled. Tours cost A$5 (U.S.$3.25) for adults and A$2.50 (U.S.$1.63) for children. To get there, take a train from the Flinders Street Station to Richmond Station and catch the special Tennis Center tram from there.

7 Shopping

Ask almost any Melbournite to help you plan your time in the city, and they'll tell you to shop 'til you drop. All of Australia regards Melbourne as a shopping mecca—it's got everything, from famous fashion houses to major department stores and unusual souvenir shops. If you're coming from Sydney, I say, save your money until you get to Melbourne, and then indulge!

Start at the magnificent city arcades, such as the **Block Arcade** (running between Collins and Little Collins streets), which has more than 30 shops, including the historic Hopetoun Tea Rooms (see "Dining," above), and the **Royal Arcade** (stretching from Little Collins Street to the Bourke Street Mall). Then hit the courts and lanes around Swanston Street and the huge **Melbourne Central** shopping complex between Latrobe and Lonsdale streets.

Next, fan out across the city, taking in **Chapel Street** in South Yarra, for its Australian fashions; and **The Jam Factory,** 500 Chapel St., South Yarra (☎ **03/9826 0537;** www.jamfactory.com.au), which is a series of buildings with a range of shops and food outlets, including a branch of the U.S.-based Borders Books, as well as 16 cinema screens. Get there on tram no. 8, or no. 72 from Swanston Street.

There's also **Toorak Road** in Toorak, for Gucci and other high-fashion names; Bridge Road in Richmond for budget fashions; **Lygon Street** in Carlton for Italian fashion, footwear, and accessories; and **Brunswick Street** in Fitzroy for a more alternative scene.

Serious shoppers might like to contact **Shopping Spree Tours** (☎ **03/9596 6600**), a company that takes you to all those exclusive and alternative shopping venues, manufacturers, and importers you wouldn't be likely to find by yourself. Tours depart Monday to Saturday at 8:30am and cost A$60 (U.S.$39) per person including lunch and a visit to the Rialto Observation Deck.

MELBOURNE SHOPPING FROM A TO Z
ABORIGINAL CRAFTS

The Aboriginal Gallery of the Dreaming. 73–77 Bourke St., City. ☎ **03/9650 3277.**

This place stocks an extensive range of acrylic dot paintings and represents more than 120 artists. Boomerangs, didgeridoos, pottery, jewelry, bark paintings, prints, books, and music are also available.

Aboriginal Handcrafts. Mezzanine floor, 130 Little Collins St. ☎ **03/9650 4717.**

Didgeridoos, bark paintings, boomerangs, and so forth are sold here, with the profits going to Aboriginal colleges.

CRAFTS

An interesting Art & Crafts Market, is held on The Esplanade in St. Kilda on Sunday from 9am to 4pm. Take tram 16 from Swanston Street or no. 96 from Bourke Street.

The Australian Geographic Shop. Shop 130, Melbourne Central, 300 Londsdale St. ☎ **03/9639 2478.**

Head here for high quality Australiana, including crafts, books, and various gadgets.

DEPARTMENT STORES

Daimaru. In the Melbourne Central complex. ☎ **03/9660 6666.**

With 6 floors of merchandise, including Asian foodstuffs and top-label fashions, Daimaru is giving more established department stores a run for shoppers' money.

David Jones. 310 Bourke St. Mall, City. ☎ **03/9643 2222.**

Like Myer, its direct competition, David Jones (or DJ's as it's affectionately known) also spans 2 blocks and offers similar goods.

Myer. 314 Bourke St. Mall, City. ☎ **03/9661 1111.**

The grand dame of Melbourne's department stores has 12 floors of household goods, perfume, jewelry, and fashions stretching over 2 blocks. (It claims to be the fifth largest store in the world.) There's a good food section on the ground floor offering, among other things, good sushi.

FASHION

Of course, you can always head to one of the major department stores (see above) if you're looking for fashions. High fashion boutiques also line the eastern stretch of Collins Street between the Grand Hyatt and the Hotel Sofitel, and Chapel Street in South Yarra.

In addition, many thousands of retail shops and factory outlets are dotted around the city, many of them concentrated on Bridge Road near Punt Road and Swan Street near Church Street in Richmond. You'll be able to find designer clothes, many just last season's fashions, at a fraction of the original price.

Country Road. 252 Toorak Rd., and other sites, including Chapel St., South Yarra. ☎ **1800/801 911** in Australia or 03/9824 0133.

County Road is one of Australia's best-known names for men's and women's fashion. The cool, classic looks don't come cheap, but the quality is worth it. County Road also sells designer cooking equipment and house wares.

Mortisha's. Shop 8–10, Royal Arcade, City. ☎ **03/9654 1586.**

The Chocolate Tour

Love chocolate? Then go for the **Chocolate Indulgence Walk** by calling ☎ **03/ 9815 1228** and/or the **Chocolates & Other Desserts Walk** (☎ **0412/158 017**). The former takes you on a tasting tour of Cadbury's, Myer, New Zealand Natural Ice Creamery, Chocolate Box, and Darrell Lea, and finishes off over chocolate cake at a cafe. This 2-hour tour leaves every Saturday at 12:30pm and costs A$22 (U.S.$14.30) for adults (children under 6 are free). The latter includes sampling plenty of ice cream and chocolates as you tour kitchens and talk to chefs. The tour finishes with tea at the Grand Hyatt. This tour leaves every Saturday at 2:30pm and also costs A$22 (U.S.$14.30). A third tour has been added, the **Coffee and Café Walk,** during which you try coffee and pastries at some of Melbourne's grooviest cafes. This tour also costs A$22 (U.S.$14.30). Bookings are essential.

Looking for something to wear to your next Goth party? Then don't miss this satin-lined, coffin-like store selling everything from vampy velvet dresses to original bridal wear. You can also find some very unusual jewelry and accessories to complete your Addams Family look.

Paddington Coat Factory. 461–463 Chapel St., South Yarra. ☎ **03/9827 4004.**

Exquisite, high-fashion clothes made by young Australian designers—such as Andrea Yasmin, Susie Mooratoff, and Lara Agnew—go for between A$39 and A$500 (U.S.$25.35–$325) at this Melbourne sister store of the one in Sydney.

Overseas Designer Warehouse. 18 Ellis St., South Yarra (off Chapel St., between Toorak and Commercial rds.). ☎ **03/9824 0399.**

This place sells end-of-run and last season's high fashions. The stuff is still pretty expensive, but you can find a few bargains if you really search.

R.M. Williams. In the Central Melbourne complex. ☎ **03/9663 7126.**

Head here for genuine Australian gear: great boots, Driza-bone coats, and Akubra hats.

Saba. 132 Bourke St., City. ☎ **03/9654 6176.**

Australian designer Joseph Saba has several very vogue, very expensive boutiques for men and women in Melbourne, including one for each sex on Chapel Street (nos. 538 and 548) in South Yarra. This store caters to both men and women.

Sam Bear. 225 Russell St., City. ☎ **03/9663 2191.**

Sam Bear is another good bet for Outback-style fashions: Driza-bone coats, Akubra bush hats, R.M. Williams boots and clothing, and Blundstone boots (my favorite). They also sell a solid range of camping equipment.

Surf, Dive 'N Ski Australia. The Jam Factory, Chapel St., South Yarra. ☎ **03/9826 4071.**

As well as surfboards, boogie boards, and sunglasses, this store stocks a wide range of hip and happening beach wear—all at reasonable prices. All the big names in Australian surf wear can be found here, including Ripcurl, Quicksilver, and Billabong.

Vegan Wares. 78 Smith St., Collingwood. ☎ **03/9417 0230.**

Instead of leather, Vegan Wares uses microfiber to create tough, stylish shoes, hand-bags, and belts. It's not just for vegetarians; carnivores enjoy browsing here, too.

FOODSTUFFS

Haigh's Chocolates. 26 Collins St., ☎ **03/9650 2114**, and Shop 26, the Block Arcade, 282 Collins St., ☎ **03/9654 7673.**

Indulge in some 50 manifestations of Australia's best chocolate, from milk to dark, fruit flavored, and shaped. I recommend the Sparkling Shiraz truffle for a serious treat.

Suga-Melbourne Candy Kitchen. Shop 20, Royal Arcade, City. ☎ **03/9663 5654.**

If you have a sweet tooth, you're likely to spend a fortune at this traditional little candy shop that makes its goodies right before your very eyes. Rock candy is a specialty, and you can get your name (or the name of someone back home) spelled out in its center.

JEWELRY

Altman & Cherny. 120 Exhibition St., at the corner of Little Collins St. ☎ **03/9650 9685.**

Even if you're not in the market to buy, it's worth coming here to check out "Olympic Australia," the largest precious gem opal in the world. It was found in Coober Pedy in South Australia in 1956 and is valued at U.S.$1.6 million. The store offers tax-free shopping for tourists armed with a passport and international airline ticket.

Dinosaur Designs. 562 Chapel St., South Yarra. ☎ **03/9827 2600.**

Dinosaur Designs is taking the jewelry design world by storm with its range of very artistic jewelry made out of resin. The shop has modern housewares as well. None of it's cheap, but the odd item won't break the bank.

Portobello Lane of South Yarra. 405 Chapel St., South Yarra. ☎ **03/9827 5708.**

Proprietor Robyn Meate specializes in locally produced and imported sterling silver jewelry with lots of beads and glass. Some of the designs are quite intricate. Pieces cost from A$40 to $200 (U.S.$26–$130).

8 Melbourne After Dark

Melbourne can be an exciting place once the sun has set. The pubs here are far better than in Sydney, though they are definitely split between the very trendy and the very down to earth. Friday and Saturday nights will see most pubs packed to the rafters, and at lunchtimes those that serve food are pretty popular, too. To find out what's hot and happening, check the entertainment guide included in *The Age* each Friday.

THE PERFORMING ARTS

Melbourne is the most dynamic city in Australia for the performing arts. Its theaters offer the whole gamut from offbeat independent productions to large-scale Broadway-style musicals. The city also hosts prestigious festivals, with the annual **Melbourne Fringe Festival** (held the first 3 weeks in October) and the annual **Melbourne International Comedy Festival** (from the end of March to roughly the end of April) attracting the best of Australian and international talent. If you are in town during these times you'll be well advised to pick up a few tickets (hotel rooms might also be more difficult to find, as people arrive from all over Australia and beyond).

The Melbourne International Comedy Festival sees venues all over the city putting on performances, while the Fringe Festival sees the streets, pubs, theatres and restaurants playing host to everyone from jugglers and fire eaters to musicians and independent productions covering all art forms. For more information check their websites at www.melbournefringe.org.au and www.comedyfestival.com.au.

Another good time to plan your visit is during the annual **Melbourne International Film Festival** (from mid-July to the end of the first week in August), when new releases, shorts and avant garde movies are shown at varying venues around the city. Look up the schedules on the net at www.melbournefilmfestival.com.au.

For information on upcoming theatre productions and reviews check out www.stageleft.com.au.

The best place to buy tickets over the net for everything from theatre to major sporting events, as well as obtain details on schedules, is via **TicketMaster** (www.ticket master.com.au). Otherwise contact them on ☎ **1800/062 849** or 13 28 849 in Australia, or 613 9299 9079 (international number).

THE HEART OF MELBOURNE'S CULTURAL LIFE

Victorian Arts Centre. 100 St. Kilda Rd. ☎ **03/9281 8000,** or 13 61 66 for ticket purchase. www.artscentre.net.au. Tickets for State Theatre A$40–$110 (U.S.$26–$71.50); Playhouse and Fairfax A$30–$59 (U.S.$19.50–$38.35); Concert Hall A$40–$80 (U.S.$26–$52).

The towering spire atop the Theaters Building of the Victorian Arts Center, on the banks of the Yarra River, crowns the city's leading performing arts complex. Beneath it, the State Theatre, the Playhouse, and the Fairfax present performances that represent the focal point of Melbourne's cultural life.

The State Theater, seating 2,079 on three levels, can accommodate elaborate productions of opera, ballet, musicals, and more. **The Playhouse** is a smaller venue that often hosts the Melbourne Theatre Company. **The Fairfax** is more intimate still, and is often used for experimental theater or cabaret.

Adjacent to the Theaters Building is the **Melbourne Concert Hall,** home of the Melbourne Symphony Orchestra and the State Orchestra of Victoria, and often host to visiting orchestras. Many international stars have graced this stage, which is known for its excellent acoustics.

Guided 1-hour tours of the Concert Hall and theaters are offered Monday to Saturday at noon and 2:30pm and Saturday at 10:30pm and noon. They cost A$10 (U.S.$6.50) for adults, A$7.50 (U.S.$4.88) for children, and A$23 (U.S.$14.95) for families. Backstage tours on Sunday at 12:15pm cost A$13.50 (U.S.$8.78). Children under 11 are not allowed. Call ☎ **03/9281 8000** between 9:30am and 5pm for information.

HALF-PRICE TICKETS

Buy your tickets for entertainment events, including opera, dance, and drama, on the day of the performance from the **Half-Tix Kiosk** in Bourke Street Mall (☎ **03/9650 9420**). The booth is open Monday from 10am to 2pm, Tuesday to Thursday from 11am to 6pm, Friday from 11am to 6:30pm, and Saturday from 10am to 2pm. Tickets must be paid for in cash. The available shows are displayed each day on the booth door, and you can't get show information over the phone.

ADDITIONAL VENUES & THEATERS

Check *The Age* to see what productions are scheduled during your visit. Odds are that the leading shows will be produced in one of the following venues:

✪ **The Comedy Club.** Level 1, 380 Lygon St., Carlton. ☎ **03/9348 1622.** Dinner and show Fri–Sat A$40–$45 (U.S.$26–$29.25) depending on performer; show only Thurs–Sat approximately A$20 (U.S.$13).

The Comedy Club is another Melbourne institution. Come here to see local and international comedy acts, musicals, and special shows.

Comedy Theatre. 240 Exhibition St., City. ☎ **03/9209 9000.**

The Comedy Theatre, with its ornate Spanish Rococo interior, manages to feel intimate even though it seats more than 1,000 people. Plays and musicals usually fill the bill, but dance companies and comedians also appear.

The Forum Theatre. 154 Flinders St., City. ☎ **03/9299 9700.**

The Forum hosts well-known bands and international comedians. Tables and chairs are set up in cabaret-style booths, from which you can order drinks and meals from the bar.

Her Majesty's Theatre. 219 Exhibition St., City. ☎ **03/9663 3211.**

A fire destroyed the original theater here, but the current structure still retains the original facade and the art deco interior added during a 1936 renovation. Musicals, such as the Australian premier of *Chicago*, frequent the boards.

The Princess Theatre. 163 Spring St., City. ☎ **03/9299 9800.**

This huge facility hosts extravaganza productions. The theater opened its doors in 1886, and it still retains a dramatic marble staircase and ornate plaster ceilings.

The Regent Theatre. 191 Collins St., City. ☎ **03/9299 9800.**

Built in 1929, the Regent fell into disrepair, and its stage was dark for 25 years. Now, after a recent A$35 million (U.S.$22.35 million) renovation, it's been restored to its former glory. Tickets are available in the United States through ATS Tours at ☎ **800/423-2880.** The theater offers a range of dining packages.

Sydney Myer Music Bowl. King's Domain, Alexandra Ave., City. ☎ **03/9281 8360.**

This enormous outdoor entertainment center is run under the auspices of the Victorian Arts Center Trust and hosts opera, jazz, and ballet in the warmer months (and ice skating in the winter!). It underwent extensive renovations in 2000.

THE CLUB & MUSIC SCENE

Melbourne's nightclub scene is centered along King Street, though "in" places come and go month by month. It's best just to follow the crowds. Otherwise, the following options are more enduring in their appeal.

✪ **Bobby McGee's Entertainment Lounge.** In the Rydges Melbourne Hotel, 186 Exhibition St. ☎ **03/9639 0630.** Cover A$5 (U.S.$3.25) Mon and Thurs–Sat after 8pm; free for hotel guests.

If you want a fun night out, head for the restaurant section of Bobby McGee's, then hit the dance floor at the disco. The restaurant has good American-style food served by waiters in fancy dress, while the disco is open from 5pm to the wee hours (the music, a mix of the popular dance hits, starts pounding at 9pm). The disco is popular with the 22-to-35 crowd after work, while the younger arrives after 10pm. You'll see lots of business suits on Thursday and Friday nights; dress is casual but smart on other nights.

Chasers. 386 Chapel St, South Yarra. ☎ **03/9827 6615.**

One for the twenty-somethings, Chasers goes wild to techno and retro in a spacious main dance room.

Metro. 20 Bourke St, City. ☎ **03/9663 4288.**

An institution on the Melbourne clubbing scene, Metro is large and stylish and popular for its dance, pop and alternative sounds. It reopened in November 2000 after a successful revamp, and has DJs, live bands, along with video games, pool and karaoke.

Monsoon's Entertainment Studio. In the Grand Hyatt Melbourne, 123 Collins St. ☎ **03/9657 1234.** Cover A$15 (U.S.$9.75); free for hotel guests.

Dress up a bit if you want to blend in with the crowd at the upscale Monsoons. Hotel guests and well-heeled locals dance to Top 40 tunes, or check out visiting jazz or cabaret performers on Friday and Saturday nights (Thursday night is funk night). One Sunday and Wednesday every month the nightclub has special theme nights.

Revolver. 229 Chapel St, Prahan. ☎ **03/9521 5985.**

Mostly techno music, though bands play on weekends with dancing later.

WHERE TO SHARE A PINT

Something fun to do if you want a few drinks and to meet a few people is to take one of the **City Pub Walks** (☎ **03/9384 0655,** or 0412/085 661). The 2½ to 3-hour walks stop off a variety of interesting pubs and bars where you can sample the local brews (at your own expense). Tours leave from "under the clocks" at Flinders Railway Station at 6:30pm Tuesday and Thursday.

Bridie O'Reillys. 62 Little Collins St. (just off Exhibition St.). ☎ **03/9650 0840.**

Bridie O'Reillys is one of Melbourne's best Irish pubs, complete with traditional dark wood decor and good beer. The two-level pub has 19 different beers on tap (7 of them Irish). There is live Irish music every night from around 9pm. The place gets quite crowded on weekends.

The Charles Dickens Tavern. 290 Collins St., City (between Elizabeth and Swanston sts.). ☎ **03/9654 1821.**

Come here for a touch of Olde England in the heart of the city. The homey pub has two bars and a restaurant serving good pub grub (traditional roasts and pies as well as some lighter dishes).

Cricketers Bar. In the Windsor Hotel, 103 Spring St. ☎ **03/9653 0653.**

Locals come to this popular English-style pub in this five-star hotel to lift a glass surrounded by the relics of Australia's summer passion. Glass cases are packed full of cricket bats, pads, and stumps, whereas the plush green carpets and solid mahogany woodwork give the place a touch of class.

The Esplanade Hotel. 11 Upper Esplanande, St Kilda. ☎ **9534 0211.**

Long established as a pub-rock and serious drinking venue, this fun place offers bands most nights—free in the front bar, and with a small cover charge out back.

The Mitre Tavern. 5 Bank Place (between Queen and William sts. and Collins and Little Collins sts.). ☎ **03/9670 5644.**

This place is almost as good as a traditional English pub—if they'd only put some good carpets on the floor. Still, it's atmospheric and centrally located. The outdoor courtyard is perfect for lunch on a sunny day.

The Night Cat. 141 Johnston St, Fitzroy. ☎ **03/9417 0090.**

Anyone for cocktails?

For a touch of sophistication and spectacular views, you can drop into the cocktail bar on the 35th floor of the **Hotel Sofitel,** at 25 Collins St. (☎ **03/9653 0000**). Otherwise, the **Windsor Hotel,** at 103 Spring St. (☎ **03/9653 0653**) offers drinks and cocktails in an atmosphere of Old World charm.

A stylish place offering jazz or lounge music most nights, the Night Cat stays open late but gets pretty crowded, so go early to get a table.

The Prince St. Kilda. 29 Fitzroy St., St. Kilda. ☎ **03/9536 1111.**

This pub is a legend among the locals. Though it was recently refurbished, it has kept its rough-at-the-edges appearance. Bands play most nights, some of them big names.

The Punters Club. 376 Brunswick St, Fitzroy. ☎ **03/9417 3006.**

There are plenty of pubs on Brunswick Street to choose from, but if you're into music and young crowds you'll probably end up at this grungy bar along with everyone else. With its nicotine-stained ceilings, dingy interior and bar stools it's nothing special to look at, but has a good atmosphere, and a back section which often features live up-and-coming bands for a cover charge of around $A10 (U.S.$6.50).

Young & Jacksons. At the corner of Flinders and Swanston sts. ☎ **03/9650 3884.**

You probably won't think much of the rough-and-tumble downstairs here, but you'll want to head upstairs, anyway, to get a peek at the naked *Chloe*. The famous painting was brought to Melbourne for the Great Exhibition in 1880. The pub, which was built in 1853 and started selling beer in 1861, has a few years on Chloe, who was painted in Paris in 1875. She has a special place in the hearts of customers and has spawned hundreds of copies that reside in far-flung places worldwide.

THE CASINO

Crown Casino. Clarendon St., Southbank. ☎ **03/9292 6868.**

Australia's largest casino is a plush affair open 24 hours. You'll find all the usual roulette and blackjack tables and so on, as well as an array of poker machines. There are some 25 restaurants and 40 bars on the premises.

9 Side Trips from Melbourne

DANDENONG RANGES

40km (25 miles) E of Melbourne

Melburnites traditionally do a "day in the Dandenongs" from time to time, topping off their getaway with Devonshire tea with scones and jam at one of the many cafes en route. Up in the cool, high country you'll find native bush, famous gardens, the Dandenong Ranges National Park, historic attractions such as the Puffing Billy vintage steam train, and plenty of restaurants and cozy B&Bs. **The Dandenong Ranges National Park** is one of the state's oldest, having been set aside in 1882 to protect its Mountain Ash forests and lush tree-fern gullies.

Auswalk, P.O. Box 516, Jindabyne, NSW 2627 (☎ **02/6457 2220;** fax 02/6457 2206; monica@auswalk.com.au) offers a 4-day/3-night, self-guided tour of the Dandenongs for two or more people, including accommodations, most meals, a ride on the Puffing Billy steam train (see below), national park entrance fees, vehicle transfers, and an itinerary and maps. The tour costs around A$590 (U.S.$383.50) per person, but could be less, depending on the season.

Parkwood Personalised Tours (☎ **03 5334 2428;** www.oztour.com; info@oztour.com) run personalized day- and multi-day tours of the Yarra Valley as well as other places in Victoria, and the Great Ocean Road, staying at quaint B&B guest houses or boutique hotels, from $60 (U.S.$39) per hour.

GETTING THERE To get to the area, take the **Burwood Highway** from Melbourne, then the **Mt. Dandenong Tourist Road,** which starts at Upper Ferntree

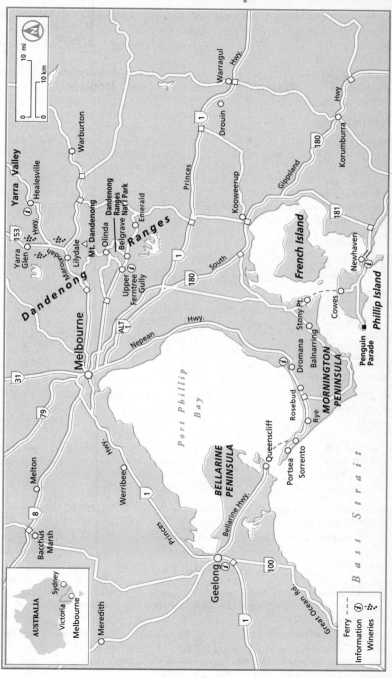

Warragul

Hwy.

Hwy.

Drouin

Princes

180

Korumburra

Gippsland

181

Kooweerup

Newhaven

French Island

Phillip Island

Warburton

Healesville

Yarra Valley

Emerald

Cowes

Olinda

Dandenong Ranges

Belgrave Nat'l Park

South

Penguin Parade

Phillip Island

Mt. Dandenong

Lilydale

Stony Pt.

HWY.

153

Yarra Glen

Maroondah

Dandenong Ranges

Upper Ferntree Gully

180

Dromana

Balnarring

ALT 1

Nepean

Hwy.

MORNINGTON PENINSULA

Melbourne

Rosebud

Rye

31

Port Phillip Bay

Queenscliff

79

BELLARINE PENINSULA

Portsea

Sorrento

Melton

Hwy.

B a s s   S t r a i t

8

Werribee

1

Bellarine Hwy.

Bacchus Marsh

Princes

Geelong

100

Great Ocean Rd.

AUSTRALIA

Sydney

Victoria

Melbourne

Meredith

1

Ferry

Information

Wineries

Gully and then winds its way through the villages of Sassafras, Olinda, Mount Dandenong, and Kalorama to Montrose. If you take a turnoff to Sherbrook, or extend your journey into a loop taking in Seville, Woori Yallock, Emerald, and Belgrave you'll see a fair slice of the local scenery.

VISITOR INFORMATION The Dandenong Ranges & Knox Visitor Information Center, 1211 Burwood Hwy., Upper Ferntree Gully, VIC 3156 (☎ **1800/645 505** in Australia, or 03/9758 7522; fax 03/9758 7533) is open daily from 9am to 5pm.

NATURE WALKS

Most people come here to get out of the city for a pleasant bushwalk (hike), so in that way it's the equivalent of Sydney's Blue Mountains. Some of the better walks include the easy 2.5-kilometer (1½-mile) stroll from the Sherbrook Picnic Ground through the forest, and the **Thousand Steps and the Kokoda Track Memorial Walk,** a challenging rain forest track from the Fern Tree Gully Picnic Ground up One Tree Hill. Along the way are plaques commemorating Australian troops who fought and died in Papua New Guinea in World War II.

FOR GARDENING BUFFS

National Rhododendron Gardens. The Georgian Rd., Olinda. ☎ **03/9751 1980.** Admission Sept–Nov A$6.50 (U.S.$4.23) adults, A$2 (U.S.$1.30) children 12–16, A$15 (U.S.$ 9.75) family of 5; Dec–Aug A$5 (U.S.$3.25) adults, A$2 (U.S.$1.30) children, A$12 (U.S.$7.80) family. Closed Christmas Day. Train to Croydon and then bus no. 688 to the gardens.

From September to November, thousands of rhododendrons and azaleas burst into bloom in these magnificent gardens. There are 103 lovely acres in all, with a 3-kilometer (2-mile) walking path leading past flowering exotics and native trees as well as great vistas over the Yarra Valley. A tearoom is open every day during spring and on weekends at other times. Visitors flock here in summer for the glorious walks, and again in autumn when the leaves are turning.

William Ricketts Sanctuary. Mt. Dandenong Tourist Rd., Mt. Dandenong. ☎ **03/9751 1300.** Admission A$5.60 (U.S.$3.70) adults, A$2.20 (U.S.$1.43) children 10–16, A$13.50 (U.S.$8.78) families of 5. Daily 10am–4:30pm. Closed Christmas. Train to Croydon then bus no. 688 to the sanctuary.

This wonderful garden, set in a forest of mountain ash, features clay figures representing the Aboriginal Dreamtime. The sculptures were created over the life of sculptor William Ricketts, who died in 1993 at the age of 94. The garden encompasses fern gullies and waterfalls over 33 acres, though the sculptures are on just 2 acres.

Bonsai Farm. Mt. Dandenong Tourist Rd., Mt. Dandenong. ☎ **03/9751 1150.** Free admission. Wed–Sun 11am–5pm. Transportation: See William Ricketts Sanctuary above.

If you don't like to crane your neck when looking at trees, then visit this large display of petite bonsais. Some of them are many decades old and cost a pretty penny.

Tesselaar's Bulbs and Flowers. 357 Monbulk Rd., Silvan. ☎ **03/9737 9305.** Admission during tulip festival, A$9.50 (U.S.$6.18) for adults, children under 16 free with adult; free for everyone rest of the year. During tulip festival (approx. Sept 12–Oct 11) daily 10am–5pm; rest of year Mon–Fri 8am–4:30pm, Sat–Sun 1–5pm. Take the train to Lilydale and then bus no. 679.

There are literally tens of thousands of flowers on display here, all putting on a flamboyantly colorful show in the spring (September and October). Expect to see a dazzling variety of tulips, daffodils, rhododendrons, azaleas, fuschias, and ranunculi. Bulbs are on sale at discount prices at other times.

FOR TRAIN BUFFS

Puffing Billy Railway. Belgrave Station, Belgrave. ☎ **03/9754 6800** for 24-hr. recorded information. www.puffingbilly.com.au. Admission A$18 (U.S.$11.70) adults, A$10 (U.S.$6.50) children 4–16, A$51 (U.S.$33.15) families of 5. Operates daily except Christmas. Train from Flinders Street Station in Melbourne to Belgrave; the Puffing Billy station is a short walk away.

For 101 years, the Puffing Billy steam railway has been chugging over a 13-kilometer (8-mile) track from Belgrave to Emerald Lake. Passengers take trips on open carriages and are treated to lovely views as the train passes through forests and fern gullies and over a National Trust-classified wooden trestle bridge. Trips take around an hour each way. Trains leave at 10:30am, 11:15am, noon, and at 2:30pm on weekdays; and at 10:30am, 11:45pm, 1:30pm, and 3:15pm on Saturday and Sunday. A further stretch of track to Gembrook was opened in 1998. Daily trips to Gembrook take an extra 45 minutes and cost A$25 (U.S.$16.25) for adults, A$14 ($9.10) for children, and A$72 (U.S.$46.80) for families. Night trains also run on occasional Saturday nights.

WHERE TO DINE

Churinga Café. 1381 Mt. Dandenong Tourist Rd., Mt. Dandenong. ☎ **03/9751 1242.** Main course A$12.95–$13.95 (U.S.$8.42–$9.07). AE, BC, DC, MC, V. Sat–Wed 10:30am–4:30pm. CAFE.

This is a nice place for a quick lunch or morning or afternoon tea. It has nice gardens and is just across from the William Ricketts Sanctuary. You can get everything here from curries to traditional British fare. Devonshire tea costs A$6 (U.S.$3.90).

Wild Oak Café. 232 Ridge Rd., Mt. Dandenong. ☎ **03/9751 2033.** Main courses A$16–$19 (U.S.$10.40–$12.35). BC, DC, MC, V. Daily 10am–10pm. MODERN AUSTRALIAN.

For good home cooking, you can't beat this cozy cafe. The food includes the likes of char-grilled steak, smoked Atlantic salmon risotto, Linguini with prawns, and Cajun chicken. The restaurant has a few vegetarian selections and a roaring log fire in winter.

YARRA VALLEY

61km (38 miles) E of Melbourne

The Yarra Valley is a well-known winegrowing region just east of Melbourne. It's dotted with villages, historic houses, gardens, craft shops, antique centers, and restaurants, as well as dozens of wineries. There are some good bushwalks around here and the Healesville Sanctuary, one of the best places in Australia to see native animals.

ESSENTIALS

GETTING THERE   **McKenzie's Bus Lines** (☎ **03/9853 6264**) operates a bus service from Lilydale Railway Station to Healesville (catch a train from Melbourne's Spencer Street Station to Lilyvale; the trip takes about an hour). Buses connect with trains approximately 12 times a day; call for exact connection times.

If you're driving, pick up a detailed map of the area from the **Royal Automotive Club of Victoria** (☎ **03/9790 3333**) in Melbourne. Maps here are free if you're a member of an auto club in your home country, but remember to bring along your membership card. Alternatively, you can pick up a map at the tourist office. Take the Maroondah Highway from Melbourne to Lilydale and on to Healesville. The trip takes around an hour and 15 minutes.

VISITOR INFORMATION   Pick up details on what to see and where to stay at the **Yarra Valley Visitor Information Center,** Old Court House, Harker Street, Healesville (☎ **03/5962 2600;** fax 03/5962 2040). It's open daily from 9am to 5pm.

EXPLORING THE VALLEY

There are three principal roads in the valley: the Melba Highway, Maroondah Highway, and Myers Creek Road, which together form a triangle. Within the triangle are three smaller roads, the Healesville Yarra Glen Road, Old Healesville Road, and Chum Creek Road, which all access wineries. Most people start their tour of the Yarra Valley from Lilydale and take in several cellar door tastings at vineyards along the route.

Balloon Aloft (☎ **1800/028 568** in Australia) offers dawn balloon rides over the wineries for A$195 (U.S.$126.75) for adults, A$130 (U.S.$84.50) for children over 8. The flight includes a champagne breakfast. **Peregrine Adventures** (☎ **03/9662 2800;** www.peregrine.net.au/home_peregrine.asp; travelcentre@peregrine.net.au) also has balloon flights over the valley, with free pickup for A$195 (U.S.$126.75) on weekends and A$175 (U.S.$113.75) on weekdays. Peregrine can also arrange accommodations.

✪ **Healesville Sanctuary.** Badger Creek Rd., Healesville. ☎ **03/5957 2800.** Fax 03/5957 2870. www.zoo.org.au. Admission A$16.40 (U.S.$10.66) adults, A$12.20 (U.S.$7.93) concession, A$8.10 (U.S.$5.27) children, A$44.30 (U.S.$28.80) family, up to 4 kids. Daily 9am–5pm. Train from Flinders Street Station to Lilydale, then bus no. 685 to the sanctuary.

Forget about seeing animals in cages—this preserve is a great place to spot native animals in almost natural surroundings. You can see wedge-tailed eagles, dingoes, koalas, wombats, reptiles, and more while strolling through the peppermint-scented gum forest, which rings with the chiming of bellbirds. Sir Colin McKenzie, who set it up as a center to preserve endangered species and educate the public, started the sanctuary in 1921. There's a gift shop, a cafe serving light meals, and picnic grounds.

NICE PLACES TO STAY & DINE

✪ **Melba Lodge.** 939 Melba Highway, Yarra Glen, VIC 3775. ☎ **03/9730 1511.** Fax 03/9730 1566. www.melbalodge.citysearch.com.au. melba@onthe.net.au. 6 units. A/C TV. A$150 (U.S.$97.50) Queen room; A$180 (U.S.$117) King room. Rates include cooked breakfast. AE, BC, DC, MC, V. Transportation: See the Healesville Sanctuary above.

These stylish, modern accommodations opened in Yarra Glen, in the heart of the Yarra Valley wine region, in early 1999. Of the six luxurious bedrooms, four have queen-size beds and two have king-size beds and a spa; all have private bathrooms. There's a comfortable lounge with an open fire. The lodge is only a few minutes' walk from historic Yarra Glen, which has antique shops and a craft market. There are plenty of restaurants and wineries around, and it's a short drive to the Healesville Sanctuary.

Sanctuary House Motel Healesville. Badger Creek Rd., (P.O. Box 162 Healesville, VIC 3777). ☎ **03/5962 5148.** Fax 03/5962 5392. 12 units. A/C TV. A$70–A$75 (U.S.$45.50–48.75) double. Extra adult A$20 (U.S.$13); extra child A$10 (U.S.$6.50). AE, BC, DC, MC, V. Transportation: See the Healesville Sanctuary above.

This place is very handy for visiting the sanctuary and even better if you want to relax and sample some good Yarra Valley wine. Just 400 meters (440 yds.) from the Healesville Sanctuary, Sanctuary House is set in some 10 acres of beautiful bushland. The rooms are motel-style and come with all the essentials. On the grounds are a pool, a Jacuzzi, a sauna, a half-court tennis court, a game room, a phone booth, and a casual restaurant serving three-course homecooked meals.

✪ PHILLIP ISLAND: PENGUINS ON PARADE

139km (86 miles) S of Melbourne

Phillip Island's penguin parade, which you can see every evening at dusk, is one of Australia's most popular attractions. There are less crowded places in Australia where you can watch penguins (Kangaroo Island in South Australia for one), but at least the little guys and their nesting holes are protected from the throngs of curious tourists by guides and boardwalks. Nevertheless, the commercialism of the Penguin Parade puts a lot of people off—busloads of tourists squashed into a sort of amphitheatre is hardly being at one with nature. Phillip Island also offers nice beaches, good bushwalking, and a seagull rookery. If you have the time, you could spend at least two days here.

ESSENTIALS

GETTING THERE   Most visitors come to Phillip Island on a day trip from Melbourne and arrive in time for the Penguin Parade and dinner. Several tour companies run daytrips. Among them are **Gray Line** (☎ **03/9663 4455**), which operates penguin trips daily departing Melbourne at 1:30pm and returning at around 11:30pm. Tours cost A$79.50 (U.S.$51.68) for adults and A$39.75 (U.S.$25.84) for children. Gray Line also offers full-day trips including the Dandenong Ranges and a ride on the Puffing Billy Steam Train.

Down Under Day Tours (☎ **03/9650 2600**), offers a half-day tour for A$79.50 (U.S.$51.68) for adults and A$39.50 (U.S.$25.68) for children; tours depart Melbourne at 1:30pm and return at 11:30pm. It also offers a day-long trip that combines a Melbourne sightseeing tour with the penguin tour for A$106 (U.S.$68.90) for adults, and A$53 (U.S.$34.45) for children, and a half-day combined Dandenong Ranges/Phillip Island tour costing A$96 (U.S.$62.40) for adults and A$48 (U.S.$31.20) for children.

An excellent budget option is a half-day trip with **Melbourne Sightseeing** (☎ **03/9663 3388**). Tours depart Melbourne daily at 1:30pm and include visits to a cattle farm where you can hand feed kangaroos, the Koala Conservation Centre, a seal colony, as well as the Penguin Parade. The coach returns to Melbourne at 10:30pm. The trip costs A$75 (U.S.$48.75) for adults (A$49/U.S.$31.85 with a YHA card) and A$38 (U.S.$24.70) for children. For the same price, an express bus leaves Melbourne at 5:30pm (returning at 11pm) and travels directly to the Penguin Parade.

Auswalk, P.O. Box 516, Jindabyne, NSW 2627 (☎ **02/6457 2220;** fax: 02/6457 2206; monica@auswalk.com.au), offers a 4-night self-guided tour of Phillip Island for two or more people for A$760 (U.S.$494) per person. The price includes accommodations, most meals, park and entrance fees to the main places of interest, some vehicle transfers, an itinerary, and maps.

If you're driving yourself, it's an easy 2-hour trip from Melbourne along the South Gippsland and Bass Highways. A bridge connects the highway to the mainland.

V/Line trains (☎ **13 22 32** in Australia, or 03/9619 5000) run in summer from Flinders Street Station to Phillip Island via Dandenong. The trip takes 2 hours and 15 minutes and costs A$13.40 (U.S.$8.71).

VISITOR INFORMATION   The **Phillip Island Information Center,** Phillip Island Tourist Road, Newhaven (☎ **1300/366 422** in Australia or 03/5956 7447), is an attraction in itself, with interactive computer displays, relevant information, dioramas giving visitors a glimpse into the penguin's world, and a small theater. It's open daily 9am to 5pm (6pm in the summer).

EXPLORING THE AREA

Visitors approach the island from the east, passing through the town of Newhaven. Just a little past Newhaven is the Phillip Island Information Center.

The island's main town, **Cowes** (pop. 2,400), is on the far north coast. It's worth taking a stroll along its Esplanade. The Penguin Parade is on the far southwest coast.

The Penguin Parade, Vistor Centre, Koala Conservation Centre, Churchill Island and Seal Rocks Seal Life Centre all require admission fees from A$3.20 to $12.50 (U.S.$2.08–$8.13). But a **Re-discover Nature Ticket** gets you into the Penguin Parade, Koala Conservation Centre and Churchill Island for A$19 (U.S.$12.35) adults, A$9.80 (U.S.$6.37) children 4 to 16 and A$45.50 (U.S.$29.58) family; while a **Four Park Pass** (including Seal Rocks) runs A$28.80 (U.S.$18.72), A$13.50 (U.S.$8.78), and A$74 (U.S.$48.20). Ask about student and senior rates. Tickets can be purchased at the Visitor Centre or by phone ☎ **03/5951 2800** from Australia, or 613/5951 2800 from outside Australia.

The tip of the west coast of the Summerland Peninsula ends in a particularly interesting rock formation called **The Nobbies.** This strange-looking outcropping can be reached at low tide by a basalt causeway. You'll get some spectacular views of the coastline and two offshore islands from here. On the farthest of these islands is a population of up to 12,000 Australian fur seals, the largest colony in Australia (bring your binoculars). This area is also home to thousands of nesting silver gulls.

On the north coast you can explore **Rhyll Inlet,** an intertidal mangrove wetland, where you can see wading birds such as spoonbills, oystercatchers, herons, egrets, cormorants, and the rare bar-tailed godwit and the whimbrel.

Birdwatchers also love **Swan Lake,** an important breeding habitat for wetland birds.

Elsewhere, walking trails lead through heath and pink granite to **Cape Woolamai,** the island's highest point, where there are fabulous coastal views. From September to April the cape is home to thousands of short-tailed shearwaters, or "muttonbirds."

If you really want to see the island (not just the parade), consider one of the 15 tours offered by Mike Cleeland and his **Island Nature Tours,** RMB 6080, Cowes, Phillip Island, VIC 3922 (☎ **03/5956 7883**).

Phillip Island Penguin Reserve. Summerland Beach, Phillip Island. ☎ **03/5956 8300** or 613 5951 2800 outside Australia. Admission to visitor center and Penguin Parade: A$12.50 (U.S.$8.13) adults, A$6.50 (U.S.$4.23) children from 4–16, A$31.40 (U.S.$20.41) families, up to 4 children. Visitor center opens 10am; penguins arrive at sunset. Reservations for the Penguin Parade are essential in summer, and on weekends and public holidays throughout the year.

The Penguin Parade takes place every night of the year at dusk, when hundreds of Little Penguins appear at the water's edge, gather together in the shallows, and waddle up the beach toward their burrows in the dunes. They're the smallest of the world's 17 species of penguins, standing just 33 centimeters (13 in.) high, and they're the only penguins that breed on the Australian mainland. Fences and viewing stands were erected in the 1960s to protect the nesting areas. Flash photography is banned because it scares the birds. Wear a sweater or jacket, since it gets chilly after the sun goes down. A kiosk selling food opens an hour before the penguins turn up.

If you get to Phillip Island on your own and don't have your own car, the **Penguin Parade Bus** (☎ **03/5952 1042,** or 04/1736 0370) will pick you up from your accommodation in time to see the action. The round-trip price is A$19 (U.S.$12.35) for adults and A$11 (U.S.$7.15) for children, including a ticket for the Penguin Parade.

Koala Conservation Centre. At Fiveways on the Phillip Island Tourist Road, about 10km (6.2 miles) from the Newhaven bridge. ☎ **03/5956 8300.** A$5.40 (U.S.$3.51) adults, A$2.20 (U.S.$1.43) children 4–16, A$13 (U.S.$8.45) family, up to 4 kids. Daily 10am–5pm.

Koalas were introduced to Phillip Island in the 1880s and at first they thrived in the predator-free environment. However, overpopulation, the introduction of foxes and dogs, and the clearing of land for farmland, townships and roads, have taken their toll. You can still see a few koalas in the wild, but the best place to find them is at this sanctuary, set up for research and breeding. Visitors can get quite close to them, especially on the elevated boardwalk, which lets you peek into their treetop homes. For the best viewing come around 4pm, when the ordinarily sleepy koalas are on the move.

WHERE TO STAY

Penguin Hill Country House B&B. At Backbeach and Ventnor rds. (RMB 1093, Cowes, Phillip Island, VIC 3922). ☎ /fax **03/5956 8777.** 3 units. A$125 (U.S.$81.25) double. Rates include cooked breakfast. BC, MC, V. Not suitable for children.

This private home with views over sheep paddocks to Bass Strait is within walking distance of the Penguin Parade. Each room has good views and is stocked with antiques (as is much of the house) and queen-size beds. Two have an attached bathroom with shower, and the third has a private bathroom across the hall. There's a TV and a phone in the cozy lounge. The hosts can pick you up from Cowes.

Rothsaye on Lovers Walk. 2 Roy Ct., Cowes 3922. ☎ /fax **03/5952 2057.** www.rothsaye. com. rothsaye@nex.net.au. 2 suites, 1 cottage. A$125–$145 (U.S.$81.25–$94.25) suite; A$130–$150 (U.S.$84.50–$97.50) cottage. BC, MC, V. Children not allowed.

The penguins are just down the road and the beach is right on the doorstep—who could ask for anything more? The two suites here are adjuncts to the owner's home and the one-bedroom cottage is set slightly apart. All rooms are very nice and come with antiques and king-size beds. You also get a fruit basket, free fishing gear, beach chairs and umbrellas, magazines, and fresh flowers. Lovers Walk, a romantic floodlit path, leads from the doorstep to the center of Cowes. The owners also have a new beachside property nearby called Abaleigh on Lovers Walk. The apartments there come with a kitchen, BBQ and good water views. They cost A$205 (U.S.$133.25) a night.

AROUND PORT PHILLIP BAY

West of Melbourne, the **Princes Freeway** (or M1) heads toward Geelong via a bypass at Werribee. To the east of Melbourne, the **Nepean Highway** travels along the coast to the Mornington Peninsula as far as Portsea. If you have time to stay the night, you can combine the two options, heading first down to the Mornington Peninsula (see below) and then taking the car and passenger ferry from Sorrento to Queenscliff (see below).

WERRIBEE

This small country town is located 32 kilometers (20 miles) southwest of Melbourne, a 30-minute drive away along the Princes Freeway. Trains run from Melbourne to Werribee station; a taxi from the station to the zoo will cost around A$5 (U.S.$3.25).

Victoria's Open Range Zoo at Werribee. K Rd., Werribee. ☎ **03/9731 9600.** www.zoo.org.au. Admission A$16.40 (U.S.$10.66) adults, A$12.20 (U.S.$7.93) concession, A$8.10 (U.S.$5.27) children, A$44.30 (U.S.$28.60) family. Daily 9am–5pm (the entrance gate closes at 3:30pm). Safari tours hourly 10am–4pm.

From your zebra-striped safari bus, you can almost touch the mainly African animals that wander over the plains—no cages here. This high-caliber open-air zoo is associated with the Melbourne Zoo. There is also a walkthrough section featuring African cats, including cheetahs, and monkeys. The safari bus tour takes 50 minutes.

Werribee Park Mansion. K Rd., Werribee. ☎ **13 19 63** in Australia or 03/9741 2444. Fax 03/9742 9623. Free park and picnic grounds; admission to mansion A$11 (U.S.$7.15) adults, A$6.50 (U.S.$4.23) concession, A$5.50 (U.S.$3.58) children 5–15, A$28.60 (U.S.$18.59) families. Nov–March daily 10am–5pm; Apr–Oct daily 10am–4pm. Closed Christmas.

Known as "the palace in the paddock," this 60-room Italianate mansion was built in 1877. It was quite the extravagant project in its day. In addition to touring the house, you can stroll around the grounds and have a picnic; it's surrounded by 325 acres of bushland fronting the Werribee River. You can also pre-arrange to take one of the popular carriage rides through the property. Allow one to two hours.

GEELONG

Victoria's second largest city, Geelong, lies 72 kilometers (45 miles) southwest of Melbourne. It's an industrial center, not really of note to visitors except as the home of the National Wool Museum. Geelong is a 45-minute drive from Melbourne. There's a regular train service, and the museum is a couple of blocks from the station.

You can pick up brochures and book accommodations through the **Geelong Great Ocean Road Visitor Information Center,** Stead Park, Princes Highway, Geelong (☎ **1800/620 888** in Australia, or 03/5275 5797; www.greatoceanrd.org.au). The office is open daily from 9am to 5pm.

National Wool Museum. 26 Moorabool St., Geelong. ☎ **1800/620 888** in Australia or 03/5227 0701. A$8 (U.S.$5.20) adults, A$6.50 (U.S.$4.23) concession, A$4 (U.S.$2.60) children under 16, A$22 (U.S.$14.30) families. Daily 9:30am–5pm. Closed Christmas and Good Friday.

In colonial Australia, the sheep was the lifeblood of the nation, providing food and warm wool, profits to the landlords, and jobs to shearers, stockmen, and farmhands. This fascinating museum tells the story, from how sheepdogs work to how the sheep are sheared. You'll also see an interesting collection of gadgets used to create products from wool. There is also a reconstructed shearers' hut and a 1920s mill workers' cottage, a specialty wool store, a gift shop, and a bistro. Allow up to two hours.

THE MORNINGTON PENINSULA

The Mornington Peninsula, a scenic 40-kilometer-long (25-mile-long) stretch of windswept coastline and hinterland 80 kilometers (50 miles) south of Melbourne, is one of Melbourne's favorite day-trip and weekend destinations. The coast is lined with good beaches and thick bush consisting almost entirely of tea trees (early colonists used it as a tea substitute). The **Cape Shanck Coastal Park** stretches along the peninsula's Bass Strait foreshore from Portsea to Cape Schank. It's home to gray kangaroos, bandicoots, echidnas, native rats, mice, reptiles, bats, and many forest and ocean birds. The park has many interconnecting walking tracks providing access to remote beaches.

Along the route south you could stop off at the **Morning Peninsula Regional Gallery,** 4 Vancouver St., Mornington (☎ **03/5975 4395**), to check out the work of famous Australian artists (open Tues–Sun 10am–5pm), or visit **Arthurs Seat State Park** to take a short hike or ride a chairlift to a 1000-foot summit offering glorious views over the surrounding bush. At **Sorrento,** take time out to spot pelicans on the jetty, or visit the town's many galleries.

Also on the Mornington Peninsula is Australia's oldest and most famous maze, **Ashcombe Maze & Water Gardens,** Red Hill Road, Shoreham (☎ **03/5989 8387**), which also has extensive water and woodland gardens. Get lost in a rose maze made out of 1,300 bushes, spectacular when in full bloom during the spring and summer.

There's also pleasant cafe with indoor and outdoor dining. The park is open daily from 10am to 5pm; admission is A$7 (U.S.$4.55) for adults, and A$4 (U.S.$2.60) for children.

GETTING THERE   From Melbourne, take the Mornington Peninsula Freeway to Rosebud, and then the Point Nepean Road. If you want to cross Port Phillip Bay from Sorrento to Queenscliff, take the **Queenscliff Sea Road Ferry** (☎ **03/5258 3255;** fax 03/5258 1877), which operates daily every 2 hours from 8am to 6pm (there's an 8pm ferry on Fri and Sat from mid-Sept–mid-Dec and daily mid-Dec–Easter Thursday). Ferries from Queenscliff operate from 7am to 5pm (plus a 7pm ferry on days listed above). The fare is A$32 to $34 (U.S.$20.80–$22.10) for cars depending on season, plus A$3 (U.S.$1.95) for adults, A$2 (U.S.$1.30) for children 5 to 15, and A$1 (U.S.65¢) for children 4 and under. Passenger-only fares are A$7 (U.S.$4.55) for adults, A$5 (U.S.$3.25) for children 5 to 15, and A$1 (U.S.65¢) for children under 4. The crossing takes 35 to 40 minutes.

VISITOR INFORMATION   The Peninsula Visitor Information Center, Point Nepean Road, Dromana (☎ **1800/804 009** in Australia, or 03/5987 3078), has plenty of maps and information and can also help book accommodations. It's open daily from 9am to 5pm. You can get more information on this and all the other Victorian National Parks on ☎ **13 19 63,** or from the website at www.parkweb. vic.gov.au/.

WHERE TO STAY & DINE

The Portsea Hotel. 3746 Point Nepean Rd., Portsea, Vic 3944. ☎ **03/5984 2213.** Fax 03/5984 4066. www.portseahotel.com.au. 34 units, 8 with bathroom. A$115.50 (U.S.$75.08) double without bathroom; A$143 (U.S.$92.95) double with bathroom; A$176 (U.S.$114.40) bay view suite. Rates are around 20% cheaper in winter. AE, BC, DC, MC. V.

The rooms in this typical Australian motel on the seafront are done up with country-style furnishings. The standard twin rooms are quite basic and all share bathrooms. None has a TV, but all have tea- and coffee-making facilities. En suite doubles have a double bed and TV, and an attached bathroom with shower. There's a reasonable bistro and three bars downstairs, as well as a terraced beer garden and another outdoor bar.

13

Victoria

by Marc Llewellyn

Australia's southernmost mainland state is astoundingly diverse. Within its boundaries are 35 national parks, encompassing every possible terrain, from rain forest and snowcapped mountain ranges to sunbaked Outback desert and a coast where waves crash dramatically onto rugged sandstone outcroppings.

Melbourne (see chapter 12) may be this rugged state's heart, but the mighty Murray River, which separates Victoria from New South Wales, is its lifeblood, providing irrigation for vast tracks of semi-desert land.

Most visitors to Victoria start out exploring Melbourne, and then visit a few local wineries, before heading for the gold fields around the historic city of Ballarat. Lots of them only experience a fraction of Victoria out the window of their rental car, but this wonderful and not overly touristed region is worth spending some quality time on.

Visitors with more time might make their way inland to the mountains (perhaps for skiing or bushwalking at Mt. Hotham or Falls Creek), or they seek out the wilderness of the Snowy River National Park. Others head to the Outback, to the Grampians National Park, and to Mildura through open deserts and past pink lakes and red sand dunes.

Lots of options await you, and because much of it is out in the country, you'll find prices for accommodations very affordable. Whatever itinerary you choose, you're sure to find adventure and dramatic scenery.

See "Side Trips from Melbourne" in chapter 12 for information on Phillip Island, the Mornington Peninsula, the Dandenong Ranges, and the Yarra Valley.

EXPLORING THE STATE

VISITOR INFORMATION Pick up brochures and maps at the **Victorian Visitors Information Centre** (see chapter 12), or call the **Victorian Tourism Information Service** (☎ **13 28 42**) from anywhere in Australia to talk to a consultant about your plans. The service, open daily from 8am to 6pm, will also send out brochures. If you need information along the way, look for blue road signs with a yellow information symbol.

GETTING THERE V/Line (☎ **13 61 96** in Victoria, 13 22 32 in NSW, or 03/9619 5000) runs a limited network of trains to various places in Victoria, continuing trips to most major centers with

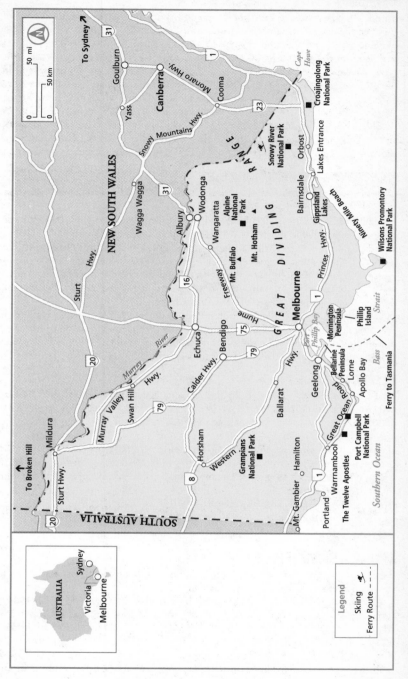

Legend

Skiing
Ferry Route ─ ─ ─

connecting buses. Several bus companies connect Melbourne with regional areas of Victoria; the biggest operators are **Greyhound Pioneer** (☎ **13 20 30** in Australia, or 03/9600 1687) and **McCafferty's** (☎ **13 14 99** in Australia or 03/9670 2533).

One of Australia's most famous train trips is aboard *The Ghan.* It leaves Melbourne every Wednesday at 10:30pm, arrives in Adelaide at 10:10am on Thursday, and in Alice Springs at 10am on Friday. (While the Melbourne—Alice service only goes once a week, there is a daily service from Melbourne to Adelaide, which can link up to the Sydney—Alice *Ghan* service.) The one-way fare to Alice Springs is A$1,029 (U.S$668.85) in first class, A$780 (U.S$507) in holiday class (also with a sleeper), and A$292 (U.S$189.80) in coach class (in a recliner chair). Contact **Great Southern Railway** (☎ **13 21 47** in Australia, or 08/8213 4592; www.gsr.com.au) for details.

1 Ballarat: Gold-Rush City

113km (70 miles) W of Melbourne

Ballarat, Victoria's largest inland city (pop. 90,000), is all about gold. In 1851, two prospectors found gold nuggets at a place known as, ironically, Poverty Point. Within a year, 20,000 people had arrived and Australia's El Dorado gold rush had begun.

In 1858, the second-largest chunk of gold discovered in Australia (the Welcome Nugget) was found, but by the early 1860s, most of the easily obtainable yellow metal was gone. Larger operators continued digging until 1918, and by then Ballarat had developed enough industry to survive without mining.

Today, you can still see the gold rush's effects in the impressive buildings, built from the miners' fortunes, lining Ballarat's streets. If you're interested in seeing another former mining town, head 1½ hours north to Bendigo, a small city filled with elaborate public buildings constructed with the gains from the gold rush.

ESSENTIALS

GETTING THERE From Melbourne, Ballarat is a 1½-hour drive via the Great Western Highway. **V/Line** (☎ **13 61 96** in Victoria, 13 22 32 in NSW, or 03/9619 5000) runs trains between the cities every day, and the trip takes less than 2 hours. The one-way fare is A$15.20 (U.S$9.88) for adults, A$7.60 (U.S$4.94) for children. Ask about family fares. A bus connects the train station with the town center.

Several sightseeing companies offer day trips from Melbourne. **Melbourne Sightseeing** (☎ **03/9663 3388**) offers one of the most affordable choices, a full-day tour that costs A$88 (U.S$57.20) for adults and A$44 (U.S$28.60) for children.

VISITOR INFORMATION The **Ballarat Visitor Information Centre** at 39 Sturt St. (at Albert Street), Ballarat, VIC 3350 (☎ **1800/648 450** in Australia or 03/5320 5741; fax 03/5332 7977; www.ballarat.com), is open daily from 9am to 5pm.

SEEING THE SIGHTS

Ballarat contains many reminders of the gold-rush era, but it all really comes to life in the colonial-era re-creation on Sovereign Hill.

✪ **Sovereign Hill Goldmining Township,** Bradshaw St. (☎ **03/5331 1944**). Admission (including mine tour and admission to Gold Museum) A$25 (U.S$16.25) adults, A$12 (U.S$7.80) children 5 to 15, A$65 (U.S$42.25) families (2 adults and up to 4 children), free for children under 5. Daily 10am to 5pm. Closed Christmas. Bus: From Ballarat, catch the Buninyong bus.

Australia's best outdoor museum transports you back to the 1850s and the heady days of the gold rush. More than 40 stone-and-wood reproduction buildings, including shops and businesses on the recreated Main Street, sit on this 60-acre former gold-mining site. There are also tent camps around the diggings on the lowest part of the site, which would have been the outskirts of town. There are lots to see and do here, so expect to spend at least 4 hours.

The Township bustles with actors in period costumes going about their daily business. In addition to seeing how miners and their families lived, visitors can pan for real gold, watch lessons in Victorian classrooms, ride in horse drawn carriages, and watch potters, blacksmiths, and tanners make their wares.

On top of Sovereign Hill are the mineshafts and their pithead equipment. The fascinating tour of a typical underground gold mine takes around 45 minutes.

The Voyage to Discovery museum has various artifacts from the gold rush, dioramas of mining scenes, and interactive computer displays. A restaurant and several cafes, coffee shops, and souvenir stores can be found around the site.

The Gold Museum. Bradshaw St. (opposite Sovereign Hill), Ballarat. ☎ **03/5337 1107.** Admission included with Sovereign Hill ticket; otherwise A$6.30 (U.S$4.10) adults, A$3.10 (U.S$2.02) children; daily 10am–5:30pm.

This interesting museum houses a large collection of gold nuggets found at Ballarat, as well as alluvial deposits, gold ornaments, and coins. There are also gallery displays relating to the history of gold mining in the area. Allow about 1 hour.

✪ Blood on the Southern Cross. At Sovereign Hill, Bradshaw St. ☎ **03/5333 5777.** Fax 03/5332 9740. Reservations required. Admission A$29 (U.S$18.85) adults, A$15 (U.S$9.75) children 5–15, A$79.50 (U.S$51.68) family. Other packages include daytime entry to Sovereign Hill: A$48.50 (U.S$31.53) for adults, A$25 (U.S$16.25) children, A$136 (U.S$88.40) families. Call for information about other packages. 2 shows nightly Mon–Sat (times vary seasonally). Closed early Aug.

This 80-minute show re-creates the Eureka Uprising, one of the most important events in Australia's history, in a breathtaking light-and-sound show that covers Sovereign Hill's 25 hectares (62 acres). Bring something warm to wear, because it can get chilly.

After gold was discovered, the government devised a system of gold licenses, charging miners a monthly fee, even if they came up empty-handed. The miners had to buy a new license every month, and corrupt goldfield police (many of whom were former convicts) instituted a vicious campaign to extract the money.

When license checks intensified in 1854, even though most of the surface gold was gone, resentment flared, and prospectors began demanding political reforms, such as the right to vote, parliamentary elections, and secret ballots.

The situation exploded when the Eureka Hotel's owner murdered a miner but was set free by the government. The hotel was burned down in revenge, and more than 20,000 prospectors joined together, burned their licenses in a huge bonfire, and built a stockade over which they raised a flag.

Troops arrived at the "Eureka Stockade" the next month, but only 150 miners remained. The stockade was attacked and in the skirmish, 24 miners were killed and 30 wounded. The uprising forced the government to act: The licenses were replaced with "miners rights" and cheaper fees, and the vote was introduced to Victoria.

Eureka Stockade Centre. Eureka St. ☎ **03/5333 1854.** Admission A$8.80 (U.S$5.72) adults, A$4.60 (U.S$2.99) children, A$24.20 (U.S$15.73) families of 6. Daily 9am–5pm. Closed Christmas and Mon except public holidays.

You can't miss this building with its huge sail, signifying the flag of the Southern Cross, which was raised above the miners' stockade. Relive the battle through multimedia displays. The Contemplation Room, where you are asked to think about Australian history while listening to a trickling water soundscape, is a bit hokey for me.

Ballarat Fine Art Gallery. 40 Lydiard St. N., Ballarat. ☎ **03/5331 5622.** Admission A$4 (U.S.$2.60) adults, A$2 (U.S.$1.30) students, A$1 (U.S.65¢) children 6–16. Daily 10:30am–5pm. Closed Good Friday and Christmas.

After you've learned the story of the Eureka uprising (see above), you may find it moving to come here and see the original Eureka flag. This provincial gallery also houses a large collection of Australian art, including works by Sydney Nolan, Fred Williams, and Russell Drysdale. Look out for Tom Roberts' *Charcoal Burners* and Phillip Fox's *Love Story.*

WHERE TO STAY

The Ansonia. 32 Lydiard St. S., Ballarat 3350. ☎ **03/5332 4678.** Fax 03/5332 4698. www.ballarat.com/ansonia.htm. ansonia@ansonia.ballarat.net.au. 20 units. TV TEL. A$130 (U.S.$84.50) double, A$145 (U.S.$94.25) executive double; A$150 (U.S.$97.50) suite; A$210 (U.S.$136.50) family room; A$210 (U.S.$136.50) apt. AE, BC, DC, MC, V. Free parking.

This boutique hotel in a restored Victorian building sports a glass atrium that runs the length of the property and is filled with plants and wicker chairs. Studio rooms are simply but comfortably furnished, and have nice polished floorboards. The executive doubles are larger and a little plusher. The two family rooms can sleep four people in two bedrooms. There is a comfortable library and sitting room, and plenty of flowers and art are scattered everywhere. Smoking is not allowed on the property.

   The restaurant acts as more of a cafe during the day and a Mediterranean-style restaurant at night. It serves up such fare as homemade pies, soups, curries, meat dishes, and a great gorgonzola soufflé on a bed of forest mushrooms.

   ✪ Ballarat Heritage Homestay. 185 Victoria St. (P.O. Box 1360, Ballarat Mail Centre, VIC 3354). ☎ **1800/813 369** in Australia, or 03/5332 8296. Fax 03/5331 3358. 5 cottages, 1 B&B unit. TV TEL (available on request). A$275–$350 (U.S.$178.75–$227.50) for 2 people for 2-night weekend stay; A$135–$160 (U.S.$87.75–$104) weekday night. Rates include breakfast. Extra adult A$30 (U.S.$19.50); extra child under 18 A$15 (U.S.$9.75). AE, BC, DC, MC, V.

If you'd enjoy staying in a historic cottage, you might want to try Ballarat Heritage Homestay. Some of these Victorian and Edwardian cottages date back to the gold-rush days. All of them are very different. Three cottages have claw-foot tubs, and one has a Jacuzzi. Generally there's a queen, a double, and two singles in each cottage.

The Sovereign Hill Lodge. Magpie St., Ballarat, VIC 3350. ☎ **03/5333 3409.** Fax 03/5333 5861. istiff@sovereignhill.austasia.net. A/C TV TEL. A$115 (U.S.$74.75) double or family room; A$126–$142 (U.S.$81.90–$92.30) heritage room. Extra person A$12.50 (U.S.$8.13). Ask about packages. AE, BC, DC, JCB, MC, V. Free parking.

The colonial-style wooden buildings adjacent to the Sovereign Hill Goldmining Township were built to resemble an 1850s Government Camp that was used to control (and tax) the mine fields. The Residence building has rooms with queen size beds and a set of single bunks, and the Offices building has heritage rooms with four-poster beds and plenty of Baltic pine furnishings, some with Jacuzzis. There are eight double rooms in the Superintendent's house, while the Barracks houses dorm rooms that sleep up to eight people (A$16/U.S.$10.40 for YHA members; A$18/U.S.$11.70 for non-members). There's a bar, 24-hour reception, and a game room on the grounds. Guests get a 10% discount off entry to Sovereign Hill.

WHERE TO DINE

Lake Pavilion Restaurant Café. Wendouree Parade (across from the Botanical Gardens). ☎ **03/5334 1811.** Main courses around A$11 (U.S$7.15). AE, BC, MC, V. Daily 9am–6pm. Bus: 15 Mon–Sat. INTERNATIONAL.

I like this restaurant across from the Botanical Gardens on the shores of Lake Wendouree. The Lake Pavilion was constructed in 1890 and still has that old-world atmosphere, with polished floorboards and high ceilings. You can eat indoors or outside, but either way you have good views across the gardens and the lake. The menu includes pizzas, focaccia sandwiches, pasta dishes, salads, steaks, and seafood. It's licensed but you can BYO wine. A kiosk adjacent to the restaurant sells cheap snacks.

Robin Hood Family Bistro. 33 Peel St. N. ☎ **03/5331 3348.** Reservations recommended Fri–Sat. Main courses A$8–$20 (U.S.$5.20–$13). AE, BC, DC, MC, V. Daily 11:30am–2pm and 5:30–8pm. BISTRO.

The Robin Hood is located in a big old pub—not exactly a place where you'd expect to find a bistro catering to healthy eating. The bistro, though, is a past winner of the Real Meal Award, handed out by the Australian Hoteliers Association and aimed at promoting healthier pub food. Everything here is made with low-fat/low-cholesterol ingredients. On the menu you'll find steak-and-kidney pie, beef curry, and several types of steak. Not healthy so far, perhaps, but there's an extensive salad bar, and all main courses come with a healthy dollop of vegetables.

2 The Great Ocean Road: One of the World's Most Scenic Drives

Geelong: 75km (46½ miles) SW of Melbourne; Torquay: 94km (58 miles) SW of Melbourne; Port Campbell National Park: 285km (177 miles) SW of Melbourne; Peterborough: 200km (160 miles) SW of Melbourne

✪ **The Great Ocean Road**—which hugs the coast from Torquay, and onwards through Anglesea, Lorne, Apollo Bay, and Port Campbell, until it ends at Peterborough—is one of Australia's most spectacular drives (many say it's the best). The scenery along the 106-kilometer (64½-mile) route includes huge cliffs, ocean vistas, beaches, rain forests, and some incredible rock formations. The settlements along the highway are small, but they offer a number of accommodation choices.

The best way to travel along the Great Ocean Road is to drive at a leisurely pace, stopping off wherever your fancy takes you. The main attractions are in coastal Port Campbell National Park, so don't be surprised if you're not overly impressed until you get there. If you are traveling to Adelaide, you could stop off for 1 night along the Great Ocean Road, and spend another in the Coorong in South Australia (see chapter 11).

ESSENTIALS

ORGANIZED TOURS   Melbourne Sightseeing (☎ 03/9663 3388) offers a bus trip featuring the highlights of the Great Ocean Road. The buses leave from Melbourne daily at 8:15am and return at 8:30pm—which is a journey I wouldn't like to attempt in a day. Tours cost A$97 (U.S.$63.05) for adults (A$54/U.S.$35.10 if you have a YHA card), and A$49 (U.S.$31.85) for children. The trip can be stretched out over 2 days with overnight accommodation; the price for the overnight trip ranges between A$136 and $170 (U.S.$88.40–$110.50) depending on property. **Grayline Sightseeing Tours** (☎ 03/9663 4455) also has daily trips that cost A$102 (U.S.$66.30) for adults and A$51 (U.S.$33.15) for children.

Another option worth considering is a 2-day excursion with **Let's Go Bush Tours** (☎ 03/9662 3969), which departs Melbourne every Wednesday and Saturday. The trip is less rushed than other, and you get to stay in the company's own house situated on the highest point of the Great Ocean Road. The trip costs A$99 (U.S.$64.35), including dinner, breakfast, and accommodation.

Wild-Life Tours (☎ **1300 650 288** in Australia, and 03/9747 1882; www.wildlife tours.com.au; wildlife@eisa.net.ay) also offers a 3-day Great Ocean Road tour, including a visit to The Grampians, for A$129 (U.S.$83.85). The company also offers a 2-day trip from Melbourne to Adelaide along the Great Ocean Road for A$129 (U.S.$83.85) one-way. Prices do not include accommodation or food. Discounts apply.

V/Line (☎ **13 61 96** in Victoria, or 13 22 32 in NSW, or 03/9619 5000) runs a combined train/coach Coast Link service as far as Warrnambool, via Geelong, Lorne, Apollo Bay, and Port Campbell. The train leaves Melbourne every day at 8:50am, 12:40pm, and 6:08pm but check before turning up—you then transfer onto a bus at Geelong. The bus tours the Great Ocean Road, stopping off at various lookout points (and for lunch) and then carries on to Warrnambool. The round-trip costs A$52.80 (U.S.$34.32) for adults and A$26.40 (U.S.$17.16) for children on Tues, Wed and Thurs, and A$75.40 (U.S.$49.01) for adults and A$37.70 (U.S.$24.51) for children other days. Ask about "family saver" fares.

VISITOR INFORMATION   Most places along the route have their own information centers. If you're coming from Melbourne, stop at the **Geelong & Great Ocean Road Visitors Centre,** Stead Park, Princess Highway, Geelong, VIC 3220 (☎ /fax **03/ 5275 5797;** www.greatoceanroad.org.au). You can book accommodations here, which you should do in advance, especially in summer. There's also a visitor center at the **National Wool Museum,** 26 Moorabool St., Geelong (☎ **1800/620 888** in Australia or 03/5222 2900).

Along the route, the **Park Information Centre,** at Port Campbell National Park, Norris Street, Port Campbell (☎ **03/5598 6382**), is also a good place to pick up brochures. It also has some interesting displays and an audiovisual show of the area. It's open from 10am to 4.30pm daily.

If you're approaching from the north, visit the **Camperdown Visitor Information Centre,** "Court House," Manifold Street, Princes Highway, Camperdown (☎ **03/ 5593 3390**). It's open Monday to Friday from 9:30am to 5pm, Saturday from 9:30am to 4pm, and Sunday from 11am to 4pm.

EXPLORING THE COASTAL ROAD

Along the route you might want to stop off at **Torquay,** a township dedicated to surfing. The main surf beach here is much nicer than the one farther down the coast in Lorne. While in Torquay, you might want to stop off at **Surfworld,** Surfcoast Plaza Beach Road in West Torquay (☎ **03/5261 4606**), which has interactive exhibits dealing with surfboard design and surfing history and the world's best surfers captured on video. Admission is A$6.50 (U.S.$4.23) for adults, A$4.50 (U.S.$2.93) for children, and A$17.50 (U.S.$11.38) for families. Bells Beach, just down the road, is world famous in surfing circles for its perfect waves.

Lorne has some nice boutiques and is a good place to stop off for lunch or stay the night. The stretch from Lorne to Apollo Bay is one of the most spectacular sections of the route, as the road narrows and twists and turns along a cliff edge with the ocean on the other side. **Apollo Bay** itself is a pleasant town that was once a whaling station. It has good sandy beaches and is much more low-key than Lorne.

Next, you come to the **Angahook-Lorne State Park,** which protects most of the coastal section of the Otway Ranges from Aireys Inlet, just south of Anglesea, to Kennett River. It has plenty of well-marked rain-forest walks and picnic areas at Shelly Beach, Elliot River, and Blanket Bay. There's plenty of wildlife around here.

About 13 kilometers (8 miles) past Apollo Bay, just off the main road, you can take a stroll through the rain forest on the **Maits Rest Rainforest Boardwalk.** A little farther along the main road an unsealed road leads north past Hopetoun Falls and Beauchamp Falls to the settlement of **Beech Forest.** Seven kilometers farther along the main road another unsealed road heads south for 15 kilometers (9 miles) to a windswept headland and the **Cape Otway Lighthouse.** Built by convicts in 1848, the 100-meter-tall lighthouse is open to tourists. Admission is A$6.50 (U.S.$4.23) for adults and A$3.50 (U.S.$2.28) for children. It's open daily from 9am to 5pm. Ask about guided tours.

Back on the main road again, your route heads inland through an area known as **Horden Vale,** before running to the sea again at **Glenaire** (there's good surfing and camping at Johanna, 6 kilometers north of here). Then the Great Ocean Road heads north again to **Lavers Hill,** a former timber town. Five kilometers southwest of Lavers Hill is the small **Melba Gully State Park,** where you can spot glowworms at night and walk along routes of rainforest ferns. Keep an eye out for one of the last giant gum trees that escaped the loggers—it's some 27 meters (88½ ft.) in circumference and is estimated to be more than 300 years old.

The next place of note is **Moonlight Head,** which marks the start of the "Shipwreck Coast"—a 120-kilometer (74-mile) stretch of coastline running to Port Fairy that claimed more than 80 ships in only 40 years at the end of the 19th century and the beginning of the 20th.

Just past Princetown starts the biggest attraction of the entire trip, the ✪ **Port Campbell National Park,** which with its sheer cliffs and coastal rock sculptures is one of the most immediately recognizable images of natural Australia. You can't miss the **Twelve Apostles,** a series of rock pillars that stand in the foam just offshore. Other attractions are the **Blowhole,** which throws up huge sprays of water; the **Grotto,** a baroque rock formation intricately carved by the waves; London Bridge, which looked quite like the real thing until the center crashed into the sea in 1990, leaving a bunch of tourists stranded on the wrong end; and the **Loch Ard Gorge.**

Port Fairy, a lovely fishing town once known as Belfast by Irish immigrants who settled here to escape the potato famine, is also on the Shipwreck Coast.

Not far past the town of Peterborough the Great Ocean Road heads inland to Warrnambool to eventually join the Princes Highway heading toward Adelaide.

WHERE TO STAY ALONG THE WAY

The **Great Ocean Road Accommodation Centre,** 136 Mountjoy Parade, Lorne, VIC 3232 (☎ **03/5289 1800**), rents out cottages and units along the route.

IN LORNE

Lorne is a good option for a night's rest. Though the beach and water are nothing special, there are plenty of restaurants.

Great Ocean Road Cottages. 10 Erskine Ave. (P.O. Box 60), Lorne, VIC 3232. ☎ **03/5289 1070.** Fax 03/5289 2508. greatoceanrdcots@iprimus.com.au. 10 cottages, 7 apts, dorms sleep 33. A$195 (U.S.$126.75) cottages summer, A$115 (U.S.$74.75) off-season. A$110–$160 (U.S.$71.50–$104) standard apts, depending on season. A$180–$200 (U.S.$117–$130) spa apts, depending on season. A$255–$295 (U.S.$165.75–$191.75) suite. AE, BC, DC, MC, V.

This complex has it all, although with so many people around (and quite a few children), it can be a little noisy in summer. There's a set of self-contained cottages, set away from each other in a quiet patch of bushland, about a 5-minute walk from the town center. Each cottage is a two-story wooden hut with a double bed, two twin beds, and a pullout mattress. There's also a bathroom and a full kitchen. Just down the road is **Waverley House,** a historic mansion that has been divided into seven apartments. All of them are nice, but they vary enormously.

Also on the property is **Great Ocean Road Backpackers,** which offers dorm-style accommodation for A$18 to $21 (U.S.$11.70–$13.65) YHA members. They have a few family rooms (discounts apply to all backpacker beds for YHA members).

IN APOLLO BAY

Bayside Gardens. 219 Great Ocean Rd., Apollo Bay, VIC 3233. ☎ /fax **03/5237 6248.** 10 units. TV. A$70–$110 (U.S.$45.50–$71.50) 1-bedroom apts. Higher rates apply Christmas, Jan, Easter, and public holidays. Minimum 1-week stay in Jan. BC, MC, V.

Right opposite the beach, with good ocean views from the front rooms, Bayside Gardens is a pleasant place to stay—and you can save money on meals by cooking in your own kitchen. The units all have a separate bedroom with a double bed, a lounge area, a full kitchen, and an attached bathroom with shower. Rooms at the front can be noisy if you're not used to living beside an ocean. There are wood fires in some of the units, and all rooms are centrally heated. Wash your clothes at the coin-op laundry and fry your fish on the barbecues scattered around in the 1½-acre grounds. It's a 10-minute walk to town.

IN PORT CAMPBELL

✪ Macka's Farm. RSD 2305 Princetown Rd., Princetown, VIC 3269. ☎ **03/5598 8261.** Fax 03/5598 8201. mackas@netcam.com.au. 3 units. A$85–$100 (U.S.$55.25–$65) double, depending on season. Extra person A$15 (U.S.$9.75). BC, MC. V.

This working farm is located 4 kilometers (2½ miles) inland from the Twelve Apostles (continue on from the Twelve Apostles for 2 kilometers (1¼ miles) and turn off at the sign for Macka's farm—it's another 4 kilometers (2½ miles) from there). The units all have kitchens, so you can cook up your own feast. Otherwise you can order meals by prior arrangement outside peak season, or visit one of the nearby restaurants. Rooms sleep between six and eight people in a mixture of singles and doubles. There's no TV, but who needs it when there are lots of pigs, cows, ducks, and chickens running around. Overall, it's a great farm experience.

WHERE TO DINE IN LORNE

Arab Restaurant. Mount Joy Parade. ☎ **03/5289 1435.** Reservations recommended. Main courses A$10.50–$18.50 (U.S.$6.83–$12.03). AE, BC, DC, MC, V. Mon–Fri 9am–9pm, Sat 8am–11pm, Sun 7:30am–10pm. Closed Christmas. INTERNATIONAL.

This popular bistro serves some of the best food along this part of the coast. The house specialty is chicken Kiev, but you can also tuck into dishes such as the fish of the day or chicken schnitzel. The apple crumble is delicious.

✪ Marks. Mount Joy Parade. ☎ **03/5289 2787.** Main courses A$9–$17.50 (U.S.$5.85–$11.38). AE, BC, DC, MC, V. Daily noon–2:30pm (only Sat–Sun in winter) and 6–8:30pm. INTERNATIONAL.

Lorne's best restaurant is a classy joint with simple wooden chairs and tables set in an elegant fashion in a cool, yellow-walled interior. Dishes include fried calamari salad, spicy octopus, risotto, and the intriguing oven-baked vine-wrapped goat cheese and macadamia nut parcel on eggplant pâté with red capsicum puree. The bar is open for coffee and drinks all day.

Ozone Milk Bar. Mount Joy Parade. ☎ **03/5289 1780.** Menu items A$1.80–$4 (U.S.$1.17–$2.60). No credit cards. Daily 7am–6pm (to 11pm Christmas to the end of Jan). AUSTRALIAN MILK BAR.

An Ozzie icon, the milk bar is a kind of downmarket cafe selling everything from milk shakes and pies to newspapers. This one sells good pies and quiche, a limp-looking and bland-tasting veggie burger, chicken fillet burgers, cookies, ice cream, and small homemade cakes. The milk shakes are particularly good. You can sit inside or around small tables outside. There's a Thai place next door, but it's very unwelcoming.

3 The Murray River

Mildura: 544km (337 miles) NW of Melbourne; Albury-Wadonga: 305km (189 miles) N of Melbourne; Echuca: 210km (130 miles) N of Melbourne

✪ **The Murray** is Australia's version of the Mississippi River. Though it's a rushing torrent of white water at its source in the Snowy Mountains, it becomes slow moving and muddy brown by the time it becomes the meandering border between Victoria and New South Wales. The Murray is watered by the Darling River, which starts off in Queensland, and together the two combine to make Australia's longest river.

Aborigines once used the Murray as a source of food and transportation, and later the water was plied by paddle steamers, laden with wool and crops from the land it helped irrigate. In 1842, the Murray was "discovered" by explorers Hamilton Hume and William Howell on the first overland trek from Sydney to Port Phillip, near Melbourne. As Hume later wrote, on their trek the explorers "suddenly arrived at the bank of a very fine river—at least 200 feet wide, apparently deep, the bank being 8 or 9 feet above the level, which is overflowed at the time of flood . . . In the solid wood of a healthy tree I carved my name." You can still see the carved initials on a tree standing by the riverbank in Albury, on the border between the two states.

ESSENTIALS

GETTING THERE   Most visitors cross the river during an overland drive between cities. There are two routes to get to the Murray from Melbourne: Either take the Calder Highway to Mildura, which is a 6-hour drive, or take the 2½-hour route down the Midland Highway to Echuca. Traveling from Melbourne to Mildura is only practical if you're continuing on to Broken Hill, which is 297 kilometers (184 miles) north of Mildura. Those in a hurry to get to Sydney can travel via the river-straddling twin towns of Albury-Wadonga on the Hume Highway (about a 12-hr. trip with short stops).

V/Line (☎ **13 61 96** in Victoria, 13 22 32 in NSW, or 03/9619 5000) runs regular train services to Mildura, Echuca, and Albury-Wadonga.

VISITOR INFORMATION   The **Echuca and Moama and District Visitor Information Centre,** 2 Heygarth St., Echuca, VIC 3564 (☎ **03/5480 7555,** or 1800/804 446 in Australia; fax 03/5482 6413; www.echucamoama.com; emt@origin.net.au) has plenty of maps and detailed information about local accommodations and river cruises. It's open daily from 9am to 5pm. The **Mildura Visitor Information & Booking Centre,** 180–190 Deakin Ave., Mildura, VIC 3502 (☎ **1800/039 043** or 03/5021 4424; fax 03/5021 1836; tourism@mildura.vic.gov.au), offers similar services. It's open Monday to Friday from 9am to 5:30pm and weekends from 9am to 5pm. If you're passing through Albury, you might want to contact the **Gateway Visitors Information Centre,** Gateway Village, Lincoln Causeway, Wadonga, VIC 3690 (☎ **02/6041 3875** or 1800/800 743; fax 02/6021 0322), open daily from 9am to 5pm.

RIVER CRUISES & OTHER FUN STUFF

IN MILDURA   Mildura is one of Australia's most important fruit-growing areas. There was a time, however, when this was just semi-arid red dust country. The area bloomed due to a little ingenuity and, of course, the Murray. The original irrigation system consisted of two imported English water pumps and the manual labor of hundreds of newly arrived immigrants, who were put to work clearing the scrub and digging channels through the new fields: Today, the hungry land soaks up the water.

Several paddle steamers leave from Mildura wharf. One of the nicest boats is the *PS Melbourne* (☎ **03/5023 2200;** fax 03/5021 3017), built in 1912 and is still powered by steam. It offers 2-hour trips leaving 10:50am and 1:50pm. The fare is A$18.50 (U.S.$12.03) for adults and A$7.50 (U.S.$4.88) for children. Children under 5 are free.

PS Melbourne's sister ship, the *Rothbury,* was built in 1881, but its steam-driven engine has been replaced by a conventional engine. It goes on a winery cruise every Thursday from 10:30am to 3:30pm, stopping at a winery for tastings and a barbecue lunch. The trip costs A$42 (U.S.$27.30) for adults and A$20 (U.S.$13) for children. The *Rothbury* has dinner cruises every Thursday from 7 to 10pm for the same price for A$40 (U.S.$26) for adults and A418 for children. You can take the paddleboat to the Golden River Zoo (see below) during school holiday periods leaving Mildura Wharf at 9:50am on Wednesday morning (returning at 3pm). The trip costs A$32 (U.S$20.80) for adults and A$16 (U.S$10.40) for children under 5 to 14, including zoo.

On dry land, the **Golden River Zoo,** Flora Avenue, Mildura (☎ **03/5023 5540,** www.goldenriverzoo.com.au) is a pleasant place to see native animals. The zoo fronts onto the river 4 kilometers (2½ miles) from the city center down 11th Street. The animals here virtually follow you around (to be fed) as you walk through their enclosures. Admission is A$15 (U.S.$9.75) for adults and A$8 (U.S.$5.20) for children, including a free barbecue lunch at noon and a free tractor-train ride to the river at 1:30pm and an animal show. The zoo is open daily, except Christmas Day, from 10am to 5pm.

IN ECHUCA In Echuca, another paddle steamer option is the *Emmylou* (☎ **03/ 5480 2237;** fax 03/5480 2927; www.emmylou.com.au). A 2-day/2-night cruise leaves the Port of Echuca Wednesday at 6pm and returns at noon on Friday (but check sailings beforehand). The cruise includes a visit to the Barmah, an area famous for its wetlands and the largest red gum trees in the world or depending on river levels will include a stop Perricoota Station. The trip costs A$415 to 435 (U.S.$269.75– $282.75) per person, depending on cabin. Children 4 to 14 receive a 25% discount. An overnight trip also leaves on Saturday at 6pm and returns at 10am on Sunday. It costs A$195 to $210 (U.S.$126.75–$136.50) per person including breakfast; dinner is extra. The Emmylou also offers various day trips costing A$15 (U.S.$9.75) for adults and A$7.50 (U.S.$4.88) for kids for 1 hour, and A$18 (U.S.$11.70) for adults and A$9 (U.S.$5.85) for kids for 1½ hours.

The **Port of Echuca** (☎ **03/5482 4248;** fax 03/5482 6951; www.portofechuca. org.au; port@portofechuca.org.au;) is definitely worth a look. The three-level red gum wharf was built in 1865 and is still used by paddle steamers. The Port owns the *PS Adelaide,* the oldest operating wooden-hulled paddle steamer in the world (1866), **the** *PS Pevensey* (1911), and the *PS Alexander Arbuthnot* (1923). One-hour cruises on the latter two are offered daily at 10:15am, 11:30am, 1pm, 2:15pm, and 3:30pm for A$15 (U.S.$9.75) for adults and A$6.50 (U.S.$4.23) for children. You can also take a look around the wharf on a guided tour, priced at A$10 (U.S.$6.50) for adults and A$6.50 (U.S.$4.23) for children. Enquire about combined and family prices. Outside the Port, in the **Echuca Port Precinct,** there are various things to do, including horse and carriage rides and old penny arcade machines in Sharpes Magic Movies, located in an old riverboat warehouse.

If you want to get out into the Outback, then trips from Mildura with **Mallee Outback Experiences,** P.O. Box 82, Nichols Point, VIC 3501 (☎ /fax **03/5021 1621,** or mobile 0418/521 0030) are well worth the effort. The company offers two trips. The first goes to ✪ **Mungo National Park,** which is famous for its red sand dunes and shifting sands, and which I highly recommend you go and see. The second is **to Hattah National Park,** which has some gorgeous river plains, Murray River lakes, pine forests, and more mallee scrub. The Mungo trip leaves every Wednesday and Saturday, and the Hattah National Park trip every Friday. All trips cost A$55 (U.S.$35.75) for adults, A$33 (U.S.$21.45) for children, and A$132 (U.S.$85.80) for a family of five.

You can get to these two national parks on your own, but it's best to have a 4-wheel-drive vehicle—even better if you go with an experienced guide. ✪ **Mungo National Park** is a unique, arid region 110 kilometers (68 miles) northeast of Mildura, off the Stuart Highway. People come here to see "the walls of China," a strange moonscape of intricately weathered red sand. The walls edge onto Lake Mungo, which was once a huge freshwater lake during the last Ice Age, but is now dry. A 60-kilometer (37-mile) driving tour starting at the visitor center at the park's entrance takes you across the lake bed to the Walls of China. There are several short walks in the park leading off from the **visitor's center** (☎ **03/5023 1054**), and campsites at the park entrance. Just outside the park, the **Mungo Lodge** (☎ **03/5029 7297;** www.mungolodge.com.au) offers affordable motel accommodation and a casual restaurant.

WHERE TO STAY
IN MILDURA

Mildura Grand Hotel Resort. Seventh St., Mildura, VIC 3500. ☎ **1800/034 228** in Australia or 03/5023 0511.Fax 03/5022 1801. 104 units (most with shower only). A/C MINIBAR TV TEL. A$110–$176 (U.S.$71.50–$114.40) double; A$146 (U.S.$94.90) "Grand Room" double. Rates include breakfast. Ask about packages. AE, BC, DC, MC, V.

This 19th-century hotel is right in the center of Mildura, overlooking the Murray. Standard double rooms are comfortable, and many have been recently refurbished. There are 21 "Grand" rooms, which are a little bigger, and some have balconies and garden views. The State Suite (A$250/U.S.$162.50 per night) has also been refurbished and matches anything you're likely to find in a five-star hotel. If money's no object, you could indulge in the luxurious Presidential Suite for a mere A$420 (U.S.$273) a night.

Guests have use of laundry facilities, a pool, a sauna, a hot tub, a game room, a pool room, and five restaurants, including the excellent Stefano's, which serves Italian cuisine with zingy Asian accents.

IN ECHUCA

Echuca Gardens B&B and YHA. 103 Mitchell St., Echuca, VIC 3564. ☎ **03/5480 6522.** Mobile 0419 881 054, Fax 03/5482 6951. 6 units (3 in B&B and 3 in hostel). B&B room A$130 (U.S.$84.50) weekends, A$100 (U.S.$65) weekdays; rates include breakfast. BC, MC, V.

There are evening gatherings around the piano at this popular two-story log cabin B&B, as well as a pretty neat hot tub in the front yard surrounded by murals and landscaped water gardens. Rooms are decorated in native flower themes, and all of them have balconies. Two rooms have showers in the bathroom, and another has a shower on the second floor. It's a short stroll from the B&B to either the river or a state forest. The YHA has a basic twin room inside and three tent-like cabins outside, one with a double bed and the other with two singles. There are also three basic dorm rooms with beds going for A$18 (U.S.$11.70) for YHA members and A$21.50 (U.S.$13.98) non members.

IN ALBURY

Hume Country Golf Club Motor Inn. 736 Logan Rd., Albury, NSW 2640. ☎ **02/6025 8233.** Fax 02/6040 4999. humegolfmotel@primus.com.au. 25 units. A/C TV TEL. A$82 (U.S.$53.30) double; A$90 (U.S.$58.50) family room; A$115 (U.S.$74.75) suite. Extra person A$10 (U.S.$6.50). AE, BC, DC, MC, V.

This is a good place to stop if you're making the long trip north to Sydney. Just on the New South Wales side of the border, this motor inn has typical rooms with everything you'd expect, plus a toaster. There are also two very large family rooms, one sleeping five the other seven. Suites are also large and come with a Jacuzzi tub. All rooms overlook the 27-hole golf course, where a round of golf costs A$18 (U.S.$11.70).

4 The Southeast Coast

The Princes Highway wanders down the coast from Sydney just past Eden, then darts across into Victoria, passing through the logging town of Orbost, dipping down toward Lakes Entrance. The highway continues to the southwest, swooping over to Melbourne.

This region's most interesting sights are **Wilsons Promontory National Park,** and—to a lesser extent—Lakes Entrance and the **Snowy River National Park.**

✪ WILSONS PROMONTORY NATIONAL PARK

200km (124 miles) SE of Melbourne.

"The Prom," as it's called, is Victoria's best-loved national park. Dipping down into Bass Strait, the park—which was named after a prominent London businessman—marks the southernmost point on Australia's mainland. It's thought that a land bridge once joined it to Tasmania. The best time to visit the park is from late September to early December, when all the bush flowers are in bloom.

Visitors come for the spectacular granite mountains, the thick forests and vast plains, and some of the country's best beaches. Wildlife abounds in the park, including plenty of koalas, kangaroos, wallabies, possums, echidnas, wombats, and emus. You can hand-feed crimson rosellas at the capital of the Prom, Tidal River, but you'll find little more here than the national park's **Tourist Information Center** (☎ 1800/ 350 552 in Australia or 03/5680 9555) and camping and caravan grounds. There are plenty of trails leading away into the mountains: Following the longer trails can turn into a 2- or 3-day excursion, though shorter day hikes are possible. One of the best trails is the 1-hour **Mt. Oberon walk,** which starts from the Mt. Oberon parking lot and offers superb views. Visitors also rave about the **Squeaky Beach Nature Walk,** a 1½-hour walk from Tidal River to the next bay and back.

There are 30 beaches in the park, some of which are easily accessible. **Norman's Beach** in Tidal River is the most popular, and it's the only one recommended for swimming. No snorkeling or lifeguards at these beaches, but they're gorgeous.

Park entry costs A$9 (U.S.$5.85) for cars, which you pay at the park entrance, 30 kilometers (18 miles) north of Tidal River. The gate is open 24 hours, but if you arrive late and the collection station is closed, pay the following morning at Tidal River.

GETTING THERE From Melbourne, take the **South Gippsland Highway** (B440), turning south at Meeniyan and again at Fish Creek or Foster. The route is well sign-posted. Tidal River is 30 kilometers inside the park boundary.

There's no public transportation to the park. You can take the **V/Line bus** from Melbourne to Foster (fare: A$21.30/U.S.$13.85), 60 kilometers (37 miles) north of the park. In Foster, you can stay at the **Foster Backpackers Hostel,** 17 Pioneer St.,

Foster, VIC 3960 (☎ **03/5682 2614**). It's basically a private home with a few spare rooms; the two doubles cost A$44 (U.S.$28.60), and dorm beds go for A$19 (U.S.$12.35). There are also 2 self-contained apartments for $55 (U.S.$35.75). The owner offers transport to Tidal River for A$22 (U.S.$14.30) each way; the trip takes around 45 minutes.

WHERE TO STAY

The park's **Tourist Information Center** rents 17 self-contained cabins for A$118.50 to $129.50 (U.S.$77.03–$84.18) a night for two—depending on season—(they can accommodate up to six; each extra adult is A$17.20 (U.S.$11.18) and child A$11 (U.S.$7.15). There are five "Lorikeet" units at A$58.30 to $93 (U.S.$37.90–$60.45) a night for two and A$93.50 to $134 (U.S.$60.78–$87.10) for three or four (higher prices in summer). For bookings call ☎ **03/5680 9500** or fax 03/568 09516.

Waratah Park Country House. Thomson Rd., Waratah Bay, VIC 3959. ☎ **03/5683 2575.** Fax 03/5683 2275. 6 units. A/C TV TEL. A$78 (U.S.$50.70) including breakfast; A$115 (U.S.$74.75) Sun–Thurs (including 4-course dinner and breakfast); A$270 (U.S.$175.50) for weekend package including 2 nights' lodgings, 2 breakfasts, and 2 4-course dinners. All rates are per person. AE, BC, MC, V.

If you don't feel like roughing it, this is the only place within the park that will do. Rooms, with king-size beds and double spas, offer stunning views over Wilsons Promontory and a dozen or so islands. The food here is excellent, too. The hotel is also next to the new Cape Liptrap Coastal Park, home to some 120 species of birds.

It's a very friendly place and the hosts will sit down with you and go through the things you want to do while in the area. A V/Line coach operates from Melbourne to Fish Creek, and the owner will pick you up from the bus station.

LAKES ENTRANCE
316km (189½ miles) E of Melbourne; 792km (491 miles) SW of Sydney

Lakes Entrance (pop. 4,200) is Victoria's fishing capital and a popular summer resort town. People come here for three things: the surrounding **national parks;** the vast **Gippsland Lakes** (Australia's largest enclosed waterway, separated from the coast by sand spits and dunes crossed by walkways); and the **beaches,** the most famous of which is Ninety Mile Beach. Most of Ninety Mile Beach is encompassed within the Gippsland Lakes Coastal Park—a bird-lovers paradise. Lake Entrance's beaches never get crowded, so grab a blanket and head for your own personal stretch of white sand.

The town is situated at the eastern end of the lake system, and attracts lots of anglers, windsurfers, boaters, and water-skiers. If you're hurrying on down to Melbourne from Sydney, you might want to pull over here and admire the ocean views from **Jemmy Point,** 2 kilometers (1 mile) west of town on the Princes Highway.

GETTING THERE V/Line (☎ **13 61 96** in Victoria, 13 22 32 in NSW, or 03/9619 5000) operates daily buses from Melbourne to Bairnsdale for around A$34.20 (U.S$22.23), with a connection to Lakes Entrance for an additional A$7.10 (U.S$4.62).

VISITOR INFORMATION The **Lakes Entrance Visitor Information Centre** (☎ **03/5155 1966;** fax 03/5155 3772) is on the Princes Highway, just as you enter the town from the west.

WHERE TO STAY

Abel Tasman Motor Lodge. 643 Esplanade (Princes Hwy.), Lakes Entrance, VIC 3909. ☎ **03/5155 1655.** Fax 03/5155 1603. www.lakes-entrance.com/abeltasman/Default.htm. a.tas@net-tech.com.au. 16 units (2 with spa). A/C TV TEL. A$72–$120 (U.S.$46.80–$78) standard double; A$90–$140 (U.S.$58.50–$91) double with spa; A$110–$187 (U.S.$71.50–$121.55) apt. Rates are highest Christmas to the end of Jan, Easter, and long weekends. AE, BC, DC, MC, V.

The rooms at this modern motel, which was totally refurbished in 1998, are the best in Lakes Entrance. Furnished in motel style, standard rooms on the top floor also have private balconies. All have views across the lake. The apartments were built in 1998, and are classy. Guests have the use of a pool, barbecues, and a coin-op laundry.

Dejà Vu. Clara St. (P.O. Box 750), Lakes Entrance, VIC 3909. ☎ **03/5155 4330.** Fax 03/5155 3718. www.dejavu.com.au. dejavu@dejavu.com.au. 6 units. TV. A$135 (U.S.$87.75) standard double; A$175–$200 (U.S.$113.75–$130) spa double. Rates include cooked breakfast. Ask about midweek packages. BC, DC, JCB, MC, V.

This waterfront retreat is set in 6 acres of rain forest and wetlands and has panoramic ocean views. Rooms are large and comfortable (four have Jacuzzis), each with a sitting room and a balcony (from which you might spot pelicans, black swans, and other feathered friends). There is also a meditation room, and massages are available. Seafood platter meals are served on your balcony, or you can paddle a canoe the 2 minutes it takes to get to the shops and restaurants in town. Tours of the area can be arranged. There's also a waterfront apartment suitable for two couples with its own beach costing A$240 (U.S.$156) for four people or A$145 (U.S.$94.25) for one couple. A minimum 2-night stay is required in the apartment, and the rates include breakfast provisions. Cruises are available by arrangement, and a happy hour cruise provides light refreshments or a full dinner cruise is available.

5 The High Country

Victoria's High Country is made up of the hills and mountains of the **Great Dividing Range,** which runs from Queensland, through New South Wales, to just before Ballarat, where it drops away and reappears in the mountains of the Grampians, in the western part of Victoria. The range separates inland Australia from the greener coastal belt. The highest mountain in the Victorian segment of the range is **Mt. Bogong,** which at just 1,988 meters (6,621 ft.) is minuscule by world mountain standards.

The main attractions of the High Country are its natural features, which include moorland and typical mountainous alpine scenery. It's also popular for its outdoor activities, including hiking, canoeing, white-water rafting, and rock climbing. The High Country is also the home of the **Victorian ski fields,** based around Mt. Buller, Mt. Stirling, Falls Creek, Mt. Buffalo, and Mt. Hotham. If you plan to go walking here make sure you have plenty of water and sunscreen, as well as a tent and a good-quality sleeping bag. As in any alpine region temperatures can plummet dramatically. In summer, days can be very hot, and nights very cold.

✪ SNOWY RIVER NATIONAL PARK
390km (242 miles) NE of Melbourne

The Snowy River National Park, with its lovely river scenery and magnificent gorges, protects Victoria's largest forest wilderness areas. The Snowy River was once a torrent worthy of Banjo Patterson's famous poem, but since Snowy Mountain Hydro-Electric came along and erected a series of dams, it's become a mere trickle of its former self.

GETTING THERE & GETTING AROUND   There are two main access roads to the park, the **Gelantipy Road** from Buchan and **the Bonang Freeway** from the logging township of Orbost. **MacKillop's Road** (also known as Deddick River Road) runs across the park's northern border from Bonang to a little south of Wulgulmerang.

Around MacKillop's Bridge, along MacKillop's Road, is some spectacular scenery, and the park's best campgrounds, set beside some nice swimming holes and sandy river beaches. **The Barry Way** leads through the main township of Buchan, where you'll find some of Australia's best caves.

VISTOR INFORMATION   The main place to get information on Snowy River National Park and Alpine National Park is **the Buchan Caves Information Centre,** in the Buchan Caves complex. It's open daily from 9am to 4:00pm (closed Christmas). Otherwise, call **Parks Victoria** (☎ **13 19 63** in Victoria, or 03/5155 9264).

EXPLORING THE BUCHAN CAVES

The ✪ **Buchan Caves** (☎ **03/5155 9264**) are set in a scenic valley that is particularly beautiful in autumn, when all the European trees are losing their leaves. Tourists can visit the Royal and Fairy caves (which are quite similar), with their fabulous stalactites and stalagmites. There are several tours daily: April to September at 11am, 1pm, and 3pm; October to March at 10am, 11:15am, 1pm, 2:15pm, and 3:30pm. Entry to one cave costs A$10 (U.S.$6.50) for adults, A$5 (U.S.$3.25) for children ages 5 to 16, and A$25 (U.S.$16.25) for families of five.

To reach the caves from the Princes Highway, turn off at Nowa Nowa (it's well signposted), or if you're coming south from Jindabyne in New South Wales (see chapter 6) follow the Barry Way, which runs alongside the Snowy River.

Want to Feel like the Man from Snowy River? **Snowy Mountain Rider Tours,** Karoonda Park, Gelantipy (☎ **03/5155 0220;** fax 03/5155 0308), offers half-day rides in the Snowy River National Park for A$60 (U.S$39), and full-day tours for A$120 (U.S.$78) including lunch. A 4-day trip, including camping and all meals, costs A$520 (U.S.$338). The company also arranges rafting on Snowy River for A$120 (U.S.$78) a day including lunch.

✪ ALPINE NATIONAL PARK

333km (200 miles) NE of Melbourne, 670km (402 miles) SW of Sydney

Victoria's largest national park at 646,000 hectares (2494 sq. miles), the Alpine National Park connects the High Country of New South Wales and the ACT. The park's scenery is spectacular, encompassing most of the state's highest mountains, wild rivers, impressive escarpments, forests, and high plains. The flora is diverse with 1,100 plant species within the park's boundaries, including 12 not found anywhere else. Walking here is good in spring and summer, when the **Bogong High Plains** are covered in wildflowers. Other impressive trails include the 5.7-kilometer (3½-mile) route through Bryce Gorge to **The Bluff,** a 200-meter (356 ft.) high, rocky escarpment with panoramic views. Of the numerous other walking tracks in the park, the most well known is the **Alpine Walking Track,** which bisects the park for 400 kilometers (240 miles) from Walhalla to the township of Tom Groggin, on the New South Wales border. There are plenty of access roads into the park, though some close in winter.

If you are a keen walker you can strap on your boots and see the area by foot. **Ecotrek** (☎ **08/8383 7198;** fax 08/8383 7377; ecotrek@ozemail.com.au) offers an 8-day Bogong Alpine Traverse trek, including 4 nights camping and 3 nights in ski lodges. You carry your own pack, but the pain is worth it for the incredible panoramic views of peaks, plains, and forested valleys. The trek costs A$1,150 (U.S.$747.50), including round-trip transport to Melbourne. The company also offers a 5-day trek that involves camping and day walks through extremely rugged country. It costs A$630 (U.S.$409.50), including round-trip transport to Melbourne.

Another option is taking a horse trek through the area. One of the best operators is **Stoney's Bluff & Beyond Rides** (☎ **03/5775 2212;** www.stoneys.com.au).

GETTING THERE   The Alpine National Park can be accessed by several routes from Melbourne, including the **Great Alpine Road** (B500), the **Kiewa Valley Highway** (C531), and the **Lincoln Road** from Heyfield. Get to The Bluff from Mansfield along the Maroodah Highway.

HITTING THE SLOPES: THE HIGH COUNTRY SKI RESORTS

Most of the Victoria's **○ ski areas** are in, or on the edge of, the Alpine National Park (see above). The ski season in the Victorian High Country lasts from June to October, with July and August being the most popular months.

MT. HOTHAM

373km (231 miles) NE of Melbourne

Mt. Hotham (1,750m/5,740 ft.) is an intimate ski resort significantly smaller than those at Falls Creek (see below). There are eight lifts; and runs from beginners to advanced. It also offers some good off-piste (off-trail) cross-country skiing, including a route across the Bogong High Plains to Falls Creek. Some of the lifts are quite far apart, although there's a free "zoo cart" and bus transport system in winter along the main road. Resort entry costs A$18 (U.S.$11.70) per car for a day, payable at the resort entry gates, or at the Mount Hotham Resort Management office (see "Visitor Information," below). Ski tickets are available from **Mount Hotham Skiing Company** (☏ **03/5759 4444**). Full-day lift tickets cost A$64 (U.S.$41.60) for adults and A$33 (U.S.$21.45) for children. Combined lift and ski lesson tickets cost A$87 (U.S.$56.55) for adults and A$59 (U.S.$38.35) for children.

GETTING THERE   From Melbourne, take the Hume Highway via Harrietville, or the Princes Highway via Omeo. The trip takes around 5½ hours (the trip is slightly quicker on the Hume Highway).

Trekset Mount Hotham Snow Service (☏ **03/9370 9055**), runs buses to Mt. Hotham daily during the ski season departing Melbourne's Spencer Street Coach Terminal at 9am. The trip takes 6 hours and costs A$70 (U.S.$45.50) one-way or A$105 (U.S.$68.25) round-trip. You need to book in advance.

VISITOR INFORMATION   **Mount Hotham Resort Management,** Great Alpine Road, Mt. Hotham (☏ **03/5759 3550**), is as close as you'll come to an information office. It has plenty of brochures. It's open daily from 8am to 5pm in during the ski season, and Monday to Friday from 9am to 5pm at other times.

Where to Stay   The **Mt. Hotham Accommodation Service** (☏ **1800/032 061** in Australia; www.mthothamaccommodation.com.au; hotham@netc.net.com), can book rooms and advise you on special deals during both off-peak and peak periods. Another option is **Mt. Hotham Central Reservations** (☏ **1800/032 061** in Australia; www.hotham.net.au). During the ski season, most places will want you to book for an entire week. Prices are significantly lower in the non-ski season.

○ FALLS CREEK

375km (225 miles) NE of Melbourne

One of Victoria's best ski resorts, and my favorite, Falls Creek is situated on the edge of the Bogong High Plains overlooking the Kiewa Valley. This compact alpine village is the only one in Australia where you can ski from your lodge to the lifts and back again from the ski slopes. The nightlife is also very good in the ski season, with plenty of party options as well as a range of walk-in lodge restaurants.

The ski fields are split into two parts, the **Village Bowl** and **Sun Valley,** with 22 lifts in all. There are plenty of intermediate and advanced runs, as well as a sprinkling for beginners. Plans were afoot to create Australia's only double-black-diamond ski run by the 2001 ski season. You'll also find some of Australia's best cross-country skiing here; Australia's major cross-country skiing event, the **Kangaroo Hoppet,** is held here on the last Saturday in August every year. Entry to the resort costs A$6 (U.S.$3.90). Full-day lift tickets cost A$64 (U.S.$41.60) for adults and A$33 (U.S.$21.45) for children. Combined lift and ski lesson tickets cost from A$37 (U.S.$24.05) for adults and from A$29 (U.S.$18.85) for children. Call the **Falls Creek Ski Lifts** (☎ 03/5758 3280; fax 03/5758 3416) for details. The ski lifts can also organize accommodation options.

Falls Creek is also a pleasant place to visit in summer, when you can go bushwalking, horseback riding, and trout fishing. **Angling Expeditions** (☎/fax 03/5754 1466) is the best option for fly-fishing for trout in the alpine area during spring, summer, and fall. Trips last from 3 hours to all day and are suitable for everyone from beginners to experts. Overnight trips are also available. Horseback riding operators include **Falls Creek Trail Rides** (☎ 03/5758 3655) and **Bogong Horseback Adventures** (☎ 03/5754 4849).

GETTING THERE   **Pyles Coaches** (☎ 03/5754 4024) runs buses to the ski resort from Melbourne every day during the ski season (from the end of June to the end of September), departing Melbourne at 9am and Falls Creek at 5pm. The round-trip fare is A$100 (U.S.$65) for adults and A$75 (U.S.$48.75) for children and includes the resort entrance fee. They also runs buses to and from Albury just over the border in New South Wales, and between Mt. Beauty and Falls Creek. Bookings are essential.

Alternatively, **Eastern Australia Airlines** (book through Qantas) flies to Albury, a 1½-hour drive from Falls Creek. Avis, **Budget, Thrifty,** and **Hertz** have desks at Albury airport.

If you're driving from Melbourne take the **Hume Highway** to Wangaratta, and then through Myrtleford and Mt. Beauty to Falls Creek. The trip takes around 4½ hours. From Sydney take the Hume Highway to Albury-Wodonga and follow the signs to Mt. Beauty and the snowfields. If you arrive in the ski season, a resort worker will direct you to a car park, and bring you back to the resort entrance, from where you can take a caterpillar-tracked "troop-carrier" to your hotel, or attempt the probably short, but slippery, walk yourself.

VISITOR INFORMATION   **The Falls Creek Information Centre** at 1 Bogong High Plains Rd., Falls Creek (☎ 03/5758 3490), is open daily from 8am to 5pm. Buy your lift tickets in the booth next door, between mid-June and October.

Where to Stay & Dine

Falls Creek is a year-round resort, with a good range of accommodations available at all times, though it tends to fill up fast during the ski season. As you might expect room rates are significantly higher during the ski season. **The Falls Creek Reservation Centre** (☎ 1800/45 35 25 in Australia, or 03/5758 3100; fax 03/5758 3337, www.fallscreek.net; accom@fallscreek.albury.net.au) can tell you what deals are on offer and can book rooms for you. The cheapest winter option is the very basic **Frying Pan Inn,** P.O. Box 55, Falls Creek, VIC 3699 (☎ 03/5758 3390; fax 03/5758 3416), which is located right in the village next to the ski lifts. Bunks in four or six-bed rooms cost A$58 (U.S.$37.70) per night Sunday to Thursday, and A$68 (U.S.$44.20) Friday to Saturday, in the ski season. Packages are available.

✪ **Feathertop Alpine Lodge.** Parallel St. (P.O. Box 259), Falls Creek, VIC 3699. ☎ 03/5758 3232. Fax 03/5758 3514. www.ski.com.au/feathertop. feathertop@fallscreek.albury. net.au. 10 units. Winter A$95–$165 (U.S.$61.75–$107.25); summer A$70 (U.S.$45.50). Rates are per person and include dinner and breakfast. AE, BC, MC, V.

I really like this old-fashioned ski lodge nestled among the gum trees. Hosts Pip and Mark Whittaker have made it into one of the friendliest getaways in the mountains, and its small size makes it easy to get to know a few of the other guests. Rooms are functional yet cozy, and sleep two to four people. All have showers. The lounge is large and comfortable with good views, a well-stocked bar, and a library. The restaurant has good reputation for country cooking. Relax after a day on the slopes or the walking trails in the sauna or swimming pool. There's a guest laundry and a drying room, too.

Summit Ridge Alpine Lodge. Schuss St., Falls Creek, VIC 3699. ☎ **03/5758 3800.** Fax 03/5758 3833. sunridge@fallscreek.albury.net.au. Winter A$110–$195 (U.S.$71.50–$126.75) queen room per person; A$120–$210 (U.S.$78–$136.50) mezzanine suite. Summer A$100 (U.S.$65) mezzanine suite per person. AE, BC, DC, MC, V. Rates include breakfast and dinner. Children 5–14 25% off adult rate. Children under 5 not allowed.

Summit Ridge is a four-star property made from local rock and timber. It caters to discerning guests. All rooms are nice, if a little stark. The mezzanine suites are split-level with the bedroom upstairs; they have king-size beds and an attached bathroom with tub. There's a large lounge and dining room on the ground floor and a small library on the second. If the mist holds out there are some fine valley views. The hosts pay a lot of attention to detail, and the homemade bread is worth an early rise. The restaurant excels in fine dining. The owner can take you out on early-morning ski runs.

✪ MT. BUFFALO NATIONAL PARK

350km (210 miles) NE of Melbourne

Based around Mt. Buffalo, this is the oldest national park in the Victorian High Country, declared in 1898. The scenery around here is spectacular, with huge granite outcrops and plenty of waterfalls. As you ascend the mountain you pass through dramatic vegetation changes, from tall snow gum forests to sub-alpine grasslands. In summer, carpets of silver snow daisies, royal bluebells, and yellow Billy Button flowers bloom on the plateau. Animals and birds here include wallabies and wombats, cockatoos, lyrebirds, and mobs of crimson rosellas, which congregate around the campsite at Lake Catani (popular for swimming and canoeing). Other popular sports around and about include advanced hang-gliding and some very serious rock climbing. There are also more than 90 kilometers (54 miles) of walking tracks. Mt. Buffalo is also home to Victoria's smallest ski resort, with just five lifts, and a vertical drop of 157 meters (515 ft.). There are also 11 kilometers (6½ miles) of marked cross-country ski trails. The entry park to Mt. Buffalo ski resort is A$10 (U.S.$6.50) per car. Full-day lift tickets cost around A$35 (U.S.$22.75) for adults, and A$21 (U.S.$13.65) for children under 15, and A$10 (U.S.$6.50) for children under 8. Combination lift and ski lesson packages cost A$37 to $49 (U.S.$24.05–$31.85) for adults, and A$27 to $34 (U.S.$17.55–$22.10) for children. Buy lift tickets at the park offices (☎ **13 19 63** in Victoria, or 03/5756 2328) or between 9am and 3pm.

GETTING THERE From Melbourne take the Hume Freeway (M31) to Wangaratta, then follow the Great Alpine Road to Porepunkah. From there follow the Mount Buffalo Tourist Road.

VISITOR INFORMATION The nearest visitor information center is in the town of Bright. Find the **Bright Visitor Information Centre** at 1A Delaney Ave., Bright (☎ **03/5755 2275**).

Where to Stay

✪ **Mt. Buffalo Chalet.** Mt. Buffalo National Park, VIC 3740. ☎ **1800/037 038** in Australia or 03/5755 1500. Fax 03/5755 1892. 97 units, 72 with bathroom (some with shower only). A$119 (U.S.$77.35) guest house without bathroom; A$145 (U.S.$94.25) room with bathroom; A$170 (U.S.$110.50) view room with bathroom; A$185 (U.S.$120.25) suite. Rates are per person and all meals, guided walks, evening activities, and park entry. Higher rates Christmas to mid-Jan and Easter weekend. AE, BC, DC, MC, V.

This rambling mountain guesthouse was built in 1910 and retains an old-world feel. Guesthouse rooms, which have a mixture of double, twin, and bunk beds, are period style, reminiscent of the 1930s. They have tea and coffee facilities but no TV. View rooms have better furnishings and views across the valley. There's a large lounge and a game room, both with fireplaces. You'll also find a sauna, a spa, tennis courts, a cafe, and a bar. During summer the chalet operates canoeing, mountain biking, and abseiling. Meals are available for non-guests for A$35 (U.S.$22.75) for three courses.

6 The Northwest: Grampians National Park

260km (161 miles) NW of Melbourne

One of Victoria's most popular attractions, the Grampians National Park rises some 1,000 meters (3,280 ft.) from the plains, appearing from the distance like some kind of monumental island. The park, which is an ecological meeting place of Victoria's western volcanic plains and the forested Great Dividing Range, contains one-third of all the wildflowers native to Victoria and most of the surviving Aboriginal rock art in southeastern Australia. Almost 200 species of birds, 35 species of mammals, 28 of reptiles, 11 of amphibians, and 6 species of freshwater fish have been discovered here. Kangaroos, koalas, emus, gliders, and echidnas can be easily spotted.

There are some awesome sites in the Grampians, including **Reeds Lookout** and **The Balconies,** which are both accessible by road, and the **Wonderland Range,** which offers walking tracks leading past striking rock formations and massive cliffs to waterfalls and more spectacular lookouts.

The main town in the Grampians is **Halls Gap,** which is situated in a valley between the southern tip of the Mt. Difficult Range and the northern tip of the Mt. William Range. It's a good place to stock up on supplies. The Wonderland Range, with its stunning scenery, is close to Halls Gap, too. There are plenty of short strolls and longer bushwalks available.

A must-do stop on the park is the **Brambuk Aboriginal Living Cultural Centre** (☎ **03/5356 4452**), adjacent to the park visitor center (see below). It offers an excellent introduction to the area's Aboriginal history and accessible rock art sites. A 15-minute movie highlighting the local Aboriginal history costs A$4 (U.S.$2.60) for adults and A$2.50 (U.S.$1.63) for children. Otherwise, entrance to the center is free. The center is open daily from 10am to 5pm.

ESSENTIALS

GETTING THERE By car, the park is accessed from the **Western Highway** at Ararat, Stawell (pronounced *Storl*), or Horsham. Alternatively, you can access the southern entrance from the Glenelg Highway at Dunkeld. The western areas of the park are reached from the Henty Highway (A200).

V/Line (☎ **13 61 96** in Victoria, 13 22 32 in NSW, or 03/9619 5000) has a daily train and bus service to Halls Gap from Melbourne (the train goes to Stawell, and a connecting bus takes you to your destination). The trip takes around 4 hours.

GETTING AROUND Sealed roads include the **Grampians Tourist Road,** which cuts through the park from Dunkeld to Halls Gap; the **Mt. Victory Road** from Halls Gap to Wartook, and the **Roses Gap Road,** which runs from Wartook across to Dadswells Bridge on the Western Highway. Many other roads in the park are unsealed, but most are passable with a 2WD car.

Grampians National Park Tours (☎ **03/5356 6221**) offers all-day, 4WD tours of the park, stopping off at Aboriginal rock art sites, waterfalls, and lookouts. There's not much walking involved, but you certainly get the chance to spot native animals and ferret around among the native flora. The tour includes lunch and morning and afternoon tea and costs A$75 (U.S.$48.75).

Auswalk, P.O. Box 516, Jindabyne, NSW 2627 (☎ **02/6457 2220;** fax 02/6457 2206; www.auswalk.com.au), organizes self-guided tours through the park. A 6-night tour for two or more people costs A$1,090 (U.S.$708.50) per person including accommodation, most meals, national-park fees, some vehicle transfers, a half-day 4WD tour, an itinerary, and maps.

VISITOR INFORMATION The Grampians National Park Visitor Centre (☎ **03/5356 4379**), 2.5 kilometers (1½ miles) south of Halls Gap, is open daily from 9am to 5pm. It has plenty of maps and brochures, and the rangers can advise you on walking trails and camping spots.

WHERE TO STAY

You can hire a caravan or a cabin for the night at **Halls Gap Caravan Park** (☎ **03/ 5356 4251**). Caravans cost A$39.50 to $45.10 (U.S.$25.68–$29.32) and cabins A$49.50 to $61.60 (U.S.$32.18–$40.04)—depending on season. They also offer self-contained units from A$61.60 to $99 (U.S.$40.04–$64.35), and log cabins from A$126.50 to $137.50 (U.S.$82.23–$89.38). Another option is the **Halls Gap Lake-side Caravan Park** (☎ **03/5356 4281**), which is 5 kilometers (3 miles) from town on the shores of Lake Bellfield. Cabins cost A$45 to $95 (U.S.$29.25–$61.75) depending on rooms and season.

The Mountain Grand Guesthouse and Business Retreat. Grampians Tourist Rd. ☎ **03/ 5356 4232.** Fax 03/5356 4254. mtgrand@netconnect.co.au. 10 units. A/C. A$108 (U.S.$70.20) double, minimum 2-night on weekend. Ask about the fully-inclusive indulgence package. Rates include breakfast. AE, BC, DC, MC, V.

A couple of years ago, this old-fashioned guesthouse was pretty run down, but recent refurbishment by the new owners has brought it up to a comfortable 3½-star standard. These days it's promoting itself as a business retreat, and as such tourists who turn up get all the benefits of those added little corporate extras, such as exceptional service. The guest house specializes in a weekend getaway package costing A$90 (U.S.$58.50) per person twin share, with a Devonshire tea, a three-course dinner, a buffet breakfast, a gourmet picnic lunch, and champagne and chocolates thrown in.

The rooms are small, but furnished with nice country-style furniture and double beds. All have an attached bathroom. Larger family rooms, some of which have a spa, were renovated in 1999. There are several lounge rooms and "conversion nooks," all with TVs, a guest laundry, a bar, a cafe, and a restaurant serving good home-cooked meals.

Canberra 14

by Marc Llewellyn

If you mention you're heading to Canberra (pronounced *Can*-bra), most Australians will say, "Why bother?" Even many Canberrans admit that the Australian Capital Territory (ACT) is a great place to live but they wouldn't want to visit.

What is it about Canberra that draws so much lackluster comment? Simply put, Australians aren't used to having things so nice and ordered. In many ways, Canberra is like Washington, D.C., or any town that was a planned community from the start. Some see its virtues as bland: The roads are wide and in good order, the buildings are modern, and the suburbs are pleasant and leafy. Canberra is also the seat of government and the home of thousands of civil servants—enough to make almost any free-thinking, individualist Aussie with a hint of convict in him or her to shudder.

But to me, Canberra's differences are the very things that make it special. The streets aren't clogged with traffic, and there are plenty of opportunities for safe biking—try that in almost any other city center and you'll find out how difficult it is. There are open spaces, parklands, and fascinating monuments, and an awful lot to see and do—from museum and gallery hopping to ballooning with a champagne glass in your hand or boating on Lake Burley Griffin. You can certainly pack a lot in a few days' visit.

Canberra was born after the Commonwealth of Australia was officially created in 1901. Melbourne and Sydney, even then jockeying for pre-eminence, each put in their bid to become the new federal capital. In the end, Australian leaders decided to follow the example of their U.S. counterparts by creating a federal district; in 1908 they chose an undeveloped area between the two cities.

Designing the new capital fell to Chicago landscape architect Walter Burley Griffin, a contemporary of Frank Lloyd Wright. The city he mapped out was christened Canberra (a local Aboriginal word meaning "meeting place"), and by 1927, the first meeting of parliament took place. The business of government was underway.

1 Orientation

ARRIVING

BY PLANE **Qantas** (☎ **13 13 13** in Australia, or 02/9691 3636) and **Kendell** (book through Ansett ☎ **13 13 00** in Australia) offer daily service to Canberra. **The Canberra Airport** is about 10 minutes from the city center. It has car-rental desks, gift shop, news-stand, currency exchange, a bar, and bistro. Stamps are sold at the newsagent and there is also a mailbox. The airport lacks lockers, showers, and a post office. **Canberra City Sites and Tours** (☎ **02/6294 3171,** or mobile phone 041/262 5552) meets most planes, but phone them before you arrive. They charge A$6 (U.S.$3.90) per person for a trip to city center hotels.

BY TRAIN   A nice way to see some countryside is to take the train. **Countrylink** (☎ **13 22 32** in Australia; www.countrylink.nsw.gov.au) runs three *Canberra Xplorer* trains daily between Sydney and Canberra. The 4-hour trip costs A$67.10 (U.S.$43.62) in first class and A$47.30 (U.S.$30.75) in economy; children are charged half price, and a return trip costs double. Many people make use of **Countrylink** transport/hotel packages (call Countrylink Holidays on ☎ **13 28 29**), which can save you a bit of money. There's a range of hotels to choose from costing between A$85 to $186 (U.S.$55.25–$120.90) a night for a couple, and if you book in advance (they recommend two weeks), you can save up to 40% on the train fare (through a Rail Escape package), too. The Countrylink office is at Wynyard CityRail Station.

From Melbourne, the **Canberra Link**—run by **V/Line** (☎ **136 196** in Australia) involves a 5-hour bus trip and a 3½-hour train trip: it costs A$55 (U.S.$35.75) for adults and A$34 (U.S.$22.10) for children and students.

Canberra Railway Station (☎ **02/6239 7039**) is on Wentworth Avenue, Kingston, about 5 kilometers (3 miles) southeast of the city center.

BY BUS   Greyhound Pioneer (☎ **13 20 30** in Australia, or 07/3258 1600; www.greyhound.com.au) runs six services a day from Sydney to Canberra. Tickets cost A$30 (U.S.$19.50) for adults, A$20 (U.S.$13) for students with an ISAC card, and A$15 (U.S.$9.75) for children; the trip takes 4 to 4½ hours. From Melbourne, tickets to Canberra cost A$49 (U.S.$31.85) for adults, A$44 (U.S.$28.60) for students, and A$39 (U.S.$25.35) for children, and the trip takes around 10 hours. (Advanced purchase fares can save you up to 35%)

Murrays Australia (☎ **13 22 51** in Australia, or 02/9252 3590) runs three services a day from Sydney to Canberra for A$35.20 (U.S.$22.88) for adults and A$18.70 (U.S.$12.16) for children. Ask for YHA member discounts. Several sightseeing companies in Sydney, including **AAT King's, Murrays,** and **Australia Pacific Tours,** offer day trips to Canberra.

Intercity buses arrive at **Jolimont Tourist Centre,** at the corner of Northbourne Avenue and Alinga Street, in Canberra City.

BY CAR   The ACT is surrounded by the state of New South Wales. Sydney is 306 kilometers (190 miles) northeast and Melbourne is 651 kilometers (404 miles) southwest of Canberra. If you drive from Sydney via the Hume and Federal Highways, the trip will take 3½ to 4 hours. From Melbourne, take the Hume Highway to Yass, then switch to the Barton Highway; the trip will take about eight hours.

VISITOR INFORMATION

The Canberra Visitors' Centre, 330 Northbourne Ave., Dickson (☎ **1800/026 166** in Australia, or 02/6205 0044; fax 02/6205 0776; www.canberratourism.com.au;), dispenses information and books accommodations. The office is open Monday to Friday from 9am to 5:30pm, and Saturday and Sunday from 9am to 4pm.

SPECIAL EVENTS   A host of free events—from concerts to competitions—are part of the annual **Canberra National Multicultural Festival** held in the first 3 weeks of March. The fun includes Canberra Day (a local holiday—always the third Monday in March), a hot-air balloon fiesta, fireworks, food and wine promotions, plenty of music, and a large range of activities organized by Australia's large ethnic mix. Visitors

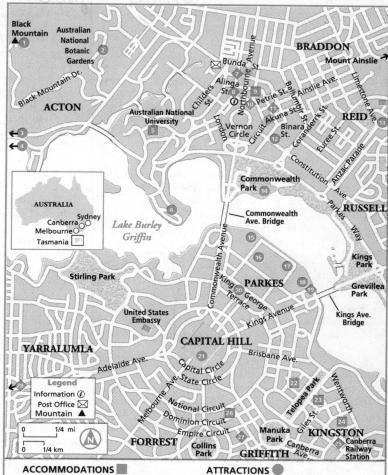

Wadden Farmes

Black Mountain ▲ 1
Australian National Botanic Gardens 2
BRADDON
Mount Ainslie →

Bunda St.
Alinga St.
Northbourne Avenue
Ballumbir St.
Petrie St.
Ainslie Ave.
Limestone Ave.
ACTON
Childers St.
London Circuit
Vernon Circle
Akuna St.
Binara St.
Coranderrk St.
Euree St.
REID
Australian National University 5
Anzac Parade
Constitution Ave.
RUSSELL
Commonwealth Park 14
Commonwealth Ave. Bridge
AUSTRALIA
Sydney
Canberra
Melbourne
Tasmania
Lake Burley Griffin
Parkes Way
Commonwealth Avenue
Kings Park
Stirling Park
King George Terrace
PARKES
Grevillea Park
Kings Ave. Bridge
United States Embassy
Kings Avenue
CAPITAL HILL
Adelaide Ave.
Capital Circle
State Circle
Brisbane Ave.
YARRALUMLA
21
Melbourne Ave.
National Circuit
Dominion Circuit
Empire Circuit
22
Telopea Park
Giles St.
Wentworth
23
24
KINGSTON
26
Manuka Park
FORREST
Collins Park
27
GRIFFITH
Canberra Ave.
25
Canberra Railway Station

Legend
Information ⓘ
Post Office ✉
Mountain ▲
0   1/4 mi
0   1/4 km

ACCOMMODATIONS ■
The Brassey of Canberra **22**
City Walk Hotel **9**
Forest Inn and Apartments **26**
Kingston Court Apartments **23**
University House **5**
Victor Lodge **24**

DINING ◆
Caffe Della Piazza **7**
Chairman and Yip **11**
The Exhibition Restaurant **19**
Little Saigon **8**
The Palette Café **28**
Portia's Place **25**
Tosolini's **10**
The Tryst **27**

ATTRACTIONS ●
Australian Institute of Sport **3**
Australian National Botanic Gardens **2**
Australian War Memorial **13**
Casino Canberra **12**
High Court of Australia **17**
National Capital Exhibition **14**
National Gallery of Australia **18**
National Library of Australia **15**
National Museum of Australia **6**
Old Parliament House **20**
Parliament House **21**
Questacon—The National Science and Technology Centre **16**
Telstra Tower **1**
Treloar Technology Center **4**

could find it a little more difficult to book accommodations during this time, but you should always be able to find something.

CITY LAYOUT

The first thing that strikes a visitor to Canberra is its park-like feel (amazing, since there was barely a tree on the original site). Half a dozen avenues radiate from Capital Hill, where the Parliament House stands. Each of these broad, tree-shaded streets leads to a traffic circle, from which more streets emanate. Around each hub, the streets form a pattern of concentric circles—not the easiest layout for visitors to navigate.

Another of Canberra's most notable features is **Lake Burley Griffin,** a manmade lake created by damming the Molonglo River. The centerpiece of the lake is the **Captain Cook Memorial Jet,** a spire of water that reaches 147 meters (162 yd.) into the air. Wedged between Commonwealth Avenue and Kings Avenue is the suburb of Parkes, also known as the **National Triangle.** Here you'll find many of the city's most impressive attractions, such as the National Gallery of Australia, the High Court of Australia, and the National Science and Technology Center (all sites here can be accessed via www.nationaltriangle.com.au/tri).

Canberra's main shopping district is on the other side of the lake, centered around Northbourne Avenue, one of the city's main thoroughfares. Officially labeled **Canberra City,** this area is more commonly known as **"Civic."** Northeast of Civic is **Mount Ainslie,** with the Australian War Memorial at its foot; from its summit there are spectacular views of the city and beyond. Another good lookout point is from the top of the **Telstra Tower** on Black Mountain, reached by Black Mountain Drive. The embassies and consulates are concentrated in the suburb of Yarralumla, east of Capital Hill, while most of the other suburbs are filled with homes and small retail areas.

2 Getting Around

BY CAR   **Advantage Car Rentals,** 74 Northbourne Ave. (corner of Barry Drive), (☎ **02/6257 6888,** or 1800 504 460 in Australia) has cars from A$35 (U.S.$22.75) per day, including 200 kilometers (124 miles) per day. **Budget** (☎ **02/6257 1305**), Hertz (☎ **02/6249 6211**), and **Thrifty (02/6248 9081**) have desks at the airport.

If you have your own wheels, you can follow one or more of the six tourist drives marked with signs; pick up details from the Canberra Visitors' Centre.

BY TAXI   Canberra's only taxi company is **Canberra Cabs** (☎ **13 22 27**).

BY BUS   Canberra's bus system is coordinated by **ACTION** (☎ **02/6207 7611;** www.action.act.gov.au). The central bus terminal is on Alinga Street, in Civic. 200 Scollay St, Tuggeranong, ACT. Bus fare is determined by zone. Canberra is divided into three zones; the city center is in Zone One, which will cost A$2.30 (U.S.$1.50) for adults one-way and A$1.70 (U.S.$1.11) for children 5 to 15. If you travel through more than one zone it will cost A$4.40 (U.S.$2.86) for adults and A$2.20 (U.S.$1.43) for children. Ask the driver when you board the bus how much you should pay.

Weekly tickets cost A$19.80 (U.S.$12.87) for Zone One and A$38 (U.S.$24.70) all three zones; children are half price. Ten-Ride tickets also cost A$19.80 (U.S.$12.87). Purchase all tickets on the bus, or from most newsagents and ACTION interchanges.

For timetable information, call ACTION Monday to Friday from 6:30am to 11:30pm, Saturday from 7:30am to 11pm, and Sunday from 8:30am to 6pm. Pick up bus route maps at bus interchanges, newsagents, and the Canberra Visitors' Center.

Canberra City Sighseeing Tours (☎ **0500 505 012**) pulls in at 11 attractions around the city. Visitors can get off and on when they like. An all-day ticket costs A$25 (U.S.$16.25) for adults and A$12.50 (U.S.$8.13) for children.

BY BICYCLE Canberra is unique in Australia for its extensive system of cycle tracks—some 120 kilometers (74 miles) of them—which makes sightseeing on two wheels a pleasurable experience. See "Outdoor Pursuits," later in this chapter for details on bike rental.

Fast Facts: Canberra

American Express The office at Centerpoint, Shop 1, 185 City Walk (at the corner of Petrie Plaza), Civic (☎ **02/6247 2333**), is open Monday through Friday from 9am to 5pm, and Saturday from 9am to noon.

Business Hours Banks are generally open Monday through Thursday from 9:30am to 4pm and Friday from 9:30am to 5pm. Stores and offices are open Monday to Friday from 9am to 5:30pm. Many shops stay open on weekends and until 9pm Fridays.

Climate The best time to visit Canberra is in spring (Sept–Nov) or autumn (Mar–May). Summers are hot and winters can get pretty cold.

Currency Exchange Cash traveler's checks at banks, at American Express (see above), or at **Thomas Cook,** at the Petrie Plaza entrance of the Canberra Centre (☎ **02/6257 2222**), Monday through Friday from 9am to 5pm and Saturday from 9:30am to 12:30pm.

Dentist Canberra lacks a dental emergency referral service. A reputable dentist in the center of town is **Lachland B. Lewis,** Level 3, 40 Allara St., Civic (☎ **02/ 6257 2777** after hours, and 02/6295 2319 or 02/6295 9495 weekends).

Doctor The **Capital Medical Centre,** 2 Mort St., Civic (☎ **02/6257 3766**), is open Monday through Friday from 8:30am to 4:30pm. **The Travellers' Medical & Vaccination Centre,** Level 1, City Walk Arcade, 2 Mort St. Now located at Level 5, 8-10 Hobart Place, (☎ **02/6257 7154**) offers vaccinations and travel medicines. Standard consultations cost around A$39 (U.S.$25.35).

E-mail The **National Library,** Parkes Place, Parkes (☎ **02/6262 1111**), has e-mail facilities available Monday through Thursday 9am to 5pm daily.

Embassies/Consulates The **British High Commission** is located at Old Parliament House Annex, Parkes (☎ **02/6270 6666**). **The Canadian High Commission** is at Commonwealth Ave., Yarralumla (☎ **02/6270 4000**); the **U.S. Embassy** is found at Moonah Place, Yarralumla (☎ **02/6214 5600**); and the **New Zealand High Commission** is at Commonwealth Ave., Yarralumla (☎ **02/ 6270 4211**).

Emergencies Call ☎ **000** for an ambulance, the police, or the fire department.

Eyeglasses For repairs, glasses and contact lenses try **OPSM Express,** shop 5, Lower Ground Floor, The Canberra Centre, Civic. (☎ **02/6249 7344**). It's open 9am to 5:30pm weekdays (to 9pm on Fri),and 9am to 4pm on Saturday.

Hospitals For medical attention, go to the **Canberra Hospital,** Yamba Drive, Garran (☎ **6244 2222**), or call the **Accident & Emergency Department** on ☎ **02/6244 2324** (24 hr.).

Hot Lines Rape Crisis Centre (☎ 02/6247 2525); Drug/Alcohol Crisis Line (☎ 02/6205 4545 24 hours); Lifeline Crisis Councelling (☎ 13 11 14); Salvation Army Councelling Service (☎ 02/9331 6000). Poison Information Centre (☎ 02/6285 2852); National Roads & Motorists Association (NRMA) (☎ 13 21 32).

Photographic Needs Fletchers Fotographics, Shop 2, 38 Akuna St., Civic (☎ 02/6247 8460), is the best place to buy camera gear and films. They also repair cameras and sell second-hand equipment.

Pharmacies The Canberra Centre Pharmacy, Civic (☎ 02/6249 8074) is open general shopping hours.

Post Office The Canberra GPO, 53-73 Alinga St, Civic (☎ 02/6209 1680), is open Monday to Friday from 8:30am to 5:30pm. The *Poste Restante* address is c/o Canberra GPO, ACT 2601.

Restrooms Found near the city bus exchange, City Hall, London Circuit.

Transit Information ACTION timetable information is at ☎ 02/6207 7611.

3 Accommodations You Can Afford

Canberra has a good scattering of places to stay, and generally accommodations are much cheaper than in most other state capitals. Many people travel to Canberra during the week, so many hotels offer cheaper weekend rates to put heads on beds. You should always ask about special deals. The rates given below are rack rates, or what the hotels hope they'll get on a good day—you can often get a room for less.

⭐ **The Brassey of Canberra.** Belmore Gardens, Barton, ACT 2600. ☎ **02/6273 3766.** Fax 02/6273 2791. www.brassey.net.au. info@brassey.net.au. 81 units. MINIBAR TV TEL. A$124 (U.S.$80.60) double, A$152 (U.S.$98.80) for a family room; A$146 (U.S.$94.90) heritage double, or A$195 (U.S.$126.75) for a heritage family room; A$185 (U.S.$120.25) suite. Rates include full breakfast. AE, BC, DC, MC, V. Free parking. Bus: 36 (get off outside the National Press Club).

Rooms in this 1927 heritage-listed building, formerly a boarding house for visiting government officials, are large, quiet, and somewhat plush. The garden bar and piano lounge are popular. Other good points include its proximity to Parliament House and other attractions, and the hearty breakfasts. The hotel underwent renovations in early 2000, which included remodeling many of the doubles into larger heritage rooms.

City Walk Hotel. 2 Mort St., Civic, ACT 2601. ☎ **02/6257 0124.** Fax 02/6257 0116. citywalk@ozemail.com. 55 units, 18 with bathroom (shower only). A$45 (U.S.$29.25) single without bathroom; A$65 (U.S.$42.25) single with bathroom; A$60 (U.S.$39) double without bathroom; A$70 (U.S.$45.50) double with bathroom; A$95–$125 (U.S.$61.75–$81.25) family room. Extra adult A$12 (U.S.$7.80); extra child is free. A$21–$23 (U.S.$13.65–$14.95) dorm bed. BC, MC, V.

You can hardly get closer to the city center than at this former YWCA-turned-budget-travel hotel. Being right near the Jolimont Tourist Centre bus interchange, it picks up a lot of business from backpackers and budget travelers arriving by bus from other parts of the country. The rooms are pretty basic, but clean. There are five double rooms with shared bathrooms, though three of these also have two extra single beds. Six rooms have air-conditioning. All rooms with bathrooms have their own TV. Family rooms sleep up to seven people, all in one room (one has its own kitchen). There is also a guest lounge, a laundry, a kitchen, a communal telephone, an air-conditioned common room with TV and video, and tea- and coffee-making facilities.

Forest Inn and Apartments. 30 National Circuit, Forrest, ACT 2603. ☎ **1800/676 372** in Australia or 02/6295 3433. Fax 02/6295 2119. www.forestinn.com. reservations@forestinn.

com. 102 units. A/C TV TEL. A$105 (U.S.$68.25) motel room; A$150 (U.S.$97.50) 1-bedroom-apt; A$167 (U.S.$108.55) 2-bedroom apt. AE, BC, DC, MC, V. Free parking. Bus: 39 (get off at the Rydges Hotel).

The Forest Inn is far from fancy, but it's close to the Manuka shops and restaurants and Parliament House. The outside of this 1960s property looks tacky, but the interior has recently been refurbished. The motel-style rooms are small and colorless, but clean; the apartments are nicer and have full-size kitchens, so for the same price I'd go for one of these. Two-bedroom apartments are perfect for families, and even the 1-bedroom apartments have a single bed in the living room.

✪ **Kingston Court Apartments.** 4 Tench St., Kingston, ACT 2604. ☎ **02/6295 2244.** Fax 02/6295 5300. www.kingstonterrace.com.au. 36 units. A/C TV TEL. A$125 (U.S.$81.25) apt for 2. Extra adult A$15 (U.S.$9.75); extra child A$7 (U.S.$4.55). AE, BC, DC, MC, V. Free parking. Bus: 38.

Kingston Court, situated about 1 kilometer (½ mile) from the Parliamentary Triangle and 6 kilometers (3½ miles) from Civic, is a good option if you're looking for the comforts of home. The apartments are modern and spacious and come with a full kitchen, washing machine and dryer, a balcony, and a courtyard. There is also a pool, gas barbecue, and a half-court tennis court on the grounds. The rooms underwent a full renovation in 2000.

Victor Lodge. 29 Dawes St., Kingston, ACT 2604. ☎ **02/6295 7777.** Fax 02/6295 2466. www.victorlodge.com.au. 28 units, 29 units none with bathroom. A$59 (U.S.$38.35) double;. A$23 (U.S.$14.95) dorm bed. Rates include continental breakfast. BC, MC, V. Free parking. Bus: 38, 39, 50.

Backpackers, parliamentary staff, and budget travelers frequent this friendly place, situated right next to Kingston shops and about a 15-minute drive from the city center. Rooms vary from dorms with three, four or five beds, to modern, simple doubles. There are communal showers and toilets, a laundry, a guest refrigerator, a TV room, free tea and coffee, and a courtyard. The staff picks up guests from the train and bus stations daily and drops off guests in town every morning. It's a nice place, but you'll have to decide whether or not you want to put up with the short trek into the city. Bike rental costs A$12 (U.S.$7.80) for a full day and A$8 (U.S.$5.20) for a half day after 2pm.

The owners also own the Best Western motel next door, which has standby rates of A$85 (U.S.$55.25) for a double. Apparently, long-suffering parents often dump their teenage kids at the lodge and live it up at the motel.

✪ **University House.** The hotel at the Australian National University, Balmain Crescent, Acton (GPO Box 1535, Canberra, ACT 2601). ☎ **1800/814 864** in Australia, or 02/6249 5211. Fax 02/6249 5252. 100 units. TV TEL. A$106 (U.S.$68.90) twin; A$111 (U.S.$72.15) suite; A$116 (U.S.$75.40) 1-bedroom apt; A$161 (U.S.$104.65) 2-bedroom apt. Ask about packages, especially during low season. AE, BC, DC, MC, V. Free security parking. Bus: 34.

University House, situated less than 2 kilometers (1¼ miles) from the city center, offers a pleasant alternative to run-of-the-mill hotels in a similar price bracket. Large twin rooms come with two single beds; suites have a sitting room and a queen size bed; the 1-bedroom apartments have queen-size beds, a sitting room, and kitchenette; the 2-bedroom apartments are huge, with large bedrooms, a dining room, a lounge room, and full kitchen. All units have bathrooms with a shower and a tub. Meals are served in Boffins Restaurant and the Cellar Café dinner Monday to Friday. Breakfast, babysitting, and bicycles are available. University House also has tennis courts and easy access to walking and jogging tracks.

4 Great Deals on Dining

✪ **Caffe Della Piazza.** 19 Garema Place, Civic. ☎ **02/6248 9711.** Reservations recommended. Main courses A$6.50–$17.50 (U.S.$4.23–$11.38). AE, BC, DC, MC, V. Daily 10:30am–midnight. ITALIAN/CAFE.

Good eating isn't hard to find in Canberra, but this place is up there with the best. It's won several awards for its Italian-inspired cooking, including the catering industries award for the best restaurant in the state (nothing like being judged by your peers). The restaurant offers both indoor and outdoor dining in pleasant surrounds, and is a good place to pop in for a light meal and a coffee, or something more substantial. Pastas here cost around A$11 (U.S.$7.15), and the best seller is chicken breast strips in a machiato sauce. You need to book early on Friday or Saturday evenings.

✪ **The Exhibition Restaurant.** Sculpture Garden of the National Gallery of Australia, Parkes. ☎ **02/6273 2836.** Reservations recommended. Main courses lunch A$20 (U.S.$13); set dinner menus A$38 (U.S.$24.70) 2-courses, A$48 (U.S.$31.20) 3-courses. AE, BC, DC, MC, V. Daily noon–2:30pm; Thurs-Sat 6:30pm–10pm. MODERN AUSTRALIAN.

The Exhibition Restaurant (formally the Mirrabook) sits on a lake edged with rushes and sculptures and full of goldfish. Add smoke machines (they call it a fog sculpture) on the far bank to send mysterious white eddies across the lake's surface toward your lakeside table, and you have a charming fantasy world in which to dine. The menu is small, with only a choice of four first courses, mains and desserts. Mains could include roasted pheasant, pan-fried lamb loin stuffed with an almond mousse, a vegetarian option and a veal fillet. The lemon meringue pie with a rhubarb base is a firm favorite.

Little Saigon. Alinga St. and Northbourne Ave., Civic. ☎ **02/6230 5003.** Main courses A$12–$15 (U.S.$7.80–$9.75). AE, BC, DC, MC, V. Daily 10am–3pm and 5–10:30pm. VIETNAMESE.

This spacious restaurant has minimalist decor and floor-to-ceiling windows offering views of the busy city center. Tables are set up on either side of an indoor pond, and there's a bar in the back of the restaurant. The menu is vast, with lots of noodle dishes as well as spicy seafood, duck, chicken, pork, beef, and lamb selections. The top seller is the lemongrass and chili chicken.

✪ **The Palette Cafe.** Beaver Gallery, 81 Denison St., Deakin. ☎ **02/6282 8416.** Main courses A$12–$18 (U.S.$7.80–$11.70). AE, BC, MC, V. Daily 10am–5pm. CAFE/MODERN AUSTRALIAN.

This is a great choice for lunch, especially since it's in the same building as Canberra's largest private art gallery. You can either eat inside, surrounded by artwork, or claim a table outside in the sunny courtyard. Standout dishes include grilled asparagus spears with Japanese scallops and almond hollandaise, and the chili-salted baby octopus. The Caesar salads are particularly good, as are the field mushrooms with a sauce of soy, Japanese rice wine, honey, and coriander. The etchings, paintings, and sculptures on display are of high quality and are well priced.

Portia's Place. 11 Kennedy St., Kingston. ☎ **02/6239 7970.** Main courses A$9.80–$18.80 (U.S.$6.37–$12.22). AE, BC, DC, MC, V. Daily noon–2:30pm; Sun–Wed 5–10pm, Thurs-Sat 5–10:30pm. CANTONESE/MALAYSIAN/PEKING

A small restaurant serving up excellent traditional cookery, Portia's Place often fills up early and does a roaring lunchtime trade. The best things on the menu are the shang tung sauce lamb ribs, the King Island fillet steak in pepper sauce, the flaming pork (brought to your table wrapped in foil and bursting with flames), and the Queensland trout stir-fried with snow peas.

⭐ **Tosolini's.** Corner of London Circuit at East Row, Civic. ☎ **02/6247 4317.** Main courses A$14.50–$18 (U.S.$9.43–$11.70). AE, BC, MC, DC, V. Daily 7:30am–5pm (Tues–Sat until 10:30pm). CAFE/MODERN AUSTRALIAN.

Since it's situated right next to the busy central bus terminal and close to the major shopping areas, Tosolini's really pulls in the passing crowd. You can sit out on the sidewalk terrace and watch the world go by. The eggs Benedict served here at breakfast could be the best A$7.50 (U.S.$4.88) you've ever spent. Lunchtime fare is almost as good. Both the battered flathead and the pan-fried broadbill (both local fish) are tasty, but Tosolini's really made its name with its pastas and focaccias.

⭐ **The Tryst.** Bougainville St., Manuka. ☎ **02/6239 4422.** Reservations recommended. Main courses A$15–$23 (U.S.$9.75–$14.95). AE, BC, DC, MC, V. Daily noon–2:30pm; Mon–Sat 6–10pm. MODERN AUSTRALIAN.

The personal touches and the service really shine through at The Tryst, and the food is consistently delicious. The restaurant is tastefully decorated in an upscale cafe style, with the kitchen staff on show as they rustle up some of the capital's best tucker. It's also relaxed, feeling more communal than intimate on busy nights. My favorite dish is the Atlantic salmon served with *beurre blanc* sauce and potatoes, but other popular dishes include the eye fillet steak, and the pumpkin risotto. If you have room left for dessert, don't miss out on the sticky date pudding served with hot butterscotch sauce, pralines, and ice cream—it's as good as it sounds. Otherwise, the long list of daily specials that complement the extensive menu could keep you busy for weeks.

WORTH A SPLURGE

⭐ **Chairman and Yip.** 108 Bunda St., Civic. ☎ **02/6248 7109.** Reservations required. Main courses A$16–$22 (U.S.$10.40–$14.30). AE, BC, MC, DC, V. Sun–Fri noon–3pm; daily 6–11pm. ASIAN AUSTRALIAN.

Without doubt, this is Canberra's best restaurant. Upbeat and popular with political bigwigs, it really is the place to see and be seen. The fish specials are good and spicy, with combinations of chili, coriander, lemongrass, and *galangal* perking up your taste buds. I always go for the prawns with homemade chili jam, served on vermicelli noodles with mango salsa. Abalone and lobster also find their way onto the menu. The pannacotta is the signature dessert.

5 Seeing the Sights

Australian Institute of Sport. Leverrier Crescent, Bruce. ☎ **02/6252 1111** (now 02/ 6214 1111) Admission A$8 (U.S.$5.20) adults, A$4 (U.S.$2.60) children, A$20 (U.S.$13) families; tours leave the AIS shop Mon–Fri at 11:30am and 2:30pm, and Sat–Sun at 10am, 11:30am, 1pm, and 2:30pm. Bus: 80 from city center.

This institution provides first-class training and facilities for Australia's elite athletes. Tours, led by one of the institute's athletes, include visits to the gymnasium, basketball courts, and Olympic swimming pool to see training in progress. There is also a fascinating interactive sports display where visitors can test their sporting skills.

⭐ **Australian War Memorial.** At the head of Anzac Parade on Limestone Ave. ☎ **02/ 6243 4211.** Free admission. Daily 10am–5pm (when the Last Post is played). Closed Christmas. Guided tours at 10am, 10:30am, 11am, 1:30pm, and 2pm. Bus: 233, 302, 303, 362, 436, or 901.

This monument to Australian troops who gave their lives for their country is truly moving. Artifacts and displays tell the story of Australia's conflicts abroad. You won't soon forget the exhibition on Gallipoli, the bloody World War I battle in which so

National Museum of Australia, Acton Peninsula.

Opened in March, 2001 to coincide with the centenary of Australian Federation, the **National Museum of Australia** (☎ **02/6208 5000;** www.nma.gov.au) was an immediate hit, welcoming its 250,000th visitor to its state-of-the-art facility by May 17. Located on the banks of Lake Burley Griffin, the museum's programs and exhibits are based on three themes: Australian society and its history since 1788; the interaction of people with the Australian environment; and Aboriginal and Torres Strait Islander cultures and histories. The collection includes some 80,000 stone tools and Australia's largest collection of bark paintings, spanning two centuries and the width and breadth of Australia. The NMA is open daily, except Christmas, from 9am–5pm. General admission is free, with fees charged for some special exhibits. The museum is located on route 34 of the Action Bus, and on Saturday and Sunday, a free shuttle bus runs from city center.

many Anzac (Australian and New Zealand Army Corps) servicemen were slaughtered. The Hall of Memory is the focus of the memorial, where the Unknown Soldier lies entombed, his remains brought back from a WWI battlefield in 1993. The Memorial also holds one of the largest collections of Australian art in the world, including major works by Tom Roberts, Arthur Streeton, and Grace Cossington-Smith. Exhibits include a film showing the surrender of Singapore projected onto the table on which the surrender was signed and a simulated ride aboard an original Lancaster bomber.

✪ **Canberra Deep Space Communication Complex.** Tidbinbilla, 39km (23¼ miles) southwest of Civic. ☎ **02/6201 7880.** www.cdscc.nasa.gov. Free admission. Summer daily 9am–8pm; rest of year daily 9am–5pm. No public bus service, but several tour companies offer programs that include the complex.

This information center, which stands beside huge tracking dishes, is a must for anyone interested in space. There are plenty of models, audio-visual recordings, and displays, including a space suit, space food, and film footage of the Apollo moon landings. The complex is still active and is tracking and recording results from the Mars Pathfinder, Voyager 1 and 2, and the Cassini, Soho, Galileo, and Ulysses space exploration projects, as well as providing a vital link with NASA spacecraft. This is a great stop off on the way back from the Tidbinbilla Nature Reserve just up the road (see below).

High Court of Australia. Overlooking Lake Burley Griffin, Parkes Place. ☎ **02/6270 6811.** www.hcourt.gov.au. Free admission. Mon–Fri 9:45am–4:30pm. Closed public holidays. Bus: 34.

The High Court, an impressive concrete-and-glass building overlooks Lake Burley Griffin next to the National Gallery of Australia. Elizabeth II opened it in 1980. It is home to the highest court in Australia's judicial system and contains three courtrooms, a video display, and a huge seven-story public hall. When court is in session, visitors can observe the proceedings from the public gallery. Call or email for session details.

National Capital Exhibition. On the lake shore at Regatta Point in Commonwealth Park. ☎ **02/6257 1068.** Free admission. Daily 9am–6pm (5pm in winter).

If you want to find out more about Canberra's beginnings—and get a memorable view of Lake Burley Griffin, the Captain Cook Memorial Water Jet, and the Carillon in the bargain—then head here. The displays are well done, and there's a film that provides and overview of the city's design.

National Gallery of Australia. Parkes Place. ☎ **02/6240 6502.** Free admission (except for major touring exhibitions). Daily 10am–5pm. Guided tours daily at 11am and 2pm; Thurs and Sun at 11am there's a free tour focusing on Aboriginal art. Bus: 36 and 39 from Old Parliament House, or 34 from Parkes Place in front of the High Court.

Linked to the High Court by a pedestrian bridge, the National Gallery showcases both Australian and international art. The permanent collection and traveling exhibitions are displayed in 11 separate galleries. You'll find paintings by big names such as Claude Monet and Jackson Pollock, and Australian painters Arthur Boyd, Sidney Nolan, Arthur Streeton, Charles Condor, Tom Roberts, and Albert Tucker. The exhibition of Tiwi islander burial poles in the foyer is also interesting (the Tiwi Islands include Melville and Bathurst islands off Darwin), and there's a large collection of Aboriginal bark paintings from central Australia. A sculpture garden surrounding the gallery has 24 sculptures and is always open to the public.

Old Parliament House. On King George Terrace, midway between the new Parliament House (below) and the lake. ☎ **02/6273 4723.** Admission A$2 (U.S.$1.30) adults, A$1 (U.S.65¢) children, A$5 (U.S.$3.25) family. Daily 9am–5pm. Bus: 39.

The seat of government from 1927 to 1988, the Old Parliament House is now home to exhibitions from the National Museum and the Australian Archives. The National Portrait Gallery is also here, and on the lawn is the Aboriginal Tent Embassy, which was set up in 1972 in a bid to persuade the authorities to recognize the land ownership claims of Aboriginal and Torres Strait Islander people. The red, black, and yellow Aboriginal flag first came to prominence here. Interestingly, the Australian Heritage Commission now recognizes the campsite as a place of special cultural significance.

Parliament House. Capital Hill. ☎ **02/6277 5399.** Free admission. Daily 9am–5pm. Closed Christmas. Bus: 39.

Conceived by American architect Walter Burley Griffin in 1912, but not built until 1988, Canberra's centerpoint was designed to blend organically into its setting at the top of Capital Hill; only a national flag supported by a giant four-footed flag pole rises above the peak of the hill. In good weather, picnickers crowd the grass that covers the roof, where the view is spectacular. Inside are more than 3,000 works of Australian arts and crafts, and extensive areas of the building are open to the general public. Be sure to look for "Meeting Place," a mosaic by Michael Tjakamarra Nelson, which represents a gathering of various Aboriginal tribes, and can be found just inside the main entrance. There's also a 20-meter (22-yd.) tapestry by Arthur Boyd in the Great Hall on the first floor and one of the four known versions of the Magna Carta in the Great

Up, Up & Away

Balloon Aloft (☎ **02/6285 1540**) offers fabulous 45-minute sunrise flights over Canberra Monday to Friday for A$155 (U.S.$100.75) for adults and A$100 (U.S.$65) for children 6 to 12, including a champagne breakfast on touchdown. On weekends an hour-long trip is A$220 (U.S.$143) for adults, A$140 (U.S.$91) for children, including breakfast at the Hyatt Hotel. It costs A$25 (U.S.$16.25), less if you don't want breakfast. **Dawn Drifters** (☎ **02/6285 4450;** fax 02/6281 5315; www.dawndrifters.com.au) will also send you soaring over the city. One-hour champagne flights with breakfast cost A$155 (U.S.$100.75) for adults Monday to Friday and A$195 (U.S.$126.75) on weekends and holidays. Children go for 40% of the adult price. Breakfast is A$15 (U.S.$9.75) extra.

The Wines of ACT

National Capital Wine Tours (☎ **02/6231 3330**) offers wine-tasting trips with gourmet lunches on Saturdays and Sundays for A$59 (U.S.$38.35), including hotel pickup. Tours leave at 10am and return at 4pm and visit three local wineries.

Hall directly beneath the flagpole. Free 50-minute guided tours are offered throughout the day.

Parliament usually is in session Monday to Thursday between mid-February and late June, and mid-August to mid-December. Both the lower house—the **House of Representatives** (where the prime minister sits)—and the upper house—the **Senate**—have public viewing galleries. The best time to see the action is during Question Time, which starts at 2pm in the lower house. If you turn up early enough, you might be lucky and get a seat; otherwise make reservations for gallery tickets via the **sergeant-at-arms** (☎ **02/6277 4889**), at least a day in advance. Free tours of the building go for 45 minutes and start at 9am (then follow every 30 min.).

Questacon—The National Science and Technology Centre. King Edward Terrace, Parkes. ☎ **02/6270 2800.** Admission A$10 (U.S.$6.50) adults, A$5 (U.S.$3.25) children, A$6.50 (U.S.$4.23) students, A$28 (U.S.$18.20) families. Daily 10am–5pm. Closed Christmas. Bus: 34.

Questacon offers some 170 hands-on exhibits that can keep you and your inner child occupied for hours. Exhibits are clustered into six galleries, each representing a different aspect of science. The artificial earthquake is a big attraction. The center is great for kids, but give it a miss if you've already visited the Powerhouse Museum in Sydney (see chapter 4).

Telstra Tower. Black Mountain Dr. ☎ **02/6248 1911.** Admission A$3 (U.S.$1.95) adults, A$1 (U.S.65¢) children. Daily 9am–10pm. No bus service.

The tower, which rises 195 meters (644 ft.) above the summit of Black Mountain, has both open-air and enclosed viewing galleries that provide magnificent 360° views over Canberra and the countryside. Those who dine in the pricey, revolving **Tower Restaurant** (☎ **02/6248 7096**) are entitled to a refund of their admission charge.

Tidbinbilla Nature Reserve. Tidbinbilla. ☎ **02/6237 5120.** Admission A$8 (U.S.$5.20) per vehicle day. Daily 9am–6pm (8pm in summer). Visitor center Mon–Fri 9am–4:30pm, Sat–Sun 9am–5:30pm. No public bus service, but several tour companies offer programs that include the reserve.

This is a great place to see native animals such as kangaroos, wallabies, koalas, platypus, and birds in their natural environment. Unlike other wildlife parks around the country, this one has plenty of space, so you may have to look hard to spot the animals. (On a recent quick visit, I saw a few birds and not much else, but on previous visits I've almost been stomped by kangaroos.) A guide is available from the visitor's center. If you want to be sure to spot some animals, contact **Round About Tours** (☎ **02/6259 5999**), which runs day tours of the reserve for A$55 (U.S.$35.75), including a picnic lunch and afternoon tea. It also offers kangaroo-spotting night tours for A$20 (U.S.$13).

Treloar Technology Centre. Corner of Vickers and Callan sts. ☎ **02/6243 4450.** Admission A$3 (U.S.$1.95) to walkway above exhibition floor. Floor tours A$15 (U.S.$9.75) adults, A$10 (U.S.$6.50) children (1 week advance notice required). Sun and Wed 11am–4pm (other times by appointment). Bus: 312–317 from city to Belconnen, and 48 from there.

Aviation buffs will want to book a floor tour of this facility, which should be done well in advance. Last time I was there, the technicians were stripping down a Lancaster bomber. Also on display are plenty of war relics: German V1 and V2 rockets, a Gallipoli landing craft, a Soviet T34 tank, Vietnam War helicopters, a Korean War Meteor, a Japanese Zero once flown by the 4th-ranked Japanese Ace (with 68 kills to his credit), miniature submarines, a Messerschmitt 163b Komet, and much more.

BOTANIC GARDENS & A NEARBY NATIONAL PARK

The ✪ **Australian National Botanic Gardens,** Clunies Ross Street, Black Mountain, Acton (☎ **02/6250 9540**), are home to the best collection of Australian native plants anywhere. The gardens are situated on 125 acres on the slopes of Black Mountain and feature a Eucalyptus Lawn with more than 600 species of eucalyptus, a rain forest area, a Tasmanian alpine garden, and self-guided walking tracks. Free guided tours depart from the visitor center at 11am on weekdays and 11am and 2pm on weekends. The gardens are open daily from 9am to 5pm (8pm in summer). The visitor center is open daily from 9:30am to 4:30pm. There's no bus service to the gardens.

The ✪ **Namadgi National Park** covers almost half of the Australian Capital Territory. Parts of the park, which has high rolling plateaus, good trout-fishing streams, and dense forest, are just 30 kilometers (19 miles) from Canberra. Marked hiking tracks can be found throughout the park. Spring is the best time of year to visit for the prolific display of bush flowers. In the past, sections of the park were cleared for sheep grazing, but these days the pastures are popular with hundreds of gray kangaroos (they're easiest to spot in the early morning and late afternoon). At Yankee Hat, off the Nass/Boboyan Road, is an Aboriginal rock art site. The **Namadgi Visitors Center** (☎ **02/6207 2900**), on the Nass/Boboyan Road, 3 kilometers (1¾ miles) south of the township of Tharwa, has maps and information on walking trails.

6 Outdoor Pursuits

BIKING   With 120 kilometers (74 miles) of bike paths, Canberra is made for exploring on two wheels. Rent a bike from **Mr. Spoke's Bike Hire** on Barrine Drive near the ferry terminal in Acton (☎ **02/6257 1188**). Bikes for adults cost A$10 (U.S.$6.50) for the first hour and A$9 (U.S.$5.85) for each hour afterwards; rates are A$9 (U.S.$5.85) for kids, going down to A$8 (U.S.$5.20) for each subsequent hour.

BOATING   **Burley Griffin Boat Hire,** on Barrine Drive near the ferry terminal in Acton (☎ **02/6249 6861**), rents paddle boats for A$20 (U.S.$13) per hour and canoes for A$14 (U.S.$9.10) per hour. **Row'n' Ride**, near the MacDermott Place Boat Ramp, Belconnen (☎ **02/6254 7838**), is open on weekends and school and public holidays and offers canoes from A$9 (U.S.$5.85) per hour, kayaks for A$10 (U.S.$6.50) per hour, and mountain bikes for A$9 (U.S.$5.85) per hour.

GLIDING   The **Canberra Gliding Club** (☎ **02/6257 1494** or 02/6452 3994) offers joy flights and trial instructional flights on weekends and public holidays from the Bunyan Airfield. Flights cost A$60 (U.S.$39).

GOLF   With 11 golf courses, Canberra offers varied opportunities for keen golfers. The nearest to the city center is the **Yowani Country Club** on the Federal Highway in the suburb of Lyneham (☎ **02/6241 3377**). Greens fees are A$28 (U.S.$18.20) for 18 holes and A$17 (U.S.$11.05) for 9 holes. Club rental costs an additional A$10 to $25 (U.S.$6.50–$16.25). Dress restrictions apply, and advance reservations are essential. **The Federal Golf Course,** Red Hills Lookout Rd., Red Hill (☎ **02/6281 1888**), is regarded as the area's most challenging. Non-members are welcome on most weekdays. Greens fees are A$50 (U.S.$32.50) for 18 holes. **The Royal Canberra Golf Course** is the most exclusive, costing A$120 (U.S.$78) for 18 holes. Guests, who must be a member of another golf club, are more likely to get a game on Mondays and Thursdays.

HORSEBACK RIDING   National Equestrian Centre, 919 Cotter Rd., Weston Creek, Canberra (☎ **02/6288 5555**), 15 minutes from Parliament House, offers trail rides through rolling rural countryside hopping with kangaroos and cattle. Rides cost from A$23.10 (U.S.$15.02) for 1 hour, with discounts for longer rides.

SWIMMING   The indoor heated pool at the **Australian Institute of Sport** (☎ **02/6214 1281**), on Leverrier Crescent in Bruce, a short drive northwest of Civic, is open to the public at certain times during the day (call ahead to check schedules). Adults pay A$3.50 (U.S.$2.28) to swim, and children pay A$2 (U.S.$1.30). It's compulsory to wear swimming caps, which can be bought there for A$2.50 (U.S.$1.63). It costs A$6 (U.S.$3.90) to use the pool, spa, and sauna.

TENNIS   **The National Tennis and Squash Centre,** Federal Highway, Lyneham (☎ **02/6247 0929**), has squash courts available for A$11.50 to $15.50 (U.S.$7.48–$10.08) per hour, depending on when you want to play. Tennis courts can be booked for A$9.50 to $14.50 (U.S.$6.18–$9.43). The Australian Institute of Sport (see above) also rents courts for A$8 (U.S.$5.20) per hour.

7 Shopping

The Canberra Centre, 4 square blocks between City Walk and Ballumbir Street between Petrie and Akuna Streets in Civic, is the place to shop till you drop. You can spend hours browsing through the boutiques or the department stores in the three-story atrium. The **City Market** section, which includes a bakery, fruit and vegetable sellers, a deli, and more, is the place to take a break; it's open Monday to Thursday from 9am to 6pm, Friday from 9am to 9pm, and Saturday and Sunday from 9am to 5pm.

The centrally located **Gorman House Markets,** Ainslie Avenue (☎ **02/6249 7377**), are spread around the courtyard of a heritage building. You can pick up good arts and crafts here, as well as clothing, jewelry, essential oils, books, and second-hand clothes. The markets are open Saturday from 10am to 4pm.

8 Canberra After Dark

The "Good Time" section in Thursday's *Canberra Times* has listings on what's on offer around town.

Of the pubs in town, the best in the city center are the British-style **Wig & Pen,** on the corner of Limestone and Alinga Street (☎ **02/6248 0171**); the very popular **Moosehead's Pub,** at 105 London Circuit in the south of the city (☎ **02/6257 6496**); the **Phoenix,** at 21 East Row (☎ **02/6247 1606**), which has live music upstairs for a small cover charge; and **P.J. O'Reileys** (☎ **02/6230 4752**) on the corner of West Row and Alinga Street, an authentic-style Irish pub.

If you're looking to roll the dice, the **Casino Canberra,** in Glebe Park, 21 Binara St., Civic (☎ **1800/806 833** in Australia or 02/6257 7074), is a small, older-style casino with all the usual games from noon to 6am. A dress code prohibits leisurewear, running shoes, and denim, but overall it's a casual place to lose some money.

Tasmania

by Marc Llewellyn

The very name "Tasmania" sounds exotic. It suggests an unspoiled place, with vast stretches of wilderness roamed by strange creatures like the Tasmanian Devil. Long thought of as literally the ends of the earth, many mainland residents still half-jokingly refer to their "country cousins" as rednecks. In truth, most Tasmanians are hospitable and friendly people, lacking the harsh edge that big cities can foster. Most also care passionately for the magnificent environment they've inherited.

Visitors to Tasmania are surprised by its size, though in comparison to the rest of Australia, the distances are more manageable. Dense rain forests, stony mountain peaks, alpine meadows, pine plantations, eucalyptus stands, and stretches of farmland are all easily accessible, but be prepared for several hours of concentrated driving to get you between the main attractions. Tasmania's main drawing cards are twofold. First, there's the natural environment. More than 20% of the island has been declared a World Heritage Area, and nearly a third of the island is protected within its 14 national parks. Wherever you go, wilderness is always within reach, and you can change out of your city clothes and step out into the bush to get the best out of it.

Tasmania's second drawing card is its history. Remains of the Aboriginal people who lived here for tens of thousands of years are evident in isolated rock paintings, engraving, stories, and a general feeling of spirituality that pervades places where modern civilization has not yet reached.

Europeans discovered Tasmania (or Van Diemen's Land, as it was known) in 1642, when the seafarer Abel Tasman set anchor off its southwest coast, although it wasn't identified as an island until 1798. Tasmania soon made its mark as a dumping ground for convicts, often transported for petty crimes committed in their homeland. The brutal system of control, still evident in the ruins at Port Arthur, soon spilled over into persecution of the native population. Tragically, the last full-blooded Tasmanian Aborigine died in 1876, just 15 years after the last convict transportation. Most of the rest had already died of disease and maltreatment at the hands of the settlers.

EXPLORING TASMANIA

VISITOR INFORMATION   The Tasmanian Travel and Information Centre (☎ **1800/806 846** in Australia, or 03/6230 8233; www. tourism.tas.gov.au; tasinfo@tourism.tas.gov.au), operates visitor centers located in more than 30 towns throughout the state. It can arrange travel passes, ferry and bus tickets, car rental, cruises, and accommodations.

Pick up a copy of *Travelways,* Tourism Tasmania's excellent tourist tabloid, for details on transport, accommodations, restaurants, and attractions around Tasmania.

WHEN TO GO   The best time to visit Tasmania is between mid-September and May, when the weather is at its best. By April, nights are getting cold, the days are getting shorter and the deciduous trees are starting to turn golden. Winters (June–Aug), especially in the high country, can be quite harsh—though that's the best time to curl up in front of a blazing log fire. The east coast is generally milder than the west, which is buffered by the "Roaring 40s"—the winds that blow across the ocean and the 40° meridian, from as far away as Argentina. December to February is the busiest time for tourism, and public and school holidays. Unlike the rest of Australia, Tasmanian schools have three terms: from the 2nd week in February to the last week in May; the 3rd week in June to the 1st week in September; and the 4th week in September to the 1st week in December.

GETTING THERE   The quickest way to get to Tasmania is by air. **Qantas** (☎ **13 13 13** in Australia, or 02/9691 3636) and **Ansett** (☎ **13 13 00** in Australia) offer daily service to Hobart and Launceston. Trips to Launceston are generally cheaper.

A more adventurous way to reach Tasmania is to take a boat across Bass Strait from the mainland. The quickest of these is the **DevilCat,** Australia's largest high-speed catamaran, which runs between Melbourne's Station Pier and George Town on Tasmania's north coast (trip time: 6 hr.). Ferries depart Melbourne at 8:30am Tuesday, Thursday, and Saturday, arriving in George Town at 2:30pm. Return ferries depart George Town Wednesday, Friday, and Sunday at 2pm, arriving in Melbourne at 8pm. Prices start at A$290 (U.S.$188.50) round-trip in winter and A$350 (U.S.$227.50) in summer. Contact **TT-Line** (☎ **03/9206 6211;** www.tt-line.com.au). **Tasmanian Redline Coaches** (☎ **03/6336 1446,** or 1300 360 000 from within Tasmania; red-linecoach@bigpond.com.au) link George Town with Launceston, 35 minutes away.

The car and passenger ferry *Spirit of Tasmania* plies the Tasman Sea between Melbourne's Station Pier and Devonport on the island's northwest coast. The ferry, which can hold 1,300 passengers, has a dining room, a buffet bistro, cafeteria, pool, a sauna, and a disco. The ferry departs Melbourne every Monday at 7:30pm, Wednesday, and Friday at 6pm and Sunday at 9am and arrives in Devonport the next morning at 8:30am. (The Sunday sailing only runs when the ferry is heavily booked at other times.) Return trips leave Devonport every Saturday at 4pm, Monday at 2am, and Tuesday and Thursday at 6pm. Return adult fares for the cheapest berth start at A$348 (U.S.$226.20) in winter and rise to A$404 (U.S.$262.60) in summer. To transport a car costs an extra A$80 (U.S.$52) return in peak season, and A$60 (U.S.$39) return in winter. Prices are highest during the school holiday periods of mid-December to January, and during the two weeks over Easter. Make reservations

Staying Connected

Tasmania might be "the ends of the earth," but you can still check your e-mail. In Hobart, there's **Internet Central-Tas Access,** Level 1, 29 Elizabeth St, Hobart, (☎ **03/6210 6210;** info@tassie.net.au). They have a branch in Launceton at Level 3, 16 Paterson Street, ☎ 03/6345 4444. Also in Launceston, there's **iCaf 22,** The Quadrant Mall, (☎ **03/6334 6815;** icaf@tassie.net; and the **Mallee Grill** at Andy's Backpackers Hostel, 1 Tamar St. (☎ **03/6331 4513;** andy@andys.com.au).

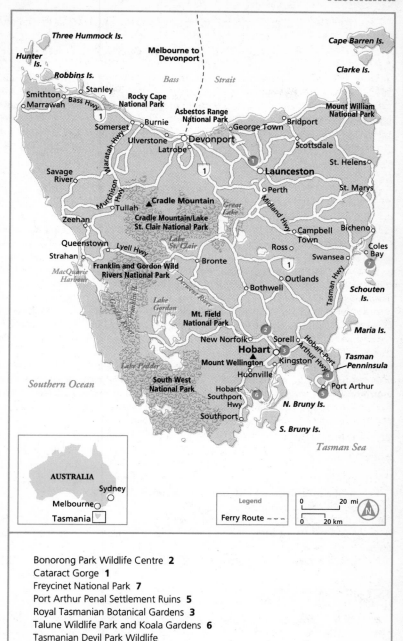

Three Hummock Is.

Hunter Is.

Robbins Is.

Cape Barren Is.

Clarke Is.

Melbourne to Devonport

Bass Strait

Smithton
Marrawah
Stanley
Bass Hwy
Somerset
Rocky Cape National Park
Burnie
Asbestos Range National Park
Ulverstone
Latrobe
Devonport
George Town
Bridport
Mount William National Park
Scottsdale

Savage River

Waratah Hwy

Murchison Hwy

Cradle Mountain

Tullah

Cradle Mountain/Lake St. Clair National Park

Zeehan

Queenstown

Strahan

Lyell Hwy

Lake St. Clair

Great Lake

Franklin and Gordon Wild Rivers National Park

MacQuarie Harbour

Bronte

Lake Gordon

Lake Pedder

Gordon River

Franklin River

Derwent River

Mt. Field National Park

New Norfolk

Hobart

Mount Wellington

South West National Park

Hobart-Southport Hwy

Southport

Southern Ocean

Launceston

Perth

St. Helens

St. Marys

Campbell Town

Ross

Midland Hwy

Bicheno

Coles Bay

Swansea

Outlands

Bothwell

Tasman Hwy

Schouten Is.

Maria Is.

Sorell

Arthur Hwy

Hobart-Port

Kingston

Huonville

Tasman Penninsula

Port Arthur

N. Bruny Is.

S. Bruny Is.

Tasman Sea

AUSTRALIA

Sydney

Melbourne

Tasmania

Legend

Ferry Route - - -

0   20 mi
0   20 km

N

Bonorong Park Wildlife Centre **2**
Cataract Gorge **1**
Freycinet National Park **7**
Port Arthur Penal Settlement Ruins **5**
Royal Tasmanian Botanical Gardens **3**
Talune Wildlife Park and Koala Gardens **6**
Tasmanian Devil Park Wildlife
   Rescue Centre **4**

through TT-Line (see above). You can also book tickets from **Inta-Aussie** at ☎ **800/ 531-9222** in the United States or Canada.

Tasmanian Redline Coaches (☎ **03/6336 1446**) connect with each ferry. Standard single fares are A$34.80 (U.S.$22.60) for adults and A$17.40 (U.S.$11.31) for children 15 years and under to Hobart, and A$14.40 (U.S.$9.36) for adults and A$7.20 (U.S.$4.68) for children to Launceston.

McCafferty's (☎ **13 14 99** in Australia) can organize coach travel from the eastern mainland states, with transfers to Tasmania by ferry.

GETTING AROUND Regional airline **Tasair** (☎ **1800/062 900** in Australia; www.tasair.com.au) flies to most major settlements in Tasmania. **Par Avion** (☎ **03/ 6248 5390;** www.paravion.com.au) concentrates on the southwest World Heritage areas of the state and also operates tours.

Bus service is provided by **Tasmanian Redline Coaches** (☎ **1800/030 033** in Australia or 03/6336 1446), **TWT Tassie Link** (☎ **03/6272 7300,** or 1300 300 520 in Australia; www.tassie.net.au/wildtour), **Tasmanian Tours & Travel Tigerland** (☎ **03/6231 3511,** 03/6272 6611; fax 03/6272 7555), and **Hobart Coaches** (☎ **1800/030 620** in Australia, or 03/6234 4077; fax 03/6234 8575). The cheapest way to get around by coach is to buy a **Tassie Link Explorer Pass,** which can be used on all TWT Tassie Link routes. Passes come in four categories: A 7-day pass good for travel within 10 days is A$130 (U.S.$84.50); a 10-day pass good for travel within 15 days is A$160 (U.S.$104); a 14-day pass good for travel within 20 days is A$190 (U.S.$123.50); and a 21-day pass for travel within 30 days is A$220 (U.S.$143). Passes are available through **TWT Tassie Link,** Hobart Head Office, 212 Main Rd, Moonah, ☎ **1300/300 520** or 03/6272 7300. Tasmanian Travel and Information Centers and the *Spirit of Tasmania* also sell the passes.

Driving a car from Devonport on the north coast to Hobart on the south coast takes less than four hours. From Hobart to Strahan on the west coast also takes around four hours, while the journey from Launceston to Hobart takes about 2 hours. **The Royal Automobile Club of Tasmania (RACT),** at Murray and Patrick streets in Hobart (☎ **13 27 22** in Tasmania), can supply you with touring maps.

TOUR OPERATORS Dozens of outfits run organized hiking, horse trekking, sailing, caving, fishing, bushwalking, diving, cycling, rafting, climbing, kayaking, or canoeing trips. For a full listing, see the "Outdoor Adventure" section of *Travelways,* the Tasmanian tourist board's publication (see "Visitor Information," above).

One of the best operators is **Tasmania Adventure Tours** (☎ **1300/654 604** in Australia). They offer a 3-day East Coast Explorer tour from Devonport, taking in Launceston, Freycinet National Park, and Port Arthur, before finishing in Hobart. The tour costs A$320 (U.S.$208). Their 3-day Wild and Green West Coast Tour departs Hobart and goes to Mount Field National Park, Strahan, Tullah and Cradle Mountain National Park before ending in Devonport. This tour costs A$340 (U.S.$221). Their

---

Driving Safety Tips

Driving in Tasmania can be dangerous; there are more accidents involving tourists on Tasmania's roads than just about anywhere else in Australia. Many roads are narrow and bends can be tight, especially in the mountainous inland—where you may also come across black ice early in the morning or anytime in winter. Marsupials are also common around dusk, and hitting or swerving to avoid them has caused countless crashes.

National Park Entry Fees

A **Tassie Holiday Pass** costs A$30 (U.S.$19.50) and allows entry for a car and passengers to all Tasmania's 18 National Parks for a period of two months. Valid for the same period is a **Backpackers Pass** available to pedestrians, cyclists and motor-cyclists for A$12 (U.S.$7.80). Occasional users can buy a 24-hour pass costing A$9 (U.S.$5.85) per car, while walkers, cyclists, motorcyclists and coach passengers pay A$3 (U.S.$1.95) per day. Passes are available at all major national parks and Tasmanian Visitor Information Centres. For more information contact the **Parks and Wildlife Service** at ☎ **03/6233 8203,** www.parks.tas.gov.au.

6-day Taste of Tasmania Tour takes in all the attractions in their other two tours, and ends up in Hobart. This tour costs A$630 (U.S.$409.50). Ring for departure days.

Peregrin Adventures (☎ 03/9662 2800; fax 03/9663 8618; www.peregrine.net. au) run rafting tours of the Franklin River, which carves its way through some of the most beautiful, rugged, and inaccessible wilderness in the world. Two other good operators are **Rafting Tasmania** (☎ **03/6239 1080;** fax 03/6239 1090; www. tasmanianadventures.com.au) and the **Roaring 40's Ocean Kayaking Company** (☎ **1800/653 712** in Australia); both companies offer paddling expeditions lasting from one to 11 days. **Tasmanian Expeditions,** based in Launceston (☎ **1800/030 230** in Australia or 03/6334 3477; fax 03/6334 3463; www.tas-ex.com; tazzie@ tassie.net.au), runs a whole range of cycling, trekking, and rafting trips around the country, some starting or finishing in Hobart.

SUGGESTED ITINERARIES   Planning my first trip to Tasmania, I'd pack walk-ing boots, raincoat, and shorts, and head first to Launceston or Hobart, the island's two main cities. I'd take in **Freycinet National Park** for its wonderful scenery and wildlife, stop in at **Port Arthur** for its beautiful setting and disturbing convict past, and head to the central highlands for a tramp around **Cradle Mountain.** If I had more time, I'd drive to **Strahan** on the far west coast to discover the great southwest wilder-ness, go trout fishing in the central lakes, and head off to the coastal towns of the north.

1 Hobart

198km (123 miles) S of Launceston

Tasmania's capital (pop. 126,000), the second-oldest settlement in Australia, is well worth visiting for a couple of days. Hobart's main features are its wonderful harbor and the colonial cottages that line the narrow lanes of Battery Point. As with Sydney, Hobart's harbor is the city's focal point, attracting yachts from all over the world. Down by the waterfront, picturesque Salamanca Place bursts with galleries, pubs, cafes, and an excellent market on Saturdays. European settlement at Hobart took place in 1804, a year after Tasmania's first colony was set up at Risdon (10km/6 miles up the Derwent River). It was known as Hobart Town until 1881.

ESSENTIALS

GETTING THERE   **Qantas** (☎ **13 13 13** in Australia, or 02/9691 3636), and **Ansett** (☎ **13 13 00** in Australia) carries passengers from the mainland. The trip from the airport to the city center takes about 20 minutes and costs about A$25 (U.S.$16.25) by taxi and A$7.50 (U.S.$4.88) by **Tasmanian Redline Coaches** (☎ **03/6336 1446**). Coaches drop you off at the Collins Street bus terminal or at any central city hotel.

Car rental offices at the airport include **Hertz** (☎ 03/6237 1155), **Advance** (☎ 1800/030 118 in Australia; www.advancecars.com.au); **Avis** (☎ 03/6248 5424), **Budget** (☎ 03/6248 5333, or 1300/362 848 in Australia), and **Thrifty** (☎ 1800/030 730 in Australia, or 03/6234 1341). Cars cost around A$50 (U.S.$32.50) for 1 day, A$45 (U.S.$22.25) per day for 2 days, A$40 (U.S.$26) per day for 4 days, and A$35 (U.S.$22.75) per day for a week or more.

VISITOR INFORMATION Information is available from the **Tasmanian Travel and Information Centre,** at Davey and Elizabeth Streets (☎ 03/6230 8233). It's open Monday through Friday from 8:30am to 5:15pm, Saturday and public holidays from 9am to 4pm, and Sunday from 9am to 1pm (longer hours in summer). You can also obtain information by calling ☎ 1800/806 846 in the rest of Australia.

You can pick up information on the State's National Parks at the **Lands Information Bureau,** 134 Macquarie St., (☎ 03/6233 8011).

CITY LAYOUT Hobart straddles the Derwent River on the south coast of the Tasmania. Salamanca Place and nearby Battery Point abut Sullivan's Cove, home to hundreds of yachts. The row of sandstone warehouses that dominate Salamanca Place date back to the city's importance as a whaling base in the 1830s. Tucked away behind Princes Wharf, Battery Point is the city's historic district, and in colonial times was the home of sailors, fishermen, whalers, coopers, merchants, shipwrights, and master mariners. The open ocean is about 50 kilometers (31 miles) farther down the river, though the Derwent empties out into Storm Bay, just 20 kilometers (12 miles) downstream. The central business district is on the west side of the water, with the main thoroughfares—Campbell, Argyle, Elizabeth, Murray, and Harrington streets—sloping down to the busy harbor. The Tasman Bridge and regular passenger ferries reach across the Derwent River. Set back from the city, but overlooking it, is the 1,270-meter-tall (4,191 ft.) Mount Wellington.

GETTING AROUND Central Hobart is small, and most of the attractions are in easy walking distance. **Metro Tasmania** (☎ 03/6233 4232) operates a system of public metro buses throughout the city and suburban areas. Single tickets cost from A$1.20 to $2.80 (U.S.78¢–$1.82) depending on how far you're going. **Day Tripper** tickets can be used between 9am and 4:30pm and after 6pm during the week and all day on weekends; they cost A$1.90 (U.S.$1.24). Purchase tickets from bus drivers. If you plan on busing about, stop off at the Metro Shop situated in the General Post Office building on the corner of Elizabeth and Macquarie streets and pick up a timetable, brochures, and sightseeing information.

The **Roche-O'May** ferry company (☎ 03/6223 1914; fax 03/6224 8333) operates lunch and dinner cruises on the *Cartela,* a wood-hulled, former steam-powered ferry built in Hobart in 1912; as well as passenger ferry service on the *Wanderer,* which stops at the Wrest Point Casino, the Royal Tasmanian Botanical Gardens, Sullivan's Cove, and the suburb of Belle Reeve. The first ferry leaves from Brooke Street Pier on Franklin Wharf at 10:30am, with other trips heading out every 1½ hours until 3pm

Parking is difficult in the city center and the one-way streets can drive you crazy.

SPECIAL EVENTS The **Sydney-to-Hobart Yacht Race,** starting in Sydney on December 26, fills the Constitution Dock Marina and harbor area close to overflowing with spectators and party-goers when the ships eventually turn up in Tasmania. The race takes anywhere from 2 to 4 days, and the sailors and fans stay on to celebrate New Year's Eve in Hobart. Food and wine lovers indulge themselves after the race during the two-month-long **Hobart Summer Festival,** which starts around December 28.

Hobart

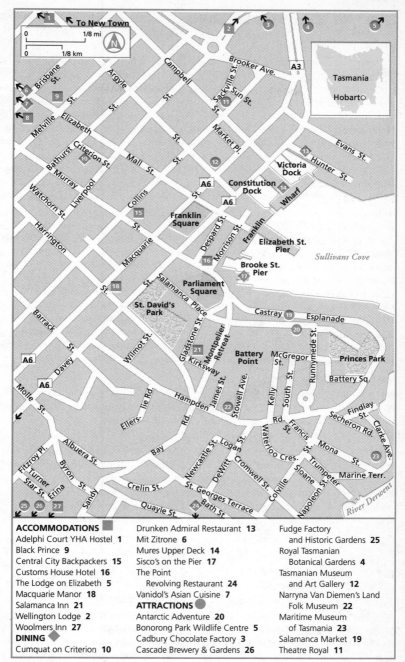

To New Town

0   1/8 mi
0   1/8 km

N

Brisbane St.

Argyle

Campbell

Brooker Ave.

Sackville St.

Sun St.

A3

Tasmania

Hobart

Melville

Elizabeth

St.

Market Pl.

Evans St.

Hunter St.

Victoria Dock

Bathurst   Criterion St.

Murray

Mall St.

St.

Constitution Dock

Wharf

Watchorn St.

Liverpool

Collins

St.

A6

A6

Harrington

St.

Franklin Square

Despard St.

Morrison St.

Franklin

Elizabeth St. Pier

Sullivans Cove

Macquarie

Brooke St. Pier

Barrack

Salamanca Place

Parliament Square

St. David's Park

Castray   Esplanade

Wilmot St.

Gladstone St.

Montpelier Retreat

Kirksway

Battery Point

McGregor St.

Runnymede St.

Princes Park

Davey

Molle St.

A6

A6

Kelly

South St.

Battery Sq.

Hampden

James St.

Stowell Ave.

Waterloo Cres.

Findlay St.

Secheron Rd.

Clarke Ave.

Ellers   Ile Rd.

Bay

Rd.

Rd.   Francis   St.

Mona   St.

Marine Terr.

Fitzroy Pl.

Turner   Byron St.

Albuera St.

Sandy

Newcastle St.

Logan   St.

DeWitt

Cromwell St.

Colville

Sloane   St.

Trumpeter

Star St.   Erina

Crelin St.

St. Georges Terrace

Bath St.

Quayle St.

Napoleon

River Derwent

ACCOMMODATIONS
Adelphi Court YHA Hostel **1**
Black Prince **9**
Central City Backpackers **15**
Customs House Hotel **16**
The Lodge on Elizabeth **5**
Macquarie Manor **18**
Salamanca Inn **21**
Wellington Lodge **2**
Woolmers Inn **27**
DINING
Cumquat on Criterion **10**

Drunken Admiral Restaurant **13**
Mit Zitrone **6**
Mures Upper Deck **14**
Sisco's on the Pier **17**
The Point
   Revolving Restaurant **24**
Vanidol's Asian Cuisine **7**
ATTRACTIONS
Antarctic Adventure **20**
Bonorong Park Wildlife Centre **5**
Cadbury Chocolate Factory **3**
Cascade Brewery & Gardens **26**

Fudge Factory
   and Historic Gardens **25**
Royal Tasmanian
   Botanical Gardens **4**
Tasmanian Museum
   and Art Gallery **12**
Narryna Van Diemen's Land
   Folk Museum **22**
Maritime Museum
   of Tasmania **23**
Salamanca Market **19**
Theatre Royal **11**

ENJOYING THE CITY & ENVIRONS

Simply strolling around the harbor and popping into the shops at Salamanca Place can keep you nicely occupied.

Also take a look around **Battery Point,** an area chock full of colonial stone cottages. The area gets its name from a battery of guns set up on the promontory in 1818 to defend the town against potential invaders (particularly the French). Today, there are plenty of tearooms, antique shops, cozy restaurants, and atmospheric pubs interspersed between grand dwellings. One of the houses worth looking into is the **Narryna Van Diemen's Land Folk Museum,** 103 Hampden Rd. (☎ **03/6234 2791**), which depicts the life of upper class pioneers. It's open Tuesday to Friday from 10:30am to 5pm and Saturday and Sunday from 2 to 5pm (closed July). Admission is A$5 (U.S.$3.25) for adults and A$2 (U.S.$1.30) for children. Also in this area is the **Maritime Museum of Tasmania,** 16 Argyle St ☎ **03/6234 1427,** one of the best museums of its type in Australia. It's open daily from 10am to 5pm, and admission is A$6 (U.S.$3.90) for adults, A$4 (U.S.$2.60) for children 4 to 16, and A$16 (U.S.$10.40) for a family.

The National Trust (☎ **03/6223 7570**) offers a 3-hour Battery Point Heritage Walk leaving at 9:30am every Saturday from the wishing well in Franklin Square. It costs A$11 (U.S.$7.15) for adults and A$3 (U.S.$1.95) for children 6 to 16 and includes morning tea.

For magnificent views over Hobart and a fair-sized chunk of Tasmania, drive to **The Pinnacle** on top of Mount Wellington, about 40 minutes from the city center. Take a warm coat, as the wind in this alpine area can bite. An extensive network of walking trails offers good hiking around the mountain. Pick up a copy of Mt. Wellington Day Walk Map and Notes from the **Department of Environment Tasmap Centre,** on the ground floor of the Lands Building, 134 Macquarie St. (☎ **03/6233 3382**).

THE TOP ATTRACTIONS

⭐ **Antarctic Adventure.** Salamanca Square. ☎ **03/6220 8220.** Admission A$16 (U.S.$10.40) adults, A$13 (U.S.$8.45) students, A$8 (U.S.$5.20) children 4–13, A$40 (U.S.$26) families. Daily 10am–5pm. Closed Christmas.

Hobart is the last port of call for expeditions to Antarctica. You can experience the cold continent yourself at this recommended attraction. It doesn't look like much at first, but I promise you'll be sucked in. You can experience an Antarctic blizzard, climb all over heavy machinery, experience a downhill ski simulator (I'm not sure how that fits in), and get computer access to Antarctic weather conditions and communications. The photos and other displays are also interesting. The irresistible stuffed huskies in the souvenir shop will take a hefty bite out of your wallet. Allow 1 to 2 hours.

Bonorong Park Wildlife Centre. Briggs Rd., Brighton. ☎ **03/6268 1184.** Admission A$8 (U.S.$5.20) adults, A$4 (U.S.$2.60) children under 15. Daily 9am–5pm. Closed Christmas Day. Bus to Glenorchy from the central bus terminal in Hobart (about 10 min.), then take bus 125 or 126 to the park. Drive north on route 1 to Brighton; it's about 25 min. north of Hobart and well signposted.

I don't think I've ever seen so many wallabies in one place as I saw here—they were hopping all over. There are lots of other native animals around, including snakes, koalas, Tasmanian devils, and wombats. The Bush Tucker shed serves lunch, billy teas (tea brewed in a metal pot with a gum leaf thrown in), and damper (Australian-style campfire bread). Koala cuddling isn't allowed in Tasmania, but if you're around at feeding times it's possible to stroke one—they're not as shy as you might think. Feeding times are 12:30pm and 3pm. The park is on the side of a hill, so travelers in wheelchairs and anyone who likes things flat are likely to fare badly. Allow 1 hour.

Cadbury Chocolate Factory. Claremont, 12km (7 miles) north of Hobart. ☎ **1800/627 367** in Australia or 03/6249 0333. Tours A$10 (U.S.$6.50) adults, A$5 (U.S.$3.25) children, A$25 (U.S.$16.25) families. Mon–Fri 8am (summer only), 9am, 9:30am, 10:30am, and 1pm.

Eat chocolates till they make you sick on this Willy Wonka–type trip. Book well ahead, because chocolate tours are very popular. See "Organized Tours" below for information on how to get there by boat.

Cascade Brewery Tours. Cascade Rd. ☎ **03/6221 8300.** Tours A$7.50 (U.S.$4.88) adults, A$1.50 (U.S.98¢) children 5–16. Mon–Fri 9:30am and 1pm. Closed public holidays. Reservations required. Bus: 44, 46, and 49; get off at stop 18.

Cascade Premium is one of the best beers in the country, in my opinion. To see how this heady amber nectar is produced, head to Australia's oldest brewery for a fascinating 2-hour tour, which includes a stroll through the grand old Woodstock Gardens behind the factory.

✪ **Fudge Factory and Historic Garden Tours.** Island Produce Confectionery, 16 Degraves St., South Hobart. ☎ **03/6223 3233.** Tours A$6 (U.S.$3.90) adults, A$3 (U.S.$1.95) children, A$15 (U.S.$9.75) families. Mon–Fri 8am–4pm. Tours begin at 10:30am (and 1:30pm during summer) Mon–Fri, reservations essential. (You can look around the gardens for free anytime if you make a purchase in the shop.) Bus: 44, 46, or 49 to South Hobart and Cascade Rd.; get off at stop 16.

This is an interesting stopover if you're visiting either the Cascade Brewery or Mount Wellington. Not only do you get a trip around a very successful fudge factory, but also a guided tour around the remains of the women's prison next door. The tales told will make the hairs on your neck stand on end—like the fact that 17 out of every 20 children born within the walls of the institution died soon after birth, and that women who died were simply tossed into an unmarked mass grave. All the proceeds of the tour go into preserving the prison. Allow 1½ hours.

Royal Tasmanian Botanical Gardens. On the Queens Domain near Government House. ☎ **03/6234 6299.** Admission: gardens, free; conservatory A$2 (U.S.$1.30) donation. Daily 8am–6:30pm (until 4:45pm in winter). Bus: 17.

Established in 1818, these gardens are known for English-style plant and tree layouts, a Japanese garden dominated by a miniature Mt. Fuji, and colorful seasonal blooming plants housed in the conservatory. A restaurant provides lunch and teas. Also here is a **Botanical Discovery Centre** (admission A$2/U.S.$1.30) and a Sub-Antarctic plant house. Allow 1 to 2 hours.

✪ **Tasmanian Museum and Art Gallery.** 40 Macquarie St. ☎ **03/6223 1422.** Free admission. Daily 10am–5pm.

Come here to find out more about Tasmania's Aboriginal heritage, its history since settlement, and the island's wildlife. The pride of the collection is *The Conciliation* by Benjamin Duttereau, as important in historical significance in Australia as Tom Roberts' *Shearing of the Rams,* in the National Gallery of Victoria in Melbourne. Traveling art exhibitions are mounted from time to time, but paintings of the colonial era are always on display. The art gallery has a particularly impressive collection of paintings by Tom Roberts and by several convict artists. Allow 1 to 2 hours.

ORGANIZED TOURS

You'll get a good introduction to the city on the **Hobart Historic Walk** (☎ **03/6225 4806;** fax 03/6225 4807), a 2-hour leisurely stroll through historic Sullivan's Cove and Battery Point. Tours start at 10am daily from September to May and on request from

June to August and cost A$17 (U.S.$11.05) for adults. Children under 12 are free. There is a minimum of six people for a walk to go ahead and group discounts are available.

Several companies run boat tours of the harbor. **Captain Fells Ferries** (☎ **03/6223 5893;** fax 03/6223 5170) offers a wide range of morning tea, lunch, afternoon, and dinner cruises. The company also runs **Cadbury Factory Tours,** which include coach transfers, a tour of the factory, a harbor cruise, and a 2-course lunch for A$32 (U.S.$20.80) for adults and A$18 (U.S.$11.70) for children; these tours leave at 9:45am Monday through Thursday. Cruises depart from Franklin Wharf behind the wooden sales booths beside Elizabeth Street Wharf at the bottom of Elizabeth Street.

The Cruise Company (☎ **03/6234 9294;** fax 03/6234 6393) operates river trips along the Derwent to the Cadbury Chocolate Factory. Cruises depart at 10am Monday to Friday, returning at 2:30pm, and cost A$33 (U.S.$21.45) for adults, A$16 (U.S.$10.40) for children 5 to 15, and A$93 (U.S.$60.45) for a family, including entry and a guided tour of the factory. Children under 5 are free. The boat leaves from Brooke Street Pier. Also available is the 2-hour **Ironpot Cruise** (to the lighthouse of that name at the mouth of the Derwent). The scenic tour of the river leaves Brooke Street Pier at 2pm every Saturday and costs A$20 (U.S.$13) for adults; free for children under 15.

THE SHOPPING SCENE

If you are in Hobart on a Saturday don't miss the ✪ **Salamanca Market,** in Salamanca Place—it's one of the best markets in Australia. Some 200 stalls offer everything from fruit and vegetables to crafts made from pottery, glass, and native woods. The market is open from 8:30am to 3pm.

Salamanca Place itself has plenty of craft and souvenir shops that are worth exploring, though you pay for the privilege of buying them in such a fashionable, area. You could try **The Salamanca Collection** (☎ 03/6224 1341) for good quality decorative arts, while the **Handmark Gallery,** 77 Salamanca Place (☎ **03/6223 7895**), has a fine selection of wooden jewelry boxes and Art Deco-style jewelry and pottery. The best bookshop in town is a beauty and sells a large range of new and secondhand books, many relating to Tasmania. Find the **Hobart Bookshop** at 22 Salamanca Square (☎ **03/6223 1803**). For great chocolate and the best licorice, head to **Darrell Lea,** shop 36 in the Cat & Fiddle Arcade between Collins and Liverpool streets. There are plenty of other interesting shops here, too.

Store hours are Monday through Thursday from 9am to 6pm, Friday from 9am to 9pm, and Saturday from 9am to noon.

WHERE TO STAY

Hobart has some of the best hotels, guesthouses, and B&Bs in Australia. For something different, you can stay with a Tasmanian family either in town or at a farm in the country or arrange accommodations in one of the many boutique B&Bs found throughout Tasmania. Contact **Heritage Tasmania Pty Ltd.,** P.O. Box 780, Sandy Bay, TAS 7005. (☎ **03/6233 5511;** fax 03/6233 5510). Nightly bed-and-breakfast rates range from about A$60 (U.S.$39) to around A$160 (U.S.$104) for a double.

There are 20 YHA youth hostels in Tasmania, including ones in Devonport (☎ **03/6424 5696**), Bicheno (☎ **03/6375 1293**), Coles Bay (☎ **03/6257 0115**), Mt Field National Park (☎ **03/6288 1369**), Stanley (☎ **6458 1266**) and Strahan (☎ **03/6471 7255**). Most have dorms as well as inexpensive double rooms.

Adelphi Court YHA Hostel. 17 Stoke St., New Town (postal address: YHA Tasmania, G.P.O. Box 174, Hobart, TAS 7001). ☎ **03/6228 4829.** Fax 03/6278 2047. www.yha.com.au.

25 units, 2 with bathroom. A$53 (U.S.$34.50) per person twin/double without bathroom; A$63 (U.S.$40.95) double with bathroom. A$20 (U.S.$13) dorm bed. Non-YHA members pay A$3.50 ($2.28) per person extra. BC, MC, V. Free parking. Bus: 15 or 16 from Argyle St. to stop no. 8A, or any bus from Stop E at Elizabeth Street Mall to bus stop no 13.

The Adelphi, is a typical clean and friendly Australian youth hostel. All dorm rooms sleep four people. It has a large game and TV room, a tour-booking desk, a kiosk, a communal kitchen, a dining room serving breakfasts, a laundry, and a barbecue area. It's located 3 kilometers (less than 2 miles) from the city center.

Black Prince. 145 Elizabeth St. Hobart, TAS 7000. ☎ **03/6234 3501.** Fax 03/6234 3502. 10 units. TV. A$56 (U.S.$36.40) standard double, including breakfast. AE, BC, DC, MC, V.

If you're looking for a place centrally located, clean, and unfussy, then I recommend the Black Prince, an American-influenced pub with a 1950s bent. All rooms come with a shower and bathtub, and a TV. Room 8 is the landlord's favorite, because "it's nearer to the stairs so you don't have to walk too far" (presumably beneficial when you've had a few beers). Downstairs, the American-style bar called Joe's Garage is popular, especially on weekends. The restaurant serves budget-priced steaks and chicken dishes. Lunch is offered from Monday to Friday, and dinner Monday to Saturday.

Central City Backpackers. 138 Collins St., Hobart, TAS 7000. ☎ **1800/811 507** in Australia, or 03/6224 2404. Fax 03/6224 2316. www.centralbackpackers.com.au. 80 units. A$22 (U.S.$14.30) twin per person; A$34 (U.S.$22.10); A$44 (U.S.$28.60) double. A$18 (U.S.$11.70) dorm bed. Cash or traveller's checks only. 2-min. walk from central bus terminal.

This place is typical of backpacker-type accommodations—cheap and cheerful, a little frayed around the edges, but right in the heart of things. The central shopping district is right outside the door, and it's only a short walk to the harbor. There is a common room with E-mail and internet access; and a pool table, a fully equipped kitchen, a dining room, a bar open in summer, and laundry facilities on the premises.

Customs House Hotel. 1 Murray St., Hobart, TAS 7000. ☎ **03/6234 6645.** Fax 03/6223 8750. 13 units, 2 with bathroom. A$65 (U.S.$42.25) double without bathroom; A$70 (U.S.$45.50) double with bathroom. Rates include continental breakfast. AE, BC, DC, MC, V.

You won't find a better value than the rooms above this historic sandstone pub on the waterfront. Built in 1846, the property offers simple, colonial-style rooms. Four have water views overlooking the old sailing ship the *May Queen*, which used to carry wood up the Derwent River. Other rooms look across Parliament House. Guests make the best of a shared TV room. Downstairs, a friendly public bar overlooks the water, and at the back of the building is a popular seafood restaurant known for its scallops.

✪ The Lodge on Elizabeth. 249 Elizabeth St., Hobart, TAS 7000. ☎ **03/6231 3830.** Fax 03/6234 2566. 13 units (some with shower only). A$115 (U.S.$74.75) standard double; A$125 (U.S.$81.25) deluxe double. AE, BC, DC, MC, V.

The Lodge on Elizabeth is located in the second-oldest building in Tasmania, with some parts of it dating back to 1810. Originally a gentleman's residence, it later became the first private boy's school in Tasmania. It's well situated just a 12-minute walk from Salamanca Place and is surrounded by restaurants. All rooms are decorated with antiques, and many are quite romantic, with four-poster beds. Standard rooms have just a shower, while the deluxe rooms come with more antiques and a large granite bathroom with a tub. Complimentary drinks are served in the communal living room in the evenings, and a good continental breakfast buffet goes for A$9.50 (U.S.$6.18).

Salamanca Inn. 10 Gladstone St., Hobart, TAS 7000. ☎ **1800/030 944** in Australia or 03/6223 3300. Fax 03/6223 7167. www.salamancainn.com.au. salamancainn@southcom.com.au. 68 units. MINIBAR TV TEL. A$176 (U.S.$114.40) 1-bedroom apt; A$198 (U.S.$128.70)

2-bedroom suite; A$240 (U.S.$156) 2-bedroom deluxe suite. Extra adult A$25 (U.S.$16.25); extra child 3–14 A$15 (U.S.$9.75). Ask about weekend and long-stay packages. AE, BC, DC, MC, V. Free parking. Bus: Sandy Bay Road.

Conveniently located right on the edge of the central business district and toward the waterfront near Battery Point, Salamanca Inn features modern and pleasant apartments. Many were fully refurbished in 1998 and now feature queen-size beds, modern leather couches, Tasmanian oak furniture, galley-style kitchens, and spacious living areas. The more expensive suites are even more plush. On the premises are a complimentary self-service laundry, a rooftop heated pool, a spa, and a restaurant. Room service and babysitting is available, and free inhouse videos are provided.

Wellington Lodge. 7 Scott St., Hobart, TAS 7000. ☎ **03/6231 0614.** Fax 03/6234 1551. 4 units, 2 with bathroom (shower only). (4 rooms, 2 with ensuite, 2 with private bathroom, all with shower and 2 with bathroom. TV. A$85–$110 (U.S.$55.25–$71.50) double. Extra person A$30 (U.S.$19.50). Rates include full breakfast. BC, MC, V. Free off street parking. The airport bus will drop you off here, as will any bus to the Aquatic Center. Free parking. Children under 11 not accepted. (10 min. walk to city centre)

This charming Victorian-style townhouse (ca. 1885) is just a 10-minute walk (through Hobart's Rose Garden) from the main shopping area and Salamanca Place. It was refurbished in 1997 and stocked with period antiques. Two rooms have their own shower attached; the other two have separate private bathrooms. All rooms have wicker chairs and a hair dryer. Complimentary port is served every evening in the guest lounge. Smoking is not permitted.

Woolmers Inn. 123–127 Sandy Bay Rd., Hobart, TAS 7000. ☎ **1800/030 780** in Australia or 03/6223 7355. Fax 03/6223 1981. 36 units. TV TEL. A$99 (U.S.$64.35) 1-bedroom apt; A$130 (U.S.$84.50) 2-bedroom apt. Extra adult A$15 (U.S.$9.75); extra child A$8 (U.S.$5.20). Rates 10% higher Christmas/Jan. AE, BC, DC, MC, V. Free parking. Bus: Catch the Sandy Bay bus from Elizabeth Street Mall on Elizabeth St.

Situated 2 kilometers (1¼ miles) south of the city, Woolmers Inn offers cozy one- or two-bedroom units with fully equipped kitchens. All units have a VCR. One unit is suitable for travelers with disabilities. Sandy Bay is Hobart's main suburb; it's halfway between the casino and the city (within walking distance of Salamanca Place) and features a "golden mile" of boutique shopping. You'll find a coin-op laundry and a travel center on the property. The inn was upgraded throughout 1999 and went from a three-star to a four-star rating.

WORTH A SPLURGE

✪ **Macquarie Manor.** 172 Macquarie St., TAS 7000. ☎ **1800/243 044** in Australia or 03/6224 4999. Fax 03/6224 4333. 18 units, most with shower only. MINIBAR TV TEL. A$140 (U.S.$91) Heritage room; A$170 (U.S.$110.50) Heritage suite; A$185 (U.S.$120.25) Macquarie suite. Rates include full breakfast. AE, BC, DC, MC, V. Free parking. 2 blocks from central bus terminal.

As soon as you walk into this place you'll know you want to stay. Macquarie Manor was built in 1875 as a doctor's surgery and residence. Extra rooms were added in 1950. Thick carpets and double-glazed windows keep the place quiet, even though the Manor is on the main road. Rooms, which vary enormously, are comfortable and elegantly furnished. One room is suitable for people with disabilities. The staff is friendly and will be happy to escort you around the premises in search of your favorite room. Check out the dining room, and the drawing room complete with old couches and grand piano. Parking is just to the left down the side of the main building. Smoking is not permitted.

WHERE TO DINE

Tasmania is known for its fresh seafood, including oysters, crab, crayfish, salmon, and trout. Once cheap, in recent years prices have crept up to match or even surpass those on the mainland. Generally though, the food is good quality—as long as you avoid some of the cheaper fish-and-chip joints on the waterfront (Flippers on Constitution Dock is an exception).

✪ **Cumquat on Criterion.** 10 Criterion St. ☎ **03/6234 5858.** Reservations recommended. Main courses A$7.50–$15 (U.S.$4.88–$9.75). No credit cards. Mon–Fri 8am–6pm. MIXED ASIAN/AUSTRALIAN.

This cafe is an excellent breakfast venue, offering everything from egg on toast to traditional porridge with brown sugar. On the menu for lunch and dinner you could find Thai beef curry, *laksa*, a daily risotto, and chermoula marinated fish. The desserts can be great. Vegetarians and vegans, and those on a gluten-free diet, are very well catered for, as well as the carnivores.

✪ **Drunken Admiral Restaurant.** 17–19 Hunter St. ☎ **03/6234 1903.** Reservations required. Main courses A$13.50–$22.90 (U.S.$8.78–$14.89). AE, BC, DC, MC, V. Daily 6pm–late. SEAFOOD.

The Drunken Admiral, opposite the Hotel Grand Chancellor on the waterfront, is an extremely popular spot with tourists, and can get quite raucous on busy evenings. The main attraction is its famous seafood chowder, swimming with anything that was on sale at the docks that morning. The large Yachties seafood grill is made up of plenty of squid, scallops, fish, mussels, and prawns, but there are plenty of simpler fish dishes on the menu, too. Otherwise, splash out on Sperm Whale Sally's Shellfish Platter, or perhaps Captain Nimrod's Depth Charge Platter. The salad bar is spread in a sailing dingy and can be raided as often as you want, but it's rather uninteresting.

✪ **Mit Zitrone.** 333 Elizabeth St., North Hobart. ☎ **03/6234 8113.** Reservations recommended. Main courses A$15.50–$17 (U.S.$10.08–$11.05). AE, BC, DC, MC, V. Mon–Sat 10am–2pm; Tues–Sat 6–10pm. MODERN AUSTRALIAN.

Chef and owner Chris Jackman has earned quite a reputation in Tasmania. His twice-cooked eggs with chili-palm sugar are a huge seller, while the hot smoked blue-eye cod with ginger and wok-fried greens, and the chicken and mushroom sausages with wide noodles, spinach, and anchovy sauce are sensational. The informal restaurant, which is basically an old shop, has bright yellow citrus walls and wooden floors and furniture. You can also drop in for coffee and cake.

✪ **Mures Upper Deck.** Between Victoria and Constitution Docks, Hobart. ☎ **03/6231 2121.** Reservations recommended. Main courses A$19.50–$25 (U.S.$12.68–$16.25). AE, BC, DC, MC, V. Daily noon–10pm. SEAFOOD.

This bustling waterfront restaurant offers great views of bobbing yachts as well as fine seafood caught on the owner's own fishing boats. I recommend starting with a bowl of potato soup, or the signature Mures Oysters topped with smoked salmon, sour cream, and salmon caviar. The most popular main courses are the blue-eye fillet Martinique—a Creole-inspired sweet fish curry with coconut cream and banana sauce—or the giant seafood platter for two. The best summer dessert is the restaurant's famous pudding, which almost bursts with berries. In winter, try the Granny Leatherwood Pudding—made of apples and Australian leatherwood honey, served with cinnamon ice cream. The complex also includes Lower Deck, a popular self-service family restaurant where you can dine well for under A$15 (U.S.$9.75).

The Point Revolving Restaurant. In the Wrest Point Hotel Casino, 410 Sandy Bay Rd. ☎ **03/6225 0112.** Reservations recommended. Main courses from A$11.50 (U.S.$7.48) lunch; from A$17 (U.S.$11.05) dinner. Set 3-course lunch menu A$25.50 (U.S.$16.58); set 3-course dinner menu A$43 (U.S.$27.95) Fri–Sat, A$34 (U.S.$22.10) Sun–Thurs. AE, BC, DC, MC, V. Daily noon–2pm and 6:30–9:30pm. TASMANIAN/AUSTRALIAN.

This revolving restaurant on the 17th floor of the Wrest Point Hotel Casino is known for its spectacular harbor and mountain views. Criticism of its consistency has led to a complete review of its cuisine over the last couple of years, but fortunately its specialties—prawns flambé in a curry sauce and the Caesar salad—have remained through regular menu upgrades. The crèpes Suzette is a wonderful signature dessert. The service is friendly and relaxed. This place is packed on weekends. The cheaper set dinner course has fewer options.

Sisco's on the Pier. Upper Level, Murray Street Pier. ☎ **03/6223 2059.** Reservations recommended. Main courses A$17–$18 (U.S.$11.05–$11.70). AE, BC, DC, MC V. Mon–Fri noon–3pm; Mon–Sat 6–12pm. SPANISH/MEDITERRANEAN/INTERNATIONAL

Sisco's has undergone a transformation from a typical Spanish eatery with roving guitar players to a more upmarket international affair in recent years. Today it's known for its paella, Morton Bay bugs (a kind of small crayfish) with chocolate, garlic prawns with squid ink spaghetti, and char-grilled octopus. The restaurant is light and bright with a large outdoor balcony.

Vanidol's Asian Cuisine. 353 Elizabeth St., North Hobart. ☎ **03/6234 9307.** Reservations recommended. Main courses A$11.90–$16.50 (U.S.$7.74–$10.73). Tues–Sun 6–11pm. AE, BC, MC, V. ASIAN.

Another restaurant popular with locals and tourists, Vanidol's serves up a variety of Thai, Indonesian, and Indian dishes (though it's better to stick to one form of cuisine instead of swapping between styles). The beef salad with basil, chili, and mint is very good, as are the barbecued prawns with a sweet tamarind sauce. The fish cooked in a light red curry sauce is another specialty. Smoking is not permitted between 6 and 9pm.

HOBART AFTER DARK

Built in 1837, the 747-seat **Theatre Royal,** 29 Campbell St. (☎ **03/6233 2299**), is the oldest remaining live theater in the country. It's known for its excellent acoustics and its classical Victorian decor. Ticket prices vary depending on the performance, but A$25 (U.S.$16.25) is average.

If the play's not the thing, then consider the **Hobart Historic Pub Tour** (☎ **03/ 6225 4806;** fax 03/6225 4807), which traces the city's development through hotel drinking holes—an important part of life in Hobart early last century. The 2-hour tour takes in four pubs; visitors enjoy a drink in each as guides give a lively account of the building's unique place in Hobart's drinking history. Tours depart Sunday to Thursday at 5pm, and cost A$35 (U.S.$22.75) including a drink at each pub.

Opened in 1829 as a tavern and a brothel frequented by whalers, **Knopwood's Retreat,** 39 Salamanca Place (☎ **03/6223 5808**) is still a raucous place on Friday and Saturday evenings, when crowds cram the historic interior and spill out onto the streets. Light lunches are popular throughout the week, and occasionally you'll find jazz or blues on the menu.

My favorite drinking hole in Hobart is **Irish Murphy's,** 21 Salamanca Place (☎ **03/6223 1119**), an atmospheric pub with stonewalls and lots of dark wood. Local bands play Friday and Saturday evenings.

If you want to tempt Lady Luck, head to the **Wrest Point Casino,** in the Wrest Point Hotel, 410 Sandy Bay Rd. (☎ **03/6225 0112**), Australia's first legal gambling club. Smart, casual attire required (collared shirts for men).

A SIDE TRIP TO MOUNT FIELD NATIONAL PARK
80km (50 miles) NW of Hobart

✪ **Mount Field National Park** is one of the prettiest in Tasmania. It was proclaimed a national park in 1916 to protect a plateau dominated by dolerite-capped mountains and glaciated valleys. **Mount Field West** is the highest point at 1,417 meters (4,648 ft.), and in the central and western regions of the park there are examples of lakes and tarns formed in the ice age of 30,000 years ago. The mountainous regions support alpine moorlands of cushion plants, pineapple and sword grass, *waratahs* and giant *pandani*. You can get a good look at these changing environments on a 16 kilometer (10 miles) drive from the park entrance to Lake Dobson along an unsealed and often highly corrugated road, which is not suitable for conventional vehicles in winter or after heavy rain.

Bennett's and rufous wallabies are common in the park, as are wombats, barred bandicoots, Tasmanian devils, and quolls. Platypus inhabit the lakes. Birds sighted include black cockatoos, olive whistlers, green rosellas, honeyeaters, currawongs, wedge-tailed eagles and lyrebirds, which were introduced from Victoria in the 1930s. Also here are rare Native Hens, Yellow Wattlebirds, and Dusky Robins.

There are walking tracks throughout the park, including one to Tasmania's most photographed waterfall, the spectacular 45 meters (147 ft.) **Russell Falls,** near the park's entrance. The walk to the falls along a sealed, wheelchair-accessible track takes 15 minutes and passes ferns and forests, with some of Tasmania's tallest trees, mighty swamp gums up to 85 meters (278 ft.) tall.

Contact the **Park Ranger** at ☎ **03/6288 1149.**

GETTING THERE   Tasmanian Redline Coaches (☎ **03/6336 1446**) runs day tours to the park from Hobart and **TWT Tassie Link** offers a daily service from December to March for A$35 (U.S.$22.75) one-way. By car, take the Lyall Highway from Hobart to the Gordon River and follow the signs after the township of Westerway.

TASMANIA BY RAFT

A good way to experience Tasmania's natural beauty is to take a raft trip with **Rafting Tasmania,** P.O. Box 403, Sandy Bay, Tasmania 7006 (☎ **03/6239 1080;** fax 03/6239 1090; raftingtas@oze-mail.com.au).

The company supplies all equipment, including high-quality rubber rafts for four or more people, trained guides, and camping gear. The Franklin River is the company's specialty, and they have trips lasting 4, 7, and 10 days departing from Hobart. Each trip leaves on specific dates between mid-November and the first week or so of April, so you'll have to make plans in advance, or take potluck when you arrive. The Franklin River offers a real wilderness experience, with gorges, waterfalls, rain forests, pebble beaches, limestone cliffs, and rapids on the way. Trips cost A$950 (U.S.$617.50) for 4 days, A$1,250 (U.S.$812.50) for 7 days, and A$1,650 (U.S.$1, 072.50) for 10 days.

An alternative is to take the company's one-day rafting trip down the **Picton River,** not too far from Hobart. This trips costs A$115 (U.S.$74.75) and leaves Hobart Sundays year-round, and Tuesdays and Fridays between November and March.

WHERE TO STAY

National Park Hotel. 2366 Gordon River Road, National Park, TAS 7140. ☎ **03/6288 1103.** 7 units, none with bathroom. A$60 (U.S.$39) double. Rates include full breakfast. BC, MC, V.

Located 300 meters (320 yd.) inside the national park, this typical one-story Aussie hotel has basic rooms with free tea- and coffee-making facilities; some rooms have a sink. There's a TV in the lounge bar. The hotel can book horseback riding expeditions within the park, and there's a golf course nearby.

Russell Falls Holiday Cottages. Lake Dobson Rd., National Park, TAS 7140. ☎ **03/6288 1198.** 4 units. TV. A$50 (U.S.$32.50) for 2 people. Extra adult A$12 (U.S.$7.80); extra child under 16 A$7 (U.S.$4.55). BC, MC, V.

These cottages are right at the entrance to the national park in a rural setting with rolling fields. Each is spacious and comfortable, with an attached toilet and shower and an open kitchen, lounge, and dining area. All cottages come with a TV and gas heating.

2 Port Arthur: Discovering Tasmania's Convict Heritage

102km (63 miles) south east of Hobart

✪ **Port Arthur,** on the Tasman Peninsula, is one of Australia's prettiest harbors and houses the remains of Tasmania's largest penal colony—essentially Australia's version of Devil's Island. It's the state's top tourist destination, and you really should plan to spend at least a whole day in this incredibly picturesque, yet haunting, place.

From 1830 to 1877, Port Arthur was one of the harshest institutions of its type anywhere in the world. It was built to house the settlement's most notorious prisoners, often prisoners who had escaped into the bush from lesser institutions. Nearly 13,000 convicts found their way here, and nearly 2,000 died while incarcerated. Port Arthur was, and still is, connected to the rest of Tasmania by a narrow strip of land called **Eaglehawk Neck.** Guards and rows of dogs kept watch over this narrow path, while the authorities circulated rumors that the waters around the peninsula were shark infested. Only a few convicts ever managed to escape, and most either perished in the bush or were tracked down and hanged. Look out for the blowhole and other coastal formations, including **Tasman's Arch, Devil's Kitchen,** and the **Tessellated Pavement,** as you pass through Eaglehawk Neck.

ESSENTIALS

GETTING THERE   Port Arthur is a 1½-hour drive from Hobart via the Lyell and Arthur highways. **Tasmanian Tours & Travel Tigerland** (☎ **03/6231 3511** or 03/6272 6611; fax 03/6272 7555; www.tigerline.com.au) runs trips from Hobart to Port Arthur every day; tours depart from 199 Collins St. at 9am and return around 5:30pm. Tours cost between A$50 (U.S.$32.50) and A$60 (U.S.$39) for adults; and A$32 to 37 (U.S.$20.80–$24.05) for children 4 to 16, depending on which tour you take. Children under 4 are free. Both trips include a guided tour of the Port Arthur site.

Something Spooky

Excellent **Ghost Tours** of Port Arthur by lantern (reservations are essential; call ☎ **1800/659 101** in Australia) leave nightly. Up to 10 tours are run after dark each night, depending on demand. Count on tours at 9pm and 9:30pm in summer, and 6:30pm and 8:30 pm in winter. Tours cost A$13 (U.S.$8.45) for adults, A$8 (U.S.$5.20) for children. (Family tickets, 2 adults and up to 6 children are A$34/U.S.$22.10).

Unlike "Taz" in the Warner Bros. cartoons, Tasmanian devils don't spin around. They are, however, voracious scavengers and will eat just about anything meaty they come across. Tough and stocky, these black and white marsupials sleep much of the day and come out to prowl at night. They often clash over carcasses and let out strings of abusive grunts, squeals and growls—which early settlers thought resembled the noises the devil would make. A website about Tasmanian devils is at www.parks.tas.gov.au/wildlife/mammals/devil.html.

Experience Tasmania (☎ **03/6234 3336;** fax 03/6234 3166) also runs coach trips from Hobart to Port Arthur every Monday, Wednesday, Friday, and Sunday, leaving the Cruise Company ferry offices on Franklin Wharf at 9:15am and returning around 5pm. Tours cost A$50 (U.S.$32.50), A$60 (U.S.$39) or A$65 (U.S.$42.25) for adults; and A$32 (U.S.$20.80), A$37 (U.S.$24.05) or A$40 (U.S.$26) for children 5 to 16. Children under 5 are free. All trips include a guided tour of the prison complex.

EXPLORING THE SITE

The ✪ **Port Arthur Historic Site** (☎ **03/6251 2310;** fax 03/6251 2311, is large and scattered with some 30 19th-century buildings (most were damaged during bushfires in 1877, shortly after the property ceased to be a penal institution). You can tour the remains of the church, guard tower, model prison, and several other buildings. It's best to tour the area with a guide, who can graphically describe what the buildings were originally used for. Don't miss the fascinating museum in the old lunatic asylum, which has a scale model of the prison complex, as well as leg irons and chains.

The site is open daily from 9am to 5pm; admission is A$18 (U.S.$11.70) for adults, A$9 (U.S.$5.85) for children 4 to 7. Admission includes a walking tour and a boat cruise around the harbor leaving eight times daily in summer. There is also a separate cruise to the **Isle of the Dead** off the coast of Port Arthur twice a day; some 1,769 convicts and 180 free settlers were buried here, mostly in mass graves with no headstones. The cruise costs an extra A$5 (U.S.$3.25) per person.

A new **Visitor Centre** opened in January 1999. The main feature is a fabulous Interpretive Gallery, which takes visitors through the process of sentencing in England to transportation to Van Dieman's Land. The gallery contains a courtroom, a section of a transport ship's hull, a blacksmith's shop, a lunatic asylum, and much more. Allow between 3 and 4 hours to explore the site and the gallery.

EN ROUTE TO PORT ARTHUR

On the way to Port Arthur you might want to stop off at the historic village of Richmond and at the **Tasmanian Devil Park Wildlife Rescue Centre.**

Richmond is 26 kilometers (16 miles) northeast of Hobart and the site of the country's oldest bridge (1823), the best-preserved convict jail in Australia (1825), and several churches, including St John's Church (1836)—the oldest Catholic church in the country. Richmond also has plenty of tearooms, galleries, and antique stores.

Eighty kilometers (50 miles) from Hobart is the **Tasmanian Devil Park Wildlife Rescue Centre,** Port Arthur Highway, Taranna, (☎ **03/6250 3230;** fax 03/6230 3406), which houses orphaned or injured native animals, including Tasmanian devils, quolls, kangaroos, eagles, and owls. The park is open daily from 9am to 5pm. Admission is A$12 (U.S.$7.80) for adults; A$6 (U.S.$3.90) for children; and A$30

(U.S.$19.50) for a family. Tasmanian Devils are fed daily at 10am and 11am.and 5pm The adjoining **World Tiger Snake Centre,** a unique medical research project, contains some 1,500 highly venomous snakes.

WHERE TO STAY & DINE

Port Arthur Motor Inn. Port Arthur Historic Site, Arthur Hwy., Port Arthur, TAS 7182. ☎ **1800/030 747** in Australia or 03/6250 2101. Fax 03/6250 2417. portarthur@ fc-hotels.com.au. 35 units. MINIBAR TV TEL. A$110 (U.S.$71.50) double. Extra person A$15 (U.S.$9.75). Children 11 and under stay free in parents' room. AE, BC, DC, MC, V. Free parking. Bus: Hobart Coaches run from Hobart on weekdays.

If you decide to stop over rather than drive all the way back to Hobart (remember marsupials get killed all the time on the roads at night—and they can do a lot of damage to a rental car), this is a good choice. The rooms are attractive and overlook the historic site. There is also a self-service laundry and a kids' playground. Port Arthur ghost tour packages are available from here. The restaurant here is quite formal, with main courses costing between A$12 and A$19 (U.S.$7.80 and $12.35).

3 Freycinet National Park

206km (129miles) NE of Hobart; 214km (134 miles) SW of Launceston

If you only have time to visit one place in Tasmania, make sure it's ✪ **Freycinet National Park.** The Freycinet Peninsula hangs down off the eastern coast of Tasmania. It's a place of pink granite peaks, spectacular white beaches, wetlands, heathlands, coastal dunes, and eucalyptus forests. Come here to spot sea eagles, wallabies, seals, pods of dolphins, and humpback and southern right whales during their migration to and from the warmer waters of northern New South Wales from May to August. The township of **Coles Bay** is the main staging post, and there are many bushwalks in the area. **The Moulting Lagoon Game Reserve**—an important breeding ground for black swans and wild ducks—is signposted along the highway into Coles Bay from Bicheno. Some 10,000 black swans inhabit the lake, so it's very rare not to see them. Six kilometers (3¾ miles) outside town, and inside the national park is the **Cape Tourville Lighthouse,** from which there are extensive views north and south along the coast and out across several of the small islands in the Tasman Ocean.

The walk to the spectacular **Wineglass Bay,** named as one of the world's top 10 beaches by *Outside* magazine, will be one of the nicest you'll ever do.

ESSENTIALS

GETTING THERE Tasmanian Redline Coaches (☎ **03/6336 1446**) run between Hobart (199 Collins St.) and Bicheno, leaving Hobart at 10am on Monday and Wednesday, 12:30pm on Tuesday and Thursday, 2pm on Friday, and 10:30am on Sunday. The trip takes about 4½ hours. From Launceston (112 George St.) buses leave at 2pm Monday to Thursday, at 3:45pm on Friday, and 11am on Sunday, and take less than 3 hours. From Bicheno catch a local bus run by **Bicheno Coach Services** (☎ **03/6257 0293,** or mobile 0419 570 293). Buses leave at 9am and 3pm every day (except Sat when there's no 3pm service). Buses also meet every coach from Hobart or Launceston, but you need to book in advance. **TWT Tassie Link** (☎ **03/6272 7300**) runs buses from Launceston to Bicheno on Monday, Wednesday, Friday, and Sunday leaving at 8:30am.

From Hobart it's about a 3-hour drive to the park.

VISITOR INFORMATION The Visitor Information Centre (☎ **03/6375 1333;** fax 03/6375 1533) on the Tasman Highway at Bicheno can arrange tour bookings.

Otherwise, the **Tasmanian Travel and Information Centre** in Hobart (☎ **03/6230 8383**) can supply you with maps and details. Daily entry to the park costs A$9 (U.S.$5.85) per vehicle.

EXPLORING THE PARK

If you only have time to do one walk, then head out from **Freycinet Lodge** on the 30-minute uphill hike past beautiful pink granite outcrops to **Wineglass Bay Lookout** for breathtaking views. You can then head down to Wineglass Bay itself and back up again. The walk takes around 2½ hours. A longer walk takes you along the length of **Hazards Beach,** where you'll find plenty of shell middens—seashell refuge heaps—left behind by the Aborigines who once lived here. This walk takes 6 hours.

Tasmanian Expeditions (☎ **1800/030 230** in Australia, 03/6334 3477; fax 03/6334 3463; www.tas-ex.com; tazzie@tassie.net.au) offers a three-day trip from Launceston and back that includes two nights in cabins at Coles Bay. The trip includes guided walks to Wineglass Bay and Mt. Amor. The company also offers 6- and 12-night walking, rafting, and cycling trips.

Not to be missed is a trip aboard **Freycinet Sea Charter's** vessel *Kahala* (☎ **03/ 6257 0355;** fax 03/6375 1461), which offers whale-watching between June and September, bay and game fishing, dolphin watching, diving, scenic and marine wildlife cruises, and sunset cruises. Half day cruises cost A$60 (U.S.$39) per person with a minimum of four adults onboard. Full day cruises cost A$100 (U.S.$65) per person.

WHERE TO STAY & DINE

Camping is available in the national park itself for A$10 (U.S.$6.50) a tent, though water is scarce. For inquiries, call the **Parks and Wildlife Service** (☎ **03/6257 0107**).

✪ **Freycinet Lodge.** Freycinet National Park, Coles Bay 7215. ☎ **03/6257 0101.** Fax 03/6257 0278. www.freycinetlodge.com.au. info@freycinetlodge.com.au. 60 units. A$160 (U.S.$104) standard cabin; A$200 (U.S.$130) spa cabin. AE, BC, DC, MC, V.

I can't praise the eco-friendly lodge enough. Comfortable one- and two-room cabins are spread unobtrusively through the bush and connected by raised walking tracks. Each has a balcony, and some have a huge spa. The main part of the lodge houses a lounge room and an excellent restaurant that sweeps out onto a verandah overlooking the limpid green waters of Great Oyster Bay. From here it's an easy stroll to the start of the Wineglass Bay walk, and the lodge is right next to the white sands of Hazards Beach.

4 Hobart to Launceston: The Heritage Highway

By the 1820s, several garrison towns had been built between Launceston and Hobart, and by the middle of the 19th century, convict labor had produced what was considered to be the finest highway of its time in Australia. Today, many of the towns along the route retain examples of Georgian and Victorian architecture. It takes about 2 hours to drive between Launceston and Hobart on the Heritage Highway (officially known as the **A1,** or the Midland Highway) but you really need 2 days to fully explore.

OATLANDS

84 km north of Hobart; 117 km south of Launceston

Oatlands, a former military garrison, has the largest number of colonial-era sandstone buildings of any village in Australia. Eighty-seven of them are on Main St, the most notable the convict-built **courthouse** (1829) and **Callington Mill** (1837), once the largest flour producer in the region. This site consists of a windmill, a granary, the steam mill, a stable and the miller's cottage. There are pleasant picnic grounds along the lakefront, and waterfowl breed in the lake's marshland wildlife sanctuary.

For additional information on the area, stop by the **Central Tasmania Tourism Centre,** 77 High St, Oatlands ☎ **03/6254 1212;** it's open daily from 9am to 5pm.

✪ ROSS
121 km north of Hobart; 78 km south of Launceston

One of Tasmania's best preserved historic villages, picturesque Ross was established as a garrison town in 1812 on a strategically important crossing point on the Macquarie River. Ross Bridge, the third oldest in Australia, was built in 1836 to replace an earlier one made of logs. The bridge is decorated with Celtic symbols, animals and faces of notable people of the time. It is lit up at night, and there are good views of it from a dirt track that runs alongside the river's north bank.

The town's main crossroads is edged by four historic buildings, humorously known as "temptation" (represented by the **Man-o'-Ross Hotel,** "salvation" (the Catholic church), "recreation" (the town hall) and "damnation" (the old gaol). The **Ross Female Factory,** built in the early 1840s, consists of ruins, a few interpretive signs and a model of the original site and buildings inside the original Overseer's Cottage. Entry is free. Women convicts were imprisoned here from 1847 to 1854.

At the **Tasmanian Wool Centre** and tourist information center on Church Street (☎ **03/6381 5466**), there is an exhibition detailing the growth of the region and the wool industry since settlement. It's open daily from 9am to 5 pm (until 6 pm Jan–Mar), and entry costs A$4 (U.S.$2.60) for adults; A$2 (U.S.$1.30) for children, and A$10 (U.S.$6.50) for a family.

WHERE TO STAY & DINE
✪ Colonial Cottages of Ross. 12 Church Street, Ross, Tasmania 7209. ☎ **03/6381 5354.** Fax 03/6381 5408. tim@tasmania.com. 4 cottages. TV. A$110–$130 (U.S.$71.50–$84.50) for 2, depending on cottage and season. Extra person A$20–$30 (U.S.$13–$19.500). BC, MC, V.

Stay in one of these delightful historic cottages to feel the part of a colonial settler in Tasmania. **Apple Dumpling Cottage** (ca. 1880) is a two-bedroom wooden cottage, sleeping four, with sandstone fireplaces, on the edge of the village in a rural setting. The spacious **Church Mouse Cottage** (ca. 1840), set in an old Sunday School, sleeps just two. **Captain Samuel's Cottage** (ca. 1830) accommodates six people in three bedrooms, with two double and two single beds. Finally, Hudson Cottage (ca. 1850) sleeps four. All cottages have modern bathroom and kitchen facilities.

The Ross Village Bakery and Inn. 15 church Street, Ross, Tasmania 7209. ☎ **03/6381 5246.** Fax 03/6381 5360. 4 units. A$95 (U.S.$61.75). AE, MC, V.

This old coaching inn, built in 1832, offers four homey rooms done out old English style. One room has a double bed, another a double and two singles, and a third a double which opens up onto a fourth with two singles (suitable as a family room). A separate lounge has a TV and free tea, coffee, sherry and cakes. The bakery on the premises is an excellent place for lunch, serving up things like filled baked potatoes and some of the best pies in Australia, baked in a wood-fired oven dating from 1860.

LONGFORD
27 km (16¾ miles) south of Launceston; 188 km (116½ miles) north of Hobart

About 6 kilometers (3¾ miles) west of the Midland Highway, Longford is best known for its Georgian architecture, much of which was built using convict labor. "The Path to History" brochure, available at the visitor center, is great for a self-guided tour of many of the colonial buildings. **Longford Visitor Information Centre** (☎ **03/6391 1181**), at 3 Malborough St., is open from 10am to 5pm daily.

Major attractions south of Longford (follow Wellington Street out of town) are the historic houses of ✪ **Woolmers** and ✪ **Brickendon,** both established by Thomas Archer who became a major landowner in the area. The oldest part of the Woolmers homestead dates from 1818, and a "new" Italianate front was added in 1845. At its peak, the estate consisted of 24,000 acres, but much of it was seized by the Government in 1911 and 1945 and given to settlers and returned soldiers. The great thing about Woolmers is that all its contents are original to the house. The out-buildings and gardens—and the outlook across the fields and English trees—are worth coming to see if you miss out on the guided tours, which are the only way to see inside the house. There's a restaurant on site and three cottages available for tourist accommodation. Woolmers (☎ **03/6391 2230**) is open from 10am to 4:30pm daily, with guided tours at 11am, 12:30pm, 2pm, and 3:30pm. Admission costs A$10 (U.S.$6.50) for adults, A$2.50 (U.S.$1.63) for children, and A$25 (U.S.$16.25) a family.

Thomas Archer's older brother, William, built Brickendon in 1829. The house itself is not open to the general public, but the gardens and convict-made buildings that surround it are. There are 16 of these buildings, including Dutch barns, a blacksmith shop, cook's house, gothic chapel, poultry shed, and a shearing shed. The gardens were established in the 1830s and planted with exotic trees from around the world. Today, the property is still the center of a working farm, so there are plenty of animals about. You can stay in one of the historic worker's cottages or farm cottages for between A$130 (U.S.$84.50) and A$150 (U.S.$97.50) a night. **Brickendon** (☎ **03/6391 1251**) is open Wednesday to Sunday 9:30am to 5pm. Entry costs A$7.50 (U.S.$4.88) for adults, A$3.50 (U.S.$2.28) for children, and A$20 (U.S.$13) a family.

Another historic house of note is ✪ **Clarendon,** located 12 kilometers (7½ miles) off the Heritage Highway via Evandale on the B41. Regarded as one of the great Georgian houses of Australia, Clarendon (☎ **03/6398 6220**) was completed in 1838 for woolgrower and merchant James Cox. Set on the banks of the South Esk River, Clarendon has extensive formal gardens featuring rows of giant elm trees. It was restored to its original appearance in 1974, with the addition of a portico and parapet. Most of the furniture and knick-knacks came from other Tasmanian collections, but they give you a good insight into the life of a 19th century landowner. The collection of dolls and children's toys on the second floor and the period dresses are fascinating. It's open daily 10 am to 5 pm (4 pm June, July and Aug). Entry costs A$7 (U.S.$4.55) for adults, A$5 (U.S.$3.25) for children under 16, and A$14 (U.S.$9.10) a family.

5 Launceston

198km (123 miles) N of Hobart

Tasmania's second city is Australia's third oldest, after Sydney and Hobart. Situated at the head of the Tamar River, 50 kilometers (31 miles) inland from the state's north coast, and surrounded by delightful undulating farmland, ✪ **Launceston** is a pleasant city crammed with elegant Victorian and Georgian architecture and plenty of remnants from convict days. Unfortunately, short-sighted local and state government officials are gradually allowing the chipping away of its great architectural heritage in favor of the usual parking garages and ugly concrete monoliths. However, Launceston (pop. 104,000) is still one of Australia's most beautiful cities and has plenty of delightful parks and churches. It's well placed as the gateway to the wineries of the

Tamar Valley, the highlands and alpine lakes of the north, and the stunning beaches to the east.

ESSENTIALS

GETTING THERE   **Qantas** (☎ **13 13 13** in Australia or 02/9691 3636) flies to Launceston from Melbourne and Sydney, and **Ansett** (☎ **13 13 00** in Australia) offers service from Melbourne.

Tasmanian Redline Coaches depart Hobart for Launceston several times daily (trip time: around 2 hr., 40 min.). The one-way fare is A$19 (U.S.$12.35). Launceston is 1½ hours from Devonport if you take the *Spirit of Tasmania* ferry across Bass Strait to Devonport. The bus ride from Devonport costs around A$13 (U.S.$8.45).

The drive from Hobart to Launceston takes just over 2 hours on Highway 1.

VISITOR INFORMATION   **The Gateway Tasmania Travel Centre** on the corner of St. John and Paterson streets (☎ **03/6336 3133;** fax 03/6336 3118; gateway.tas@microtech.com.au) is open Monday through Friday from 9am to 5pm, Saturday from 9am to 3pm, and Sunday and public holidays from 9am to noon.

CITY LAYOUT   The main pedestrian shopping mall, **Brisbane Street,** along with St. John and Charles streets on either side, forms the heart of the central area. The Victorian-Italianate **Town Hall** is 2 blocks north on Civic Square, and opposite the red brick Post Office building dating from 1889. The Tamar River slips quietly past the city's northern edge and is crossed at two points by Charles Bridge and Tamar Street. **City Park,** to the northeast of the central business district, is a nice place for a stroll.

EXPLORING THE CITY & ENVIRONS

Launceston is easily explored on foot. We recommend a stroll with ✪ **Launceston Historic Walks**, (☎ **03/6331 3679;** harris.m@bigpond.com), which leave from the Gateway Tasmania Travel Centre Monday to Friday at 9:45am (weekend walks can also be arranged). The hour-long walk gives a fascinating insight into Launceston's history and costs A$10 (U.S.$6.50). **City Sights** (☎ **03/6336 3122**), on the corner of St. John and Paterson streets, runs city tours daily by replica tram. Tours cost A$23 (U.S.$14.95) for adults and A$16 (U.S.$10.40) for children under 16.

A must see is ✪ **Cataract Gorge,** the result of violent earthquakes that rattled Tasmania some 40 million years ago. It's a wonderfully scenic area just 10 minutes from Launceston. The South Esk River flows through the gorge and collects in a small lake traversed by a striking yellow suspension bridge and the longest single span chair lift in the world. The chair lift (☎ **03/6331 5915**) is open daily from 9am to 4:30pm (except from June 23–Aug 11, when it operates on Sat and Sun only), and costs A$5 (U.S.$3.25) for adults and A$3 (U.S.$1.95) for children under 16. Outdoor concerts are sometimes held on the lake bank. The hike to the **Duck Reach Power Station** takes about 45 minutes. Take good footwear and a raincoat. Other walks in the area are shorter and easier. **The Gorge Restaurant** (☎ **03/6331 3330**) and the kiosk next door serve meals with glorious views from the outdoor tables.

Tamar River Cruises (☎ **03/6334 9900**) offers lunch, afternoon, and evening buffet dinner cruises up the Tamar River from Home Point Wharf in Launceston.

Mountain biking is popular in this area. Contact **Tasmanian Expeditions** (☎ **1800/030 230** in Australia, or 03/6334 3477; www.tas-ex.com/tas-ex); for information on their 4- to 7-day trips along the east coast in summer.

You can rent bicycles from the **youth hostel** at 36 Thistle St. (☎ **03/6344 9779**) for A$11 (U.S.$7.15) per day for a touring bike or A$18 (U.S.$11.70) per day for a mountain bike. (You can also hire bushwalking equipment including boots, tents, sleeping bags and stoves etc.).

How to Catch a Tiger

The Tasmanian Tiger, also called the *Thylacine*, is difficult to spot. For one thing it prefers living in dense forests. Secondly, the lightly built dog-sized marsupials are shy, and extremely rare (officially it's considered extinct, the last one dying in captivity in a Hobart zoo in 1936). However, keep your camera handy, because there have been over 400 sightings since then, the last in January 1995 when a Parks and Wildlife Service officer saw one in eastern Tasmania. Tigers were relatively common until they were accused of threatening sheep and a bounty was put on their heads at the beginning of the 20th century. If you need details before you start your hunt, check out the skins and stuffed example at the Tasmanian Museum and Art gallery in Hobart, or the Queen Victoria Museum in Launceton.

Interestingly, in mid-1999 the Australian Museum in Sydney announced that it had plans to clone the tiger from a specimen preserved in alcohol, which had its DNA intact. It is only one of two such preserved specimens in existence.

The **Trevallyn State Recreation Area,** on the outskirts of Launceston off Reatta Road, is a manmade lake surrounded by a beautiful wildlife reserve with several walking tracks. There are also barbecue facilities, picnic areas, and even a beach.

OTHER ATTRACTIONS

Aquarius Roman Baths. 127 George St., ☎ **03/6331 2255.** Admission to baths and hot rooms A$20 (U.S.$13) for 1, A$30 (U.S.$19.50) for 2. Treatments extra. Mon–Fri 8:30am–10pm, Sat–Sun 9am–6pm.

Adorned with gold, Italian marble, and works of art, this remarkable Romanesque structure is worth visiting just for the architectural experience. Indulge in warm, hot, and cold water baths; visit the steam room; or get a massage or a beauty makeover.

The Old Umbrella Shop. 60 George St. ☎ **03/6331 9248.** Free admission. Mon–Fri 9am–5pm, Sat 9am–noon.

Built in the 1860s, this shop is the last genuine period store in Tasmania and has been operated by the same family since the turn of the 20th century. Umbrellas spanning the last 100 years are on display, while modern "brollies" are for sale. Allow 15 minutes.

National Automobile Museum of Tasmania. 86 Cimitiere St. ☎ **03/6334 8888.** Admission A$7.50 (U.S.$4.88) adults, A$4 (U.S.$2.60) children under 16, A$19 (U.S.$12.35) families. Daily 9am–5pm summer, 10am–4pm winter. Closed Christmas.

More than 80 classic automobiles and motorbikes are on display here, some unique to this exhibition. Children particularly enjoy the model car collection.

The Penny Royal World & Gunpowder Mill. Off Bridge Rd. ☎ **03/6331 6699.** Admission A$19.50 (U.S.$12.68) adults, A$9.50 (U.S.$6.18) children. Also family 2 adults up to 6 children is A$49.50 (U.S.$32.18) Daily 9am–4:30pm. Closed Christmas.

This amusement park, with its sailboat, barges and trams, and historic gunpowder mills, is large enough to occupy an entire day. Admission also includes a tram ride and a trip up Cataract Gorge and the Tamar River on the paddle steamer *MV Lady Stelfox.*

The Queen Victoria Museum & Art Gallery. Corner of Wellington and Paterson sts. ☎ **03/6323 3777.** Free admission. Mon–Sat 10am–5pm, Sun 2–5pm.

Opened in honor of Queen Victoria's Golden Jubilee in 1891, this museum houses a large collection of stuffed wildlife, including the supposedly extinct Tasmanian Tiger, or Thylacine. There are also temporary exhibits and historical items. Allow an hour.

Waverley Woollen Mills. Waverley Rd. ☎ **03/6339 1106.** Tours A$4 (U.S.$2.60) adults, A$2 (U.S.$1.30) children, A$12 (U.S.$7.80) families. Tours daily 9am–4pm (there's usually a 20-min. wait).

Established in 1874 on a site 5 kilometers (3 miles) northeast of town, this mill still uses a waterwheel to turn the looms for wool blankets and rugs. Tours show how the process works. Everything from woolen hats to ties is sold on the premises. Allow an hour.

WHERE TO STAY

Innkeepers Colonial Motor Inn. 31 Elizabeth St., Launceston, TAS 7250. ☎ **03/6331 6588.** Fax 03/6334 2765. 63 units. A/C MINIBAR TV TEL. A$120 (U.S.$78) double; A$195 (U.S.$126.75) suite. Extra person A$15 (U.S.$9.75). Lower weekend rates. Children under 3 stay free in parents' room. AE, BC, DC, MC, V. Free parking.

Those who desire tried-and-true motel lodging will feel at home at the Colonial, a place that combines old-world ambience with modern facilities. The rooms are large and have attractive furnishings. The Old Grammar School next door has been incorporated into the complex, with the Quill and Cane Restaurant operating in what once was a schoolroom, and Three Steps On George, Launceston's liveliest nightspot, in the former boys' gym. Rooms are fairly standard and attract a large corporate clientele.

Hillview House. 193 George St., Launceston, TAS 7250. ☎ **03/6331 7388.** Fax 03/6331 7388. 9 units. A$90 (U.S.$58.50) double; A$105 (U.S.$68.25) family room for 3. Rates include full breakfast. MC, V.

The rooms at this restored farmhouse are not fancy, but quite comfortable. They come with a double bed, a TV, and a shower. The family room has an extra single bed; it's the nicest room and has the best views. The hotel overlooks the city, and the verandah and colonial dining room have extensive views of the city and the Tamar River.

Hotel Tasmania. 191 Charles St., Launceston, TAS 7250. ☎ **03/6331 7355.** Fax 03/6331 5589. 18 units. A$58 (U.S.$37.70) double. Rates include continental breakfast. Extra person A$17 (U.S.$11.05). BC, MC, V. Free on-street parking.

Situated right in the heart of town, this hotel offers simple rooms with modern furnishings, a TV, coffee- and tea-making facilities, and attached showers. All the rooms were renovated in 1998, which helped win the hotel the Australian Hoteliers Association's award for the best budget pub-style accommodation in Tasmania. Downstairs there's a saloon-style bar with a cowboy theme. There's also a bistro.

Lloyd's Hotel. 23 George St., Launceston, TAS 7250. ☎ **03/6331 4966.** Fax 03/6331 5589. 18 units (some with shower only). A$54 (U.S.$35.10) double. Rates include full breakfast. Extra person A$20 (U.S.$13). BC, MC, V. Free parking.

This older-style property offers comfortable lodging. It's centrally located, and the owners are friendly, interesting, and have traveled extensively, mainly through the

Outdoor Shopping

If you're in Launceston on a Sunday, try to visit the **York Town Square Market,** at the rear of the Launceston International Hotel. There are plenty of craft items on sale. The market is open from 9am to 5pm.

United States. Each room comes with a refrigerator, and tea- and coffee-making facilities. Most rooms have a TV.

✪ **Waratah on York.** 12 York St., Launceston, TAS 7250 ☎ **03/6331 2081.** Fax 03/6331 9200. waratahonyork@bigpond.com. 9 units. TV TEL. A$148 (U.S.$96.20) standard double; A$168 (U.S.$109.20) spa room; A$198 (U.S.$128.70) executive spa suite. Rates include continental breakfast. AE, BC, DC, MC, V. Free off-street parking.

The Waratah on York is a carefully renovated Victorian mansion, originally built in 1862 for Alexander Webster, an ironmonger by trade and mayor of Launceston in the 1860s and 70s. The current owners have spent considerable time and energy restoring the property to its former glory. Some of the original features—pressed brass ceiling roses and a staircase with a cast-iron balustrade—remain, while others have been faithfully recreated. Of the nine rooms, six come with a spa, one with a private balcony, and another with a private sunroom. All have high ceilings, large-screen TVs, hair dryers, and ornate (but nonfunctional) fireplaces. The executive rooms have four-poster beds and sweeping views down upon the Tamar River. There's also a comfortable lounge with an open fireplace and a bar.

WORTH A SPLURGE

✪ **York Mansions.** 9–11 York St., Launceston, TAS 7250. ☎ **03/6334 2933.** Fax 03/6334 2870. www.yorkmansions.com.au. yorkmansions@tassie.net.au. 5 units. TV TEL. A$176 (U.S.$114.40) 2-bedroom apt; A$45 (U.S.$29.25) extra person; A$216 (U.S.$140.40) 3-bedroom apt, A$45–$50 (U.S.$29.25–$32.50) extra person. Rates include breakfast provisions. AE, BC, DC, MC, V. Free parking.

If you feel that where you stay is as important to your visit as what you see, then you must stay here. Within the walls of the National Trust—classified York Mansions, built in 1840—are five spacious apartments, each with an individual character. The **Duke of York** apartment is fashioned after a gentleman's drawing room, with rich leather sofa, antiques, and an extensive collection of historic books. The light and airy **Duchess of York** unit has hand painted silk panels. Each apartment is self-contained and has its own kitchen, dining room, living room, bedrooms, bathroom, and laundry. A CD player and large-screen TV add modern touches. The ingredients for a hearty breakfast can be found in the refrigerator. There's also a delightful cottage garden.

WHERE TO DINE

You'll find most places to eat in Launceston don't have a fixed closing time, instead they close up shop when the last customer has been served and has eaten.

✪ **Fee & Me Restaurant.** Corner of Charles and Frederick sts. ☎ **03/6331 3195.** Reservations recommended. A$42 (U.S.$27.30) for 3 courses, A$48 (U.S.$31.20) for 4 courses, A$50 (U.S.$32.50) for 5 courses. AE, BC, DC, MC, V. Mon–Sat 7pm–late. MODERN AUSTRALIAN.

What is perhaps Launceston's best restaurant is found in a grand old mansion. The menu is structured so that diners choose a selection from five categories, moving from light to rich. An extensive wine list has been designed to complement each course. The menu change very frequently, but a five-course meal could go something like this: Tasmanian smoked salmon with salad, capers, and a soft poached egg; followed by chili oysters with a coconut sauce and vermicelli noodles; then ricotta and goat cheese gnocchi with creamed tomato and red capsicum; followed by Asian-style duck on bok choy with a citrus sauce; topped off with a coffee and chicory soufflé.

Konditorei Cafe Manfred. 106 George St. ☎ **03/6334 2490.** Reservations not accepted. Light meals A$4–$5 (U.S.$2.60–$3.25); main courses A$9–$18 (U.S.$5.85–$11.70). AE, BC, DC, MC, V. Mon–Thurs 9am–5:30pm, Fri 9am–late, Sat 10am–late. PATISSERIE.

This German patisserie has moved to larger premises to keep up with demand for its sensational cakes and breads. It's also added an a la carte restaurant serving the pastas and steaks. Light meals include croissants, salads, and cakes. You can eat in or outside.

O'Keefe's Hotel. 124 George St. ☎ **03/6331 4015.** Reservations recommended. Main courses A$10.50–$14.50 (U.S.$6.83–$9.43). AE, BC, MC, V. Daily 11:30am–2pm and 5:30pm–late. ASIAN/TASMANIAN.

This pub-based eatery earns high praise for its variety of well-prepared dishes. You can choose such delicacies as Thai curry and *laksa*, seafood dishes like scallops, prawns, and sushi, and plenty of pastas and grills. There's also a range of good salads.

✪ **Shrimps.** 72 George St. (at the corner of Paterson St.) ☎ **03/6334 0584.** Reservations recommended. Main courses A$14–$19 (U.S.$9.10–$12.35). AE, BC, DC, MC, V. Mon–Sat noon–2pm and 6:30pm–late. SEAFOOD.

Shrimps offers the best selection of seafood in Launceston. Built in 1824 by convict labor, it has a classic Georgian exterior. Tables are small and well spaced, and the best meals are off the blackboard menu, which generally includes at least eight fish dishes. Usually available are wonderful Tasmanian mussels, whitebait, Thai-style fishcakes, and freshly split oysters. Everything is very fresh and seasonal.

TWO CAFES

✪ **Croplines Coffee Bar.** Brisbane Court, off Brisbane St. ☎ **03/6331 4023.** Coffees and teas A$1.60–$2.40 (U.S.$1.04–$1.56). Cakes under A$2 (U.S.$1.30). AE, BC, MC, V. Daily 8am–5:30pm.

If you crave good coffee, head here. It's a bit hard to find, and you may have to ask for directions, but basically it's behind the old Brisbane Arcade. The owners are dedicated to coffee, grinding their beans on the premises daily. If coffee's not your cup of tea, then try the hot chocolate—it's the best I've tasted.

✪ **Star Bar Cafe.** 113 Charles St. ☎ **03/6331 9659.** Reservations recommended. Main courses A$10.50–$17.50 (U.S.$6.83–$11.38). AE, BC, MC, V. Mon–Wed 11am–11pm, Thurs–Sat 11am–midnight, Sunday noon–10pm. MEDITERRANEAN.

Many consider this Tasmania's best bistro. It offers a range of dishes, such as *mee goreng*, beetroot, and quail risotto; grilled octopus, steaks, and chicken livers; as well as popular pizzas and breads cooked in the large wood-fired oven. In winter, guests congregate around a large open fire.

6 Cradle Mountain & Lake St. Clair National Park

85km (53 miles) S of Devonport; 175km (107 miles) NW of Hobart

The national park and World Heritage area that encompasses both ✪ Cradle Mountain and Lake St. Clair is one of the most spectacular regions in Australia and, after Hobart and Port Arthur, the most visited place in Tasmania. The 1,545-meter (5,199-ft.) mountain dominates the north part of the island, and the long, deep lake is to its south. Between them lie more slopes, button grass plains, majestic alpine forests, lakes filled with trout, and several rivers. Mount Ossa, in the center of the park, is Tasmania's highest point at 1,617 meters (5,336 ft.). The Overland Track (see below), links Cradle Mountain with Lake St. Clair and is the best known of Australia's walking trails. Another option in the area is a visit to the Walls of Jerusalem National Park, a high alpine area with spectacular granite walls, small lakes, and old-growth forest.

ESSENTIALS

GETTING THERE   **TWT Tassie Link** (☎ 03/6272 7300; fax 03/6334 2029) runs buses to Cradle Mountain from Hobart, Launceston, Devonport, and Strahan. Round-trip coach transfers from Launceston cost A$69 (U.S.$44.85) and leave daily in the summer at 8:30am. A special Overland Track service drops off passengers at the beginning of the walk and picks them up at the end and costs A$69 (U.S.$44.85) round-trip from Hobart. All coaches have commentary on board.

    Maxwells Cradle Mountain-Lake St. Clair Charter Bus and Taxi Service (☎/fax 03/6492 1431) runs buses from Devonport and Launceston to Cradle Mountain from A$35 (U.S.$22.75), depending on the number of passengers. The buses also travel to other areas nearby, such as the Walls of Jerusalem, and Lake St. Clair. Buses also run from Cradle Mountain campground to the start of the Overland Track.

    Motorists enter the park via the Lyall Highway from Hobart, via Deloraine or Poatina from Launceston, and via Sheffield or Wilmot from Devonport. Both Cradle Mountain and Lake St. Clair are well signposted.

VISITOR INFORMATION   The park headquarters, **Cradle Mountain Visitor Centre** (☎ 03/6492 1133; fax 03/64 921120; www.parks.tas.gov.au), on the northern edge of the national park just outside Cradle Mountain Lodge, offers the best information on local walks and treks. It's open 8am to 5pm (6pm in summer) daily.

EXPLORING THE PARK

Cradle Mountain Lodge (see "Where to Stay & Dine," below) runs a program of guided walks, abseiling, rock-climbing, and trout-fishing excursions for guests. There are also plenty of trails in the area that can be attempted by people equipped with directions from the staff at the park headquarters (see "Visitor Information," above). Be warned, though, that the weather changes quickly in the high country; so go prepared with wet-weather gear and always tell someone where you are headed. Of the shorter walks, the stroll to Pencil Pines and the 5-kilometer (3-mile) walk to Dove Lake are the most pleasant.

    Between June and October it's sometimes possible to cross-country ski in the park.

HIKING THE OVERLAND TRACK

The most well known hiking trail in Australia is the ✪ **Overland Track,** an 85-kilometer (53-mile) route between Cradle Mountain and Lake St. Clair. The trek takes between 5 to 10 days and goes through high alpine plateaus, buttongrass plains, heathland, dense rain forests and passes glacial lakes, ice-carved crags, and waterfalls. The trek gives you a good look at the wild beauty of Tasmania's pristine wilderness, and although the first day is tough walking, you soon get into the rhythm. After climbing to Pelion Gap, the track descends southwards toward the towering myrtle forests on the shores of Lake St Clair. There are many rewarding side trips, including the one-day ascent of Mt. Ossa (1,617m/5,305 ft.), Tasmania's highest peak.

    Several companies offer guided walks of the Overland Track from October to April, although simple public huts, on a first-come-first-served basis, and camping areas are available for those who wish to do it solo. Every summer up to 200 people a day start the trek. Most trekking companies employ at least two guides who carry tents and cooking gear, while you carry your sleeping bag, lunch, and personal belongings. Wet-weather gear is essential as heavy downpours can be frequent, and make sure your boots are well worn in to avoid blisters.

    ✪ **Tasmanian Expeditions** (☎ 1800/030 230 in Australia, or 03/6334 3477; fax 03/6334 3463; www.tas-ex.com/tas-ex) offers 3-day walking tours around Cradle Mountain, staying at Waldheim Cabins. The tours depart from Launceston and cost

A$430 (U.S.$279.50), all-inclusive. Trips leave every Sunday and Wednesday between November and April, with extra trips from Christmas to the end of January. The company also offers a full 8-day trek on the Overland Track for A$995 (U.S.$646.75) all-inclusive from Launceston (wet-weather gear costs A$55/U.S.$35.75 extra to rent). These trips depart every Saturday between November and April, with extra trips from late December through January. Another trip, a 6-day Cradle Mountain and Walls of Jerusalem National Park trip, includes 3 nights' wilderness camping and 3 nights in a cabin. It costs A$840 (U.S.$546) and leaves every Sunday between October and April. Many people have reported this trek to be the highlight of their trip to Australia.

⭘ **Craclair Tours** ☎ and fax **03/6424 7833;** www.southcom.com.au/~craclair; craclair@southcom.com.au), also offers an 8-day Overland Track tour, including 5 nights of camping, between October and mid-April (leaving every Sun and Wed) for A$1,085 (U.S.$705.25).

Another alternative is to go on an organized trek with ⭘ **Cradle Mountain Huts** (P.O. Box 1879, Launceston, TAS 7250. ☎ **03/6331 2006;** fax 03/6331 5525; cradle@tassie.net.au). The huts are heated and well equipped. 6-day walks cost A$1,450 (U.S.$942.50) for adults and A$1,350 (U.S.$877.50) for children 12 to 16; rates are all-inclusive and include transfers to and from Launceston. Children under 12 are not permitted. The huts have showers, a main living area, and a full kitchen. You get a good three-course meal every night. The treks leave every day between Christmas Day and early February, and around 5 times a week between November and April.

WHERE TO STAY & DINE

⭘ **Cradle Mountain Lodge.** GPO Box 478, Sydney, NSW 2001. ☎ **800/225-9849** in the U.S 13 24 69 in Australia, 0171/805-3875 in the U.K., or 03/6492 1303. Fax 02/9299 2477. www.poresorts.com.au. 96 self-contained cabins. Pencil Pine cabins A$186 (U.S.$120.90) per cabin; spa cabins A$240 (U.S.$156) per cabin. Extra person A$26 (U.S.$16.90). Children under 3 stay free in parents' room. Ask about special winter packages. AE, BC, DC, MC, V. Free parking.

If you like luxury with your rain forests, then this award-winning lodge is the place for you. Cradle Mountain Lodge is simply marvelous. Just minutes from your bed are the giant buttresses of 1,500-year-old trees, moss forests, craggy mountain ridges, pools and lakes, and hoards of scampering marsupials. The cabins are comfortable, the food excellent, the staff friendly, and the open fireplaces well worth cuddling up in front of. Each modern wood cabin has a pot-bellied stove as well as an electric heater for chilly evenings, a shower, and a small kitchen. There are no telephones or TV in the rooms—but who needs them! Spa cabins come with carpets, a spa tub, and a balcony offering a variety of scenic views. Some have a separate bedroom. Two cabins have limited facilities for travelers with disabilities. Guests have the use of the casual and comfortable main lodge where there is a large dining room, a lounge with TV and VCR, cozy bars, a tavern, and a cafe. Almost every room in the lodge has a blazing log fire.

Waldheim Cabins. Cradle Mountain Visitor Centre, P.O. Box 20, Sheffield, TAS 7306. ☎ **03/6492 1110.** Fax 03/6492 1120. 8 cabins, none with bathroom. A$60.50 (U.S.$39.33) 4-berth cabin for 2; A$71.50 (U.S.$46.48) 6-berth cabin for up to 3; A$82.50 (U.S.$53.63) 8-berth cabin for up to 3. Additional adult A$20.90 (U.S.$13.59); additional child A$9.90 (U.S.$6.44). BC, MC, V. Collect cabin keys from the National Park Visitor Centre, just inside the boundary of the national park, between 8am and 5:30pm daily.

If you want a real wilderness experience then head for these cabins run by the Parks and Wildlife Service and located just 5 kilometers (3.1 miles) from Cradle Mountain Lodge. Nestled between button grass plains and temperate rain forest, they are simple and affordable and offer good access to plenty of walking tracks. Each cabin is equipped with heating, single bunk beds, basic cooking utensils, crockery, cutlery and a gas stove. They are serviced by two composting toilets and showers. Generated power is provided for lighting between 6pm and 11pm only. Stores and fuel can be bought at Cradle Mountain Lodge. Bring your own bed linen and toiletries.

LAKE ST. CLAIR

Australia's deepest natural freshwater lake, ✪ **Lake St. Clair,** is a narrow, 15 kilometers (9.3 miles) long waterway, fully enclosed within the Cradle Mountain-Lake St Clair National Park. On the lake's southern edge is Cynthia Bay, site of an informative ranger station where you must register if you're attempting the Overland Track from this end, a restaurant, cabin accommodation and a backpackers' hostel (the latter are operated by **Lakeside St Clair** on ☎ **03/6289 1137**). National **park rangers** run several tours between Boxing Day and the end of February, including spotlighting tours and guided walks around the local area. Call ahead for details (☎ **03/6289 1172**).

At the kiosk near the ranger station you can book a seat on the small MV *Idaclair* ferry, which stops off at Echo Point and Narcissus Bay at the lake's northern tip. From Echo Point the walk back to Cynthia Bay along the lakeshore takes 3 to 4 hours (5–6 hr. from Narcissus Bay). Other walks include a 1½-hour Woodland Nature Walk and the 45-minute Watersmeet Track, which both run to and from the ranger station and take in pockets of rainforest and sphagnum moorland.

The MV *Idaclair* departs Cynthia Bay at 9am, 12:30pm, and 3pm. (a minimum of four people required for the ferry to run, but in summer that's not usually a problem). Tickets cost A$15 (U.S.$9.75) one-way for adults, and A$10 (U.S.$6.50) for children 4 to 14. The trip time to Narcissus Bay is 30 minutes. A scenic cruise (basically a return to Cynthia Bay) costs A$20 (U.S.$13) for adults and A$12 (U.S.$7.80) for children.

7 The West Coast

STRAHAN
296km (184 miles) NW of Hobart; 245km (152 miles) SW of Devonport

Tasmania's west coast is wild and mountainous with a scattering of mining and logging towns and plenty of wilderness. The pristine Franklin and Gordon rivers tumble through World Heritage Areas once bitterly contested by loggers, politicians, and environmentalists, whereas the bare, poisoned hills that make up the eerily beautiful "moonscape" of Queenstown show the results of intensive mining and industrial activity. ✪ **Strahan** (pronounced *Strawn*), the only town of any size in the area, is the starting point for cruises up the Gordon River and ventures into the rain forest.

ESSENTIALS

GETTING THERE   **TWT Tassie Link** (☎ **03/6272 7300**) runs coaches between Strahan and Launceston, Devonport, and Cradle Mountain every Tuesday, Thursday, and Saturday (and also Sun to and from Hobart). The trip from Launceston takes over 8 hours. The drive from Hobart to Strahan takes about 4½ hours without stops. From Devonport, allow 3½ hours. Although the roads are good, they twist and turn quite dramatically and are particularly hazardous at night when marsupial animals come out to feed.

The cheapest way to travel between these places is via bus with a **Tassie Wilderness Pass.** Contact TWT Tassie Link at the number listed above, or check the various rates and timetables for passes and tours at www.tassie.net.au/wildtour/wildpasf.htm.

VISITOR INFORMATION **Strahan Visitors Centre,** on The Esplanade (☎ **03/6471 7622;** fax 03/6471 7533), is open daily from 10am to 6pm in winter and to 8pm in spring and summer. It has good information on local activities.

CRUISING THE RIVERS & OTHER ADVENTURES

Gordon River Cruises, P.O. Box 40, Strahan, TAS 7468 (☎ **03/6471 7187;** fax 03/6471 7317) offers a half-day trips daily in the first 3 weeks of January, and a full-day trip from October 1 to the end of May. Cruises cross Macquarie Harbour and head up the Gordon River past **Sarah Island,** where convicts used to log valuable Huon pine. A stop is made at Heritage Landing, where you can get a taste of the rain forest on a half-hour walk. The full-day cruise in the high season (Oct–May) includes lunch and a guided tour through the Sarah Island convict ruins. Cruises depart from the Main Wharf on The Esplanade, in the town center.

World Heritage Cruises (☎ **03/6471 7174;** fax 03/6471 7431; www.world heritagecruises.com.au) offers daily all year round leaving Strahan Wharf at 9am and returning at 3:30pm. The company's *MV Wanderer III* stops at Sarah Island, Heritage Landing, and the salmon and trout farm at Liberty Point. Meals and drinks are available on board.

West Coast Yacht Charters (☎ **03/6471 7422**) runs fishing trips from 9am to noon for A$40/U.S.$26) (negotiable) with fishing gear, bait, and morning tea included; crayfish dinner and fishing cruises from 6 to 8:30pm for A$50 (U.S.$32.50); and 2-day, 2-night sailing cruises for A$320 (U.S.$208) all-inclusive. (Bed and Breakfast Available)

Cruises are the main attraction, but you can also enjoy jetboat rides, flightseeing in a seaplane that lands on the Gordon River, helicopter flights, and 4WD tours.

MINE TOURS & OTHER ATTRACTIONS

Zeehan's West Coast Pioneers Memorial Museum (☎ **03/6471 6225**), 42 kilometers (26 miles) north of Strahan, is worth a visit for its mining relics and fascinating local history. It's open daily from 8:30am to 5pm from April 1 to October 1, and until 6pm at other times. Admission is A$5 (U.S.$3.25) for adults, A$3 (U.S.$1.95) for children, and A$10 (U.S.$6.50) for families.

Worth seeing too are the 103 meters (338 ft.) **Montezuma Falls,** the highest falls in Tasmania. A highly recommended 5 kilometers (3 miles) walk to the falls starts off at the Montezuma Falls signpost at Williamstown, 5 kilometers (3 miles) south of Rosebery. The walk is mostly through rainforest following an old railway track. It's flat and easy, though it can be slippery at times; the journey takes about 3 hours return. **Hays Bus Service** (☎ **03/6473 1247**) runs 4WD trips to the falls if you don't fancy the walk. The trip takes around 3 hours (it's slow going along that track) and costs A$44 (U.S.$28.60) including lunch. Ring in advance for times.

The **Queenstown Chairlift** in Queenstown is also interesting. It's open daily from 8am to 6pm and costs A$6 (U.S.$3.90) for adults, A$4 (U.S.$ 2.60) for children, and A$15 (U.S.$9.75) for families. The chairlift offers panoramic views across the surrounding starkness of the hillsides. The ride takes 15 minutes to the top of the 537-m (1,761 ft.) Limestone Quarry Hill. You can walk around on top before coming back down. There's a cafe in the chairlift building.

✪ **Lyell Tours** (☎ **03/6471 2388;** fax 03/6471 2222) runs surface and underground tours of a **Queenstown mine,** operated by Copper Mines of Tasmania (CMT). The 1-hour surface tour takes in the enormous open-cut mine, the lunar landscape around Queenstown its main street. The tour leaves from the company's offices below the Empire Hotel in Driffield Street, Queenstown. They run at 9:15am and 4pm and cost A$12 (U.S.$7.80) for adults and A$6.50 (U.S.$4.23) for children. The company's underground tour of the mine (3½ hr.) starts at 8:30am and 1:30pm. It really is world class. Visitors dress as miners and get taken 5 kilometers (3 miles) underground in a cage. It costs A$50 (U.S.$32.50) per person, and there's a maximum of seven people. Children under 12 are not allowed. The company also runs an excellent **Bird River Rainforest Tour,** taking in some of Australia's most spectacular rainforest. The 4½-hour tour leaves at 8:30am and 2pm daily and costs A$60 (U.S.$39) for adults and A$40 (U.S.$26) for children.

DUNE BUGGY RIDES

What's more fun than scooting across the sand in a dune buggy? **Four-Wheelers** (☎ **03/6471 7622,** or mobile 0419/508 175; fax 03/6471 7020) offers exhilarating, 40-minute rides across the ✪ **Henty Sand Dunes,** about 10 minutes north of Strahan. Trips cost just A$30 (U.S.$19.50) for one adult and A$55 (U.S.$35.75) for two. Longer trips are also offered outside the hot summer months.

WHERE TO STAY

Franklin Manor. The Esplanade, Strahan, TAS 7468. ☎ **03/6471 7311.** Fax 03/6471 7267. 18 units, including 4 cottages. TV TEL. A$150 (U.S.$97.50) standard double; A$170 (U.S.$110.50) deluxe double or cottage. Rates include breakfast. AE, BC, DC, MC, V. Ask about winter deals.

Built in 1886 as the home of the harbormaster, this old mansion was abandoned and known as a local "haunted house" by the 1960s. Completely restored in the late 80s, it has become a self-described "casual boutique hotel." Standard rooms have queen-size beds, while deluxe rooms have king-size ones. The main lounge is comfortable and warmed by a log fire. The simple Huon pine bar in the foyer and the wine cellar operate on the honor system. A three-course dinner costs A$39 (U.S.$25.35) per person. The specialties are salmon, duck, and lobster, with venison and wallaby served in winter.

Gordon Gateway Chalets. Grining St., Strahan, TAS 7468. ☎ **03/6471 7165.** Fax 03/6471 7588. 12 units. TV. Jan–Apr A$110 (U.S.$71.50) studio double. May–Dec A$72 (U.S.$46.80) studio double. Sept 1–Apr 30 A$150 (U.S.$97.50) 2-bedroom. May 1–Aug 31 A$125 (U.S.$81.25) 2-bedroom. BC, MC, V.

These modern self-contained units are on a hill with views of the harbor and Strahan Township. Each has cooking facilities, so you can save on meals. The two-bedroom apartments have a bathtub, and the studios have a shower. Breakfast is provided on request for A$8.50 (U.S.$5.53) per person. Guests have the use of a self-service laundry, a barbecue area, and children's playground. One unit has facilities for travelers with disabilities.

8 Northwest Coast

STANLEY

140km (90 miles) west of Devonport; 430km (270 miles) north west of Hobart.

Among the least well-known areas of Tasmania, the coastline east of Devonport can throw up some surprises. Not least of them is "The Nut," a kind of miniature Ayers Rock rising out from the sea and towering above the township of Stanley. The Nut is the 152-meter (500 ft.) remains of a volcanic plug that forced its way through a crack in the earth's crust some 12 million years ago. You can walk to the top in about 20 minutes or take a chairlift up for A$6 (U.S.$3.90) for adults, A$4 (U.S.$2.60) for children, and A$15 (U.S.$9.75) for a family. A warning, though, don't attempt riding the chairlift back down again if you're afraid of heights—the descent is incredibly steep and there's no getting off! There's a small buggy up top that will take you on a tour of The Nut for A$5 (U.S.$3.25). Children under 10 are free.

WHERE TO STAY

✪ **The Old Cable Station.** Highfield Lane, Stanley, TAS 7331. ☎ **03/6458 1312.** Fax. 03/6458 2009. 4 units (1 with spa). A$90–$120 (U.S.$58.50–$78) double. Rates include continental breakfast. AE, BC, MC, V.

Darryl Stafford—an ex-logger—and his wife Heather have turned the former exchange building for the telephone line coming over from the mainline into a very cozy B&B. The rooms are nice and comfortable; there are TVs in two rooms, but you'll probably spend all your time in the lounge room chatting around the fire anyway. Darryl is as Aussie as you can get and will keep you entranced for hours with his stories. He also runs penguin-spotting tours for A$12 (U.S.$7.80) for adults and A$5 (U.S.$3.25) for children between September and the end of March, and seal tours daily weather permitting for A$35 (U.S.$22.75). Home-cooked dinners are served daily in the restaurant and cost A$25 (U.S.$16.25) for two courses.

WHERE TO DINE

Hursey Seafoods. 2 Alexander Terrace, Stanley. ☎ **03/6458 1103.** Main course in cafe A$10 (U.S.$6.50), and around A$15 (U.S.$9.75) in restaurant. MC, V. Takeaway/cafe 9am–6pm; restaurant 6–10pm. SEAFOOD.

There are plenty of people around who rate this little place as having the best seafood in Australia. Downstairs, it's a casual cafe, where you choose what you want from fish tanks, while upstairs it's a more formal restaurant. An unusual specialty is muttonbird (shearwater), an oily seabird that you either like seeing flying around or like seeing on your plate. You can't have it both ways.

9 The Central Highlands Lakes

Tasmania's extensive hydroelectric schemes have transformed the island state, creating the ✪ **Central Highlands Lakes,** all seeded with trout. Some of the most popular trout fishing and recreation lakes are Arthur's Lake, Great Lake, Lake Sorell and Lake St. Clair—the deepest lake in Australia. The Bronte system of lakes, between Bronte Park and Tarraleah are also favorites, especially because they are about half way between Strahan and Hobart and offer accommodation options. The lakes around here hold some of the biggest wild brown and rainbow trout in the world. Monsters of well over 9 pounds are not uncommon, while anglers frequently land 5- to 6-pound fish. The water is clear and shallow, making spotting the trout an easy affair.

To fish, you need an angling license costing $12 (U.S.$7.80) for 1 day, $20 (U.S.$13) for 3 days, $35 (U.S.$22.75) for 2 weeks and $45 (U.S.$29.25) for a full season. The trout-fishing season is from the beginning of August to the end of April. Call **Inland Fisheries** (☎ **03/6233 4140**), or pick up a license at a tourist office, aboard the *Spirit of Tasmania*, in tackle shops, and general stores in small towns.

For more information on trout guiding services contact the **Tasmanian Professional Trout Guides Association** (☎ **03/6229 5896**; tastroutguides@vision.net.au).

WHERE TO STAY
BRONTE PARK

Bronte Park Highland Village. Bronte Park, TAS 7140. Tel. **03/6289 1126.** Fax 03/6289 1109. 17 cottages, 12 rooms in chalet, 9 hostel rooms. A$65 (U.S.$42.25) standard cottages, A$12 (U.S.$7.80) extra adult, A$5 (U.S.$3.25) extra child; A$88 (U.S.$57.20) superior cottages, A$17 (U.S.$11.05) extra adult, A$10 (U.S.$6.50) extra child. A$66 (U.S.$42.90) standard ensuite rooms, A$15 (U.S.$9.75) extra adult, A$10 (U.S.$6.50) extra child; A$75 (U.S.$48.75) superior ensuite rooms. A$120 (U.S.$78) Spa cottage. Ask about specials. AE, BC, DC, MC, V. Free parking.

Village by name, village by nature, Bronte Park offers everything for a passer-through or for those after the local trout. Cottages are self-contained and comfortably warmed by log fires, and can sleep between four and ten. Chalet rooms within the main house are old pub-style in appearance, with attached bathrooms. The spa cottage has a double and two singles and is rated as four star. Caravans and camping facilities are also on site. The main building has a gift shop, a good restaurant a family bar, even bigger log fires, a TV room and game room. The village store acts as a post office, a service station and takeaway. You can also hire your trout fishing gear here. Find Bronte Park just off the Lyell Highway between Queenstown and Hobart.

TULLAH

90km (56 miles) northeast of Strahan and 64km (102 miles) south of Devonport.

Tullah Lakeside Chalet. Farrell St., Tullah TAS 7321. ☎ **03/6473 4121.** Fax 03/6473 4130. 51 units. A$55 (U.S.$35.75) standard double, A$75 (U.S.$48.75) superior double, A$90 (U.S.$58.50) Lakeside double. Extra child 2–12 A$10 (U.S.$6.50). AE, BC, DC, MC,V.

This place is a good stop over for lunch on the way to and from the north coast from Strahan, or an excellent base from which to discover Tasmania's lake district. Standard rooms are cheap and cheerful, although quite small, and come with a double bed and a shower. Superior rooms are slightly larger and come with a queen size bed. Guests also have the use of a laundry, a kitchenette, and a TV lounge. Devonshire teas, for A$5 (U.S.$3.25), are available in the bar or dining room or in front of the huge fireplace. Lunch and dinner menus could include marinated quail as a starter, and spinach and ricotta cannelloni or a big chunk of salmon served with a simple salad and French fries for a main course. Mains go for between A$12 (U.S.$7.80) and A$18 (U.S.$11.70).

The Chalet runs horse riding tours, trout-fishing tours, boating trips on the lake, and horse and wagon rides around the village. Mountain bikes and canoes are also available for hire. Among the most popular walks in the area are the 5-hour return hike to the top of **Mount Murchison,** which offers 360°-degree views as far as the coast, Queenstown and to Cradle Mountain-Lake St. Clair National Park; and the 3-hour walk to the top of Mount Farrel, which overlooks Tullah and Lake Rosebury. Ask at the chalet for directions. **Hays Bus Service** (☎ **03/6473 1247**) runs half-day and full-day trout fishing tours of the area's lakes.

Appendix:
Australia in Depth

by Marc Llewellyn

The land "Down Under" is a modern nation coming to terms with its identity. The umbilical cord with mother England has been cut, and the nation is still trying to find its position within Asia.

One thing it realized early, though, was the importance of tourism. Millions of visitors flock to Australia every year. You'll generally find people to be helpful and friendly, and services, tours, and food and drink to rival any in the world. Then there's the landscape, the native Australian culture, the sunshine, the animals, and some world-class cities—what more could you ask?

1 Australia's Natural World

THE LAND OF THE NEVER-NEVER

People who have never visited Australia always wonder why such a huge country has a population of only 19 million people. The truth is, Australia can barely support that many. The majority of it is harsh Outback country, characterized by salt bush plains, arid crags, shifting sand deserts, and salt lake country. The soil is poor in the Outback; it hardly ever rains, and the rivers barely make it to the ocean. People survive where they can in this great arid land because of one thing—the Great Artesian Basin. This saucer-shaped geological structure forms about one fifth of the land mass, stretching over much of inland New South Wales, Queensland, South Australia, and the Northern Territory. Beneath it are underground water supplies stored during Jurassic and Cretaceous times (66–208 million years ago), when the area was much like the Amazon basin is today. The water is brought to the surface under pressure, allowing sheep, cattle, and humans a respite from the dryness.

About 90% of Australia's 19 million people live in an area that covers only 2.6% of the continent. Climatic and physical land conditions ensure that the only relatively decent rainfall occurs along a thin strip of land around Australia's coastal fringe. The green rim found on Australia's eastern side is caused by the Great Dividing Range, a line of hills thrust up some 80 million years ago. The divide reaches from southeastern Victoria right up to Cairns in northern Queensland. The Blue Mountains, inland from Sydney, and the Snowy Mountains to the south both form part of it. Clouds gather over the mountains and move to the sea, dropping rain over the lower slopes and the green edge. The coastal lands that skirt the rest of the continent also have a higher rainfall than the center, with added drainage from the inland plateaus. The far north territories of Australia benefit from monsoonal rains.

The Queensland coast is blessed with one of the greatest natural attractions in the world. The Great Barrier Reef stretches some 2,000 kilometers (1,240 miles) from off Gladstone in Queensland, to the Gulf of Papua, near New Guinea. It's not more than 8,000 years old, though many fear that rising sea waters, caused by global warming, will cause its demise. As it is, the non-native Crown of Thorns starfish and a bleaching process believed to be the result of excessive nutrients flowing into the sea from Australia's farming land, is already causing significant damage. The reef is covered in chapter 7.

AUSTRALIA'S FLORA & FAUNA

PLANT LIFE   Just two genera of plants—**acacias** and **eucalypts**—dominate more than 75% of Australia. In general, eucalyptus (or gum trees) dominate a broad band around the coast, while acacias flourish in the dry central regions. Here and there, patches of rain forest cling to the higher slopes, draped with strangler figs, staghorn ferns, and native orchids. If you travel through the Outback, you'll see vast expanses of grassy tufts called spinifex, complimented in places by knee-high salt bush, or blue bush. If you go hiking (or *bushwalking*, as the Aussies call it) around the coastal regions, you're likely to come across flowering banksias (the yellow ones look like and smell like corn on the cob), as well as grevillias, bottlebrushes, and a whole host of tiny flowers that reach their peak in springtime.

NATIVE ANIMALS   Australia's isolation from the rest of the world over millions of years has led to the evolution of forms of life found nowhere else. Probably the strangest is the **platypus.** This monotreme, or egg-laying marsupial, has webbed feet, a duck-like bill, and a tail like a beaver's. It lays eggs, and the young suckle from their mother. When a specimen was first brought to Europe, skeptical scientists insisted it was a fake—a concoction of several animals sewn together. You will probably never see this shy, nocturnal creature in the wild, though there are a few at Sydney's Taronga Zoo.

Another strange one is the **koala.** This fluffy marsupial eats virtually indigestible gum leaves and sleeps about 20 hours a day. There's just one species, though those found in Victoria are substantially larger than their brethren in more northern climes.

Australia is also famous for its **kangaroos.** There are 45 different kinds of kangaroos and wallabies in all, ranging in scale from small rat-sized kangaroos to the man-size Red kangaroos.

The animal you're most likely to come across in your trip is the **possum,** named by Captain James Cook after the North American "opossum," which he thought they resembled (in fact they are not related). The brushtail possum is commonly found in suburban gardens, including those in Sydney. Then there's is the **wombat.** There are four species of this bulky burrower in Australia, but the most frequently found is the common wombat. You might come across the smaller hairy-nosed wombat in South Australia and Western Australia.

The **dingo,** thought by many to be a native of Australia, was in fact introduced—probably by the Aborigines. They vary in color from yellow to a russet red, and are heavily persecuted by farmers.

Commonly seen **birds** include the fairy penguin along the coast, black swans, parrots and cockatoos, and honeyeaters. **Tasmanian devils** can be found in (you guessed it) the island/state of Tasmania.

DANGEROUS NATIVES **Snakes** are common in Australia, but you will rarely see one. The most dangerous land snake is the taipan, which hides in the grasslands in northern Australia—one bite contains enough venom to kill up to 200 sheep. If by the remotest chance you are bitten, you must immediately demobilize the limb, wrapping it quite tightly (but not tight enough to restrict the blood flow) with a cloth or bandage, and head to the nearest hospital where antivenin should be available.

There are two types of **crocodile** in Australia: the harmless freshwater crocodile, which grows to three meters (9.8 ft.); and the dangerous estuarine (or saltwater) crocodile, which reaches 5 to 7 meters (16.4–23 ft.). Freshwater crocs eat fish; estuarine crocs aren't so picky. Never swim in, or stand on the bank of, any river, swamp, or pool in northern Australia unless you know for *certain* it's croc free.

Spiders are common all over Australia, with the funnel web spider and the red-back spider the most aggressive. Funnel webs live in holes in the ground (they spin their webs around a hole's entrance) and stand on their back legs to attack. Red-backs have a habit of resting under toilet seats and in car trunks, generally outside the main cities. Caution is a good policy.

If you go bushwalking, check your whole body carefully. **Ticks** are common, especially in eastern Australia, and can cause severe itching and fever. If you find one attached to you, dab it with methylated spirits or some other noxious chemical. Wait for a while, then pull it gently out with tweezers, carefully ensuring you don't leave its head buried inside the wound.

Fish to avoid are stingrays, porcupine fish, stonefish, lionfish, and puffer fish. Never touch an **octopus** if it has blue rings on it, or a cone shell, and be wary of the painful and sometimes deadly tentacles of the box **jellyfish** found along the northern Queensland coast in summer. If you happen to touch one of these, pour vinegar over the affected site immediately—local councils leave bottles of vinegar on the beach. Vinegar deactivates the stinging cells that haven't already affected you, but doesn't affect the ones that already have.

In Sydney, you might come across "stingers" or "blue bottles" as they are also called. These long-tentacled blue jellyfish can inflict a very nasty stinging burn that can last for hours. Sometimes you'll see warning signs on patrolled beaches. The best remedy if you are severely stung is to wash the affected water with fresh water and have a very hot bath or shower.

Otherwise, enjoy yourself!

THE FERAL THREAT Australia has become a very different place since the arrival of the white man. The introduction of non-indigenous species of animals has caused two-thirds of the mammal species in the arid regions to become endangered or extinct. **Rabbits** eat almost anything that grows, and compete with native animals and change the nature of the land. Domestic **cats** gone wild and foxes have devastated marsupial populations and taken a heavy toll on native bats and birds as well. Roaming the drier country in the millions, turning it into dust, are feral **goats,** which prefer to rest up in rocky places, forcing the endangered yellow-footed rock wallaby out of its hiding places and into the talons of wedge-tailed eagles. A **pig** will eat native water birds and eggs, but their sheer numbers (millions) also cause serious damage with their wallowing and digging. Feral **horses,** nicknamed "brumbies" in Australia, together with wild **donkeys** and **camels,** compete for water with native animals and scar the land with their hooves. Roaming the wetlands and forests of northern and central Australia are hundreds of thousands of **buffalo,** which heavily impact on waterways and wetlands, turning pools into mud. **Cane**

toads, introduced in Queensland in the 1930s to eat beetles, have infested the state, and are now found in New South Wales and the Northern Territory. Secreting poison from their neck glands, the amphibians are suspect in the declining numbers of quolls (wild cats) and goannas (lizards).

2 The People of Oz

Heavy immigration has led to people from some 165 nations making Australia their home. In general, relations between the ethnic groups have been peaceful. Today. Australia is an example of a multicultural society, despite an increasingly vocal minority that believes that Australia has come too far in welcoming people from races other than their own.

THE ABORIGINES   When Captain James Cook landed at Botany Bay in 1770 to claim the land for the British Empire, at least 300,000 Aborigines were already on the continent. Whether you believe a version of history that suggests the Aboriginal people were descendants of migrants from Indonesia to the north, or the Aboriginal belief that they have occupied Australia since the beginning of time, there is scientific evidence that people were using fire for cooking in present-day New South Wales at least 120,000 years ago.

At the time of the white "invasion" of their lands, there were at least 600 different, largely nomadic tribal communities, each linked to their ancestral land by "sacred sites" (certain features of the land, such as hills or rock formations). They were hunter-gatherers, spending about 20 hours a week harvesting the resources of the land, rivers, and the ocean. A complex social and belief system, as well as the practicalities of life, such as making utensils, weapons, and unique musical instruments such as didgeridoos, and clapsticks, took up much of the rest of the time.

The basis of Aboriginal spirituality rests in the Dreamtime stories, in which everything: land, stars, mountains, the moon, the sun, the oceans, water holes, animals and humans, were created by spirits. Much Aboriginal art is related to their land, and the sacred sites that are home to the Dreamtime spirits. Some Aboriginal groups believe these spirits came in giant human form, others believed they were animals, still more that they were huge snakes. Some even believe in a single Western God-like figure. According to Aboriginal custom, individuals can draw on the power of the Dreamtime spirits by reenacting various stories and practicing certain ceremonies.

Aboriginal groups had encountered people from other lands before the British arrived. Dutch records from 1451 show that the Macassans, from islands now belonging to Indonesia, had a long relationship trading Dutch glass, smoking pipes, and alcohol for edible sea slugs from Australia's northern coastal waters. Dutch, Portuguese, French, and Chinese vessels also encountered Australia—with the Dutch fashion for pointy beards catching on through northern Australia long before the invasion of 1770.

When the British came, bringing their diseases with them, coastal communities were virtually wiped out by smallpox. Even as late as the 1950s, large numbers of Aborigines in remote regions of South Australia and the Northern Territory succumbed to deadly influenza and measles outbreaks.

Though relationships between the settlers and local Aborigines were initially peaceful, conflicts over land and food soon led to skirmishes in which Aborigines were massacred and settlers and convicts attacked—Governor Phillip was speared in the back by an Aborigine in 1790.

Within a few years, some 10,000 Aborigines, and 1,000 Europeans were killed in Queensland alone, while in Tasmania, a campaign to rid the island entirely of local Aborigines was ultimately successful, with the last full-blooded Tasmanian Aborigine dying in 1876. By start of the 20th Century, the Aboriginal people were considered a dying race. Most left alive lived in government-owned reserves or Church-controlled missions.

Massacres of Aborigines continued to go largely or wholly unpunished into the 1920s, while from the late 1930s until the 1970s, it was government policy to remove light-skinned Aboriginal children from their families, in the belief that bringing them up "as whites" would make them "better" Australian citizens. Many children of the "stolen generation" were brought up in white foster homes or church refuges and never reunited with their biological families—many with living parents were told that their parents were dead. No one knows how many children were removed, though some statistics suggest between one-third and half of all Aboriginal children were separated from their parents. An Australian Bureau of Statistics report revealed that 10 percent of all Aboriginal people aged over 25 in 1994 had been removed.

Today, there are some 283,000 Aborigines in Australia, and a great divide still exists between them and the rest of the population. Their life expectancy can be twenty times lower than other Australians, with death rates between two and four times higher. A higher percentage of Aboriginal people than in the general population fill Australian prisons, and despite a Royal Commission into Aboriginal Deaths in Custody, Aborigines continue to die while incarcerated.

A landmark in Aboriginal affairs occurred in 1992 when the High Court determined that Australia was not an empty land (*terra nullius*) as it had been seen officially since the British invasion. The "Mabo" decision resulted in the 1993 Native Title Act, which allowed Aboriginal groups, and the ethnically distinct people living in the Torres Strait islands off northern Queensland, to claim government-owned land if they could prove continual association with it since 1788. The later "Wik" decision determined that Aborigines could make claims on Government land leased to agriculturists.

The federal government, led by the right-leaning Prime Minister John Howard, curtailed these rights following pressure from farming and mining interests.

Issues currently facing the Aboriginal population include harsh mandatory sentencing laws, enacted in West Australia and the Northern Territory state governments in 1996 and 1997 respectively, came to the forefront of international attention in 2000.

The Aboriginal community perceived the laws as targeting them. When a 15-year-old Aboriginal boy allegedly committed suicide less than a week before he was due to be released from a Northern Territory prison in 2000, and a 21-year-old Aboriginal youth was imprisoned for a year for stealing A$23-worth of fruit cordial and biscuits, Aboriginal people protested, activists of all colors came out in support, and even the United Nations weighed in with criticism.

Added to this was the simmering issue of the federal government's decision not to apologize to the Aboriginal people for the "stolen generation." In March 2000, a government-sponsored report stated there was never a "stolen generation," and according to respected researchers on both sides of the fence, went on to markedly underestimate the amount of people personally affected.

Prior to the Sydney 2000 Olympic Games, a popular movement involving people of all colors and classes called for reconciliation and an apology to the Aboriginal people. In Sydney, an estimated 250,000 people marched across the Sydney Harbour Bridge. The Liberal (read "conservative") Government refused to bow to public pressure. Despite Aboriginal threats of boycotts and rallies during the Olympics, the Games passed without major disturbance, and a worldwide audience watched as Aboriginal runner Cathy Freeman lit the Olympic cauldron.

THE REST OF AUSTRALIA "White" Australia was always used to distinguish the Anglo-Saxon population from that of the Aboriginal population. These days, though, a walk through any of the major cities would show that things have changed dramatically. About 100,000 people emigrate to Australia each year. Of these, about 12% were born in the U.K. or Ireland, 11% in New Zealand, and more than 21% in China, Hong Kong, Vietnam, or the Philippines. Waves of immigration have brought in millions of people since the end of World War II. The 1996 census showed more than a quarter of a million Australia residents were born in Italy, for example, some 186,000 in the former Yugoslavia, 144,000 in Greece, 118,000 in Germany, and 103,000 in China. So what's the typical Australian like? Well, he's hardly Crocodile Dundee.

3 History 101

IN THE BEGINNING In the beginning there was the Dreamtime, according to the Aborigines of Australia. Between then and now, perhaps, the supercontinent referred to as Pangaea split into two continents called Laurasia and Gondwanaland. Over millions of years, continental drift carried the land masses apart. Laurasia gradually broke up and formed North America, Europe, and most of Asia. Meanwhile, Gondwanaland divided into South America, Africa, India, Australia and New Guinea, and Antarctica. Giant marsupials evolved to roam the continent of Australia: Among them were a plant-eating animal that looked like a wombat the size of a rhinoceros; a giant kangaroo standing 3 meters (10 ft.) high; a giant wombat the size of a donkey; and a flightless bird the same size as an emu, but four times heavier. The last of these giant marsupials are believed to have died out some 40,000 years ago.

EARLY EXPLORERS The existence of Australia had been in the minds of Europeans since the Greek astronomer Ptolemy drew a map of the world in about A.D. 150 showing a large land mass in the south, which he believed had to be there to balance out the land in the northern hemisphere. He called it *Terra Australia Incognita*—the unknown south land.

Evidence suggests Portuguese ships reached Australia as early as 1536. In 1606, William Jansz was sent by the Dutch East India Company to find a new route to the Spice Islands, and to find New Guinea, which was supposed to be rich in gold. He landed on the north coast of Queensland, and fought with local

Dateline

- **120,000** B.C. Evidence suggests Aborigines living in Australia.
- **60,000** B.C. Aborigines living in Arnham Land in the far north fashion stone tools.
- **1606** Dutch explorer Willem Jansz lands on far north coast of Van Diemen's Land (Tasmania).
- **1622** First English ship to reach Australia wrecks on the west coast.
- **1642** Abel Tasman charts the Tasmanian coast.
- **1770** Capt. James Cook lands at Botany Bay.
- **1787** Capt. Arthur Phillip's First Fleet leaves England with convicts aboard.
- **1788** Captain Phillip raises British flag at Port Jackson (Sydney Harbour).
- **1788–1868** Convicts are transported from England to the colony of Australia.
- **1793** The first free settlers arrive.
- **1813** Explorers Blaxland, Wentworth, and Lawson cross the Blue Mountains.
- **1830** Governor Arthur lines up 5,000 settlers across Van Diemen's Land to walk the length of the island to

continues

capture and rid it of all Aborigines.

- 1841 Explorer Edward Eyre travels overland from Adelaide to Perth.
- 1850 Gold discovered in Bathurst, New South Wales.
- 1852 Gold rush begins in Ballarat, Victoria.
- 1853 The last convict arrives in Van Diemen's Land and to celebrate the colony is renamed Tasmania after Abel Tasman.
- 1860 The white population of Australia reaches more than one million.
- 1861 Explorer John Stuart travels overland from Adelaide to Northern Territory coast.
- 1861 Explorers Burke and Wills perish at Coopers Creek.
- 1872 England and Australia exchange their first telephone call.
- 1875 Silver found at Broken Hill, New South Wales.
- 1880 Bushranger Ned Kelly hanged.
- 1886 The Duke of Edinburgh wounded by a shot in the back in Sydney.
- 1892 Massive gold reef found at Kalgoorlie, Western Australia.
- **1895** Banjo Patterson's *The Man from Snowy River* published.
- 1889 Australian troops fight in the Boer War in South Africa.
- 1901 The six states join together to become the Commonwealth of Australia.
- 1902 Women gain the right to vote.
- 1908 Canberra is chosen as the site for the federal capital.
- 1911 Australian (non-Aboriginal) population reaches 4,455,005.
- 1915 Australian and New Zealand troops massacred at Gallipoli.
- 1920 Qantas airline founded.

Aborigines. Between 1616 and 1640, more Dutch ships made contact with Australia as they hugged the west coast of what they called "New Holland," sailing with the *westerlies* (west winds) from the Cape of Good Hope.

In 1642, the Dutch East India Company, through the Governor General of the Indies, Anthony Van Diemen, sent Abel Tasman to search and map the great south land. During two voyages, he charted the northern Australian coastline and discovered Tasmania, which he named Van Diemen's Land after the Governor General.

THE ARRIVAL OF THE BRITISH In 1697, English pirate William Dampier published a book about his adventures. In it, he mentions Shark Beach on the northwest coast of Australia as the place his ship made its repairs after robbing ships on the Pacific Ocean. Sent to further explore by England's King William III, Dampier returned and reported that he found little to recommend.

Captain James Cook turned up in 1770, and charted the whole east coast in his ship HMS *Endeavor.* He claimed it for Britain and named it New South Wales, probably as a favor to Thomas Pennant, a Welsh patriot and botanist. On the April 29, Cook landed at Botany Bay, which he named after the discovery of scores of plants hitherto unknown to science. Turning northwards, Cook passed an entrance to a possible harbor where he noted there appeared to be safe anchorage. He named it Port Jackson after the Secretary to the Admiralty, George Jackson. Back in Britain, King George III was convinced Australia could make a good colony. It would also reduce Britain's overflowing prison population, as England could no longer transport convicts to the United States of America following the War of Independence.

The First Fleet left England in May 1787, made up of 11 store and transport ships (none of them was bigger than the passenger ferries that ply modern-day Sydney Harbour from Circular Quay to Manly) led by Arthur Phillip. Aboard were 1,480 people, including 759 convicts. Phillip's flagship, *The Supply,* reached Botany Bay in January 1788, but Phillip decided the soil was poor and the surrounds too swampy. On 26th January, now celebrated as Australia Day, he settled for Port Jackson (Sydney Harbour) instead.

SETTLING DOWN The convicts were immediately put to work clearing land, planting crops, and constructing buildings. The early food harvests were failures, and by early 1790, the fledgling colony was facing starvation.

Phillip decided to give some convicts pardons for good behavior and service, and even grant small land parcels to those who were really industrious. In 1795, coal was discovered; in 1810 Governor Macquarie began extensive city building projects; and in 1813 the explorers Blaxland, Wentworth, and Lawson forged a passage over the Blue Mountains to the fertile plains beyond.

When gold was discovered in Victoria in 1852, and in Western Australia twelve years later, hundreds of thousands of immigrants from Europe, America, and China flooded into the country in search of their fortunes. By 1860, more than a million non-Aboriginal people were living in Australia.

The last 10,000 convicts were transported to Western Australia between 1850 and 1868, bringing the total shipped out to Australia to 168,000.

FEDERATION & THE GREAT WARS On January 1, 1901, the six states that made up Australia proclaimed themselves to be part of one nation, and the Commonwealth of Australia was formed. In the same ceremony, the first Governor General was sworn in as the representative of the Queen, who remained head of state. In 1914, Australia joined the mother country in war. In April the following year, the Australian and New Zealand Army Corps (ANZAC) formed a beachhead on the peninsula of Gallipoli in Turkey. The Turkish troops had been pre-warned, and eight months of fighting ended with 8,587 Australian dead and more than 19,000 wounded.

Australians fought in World War II in North Africa, Greece, and the Middle East. In March 1942, Japanese aircraft bombed Broome in Western Australia and Darwin in the Northern Territory. In May 1942, Japanese midget submarines entered Sydney Harbour and torpedoed a ferry before being destroyed. Later that year, Australian volunteers fought through the jungles of Papua New Guinea on the Kokoda Trail against superior Japanese forces. Australian troops fought alongside Americans in subsequent wars in Korea and Vietnam and sent military support to the Persian Gulf conflicts.

- 1927 The federal capital is moved from Melbourne to Canberra.
- 1931 The first airmail letters are delivered to England by Charles Kingsford Smith and Charles Ulm.
- 1931 The Arnham Land Aboriginal Reserve is proclaimed.
- 1932 The Sydney Harbour Bridge opens.
- 1942 Darwin bombed, and Japanese mini-submarines found in Sydney Harbour.
- 1942 Australian volunteers hold back Japanese invasion of New Guinea on the Kokoda Trail—Australia's Alamo.
- 1950 Australian troops fight alongside Americans in Korea.
- 1953 British nuclear tests at Emu in South Australia lead to a radioactive cloud killing and injuring many Aborigines.
- 1956 Olympic Games held in Melbourne.
- 1957 British atomic tests conducted at Maralinga, South Australia. Aborigines again affected by radiation.
- 1962 Commonwealth government gives Aborigines the right to vote.
- 1965 Australian troops start fighting in Vietnam.
- 1967 Aborigines granted Australian citizenship and are counted in census.
- 1968 Australia's population passes 12 million following heavy immigration.
- 1971 Australia pulls out of Vietnam following mass demonstrations.
- 1971 The black, red, and yellow Aboriginal flag flown for the first time.
- 1972 White Australia policy formally ended.
- 1972 Aboriginal Tent Embassy erected outside Parliament House in Canberra.

continues

- 1973 The Sydney Opera House completed.
- 1974 Cyclone Tracy devastates Darwin.
- 1976 The Aboriginal Land Rights (Northern Territory) Act gives some land back to native people.
- 1983 Ayers Rock given back to local Aborigines, who rename it Uluru.
- 1983 Australia wins the Americas Cup, ending 112 years of American domination of the event.
- 1984 *Advance Australia Fair* made Australian national anthem following referendum.
- 1986 Queen Elizabeth II severs the Australian Constitution from Great Britain's.
- 1988 Aborigines demonstrate as Australia celebrates its Bicentennial with a re-enactment of the First Fleet's entry into Sydney Harbour.
- 1991 Australia's population reaches 17 million.
- 1993 Sydney chosen as the site of 2000 Olympics.
- 1994 High Court *Mabo* decision overturns the principle of *Terra Nullius*, which suggested Australia was unoccupied at time of white settlement.
- 1995 Australians protest as France explodes nuclear weapons in the South Pacific.
- 1996 Severe bushfires destroy many national parks and charcoal leaves rain down across Sydney.
- 1996 Gunman Martin Bryant kills 35 people in Port Arthur, Tasmania.
- 1996 High Court hands down *Wik* decision, which allows Aborigines the right to claim some Commonwealth land.
- 1998 Prime Minister John Howard attempts to reverse *Wik* in favor of lease-holding pastoralists.

RECENT TIMES Following World War II, mass immigration to Australia, primarily from Europe, boosted the population. In 1974 the left-of-center Whitlam government put an end to the White Australia policy that had largely restricted black and Asian immigration since 1901. In 1986 the official umbilical cord to Britain was cut when the Australian Constitution was separated from that of its motherland. Australia had begun the march to complete independence.

In 1992 the High Court handed down the "Mabo" decision that ruled that Aborigines had a right to claim government-owned land if they could prove a continued connection with it. The following year, huge crowds filled Sydney's Circular Quay to hear that the city had won the 2000 Olympic Games.

The Olympic city built new venues. A new expressway and train link were built to connect the spruced-up airport to the city center, and Sydney welcomed thousands of international visitors to the two-week extravaganza starting in September, 2000. The Games put medal-winning Australian athletes Cathy Freeman and swimmer Ian Thorpe in the spotlight, and spurred a new wave of interest and tourism in the Land Down Under.

4 Oz Art

The Aborigines might not have created the original art in Australia. Ancient, strange-looking stick figures, totally dissimilar to the Aboriginal cave paintings that are found on rock overhangs across the country, were discovered in Western Australia. We'll probably never know who painted them, but we know a bit about what remains of age-old Aboriginal artistic creations. Using natural pigments from charcoal, clays, plants, and ochre from iron ore, the Aboriginal people created long-lasting art. Often, they would spray paint from their mouths over their hands to leave a stencil mark on a wall—the painting would show that they belonged to that land. Some paintings told stories of the Dreamtime, some marked sacred places, and others were used as maps to show what animals were around and where the water holes were. They also used quartz to chip at rocks, forming picture engravings, some of which still survive. In our time, Aboriginal people have taken to portraying their inner life and tribal land maps on canvas. Many of the best paintings cost a fortune and are sold to collectors from all over the world.

Colonial art got off to a false start in Australia, with many artists trying to produce paintings with the same heavy, gloomy light found in Europe. Yet, unlike Europe, the light in Australia is blinding, and the landscapes bleached. It wasn't until late in the 19th century that the impressionist Arthur Streeton started to paint Australian landscapes in their own light.

In the first decades of the 20th century, Australia's male artists were busily painting rural scenes with woolsheds and sheep, while female artists were traveling overseas and bringing back European Modernism with them. Two painters of this period are Margaret Preston and Grace Cossington-Smith. In the 1930s and 40s a host of influential artists appeared, the best known being Sydney Nolan—most famous for a series of paintings based on the bushranger Ned Kelly and the World War I assault on Gallipoli. John Olson and Arthur Boyd emerged as key figures of the 1960s. Olson looked for the essence behind things in a landscape, and Boyd often placed Aboriginal and biblical figures in a landscape. Another noted Australian artist is Tony Tuckson; his paintings bring Australian art almost full circle, with his work showing a very strong Aboriginal influence.

- **1998** The right-wing One Nation Party, led by former fish-and-chip shop owner Pauline Hanson, holds the balance of power in Queensland elections on a platform of anti-immigration and anti-Aboriginal policies.
- **1999** Australia votes on whether to shake off its ties with the Queen and become a republic. However, the "yes" option on the ballot states that politicians will elect the President, not the people. Australians, including many Republicans who are angry with the wording, vote against the proposal.
- **2000** A 10% Goods and Services tax becomes part of everyday life in Australia. In response, business and consumer confidence evaporates, and the country is jolted into an economic downturn.
- **2000** The Sydney Olympics held.

5 Aussie Eats & Drinks

THE EATS

It took a long time for the average Australian to realize there was more to food than English-style sausage and mashed potatoes, "meat and three veg," and a Sunday roast. It wasn't so long ago that spaghetti was something foreigners ate, and vegetables like zucchini and eggplant were considered exotic. Then came mass immigration, and with it, all sorts of foods that people had only read about in *National Geographic*.

The first big wave of Italian immigrants in the 1950s caused a national scandal. The great Aussie dream was to have a quarter-acre block of land with a Hills Hoist (a circular revolving clothesline) in the backyard. When Italians started hanging their fresh pasta out to dry on this Aussie icon, it caused a national uproar, and some clamored for the new arrivals to be shipped back. As Australia matured, Southern European cuisine became more popular, until olive oil was sizzling in frying pans the way only lard had previously done.

In the 1980s, waves of Asian immigrants hit Australia's shores. Suddenly, everyone was cooking with woks, and newly discovered spices and herbs were causing a sensation. These days, this fusion of flavors and styles has melded into what's now commonly referred to as "Modern Australian"—a distinctive cuisine blending the spices of the east with the flavors of the west.

Witchetty Grubs, Lilli-Pillies & Other Good Things to Eat

Soon after the First Fleet of convicts and settlers landed in Sydney Cove on January 26, 1788, they starved. They thought the Australian bush was empty of nourishment, despite evidence to the contrary in the well-fed, healthy and happy Aboriginals all around them. Only in the past 10 years or so, a mere 200 years after landing, have Europeans finally started to wake up to the dazzling variety and wonderful tastes of "bush tucker," as native Aussie food is tagged. These days bush tucker is all the rage and it's a rare fashionable restaurant that does not have wattle-seed, lemon myrtle or some other native taste sensation worked into its menu.

To help you make sense of unusual items on the menu, below is a list of those foods you may encounter in trendy restaurants around the country:

Bush Tucker	Explanation
Bunya nuts	Crunchy nuts of the bunya pine, about the same size as a macadamia
Bush tomatoes	Dry, small darkish fruits more like raisins in look and taste
Cranberries (native)	Small berry that tastes a bit like an apple
Kangaroo	You know what this one is. Kangaroo is a red meat with a strong gamey flavor. Tender when correctly prepared, tough when it is not. It is excellent smoked.
Illawarra plums	Dark berry with a rich strong tangy taste
Kakadu plum	Wonderfully sharp tangy green fruit that boasts the highest recorded Vitamin C level of any food

Aboriginal people have been living off the land for tens of thousands of years, but it was only recently that Australian restaurateurs began looking into native foods ("bush tucker"). Kangaroo is now a common sight on menus, with wallaby, emu, and crocodile also making regular appearances—though many Australians blanch when faced with eating the wildlife.

Native berries and nuts, such as the *quandong* (a tart-tasting fruit the size of a grape) and the now world-famous macadamia nut, commonly find their way into new wave Australian cuisine. Australia's introduced species have also become semi-popular eating, with Northern Territory buffalo, in particular, lumbering onto restaurant menus.

THE DRINKS

THE AMBER NECTAR   The great Aussie drink is a "*tinnie*" (a can) of beer. Barbecues would not be the same without a case of tinnies, or "*stubbies*" (small bottles). In the hotter parts of the country, you may be offered a polystyrene cup in which to place your beer to keep it cool.

Australian beers vary considerably in quality, but, of course, there's no accounting for tastes. Among the most popular are Victoria Bitter (known as 'VB'), XXXX (pronounced "four ex"), Fosters, and various brews produced by

Lemon aspen	Citrusy light yellow fruit with a sharp tangy flavor
Lemon myrtle	Gum leaves with a fresh lemony tang; often used to flavor white meat
Lilly-pilly	Delicious juicy sweet pink berry; also called a riberry
Macadamia nuts	Sweet white nut. Macadamias come from Australia, not Hawaii.
Paperbark	Not a food but the bark of the melaleuca (*me-la-loo-ka*) tree. Good for wrapping fish and veggies in to steam them.
Quandong	A tart, tangy native peach
Rosella	Spiky red petals of a flower with a rich berry flavor; traditionally used by Europeans to make rosella jam
Wattle-seed	Roasted ground acacia seeds that taste a little like bitter coffee; commonly used by Europeans in pasta or desserts
Wild limes	Smaller and more sour than regular limes; good in salads.

One ingredient you probably will not see on restaurant menus is witchetty grubs, because most people are too squeamish to eat these fat slimy white critters. They live in the soil or dead tree trunks and are a common protein source for Aboriginals. If you are offered one to eat in the Outback, you can do what most folks do and freak out, or eat the thing and enjoy its pleasantly nutty taste as a reward for your bravery!

the Tooheys company. All are popular in cans, bottles, or on tap (draft). My favorite beer is Cascade, a German-style beer that you will usually find only in a bottle. It's light in color, strong in taste, and made from Tasmanian water straight off a mountain. If you want to get plastered, try Coopers—it's rather cloudy in looks, very strong, and usually ends up causing a terrific hangover. Most Australian beers range from 4.8% to 5.2% alcohol.

In New South Wales, beer is served by the glass in a "schooner" and a smaller "midi"—though in a few places it's sold in British measurements, by pints and half pints. In Victoria you should ask for a "pot," or the less copious "glass." In South Australia a "schooner" is the size of a NSW "midi," and in West Australia a "midi" is the same size as a New South Wales midi, but a glass about half its size is a "pony." Confused? My advice is to ask for a beer and gesture with your hands to show whether you want a small or a large one.

THE VINO   Australian winemaking has come a long way since the first grape vines were brought to Australia in 1788. These days, more than 550 major companies and small winemakers produce wine commercially in Australia. Vintages from Down Under consistently beat competitors from other wine-producing nations in international shows. The demand for Australian wine overseas has increased so dramatically in the past few years that domestic prices have risen, and new vineyards are being planted at a frantic pace.

Australian wines are generally named after the grape varieties from which they are made. Of the white wines, both the fruity chardonnay and riesling varieties; the "herbaceous," or "grassy" sauvignon blanc; and the dry semillon are big favorites. Of the reds, the dry cabernet sauvignon, the fruity merlot, the burgundy-type pinot noir, and the big and bold shiraz come out tops.

6 The After-Dark Scene

If you have an opportunity to see a performance in the Sydney Opera House, jump at it. The "House" is actually not that impressive inside, but the walk back after the show towards the ferry terminals at Circular Quay, with Sydney Harbour Bridge lit up to your right and the departing crowd all around you debating the best part of this play or who dropped a beat in that performance—well, its like riding around the pyramids on a horse, or hearing Gershwin while on the streets of New York.

If you like your after-dark entertainment less highbrow, we can manage that, too. Australians can be party animals when they're in the mood. Whether it's a few beers around the barbecue, a few bottles of red at dinner with friends, or an all-night rage in a dance club, they're always on the lookout for the next event. You'll find that alcohol plays a big part in the Aussie culture.

PUBS   Traditional Australian pubs are uniquely ugly by tradition. The walls are often tiled like a bathroom (so you can hose them down at the end of the night), and the bar area is an often far-too-large circular contraption that pins thirsty patrons onto uncomfortable bar stools around its edge. Traditionally, too, the Aussie pub was also the local hotel (you'll often hear pubs referred to as "hotels"). It was a sign of the times, when the only place to stay as a traveler, or to recover from a hangover, was the hostelry above the bar. (It's fortunate that the Irish are slowly infiltrating the pub scene, bringing with them more comfortable venues, with a bit more atmosphere. If you spot a shamrock on a pub-lined street, make a beeline for it.) That said, Aussies are friendly pubgoers. They chat away merrily (often disconcertingly in the bathroom), shake hands after playing pool, and are generally jolly drunks.

Pub opening times vary depending on their licenses, but most are open from around 10am to midnight most nights, with many extending their drinking hours to the small hours on Friday and Saturday nights. A few pubs in major cities are open 24 hours.

CASINOS & CLUBS   Most Australian capital cities have a casino to soak up any spare cash you might have. Generally, casinos stay open until the wee hours and impose a "smart but casual" dress code (jeans are allowed).

If you're not ready to hit the high-stakes tables of a casino, you can patronize a traditional Aussie "club" instead. Every town and city has at least one, and often several, of these ostensibly "private" clubs, which are usually ex-servicemen's clubs, workers' clubs, bowling clubs, ethnic clubs, or sporting "leagues" clubs. Most offer essentially the same things—cheap drinks, a bistro, sometimes a quality restaurant, plenty of "pokies" (poker machines, or "one-armed-bandits"), and a billiards table or two. On weekends, there might be entertainment or a disco. Some clubs can be enormous, with tens of thousands of registered members and a huge patronage every day of the week. The club is the social heart of many small towns. Non-members must sign a form when they enter the club to comply with government licensing laws.

7 Australia in Print & on the Silver Screen

BOOKS

One of the best ways to get to the heart of a nation is to read its books. The earliest Australian literature consists mostly of poems and chanties that go on about how difficult it was to travel all the way over to the new land to find it full of flies, dusty plains, and hard work. Of the 19th-century writers, the one that stands head and shoulders above anyone else is the poet "Banjo" Patterson whose epic poem *The Man from Snowy River* hit the best-seller list in 1895 (and was later made into a film).

The big names of this century include Miles Franklin, who wrote *My Brilliant Career* (1901), which tells the story of a young woman faced with the dilemma of choosing between marriage and a career (and another outstanding film). Outback adventures were at the heart of three classic Australian books. Colleen McCullough's *Thorn Birds* is a romantic epic about a Catholic priest who falls in love with a girl; *We of the Never Never* by Mrs. Aeneas Gunn, tells the story of a young woman who leaves Melbourne to live on a cattle station in the Northern Territory; and *Walkabout* by James V. Marshall shows the relationship between an Aboriginal and two children who get lost in the bush. It was later made into one of Australia's most acclaimed movies.

Novelist Patrick White won the Nobel Prize for Literature in 1973 for *The Eye of the Storm*. Though not Australian, D. H. Lawrence spent a lot of time Down Under, and his novel *Kangaroo* is worth a read.

Travel writer Bruce Chatwin got to the heart of Australia with his book *Songlines*, while another travel scribe, Jan Morris, summed up the Emerald City well in her book *Sydney*. If you can find it, *The Long Farewell* by Don Charlwood tells amazing first-hand diary accounts of long journeys from Europe to Australia in the last century. A good historical account of the early days of settlement is Geoffrey Blainey's *The Tyranny of Distance*, first published in 1966. Robert Hughes's *The Fatal Shore: The Epic of Australia's Founding*, is a bestselling non-fiction study of the country's early days.

Modern novelists of note include David Ireland, Elizabeth Jolley, Helen Garner, Sue Woolfe, and Peter Carey, whose *True History of the Kelly Gang*, a fictionalized autobiography of the outlaw Ned Kelly was a best-seller in 2001, winning the prestigious Booker Prize.

FILMS

Australia's movie industry has never been a slouch when it comes to producing beautifully made, intelligent dramas, as well as a quirky, offbeat comedies. All the films below are available on video. If you plan to buy any of them in Australia, note that Australia uses the PAL system, while the United States used the NTSC system; which means you'll have to get your videos converted.

COMEDY

- *The Adventures of Priscilla, Queen of the Desert* (1994). Terrence Stamp, Hugo Weaving, and Guy Pearce stars as three drag queens who set out from Sydney in a bus called Priscilla to work their way across Australia. Their outrageous exploits made the movie far from a drag. The costumes won an Oscar.
- *Babe* (1994). Starring a young pig, this cute and moving porcine masterpiece cried out for a string of Oscars when it hit the world's screens. Indulge yourself in a movie that caused a generation of children to push aside their bacon.

- *Bad Boy Bubby* (1994). Starring Nick Hope, this strange comedy-drama is about a man in his 30s who's never left his mother's apartment. When he finally finds his way out he finds he has a fascination for disposing of cats and people by winding them up in plastic food wrap.
- *Cane Toads, An Unnatural History* (1987). This darkly funny documentary illustrates the love/hate (mostly hate) relationship Australians have with this prolific, non-indigenous creature that has wreaked environmental havoc.
- *Malcolm* (1986). Colin Friels and John Hargreaves are excellent in this offbeat film about a slow-witted man who is a genius at inventing mechanical gadgets.
- *Muriel's Wedding* (1994). Toni Collette, Rachel Griffith, and Bill Hunter combine in this quirky comedy about a plain-looking girl from suburbia who leaves it all behind to find the man of her dreams in the big city. Delves into the Australian love of the music of Abba.
- *Reckless Kelly* (1993). Yahoo Serious plays a wacky version of the notorious Australian bush-ranging bandit Ned Kelly. Yahoo's 1988 hit *Young Einstein* was a strange tail of a Tasmanian apple farmer who plans to split the beer atom.
- *Strictly Ballroom* (1992). Paul Mercurio hotfoots it around the ballroom dance floor as he breaks all tradition by introducing his own steps. It's a romantic comedy well worth watching.

DRAMA

- *The Boys* (1998). Brutally realistic, this film tells of the events leading up to a horrendous crime. It shows the underbelly of Australian society.
- *Breaker Morant* (1980). Aussie icons Edward Woodward, Jack Thompson, and Bryan Brown star in a true story of three mates who find themselves in the Boer War. Many consider this to be one of the best dramas ever made.
- *Gallipoli* (1981). Mel Gibson and Mark Lee are two young runners who join the army amidst the jingoism surrounding World War I. They find themselves facing their toughest moment when going over the top of the trenches means running for their lives.
- *High Tide* (1988). Gillian Armstrong and Judy Davis pair up once more as Davis portrays a backup singer for an Elvis impersonator who returns to her roots in a small coastal Australian town and is reunited with the daughter she left behind.
- *The Man from Snowy River* (1982). Kirk Douglas and Jack Thompson ride the ranges in a remake of Banjo Patterson's famous poem about the chase of an escaped colt.
- *Mad Max* (1979). The first of three films set in a futuristic world controlled by roving gangs. Mel Gibson came of age as an ex-cop. The other films in the trilogy are *The Road Warrior*, and the best, *Beyond Thunderdome*.
- *My Brilliant Career* (1979). Award-winning film based on Miles Franklin's novel, directed by Gillian Armstrong, garnered an Oscar nomination for Judy Davis.
- *Picnic at Hanging Rock* (1975). Rachel Roberts is one of three girls and a teacher who disappear while on a school trip into the bush. The images are hauntingly beautiful.

- *Proof* (1991). Hugo Weaving, Genevieve Picot, and Russell Crowe in an eccentric drama about a blind photographer who composes his shots through the eyes of a young kitchen hand. When his assistant falls in love with his housemaid the problems really begin.
- *Romper Stomper* (1992). Pre-*Gladiator* Russell Crowe is a skinhead who, with his gang, takes to beating up Melbourne's Asian youth. It was controversial and is very violent, but an interesting study of a youth culture.
- *Storm Boy* (1976). Set in The Coorong in South Australia, this delightful film stars Greg Rowe as a kid who develops a friendship with a pelican and an Aborigine (played by David Gulpilil) who teaches him how to love his environment.
- *Walkabout* (1976). Jenny Agutter and David Gulpilil are the stars of this visually evocative movie about a young girl and her brother who get lost in the desert and are befriended by a traditional Aborigine.

Index

Aboriginal Art and Culture Centre (Alice Springs), 8, 358, 359, 361, 363

Aborigines (Aboriginal culture), 625–627
Adelaide, 482
Alice Springs, 359
arts and crafts, 141–142, 363, 390, 400, 419, 445–446, 538, 630–631
Ayers Rock, 376
best places to learn about, 8
Brambuk Aboriginal Living Cultural Centre, 573
Melbourne, 532
Mootwingee National Park, 199
N'Dhala Gorge Nature Park, 371
Port Douglas, 276
Queensland, 239
Tjapukai Aboriginal Cultural Park (Cairns), 254–255
tours, 2, 361, 373, 377, 399, 405

Abseiling (rappelling), 3, 39, 159, 160, 225

Accommodations, 10–12, 22–23, 62–65

Active vacations, 37–43

Adelaide, 469–487
accommodations, 476–479
layout of, 473
nightlife, 486–487
organized tours, 483
outdoor activities, 484–485
restaurants, 479–482
shopping, 485–486
side trips from, 487–494
sights and attractions, 482–484
transportation, 473–474
traveling to, 471–473
visitor information, 473

Adelaide Festival Centre, 486
Adelaide Festival of Arts, 36, 472
Adelaide Hills, 491–494
Adelaide Zoo, 483
Admiral's Arch, 499
Aerial tours (scenic flights), 373, 375, 379, 402, 405, 410, 411, 414, 424, 505, 506
Airfares, 22, 50–52
Airlie Beach, 293, 296, 298, 300–303
Airlines, 49–53
Air passes, 52–53
Alexander, Lake, 391
Alice Springs, 355–368
Aboriginal tours, 361
accommodations, 364–366
layout of, 358
organized tours, 361
outdoor activities, 362
restaurants, 366–368
road trips from, 368–372
shopping, 363
sights and attractions, 358–361
special events, 358
transportation, 358
traveling to, 356
visitor information, 358

Alice Springs Cultural Precinct, 358–359
Alice Springs Desert Park, 359–360
Alpine National Park, 569
American Express, 65, 85, 209, 430, 474, 518, 579
American River, 497, 501–502
Amigo's Castle, 202
AMP Centrepoint Tower (Sydney), 123
Amusement parks. See Theme parks

Anangu Tours (Ayers Rock), 8, 377
Angahook-Lorne State Park, 560
Angaston, 487, 489–491
Ansett Australia, 18
Antarctic Adventure (Hobart), 596
Anzac Memorial (Sydney), 130
Apollo Bay, 560, 562
Aqua (Perth), 440
Aquarium, Melbourne, 532
Aquarium, Sydney, 122–123, 132, 137, 146
Aquarius Roman Baths (Launceston), 611
Archibald Fountain (Sydney), 130
Argyle Cut (Sydney), 135
Arltunga Historical Reserve, 371
Arnhem Plateau, 405
Artesian Bore Baths, 202
Art galleries, 142, 146, 198, 363, 419, 445–446, 552. See also Arts and crafts
Art Gallery of New South Wales (Sydney), 127
Art Gallery of South Australia (Adelaide), 482
Art Gallery of Western Australia (Perth), 438
Arthurs Seat State Park, 552
Arts and crafts, 143, 181, 202, 259, 457, 485, 538
Aboriginal, 141–142, 363, 390, 400, 419, 445–446, 538, 630–631
Ashcombe Maze and Water Gardens (Shoreham), 552
Atherden Street (Sydney), 135
ATMs (automated-teller machines), 31–32

Australasian Steam Navigation Company Building (Sydney), 133
Australia Day, 35
Australian Aviation Heritage Centre (Darwin), 10, 390
Australian Butterfly Sanctuary (Kuranda), 4, 260
Australian Capital Territory (ACT), 20, 575
Australian Chamber Orchestra (Sydney), 148
Australian Institute of Sport (Canberra), 583
Australian Museum (Sydney), 128
Australian National Botanic Gardens (Acton), 587
Australian Prospectors and Miners Hall of Fame (Kalgoorlie), 461
Australian Reptile Park (Sydney), 124
Australian Stockman's Hall of Fame and Outback Heritage Centre (Longreach), 347
Australian Surf Life Saving Championships (Kurrawa Beach), 36
Australian War Memorial (Canberra), 10, 583–584
Australian Woolshed (Brisbane), 221–222
Australia Zoo (Beerwah), 325
Auto racing, 36–37, 536
Avon Valley Historical Rose Garden (York), 452
Ayers Rock, 2. *See also* Uluru-Kata Tjuta National Park
Ayers Rock Observatory, 381

B abysitters, Sydney, 85
Backpacker lodges, 12, 23, 24, 64
Backpackers' hostels. *See* Hostels
Bali Hai, 298
Ballarat, 556–559
Ballarat Fine Art Gallery, 558
Ballooning, 171
Balmain (Sydney), 79
Balmoral (Sydney), 127
Barossa, the (Barossa and Eden valleys), 3, 469, 487–491
Barrenjoey Lighthouse (Sydney), 127

Barrington Tops National Park, 168
Barron Falls, 258, 259
Barron River, 261
Bartle Frere, Mt., 260
Batemans Bay, 191–192
Bay Islands, 233
Beaches, 6, 43. *See also specific beaches, regions, and coasts*
Bed-&-breakfast inns, 63
Beech Forest, 561
Beer, 632–633
Bellingen, 181
Belongil Beach, 185
Berry Farm (near Margaret River), 456
Bevan's Black Opal and Cactus Nursery, 202
Bicentennial Park (Sydney), 130
Big Banana Theme Park (near Coffs Harbour), 180
Big Pineapple (near Nambour), 324
Biking and mountain biking, 39, 138, 160, 171, 225, 261, 274, 277, 362, 443, 484, 535, 587
tours, 42
Billabong Koala and Wildlife Park (Port Macquarie), 178–179
Billabong Sanctuary (Townsville), 288
Birdsville Track, 503
Bird-watching, 39–40, 180, 259, 260, 334–335, 342, 410, 550, 606, 623
Birdworld (Kuranda), 259
Birrabeen, Lake, 319
Blackall Ranges, 325
Blackheath, 165–166
Blood on the Southern Cross (Ballarat), 557
Bloomfield Falls, 274
Blowholes, Kiama, 189
Blue bottles (marine stingers), 6, 125, 126, 240, 267, 272, 282, 288, 291, 294, 296, 386, 418, 440, 624
Blue Mountains, 3, 7, 131, 156–167
guided tours from Sydney, 158
outdoor activities, 158–160
visitor information, 157–158

Boat tours and cruises. *See also* Dolphins and dolphin-watching; Whales and whale watching
Batemans Bay, 191
Bay Islands, 233
Brisbane, 224
Daintree River, 275
Dunk Island, 284
Gold Coast, 335
Great Barrier Reef, 244–248, 268, 274
Green Island, 257
Kakadu National Park, 399
Kuranda, 259
Lone Pine, 220
Longreach, 348
Magnetic Island, 291
Murray River, 563–564
Nitmiluk National Park, 404
Ord River, 411
Port Macquarie, 179
Port Stephens, 176
Shark Bay, 464–465
Sydney, 136–137
Tasmania, 594, 598, 607, 610, 618
Whitsunday Islands, 294, 297–298, 300
Bonaparte Archipelago, 408
Bond Gap, 368
Bondi Beach (Sydney), 78, 97, 113–114, 126, 139
Bonorong Park Wildlife Centre (Hobart), 596
Bonsai Farm (Mt. Dandenong), 546
Books about Australia, 635
Boranup Drive, 457
Botanic Gardens (Adelaide), 483
Botanic Gardens at Mt. Coot-tha, Brisbane, 222–223
Bouderee National Park, 189–190
Brickendon (Longford), 609
Brisbane, 203–234
accommodations, 212–216
casino, 230
layout of, 206
neighborhoods, 207
nightlife, 227–230
organized tours, 224–225
outdoor activities, 225–226
performing arts, 227–228
pubs and bars, 229–230
restaurants, 216–219
river cruises, 224

Brisbane, 203–234 *(cont.)*
  shopping, 226–227
  sights and attractions, 220–225
  spectator sports, 226
  street maps, 206–207
  strolls, 223–224
  transportation, 208–209
  traveling to, 204, 206
  visitor information, 206
Brisbane Botanic Gardens at Mt. Coot-tha, 222–223
Broadbeach, 331
Broken Heads Nature Reserve, 185
Broken Hill, 5, 9, 196–201
Bronte Beach (Sydney), 126
Broome, 9, 407, 416–420
Broome Bird Observatory, 410
Buccaneer Archipelago, 408
Buchan Caves, 569
Buley Rockhole, 395
Bulimba, 207
Bundaberg, 315–316
Bundeena, 132
Bundegi Beach, 467
Bungee jumping, 261, 281, 335–336
Bungle Bungles (Purnululu National Park), 413–414
Burleigh Heads, 331
Burning Palms Beach, 132
Bush Two-Up School (Kalgoorlie), 461
Bushwalking (hiking), 38–39
  Adelaide, 484
  Alice Springs, 362
  best places for, 7–8
  Blue Mountains, 158–159
  Brisbane, 226
  Cradle Mountain National Park, 4
  Dandenong Ranges, 546
  Kakadu National Park, 401
  Katherine, 405
  the Kimberley, 410
  Kings Canyon, 372–373
  Mission Beach, 283
  near Sydney, 131
  safety tips, 43
  tours, 42
  Uluru, 378
  Whitsunday Islands, 300
Business hours, 65
  Sydney, 85–86
Butterflies, 4, 258, 260, 275, 284, 532
Byron Bay, 184–187

Cable Beach, 6, 418
Cadbury Chocolate Factory (near Hobart), 597
Cadmans Cottage (Sydney), 133
Cairns, 7, 239, 251–271
  accommodations, 263–269
  day trips to Great Barrier Reef from, 245–246, 249
  layout of, 254
  outdoor activities, 260–262
  rain forests, 260
  restaurants, 269–271
  side trip to Kuranda, 257–260
  transportation, 254
  traveling to, 251–252
  visitor information, 252
Cairns Regional Gallery, 255
Calendar of events, 35–37
Caloundra, 320, 322
Camel trekking and safaris, 3, 40, 362, 379, 418, 505
Cammoo Caves, 308
Campbell's Storehouse (Sydney), 135
Campervans, 58
Camping, 42, 47, 65, 131, 190, 306–307, 320, 345, 355, 396, 401–402
Canberra, 575–588
  accommodations, 580–581
  layout of, 578
  nightlife, 588
  outdoor activities, 587–588
  restaurants, 582–583
  shopping, 588
  sights and attractions, 583–587
  transportation, 578–579
  traveling to, 575–576
  visitor information, 576
Canberra Deep Space Communication Complex, 584
Canberra National Multicultural Festival, 576, 578
Canoeing, 3, 40, 42, 140, 299, 386, 404–406, 411, 443, 457, 587, 592
Canyoning, 159, 160, 167
Cape Byron Lighthouse, 185
Cape du Couedic, 499
Cape Mentelle (near Margaret River), 455

Cape Moreton lighthouse, 232
Cape Otway Lighthouse, 561
Cape Shanck Coastal Park, 552
Cape-to-Cape, 8, 457
Cape Tribulation National Park, 272–275
Cape Woolamai, 550
Capricorn Coast, 307
Caravan parks, 65, 172
Car rentals, 56–58
Cars and driving, 56–62
Cascade Brewery Tours (Hobart), 597
Casinos, 154, 230, 340, 394, 447, 487, 544, 588, 602, 634
Castle Rock, 286
Casuarina Beach, 391
Cataract Gorge, 610
Cathedrals (cliffs), 319
Caversham Wildlife Park, 450
Caves (caving), 40, 160, 167, 308, 406, 456, 457, 569, 592
Caves Beach, 190
CaveWorks (Lake Cave), 456
Centennial Park (Sydney), 130
Central Highlands Lakes, 620–621
Central Tilba, 9, 192
Cessnock, 168, 169, 171, 172, 174
Champagne Pools, 319
Charters Towers, 286
Children, families with. *See* Families with children
Chinatown (Melbourne), 514–515
Chinese Garden (Sydney), 122
City Hall (Brisbane), 222
Clarendon (Longford), 609
Clare Valley, 487
Clarke's Beach, 185
Cleland Wildlife Park, 494
Cliff Walk (Blackheath), 166
Clocktower Building (Sydney), 135
Clovelly Beach (Sydney), 126
Club Crocodile Long Island, 298, 299, 303–304
Cobblers Beach (Sydney), 127
Coffs Harbour, 179–183
Coffs Harbour Zoo, 180
Cohunu Koala Park (Perth), 438–439
Coles Bay, 606

Combo Waterhole Conservation Park, 349
Consolidators (bucket shops), 21, 22, 50
Consulates, 66
Coober Pedy, 9, 506–508
Coochiemudlo Island, 234
Coogee (Sydney), 126
Cook's Cottage (Melbourne), 535
Coolangatta, 331
Coolgardie, 459–462
Coolgardie Camel Farm (Coolgardie), 462
Cooloola National Park (Great Sandy National Park), 323–324
Coonawarra, 487
Coorong, 469, 508–510
Coral Bay, 466
Coroners Court (Sydney), 133
Corroboree Rock, 371
Cotters Market (Townsville), 288
Cottesloe Beach, 440
Cowaramup, 455, 458
Cowes, 549
Crackenback Chairlift, 194
Cradle Mountain-Lake St. Clair National Park, 4, 614–617
Credit cards, 32
Cricket, 140, 226, 445, 485, 536
Crocodiles, 40, 43, 61, 124, 254, 309, 325, 335, 384, 386, 389, 396, 398–401, 410, 411, 416
    Crocodylus Park (Darwin), 389
    Hartley's Creek Crocodile Farm (Cairns), 256
    Malcolm Douglas Broome Crocodile Park (near Broome), 419
    Original Jumping Crocodiles (near Beatrice Hill), 399
Crocodylus Park (Darwin), 389
Cultural Centre (Ayers Rock), 376
Currency and currency exchange, 31, 32
Currumbin Wildlife Sanctuary, 4, 334–335
Customs House (Sydney), 128
Customs regulations, 30
Cutta Cutta Caves, 406
Cycling. See Biking

D aintree National Park, 275
Daintree Rain Forest, 251, 271, 275
Daintree River, 275
Dandenong Ranges National Park, 544, 546
Darwin, 386–396
Darwin Botanic Gardens, 389
David Fleay Wildlife Park (West Burleigh), 335
Daydream Island, 298, 299, 301
Delprat's Mine (Broken Hill), 198
Derby, 414
Devil's Marbles Conservation Reserve, 381
Didgeridoo University (Alice Springs), 359
Dingoes, 124, 125, 180, 256, 335, 438, 440, 495, 503, 548, 623
Dinosaurs, 345, 347, 349, 418, 440
Disabilities, travelers with, 46–47
Dolphins and dolphin-watching, 176, 182, 190, 232, 464
Dorrigo National Park, 181
Drayton Family Wines (Pokolbin), 170
Dreamtime Cultural Centre (near Rockhampton), 308
Dreamworld (Coomera), 333
Dromedary, Mount, 192, 193
Dune buggy rides (Strahan), 619
Dunk Island, 281, 284
Dunwich, 232

E ast Macdonnell Ranges, 371
East Point Military Museum, 390
Echuca, 563–565
Eco-tours, 234, 300, 377, 405, 406
Eden, 193
Eden Killer Whale Museum, 193
Edith Falls, 405
Edmund Kennedy track, 283
Electricity, 66
Eli Creek, 319
Elizabeth Bay House (Sydney), 128

Ellalong, 172
Ellery Creek Big Hole, 368–369
Ellis Beach, 262
El Questro Station, 412, 414
Elsey National Park, 406
Elsey Station, 6, 8, 406
Embassies and consulates, 66, 86, 579
Emergencies, 66
Emily Gap, 371
Entry requirements, 28–30
Escorted tours, 48, 49
Esplanade, The (Cairns), 239
Etiquette, 66
Eumundi Markets, 325
Eureka Stockade Centre (Ballarat), 557
Exmouth, 466

F alls Creek, 570–571
Families with children. See also Theme parks; Zoos
    information and resources, 47
    restaurants
        Brisbane, 219
        Sydney, 105
    Sydney sights and attractions, 132
Fannie Bay, 389
Farmstays, 64
Featherdale Wildlife Park (Sydney), 125, 132
Ferries and jetcats, Sydney, 83–84
Film Festival, Melbourne International, 541
Film Festival, Sydney, 36
Finke Gorge National Park, 5, 370–371
Fishing, 40, 180, 191, 192, 248, 261, 300, 319, 390–391, 401, 419, 444, 448, 468, 500
Fitzroy Island, 257, 268
Flaxton Gardens, 326
Flecker Botanic Gardens (near Cairns), 239, 255
Flightseeing tours. See Aerial tours
Flinders Chase National Park, 498
Flinders Ranges National Park, 469, 503–506
Florence Falls, 395, 396
Floriade (Canberra), 36

Fogg Dam Conservation Reserve, 398
Food, 631–632
Football, Australian Rules, 140, 226, 445, 485, 535, 536
Forest Glen Deer Sanctuary (Forest Glen), 324–325
Fort Denison (Sydney), 131
Foundation Park (Sydney), 135
Four Mile Beach, 6, 271, 272, 276–278
Four-wheel-driving (rentals, tours, and safaris), 41–43, 181, 192, 274, 275, 300–301, 320, 324, 343, 369, 386, 397, 398, 401, 408, 414, 417, 461, 464, 468, 506, 508, 574
    for beginners, 318
    rentals, 57, 318
    tips for, 61
Francois Peron National Park, 465
Franklin River, 603
Fraser Island, 239, 307, 317–320
Fremantle, 428, 441–443
    accommodations, 433–434
    restaurants, 438
Fremantle Arts Centre, 442
Fremantle History Museum, 442
Fremantle Prison, 442
Freycinet National Park, 8, 606–607
Frontier Camel Farm (Alice Springs), 360
Fudge Factory and Historic Garden Tours (Hobart), 597

Gantheaume Point, 418
Garrison Church (Sydney), 135
Gasoline (petrol), 58–59
Gawler, 487
Gay Games VI (Sydney), 37
Gays and lesbians
    information and resources, 47
    Sydney, 35, 37, 151
Geelong, 552
Geikie Gorge National Park, 416
Gibb River Road, 414
Ginger Factory (Yandina), 324

Gippsland Lakes, 567
Gladstone, 311–312
Glass House Mountains, 158, 326
Glenaire, 561
Glenelg, 484
Glengarry opal fields, 201
Glen Helen Gorge, 369
Gold Coast, 328–345
Gold Coast Highway, 331
Golden River Zoo (Mildura), 564
Goldfields, 459–462
Goldfields Exhibition (Coolgardie), 461
Gold mining and prospecting, 180, 459–461, 556, 557
Gold Museum (Ballarat), 557
Gold Treasury Museum (Melbourne), 534
Golf, 35, 40–41, 139, 192, 193, 200, 261, 276–277, 336, 362, 444, 484–485, 536, 587–588
Goolang River, 182
Government House (Sydney), 130
Grampians National Park, 573–574
Grawin opal fields, 201
Great Barrier Reef, 2, 15, 241–251, 274
    day trips to, 244–248
    gateways to, 242, 244
    safety warnings, 244
    snorkeling and diving, 242, 247–251
Great Dividing Range, 568, 573, 622
Great Keppel Island, 307, 309–311
Great Ocean Road, 3, 559–563
Great Sandy National Park (Cooloola National Park), 323–324
Green Island, 7, 247, 256–257
Greenpatch, 190
Gunlom Falls, 401

Hahndorf, 9, 492–493
Halls Gap, 573
Hamelin Pool Historic Telegraph Station (Monkey Mia), 465

Hamilton Island, 299
Hannans North Historic Mining Reserve (Kalgoorlie), 460–461
Hartley's Creek Crocodile Farm (Cairns), 256
Hattah National Park, 565
Healesville Sanctuary, 548
Health insurance, 44–46
Heineken Classic (Melbourne), 35
Henley-on-Todd Regatta (Alice Springs), 36, 358
Heritage Highway, 607–609
Heritage Park (Woodside), 492
Hermannsburg Historical Precinct, 370
Heron Island, 307, 312–315
Heysen Trail, 484, 491, 504
High Country (Victoria), 568–573
High Court of Australia (Canberra), 584
Hiking. See Bushwalking
History of Australia, 627–630
Hobart, 593–604
Hole in the Wall Beach, 190
Holidays, 34–35
Holloways, 262
Homebush Bay, 79
Homeowner's insurance, 45
Honda Indy 300 Carnival, 36–37
Hook Island, 299, 303, 304
Horden Vale, 561
Horseback riding, 41, 166, 176, 181, 196, 277, 588
Horse racing, 37, 140, 493, 537
Horse trekking, 3
Hostels, 12, 21, 23, 24, 64–65
Hot-air ballooning, 171, 261, 362, 535, 548, 585
Hotham, Mt., 570
Houghton's (Middle Swan), 450
Hunter Estate Winery (Pokolbin), 170
Hunter Valley, 168–175
Huskisson, 190
Hyams Beach, 6, 190
Hyde Park (Sydney), 130
Hyde Park Barracks Museum (Sydney), 123
Hydro Majestic Hotel (Medlow Bath), 165

I lfracombe, 348
Indian Head, 319
Indo Pacific Marine Research
   Centre (Darwin), 390
Information sources, 27–28
In-line skating, 139, 226, 536
Insurance, 21, 44–46, 57
International Student
   Identification Card (ISIC),
   21, 48
Internet access, 87, 212,
   476, 518–519, 590
Isle of the Dead, 605

J amison Valley, 161
Jellyfish (marine stingers), 6,
   125, 126, 240, 267, 272,
   282, 288, 291, 294, 296,
   386, 418, 440, 624
Jenolan Caves, 166–167
Jervis Bay, 4, 189–191
Jessie Gap, 371
Jet lag, 51
Jet skiing, 261, 262, 276,
   292, 293, 296, 299,
   301, 323
Jewel Cave, 456
Jim Jim Falls, 400
Jindabyne, 194, 195
Jogging, 139, 226, 484
Johnstone River, 261
Julian Rocks, 185

K akadu National Park, 2,
   5, 8, 396–403
Kalgoorlie, 9, 459–462
Kangaroo Island, 5, 484,
   494–503
Kangaroos, 60–61, 124, 125,
   173, 178, 180, 189, 190,
   220, 221, 256, 260, 275,
   288, 309, 324, 389, 438,
   440, 483, 492, 494, 623
     Kangaroo Island, 494, 495,
        498, 499
Katherine, 403–407
Katherine Gorge (Nitmiluk
   National Park), 403–405
Katherine Hot Springs, 406
Katoomba, 160–164
Kershaw Gardens
   (Rockhampton), 309
Kewarra Beach, 262
Kiama, 189

Kimberley, the, 2, 407–420
Kingfisher Bay Resort, 239
Kings Canyon, 5, 18, 355,
   370, 372–374
Kingscote, 497, 500, 501
Kings Park and Botanic
   Garden (Perth), 439
Kiwi Down Under Farm
   (Coffs Harbour), 181
Koala Conservation Centre
   (Phillip Island), 550–551
Koala Park (Sydney), 125
Koalas, 5, 124, 132, 175,
   180, 220, 221, 239, 256,
   286, 290, 299, 309, 324,
   440, 450, 494, 498, 530,
   548, 551, 566, 573, 586,
   596, 623
     Billabong Koala and
        Wildlife Park (Port
        Macquarie), 178–179
     Cohunu Koala Park (Perth),
        438–439
     Kangaroo Island, 498, 499
     Koala Conservation Centre
        (Phillip Island), 550–551
     Koala Park (Sydney), 125
     Lone Pine Koala Sanctuary
        (Brisbane), 4, 220
Kondalilla Falls, 326
Kosciuszko, Mount, 194
Kosciuszko National Park,
   194, 196
Kununurra, 407, 410–413
Kuranda, 257–260
Ku-ring-gai Chase National
   Park, 131
Ku-ring-gai Wildflower
   Garden (St. Ives), 131

L ady Elliot Island, 307,
   316–317
Lady Jane Bay (Sydney), 127
Lakes Entrance, 567–568
Lamington National Park, 4,
   7, 340, 342–344
Larapinta Trail, 8, 362
Lark Quarry Conservation
   Park, 349
Lathami Conservation
   Park, 500
Latrobe's Cottage
   (Melbourne), 535
Launceston, 9–10, 609–614
Lavers Hill, 561
Lawn Hill National Park, 350

Leeuwin Estate (Margaret
   River), 455
Leura, 164
Licuala Fan Palm track, 283
Lightning Ridge, 201–202
Lindemans (Pokolbin), 170
Liquor laws, 66
Litchfield National Park,
   395–396
Living Desert Nature Park
   (near Broken Hill), 199
Lofty, Mt., 494
Lone Pine Koala Sanctuary
   (Brisbane), 4, 220
Longford, 608–609
Longreach, 346–348
Lorne, 560–562
Lost City, 372
Low Isles, 274

M acDonnell Ranges, 5, 8,
   356, 368–372
McGuigan Brothers Winery
   (Pokolbin), 170
McKenzie, Lake, 319
McWilliams Mount Pleasant
   (Pokolbin), 170
Magic Mountain amusement
   park (Glenelg), 484
Magnetic Island, 281,
   290–292
Mail and post offices, 67
Main Beach (Byron Bay), 185
Main Beach (Gold Coast), 331
Main Beach (Sunshine
   Coast), 6
Mala Walk, 378
Malcolm Douglas Broome
   Crocodile Park (near
   Broome), 419
Maleny, 326
Mammoth Cave, 456
Mamukala wetlands, 401
Mangarrayi People
   (Katherine), 8, 406
Mangrove Boardwalk
   (Brisbane), 222
Manly (Sydney), 79, 97–99,
   114–115, 126, 130–131
Manly to Spit Bridge Scenic
   Walkway (Sydney),
   130–131
Manyalluluk Aboriginal
   community, 405
Mapleton, 325–326

Mapleton Falls, 326

Margaret River, 3, 454–456, 458–459

Marineland Melanesia (Green Island), 256–257

Mariners Church (Sydney), 133

Marine stingers (jellyfish; blue bottles), 6, 125, 126, 240, 267, 272, 282, 288, 291, 294, 296, 386, 418, 440, 624

Maritime Museum, Australian National (Sydney), 10, 121–122, 132

Maritime Museum of Tasmania (Hobart), 596

Maroochydore, 322

Marrdja Botanical Walk, 274

Mataranka, 382, 406

Mataranka Falls, 406

Mataranka Thermal Pools, 406

MCA (Museum of Contemporary Art) (Sydney), 123

Medical insurance, 44–46

Medlow Bath, 165

Melba Gully State Park, 561

Melba's Chocolate Factory (Woodside), 492

Melbourne, 511–553
    accommodations, 519–524
    Carlton, 515
        accommodations, 522
        restaurants, 528
    Chinatown, 514–515
    City Center, 514
        accommodations, 519–522
        restaurants, 526–528
        strolling, 516
    Fitzroy, 515
        accommodations, 523
        restaurant, 528–529
    layout of, 514
    neighborhoods, 514–516
    nightlife and entertainment, 540–544
    outdoor activities, 535–536
    pubs, 543–544
    restaurants, 524–530
    Richmond, 515
    St. Kilda, 515
        accommodations, 523–524
        restaurants, 529
    shopping, 537–540

side trips from, 544–553

sights and attractions, 530–535

Southgate, 515

South Yarra/Prahan, 515
    accommodations, 524
    restaurants, 529–530

spectator sports, 536

transportation, 516–518

traveling to, 512–514

visitor information, 514

Melbourne Aquarium, 532

Melbourne Cup, 37

Melbourne International Comedy Festival, 540

Melbourne International Film Festival, 541

Melbourne Zoo, 530, 532

Mereenie Loop Road, 370

Merimbula, 193–194

Migration Museum (Adelaide), 10, 482

Mildura, 563–565

Mindil Beach Markets, 14, 393

Mission Beach, 6, 9, 281–286
    day trips to Great Barrier Reef, 246–247, 250

Money, 31–32

Money-saving tips and discounts, 20–25

Monkey Mia (Shark Bay), 5, 462–465

Mon Repos Beach, 314

Mon Repos Turtle Rookery, 4, 314

Montague Island, 4, 192

Montezuma Falls, 618

Montville, 326

Mooloolaba, 322–324, 327

Moondyne Cave, 456

Moonlight Head, 561

Mootwingee National Park, 199

Moreton Bay and islands, 230–234

Moreton Island, 232–233

Mornington Peninsula, 552–553

Mossman Gorge, 274, 275

Motorcycle tours, 138, 161, 373, 379

Moulting Lagoon Game Reserve, 606

Mt. Buffalo National Park, 572–573

Mt. Etna Caves National Park, 308

Mt. Isa, 350–351

Mt. Isa Mine Tours, 351

Mount Field National Park, 603

Mount View Estate, 170

Movies, Australian, 635–637

Mrs. Macquarie's Chair (Sydney), 130

Mumbulla Mountain, 192

Mungo National Park, 565

Murray River, 563–566

Murwillumbah, 187–188

Museum and Art Gallery of the Northern Territory (Fannie Bay), 389–390

Museum of Contemporary Art (MCA) (Sydney), 123

Museum of Sydney, 128–129

Museum of the Goldfields (Kalgoorlie), 461

Museum of Tropical Queensland (Townsville), 286, 287–288

Museums, best, 10

Mutton Bird Island, 180

Mylor, 492

Namadgi National Park, 587

Nambour, 322, 324, 325

Narooma, 192–193

National Automobile Museum of Tasmania (Launceston), 611

National Capital Exhibition (Canberra), 584

National Gallery of Australia (Canberra), 585

National Gallery of Victoria (Melbourne), 532

National Maritime Museum (Sydney), 10, 121–122, 132

National Museum of Australia (Canberra), 584

National Pass Walk, 164

National Pioneer Women's Hall of Fame (Alice Springs), 360

National Rhododendron Gardens (Olinda), 546

National Wool Museum (Geelong), 552

Native Guide Safari Tours, 8, 276

N'Dhala Gorge Nature
    Park, 371
Nelson Bay, 175–177
New Norcia, 453–454
New South Wales, 15, 18,
    155–202
        Outback, 196–202
        transportation, 155–156
        visitor information, 155
Newspapers and
    magazines, 67
Newstead House
    (Brisbane), 223
Newtown (Sydney),
    restaurants, 112–113
New Year's Eve, 35
Ngilgi Cave, 456
Nimbin, 185
Ningaloo Reef, 7, 463
Nitmiluk National Park,
    403–405
Nobbies, The, 550
Noosa (Noosa Heads), 320,
    322, 323, 326–328
Noosa National Park, 323
Noosaville, 322, 323, 328
Norman's Beach, 566
North Gorge Headlands
    Walk, 232
North Stradbroke Island,
    230, 232
North Sydney, 78–79
    restaurants, 115
Northwest Cape, 5, 466–468
Nourlangie Rock, 400
Nuriootpa, 487–489
Nymboida River, 41, 179,
    181–182

O akbank, 493
Oatlands, 607–608
Oceanworld (Sydney),
    125, 132
Old Gaol and Court House
    (York), 452
Old Gum Tree (Glenelg), 484
Old Melbourne Gaol, 532
Old Parliament House
    (Canberra), 585
Old Sydney Town, 123
Old Umbrella Shop
    (Launceston), 611
Olga, Mt. (the Olgas; Kata
    Tjuta), 2, 379
Oliver Hill (Rottnest
    Island), 449

Olsen's Capricorn Caverns
    (Rockhampton), 308
Oodnadatta Track, 503
Opals, 147, 199, 201, 202,
    257, 390, 446, 485,
    506, 540
Opera Australia (Sydney),
    148, 507
Opera House, Sydney,
    117, 120
Opera Queensland
    (Brisbane), 228
Ord River, 40, 410–412
Original Jumping Crocodiles
    (near Beatrice Hill), 399
Orlando (Rowland Flat), 488
Ormiston Gorge and
    Pound, 369
Otford, 132
Outback, the, 196–202,
    345–351, 503–508
        best places to experience,
        5–6
Outback pub at Daly
    Waters, 382
Outfitters and adventure-
    travel operators, 41–42
Overland Track, 615

P acific Highway,
    178–188
Package tours, 22, 48–49
Paddington, 207, 226–227
Palm Beach (Sydney), 6, 127
Palm Cove, 262
Palm Valley, 370
Parasailing, 139, 261,
    276, 299
Parliament, Queensland, 222
Parliament House
    (Brisbane), 223
Parliament House
    (Canberra), 585–586
Parndana, 502
Pearl Luggers (Broome), 418
Penfolds (Nuriootpa), 488
Penguins, 3, 4, 20, 123, 444,
    500, 530, 532, 548–550
Penneshaw, 497, 500,
    502–503
Penny Royal World and
    Gunpowder Mill
    (Launceston), 611
Perth, 425–447
    accommodations, 431–434
    beaches, 440–441

layout of, 426
maps, 428
neighborhoods, 428
nightlife, 446–447
outdoor activities, 443–445
restaurants, 434–438
shopping, 445–446
side trips from, 447–454
sights and attractions,
    438–440
spectator sports, 445
tours and cruises, 443
transportation, 428–430
traveling to, 425–426
visitor information, 426
Perth International Arts
    Festival, 447
Perth Mint, 439
Perth Zoo, 439–440
Peterson's Champagne
    House (Pokolbin), 170
Peterson's Vineyard (Mount
    View), 170
Petrol (gasoline), 58–59
Phillip Bay, 551–552
Phillip Island, 548–551
Phillip Island Penguin
    Reserve, 550
Picton River, 603
Pine Creek, 382
Platypus, 124, 260, 335, 492,
    495, 498, 499, 530, 586,
    603, 623
Point Lookout (North
    Stradbroke Island), 232
Point Lookout (near
    Leura), 164
Pokolbin, 168–175
Police, 67
Port Adelaide, 473
Port Arthur, 604–606
Port Campbell, 562
Port Campbell National
    Park, 561
Port Dock Railway Museum
    (Adelaide), 483
Port Douglas, 6–7, 271–281
Port Fairy, 561
Port Macquarie, 178–179
Port of Echuca, 564
Port Stephens Bay, 175–178
Possum, 189, 220, 256, 260,
    324, 335, 340, 342, 344,
    492, 495, 499, 566, 623
Powerhouse Museum
    (Sydney), 122
Princes Highway, 188–194

Pubs with accommodations, 63–64

Puffing Billy Railway (Belgrave), 547

Purnululu National Park (Bungle Bungles), 413–414

Pylon Lookout (Sydney), 121

Q antas Australian Formula One Grand Prix (Melbourne), 36

Qantas Founders Outback Museum (Longreach), 348

Queensland, 18, 235–351. *See also* Great Barrier Reef
  coast, 239–241
  free (or almost free) sights and activities in, 239
  Outback, 345–351
  seasons, 240
  three-day tour of, 238
  transportation, 240–241
  visitor information, 239–240

Queensland Art Gallery (Brisbane), 221, 222

Queensland Cultural Centre (Brisbane), 221

Queensland Museum (Brisbane), 221

Queensland Museum Theater (Brisbane), 222

Queensland Orchestra (Brisbane), 228

Queensland Performing Arts Complex (Brisbane), 221

Queenstown mine, 618–619

Queen Victoria Markets (Melbourne), 533

Queen Victoria Museum and Art Gallery (Launceston), 611–612

Questacon-The National Science and Technology Centre (Canberra), 586

R afting, 603. *See also* White-water rafting
  Blue Mountains, 159

Railway Station Museum (Coolgardie), 461

Rainbow Beach, 320

Rainforestation Nature Park (Kuranda), 259–260

Rainforest Habitat wildlife sanctuary, 275

Rain forests, 181, 185, 186, 226, 238, 239, 257, 259, 272, 277, 279, 281, 283–285, 299, 309, 326, 340, 341, 395, 546, 561, 618. *See also* Daintree Rain Forest; Lamington National Park

Ranger Uranium Mine, 399

Rappelling (abseiling), 3, 39, 159, 160, 225

Ravenswood, 286

Red Centre, 18–19, 352–382

Reef HQ (Townsville), 287

Regions of Australia, 15–20

Renner Springs, 382

Residency Museum (York), 452

Restaurants, best, 12–14

Rhyll Inlet, 550

Rialto Towers Observation Desk (Melbourne), 533

Richmond (Melbourne), 515

Richmond (village), 605

Rippon Lea House Museum and Historic Garden (Melbourne), 534

River cruises. *See* Boat tours and cruises

Riversleigh Fossil Centre (Mt. Isa), 351

Road trains, 61

Rock climbing, 42, 160, 225, 378, 405, 457, 572

Rockford (Tanunda), 488–489

Rockhampton, 307–309

Rockhampton Botanic Gardens, 309

Rocks, The (Sydney), 75, 89, 92, 104–107, 132–136

Ron McKauge Walk (Cairns), 262

Ross, 608

Rothbury Estate (Pokolbin), 170

Rottnest Island, 7, 425, 447–450

Roundhouse (Fremantle), 442–443

Royal Botanic Gardens (Melbourne), 534–535

Royal Botanic Gardens (Sydney), 130

Royal Flying Doctor Base (Mt. Isa), 351

Royal Flying Doctor Service (RFDS) (Alice Springs), 360

Royal Flying Doctor Service (RFDS) (Kalgoorlie), 461

Royal Flying Doctor Service base (Broken Hill), 198

Royal Flying Doctor Visitors Centre (Cairns), 255–256

Royal National Park, 131–132

Royal Tasmanian Botanical Gardens (Hobart), 597

Runnymeade, 173

Russell Falls, 603

S afety, 67
  driving, 60–62
  outdoor activities and, 42–43

Sailing (yachting), 2, 37, 41, 140, 141, 234, 291, 296–298, 301, 444. *See also* Boat tours and cruises

Sailors' Home (Sydney), 133

St. Clair, Lake, 617

St. Helena Island, 233

St. James Church (Sydney), 128

St. John's Anglican Cathedral (Brisbane), 222

St. Mary's Cathedral (Sydney), 128

St. Patrick's Cathedral (Melbourne), 533

St. Pauls Cathedral (Melbourne), 533

Sandalford, 450

Sandalford (Caversham), 450

Sandy Creek Falls, 395

Scarborough Beach, 428, 440–441

Scenic Railway (Blue Mountains), 161

School of Distance Education (Longreach), 347–348

School of the Air (Alice Springs), 361

School of the Air (Broken Hill), 198

School of the Air (Katherine), 406

Sciencentre (Brisbane), 223

Scuba diving, 37, 138, 180, 185, 192, 242, 244, 247–251, 257, 274, 293, 298, 315, 444, 448, 467. *See also specific locations*
  best places for, 6–7
  courses, 250–251, 315, 467

Sea kayaking, 3, 40, 42, 257, 283, 284, 301, 323, 443–444
Seal Bay (Kangaroo Island), 499–500
Sea lions, 3
Seasons, 32–34
Sea World (Main Beach), 332, 333
Seniors, 47
Seppelts (Seppeltsfield), 489
Serpentine Gorge, 369
75 Mile Beach, 319
Shark Bay (Monkey Mia), 462–465
Shark Museum (Glenelg), 484
Sharks, 126, 132, 287, 324, 333, 440
    whale, 19, 462, 467
Shell Beach, 465
Shelly Beach (Sydney), 127
Shoal Bay, 175
Shopping, money-saving tips and discounts, 25
Silverton, 199
Silver Tree (Broken Hill), 198
Simpson's Gap, 368
Singles, 47–48
Skiing, 3
    Snowy Mountains, 194–195
    tours, 41–42
    Victoria, 570–573
Skyrail Rainforest Cableway, 257–258
Skyway (Blue Mountains), 161
Smiths Beach, 457
Smoking, 44
Snakes, 309, 315, 596, 606, 624
Snorkeling, 242, 247–251, 257, 274, 297–298, 444, 448, 467–468. See also specific locations
    best places for, 6–7
Snowy Mountains, 3, 194–196
Snowy River National Park, 568, 569
Sorrento, 552
South Australia, 19–20, 469–510
    Outback, 503–508
South Australian Maritime Museum (Adelaide), 482
South Australian Museum (Adelaide), 482

South Bank Parklands (Brisbane), 220–222
Southeast Coast, 566–568
South Molle Island, 299, 303, 305
South Stradbroke Island, 232
Sovereign Hill Goldmining Township (Ballarat), 556–557
Spiders, 43, 389, 624
Standley Chasm, 368
Stanley, 619–620
State Houses of Parliament (Melbourne), 534
State Library of NSW (Sydney), 129
Stolen luggage, 45
Strahan, 617–619
Strand, The, 288
Strzelecki Track, 503
Students, 48
Suez Canal (Sydney), 135–136
Sun, exposure to the, 45
Sun-Herald City to Surf (Sydney), 36
Sunshine Beach, 323
Sunshine Coast, 320–328
Super Pit open-cut mine (Kalgoorlie), 459, 461
Surfers Paradise, 331
Surfers Paradise Beach, 6
Surfing, 3, 41, 43, 139, 141, 178, 184, 323, 444–445, 448, 457, 560, 561
Surfworld (Torquay), 560
Survivor 2-The Australian Outback (TV show), 346
Susannah Place (Sydney), 135
Swan Lake, 550
Swan Valley, 450–451
Swimming, 139–140, 288, 588
Sydney, 2, 70–154
    accommodations, 88–99
    Balmain, 79
    bars, 151–153
    beaches, 70, 72, 125–127
        nude, 127
    Bondi and southern beaches, 78, 113–114
        accommodations, 97
    business hours, 85–86
    cafes, 111–112
    casino, 154
    Central (Central Station), 78
        accommodations, 96

Circular Quay, 75
    restaurants, 102–104
currency exchange, 86
Darling Harbour, 75
    accommodations, 92
    restaurants, 108–109
    sights and attractions, 121–123
Darlinghurst, 78
    accommodations, 95
emergencies, 86
gays and lesbians, 35, 37
    clubs, 151
Glebe, 78
    accommodations, 96
harbor cruises, 117, 136–137, 140
Homebush Bay, 79
hospitals, 86
hot lines, 87
Internet access, 87
Kings Cross and suburbs beyond, 75, 78
    accommodations, 92–95
    restaurants, 109–111
layout of, 74–75
lost property, 87
luggage storage, 87
Manly and northern beaches, 79
    accommodations, 97–99
    restaurants, 114–115
motorcycle tours, 138
movies, 153–154
neighborhoods, 75, 78–79
newspapers, 87
Newtown, 78
    restaurants, 112–113
nightlife and entertainment, 147–154
North Shore (Mosman), 79
    accommodations, 99
North Sydney, 78–79
    restaurants, 115
organized tours, 136–138
outdoor activities, 138–140
Paddington/Oxford Street, 78
    restaurants, 111
parks and gardens, 130–132
performing arts, 148–149
picnics, 104
post office, 87–88

Sydney, 2, 70–154 *(cont.)*
  restaurants, 99–115
    ethnic, 112–113
    family-friendly, 105
    seafood, 109
  restrooms, 88
  The Rocks, 75
    accommodations,
      89, 92
    restaurants, 104–107
    self-guided walk,
      132–136
  safety, 88
  shopping, 141–147
  sights and attractions
    for kids, 132
    money-saving tips, 117
    suggested itineraries,
      116–117
  spectator sports, 140–141
  taxes, 88
  telephones, 88
  Town Hall, 75
    restaurants, 107–108
  transportation, 79–85
    buses, 82–83
    by car, 85
    CityRail, 84
    ferries and jetcats,
      83–84
    money-saving passes,
      79, 82
    monorail, 84
    taxis, 84–85
    trams, 84
    transit information, 82
    water taxis, 85
  traveling to, 72–74
  visitor information, 74
  walking tours, 137–138
  Watsons Bay, 78
Sydney Aquarium, 122–123,
  132, 137, 146
Sydney Festival, 35, 149
Sydney Film Festival, 36
Sydney Gay and Lesbian
  Mardi Gras, 35
Sydney Harbour (Port
  Jackson), 120–121
    beaches north of, 126–127
    beaches south of, 126
Sydney Harbour Bridge,
  121, 122
Sydney Harbour National
  Park, 127, 130–131
Sydney International Aquatic
  and Athletic Centres, 123

Sydney Jewish Museum, 129
Sydney Observatory, 129
Sydney Opera House, 117
Sydney Symphony
  Orchestra, 148
Sydney-to-Hobart Yacht
  Race, 37, 594
Sydney Visitor Centre, 133

Tabletop Range, 395
Tamarama (Sydney), 126, 139
Tamborine, Mt., 341
Tamburlaine (Pokolbin), 171
Tamworth Country Music
  Festival, 35
Tandanya Aboriginal
  Cultural Institute
  (Adelaide), 9, 483
Tangalooma Wild Dolphin
  Resort (Moreton), 232
Tanunda, 487, 488, 491
Taronga Zoo (Sydney),
  124–125, 132
Tasmania, 3, 20, 589–621
  suggested itineraries, 593
  tour operators, 592–593
  transportation, 592
  traveling to, 590, 592
  visitor information,
    589–590
  when to go, 590
Tasmanian Devil Park
  Wildlife Rescue Centre
  (Taranna), 605–606
Tasmanian devils, 180, 220,
  440, 494, 596, 603, 605,
  606, 623
Tasmanian Museum and Art
  Gallery (Hobart), 597
Taxes, 67
Telegraph Station Historical
  Reserve (Alice Springs),
  10, 360
Telephone, 67–69
Telstra Tower (Canberra), 586
Tennant Creek, 381–382
Tennis, 140, 536, 537, 588
Territory Wildlife Park, 389
Tesselaar's Bulbs and
  Flowers (Silvan), 546
Theater, 148, 228, 486, 535,
  540–542
Theme parks, 124, 180, 221,
  247, 324, 330, 332–334
Thomson Bay, 449
Thomson River, 348

Thredbo Village, 194–196
Three Brothers, 165
Three Sisters, 161
Tidbinbilla Nature
  Reserve, 586
Time zones, 69
Tinklers (Pokolbin), 171
Tipping, 69
Tjapukai Aboriginal Cultural
  Park (Cairns), 8,
  254–255, 258
Tnorala (Gosse Bluff)
  Conservation Reserve, 370
Top End, 3, 19, 383–420
  tour operators, 386
  transportation, 384, 386
  visitor information,
    383–384
  when to go, 384
Torquay, 560
Tourist information, 27–28
Tours
  Aboriginal, 2, 361, 373, 377
  Aboriginal culture, 2, 361,
    373, 377, 399, 405
  adventure-travel operators,
    41–42
  aerial (scenic flights), 373,
    375, 379, 402, 411, 424,
    505, 506
  eco-, 234, 300, 377,
    405, 406
  escorted, 48, 49
  money-saving tips and
    discounts, 24–25
  package, 22, 48–49
Town Beach (Broome), 419
Townsville, 247, 250,
  286–292
Train travel, 53–55
  Kuranda Scenic
    Railway, 258
  road trains, 61
  Scenic Railway (Blue
    Mountains), 161
Transportation, 51–62
  money-saving tips and
    discounts, 23–24
Traveler's checks, 32
Travel insurance, 21, 45–46
Treloar Technology Centre
  (Canberra), 586–587
Trephina Gorge Nature
  Park, 371
Trigg Beach, 441
Trinity Beach, 262
Tropical Fruit World (near
  Murwillumbah), 187–188

Tullah, 621
Tully River, 3, 261, 281, 283
Tunnel Creek National Park, 415–416
Turquoise Bay, 467
Turtles, 125, 220, 232, 241, 268, 307, 309, 312–314, 316, 440, 463, 465, 467, 468
Tweed Heads, 331
Twelve Apostles, 561
Twin Falls, 400
Tyrell's (Pokolbin), 171

U birr Rock, 400
Uluru, 354
Uluru-Kata Tjuta National Park (Ayers Rock/ The Olgas), 5, 374–381. *See also* Ayers Rock
Umbarra Aboriginal Cultural Centre (Wallaga Lake), 8, 192
Underwater World (Mooloolaba), 324

V alley of the Waters, 164
Vasey Esplanade, 262
Vasse, 455, 458, 459
Vasse Felix (Cowaramup), 455
Vaucluse House (Sydney), 129
Victoria, 20, 554–574
 traveling to, 554, 556
 visitor information, 554
Victorian Alps, 3
Victorian Arts Centre (Melbourne), 541
Victoria's Open Range Zoo at Werribee, 551
Vincentia, 190
Visitor information, 27–28
Voyager Estate (Margaret River), 456

W ait-A-While Environ- mental Tours, 4, 260
Wallabies, 124, 125, 131, 132, 220, 291, 298, 324, 335, 340, 342, 368, 389, 414, 438, 465, 468, 492, 494, 495, 498–501, 530, 566, 572, 586, 596, 603, 606, 623

Waltzing Matilda Centre (Winton), 349
Wanggoolba Creek, 319
Wangi Falls, 395, 396
Warden Finnerty's Residence (Coolgardie), 462
Warner Bros. Movie World (Oxenford), 334
Warning, Mount, 188
Warradjan Aboriginal Cultural Park (Kakadu National Park), 10, 400
Warrawong Sanctuary (Mylor), 492
Watarrka National Park, 372
Wategos Beach, 185
Water, drinking, 69, 272, 386
Waterskiing, 276, 291, 293, 299
Watsons Bay (Sydney), 78, 131
Waverley Woollen Mills (Launceston), 612
Weather, 69
Websites, travel-planning and booking, 25–27
Wentworth Falls, 164–165
Werribee, 551–552
Werribee Park Mansion, 552
Western Australia, 19, 421–468
Western Australian Maritime Museum (Fremantle), 443
Western Australian Museum (Perth), 10, 440
West MacDonnell National Park, 368–369
Wet 'n' Wild (Oxenford), 334
Wet Tropics, 260
Wet Tropics rain forests, 2, 239, 251, 260, 275
Whales and whale-watching, 176, 182, 192, 193, 300, 319, 457
Whale sharks, 19, 462, 467
White Cliffs, 199
Whitehaven Beach, 6, 299
White-water rafting, 3, 41, 42, 181–182, 261, 283, 443–444
Whitsunday Coast and Islands, 2, 7, 293–307
 camping, 306–307
 day trips to Great Barrier Reef from, 248, 250
 exploring, 297–300
 outdoor activities, 300–301

resorts, 303–306
 transportation, 294
 traveling to, 293–294
 visitor information, 294
Wildflowers, 3, 8, 175, 194, 421, 424, 454, 503, 569, 573
Wildlife, 30, 623–625. *See also* Bird-watching; Dolphins and dolphin- watching; Whales and whale watching; Zoos; *And specific wildlife, wildlife parks and reserves*
 best places to view, 4–5
 safety tips, 43–44
Wild World (Cairns), 256
William Creek, 508
William Ricketts Sanctuary (Mt. Dandenong), 546
Williams Esplanade, 262
Willie Creek Pearl Farm, 418–419
Wilpena Pound, 504
Wilsons Promontory National Park, 566
Windjana Gorge National Park, 415–416
Window on the Wetlands Visitor Centre, 398
Windsurfing, 140, 234, 299, 301, 303
Wineglass Bay, 606
Wines and vineyards, 633–634
 the Barossa, 488–489
 Canberra, 586
 Clare Valley, 487
 the Coonawarra, 487
 Hunter Valley, 169–171
 Margaret River, 455–456
 Mount Tamborine, 341
 Swan Valley, 450–451
Winton, 349–350
Wolf Blass (Nuriootpa), 489
Wollongong, 132
Wombats, 4, 124, 125, 178, 180, 220, 324, 335, 438, 440, 509, 530, 548, 566, 572, 596, 603, 623
Wonderland Sydney, 124
Wonga Beach, 277
Woodbridge (West Midland), 450–451
Woodside, 492

Woolmers (Longford), 609
Woongarra Marine Park
  (Bundaberg), 315
World War II oil storage
  tunnels (Darwin), 390

Y alumba (Angaston), 489
Yamatji Bitja Aboriginal
  Bush Tours (Kalgoorlie),
  9, 461

Yarra Valley, 547–548
Yellow Water Billabong, 399
Yongala wreck, 7
York, 451–453
Yorkeys Knob, 262
York Motor Museum, 10, 452
Youth hostels. *See* Hostels

Z eehan's West Coast
  Pioneers Memorial
  Museum (Strahan), 618
Zoos, 124, 132, 146, 180,
  325, 439–440, 483, 530,
  551, 564

FROMMER'S® COMPLETE TRAVEL GUIDES

Alaska
Amsterdam
Argentina & Chile
Arizona
Atlanta
Australia
Austria
Bahamas
Barcelona, Madrid & Seville
Beijing
Belgium, Holland & Luxembourg
Bermuda
Boston
British Columbia & the Canadian Rockies
Budapest & the Best of Hungary
California
Canada
Cancún, Cozumel & the Yucatán
Cape Cod, Nantucket & Martha's Vineyard
Caribbean
Caribbean Cruises & Ports of Call
Caribbean Ports of Call
Carolinas & Georgia
Chicago
China
Colorado
Costa Rica
Denmark
Denver, Boulder & Colorado Springs
England
Europe
European Cruises & Ports of Call
Florida
France

Germany
Great Britain
Greece
Greek Islands
Hawaii
Hong Kong
Honolulu, Waikiki & Oahu
Ireland
Israel
Italy
Jamaica
Japan
Las Vegas
London
Los Angeles
Maryland & Delaware
Maui
Mexico
Montana & Wyoming
Montréal & Québec City
Munich & the Bavarian Alps
Nashville & Memphis
Nepal
New England
New Mexico
New Orleans
New York City
New Zealand
Nova Scotia, New Brunswick & Prince Edward Island
Oregon
Paris
Philadelphia & the Amish Country
Portugal
Prague & the Best of the Czech Republic

Provence & the Riviera
Puerto Rico
Rome
San Antonio & Austin
San Diego
San Francisco
Santa Fe, Taos & Albuquerque
Scandinavia
Scotland
Seattle & Portland
Shanghai
Singapore & Malaysia
South Africa
South America
Southeast Asia
South Florida
South Pacific
Spain
Sweden
Switzerland
Texas
Thailand
Tokyo
Toronto
Tuscany & Umbria
USA
Utah
Vancouver & Victoria
Vermont, New Hampshire & Maine
Vienna & the Danube Valley
Virgin Islands
Virginia
Walt Disney World & Orlando
Washington, D.C.
Washington State

FROMMER'S® DOLLAR-A-DAY GUIDES

Australia from $50 a Day
California from $70 a Day
Caribbean from $70 a Day
England from $75 a Day
Europe from $70 a Day

Florida from $70 a Day
Hawaii from $80 a Day
Ireland from $60 a Day
Italy from $70 a Day
London from $85 a Day

New York from $90 a Day
Paris from $80 a Day
San Francisco from $70 a Day
Washington, D.C., from $80 a Day

FROMMER'S® PORTABLE GUIDES

Acapulco, Ixtapa & Zihuatanejo
Alaska Cruises & Ports of Call
Amsterdam
Aruba
Australia's Great Barrier Reef
Bahamas
Baja & Los Cabos
Berlin
Big Island of Hawaii
Boston
California Wine Country
Cancún
Charleston & Savannah
Chicago
Disneyland

Dublin
Florence
Frankfurt
Hong Kong
Houston
Las Vegas
London
Los Angeles
Maine Coast
Maui
Miami
New Orleans
New York City
Paris

Phoenix & Scottsdale
Portland
Puerto Rico
Puerto Vallarta, Manzanillo & Guadalajara
San Diego
San Francisco
Seattle
Sydney
Tampa & St. Petersburg
Vancouver
Venice
Virgin Islands
Washington, D.C.

FROMMER'S® NATIONAL PARK GUIDES

Family Vacations in the National Parks
Grand Canyon

National Parks of the American West
Rocky Mountain
Yellowstone & Grand Teton

Yosemite & Sequoia/ Kings Canyon
Zion & Bryce Canyon

FROMMER'S® MEMORABLE WALKS

Chicago
London

New York
Paris

San Francisco

FROMMER'S® GREAT OUTDOOR GUIDES

Arizona & New Mexico
New England

Northern California
Southern New England

Vermont & New Hampshire

SUZY GERSHMAN'S BORN TO SHOP GUIDES

Born to Shop: France
Born to Shop: Hong Kong,
   Shanghai & Beijing

Born to Shop: Italy
Born to Shop: London

Born to Shop: New York
Born to Shop: Paris

FROMMER'S® IRREVERENT GUIDES

Amsterdam
Boston
Chicago
Las Vegas
London

Los Angeles
Manhattan
New Orleans
Paris
Rome

San Francisco
Seattle & Portland
Vancouver
Walt Disney World
Washington, D.C.

FROMMER'S® BEST-LOVED DRIVING TOURS

Britain
California
Florida
France

Germany
Ireland
Italy

New England
Scotland
Spain

HANGING OUT™ GUIDES

Hanging Out in England
Hanging Out in Europe

Hanging Out in France
Hanging Out in Ireland

Hanging Out in Italy
Hanging Out in Spain

THE UNOFFICIAL GUIDES®

Bed & Breakfasts and Country
   Inns in:
      California
      New England
      Northwest
      Rockies
      Southeast
Beyond Disney
Branson, Missouri
California with Kids
Chicago
Cruises
Disneyland

Florida with Kids
Golf Vacations in the
   Eastern U.S.
The Great Smokey &
   Blue Ridge Mountains
Inside Disney
Hawaii
Las Vegas
London
Mid-Atlantic with Kids
Mini Las Vegas
Mini-Mickey
New England & New York
   with Kids

New Orleans
New York City
Paris
San Francisco
Skiing in the West
Southeast with Kids
Walt Disney World
Walt Disney World for
   Grown-ups
Walt Disney World for Kids
Washington, D.C.
World's Best Diving Vacations

SPECIAL-INTEREST TITLES

Frommer's Adventure Guide to Australia & New
   Zealand
Frommer's Adventure Guide to Central America
Frommer's Adventure Guide to India & Pakistan
Frommer's Adventure Guide to South America
Frommer's Adventure Guide to Southeast Asia
Frommer's Adventure Guide to Southern Africa
Frommer's Britain's Best Bed & Breakfasts and
   Country Inns
Frommer's France's Best Bed & Breakfasts and
   Country Inns
Frommer's Italy's Best Bed & Breakfasts and Country
   Inns
Frommer's Caribbean Hideaways

Frommer's Exploring America by RV
Frommer's Gay & Lesbian Europe
Frommer's The Moon
Frommer's New York City with Kids
Frommer's Road Atlas Britain
Frommer's Road Atlas Europe
Frommer's Washington, D.C., with Kids
Frommer's What the Airlines Never Tell You
Israel Past & Present
The New York Times' Guide to Unforgettable
   Weekends
Places Rated Almanac
Retirement Places Rated

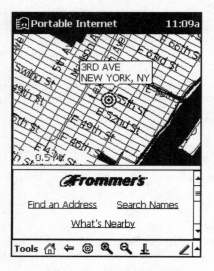